October 22–26, 2012
Santa Monica, California, USA

Association for
Computing Machinery

Advancing Computing as a Science & Profession

ICMI'12

Proceedings of the ACM International Conference on
Multimodal Interaction

Sponsored by:

ACM SIGCHI

Supported by:

Openstream, USC ICT, PASCAL2, Microsoft Research, Nuance and Disney Research

Association for
Computing Machinery

Advancing Computing as a Science & Profession

The Association for Computing Machinery
2 Penn Plaza, Suite 701
New York, New York 10121-0701

ISBN: 978-1-4503-1467-1 (Digital)

ISBN: 978-1-4503-1927-0 (Print)

Additional copies may be ordered prepaid from:

ACM Order Department
PO Box 30777
New York, NY 10087-0777, USA

Phone: 1-800-342-6626 (USA and Canada)
+1-212-626-0500 (Global)
Fax: +1-212-944-1318
E-mail: acmhelp@acm.org
Hours of Operation: 8:30 am – 4:30 pm ET

Printed in the USA

ICMI 2012 Chairs' Welcome

Welcome to Santa Monica and to the 14th edition of the International Conference on Multimodal Interaction, ICMI 2012. ICMI is the premier international forum for multidisciplinary research on multimodal human-human and human-computer interaction, interfaces, and system development.

We had a record number of submissions this year: 147 (74 long papers, 49 short papers, 5 special session papers and 19 demo papers). From these submissions, we accepted 15 papers for long oral presentation (20.3% acceptance rate), 10 papers for short oral presentation (20.4% acceptance rate) and 19 papers presented as posters. We have a total acceptance rate of 35.8% for all short and long papers. 12 of the 19 demo papers were accepted. All 5 special session papers were directly invited by the organizers and the papers were all accepted. In addition, the program includes three invited Keynote talks.

One of the two novelties introduced at ICMI this year is the Multimodal Grand Challenges. Developing systems that can robustly understand human-human communication or respond to human input requires identifying the best algorithms and their failure modes. In fields such as computer vision, speech recognition, and computational linguistics, the availability of datasets and common tasks have led to great progress. This year, we accepted four challenge workshops: the Audio-Visual Emotion Challenge (AVEC), the Haptic Voice Recognition challenge, the D-META challenge and Brain-Computer Interface challenge. Stefanie Telex and Daniel Gatica-Perez are co-chairing the grand challenge this year. All four Grand Challenges will be presented on Monday, October 22nd, and a summary session will be happening on Wednesday, October 24th, afternoon during the main conference.

The second novelty at ICMI this year is the Doctoral Consortium—a separate, one-day event to take place on Monday, October 22nd, co-chaired by Bilge Mutlu and Carlos Busso. The goal of the Doctoral Consortium is to provide Ph.D. students with an opportunity to present their work to a group of mentors and peers from a diverse set of academic and industrial backgrounds and institutions, to receive feedback on their doctoral research plan and progress, and to build a cohort of young researchers interested in designing multimodal interfaces. All accepted students receive a travel grant to attend the conference. From among 25 applications, 14 students were accepted for participation and to receive travel funding. The organizers thank the National Science Foundation (award IIS-1249319) and conference sponsors for financial support.

The review process was organized using the PCS submission and review system, which ICMI has used in the past. The quality of the review process was high thanks to 26 Area Chairs (ACs) who helped the Program Chairs in defining the Program Committee, and in finding excellent reviewers for each paper. Once reviews were submitted, the ACs provided meta-reviews for all papers which, along with the reviews, were sent to the authors for a rebuttal — a step which allows authors to clarify their intentions and results in higher quality final papers. In a final step, all papers and their reviews were discussed by the Program Chairs on a two-day remote meeting in order to decide on the list of accepted submissions.

The program was formed by grouping papers into main topics of interest for this year's conference. Following the trend in previous ICMI events and many other academic meetings, to minimize paper consumption we decided to distribute the conference proceedings on USB Flash Drives. The program chairs pre-selected the top-ranked paper submissions based on reviewers and area chairs comments. The Best Paper Award committee reviewed these top-ranked papers carefully, identified award finalists (marked in the technical program), and selected the recipients of the Best Student Paper Award and the Best Paper Award. The final award decisions will be announced at the conference banquet.

As in previous events, ICMI-2012 has been organized with the support of ACM and SIGCHI. In addition, considerable support has been provided by our generous sponsors. We have one sponsor at the multimodal level (OpenStream), two bimodal sponsors (ICT, and PASCAL2), and three unimodal sponsors (Microsoft Research, Nuance and Disney Research). We are grateful for the support extended by all these organizations and we hope that ICMI will continue to benefit from their generous support in the years to come.

The chairs would like to thank our colleagues in the conference organization committee for their tireless effort bringing this meeting together. We are thankful to Alesia Egan who served as the local organizer and the treasurer. Finally our thanks are extended to all program committee members and volunteer reviewers who contributed their effort to the review process and made it possible to develop such a high quality technical program. Last, but not least, we would like to thank you: the authors and attendees. Thank you for your work and your time. We hope you find a meeting filled with new ideas, old colleagues and future collaborators!

ICMI 2012 Technical Program Chairs

Justine Cassell
Carnegie Mellon University, USA

Anton Nijholt
University of Twente, The Netherlands

Julien Epps
The University of New South Wales, Australia

ICMI 2012 General Chairs

Louis-Philippe Morency
University of Southern California, USA

Dan Bohus
Microsoft Research, USA

Hamid Aghajan
Stanford University, USA

Table of Contents

Demo Session 1

Session Chairs: Ramón López-Cózar Delgado *(University of Granada)*, Wolfgang Minker *(University of Ulm)*

Poster Session 1

Session Chair: Julien Epps *(The University of New South Wales)*

Oral Session 3: Vision

Session Chair: Louis-Philippe Morency *(University of Southern California)*

Keynote 2
Session Chair: TBA

Oral Session 4: Special Session: Child-Computer Interaction
Session Chair: Anton Nijholt *(University of Twente)*

Oral Session 5: Gestures
Session Chair: Kristiina Jokinen *(University of Helsinki)*

Demo Session 2
Session Chairs: Ramón López-Cózar Delgado *(University of Granada)*, Wolfgang Minker *(University of Ulm)*

Poster Session 2: Doctoral Spotlight Session

Session Chairs: Carlos Busso *(University of Texas – Dallas)*, Bilge Mutlu *(University of Wisconsin – Madison)*

Grand Challenge Overview

Session Chairs: Daniel Gatica-Perez *(IDIAP Research Institute)*,
Stefanie Tellex *(Massachusetts Institute of Technology)*

Keynote 3

Session Chair: Stephen Fairclough *(Liverpool John Moores University)*

Oral Session 6: Touch / Taste

Session Chair: Sidney D'Mello *(University of Notre Dame)*

Oral Session 7: Multimodal Interaction

Session Chair: Kenji Mase *(Nagoya University)*

Challenge 1: 2nd International Audio/Visual Emotion Challenge and Workshop – AVEC 2012

Session Chairs: Björn Schuller *(Technische Universität München)*, Michel Valstar *(University of Nottingham)*, Roddy Cowie *(Queen's University Belfast)*, Maja Pantic *(Imperial College London)*

Challenge 2: Haptic Voice Recognition Grand Challenge

Session Chairs: Khe Chai Sim, Shengdong Zhao *(National University of Singapore)*, Kai Yu *(Cambridge University)*, Hank Liao *(Google Inc.)*

Challenge 3: BCI Grand Challenge: Brain-Computer Interfaces as Intelligent Sensors for Enhancing Human-Computer Interaction

Session Chairs: Femke Nijboer, Mannes Poel, Anton Nijholt, Egon L. van den Broek *(University of Twente)*, Stephen Fairclough *(Liverpool John Moores University)*

Workshop Overview

Session Chairs: Toyoaki Nishida *(Kyoto University)*, Rainer Stiefelhagen *(Karlsruhe Institute of Technology)*

ICMI 2012 Organization

General Chairs:	Louis-Philippe Morency *(University of Southern California, USA)* Dan Bohus *(Microsoft Research, USA)* Hamid Aghajan *(Stanford University, USA)*
Program Chairs:	Justine Cassell *(Carnegie Mellon University, USA)* Anton Nijholt *(University of Twente, Netherlands)* Julien Epps *(The University of New South Wales, Australia)*
Workshop Chairs:	Rainer Stiefelhagen *(Karlsruhe Institute of Technology, Germany)* Toyoaki Nishida *(Kyoto University, Japan)*
Publication Chairs:	Ginevra Castellano *(University of Birmingham, UK)* Kenji Mase *(Nagoya University, Japan)*
Demo Chairs:	Wolfgang Minker *(Ulm University, Germany)* Ramón López-Cózar Delgado *(University of Granada, Spain)*
Doctoral Consortium Chairs:	Carlos Busso *(University of Texas at Dallas, USA)* Bilge Mutlu *(University of Wisconsin-Madison, USA)*
Multimodal Grand Challenge Chairs:	Daniel Gatica-Perez *(IDIAP, Switzerland)* Stefanie Tellex *(MIT, USA)*
Publicity Chairs:	Kazuhiro Otsuka *(NTT, Japan)* Michael Johnston *(AT&T Labs, USA)*
Sponsorship Chairs:	Nicu Sebe *(University of Trento, Italy)* Patrick Ehlen *(AT&T, USA)*
Local Organization Chair:	Alesia Egan *(University of Southern California, USA)*
Treasurer:	Alesia Egan *(University of Southern California, USA)*
Web Chair:	Chih-Wei Chen *(Stanford University, USA)*
Advisory Board Chair:	Fabio Pianesi *(FBK, Trento, Italy)*
Advisory Board:	Samy Benjio *(Google)* Hervé Bourlard *(IDIAP, Switzerland)* Jean Carletta *(University of Edinburgh)* James L. Crowley *(INRIA Grenoble Rhone Alpes, France)* Trevor Darrell *(UCB/ICSI, USA)* Sadaoki Furui *(Tokyo Institute of Technology, Japan)* Yuri Ivanov *(MERL, USA)*

ICMI 2012 Additional Reviewers

Xavier Alameda-Pineda
Denis Aleshin
Amir Aly
Dimitra Anastasiou
JesÚs Andrés-Ferrer
Sean Andrist
Ricardo Ron Angevin
Xavier Anguera
Lisa Anthony
Oya Aran
Mobalaji Ayoade
Mohammad Azhar
Siley Ba
Gérard Bailly
Marian Bartlett
Patrick Baudisch
Tilman Becker
Yacine Bellik
Kirsten Bergmann
Cindy Bethel
Nadia Bianchi-Berthouze
Ralph Biedert
John N.A. Brown
Frank Broz
Gerd Bruder
Stéphanie Buisine
Harm Buisman
Andreas Bulling
Hendrik Buschmeier
Carlos Busso
Maya Cakmak
Zoraida Callejas
Rafael Calvo
Jorge Cardoso
George Caridakis
Francisco Casacuberta
Ginevra Castellano
Jessica Cauchard
Marc Cavazza
Crystal Chao
Mohamed Chetouani
Keith Cheverst
Gokul Chittaranjan
Seungmoon Choi
Céline Clavel
Alexis Clay
Maureen Clerc
Paul Coulton
James Crowley
Sanchez Cortez Dairazalia
Ionut Damian
Iwan de Kok
Celso de Melo
Ramon Lopez-Cozar Delgado
Cenk Demiroglu
Hamdi Dibeklioglu
Ferran Diego
Trinh-Minh-Tri Do
Bruno Dumas
Stephen Dunne
Jens Edlund
Eleni Efthimiou
Rana El Kaliouby
Gwenn Englebienne
Sibylle Enz
Julien Epps
Dominik Ertl
Engin Erzin
Anna Esposito
Florian Eyben
Stephen Fairclough
Alireza Fathi
Pierre-Alexandre Favier
Benedict Fehringer
Gaelle Ferre
Pable Figueroa
Maurizio Filippone
Samantha Finkelstein
Patrick Gebhard
Laurent George
Kallirroi Georgila
Gary Geunbae Lee
Sylvie Gibet
Gianluca Giorgolo
Tom Giraud
Michael Gleicher
David Griol
Cuntai Guan
Hatice Gunes
Hayrettin Gürkök
Joakim Gustafson
Joakim Gustafson
Abdenour Hadid
Brahim Hamadicharef
Zakia Hammal
Nick Hawes
Patrick Healey
Tobias Heinroth
Paul Heisterkamp
Wilko Heuten
David House
Chien-Ming Huan
Hayley Hung
Wolfgang Hürst
José Iñesta
Kotsia Irene
Charles Isbell
Stewart James
Takatalo Jari
David A.G. Jáuregui
Dinesh Babu Jayagopi
Yi Ji
Wei Ji
Kyle Johnsen
J. Adam Jones
Mike Just
Gerrit Kahl
Takayuki Kanda
Maurits Kaptein
Kostas Karpouzis
Taemie Kim
Felix Kistler
Kiyoshi Kiyokawa
Andreas Kleinsmith
Sebastian Koenig
Sven Kratz
Christian Kray
Geert-Jan Kruijff
David Krum
Tsvi Kuflik
Katja Kurdyukova
Denis Lalanne
Joel Lanir
Eric Larson
Marc Erich Latoschik
Anamary Leal
Robert Leeb
Luis Leiva
Bruno Lepri
Haifeng Li
Peter Ljunglof
Katrin Lohan
Manja Lohse
Karljohan Lundin Palmerius

Mathew Magimai Doss
Charlotte Magnusson
Päivi Majaranta
Maurizio Manzini
Maud Marchal
Daniel Martin-Albo
Jeremie Mattout
Ross Mead
Gregor Mehlmann
Helen Meng
Cetin Mericli
Nicholas Micallef
Florian Michahelles
Teruhisa Misu
Betty Mohler
Jonas Moll
Melody Moore
Lee Morton
Konstantinos Moustakas
Franck Multon
Yukie Nagai
Satoshi Nakamura
Yukiko Nakano
Costanza Navarretta
Robert Nebelrath
Michael Neff
Sigrid Norris
David Novick
Petteri Nurmi
Ian Oakley
Mohammad Obaid
Magalie Ochs
Eva Oliveira
Roeland Ordelmans
Kazuhiro Otsuka
Sharon Oviatt
Derya Ozkan
Tim Paek
Ana Paiva
Maja Pantic
Roberto Paredes
Hari Parthasarathi
Olivier Patrick
Tabitha Peck
Veronica Perez-Rosas
Fabio Pianesi
Martin Pielot
Thomas Ploetz
Mannes Poel
Isabella Poggi
Ronald Poppe
Benjamin Poppinga
Robert Porzel
Gerasimos Potamianos
Matthew Purver
Bogdan Raducanu
Irene Rae
Andrew Raij
Kirsten Rassmus-Grohn
Antoine Raux
Norbert Reithinger
Steve Renals
Boris Reuderink
Laurel D. Riek
Fabien Ringeval
Mikko Rissanen
Teather Robert
Peter Robinson
Luis Rodríguez
Michael Rohs
Agata Rozga
Lukas Rybok
Selma Sabanovic
Amir Sadeghipour
Maha Salem
Antonios Saravanos
Dominique Scapin
Tatjana Scheffler
Stefan Scherer
Reinhold Scherer
Gianluca Schiavo
Albrecht Schmidt
Alexander Schmitt
Michael Schmitz
Johannes Schöning
Christian Schulz
Tim Schwartz
Nicu Sebe
Hui Shi
Candace Sidner
Mohammad Soleymani
Erin Solovey
Daniel Sonntag
Richard Souvenir
Stefano Squartini
Christoph Stahl
Stefan Steidl
Frank Steinicke
Rainer Stiefelhagen
Ramanathan Subramanian
Sriram Subramanian
David Suendermann
Dag Sverre Syrdal
Mark ter Maat
Allison Terrell
Thad Starner
Mariet Theune
Edison Thomaz
Andrea Thomaz
Marko Tkalcic
Alejandro Héctor Toselli
Hideaki Touyama
David Traum
Khiet Truong
Matthew Turk
Stephen Uzor
Roberto Valenti
Michel Valstar
Kees van Deemter
Egon L, van den Broek
Jan van Gemert
Herwin van Welbergen
Giovanna Varni
Radu-Daniel Vatavu
Theresa Vaughan
Gualtiero Volpe
Astrid von der Putten
Danli Wang
Rainer Wasinger
Michael Weber
Ina Wechsung
Felix Weninger
Julie Rico Williamson
Marcelo Worsley
Danny Wyatt
Bo Xiao
Ming-Hsuan Yang
Georgios Yannakakis
Sumi Yasuyuki
Chen Yu
Zeynep Yücel
Thorsten Zander
Yin Zhou
Gottfried Zimmermann
Job Zwiers

ICMI 2012 Sponsor & Supporters

Sponsor: SIGCHI

Multimodal Supporter: Openstream®
Making Communications Smarter

Bimodal Supporters: USC ICT
INSTITUTE FOR CREATIVE TECHNOLOGIES

PASCAL2
Pattern Analysis, Statistical Modelling and Computational Learning

Unimodal Supporters: Microsoft Research

NUANCE®

Disney Research

The Co-Operative, Transformative Organization of Human Action and Knowledge

Charles Goodwin
Applied Linguistics, UCLA
P3300 Rolfe Hall
Los Angeles CA 90095-1531
cgoodwin@humnet.ucla.edu

ABSTRACT

Human action is built by actively and simultaneously combining materials with intrinsically different properties into situated contextual configurations where they can mutually elaborate each other to create a whole that is both different from, and greater than, any of its constitutive parts. These resources include many different kinds of lexical and syntactic structures, prosody, gesture, embodied participation frameworks, sequential organization, and different kinds of materials in the environment, including tools created by others that structure local perception. The simultaneous use of different kinds of resources to build single actions has a number of consequences. First, different actors can contribute different kinds of materials that are implicated in the construction of a single action. For example embodied visual displays by hearers operate simultaneously on emerging talk by a speaker so that both the utterance and the turn have intrinsic organization that is both multi-party and multimodal. Someone with aphasia who is unable to produce lexical and syntactic structure can nonetheless contribute crucial prosodic and sequential materials to a local action, while appropriating the lexical contributions of others, and thus become a powerful speaker in conversation, despite catastrophically impoverished language. One effect of this simultaneous, distributed heterogeneity is that frequently the organization of action cannot be easily equated with the activities of single individuals, such as the person speaking at the moment, or with phenomena within a single medium such as talk. Second, subsequent action is frequently built through systematic transformations of the different kinds of materials provided by a prior action. In this process some elements of the prior contextual configuration, such as the encompassing participation framework, may remain unchanged, while others undergo significant modification. A punctual perspective on action, in which separate actions discretely follow one another, thus becomes more complex when action is seen to emerge within an unfolding mosaic of disparate materials and time frames which make possible not only systematic change, but also more enduring frameworks that provide crucial continuity. Third, the distributed, compositional structure of action provides a framework for developing the skills of newcomers within structured collaborative action. Fourth, human tools differ from the tools of other animals in that, like actions in talk, they are built by combining unlike materials into a whole not found in any of the individual parts (for example using a stone, a piece of wood and leather thongs to make an ax). This same combinatorial heterogeneity sits at the heart of human action in interaction, including language use. It creates within the unfolding organization of situated activity itself the distinctive forms of transformative collaborative action in the world, including socially organized perceptual and cognitive structures and the mutual alignment of bodies to each other, which constitutes us as humans.

ICMI '12, October 22–26, 2012, Santa Monica, California, USA.
ACM 978-1-4503-1467-1/12/10.

ACM Classification Keywords

H.5.2 [Information Interfaces and Presentation]: User Interfaces - Interaction styles.

Author Keywords

Co-operative action, talk-in-interaction, embodiment, distributed cognition, situated activity.

BIOGRAPHY

Charles Goodwin is Professor of Applied Linguistics at UCLA. He received his Ph.D. from the Annenberg School of Communications, University of Pennsylvania, 1977, and a Doctor of Philosophy Honoris Causa from the Faculty of Arts and Sciences, Linköping University in 2009. His interests include video analysis of talk-in-interaction (including study of the discursive practices used by hearers and speakers to construct utterances, stories, and other forms of talk), grammar in context, cognition in the lived social world, gesture, gaze and embodiment as interactively organized social practices, aphasia in discourse, language in the professions and the ethnography of science. He has been involved in numerous studies including family interaction in the United States, the work of oceanographers in the mouth of Amazon, archaeologists in the United States and Argentina, geologists in the back country of Yellowstone, the organization of talk, vision and embodied action in the midst of surgery, and how a man with severe aphasia is able to function as a powerful speaker in conversation. As part of the Workplace Project at Xerox PARC he investigated cognition and talk-in-interaction in complex work setting.

His publications include Embodied Interaction: Language and Body in the Material World (edited with Jürgen Streeck and Curtis LeBaron (Cambridge U. Press), Rethinking Context (Cambridge University Press) (co-edited with Alessandro Duranti), Conversation and Brain Damage (Oxford U. Press) Conversational Organization, (Academic Press), Il Senso del Vedere: Pratiche Sociali della Significazione (Melterri Editore) "Professional Vision" (American Anthropologist) "Action and Embodiment" (Journal of Pragmatics), "Constructing Meaning Through Prosody in Aphasia" (Prosody in Interaction ed. by Barth-Weingarten, et. al.), "Ensembles of Emotion" (with M.H. Goodwin, et. al in Emotion in Interaction, edited by Sorjonen and Perakyla), "How geoscientists think and learn" (with Kastens et. al, EOS Transactions, American Geophysical Union), "Can you see the cystic artery yet?" with Koschmann et. al, Journal of Pragmatics.

Two People Walk Into a Bar: Dynamic Multi-Party Social Interaction with a Robot Agent

Mary Ellen Foster[1,*] Andre Gaschler[2] Manuel Giuliani[2]
Amy Isard[3] Maria Pateraki[4] Ronald P.A. Petrick[3]
[1] School of Mathematical and Computer Sciences, Heriot-Watt University, Edinburgh, UK
[2] fortiss GmbH, Munich, Germany [3] School of Informatics, University of Edinburgh, Edinburgh, UK
[4] Foundation for Research and Technology – Hellas (FORTH), Heraklion, Crete, Greece
M.E.Foster@hw.ac.uk {gaschler,giuliani}@fortiss.org
{amyi,rpetrick}@inf.ed.ac.uk pateraki@ics.forth.gr

ABSTRACT

We introduce a humanoid robot bartender that is capable of dealing with multiple customers in a dynamic, multi-party social setting. The robot system incorporates state-of-the-art components for computer vision, linguistic processing, state management, high-level reasoning, and robot control. In a user evaluation, 31 participants interacted with the bartender in a range of social situations. Most customers successfully obtained a drink from the bartender in all scenarios, and the factors that had the greatest impact on subjective satisfaction were task success and dialogue efficiency.

Categories and Subject Descriptors: H.5.1 [Information Interfaces and Presentation]: Multimedia Information Systems – Evaluation/methodology; I.2.9 [Artificial intelligence]: Robotics – Operator interfaces

General Terms: Human Factors

Keywords: Social robotics, Multi-party interaction

1. INTRODUCTION

A robot interacting with humans in the real world must be able to deal with situations in which socially appropriate interaction is vital. It is not enough simply to achieve task-based goals: the robot must also be able to satisfy the social goals and obligations that arise during the course of human-robot interaction. In the JAMES project, we are addressing this issue by developing a robot bartender (Figure 1) which is able to deal with multiple customers in a dynamic setting. Interactions in the context of a bartending scenario incorporate a mixture of task-based aspects (e.g., ordering and paying for drinks) and social aspects (e.g., engaging in social conversation, managing multiple transactions), both of which present challenges: the robot bartender must be able to recognise, understand and respond appropriately to both the social and the task-based needs of the humans that it encounters, and to successfully distinguish between the two types.

*The author names are listed in alphabetical order.

ICMI'12, October 22–26, 2012, Santa Monica, California, USA.

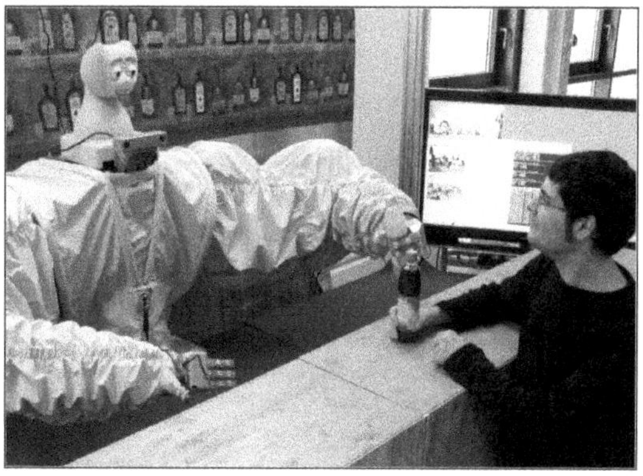

Figure 1: The JAMES robot bartender

Interaction 1 (Socially inappropriate)	**Interaction 2 (Socially appropriate)**
One person, A, approaches the bar and turns towards the bartender	
Robot (to A): How can I help you?	Robot (to A): How can I help you?
A: A pint of cider, please.	A: A pint of cider, please.
A second person, B, approaches the bar and turns towards the bartender	
Robot (to B): How can I help you?	Robot (to B): One moment, please.
B: I'd like a pint of beer.	Robot: (Serves A)
Robot: (Serves B)	Robot (to B): Thanks for waiting. How can I help you?
Robot: (Serves A)	B: I'd like a pint of beer.
	Robot: (Serves B)

Figure 2: Social interaction in a bar setting

As a concrete example, consider the bartender interactions shown in Figure 2. At the end of both interactions, the needs of both customers A and B have been successfully met: each has made a request and has been served by the bartender. However, the second interaction is clearly more appropriate than the first. Not only are the customers served in the same sequence that they made their requests, but the robot also interacts with customer B in a more socially acceptable manner, by acknowledging B's arrival and completing the existing transaction before dealing with a new request. This demonstrates that, while many human-robot interactions may lead to the same goal at the task level, the quality of those interactions can be greatly enhanced by getting the "people skills" right.

Even a simple scenario like this one poses state-of-the-art challenges: the vision system must accurately track the locations and body postures of the two agents; the speech recogniser must be able to detect and deal with speech from multiple users in an open setting; the reasoning components must determine that each cus tomer requires attention and should choose appropriate behaviours to deal with both of them; while the output components must select and coordinate actions for all of the output channels that correctly realise the high-level plans, including both communicative actions and behaviours of the robot manipulators.

This work fits into the active research area of *social robotics*: "the study of robots that interact and communicate with themselves, with humans, and with their environment, within the social and cultural structure attached to their roles." [12]. Most current social robots play the role of a companion, often in a long-term, one-on-one relationship with the user [e.g., 7–9]. In this context, the primary goal for the robot is to build a relationship with the user through social interaction: the robot is primarily an interactive partner, and any task-based behaviour is secondary to this overall goal.

We address a style of interaction which is distinctive in two main ways. First, while most existing social robots deal primarily with one-on-one interactive situations, the robot bartender must deal with dynamic, multi-party scenarios: people constantly enter and leave the scene, so the robot must constantly choose appropriate social behaviour while interacting with a series of new partners. Second, while existing social robotics projects (even those that deal with multiple partners such as [24, 25]) generally take social interaction as the primary goal, the robot bartender supports social communication in the context of a cooperative, task-based interaction. Also, existing "robot bartenders" [e.g., 14, 23] focus on the physical tasks associated with bartending (i.e., actually preparing and serving drinks), and fail to consider the social context.

Our robot bartender is most similar to the multimodal interactive kiosk described by Bohus and Horvitz [6], which handles situated, open-world, multimodal dialogue in scenarios such as a reception desk. Their system incorporates models of multi-party engagement, turn-taking, and intention recognition, and has been evaluated in a series of real-world and laboratory studies. The robot bartender extends this work by adding physical embodiment, which has been shown to have a large effect on social interaction: for example, physical agents have been found to be more appealing, perceptive, and helpful than virtual agents [36], and to result in more positive and natural interactions [2, 22].

2. SYSTEM DETAILS

As shown in Figure 1, the bartender robot consists of two manipulator arms with humanoid hands mounted in a position to resemble human arms, along with an animatronic talking head. The software architecture (Figure 3) uses a standard three-layer structure: low-level components deal with modality-specific, highly detailed information such as spatial coordinates, speech-recognition hypotheses, and robot arm trajectories; the mid-level components deal with abstract, cross-modal representations of states and events; while the high-level components reason about the most abstract structures, such as knowledge and actions represented in a logical form.

On the input side, the low-level components include a vision system (Section 2.1), which tracks the real-time location of all people in the scene as well as their body language, along with a linguistic processing system (Section 2.2) combining a speech recogniser with a natural language parser to create symbolic representations of the spoken contributions of all users. The low level also includes output components (Section 2.5) that control the animatronic talking head (which produces synthesised speech, facial expressions, and gaze behaviour) and the robot arms and hands (which can point at and manipulate objects), along with a robot simulator.

The primary mid-level input component is the social state manager (Section 2.3), which combines information from the low-level input components to estimate the real-time social and communicative state of all users. On the output side, the output planner (Section 2.2) both translates the selected communicative and task-based acts into specific action sequences for the low-level components and also coordinates the execution of those sequences.

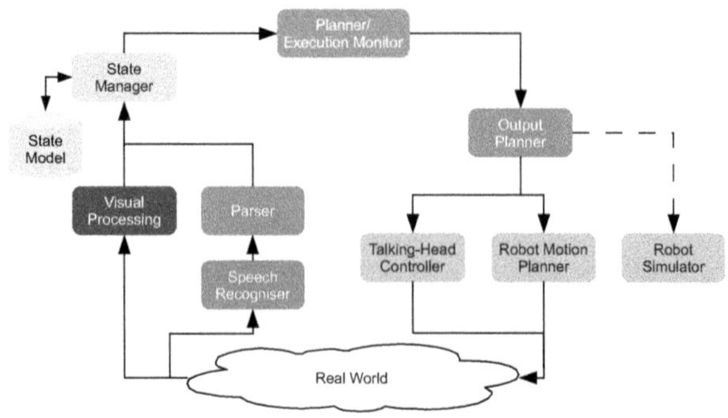

Figure 3: System architecture

Finally, the high level includes a knowledge-level planning component (Section 2.4) that generates plans for the robot to achieve its goals, where the plans include a mixture of domain actions (e.g., manipulating objects in the world), sensing actions (e.g., using the robot arms to test object properties), and communicative actions (e.g., getting a customer's drink request). The high-level system also includes a plan execution monitor which tracks the execution of the plan steps by monitoring the state of the world and updates the state of the plan and/or re-plans as necessary.

2.1 Visual processing

The vision module utilises input from visual sensors to detect and track in real time the faces and hands of people in the scene and to extract their 3D position, and also to derive each person's focus of attention via torso orientation.

To detect and track faces and hands we employ and extend a blob-tracking approach [3], according to which foreground, skin-coloured pixels are identified according to their colour and grouped together into skin-coloured blobs. Information about the location and shape of each tracked blob is maintained by means of a set of pixel hypotheses which are initially sampled from the observed blobs and are propagated from frame to frame according to linear object dynamics computed by a Kalman filter. The distribution of the propagated pixel hypotheses provides a representation for the uncertainty in both the position and the shape of the tracked object.

Moreover, an incremental classifier has been developed [4, 26] which extends the above blob tracking approach and which is used to maintain and continuously update a belief about whether a tracked hypothesis of a skin blob corresponds to a facial region, a left hand or a right hand. For this purpose, we use a simple yet robust feature set which conveys information about the shape of each tracked blob, its motion characteristics, and its relative location with respect to other blobs. The class of each track is determined by incrementally improving a belief state based on the previous belief state and the likelihood of the currently observed feature set. To derive the 3D position of the centroids of coloured regions, we apply the above tracking approach to precalibrated stereo images, establish correspondences of the detected coloured regions in the stereo images by using simple, computationally inexpensive techniques [1], and extract the 3D positions in a world-centred coordinate system. Figure 4 shows the output of the face and hand tracking process.

Also of interest in this domain is the focus of attention of a person approaching the bar, which is derived from information on torso orientation (arm tracking). For the torso orientation, a tracking approach is used [34] to track both arms (four parameters for

Figure 4: Output of face and hand tracking

```
<lf>
  <node id="w1" pred="can-verb" mood="int" tense="pres"
        voice="active">
    <rel name="Body">
      <node id="w3" pred="get-verb">
        <rel name="ArgOne">
          <node id="w2" pred="pron" num="sg" pers="1st"/>
        </rel>
        <rel name="ArgTwo">
          <node id="w5" pred="coke" det="indef" num="sg"/>
        </rel>
      </node>
    </rel>
    <rel name="HasProp">
      <node id="w0" pred="please"/>
    </rel>
  </node>
</lf>
```

Figure 5: OpenCCG logical form for "Please can I get a Coke?"

each arm) as well as the orientation of the human torso (one parameter). To reduce the complexity of the problem and to achieve real-time performance, the model space is split into three different partitions and tracking is performed separately in each of them. More specifically, a Hidden Markov Model tracks the orientation of the human torso in the 1D space of all possible orientations, and two different sets of particles are used to track the four degrees.

In later versions of the system, the vision module will detect and track objects used in different human actions—such as pointing, looking at, grabbing, and holding an object—by extending the blob-tracking approach to handle multiple colour-classes. An additional attentive cue, that of head pose estimation based on Least-Squares Matching [27], will be fused with torso orientation to improve extraction of focus of attention and to handle cases when the user only rotates the head towards the robot to seek attention. Complementary cues from visual speech detection and facial expression recognition will also be integrated in future versions of the system.

2.2 Linguistic interaction

The linguistic interaction in the system is carried out by components which recognise, understand, and generate embodied natural language. First we describe the components which deal with recognising the user's spoken input: speech recognition and natural language interpretation; we then turn to the components which create the system's spoken output and pass it on to the actuators along with the outputs for the other modalities: natural language generation and the multimodal output generator.

The speech recognition uses the Microsoft Kinect and the associated Microsoft Speech API. We use a grammar in the SRGS format [15] to constrain the recognition and achieve more reliable recognition results, and the output is a list of hypotheses with associated confidence values, along with source localisation information

```
<output>
  <gesture-list>
    <gesture type="Smile"/>
  </gesture-list>
  <action-list>
    <action type="give">
      <object type="drink" name="juice" id="A1"/>
      <person id="id5"/>
    </action>
  </action-list>
  <speech-list>
    <speech type="inform" politeness="4">
      <person id="id5"/>
      <pred type="hand-over">
        <object type="drink" name="juice" id="A1"/>
      </pred>
    </speech>
  </speech-list>
</output>
```

Figure 6: XML for multimodal presentation planning

from the Kinect. To avoid attempting to process the system speech, recognition is not carried out while the robot is speaking. Because we have a relatively constrained grammar, if customers say something which is outside our domain (e.g. "what time is it"), we are likely to get a very low recognition score, and the hypotheses may all be rejected as being below the Speech API's built-in threshold, and therefore not be passed on. In most cases, the top hypothesis is passed to the natural language interpretation module which parses it to provide syntactic and semantic information, using a bi-directional OpenCCG grammar [39] which is also used for the natural language generation. The resulting logical form is passed on to the state management component. The example shown in Figure 5 is produced by the spoken input "Please can I get a Coke?"

On the output side, the multimodal output component receives from the planner an XML representation of the system actions to be carried out by the robot talking head and arms, such as the one in Figure 6. This example would cause the robot to smile while handing a juice to the customer and saying "here is your drink." The verbal output is specified in a format [17] based on Rhetorical Structure Theory (RST) [21] and is used to create a logical form which is then realised by using the OpenCCG grammar mentioned above. The speech output and facial expressions are sent to the talking head, and the gestures to the robot arms.

In subsequent versions of the robot bartender, the coverage of the OpenCCG grammar will be expanded to cover the input and output requirements of the more complex scenarios, and the multimodal output component will also be enhanced to allow more precise timing among the various components of a multimodal output turn.

2.3 State management

The primary role of the state manager is to turn the continuous stream of messages produced by the low-level input and output components into a discrete representation of the world, the robot, and all entities in the scene, combining social, dialogue, and task-based properties. The resulting state is used in two distinct ways in the system processing. On the one hand, the state manager provides a persistent, queryable interface to the state: for example, it stores the world coordinates of all entities as reported by the vision system so that the robot is able to correctly look at a particular agent when needed. On the other hand, it also informs the high-level reasoning components whenever there is a relevant change to the state.

In the current system, the state manager is rule-based. One set of rules infers user social states (e.g., seeking attention) based on the low-level sensor data, using guidelines derived from the study of human-human interactions in the bartender domain [16]: in particular, an agent is considered to be seeking attention if they are close to the bar and oriented towards the bartender. The state manager also incorporates rules that map from the logical forms produced by the parser into communicative acts (e.g., drink orders), and that use the source localisation from the speech recogniser together with the vision properties to determine which customer is likely to be speaking. A final set of rules determine when new state reports are published, which helps control turn-taking in the system. Details on the representations used in the state manager are given in [30].

In subsequent versions of the system, the state manager will be enhanced to process more complex messages from the updated input and output components, taking into account the associated confidence scores, and also to deal with the more complex state representations that will be required by the updated high-level reasoning system. To address this, we will draw on recent work in social signal processing [35] by training supervised learning classifiers on data gathered from humans interacting with both real and artificial bartenders, using methods similar to those employed by [6, 18].

2.4 High-level planning and monitoring

The high-level planning component uses state reports from the state manager to generate sequences of actions which are sent to the output planner for execution on the robot as speech, head gestures, and arm movements. This component also monitors the execution of such actions, through subsequent state reports, to ensure the system's high-level goals are being met. When failures or plan divergences are detected, actions are replanned as necessary.

To control action selection, we use a knowledge-level planner called PKS (Planning with Knowledge and Sensing) [28, 29] which builds plans in the presence of incomplete information and sensing, by reasoning about how its knowledge state changes due to action. PKS's knowledge state is represented symbolically by a set of five databases, each of which models a particular type of information, interpreted in a modal logic of knowledge. Actions can modify any of the databases in a STRIPS-like [10] manner through additions or deletions which produce changes in the planner's knowledge. To ensure efficient reasoning, PKS restricts the knowledge it can represent while ensuring it is expressive enough to model many types of information that arise in common planning scenarios.

Like other symbolic planners, PKS requires a definition of the actions available to it, initial (knowledge) state, and a goal to be achieved. A plan is successful provided it transforms the initial state to a state where the goals are satisfied. In the bartending scenario, the domain includes definitions for eight parameterised actions, including `greet(?a)` (greet an agent `?a`), `ask-drink(?a)` (ask an agent `?a` for a drink order), `serve(?a,?d)` (serve drink `?d` to agent `?a`), `wait(?a)` (tell agent `?a` to wait), `ack-wait(?a)` (thank agent `?a` for waiting), `ack-thanks(?a)` (respond to an agent `?a` that thanks the bartender), `not-understand(?a)` (alert agent `?a` that their response was not understood), and `bye(?a)` (end an interaction with agent `?a`). These actions are described at an abstract level and include a mix of task, sensory, and linguistic acts.

Unlike many systems that include speech as an input and output modality, we do not use a dedicated dialogue or interaction manager (e.g., TrindiKit [19]). Instead, the planner is a general-purpose problem solving engine, rather than a specialised tool that has been optimised for dialogue. As a result, all actions (linguistic or otherwise) are treated in a similar fashion during plan generation.

The initial state is not hardcoded. Instead, the planner uses the state information passed to it from the state manager. The planner's goal is simply to serve each agent it knows about. This goal is viewed as a rolling target which is reassessed each time it receives a state report from the state manager. For instance, if the appearance of an agent `A1` is reported to the planner as an initial state report, the planner will build a plan of the following form to serve the agent:

`greet(A1),`	[Greet agent `A1`]
`ask-drink(A1),`	[Ask `A1` for a drink order]
`serve(A1,drink(A1)),`	[Give the ordered drink to `A1`]
`bye(A1).`	[Finish the transaction with `A1`]

(`drink(A1)` is a placeholder for the actual drink ordered by `A1`.)

When a plan has been built, it is post-processed by mapping each action into an RST structure (Figure 6) that explicitly encodes the speech, gesture, and robot parts. Actions are then sent to the output planner, one at a time, for eventual execution in the world.

Once action execution has begun, an execution monitor assesses plan correctness, by comparing subsequent state manager reports against the states predicted by the planner. In the case of disagreement, for instance due to unexpected outcomes like action failure, the planner is invoked to construct a new plan using the current state as its initial state. This method is particularly useful for responding to unexpected actions by agents interacting with the bartender.

For example, if the planner receives a report that `A1`'s response to `ask-drink(A1)` was not understood, it will attempt to build a new plan. One possible result is a modified version of the original plan that first informs the agent they were not understood before repeating `ask-drink(A1)` and continuing with the rest of the plan:

`not-understand(A1),`	[Inform `A1` they were not understood]
`ask-drink(A1),`	[Ask `A1` for a drink order]
...continue with plan...	

Another useful consequence of this approach is that certain types of over-answering by the interacting agent can be handled by the execution monitor through replanning. For instance, if a `greet(A1)` action by the bartender causes `A1` to respond with a drink order, replanning will construct a new plan that omits the `ask-drink(A1)` action and instead proceeds to serve the drink.

The planner can also deal with multiple agents, as in Figure 2. For instance, with two agents, `A1` and `A2`, one possible plan is:

`wait(A2),`	[Tell agent `A2` to wait]
`greet(A1),`	[Greet agent `A1`]
`ask-drink(A1),`	[Ask `A1` for a drink order]
`serve(A1,drink(A1)),`	[Give the ordered drink to `A1`]
`bye(A1),`	[Finish the transaction with `A1`]
`ack-wait(A2),`	[Thank agent `A2` for waiting]
`ask-drink(A2),`	[Ask `A2` for a drink order]
`serve(A2,drink(A2)),`	[Give the ordered drink to `A2`]
`bye(A2).`	[Finish the transaction with `A2`]

Agent `A2` is first told to wait and then `A1`'s drink order is taken and the drink is served. After ending `A1`'s transaction, `A2` is thanked for waiting and the drink ordering process is repeated for `A2`.

In the initial version of the bartender domain, the planner only builds simple sequences of actions (i.e., linear plans). In the next version of the system, we will consider plans with contingencies (i.e., plans with branches), in an attempt to construct more robust plans. More details on the bartending domain are provided in [30].

2.5 Robot behaviours

The talking head and the robot arms are controlled by separate software modules. The talking-head controller provides basic behaviours that are called by the output planner when needed. In this study, we used the following behaviours: lip-synchronised speech output of generated sentences, display of emotions (including smiling and frowning), nodding and shaking the head, and turning the head towards an agent or a neutral position. Furthermore, the talking-head controller informs the rest of the system when speech starts and ends and when it executes a facial expression or head gesture. This information is used to stop speech recognition when the robot was talking to prevent recognition from analysing the robot's utterances, and also to help control turn-taking.

The robot motion planner and simulator components provide a common interface for grasp and place commands from a set of predefined locations. The motion planner generates smooth trajectories and controls the two robot arms in real-time. The simulator shares the same implementation and produces identical trajectories—its single difference lies in the robot hardware abstraction, as it visualises the robot setup and its environment in 3D, allowing the rest of the system to be tested independent of the robot hardware.

Motion planning and robot control make use of the Robotics Library [31, 33]. To create a robust system with deterministic behaviour, we implemented a simple grasping strategy that moves the tool centre point to the desired location with a fixed tool centre orientation. Since the humanoid hands are driven by series elastic actuators and coated with non-slip urethane, we can easily achieve a robust grasp with a simple torque-limited position controller. With this grasping scheme, the robot can grasp various types of bottles of different sizes and materials. For motion planning, locations and via-points are transformed into joint space by the closed-form inverse kinematics given in the Robotics Library. Then, smooth trajectories are generated by quintic polynomial interpolation. For via-points, a tangential velocity is chosen based on the positions of the previous and the next point. Since the number of locations and robot behaviours is limited in the current version, we can enumerate and check all trajectories for collisions with the static environment, checking for collisions at compile time.

In later versions of the bartender, the range of robot actions will be expanded to allow the robot to pick up, put down, and hand over a range of objects at any location; the talking-head actions will also be expanded to cover more complex interaction scenarios.

3. USER EVALUATION

To evaluate the robot bartender, we carried out a user study in which participants enacted variations on the drink-ordering scenario shown in Figure 2 and then answered a short questionnaire regarding their experience of interacting with the bartender. In addition to the questionnaire, we also gathered a range of other measures assessing the quality of the interaction based on data gathered from the system log files. This study serves two purposes: on the one hand, the results provide a useful assessment of the quality of the initial robot bartender system, and one which can serve as a baseline for future evaluations. On the other hand, the study also acts as a formative assessment of the system components, guiding the development of enhanced versions.

3.1 Participants

31 participants (22 male), drawn from university departments outside the robotics group, took part in this experiment. The mean age of the participants was 27.9 (range 21–50), and their mean self-rating of experience with human-robot interaction systems was 2.29 on a scale of 1–5. Neither of these demographic factors had any effect on the study results presented below.

3.2 Scenario

The study took place in a lab, with lighting and background noise controlled as far as possible. Each participant ordered a drink from the robot bartender in the following three scenarios:

1. The participant approached the bartender alone.
2. The participant approached the bartender with a confederate also in view of the cameras but not attempting to attract the bartender's attention.
3. The participant and a confederate both approached the bartender together.

The interactions were similar to that shown in Figure 2. Note that a minimal successful drink-ordering transaction requires three system turns: a greeting from the bartender, serving the drink, and a good-bye from the robot. The transaction could also include any number of requests for the customer's drink order. Each participant was given a list of the possible drinks that could be ordered (water, juice, or Coke), but was not given any further instructions. The robot was static until approached by a customer, and the confederate did not attempt to speak at the same time as the participant. After the three scenarios were completed, the participant completed a short computer-based questionnaire.

3.3 Dependent measures

We gathered two classes of dependent measures: objective measures derived from the system logs and video recordings, and subjective measures gathered from the questionnaire.

3.3.1 Objective measures

The objective measures were divided into three categories, based on those used in the PARADISE framework [37]. To assess **task success** in this scenario, we checked whether customers were correctly detected to be seeking attention, and whether each customer who wanted a drink received one. The **dialogue quality** measures counted the number of attempted user turns that fell below the speech-recognition confidence threshold (see Section 2.2), and the number of timeouts (i.e., moments where the user failed to provide a recognised input when one was expected). Finally, the **dialogue efficiency** measures concentrated on the timing: the time taken for the bartender to acknowledge a customer's bid for attention, the number of system turns, the number of times the robot asked the customer for a drink order, and the duration of the transaction.

3.3.2 Subjective measures

The subjective questionnaire began by asking the participant to rate each of the three interactions on a scale of 1–10, and then asked them to rate the robot and their experience of using it on a number of scales. The survey was based on the GODSPEED questionnaire [5], which is designed to be a standard user measurement tool for human-robot interaction. The survey measured user opinions of the robot on five scales: anthropomorphism (five items), animacy (six items), likeability (six items), perceived intelligence (five items), and perceived safety (three items); the items in the different categories were interleaved. All responses were given on a five-point semantic differential scale, with lower scores corresponding in each case to a more negative assessment of the robot or the interaction.

3.4 Results

3.4.1 Objective results

Table 1a shows the task success results, divided by the scenario. For all 31 participants, the robot detected and attempted to serve the first customer in all scenarios. In scenario 2, the confederate was—correctly—never considered to need attention. In scenario 3, the system detected the second customer in 18 trials, and determined that they wanted attention in 16 trials: the remaining customers were not detected due to a combination of technical vision problems and state-manager rule failure. Overall, of the 109 customers who were determined to need attention, 104 managed to order a drink. All of the unsuccessful transactions were due to technical problems that led to user inputs not being processed.

Scen.	Measure	Count	%
1	Drink served	31/31	100.0
2	Drink served	28/31	90.3
3	Drink #1 served	30/31	96.8
	Drink #2 served	15/16	93.8

(a) Task success

	Mean	Std dev	Min	Max
Low ASR	2.26	1.67	0	6
Timeouts	0.94	2.20	0	11
Response time (ms)	658	2443	9	17920
System turns	5.84	2.87	3	22
Order requests	2.37	2.99	0	20
Duration (s)	49.4	29.6	24.4	164.6

(b) Dialogue quality and efficiency

Table 1: Objective results

Scen.	Mean	Std dev	Min	Max
1	6.65	2.95	2	10
2	6.55	2.79	1	10
3	4.22	3.16	1	10

(a) Scenario quality

Category	Cronbach's α	Mean	Std dev
Anthropomorphism	0.79	2.39	0.75
Animacy	0.83	2.57	0.77
Likeability	0.93	3.73	0.93
Perceived Intelligence	0.84	3.16	0.77
Perceived Safety	0.68	3.56	0.60

(b) GODSPEED questionnaire

Table 2: Subjective results

The results for dialogue quality are shown in the top rows of Table 1b, averaged across all of the 109 drink-ordering transactions. Most transactions included at least one attempted user turn that fell below the ASR confidence threshold, and many also included at least one timeout. Despite this, 74 transactions proceeded with no timeouts; the transactions with a large number of timeouts (≥ 10) were due to input-processing failures as mentioned above.

The bottom rows of Table 1b show the results on the dialogue efficiency measures, again averaged across the 109 transactions. The robot was generally very responsive, often reacting to an attention bid in less than 10 milliseconds; longer response times reflect transactions where the second customer bid for attention while the first drink was being served, and therefore had to wait to be acknowledged. To put these results into context, consider that that a minimal drink-ordering transaction required 3–4 system turns, while the robot arm took 22 seconds to serve a drink. In other words, while many transactions were as efficient as possible, there were also some that took much longer than required.

3.4.2 Subjective results

Table 2a shows the users' judgements of the overall quality of the interaction in the three scenarios, on a scale of 1–10. In general, the participants gave moderately positive ratings to the first two scenarios, and a somewhat more negative rating to the third (two-customer) scenario. There was little correlation among the users' responses to the three judgements ($\alpha = 0.34$).

The overall results from the GODSPEED questionnaire are shown in Table 2b. For each subset of items, we first computed Cronbach's alpha as a measure of internal consistency: as shown in the first column of the table, the consistency for all item categories generally fell into the acceptable range ($\alpha \gtrsim 0.70$). The remaining columns of the table summarise the user responses to each group of questions. The mean responses for anthropomorphism and animacy were around the middle of the five-point semantic differential scale, while the findings for likeability, perceived intelligence, and perceived safety were somewhat above the middle.

Scen.	Function	R^2	Significance
1	$6.65 - 1.54 * \mathcal{N}(\text{SysTurns})$	0.25	SysTurns: $p < 0.01$
2	$6.55 - 1.35 * \mathcal{N}(\text{SysTurns})$	0.21	SysTurns: $p < 0.01$
3	$4.23 + 1.34 * \mathcal{N}(\text{Serve3-2}) - 0.91 * \mathcal{N}(\text{Duration})$	0.10	Serve3-2: $p < 0.05$, Duration: $p \approx 0.14$

Table 3: Predictor functions for scenario quality

3.4.3 Comparing objective and subjective measures

In the preceding sections, we considered a number of objective and subjective measures, all of which varied widely across participants and across trials. We therefore investigated which of the objective measures had the largest effect on users' subjective reactions. Being able to predict subjective user satisfaction from more easily-measured objective properties can be very useful for developers of interactive systems: in addition to making it possible to evaluate systems based on automatically available data without the need for extensive experiments with users, such a performance function can also be used in an online, incremental manner to adapt system behaviour to avoid entering a state that is likely to reduce user satisfaction [20], or can be used as a reward function in a reinforcement-learning scenario [38].

We employed the procedure used in the PARADISE evaluation framework [37] to explore the relationship between the subjective and objective factors. The PARADISE model uses iterative, stepwise multiple linear regression to predict subjective user satisfaction based on objective measures representing the performance dimensions of task success, dialogue quality, and dialogue efficiency, resulting in a predictor function of the following form:

$$Satisfaction = \sum_{i=1}^{n} w_i * \mathcal{N}(m_i)$$

The m_i terms represent the value of each measure, while the $\mathcal{N}$ function transforms each measure into a normal distribution using z-score normalisation. Stepwise linear regression produces coefficients (w_i) describing the relative contribution of each predictor to the user satisfaction. If a predictor does not contribute significantly, its w_i value becomes zero after the stepwise process.

We first used the PARADISE procedure to generate predictor functions for the scenario judgements (Table 2a), using the objective results from the relevant scenario as initial factors. The resulting functions are shown in Table 3. The R^2 column indicates the percentage of the variance that is explained by the predictor function, while the *Significance* column gives significance values for each term in the function. The functions for the first two scenarios are very similar: in both cases, the only significant predictor was the number of system turns, which had a negative effect on the judgement, explaining over 20% of the variance. For Scenario 3, the main factors were whether the second customer got served (which had a positive effect), and the duration (which had a negative effect); this function also explains less of the variance (10%).

We then used a similar procedure to generate predictor functions for the responses to the rest of the questionnaire. The objective measures described in Section 3.4.1 were computed on the basis of individual transactions, while each participant provided a single set of responses to the questionnaire; for the purposes of the regression

Category	Function	R^2	Significance
Anthropomorphism	$2.39 - 2.69 * \mathcal{N}(\text{ServeMean}) + 2.20 * \mathcal{N}(\text{Serve3-1}) + 1.96 * \mathcal{N}(\text{Serve2}) + 0.33 * \mathcal{N}(\text{RespTimeMean})$	0.20	RespTimeMean: $p < 0.05$, Serve3-1: $p < 0.05$, Serve2: $p < 0.05$, ServeMean: $p < 0.05$
Animacy	$2.57 - 2.51 * \mathcal{N}(\text{ServeMean}) + 1.94 * \mathcal{N}(\text{Serve2}) + 1.88 * \mathcal{N}(\text{Serve3-1})$	0.09	Serve2: $p < 0.05$, Serve3-1: $p \approx 0.06$, ServeMean: $p \approx 0.07$
Likeability	$3.73 - 3.44 * \mathcal{N}(\text{ServeMean}) + 2.77 * \mathcal{N}(\text{Serve2}) + 2.48 * \mathcal{N}(\text{Serve3-1})$	0.25	Serve2: $p < 0.05$, Serve3-1: $p < 0.05$, ServeMean: $p < 0.05$
Perceived Intelligence	$3.16 - 3.62 * \mathcal{N}(\text{ServeMean}) + 2.75 * \mathcal{N}(\text{Serve2}) + 2.75 * \mathcal{N}(\text{Serve3-1}) + 0.24 * \mathcal{N}(\text{Serve3-2}) - 0.23 * \mathcal{N}(\text{LowASRMean})$	0.29	Serve2: $p < 0.01$, Serve3-1: $p < 0.01$, ServeMean: $p < 0.01$, Serve3-2: $p \approx 0.08$, LowASRMean: $p \approx 0.08$
Perceived Safety	$3.56 - 2.91 * \mathcal{N}(\text{ServeMean}) + 2.21 * \mathcal{N}(\text{Serve3-1}) + 1.94 * \mathcal{N}(\text{Serve2}) + 1.28 * \mathcal{N}(\text{DurationMean}) - 1.15 * \mathcal{N}(\text{OrderReqMean}) - 0.52 * \mathcal{N}(\text{Serve3-2}) - 0.21 * \mathcal{N}(\text{LowASRMean})$	0.31	DurationMean: $p < 0.05$, Serve3-2: $p < 0.05$, Serve3-1: $p < 0.05$, ServeMean: $p < 0.05$, Serve2: $p \approx 0.06$, OrderMean: $p \approx 0.09$, LowASRMean: $p \approx 0.16$

Table 4: Predictor functions for GODSPEED questionnaire categories

analysis, we therefore used the per-participant means as predictors. Table 4 shows the predictor functions that were derived for each of the classes of subjective measures in this study. For most categories, the main factor was the task success: in almost all cases, the scores tended to be higher when drinks were successfully served in Scenarios 2 and 3, with a negative weight on the mean success score compensating for participants for whom both scenarios were successful. Other factors such as the response time and the number of order requests also appear in some functions, but with much lower weights. Most of the predictor functions explain 20-30% of the variance in the questionnaire scores, with the exception of the function for animacy which explains less than 10%.

3.5 Discussion

The overall objective results of this study indicate that the system was generally successful at detecting customers who wanted attention and at serving their drinks. Despite the minimal instructions given to the participants, nearly all of them succeeded in attracting the bartender's attention and ordering a drink. The failures were largely due to easily remedied, low-level technical problems (such as threshold settings or modules behaving improperly) rather than to any higher-level problem with the overall system. While the results for dialogue quality and efficiency suggest that there is room for improvement, it is encouraging that many drink-ordering transactions were successful.

The subjective results are also encouraging: despite the simplicity of the scenario, participants gave the system positive scores for likeability and perceived intelligence, and also gave an overall positive assessment of the interactions in Scenarios 1 and 2. The PARADISE evaluation found that the main contributors to the subjective judgements were task success and dialogue efficiency. The R^2 values for the predictor functions, while in line with those from similar studies [e.g., 13, 20, 38], were generally low, indicating that the users' subjective judgements were also affected by factors other than the objective measures considered here. We are currently analysing the video recordings of the interactions and will use these recordings as the basis for additional measures such as the word error rate from the speech recogniser; we expect that adding such measures will increase the R^2 values.

4. CONCLUSIONS AND FUTURE WORK

We have presented a robot bartender that is designed to work in dynamic, multi-party social situations and have described the architecture and components of the system. We then presented the findings from a user evaluation of the integrated system. The results of this study confirm that users were generally able to order a drink from the bartender in a range of social situations, and also suggest that the main factors influencing the users' subjective opinions were the task success and the dialogue efficiency. These findings provide a baseline for use in follow-up evaluations, and also suggest the areas to focus on for subsequent versions of the system.

Short-term updates to the system include improving the robustness of the input processing to decrease the amount of user speech that is discarded and to increase the number of customers that are detected. We are also currently integrating an alternative high-level decision-making component that uses a policy trained through reinforcement learning to select appropriate system behaviour based on states inferred from the low-level input sensors, using techniques similar to those employed in [11, 32].

In the next user evaluation, we will assess the impact of the social behaviours directly by implementing a version of the system that behaves as in Interaction 1 in Figure 2 and comparing it to the current system. We will also compare the system using the trained RL policy to the current system. A limitation of the current study is that the scenarios were always presented in the same order. The main goal of this study was to test the initial integrated system in a range of conditions, so we do not think that this compromises the overall results; however, we will be sure to counterbalance the scenario order in follow-up studies. Also, in this study participants filled out the full GODSPEED questionnaire series once at the end of all the interactions. In future studies, we will select items from the series that are particularly relevant to the bartender scenario, such as perceived intelligence. Using a shorter questionnaire would also the participants to rate each interaction individually, which would also allow for finer-grained analysis of the results.

In the longer term, we will update all of the components of the system to allow it to support more complex scenarios involving larger numbers of customers in more dynamic scenarios, including customers in groups and dialogues incorporating more of the ordering phenomena found in natural bar interactions [16], such as follow-up questions from the bartender and taking payment. This will involve enhancements to all of the system components as described in Section 2. The updated system will be evaluated in a study similar to this one; the more complex scenarios should also allow the human-robot interactions behaviour to be compared with those found in the human-human data.

5. ACKNOWLEDGEMENTS

The research leading to these results has received funding from the European Union's Seventh Framework Programme (FP7/2007–2013) under grant agreement no. 270435, JAMES: Joint Action for Multimodal Embodied Social Systems, http://james-project.eu/. We thank the ICMI reviewers for their constructive comments, and our JAMES colleagues for useful discussion and collaboration.

6. REFERENCES

[1] A. Argyros and M. Lourakis. 3D tracking of skin-colored regions by a moving stereoscopic observer. *Applied Optics*, 43(2):366–378, Jan. 2004.

[2] W. Bainbridge, J. Hart, E. Kim, and B. Scassellati. The benefits of interactions with physically present robots over video-displayed agents. *International Journal of Social Robotics*, 3:41–52, 2011. doi: 10.1007/s12369-010-0082-7.

[3] H. Baltzakis and A. Argyros. Propagation of pixel hypotheses for multiple objects tracking. In *Proceedings of ISVC 2009*, Nov. 2009.

[4] H. Baltzakis, M. Pateraki, and P. Trahanias. Visual tracking of hands, faces and facial features of multiple persons. *Machine Vision and Applications*, pages 1–17, 2012. doi: 10.1007/s00138-012-0409-5.

[5] C. Bartneck, D. Kulić, E. Croft, and S. Zoghbi. Measurement instruments for the anthropomorphism, animacy, likeability, perceived intelligence, and perceived safety of robots. *International Journal of Social Robotics*, 1:71–81, 2009. doi: 10.1007/s12369-008-0001-3.

[6] D. Bohus and E. Horvitz. Dialog in the open world: platform and applications. In *Proceedings of ICMI-MLMI 2009*, pages 31–38, Nov. 2009. doi: 10.1145/1647314.1647323.

[7] C. Breazeal. Socially intelligent robots. *interactions*, 12(2):19–22, 2005. doi: 10.1145/1052438.1052455.

[8] G. Castellano, I. Leite, A. Pereira, C. Martinho, A. Paiva, and P. W. McOwan. Affect recognition for interactive companions: challenges and design in real world scenarios. *Journal on Multimodal User Interfaces*, 3(1):89–98, 2010. doi: 10.1007/s12193-009-0033-5.

[9] K. Dautenhahn. Socially intelligent robots: dimensions of human-robot interaction. *Philosophical Transactions of the Royal Society B: Biological Sciences*, 362(1480):679–704, 2007. doi: 10.1098/rstb.2006.2004.

[10] R. E. Fikes and N. J. Nilsson. STRIPS: A new approach to the application of theorem proving to problem solving. *Artificial Intelligence*, 2:189–208, 1971. doi: 10.1016/0004-3702(71)90010-5.

[11] M. Frampton and O. Lemon. Recent research advances in reinforcement learning in spoken dialogue systems. *The Knowledge Engineering Review*, 24(4):375–408, 2009. doi: 10.1017/S0269888909990166.

[12] S. S. Ge and M. J. Matarić. Preface. *International Journal of Social Robotics*, 1(1):1–2, 2009. doi: 10.1007/s12369-008-0010-2.

[13] M. Giuliani, M. E. Foster, A. Isard, C. Matheson, J. Oberlander, and A. Knoll. Situated reference in a hybrid human-robot interaction system. In *Proceedings of INLG 2010*, 2010.

[14] T. Horf, R. Roller, and S. Wilske. MiCo: The robotic bartender for mini-cocktails. http://www.coli.uni-saarland.de/courses/lego-04/page.php?id=barkeeper, 2004.

[15] A. Hunt and S. McGlashan. Speech recognition grammar specification version 1.0. W3C recommendation, W3C, Mar. 2004.

[16] K. Huth. Wie man ein Bier bestellt. Master's thesis, Universität Bielefeld, 2011.

[17] A. Isard and C. Matheson. Rhetorical structure for natural language generation in dialogue. In *Proceedings of SemDial 2012*, 2012.

[18] A. Kapoor, W. Burleson, and R. W. Picard. Automatic prediction of frustration. *International Journal of Human-Computer Studies*, 65 (8):724–736, 2007. doi: 10.1016/j.ijhcs.2007.02.003.

[19] S. Larsson and D. Traum. Information state and dialogue management in the TRINDI dialogue move engine toolkit. *Natural Language Engineering*, 6(3&4):323–340, 2000. doi: 10.1017/S1351324900002539.

[20] D. J. Litman and S. Pan. Designing and evaluating an adaptive spoken dialogue system. *User Modeling and User-Adapted Interaction*, 12(2–3):111–137, 2002.

[21] W. C. Mann and S. A. Thompson. Rhetorical structure theory: Toward a functional theory of text organization. *Text*, 8(3):243–281, 1988.

[22] E. Márquez Segura, M. Kriegel, R. Aylett, A. Deshmukh, and H. Cramer. How do you like me in this: User embodiment preferences for companion agents. In *Proceedings of IVA 2012*, Sept. 2012.

[23] T. Masuda and D. Misaki. Development of Japanese green tea serving robot "T-Bartender". In *Proceedings of ICMA 2005*, volume 2, pages 1069–1074, July 2005. doi: 10.1109/ICMA.2005.1626700.

[24] Y. Matsusaka, T. Tojo, and T. Kobayashi. Conversation robot participating in group conversation. *IEICE Transactions on Information and Systems*, 86(1):26–36, 2003.

[25] B. Mutlu, T. Shiwa, T. Kanda, H. Ishiguro, and N. Hagita. Footing in human-robot conversations: how robots might shape participant roles using gaze cues. In *Proceedings of HRI 2009*, pages 61–68, 2009. doi: 10.1145/1514095.1514109.

[26] M. Pateraki, H. Baltzakis, and T. P. Visual tracking of hands, faces and facial features as a basis for human-robot communication. In *Proceedings of the IROS 2011 Workshop on Visual Tracking and Omnidirectional Vision*, September 2011.

[27] M. Pateraki, H. Baltzakis, and P. Trahanias. Using Dempster's rule of combination to robustly estimate pointed targets. In *Proceedings of ICRA 2012*, May 2012.

[28] R. P. A. Petrick and F. Bacchus. A knowledge-based approach to planning with incomplete information and sensing. In *Proceedings of AIPS-2002*, pages 212–221, Apr. 2002.

[29] R. P. A. Petrick and F. Bacchus. Extending the knowledge-based approach to planning with incomplete information and sensing. In *Proceedings of KR-2004*, pages 613–622, June 2004.

[30] R. P. A. Petrick and M. E. Foster. What would you like to drink? recognising and planning with social states in a robot bartender domain. In *Proceedings of CogRob 2012*, 2012.

[31] M. Rickert. *Efficient Motion Planning for Intuitive Task Execution in Modular Manipulation Systems*. Dissertation, Technische Universität München, 2011.

[32] V. Rieser and O. Lemon. *Reinforcement Learning for Adaptive Dialogue Systems: A Data-driven Methodology for Dialogue Management and Natural Language Generation*. Springer, 2011. doi: 10.1007/978-3-642-24942-6.

[33] Robotics Library. URL http://roblib.sf.net/.

[34] M. Sigalas, H. Baltzakis, and P. Trahanias. Visual tracking of independently moving body and arms. In *Proceedings of IROS '09*, Oct. 2009.

[35] A. Vinciarelli, M. Pantic, and H. Bourlard. Social signal processing: Survey of an emerging domain. *Image and Vision Computing*, 27 (12):1743–1759, 2009. doi: 10.1016/j.imavis.2008.11.007.

[36] J. Wainer, D. J. Feil-Seifer, D. A. Shell, and M. J. Matarić. Embodiment and human-robot interaction: A task-based perspective. In *Proceedings of IEEE RO-MAN 2007*, pages 872–877, Aug. 2007. doi: 10.1109/ROMAN.2007.4415207.

[37] M. Walker, C. Kamm, and D. Litman. Towards developing general models of usability with PARADISE. *Natural Language Engineering*, 6(3&4):363–377, 2000. doi: 10.1017/S1351324900002503.

[38] M. A. Walker. An application of reinforcement learning to dialogue strategy selection in a spoken dialogue system for email. *Journal of Artificial Intelligence Research*, 12:387–416, 2000.

[39] M. White. Efficient realization of coordinate structures in Combinatory Categorial Grammar. *Research on Language and Computation*, 4(1):39–75, 2006. doi: 10.1007/s11168-006-9010-2.

Changes in Verbal and Nonverbal Conversational Behavior in Long-Term Interaction

Daniel Schulman
College of Computer and Information Science
Northeastern University
Boston, MA
schulman@ccs.neu.edu

Timothy Bickmore
College of Computer and Information Science
Northeastern University
Boston, MA
bickmore@ccs.neu.edu

ABSTRACT

We present an empirical investigation of conversational behavior in dyadic interaction spanning multiple conversations, in the context of a developing interpersonal relationship between a health counselor and her clients. Using a longitudinal video corpus of behavior change counseling conversations, we show systematic changes in verbal and nonverbal behavior during greetings (within the first minute of conversations). Both the number of prior conversations and self-reported assessments of the strength of the interpersonal relationship are predictive of changes in verbal and nonverbal behavior.

We present a model and implementation of nonverbal behavior generation for conversational agents that incorporates these findings, and discuss how the results can be applied to multimodal recognition of conversational behavior over time.

Categories and Subject Descriptors

H.5.2 [**Information Interfaces and Presentations**]: User Interfaces—*Graphical user interfaces, Interaction styles, Natural language, Theory and methods*

General Terms

Design, Experimentation, Human Factors

Keywords

conversational agent, long-term interaction, multimodal interaction

1. INTRODUCTION

As conversational agents spend more time with people and work in roles in which multiple interactions are required (such as in education or counseling), it is important that the multimodal interactions they have with users are as natural as possible — not only within a given conversation but between conversations over time. This is not only important to provide users with an experience that is as natural and similar to their interactions with other people as possible, but may be crucial if agents are to succeed in those roles that require long-term interactions. Longitudinal adaptations in multimodal conversational behavior may be key for maintaining user engagement over time, such as retention in a year-long health behavior change intervention, or cognitive involvement in the fiftieth lesson that a pedagogical agent delivers.

To inform the design of such agents, we are interested in studying verbal and nonverbal behavior in face-to-face conversation between people — including such things as hand gestures, gaze cues, and posture shifts — focusing on how this behavior changes over time as a function of interaction history and the nature of the evolving interpersonal relationship between the interactants. Interaction history includes the number, pattern, and purpose of the series of conversations two interactants have had. Interpersonal relationship includes such longitudinal constructs as trust, intimacy, and working relationship (such as therapeutic alliance in healthcare). These two variables — history and relationship — are related, but often separate factors in influencing the behavior of dyads over time [31].

An understanding of longitudinal changes in human conversational behavior is also important for building multimodal interfaces that can recognize subtle variations in user behavior that signal changes in cognitive engagement, trust, or therapeutic alliance, or which indicate that a user is about to discontinue use of a system (e.g., withdraw from an online course or drop out of a weight loss program).

In this paper, we present an observational study of conversational behavior in a longitudinal video corpus of dyadic interaction between a health counselor and her clients. We focus on behavior occurring within conversation openings, defined here as the first minute of conversations. Openings are a particularly important segment of conversation, in which effects of relationship status may be most pronounced. At the beginning of a conversation, participants' beliefs about their interpersonal relationship may be communicated and/or negotiated [11]. Prior studies that have examined differences in behavior across multiple conversation showed that such differences were larger at the beginning of conversations [25, 26].

Our analyses yield models that predict certain patterns of nonverbal behavior based on interaction history and relationship status. We then describe a model and implementation of behavior generation for conversational agents which incorporates these results, and discuss future work and im-

ICMI'12, October 22–26, 2012, Santa Monica, California, USA.
Copyright 2012 ACM 978-1-4503-1467-1/12/10 ...$15.00.

plications for multimodal recognition of nonverbal conversational behavior over time.

2. BACKGROUND AND RELATED WORK

2.1 Conversational Behavior in Long-Term Interaction

Several prior studies have reported differences in behavior in dialogue between interactants who have had a substantial number of prior conversations, and those who have had few or none. Most such work is cross-sectional and compares, for example, dyads of friends with (different) dyads of strangers. A cross-sectional study may show differences between friends and strangers, but has limited ability to show a pattern of change over time. Cross-sectional studies also cannot separate changes over time from differences between dyads. For example, a difference in nonverbal behavior between friends and strangers may be explained as either a change that occurs as people become friends, or as a baseline difference that predicts whether a dyad will become friends.

Planalp and Benson showed that observers are able to discriminate, with 79% accuracy, audiotaped conversations between friends from conversations between acquaintances. When asked what cues they used, observers reported that friends referred more often to mutual knowledge, showed higher content intimacy, sounded more relaxed, interrupted each other more often, and had more equal distribution of floor time, compared to acquaintances [21].

Cassell et al. compared direction-giving dialogues between friends and between strangers in a cross-sectional study [7]. Strangers used more explicit acknowledgments than friends when giving or receiving information. Strangers also used more nonverbal behavior related to coordination: head nods and mutual gaze were more likely to occur during acknowledgments.

Tickle-Degnen and Rosenthal propose a model of dyadic rapport that deepens over time [30, 31], and consists of three components: mutual attentiveness, positivity, and coordination. The relative importance of these components is predicted to vary throughout the course of the relationship, with coordination increasing and positivity decreasing. They suggest that components of rapport can be observed via correlates in nonverbal behavior. A meta-analysis indicated that a participants' evaluation of their partner's level of positivity was positively associated with the partners' nonverbal behaviors including forward trunk leaning, smiling, nodding, direct body orientation, and uncrossed arms.

In a series of observational studies, Schulman and Bickmore report changes in verbal and nonverbal behavior across multiple conversations. While longitudinal, these studies examine only a limited range of behaviors relative to the present study. Participants had faster articulation rates on discourse markers in later conversations [25]. Participants also used more posture shifts at the beginning of a conversation than the end, and this decrease was significantly more rapid in later conversations [26].

2.2 Conversational Agents in Long-Term Interaction

Bickmore introduced and explored the concept of "relational agents": computer agents designed to form long-term social-emotional relationships with their users [4]. As an implementation of this concept, he created a conversational agent that used various conversational behaviors intended to promote an interpersonal relationship with a user, including small talk [24], humor, empathetic messages, and reciprocal self-disclosure [2]. Bickmore's relational agent implementation was focused on identifying particular messages which, when delivered appropriately during conversation, would promote a strong user-agent relationship.

Several researchers have demonstrated (e.g., [12]) that the nonverbal behavior of agents can affect user-agent rapport, focusing on short-term rapport within a single conversation. The nonverbal behaviors associated with improved rapport may change across multiple conversations [31, 29], suggesting that this work could be meaningfully extended toward long-term interaction.

3. THE EXERCISE COUNSELING CORPUS

Our corpus for this work is a longitudinal video corpus of weekly face-to-face conversations between a human counselor (a certified exercise trainer) and clients (Figure 1). The corpus contains up to six sessions per client, resulting in 32 conversations (mean duration 15.6 minutes), comprising approximately 8.3 hours of recorded video and approximately 100,000 words of spoken dialogue.

This data was collected with the goal of modeling changes in verbal and nonverbal behavior — including both the counselor's behavior and the client's — which occur across these six sessions. Behavior change counseling is an area for which conversational agents have been repeatedly applied (e.g., [4]), and nonverbal behavior is associated with the development of the client-counselor relationship [29].

We recruited clients (N=6, 5 female) who stated they did not currently exercise regularly. The same counselor conducted all conversations, and in each conversation attempted to encourage the client to increase his or her daily physical activity. All conversations were held in the same room, with both client and counselor seated in office chairs, and were videotaped from three angles. The participants were informed the conversations would be videotaped and examined, but were not told what behaviors were being investigated.

After each conversation, both partcipants completed (separately) questionnaires to assess their interpersonal relationship. We used the short revised Working Alliance Inventory (WAI-SR) [13]. This instrument is an assessment of therapeutic alliance [5], a model of interpersonal relationship specific to counseling and psychotherapy, and including components of agreement on overall goals of counseling, specific tasks, and interpersonal bond or rapport. Strong therapeutic alliance is predictive of positive counseling outcomes [17].

There is evidence of the development of strong counselor-client interpersonal relationships over time: therapeutic alliance increases across sessions, both as reported by clients (from mean 3.7 in the first session to mean 4.7 in the last, on a 1–5 scale), and by the counselor (from 2.6 to 3.8).

4. METHODS

The goal of our analysis was to identify whether there were systematic changes in counselor and client nonverbal behavior across conversations, as a function of interaction history (the number of conversations, and whether the current conversation is the last), relationship strength (mea-

Figure 1: The Exercise Counseling Corpus: Samples from 1st, 3rd, and 6th conversations

sured by therapeutic alliance), or both. We did not attempt to account for all variability in behavior, and substantial unexplained variability remains after our analysis.

A one-minute segment of each conversation was selected, beginning from the first point at which both participants were judged to be fully seated; participants sat facing each other immediately after entering the room in all conversations. The resulting 32 minutes of video were manually annotated for various nonverbal behaviors (detailed below) using ANVIL [14]. A word-aligned orthographic transcription of the corpus, performed for previous work [25], was used to identify segments where each participant was speaking.

4.1 Outcome Variables

We chose the following set of outcome variables for analysis based on those behaviors which prior work suggested might show changes associated with varying interpersonal relationship:

- *The proportion of time spent speaking*: friends are reported to share speaking time more equally than strangers [21].
- *The number of gaze-aways during speech*: the amount of gaze-away during speech is reported to be associated with topic intimacy [1].
- *The proportion of time, when not speaking, spent nodding*: friends are reported to use less nodding for acknowledgement than strangers [7]. Restricting to time when not speaking controls for varying opportunity to show acknowledgment in different videos.
- *The proportion of time spent smiling or frowning*, or more generally with the mouth in a non-neutral position: increased facial expressivity is associated with higher immediacy [3].
- *The proportion of time spent performing self-adaptors, when not speaking*: the use of self-adaptors — self-touching gestures that do not signal meaning in conversation, and often serve to release bodily tension — is associated with perceptions of anxiety [32]. A qualitative inspection of the corpus indicated that most self-adaptors occurred when not speaking.
- *The proportion of time spent performing gestures (other than self-adaptors), during speech*: frequent and expressive gestures are associated with immediacy [3], and most hand gestures co-occur with speech.
- *The proportion of time spent with eyebrows raised or lowered, during speech*: eyebrows raises and frowns are a component of displays of affect and other facial expressivity, associated with immediacy.

A preliminary analysis indicated no significant changes in behavior within a single one-minute video. Therefore, all outcome variables are aggregates of behaviors over a video clip.

4.2 Coding of Nonverbal Behavior

The following behaviors were coded in order to determine values for the outcome variables for each of the 32 one-minute video clips.

Gaze.

An event was coded whenever a participant looked away from the partner's eyes, in any direction (up, down, or sideways).

Eyebrows.

An event was coded whenever a participant raised or lowered his or her eyebrows away from a neutral facial expression.

Head Movement.

An event was coded for any head movement which caused any part of the head to move at least two inches in any direction. However, nodding, shaking, and other rhythmic and repetitive movements were always coded. Each event was categorized as one of: nod (up-and-down movement), jerk (single quick upward movement), back (movement away from the partner), forward (toward the partner), turn (rotation either left or right), or tilt (leaning to either side).

Mouth Shape.

An event was coded whenever a participant's mouth took a shape that differed from a neutral facial expression (e.g.,

Table 1: Interrater reliability for coding of nonverbal behavior

Behavior	Cohen's κ
Gaze-away	0.71
Eyebrows	0.65
Head movement (occurrence)[a]	*0.68*
Head movement (categorized)	0.67
Mouth	0.81
Gesture (occurrence)[a]	*0.71*
Gesture (categorized)[a]	*0.57*
Gesture (self-adaptor)[b]	0.91

[a] not used in subsequent analysis
[b] a composite of several categories

corners up or down, lips protruded or retracted), other than to open during speech.

Hand Gesture.
Based on semiotic categories as described by McNeill [19], gestures were coded as deictic, iconic, emblematic, beat, self-adaptor, or "other".

4.3 Interrater Reliability

Three randomly-selected videos, containing sessions with three different clients, were coded separately by the primary author and by a second coder who was not involved in the development of the coding manual. The start and end times of all coded events were aligned to the nearest quarter second, and Cohen's κ was computed, treating a quarter second segment as one observation. Reliability was considered acceptable when $\kappa \geq 0.65$.

Table 1 summarizes the results. For head movement and hand gesture, Cohen's κ is reported separately for coding the occurrence of an event at the same time, and for coding the same event category at the same time. Reliability was low for categorized hand gestures: beat, iconic, and deictic gestures were all frequently confused, and emblematic gestures were rare. Combining all categories other than "adaptor" yielded good reliability, and all subsequent analysis uses only the categories of self-adaptor and non-adaptor gestures.

4.4 Analysis

For each outcome variable listed in 4.1, we fit a series of regression models. Ordinary linear regression is inappropriate here, as it assumes that observations are independent, whereas here conversations are grouped within dyads. We use generalized linear mixed-effect regression [18], an extension of ordinary linear regression that accounts for grouped data by adding "random effects", or per-group means that are assumed to be normally distributed around the population mean. We treat counselor and client behavior as separate but correlated per-conversation outcome variables, and include separate per-dyad means for the counselor and client, which may also be correlated.

We considered four variants of this model for each behavior, differing in the set of predictors included. All models include two predictors, modeling change over time: the number of prior conversations, and whether the current conversation is the last conversation for that dyad.[1] From this basic model, we consider:

A. The predictors above, with the added assumption that the effect of these predictors is the same on the counselor and the client.

B. As in A, and including self-reported therapeutic alliance from the previous conversation.

C. As in A, but with no assumption that effects on the client and counselor are the same.

D. As in B, but with no assumption that effects on the client and counselor are the same.

The models were fit to the data using Bayesian estimation with weak prior distributions: normal distributions with high variance (10^{10}) for fixed effects of parameters and inverse Wishart distributions (3 d.f.) for the dyad-level and conversation-level covariance matrices. Models were compared using the Deviance Information Criterion (DIC) [28].

The number of gaze-aways during speech was modeled as a Poisson-distributed count outcome with an added Gaussian random effect to allow for overdispersion [6]. For all other behaviors, the proportion of time during which the behavior was observed was modeled as a Gaussian-distributed outcome, following two transformations: first, by "squeezing" all values toward 0.5 slightly to avoid proportions exactly equal to 0 or 1 [27], and then by applying the inverse logit function:

$$y' = \text{logit}^{-1}\left(\frac{y * (N-1) + 0.5}{N}\right)$$

where $N = 64$ is the total number of observations.

All results are based on Markov Chain Monte Carlo simulation, performed using JAGS [22] and R 2.13.1 [23]. For each model and each behavior, 1000 samples were drawn from each of 3 different runs, and convergence was tested with Gelman-Rubin [10] diagnostics.

5. RESULTS

Table 2 gives descriptive statistics for each outcome variables, and the best-fitting regression models are summarized in Table 3. Gaze-aways, nodding, and smiling and frowning were best predicted by models in which interaction history and relationship strength have the same effect on counselor and client behavior. However, the proportion of time spent speaking, the use of both self-adaptor and non-adaptor gestures, and eyebrow raises and frowns were best predicted by models in which effects on the counselor and client differed.

Gaze.
The number of gaze-aways during speech is predicted about equally well by models with and without therapeutic alliance, although both give similar predictions: There is an increase in the rate of gaze-aways over time, which reverses in the last session (Figure 2).

[1] This predictor was added after observing that the final sessions appeared qualitatively different from others in the corpus. Omitting these sessions gives estimates similar to Table 3, although the interaction of therapeutic alliance and number of conversations on nodding (Figure 3) is only near-significant.

Table 3: Regression coefficients for best-fitting models. Bolded coefficients indicate a 95% credible interval which excludes 0.

Behavior	Mouth	Gaze	Nod	Speech	Adaptor	Gesture	Brows
Model	A	A	B	C	C	C	C
Intercept (counselor)	-0.43	**-3.74**	**-1.48**	**-1.00**	**-3.24**	**-2.85**	**-3.48**
Intercept (client)	-0.37	**-2.84**	**-2.30**	0.04	**-2.78**	**-2.75**	**-2.86**
Session (counselor)	-0.16	**0.20**	0.06	**-0.27**	**0.29**	**-0.37**	**-0.34**
Session (client)				**0.13**	-0.06	0.14	0.14
Last Session (counselor)	**0.97**	**-0.80**	-0.44	**0.93**	-0.31	1.20	0.65
Last Session (client)				-0.36	-1.15	0.28	0.28
Alliance			**-0.28**				
Alliance×Session			**0.06**				
σ_{dyad} (counselor)	0.78	0.62	0.53	0.55	0.56	0.64	0.62
σ_{dyad} (client)	0.95	0.78	0.91	0.54	1.21	0.82	0.70
ρ_{dyad}	**0.60**	-0.02	0.23	-0.00	0.03	-0.03	-0.10
σ_{conv} (counselor)	0.56	0.56	0.45	0.65	0.93	0.92	1.06
σ_{conv} (client)	0.96	0.40	0.87	0.39	1.35	1.11	1.21
ρ_{conv}	**0.66**	0.03	0.07	**-0.62**	0.10	-0.19	**-0.33**

Table 2: Descriptive statistics for all behaviors

	Counselor		Client		Overall	
	Mean	SD	Mean	SD	Mean	SD
Mouth[a]	0.35	0.18	0.37	0.24	0.36	0.21
Gaze-Away[b]	0.04	0.06	0.11	0.08	0.08	0.08
Nod[c]	0.24	0.08	0.14	0.10	0.19	0.10
Speech[a]	0.20	0.10	0.57	0.12	0.39	0.21
Adaptor[c]	0.09	0.07	0.11	0.18	0.10	0.14
Gesture[d]	0.04	0.04	0.12	0.11	0.08	0.09
Brows[d]	0.02	0.05	0.10	0.09	0.06	0.08

[a] Proportion of time
[b] Count of events during speech
[c] Proportion of time not speaking
[d] Proportion of time speaking

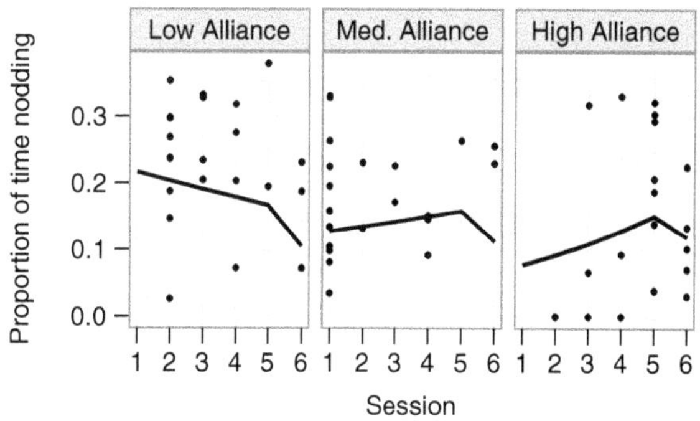

Figure 3: Nodding when not speaking, by session and alliance. The lines are model-based predictions for the average participant, at 25th, 50th, and 75th percentile therapeutic alliance.

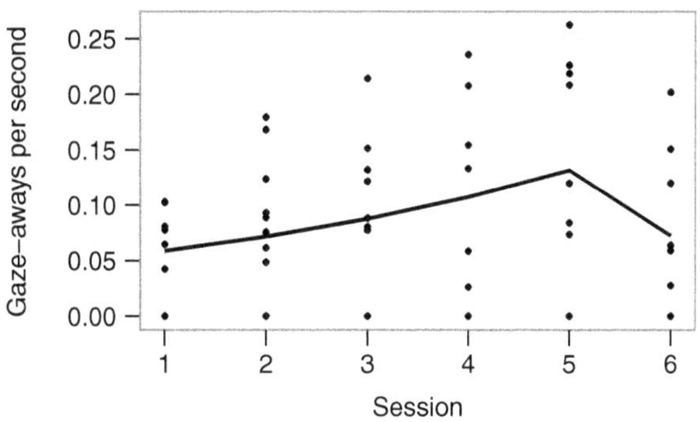

Figure 2: Gaze-aways during speech, by session. There were multiple observations of no gaze-aways by a participant: 6 in first sessions, and 3–4 in each of second through last sessions. The line is the model-based prediction for the average participant.

Nodding.
The proportion of time spent nodding was best predicted by a model which included therapeutic alliance. Participants nodded less when they reported higher therapeutic alliance, but this effect was moderated by the number of sessions: in later sessions, all participants tended to nod more. There was a non-significant trend toward less nodding in the last session (Figure 3).

Mouth.
Participants used fewer non-neutral mouth positions in later sessions, but reversed this trend in the last session (Figure 4).

Speech.
The counselor spoke less in later sessions, and the clients spoke more, but this reversed in the last session for the counselor and there was a non-significant trend for it to reverse for the client.

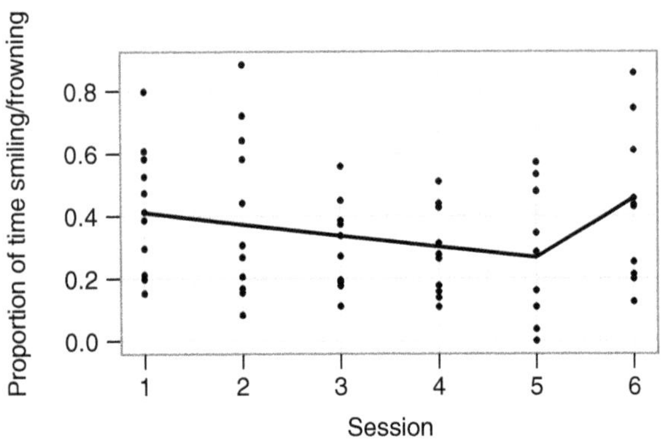

Figure 4: Occurrence of non-neutral mouth positions, by session. The line is the model-based prediction for the average participant.

Self-Adaptors.

The counselor used more self-adaptors in later sessions, but there was no significant trend for clients

Hand Gestures.

The counselor performed fewer non-adaptor gestures in later conversations, but reversed this trend in the last session. There was no significant trend for clients.

Eyebrow Movement.

The proportion of time spent performing eyebrow raises or lowering was predicted poorly by every model. No systematic trends were observed.

6. DISCUSSION

We show significant longitudinal differences in most behaviors investigated. In later conversations, gaze-aways during speech are more common, and less time is spent smiling and frowning. Participants nod more when they report lower therapeutic alliance. The counselor decreases speaking time while the client increases. Most trends reverse in the last conversation.

The results presented here do not fully agree with previous work. Prior (cross-sectional) studies have reported that friends share speaking time more equally than strangers, whereas here the counselor speaks less initially and further decreases her speaking time in later conversations. This may be due to the nature of the conversational task, which is focused on the client's attitudes and behavior.

Our finding of less smiling and frowning over time is broadly in agreement with Tickle-Degnen's model of rapport [31]: positivity is more important in early conversations. In an informal examination of the corpus (during coding) we noted that few of the smiles coded are Duchenne smiles [9]. We conjecture that "performing" appropriately-valenced facial expressions as an indication of empathy may be important for rapport in early conversations.

Cassell et al. report that friends use fewer nods for acknowledgments than strangers [7]. We report an effect of relationship strength: stronger self-reported relationship is associated with less nodding, particularly in early conversations. We conjecture that Cassell et al.'s study, which is cross-sectional, is showing differences between dyads rather than change over time: dyads with a strong relationship (associated with less nodding) are more likely to become and remain friends.

The results we report on the use of hand gesture, including both self-adaptors and other gestures, are difficult to generalize. We see significant change for the counselor only, and these results may blend general and idiosyncratic factors: they may be useful for developing models of this particular counselor rather than more general models of human behavior.

Across nearly all behavior, we report a pattern where the observed change over time reverses in the last conversation. We note that participants were always aware that the sixth conversation was their last, and all dyads had an explicit discussion about the end of their relationship. We conjecture that a final interaction, like an initial interaction, has increased uncertainty about the participants' interpersonal relationship, and this uncertainty is associated with changes in behavior.

7. TOWARD BEHAVIOR GENERATION FOR LONG-TERM INTERACTION

Multiple approaches to behavior generation have been explored, including rule-based (BEAT [8] and NVBG [16]), probabilistic generation from a model of an annotated corpus [20], or generation as part of grammar-based natural language generation [15]. In this section, we explore the feasibility of implementing our reported findings in a generation system.

Our approach is to implement these findings as adjustments to the probability of generating a behavior event. This can be done with any underlying behavior generation system that outputs generation probabilities for each behavior event (or can be modified to do so). However, we make some additional assumptions: First, we assume that the results found here hold constant throughout a conversation. Second, we assume that these results combine additively with other predictors of behavior. This second assumption allows us to implement these findings as simple adjustments, ignoring how the baseline probability is generated.

As a proof of concept, we have implemented "Rhythm", a simple rule-based nonverbal behavior generator. Rhythm inputs the text of agent utterances, annotated with relevant contextual information (e.g., the number of previous conversations), and outputs synchronized nonverbal behavior annotations. The baseline probability of generating a behavior event (p, below) is produced by rules given in other work. Rhythm currently implements the following longitudinal changes:

- The probability of generating a smile or frown changes as a function of the interaction history, where s is the number of prior conversations, and f is 1 if the agent believes this is a final conversation and 0 otherwise:

$$p' = \text{logit}^{-1}(\text{logit}(p) - 0.16s + 0.97f)$$

- The probability of generating a gaze-away changes as a function of interaction history:

$$p' = 1 - (1 - p)^{\exp(0.2s - 0.8f)}$$

- The probability of generating a headnod changes as a function of interaction history and the agent's be-

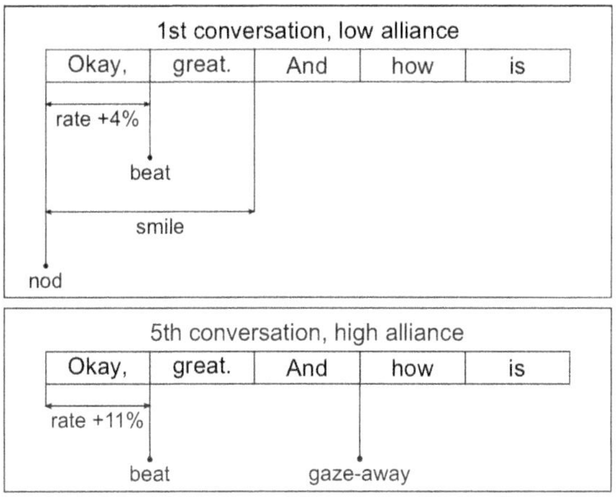

Figure 5: Sample behavior generation for the utterance "Okay, great. And how is your exercise going?"

liefs about the strength of the user-agent relationship, where a is therapeutic alliance, standardized to a z-score:

$$p' = \text{logit}^{-1}(\text{logit}(p) + 0.06s - 0.44f - 0.28a + 0.06sa)$$

- Following [26], the probability of generating a posture shift changes as a function of interaction history and minutes from conversation start (m):

$$p' = \text{logit}^{-1}(\text{logit}(p) + 0.16s - 0.03m - 0.02sm)$$

In addition, following [25], the articulation rate of discourse markers increases in later conversations. Figure 5 shows an example of behavior generated by Rhythm, on identical sentences, in the context of a first conversation between a dyad with high therapeutic alliance, and a fifth conversation between a dyad with low therapeutic alliance. In the first conversation, Rhythm generates a head nod and a smile, which do not appear in the fifth. In the fifth conversation, the articulation rate on the first word ("Okay") is increased, and an additional gaze-away is generated.

8. CONCLUSIONS AND FUTURE WORK

We have described systematic changes in nonverbal behavior that occur over time, and are also associated with changes in relationship quality independent of time. These findings have been implemented in a nonverbal behavior generation system. We plan to conduct a longitudinal evaluation study which is intended to validate this generation model, to (partially) validate these findings in a larger population, and to examine the effect of these changes across multiple conversations on user-agent rapport, user engagement, and the perceived behavioral realism of an agent.

The findings raise potential research issues both for applications focused on the generation of realistic conversational behavior, and those focused on the multimodal recognition of conversational behavior in the context of long-term human-agent interaction. Models which assume that a single interaction is representative of *all* interactions may give misleading results. For example, our results indicate a greater tendency to gaze away from a conversation partner in later conversations; a model of engagement based on gaze might interpret this change (possibly erroneously) as decreased engagement.

The difference between a final conversation and earlier conversations was an unexpected finding that does not, to our knowledge, appear in prior work, and it merits further investigation. Under the assumption that these changes occur because participants know the session will end their relationship, we suggest a new research question: will other changes in the nature of a conversational task or the nature of an interpersonal relationship (for example, from a professional and impersonal relationship to a friendship) produce similar effects? As very long-term user-agent interaction is explored, such changes may become more common.

Our results show that conversational behavior in long-term interaction is a complex product of the people involved and multiple aspects of their interpersonal relationship. The findings reported could be investigated largely because of features of the exercise counseling corpus relative to those used in other work: conversations in the corpus vary on multiple dimensions, including the participants involved and the history of their interaction, and the corpus is augmented with self-report measures of interpersonal relationship. Validating these results in a larger population — and extending them to other aspects of long-term interaction — will require very large, high-quality, and well-annotated corpora of face-to-face conversation. The exercise counseling corpus, at 8 hours of video, is small enough to limit the research questions that can be investigated, but already large enough to make manual annotation a major effort. Automated and semi-automated annotation will be necessary for further research in this area.

This work illustrates that producing realistic behavior in conversational agents should take many new contextual factors into account, including characteristics of the user, the agent, their relationship, and the conversational task.

9. ACKNOWLEDGEMENTS

The authors thank Jenna Zaffini for her work in collecting the corpus, Kshitij Lohani for assistance in coding, and to the members of the Relational Agents Group for much help and useful discussion.

This material is based upon work supported by the National Science Foundation under Grant No. ISS-0545932. Any opinions, findings, and conclusions or recommendations expressed in this material are those of the authors and do not necessarily reflect the views of the National Science Foundation.

10. REFERENCES

[1] A. Abele. Functions of gaze in social interaction: Communication and monitoring. *Journal of Nonverbal Behavior*, 10(2):83–101, June 1986.

[2] I. Altman and D. Taylor. *Social penetration: The development of interpersonal relationships.* Holt, Rinehart and Winston, 1973.

[3] P. A. Andersen. Nonverbal immediacy in interpersonal communication. In A. W. Siegman and S. Feldstein, editors, *Multichannel Integrations of Nonverbal Behavior*, pages 1–36. Lawrence Erlbaum, Hillsdale, NJ, 1985.

[4] T. Bickmore. *Relational Agents: Effecting Change through Human-Computer Relationships.* PhD thesis,

Massachusetts Institute of Technology, Cambridge, MA, 2003.
[5] E. S. Bordin. Theory and research on the therapeutic working alliance: New directions. In A. O. Horvath and L. S. Greenberg, editors, *The Working Alliance: Theory, Research, and Practice*, chapter 1, pages 13–37. Wiley, New York, NY, 1994.
[6] N. E. Breslow. Extra-Poisson variation in Log-Linear models. *Applied Statistics*, 33(1):38+, 1984.
[7] J. Cassell, A. J. Gill, and P. A. Tepper. Coordination in conversation and rapport. In *Workshop on Embodied Language Processing*, pages 41–50. Association for Computational Linguistics, June 2007.
[8] J. Cassell, H. H. Vilhjálmsson, and T. Bickmore. BEAT: the behavior expression animation toolkit. In *Proceedings of the 28th annual conference on Computer graphics and interactive techniques*, SIGGRAPH '01, pages 477–486, New York, NY, USA, 2001. ACM.
[9] P. Ekman, R. J. Davidson, and W. V. Friesen. The Duchenne smile: Emotional expression and brain physiology II. *Journal of Personality and Social Psychology*, 58(2):342–353, 1990.
[10] A. Gelman and D. B. Rubin. Inference from iterative simulation using multiple sequences. *Statistical Science*, 7(4):457–472, Nov. 1992.
[11] E. Goffman. *Relations in public; microstudies of the public order.* Basic Books, 1971.
[12] J. Gratch, A. Okhmatovskaia, F. Lamothe, S. Marsella, M. Morales, R. van der Werf, and L.-P. Morency. Virtual rapport. In J. Gratch, M. Young, R. Aylett, D. Ballin, and P. Olivier, editors, *Intelligent Virtual Agents*, volume 4133, chapter 2, pages 14–27. Springer Berlin Heidelberg, Berlin, Heidelberg, 2006.
[13] R. L. Hatcher and A. J. Gillaspy. Development and validation of a revised short version of the working alliance inventory. *Psychotherapy Research*, 16(1):12–25, Jan. 2006.
[14] M. Kipp. ANVIL — a generic annotation tool for multimodal dialogue. *Proceedings of the 7th European Conference on Speech Communication and Technology (Eurospeech)*, pages 1367–1370, 2001.
[15] S. Kopp, P. Tepper, and J. Cassell. Towards integrated microplanning of language and iconic gesture for multimodal output. In *Proceedings of the 6th international conference on Multimodal interfaces*, ICMI '04, pages 97–104, New York, NY, USA, 2004. ACM.
[16] J. Lee and S. Marsella. Nonverbal behavior generator for embodied conversational agents. In J. Gratch, M. Young, R. Aylett, D. Ballin, and P. Olivier, editors, *Intelligent Virtual Agents*, volume 4133, chapter 20, pages 243–255. Springer Berlin Heidelberg, Berlin, Heidelberg, 2006.
[17] D. J. Martin, J. P. Garske, and M. K. Davis. Relation of the therapeutic alliance with outcome and other variables: a meta-analytic review. *Journal of consulting and clinical psychology*, 68(3):438–450, 2000.
[18] C. E. McCulloch and J. M. Neuhaus. Generalized linear mixed models. In *Encyclopedia of Biostatistics.* John Wiley & Sons, Ltd, 2005.
[19] D. McNeill. *Hand and Mind: What Gestures Reveal about Thought.* University Of Chicago Press, Aug. 1992.
[20] M. Neff, M. Kipp, I. Albrecht, and H. P. Seidel. Gesture modeling and animation based on a probabilistic re-creation of speaker style. *ACM Trans. Graph.*, 27(1):1–24, 2008.
[21] S. Planalp and A. Benson. Friends' and acquaintances' conversations I: Perceived differences. *Journal of Social and Personal Relationships*, 9(4):483–506, Nov. 1992.
[22] M. Plummer. JAGS: A program for analysis of Bayesian graphical models using Gibbs sampling. In *Proceedings of the 3rd International Workshop on Distributed Statistical Computing*, 2003.
[23] R Development Core Team. *R: A Language and Environment for Statistical Computing.* R Foundation for Statistical Computing, Vienna, Austria, 2009.
[24] K. P. Schneider. *Small talk: Analyzing phatic discourse.* Hitzeroth, 1988.
[25] D. Schulman and T. Bickmore. Modeling behavioral manifestations of coordination and rapport over multiple conversations. In J. Allbeck, N. Badler, T. Bickmore, C. Pelachaud, and A. Safonova, editors, *Intelligent Virtual Agents*, volume 6356 of *Lecture Notes in Computer Science*, chapter 14, pages 132–138. Springer Berlin / Heidelberg, Berlin, Heidelberg, 2010.
[26] D. Schulman and T. Bickmore. Posture, relationship, and discourse structure. In H. Vilhjálmsson, S. Kopp, S. Marsella, and K. Thórisson, editors, *Intelligent Virtual Agents*, volume 6895 of *Lecture Notes in Computer Science*, pages 106–112, Berlin, Heidelberg, 2011. Springer Berlin / Heidelberg.
[27] M. Smithson and J. Verkuilen. A better lemon squeezer? maximum-likelihood regression with beta-distributed dependent variables. *Psychological Methods*, 11(1):54–71, Mar. 2006.
[28] D. J. Spiegelhalter, N. G. Best, B. P. Carlin, and A. Van Der Linde. Bayesian measures of model complexity and fit. *Journal of the Royal Statistical Society: Series B (Statistical Methodology)*, 64(4):583–639, Oct. 2002.
[29] L. Tickle-Degnen and E. Gavett. Changes in nonverbal behavior during the development of therapeutic relationships. In P. Philippot, R. S. Feldman, and E. J. Coats, editors, *Nonverbal behavior in clinical settings*, chapter 4, pages 75–110. Oxford University Press, New York, NY, USA, 2003.
[30] L. Tickle-Degnen and R. Rosenthal. Group rapport and nonverbal behavior. In C. Hendrick, editor, *Group processes and intergroup relations*, volume 9 of *Review of Personality and Social Psychology*, pages 113–136. Sage, Newbury Park, CA, 1987.
[31] L. Tickle-Degnen and R. Rosenthal. The nature of rapport and its nonverbal correlates. *Psychological Inquiry: An International Journal for the Advancement of Psychological Theory*, 1(4):285–293, 1990.
[32] P. H. Waxer. Nonverbal cues for anxiety: an examination of emotional leakage. *Journal of abnormal psychology*, 86(3):306–314, June 1977.

I Already Know Your Answer: Using Nonverbal Behaviors to Predict Immediate Outcomes in a Dyadic Negotiation

Sunghyun Park, Jonathan Gratch, and Louis-Philippe Morency
Institute for Creative Technologies
University of Southern California
12015 Waterfront Drive, Playa Vista, CA 90094
{park, gratch, morency} @ict.usc.edu

ABSTRACT

Be it in our workplace or with our family or friends, negotiation comprises a fundamental fabric of our everyday life, and it is apparent that a system that can automatically predict negotiation outcomes will have substantial implications. In this paper, we focus on finding nonverbal behaviors that are predictive of immediate outcomes (acceptances or rejections of proposals) in a dyadic negotiation. Looking at the nonverbal behaviors of the respondent alone would be inadequate since ample predictive information could also reside in the behaviors of the proposer, as well as the past history between the two parties. With this intuition in mind, we show that a more accurate prediction can be achieved by considering all the three sources (multimodal) of information together. We evaluate our approach on a face-to-face negotiation dataset consisting of 42 dyadic interactions and show that integrating all three sources of information outperforms each individual predictor.

Categories and Subject Descriptors

H.1.2 [**Models and Principles**]: User/Machine Systems – *human information processing.*
H.4.0 [**Information Systems Applications**]: General.
I.2.1 [**Artificial Intelligence**]: Applications and Expert Systems.
I.5.4 [**Pattern Recognition**]: Applications – *signal processing.*

General Terms

Algorithms, Experimentation, Human Factors, Theory.

Keywords

Negotiation, Machine Learning, Multimodal, Behavior Prediction, Human Communication, Social Behavior.

1. INTRODUCTION

Negotiation is a complex and dynamic process in which two or more parties, often having non-identical preferences or agenda, work together to reach a mutual agreement. Be it in our workplace or with our family or friends, negotiation comprises such a fundamental fabric of our everyday life that we sometimes engage in the act without even being consciously aware of it. It is then apparent that a system that can automatically predict negotiation outcomes will have substantial implications. For instance, such a system could function as a real-time decision support tool to directly help a person during a negotiation process or it could be useful in training a person to be a better negotiator.

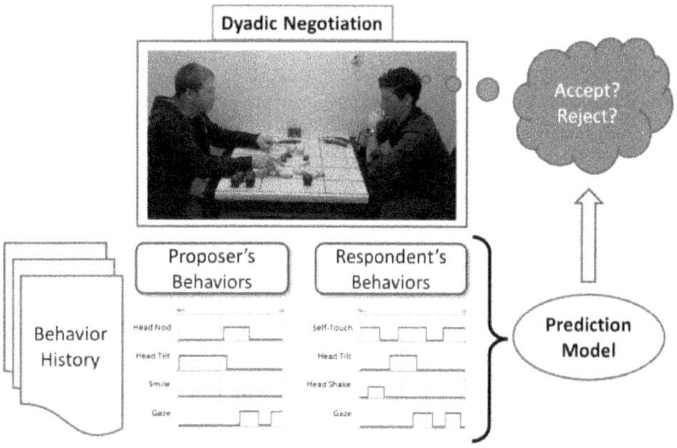

Figure 1. Multimodal factors for immediate negotiation outcome predictions including the nonverbal behaviors of the proposer and of the respondent, as well as the history information between the two parties.

Negotiation has long been and still is an active topic for research, and the reader can find a brief history of the psychological study of negotiation in [6]. For researchers endorsing a traditional cognitive view, negotiation is essentially a decision-making process, the people involved dispassionate negotiators, and the outcome a result of dynamics governed by rational strategies. There are also researchers who put more emphasis on affective aspects [11]. Some have tried to understand the general role of affect in different stages of negotiation [5] while others have investigated the influence of mood [3, 8], emotion [1, 20], and personality [4]. In addition, researchers focusing on social contexts further deepen our understanding of negotiation dynamics [14, 18].

The affective and social perspectives of negotiation give intuitions that nonverbal behaviors can give clues to the ongoing state of a negotiation process. Ambady and Rosenthal [2] showed that much inference is possible just by observing "thin slices" of nonverbal behaviors, and Curhan and Pentland [10] applied the idea in a simulated employment negotiation scenario where they found that certain speech features within the first five minutes of negotiation were predictive of the overall negotiation outcome in the end.

Although negotiation research abounds in literature, there is still limited work that investigated nonverbal behaviors in the context of negotiation, let alone computational models. In this paper, our main focus is on finding nonverbal behaviors that are related to negotiation outcomes and exploring the possibility of building an automatic system for the outcome predictions. Moreover, whereas Curhan and Pentland's work was on predicting the overall negotiation outcomes in the end, we focus on making shallow predictions of immediate outcomes (acceptances or rejections) for individual proposals made during negotiation.

2. NONVERBAL FACTORS IN FACE-TO-FACE NEGOTIATION

To predict whether the respondent will accept or reject a proposal during negotiation, looking at the nonverbal behaviors of the respondent alone would be inadequate since ample predictive information could also reside in the behaviors of the proposer, as well as the past history between the two parties (see Figure 1).

2.1 Proposer's and Respondent's Behaviors

In a business negotiation setting, Niemeier et al. [19] investigated various nonverbal communication channels including proxemics, body postures, gestures, facial expressions and paralanguage, arguing that they could hint at the emotional attitudes of the negotiators. In a study of cooperativeness and competitiveness during negotiation, Johnson [16, 17] similarly found that cooperativeness is expressed through "warm" behaviors including a soft tone of voice, smiles, interested facial expressions, direct eye contact, open gestures, close spatial distance, and an occasional soft touch, while competitiveness is expressed through "cold" behaviors including tense postures, avoidance of eye contact, closed gestures, distant spatial distance, and avoidance of touching.

Head movements can also provide rich information. For instance, the proposer could show eagerness by nodding his head while staring at the respondent, giving more emotional burden to the respondent if not accepting the offer. Similarly, the respondent could shake his head while listening to the proposal or tilt his head in confusion. Another interesting nonverbal behavior in the context of negotiation is self-touching, which Ekman et al. [13] call a type of adaptors. According to Harrigan et al. [15], the overall consensus is that negative affect, such as anxiety or discomfort, triggers self-touching behaviors.

2.2 History

The history information can be thought of as capturing the ongoing relationship between the negotiators. For instance, in the absence of other contexts, if the respondent has mostly rejected the proposer's offers in the past, it would mean something quite different from the opposite case. Moreover, reciprocity can be a good predictor of the outcomes in mixed-motive settings [12].

3. DATASET

In total, 84 undergraduate business students (40 males and 44 females) participated in 42 dyadic negotiation sessions, of which one dyad was discarded because the participants deviated from the experimental procedure. Each session involved same-sex participants to eliminate the influence of gender, and 3 video cameras were placed unobtrusively to record a near-frontal view of each negotiator, as well as an overall side view of the interaction.

In each session, two participants sat face-to-face across each other at opposite ends of a table, on which several types of plastic fruits or vegetables were placed. The participants were randomly assigned to represent one of two different restaurants, which had different pay-off matrices associated with the items on the table. Each participant was told only the pay-off matrix of his/her assigned restaurant, and the participants had 12 minutes to negotiate on how to distribute the items on the table. As an incentive, each participant could receive up to $50 depending on the final points earned by each participant for his/her restaurant.

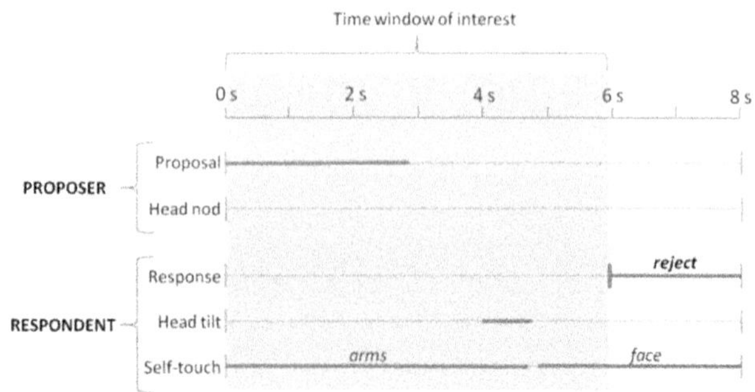

Figure 2. An example of a rejected proposal-response event.

The annotations of nonverbal behaviors were done with ELAN software [7]. Below is a summary of the annotations made.

- *Proposal-response event:* For each negotiation session, all the events of proposal-response pairs were identified. A proposal is defined as an utterance made with a clear offer related to negotiating the items, and if it is followed by a clear utterance of acceptance or rejection, we group the start of the proposal until the end of the matching response as a proposal-response event. A total of 253 proposal-response events were identified, out of which 190 were accepted proposals and 63 were rejected proposals.

Within the time window of each proposal-response event identified, the following nonverbal behaviors were annotated for both of the negotiators in a dyad.

- *Head nod*: Whether there is a vertical downward (or repeated upward and downward) movement of the head.
- *Head shake*: Whether there is a repeated horizontal left and right movement of the head.
- *Head tilt*: Whether there is a rotation of the head to the left or to the right. With a frontal view of the face in 3D coordinates, rotation around the z-axis.
- *Gaze*: Whether the gaze of a negotiator is directed toward the other party, toward the table, or somewhere else.
- *Smile*: Whether a negotiator is smiling or not.
- *Self-touch*: Whether a negotiator is touching his/her own body with his/her hands (e.g. touching the face with the hand). Only the upper portion of the body was visible in the videos.

4. AUTOMATIC PREDICTIONS OF NEGOTIATION OUTCOMES

Our goal is to predict whether the respondent will accept or reject a given proposal. Thus, for each proposal-response event, we are only interested in the nonverbal behaviors within the time window from the start of the proposal until the start of the response (see Figure 2). This time window is called the *time window of interest* henceforth.

4.1 Feature Encoding

Each of the annotated nonverbal behaviors defined in Section 3 was converted into binary features. For example, the proposer's binary smile feature will be whether the proposer smiled or not within the *time window of interest*. We encoded the binary features for both the proposer's and the respondent's nonverbal behaviors. We also added another feature called *binary response time* to the respondent's feature set.

- *Binary response time*: For each proposal-response event, the response time was computed as *the time when the respondent started uttering acceptance or rejection* minus *the time when the proposer finished uttering his/her proposal*. After taking the means of the response times for all accepted and for all rejected cases, the midpoint of the two means was found and used as a threshold (1.4 seconds in our experiments). Using this threshold, the response time in each proposal-response event was converted into a binary feature. (*The time when the respondent started uttering acceptance or rejection* was also his/her first utterance made in the proposal-response event for about 89% of the time, which means something for implementing real-time systems).

To capture the history information, we used the following 2 features.

- *Negotiation history*: The total net response history of the respondent at the time of the proposal-response event (+1 and -1 for each previous acceptance and rejection respectively). Normalized to z-scores.

- *Response time history*: The mean of all the previous response times of the respondent at the time of the proposal-response event. This feature could help better understand the *binary response time* feature by providing the general response time characteristic / habit of each negotiator. Normalized to z-scores.

We note that the features were extracted from all the three sources of information (the proposer's nonverbal behaviors, the respondent's nonverbal behaviors, and history). No acoustic features were used because the video cameras, which were used to record the negotiation interactions, yielded poor audio quality.

4.2 Prediction Model and Experimental Methodology

For the prediction model, a support vector machine (SVM) classifier with the radial basis function kernel was trained and tested using Chang and Lin's LIBSVM library [9]. A subset of features were selected to be included in each source of information (proposer, respondent, and history) based on the prediction performance as individual features and also as a group. Also, various explorative methods have been performed including greedy forward feature subset selection.

In order to make balanced sample sets for predictor (classifier) training and testing, all of the 63 samples of the rejected proposal-response events were combined with 63 randomly selected samples of the accepted events, and 3 such randomly balanced sets were created. Each randomly balanced set was again randomly separated into 4 folds with almost an equal number of accept and reject samples. It is worth noting that no 2 folds contained the samples from the same negotiation session. In other words, the 4 folds were created such that they were all session-independent to one another. Then, 4-fold testing hold-out validation was performed with 1 hold-out fold for validation to find the optimal parameters using a grid search technique and another hold-out fold for testing. All the prediction results were averaged over 12 test results (3 sets × 4-fold cross-validation).

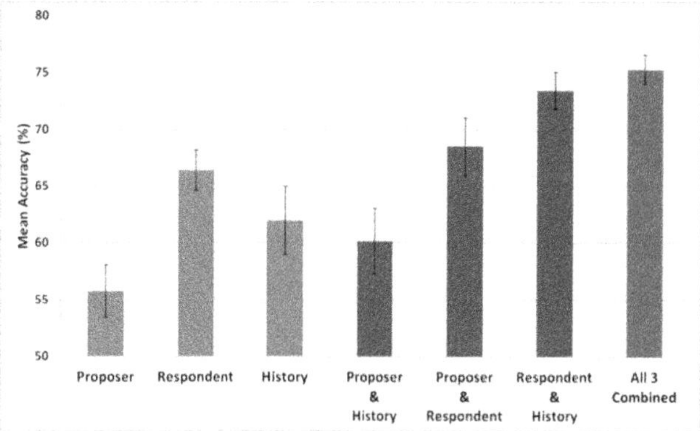

Figure 3. Mean accuracies of negotiation outcome predictions using multimodal (multi-source) features. The error bars show standard errors.

5. RESULTS AND DISCUSSIONS

Figure 3 shows the results of prediction accuracies for using different combinations of the 3 sources of information, and a general trend of performance improvement was evident when combining more modalities (note that chance is 50%). Except for the combination of the proposer and history features, all the other possible combinations of different sources of information showed significant improvements over using an individual source alone. Especially, using all the three sources of information together yielded the best result with the accuracy of over 75%, which emphasizes the importance of taking into account all the three sources of information for making negotiation outcome predictions. Paired-sample t-tests showed that the differences between the results of the 3-source classifier and those of all other classifiers were statistically significant at $p < 0.01$, except for the respondent+history classifier which was still at $p < 0.05$. In addition, the respondent+history classifier's performance was statistically significant over the individual classifiers using just the respondent ($p < 0.01$) or the history ($p < 0.05$) information. The proposer+respondent classifier's accuracy was also statistically significant at $p < 0.01$ compared to the classifier with just the proposer's information.

The prediction results using individual features from each source of information (proposer's behaviors, respondent's behaviors, and history information) are summarized in Table 1. From the proposer's behaviors, head tilt was slightly predictive of the outcome. Although head nod performed at chance, the prediction made by combining the two features together was higher than that made with head tilt alone. From the respondent's nonverbal behaviors, the *binary response time*, self-touch and head tilt were all very useful in the outcome predictions. When the three features were combined together, the prediction rate notably improved to over 66%. Lastly, both of the two history features also proved useful in the predictions.

Although not shown here, head nod and head shake behaviors of the respondent, if experimented individually, also yielded prediction accuracies of close to 57%. However, they did not perform too well when combined with other features together. In addition, a lot of head nods and shakes occurred too close to actual responses, which defeats the purpose of making the predictions in the first place. Smiles were not useful because

Table 1. Negotiation outcome predictions using individual features.

Source	Feature	Accuracy (%)	F_1
Proposer	Head Nod	50.00	0.3532
	Head Tilt	54.17	0.4549
	Combined	**55.73**	**0.5047**
Respondent	Head Tilt	58.33	0.5275
	Self-Touch	56.51	0.4933
	Binary Resp. Time	60.16	0.5572
	Combined	**66.41**	**0.6579**
History	Neg. History	63.02	0.6229
	Resp. Time History	59.64	0.5748
	Combined	**61.98**	**0.6156**

people tend to smile in so many different situations (with happy smiles, polite smiles, embarrassed smiles, etc.), and gaze was also not useful in our scenario possibly because the participants mostly had their eyes on the negotiating items on the table.

From the proposer's nonverbal behaviors, head tilt seems to indicate the proposer's lack of confidence (thus more likely to be rejected) of the respondent's answer as the proposal is being made. From the respondent's behaviors, the reason that the *binary response time* feature is useful seems clear. The more the respondent likes a proposal, the sooner he/she accepts it. As for self-touch, it seems to hint at the respondent's discomfort either of the proposal or of the fact that he/she will soon reject it. Head tilt of the respondent might mean that he/she needs to think more deeply about the proposal, which eventually could yield more rejections than acceptances. From the history information, the result of the *negotiation history* feature is interesting because it seems to capture the relationship between the negotiators in a dyad. The more someone rejected your proposals, the more you can expect him/her to reject your offers in the future. In the context of our experimental scenario, the feature might have captured the cooperativeness or competiveness between the negotiators.

6. CONCLUSION AND FUTURE WORK

In this paper, we showed that it is important to consider multiple sources of information (especially nonverbal behaviors) to predict a proposal's immediate outcome (acceptance or rejection) during a dyadic negotiation. For future work, more nonverbal behaviors in negotiation contexts could be explored, and the influence of another source of information, namely mutual behaviors, could also be examined. Our results suggest that machine analysis of human negotiations have potential to add fundamental insight into how people negotiate and provide practical tools to benefit human negotiators.

7. ACKNOWLEDGMENT

This material is based upon work supported by the National Science Foundation under Grant No. 0917321 and the U.S. Army Research, Development, and Engineering Command. Any opinions, findings, and conclusions or recommendations expressed in this material are those of the author(s) and do not necessarily reflect the views of the National Science Foundation or the Government.

8. REFERENCES

[1] Allred, K., Mallozzi, J., Matsui, F., and Raia, C. 1997. The influence of anger and compassion on negotiation performance. *Org. Beh. and Hum. Dec. Proc.* 70, 3, 175-187.

[2] Ambady, N. and Rosenthal, R. 1992. Thin slices of expressive behavior as predictors of interpersonal consequences: A meta-analysis. *Psychological Bulletin* 111, 2, 256-274.

[3] Baron, R. 1990. Environmentally induced positive affect: Its impact on self-efficacy, task performance, negotiation, and conflict. *Jour. of Applied Soc. Psyc.* 20, 5, 368-384.

[4] Barry, B. and Friedman, R. 1998. Bargainer characteristics in distributive and integrative negotiation. *Journal of Personality and Social Psyc.* 74, 2, 345-359.

[5] Barry, B. and Oliver, R. 1996. Affect in dyadic negotiation: A model and propositions. *Organizational Behavior and Human Decision Processes* 67, 2, 127-143.

[6] Bazerman, M., Curhan, J., Moore, D., and Valley, K. 2000. Negotiation. *Annual Review of Psychology* 51, 279-314.

[7] Brugman, H. and Russel, A. 2004. Annotating multimedia / multi-modal resources with ELAN. In *Proc. of the Fourth Int'l. Conf. on Lang. Res. and Eval.* LREC 2004. 2065-2068.

[8] Carnevale, P. and Isen, A. 1986. The influence of positive affect and visual access on the discovery of integrative solutions in bilateral negotiation. *Org. Beh. and Hum. Dec. Proc.* 37, 1, 1-13.

[9] Chang, C.-C. and Lin, C.-J. 2011. LIBSVM: A library for support vector machines. *ACM Trans. on Intelligent Systems and Technology (TIST)* 2, 3, 27:1 - 27:27.

[10] Curhan, J. and Pentland, A. 2007. Thin slices of negotiation: Predicting outcomes from conversational dynamics within the first 5 minutes. *Jour. of Applied Psyc.* 92, 3, 802-811.

[11] Druckman, D., and Olekalns, M. 2008. Emotions in negotiation. *Group Decision and Negotiation* 17, 1, 1-11.

[12] Dufwenberg, M. and Kirchsteiger, G. 2004. A theory of sequential reciprocity. *Games and Eco. Beh.* 47, 2, 268-298.

[13] Ekman, P. and Friesen, W. 1969. The repertoire of nonverbal behavior. *Semiotica* 1, 49-98.

[14] Greenhalgh, L., and Chapman, D. 1998. Negotiator relationships. *Group Dec. & Neg.* 7, 6, 465-489.

[15] Harrigan, J., Kues, J., and Weber, J. 1986. Impressions of hand movements: Self-touching and gestures. *Perceptual and Motor Skills* 63, 2, 503-516.

[16] Johnson, D. 1971. Effects of warmth of interaction, accuracy of understanding, and the proposal of compromises on listener's behavior. *Jour. of Couns. Psyc.* 18, 3, 207-216.

[17] Johnson, D., McCarty, K., and Allen, T. 1976. Congruent and contradictory verbal and nonverbal communications of cooperativeness and competitiveness in negotiations. *Communication Research* 3, 275-292.

[18] Kramer, R. and Messick, D. 1995. *Negotiation as a Social Process*. Thousand Oaks, CA, US: Sage Publications, Inc.

[19] Niemeier, S. 1997. Nonverbal expressions of emotions in a business negotiation. In *The Language of Emotions*, S. Niemeier and R. Dirven, Eds. John Benjamins Publishing Company, Amsterdam/Philadelphia, 277-306.

[20] Van Kleef, G., De Dreu, C., and Manstead, A. 2004. The interpersonal effects of emotions in negotiations. *Journal of Personality and Social Psyc.* 87, 4, 510-528.

Modeling Dominance Effects on Nonverbal Behaviors Using Granger Causality

Kyriaki Kalimeri
University of Trento, CIMEC
Bruno Kessler Foundation
kalimeri@fbk.eu

Bruno Lepri
Bruno Kessler Foundation
MIT Media Lab
lepri@fbk.eu

Oya Aran
Idiap Research Institute
oaran@idiap.ch

Dinesh Babu Jayagopi
Idiap Research Institute
djaya@idiap.ch

Daniel Gatica-Perez
Idiap Research Institute
Ecole Polytechnique Federal de Lausanne (EPFL)
gatica@idiap.ch

Fabio Pianesi
Bruno Kessler Foundation
pianesi@fbk.eu

ABSTRACT

In this paper we modeled the effects that dominant people might induce on the nonverbal behavior (speech energy and body motion) of the other meeting participants using Granger causality technique. Our initial hypothesis that more dominant people have generalized higher influence was not validated when using the DOME-AMI corpus as data source. However, from the correlational analysis some interesting patterns emerged: contradicting our initial hypothesis dominant individuals are not accounting for the majority of the causal flow in a social interaction. Moreover, they seem to have more intense causal effects as their causal density was significantly higher. Finally dominant individuals tend to respond to the causal effects more often with complementarity than with mimicry.

Categories and Subject Descriptors

I.5.1 [**Computing Methodologies**]: PATTERN RECOGNITION—*Models*

Keywords

Social and Group Interaction, Multimodal Fusion and Integration, Granger Causality

1. INTRODUCTION

One of the basic mechanisms of social interaction and one of the fundamental dimensions for analyzing the group dynamics and the formation of a group social structure is dominance [6]. In social psychology, dominance is usually seen in two ways: (i) as a personality characteristic (a trait) [13] or (ii) a sign of a person's hierarchical position within a group [13]. Several social psychology studies have shown that individuals higher in trait dominance tend to attain more influence in face-to-face interactions [3, 17]. In the last years dominance aroused much interest in the domain of social interaction from sensor data [1]. Different researchers have dealt with the automatic detection of the most dominant person and/or of the least dominant person in small group interactions (e.g. meetings) using nonverbal acoustic and visual cues [10, 11]. Some studies in social psychology [19] confirm that people can respond to dominant behaviors with either mimicry or complementarity behaviors, where the former amounts to a reproduction of the behavior of the dominant person and the latter to an opposite behavior. Recently, some works have started to deal with the automatic detection of mimicry. In [18] the way in which visual and vocal behaviors displayed by two interlocutors can be used to detect and identify visual and vocal mimicry was investigated. On the visual side, they detected the existence of a correlation between the motion intensities of two interacting persons. They were also able to detect similar correlations between vocal features showing that people change their vocal style while interacting with others and that the change is in the direction of mimicry. However, according to Chartrand and Bargh [5], mere correlational approaches are not enough to conclude that person X is mimicking (or complementing) person Y; rather, they can only inform whether X and Y are displaying similar or contrasting behavioural patterns. In order to conclude for the presence of true mimicry/complementarity, a causal relationship must be proven in which the display of a particular behaviour and then person Y mimics (or complements) that behaviour.

In this work, our goal is to automatically model the causal effects that people displaying dominant nonverbal behaviors have on the nonverbal behaviors of the other participants. In order to investigate these effects, we apply Granger causality, an approach that detects and estimates the direction of causal influence in time series analysis. To exemplify this approach, in this work we focus on peoples' nonverbal activity, both vocal and kinesic, detected by means of acoustic and visual cues and the way that affects the nonverbal behavior of other group members. Granger causality [9] is a promising approach to this end: widely used in neuroscience to infer the existence of causal relationships among neural circuits and model causal relationships among temporal se-

ICMI'12, October 22–26, 2012, Santa Monica, California, USA.

ries. To our knowledge, it has been seldom applied to the automatic analysis of human behavior [14, 12] and to social behavior, in particular.

2. THE DOME CORPUS

In our work we exploited a multimodal corpus, DOME, which includes small group conversations with dominance annotations [2].
It contains five-minute non-overlapping slices selected from a subset of meetings of the popular Augmented Multi-party Interaction (AMI) corpus. The DOME corpus has been presented in [2] and used in previous studies for the modeling of dominance based on automatically extracted audio-visual nonverbal cues [1, 11]. Each meeting has four participants. Meetings in the AMI corpus were carried out in a multi-sensor meeting room which contained a table for four participants, a slide screen and a white board. The audio was recorded via several microphones: two circular microphone arrays on the ceiling and on the table, headset and lapel microphones. The video was recorded via seven cameras (see Figure 1 for sample screen shots).

Figure 1: Screen shots from the corpus from the available close-up cameras.

The entire DOME corpus consists of two subsets of meetings, corresponding to 10 hours of meeting data. Following the "thin slice" approach, every meeting has been divided in five-minute non-overlapping meeting segments. The first subset, M1, which is used in this study, contains 58 five-minute meeting segments. The segments were selected from 11 scenario meetings in AMI corpus.

Each meeting segment is annotated by three annotators, who used their own judgements on dominance to rank the meeting participants. No prior definition of dominance is given to the annotators. Each annotator ranked each meeting participant from 1 to 4, with 1 representing the most dominant person, and 4 representing the least dominant person in the meeting. The annotations have been analyzed to assess the agreement between the annotators for the most and least dominant participants. A detailed analysis of the corpus and the annotations can be found in [2].

3. AUDIO-VISUAL CUES EXTRACTION

A solid body of work in social psychology and social computing has documented the role that nonverbal communicative cues play in the expression and perception of dominant behavior [13, 6]. We focus on peoples' nonverbal activity detected by means of acoustic and visual cues and the way that affect the nonverbal behavior of other group members. To this end, we extracted two features: speaking energy and body motion activity.

3.1 Acoustic Cues

The speaking energy was extracted from the four close-talk microphones attached to each of the meeting participants, one per person. In particular, we computed a speaker energy value for each participant using a sliding window at each time step as described in [21]. The value of speaking energy was extracted using the root mean square amplitude of the audio signal over a sliding time window for each audio track. A window of 40 ms was used with a 10 ms time shift.

3.2 Visual Cues

To estimate the nonverbal kinesic behavior of the participants, we have used compressed domain processing [20] in order to extract the motion from the skin colored regions. The motion vectors and residual coding bit rate features are extracted from compressed domain videos. A motion vector of a source block in frame t indicates which predictor block from frame $t-1$ is to be used. The extracted motion vectors are further filtered and for each motion vector a confidence measure is computed by using DCT coefficients that measure the amount of local texture and only the vectors with high confidence are kept. In order to capture finer motion, such as moving lips, etc., we use the residual coding bitrate. After motion compensation, the DCT coefficients of the residual signal, which is the difference between the block to be encoded and its prediction from the reference frame, are quantized and entropy coded. The residual coding bitrate is the number of bits used to encode this transformed residual signal.In combination with the motion vector magnitude, the residual coding bitrate provides complementary evidence for visual activity. The skin-colored blocks in the compressed domain are detected using a Gaussian mixture model to identify hand and head regions of participants, and motion features are computed only on these blocks. We further normalized the motion vector magnitudes and residual coding bitrate, with respect to the average participant and overall activity in the meeting [11]. The final feature representing the amount of motion is computed as the average of normalized motion vector magnitude and residual coding bit rate, and indicates the compressed domain activity levels for the participant for each time frame, with 25 fps frame rate.

4. MODELING DOMINANCE EFFECTS

To understand the direction of the influence flow in social interactions, it is of fundamental importance to distinguish the driver from the recipient. One of the most prominent methods to estimate the direction of the causal influence in time series analysis is the Granger Causality(GC) [9]. This method is based on asymmetric prediction accuracies of one time series on the future of another. In detail, let two time series X_1 and X_2 be defined as,

$$X_1(t) = \Sigma_{j=1}^{p} A_{11,j} X_1(t-j) + \Sigma_{j=1}^{p} A_{21,j} X_2(t-j) + \xi_1(t) \quad (1)$$

$$X_2(t) = \Sigma_{j=1}^{p} A_{21,j} X_1(t-j) + \Sigma_{j=1}^{p} A_{22,j} X_2(t-j) + \xi_2(t) \quad (2)$$

where A is the matrix containing the coefficients of the model and ξ_1,ξ_2 are the residuals of X_1 and X_2 respectively. A time series X_1, is said to Granger-cause X_2 if the inclusion of past observations of X_1 reduces the prediction error of X_2 in a linear regression model of X_2 and X_1, as compared to a model including only the previous observations of X_2. An important aspect of GC is its generalizability to the multivariate case in which the GC of X_1 on X_2 is tested in the context of multiple additional variables (in our scenario the other two meeting participants denoted by W and Z). In this case, X_1 is said to Granger-cause X_2 if knowing X_1 reduces the variance in X_2's prediction error when all the other variables are also included in the model [8].

In our case we defined two systems, one in which the time series X_1, X_2, X_3, X_4 of the system $\mathbf{X}$ refer to the body movement of each of our subjects and a second one in which the time series refer to their speaking activity as described above. To remove every linear trend from the data, all series have been de-trended and their temporal mean has been removed as an initial preprocessing step. We estimated the best order of the multivariate autoregressive model (MVAR) using the Bayesian Information Criterion (BIC) [15]. The estimated model was further checked both (i) to control whether it accounted for a sufficient amount of variance in the data and (ii) using the Durbin-Watson [7] test to validate whether its residuals are serially uncorrelated. Then, once the set of significant lagged values for X_2 is found, the regression is augmented with lagged levels of X_1. Having estimated the G-causality magnitudes, their statistical significance was evaluated via an F-test on the null hypothesis that the coefficients $A_{i,j}$ are zero. If the coefficients in the corresponding $A_{i,j}$ were jointly significantly different from zero, then the causal interaction was considered to be statistically significant. To correct the tests from multiple comparisons, the Bonferroni correction [4] approach was chosen thresholded at $\frac{P}{n(n-1)}$, with P=0.01.

Let our group of participants be a small causal network of four interacting nodes. In causal networks, the nodes represent variables and the directed edges represent causal interactions. A measure of the causal interactivity of a system $\boldsymbol{X}$ is the causal density [16], which is defined as the mean of all pairwise G-causalities between system elements, conditioned on the system's statistically significant interactions.

$$cd(X) \equiv \frac{1}{n(n-1)} \Sigma_{i \neq j} F_{X_i \rightarrow X_j | X_{[ij]}}$$

where $X_{[ij]}$ is the network from which the variables X_i and X_j are omitted. For each of our nodes (i.e. each subject), we estimate the unit causal density $cd_u(i)$ which is the summed causal interactions involving a node i normalized by the number of nodes. Furthermore, to identify nodes with distinctive causal effects on the network dynamics, we estimated the *causal flow* of a subject X_1. The causal flow is defined as the difference between the in-degree and the out-degree of a given node. Therefore, a subject with a high positive causal flow exerts a strong causal influence on the meeting and it can be called a causal *source*. On the other side, a subject with a highly negative causal flow can be called a causal *sink*. From the GC relationships in the causal network, we are only able to determine if the speech/body activity of subject X_1 has a causal effect on the speech/body activity of subject X_2; however, we are not able to discriminate between mimicry and complementarity effects.

5. RESULTS

Initially, we focus our attention on the relationships between influence, behavior and the dominance scores. Our expectation was that more dominant people have generalized higher influence, measured in terms of higher density, positive and higher flow and higher out-flow. For both modalities we computed the Spearman rank correlation between the causal flow and the dominance scores obtained by the 3 annotators. The four participants were ranked according to their score for the different measurements on a slice by slice time basis. In Figure 2, both the distributions for the bodily activity (blue bars), the speech activity (red bars) and the combination of the normalized causal effect of the two modalities (green bars) suggest a tendency of the most dominant people to adapt to the nonverbal behavioral manifestation of the other participants. This evidence is against our initial hypothesis as we expected the less dominant participants to manifest this kind of behavior.

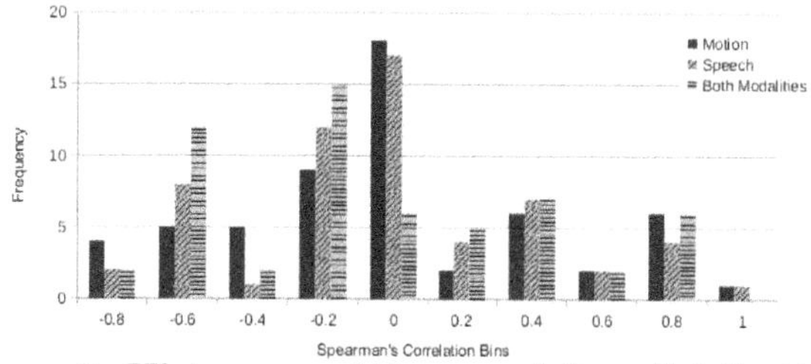

Figure 2: Histogram of the causal flow distribution. From left to right: In blue the bodily activity, in red the speaking activity and in green the joint contribution correlations

Similarly, for both modalities we computed the Spearman rank correlation between the causal density and the dominance scores obtained by the 3 annotators. Again, all ranks are computed on a slice by time slice basis. In Figure 3, the pattern of the causal density has interestingly changed, showing an increase of the positive correlations for both modalities.

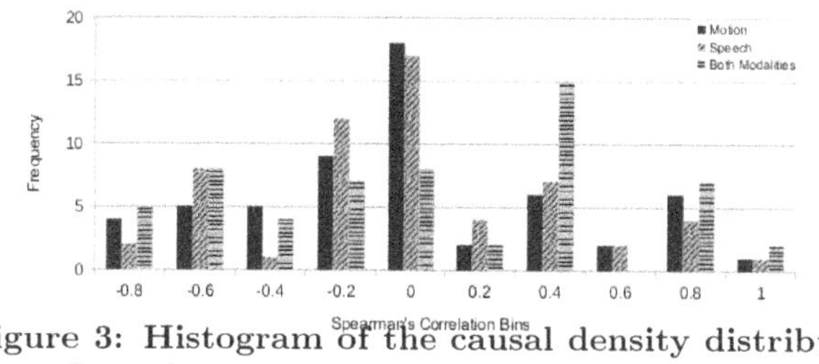

Figure 3: Histogram of the causal density distribution. From left to right: In blue the bodily activity, in red the speaking activity and in green the joint contribution correlations

In both Figure 2 and Figure 3 the peak of the distributions is zero because of the fact that we have considered only the measurements that were statistically significant considering all the others to be zero. As emerges from the correlations between the causality flow and the dominance annotation ranking the most dominant people are not usually the ones that account for the highest quantity of causal flow, in contrast with our initial hypothesis. In order to assess the phenomena of mimicry and complementarity, we investigated the correlation between the time series of the subjects for which we found some significant causal effect. For example, once determined that subject X_1 Granger-causes X_2, we checked if the histogram of the correlation between the time series X_1 and the time series X_2 is positive, possibly suggesting mimicry effects, or is negative, suggesting complementarity ones. The patterns that emerged showed a tendency of the most dominant individuals to reply with complementarity as in most of the cases the correlation was negative. Out of 51 cases we classified 20 mimicry responses and 31 complementarity ones.

6. CONCLUSIONS

In this paper we have employed Granger Causality in the analysis of the effects dominant behavior might on the nonverbal behavior of others in a small group interaction and we further characterized them according to their potential relation to mimicry and complementarity patterns. Using the DOME meeting corpus, the patterns emerged from the correlational analysis are interesting, contradicting our initial hypothesis that dominant individuals do not appear to account for the majority of the causal flow in social interactions, confirming the findings of [12] obtained from the analysis of accelerometer data on a dataset of brainstorming and problem solving tasks. Moreover, dominant individuals seem to have more intense causal effects as their causal density was significantly higher while they tend to respond to the causal effects more often with behavior we hypothesize to be related to complementarity rather than mimicry. The importance of this study lies on the novelty of the proposed model that takes into consideration the causal effects dominant subjects' nonverbal behavior has on the behavior of the other parties of a social interaction, rendering it a promising approach to the potential assessment of more complex behaviors. However, further analysis needs to be carried out in order to confirm the validity of these findings.

7. ACKNOWLEDGEMENTS

Bruno Lepri's research was funded by the Marie Curie-COFUND-7th Framework PERSI project. Oya Aran's research was funded by the Swiss National Science Foundation Ambizione project SOBE ($PZ00P2\_136811$). D. Jayagopi and D. Gatica-Perez thank the support of the SNSF NCCR IM2.

8. REFERENCES

[1] O. Aran and D. Gatica-Perez. Fusing Audio-Visual Nonverbal Cues to Detect Dominant People in Group Conversations. *2010 20th International Conference on Pattern Recognition*, 0:3687–3690, 2010.

[2] O. Aran, H. Hung, and D. Gatica-Perez. A Multimodal Corpus for Studying Dominance in Small Group Conversations. In *LREC workshop on Multimodal Corpora, Malta (LREC MMC'10)*, 2010.

[3] E. J. Aries, C. Gold, and R. H. Weigel. Dispositional and situational influences on dominance behavior in small groups. *Journal of Personality and Social Psychology*, 44(4):779–786, 1983.

[4] Y. Benjamini and Y. Hochberg. Controlling the False Discovery Rate: A Practical and Powerful Approach to Multiple Testing. *Journal of the Royal Statistical Society. Series B (Methodological)*, 57(1):289–300, 1995.

[5] T. L. Chartrand and J. A. Bargh. The chameleon effect: the perception-behavior link and social interaction. *Journal of Personality and Social Psychology*, 76(6):893–910, 1999.

[6] N. E. Dunbar and J. K. Burgoon. Measuring nonverbal dominance. *The sourcebook of nonverbal measures going beyond words*, page 361, 2005.

[7] J. Durbin and G. Watson. Testing for serial correlation in least squares regression.I. *Biometrika*, 37(3):409–428, 1950.

[8] J. Geweke. Measurement of Linear Dependence and Feedback Between Multiple Time Series. *Journal of the American Statistical Association*, 77(378):304–313, 1982.

[9] C. W. J. Granger. Investigating causal relations by econometric models and cross-spectral methods. *Econometrica*, 37(3):424–438, 1969.

[10] H. Hung, D. Jayagopi, C. Yeo, G. Friedland, S. Ba, J.-M. Odobez, K. Ramchandran, N. Mirghafori, and D. Gatica-Perez. Using audio and video features to classify the most dominant person in a group meeting. In *Proceedings of the 15th international conference on Multimedia*, pages 835–838. ACM Press, 2007.

[11] D. B. Jayagopi, H. Hung, C. Yeo, and D. Gatica-Perez. Modeling Dominance in Group Conversations Using Nonverbal Activity Cues. *IEEE Transactions on Audio, Speech {&} Language Processing*, 17(3):501–513, 2009.

[12] K. Kalimeri, B. Lepri, T. Kim, F. Pianesi, and A. Pentland. Automatic modeling of dominance effects using granger causality. In *HBU*, pages 124–133, 2011.

[13] M. S. Mast. Dominance as Expressed and Inferred Through Speaking Time. *Human Communication Research*, 28(3):420–450, 2002.

[14] K. Prabhakar, S. M. Oh, P. Wang, G. D. Abowd, and J. M. Rehg. Temporal causality for the analysis of visual events. In *CVPR*, pages 1967–1974, 2010.

[15] G. Schwarz. Estimating the Dimension of a Model. *The Annals of Statistics*, 6(2):461–464, 1978.

[16] A. K. Seth. A MATLAB toolbox for Granger causal connectivity analysis. *Journal of Neuroscience Methods*, 186(2):262–273, 2010.

[17] J. A. Smith and R. J. Foti. A pattern approach to the study of leader emergence. *The Leadership Quarterly*, 9(2):147–160, 1998.

[18] X. Sun, J. Lichtenauer, M. F. Valstar, A. Nijholt, and M. Pantic. A multimodal database for mimicry analysis. In *Proceedings of the 4th Bi-Annual International Conference of the HUMAINE Association on Affective Computing and Intelligent Interaction (ACII2011)*, Memphis, Tennessee, USA, October 2011.

[19] L. Z. Tiedens and A. R. Fragale. Power moves: complementarity in dominant and submissive nonverbal behavior. Technical Report 3, Graduate School of Business, Stanford University, California 94305-5015, USA. ltiedens@stanford.edu, 2003.

[20] C. Yeo, P. Ahammad, K. Ramchandran, and S. Sastry. High-speed action recognition and localization in compressed domain videos. *IEEE Transactions on Circuits and Systems for Video Technology*, 18(8):1006–1015, 2008.

[21] D. Zhang, D. Gatica-Perez, S. Bengio, and I. McCowan. Modeling individual and group actions in meetings with layered HMMs. *IEEE Transactions on Multimedia*, 8(3):509 – 520, 2006.

Multimodal Human Behavior Analysis: Learning Correlation and Interaction Across Modalities

Yale Song
MIT CSAIL
Cambridge, MA 02139
yalesong@csail.mit.edu

Louis-Philippe Morency
USC ICT
Los Angeles, CA 90094
morency@ict.usc.edu

Randall Davis
MIT CSAIL
Cambridge, MA 02139
davis@csail.mit.edu

ABSTRACT

Multimodal human behavior analysis is a challenging task due to the presence of complex nonlinear correlations and interactions across modalities. We present a novel approach to this problem based on Kernel Canonical Correlation Analysis (KCCA) and Multi-view Hidden Conditional Random Fields (MV-HCRF). Our approach uses a nonlinear kernel to map multimodal data to a high-dimensional feature space and finds a new projection of the data that maximizes the correlation across modalities. We use a multi-chain structured graphical model with disjoint sets of latent variables, one set per modality, to jointly learn both view-shared and view-specific sub-structures of the projected data, capturing interaction across modalities explicitly. We evaluate our approach on a task of agreement and disagreement recognition from nonverbal audio-visual cues using the Canal 9 dataset. Experimental results show that KCCA makes capturing nonlinear hidden dynamics easier and MV-HCRF helps learning interaction across modalities.

Categories and Subject Descriptors

I.5.4 [**Pattern Recognition**]: Applications—*Signal processing*

Keywords

Multimodal signal processing; multi-view latent variable discriminative models; canonical correlation analysis; kernel methods

1. INTRODUCTION

Human communication is often accompanied by multimodal nonverbal cues, such as gestures, eye gaze, and facial expressions. These nonverbal cues play an important role in the way we communicate with others and can convey as much information as spoken language. They complement or substitute for spoken language, help to illustrate or emphasize main points, and provide a rich source of predictive information for understanding the intentions of the others. Automatic analysis of human behavior can thus benefit from harnessing multiple modalities.

From the machine learning point of view, multimodal human behavior analysis continues to be a challenging task, in part because learning the complex relationship across modalities is non-trivial. Figure 1(a) shows a pair of time-aligned sequences with audio and visual features (from [11]; details can be found in Section 4.1). When learning with this type of data, it is important to consider the correlation and interaction across modalities: An underlying correlation structure between modalities may make the amplitude of the signal from one modality different in relation to the signal from another modality, e.g., loud voice with exaggerated gestures. Also, the interaction between modalities may have certain patterns that change the direction in which each sequence may evolve over time.

In this paper, we investigate the hypothesis that transforming the original data to be maximally correlated across modalities, in a statistical sense, and capturing the interaction across modalities explicitly from the transformed data improves recognition performance on human behavior analysis. To this end, we present a novel approach to multimodal data learning that captures complex nonlinear correlations and interactions across modalities, based on KCCA [3] and MV-HCRF [10]. Our approach uses a nonlinear kernel to map multimodal data to a high-dimensional feature space and finds a new projection of the data that maximizes the correlation across modalities. Figure 1(b) shows the projected signals found by KCCA, where the relative importance of gestures 'head shake' and 'shoulder shrug' have been emphasized to make the statistical relevance between the audio and visual signals become as clear as possible. We then capture the interaction across modalities using a multi-chain structured latent variable discriminative model. The model uses disjoint sets of latent variables, one set per view, and jointly learns both view-shared and view-specific sub-structures of the projected data.

We evaluated our approach using the Canal 9 dataset [11], where the task is to recognize agreement and disagreement from nonverbal audio-visual cues. We report that using KCCA with MV-HCRF to learn correlation and interaction across modalities successfully improves recognition performance compared to baseline methods.

2. RELATED WORK

Due to its theoretical and practical importance, multimodal human behavior analysis has been a popular research topic. While audio-visual speech recognition is probably the most well known and successful example [6], multimodal affect recognition has recently been getting considerable attention [12]. Bousmalis *et al.* [1] proposed a system for spontaneous agreement and disagreement recognition based only on prosodic and gesture cues, as we did here. They used an HCRF to capture the hidden dynamics of the multimodal cues. However, their approach did not consider the correlation and interaction across modalities explicitly.

Canonical correlation analysis (CCA) has been successfully applied to multimedia content analysis [3, 13]. Hardoon *et al.* [3]

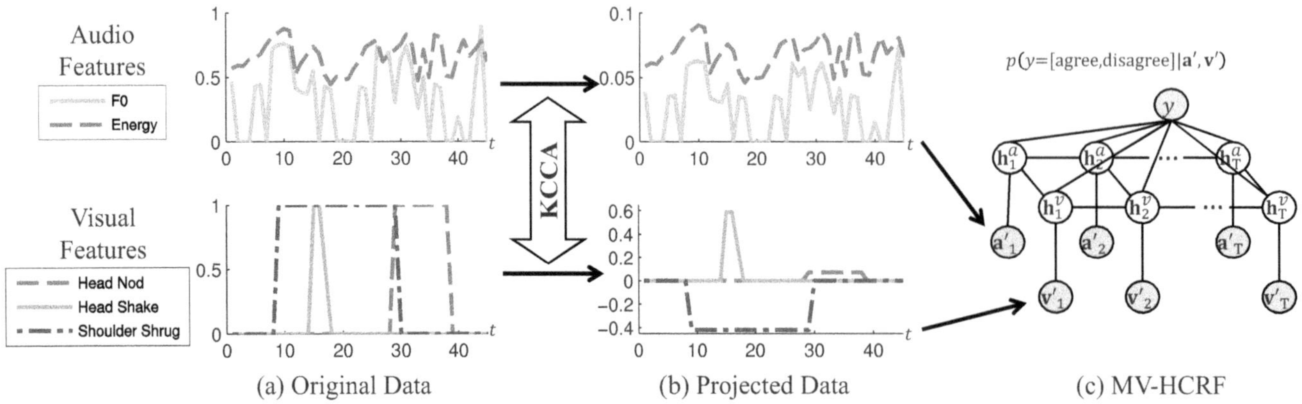

Figure 1: An overview of our approach. (a) An audio-visual observation sequence from the Canal 9 dataset [11]. KCCA uses a nonlinear kernel to map the original data to a high-dimensional feature space, and finds a new projection of the data in the feature space that maximizes the correlation between audio and visual channels. (b) The projected data shows that emphasizing the amplitude of the 'head shake' and 'shoulder shrug' gestures maximized the correlation between audio and visual channels. (c) multi-view HCRF for jointly learning both view-shared and view-specific sub-structures of the projected data. $\mathbf{a}_t$ and $\mathbf{v}_t$ are observation variables from audio and visual channels, and $\mathbf{h}_t^a$ and $\mathbf{h}_t^v$ are hidden variables for audio and visual channels.

used kernel CCA (KCCA) for learning the semantic representation of images and their associated text. However, their approach did not consider capturing hidden dynamics in the data. Latent variable discriminative models, e.g., HCRF [7], have shown promising results in human behavior analysis tasks, for their ability to capture the hidden dynamics (e.g., spatio-temporal dynamics). Recently, the multi-view counterpart [10] showed a significant improvement over single-view methods in recognizing human actions. However, their work did not learn nonlinear correlation across modalities. We extend this body of work, enabling it to modeling multimodal human behavior analysis.

3. OUR APPROACH

Consider a labeled sequential dataset $\mathcal{D} = \{(\mathbf{x}_i, y_i)\}_{i=1}^N$ where $\mathbf{x}_i$ is a multivariate observation sequence and $y_i \in \mathcal{Y}$ is a sequence label from a finite label set $\mathcal{Y}$. Since we have audio-visual data, we use the notation $\mathbf{x}_i = (\mathbf{a}_i, \mathbf{v}_i)$ where $\mathbf{a}_i \in \mathbb{R}^{n_a \times T}$ and $\mathbf{v}_i \in \mathbb{R}^{n_v \times T}$ are audio and visual sequences of length T, respectively.

Figure 1 shows an overview of our approach. We first find a new projection of the original observation sequence $\mathbf{x}' = (\mathbf{a}', \mathbf{v}')$ using KCCA [3] such that the correlation between $\mathbf{a}'$ and $\mathbf{v}'$ is maximized in the projected space (Section 3.1). Then we use this projected data as an input to MV-HCRF [10] to capture hidden dynamics and interaction between audio and visual data (Section 3.2).

3.1 KCCA

Given a set of paired samples $\{(\mathbf{a}_i, \mathbf{v}_i)\}_{i=1}^N$, $\mathbf{A} = [\mathbf{a}_1, \cdots, \mathbf{a}_N]$ and $\mathbf{V} = [\mathbf{v}_1, \cdots, \mathbf{v}_N]$, Canonical Correlation Analysis (CCA) aims to find a pair of transformations $\mathbf{w}_a$ and $\mathbf{w}_v$ such that the correlation between the corresponding projections $\rho(\mathbf{w}_a^\top \mathbf{A}, \mathbf{w}_v^\top \mathbf{V})$ is maximized. However, since CCA finds $\mathbf{w}_a$ and $\mathbf{w}_v$ that are linear in the vector space, it may not reveal nonlinear relationships in the data [9].

Kernel CCA (KCCA) [3] uses the kernel trick [9] to overcome this limitation by projecting the original data onto a high dimensional feature space before running CCA. A kernel is a function $K(\mathbf{x}_i, \mathbf{x}_j)$ that, for all $\mathbf{x}_i, \mathbf{x}_j \in \mathbb{R}$,

$$K(\mathbf{x}_i, \mathbf{x}_j) = \langle \Phi(\mathbf{x}_i), \Phi(\mathbf{x}_j) \rangle$$

where $\langle \cdot, \cdot \rangle$ denotes an inner product, and Φ is a nonlinear mapping function to a Hilbert space $\mathcal{F}$, $\Phi : \mathbf{x} \in \mathbb{R} \mapsto \Phi(\mathbf{x}) \in \mathcal{F}$.

To apply the kernel trick, the standard KCCA then rewrites $\mathbf{w}_a$ (and $\mathbf{w}_v$) as an inner product of the data $\mathbf{A}$ (and $\mathbf{V}$) with a direction α (and β),

$$\mathbf{w}_a = \mathbf{A}^\top \alpha, \quad \mathbf{w}_v = \mathbf{V}^\top \beta \tag{1}$$

If we assume that $\mathbf{a}$'s and $\mathbf{v}$'s are centered (i.e., mean zero), the goal is to maximize the correlation coefficient

$$\begin{aligned}
\rho(\cdot, \cdot) &= \max_{\mathbf{w}_a, \mathbf{w}_v} \frac{\mathbb{E}[\mathbf{w}_a^\top \mathbf{a} \mathbf{v}^\top \mathbf{w}_v]}{\sqrt{\mathbb{E}[\mathbf{w}_a^\top \mathbf{a}\mathbf{a}^\top \mathbf{w}_a]}\sqrt{\mathbb{E}[\mathbf{w}_v^\top \mathbf{v}\mathbf{v}^\top \mathbf{w}_v]}} \\
&= \max_{\mathbf{w}_a, \mathbf{w}_v} \frac{\mathbf{w}_a^\top \mathbf{A}\mathbf{V}^\top \mathbf{w}_v}{\sqrt{\mathbf{w}_a^\top \mathbf{A}\mathbf{A}^\top \mathbf{w}_a \mathbf{w}_v^\top \mathbf{V}\mathbf{V}^\top \mathbf{w}_v}} \\
&= \max_{\alpha, \beta} \frac{\alpha \mathbf{A}\mathbf{A}^\top \mathbf{V}\mathbf{V}^\top \beta}{\sqrt{\alpha \mathbf{A}\mathbf{A}^\top \mathbf{A}\mathbf{A}^\top \alpha \cdot \beta \mathbf{V}\mathbf{V}^\top \mathbf{V}\mathbf{V}^\top \beta}} \\
&= \max_{\alpha, \beta} \frac{\alpha^\top K_a K_v \beta}{\sqrt{\alpha^\top K_a^2 \alpha \cdot \beta^\top K_v^2 \beta}}.
\end{aligned} \tag{2}$$

where $K_a = K(\mathbf{A}, \mathbf{A})$ and $K_v = K(\mathbf{V}, \mathbf{V})$ are kernel matrices.

Since Equation 2 is scale invariant with respect to α and β (they cancel out), the optimization problem is equivalent to:

$$\max_{\alpha, \beta} \alpha^\top K_a K_v \beta \quad \text{subject to} \quad \alpha^\top K_a^2 \alpha = \beta^\top K_v^2 \beta = 1 \tag{3}$$

The corresponding Lagrangian dual form is

$$L(\alpha, \beta, \theta) = \alpha^\top K_a K_v \beta - \frac{\theta_\alpha}{2}(\alpha^\top K_a^2 \alpha - 1) - \frac{\theta_\beta}{2}(\beta^\top K_v^2 \beta - 1) \tag{4}$$

The solution to Equation 3 is found by taking derivatives of Equation 4 with respect to α and β, and solving a standard eigenvalue problem [5]. However, when K_a and K_v are non-invertible, as is common in practice with large datasets, problems can arise such as computational issues or degeneracy. This problem is solved by applying the partial Gram-Schmidt orthogonalization (PGSO) with a precision parameter η to reduce the dimensionality of the kernel matrices and approximate the correlation.

After we find α and β, we plug the solution back in to Equation 1 to obtain $\mathbf{w}_a$ and $\mathbf{w}_v$, and finally obtain new projections:

$$\begin{aligned} \mathbf{A}' &= [\langle \mathbf{w}_a, \mathbf{a}_1 \rangle, \cdots, \langle \mathbf{w}_a, \mathbf{a}_N \rangle] \quad (5) \\ \mathbf{V}' &= [\langle \mathbf{w}_v, \mathbf{v}_1 \rangle, \cdots, \langle \mathbf{w}_v, \mathbf{v}_N \rangle]. \end{aligned}$$

3.2 Multi-view HCRF

Given the new projection's audio-visual features $\mathbf{A}'$ and $\mathbf{V}'$ (Equation 5), the next step is to learn the hidden dynamics and interaction across modalities (see Figure 1 (b) and (c)).

A Multi-View Hidden Conditional Random Field [10] (MV-HCRF) is a conditional probability distribution that factorizes according to a multi-chain structured undirected graph $\mathcal{G} = (\mathcal{V}, \mathcal{E})$, where each chain is a discrete representation of each view. We use disjoint sets of latent variables $\mathbf{h}^a \in \mathcal{H}^a$ for audio and $\mathbf{h}^v \in \mathcal{H}^v$ for visual channel to learn both view-shared and view-specific sub-structures in audio-visual data. An MV-HCRF defines $p(y \mid \mathbf{a}', \mathbf{v}')$ as

$$p(y \mid \mathbf{a}', \mathbf{v}') = \frac{\sum_{\mathbf{h}} \exp\{\Lambda^\intercal \Phi(y, \mathbf{h}, \mathbf{a}', \mathbf{v}')\}}{\sum_{y', \mathbf{h}} \exp\{\Lambda^\intercal \Phi(y', \mathbf{h}, \mathbf{a}', \mathbf{v}')\}}$$

where $\mathbf{h} = \{\mathbf{h}^a, \mathbf{h}^v\}$ and $\Lambda = [\lambda, \omega]$ is a model parameter vector. The function $\Lambda^\intercal \Phi(y, \mathbf{h}, \mathbf{a}', \mathbf{v}')$ is factorized with feature functions $f_k(\cdot)$ and $g_k(\cdot)$ as

$$\begin{aligned} \Lambda^\intercal \Phi(y, \mathbf{h}, \mathbf{a}', \mathbf{v}') &= \sum_{s \in \mathcal{V}} \sum_k \lambda_k f_k(y, h_s, \mathbf{a}', \mathbf{v}') \\ &+ \sum_{(s,t) \in \mathcal{E}} \sum_k \omega_k g_k(y, h_s, h_t, \mathbf{a}', \mathbf{v}'). \end{aligned}$$

Following [10], we define three types of feature functions. The *label* feature function $f_k(y, h_s)$ encodes the relationship between a latent variable h_s and a label y. The *observation* feature function $f_k(h_s, \mathbf{a}', \mathbf{v}')$ encodes the relationship between a latent variable h_s and observations $\mathbf{x}$. The *edge* feature function $g_k(y, h_s, h_t)$ encodes the transition between two latent variables h_s and h_t. We use the linked topology from [10] to define the edge set $\mathcal{E}$ (shown in Figure 1(c)), which models contemporaneous connections between audio and visual observations, i.e., the concurrent latent states in the audio and visual channel mutually affect each other. Note that the $f_k(\cdot)$ are modeled under the assumption that views are conditionally independent given respective sets of latent variables, and thus encode the view-specific sub-structures. The feature function $g_k(\cdot)$ encodes both view-shared and view-specific sub-structures.

The optimal parameter set Λ^* is found by minimizing the negative conditional log-likelihood

$$\min_{\Lambda} L(\Lambda) = \frac{1}{2\sigma^2} \|\Lambda\|^2 - \sum_{i=1}^{N} \log p(y_i \mid \mathbf{a}'_i, \mathbf{v}'_i; \Lambda) \quad (6)$$

where the first term is the Gaussian prior over Λ that works as an L_2-norm regularization. We find the optimal parameters Λ^* using gradient descent with a quasi-newton optimization method, the limited-memory BFGS algorithm [5]. The marginal probability of each node is obtained by performing an inference task using the Junction Tree algorithm [2].

4. EXPERIMENT

In this section, we describe the dataset, detail our experimental methodology, and discuss our results.

4.1 Dataset

We evaluated our approach using the Canal9 dataset [11], where the task is to recognize agreement and disagreement from nonverbal audio-visual cues during spontaneous political debates. The Canal9 dataset is a collection of 72 political debates recorded by the Canal 9 TV station in Switzerland, with a total of roughly 42 hours of recordings. In each debate there is a moderator and two groups of participants who argue about a controversial political question. The dataset contains highly spontaneous verbal and non-verbal multimodal human behavior data.

In order to facilitate comparison, we used the same part of the Canal9 dataset with nonverbal audio-visual features as was selected for use in Bousmalis *et al.* [1]. This consisted of 53 episodes of agreements and 94 episodes of disagreement collected over 11 debates. Bousmalis *et al.* selected the episodes based on two criteria: (a) the verbal content clearly indicates agreement/disagreement, which ensures that the ground truth label for the episode is known; (b) the episode includes only one person, with a close-up shot of the speaker. The audio channel was encoded with 2-dimensional prosodic features, including the fundamental frequency (F0) and the energy. The visual channel was encoded with 8 gestures: *'Head Nod', 'Head Shake', 'Forefinger Raise', 'Forefinger Raise-Like', 'Forefinger Wag', 'Hand Wag', 'Hands Scissor', and 'Shoulder Shrug'*, where the presence/absence of the actions in each frame was manually annotated with binary values. We downsampled the data from the original sampling rate of 25 *kHz* to 12.5 *kHz*.

4.2 Methodology

The first step in our approach is to run KCCA to obtain a new projection of the data. We used a Gaussian RBF kernel as our kernel function $K(\mathbf{x}_i, \mathbf{x}_j) = \exp\left(- \|\mathbf{x}_i - \mathbf{x}_j\| / 2\gamma^2\right)$ because of its empirical success in the literature [9]. We validated the kernel width $\gamma = 10^k, k = [-1, 0, 1]$ and the PGSO precision parameter $\eta = [1:6]$ using grid search. The optimal parameter values were chosen based on the maximum correlation coefficient value.

Our experiments followed a leave-two-debates-out cross-validation approach, where we selected 2 debates of the 11 debates as the test split, 3 debates for the validation split, and the remaining 6 debates for the training split. This was repeated five times on the 11 debates. The F1 scores were averaged to get the final result. We chose four baseline models: Hidden Markov Models (HMM) [8], Conditional Random Fields (CRF) [4], Hidden Conditional Random Fields (HCRF) [7], and Multi-view HCRF (MV-HCRF) [10]. We compared this to our KCCA with MV-HCRF approach. Note that HMM and CRF perform per-frame classification, while HCRF and MV-HCRF perform per-sequence classification. The classification results of each model in turn were measured accordingly.

We automatically validated the hyper-parameters of all models. For all CRF-family models, we varied the L_2-norm regularization factor $\sigma = 10^k, k = [0, 1, 2]$ (see Equation 6). For HMM and HCRF, the number of hidden states were varied $|\mathcal{H}| = [2:6]$; for MV-HCRF, they were $\left(|\mathcal{H}^A|, |\mathcal{H}^V|\right) = ([2:4], [2:4])$. Since the optimization problems in HMM, HCRF and MV-HCRF are non-convex, we performed two random initializations of each model; the best model was selected based on the F1 score on the validation split. The L-BFGS solver was set to terminate after 500 iterations.

4.3 Result and Discussion

We first compared our approach to existing methods: HMM [8], CRF [4], HCRF [7], and MV-HCRF [10]. Figure 2 shows a bar plot of mean F1 scores and their standard deviations. We can see that our approach clearly outperforms all other models.

For further analysis, we investigated whether learning nonlinear correlation was important, comparing KCCA to CCA and the original data. Table 1 shows that models trained with KCCA always outperformed the others, suggesting that learning nonlinear correlation in the data was important. Figure 1(b) shows the data projected in

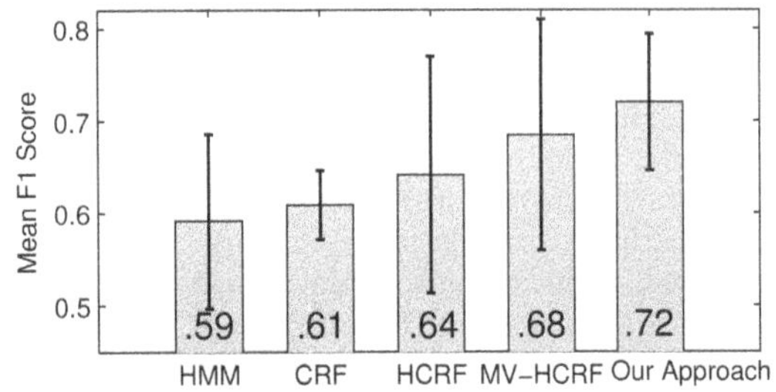

Figure 2: A bar plot of mean F1 scores with error bars showing standard deviations. This shows empirically that our approach successfully learned correlations and interactions between audio and visual features using KCCA and MV-HCRF.

Models	Original Data	CCA	KCCA
HMM	.59 (.09)	.59 (.12)	.61 (.13)
CRF	.61 (.04)	.63 (.03)	.67 (.08)
HCRF	.64 (.13)	.65 (.07)	.69 (.06)
MV-HCRF	**.68 (.13)**	**.71 (.07)**	**.72 (.07)**

Table 1: Experimental results (means and standard deviations of F1 scores) comparing KCCA to CCA and the original data. The results show that learning nonlinear correlation in the data was important in our task.

a new space found by KCCA, where the 'head shake' and 'shoulder shrug' gestures were relatively emphasized compared to 'head nod', which maximized the correlation between the audio and visual signals. We believe that this made our data more descriptive, allowing the learning algorithm to capture the hidden dynamics and interactions between modalities more effectively.

We also investigated whether our approach captures interaction between audio-visual signals successfully. We compared the models trained with a unimodal feature (audio or visual) to the models trained with audio-visual features. Table 2 shows means and standard deviations of the F1 scores. In the three single-chain models, HMM, CRF, and HCRF, there was an improvement when both audio and visual features were used, confirming that using a combination of audio and visual features for our task is indeed important. Also, MV-HCRF outperformed HMM, CRF, HCRF, showing empirically that learning interaction between audio-visual signals explicitly improved the performance.

5. CONCLUSIONS

We presented a novel approach to multimodal human behavior analysis using KCCA and MV-HCRF, and evaluated it on a task of recognizing agreement and disagreement from nonverbal audio-visual cues using the Canal9 dataset. On this dataset, we showed that preprocessing multimodal data with KCCA, by projecting the data to a new space where the correlation across modalities is maximized, helps capture complex nonlinear relationship in the data. We also showed that KCCA with MV-HCRF, which jointly learns view-shared and view-specific interactions explicitly, improves the recognition performance, showing that our approach successfully captured complex nonlinear interaction across modalities. We look forward to applying our technique to other applications in multimodal human behavior analysis for further analysis.

Models	Audio	Video	Audio+Video
HMM	.54 (.08)	.58 (.11)	**.59 (.09)**
CRF	.48 (.05)	.58 (.15)	**.61 (.04)**
HCRF	.52 (.09)	.60 (.09)	**.64 (.13)**
MV-HCRF	·	·	**.68 (.13)**
KCCA + MV-HCRF	·	·	**.72 (.07)**

Table 2: Experimental results (means and standard deviations of F1 scores) comparing unimodal (audio or video) features to the audio-visual features. The results confirms that using both audio and visual features are important in our task.

6. ACKNOWLEDGMENTS

This work was funded by ONR grant #N000140910625, NSF grant #IIS-1118018, NSF grant #IIS-1018055, and U.S. Army RDECOM.

7. REFERENCES

[1] K. Bousmalis, L.-P. Morency, and M. Pantic. Modeling hidden dynamics of multimodal cues for spontaneous agreement and disagreement recognition. In *FG*, 2011.

[2] R. G. Cowell, A. P. Dawid, S. L. Lauritzen, and D. J. Spiegelhalter. *Probabilistic Networks and Expert Systems*. Springer-Verlag, 1999.

[3] D. R. Hardoon, S. Szedmák, and J. Shawe-Taylor. Canonical correlation analysis: An overview with application to learning methods. *Neural Comp.*, 16(12):2639–2664, 2004.

[4] J. D. Lafferty, A. McCallum, and F. C. N. Pereira. Conditional random fields: Probabilistic models for segmenting and labeling sequence data. In *ICML*, 2001.

[5] J. Nocedal and S. J. Wright. *Numerical Optimization*. Springer-Verlag, 1999.

[6] G. Potamianos, C. Neti, J. Luettin, and I. Matthews. *Audio-Visual Automatic Speech Recognition: An Overview*. MIT Press, 2004.

[7] A. Quattoni, S. B. Wang, L.-P. Morency, M. Collins, and T. Darrell. Hidden conditional random fields. *TPAMI*, 29(10):1848–1852, 2007.

[8] L. R. Rabiner. *A tutorial on hidden Markov models and selected applications in speech recognition*, pages 267–296. Morgan Kaufmann Publishers Inc., 1990.

[9] B. Scholkopf and A. J. Smola. *Learning with Kernels: Support Vector Machines, Regularization, Optimization, and Beyond*. MIT Press, Cambridge, MA, USA, 2001.

[10] Y. Song, L.-P. Morency, and R. Davis. Multi-view latent variable discriminative models for action recognition. In *CVPR*, 2012.

[11] A. Vinciarelli, A. Dielmann, S. Favre, and H. Salamin. Canal9: A database of political debates for analysis of social interactions. In *ACII*, 2009.

[12] Z. Zeng, M. Pantic, G. I. Roisman, and T. S. Huang. A survey of affect recognition methods: Audio, visual, and spontaneous expressions. *TPAMI*, 31(1):39–58, 2009.

[13] H. Zhang, Y. Zhuang, and F. Wu. Cross-modal correlation learning for clustering on image-audio dataset. In *MM*, pages 273–276, 2007.

Consistent but Modest: A Meta-Analysis on Unimodal and Multimodal Affect Detection Accuracies from 30 Studies

Sidney D'Mello
University of Notre Dame
Notre Dame, IN 46556, USA
(011)-574-631-1822
sdmello@nd.edu

Jacqueline Kory
University of Notre Dame
Notre Dame, IN 46556, USA
(011)-574-631-1822
jkory@nd.edu

ABSTRACT
The recent influx of multimodal affect classifiers raises the important question of whether these classifiers yield accuracy rates that exceed their unimodal counterparts. This question was addressed by performing a meta-analysis on 30 published studies that reported both multimodal and unimodal affect detection accuracies. The results indicated that multimodal accuracies were consistently better than unimodal accuracies and yielded an average 8.12% improvement over the best unimodal classifiers. However, performance improvements were three times lower when classifiers were trained on natural or seminatural data (4.39% improvement) compared to acted data (12.1% improvement). Importantly, performance of the best unimodal classifier explained an impressive 80.6% (cross-validated) of the variance in multimodal accuracy. The results also indicated that multimodal accuracies were substantially higher than accuracies of the second-best unimodal classifiers (an average improvement of 29.4%) irrespective of the naturalness of the training data. Theoretical and applied implications of the findings are discussed.

Categories and Subject Descriptors
H.5.m [**Information Interfaces and Presentation**]: Miscellaneous.

Keywords
Affect detection, emotion detection, affective computing, multimodal affect detection, meta-analysis, review

1. INTRODUCTION
Affect detection has been, and continues to be, on the forefront of Affective Computing (AC) research. The emphasis on affect detection is reasonable because a system can never respond to users' emotions if it cannot detect their emotions. Consequently, the last 15 years have witnessed numerous efforts toward detecting affective states from a variety of modalities, such as facial expressions, acoustic-prosodic cues, body movements, gesture, contextual cues, text and discourse, physiology, and neural circuitry (see [1-3] for reviews). Although some early affect detection systems focused primarily on individual modalities and on emotional expressions portrayed by actors, several of the contemporary systems emphasize multimodal detection of naturalistic affective expressions. This suggests that the field is moving in the right direction.

Despite the impressive progress made so far, it is safe to say that there is still considerable ground to be covered before affect detectors can be integrated into everyday interfaces and devices. The field is still confronted with the persistent problems of: (a) intrusive, expensive, and noisy sensors that are largely unscalable, (b) technical challenges associated with detecting latent psychological constructs (i.e., affect) from weak signals embedded in noisy channels, (c) difficulties associated with collecting adequate and realistic training data for machine learning models, (d) challenges of incorporating top-down models of context and appraisals with bottom-up bodily- and physiological-based sensing, (e) lack of clarity of the affective phenomenon being modeled (e.g., moods vs. emotions, categorical vs. dimensional representations), (f) issues pertaining to generalizability across contexts, time, individual differences, and cultural differences, and (g) many others.

As AC researchers are well aware, this laundry list of challenges and open problems is more the norm than the exception given the difficulty of affect detection and the relative infancy of the field. Numerous innovative solutions are being developed to address several of these issues. One strategy that is gaining momentum in the literature is to alleviate the noisy signal problem (item b from the list above) by increasing the amount of available data. More specifically, several researchers are focusing on developing multimodal affect detectors with the assumption that incorporating multimodal signals will yield classification accuracies that are superior to unimodal signals. Although this assumption has obvious face validity, the results of these endeavors are somewhat mixed. When compared to the accuracies obtained by the best unimodal classifiers, some studies have reported impressive multimodal improvements (e.g., [4-8]), others have reported negligible or null improvements (e.g., [9-11]), and some have even reported negative improvements (e.g., [12-14]).

The considerable inter-study variance in the results of multimodal affect classifiers makes it difficult to appropriately gauge what advantages (if any) multimodal classification yields over unimodal classification. More importantly, is it possible to identify situations where multimodal classifiers are expected to yield impressive improvements and differentiate these from situations that result in null or negative improvements? The present paper makes an initial attempt to address these questions by analyzing multimodal and unimodal classification accuracies reported in 30 published affect detection studies.

The analyses focused on quantifying the *added value* afforded by multimodal affect classification above and beyond unimodal classification (called MM effect size). We were also interested in identifying factors that reliably predicted MM effects. Our focus is on quantifying performance rather than analyzing the different approaches used to integrate multimodal information (see [1-3] for reviews on different multimodal systems). As such, this paper should be considered to be more of a meta-analysis of the multimodal affect detection literature rather than a review or survey paper. Hence, the descriptions of the studies themselves are quite brief (Section 2), but we emphasize the data (Section 3) and various analyses on the data (Section 4).

2. SUMMARY OF STUDIES ANALYZED

Studies were selected by formally searching relevant journals (e.g., *IEEE Transactions of Affective Computing, IEEE Transactions on Multimedia*) and conference proceedings (e.g., *Affective Computing and Intelligent Interaction, Multimodal Interaction, Face and Gesture*). Informal searches for variants of the terms *"multimodal" and "affect or emotion" and "detection or classification"* were also performed via Google Scholar. Any peer-reviewed publication that reported both unimodal and multimodal affect detection accuracies in a clearly accessible format (i.e., accuracy metrics could be easily obtained from the text, tables, or figures) was included in the analysis. More recent studies were given preference over older studies. Selection bias was avoided by including the first 30 studies that satisfied these basic criteria. A summary of the studies along several dimensions is presented below.

2.1 Data type

This pertains to whether the data used to train and validate the unimodal and multimodal classifiers consisted of emotional expressions that were: (a) obtained by asking *actors* to portray various emotions (e.g., [8, 11, 12, 15-19]), (b) collected via experimental methods that *induced* specific emotions (e.g., [9, 14, 20]), (c) *naturalistic* displays of emotion (e.g., [21-24]), or (d) some blend of (b) and (c) (e.g., [13, 25-27]), henceforth referred to as *seminatural.* Approximately half of the multimodal classifiers (53.3%) were trained and validated on acted data, 20% used semi-natural data, 16.6% used natural data, and 10% induced specific emotions.

While the criteria for a dataset to be categorized as acted, natural, or induced is quite clear, the seminatural category requires some clarification. This designation was mainly applied to data sets where specific emotions were not directly induced (e.g., showing participants emotion-induction films [20]), but the interaction itself was intentionally emotionally charged, thereby increasing the likelihood that participants would respond emotionally. For example, the SEMAINE database [28] was constructed by asking participants to engage in a conversation with an avatar that had one of four affective dispositions (or personalities): angry, happy, gloomy, or pragmatic. Studies that utilized this database (e.g., [27, 29]) were categorized as seminatural because it is likely that the personality of the avatar influenced the emotions of the participant. In particular, there is considerable evidence that perceiving an emotion increases the likelihood of experiencing that emotion (i.e., emotion contagion) because of shared neural substrates that underlie perception and expression [30].

2.2 Classification task

This refers to whether the affect detector performed a categorical versus a dimensional classification. *Categorical* classification consists of discriminating between one of *k* affect labels (e.g., anger, sadness, happiness, and neutral [25]). *Dimensional* classification involved predicting activity on a particular affective dimension (e.g., valence, activation, dominance [24]). There were a number of studies that used a dimensional model to annotate affect, but proceeded with a categorical classification by dividing the dimensional affective space. These have been categorized as *mixed.* For example, Wöllmer [6] used 5 point scales to annotate valence and activation, but then performed a categorical classification by performing a tripartite split on each dimension (i.e., dividing the scale into low, medium, and high sections). Similarly, continuous activation-valence values were discretized by clustering prior to classification in [27]. A vast majority (66.7%) of the studies performed a categorical classification, while mixed (23.3%) and dimensional (10%) classifications were comparatively rare.

2.3 Affective states classified

Most of the studies focused on all or some subset of the "basic" emotions (e.g., [7, 8, 12, 25, 31]). Several studies focused on predicting valence and arousal, usually independently (e.g., [6, 10, 13, 20, 32]), but occasionally jointly in a valence-arousal space (e.g., [9, 16, 27]). Studies that focused on non-basic emotions (e.g., [22]) or on some of the less studied dimensions of expectancy and power (e.g., [13, 26]) were less frequent.

2.4 Modalities

Most of the studies analyzed facial expressions (77%) and acoustic-prosodic cues (77%). Almost a third (30%) of the studies tracked some form of body movements, postures, and gestures. Text, EEG, biosignals (i.e., ECG, EMG, GSR, etc.), eye gaze, event, and context were comparatively rare. Accordingly, audio-visual features constituted the most common multimodal systems (43.3%) followed by a trimodal face + voice + posture and gesture systems (16.7%). Overall, 73.3% of the multimodal systems were bimodal, while 26.7% were trimodal.

2.5 Multimodal Fusion Techniques

Most studies considered different multiple fusion techniques, so it is difficult to accurately estimate if a particular method or technique was more commonly used than the others. In general, many studies compared naïve feature-based fusion with decision-level fusion (e.g., [4, 12, 19, 20]), model-level fusion [7, 10, 29], and more sophisticated fusion strategies. These include mixtures of Gaussian process classification [23], string-based approaches [26], hybrid approaches that combine feature-level and decision-level fusion [9] or decision-level and model-level fusion [7], bidirectional long short-term memory neural networks [10, 29], emotion-adapted decision-level fusion [16], and meta-decision trees [31].

3. THE DATA

Table 1 provides both unimodal and multimodal classification performance scores. The 27 studies that performed a categorical classification used classification accuracy (i.e., the proportion of correctly classified instances) as the evaluation metric. In rare cases where both classification accuracy and the F1-measure was reported (e.g., [6, 10]), classification accuracy was taken to be the metric in order to increase consistency among studies. The dimensional studies typically reported a correlation coefficient, and this was taken as the performance metric.

The rightmost column (MM Effect) is the metric used to quantify multimodal performance improvement as a function of unimodal performance. If a_1 and a_2 are accuracies associated with two unimodal classifiers, and a_{12} is the multimodal accuracy, then the multimodal effect is $100 * \frac{a_{12} - max\,(a_1, a_2)}{max\,(a_1, a_2)}$. This is simply the percent improvement over the best unimodal classifier. This metric affords a unified analysis of studies that use classification accuracy and the correlation coefficient as the evaluation metric.

It is important to note two points about the data presented in Table 1. First, accuracy scores associated with the best performing classifier were used in situations where multiple classifiers were considered for the *same* classification task. For example, [20] reported both feature-level and decision-level multimodal classification accuracy rates. Decision-level fusion yielded higher accuracy rates, so only decision level fusion results were used for in the subsequent analyses.

Second, there were more data points (N = 47) than studies (N = 30) because some studies performed *multiple* classification tasks. For example, [22] developed one classifier to predict four affective states and another to predict an overlapping but different set of five affective states. Other than this exception, in general, one data point was obtained for the studies that performed a categorical classification. It was the dimensional studies that contributed multiple data points because the number of classification models increases linearly with the number of dimensions considered. For example, the study by Eyben and colleagues [26] contributed five data points because their models independently predicted five affect dimensions (i.e., activation, expectancy, intensity, power, and valence).

There was the concern that studies that contributed multiple data points would bias the MM effect distributions and the summary statistics (i.e., means and standard deviations). They would also violate independence assumptions of the inferential statistical analyzes performed on the data. Therefore, the data reported in Table 1 consists of average performance scores across multiple classification tasks within the same study. For example, the five correlation coefficients from the Eyben et al. study [26] were averaged to yield one multimodal correlation. This resulted in one data point per study. The only exception was the Lin et al. [7] study, which contributed two data points. This is because the two different data sets analyzed in that study were sufficiently unique to warrant separate consideration. It should also be noted that the Caridakis et al. [17] and Castellano et al. [15] studies used the same data set, but considered different models based on different but non-mutually exclusive subsets of the data. The second column (N) in the Table 1 presents the number of data points that were averaged to produce the aggregate scores.

Table 1. Unimodal and Multimodal Classification Accuracies

			Unimodal Performance										
Ref.	N	**Metric**	**Face**	**Voice**	**Txt**	**PosGes**	**EEG**	**Gaze**	**Context**	**Event**	**BioS**	**MM**	**MM Effect (%)**
[25] Busso	1	Acc	.851	.709								.891	4.70
[17] Caridakis	1	Acc	.596	.708		.832						.894	7.45
[15] Castellano	1	Acc	.483	.571		.671						.783	16.7
[21] Chanel	1	Acc					.560				.590	.630	6.78
[18] Cueva	1	Acc	.200	.650								.750	15.4
[22] D'Mello	2	Acc	.352			.316			.381			.487	6.83
[11] Emerich	1	Acc	.907	.877								.930	2.54
[26] Eyben	5	CC	.131	.326						.318		.403	-5.71
[13] Glodek	4	Acc	.518	.533								.501	-8.18
[12] Gunes	1	Acc	.829			1.00						.910	-9.00
[19] Gunes	1	Acc	.352			.769						.827	7.54
[8] Jiang	1	Acc	.468	.522								.665	27.4
[23] Kapoor	1	Acc	.668			.820			.572			.865	5.53
[27] Karpouzis	1	Acc	.670	.730								.820	12.3
[4] Kessous	1	Acc	.483	.571		.671						.783	16.7
[14] Khalili	1	Acc					.667				.517	.622	-6.75
[9] Kim	1	Acc		.540							.510	.550	1.85
[7] Lin(a)	1	Acc	.622	.603								.781	25.7
[7] Lin(b)	1	Acc	.714	.710								.906	27.0
[32] Litman	4	Acc		.608	.645							.660	2.63
[10] Metallinou	2	Acc	.562	.559								.630	2.52
[29] Nicolaou	2	CC	.603	.515		.502						.719	10.7
[5] Paleari	1	Acc	.321	.361								.430	19.1
[33] Rabie	1	Acc	.745	.619								.782	4.98
[24] Schuller	3	CC		.683	.685							.776	2.55
[20] Soleymani	2	Acc					.563	.689				.725	5.15
[16] Wagner	1	Acc	.480	.510		.420						.550	7.84
[6] Wollmer	2	Acc	.497	.511								.672	21.5
[31] Wu	1	Acc		.800	.809							.836	3.25
[34] Zeng	1	Acc	.390	.690								.750	8.70

N refers to the number of data points that were aggregated to produce the averages in the table. **Metric.** refers to the metric used to quantity classification accuracy. Acc. = proportion correct. Corr. = correlation coefficient. **PosGes.** refers to posture or gesture. **BioS** refers to a combination of physiological measures (e.g., EMG, ECG) but does not include EEG. **MM.** refers to multimodal performance. **MMEffect (%)** refers to the percent improvement of multimodal affect detection accuracy compared to the best unimodal classifier.

4. RESULTS

4.1 Overall Effects (MM Effect)

The distribution of MM effects is presented in Figure 1. A one-sample t-test indicated that the mean MM effect of 8.12% significantly differed from zero, $t(29) = 4.56$, $p < .001$, $d = .83$ sigma. This suggests that the multimodal classifiers yield non-zero improvements in performance (classification accuracy or correlation) compared to the best unimodal classifiers. There was also considerable variance in the MM effect distribution. MM effects ranged from -9.00% to 27.4% with a standard deviation of 9.75%. The large range and the fact that the standard deviation is greater than the mean, suggests that the *median value of 6.81%* might provide a more accurate estimate of the central tendency of the distribution.

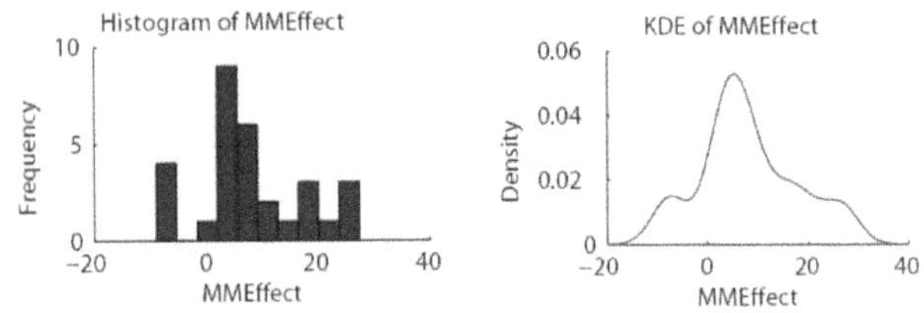

Figure 1. Histogram (left) and kernel smoothing density estimation (right) of distribution of MM effects

4.2 Relationship between Unimodal and Multimodal Accuracies

We investigated the amount of shared variance between the unimodal and multimodal classifiers by correlating accuracy of the best unimodal classifier with multimodal accuracy. This analysis focused on the 27 studies that used classification accuracy as the performance metric. There was a very robust correlation between accuracy of the best unimodal classifier and multimodal accuracy, $r(25) = .901$, $p < .001$. The correlation between multimodal accuracy and accuracy of the second-best unimodal classifier was similarly large, $r(25) = .664$, but was lower than the correlation with the best unimodal classifier. Accuracies of the best and second-best unimodal classifiers were also strongly correlated, $r(25) = .733$, $p < .001$.

To address the extent to which the best and second-best unimodal classifiers explained unique variance in predicting multimodal performance, two partial correlations were computed. First, multimodal accuracy was correlated with the best unimodal accuracy after controlling for the second-best unimodal accuracy. This correlation was statistically significant and was quite large, $r(24) = .814$, $p < .001$. Second, multimodal accuracy was correlated with the second-best unimodal accuracy after partialling out the best unimodal accuracy. This yielded a non-significant correlation, $r(24) = .011$, $p = .957$.Taken together, these results suggests that much of the variance in multimodal accuracy can be explained by accuracies of the best unimodal accuracy. The second-best unimodal classifier did not explain any additional variance.

4.3 Effects as a Function of Data Type

We analyzed how MM effects of classifiers that were trained on naturalistic affective data (natural classifiers) compared to classifiers trained on acted data (acted classifiers). This analysis was complicated by the fact that a majority (16 classifiers) used acted data, but only a handful (5 classifiers) were trained on naturalistic data. To partially address this imbalance, we merged the 5 natural classifiers with the 6 seminatural classifiers to form a new category of 11 *natural-seminatural* classifiers.

An analysis of the MM effect distributions (not shown here) for the acted and natural-seminatural classifiers indicated that each distribution had one potential outlier. These outliers were quantitatively identified as MM effects that exceeded two standard deviations from the mean. There was one outlier (-9.00%) in the distribution of acted MM effects and another (25.7%) in the distribution of natural-seminatural effects. Each outlier was replaced with the next closest value in the distribution. In particular, the -9.00% outlier was replaced with 2.54% and the 25.7% outlier was replaced with 12.3%. Paired-sample t-test on the distributions before and after outlier replacement did not yield significant differences for either the acted ($p = .333$) or the natural-seminatural distributions ($p = .341$), thereby indicating that this method of replacing outliers had no unintended effects.

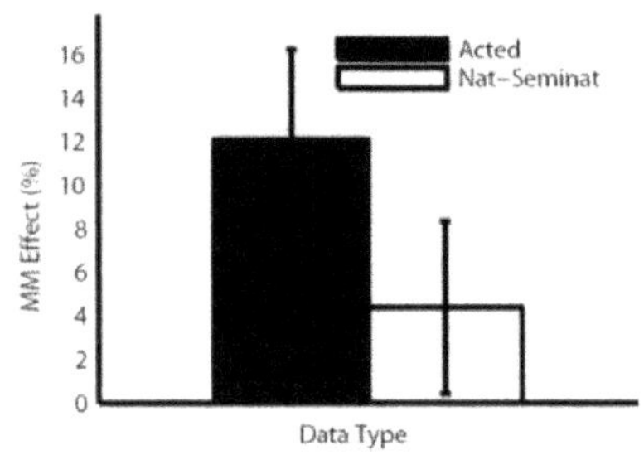

Figure 2. Comparison of data types

Figure 2 shows means and 95% confidence intervals for each effect size distribution. The mean MM effect for the acted classifiers ($M = 12.1$, $SD = 8.51$) was approximately *three times greater* than the mean MM effect for the natural-seminatural classifiers ($M = 4.39$, $SD = 6.70$). An independent samples t-test indicated that this difference was statistically significant, $t(25) = 2.51$, $p = .019$, and was consistent with a large effect ($d = 1.01$ sigma).

We investigated if the MM effects of each data type significantly differed from zero with two one-sample t-tests. A significant difference from zero was obtained for the acted MM effects, $t(15) = 5.68$, $p < .001$, $d = 1.42$ sigma. The test for the natural-seminatural distribution approached significance, $t(10) = 2.17$, $p = .055$, $d = .655$ sigma. This difference is likely to be significant with a larger sample.

4.4 Predicting Multimodal Accuracy

The results so far have indicated that multimodal accuracies were related to accuracies of the best unimodal classifiers (Section 4.2) as well as the type of data (i.e., acted vs. natural-seminatural) used to train the classifiers (Section 4.3). Could these two factors predict MM accuracy with sufficient precision to allow predictions to be made for unseen (new) MM classifiers? This question was addressed by regressing MM accuracy on the best unimodal accuracy and data type (an indicator variable with natural-seminatural as the reference group). The analysis focused on a subset of 24 systems that used classification accuracy as the performance metric and were trained on acted or natural-seminatural data. A tolerance analysis yielded tolerance values of .943, thereby alleviating any multicollinearity concerns pertaining to these two predictor variables [35].

The results yielded a significant model, $F(2, 21) = 54.9$, $p < .001$, that explained a robust amount of the variance ($R^2 = .840$). The dominant predictor was the accuracy of the best unimodal classifier ($\beta = .878$, $p < .001$). Data type was not a significant predictor of MM accuracy ($\beta = .127$, $p = .172$), ostensibly because the stronger predictor suppressed its effect. This suggests that the two predictor variables did not have an additive effect in predicting MM accuracy.

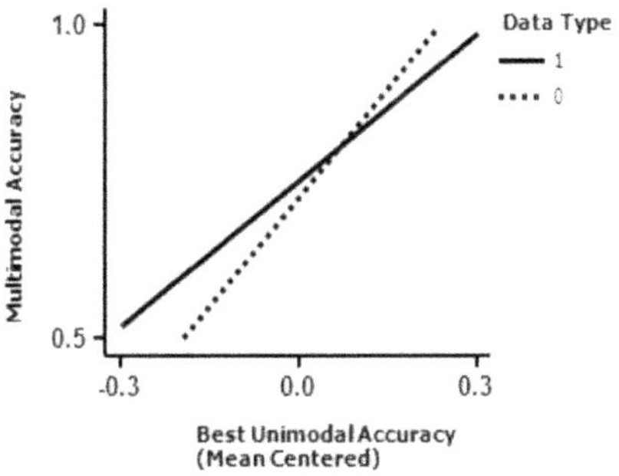

Figure 3. Data Type (1 for acted and 0 for natural-seminatural) × Best Unimodal Accuracy Interaction

We investigated if these two predictors had an interactive effect by including the *data type × best unimodal accuracy* interaction term in the regression equation. The overall model was significant, $F(3, 20) = 41.2$, $p < .001$, and yielded an R^2 of .861. The interaction term approached significance ($p = .096$) and explained an additional 2.1% of the variance. This categorical × continuous interaction indicates that the relationship between the best unimodal accuracy and MM accuracy varies by data type (see Figure 3). Specifically, accuracy of the best unimodal classifier was a better predictor of MM accuracy for the natural-seminatural classifiers ($B = 1.17$, $p < .001$) than the acted classifiers ($B = .783$, $p < .001$).

4.5 Generalizability Across Studies

The results of the previous section indicated that it was possible to predict MM accuracy primarily on the basis of the accuracy of the best unimodal classifier. The relatively small sample size raises some important generalizability issues. That is, to what extent does the regression model generalize to new studies? We addressed this question by performing a bootstrapping cross validation analysis. This is the recommended validation technique to assess generalizability and overfitting of models constructed on small data sets [36]. The analysis proceeded as follows. Training data was obtained by sampling a subset of the studies; models were fit on the training data and *training* R^2 was computed. The training models were then applied to the testing data, which consisted of the training studies plus new studies not included in the training data. Goodness of fit for the testing data (*testing* R^2) was obtained. Overfitting was computed as the difference between testing and training R^2 values. This procedure was repeated for 10,000 iterations and average R^2 values were computed. The results yielded an average training R^2 of .826 and an average testing R^2 of .806. The very small discrepancy of .020 suggests that the regression model is likely to generalize to new studies.

4.6 Second Order Effects (MM2 Effect)

Our results, for the most part, have focused on the MM effect distribution or on comparing multimodal accuracy with the best unimodal accuracy. A related question is how multimodal accuracy compares with respect to the *second-best* performing unimodal system. This question was addressed by computing an MM2 effect score according to the following equation: $100 * \frac{a_{12} - max\ 2(a_1,a_2)}{max2\ (a_1,a_2)}$ ($max2$ represents the second largest value in a series). The examination of the distribution of MM2 effects yielded three outliers (92.3%, 135%, and 275%), which were replaced with the next-closest value (62.5%) that was not an outlier.

MM2 effects ranged from 4.23% to 62.5% with a mean of 29.4% (SD = 17.6%). The median value of 28.2% was very close to the mean. A one-sample t-test indicated that the mean MM2 effect significantly differed from zero, $t(29) = 9.14$, $p < .001$, $d = .1.67$ sigma. Furthermore, a paired samples t-test indicated that the mean MM2 effect was significantly, $t(29) = 7.05$, $p < .002$, and substantially ($d = 1.29$ sigma) greater than the mean MM effect. Indeed, the mean MM2 effect (29.4%) was approximately 4 times greater than the mean MM effect (8.12%).

We also examined if the type of training data (acted vs. natural-seminatural) influenced the MM2 effects. However, unlike the results for MM effects, an independent samples t-test indicated that the mean MM2 acted effect of 32.9% (SD = 19.2) was statistically equivalent to the mean MM2 natural-seminatural effect of 27.2% (SD = 16.4%), $t(25) = .809$, $p = .426$.

4.7 Unimodal Comparisons

A long standing question in the literature is whether any one particular modality yields classification accuracies that are superior to the other modalities. This is a difficult question to address in any individual study because it is unclear if any modality advantages obtained in one study will generalize to other studies. Nineteen of the studies monitored facial and acoustic-prosodic features, so there might be sufficient data to draw some generalizations about the comparative advantages of these two modalities. Two of these 19 face-voice studies used the correlation coefficient as the performance metric, while the remaining 17 studies used classification accuracy. This analysis focused on the latter 17 studies.

The results indicated that classification accuracies associated with unimodal facial feature tracking ($M = .559$, $SD = .182$) were quantitatively lower that unimodal voice feature tracking ($M = .614$, $SD = .118$). However, a paired-samples t-test did not yield a significant modality effect, $t(17) = 1.60$, $p = .129$, $d = .39$ sigma. Nevertheless, the .39 effect size in favor of voice is indicative of a small to medium sized effect [37]. This effect might be significant with a larger sample, although this is entirely an empirical question.

As a follow-up analysis, we investigated the pattern of correlations of accuracies obtained by the face, voice, and multimodal systems that included these modalities. Both face and voice accuracies were significantly correlated with multimodal accuracy, but the voice (r (15) = .870, $p < .001$) demonstrated a stronger correlation than the face (r (15) = .614, $p = .009$). Face and voice accuracies were also related, (r (15) = .633, $p = .006$).

5. GENERAL DISCUSSION

The present study analyzed 30 published research articles that developed and validated multimodal affect classifiers. Our focus was on quantifying the improvement that multimodal classifiers afford over their unimodal counterparts. The results were illuminating in a number of respects. In this section, we summarize our major findings, discuss their theoretical implications, address limitations, and identify potential avenues for further research.

5.1 Major Findings and Applied Implications

The major findings are organized into three themes as discussed below.

Significant but modest MM effects. The results consistently revealed that MM effects were significantly greater than zero, with only four of the 30 studies reporting negative effects. This provides some initial evidence that MM classifiers do outperform their best unimodal counterparts. One caveat is the possibility of publication bias because it is likely that the papers that report positive MM effects are more likely to be published, and subsequently included in this meta-analysis, than papers that report negligible or negative effects.

The results also indicated that MM effects were somewhat modest, with the median overall effect being 6.81% (the mean was 8.12%). Importantly, the effects associated with classifiers trained on naturalistic or seminatural affect data (4.39%) were substantially lower than classifiers trained on acted data (12.1%). Since the ultimate goal of affect detection is to sense naturalistic affective expressions in real-world contexts, the 4.39% effect might represent a more accurate estimate of state-of-the-art multimodal affect detection accuracies. The question of whether this modest improvement in accuracy obtained by MM systems is worth their increased complexity is a question that is best addressed at the application-level.

Redundancy among modalities. One reason for the relatively modest MM effect, especially for the systems trained on more naturalistic data, is that there might be considerable redundancy among the different modalities. Strong correlations among the best unimodal, second-best unimodal, and MM accuracies provide some evidence to support this view. Further evidence for redundancy among modalities can be obtained by the fact that the best unimodal accuracies predicted a cross-validated 80.6% of the variance in multimodal accuracies. Indeed, impressive MM effects are not expected if the different modalities convey similar information, albeit in different ways.

Importantly, accuracy of the best unimodal classifier was a better predictor of MM accuracy for the natural-seminatural systems compared to the acted systems (see Section 4.4). This finding suggests that natural-seminatural MM systems have less room for improvement than acted systems. This finding is intuitively plausible because individuals tend to invoke a prototypical emotional response when asked to "act out" an emotion. This typically involves a higher level of coordination among the different modalities when compared to naturalistic expressions of emotion, thereby resulting in more optimistic MM effects.

Substantial second-order effects. The analysis that focused on assessing MM performance improvements over the second-best unimodal classifier yielded particularly interesting findings. The mean MM2 effect was an impressive 29.4% and was not dependent upon whether the training data was acted or natural-seminatural. Additionally, a paired-samples t-test indicated that the accuracy of the second-best unimodal system (M = .559, SD = .161) was significantly ($t(26) = -5.30$, $p < .001$) and substantially (d = 1.02 sigma) lower than accuracy of the best unimodal system (M = .674, SD = .143). Taken together, these findings suggest that although combining modalities yields modest improvements in affect detection accuracies, *considering multiple individual modalities* can have a major impact on system performance. This is because performance would be severely impacted if only one modality was modeled and in the worst case if it always happened to be the lower performing modality.

5.2 Theoretical Implications

The fact that combining multimodal accuracies yielded modest improvements has important implications for psychological theories of emotion. These theories in turn guide much of our affect detection models, so alignment of our findings with emotion theory has implications for next-generation affect detection systems.

The classical model of emotion, which was proposed by Tomkins, Ekman, Izard, and others, posits that discrete "affect programs" produce the physiological, behavioral, and subjective changes associated with a particular emotion [38-40]. According to this theory of "basic emotions," there is a specialized circuit for each basic emotion in the brain. Upon activation, this circuit triggers a host of *coordinated responses* in the mind and body. In other words, an emotion is expressed via a sophisticated synchronized response that incorporates peripheral physiology, facial expression, speech, modulations of posture, affective speech, and instrumental action. This prediction is very relevant to affect detection because it suggests that multimodal affect detection should yield accuracies that are substantially greater than the individual modalities due to this coordinated recruitment of response systems.

In contrast to this highly integrated, tightly coupled, central executive view of emotion, researchers have recently argued in favor of a disparate, loosely coupled, distributed perspective [41, 42]. According to this view, there is no central affect program that coordinates the various components of an emotional episode. Instead, these components are loosely coupled and the specific context and appraisals determine which bodily systems are activated. Therefore, coordinated bodily responses associated with particular emotions are rare. These models would accommodate the prediction that in most cases a combination of modalities might conceivably yield small improvements in classification accuracies.

We suspect that the expectation for impressive multimodal effects stems from an adherence to the classical model of emotion. However, the present data is more consistent with the alternate approach, which suggests that other than the rare cases of prototypical emotions, or in artificial experimental contexts involving acted emotions, modest MM effects might be expected.

5.3 Limitations and Future Work

There are two primary limitations to this work. The first pertains to the comprehensiveness of the studies that were analyzed. Our focus was on obtaining a reasonably large sample of studies that reported MM accuracies, rather than attempting to analyze every single study in the literature. This is defendable because one does not need to study an entire population to estimate its parameters. Furthermore, almost all of the tests of statistical significance yielded significant results, thereby suggesting that our sample size was adequate to detect the relatively large effects in our data.

The second limitation was that there was some imbalance with respect to the modalities, data, evaluation metrics, and affective states classified. For example, a majority of the studies we analyzed focused on audio-visual affect recognition, so the results are somewhat biased towards these systems. It is important to note, however, that this imbalance in our study is linked to a similar imbalance in the current state-of-the art. Specifically, most studies focus on the audio and visual modalities, while EEG, gaze, and context-based sensing are comparatively rare. Physiological-based affect sensing (i.e., biosignals) are quite popular affect detection modalities, but these are not often combined with face, voice, text, and other modalities.

This form of data imbalance was also the reason why we did not perform moderation analyses on other study-level variables (e.g., affective states classified, specific fusion methods) like we did with data type.

We are in the process of addressing these limitations in two ways. First, we are expanding the analysis to include a larger number of studies (approximately 50-100). Second, we will increase the breadth of our search of the literature to include all available MM studies on some of the less common modalities.

5.4 Concluding Remarks

The phrase "*consistent, but modest*" succinctly captures the results of this study. These MM systems were *consistently* better than their unimodal counterparts, but the improvements were *modest*, at least for the natural-seminatural systems. A fundamental question is whether these findings can be best explained by the *method* or by the *data*. In particular, are MM effects modest because our classifiers are not sufficiently sophisticated to model the intricate nonlinear time-varied relationships between the different modalities? Or are they modest because the data used to train the classifiers does not contain adequate expressions of coordination and synchronization among modalities, thereby rendering even the most sophisticated classifiers inept? The field of multimodal affect detection is too young to currently settle these issues, so the answer to this question awaits further research.

However, there is another possibility beyond the method and the data. It may be the case that the expression of naturalistic emotions is inherently a diffuse phenomenon, which will usually yield modest effects irrespective of method or data. This suggests that in addition to considering different methods and data sources, it might be useful to consider alternate models of emotion beyond the classic view described in Section 5.2. Unfortunately, almost all of the 30 studies (including our own [22]) we analyzed emphasized the method and the data at the expense of examining the affective phenomenon itself (i.e., insufficient attention to recent development in emotion theories and alternate models). Perhaps a more balanced approach that combines better data sources and innovative classifiers with more diverse emotion models represents the most promising way forward.

6. ACKNOWLEDGMENTS

This research was supported by the National Science Foundation (NSF) (ITR 0325428, HCC 0834847, DRL 1235958). Any opinions, findings and conclusions, or recommendations expressed in this paper are those of the authors and do not necessarily reflect the views of the NSF.

7. REFERENCES

[1] Calvo, R.A. and D'Mello, S.K. 2010. Affect detection: An interdisciplinary review of models, methods, and their applications. *IEEE Transactions on Affective Computing*, 1, 18-37.

[2] Zeng, Z., Pantic, M., Roisman, G. and Huang, T. 2009. A survey of affect recognition methods: Audio, visual, and spontaneous expressions. *IEEE Transactions on Pattern Analysis and Machine Intelligence*, 31, 39-58.

[3] Pantic, M. and Rothkrantz, L. 2003. Toward an affect-sensitive multimodal human-computer interaction. *Proceedings of the IEEE*, 91, 1370-1390.

[4] Kessous, L., Castellano, G. and Caridakis, G. 2010. Multimodal emotion recognition in speech-based interaction using facial expression, body gesture and acoustic analysis. *Journal on Multimodal User Interfaces*, 3, 33-48.

[5] Paleari, M., Benmokhtar, R. and Huet, B. 2009. Evidence theory-based multimodal emotion recognition. In *Proceedings of Proceedings of the 15th International Multimedia Modeling Conference (MMM '09)* (Chongqing, China, January 6-8, 2009).Springer-Verlag, Berlin, Heidelberg, 435-446.

[6] Wöllmer, M., Metallinou, A., Eyben, F., Schuller, B. and Narayanan, S.S. 2010. Context-sensitive multimodal emotion recognition from speech and facial expression using bidirectional LSTM modeling. In *Proceedings of Proceedings of the 11th Annual Conference of the International Speech Communication Association (INTERSPEECH 2010)* (Makuhari, Chiba, Japan, September 26-30, 2010). 2362-2365.

[7] Lin, J., Wu, C. and Wei, W. 2012. Error Weighted Semi-Coupled Hidden Markov Model for Audio-Visual Emotion Recognition. *IEEE Transactions on Multimedia*, 14, 142 - 156.

[8] Jiang, D., Cui, Y., Zhang, X., Fan, P., Ganzalez, I. and Sahli, H. 2011. Audio visual emotion recognition based on triple-stream dynamic bayesian network models. In *Proceedings of Fourth International Conference on Affective Computing and Intelligent Interaction* (Memphis TN, October 9-12, 2011).Springer-Verlag, Berlin Heidelberg, 609-618.

[9] Kim, J. 2007. Bimodal emotion recognition using speech and physiological changes. In Grimm, M. and Kroschel, K. eds. *Robust Speech Recognition and Understanding*, Vienna, Austria, I-Tech, 265-280.

[10] Metallinou, A., Wollmer, M., Katsamanis, A., Eyben, F., Schuller, B. and Narayanan, S. in press. Context-Sensitive Learning for Enhanced Audiovisual Emotion Classification. *IEEE Transactions on Affective Computing.*

[11] Emerich, S., Lupu, E. and Apatean, A. 2009. Emotions recognition by speech and facial expressions analysis. In *Proceedings of Proceedings of the 17th European Signal Processing Conference (EUSIPCO 2009)* (Glasgow, Scotland, August 24-28, 2009).

[12] Gunes, H. and Piccardi, M. 2005. Fusing face and body display for bi-modal emotion recognition: Single frame analysis and multi-frame post integration. In *Proceedings of First International Conference on Affective Computing and Intelligent Interaction (ACII 2005)* (Beijing, China, October 22-24, 2005).Springer-Verlag, Berlin Heidelberg, 102-111.

[13] Glodek, M., Tschechne, S., Layher, G., Schels, M., Brosch, T., Scherer, S., Kächele, M., Schmidt, M., Neumann, H. and Palm, G. 2011. Multiple Classifier Systems for the Classification of Audio-Visual Emotional States. In *Proceedings of 4th International Conference on Affective Computing and Intelligent Interaction (ACII 2011)* (Memphis, TN, October 9-12, 2011).Springer, Berlin/Heidelberg, 359-368.

[14] Khalali, Z. and Moradi, M. 2009. Emotion recognition system using brain and peripheral signals: Using correlation dimension to improve the results of EEG. In *Proceedings of Proceedings of International Joint Conference on Neural Networks* (Atlanta, GA, June 14-19, 2009).IEEE, 1571 - 1575

[15] Castellano, G., Kessous, L. and Caridakis, G. 2008. Emotion recognition through multiple modalities: face, body gesture, speech. In Peter, C. and Beale, R. eds. *Affect and Emotion in*

Human-Computer Interaction (LNCS, vol. 4868), Springer, Heidelberg, 92-103.

[16] Wagner, J., Andre, E., Lingenfelser, F., Kim, J. and Vogt, T. 2011. Exploring Fusion Methods for Multimodal Emotion Recognition with Missing Data. *IEEE Transactions on Affective Computing*, 2, 206-218.

[17] Caridakis, G., Castellano, G., Kessous, L., Raouzaiou, A., Malatesta, L., Asteriadis, S. and Karpouzis, K. 2007. Multimodal emotion recognition from expressive faces, body gestures and speech. In Boukis, C., Pnevmatikakis, L. and Polymenakos, L. eds. *International Federation for Information Processing, Volume 247, Artificial Intelligence and Innovations 2007: From Theory to Applications*, Springer, Boston, 375-388.

[18] Cueva, D., Gonçalves, R., Cozman, F. and Pereira-Barretto, M. 2011. Crawling to Improve Multimodal Emotion Detection. In *Proceedings of Proceedings of the 10th Mexican International conference on Artificial Intelligence (MICAI 2011)* (Puebla, Mexico, November 26 - December 4, 2011).Springer-Verlag, Berlin, Heidelberg, 343-350.

[19] Gunes, H. and Piccardi, M. 2009. Automatic temporal segment detection and affect recognition from face and body display. *IEEE Transactions on Systems, Man, and Cybernetics, Part B: Cybernetics*, 39, 64-84.

[20] Soleymani, M., Pantic, M. and Pun, T. in press. Multi-Modal Emotion Recognition in Response to Videos. *IEEE Transactions on Affective Computing*.

[21] Chanel, G., Rebetez, C., Bétrancourt, M. and Pun, T. 2011. Emotion assessment from physiological signals for adaptation of game difficulty. *IEEE Transactions on Systems, Man and Cybernetics, Part A: Systems and Humans*, 41, 1052-1063.

[22] D'Mello, S. and Graesser, A. 2010. Multimodal semi-automated affect detection from conversational cues, gross body language, and facial features. *User Modeling and User-adapted Interaction*, 20, 147-187.

[23] Kapoor, A. and Picard, R. 2005. Multimodal affect recognition in learning environments. In *Proceedings of Proceedings of the 13th annual ACM international conference on Multimedia* (Hilton, Singapore, November 6-11, 2005).ACM, NY, NY, 677-682.

[24] Schuller, B. 2011. Recognizing Affect from Linguistic Information in 3D Continuous Space. *IEEE Transactions on Affective Computing*, 2, 192-205.

[25] Busso, C., Deng, Z., Yildirim, S., Bulut, M., Lee, C.M., Kazemzadeh, A., Lee, S., Neumann, U. and Narayanan, S. 2004. Analysis of emotion recognition using facial expressions, speech and multimodal information. In *Proceedings of Proceedings of the 6th International Conference on Mutlmodal Interfaces (ICMI '04)* (State College, PA, October 13-15, 2004).ACM, New York, NY, 205-211.

[26] Eyben, F., Wollmer, M., Valstar, M.F., Gunes, H., Schuller, B. and Pantic, M. 2011. String-based audiovisual fusion of behavioural events for the assessment of dimensional affect. In *Proceedings of Ninth IEEE International Conference on Automatic Face and Gesture Recognition (FG 2011)* (Santa Barbara, CA, March 21-25, 2011).IEEE, Washington, DC, 322-329.

[27] Karpouzis, K., Caridakis, G., Kessous, L., Amir, N., Raouzaiou, A., Malatesta, L. and Kollias, S. 2007. Modeling naturalistic affective states via facial, vocal, and bodily expressions recognition. In Huang, T. ed. *Artifical Intelligence for Human Computing*, Springer-Verlag, Berlin Heidelberg, 91-112.

[28] McKeown, G., Valstar, M., Cowie, R., Pantic, M. and Schroder, M. 2012. The SEMAINE database: Annotated multimodal records of emotionally coloured conversations between a person and a limited agent. *IEEE Transactions on Affective Computing*, 3, 5-17.

[29] Nicolaou, M., Gunes, H. and Pantic, M. 2011. Continuous Prediction of Spontaneous Affect from Multiple Cues and Modalities in Valence& Arousal Space. *IEEE Transactions on Affective Computing*, 2, 92-105.

[30] Adolphs, R.A. 2002. Neural systems for recognizing emotions. *Current Opinion in Neurobiology*, 12, 169-177.

[31] Wu, C. and Liang, W. 2011. Emotion recognition of affective speech based on multiple classifiers using acoustic-prosodic information and semantic labels. *IEEE Transactions on Affective Computing*, 2, 10-21.

[32] Litman, D.J. and Forbes-Riley, K. 2006. Recognizing student emotions and attitudes on the basis of utterances in spoken tutoring dialogues with both human and computer tutors. *Speech Communication*, 48, 559-590.

[33] Rabie, A., Wrede, B., Vogt, T. and Hanheide, M. 2009. Evaluation and discussion of multi-modal emotion recognition. In *Proceedings of Proceedings of the Second International Conference on Computer and Electrical Engineering (ICCEE '09)* (Dubai, UAE, December 28-30, 2009).IEEE Computer Society, 598-602.

[34] Zeng, Z., Hu, Y., Roisman, G., Wen, Z., Fu, Y. and Huang, T. 2006. Audio-visual emotion recognition in adult attachment interview. In *Proceedings of Proceedings of the 8th international conference on Multimodal Interfaces (ICMI '06)* (Banff, Canada, November 2-4, 2006).ACM, New York, NY, 139-145.

[35] Allison, P.D. 1999. *Multiple regression*. Pine Forge Press, Thousand Oaks, CA.

[36] Baayen, R.H. 2008. *Analyzing linguistic data: A practical introduction to statistics using R*. Cambridge Univ Press, Cambridge.

[37] Cohen, J. 1992. A power primer. *Psychological Bulletin*, 112, 155-159.

[38] Ekman, P. 1992. An argument for basic emotions. *Cognition & Emotion*, 6, 169-200.

[39] Tomkins, S.S. 1962. *Affect Imagery Consciousness: Volume I, The Positive Affects*. Tavistock, London.

[40] Izard, C.E. 2007. Basic emotions, natural kinds, emotion schemas, and a new paradigm. *Perspectives on Psychological Science*, 2, 260-280.

[41] Coan, J.A. 2010. Emergent ghosts of the emotion machine. *Emotion Review*, 2, 274-285.

[42] Lewis, M.D. 2005. Bridging emotion theory and neurobiology through dynamic systems modeling. *Behavioral and Brain Sciences*, 28, 169-245.

Multimodal Recognition of Personality Traits in Human-Computer Collaborative Tasks

Ligia Maria Batrinca*, Bruno Lepri§, Nadia Mana¤ and Fabio Pianesi¤

*CIMeC, Univ. of Trento and FBK
Corso Bettini, 38068 Rovereto, Italy

§ FBK and MIT Media Lab
via Sommarive 18, 38123 Trento, Italy

¤ FBK
via Sommarive 18, 38123 Trento, Italy

{batrinca,lepri,mana,pianesi}@fbk.eu

ABSTRACT

The user's personality in Human-Computer Interaction (HCI) plays an important role for the overall success of the interaction. The present study focuses on automatically recognizing the Big Five personality traits from 2-5 min long videos, in which the computer interacts using different levels of collaboration, in order to elicit the manifestation of these personality traits. Emotional Stability and Extraversion are the easiest traits to automatically detect under the different collaborative settings: all the settings for Emotional Stability and intermediate and fully-non collaborative settings for Extraversion. Interestingly, Agreeableness and Conscientiousness can be detected only under a moderately non-collaborative setting. Finally, our task does not seem to activate the full range of dispositions for Creativity.

Categories and Subject Descriptors

H.1.2 [**User/Machine Systems**]: Human Information Processing; I.5.4 [**Pattern Recognition Applications**]: Computer Vision, Signal Processing; J.4 [**Computer Applications**]: Social and Behavioral Sciences – *Psychology, Sociology, Economics*.

General Terms

Algorithms, Performance, Human Factors.

Keywords

Personality recognition, Big Five, HCI, collaborative and non-collaborative behavior.

1. INTRODUCTION

Humans have the tendency to understand and explain other humans' behavior in terms of stable properties that are variously assorted on the basis of the observation of everyday behavior. In this sense, the attribution of a personality and its usage to infer about the others is a fundamental property of our naïve psychology.

Scientific psychology has maintained the importance of personality as a higher-level abstraction encompassing sets of stable dispositions towards action and towards belief and attitude formation. The concept of personality is commonly used to explain human behavior in several domains: clinical and social psychology, educational studies and so on. Most of the existing models of personality are based on traits, meant as higher level abstractions derived on the basis of factorial studies [4]. One of these models, widely used in psychological research and well-known, is the Big Five model [20].

In the field of Human-Computer Interaction (HCI), personality is a key factor [25]. Bickmore and Picard [8], as well as Nass and Brave [31], argued that matching users' personality increases the efficiency of the interaction and makes interaction more natural for the user. Nakajima et al., [30] have argued that in the context of a human-machine collaboration system, the system's personality is: a) perceived by the user and b) influencing the user's behavior.

The notion of personality has been used to improve the believability of lifelike characters. The main idea is that a virtual agent can appear more realistic if the engine that plans its actions may condition the behavior according to a given personality scheme (see for example, [2], [12], [25]).

Within the research area of socially assistive robotics [16], Tapu□ et al. [37] tackled the issue of matching the assistant robot's personality to the personality of post-stroke patients who are involved in rehabilitation therapy. However, they focused only on Extraversion/Introversion trait.

Recently, several works have explored the automatic analysis of personality ([26], [34], [23], [6], [28]), often targeting the Big Five model of personality, based on five traits (Extraversion, Agreeableness, Conscientiousness, Emotional Stability, and Creativity).

In this work we make an attempt at proceeding one step further and investigate to which degree it is possible to automatically predict all five traits of the Big Five model in a scenario that resembles the vision of HCI: a human interacting with a machine. The automatic recognition of personality poses two important challenges: a) recognize it in real-time and b) recognizing all five traits, with a satisfactory accuracy.

To date, few works address the issue of recognizing all the Big Five personality traits in a human-machine interaction context. In particular, to our knowledge, no work has yet addressed the issue of personality recognition in the assistive human-machine interaction context, given different collaborative behaviors.

For our research purposes, we have collected a special corpus. Similarly to [13], the data collection was based on a Map Task [1]. However, in our case, the interaction took place between a human and a system. So, it was a human-computer interaction and not a human-human interaction. Furthermore, the interaction was based on a distance communication via Skype, instead of a direct communication with the participants in the same room. Finally, in order to provoke possible behavioral reactions in the subjects, eliciting their personality traits, the second participant (i.e. the machine, simulated by the experimenter) played four specific behaviors (differently collaborative) during the interactions along the experimental sessions.

According to our hypotheses, collaborative behaviors elicit the manifestation of traits related to sociability and positive outcomes (e.g., Agreeableness and Extraversion), while non-collaborative behaviors may trigger anxious reactions and the manifestation of related traits (e.g., Emotional Stability/Neuroticism) in the subjects.

The rest of the paper is structured as follows: Section 2 presents the related work, whereas Section 3 provides a description of our Map Task corpus. Section 4 describes the acoustic and visual features that were manually and automatically extracted from the collected videos. This section also describes the feature selection process. In Section 5, the algorithms used to perform our binary classification task on each personality trait are presented, as well as the achieved results. An extended discussion of the results can be found in Section 6, whereas in Section 7 conclusions are drawn.

2. RELATED WORK

One of the first works addressing automatic recognition of personality was presented by Argamon and colleagues in [3]. They focused on two (Extraversion and Emotional Stability) of the five Big Five traits, measured by means of self-reports. Support vector machines (SVMs), trained on word categories based on systemic functional grammar (SMG) and relative frequency of function words, were used to recognize these two traits. Similarly, Oberlander and Nowson worked on automatic classification of author personality to detect four (Agreeableness, Conscientiousness, Extraversion and Neuroticism) of the Big Five traits on a corpus of personal weblogs [32]. They explored both Naïve Bayes classifiers and SVMs, trained on different set of n-gram features. Also Mairesse et al. [26] worked on recognition of the Big Five personality traits. According to psycholinguistic and psychosocial literature, they systematically investigated the usefulness of different sets of acoustic and textual features extracted from self-reports and observed data. The results showed that: a) prosodic features play a major role, b) Extraversion is the easiest personality trait to model from spoken language and c) the automatic recognition was closer to observed personality than to that emerging from the self-reports.

Pianesi et al. [34] provided evidence about the feasibility of multimodal analyses of personality traits and the influence of the social context. In particular, they proposed an automatic prediction of two personality traits (Extraversion and Locus of Control), based on simple non-verbal features, in a group interaction context. They started from the assumption that: a) personality shows up in the course of social interaction and b) 1-minute-long sequences of social behavior are enough to classify personality traits. The same approach was used by Lepri et al. [23], while extending the work presented in [34].

More recently, Mohammadi et al., ([28], [29]) worked on prosodic features, while showing that features may be used to predict personality assessments of human experts on a collection of 640 speech samples.

Finally, Batrinca et al. ([7], [6]) addressed the automatic detection of the Big Five personality traits from short (30-120 seconds) self-presentations. The effectiveness of 29 simple acoustic and visual non-verbal features, extracted from videos, were investigated. The results show that Conscientiousness and Emotional Stability/Neuroticism are the best recognizable traits. The lower accuracy levels for Extraversion and Agreeableness are explained through the interaction between situational characteristics and the differential activation of the behavioral dispositions underlying those traits.

3. THE MAP TASK CORPUS

3.1 Participants

In our study, we had a total of 45 subjects recruited among employees of a research centre, university students and other external people. The corpus was acquired in the Italian language.

Because of the low quality of the collected data during two experimental sessions (repetitive loss of audio and/or video signals), two subjects were left out and thus we focused on a sample of 43 subjects.

The distribution of the participants was quite balanced in terms of gender (19 female and 24 male) and age (18 people under 25 and 25 people over the age of 25). The average age of the subjects was 31, namely falling within the adult range (over 25).

3.2 Technical Setup and Recording Procedure

The subjects, involved in individual sessions, were invited to sit in front of a monitor with a webcam on its top. They used the computer mouse just to fill in an online questionnaire and to accept the Skype call (via audio only because of conflicts between Skype video and the webcam recordings) from the experimenter at the beginning of the experimental session. A clip-on microphone, worn by the subject on the shirt or sweater collar, was used to communicate with the experimenter.

At the beginning of the session, the experimenter provided each subject with the necessary details. Then she asked the subject to sign the informed consent form and to fill in an online personality questionnaire (see Section 3.4). After checking that the subjects properly wore the clip-on microphone and securing that the webcam was properly placed for frontal and central shots and for the video recording of the subject during the experimental session, the experimenter left the room for the recording room. From there, she called the subject via Skype, informing him/her that he/she could start a short self-introduction session, followed by the Map Task session.

The subject was told that he/she would be interacting with a machine and his/her task was to guide it along a path, marked on the map showed on the laptop screen. The machine was actually simulated by the experimenter by means of pre-recorded audio files (see Section 3.3).

In order to lead the subject into believing he/she was interacting with a machine, at the beginning of the Map Task session the experimenter orally simulated a connection to an automatic system by saying "Ora la connetto al sistema e l'esperimento ha inizio" (lit. "Now I am going to connect you to the system and then the experiment will start").

3.3 Map Task

Introduced by HCRC group at the Edinburgh University in 1991

[1], the Map Task is a cooperative task widely used in psychology, sociology and linguistics studies to collect spontaneous dialogues and interactions, elicited by a task solution.

In the original task, two speakers sit opposite one another, separated by a panel. Each of them has a map, not visible to the other. One speaker, designated as the Instruction Giver, has a route marked on her map (see Figure 1-a); the other speaker, designated like 'Instruction Follower', has a similar map without route. The speakers are told that their goal is to reproduce the Instruction Giver's route on the Instruction Follower's map. The maps are not identical (compare Figure 1-a and 1-b) and the speakers are told this explicitly at the beginning of their session but they do not know how the two maps differ.

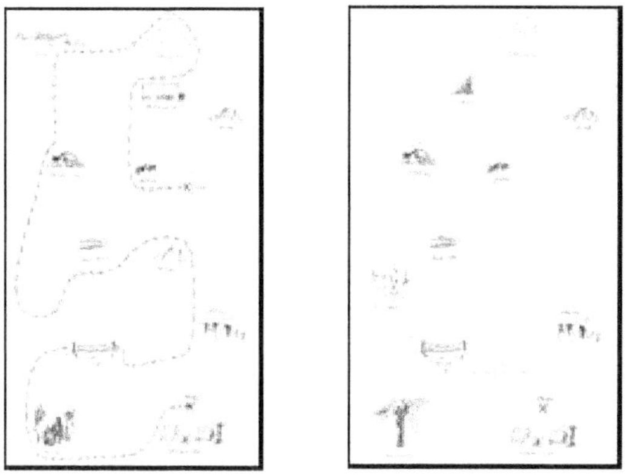

(a) **(b)**

Figure 1 - An example of two maps used by the Instruction Giver (a) and the Instruction Follower (b) in the original version of the Map Task.

In our case, the subjects played the role of the Instruction Giver. Similar to [13], their maps were changed in order to have a landscape orientation for a better visualization on the laptop screen. We also substituted all the drawings with pictures to make the elements on the map more easily recognizable (see Figure 2).

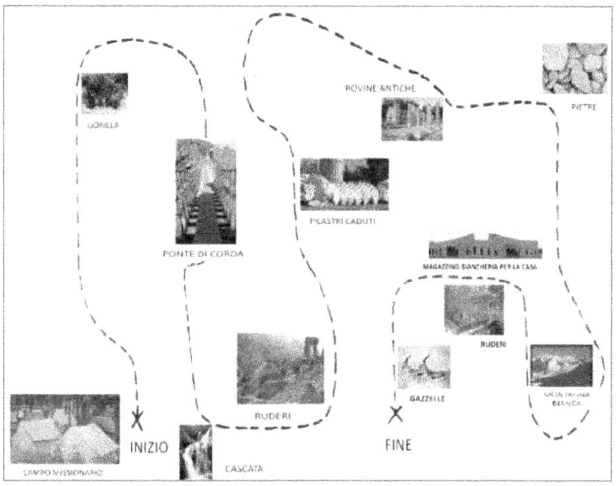

Figure 2. The map used by our participants

Different from [13], the two participants, namely the experimenter and the subject, were in separate rooms and communicated via Skype. As in the original version of the task, they both had a map with some objects: some of these objects were exactly in the same position and marked with the same label but, in order to stimulate the conversational interaction, most of them were in different positions or didn't have identical labels. Others were even different objects (e.g. a banana tree instead of gorillas close to a palm).

Unlike the original Map Task, where the final goal was to draw on the map of the Instruction Follower the same route reported on the Instruction Giver's map, in our Map Task, the Instruction Giver was told to guide the system from a point to another, according exactly to the route marked on her/his map. The system to guide was simulated by the experimenter who was playing a set of 50 pre-recorded sentences. Such sentences were properly modified to be played back in a more computer-like fashion, in order to give the impression of interacting with an actual machine.

During the interaction, the experimenter could use neutral sentences, distinguished in "positive-neutral" (e.g. *"sì", "OK", "va bene"* – lit. *"yes", "OK", "fine"*) and "negative-neutral" (e.g. *"no", "cosa?", "non ho capito"* – lit. *"no", "what?", "I don't know"*). At the same time, in order to provoke the subjects' different behavioral reactions eliciting his/her personality traits, the experimenter exhibited different behaviors, according to four different collaboration levels (CL). The experimenter's behavior went from a fully collaborative (CL1) to a fully non-collaborative one (CL4), going through two intermediate collaboration levels (CL2 and CL3). In the first case (CL1), the system was fully complying with the subject's requests (e.g. "perfetto, ho capito, va bene" – lit. "perfect, I understand, all right" – uttered with enthusiastic and trusting voice). In the exact opposite case (CL4), it was not complying with the subject's requests up to being very aggressive and offensive (e.g. "È' meglio che impari un po' a spiegarsi!" – lit. "it's better that you learn to explain!" – uttered with an aggressive voice).

All four behaviors, performed by means of four different set of specific sentences, were played along the experimental session in the same order (CL1, CL3, CL4, CL2) with each subject. The only variable was the length of each interaction modality (2-5 minutes), which varied with each subject according to his/her clearness in providing directions. A defined criteria based on which the experimenter would move to another interaction level does not exist. The switch was done based solely on the interaction between the experimenter/machine and the subject.

Since this is an exploratory work, we preferred to maintain a certain number of collaborative conditions, under the hypothesis that different levels of collaboration could elicit a larger set of reactions and facilitate the emergence of subjects' personality traits.

3.4 The Big Five Model

Given its optimal factorial structure, for our task we used the Big Five model [20], asking to the subjects to fill in the Italian version of the questionnaire.

The model owes its name to the five traits that it takes as constitutive of people's personality:

1. Extraversion vs. Introversion
   (sociable, assertive, playful vs. aloof, reserved, shy)
2. Agreeableness vs. Disagreeableness
   (friendly, cooperative vs. antagonistic, faultfinding)
3. Conscientiousness vs. Un-conscientiousness
   (self-disciplined, organized vs. inefficient, careless)
4. Emotional stability vs. Neuroticism

(calm, unemotional vs. insecure, anxious)

5. Creativity or Openness to experience
(intellectual, insightful vs. shallow, unimaginative)

In the standard questionnaire, validated on the Italian language [33], each trait is investigated through ten items assessed by means of a 1 to 7 Likert based points scale.

The final scores of the questionnaire were calculated per each personality trait, by first computing the z-scores and then orthogonalizing these values. The results (average and standard deviation values) are reported in Table 1. For completeness they are across gender but that is not used further in this study.

Table 1. Averages and standard deviations (in brackets) of Big Five scores on our corpus

	Women		Men	
	<25	≥25	<25	≥25
Extra	44.88 (10.05)	46.64 (7.3)	45.06 (9.05)	41.36 (7.59)
Agree	47.5 (3.96)	50.91 (6.3)	48.1 (9.67)	50.57 (8.58)
Consc	39.75 (9.45)	50.09 (9.05)	38.4 (9.37)	49.07 (8.08)
EmSt	35 (7.62)	36.82 (4.14)	41.4 (6.5)	46.07 (6.84)
Creat	42.25 (4.2)	44.73 (6.07)	48.8 (7.38)	47.36 (8.19)

4. EXTRACTED FEATURES

The dialogue between the subject and the computer provides a plethora of resources that can be significant for the classification of personality traits. According to the literature, we build an initial set of features considered relevant for automatically detecting the personality of the user, in a HCI context where the computer "behavior" represents an additional constant.

Similarly to ([6], [7]), we focused on acoustic and visual features. The relevance of acoustic features, such as pitch and intensity, for personality assessment, has often been pointed out ([15], [36]). Furthermore, Furnham [18] investigated how extraverted people are characterized by a particular speaking style: they talk more, louder, faster and have fewer hesitations. Others pointed out that frequency of hand movements/gestures was positively correlated with Extraversion [11]. Riggio [35] suggested that extraverts have a higher head movement frequency than introverts and they change their posture more often. Many visual cues have been correlated to Agreeableness ([18], [9]). Conscientiousness was correlated with speaking fluency, speech rate and hand movements ([3], [18], [9]).

In the following sub-sections all the features, extracted from the automatic annotations and from the audio and video signals, are described. Such features are summarized in Table 2.

4.1 Acoustic Features

In our corpus audio cues were extracted in two different ways. On one hand, pitch, intensity and statistics related to these two were extracted automatically using the Praat tool [9]. On the other hand, although manual annotations of dialogue segments can be very tedious and time consuming, we opted for them in order to enrich the corpus annotations (see Section 4.1.2).

Table 2. Extracted Features

	Label	Description	Ref
Acoustic Features	DurSpeechExp	duration of experimenter's speech	1
	DurSpeechSubj	duration of subject's speech	2
	DurOverlap	duration of the overlapping speech between the subject and the experimenter	3
	DurSilence	duration of silence	4
	MeanPitch	mean of the subject's pitch	5
	MaxPitch	maximum of the subject's pitch	6
	MinPitch	minimum of the subject's pitch	7
	MedianPitch	median of the subject's pitch	8
	StDevPitch	Standard deviation of the subject's pitch	9
	MeanInt	mean of the subject's intensity	10
	MaxInt	maximum of the subject's intensity	11
	MinInt	minimum of the subject's intensity	12
	StDevInt	standard deviation of the subject's intensity	13
Visual Features	MVMAll	Motion Vector Magnitude computed over all blocks in the frame	14
	MVMSkin	Motion Vector Magnitude computed over the skin blocks in the frame	15
	RCBAll	Residual Coding Bitrate computed on the all blocks	16
	RCB_Skin	Residual Coding Bitrate computed over the skin blocks in the frame	17
	MVMRCB_All_Av	Average between the Motion Vector Magnitude and Residual Coding Bitrate computed on all blocks in the frame	18
	MVMRCB_Skin_Av	Average between the Motion Vector Magnitude and Residual Coding Bitrate computed on the skin blocks in the frame	19
Additional Features	SubjTurns	number of speaking turns	20
	SubjLongTurns	number of speaking turns longer than 2 sec.	21

4.1.1 Speaker Diarization System

Aiming at extracting acoustic features related to the dialogue between the subject and the machine, we came across the speaker diarization problem, namely the process of partitioning an input audio stream into homogeneous segments according to the speaker identity.

However, since we know the number of speakers involved in the interaction (always two) and also their identity, we have approached the problem from a speaker recognition perspective.

We used Gaussian mixture models (GMMs), a background model and maximum a posteriori (MAP) adaptation for updating means of the Gaussian distribution in the speaker models. The background model is constructed using a speech corpus. It is based on two models: one for speech and one for silence. Adaptation process is applied to both of the models using data from the actual corpus that will be annotated (the Map Task, in our case).

In our study, we constructed the model for the experimenter by applying MAP adaptation by means of the HTK toolkit [39]. For each subject, a single speech model has been constructed by adapting the background model using speech samples collected from each of them. According to the method, we then applied Viterbi decoding to all the videos for the given subjects, again by the HTK toolkit. In this way, we obtained the automatically annotated videos with the corresponding speech label (for both the subject and the experimenter) and silence label. Finally, the annotations were converted to an ANVIL-compliant format [21], to make them visible using this annotation tool.

4.1.2 Audio Features Extracted From the Automatic Annotations

We post-edited the automatic annotations, by correcting the label of the erroneous speech segment label. From the latter annotations we derived the following set of features:

- *Turns:* computed over the entire dialogue, they refer to the number of turns of the subject. Therefore, to extract this feature, we took into consideration the number of speech segments labeled with "Subject".
- *Long Turns:* computed over the entire dialogue, they refer to the number of the subject's speech segments that are longer than 2 seconds. During the dialogues we observed events such as back-channeling, coughing or sounds unrelated/irrelevant to the dialogue. To not include these phenomena, we decided to discard turns shorter than 2 seconds. A similar approach has proven to be effective in [19].
- *Total Speaking Duration of the Subject:* captures the total amount of time in which the subject is vocally active. This feature sums the duration of all speech segments with the "Subject" label.
- *Total Speaking Duration of the Experimenter:* refers to the total amount of time in which the experimenter is speaking. This feature sums the duration of all speech segments with the "Experimenter" label.
- *Total Duration of the Overlapped Speech:* captures the total amount of time where the subject and experimenter's speech overlap.
- *Total Duration of the Silence:* for each video, we have computed the total amount of time, in which neither the subject nor the experimenter is active.

4.1.3 Audio Features Extracted Automatically

Focusing only on the subject's speech segments, pitch and acoustic intensity were automatically extracted using Praat [9]. The start and end time of each segment has been taken from the post-edited annotations. The pitch algorithm is based on the autocorrelation method. By setting the default values for the time step and pitch ceiling (600 Hz) parameters, but lowering the pitch floor from 70 Hz to 50 Hz, the algorithm uses a time step of 15 ms and a window length of 60 ms. The algorithm computes 67 pitch values per second. Going through these values, a post-processing algorithm seeks the cheapest path, ignoring values above the one set by the pitch ceiling parameter. Intensity is calculated taking into consideration the minimum periodicity frequency in the signal. The maximum, minimum, average, median and standard deviation were computed for pitch, as well as for intensity.

4.2 Visual Features

Five visual activity cues were extracted using the approach described in [19]. More precisely, for each frame where the participant is visible in the close-up view, the average *motion vector magnitude* and the *residual coding bitrat*e over all the estimated blocks and skin blocks are computed and used as a measure of individual visual activity. Motion vectors are generated from motion compensation during the video encoding; for each source block that is encoded in a predictive fashion, its motion vectors indicate which predictor block from the reference frame is to be used. A predictor block is highly correlated with the source block and hence similar to the block to be encoded. Therefore, motion vectors are usually a good approximation of optical flow, which in turn is a proxy for the underlying motion of objects in the video [14].

After motion compensation, the DCT (Discrete Cosine Transform) coefficients of the residual signal, which is the difference between the block to be encoded and its prediction from the reference frame, are quantized and entropy-coded. The residual coding bitrate is the number of bits used to encode this transformed residual signal.

Motion vector magnitude and residual coding bitrate capture different kind of information: while the motion vectors capture the rigid body motion like translation, residual coding bitrate attempts to capture the non-rigid motion. In order to compare in a meaningful way the motion vector magnitudes and the residual coding bitrate, the quantities were normalized [38]. Following [19], we also used as fifth measure the combined estimate of the visual activity, namely the average of visual activity from motion vector magnitude and from residual coding over the estimated skin blocks. In this way, both rigid and non-rigid local motions can be approximated. These features were used to detect dominant people in meeting scenario, considering that dominant people tend to move more [19].

4.3 Feature Selection

A known problem in classification tasks is to find strategies to reduce the dimensionality of the feature space in order to avoid over-fitting. In our experiments, we applied the Weka implementation of the Classifier Subset Evaluator that evaluates subsets of features using a classifier (in our case, Support Vector Machine with linear kernel) to estimate the 'merit' of a set of attributes [22]. The evaluation was performed on the datasets generated by an inner leave-one-subject-out cross validation.

This method was used jointly with a Best First search strategy, that searches the space of subsets of features by greedy hill-climbing augmented with a backtracking facility. We used the forward direction of the search that begins at the empty set of features. In the Table 3, we report the features selected for the different traits using the linear SVM subset evaluator. These features were used for running the classification tasks (see Section 5).

Table 3. Features selected using SVM (with linear kernel) subset evaluator (features' numbers refer to Table 2)

	Extr.	Agree.	Consc.	Em.Stab.	Creat.
CL1	1,9, 16,20	6,7, 12,14	1,2,6,7 9,13, 14,18	6,7,11	2,7, 19
CL2	1,10, 16,18, 21	1,4,9, 10,14	1,21	5,6,11, 18	3
CL3	14	1,3,4,5 8,9,13, 14,19, 20	1,3,4, 20	5	1,2,7, 16,17
CL4	2,10, 17,20	1,2,3,5 7,8,12, 18	1,4,5	5,17	2,11, 18,19

5. AUTOMATIC CLASSIFICATION

For our classification experiments, all personality traits' scores were quantized (Low/High) along their median values (Agreeableness = 50.45, Conscientiousness = 50.72, Creativity = 48.13, Emotional Stability = 51.69 and Extraversion = 50.25).

Classification was firstly performed by means of Support Vector Machines (SVMs) with linear kernel.

In particular, the bound-constrained SVM classification algorithm was used for the SVM classifier. The cost parameter C was estimated trough an inner leave-one-subject-out cross validation on the training set of the first fold and were then kept fixed for the outer-cross validation.

We designed 5 binary classification tasks, one per personality trait. Each binary classification task was performed for each interaction modality, CL1-CL4. The total number of experimental conditions was 20.

For each classifier, for each trait, and for each collaboration level of the interacting machine, only the features retained in the feature selection step (see Section 4.3) were used.

The leave-one-out cross-validation strategy was employed. Hence, 43 models for each personality trait were trained on 42-subject subsets, evaluating them against the remaining ones and finally averaging the results.

For comparison, we ran the same experiments described above by using SVMs with Radial Basis Function (RBF) kernels and Naïve Bayes. Since the classification using SVMs with RBF kernel and Naïve Bayes gave results not significantly different to those obtained by SVM with linear kernel algorithm, for space reason we report here only the latter ones.

6. RESULTS AND DISCUSSION

Table 4 summaries the accuracy values for each trait and for each level of collaboration (CL), as described in Section 3.3, performed by the interacting machine.

The accuracy values highlighted in bold are statistically significant, according to binomial tests that compared the observed accuracy to that of the baseline classifier that exploits the observed frequencies of the two classes. The significance was set at $p \leq 0.01$ and the resulting threshold values for accuracy where 0.67 for all the traits.

Table 4. Accuracy obtained using SVM with linear kernel

	Extr.	Agree.	Consc.	Em.Stab	Crea.
CL1	62,79	65,12	51.16	**81.30**	48,43
CL2	**81,39**	**69,77**	**69,76**	**74.41**	58,13
CL3	**74,41**	67,44	62,79	**74.41**	58,13
CL4	**72.09**	41,86	60,46	**74.41**	60,46

Extraversion and Emotional Stability are the only traits yielding, in an almost consistent way, results significantly better than the baseline.

Emotional Stability and its counterpart, Neuroticism, concern the susceptibility to negative emotions, which we one might think are elicited by the certain behaviors of the second participant in the dialogue. All four interaction modalities (CL1-CL4) seem to be fit, for the study of the manifestation of this trait. Emotional Stability/Neuroticism includes both anxious and irritable distress. The former is inner-focused and includes dispositions to anxiety, sadness and insecurity. Irritable distress, in turn, involves outer-directed hostility, anger, frustration and irritation. We can easily figure out that the task of trying to accomplish a given task, in a collaborative or non-collaborative setting, activates one of those two sets of dispositions, depending on the person's internal constitution. The behavioral signs that proved effective concerned: a) pitch in all the different conditions given by the machine's role, b) intensity (maximum of subject's intensity) while the computer was behaving in fully collaborative way (CL1) and c) body motion activity while the computer/experimenter was interacting in a fully non-collaborative way (CL4).

A good accuracy level was obtained for Extraversion too. The core of Extraversion lies in the tendency to behave in a way so as to engage, attract and enjoy social attention, *i.e.*, extraverts invest time and energy in activities that attract the attention of others ([5], [27]). One possible consequence of this view can be the explanation to why Extraversion-related disposition are activated to a greater extent in situations like the ones we are considering here. In particular, the effective behavioral signs were: a) intensity of subject's speech signal while the computer is behaving in fully non-collaborative way (CL4) and in one of the intermediate modality (CL2), b) body motion activity and c) long speaking turns in case of CL2 intermediate modality.

Agreeableness and Conscientiousness obtained a result slightly above the threshold only in the condition CL2. In particular, for Agreeableness we could hypothesize there is no coincidence that this trait is better recognized in the CL2 setting. The key might lie in the characteristics of the collaboration level. CL2, distinguished by a set of neutral-positive responses to the subject's indications, activates a pleasing attitude in the subject, while CL3 and CL4 have no bearing.

We also tested if the performance differed among the conditions given that different interaction modalities performed by the machine were significant. We did not find any statistically significant difference with the exception of CL1 for which the performance was significantly worse for Extraversion than in the three other conditions. This result calls to further investigations.

Finally, we found an interesting trend for the fully collaborative modality (CL1) which facilitated a better performance in the recognition of Emotional Stability compared to all other personality traits. The CL2 modality facilitated a better performance for classifying the Extraversion trait.

7. CONCLUSION

The goal of this paper is to contribute to the advancement the state of the art in the automatic recognition of people's personality in the context of Human-Computer Interaction. In particular, we investigated the feasibility of detecting the Big Five personality dimensions under the influence of four different behavioral settings. In doing so, we analyzed the contribution of a large set of different acoustic and visual non-verbal cues.

The main findings of our paper are the following:

a) Extraversion and Emotional Stability are the easiest traits to automatically detect under the different collaborative settings (CL1, CL2, CL3, CL4 for Emotional Stability and CL2, CL3 and CL4 for Extraversion). For the former trait, the reason could be that since the proper social context is provided, it allows us to better observe and capture the characteristics of the trait, while for the latter, which is connected to emotional reactions (e.g. distress), the interaction and the various behaviors of the machine, elicits its manifestation.

b) Our task does not seem to activate the full range of dispositions for Creativity. We have invoked the masking effect of the necessity of giving precise indications to the experimenter, implicit in the nature of the situation.

Interestingly, Agreeableness and Conscientiousness, perform better than the baseline, only under a moderately non-collaborative setting. Since the main characteristics of the Agreeableness trait are related to pleasing the interlocutor, and receiving attention and it's not a trait that exhibits antipodal behaviors, a possible explanation could be that opposite, extreme settings (fully collaborative or fully non-collaborative) do not foster conditions for a clear observation of the trait. For Conscientiousness, it is possible that only CL2-like settings are appropriate for further studies on this trait. Of course, more experiments are needed to validate this.

On the practical side, although not excellent, part of our results are encouraging and represent an important initial step towards automatic systems capable of recognizing personality under different circumstances and in different scenarios (e.g. assistive robotics, human-interaction collaborative systems). On a more theoretical side, they emphasize and demonstrate up to a certain point, the influence of the situation for a full unfolding of the behavioral dispositions tied to personality traits. Further works are needed to clarify the role played by the situations. For instance, one might follow [17], and target personality states, that is, specific behavioral episodes wherein a person behaves, e.g., more or less introvertly/extravertly, depending on situational characteristics. The distribution of personality states conditioned by the situation characteristics can then be used to reconstruct the relevant trait, reconciling the traditional focus on between-person variability with the meaningfulness of within-individual variability. To this end, a specific corpus has been collected [23].

The original hypotheses: a) differences in the interaction context are associated with difference in the way personality traits manifest and b) these can be used to better predict the traits, could not be proved to the extent of our expectations. We believe that the sample size of our data bears an influence upon our results and limits the scientific observations that would be possible to make with the behavioral conditions we employed for this paper.

More work is needed to fully explore the automatic analysis of personality traits under the considered conditions. A continuing strategy would be have a richer dataset or to consider even larger sets of non-verbal feature, as well as verbal ones (e.g., lexical choice, presence of emotion-related words; topic dynamics, etc.); and/or exploiting regression or ordinal techniques.

8. ACKNOWLEDGMENTS

Bruno Lepri's research is funded by PERSI project inside the Marie Curie COFUND – 7th Framework.

9. REFERENCES

[1] Anderson, A., Bader, M., Bard, E., Boyle, E., Doherty, G.M., Garrod, S., Isard, S., Kowtko, J., McAllister, J., Miller, J., Sotillo, C., Thompson, H.S., and Weinert, R. 1991. The HCRC Map Task Corpus. Language and Speech, 34, pp. 351-366.

[2] Andrè E., Klesen M., Gebhard P., Allen S., and Rist T. 1999. Integrating models of personality and emotions into lifelike characters. In Proc. of the International Workshop on Affect in Interactions, p. 136–149.

[3] Argamon, S., Dhawle, S., Koppel, M., and Pennbaker, J. 2005. Lexical predictors of personality type. In Proc. of Interface and the Classification Society of North America.

[4] Ashton, M.,C., and Lee, K. 2001. A theoretical basis for the major dimensions of personality. European Journal of Personality. 15:327–53.

[5] Ashton, M. C., Lee, K., and Paunonen, S. V. 2002. What is the Central Feature of Extraversion? Social Attention Versus Reward Sensitivity. Journal of Personality and Social Psychology, 83, 245-252.

[6] Batrinca, L., Lepri, B., and Pianesi, F. 2011. Multimodal recognition of personality traits during short self-presentations. In Proc. of the joint ACM workshop on Human gesture and behavior understanding, (J-HGBU '11), Scottsdale, Arizona.

[7] Batrinca, L., Mana, N., Lepri, B., Pianesi, F., and Sebe, N. 2011. Please, tell me about yourself: automatic personality assessment using short self-presentations. In Proc. of the International Conference on Multimodal Interaction.

[8] Bickmore, T.W. and. Picard, R.W. 2005. Establishing and aintaining long-term human-computer relationships. ACM Trans. Comput.-Hum. Interact., 12:293–327, June 2005.

[9] Boersma, P., and Weenik, D. – Praat: doing phonetics by computer. Computer Program, Version 5.2.05. www.praat.org

[10] Borkenau, P., and Liebler, A. 1992. Trait inferences: Sources of validity at zero acquaintance. Journal of Personality and Social Psychology, 62, 645-657.

[11] Brebner, J. 1985. Personality theory and movement. In B. D. Kirkcaldy (Ed.), Individual differences in movement (pp. 27-41). Lancaster, England: MTP Press Limited.

[12] Castelfranchi, C., and DeRosis, F. 1999 How can personality factors contribute to make agents more 'believable', Proceedings of the Workshop on Behavior Planning for Lifelike Characters and Avatars, Sitges, Spain, 25-35, 1999.

[13] Cavicchio, F., and Poesio, M. 2008. Annotation of Cooperation and Emotion in Map Task Dialogues. In Proc. of the LREC Workshop on Multimodal Corpora, pp. 376-38.

[14] Coimbra, M.T., and Davies, M. 2005. Approximating optical flow within the MPEG-2 compressed domain. In IEEE Transactions on Circuits and Systems for Video Technology, 15(1):103–107.

[15] Dewaele, J. M., and Furnham, A. 2000. Personality and speech production: a pilot study of second language learners. In Personality and Individual Difference.

[16] Feil-Seifer, D., and Mataric, M. J. 2005. Defining socially assistive robotics. In Proc. of the IEEE international Conference on rehabilitation robotics (ICORR'05), Chicago, IL, USA, pp 465–468

[17] Fleeson, W. 2001. Towards a structure- and process-integrated view of personality: Traits as density distributions of states. Journal of Personality and Social Psychology, 80, 1011-1027.

[18] Furnham, A. 1990. Language and personality. In K. R. Scherer and H. Giles and W. Robinson (Eds). Handbook of Language and Social Psychology, Winley.

[19] Jayagopi, D., Hung, H., Yeo, C., and Gatica-Perez, D. 2009. Modeling dominance in group conversations from non-verbal activity cues. In IEEE Transactions on Audio, Speech and Language Processing.

[20] John, O. P., and Srivastava, S. 1999. The Big five trait taxonomy: History, measurement and theoretical perspectives. In Pervian, L. A. & John, O. P., (Eds.) Handbook of personality theory and research. Guilford Press. New York.

[21] Kipp, M. 2001. Anvil – A generic Annotation Tool for Multimodal Dialogue. In Proceedings of the 7th European Conference on Speech Communication and Technology, Eurospeech, pp. 1367-1370.

[22] Kohavi, R. and John, G.H. 1997. Wrappers for feature subset selection. Artificial Intelligence, 97(1-2):273–324.

[23] Lepri B, Staiano J, Rigato G., Kalimeri K., Finnerty A., Pianesi F., Sebe N., and Pentland A.. 2012. The SocioMetric Badges Corpus: A Multilevel Behavioral Dataset for Social Behavior in Complex Organizations.In Proc. of ASE/IEEE SocialCom 2012

[24] Lepri, B., Mana, N., Cappelletti, A., Pianesi, F., and Zancanaro, M. 2009. Modeling the Personality of Participants during Group Interaction. In Proc. UMAP – User Modeling, Adaptation and Personalization. Trento, Italy.

[25] Liscombe, J., Venditti, J., and Hirschberg, J. 2003. Classifying subject ratings of emotional speech using acoustic features. In Proc. of Eurospeech - Interspeech 2003, p. 725–728.

[26] Mairesse, F., and Walker, M. 2006. Automatic recognition of personality in conversation. In Proc of HLT-NAACL.

[27] Mairesse, F., and Walker, M. 2006. Words mark the nerds: Computational models of personality recognition through language. In Proc. of the 28th Annual Conference of the Cognitive Science Society, pp. 543–548.

[28] Mohammadi, G. and Vinciarelli, A. 2012. Automatic Personality Perception: Prediction of Trait Attribution Based on Prosodic Features. Accepted for publications by IEEE Transactions on Affective Computing.

[29] Mohammadi, G., Vinciarelli, A., and Mortillaro, M. 2010. The Voice of Personality: Mapping Nonverbal Vocal Behavior into Trait Attributions. In Proc. of the Second International Workshop on Social Signal Processing (SSPW 2010).

[30] Nakajima, H., Nass, S.B.C., Yamada, R., Morishima, Y., and Kawaji, S. The functionality of human-machine collaboration systems mind model and social behavior. In Proc. of the IEEE Conference on Systems, Man, and Cybernetics, pp. 2381–2387. Washington, USA (2003)

[31] Nass, C. and Brave, S. 2005. Wired for Speech: How Voice Activates and Advances the Human-Computer Relationship. MIT Press, 2005.

[32] Oberlander, J. and Nowson, S. 1992. Whose thumb is it anyway? Classifying author personality from weblog text. In Proc. of the Annual Meeting of the ACL. Association for Computational Linguistics, 627-634.

[33] Perugini, M. and Di Blas, L. 2002. Analyzing Personality related Adjectives from an Eticemic Perspective: The Big Five marker Scales (BFMS) and the Italian AB5C Taxonomy. In B. De Raad and M. Perugini (eds.) Big Five Assessment, Hogrefe und Huber Publishers, Göttingen, 281-304.

[34] Pianesi, F., Mana, N., Cappelletti, A., Lepri, B., and Zancanaro 2008. Multimodal Recognition of Personality Traits in Social Interactions. In Proc. of International Conference on Multimodal Interfaces, Chania, Crete, Greece.

[35] Riggio, R., Friedman, H. 1986. Impression formation: The role of expressive behavior. In Journal of Personality and Social Psychology 50(2), 421-427.

[36] Scherer, K. R. 1979. Personality markers in speech. In K. R. Scherer and H. Giles (Eds)., Social Markers in Speech. Cambridge University Press.

[37] Tapus, A., Tapus, C., and Mataric, M. 2008. User-Robot Personality Matching and Robot Behavior Adaptation for Post-Stroke Rehabilitation Therapy. Intelligent Service Robotics Journal, Special Issue on Multidisciplinary Collaboration for Socially Assistive Robotics, 1(2):169-183.

[38] Yeo, C., and Ramchandran, K. 2008. Compressed domain video processing of meetings for activity estimation in dominance classification and slide transition detection. Technical Report UCB/EECS-2008-79, EECS Department, University of California, Berkeley, Jun 2008.

[39] Young, S., Evermann, G., Gales, M., Hain, T., Kershaw, D., Liu, X.A., Moore, G., Odell, J., Ollason, D., Povey, D., Valtchev, V., and Woodland, P. 2006. The HTK Book (for HTK Version 3.4). Cambridge University Press.

Automatic Detection of Pain Intensity

Zakia Hammal
Carnegie Mellon University
Robotics Institute,
5000 Forbes Ave
Pittsburgh, PA 15213, USA
zhammal@andrew.cmu.edu

Jeffrey F. Cohn[1,2]
(1) Carnegie Mellon University,
(2) University of Pittsburgh
210 S. Bouquet Street
Pittsburgh, PA 15213, USA
jeffcohn@cs.cmu.edu

ABSTRACT
Previous efforts suggest that occurrence of pain can be detected from the face. Can intensity of pain be detected as well? The Prkachin and Solomon Pain Intensity (PSPI) metric was used to classify four levels of pain intensity (none, trace, weak, and strong) in 25 participants with previous shoulder injury (McMaster-UNBC Pain Archive). Participants were recorded while they completed a series of movements of their affected and unaffected shoulders. From the video recordings, canonical normalized appearance of the face (CAPP) was extracted using active appearance modeling. To control for variation in face size, all CAPP were rescaled to 96x96 pixels. CAPP then was passed through a set of Log-Normal filters consisting of 7 frequencies and 15 orientations to extract 9216 features. To detect pain level, 4 support vector machines (SVMs) were separately trained for the automatic measurement of pain intensity on a frame-by-frame level using both 5-folds cross-validation and leave-one-subject-out cross-validation. F1 for each level of pain intensity ranged from 91% to 96% and from 40% to 67% for 5-folds and leave-one-subject-out cross-validation, respectively. Intra-class correlation, which assesses the consistency of continuous pain intensity between manual and automatic PSPI was 0.85 and 0.55 for 5-folds and leave-one-subject-out cross-validation, respectively, which suggests moderate to high consistency. These findings show that pain intensity can be reliably measured from facial expression in participants with orthopedic injury.

Categories and Subject Descriptors
J [**Computer Applications**]: J.3 [Life and Medical Sciences]; I.5.4 [**Pattern Recognition Applications**]; H.1.2 [**User/Machine systems**]: [Human information processing, Human Factors].

General Terms
Algorithms, Measurement, Performance, Design, Experimentation, Human Factors.

Keywords
Facial Expressions, Pain, Intensity, Active Appearance Models (AAMs), Log-Normal filters, Support Vector Machines (SVMs).

1. INTRODUCTION
Pain assessment and management are important across a wide range of disorders and treatment interventions. The assessment of pain is accomplished primarily through subjective reports of patients, caregivers, or medical staff. While convenient and useful, subjective reports have several limitations. These include inconsistent metrics, reactivity to suggestion, efforts at impression management or deception, and differences among clinicians' and sufferers' conceptualizations of pain. Further, self-report cannot be used with children or patients with certain neurological impairments, dementia, or those in transient states of consciousness or requiring breathing assistance [1]. Biomedical research has found that pain can be detected reliably from facial expression [26], [6]. Recent efforts in affective computing suggest that automatic detection of pain from facial expression is a feasible goal. Several groups have automatically distinguished pain from absence of pain [14], [1], [16], [10]. For clinical or experimental utility, pain intensity need be measured as well.

Automatic measurement of pain from the face is challenging for at least two reasons. One is the lack of training and testing data of spontaneous, un-posed and unscripted, behavioral observations in individuals that have clinically relevant pain. The other is the difficulty of face and facial features analysis and segmentation in real world settings, such as medical clinics. The recent distribution of the UNBC-McMaster Pain Archive addresses the need for well-annotated facial expression recordings during acute pain induction in a clinical setting. Using the UNBC or other data sources, several approaches have been proposed to detect occurrence of pain: [23], [14], [1], [16], [10]. Notably, [11] proposed the more demanding task of detecting ordinal pain intensity.

In the current contribution, we extend the state of the art in pain recognition by automatically detecting four levels of pain intensity consistent with the Prkachin and Solomon Pain Intensity (PSPI) metric in participants with orthopedic injuries. The PSPI [27] is a well-validated approach to manual measurement of pain that is based on the Facial Action Coding System (FACS) [9]. Pain is measured on an ordinal scale.

Previous work has found that active appearance models (AAMs) are a powerful means of analyzing spontaneous pain expression. [1][16]. These approaches use gray-scale features, however, that may be less robust to the head pose variation that is common in pain. [17]. [3] found that biologically inspired features (e.g., Gabor magnitudes) are more robust to the registration error introduced by head rotation. [14] used biologically inspired features to discriminate real from feigned pain.

In the current paper we couple AAMs with biologically inspired features to assess pain intensity in participants with significant orthopedic injury. Using video from the recently released UNBC-McMaster Should Pain Archive [18], AAMs are used to track and register rigid and non-rigid face motion [16] in each video frame. Based on this information, the canonical appearance of the face (CAPP) is extracted for each frame, rescaled to 96x96 pixels, and passed through a set of Log-Normal filters of 7 frequencies and 15 orientations [12]. The extracted spatial face representation is then aligned as a vector of 9216 features used by four SVMs trained separately for the automatic measurement of four levels of pain intensity.

The paper is organized as follows: Section 2 describes the pain intensity metric developed by Prkachin and Solomon [27]; Section 3 describes the UNBC-McMaster Shoulder Pain Expression Archive [16] used in the current paper; Section 4 describes the different steps of the proposed automatic model for pain intensity measurement; and Section 5 presents the obtained performances.

2. PRKACHIN and SOLOMON PAIN INTENSITY METRIC (PSPI)

Many efforts have been made in human behavior studies to identify reliable and valid facial indicators of pain (e.g., [26], [6], [20], [27]. In these studies pain expression is widely characterized by the activation of a small set of facial muscles and coded by a set of corresponding actions units (AUs): brow lowering (AU 4), orbital tightening (AU 6 and AU 7), levator labii raise (AU 9 and AU 10) and eye closure (AU 43) (see Figure. 1). With the exception of AU 43, which is binary, each of these actions is measured on a six-point ordinal scale (0 = absent, 5 = maximum) using FACS. In a recent study Prkachin and Solomon [27] confirmed that pain information is effectively contained in these AUs and defined pain intensity as the sum of their intensities. The Prkachin and Solomon FACS pain intensity (PSPI) scale is defined as:

$$\text{Pain} = AU4 + (AU6 || AU7) + (AU9 || AU10) + AU43 \quad (1)$$

Figure 1 shows an example of face in pain from the UNBC-McMaster Shoulder Pain Expression Archive with the corresponding AUs and their intensities. In this example, pain intensity using the PSPI metric is computed as:

Pain= Intensity (AU4) + (Max Intensity AU6 or AU7) + (Max Intensity AU9 or AU10) + Intensity (AU43)

Taking into account the intensity of each AU, the PSPI in this example is equal to 12:

Pain = 4 + Max (3, 4) + Max (2, 3) +1 = 4 + 4 + 3 + 1=12.

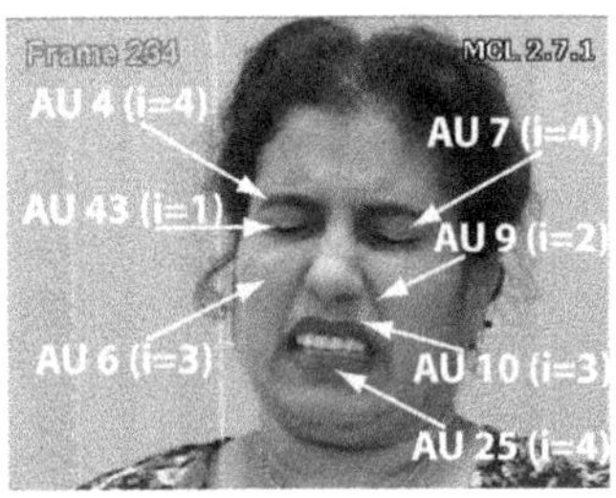

Figure 1. Example of painful face from the UNBC-McMaster Shoulder Pain Expression Archive with the corresponding Action Units and their intensities. (i= intensity of each AU).

3. DATABASE

The evaluation of the proposed model for the recognition of pain expression intensities is made on UNBC-McMaster Shoulder Pain Expression Archive [18]. The database is composed of 129 participants (63 males and 66 females) who self-identified as having problems with pain shoulder. Participants were recorded during a series of movements to test their affected and unaffected shoulder during active and passive conditions. In the active condition, participants initiated shoulder rotation on their own. In the passive condition, a physiotherapist was responsible for the movement. Sony digital cameras recorded participants' facial expressions. In the active condition, camera orientation was initially frontal; in the passive condition camera orientation was about 70° from frontal. In both conditions, moderate changes in pose were common as participants contorted in pain. Videos were captured at a resolution of 320x240 pixels, out of which the face area spanned an average of approximately 140x200 pixels [18].

Three FACS-certified coders coded facial action units on a frame-by-frame basis. Each AU was coded on a 6-level intensity dimension (from 0 = absent, 1 = trace to 5 = maximum) by one of three coders, each of whom had previously demonstrated proficiency by passing the FACS final test [27]. A fourth coder who had also demonstrated proficiency on the final test then reviewed all coding. Finally, to assess inter-observer agreement, 1738 frames selected from one affected-side trial and one unaffected-side trial of 20 participants were randomly sampled and independently coded. Inter-coder percent agreement as calculated by the Ekman-Friesen formula [8] was 95%, which compares favorably with other research in the FACS literature [27]. For a detailed description of the database, please refer to [27] and [18]. Pain intensity was finally annotated frame-by-frame using the PSPI metric described in section 2 using equation 1. Figure 2 shows examples from the UNBC-McMaster Shoulder Pain Expression Archive with the corresponding PSPI scores. In addition to the PSPI, participants completed three self-report pain measures after each test to rate the maximum pain they experienced: the sensory (SEN) and affective (AFF) verbal pain descriptors and the Visual Analog Scales (VAS).

The recently released version of the UNBC-McMaster Pain Archive includes 200 video sequences from 25 subjects in the active condition [18]. Of the 200 video sequences, 100 were for the affected shoulder, for which pain could be experienced. Of these, we used the first 53 sequences. These consisted of 16657 frames of FACS-coded video. Using equation 1 and the six-point scale of AU intensity, the PSPI could theoretically vary from 0 to 16. The obtained observer scores ranged from 0 to 12. Because some gradations of pain were sparsely represented, the PSPI scores were pooled to create a 4-point scale defined as shown in Table 1.

Table 1. Number of video frames for each level of pain.

	Pain Severity and PSPI Score			
	No pain	Trace	Weak	Strong
	0	1	2	≥ 3
Number of frames	12503	1263	1239	1652

Figure 2 shows examples of each of the four intensity levels. The following section describes the proposed machine learning method for the automatic measurement of these four levels.

4. AUTOMATC MEASUREMENT OF PAIN EXPRESSION INTENSY

4.1 Preliminary analyses

An anatomically based measure of pain intensity, the PSPI, was used to train automatic detectors of pain intensity. A preliminary question was how well the PSPI correlated with the self-report measures of pain. To evaluate the correspondence between the PSPI and participants' self-reported pain intensity, the self-report measures were compared with each other and then with the PSPI. The three self-report measures were highly inter-correlated (r= 0.94 to r = 0.96, all $p < 0.001$), which represents high consistency between self-reports of pain intensity. To compare the PSPI to the self-report measures, we considered the PSPI score as the maximum intensity over all images for each sequence. The Pearson's correlations between the PSPI and self-reported pain was $r > 0.61$ or higher, all $p < 0.001$. The obtained correlation suggests moderate to strong association between PSPI and self-reported pain intensity.

4.2 Overview

To automatically measure the intensity of pain, active appearance models (AAMs) are first used to extract the canonical appearance of the face (CAPP) [19, 16]. The obtained CAPP is then rescaled and passed through a set of Log-Normal filters [12]. The extracted features are finally given as inputs to four separate support vector machines (SVMs) trained for the automatic measurement of the four levels of pain intensity. A detailed description of the three steps is given in the following subsections.

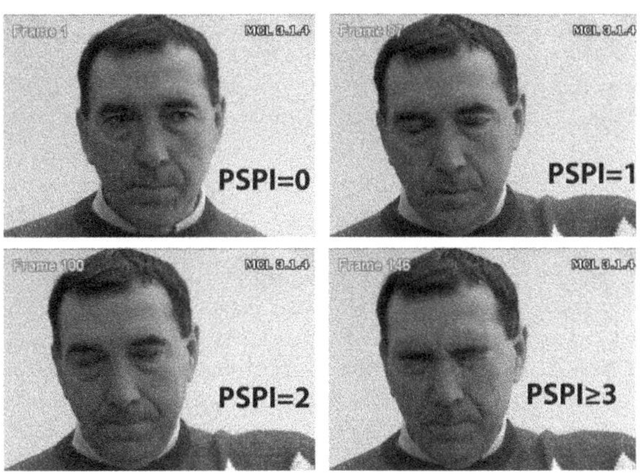

Figure 2. Examples from the UNBC-McMaster Shoulder Pain Expression Archive database with the corresponding pain intensity using the PSPI metric.

4.3 Active Appearance Model

Active appearance models (AAM) [4] have been successfully used for face tracking and facial features extraction for spontaneous facial expression analysis and recognition [19, 1, 16]. AAMs are defined by a shape component, s, and an appearance component, g, which jointly represent the shape and texture variability of the face [19]. The AAMs fit their shape and appearance components through a gradient-descent search, although other optimization methods have been employed with similar results [5].

A 2D triangulated mesh describes the shape s of an AAM. The coordinates of the mesh vertices define the shape $s = [x_1, .y_1, x_1, .y_1, ..., x_n, y_n]$, where n is the number of vertices. These vertex locations correspond to a source appearance image, from which the shape is aligned. Since AAMs allow linear shape variation, the shape s can be expressed as a base shape s_0 plus a linear combination of m shape vectors s_i :

$$s = s_0 + \sum_{i=1}^{m} p_i s_i \qquad (2)$$

where the coefficients $p = (p_1, ..., p_m)^T$ are the shape parameters. These shape parameters can typically be divided into rigid similarity parameters p_s and non-rigid object deformation parameters p_0, such that $p^T = [p_s^T, .p_0^T]$. Similarity parameters are associated with a geometric similarity transform (i.e. translation, rotation and scale). The object-specific parameters, are the residual parameters representing non-rigid geometric variations associated with the object shape (e.g., mouth opening, eyes shutting, etc.). Procrustes alignment [5] is employed to estimate the base shape s_0.

For each participant, approximately 3% of frames were manually labeled in training the AAM. All frames then were automatically aligned using a gradient descent AAM fitting algorithm described in [25]. Based on [19, 1 and 16] canonical normalized appearance CAPP (see Figure 3.b) was derived from shape and appearance parameters of the AAMs. Canonical normalized appearance a_0 refers to the situation where all the non-rigid shape variation has been normalized with respect to the base shape s_0. This is accomplished by applying a piece-wise affine warp on each triangle patch appearance in the source image so that it aligns with the base face shape s_0 [16]. CAPP features correspond to 87 × 93 synthesized grayscale face images. Figure 3.b shows an example of CAPP [16].

In a recent study of pain analysis and recognition using AAMs Lucey and collaborators [16] found that canonical normalized appearance (CAPP) gives better performances for pain recognition compared to similarity shape features. Given these results, CAPP features are investigated in the current contribution for pain intensities measurement. Additionally, energy based representation (such as Gabor amplitude) has been found to be highly discriminative for facial action recognition compared to the grayscale representation [7, 17]. Thus, rather than using the grayscale representation of the CAPP, the results of the application of a set of filters (using Log-Normal filters), is used for the automatic recognition of 4 levels of pain intensity.

4.4 Log-Normal Filters

Pain facial expression is characterized by the deformations of facial features (see section 2). Figure 2a shows an example where pain expression is characterized by a deepening and orientation change of the naso-labial furrows as well as eyes closure. The intensity of pain can be characterized by the magnitude of such deformations (such as the strong or soft appearance of nasal root wrinkles, the degree of eyes closure, etc.). These deformations can be measured directly in the energy-based representation by the magnitude of energy appearing in the face after filtering process compared to the relaxation state. For example, in Figure 3 one can see that the appearance of nasal root wrinkles (Figure 3.b) leads to high-energy magnitude after filtering process (see the whitest areas in Figure 3.c). Thus, instead of using the grayscale representation of CAPP [16], we investigated the results of an additional filtering of the CAPP. To do so, a set of biologically based Log-Normal filters [12, 24] is applied to the extracted CAPP. Log-Normal filters were originally proposed by [24] for measuring frequencies and orientations in texture images for 3D shape detection. Log-Normal filters are a good model of the complex cells found in the visual cortex V1. Notably they share specific characteristics such as: they are symmetrical on a log-frequency scale; they are well defined even at very low frequency; and they sample completely the Fourier space (interested reader can find a more detailed description of the Log-Normal filters in [24], and their application for facial feature extractions in [12]).

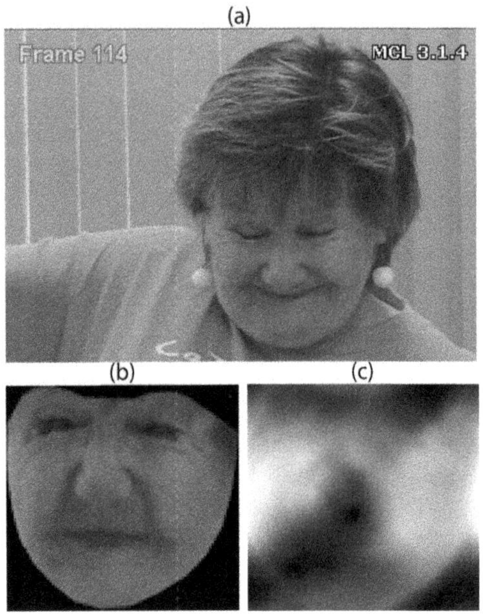

Figure 3. (a) Input frame, (b) Canonical Normalized Appearance CAPP, (c) Log-Normal filtering.

Compared with the more commonly used Gabor filters, the Log-Normal filters are chosen because they may better sample the power spectrum and are easily tuned and separable in frequencies and orientations [12]. These attributes make them well suited for detecting features (such as the naso-labial furrows in the case of pain) at different scales and orientations [12]. The Log-Normal filters are defined as follow:

$$\left|G_{i,j}(f,\theta)\right|^2 = \left|G_i(f).G_j(\theta)\right|^2 = A\frac{1}{f}.\exp\left(-\frac{1}{2}\left(\frac{\ln(f/f_i)}{\sigma_r}\right)^2\right).\exp\left(-\frac{1}{2}\left(\frac{\theta-\theta_j}{\sigma_\theta}\right)^2\right)$$

(3)

Where $G_{i,j}$ is the transfer function of the filter at the ith frequency and the jth orientation, $G_i(f)$ and $G_j(\theta)$, represents the frequency and the orientation components of the filter, respectively; f_i is the central frequency, θ_j, the central orientation $(\theta_j = (180/15).(j-1))$, σ_f, the frequency bandwidth $(\sigma_f = \sqrt{\ln(f_{i+1}/f_i)})$, σ_θ, the orientation bandwidth and A, a normalization factor. The factor $1/f$ in equation1 accounts for the decrease of energy in function of the frequency, which in average follows $1/f^{\alpha}$ power law. This factor ensures that the sampling of the spectral information of the face takes into account the specific distribution of energy of the studied face at different scales. This property ensures that the facial information is optimally sampled over the different frequency bands [12].

To compute the magnitude of the response of the Log-Normal filters, the power spectrum of the normalized CAPP is multiplied by a bank of Log-Normal filters (15 orientations and 7 central frequencies, see [24, 12] for details on the filter bank design). The inverse Fourier transform (IFFT) is then computed to recover the spatial representation of the filtered CAPP. Figure 3.c shows an example of the magnitude response after the Log-Normal filtering in the case of strong pain (PSPI >3).

4.5 Support Vector Machine Based Classification

To examine the possible description of pain intensities based on the Log-Normal filter responses, support vector machines (SVMs) [2] are used. Among other possible classifiers, SVMs are selected because they can cope with large representation spaces, are simple to train, and generalize well. SVMs are well-suited to the high dimensional representation of Log-Normal filter responses), which depend only on the number of training examples [22]. However, the training time complexity for an SVM is $O(m^3)$, where m is the number of training examples [2, 1]. A compromise between the best use of the training data and the training time is necessary for an efficient use of SVM. Previous work has shown the concurrent validity of SVMs for the recognition of spontaneous AU intensity (e.g. [22], [21]). In the current contribution, an SVM is built for each pain intensity level. Each SVM is trained on the corresponding images (see section 3) using a linear basis function. Four linear basis function SVMs are thus employed to recognize separately the four levels of pain intensity defined in section 3. Each SVM based intensity detector is trained using positive examples, which consist of the frames that the PSPI metric labeled as equal to that particular intensity. The negative examples correspond to all the other frames that the PSPI metric labeled with another intensity (see Table 1). The SVMs are trained on the (96x96=9216) pixel responses after the Log-Normal filtering process (see Figure 3.c). This process allows taking into account magnitude energy response as well as the distribution of this energy over the face (i.e. the spatial position). The generalization of the proposed SVM based models, for the recognition of pain intensity levels, to new data is evaluated by using the standard 5-folds cross-validation process and the leave-one-subject out validation process, in which all images of the test participant were excluded from training. Section 5 describes the obtained performances. In 5-folds cross-validation, train and test sets are independent with respect to frames (i.e. no frame included in training is used in testing). In leave-one-out cross-validation, train and test are independent with respect to participants. Thus, leave-one-out cross-validation affords a more rigorous test.

5. PERFORMANCES

5.1 Classification Results

In this section, the performance of the proposed SVM classifiers for the four intensity levels is evaluated. Recall, precision and F1 are used to quantify the performance of each classifier in comparison with ground truth, the PSPI. The 5-folds cross-validation in which all video frames of the training set are removed from the testing set is used first for the evaluation. The obtained performance of each SVM is reported in Table 2. The best results are obtained for no pain (PSPI=0) and strong pain (PSPI>=3). These results may be explained by the strong difference between these two intensity levels relative to intermediate ones (see Figure 2). The obtained performances are encouraging given the task difficulty.

Table 2. Performances of Pain Intensity measurement compared to the PSPI manual detection (ground truth). CR = Classification Rate (%), PR = Precision (%), F1 = F1 measure (%).

	5-folds cross validation			Leave one subject out validation		
Intensity	CR	PR	F1	CR	PR	F1
0	97	95	96	61	65	57
1	96	97	92	72	37	67
2	96	97	91	79	35	40
>=3	98	98	95	80	70	60

Five-folds cross-validation is not participant-independent. Frames from the same participant may appear in both the training and testing sets. To control for this limitation, we next performed a leave-one participant out cross-validation in which participants (i.e. all the corresponding images) of the training are removed from the testing. This validation allows exploring how the proposed method for pain intensity measurement generalizes to a new set of participants who were not part of the training set. The leave-one-subject-out validation, consists in building 25 classifiers for each one of the four levels of pain intensity and iterating the process. In the leave one subject out validation, the number of training frames from all the video sequences is prohibitively large to train a SVM, as the training time complexity for SVM is $O(m^3)$, where m is the number of training examples [2, 1]. In order to make the learning process practical, while making the best use of the training data, each video sequence is down-sampled by taking 1 of every frames [21]. The training is thus performed on only 15% of video images excluding one participant. The SVM testing is made on the left- out participant. Based only on 15% of the training data, the obtained F1 for each level of pain intensity (from 0 to 3) was 0.57, 0.67, 0.40, and 0.60, respectively.

5.2 Intra Class Correlation Coefficient

The Previous results are for category-level agreement. Here we compare consistency of the 4-level automatic measurement with the 12-level PSPI. To do so, the reliability between the proposed method and the PSPI is quantified by the intra-class correlation coefficient (ICC) [28]. Values range within a restricted interval [-1,1]. An ICC of 1 would indicate perfect consistency. The ICC is typically used to calculate the reliability of judgments. Following Mahoor [21], ICC is used to measure concurrent validity between automatic and manual coding of intensity. The ICC values between the automated measurements and the manually labeled pain intensity levels using the PSPI were 0.85 and 0.55 for 5-folds and leave-one-subject-out validation, respectively. The obtained ICC between ground truth PSPI and each of the estimated PSPIs suggest moderate to high consistency between manual and automatic measurement of pain intensity.

6. CONCLUSION AND PERSPECTIVES

We used a combination of AAM, Log-Normal filters, and SVMs to measure four levels of pain intensity in the McMaster-UNBC Pain Archive. Using both 5-folds cross-validation and leave-one-subject-out cross-validation, the results suggest that automatic pain intensity measurement in a clinical setting is a feasible task. Intra-class correlation results were within the acceptable range for behavioral measurement. Replication in shoulder-pain populations and applications to other types of pain would be next steps for future research.

The current work opens several additional directions for future investigations. One is to compare additional types of features (e.g., Gabor) and classifiers. Two is to evaluate whether pain intensity might be detected better by first detecting AU intensity and then calculating PSPI from the result. In our work, classifiers were trained to directly detect PSPI scores without first detecting individual AU intensities. Detection of AU intensity is in the early stages of research [21]. To our knowledge, no one has yet compared direct versus indirect measurement of the intensity of pain or other constructs.

Three, following previous work, we measured pain at the frame-by-frame level. However, pain expression is not static, but results from the progressive deformation of facial features over time. A next investigation would be to include dynamics when measuring pain intensity.

And four, previous work in both pain and AU detection primarily regards head pose variation as a source of registration error. However, head pose is itself a potentially informative signal. In particular, head pose changes may themselves be a good indicator of pain [18] and pain intensity. We are currently in the process of exploring the dynamic characteristics of head orientation such as (but not limited to) the speed, velocity, and acceleration of pain indicators. We believe explicit attention to dynamics is an exciting direction for further research.

7. REFERENCES

[1] Ashraf, A., B., Lucey, S., Cohn, J. F., Chen, T,., Prkachin, K. M. and Solomon, P. E. (2009). The painful face: Pain expression recognition using active appearance models," *Image and Vision Computing,* vol. 27, pp. 1788–1796, 2009.

[2] Burges, Christopher J. C.; A Tutorial on Support Vector Machines for Pattern Recognition, Data Mining and Knowledge Discovery 2:121–167, 1998

[3] Chew, S. W., Lucey, P., Lucey, S., Saragih, J., Cohn, J. F., and Sridharan, S. In the pursuit of effective affective computing: The relationship between features and registration," IEEE Transactions on Systems, Man, and Cybernetics - Part B, In press.

[4] Cootes, T., Cooper, D., Taylor, C., and Graham, G. 1995. Active shape models - their training and application. *Computer Vision and Image Understanding*, 61(1):38–59, Jan. 1995.

[5] Cootes, T., Edwards, G. and Taylor, C. 2001. Active Appearance Models, IEEE Transactions on Pattern Analysis and Machine Intelligence, vol. 23, no. 6, pp. 681–685, 2001.

[6] Craig, K. D., Prkachin, K. M., and Grunau, R. V. E. 2001. The facial expression of pain. In D. C. Turk and R. M., editors, Handbook of pain assessment. Guilford, New York, 2nd edition, 2001.

[7] Donato, G., Bartlett, M., Hager, J, Ekman, P., and Sejnowski, T. 1999. Classifying facial actions," *IEEE Transactions on Pattern Analysis and Machine Intelligence*, vol. 21, no. 10, pp. 974–989, 1999.

[8] Ekman P, Friesen WV. (1978). Manual for the Facial Action Coding System. Palo Alto, CA: Consulting Psychologists Press; 1978.

[9] Ekman, P., Friesen, W. V. and Hager, J. C. 2002. Facial action coding system: Research Nexus, Network Research Information, Salt Lake City, UT, 2002.

[10] Hammal, Z., and Kunz, M., (2012). Pain Monitoring: A Dynamic and Context-sensitive System (2012). Pattern Recognition. Volume 45, Issue 4, April 2012, Pages 1265-1280.

[11] Hammal, Z., Context based Recognition of Pain Expression Intensities. The 5th Workshop on Emotion in Human-Computer Interaction - Real World Challenges -held at the 23rd BCS HCI Group conference. Cambridge University, Cambridge, UK, September 2009. (Fraunhofer VERLAG, 2010).

[12] Hammal, Z., and Massot, C., (2011). Gabor-like Image Filtering for Transient Feature Detection and Global Energy Estimation Applied to Multi-Expression Classification. Pages 135-153. In "Communications in Computer and Information Science" (CCIS 229) (eds. P. Richard and J. Braz, Springer, CCIS 229, 2011).

[13] Kunz, M., Scharmann, S., Hemmeter, U., Schepelmann, K., & Lautenbacher, S. 2007. The facial expression of pain in patients with dementia. Pain. December 15;133(1-3):221-8, (2007).

[14] Littlewort, G.C., Bartlett, M.S. & Kang, M.S. 2007. Faces of Pain: Automated Measurement of Spontaneous Facial Expressions of Genuine and Posed Pain. Proc. ICMI, Nagoya, Aichi, Japan, November 12–15, 2007.

[15] Lehr, V.T., Zeskind, P.S., Ofenstein, J.P., Cepeda, E., Warrier, I. Aranda, J.V. 2007. Neonatal facial coding system scores and spectral characteristics of infant crying during newborn circumcision. Clin J Pain. Jun; 23(5):417-24, 2007.

[16] Lucey, P., Cohn, J. F., Howlett, J., Member, S. L., & Sridharan, S. (2011). Recognizing emotion with head pose variation: Identifying pain segments in video. *Systems, Man, and Cybernetics – Part B, 41*(3), 664-674.

[17] Lucey, P,, Lucey, S., and Cohn, J. F. (2010). Registration invariant representations for expression detection," *International Conference on Digital Image Computing: Techniques and Applications (DICTA),* December 1-3, 2010 2010.

[18] Lucey, P., Cohn, J. F., Prkachin, K. M., Solomon, P., & Matthews, I. (2012). Painful data: The UNBC-McMaster shoulder pain expression archive database," *Image, Vision, and Computing Journal,* vol. 30, pp. 197-205, 2012.

[19] Lucey, S., Ashraf, A., and Cohn, J. (2007). Investigating spontaneous facial action recognition through aam representations of the face, in Face Recognition Book, K. Kurihara, Ed. Pro Literatur Verlag, 2007.

[20] Lints-Martindale, A.C., Hadjistavropoulos, T., Barber, B., Gibso, S.J. 2007. A psychophysical investigation of the facial action coding system as an index of pain variability among older adults with and without Alzheimer's disease. Pain Nov-Dec;8(8):678-89, 2007.

[21] Mahoor, M. H., Cadavid, S., Messinger, D. S. and Cohn, J. F. (2009). A Framework for Automated Measurement of the Intensity of Non-Posed Facial Action Units. 2nd IEEE Workshop on CVPR for Human communicative Behavior analysis (CVPR4HB), Miami Beach, June 25, 2009.

[22] Marian Stewart Bartlett, M.S., Littlewort, G., Frank, M., Lainscsek, C., Fasel, I., Movellan, J., (2006). Fully Automatic Facial Action Recognition in Spontaneous Behavior. Proceedings of the 7th International Conference on Automatic Face and Gesture Recognition (FGR'06)

[23] Maruf Monwar, Md. and Siamak R. 2006. Pain Recognition Using Artificial Neural Network. Proc. of IEEE International Symposium on Signal Processing and Information Technology 2006.

[24] Massot C., Herault J., 2008. Model of Frequency Analysis in the Visual Cortex and the Shape from Texture Problem, International Journal of Computer Vision, 76(2), 2008.

[25] Matthews, I. and Baker, S. 2004. Active appearance models revisited, International Journal of Computer Vision, vol. 60, no. 2, pp. 135–164, 2004.

[26] Prkachin, K., 1992. The consistency of facial expressions of pain: a com- parison across modalities," Pain, vol. 51, pp. 297–306, 1992.

[27] Prkachin, K. M. & Solomon, P. E. 2008. The structure, reliability and validity of pain expression: Evidence from patients with shoulder pain. Pain, 139, 267-274, 2008.

[28] Shrout, P., and J. Fleiss, J. (1979). Intraclass correlations: uses in assessing rater reliability. *Psychological Bulletin,* 86(2):420–428, 1979.

FaceTube: Predicting Personality from Facial Expressions of Emotion in Online Conversational Video

Joan-Isaac Biel
Idiap Research Institute
Ecole Polytechnique Fédérale de Lausanne (EPFL)
jibiel@idiap.ch

Lucía Teijeiro-Mosquera
University of Vigo
Idiap Research Institute
luciatm@gts.uvigo.es

Daniel Gatica-Perez
Idiap Research Institute
Ecole Polytechnique Fédérale de Lausanne (EPFL)
gatica@idiap.ch

ABSTRACT

The advances in automatic facial expression recognition make possible to mine and characterize large amounts of data, opening a wide research domain on behavioral understanding. In this paper, we leverage the use of a state-of-the-art facial expression recognition technology to characterize users of a popular type of online social video, conversational vlogs. First, we propose the use of several activity cues to characterize vloggers based on frame-by-frame estimates of facial expressions of emotion. Then, we present results for the task of automatically predicting vloggers' personality impressions using facial expressions and the Big-Five traits. Our results are promising, specially for the case of the Extraversion impression, and in addition our work poses interesting questions regarding the representation of multiple natural facial expressions occurring in conversational video.

Keywords

YouTube, vlogs, facial expressions, personality prediction

Categories and Subject Descriptors

H.1.2 [**User/Machine Systems**]

1. INTRODUCTION

Conversational vlogging is a successful genre of online social video that generates an enormous amount of audiovisual behavioral content. One differential feature of vlogging is that users can combine their verbal expression of opinions, desires, and personal narratives, together with a myriad of spontaneous nonverbal cues (through face, body, and voice) captured by the audio and video channels, and all this is watched by their online audience. This people-watching-people phenomenon involves complex interpersonal perception processes, in which people watching build impressions from personal information inferred from vlogs, and based on them, may react by posting comments or sharing the videos with others. This poses questions regarding the types of impressions that are built, their reliability, and the sources of information that people use, which are important issues not only for the understanding of the production and consumption mechanisms of this social media, but also for the automatic characterization of vloggers and the prediction of interpersonal impressions based on the automatic analysis of vlog content. Due to their abundance, the variety of topics and the naturalistic conditions of vlogs we posit that facial expressions of emotion occur frequently enough (see Fig. 1) to influence personality judgements [10].

Recent research has addressed the study of interpersonal perception in vlogging, from the perspective of Big-Five personality impressions and nonverbal behavioral analysis [3, 4]. Regarding judgements of personality, Biel et al. found that Extraversion and Agreeableness are the traits judged with higher reliability in vlogging [3]. Moreover, in an attempt to address the personality prediction task from automatically extracted nonverbal cues [4], the same authors found that nonverbal cues from audio and visual activity patterns seemed useful mainly to predict Extraversion [4]. Compared to past attempts to predict personality meetings [11] and monologue video presentations [2], the results in [3, 4] emphasized that the cues conveying personality information and the specific impression that can be reliably estimated from automatic analysis are particular of each communication scenario. In addition, those authors did not investigate other possible sources of useful personal information. In other related work, the analysis of facial expressions on online video has been previously researched in [13] from the perspective of passive, mainly silent, viewing of advertising content, but to our knowledge our paper is the first attempt to deal with facial expressions in video vlogs where people are mainly talking. We address the problem of predicting vloggers personality impressions from automatically extracted facial expressions of emotion. The human face has been widely documented in the social psychology literature as an important source of information in interpersonal impressions [9, 10, 8]. People rely heavily in facial cues to make interpersonal judgements because there is a general belief that faces provide valuable information about a person's character or personality [9]. We argue that this may be specially true in the vlogging scenario, in which vloggers typically display head and shoulders in camera and faces occupy a large portion of the screen [4]. Among facial features, there is evidence that facial expressions of emotion provide information other that emotional states, influencing interpersonal impressions such as personality judgements, and that specific affective cues are in fact correlated with the possession of various personality traits [10, 8].

This paper has four contributions. First, we explore to what extent spontaneous facial expressions are found in vlogging based on a dataset of vlogs collected from YouTube

ICMI'12, October 22–26, 2012, Santa Monica, California, USA.

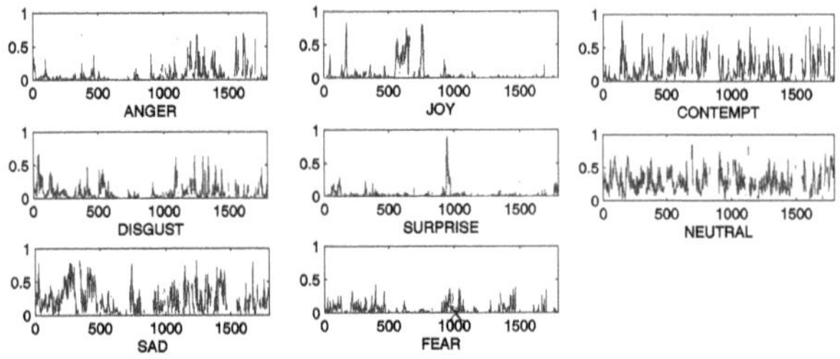

Figure 1: Example of CERT outputs for the eight universal facial expression of emotion.

and the analysis of the output obtained from processing vlogs with the Computer Expression Recognition Toolbox (CERT) [12]. Second, we study the associations between automatically extracted facial expressions of emotion and Big-Five personality judgements from vloggers to understand what specific facial expressions are most prominent for modeling each of the different impressions. Third, we do some experiments on predicting personality impressions usign different sets of facial expressions cues. Finally, we compare our results with previous results on personality prediction using nonverbal cues.

2. DATASET

Our dataset of vlogs was obtained from YouTube with a keyword-based search for "vlogs" and "vlogging", similarly to what was proposed in [4]. From this search we manually selected videos that featured a monologue scenario in which users talk in front of the camera. Then, we used a Viola-Jones face and facial feature detector to detect face, eyes, nose, and mouth [1], and selected videos were most of the frames contained all facial features detected. This preprocessing step for selecting videos aimed to minimize possible problems in the face registration step previous to the facial expression extraction (see Sec. 3.1). The final dataset contained 281 vloggers, mostly balanced in gender (53% female and 47% males). All the videos were cut to be one minute long.

We completed our dataset with annotations of personality impressions using Mechanical Turk. The task of crowdsourcing personality impressions from video watching had been attempted in previous work with comparable reliabilities to those obtained in other settings [4]. Using a short personality questionnaire [7], annotators were asked to judge the extent to which each vlogger could be described with each of the Big-Five traits: Extraversion (E), Agreeableness (A), Conscientiousness (C), Emotion Stability (ES), and Openness to Experience (O). To have more reliable estimates for personality we collected five different annotations for each vlog and aggregated the personality impressions using the average value. The ICC(1,k) reliabilities for each one of the personality impressions were .76 (E), .63 (A) .42 (C), .40 (ES), and .49 (O).

3. AUTOMATIC EXTRACTION OF FACIAL EXPRESSION CUES

In this section, we explain our approach to characterize vloggers' facial activity using the frame-by-frame estimates of a state-of-the art facial expression recognition system.

3.1 Automatic Facial Expression Analysis

Facial expression analysis has been thoroughly researched during the last two decades [6, 5] in the computer vision field. The Facial Action Coding System (FACS) developed by Ekman et al. [5] has become a standard framework for detecting facial actions and for classifying facial expressions of emotion. FACS defines the action units (AUs) that code the movement of facial muscles, and are considered the fundamental units of facial expressions. Using FACS, seven facial expressions of emotion considered as universal - Anger, Contempt, Surprise, Fear, Joy, Sad and Disgust- are uniquely defined in terms of AUs.

We processed vlogs using the Computer Expression Recognition Toolbox (CERT) [12], which is a real-time face processing software developed for facial expression understanding and constitutes a state-of-the-art in the field. CERT combines three face processing stages: face detection, feature detection, and face registration, to obtain a cropped face patch used for expression analysis. Our video selection step based on facial feature detection was targeted to prevent CERT from mis-registrations. Based on the AUs estimated using Gabor-based filters and SVM classifiers, CERT uses a multivariate logistic regressor to predict the seven expressions of emotion plus neutral expression. We use these 8 categories for the purpose of characterizing the facial expressions. In addition, we also use the smile detector output present in CERT [12].

3.2 Facial expressions activity cues

We propose a systematic method to model the frame-by-frame facial expression stream from CERT (see Fig. 1) into aggregate cues that capture different facial expression activity patterns. First, we converted the CERT output to a binary segmentation that divides the expression signal in active/inactive regions using two different approaches:

Thresholding (THR): we consider the CERT output to be activated when frame values are larger than a threshold λ. For facial emotions we choose $\lambda = .005$, which represents a rather conservative choice, whereas for smile the threshold was set up to $\lambda = 0$ by definition [12].

HMM: we used a two-state (active/inactive) Hidden Markov Model to detect the active state of the CERT output. Each output is modeled with one single Gaussian initialized with the threshold-based segmentation, while the transition probabilities are set to $\rho_{00} = \rho_{11} = 0.95$ and $\rho_{01} = \rho_{10}$.

In practice, the THR approach copes with high frequency changes, tends to give shorter and more frequent active states, and is also more sensitive to outliers. The HMM provides a smooth output, that tends to detect peaks in the CERT generated signals.

Based on these segmentations we extracted four different facial cues to measure the presence of expressions, their duration, their frequency, and the time of short segments.

Proportion of active time (PT): computed as $PT = \frac{1}{N}\sum_{i=0}^{N_r} \tau(r_i = 1)$, where $\tau(r)$ is the duration of segment r in frames, N_r is the total number of segments, and N is the total number of frames.

Number of active segments (NS): computed as $NS = \frac{1}{Nf}\sum_{i=0}^{N_r} (r_i = 1)$, where f is the frame rate.

Average duration of the expressions (AD): computed as $AD = \frac{1}{Nf}\sum_{i=0}^{N_r} \tau(r_i = 1)$ where $\tau(r_i)$ is the duration of region r in frames.

Proportion of short segments time (PTS): computed as $PTS = \frac{1}{N_r}\sum_{i=0}^{N} \tau(r_i = 1|\tau(r_i) \leq 0.001f)$, i.e., the proportion of time in segments shorter than 100ms.

	THR	HMM
E	**Anger:** PT (−.16), AD (.24), NS (−.23), PTS (.27). **Contempt:** NS (−.15). **Disgust:** PT (−.11), AD (.22), PTS (.29). **Fear:** PT (.22). **Joy:** PT (.20), AD (.21), PTS (.17). **Neutral:** NS (−.18). **Surprise:** PT (.15), AD (.11). **Smile:** PT (.25), AD (.21), PTS (.18) # Cue utilization = 18	**Anger:** PT (−.12), AD (−.13). **Contempt:** PT (−.12), AD (−.21), NS (.21), PTS (.18). **Disgust:** PT (−.07). **Fear:** NS (.30), PTS (.26), **Joy:** NS (.37). **Neutral:** (AD (−.16), NS (.17). **Sad:** NS (.23), PTS (.13). **Surprise:** NS (.26), PTS (.24). **Smile:** PT (.19), NS (.22). # Cue utilization = 18
C	**Contempt:** NS (.10), **Joy:** PT (.10), NS (.09), PTS (−.10). **Neutral:** AD (−.19), NS (.20). **Surprise:** AD (−.11), PTS (−.13). # Cue utilization = 8	- # Cue utilization = 0
O	**Anger:** PT (−.22), AD (.11), NS (−.21), PTS (.16). **Disgust:** PT (−.14), AD (.10), PTS (.14). **Fear:** PT (.22), **Joy:** PT (.12). **Surprise:** PT (.20), NS (.20) # Cue utilization = 11	**Anger:** PT (−.14). **Disgust:** NS (−.10). **Fear:** NS (.23), PTS (.19). **Smile:** PT (.10), NS (.11). **Surprise:** NS (.21), PTS (.15). # Cue utilization = 8
A	**Anger:** PT (−.17). **Joy:** PT (.17), NS (.19), PTS (−.12). **Smile:** PT (.18), AD (.11). # Cue utilization = 7	**Anger:** NS (−.19). **Disgust:** NS (−.08), PTS (−.08). **Joy:** PT (.22), **Sad:** PTS (−.09). **Smile:** AD (.14). # Cue utilization = 6
ES	**Joy:** AD (−.16), NS (.09), PTS (−14). **Smile:** PT (.07). # Cue utilization = 4	**Anger:** NS (−.13). **Disgust:** NS (−.05), PTS (−.07). **Sad:** PTS (−.11). **Smile:** AD (.08). # Cue utilization = 5

Table 1: Significant Pearson correlation effects ($p < .05$.) between Big Five personality impressions (E, C, O, A, ES) and facial expression activity cues measured from THR and HMM segmentations.

	Thr			*HMM*		
Expression	*Med*	*SD*	Q_3	*Med*	*SD*	Q_3
Anger	.47	.25	.67	.02	.21	.06
Contempt	.88	.17	.95	.42	.41	1.00
Disgust	.33	.27	.62	.01	.14	.04
Fear	.50	.26	.68	.03	.17	.09
Joy	.54	.28	.75	.03	.24	.10
Neutral	.93	.14	.98	1.00	.23	1.00
Sad	.86	.16	.94	.20	.41	1.00
Surprise	.86	.16	.94	.20	.41	1.00
Smile	.12	.15	.26	.32	.15	.41

Table 2: Median and SD values for the PT cues obtained from Thr and HMM segmentations

This activity cue was introduced to explore the characterization of facial expressions as signals of short duration.

4. RESULTS

This section is divided in four parts. First, we provide descriptive statistics of vloggers' facial expression activity. Second, we analyze the correlation between facial expressions and personality impressions. Third, we address the task of personality prediction. Finally, we compare our results to other nonverbal cues reported in previous work.

4.1 Descriptive analysis

We computed basic statistics of facial activity cues across vlogs, but for space reasons in Table 2 we only report values of the PT cues obtained from both THR and HMM segmentations (see Table 2). These measures are useful to interpret the functioning of the two approaches proposed, and have also potential for understanding the type of facial expressions that can be typically found in the vlogging scenario.

Though THR and HMM segmentations provide substantially different values for most expressions, they seem to agree on the high presence of the Neutral expression: in Table 2, around half of the vloggers seem to have neutral expressions between 93 and 100% of the time. For the THR segmentation, this result challenges the fact that, as seen from the median values, a large number of the vlogs also show large presence of other facial expressions, which indicates that the intervals in which facial expressions are active overlap. Though it may seem the case by looking at the CERT output (see Figure 1), it is unlikely that some facial expressions co-occur in time. In contrast, the HMM segmentation suggests a more realistic scenario in which the activation of facial expressions signals concurs with the activation of the neutral signal. Though median values for HMM may seem low compared to THR segmentations, the third quartile (Q_3) indicates that 25% of the vlogs still show large presence of facial expressions of emotion such as Contempt, Joy, Sadness, Surprise, and Smiles.

4.2 Correlation analysis

We now investigate the individual correlations between facial expression activity cues and personality impressions, to understand what facial expressions may be useful to infer personality judgements in vlogging (a.k.a. cue utilization). Table 1 shows the significant effects ($p<0.05$) found for cues from both THR and HMM segmentations.

As a first result, we found that Extraversion is the trait showing the largest cue utilization (18), which indicates that facial expressions of emotion are useful to build personality impressions for this trait, which is related to the evidence showed in related literature that Extraversion is typically easier to judge [3, 4]. Though Agreeableness has the second largest ICC (see Sec. 2), it does not compare to Extraversion in terms of cue utilization (6-7), and it is even lower than other traits such as Openness to Experience.

We found different interesting effects between facial expressions of emotions and personality impressions. Facial expressions of emotions with positive valence such as Joy and Smile showed almost exclusively positive effects with personality impressions. For the case of HMM, for example, smile is correlated with Extraversion (PT, $r = .19$.), and Agreeableness (AD, $r = .14$), among others. Facial expressions of negative valence, such as Anger, showed negative correlations with judgements of Extraversion (PT, $r = -.16$.), Openness to Experience (PT, $r = -.22$.), and Agreeableness (PT, $r = -.17$.). Whereas Contempt or Surprise have both negative and positive effects, see for example Contempt and Extraversion impressions (NS, $r = -.15$.) compared to Conscientiousness (NS, $r = .10$).

We also saw differences between effects in cues computed from THR and HMM segmentations. Whereas most values of PT show same sign effects, some values for AD, NS, and PTS indicate different sign effects. Though this is clearly

Feature Set	E	C	OE	A	ES
THR	.17	.07	.12	.06	.05
HMM	.16	.07	.12	.06	.05
THR+HMM	.20	.05	.09	.07	.03
THR_Sel	.20	.07	.10	.06	.07
HMM_Sel	.16	-	.07	.05	.05
THR_Sel+HMM_Sel	.22	.06	.08	.07	.03

Table 3: Big-Five personality traits prediction results (in mean R-squared) for feature sets obtained from segmentations using THR and HMMs.

Feature Set	E	C	OE	A	ES
Audio	.37	.05	.06	.05	.02
Visual	.13	.04	.05	.02	.03
THR_Sel+HMM_Sel	.22	.06	.08	.07	.03

Table 4: Big-Five personality traits prediction results (in mean R-squared) for audio, visual, multimodal, and facial expression features.

consecuence of the two different segmentation approaches, it needs to be investigated in more detail.

4.3 Regression Analysis

We addressed the task of personality impression prediction with regression tasks targeted to predict the score of each one of the personality traits. We used support vector regression and followed a cross-validation approach by dividing the 281 samples in 10 folds, and using, at each resampling iteration, one fold for testing and the other 9 folds for training. Each time a model was trained, the parameters were optimized on the basis of another inner 10-fold cross validation.

We evaluated several models with distinct feature sets and different kernels. Results in Table 3 show R-squared prediction performance for experiments with a radial kernel (which provided only slightly better performance than other kernels). The three first rows of the table are experiments including all the cues, while the three last rows are experiments using significant cues from Table 1.

Not surprisingly, the best results are obtained for the Extraversion trait followed by Openness to Experience, which are the traits with large cue utilization. We observed that by using significant cues from the THR segmentation (THR_Sel) we obtained better performances than using significant cues from the HMM (HMM_Sel). In addition, the results suggest that combining cues from both segmentations may also help to improve results, at least for Extraversion. For the rest, the performance of HMMs and THR segmentations is comparable. Thus, we note that whereas HMM may be useful to interpret the presence and absence of facial expressions (see Section 4.1), it does not provide any advantage in terms of predictive performance, compared to using cues obtained from the THR segmentation.

4.4 Facial expressions vs. other cues

We were interested to assess the performance of facial expression activity cues to other cues used in previous work, and therefore, for comparative results, we have replicated regression experiments using the set of nonverbal features reported in [4]. Table 4 shows the result of predicting personality for our dataset, using three different sets of cues. As a first result, we found that the facial expression activity cues (THR_Sel+HMM_Sel) provided better performance than the visual activity cues (visual) used in [4], which estimate the total amount of the visual activity in vlogs. The result is relevant because both sets of cues extract information from the visual channel. However, the facial-based performance seems to be far from the one obtained from the audio, specially using prosodic cues.

5. CONCLUSIONS

We presented what to our knowledge is the first attempt to use fully automatic facial expression for the prediction of personality traits in vlogs. We used a state-of-the art automatic facial expression recognizer to process a sample of vlogs collected from YouTube and we modeled the presence of facial expressions using both a threshold and HMM-based methods to compute facial activity cues.

Overall, the results indicate that some facial expressions of emotion are indeed related to personality judgements, and that they are useful to predict impressions of Extraversion with better performance than using previously reported cues from visual activity and pose. We also found that, whereas the HMM segmentation seems to provide a more realistic characterization of the activation of facial expressions result in comparable, slightly lower performances than the threshold-based approach.

Acknowledgments This research was funded by the SNSF NCCR IM2 and Spanish Ministry of Education. We thank the Machine Perception Lab at UCSD for sharing CERT.

6. REFERENCES

[1] E. Agulla, E. Rua, J. Castro, D. Jimenez, and L. Rifon. Multimodal biometrics-based student attendance measurement in learning management systems. In *Proc. IEEE ISM*, 2009.

[2] L. Batrinca, N. Mana, B. Lepri, F. Pianesi, and N. Sebe. Please, tell me about yourself: Automatic assessment using short self-presentations. In *Proc. ICMI-MLMI*, 2011.

[3] J.-I. Biel, O. Aran, and D. Gatica-Perez. You are known by how you vlog: Personality impressions and nonverbal behavior in youtube. In *Proc. AAAI ICWSM*, 2011.

[4] J.-I. Biel and D. Gatica-Perez. The youtube lens: Crowdsourced personality impressions and audiovisual analysis of vlogs. *IEEE Trans. on Multimedia*, 2012.

[5] G. Donato, M. Bartlett, J. Hager, P. Ekman, and T. Sejnowski. Classifying facial actions. *IEEE Trans. on PAMI*, 21(10):974–989, 1999.

[6] B. Fasel and J. Luettin. Automatic facial expression analysis: a survey. *Pattern Recognition*, 36(1):259 – 275, 2003.

[7] S. D. Gosling, P. J. Rentfrow, and W. B. Swann. A very brief measure of the big-five personality domains. *J. of Research in Personality*, 37:504–528, 2003.

[8] J. A. Hall, S. D. Gunnery, and S. A. Andrzejewski. Nonverbal emotion displays, communication modality, and the judgment of personality. *J. of Research on Personality*, 45(1):77 – 83, 2011.

[9] M. L. Knapp and J. Hall. *Nonverbal communication in human interaction*. Holt, Rinehart and Winston, New York, 2005.

[10] B. Knutson. Facial expressions of emotion influence interpersonal trait inferences. *J. of Nonverbal Behavior*, 20(3):165 – 182, 1996.

[11] B. Lepri, N. Mana, A. Cappelletti, F. Pianesi, and M. Zancanaro. Modeling the personality of participants during group interactions. In *Proc. UMAP*, 2009.

[12] G. Littlewort, J. Whitehill, T. Wu, I. Fasel, M. Frank, J. Movellan, and M. Bartlett. The computer expression recognition toolbox (CERT). In *Proc. IEEE FG*, 2011.

[13] D. McDuff, R. el Kaliouby, and R. Picard. Crowdsourced data collection of facial responses. *Proc. ICMI*, 2011.

The Blue One to the Left: Enabling Expressive User Interaction in a Multimodal Interface for Object Selection in Virtual 3D Environments

Pulkit Budhiraja and Sriganesh Madhvanath
Hewlett-Packard Labs, India
24 Salarpuria Arena, Hosur Main Road, Adugodi
Bangalore 560030, INDIA
+91 80 33829169
pulkit.budhiraja@gmail.com, srig@hp.com

ABSTRACT

Interaction with virtual 3D environments comes with a host of challenges. For instance, because 3D objects tend to occlude one another, performing object selection by pointing gestures is problematic, and more so when there are many objects in the scene. In the real world we tend to use speech to clarify our intent, by referring to distinctive attributes of the object and/or its absolute or relative location in space. Multimodal interactive systems involving speech and gesture have generally relied on speech for commands and deictic gestures for indicating the target object. In this paper, we present a system which allows object references to be made using gestures and speech, and supports a variety of expressions inspired by real-world usage.

Categories and Subject Descriptors

H.5.2 **[Information Interfaces and Presentation]:** User Interfaces – *Interaction Styles.*

General Terms

Design, Human Factors

Keywords

Multimodal interface, selection, virtual 3D environment

1. INTRODUCTION

Multimodal interactive systems involving speech and gesture have generally relied on speech for commands and deictic hand or touch gestures for indicating the target object. The use of gestures for pointing becomes problematic when there are a large number of objects close together, and gets worse when applied to virtual 3D environments wherein 3D objects tend to occlude one another. In the real world we tend to use speech to clarify our intent, by referring to distinctive attributes of the object (e.g. "*the big blue book*") and/or its absolute or relative location in space (e.g "*the one in the left corner*").

In this paper, we present a system which allows object references to be made using a variety of expressions that we use to refer to objects in the real world, for instance: (i) using speech and gesture in combination, (ii) using visible attributes, of objects, (iii) indirect references involving spatial relations, (iv) references to spatial regions, and (v) anaphoric references.

The intent of supporting multiple ways of referring to objects is to give the user freedom to use the most convenient option to refer to an object in a particular scenario, rather than being constrained to follow a specific command syntax or interaction technique.

ICMI '12, October 22–26, 2012, Santa Monica, California, USA.
ACM 978-1-4503-1467-1/12/10.

2. RELATED WORK

Related work in the field of multimodal object reference includes Peter Gorniak's *Bishop*, which understands natural language references to objects in a spatial scene [5]. Edward Tse's *speech-filtered bubble ray* uses speech as a filter for selecting objects in a densely packed area on a wall display using pointing gestures [1]. Landragin's work focuses on classifying objects under multiple reference domains based on their visual perception, and gestures and language used in a dialogue [3]. Our system is greatly inspired by work of Makalic and Zuckerman, which focuses on probabilistic reference disambiguation for spoken dialogue [2][4].

3. INTERFACE AND INTERACTIONS

The physical setup of the system includes a large display attached to a Windows PC (Fig.1). A 3D scene is rendered by computer graphics software called *Blender*. Hand gestures are captured using a *Microsoft Kinect* depth camera. Speech is captured using a headset microphone. The user stands at a distance of 4-6" from the display to interact with the system.

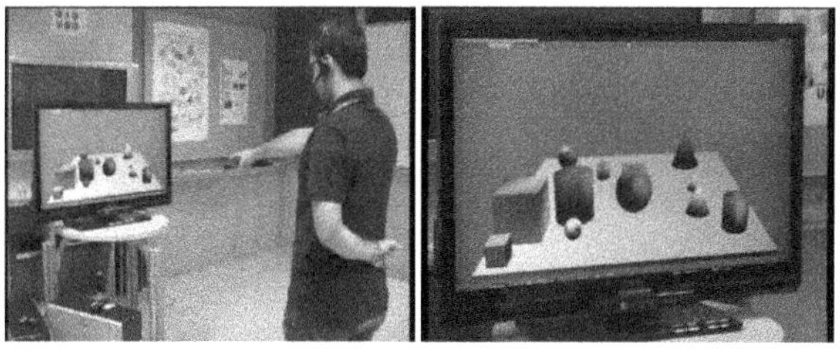

Figure 1. Physical setup and 3D scene

The 3D scene in the present version comprises of simple objects such as cubes, cylinders, cones and spheres which may differ in size and color. The present version only allows selection of objects, and of one object at a time. However the design is extensible in order to allow selection of groups of objects, as well as other commands such as deletion, movement and so on.

The system supports object selection through speech using restricted natural language and/or gestures. The system provides the user with multiple ways of interacting with the scene. References to objects may be made using speech or both speech and gesture. The system also attempts to understand grammatically incorrect utterances. The following types of object references can be understood by the system:

Object Attributes The user can refer to an object using one or more visible attributes such as color, shape, size, e.g. "*the big blue cone*" as well as its spatial location (by pointing). The user has the freedom to choose as many attributes as he/she desires to specify the object. The system uses these attributes to obtain an unambiguous reference to the target object.

Spatial Regions The number of objects to be considered can be filtered by making a reference about the region of the target object, e.g. "*the blue one to the left*". The system compares an object's position in the scene with a reference point depending upon the region specified. For example, for "*left*" the leftmost point of the scene is taken as the reference point. The system supports references to *left*, *right*, *front*, *back*, *center* and *corner*.

Spatial Relations For objects that are difficult to refer to directly, an indirect reference with respect to another object can be made, e.g. "*the object behind the green cone*". Indirect references can also be with respect to the currently selected object, e.g. "*the blue cone behind that one*". The system can resolve the different meanings of reference depending upon the context of the utterance. The system supports a variety of spatial relations between the two objects, such as *left*, *right*, *front*, *back*, *behind*, *ahead*, *near*, *next*.

The system also allows the user to rotate the scene using speech or gesture commands. A video demonstration of the system can be seen at http://vimeo.com/44531259.

4. SYSTEM DESIGN

Abstract information about all the objects in the scene is known to the system (Fig. 2). The *User Display Application* (*Blender*) renders the scene using this information. In order to interpret interactions, the system analyzes multiple transcripts of the speech and employs a probabilistic semantic engine to assess the meaning of spoken utterance. The probabilistic approach of understanding an utterance enables the system to handle ambiguity and speech recognition errors.

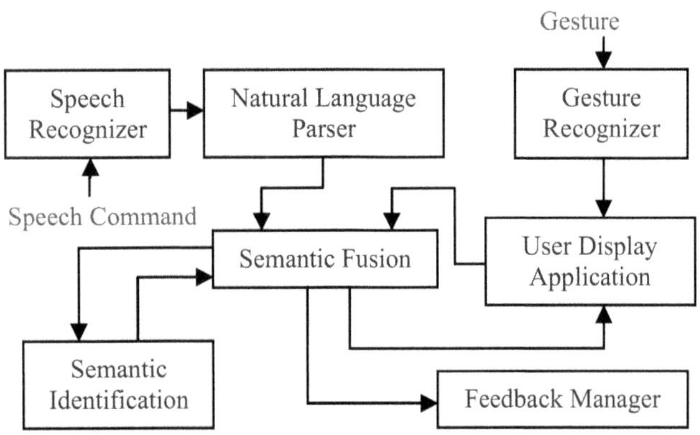

Figure 2. System design

The *Speech Recognizer* (*Microsoft SAPI*) returns multiple interpretations of the spoken utterance, each with its confidence score. The *Natural Language Parser* (*Stanford NLP*) returns a parse tree for each interpretation. The *Gesture Recognizer* sends the screen coordinates of the user's pointing hand to the User Display Application. These coordinates are mapped to a pointer in the scene for visual feedback. The parse trees and hand coordinates are sent to the *Semantic Fusion* component.

Semantic Fusion Semantic Fusion encompasses temporal and semantic fusion of speech and pointing gestures. On-screen locations of objects referred to by pointing are determined by averaging the hand coordinates corresponding to spoken keywords such as "*this*" or "*that*" in the utterance.

The verb phrase, noun phrases and prepositional phrases in the parse tree are examined to extract information about the action, attributes of the target object and (in case of indirect reference) referred object and the spatial relation between them. This information is represented in a graph-like data structure. Multiple such graphs are generated corresponding to alternative parse trees, and sent to the *Semantic Identification* component to resolve object references in the interaction, to objects present in the scene.

Semantic Identification The Semantic Identification component tries to match the attributes of each of the objects in the scene, e.g. color, shape, size and location, with those extracted from the parse tree, and returns a likelihood score. If the target object is to be restricted to a particular region, the identification layer assigns a score to a candidate object by comparing a specific feature dimension (depending upon the region specified) with the absolute dimensions of the scene using a Gaussian function (Fig. 3). In the case of indirect references, the spatial relation between the candidate target object and the candidate referred object is evaluated. The target object from the graph having the best combined likelihood score is selected as the result.

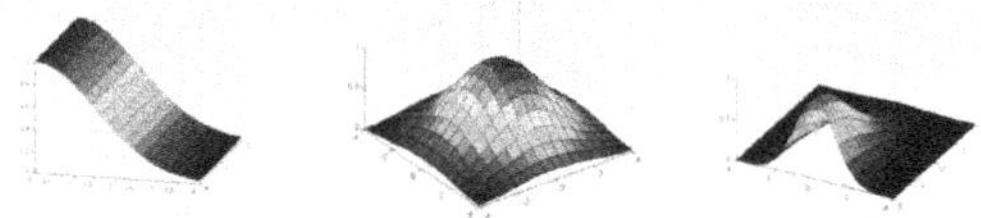

Figure 3. From left to right: Probability distributions for spatial regions *left* and *center*, and spatial relation *behind*

5. SUMMARY AND NEXT STEPS

In this paper, we have described a prototype system for interacting with virtual 3D environments that supports expressive object references made using gestures and speech. The system is presently limited in the types of objects that can be present in the scene, and the attributes that may be used to refer to them (shape, color and size). These restrictions would need to be addressed for creating useful real-world applications. In terms of possible actions beyond selection; movement, rotation, deletion, etc. can be added to the system, requiring the semantic fusion and semantic identification logic to be suitably extended. The user interface of the application can be further improved by adding the ability to zoom and pan using speech, gestures or both.

6. REFERENCES

[1] Edward Tse, Mark Hancock, and Saul Greenberg. 2007. Speech-filtered bubble ray: improving target acquisition on display walls. In *Proc 9th Intl Conf on Multimodal Interfaces* (ICMI '07)

[2] Enes Makalic, Ingrid Zukerman, Michael Niemann, and Daniel Schmidt. 2008. A Probabilistic Model for Understanding Composite Spoken Descriptions. In *Proc 10th Pacific Rim Intl Conf on AI* (PRICAI '08)

[3] Frédéric Landragin. 2006. Visual perception, language and gesture: a model for their understanding in multimodal dialogue systems. *Signal Processing* 86, 12

[4] Ingrid Zukerman, Enes Makalic, Michael Niemann, and Sarah George. 2008. A Probabilistic Approach to the Interpretation of Spoken Utterances. In *Proc 10th Pacific Rim Intl Conf on AI* (PRICAI '08)

[5] Peter Gorniak and Deb Roy. 2003. A visually grounded natural language interface for reference to spatial scenes. In *Proc 5th Intl Conf on Multimodal interfaces* (ICMI '03)

Pixene: Creating Memories while Sharing Photos

Ramadevi Vennelakanti, Sriganesh Madhvanath, Anbumani Subramanian,
Ajith Sowndararajan, Arun David, Prasenjit Dey
Hewlett-Packard Labs, India
24 Salarpuria Arena, Hosur Main Road, Adugodi
Bangalore 560030, INDIA
{rama.v, srig, anbumani, ajith.sowndararajan, arun.david, pdey}@hp.com

ABSTRACT
In this paper we describe Pixene, a photo sharing system that focuses on the capture and subsequent visualization and consumption of *interactions around shared photos*, where the sharing may be with physically co-present friends and family, or online with one's social network. In the former scenario, the interactions may be richly multimodal and involve pointing and spoken comments. Remote interaction is primarily in the form of 'like's and text comments on social networking sites. Pixene thus acts as a common repository for interactions over photos and brings interactions from a co-located and online photo sharing into a single platform. Pixene also provides a rich photo browsing experience that allows users to view not only the photographs but also the interaction history around them, e.g. who saw it, who did they see it with, what they said in association with different regions of interest, comments and 'like's. In this paper, we describe the features and system design of Pixene.

Categories and Subject Descriptors
H.5.2 [User Interfaces]: User interface management systems; Voice I/O; Natural language; D.2.2 [Software Engineering]: Design Tools and Techniques - user interfaces;

General Terms
Interaction metadata, User Interface Design,

Keywords
Photo sharing, interaction metadata, tagging, multimodal

1. INTRODUCTION
Co-located photo sharing with family and friends is a familiar experience. A co-located photo sharing session contains rich interaction information such as who saw it with whom, what were the comments made, what specific regions of the photograph were pointed at while making those comments, and so on. Multimodal interaction metadata [1] is created when these interactions and information available is captured implicitly and made available for future use. This interaction metadata can be used to organize photo collections better by enabling filtering mechanisms based on number of views, who viewed etc. Over time, such interaction metadata can also be used to create an interaction history of the photograph and aid in capturing memories, storytelling and serendipitous discovery. On the other hand, online social networking and photo sharing sites such as Facebook allow for the capture of text tags, comments and 'likes' for shared photographs, from one's extended social network.

ICMI'12, October 22–26, 2012, Santa Monica, California, USA.
ACM 978-1-4503-1467-1/12/10.

Pixene is a photo sharing system that bridges the domains of co-located and online photo sharing. It enables the capture of multimodal interaction metadata (called 'Pixene metadata') as it is created during a co-located multiuser photo sharing scenario. It also captures comments and 'like's made when the same photograph is shared online via Pixene. It thus enables the unique experience of browsing and navigating through photographs, and their historic interaction metadata from all sources.

We describe below the Pixene system in terms of its system design and user interface design, and describe briefly the interaction experiences it enables.

2. SYSTEM DESIGN
The main components of the Pixene system are the *User Interface*, the *Co-located metadata capture subsystem*, the *Online metadata capture subsystem*, and the *Pixene metadata repository.*

Fig. 1 shows the *Co-located metadata capture subsystem.* Various sensors available on a personal computer are used to create 'Pixene metadata', which in turn captures details of co-located multimodal interactions with photos and videos in a user's personal photo collection. These interactions typically involve multiple viewers commenting on photographs they are viewing while simultaneously pointing at regions of interest. A microphone is used to capture the audio conversations in an interaction. A web camera is used to detect faces in real-time using the OpenCV face detection [3], and recognize faces from a small library of registered faces, using an existing in-house face recognition algorithm. Mouse or touch input is used to determine regions of interest within the photo, as shown in Fig. 2.

The described system design enables capture of a variety of interaction metadata: the number of users viewing the photographs, the identity of the viewers (if registered with the system), the date, time and duration of view of each photograph, the specific regions of interest in a photograph that were pointed at, speech associated with that specific region of interest, etc.

The *Online metadata capture subsystem* allows the posting of photos to social networking and photo sharing sites, and periodically downloading metadata such as 'like's and comments made on them. The current prototype also supports Facebook sync as an example but can be easily extended to other social networking and photo sharing sites as well.

The *Pixene metadata repository* is implemented as a relational database. For each media object in the user's collection, an interaction history is maintained in the form of time stamped interaction events, which may be *co-located* or *online.* Interaction metadata captured and created over time enables unique photo navigation and browsing experiences, and may also be selectively retrieved subsequently using SQL queries.

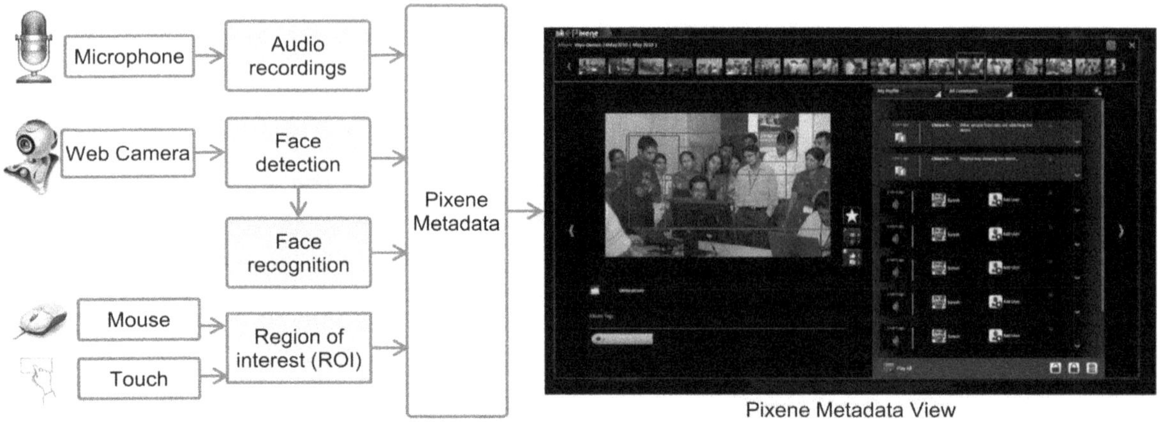

Figure 1 Pixene metadata creation and visualization

3. PIXENE USER INTERFACE DESIGN

The Pixene user interface allows users to navigate through their photo collection and provides a unified view of the interaction metadata (both co-located and online) associated with each photograph. The interface also supports filters (e.g. based on text tags, "viewed by") and alternative sort orders (e.g. based on popularity - a composite metric based on duration of views and number of comments, most commented, etc), apart from the default time line view.

The interface supports implicit as well as explicit ways of gathering interaction metadata while browsing photos. In the implicit mode, users' interactions are captured by monitoring the microphone for speech activity as well as mouse/touch actions across the photograph, and associating the speech activity with mouse/touch activity (if present). In order to reduce sensitivity to ambient, non-system-directed audio, speech is recorded only if at least one frontal face is detected. Interaction metadata may also be captured in an explicit manner, wherein the user marks regions of interest on a photograph and records voice comments for each region of interest (Fig. 2).

Figure 2 Tagging regions of interest

Pixene's metadata view (Fig. 1) provides a reverse-chronological view of the interaction history of the photograph, which includes both co-located and online events (referred to simply as "comments" in the interface). When a co-located event is selected, the audio comment is played and the associated region of interest in the photograph (if any) is displayed. The user can also touch the photograph directly to access any audio comments associated with that region of the photograph. Finally, the 'play all' mode uses the 'play list' metaphor to play all of the voice comments in sequence, while simultaneously highlighting the regions in the photograph that the comments were associated with.

Family photo collections are often stored on a single shared family PC, however different family members may share the same photos with different groups of people (e.g. extended family vs teenage son's friends), and wish to keep the resulting interactions separate. Therefore Pixene supports multiple user accounts and the notion of ownership of interaction metadata. Comments are owned by the user who happens to be logged in, and can be made private or public (a Guest mode allows photos to be shared with the need for login). User accounts can be mapped to Facebook accounts to enable selected photos to be posted to Facebook and comments to be downloaded into the Pixene metadata repository.

4. CONCLUSION AND NEXT STEPS

We have a working prototype for a touch and mouse click based interaction and a video demo of the same is available for view [3]. While the current implementation is touch and mouse based it has been tested for distance interaction enabled via free hand visual gestures (using Kinect) and input devices such as the wiiMote.

While the current prototype deals with photos, other media types such as video, documents can easily be included making it amenable for personal and enterprise use as well. The current prototype assumes the photos and their metadata are stored locally; potentially they may be hosted on the cloud as well.

5. ACKNOWLEDGMENTS

We acknowledge the contribution of our development team and interns whose effort and ideas help build Pixene.

6. REFERENCES

[1] Vennelakanti, R., Dey, P., Shekhawat. A., and Pisupati. P. 2011. The picture says it all! Multimodal interactions and interaction metadata. In *Proceedings of the 13th international conference on multimodal interfaces* (ICMI '11). ACM, Alicante, Spain

[2] http://opencv.willowgarage.com/wiki/FaceDetection/

[3] http://www.hpl.hp.com/india/research/Pixene.html

Designing Multiuser Multimodal Gestural Interactions for the Living Room

Sriganesh Madhvanath, Ramadevi Vennelakanti, Anbumani Subramanian,
Ankit Shekhawat*, Prasenjit Dey, Amit Ranjan
Hewlett-Packard Labs India
24 Salarpuria Arena, Hosur Main Road,
Bangalore 560030
{srig, rama.vennelakanti, anbumani, pdey, amitr}@hp.com

ABSTRACT
Most work in the space of multimodal and gestural interaction has focused on single user productivity tasks. The design of multimodal, freehand gestural interaction for multiuser lean-back scenarios is a relatively nascent area that has come into focus because of the availability of commodity depth cameras. In this paper, we describe our approach to designing multimodal gestural interaction for multiuser photo browsing in the living room, typically a shared experience with friends and family. We believe that our learnings from this process will add value to the efforts of other researchers and designers interested in this design space.

Categories and Subject Descriptors
H5.m. Information interfaces and presentation (e.g., HCI): Miscellaneous. D.2.2 [Software Engineering]: Design Tools and Techniques - user interfaces;

General Terms
Design, Experimentation, Human Factors

Keywords
Multiuser, Multimodal, Gestural interaction

1. INTRODUCTION
Interactions in the living room have for decades focused on a single input device – the remote control. With the wider availability of depth cameras and microphones, gestural and multimodal interactions are beginning to be seriously explored as alternative interaction methods. The scenario we consider in this paper is that of a group of friends sharing photographs on a large TV display. Such interactions happen at a distance of six feet and over, are potentially multimodal involving freehand gestures and speech, and may be initiated and driven by any of the users present. In this paper we describe, in brief, our approach to the design of such interaction experiences and the prototype we have built to realize them.

2. EXPERIENCE DESIGN
A full featured photo application allows browsing, sharing, editing, and organizing of photos. We focused on photo browsing, a passive consumption activity that is typically a shared experience. Our design goal was to enable a "10-foot" multi-user interface that could enable users to use (multimodal) hand gestures to navigate a collection of photo albums, drill down to specific albums and individual photos, zoom, rotate, audio-tag and rate photos. We also wished to maintain an interaction history for each photo by recording the identity of the interacting user, and the timestamp and duration of interaction. Here we discuss the key elements of the design.

Gesture Vocabulary: As gestural interfaces have matured, researchers have created frameworks for designing gesture vocabularies [3]. In our work, we defined some key principles for the gesture vocabulary to satisfy in order to be usable: (i) the gestures should be limited, distinct, and easy to perform and recall, (ii) the use of a gesture may be extended by combining it with short spoken "qualifiers", and (iii) the meaning of a (multimodal) gesture should be determined by the application context. An initial gesture vocabulary was arrived at through a process of trying out different gestures that we felt best conveyed the intended action, while being stable and distinct enough for a depth-camera based computer vision system to be able to reliably recognize. The latter was an important concern especially given that the human hand is an extremely articulate object capable of self-occlusion, and the depth camera has only one view of the users' hands. Our final gesture set consisted of gestures for *swipe left / right, open, point, escape, zoom in / out, pan & scroll* and *rotate*.

We conducted a Wizard-of-Oz study to ascertain the recall, learnability and ease of use of the gesture vocabulary in the context of a photo browsing task we set the participants. The participants learned the gesture vocabulary by watching a short training video of the gestures being performed. The study was observational in nature and the findings qualitative. The key learning from this study was while most of the gestures were easy to recall and perform; they were modified from their "ideal" form with use, along three dimensions – *hand pose*, *translation direction* and *translation distance*. We also found that users spontaneously repeated the gesture when the system (wizard) was slow to respond, and used speech along with gesture when the gesture "failed" repeatedly. We subsequently added gestures for rating photos (*thumb up and down*) and speech qualifiers to existing gestures to create different but related behaviors, e.g., a *zoom* gesture could be qualified by saying "restore" to restore the photo to its original size.

Engagement: Rather than have a user make an explicit "engagement gesture" (e.g. wave) to indicate his/her intent to interact, we adopted a touch screen-like model of "instantaneous engagement". Any gesture performed with the hand extended out - outside a virtual *action bubble* centered at the user's torso, was treated as input into the system. In order to further reduce false positives, we required that the user be in front of the display with his/her face facing the display. This was checked using face detection with a webcam placed above the display.

---

*While at HP Labs India

ICMI'12, October 22–26, 2012, Santa Monica, California, USA.
ACM 978-1-4503-1467-1/12/10.

Figure 1. RGB and depth camera views of a multi-user interaction and the gesture recognition system feedback

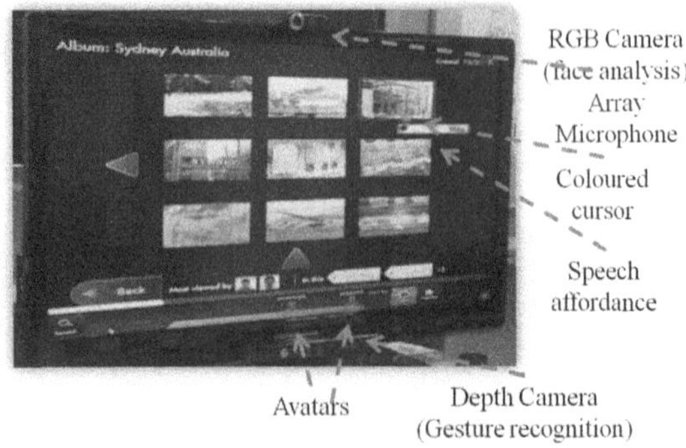

Figure 2. Technology components and user-interface indicating user presence and feedback

Presence and Interaction Feedback: The presence of users in front of the system (detected using the depth camera, and identified using the web camera) was indicated using avatars at the bottom of the screen. Each user was assigned a unique color by the system, and onset of engagement was indicated by displaying a cursor of the same color and making the avatar larger and brighter. The cursor disappeared as soon as the user stopped gesturing by retracting his/her hand towards his/her body - inside his/her action bubble (Fig. 1). When the user starts to perform different gestures such as two-handed zoom, or thumbs-up to rate a photo, the cursor icon changes (keeping the color unchanged) to indicate the operation in progress. Sounds were used to accentuate key events, such as (dis-) engagement, opening an album, increasing likes for a photo, etc.

Affordances: Conveying the affordances of a multimodal interface becomes critical in the absence of GUI-like dropdown menus. We experimented with multiple models, and eventually used a model of displaying all contextually relevant (multimodal) gestures in an iconic form at the start of the interaction.

Control Passing: In the absence of a single input device (e.g. remote control) to channel commands from multiple simultaneous users, we designed a control passing mechanism that allows users complete and independent control of non-disruptive interactions (e.g. pointing to something of interest) while enforcing turn-taking for disruptive interactions (e.g. going to the next photo or exiting the album).

3. PROTOTYPE

The interface described was prototyped in the form of a Windows application running on a desktop PC connected to a 42" TV display (Fig. 2). Depth images from a Kinect depth camera were analyzed to extract user torsos (for presence), detect (dis-) engagement using the action bubble, detect hands (confirmed using a skin color check) and interpret single and two-handed gestures such as *hover, swipe* and *zoom* as well as hand poses such as *point*, *palm* and *thumbs up/down* [4].

We used Microsoft SAPI for speech recognition using a separate 2-microphone array. The microphone array was also used to detect the direction of speech, and thereby identify the active speaker (and ignore background noise). A Logitech HD web camera was used for face detection and face recognition (from among a small set of registered users) [2].

The interpreted results from these input and user context modalities were processed in real-time using our MIST Multimodal Interaction Framework [1]. The framework uses a unification-based approach to fuse these events from multiple users temporally and semantically according to the defined multimodal interaction vocabulary, to generate appropriate application behavior. Additional details of these technology components may be found in the cited references.

The prototype was tested with as many as five simultaneously interacting users, and it achieved system response times (from interaction to application response) of < 150 msec, empirically observed to be sufficient to support real-time interaction.

4. SUMMARY

In this paper, we have outlined key aspects of the multiuser multimodal interaction experience we created for lean-back media consumption in the living room. The resulting system is complex in its construction and uses a gamut of technologies such as freehand gesture recognition, speech recognition, active speaker detection, and face detection, to interpret both explicit gesture and speech input, and implicit user context such as user attention and identity, and fuses them in real-time.

We have described how we designed and built a system that supports multi user multimodal gestural interactions from a distance. The current system was designed and built to enable co-located photo sharing in the living room, our design process needs further validation with additional use cases. Work is also required to address failures (system failing to recognize a gesture, hand pose, speech qualifier, or user) and provide recovery mechanisms.

5. REFERENCES

[1] Dey, P., Madhvanath, S., Ranjan, A. and Das, S. 2011. An Exploration of Gesture-Speech Multimodal Patterns for Touch Interfaces. *3rd International Conference on Human Computer Interaction,* April 7 – 10 2011, Bangalore, India.

[2] Dey, P., Selvaraj, M. and Lee, B. 2011. Robust User Context Analysis for Multimodal Interfaces. *ICMI 2011: 13th International Conference on Multimodal Interaction,* November 14-18, 2011, Alicante, Spain.

[3] Perron, L. 2007. What gestures to perform a collaborative storytelling? *In ICVS'07: Proc. 4th Intl. Conf. on virtual storytelling: Using virtual reality technologies for storytelling* (2007).

[4] Suryanarayan, P., Subramanian, A. and Mandalapu, D. 2010. 'Dynamic Hand Pose Recognition Using Depth Data'. *20th International Conference on Pattern Recognition (ICPR)*, Istanbul, Turkey, August 23-26, 2010

[5] http://www.hpl.hp.com/india/research/MMI.html

Using Explanations for Runtime Dialogue Adaptation

Florian Nothdurft
Institute of Communications Engineering
University of Ulm, Germany
florian.nothdurft@uni-ulm.de

Frank Honold
Institute of Media Informatics
University of Ulm, Germany
frank.honold@uni-ulm.de

Peter Kurzok
Institute of Artificial Intelligence
University of Ulm, Germany
peter.kurzok@uni-ulm.de

ABSTRACT

In this demo paper we present a system that is capable of adapting the dialogue between human and so-called companion systems in real-time. Companion systems are continually available, co-operative, and reliable assistants which adapt to a user's capabilities, preferences, requirements, and current needs. Typically state-of-the art Human-Computer interfaces adapt the interaction only to pre-defined levels of expertise like novice, intermediate or expert. In contrast, the presented system adapts the structure and content of the interaction to each user by including explanations to prepare him for upcoming tasks he has to solve together with the companion system.

Categories and Subject Descriptors

H.5.2 [**Information Interfaces and Presentation**]: User-centered design, Natural language, Training help and documentation

General Terms

Design, Human Factors

Keywords

Multimodal Dialogue System, Dialogue Modeling, Adaptivity, Human-Machine-Interaction

1. INTRODUCTION

The demonstrated work is part of a so-called companion system (see figure 1). Companion Systems assist the user in everyday life, in daily recurring as well as in not habitual tasks. By the term companion system we do not only refer the software architecture as coined by Forbus and Hinrichs [1] but also the technical realization of such a system.

One of the main aspects in companion systems is to evolve the capabilities of solving problems collaboratively with the user. However, solving complex problems together with a companion system is only feasible if the human user interprets and understands the machine correctly. This means that an optimal human-machine-interaction (HMI) has to be tailored to the capabilities and knowledge of each respective user. Therefore, the demonstrated system uses user-adaptive explanations to prevent misunderstandings in the

ICMI'12, October 22–26, 2012, Santa Monica, California, USA.
ACM 978-1-4503-1467-1/12/10.

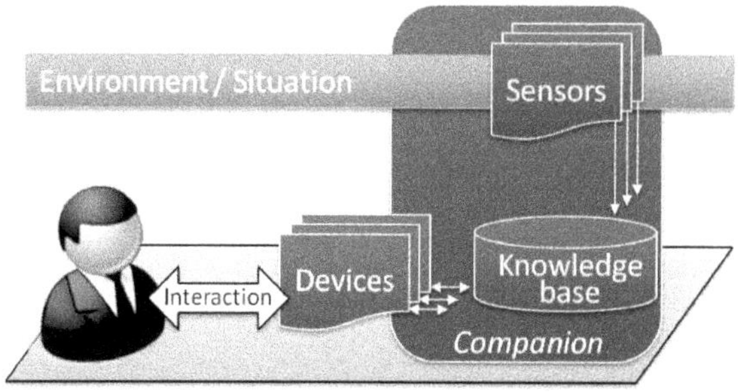

Figure 1: Overview of a companion system

HMI. The main idea is to improve the interaction by providing explanations only when necessary and in the appropriate complexity for each user. For example, if a user has to connect a Blu-ray player and an amplifier via HDMI cable, and knows what an amplifier and a Blu-ray player is, the provided explanation for this task will explain in detail the HDMI cable, but not the amplifier or the Blu-ray player. Compared to the traditional approach of adapting the interaction to general levels of user expertise this approach is more exact and flexible.

2. SYSTEM OVERVIEW

The predefined course of interaction in our system is adapted and extended to the individual needs of the user during runtime using multimodal explanations. For this the predefined interaction dialogues are checked against the current user knowledge model. If the user knowledge is not sufficient, the predefined dialogue is updated to better fit the user's knowledge model or new explanations are included accordingly. The generated explanation dialogue steps can consist of text, spoken text and pictures. These ad-hoc generated explanations can be presented to the user on different devices and the user can interact with them in a multimodal way by speech, gestures, touch or point-to-click (see figure 2). In the remainder we will introduce how the system determines the necessity for dialogue adaptation, how this adaptation is generated and how it is included into the running dialogue.

3. DIALOGUE ADAPTATION

The course of actions the user has to fulfill in order to solve the task he wants to accomplish or the problem he is facing is represented by so-called dialogue steps. These split

Figure 2: The user interacts with a pointing guesture with the system

the overall task or problem into smaller pieces. Each of these steps is represented as a relation with the name of the task and its appendant concepts as its arguments. As our main goal is to prevent task failure we have to ensure that the upcoming or current tasks and appendant concepts do not exceed the user's knowledge. In this knowledge model we distinguish between declarative knowledge and procedural knowledge. The former can be used to describe the being of things (i.e., appearance, purpose). Possessing declarative knowledge about something does not necessarily mean to be able to use this knowledge for a task or action (see 3 for a graphical representation of the xml schema). In comparison to that procedural knowledge can be applied to a task. Procedural knowledge provides the knowledge on how to execute a task or on how to solve a problem. Since knowledge is not a static concept, but fades away over time, so does knowledge in our user knowledge model.

For example, in a task represented in a relation as *connect(TV, Receiver, HDMI)*, the knowledge level of the action *connect* as well as the concepts *TV*, *Receiver* and *HDMI* are modeled separately as well as the complete unique relation. These knowledge objects are modeled in a five-step scale representing the level of knowledge. This means that compared to other systems the knowledge is modeled in small pieces instead of in only one general level. Therefore the model is more realistic and exact.

However, contained knowledge levels are not true or false, but are represented with a probability value ranging from 0 to 1. This is due to the fact, that the system can only make an assumption of the knowledge level of the user by observation. Occurring events during dialogue influence the probability value of relevant contained data objects. These events may be, for example, given explanations, failed actions or elapsed time. Contained is for example not only which task the user did execute, but which entities were used for this task and if the task completion was successful. During the dialogue we check if the knowledge levels of the dialogue step constituents guarantee task completion with a sufficiently high probability. However, if the probabilities of success are too low the explanation manager is notified via an explanation request to generate an explanation which enables the user to execute the dialogue step successfully and to guarantee that the user's model will be congruent to the minimum requirements of the upcoming tasks.

The explanation manager then selects which type of explanation is the appropriate one for the current lack of knowledge. As the dialogue step consists of several parts, so does

Figure 3: An excerpt of the person model schema.

the explanation. Each task and concept is analyzed to generate a summarized explanation. The explanation manager sends pictures, text or text meant to be spoken to the fission engine which decides by modality arbitration on which device and how the content should be presented. This means that the dialogue steps and content itself are modality independent. The explanation manager activates also possible input listeners to enable the user to interact with the presented interaction step. Some listeners are predefined and can be referenced. For example, a simple confirmation interaction as *okay* is reusable in most interaction steps.

4. OUTLINE OF THE DEMONSTRATION

In order to demonstrate the described work, we recorded a video of two different users interacting with the system. It shows how the course and content of the dialogue is adapted depending on the current user knowledge model. In the first run of the interaction the user is a novice for some knowledge model constituents and therefore gets detailed instructions and explanations for them. In the second run the user is an expert in all constituents and therefore does not need detailed instructions. A high-quality version of the video can be found at:
`companion.informatik.uni-ulm.de/icmi2012/RDAFI.mp4`.

5. CONCLUSIONS

In this work we described a running prototype which enables a multimodal dialogue system to adapt during runtime to the individual needs and requirements of users. The interaction consists of multimodal input via gestures, speech or touch and output via text, spoken text and pictures.

6. ACKNOWLEDGMENTS

This work was supported by the Transregional Collaborative Research Centre SFB/TRR 62 "Companion-Technology for Cognitive Technical Systems" which is funded by the German Research Foundation (DFG).

7. REFERENCES

[1] K. D. Forbus and T. R. Hinrichs. Companion cognitive systems a step toward human-level ai. *AI Magazine*, 27:83–95, 2006.

NeuroDialog: An EEG-Enabled Spoken Dialog Interface

Seshadri Sridharan, Yun-Nung Chen, Kai-Min Chang, Alexander I. Rudnicky
Language Technologies Institute, Carnegie Mellon University
5000 Forbes Ave., Pittsburgh, PA 15213-3891, USA
{seshadrs,yvchen,kkchang,air}@cs.cmu.edu

ABSTRACT
Understanding user intent is a difficult problem in Dialog Systems, as they often need to make decisions under uncertainty. Using an inexpensive, consumer grade EEG sensor and a Wizard -of-Oz dialog system, we show that it is possible to detect system misunderstanding even before the user reacts vocally. We also present the design and implementation details of *NeuroDialog*, a proof-of-concept dialog system that uses an EEG based predictive model to detect system misrecognitions during live interaction.

Categories and Subject Descriptors
H.5.2 [**User Interfaces**]: User interface management systems; Voice I/O; Natural Language; I.2.7 [**Natural Language Processing**]: Speech recognition and synthesis.

General Terms
Experimentation, Languages.

Keywords
Brain-computer interaction (BCI), electroencephalogram (EEG).

1. INTRODUCTION
Traditionally, dialog systems base their decisions solely on the acoustic signal. Although vision based multi-modal systems exist, detecting dialog critical metrics such as user frustration, attention, fatigue etc. visually is nonviable. Awareness of the user's state of mind can help interactive systems act in accordance with user goals. Given the advances in brain computer interaction (BCI) research [1] and the recent availability of low cost sensors for electroencephalography (EEG), we can now interface neural signals to dialog systems as a secondary sensory stream that helps augment system perception.

Misrecognition of speech, incorrect parsing and mistaking user intent are common problems in dialog systems. Bulyoka et al showed that detecting errors in advance and adjusting the response strategy could improve the performance of spoken dialog systems. By monitoring the user's brain activity, it is possible to detect system mistakes as they happen, which could trigger error-rectifying mechanisms. In this paper, we describe such a spoken dialog system that tailors responses to user's EEG signal.

ICMI'12, October 22–26, 2012, Santa Monica, California, USA.
ACM 978-1-4503-1467-1/12/10.

2. DIALOG INTERACTION
A Wizard-of-Oz spoken dialog system (Figure 1) is used to collect EEG data. A Wizard controls the dialog interaction remotely, while the participant interacts with a dialog interface, designed based on the process monitor in the Olympus framework [3]. The interactions are scripted, where in each interaction a query is made for a particular place in the local neighborhood. Figure 2 shows examples of a correctly recognized and a misunderstood interaction. The System's speech response and the text-output (TTY) are the auditory and visual cues to the user about possible misunderstanding. The EEG signal over the period between these cues and the user-confirmation is considered.

Six adults from our laboratory participated in this pilot study. The participants interacted with the Wizard system while wearing a wireless single-channel BrainBand [4] EEG headset that measured their frontal lobe activity (Figure 3). No participants reported discomfort while wearing the EEG sensor. Besides the timestamps from the dialog interaction, we used the headset to collect the following signal streams: a) the raw EEG signal sampled at 512 Hz, b) proprietary "attention" and "meditation" measures reported at 1 Hz, c) power spectrum reported at 8 Hz, consisting of Delta (1-3Hz), Theta (4-7Hz), Alpha (8-11Hz), Beta (12-29Hz), and Gamma (30-100Hz) frequency bands, and d) an indicator of signal quality reported at 1 Hz. To remove potential EMG artifacts, Neurosky [4] applies a 3-100Hz band-pass filter to the raw EEG signal.

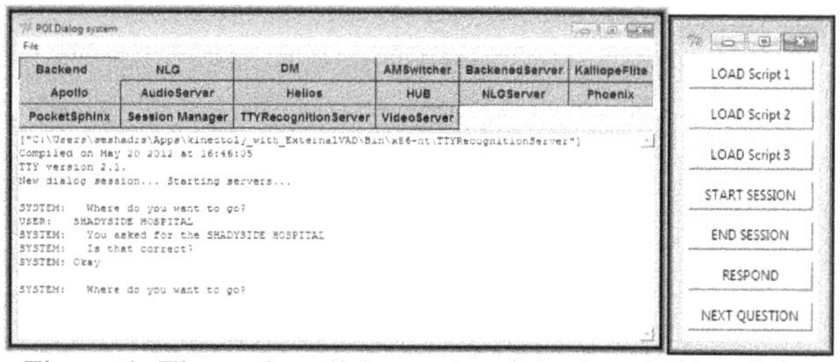

Figure 1: The spoken dialog system interface (left) and the Wizard-of-Oz's command interface (right)

SYSTEM:	Where do you want to go?	*SYSTEM*:	Where do you want to go?
USER:	I want to go to HOMEWOOD.	*USER*:	I want to go to BEACON.
TTY:	I want to go to HOMEWOOD.	*TTY*:	I want to go to BAYARD.
SYSTEM:	You asked for HOMEWOOD.	*SYSTEM*:	You asked for BAYARD.
SYSTEM:	Is that correct?	*SYSTEM*:	Is that correct?
USER:	Yes.	*USER*:	No.
SYSTEM:	Okay.	*SYSTEM*:	Okay.

Figure 2: Example interactions with correct recognition (left) and incorrect recognition (right)

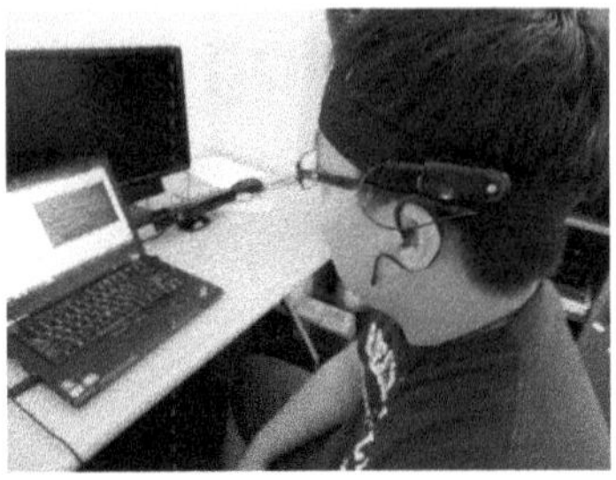

Figure 3: Participant wearing the BrainBand EEG sensor.

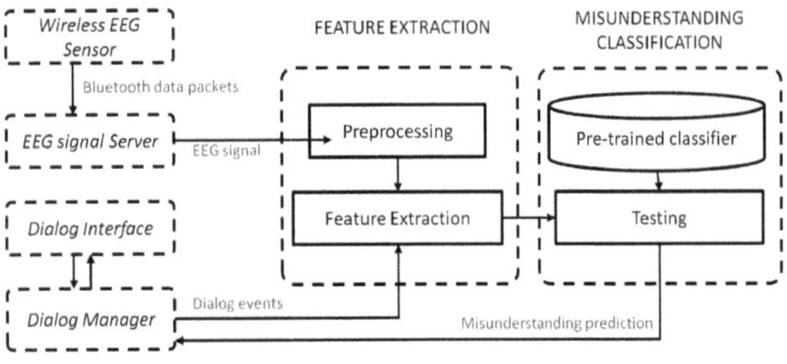

Figure 4: *NeuroDialog* system architecture

We trained a Gaussian Naïve Bayes classifier to detect system misunderstanding based on the brain activity. Initial results of our predictive models on the 360 aggregate dialog interactions we collected were encouraging. We observed a statistically significant average accuracy of 61% for the user-dependent classification task. In the *NeuroDialog* system, we use a similarly trained classifier.

3. NEURODIALOG SYSTEM

The *NeuroDialog* system has the same interface and dialog-task as the Wizard-of-Oz system, except that 1) there is no wizard involved, instead, the system misunderstands the user with a binomial probability of 50% over a predetermined query order that the user follows; and 2) there is no explicit system confirmation, instead, the system directly tailors its response to the EEG based misunderstanding prediction. The architecture schema of the system is shown in Figure 4. The wireless EEG sensor sends Bluetooth data packets to an EEG-signal server that runs locally. The signal stream from this server is preprocessed and stored in a buffer. Timestamps from the asynchronous dialog events from the dialog manager are used to extract the EEG signal over a particular period following the system's initial answer to the user query. Features extracted from this data are sent to the pre-trained classifier model for testing, and the signal buffer is emptied. The classifier's prediction on system misunderstanding and its confidence measure are sent back to the dialog manager.

The system adapts its response to user query depending on the classifier's prediction and the confidence interval. For high confidence of correct system recognition, the system proceeds with the dialog. When the classifier is adequately confident about the misunderstanding, the response ranges from "Could you please repeat? I misheard that." to "I think I may have got you wrong." At the end of the dialog session, we also generate a visualization of the trend in the attention, meditation and normalized signals for the right and wrong system understandings (Figure 5) along with the annotations of the dialog events.

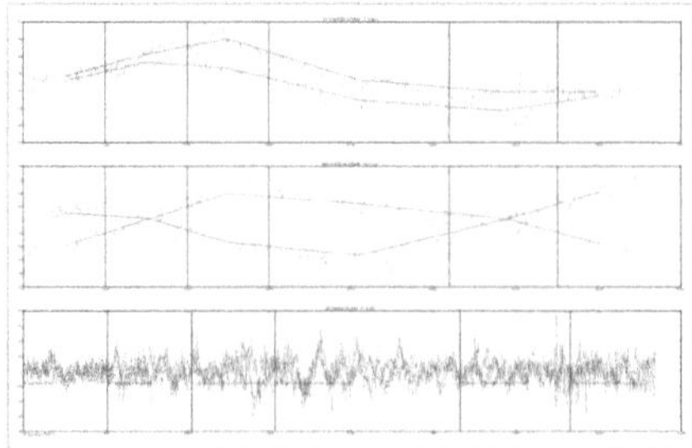

Figure 5: Trend in attention, meditation and raw signal for right (green) and wrong (red) answers for a user.

4. APPLICATIONS IN DIALOG

In a dialog system, the misunderstanding model can act as a sensory mechanism that aids it to act in accordance with the user's goal, without additional effort from the user. The classifier's prediction could be used as a confidence metric while the system advances to the next level of the dialog. A live classifier could publish its predictions to the dialog manager, which in turn could use the metric to make informed decisions. Collecting misunderstanding labels for the EEG data based on the dialog outcomes can be used to learn better predictive models with time.

From the user perspective, the ability to detect misunderstanding can potentially avoid many barge-in situations, where the system could initiate error-rectifying mechanisms before the barge-in event. The system may even skip multiple confirmation steps, common in dialog systems, saving time for the user. For example, in time sensitive applications where explicit user validation is expensive, such as gaming systems or command interfaces, the system can base its immediate decisions on the classifier confidence. As the next phase of our work, we will evaluate the impact of our system on dialog using objective metrics such as reduction in dialog length, barge-in events, as well as subjective metrics such as user satisfaction surveys, etc.

5. CONCLUSION

We present a Wizard-of-Oz dialog system capable of EEG data collection for training a system misunderstanding classifier. We also detail the design of our proof-of-concept multimodal system *NeuroDialog* that responds based on the predictions of a pre-trained system misunderstanding classifier. This predictive ability can be used to develop effective strategies to build perceptive dialog systems.

6. REFERENCES

[1] A. Nijholt and et al., *Brain-Computer Interaction: Can Multimodality Help?*. In *ICMI,* 2011.

[2] I. Bulykoa and et al., *Error-correction detection and response generation in a spoken dialog system.* In *Speech Communication*, 2005.

[3] B. Dan and et al., *Olympus: An Open sourse framework for converational spoken language research.* In *Dialog Technology workshop at HLT/NAACL*, 2007.

[4] NeuroSky, Brain Wave Signal (EEG): NeuroSky. Inc Neurosky, 2009.

[5] D. L. Donoho, *De-noising by soft-thresholding.* IEEE Trans. on Infomation Theory, 1995.

Companion Technology for Multimodal Interaction

Frank Honold
Institute of Media Informatics
Ulm University
89069 Um, Germany
frank.honold@uni-ulm.de

Felix Schüssel
Institute of Media Informatics
Ulm University
89069 Um, Germany
felix.schuessel@uni-ulm.de

Florian Nothdurft
Institute of Communications Engineering
Ulm University
89081 Um, Germany
florian.nothdurft@uni-ulm.de

Peter Kurzok
Institute of Artificial Intelligence
Ulm University
89069 Um, Germany
peter.kurzok@uni-ulm.de

ABSTRACT

We present a context adaptive approach for multimodal interaction for the use in cognitive technical systems, so called *Companion Systems*. Such systems yield properties of multimodality, individuality, adaptability, availability, cooperativeness and trustworthiness. These characteristics represent a new type of interactive systems that are not only practical and efficient to operate, but as well agreeable, hence the term "companion". Companion technology has to consider the entire situation of the user, machine, and environment. The presented prototype depicts a system that offers assistance in the task of wiring the components of a home cinema system. The user interface for this task is not predefined, but built on the fly by dedicated fission and fusion components, thereby adapting the system's multimodal output and input capabilities to the user and the environment.

Categories and Subject Descriptors

H.5.2 [**Information Interfaces and Presentation**]: User Interfaces—*Theory and methods, Graphical user interfaces, Interaction styles*

General Terms

Design, Theory

Keywords

Companion Technology, HCI, Multimodal Fission, Multimodal Fusion

1. INTRODUCTION

When envisioning future technical systems there is a common ground for the main characteristics needed: Future technical systems shall be continually available, cooperative and reliable assistants that provide their functionality in a completely individualized way. Users should trust these systems and experience them as competent and empathic partners. These so-called *Companion Systems* are cognitive technical systems which attempt to adapt their behavior to the users' preferences, needs, capabilities, emotional state and situation.

ICMI'12, October 22–26, 2012, Santa Monica, California, USA.
ACM 978-1-4503-1467-1/12/10.

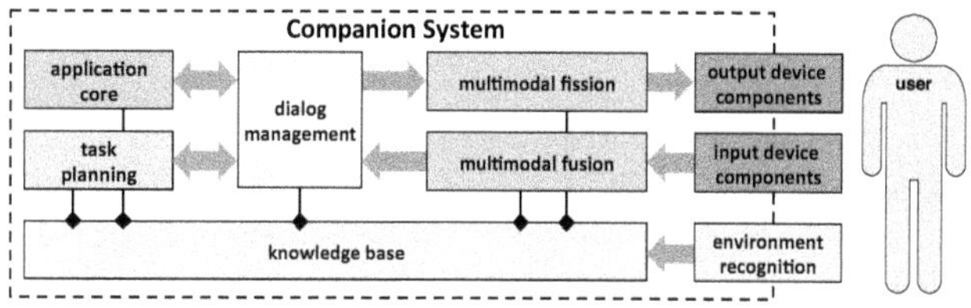

Figure 1: Overview of the system's output and input processing chains in the human computer interaction loop.

2. SYSTEM OVERVIEW

Within our collaborative research center we developed technical components to realize a multi-sensor companion system. A simplified architecture scheme is depicted in Figure 1. Such a system is aware of its user and its surroundings as described in [5]. With the need of permanent availability, such a system has to offer a very flexible interaction and UI concept, to be able to realize a proper UI via diverse device components in any given situation. Focusing on the system's adaptive communication concept, the user's preferences, needs, capabilities, emotional state, and situation must be taken into account.

The presented prototype envisions a scenario in which a companion system assists a user in setting-up a new home theater system. All knowledge about the components to be wired together and the possible cable types to do this, is stored in the system's knowledge base. Upon the task planning has identified the necessary task order, the next action to be carried out by the user is handed over to the dialog management. Within this component, the required system outputs and user inputs are composed in an abstract and modality independent manner. The shown implementation demonstrates the capabilities of the fusion and fission components, therefore the aforementioned results of task planning and dialog management are existent in a predefined yet abstract dialog model. Using this information, the multimodal fission component uses a probabilistic reasoning strategy of modality arbitration under uncertainty to provide the

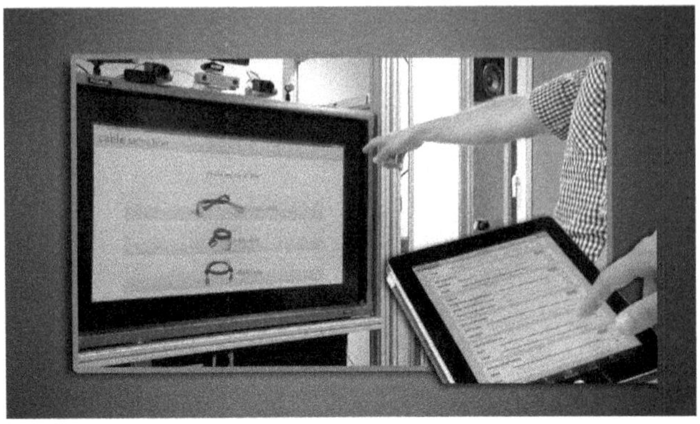

Figure 2: A user interacting with the prototype of a companion system within our research lab. The system's permanent UI adaption is influenced by environmental sensors or, for test cases, via changing parameters on a simulating tabled.

user with a situation adaptive and individual interface. At the same time, the multimodal fusion component relies on belief theory to keep track of the user's actions observed by multimodal sensors (e. g. speech and gesture recognition) and provides the dialog management with the most probable interpretations. Figure 2 shows a photograph of a user interacting with the presented prototype running in our consortium's research lab.

In our demonstration scenario we can semantically combine gestures an deictic references to select arbitrary items via the utterance "this one" while performing a pointing gesture. The user and surroundings models can be manipulated via an external tablet as depicted in Figure 2. A change in the models results in an ad-hoc change of the UI, resp. the offered interaction concept.

3. MULTIMODAL FISSION

The process of modality arbitration is carried out by a multimodal fission component. Using an extensible rule set, the best way to output the given information in the current situation and the currently available devices is computed and realized. Our model-based implementation extends the often theoretical approaches of the state of the art and introduces probabilistic reasoning to integrate uncertain and ambiguous knowledge (cf. [1, 3]). It is designed to easily integrate new reasoning knowledge at runtime. With respect to the reasoning time, the presented approach is qualified to be used in interactive systems with real-time requirements, as shown in the prototype.

4. MULTIMODAL FUSION

The multimodal fusion component is based on an approach proposed by Reddy and Basir in the robotic domain [2] using Smets' transferable belief model (TBM) [4] that is extended to the broader context of GUI-based applications.

By using a common meaning representation derived from the fission output, multiple parallel fusions, and temporal fading of events, Reddy and Basir's concept is extended to account for the increased complexity imposed by the focused domain of companion technology. The system allows the user to interact in a natural, and where applicable, multimodal way. At the same time the robustness of input recognition is increased by the combination, disambiguation, reinforcement, and conflict detection capabilities of the adapted TBM.

5. OUTLINE OF THE DEMONSTRATION

In order to show the multimodal features of the prototype, we recorded a video showing two different user types that are assisted by the companion system in connecting the various components of a home cinema system by different cables. The video can be found at `http://companion.informatik.uni-ulm.de/icmi2012/MultimodalInteraction.mp4`.

6. CONCLUSIONS

Our presented system is ready to enable multimodal interaction. We can demonstrate a probabilistic fission module as well as a fusion concept, which is based on the theory of transferable belief models. Our plug-and play concept, in combination with a model driven UI generation process, allows us to use different input and output devices. In terms of scalability we can demonstrate this with the use of various mobile clients (laptops) at runtime. We will show gesture and speech recognition as well as model driven GUI generation and speech synthesis.

7. ACKNOWLEDGMENTS

This work is originated in the Transregional Collaborative Research Center SFB/TRR 62 "Companion-Technology for Cognitive Technical Systems" funded by the German Research Foundation (DFG).

8. REFERENCES

[1] D. Costa and C. Duarte. Adapting multimodal fission to user's abilities. In *Proceedings of the 6th international conference on Universal access in human-computer interaction: design for all and eInclusion - Volume Part I*, UAHCI'11, pages 347–356, Berlin, Heidelberg, 2011. Springer-Verlag.

[2] B. S. Reddy and O. A. Basir. Concept-based evidential reasoning for multimodal fusion in human-computer interaction. *Appl. Soft Comput.*, 10(2):567–577, Mar. 2010.

[3] C. Rousseau, Y. Bellik, F. Vernier, and D. Bazalgette. A framework for the intelligent multimodal presentation of information. *Signal Process.*, 86(12):3696–3713, 2006.

[4] P. Smets. Data fusion in the transferable belief model. In *Proc. of the Third International Conference on Information Fusion. FUSION 2000.*, pages PS21 – PS33, July 2000.

[5] A. Wendemuth and S. Biundo. A companion technology for cognitive technical systems. In A. Esposito, A. Vinciarelli, R. Hoffman, and V. C. Müller, editors, *Proceedings of the EUCogII-SSPNET-COST2102 International Conference (2011)*, LNCS Proceedings on Cognitive Behavioural Systems, Dresden, 2012.

IrisTK: a Statechart-based Toolkit for Multi-party Face-to-face Interaction

Gabriel Skantze
KTH Speech Music and Hearing
Stockholm, Sweden
gabriel@speech.kth.se

Samer Al Moubayed
KTH Speech Music and Hearing
Stockholm, Sweden
sameram@kth.se

ABSTRACT
In this paper, we present IrisTK - a toolkit for rapid development of real-time systems for multi-party face-to-face interaction. The toolkit consists of a message passing system, a set of modules for multi-modal input and output, and a dialog authoring language based on the notion of statecharts. The toolkit has been applied to a large scale study in a public museum setting, where the back-projected robot head Furhat interacted with the visitors in multi-party dialog.

Categories and Subject Descriptors
H.5.2 [**Information Interfaces and Presentation**] : User Interfaces – Natural Language; D.2.2 [**Software Engineering**] Design Tools and Techniques – State diagrams; D.2.11 [**Software Engineering**] Software Architectures – Languages

Keywords
Multi-party interation, Gaze, Gesture, Speech, Spoken dialog, Multimodal systems, Statecharts

1. INTRODUCTION
Spoken dialog technology has for a long time focused on the linguistic interaction, and not as much on the physical space where the interaction takes place. Applications such as ticket booking over the telephone assume that the system interacts with a single user, and that the system and user are not physically co-located. While embodied conversational agents (ECAs) assume some sort of co-location, the ECA is still located behind a display, and the user's physical location in relation to the agent is most often not taken into account. However, there are many recent efforts at locating the interaction in a physical space which is shared between system agent and the users. An example of this is [1], where a virtual receptionist is presented which interacts with several users in a multi-party dialog. The animated agent is still presented on a screen, but the system uses visual input to detect the users' attentional states, and direct the system's attention in order to regulate the interaction. A related field of research is human-robot interaction, where the physical space in which the interaction takes place is of great importance [2].

ICMI '12, October 22–26, 2012, Santa Monica, California, USA.

One enabling factor behind this development is the advances in visual processing techniques (such as face detection and body tracking) that are needed to fully model face-to-face interaction, and the cheap commercial products this has resulted in, such as Microsoft Kinect[1]. This allows a wide audience of researchers and developers to experiment with multimodal interfaces. However, the combination of all these techniques together with spoken dialog technology is not trivial. Face-to-face interaction involves a large amount of real-time events that need to be orchestrated in order to handle phenomena such as overlaps, interruptions, coordination of headpose and gaze in turn-taking, etc. Also, the knowledge to develop and put together all necessary modules is of a very interdisciplinary nature. This calls for a dialog system toolkit for multi-party face-to-face interaction, which provides necessary modules for multimodal input and output and allows the developer or researcher to author the dialog flow in a way that is simple to understand for the novice, yet powerful enough to model more sophisticated behaviors. Such a toolkit should define clear interfaces to make it easy for a researcher who is interested in a specific aspect (such as the use of headpose and gaze in interaction) to adjust specific modules and easily adapt the dialog flow, without being an expert on dialog systems or body tracking. In this paper we present an effort towards developing such a toolkit, called *IrisTK*.

We will start the exposition by describing a challenging setting where IrisTK has been applied: a museum setup where the robot head Furhat interacted with the visitors in multi-party dialog. Over four days the exhibition was seen by thousands of visitors, resulting in a corpus of about 10.000 user utterances. This real-life complex example not only indicates the stability of the toolkit, but also helps us to exemplify many of its features. We will then continue by describing the general principles of the events that are sent in the system and the modules that were used in the exhibition. After this, we will describe the dialog authoring language *IrisFlow* that has been developed as part of the toolkit. We end with a comparison with related work and a discussion on our current and future work.

2. FURHAT AT ROBOTVILLE
The development of IrisTK is part of the IURO project[2], which aims at exploring how robots can be endowed with capabilities for obtaining missing information from humans through spoken interaction. The test scenario for the project is to build a robot that can autonomously navigate in a real urban environment, approach crowds of pedestrians, and enquire them for route directions. In December 2011, the IURO project was invited to take part in the Robotville exhibition at the London Science Museum, showcasing some of the most advanced robots currently being developed in

[1] http://kinectforwindows.org/
[2] http://www.iuro-project.eu/

Europe. In order to explore how a robot can gather information from humans through multi-party dialog, we put the interactive robot head Furhat [3] on display. During the four days of the exhibition, Furhat's task was to collect information on peoples' beliefs about the future of robots, in the form of a survey.

There are several examples of multimodal dialog systems put to the test in public settings [4,5,6]. Allowing spoken interaction in a public setting is indeed a very challenging task – the system needs to cope with a lot of noise and crowds of people wanting to interact at the same time. To make the task feasible, different restrictions are often applied. One example is the virtual museum guide Max [5], which only allowed written input. Another example is the museum guides Ada and Grace [6], which did not allow the visitors to talk to the agents directly, but instead used a "handler" who spoke to the system, that is, a person who knew the limitations of the system and "translated" the visitors' questions. Also, in that system, the dialogue was very simplistic – basically a mapping of questions to answers independent of any dialog context. What makes the Furhat at Robotville exhibition special, apart from allowing the visitors to talk directly to the system, is that the visitors interacted with the system in a multi-party dialog, allowing several visitors to talk to the system at the same time. While there are examples of systems that have engaged in multi-party dialogue in more controlled settings, such as the virtual receptionist presented in [1], we are not aware of any other multi-party dialogue system put to the test in a public setting, interacting with a large number of users.

Most studies on more sophisticated multi-party interaction (such as [1]) have utilized an embodied conversational agent presented on a flat screen. This may be problematic, however, due to the phenomenon known as the Mona Lisa effect [7]: Since the agent is not spatially co-present with the user, it is impossible to establish exclusive mutual gaze with one of the observers – either all observers will perceive the agent as looking at them, or no one will. While mechanical robot heads are indeed spatially and physically co-present with the user, they are expensive to build, inflexible and potentially noisy. The robot head Furhat that we have used here [3], shown in Figure 1, can be regarded as a middle-ground between a mechanical robot head and animated agents. Using a micro projector, the facial animation is projected on a three-dimensional mask that is a 3D printout of the same head model used in the animation software. The head is then mounted on a neck (a pan-tilt unit), which allows the use of both headpose and gaze to direct attention. It has previously been shown in an experimental setting that such a 3D projection increases the system's ability to regulate turn-taking in multi-party dialog, as compared to a 2D screen [8].

The setting of a public exhibition in a museum poses considerable challenges to a multimodal dialog system. In order to engage in a multi-party, situated interaction, the system not only needs to cope with the extremely noisy environment, but also be able to sense when visitors are present. For robustness reasons, we used two handheld close-range microphones put on podiums with short leads, forcing visitors to walk up to one of the microphones whenever they wanted to speak to Furhat. To sense whether someone was standing close to a microphone, ultrasound proximity sensors were mounted on the podiums. Furhat and the two podiums formed an equilateral triangle with sides of about 1.5 meter. On the wall next to Furhat, a screen was mounted with charts showing the real-time results of the survey. The purpose of this was to make the whole exhibition more interesting for the visitors. A snapshot of the setup can be seen in Figure 2.

An example dialog is shown in Table 1, which illustrates a number of typical interaction patterns. As soon as Furhat was approached by a visitor, Furhat immediately took the initiative and started to ask questions, as can be seen in turn 1-4. When the system understood an answer, it gave some relevant feedback (as in turn 6), but if it did not understand, it simply continued (as in turn 9 and 17). All answers were recorded and information about the corresponding questions was logged, which made it possible to annotate all answers later on. After each question, the system also made an *elaboration request* (as in turn 6 and 15). All utterances from the system (including questions) were randomly selected from a set of possible utterances, resulting in a varied output.

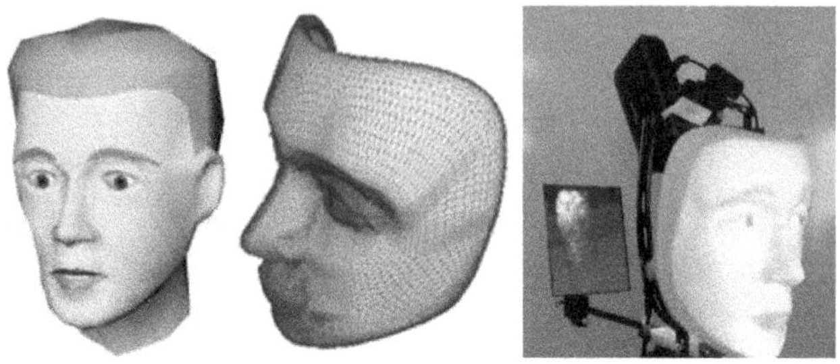

Figure 1: The 3D animation model used for Furhat (left), the mask (middle) and the projection (right).

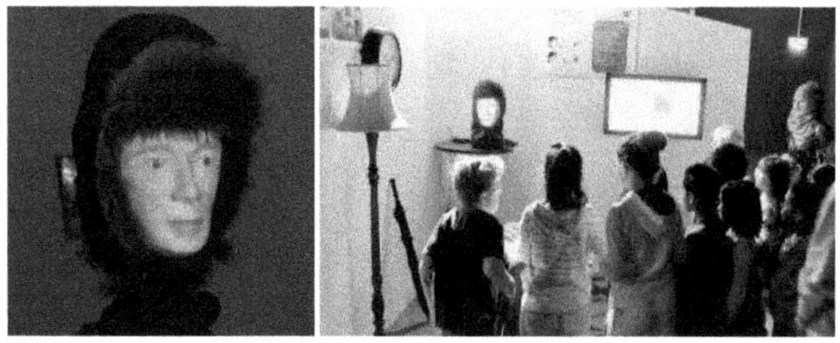

Figure 2: Furhat at Robotville.

With two users present, Furhat could either ask a *directed question* – with the head posed in direction towards the addressee, and eyes looking forward (establishing eye-contact) – or an *open question* to both of them – with the head directed between the users, while alternating gaze between them (as in turn 17). Furhat then turned to the person who answered the question. When speech was detected in both microphones at the same time, the audio levels were compared in order to choose who to attend to. If a question was directed to one of the users and the other user tried to take the turn, Furhat would acknowledge this by shifting the gaze towards this user and say something like "could you please wait a second", while keeping the head directed towards the original user. Furhat would then shift the gaze back and continue with the interaction he was previously involved with (as in turn 11). Another option for Furhat in the multi-party setting was to follow up an elaboration request with an *agreement request*, by turning to the other interlocutor (as in turn 13). This could sometimes result in longer sequences on the same topic, such as the one shown in turn 9-16: question-elaboration-agreement-elaboration.

Although Furhat always started the interactions by asking questions from the survey, it was also possible for the visitors to ask questions (as in turn 18) and thereby shift the topic for the dialog. This would trigger Furhat into awaiting further questions, resulting in mixed-initiative interaction patterns. After answering some questions, or after too many non-understandings, Furhat again tried to get the initiative and ask questions from the survey.

Over the four days of the exhibition, the system ran continuously without any problems, which indicates the robustness of the toolkit. This setup allowed us to collect a corpus of about 10.000 user utterances and to perform large-scale experiments in which we could investigate how people respond to a survey robot and how the 3D design of Furhat allows for accurate turn-taking regulation in a multi-party setting [9]. We also selected 86 visitors who actively interacted with the robotic head, and asked them to fill in a short questionnaire on their impression of the conversation, using a 5-point Likert scale. The participants' overall impression of the system was very positive. The results indicated that they liked Furhat (mean = 4.08, SD .76), they enjoyed talking to the robot (mean = 4.13, SD .84), and they liked Furhat's response behavior (mean = 3.80, SD .71). For a more detailed analysis, see [10].

Table 1: Example interaction. ASR results shown in brackets, using S: SRGS or D: Dictation grammar.

1. U1	*(Approaching microphone 1)*
2. F	*(Looking up at U1)* Hi there. Could you perhaps help me?
3. U1	Yes [S: **yes**]
4. F	I have some questions for you. When do you think robots will beat humans in football?
5. U1	Maybe in 10 years [D: that see **in 10 years**]
6. F	That soon! Could you elaborate on that?
7. U1	Well, they are already pretty good at it [D: while they are already predicted owners]
8. U2	*(Approaching microphone 2)*
9. F	*(Still looking at U1)* Yeah... I have another question for you. Would you like robots to be like humans?
10. U2	Yes, absolutely [D: **yes** that see]
11. F	*(Turning to U2 with gaze only)* Could you just wait a second? *(Looking back at U1)* I'm sorry, where were we. Would you like robots to be like humans?
12. U1	Sure [S: **sure**]
13. F	Yeah? *(Turning the head towards User-2)* Do you agree?
14. U2	No [S: **no**]
15. F	Mhm. Could you say something more about that?
16. U2	Well, I want robots to be like robots [D: I want robots to be like Reynolds]
17. F	Yeah... *(Posing head between users, shifting gaze back and forth between them)* I have another question for you. When do you think robots will serve hamburgers at McDonalds?
18. U1	Do I need an umbrella? [S: **do I need an umbrella**]
19. F	*(Turning to U1)* What do you think, you are in London! Maybe you have another question for me?

3. ARCHITECTURE AND EVENTS

The system consists of a set of modules which produce and consume events. The three basic types of events are *action*, *sense* and *monitor*. *Action* represents things that the system should do, such as saying something, producing a gesture or turning the head. *Sense* represents things that the system perceives (such as a user saying something or approaching Furhat). *Monitor* represents feedback sensations that modules are required to produce when performing an action. Such signals are essential to real-time systems, since they allow other modules to know when actions have been performed or are about to be performed, which facilitates synchronization, sequencing and interruptions of actions (for example if the utterance the system is producing needs to be interrupted because the user is leaving the interaction in the middle of it).

Figure 3 gives an abstract view of the general types of modules and events in the system. *Sensor* modules (such as cameras and microphones) produce low level sensations. Based on this, *interpreter* modules (parsing, gesture recognition, etc) produce high level sensations. The *controller* takes this high level sensation and produces a high level action. This is in turn broken down by *generator* modules (natural language generation, gesture synthesis, etc) into low level actions which are executed by *actuator* modules (motors, facial animation, etc). Of course, a controller does not have to operate on a high level; it may also directly map low level sensations to low level actions. It is also important to note that a single module can serve many of these roles at the same time, and that there can be several components that serve each role.

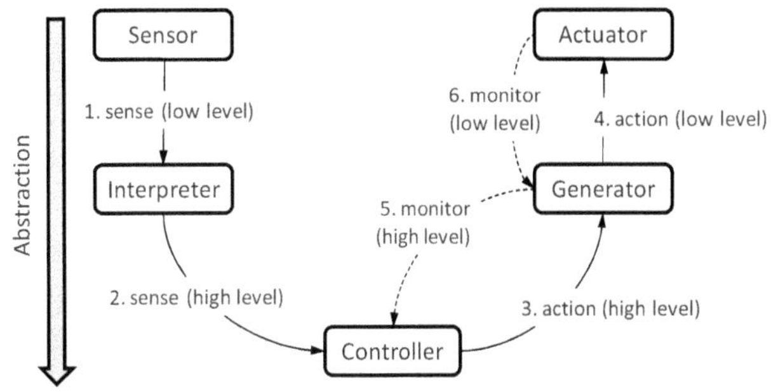

Figure 3: Types of modules and events.

The modules can run on the same computer in a single process or distributed over several processes and computers, using sockets to communicate, which allows for platform and programming language independence. All messages have a corresponding XML representation for serialization. By default, all messages that a module produces are sent to all other modules, but this can be changed in order to optimize the system.

4. EXAMPLE MODULES

We have implemented a range of modules for IrisTK that allows for face-to-face interaction. In this section we will describe these and the events that they produce, or may trigger them into action. A general principle behind all events is *symmetry* – a system might sense *speech* from a user, but also issue an action to produce *speech* as a response to this, which in turn will result in a *speech* monitor event by the module that realizes this action. This means that we represent speech from the system and speech from the users in a similar way.

4.1 Input: User locations

In order to participate in a multi-party face-to-face interaction, the system needs to be able to detect potential interlocutors. This includes both their locations and their identities. Identities might either be global (across sessions, for example by use of face recognition), or local (stable only during one session).We have explored different types of sensors for this, and incorporated them into IrisTK.

A simple and robust way of detecting the users' location, which was done for the Robotville exhibition, is to use off-the-shelf ultrasound proximity sensors. This requires that the possible locations are predefined. The proximity sensor can provide an estimate of the distance to the user, but not any hints to the user's identity.

A more advanced and flexible (but less robust) solution is to use Microsoft Kinect. Using a depth camera and skeletal tracking software, Kinect can track up to two people at the same time and provide the 3D coordinates of the body parts. Kinect can provide local identities of the bodies. We have implemented a module for the toolkit which uses Kinect to identify and track the users.

Another solution that we have used, which is more stable than Kinect and allows for more participants, is to use a regular camera and the face tracking software SHORE developed by Frauenhofer IIS [11]. The users are given wireless handheld microphones with colored markers. This allows the visual processing software to easily identify them (see Figure 4). If a face is detected close to the microphone, this indicates that a user is ready to talk to the system. It is also possible to detect if the users' heads are oriented towards the system agent (as an indication of their attentional state).

The basic event that is produced by these modules is `sense.body`. The message might include a predefined location (as is the case with the proximity sensor), or precise coordinates of the users, their body parts (head, hands, microphones, etc) and the rotation of the head, depending on the capabilities of the specific module.

Figure 4: Microphone and face detection.

4.2 Input: Speech understanding

For speech recognition, we have been using the Windows 7 ASR. By running several ASR modules in parallel, it is possible to process speech from several microphones simultaneously (as was done in the Robotville exhibition). Each ASR engine can also use parallel language models: context-free grammars with semantic tags (SRGS[3]), tailored for the domain, and an open dictation model (as shown in Table 1). This makes it possible to handle "out-of-grammar" utterances to some extent. To interpret the dictation results, we have implemented a robust parser that uses the SRGS grammar to find islands of matching fragments (similar to [12]).

The speech recognition is started by issuing an `action.listen` event. It is possible to specify the location where the system should listen (which will only trigger the associated ASR module). It is also possible to re-weight the language models used, depending on the state of the interaction. At the start and end of speech, the speech recognizer produces `sense.speech` events. The end-of-speech event contains the recognized text and the semantic interpretation, as specified in the SRGS grammar, according to the SISR standard[4], which allows for a nestled key-value structure. All nodes in the result are associated with confidence scores.

Another possibility that we have explored is to use the microphone array in Microsoft Kinect, which allows the use of ASR without handheld microphones (at the cost of a lower ASR performance). The microphone array can also be used to determine the users' locations using built-in beam-forming algorithms.

4.3 Output: Furhat

To control Furhat (Figure 1) within IrisTK, two modules have been implemented, a *face* module and a *neck* module.

The face module handles the facial animation and speech synthesis. For speech synthesis, we use the CereVoice system developed by CereProc[5], lip-synchronized with the facial animation. The module listens for `action.speech` events, which includes the text to be said, annotated with SSML[6]. Feedback sensations are produced at the start and end of the utterance. The eye rotation (and thereby the gaze) of Furhat is controlled by `action.gaze` events. It is also possible to trigger predefined gestures in Furhat's face (such as smiling or raising the eyebrows) using `action.gesture` events. Currently, we only have a set of predefined gestures, but this could eventually be extended with a more powerful markup language, such as BML [13].

The neck module controls the pan-tilt unit and listens for `action.headpose` events. Both this event and the `action.gaze` event allows for duration to be set (in milliseconds). This makes it possible to coordinate different movements. For example, by moving the neck and gaze in opposite directions with the same duration parameters, Furhat can keep the gaze at a fixed target while moving the head.

4.4 Attention manager

The task of the Attention manager (AM) is to build a situation model and keep track of the users' locations and identities, and the attentional state of the system. Using this model, it can act as an interpreter and generator for events related to these issues, translating raw sensory input into higher level behaviors, and higher level action behavior into lower level actions. The AM also uses the situation model to assign id:s to the agents. Hence, the Dialog manager does not need to care about what sensory devices or actuators the system uses and can be used in different setups.

An example of how the AM and the other modules were used in the Robotville scenario is shown in Figure 5. This also illustrates the different roles that the different modules served (compare with Figure 3). As a user approaches the proximity sensor, a `sense.body` event is raised, which is then interpreted by the AM as someone entering a specific location (`sense.enter`). This in turn triggers the Dialog manager (the controller) to raise an `action.attend` event. This is caught by the AM, and is translated into `action.gaze` and `action.headpose` events. These are then consumed by the Neck and Face modules, making Furhat look up and shift the gaze towards the user. When these actions have been executed, a chain of feedback sensory events on different levels are raised (`monitor.gaze`, `monitor.headpose`, `monitor.attend`). This triggers the Dialog Manager to issue an `action.listen` event targeted towards the location where the user is standing. The ASR-1 module receives this and starts the recognizer, producing a `monitor.listen` event (as feedback) and `sense.speech` events (when the user starts and stops speaking).

---

[3] http://www.w3.org/TR/speech-grammar/

[4] http://www.w3.org/TR/semantic-interpretation/

[5] http://www.cereproc.com/

[6] http://www.w3.org/TR/speech-synthesis/.

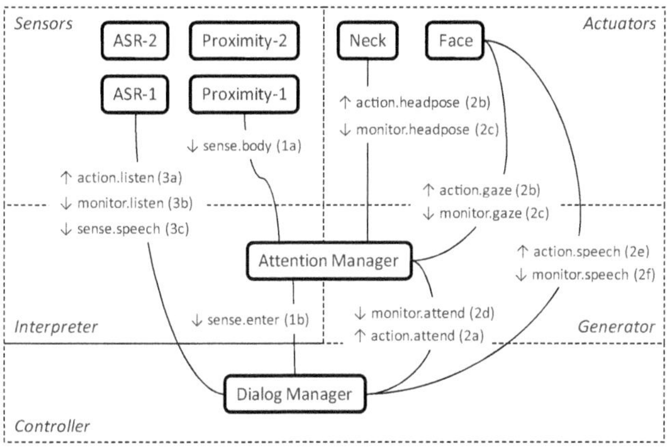

Figure 5: The flow of events between modules during the first three turns in Table 1. The numbers and letters represent the order in which the events are fired.

5. AUTHORING THE DIALOG FLOW

As can be seen in Figure 5, the central controller module (mapping sensations to actions) in the system is the Dialog manager. In this section, we will describe the formalism we use in IrisTK for authoring the behavior of the Dialog manager.

5.1 The statechart paradigm

The central problem of dialog management is that of selecting the next system action (in other words, mapping sensations to actions). The most straightforward approach is a direct mapping of the last user utterance to a system response, which may work for very simple question-answering systems [6]. However, since dialog is inherently context dependent, the selection of action often needs to depend on the current *dialog state*. Two common models which take the dialog state into account are finite state machines (FSM) and the information state update (ISU) approach [14]. FSMs are attractive in that they can be easily visualized and the flow is easy to understand. However, this only holds for simple models; the number of states and transitions can easily explode, and FSMs are therefore hard to use in, for example, mixed-initiative dialogs. In the ISU approach, the dialog state is represented as a collection of variables (the *information state*), such as the last user utterance, a stack of issues under discussion, etc. A set of rules are then applied that are conditioned on these variables and may cause other variables to change (causing other rules to apply) or result in actions that the system can take (similar to the concept of a *production system*). The ISU approach may scale better to more complex interaction patterns and domains than FSM, since the number of possible states the system can be in (in effect, all possible combinations of the variables) need not be enumerated (as is the case for FSMs). However, since these states are not explicitly defined, it may be hard to anticipate and get an overview of the system's behavior, as the number of variables and update rules grows. This also means that the state-space cannot be easily visualized, as is the case with (smaller) FSMs.

In [15], David Harel presented a powerful formalism for defining complex, reactive, event-driven systems, called *statecharts* (often referred to as Harel statecharts). When applied to dialog management, this paradigm can be regarded as a middle ground between ISU and FSM. Just like FSM, the dialog state is represented as a set of predefined states with transitions that are triggered by events. It is thereby possible for the designer to visualize the state-space and get an overview of the system's behavior. However, Harel added a number of extensions that drastically reduce the number of states and transitions needed. First, the states can be hierarchically structured; allowing the designer to define generic event handlers (i.e., transitions) on one level and more specific event handlers in the sub-states. Second, it is possible to add a *datamodel* (i.e., variables), which may affect further execution. Third, it is possible to add *guard conditions* to transitions, which are dependent on event parameters and the state of the datamodel. Fourth, transitions between states, or the entering or leaving of a state, can also be associated with *actions*, which can be used to raise internal or external events that either affect the further execution of the statechart, or give rise to actions in the other parts of the system (such as issuing the speech synthesizer to say something). Another extension that we will not discuss further in this paper is the support for concurrent states.

Statecharts has recently gained increasing interest as a model for dialog management. An XML-based representation which closely follows the original Harel statechart model, called SCXML[7], is currently being standardized by W3C. SCXML is planned to be part of the VoiceXML 3.0 standard[8], in order to allow for a more flexible control in telephone-based dialog systems. In the research community, it has been shown how SCXML can be used to model the ISU-approach to dialog management (using the *datamodel* to represent the information state) [16]. While this illustrates the flexibility of the formalism, we think that it is better to utilize the state space to directly model the different states of the dialog, in order to avoid the shortcoming of the ISU-approach discussed above.

5.2 IrisFlow – a statechart variant

While SCXML corresponds to the statechart model that Harel presented, we don't think the specification is optimal as an authoring language for dialog behavior. One of the problems that we have encountered is the handling of what Harel refers to as *activities*. These are defined as actions that take some time (i.e., that are not instantaneous), which obviously is very common for dialog systems (e.g., when the system says something or makes a gesture). In order to handle activities, the Harel statechart model assumes that each activity is associated with a state (i.e., the entering and leaving of the state are associated with the beginning and end of the activity). If an event handler needs to execute a sequence of activities (again, very common for dialog systems) and associate different event handlers with these, a new state has to be defined for each specific activity. Thus, it becomes cumbersome to manually author such behavior[9].

To make the authoring of the dialog behavior more efficient and simpler, we have defined an XML-based authoring language for dialog flow control, called *IrisFlow*, which can be regarded as a variant of Harel statecharts. The most important extension is the possibility of recursion (or context-freeness), which we think allows for a better handling of activities in dialog systems[10]. A single event handler can trigger a sequence of activities by a sequence of *parameterized state calls*. To allow this, we define two types of transitions: *goto* and *call*. While *goto* corresponds to a traditional statechart transition, *call* makes the execution model

7 http://www.w3.org/TR/scxml/

8 http://www.w3.org/TR/voicexml30/

9 In VoiceXML 3.0, the individual dialog-related activities are not executed within SCXML. Instead, a complete VoiceXML interaction is associated with a single SCXML state. Instead, we want to control all dialog behavior within the statechart and not mix models.

10 The possibility of such an extension is discussed in Harel's original article [15] (6.4).

put the current state and execution plan on a call stack before the transition takes place. The called state can then *return* to the calling state and execution plan without any explicit reference to a return point. Thus, the called state might be thought of as a *dynamic sub-state* (as opposed to the static sub-states defined by the state hierarchy).

5.3 IrisFlow example

A graphical representation of a small subset of the statechart used for the Robotville setup is shown in Figure 6. The boxing of the states illustrates the hierarchical structure. We do not show all possible transitions here, but instead the transitions that take place during the dialog in Table 1 (numbers on the arrows correspond to the different turn numbers in the scenario).

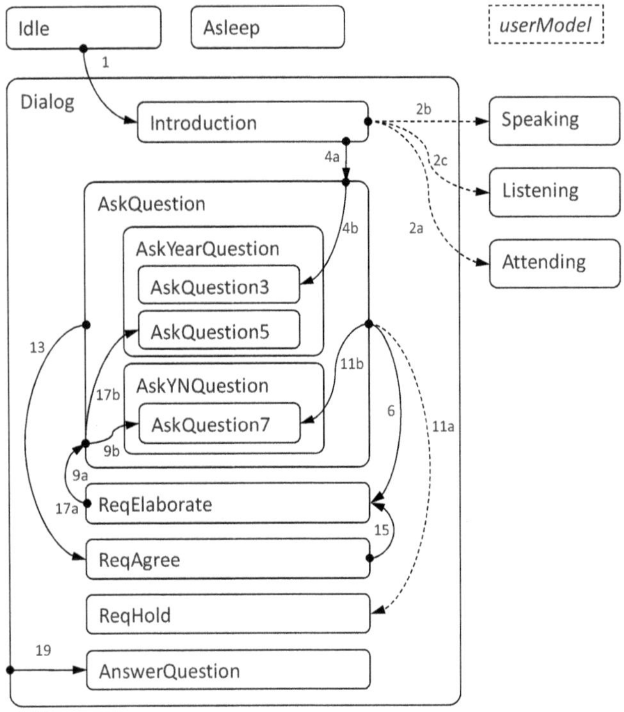

Figure 6: Fragment of the statechart for the Robotville exhibition. Arrows illustrate state transition for the example in Table 1 (solid lines=*goto*, dotted lines=*call*).

Using IrisFlow, we defined generic states, such as *Idle* and *Dialog*, with sub-states such as *Introduction* and *AskQuestion* (which in turn has sub-states such as *AskYNQuestion* and *AskYearQuestion*). The generic *Dialog* state defines event handlers to handle questions from the user regardless of the current sub-state, allowing mixed-initiative interaction. Dynamic sub-states were also defined, such as *Speaking*, *Attending* and *Listening*, with relevant event handlers. An event handler in the *Introduction* state can thus first call the *Speaking* state (asking the user a question) and then, when the speaking is completed, the *Listening* state (listening for the user's answer to the question). When in a called state (i.e., a dynamic sub-state), events are not only checked against the event handlers of the current state and its super-states, but also the event handlers of the calling states. Thus, when an event is processed and the flow is in the state *Speaking*, the event handlers of the following states will be checked (in order): *Speaking*, *Introduction*, *Dialog*. An important extension to Harel statecharts that makes the call transition useful to handle activities (that Harel also discussed in [15]; 6.1) is that transitions can be parameterized. For example, a called state can take parameters that are passed when the *call* is made (much like a function with arguments), which controls the behavior while in that state.

It is also possible to define variables on different level. As illustrated in Figure 6 (with dotted outline), a global variable called *UserModel* is also defined, which is used by the system to remember which questions it has previously asked a specific user, thus avoiding to ask the same question again. Each time the *AskQuestion* state is entered (see transition 4a, 9a and 17a in Figure 6), the UserModel is consulted to select which question should be asked next (resulting in transition 4b, 9b and 17b).

The IrisFlow statechart is authored using XML. The XML code is then compiled into Java source code, which is in turn compiled into Java byte code. Therefore, Java code can be used directly in the XML (in for example guard conditions), and there is no need for a scripting language such as JavaScript. An IrisFlow statechart (`<flow>`) contains a collection of states (`<state>`). A state, in turn, contains a collection of event handlers (`<catch>`). A small fragment of the definition of super-state *Dialog* is shown below. This defines generic event handlers that are used throughout the dialog, regardless of which specific dialog state the system may be in.

```
<state id="Dialog">
  <catch event="sense.leave"
         cond="userModel.attending(@agent)">
    <if cond=" userModel.present('loc-1')">
      <call state="Attending" param:target="'loc-1'"/>
      <goto state="AskQuestion"/>
    <elseif cond=" userModel.present('loc-2')"/>
      <call state="Attending" param:target="'loc-2'"/>
      <goto state="AskQuestion"/>
    <else/>
      <goto state="Idle" param:goodbye="true" />
    </if>
  </catch>
  <catch event="sense.speech.end"
         cond="eq(@sem.act,'req_name')">
    <call state="Speaking"
          param:text="'My name is FurHat!'" />
    <goto state="AnswerNext" />
  </catch>
</state>
```

Each event handler (`<catch>`) corresponds to the `<transition>` element in SCXML, with possible guard conditions (`cond`). However, it only specifies a sequence of actions to take when an event is caught, and the actual transition is defined as an action (`<goto>`). As can be seen, both *call* and *goto* can be parameterized (attributes in the namespace *param*). The names of external events that can be caught (such as `sense.leave`) correspond to the name of the events described in section 4 above. It is also possible to raise and catch internal events which can be defined by the dialog author. As can be seen, the *Dialog* state defines the behavior when an agent leaves the interaction (turn to the other speaker if there is one, otherwise go to the Idle state). It also handles questions from the user (such as "what is your name?"). Below is a small fragment of the *Introduction* state, which extends the *Dialog* state[11]:

```
<state id="Introduction" extends="Dialog">
  <onentry>
    <random>
      <call state="Speaking"
        param:text="'Could you perhaps help me?'"/>
      <call state="Speaking"
```

[11] The <state> elements are not nestled as in SCXML, which we think makes it easier to distribute the code over several documents and potentially allows for "multiple inheritance" (again, an extension that Harel discuss in [15], 6.2).

```
      param:text="'Would you like to help me?'"/>
    <call state="Speaking"
      param:text="'Do you want to help me?'"/>
  </random>
  <call state="Listening"
        param:grammar="'default/0.5 yn/1.0'"/>
</onentry>
<catch event="sense.speech.end"
      cond="eq(@sem.act,'no')">
  <call state="Speaking" param:text="'Okay'"/>
  <goto state="Idle" param:goodbye="true"/>
</catch>
<catch event="sense.speech.end"
      cond="eq(@sem.act,'yes')">
  <call state="Speaking" param:text="'Great!'"/>
  <goto state="AskQuestion"/>
</catch>
<onidle>
  <call state="Speaking"
      param:text="'Sorry, I didn't hear you'"/>
  <reenter/>
</onidle>
</state>
```

The *Introduction* state basically handles a simple yes/no question to the user. However, since it extends the *Dialog* state, it is still possible for the user to not answer the question but instead ask a counter-question, leave the interaction, etc., which allows for mixed-initiative. As in SCXML, the `<onentry>` is a special event handler that is triggered when the state is entered. The `<random>` element allows for a probabilistic behavior, which in this case allows for a more varied output. There is also a special event handler, `<onidle>` which is called when there are no more actions to take and no more events in the event queue (e.g., if the *Listening* call returns without triggering any event handlers). The `<reenter>` element causes the current state to be entered again.

Below is a small fragment of the *Listening* state, which is called when the system runs the speech recognizer (how the state is called can be seen in the *Introduction* state above):

```
<state id="Listening">
  <param name="timeout" default="8000"/>
  <param name="grammar" default="'default/1.0'"/>
  <onentry>
    <send event="action.gesture" param:name="'brow-up'"/>
    <send event="action.listen" param:timeout="timeout"
                                param:grammar="grammar"/>
  </onentry>
  <catch event="monitor.listen.end">
    <send event="action.gesture"
          param:name="'brow-down'"/>
    <return/>
  </catch>
</state>
```

As can be seen, the parameters that the state takes are explicitly defined with default values (`<param>`). On entry, the state issues an external event to start the recognizer and to raise the eyebrows, which signals to the user that the system is listening. When the speech recognizer ends (producing the feedback sensation `sense.listen`), the eyebrows are lowered again and the execution returns to where it left off in the calling state (`<return>`).

These examples show how the dialog behavior can be specified in a rather compact way. To implement the *Introduction* state above with SCXML, each call to the Speaking and Listening state would require their own state (a total of seven states instead of one), defined with their respective event handlers. Using IrisFlow, behavior that is specific to each activity can be defined using parameters, behavior that is specific to this collection of activities can be defined in *Introduction* state, and the general behavior when speaking can be defined in the *Speaking* state.

These examples only illustrate some basic principles; the complete IrisFlow XML used for Robotville contained 33 states (about 1600 lines of XML code).

6. DISCUSSION AND RELATED WORK

In the example presented here we only have one controller. It has been suggested [17,18] that it might be better to split the sensor-action mapping into modules that responsible for low-level actions (such as backchannels and engagement), and modules responsible for high-level actions (such as selecting the next dialog move). While we can see the benefits of such an approach when it comes to reusability of modules (e.g., the same backchannel or engagement module could be used in different applications), there is also a risk that it may result in conflicting actions being issued, especially as the complexity of the system increases. Also, since the purpose of IrisTK is to allow rapid development, all aspects of the behavior of the system should be easily authored, and it is therefore a great advantage if all control of the system actions are handled in a uniform way. We will therefore stick to a *single-controller architecture* as a best practice (although no such restrictions are enforced by the framework). When it comes to reusability, we think that the statechart-based design presented here provides an elegant solution. Super-states, such as *Dialog*, and dynamic sub-states, such as *Speaking* and *Listening*, can be defined for different kinds of dialogs (e.g., multi-party vs. dyadic) and for different setup of modules, and can then be reused across applications.

It should be noted that the example presented here is a practical system in a public setting. The states are very tightly coupled to the specific questions asked by the system, with hard-coded textual representations of the system's utterances. However, it is also possible to implement more generalized models of dialog, where the states correspond to more general discourse units such as Initiative and Response. It should also be possible to implement specific theories of dialogue, such as the Collaborative Discourse Theory [19], where the recursive state calls could be used to model Discourse Segments on different levels.

There are many other examples of research platforms for developing spoken dialog systems. One example is **TrindiKit** [14], which builds upon the ISU approach to dialog management discussed in 5.1. Another example is **RavenClaw** [20], which is based on the idea of automatically constructing a dialog model from a task model. **Jindigo** [21] is a framework targeted towards incremental dialog processing. **WAMI** [22] is a framework for multimodal systems that are to be run within a web-browser. None of these are especially targeted towards face-to-face or multiparty interaction; their primary focus is on the linguistic interaction. This does not necessarily mean that they cannot be used for this, but the frameworks do not provide useful modules for such interaction, nor have they been proven useful in such settings. More importantly, none of these frameworks are based on the statechart model for authoring the dialog flow, and are, in our opinion, not as intuitive and flexible when it comes to dialog modeling. There are of course more complex frameworks for multimodal robotic systems, such as **RT-Middleware**[12] and **ROS**[13]. While these frameworks are indeed mature and offer a range of modules, they do not have a special focus on the spoken interaction and do not provide any simple dialog authoring tools.

[12] http://www.openrtm.org/

[13] http://www.ros.org

The most well-known open standard for dialog flow authoring is perhaps **VoiceXML**. However, we do not think that VoiceXML can account for more sophisticated dialog behaviors, nor is there any support for multimodal events (beyond DTMF touchtones). While the upcoming version of the standard (3.0) has support for more flexible control, using **SCXML,** it is still unimodal. As discussed above, we also think that SCXML is less suitable for direct authoring of the dialog behavior.

7. FUTURE WORK

We are currently applying IrisTK to the final demonstrator in the IURO project: a robot that can autonomously navigate in a real urban environment, approach crowds of pedestrians, and enquire them for route directions. The statechart model has allowed us to define mixed-initiative dialog, where the system can first turn to one pedestrian and let her freely describe the route, then turn to another pedestrian and let him verify the route, segment by segment.

There are several directions in which IrisTK can be extended. Since the statechart paradigm lends itself well to visual representations, it should be possible to develop a graphical editor for designing the interaction flow, similar to the CSLU toolkit[14], but much more powerful. Another interesting extension is to allow the dialog designer to define explicit decision points in the flow (similar to the `<random>` statement), and associate rewards to specific states. Then, reinforcement learning could be used to automatically learn optimal decisions at these points when executing the statechart, by letting the system interact with real or simulated users [23].

We are also planning to release IrisTK as open source. Hopefully, this will be useful to other researchers and inspire them to contribute to the toolkit. While the focus in this paper has been on the benefits for multi-party face-to-face interaction, IrisTK can of course also be used for other kinds of dialog applications and experimental settings. To our knowledge, Furhat at Robotville is the first example of multi-party spoken interaction with a physically situated agent in a public setting. This was made possible by developing the toolkit that has been presented in this paper.

8. ACKNOWLEDGMENTS

This work is partly supported by the European Commission project IURO (Interactive Urban Robot), grant agreement no. 248314, as well as the SAVIR project (Situated Audio-Visual Interaction with Robots) funded by the Swedish Government (strategic research areas). The authors would like to thank Jonas Beskow, Joakim Gustafson, Björn Granström and Nicole Mirnig for their contribution to the Robotville exhibition.

9. REFERENCES

[1] Bohus, D., & Horvitz, E. (2010). Facilitating multiparty dialog with gaze, gesture, and speech. In *Proc ICMI 10*. Beijing, China.

[2] Kanda, T., Shiomi, M., Miyashita, Z., Ishiguro, H., & Hagita, N. (2009). An affective guide robot in a shopping mall. In *Proceedings of HRI* (pp. 173-180).

[3] Al Moubayed, S., Beskow, J., Skantze, G., & Granström, B. (2012). Furhat: A Back-projected Human-like Robot Head for Multiparty Human-Machine Interaction. In Esposito, A., Esposito, A., Vinciarelli, A., Hoffmann, R., & C. Müller, V. (Eds.), *Cognitive Behavioural Systems. Lecture Notes in Computer Science*. Springer.

[4] Gustafson, J. (2002). *Developing multimodal spoken dialogue systems. Empirical studies of spoken human-computer interaction*. Doctoral dissertation, KTH, Department of Speech, Music and Hearing, KTH, Stockholm.

[5] Kopp, S., Gesellensetter, L., Krämer, N., & Wachsmuth, I. (2005). A conversational agent as museum guide - design and evaluation of a real-world application. In *Proceedings of IVA 2005, International Working Conference on Intelligent Virtual Agents*. Berlin: Springer-Verlag.

[6] Swartout, W., Traum, D., Artstein, R., Noren, D., Debevec, P., Bronnenkant, K., Williams, J., Leuski, A., Narayanan, S., Piepol, D., Lane, C., Morie, J., Aggarwal, P., Liewer, M., Chiang, J-Y., Gerten, J., Chu, S., & White, K. (2010). Ada and Grace: Toward Realistic and Engaging Virtual Museum Guides. In *10th International Conference on Intelligent Virtual Agents (IVA)*.

[7] Al Moubayed, S., Edlund, J., & Beskow, J. (2012). Taming Mona Lisa: communicating gaze faithfully in 2D and 3D facial projections. *ACM Transactions on Interactive Intelligent Systems, 1*(2), 25.

[8] Al Moubayed, S., & Skantze, G. (2011). Turn-taking Control Using Gaze in Multiparty Human-Computer Dialogue: Effects of 2D and 3D Displays. In *Proceedings of AVSP*. Florence, Italy.

[9] Skantze, G., Al Moubayed, S., Gustafson, J., Beskow, J., & Granström, B. (in press). Furhat at Robotville: A Robot Head Harvesting the Thoughts of the Public through Multi-party Dialogue. To be published in *Proceedings of IVA-RCVA*. Santa Cruz, CA.

[10] Al Moubayed, S., Beskow, J., Granström, B., Gustafson, J., Mirning, N., Skantze, G., & Tscheligi, M. (2012). Furhat goes to Robotville: a large-scale multiparty human-robot interaction data collection in a public space. In *Proc of LREC Workshop on Multimodal Corpora*. Istanbul, Turkey.

[11] Kueblbeck, C., & Ernst, A. (2006). Face detection and tracking in video sequences using the modified census transformation. *Journal on Image and Vision Computing, 24*(6), 564-572.

[12] Skantze, G., & Edlund, J. (2004). Robust interpretation in the Higgins spoken dialogue system. In *Proceedings of ISCA Tutorial and Research Workshop (ITRW) on Robustness Issues in Conversational Interaction*. Norwich, UK.

[13] Kopp, S., Krenn, B., Marsella, S., Marshall, A., Pelachaud, C., Pirker, H., Thórisson, K., & Vilhjálmsson, H. (2006). Towards a Common Framework for Multimodal Generation in ECAs: The Behavior Markup Language. In *Proceedings of IVA* (pp. 205-217). Marina del Rey.

[14] Larsson, S., & Traum, D. R. (2000). Information state and dialogue management in the TRINDI dialogue move engine toolkit. *Natural Language Engineering: Special Issue on Best Practice in Spoken Language Dialogue Systems Engineering, 6*(3-4), 323-340.

[15] Harel, D. (1987). Statecharts: A visual formalism for complex systems. *Science of Computer Programming, 8*, 231-274.

[16] Kronlid, F., & Lager, T. (2007). Implementing the information-state update approach to dialogue management in a slightly extended scxml. In *Proceedings of the 11th International Workshop on the Semantics and Pragmatics of Dialogue (DECALOG)* (pp. 99-106).

[17] Raux, A., & Eskenazi, M. (2007). A multi-layer architecture for semi-synchronous event-driven dialogue management. In *ASRU 2007*. Kyoto, Japan..

[18] Lemon, O., Cavedon, L., & Kelly, B. (2003). Managing dialogue interaction: A multi-layered approach. In *Proceedings of the 4th SIGdial Workshop on Discourse and Dialogue* (pp. 168-177).

[19] Rich, C., Sidner, C., & Lesh, N. (2001). COLLAGEN: Applying Collaborative Discourse Theory to Human Computer Interaction. *Artificial Intelligence Magazine, 22*, 15-25.

[20] Bohus, D., & Rudnicky, A. (2009). The RavenClaw dialog management framework: Architecture and systems. *Computer Speech and Language, 23*(3), 332-361.

[21] Skantze, G. (2010). *Jindigo: a Java-based Framework for Incremental Dialogue Systems*. Technical Report, KTH, Stockholm, Sweden.

[22] Gruenstein, A., McGraw, I., & Badr, I. (2008). The WAMI toolkit for developing, deploying, and evaluating web-accessible multimodal interfaces. In *Proceedings of ICMI* (pp. 141-148). Chania, Crete, Greece.

[23] Rieser, V., & Lemon, O. (2012). *Reinforcement Learning for Adaptive Dialogue Systems*. Berlin: Springer-Verlag.

[14] http://www.cslu.ogi.edu/toolkit/

Estimating Conversational Dominance in Multiparty Interaction

Yukiko I. Nakano
Dept. of Computer and Information Science,
Seikei University
Musashino-shi, Tokyo 180-8633, Japan
y.nakano@st.seikei.ac.jp

Yuki Fukuhara
Graduate School of Science and Technology
Seikei University
Musashino-shi, Tokyo 180-8633, Japan

ABSTRACT
It is important for conversational agents that manage multiparty conversations to recognize the group dynamics existing among the users. This paper proposes a method for estimating the conversational dominance of participants in group interactions. First, we conducted a Wizard-of-Oz experiment to collect conversational speech, and motion data. Then, we analyzed various paralinguistic speech and gaze behaviors to elucidate the factors that predict conversational dominance. Finally, by exploiting the speech and gaze data as estimation parameters, we created a regression model to estimate conversational dominance, and the multiple correlation coefficient of this model was 0.85.

Categories and Subject Descriptors
H5.3 [Information Interfaces and Presentation]: Group and Organization Interfaces - Synchronous interaction.

General Terms
Human Factors; Design; Measurement.

Keywords
Conversational dominance; multiparty interaction; nonverbal information; conversational agent.

1. INTRODUCTION
In multiparty conversations, one person often plays a central role and leads the conversation, and another person in the group is often submissive and has little chance to speak. While conversational dominance is determined based on various factors, such as social status, social role, and personality, a dominant/submissive person can be identified by observing his/her verbal and nonverbal behaviors without foreknowledge of the social and personal relationships between them. Moreover, the dominance levels of the participants may affect what to say to whom in conversation. For example, to urge a group of people to make a decision, it may be effective to address a person with higher dominance. On the contrary, it may also be possible that participants take note of different perspectives by asking submissive people for their opinions. Therefore, if conversational agent systems can estimate the conversational dominance of each member of a group of users, agent's effective behaviors in managing multiparty conversations can be chosen.

Research in social psychology and communication science has analyzed the relationships between conversational dominance and verbal and nonverbal communication behaviors [3, 9, 14]. However, very few attempts have been made to create computational models of conversational dominance [16, 17, 20], and these have only used speech features to estimate conversational dominance. In this study, we focus on eye gaze information in addition to speech features in estimating conversational dominance. Participants with higher dominance may receive more attention from others, but less-dominant people may receive less. Thus, more refined analyses of the relationship between gaze behavior and conversational dominance are necessary to establish a computational model of dominance estimation. To accomplish this goal, we address the following issues:

1. Collecting conversation corpus by experimentally controlling the conversational dominance of the participants and obtaining speech audio and head-direction data to roughly estimate gaze direction;
2. Measuring conversational dominance in subjective and objective ways;
3. Analyzing the correlation between conversational dominance and various measures of eye gaze and acoustic information;
4. Establishing a regression model for the estimation of conversational dominance.

In section 2, we discuss related work investigating multiparty conversations and conversational dominance; then, in section 3, we describe the data-collection experiment conducted for this study. Section 4 provides the analysis of correlations between conversational dominance and nonverbal behaviors to determine which parameters are useful in estimating conversational dominance. In section 5, we propose an estimation model for conversational dominance and evaluate how well our model can estimate this type of dominance.

ICMI '12, October 22–26, 2012, Santa Monica, California, USA.

2. RELATED WORK

2.1 Studies in Multiparty Interaction

Compared to dialogue, in which each participant is either a speaker or a listener, participants' roles are more complex in multiparty conversations. Goffman [10] discussed the concept of participation in conversations, and based on his discussion, Clark [5] distinguished participants from overhearers. His definitions of participants include "speaker", "addressee (or hearer)", and others who are taking part in the conversation but not currently being addressed. Non-addressed participants are referred to as "side participants". All other listeners are "overhearers" who have no rights or responsibilities in a given conversation. In this study, we analyze the behaviors of participants in multiparty conversations by employing Clark's definitions of participants as speaker, hearer, and side participant.

Previous studies have shown that participants' gaze behaviors differ depending on the participant's role. People gaze more while listening (75%) than while speaking (41%) in dyadic conversations [2]. Analyzing multiparty conversations, Vertegaal [19] reported the similar result—about 1.6 times more gaze occurred while listening compared to while speaking. However, when a person begins speaking to other people, his/her gaze is distributed to all of them. In this condition, the total percentage of time engaged in gaze behavior (while speaking) rises to 59%. Vertegaal applied these findings to a design of mediated communication.

Studies on multiparty conversations with conversational agents have primarily focused on interactions between one user and multiple agents. Eichner et al. [8] developed a conversational presentation system that generates conversations between two agents to answer the user's questions. Traum et al. [18] proposed a multiparty conversational system that manages a negotiation conversation among three parties: two virtual agents and a user. Nagao et al. [15] proposed a plan-based multiparty conversation system for two users. More recently, Bohus et al. [4] proposed a method to predict users' intention of engagement in conversation in an open-world context. Huang et al. [12] proposed a quiz agent that estimates whether the users are excited about talking with the agent.

However, as far as we know, little attention has been paid to conversational dominance in computer-supported human-human as well as human-agent/robot multiparty communication.

2.2 Studies in Conversational Dominance

As a study on group interaction, Bales [3] proposed three dimensions to characterize conversational participants; dominance vs. submission, friendliness vs. unfriendliness, and instrumental control vs. emotional expressiveness. In the dominance/submission dimension, he mentioned that dominant participants are more active and extroverted, talk more, and have more power to control the entire conversation than do submissive participants.

Previous studies in social psychology have revealed that nonverbal behaviors are different depending on their conversational dominance. Dovidio [6] found that in dyadic conversations, less-dominant people are more likely to be the first to break a mutual gaze. Knapp [14] reported that higher-status people gaze roughly the same percentage of the time when listening and when speaking; whereas lower-status people gaze relatively more while listening than while speaking. Moreover, dominant people with higher status and more power initiate speech more often and control the whole interaction [3]. However, all of these studies are analysis-oriented, and they do not aim to achieve automatic prediction by applying computational models.

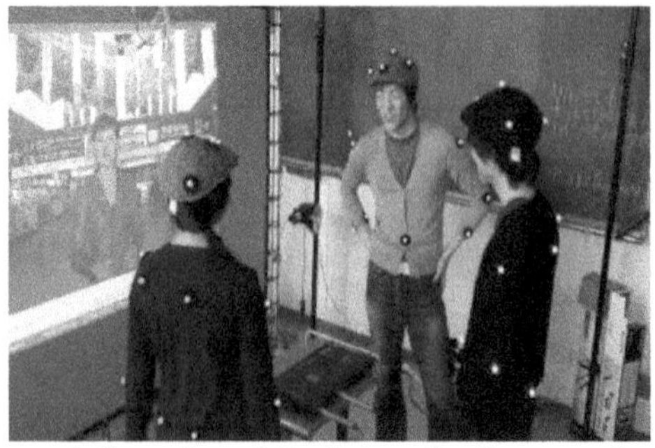

Figure 1. Snapshot of the data collection experiment

Many studies in analyzing and recognizing multiparty communication were conducted in AMI (Augmented Multi-party Interaction) project [1]. Using the AMI corpus, Rienks and Heylen [16] and Rienks et al. [17] proposed a method for estimating dominance of conversation participants in three levels: high, normal, and low. They employed several basic speech-activity features and higher-level features, such as topic changes, participant roles, turns, and interruptions, which were manually annotated by human annotators. The estimation accuracy of their model was reported to be about 70%. Although the results of that study suggest a good possibility towards automatic estimation of conversational dominance, the actual data used for estimation were manually annotated, and eye-gaze information was not used. Therefore, in this study, we will establish a computational model for the estimation of conversational dominance based on automatically obtained audio and visual data, and we will propose a fully automatic dominance estimation method.

3. EXPERIMENT

First, we conducted an experiment to collect multiparty conversations with a virtual agent in a Wizard-of-Oz setting.

3.1 Procedure

We recruited 12 subjects, who were divided into three groups. In each group, the group members were friends in the same grade (of the same age) and in the same department of a university. Therefore, we assumed that their social status was relatively uniform [11] and that their conversational dominance would not be affected by this status. In each session, three out of four people in the group participated in the conversation. Four sessions were held for each group; we collected 12 conversations in total.

Groups of three people participated in the experiment as subject groups. The task of the subject groups was to discuss and decide where they would like to go out to enjoy a weekend. To collect information about places to visit, they could ask questions to the agent displayed in front of them. The agent, which was controlled by an experimenter, answered questions and recommended some places to visit. The places to visit were changed for each session so that the contents of the conversation were different for each session. A snapshot of an experimental session is shown in Figure 1. To experimentally control the participants' attitudes toward the conversation, one subject in each session played the role of a person who could not go out that weekend. We expected this

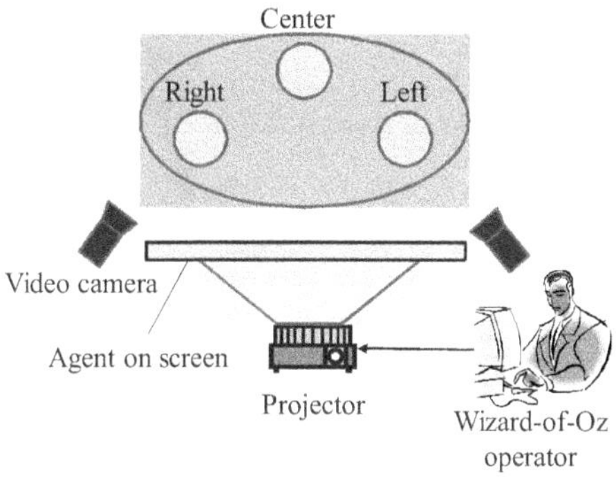

Figure 2. Configuration of the experiment

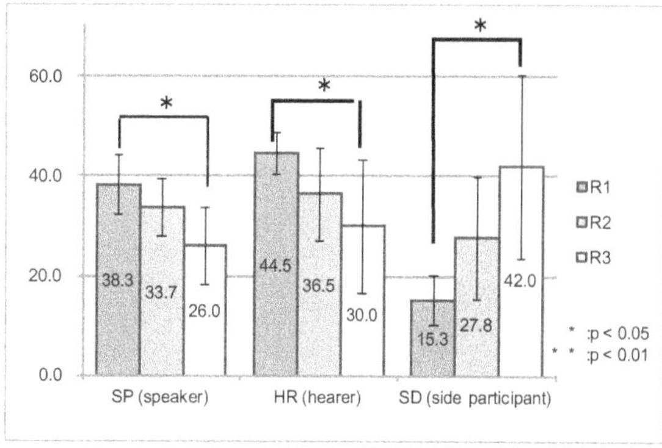

Figure 3. Distribution of participation role

person to participate in the conversation less dominantly and less positively compared to the others; he/she was estimated to have a greater possibility of becoming a side participant.

The other two subjects were assigned different goals in selecting the places. For example, one subject was instructed to go to a place with good shopping, and the other was instructed to go to a place with good scenery. Thus, the task was to resolve these conflicts and choose two places that would satisfy each member's requirements as much as possible. The roles of the subjects were changed for every session. To motivate the subjects, we instructed them that they would receive more rewards if they chose places that satisfied all the requirements.

Each session lasted 5 minutes. If the subjects decided where to go within this time, the session was terminated. After each session, we asked the subjects to rank the participants with respect to their conversational dominance.

3.2 Experimental Setting and Collected Data

The experimental setting is shown in Figure 2. The proxemics of the subjects and the position of the virtual agent are also shown in the figure. The subjects were instructed to stand around an audio interface at the same distances from each other and the screen, so that they could see each other and the agent. To record motion data, we used the NaturalPoint OptiTrack motion capture system with 10 cameras mounted on 6 poles. Each subject wore a sweater with markers for motion capturing (see Figure 1); therefore, the motion capture system measured the upper-body motions of each subject. The animated agent was displayed on a 100-inch screen in front of the subjects (Figure 1). We used the Haptek animation system to produce the agent animations. When a subject asked the agent a question, an experimenter listened to the question and chose one of the answer menus or typed some text to answer the question. Then, the spoken response was produced through the Hitachi HitVoice text-to-speech system. The agent did not display any facial expressions or gestures, but her lip movement was synchronized with her speech. The interaction was video-taped using two Hi-vision cameras. We used the EDIROL UA-1000 USB audio interface and a multi-track recoding software to synchronously record the subjects' speech sounds. We obtained the following data from the experiment:

- Video data shots from the right-front and left-front of the subjects;
- Speech sounds for each subject, synchronized with other measurements;
- Upper-body motion data, measured by a motion-capture system;
- Ranked order of dominance (1st, 2nd, and 3rd most dominant persons) for each session, reported by the subjects.

4. DATA ANALYSIS

As a preliminary step in determining the prediction parameters of conversational dominance, we investigated various nonverbal behaviors and the correlations between the ranked orders of conversational dominance, as reported by the subjects.

We first assessed the validity of the subjective rankings of dominance obtained in section 3. For each session, each participant's average dominance ranking (as per the three participants' judgments) was calculated. The participant who received the highest average ranking was referred to as the "rank 1 participant" (R1); the participant with the second highest average ranking, the "rank 2 participant" (R2); the participant with the lowest average ranking, the "rank 3 participant" (R3). The averages of ranking for R1, R2, and R3 across the entire corpus were 1.16, 2.08, and 2.75, respectively; since these are average rankings, smaller values indicate higher ranks. The average rankings clearly differ between participants who were ranked differently. To check the validity of the experimental control, we examined whether the participants assigned as not being able to go out for the weekend were actually ranked as R3. The results indicated that in 5 out of 8 sessions, the subjects who could not go out were ranked as R3. In the other three sessions, they were ranked as R2. The subjects who could not go out were never ranked as R1. Therefore, we believe that the experimental instructions successfully controlled the subjects' attitudes toward participating in the conversation.

4.1 Participation Role and Conversational Dominance

Bales [3] mentioned that a dominant person is more likely to be a speaker. Therefore, we investigated whether the distribution of participation roles are different depending on conversational dominance. First, we segmented the corpus into turns and used turns as the units of analysis. We defined a turn as the time interval from when a speaker starts speaking to when a different person takes the next turn. If there is a pause of longer than 2 seconds, after which the same speaker speaks again, we count them as different turns. Turns were automatically identified according to this definition. For each turn, three types of participation roles (speaker (SP), hearer (HR), and side participant

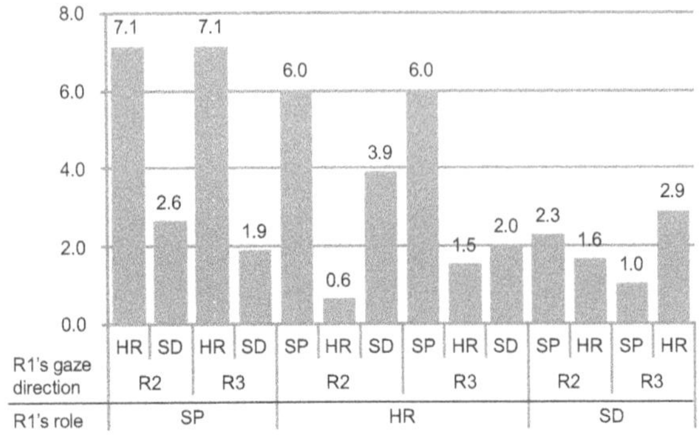

(4-a) R1's gaze direction

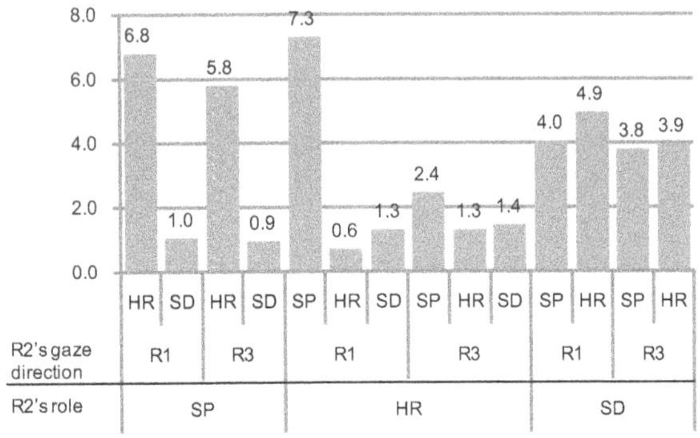

(4-b) R2's gaze direction

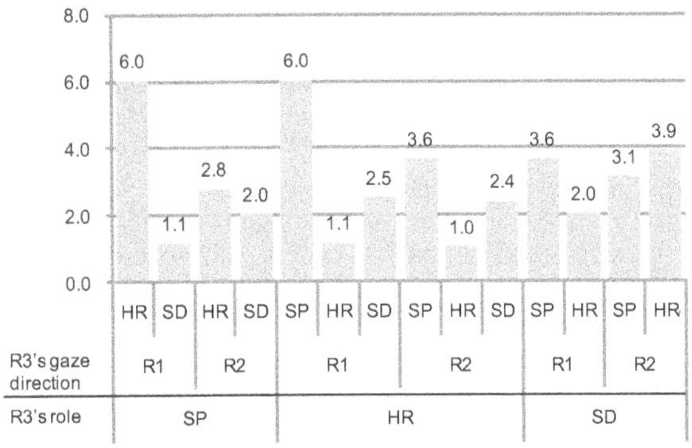

(4-c) R3's gaze direction

Figure 4. Distribution of gaze

(SD), were manually annotated. When an SP talked to the other two participants simultaneously, the HR label was assigned to both non-speaking participants.

Figure 3 shows the average percentages of each participation role for each session according to dominance ranking. R1 more frequently served as an SP, and less frequently served as an SD than the other participants. As a result of ANOVA, statistically significant differences were found in all the participation roles (SP: $F(2,21) = 6.338$ $p < 0.001$, Scheffe's post hoc test: R1 vs. R3 $p < 0.05$; HR: $F(2,21) = 4.481$ $p < 0.005$, R1 vs. R3 $p < 0.05$; SD: $F(2,21) = 7.302$ $p < 0.001$, R1 vs. R3 $p < 0.05$). These results

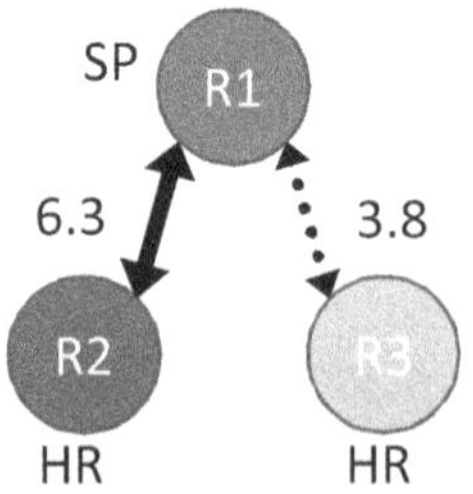

(5-a) R1 is an SP

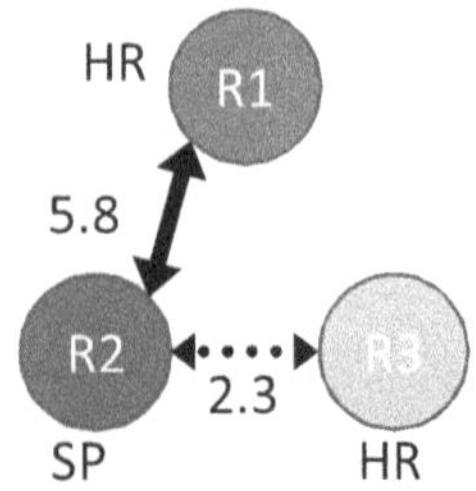

(5-b) R2 is an SP

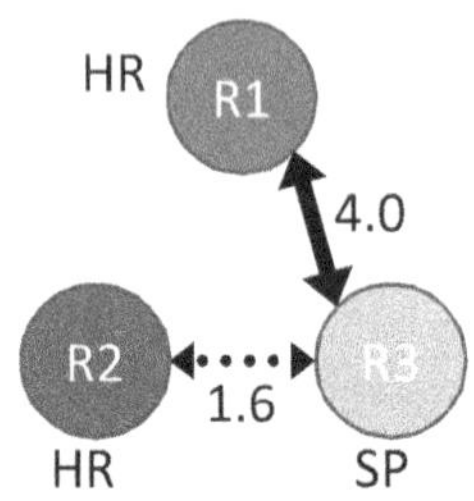

(5-c) R3 is an SP

Figure 5. Frequency of mutual gaze between a speaker (SP) and a hearer (HR)

suggest that more dominant people are likely to be SPs or HRs and less likely to be SDs. On the other hand, less dominant people are more likely to be SDs.

4.2 Eye Gaze and Conversational Dominance

Eye gaze is known to strongly affect turn taking/releasing and conversational coordination [7, 13]. This section investigates whether gaze and mutual gaze are different depending on conversational dominance.

4.2.1 Automatic Annotation of Gaze

Since manually annotating gaze direction by looking at videos is very time consuming, we estimated the gaze direction from the head motion data obtained via motion capture. A decision tree algorithm implemented in the Weka software package (J48) was applied to the following head motion data: x, y, and z positions and rotations. We prepared training data by manually annotating gaze direction (center, left, or right in Figure 2) for each participant across 5 sessions. By employing the leave-one-out method, four sessions were used for training and one for testing. We examined all the combinations of training and test sets and obtained 0.9 in F-measure for all three standing positions. Since the accuracy of the decision tree was sufficient, we decided to use this model to automatically annotate subjects' gaze directions.

4.2.2 Gaze and Received Gaze from Others

Figure 4 shows the average frequency of eye gaze per conversation with respect to dominance rankings. As shown in Figure 4-a, when R1 was an SP, he/she paid equal amount of attention to R2 and R3 as HRs (7.1 times per conversation). Even when R1 was an HR, he/she looked at R2 and R3 to the same extent (6.0). Figure 4-b shows that when R2 was an SP, he/she looked at R1 (6.8) slightly more frequently than at R3 (5.8). More distinguishably, when R2 was an HR, he/she looked much more at R1 (7.3) than at R3 (2.4) when they spoke. In addition, Figure 4-c shows that R3's gaze behaviors clearly distinguished R1 from R2. Regardless of whether R3 was an SP or an HR, he/she looked at R1 much more than at R2.

The results indicate that R1 was gazed at the most, as an SP and an HR, even though R1 himself/herself gazed at R2 and R3 equally frequently. This result is consistent with those of Knapp's [14] study of dominance. On the contrary, R2's gaze behavior distinguished R1 from R3, and R3's gaze distinguished R1 from R2. Thus, these results suggest that gaze behaviors in conversation are considerably different depending on dominance rankings; gaze behavior is therefore expected to be useful in estimating conversational dominance.

4.2.3 Amount of Mutual Gaze

In addition to gaze, we investigated whether the frequency of mutual gaze was different depending on dominance rankings. We counted gaze overlap between two participants in which they look at each other as mutual gaze. Figure 5 shows the average number of mutual gaze for each participant per conversation. As shown in Figure 5-a, when R1 was speaking, mutual gaze was established more frequently with R2 as an HR (6.3 times per conversation) than with R3 (3.8). Likewise, as shown in 5-b, when R2 was an SP, mutual gaze was more frequently established with R1 (5.8) than with R3 (2.3). These results suggest that when R1 or R2 was an SP, mutual gaze was established more frequently between them (not with R3). It is interesting that even though R1 looked at the other participants equally (as shown in Figure 4), mutual gaze was more frequently exchanged between the higher-ranked participants; R1 and R2. On the other hand, mutual gaze during R3's speaking is informative in distinguishing R1 from R2. As shown in Figure 5-c, R2 was engaged in much less mutual gaze (1.6) than R1 (4.0) when R3 was an SP.

The analysis revealed that participants with higher conversational dominance were gazed at more by other participants; further, participants with higher conversational dominance established mutual gaze with each other more frequently than with participants with lower conversational dominance. On the contrary, less dominant participants received less attention from others, and tried to establish mutual gaze with the highest ranked participant. These results suggest that information regarding individual and mutual gaze is useful in estimating conversational dominance.

4.3 Turns and Conversational Dominance

According to Bales [3], more dominant participants are expected to talk more and be more successful in terms of floor management. To investigate these points, we now focus on turn taking.

4.3.1 Number of Turns and Turn Duration

Section 4.1 used turns as the units of analysis, and the same data were used in this section. The average number of turns taken during the conversation was 18.25 for R1, 16.71 for R2, and 13.56 for R3. As a result of ANOVA, it was found that the average number of turns was different depending on the dominance ranking, and the difference was statistically significant ($F(2,21) = 5.10$, $p < 0.05$). We also conducted a Scheffe's post hoc test, and found that the difference between R1 and R3 was statistically significant ($p < 0.05$).

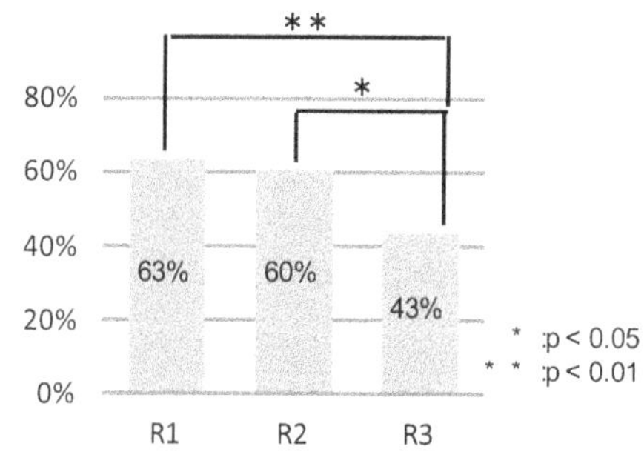

Figure 6. Turn-releasing success ratio

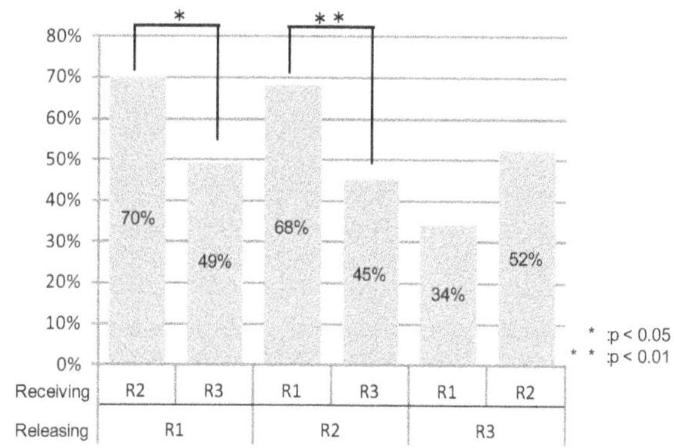

Figure 7. Turn-releasing success ratio with respect to addressee of the gaze signal

Next, we analyzed whether turn duration differed depending on conversational dominance. The average turn durations were 1.75 sec, 1.38 sec, and 1.28 sec for R1, R2, and R3, respectively. We conducted an ANOVA, and found a statistical trend that turn duration was different depending on conversational dominance ($F(2,21) = 2.96$, $p < 0.1$). Scheffe's post hoc test also found a statistical trend in the difference between R1 and R3 ($p < 0.1$).

We found that the number of turns and their duration differed depending on conversational dominance. More dominant participants took more turns, and the duration of each turn tended to be longer. On the other hand, less dominant person took fewer and shorter turns. These results suggest that the number and duration of turns are useful in estimating conversational dominance.

4.3.2 Turn-releasing Success Ratio

In previous studies [7, 13], it was found that the speaker chooses the next speaker using his/her gaze. The next speaker, who receives the turn-releasing gaze signal by establishing a mutual gaze with the current speaker, looks away for a very short period of time, and then starts speaking. This is a typical gaze exchange observed at turn taking. We investigated whether this turn taking process is different depending on the dominance of a participant in a given conversation. We calculated the turn-releasing success ratio for each participant. For each utterance, we identified the target of the current speaker's gaze during the last 1 second of his/her utterance. If the person who received the turn-releasing signal actually started speaking within 2 seconds of the signal, we counted this as the success of choosing the next speaker (or success in turn-releasing).

Figure 6 shows the turn-releasing success ratio with respect to the dominance ranking. The success ratios of R1 and R2 participants were over 60%. On the contrary, those of R3 participants was about 40%. Chi-square test indicated that the turn-releasing success ratio was different depending on the ranked order of conversational dominance ($\chi^2 = 10.7785$, $p < 0.0045$). A post hoc test using Ryan's method revealed that the difference between R1 and R3 and that between R2 and R3 were statistically significant (R1 vs. R3: $t(260) = 3.00$, $p < 0.01$; R2 vs. R3: $t(227) = 2.60$, $p < 0.05$). These results suggest that R3 was less successful in choosing the next speaker using his/her gaze.

We also analyzed whether the turn-releasing success ratio is different depending on who releases the turn to whom. As shown in Figure 7, the turn-releasing success ratios between R1 and R2 (when R1 gave a turn to R2 and when R2 gave a turn to R1) were about 70%. On the contrary, when R1 or R2 released a turn to R3 or received a turn from R3, the success ratios dropped to around 50% or lower. We applied Ryan's method to test the differences in turn-releasing success ratios, and found that the success ratio of releasing a turn from R1 to R2 was significantly higher than that from R1 to R3 ($t(129) = 2.36$, $p < 0.05$). We also found that the success ratio of releasing a turn from R2 to R1 was higher than that from R2 to R3 ($t(98) = 2.65$ $p < 0.01$). These results suggest that turn-releasing is quite successful between R1 and R2; however, less dominant person does not exchange turns smoothly with other participants. Turn-releasing success ratio is thus also a possible predictive parameter for conversational dominance.

4.3.3 Interrupting Others' Turns
In order to examine the difficulty of taking a turn, we counted the number of interruption of each participant. We counted each case when a participant started speaking while the current speaker was still talking as an interruption. The average frequencies of interruptions per conversation were 3.88, 3.57, and 4.22 for R1, R2, and R3, respectively. R3, who was the most submissive person in each conversation, most frequently interrupted others in order to grab a turn. Less dominant people need to interrupt others' turns because they cannot smoothly exchange turns with others, as found in section 4.3.2. However, the difference was not statistically significant in ANOVA, and we did not get clear results regarding interruption.

4.3.4 Taking a Turn during Silence
When a turn is not successfully released to the next speaker and no one starts speaking, a silence occurs. We assume that a person who breaks the silence in such a situation may be more dominant in the conversation. A situation was identified as a silence when no one spoke for more than 2 seconds. The average number of times that each participant took the next turn by breaking a silence was 2.25, 0.86, and 1.33 times per conversation for R1, R2, and R3, respectively. As the result of ANOVA, the difference was statistically significant ($F(2,21) = 4.37$ $p < 0.05$). Scheffe's post hoc test revealed that the difference between R1 and R2 was statistically different ($p < 0.05$). R1 more actively took the next turn when a silence occurred and normally tried to smoothly resume the conversation. Therefore, this factor is also a candidate estimation parameter for conversational dominance.

5. ESTIMATING CONVERSATIONAL DOMINANCE
This section proposes an estimation model for conversational dominance based on the empirical study described in the previous sections.

5.1 Ratings of Conversational Dominance
In section 3, conversational dominance was determined based on the subjective ranked order reported by the three participants. Since the subjects judged the dominance rankings after the conversation, this measure did not indicate the dynamic change in conversational dominance during the flow of conversation. Moreover, only very limited statistical analyses can be applied to data ranked on an ordinal scale; therefore, expressing these values on an interval scale is desirable. To resolve these problems, we needed a finer-grained measure of dominance.

Since the purpose of the conversation in the experiment was to determine where to go for a weekend, we assumed that "information requests" such as "Do you know where Kinkakuji is?", and "information providing" such as "Both of these places have nice views," were important verbal behaviors in such conversations. Information requests were used to obtain new information from others, and information providing utterances were used to give information to the other participants in order to share knowledge. Therefore, these two types of utterances are critical in accomplishing the goal of the conversation, and the person who uses such utterances is expected to lead the conversation.

Based on the discussion above, this study exploits the frequency of information providing and information requests as a measure of conversational dominance. To test the validity of our new measure of conversational dominance, we computed the Kendall tau rank correlation coefficients between the dominance rankings, as determined based on the frequency of information providing/request utterances, and the subjective rankings described in section 3. The correlation coefficient was very high ($\tau = 0.76$) and statistically significant ($Z = 4.84$, $P < 0.01$). This result clearly indicates that conversational dominance, as measured by the frequency of information providing/request utterances, is strongly correlated with human subjective judgment. Thus, we will use this new measure in creating an estimation model for conversational dominance.

5.2 Estimation Model for Conversational Dominance
We employed a linear regression model in order to estimate the degree of conversational dominance. The cumulative number of information request/providing utterances during the conversation was used as the dominance score, which was the dependent variable to be estimated by the model. The gaze and turn-taking data analyzed in section 4 were used as independent variables. Since the measurement of participation role (section 4.1) requires manual annotation, we did not use this information for estimation; instead, we only used information that can be obtained automatically from audio processing and motion captureing. Therefore, the following eight parameters were used as the independent variables:

Table 1. Standardized partial regression coefficients

Independent variable	Standardized partial regression coefficients
amount of gaze directed toward others	0.26**
amount of mutual gaze	0.49**
amount of speech	0.21**
breaking a silence	0.06**

(1) Gaze information

- *Amount of gaze at others* (sec): cumulative duration of gazing at others (section 4.2.2)
- *Amount of received gaze* (sec): cumulative duration of being gazed at by other participants (section 4.2.2)
- *Amount of mutual gaze* (sec): cumulative duration of mutual gaze with other participants (section 4.2.3)

(2) Turn-taking information

- *Amount of speech* (sec): cumulative amount of speech (or accumulated turn duration) (section 4.3.1)
- *Turn-releasing success*: cumulative number of instances of turn-releasing success (section 4.3.2)
- *Turn-releasing failure*: cumulative number of instances of turn-releasing failure (section 4.3.2)
- *Interruption*: cumulative number of instances of interrupting another's turn (section 4.3.3)
- *Breaking a silence*: cumulative number of instances of taking a turn by breaking a silence (section 4.3.4)

Note that all the parameter values are cumulative throughout the conversation. Therefore, the model estimates the dominance of each participant based on all of his/her behaviors, not just on the data for one turn. The model can update the estimations each turn.

Although we started with the eight parameters, shown above, as independent variables, some of them may contain redundant information. This might cause high correlations between the independent variables, or even multicollinearity. Multicollinearity may cause strange results: for example, even though all simple correlation values are positive, it sometimes happens that the standardized partial regression coefficients of some of the parameters are close to zero or negative. To avoid such problems, we employed a stepwise method to select independent variables for inclusion in the model. As a result, four independent variables were selected: *amount of gaze at others*, *amount of mutual gaze*, *amount of speech*, and *breaking a silence*. By using these parameters, we propose the following regression model for estimating conversational dominance. The weighting values indicate the partial regression coefficients of each parameter.

Conversational dominance = (0.80) × amount of gaze at others + (0.162) × amount of mutual gaze + (0.94) × amount of speech + (0.256) × breaking a silence + (-0.25)

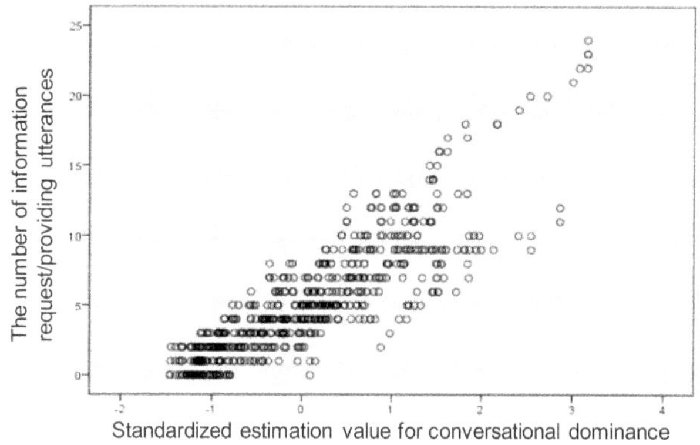

Figure 8. Correlation between the number of information request/providing utterances and the estimated degree of conversational dominance

5.3 Evaluating the Model

The estimation was made for each turn, and overall, 385 turns of data were used to create the model. The multiple correlation coefficient of this model was 0.85, which is very high. Table 1 shows the standardized partial regression coefficients for each independent variable. They were computed by applying regression analysis after standardizing all the variables to have mean 0 and variance 1. Standardized partial regression coefficients can be compared to each other even when the units of measurement of each parameter are different. The amount of mutual gaze had the largest standardized partial regression coefficient ($r = 0.49$). This parameter makes the largest contribution to the dominance estimation. The amount of gaze at others ($r = 0.26$) has the second largest contribution to the dominance estimation. These results indicate that gaze information is the most important predictor of conversational dominance. This is consistent with our findings in section 4—people who frequently establish mutual gaze have higher conversational dominance. While these two parameters had the strongest roles in the prediction, the other two parameters also made statistically significant contributions, indicating that all four parameters were useful in estimating conversational dominance. Figure 8 shows the correlation between the number of information requests/providing utterances and the standardized estimation value for conversational dominance. As shown in the figure, these two variables are strongly correlated.

The coefficient of determination, which is the square of the multiple correlation coefficient, is a standard measure for evaluating model fit. If this value is higher than 0.7, the regression model is said to fit well. The coefficient of determination of our model was 0.72, and the effectiveness of this model was statistically significant ($F(4,667) = 425.05$, $p < 0.01$), indicating that the proposed model fits very well.

As discussed above, the proposed regression model can properly estimate conversational dominance measured by the number of information requests/providing utterances. Since section 5.1 confirmed that this utterance-based method of assigning dominance ratings was highly correlated with humans' subjective judgments of dominance, we can claim that our regression model estimates conversational dominance in a similar manner to human subjects. Moreover, since this model only uses parameters that can be automatically obtained from motion-capture and speech-processing systems, fully automatic estimation of conversational dominance becomes possible by implementing this model.

6. CONCLUSION AND FUTURE WORK

With the goal of proposing a method for automatic estimation of conversational dominance, we collected and analyzed multiparty conversations among three people. We determined prediction parameters from our empirical study, and we applied the extracted parameters to a regression model. Then, we finally selected four parameters that are all statistically significant predictors of conversational dominance. The coefficient of determination of the proposed model is 0.72, which is very high.

We have already implemented the model and will test it in real-time processing. An important future direction is to consider the participants' interaction with the agent. Since this study focuses on human communication, it is necessary for future studies to design the agent's behavior to effectively control multiparty conversations according to the estimated conversational dominance levels of the participants.

7. ACKNOWLEDGMENTS

This work is partially funded by the JSPS under a Grant-in-Aid for Scientific Research on Innovative Areas (No. 23119721).

8. REFERENCES

1. *AMI (Augmented Multi-party Interaction)*. Available from: http://www.amiproject.org/.
2. Argyle, M. and Cook, M., *Gaze and Mutual Gaze*. 1976, Cambridge: Cambridge University Press.
3. Bales, R., *Interaction Process Analysis: A Method for the Study of Small Groups*. 1950, Addison Wesley.
4. Bohus, D. and Horvitz, E. *Open-World Dialog: Challenges, Directions, and Prototype*. in *IJCAI2009 Workshop on Knowledge and Reasoning in Practical Dialogue Systems*. 2009.
5. Clark, H.H., *Using Language*. 1996, Cambridge: Cambridge University Press.
6. Dovidio, J.F. and Ellyson, S.L., *Patterns of Visual Dominance Behavior in Humans*. in *Power, Dominance, and Nonverbal Behavior*, S.L. Ellyson and J.F. Dovidio, Editors. 1985, New York: Springer-Verlag. p. 129-149.
7. Duncan, S., *Some Signals and Rules for Taking Speaking Turns in Conversations*. Journal of Personality and Social Psychology, 1972. **23**(2): p. 283-292.
8. Eichner, T., et al. *Attentive Presentation Agents*. in *The 7th International Conference on Intelligent Virtual Agents (IVA)*. 2007.
9. Goetsch, G. and McFarland, D., *Models of the Distribution of Acts in Small Discussion Groups*. Social Psychology Quarterly, 1980. **43**: p. 173-183.
10. Goffman, E., *Forms of Talk*. 1981, Philadelphia, PA: University of Pennsylvania Press.
11. Hollingshead, A.B., *Four Factor Index of Social Issues*. 1975, New Haven, CT: Yale University Press.
12. Huang, H.-H., et al. *How Multiple Concurrent Users React to a Quiz Agent Attentive to the Dynamics of their Game Participation*. in *AAMAS*. 2010.
13. Kendon, A., *Some Functions of Gaze Direction in Social Interaction*. Acta Psychologica, 1967. **26**: p. 22-63.
14. Knapp, M.L. and Hall, J.A., *Nonverbal Communication in Human Interaction*. 2010, Wadsworth.
15. Nagao, K. and Takeuchi, A. *Social Interaction: Multimodal Conversation with Social Agents*. in *Twelfth National Conference on Artificial Intelligence*. 1994. Menlo Park, CA: AAAI Press.
16. Rienks, R. and Heylen, D. *Dominance Detection in Meetings Using Easily Obtainable Features*. in *2nd Joint Workshop on Multimodal Interaction and Related Machine Learning Algorithms (MLMI 2005)*. 2005. Edinburgh, Scotland.
17. Rienks, R., et al. *Detection and Application of Influence Rankings in Small Group Meetings*. in *ICMI '06 Proceedings of the 8th International Conference on Multimodal Interfaces (ICMI06)*. 2006.
18. Traum, D., et al. *Multi-party, Multi-issue, Multi-strategy Negotiation for Multi-modal Virtual Agents*. in *The 8th International Conference on Intelligent Virtual Agents (IVA08)*. 2008.
19. Vertegaal, R. *The GAZE Groupware System: Mediating Joint Attention in Multiparty Communication and Collaboration*. in *CHI 1999*. 1999.
20. Zhang, D., et al. *Learning Influence among Interacting Markov Chains*. in *NIPS (2005)*. 2005.

Learning Relevance from Natural Eye Movements in Pervasive Interfaces

Melih Kandemir[1] Samuel Kaski[1,2]

[1]Helsinki Institute for Information Technology HIIT,
Department of Information and Computer Science, Aalto University

[2]Helsinki Institute for Information Technology HIIT,
Department of Computer Science, University of Helsinki

{melih.kandemir, samuel.kaski}@aalto.fi

ABSTRACT

We study the feasibility of the following idea: Could a system learn to use the user's natural eye movements to infer relevance of real-world objects, if the user produced a set of learning data by clicking a "relevance" button during a learning session? If the answer is yes, the combination of eye tracking and machine learning would give a basis of "natural" interaction with the system by normally looking around, which would be very useful in mobile proactive setups. We measured the eye movements of the users while they were exploring an artificial art gallery. They labeled the relevant paintings by clicking a button while looking at them. The results show that a Gaussian process classifier accompanied by a time series kernel on the eye movements within an object predicts whether that object is relevant with better accuracy than dwell-time thresholding and random guessing.

Categories and Subject Descriptors

H.5.2 [**Information Interfaces and Representation**]: User interfaces—*input devices and strategies*

General Terms

Algorithms, Human Factors

Keywords

eye tracking, proactive interfaces, Midas touch, pervasive computing, ubiquitous computing, object selection, information retrieval

1. INTRODUCTION

Eye gaze is correlated with visual attention [13]. This property makes eye movements a plausible modality for human-computer interaction. The attractive prospect of hands-free control with the eyes further motivates eye gaze driven computer interaction as a very attractive research direction (see [5] for a comprehensive survey). Bolt [3] has done the pioneer work on using eye movements as an interaction modality where the user is able to select and zoom one of several video streams simultaneously playing on a computer screen.

Eye gaze-based interaction is typically designed to be done by intensively looking at visual items. A common problem is that normal attention and natural eye movements easily cause unintentional clicks, which is known as the *Midas touch* problem [12]. To avoid this, a predefined pattern of eye movements may be required for doing the actual selection of the object being looked at. Examples are looking at the item of interest longer than a threshold (dwell-time thresholding) [12], following a specific trajectory (eye gesturing) [35], looking at another copy of the item (antisaccades) [9] or at a button [33] after the item of interest. Such interfaces are desirable for people having hand disabilities and workers who need their hands for other tasks, and additionally they may suit the personal taste of some users. Some tasks such as text typing [32] can be performed by eye movements faster than using more traditional input modalities. Eye movements can also be used as a side modality to facilitate the interaction. Fast pan-zoom [28] and fast scrolling [16] are among the successful applications of gaze-supported interaction.

An alternative way of designing eye gaze-based interfaces is to build a proactive interface based on *natural eye movements*. By *natural*, we mean that the user does not need to use her eyes for any artificial behaviour, such as the ones listed above, but instead she can just look around in a natural way. A *proactive interface* [30] is a means of user interaction where the computer guesses the needs of the user and takes helpful actions without any explicit command. This concept has been used in the eye gaze-based user interaction research in various ways. Hyrskykari et al. [10] developed a text reader which automatically infers from the eye movements the words that the reader wants to look up from a dictionary. Hardoon et al. [7] introduced a text retrieval engine that constructs the queries by inferring the relevance of the words in the vocabulary from the eye movements on the previously read documents. Oyekoya et al. [20] proposed an image retrieval system working on eye movement-based queries. Kozma et al. [15] developed an eye movement-based zooming interface for image databases. Image relevances were inferred from eye movements, and then the retrieved images were displayed on zoomable nested circles. By zooming in, the user gets to see more relevant images.

In this paper, we study whether proactive interaction with real-world objects via natural eye movements is possible in pervasive

ICMI'12, October 22–26, 2012, Santa Monica, California, USA.

setups. We assume that the user is mobile and her eye movements are tracked. There are real-world objects around, and the computer the user wears is able to detect these objects and retrieve information about them. In this paper we report the first results on the feasibility of building a proactive interface for interacting with the objects. Various applications are possible given such a well-working interface. One example is *Lifelogging* [19]. A proactive interface can automatically extract a summary of a day of the user by taking snapshots of the important moments detected from her eye movements. Another example is a proactive information retrieval device that infers how interesting the real-world object being looked at, for instance the face of a person in a conversation, is to the user, and retrieves useful information such as the business card of that person in case the object is interesting enough. By default, the retrieved information will be shown only by the user's request, but if the inference of interestingness can be done accurately enough, the interface can be used even more proactively. In particular, the real-world scene can be thought of as a point-and-click interface where the items are real-world objects, and the "implicit" click commands can be inferred from the eye movements. This can also be viewed as a zero-effort solution to the Midas touch problem.

Small-effort solutions in pervasive interfaces have been proposed in several studies. Park et al. [21] used dwell-time thresholding. Baldauf et al. [2] proposed blinking for longer than two seconds. Lee et al. [17] introduced *half-blinking*. All of these methods are based on explicit commands, and hence prohibit "natural" use of the eyes. All of these studies are prototype proposals; none of them reports on analyses about the users' task performance. In a previous work that motivated this study, we observed that it is possible to infer the relevance rankings of real-world objects from eye movement patterns in augmented video to a small extent using simple machine learning techniques [14]. There we assumed that the correct answers are available *a priori* for learning, and in practice we needed to make artificial assumptions. What we propose in this paper gives the users the chance to collect the learning data in natural setups, enhancing the adaptation of the learner to the ecology it operates on.

For the feasibility study, we designed an experiment where five test subjects explored an experimental art gallery, wearing a head-mounted eye tracker. We have chosen an art gallery scenario, similar to [17, 21], to simulate a case where several objects with rich visual content are being looked at. The subjects carried a button in their hand and clicked it when they encountered an interesting ("*relevant*") painting. We then investigated how well the relevance of the paintings can be predicted from the measured eye movement patterns.

Two alternative setups are possible for predicting the relevance. The first, more difficult one, is to predict all the time, in practice for every short window of time. The second, more feasible setup is to make one prediction for each encountered object. The latter requires a pattern recognition system to be available for detecting the objects. We will investigate the accuracy of the predictions as a function of the time delay from encountering the object; the accuracy will obviously increase as a function of the delay, as new evidence accumulates. Our result is that the first setup is too difficult to be practical, even though the results are better than random, whereas in the second setup a standard Gaussian process classifier with a linear time warping kernel is able to predict the relevant paintings with a reasonable level of accuracy. Explicit eye-commands [2, 17, 21] are naturally even more accurate but since giving explicit commands by the eyes is disturbing in many contexts, this outcome encourages investigating the use of "natural" eye movements in lifelogging applications, and for building pervasive recommender systems.

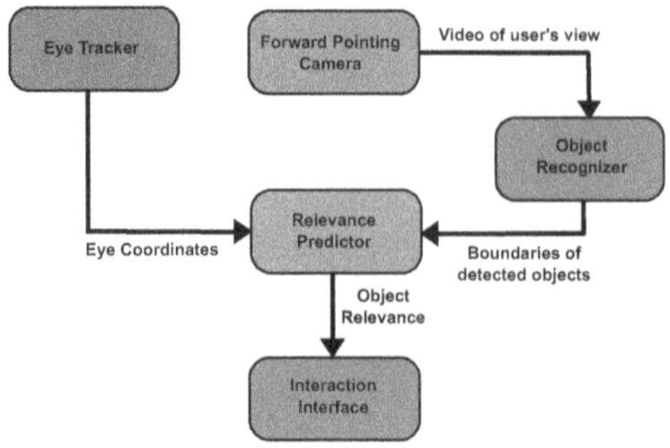

Figure 1: A systems architecture for pervasive interaction by natural eye movements.

2. PROACTIVE NATURAL INTERACTION BY EYES

We will first list the components that are needed in a processing platform as a background for the proposed eye movement-based interaction. Then we give the details of the machine learning setup that we introduce for proactive interaction, for predicting object relevances from eye movements. Based on the results, we then draw conclusions on the feasibility of pervasive proactive interaction with natural eye movements.

2.1 The Platform Architecture

The block diagram in Figure 1 shows the essential components of the pervasive interaction platform that we assume. The platform includes a mobile eye tracker for (implicit) user interaction, and a forward pointing camera for detecting objects and their locations. There is an object recognition tool for identifying the objects, their locations and boundaries in the field of view. In this study, we approximated the object boundaries by their bounding boxes for computational simplicity. Whenever the user's eyes point at an object, the *relevance predictor* computes a relevance estimate for that object from the eye trajectory in the object boundaries, using a machine learning algorithm.

The system will learn to predict relevance off-line, and the learned relevance predictor algorithm will then be used on-line in an *automatic mode* to predict relevances. In the off-line learning phase, "ground truth" relevance will need to be known for the data. We propose collecting the data in a *manual mode* where the user can mark relevant objects explicitly, using any clicking method such as dwell-time thresholding, button clicking etc. During this mode, the system will be collecting data whose labels come from the user's manual clicks. The relevance prediction algorithm can then be trained on this labeled data set, after which the relevances can in the automatic mode be predicted for new data, for which only eye movements are available. Since no explicit eye movement control is needed in the on-line mode, the user can maximally concentrate on the real world.

If the predictions are accurate enough, the relevance predictions can be used to directly trigger actions. For instance, if the object has high relevance, more information about the object can be retrieved from a database or the Internet, and presented in a non-intrusive way. Presentation options are *augmented audio* [1] or *augmented vision*, presenting information visually on data goggles.

Several pervasive interaction platforms have been introduced previously. The Touring Machine [6] is one of the pioneer studies on augmenting outdoor objects with virtual tags. The objects are clicked either by positioning them at the center of the field of view for longer than a specific time threshold, or alternatively by pointing and clicking a cursor on a trackpad that the user holds in her hand. In [27], usability of goggles for pervasive augmented reality is investigated at a conceptual level. The objects are clicked by pointing with a finger. Neither of these studies used eye movements for interaction.

Eye movements have started to be used in pervasive interaction more recently. Nilsson et al. [18] took the user commands via virtual buttons shown on the field of view. Ishiguro et al. [11] introduced a so-called *life event extraction* system that detects new objects and recognizes previously seen objects in natural scenes, and displays augmented textual information about the recognized objects. Eye movements are used for narrowing the search space to the surroundings of the point of attention. The act of looking at an object is considered a *smart lens* [25], and the object is augmented. In [1], a hardwired estimator of object relevance from *gaze intensity* (the proportion of the time an object is looked at within a fixed-length time window [22]) was used as a contextual cue for information filtering in a wearable pervasive information access system. In this paper, we complement these studies by including a new component, an adaptive relevance estimator based on fully *natural* eye movements, and carry out a quantitative analysis on the prediction performance.

2.2 Prediction of Object Relevance

The key question we investigate in this paper is how feasible is natural eye movement-based proactive interaction in wearable pervasive setups. To this end, we carry out a feasibility study with a probabilistic model that predicts real-world object relevances from natural eye movement patterns. We take the prediction performance of this model as a benchmark to measure the feasibility of the proactive eye movement-based interaction idea.

Regarding when to make the predictions we propose two options. The first, which is both difficult and computationally demanding (as will be detailed in Section 4), is to make predictions at every time instant. The second option is to predict the relevance of each *object* the user looks at. For this, we introduce the concept of *dwell session*, to be the time interval that the user's visual attention is continuously inside a particular object. Figure 2 illustrates the concept. A less time-accurate version of this concept, named as *models of interest*, has been introduced earlier as a method for partitioning the timeline by the objects being looked at [29]. It was used for fast browsing of previously recorded eye movements.

A minor technical detail is that the dwell session concept implicitly assumes that the user does not click more than once within a dwell session. In our experiments, we observed multiple clicking within a dwell session only once in 23 clicks, which we consider as a noise in the modeling. A dwell session is labeled positively if it includes any click. Hence, the extra click did not affect the label.

When making predictions during the dwell session, a trade-off needs to be made. On the one hand, the more quickly the model predicts the relevance and the system takes an appropriate action, the more the user experience potentially improves. On the other hand, a quicker prediction would necessarily be less accurate, since it will be made based on more limited observations of the eye movement pattern. In this study, we aim at quantifying this trade-off by studying performance as a function of the prediction delay from the beginning of the dwell session. For dwell sessions that last shorter than the delay period, we take the entire time series.

The data set for learning the predictor is constructed of the dwell

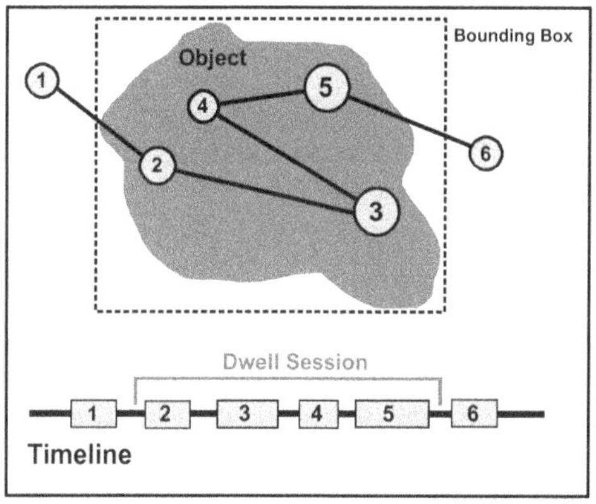

Figure 2: The concept of *dwell session* is illustrated in spatial (top figure) and time (bottom figure) domains. The green area represents the boundaries of an object in the visual scene. The dotted rectangle is the bounding box of the object, which represents its approximate boundaries detected by the system. Yellow circles are fixations numbered by their occurence order. The solid line below is the timeline going from left to right. Yellow rectangles are fixations. Fixations from 2 to 5 form a dwell session.

sessions, each being a labeled multivariate time series of eye-movement features. The time series is formed by dividing the timeline into short intervals of uniform length and representing each interval with a data vector. We preferred one second as the interval length for simplicity in calculations. A data vector is composed of the following six features:

- mean and standard deviation of saccade length in the previous three intervals,
- mean and standard deviation of fixation duration in the previous three intervals, and
- mean and standard deviation of pupil area in the previous three intervals.

The context depth was set to three seconds; the results for 2, 2.5, 3.5, and 4 seconds were similar (not shown).

The raw eye trajectory is segmented into saccades and fixations by grouping each consecutive set of targets within a radius of 25 pixels into one fixation and the jumps between fixations as saccades. In order to exploit the known correlation between fixation duration, pupil size, and mental activity [8], we include the mean and standard deviation of these measures into our feature set.

The object relevance can be predicted using any classifier that is able to operate on a data set each data point of which is a time series with an attached binary label. The kernelizeable classifiers, such as the support vector machine (SVM) [31] or the standard binary Gaussian process (GP) classifier [24], accompanied by a time series kernel are among suitable choices. We preferred the GP classifier over SVM in order to get probabilistic predictions. The results for the SVM were very similar.

Let $\mathbf{X} = [\boldsymbol{x}_1, \boldsymbol{x}_2, \cdots, \boldsymbol{x}_N]$ be a set of N dwell sessions, and $\boldsymbol{y} = [y_1, y_2, \cdots, y_N]$ be the binary vector of their ground-truth relevances. The GP classifier assumes a latent function $f \in \mathbb{R}$ between the input pattern and the output label which is governed by a Gaussian process. The sign and the magnitude of this function indicates the predicted class and the prediction confidence respectively, for binary labels $\{-1, +1\}$. The predictive distribution of the label y^* for a test pattern $\boldsymbol{x}^*$ is

$$p(y^* = +1|\mathbf{X}, \boldsymbol{y}, \boldsymbol{x}^*) = \int p(y^* = +1|f^*)\, p(f^*|\mathbf{X}, \boldsymbol{y}, \boldsymbol{x}^*) df^*$$

where

$$p(f^*|\mathbf{X}, \boldsymbol{y}, \boldsymbol{x}^*) = \int p(f^*|\mathbf{X}, \boldsymbol{x}^*, \boldsymbol{f})\, p(\boldsymbol{f}|\mathbf{X}, \boldsymbol{y}) d\boldsymbol{f}, \quad (1)$$

and the vector $\boldsymbol{f} = [f_1, f_2, \cdots, f_N]$ contains the values of the latent function for the training data points. The predictive distribution of the latent function $p(f^*|\mathbf{X}, \boldsymbol{x}^*, \boldsymbol{f})$ is the same as the predictive distribution of GP regression. By the Bayes' theorem, the posterior of the latent function can be expressed as:

$$p(\boldsymbol{f}|\mathbf{X}, \boldsymbol{y}) = \frac{p(\boldsymbol{y}|\boldsymbol{f})p(\boldsymbol{f}|\mathbf{X})}{p(\boldsymbol{y}|\mathbf{X})}.$$

Here, $\boldsymbol{f}|\mathbf{X} \sim \mathcal{GP}(\mathbf{0}, \mathbf{K})$ is the standard Gaussian process prior on the training data, where $\mathbf{K}$ is the covariance matrix with entries calculated by the kernel $k(\boldsymbol{x}, \boldsymbol{x}')$ for each pair of training samples. The likelihood function $p(y|f) = \sigma(f)$ is a sigmoid function that converts latent function values into posterior class probabilities. We used the probit function $\Phi(z) = \int_{-\infty}^{z} \mathcal{N}(\tau|0, 1)d\tau$ as the likelihood function. The denominator $p(\boldsymbol{y}|\mathbf{X})$ is the marginal likelihood, which typically appears as a constant in the inference stage, since it is not a function of $\boldsymbol{f}$. The integral in Equation 1 is intractable due to the nonlinearity of the likelihood function. We adopted the standard Laplace method [34] to solve this integral, which approximates $p(\boldsymbol{f}|\mathbf{X}, \boldsymbol{y})$ by a Normal distribution. We treat $p(y = +1|\boldsymbol{x})$ as an estimate for the relevance of the object being looked at an instant. We avoided formulating the problem as a regression problem since it would be tedious, if not impossible, to gather ground truth data for intermediate relevance levels. We made our analysis using the GPML implementation [23] of binary GP classification.

In our setting, we require a kernel that measures the similarity between two multivariate time series of possibly different lengths. One standard way of making two time series of different lengths comparable is to *align* them. An alignment can be viewed as an element-wise matching between data points of two time series. In this work, we adopt the standard linear static time-warping as the alignment method to keep the model as simple and computationally efficient as possible. More formally, the kernel function is as follows [26]:

$$k(\mathbf{X}, \mathbf{V}) = \frac{1}{L} \sum_{t=1}^{L} \phi(\boldsymbol{x}_{\psi(t)}, \boldsymbol{v}_{\theta(t)}, \sigma). \quad (2)$$

Here, the $\psi(t) = \lfloor(|\mathbf{X}|/L)t\rfloor$ and $\theta(t) = \lfloor(|\mathbf{V}|/L)t\rfloor$ are the linear time-warping functions, L is an arbitrary integer, and $\phi(\boldsymbol{x}_i, \boldsymbol{x}_j, \sigma) = \exp(-\|\boldsymbol{x}_i - \boldsymbol{x}_j\|^2/\sigma^2)$ is the radial basis function with length scale σ. We choose $L = \max(|\mathbf{X}|, |\mathbf{V}|) \times 2$. We choose σ as the square-root of the feature vector dimensionality, adopting the customary heuristic [4] coming from the fact that the total variance of a z-score normalized data set equals the feature vector dimensionality.

3. EXPERIMENTS

To test predictability of object relevance from natural eye movements, we design an experiment where the subject encounters many real-world objects within a short time interval, to ensure collecting enough data for testing. An "art gallery", where the subject explores the paintings and marks a subset of the paintings as relevant, is a suitable scenario for this goal.

3.1 Procedure and Design

The art gallery was composed of 14 colored paintings printed out on A4-sized papers and attached to the walls of a room in groups of three, five, and six paintings as shown in Figure 3. We drew lines on the floor at a distance of one meter from the paintings, and instructed the subjects not to cross them. The motivation of this setup was to get several objects into the view at the same time, so that the user would continuously be in the process of considering not only whether to click on the painting she was looking, but also whether to switch to another object in the view. There were on average 2.33 paintings simultaneously in the view, with standard deviation of 0.90. Augmented reality markers were attached to the paintings in order to identify the objects and automatically detect their boundaries from the video data. We used the software platform introduced in [1] for this task. The subjects were equipped with a mobile eye tracker, a forward-pointing camera, and a small laptop to be held in their hands. They were asked to keep their finger on the space button of the laptop throughout the experiment and click it when they were interested in a painting that they were looking at.

In order to keep the test subjects concentrated on the paintings during the experiment, we assigned them a task appropriate for visiting an art gallery. They were told that they would report in the end a list of the four best paintings. Four was chosen as a reasonable length that is large enough to demand considerable mental effort for comparing paintings and small enough to keep the entire list in mind. They started with an empty list in mind, and pushed a painting into the list by a click. If the list was already full, when clicking they replaced a chosen painting already in the list with the new one. This way, they had to keep in mind an unordered list of the best four paintings from the beginning to the end of the experiment. All subjects accomplished this memory task without any reported difficulty. The subjects were allowed to visit the painting groups multiple times. The experiment of one subject lasted 229 seconds on average with 59 seconds of standard deviation, and each subject clicked 6 to 13 times. The subjects performed 8.40 clicks on average with standard deviation of 3.44.

Five naive male undergraduate and postgraduate university students aging from 23 to 27, with mean 24.80 and standard deviation of 1.48 participated in the experiments. The test subjects volunteered and did not get paid.

3.2 Apparatus

We used an SMI iView X HED [1] model mobile eye tracker for recording the eye movements. The sampling rate of the eye tracker was 50 Hz. To ensure the stability of the recordings against head movements, the tracker was attached to a bicycle helmet. The device included a web camera with a resolution of 757×480 pixels that was placed in front of the helmet for recording the view of the user. We identified the markers and their locations by postprocessing the recorded field of view video of each test subject, using the AR software of [1].

4. RESULTS

As discussed in Section 2.2, there are two alternative setups for predicting the object relevance. We started with the first and more difficult one, of making predictions at every fixed-length short time window. When the one-second time slots within the dwell sessions of all subjects are treated as individual data points, we obtain a data set of 687 samples, only 23 of which are positively labeled (con-

[1]http://www.smivision.com/en/gaze-and-eye-tracking-systems/products/iview-x-hed.html

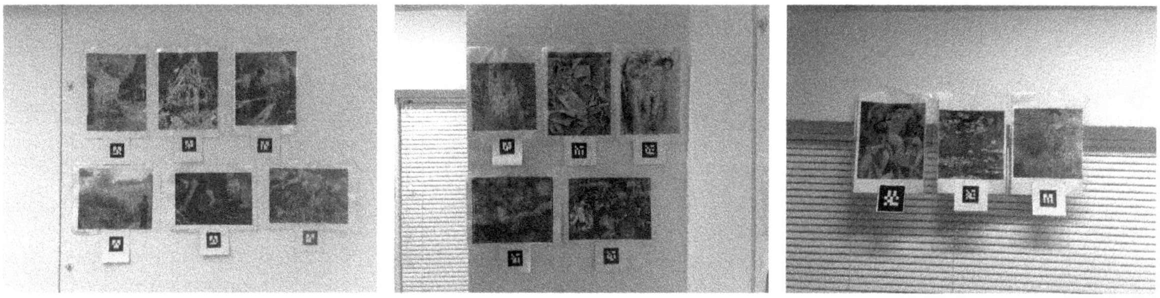

Figure 3: The experimental art gallery that consisted of three groups of paintings. In total 14 paintings from four painters were displayed.

taining clicks). We used randomly chosen 75 per cent of the data for training, and the rest for testing. We repeated this procedure for 50 splits and reported the average of these replications.

As shown in the Receiver Operating Characteristic (ROC) and the precision-recall curves in Figure 4, this learning setup delivers only a marginal improvement over uniform random guessing, which does not look promising for practical usage. One main reason behind this poor performance is likely to be that in this setup we attempt to predict the precise timing of the click (the time interval for which the relevance is known to be maximal) within the dwell session, although the change in the user's eye movement patterns based on her interest does not necessarily take place right at the click time. This difference might get detectable only when the entire dwell sessions are compared, instead of short time windows. Furthermore, the severe class imbalance makes the machine learning task difficult.

In the alternative prediction setup discussed in Section 2.2, of predicting relevance for each dwell session, the data for each prediction is a time series of short time windows during the dwell session. We again studied multi-user prediction, by pooling together the data collected from all users, as in the previous setup. This way, we have more learning data than for individual users. Our data set consists of 63 dwell sessions, 23 of which are labeled positively. The duration of the dwell sessions varied from 3 to 34 seconds. We used a randomly selected 75 per cent of the data set for training and the rest for testing. We repeated the entire analysis for 50 splits to training and test sets. All the results given in the figures below are averages over the 50 replications.

We compared our eye movement-based relevance predictor to three baselines. The first measures how long the user looks at an object (the dwell time), and predicts a click when the dwell time exceeds a threshold (which was optimized on training data using line search). This corresponds to an adaptive version of the clicking method used in [21]. This is the only existing eye movement-based relevance prediction method for pervasive scenes. The second is the standard baseline of predicting the largest class, which is not useful in practice as it would never predict non-zero relevance. The third is random guessing according to the prior probabilities of the classes (class ratio in the training data).

Figure 5 shows the prediction accuracy, area under ROC curve (AUC), and F1 score (the harmonic mean of precision and recall) of our model and the baselines as a function of prediction delay (the prediction time relative to the start of the dwell session). Our model is better than the alternatives on a grand majority of delays, and the differences are significant at each delay for one or more of the three metrics when the delay is larger than 3 seconds. Notice that F1 score is undefined for dwell-time thresholding for delays shorter than the learned threshold (12 seconds) since it constantly

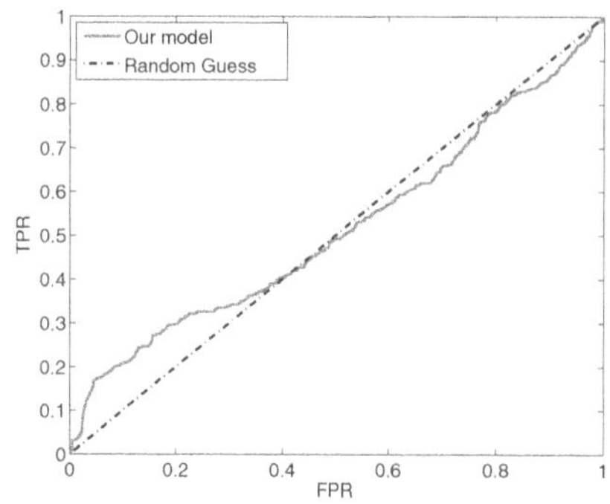

(a) ROC Curve

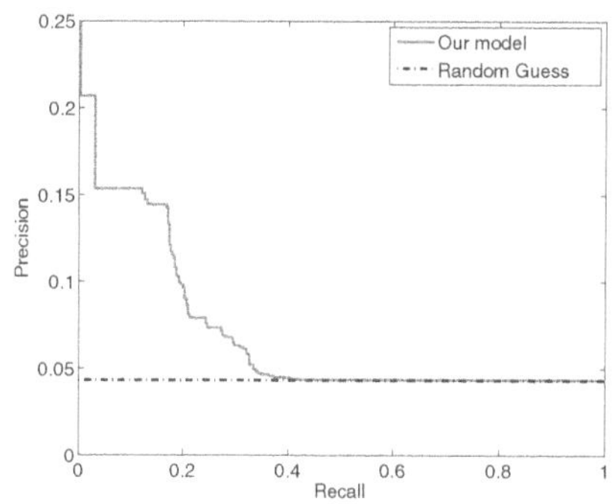

(b) Precision-recall curve

Figure 4: Predicting relevance for each short time instance is better than but close to random guessing. The ROC (a) and precision-recall curves (b) of this setup are given in solid red, and uniform random guessing with the dashed black line.

predicts zero relevance. We interpret the clear improvement of our model over random guessing and majority voting as a strong evidence to the discriminative effect of user's interest on eye movements. On the other hand, outperforming dwell-time thresholding indicates that this discriminative effect is primarily observable on *patterns* of eye movements, rather than dwell duration. It is also worthwhile to note that our model follows a rather steadily increasing trend proportional to delay in all performance metrics, which implies that prediction delay can be thought of as a user-tunable configuration parameter.

Since it is more user-friendly to make the prediction as early as possible, we take a closer look at the performance at short delays. Precision-recall curves of our model and random guessing are shown in Figure 6 for four to seven seconds of delay. Dwell-

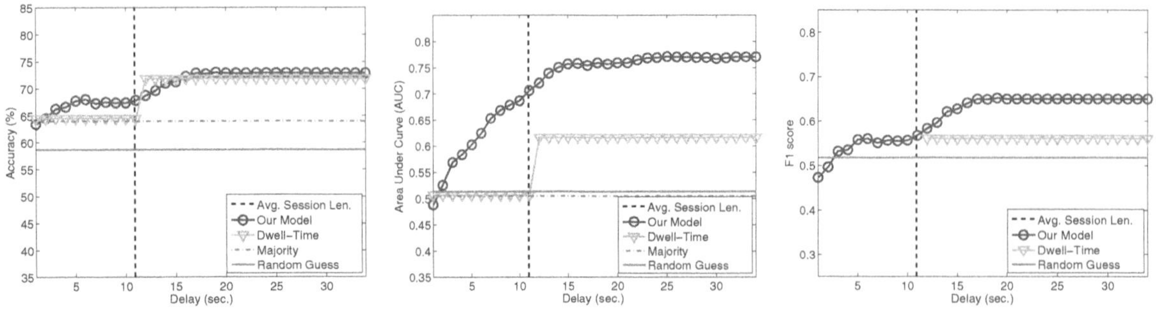

(a) Accuracy (b) Area Under ROC Curve (AUC) (c) F1 score

Figure 5: Our model predicts the relevant paintings with better accuracy than the baselines. The prediction accuracy (a), area under ROC curve (b), and F1 score (c) are plotted as a function of the prediction delay from the beginning of the dwell session, for our model (in blue circles), dwell-time thresholding (green triangles), majority voting (horizontal dashed pink line), and random guessing by class ratio (horizontal solid red line). The F1 scores of majority voting and dwell-time thresholding for delays less than the learned threshold (12 seconds) are skipped since F1 score is undefined for a predictor that constantly gives negative output. The vertical dashed black line shows the average dwell session duration. Our model's improvement over all baselines is statistically significant in at least one metric for delays larger than three seconds (Wilcoxon signed-rank test over the scores for 50 splits: $p < 0.05$).

time thresholding is not shown in the figure since it always predicts zero relevance for delays shorter than 12 seconds. The curve of our model is always above random guessing, although the improvement is marginal for very short delays. Note that the user's interest affects her eye movement patterns even at very early stages of the dwell session. This outcome encourages further research on using natural eye movement patterns for proactive interaction in future systems, as an alternative to giving explicit commands by eyes.

We present the precision-recall curves for long delays in Figure 7 for completeness. Our model outperforms both dwell-time thresholding and random guessing more clearly as the delay gets larger.

Computational efficiency of our model is adequate for online use. Off-line training of the classifier on 47 dwell sessions (corresponding to 7 minutes of eye movement data) takes approximately 16 seconds, and prediction of the click for one dwell session takes 0.25 seconds on a computer with a 2.66 GHz processor and 4 GB of main memory.

5. DISCUSSION

We made a feasibility study on building proactive user interfaces for pervasive user setups based on natural eye movements. We chose a specific use case where the user explores the paintings in an art gallery, accompanied with a wearable computer. In an off-line or manual mode, the system collects data for learning to predict relevances; these data were collected by asking the test subjects to visit the paintings and click a button while looking at the paintings that they find interesting. Using the collected data, we built a machine learning model that predicted clicks on test data with accuracy higher than that of baselines including dwell-time thresholding. The learned predictor can then be used in an on-line or automatic mode, without the button clicks.

Eye movement patterns depend heavily on the user task [36]. Hence, generalization of our early findings to other use cases and other types of real-world objects needs to be studied later. One interesting use case would be a meeting where the real-world objects are human faces and the task of the system is to bookmark the important moments of the meeting. We expect that our outcome will generalize to other domains to a large extent, since our features are not tailored to the current domain. As another direction of future research, a comprehensive user study could be carried out for finding out whether the relevance prediction performance is sufficient for smooth user experience in tasks such as automatic moment highlighting, information filtering (retrieving information only for a relevant subset of objects), and natural eye movement-based clicking. Finally, in this study, the inferences were based on partly heuristically chosen features computed from the eye movements. A psychophysics experiment to optimize the feature set could be valuable.

We believe that the big promise in using specific eyeglasses for information access comes from the prospect of being able to use fully natural and hence convenient eye movements. If the user will need to give the commands explicitly, carrying a smart phone and using its see-through camera for information access is a strong competitor (see Layar [2] and Wikitude [3] as widely known examples of pervasive augmented reality information access applications). The results in this paper are promising but more work is needed; at the current state, we would not recommend automatic "clicking" to be inferred from natural eye movements, but eye movements do already give a fair amount of relevance feedback which can be used implicitly in proactive interfaces.

6. ACKNOWLEDGMENTS

The authors belong to the Finnish Center of Excellence in Computational Inference Research (COIN). SK also belongs to PASCAL2 EU network of excellence. This study was funded by Aalto University MIDE programme. We thank Veli-Matti Saarinen and Lotta Hirvenkari for their help in conducting the experiments, and Arto Klami for his very useful discussion.

7. REFERENCES

[1] A. Ajanki, M. Billinghurst, H. Gamper, T. Järvenpää, M. Kandemir, S. Kaski, M. Koskela, M. Kurimo, J. Laaksonen, K. Puolamäki, T. Ruokolainen, and T. Tossavainen. An augmented reality interface to contextual information. *Virtual Reality*, 15(2):1–13, 2010.

[2] M. Baldauf, P. Fröhlich, and S. Hutter. Kibitzer: a wearable system for eye-gaze-based mobile urban exploration. In

[2] http://www.layar.com

[3] http://www.wikitude.org

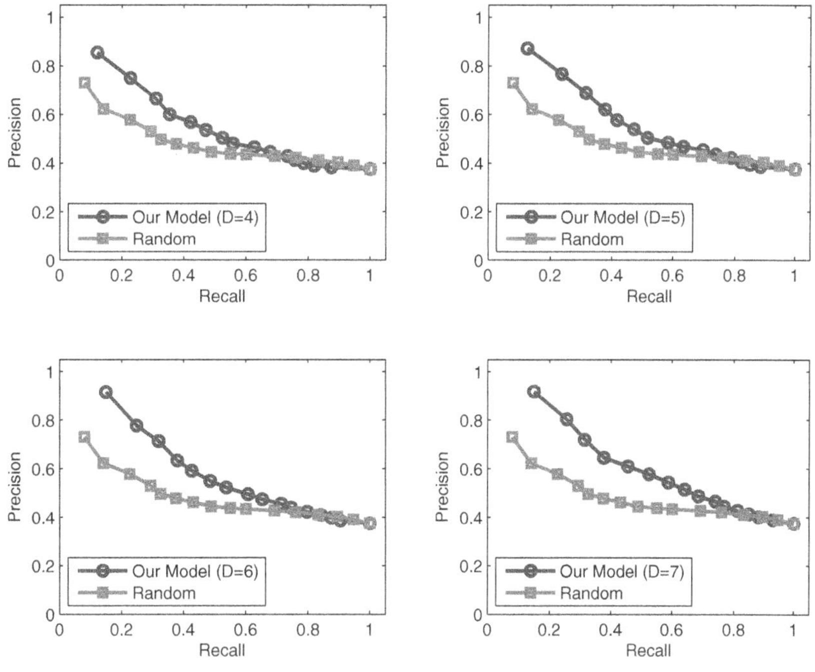

Figure 6: Retrieval performance of our model is better than random guessing for short delays. Precision-recall curves of our model (in blue circles), and random guessing by class ratio (in red squares) are given for four to seven seconds of delay (D).

Proceedings of the Augmented Human International Conference (AH), pages 9:1–9:5, New York, NY, USA, 2010. ACM.

[3] R. A. Bolt. Gaze-orchestrated dynamic windows. *SIGGRAPH Computer Graphics*, 15(3):109–119, 1981.

[4] C.-C. Chang and C.-J. Lin. *LIBSVM: a library for support vector machines*, 2001. Software available at `http://www.csie.ntu.edu.tw/~cjlin/libsvm`.

[5] A. T. Duchowski. *Eye Tracking Methodology: Theory and Practice*. Springer-Verlag Inc., New York, NY, USA, 2007.

[6] S. Feiner, B. MacIntyre, T. Höllerer, and A. Webster. A touring machine: Prototyping 3D mobile augmented reality systems for exploring the urban environment. *Personal and Ubiquitous Computing*, 1(4):208–217, 1997.

[7] D. Hardoon, J. Shawe-Taylor, A. Ajanki, K. Puolamäki, and S. Kaski. Information retrieval by inferring implicit queries from eye movements. In *Proceedings of the International Conference on Artificial Intelligence and Statistics (AISTATS '07)*, 2007.

[8] E. H. Hess and J. M. Polt. Pupil size in relation to mental activity during simple problem-solving. *Science*, 143(3611):1190–1192, 1964.

[9] A. Huckauf and M. H. Urbina. Object selection in gaze controlled systems: What you don't look at is what you get. *ACM Transactions on Applied Perception*, 8(13):1–14, 2011.

[10] A. Hyrskykari, P. Majaranta, and K.-J. Räihä. Proactive response to eye movements. In *Proceedings of INTERACT - IFIP Conference on Human-Computer Interaction*, pages 129–136. IOS Press, 2003.

[11] Y. Ishiguro, A. Mujibiya, T. Miyaki, and J. Rekimoto. Aided eyes: eye activity sensing for daily life. In *Proceedings of the Augmented Human International Conference (AH)*, pages 1–7, New York, NY, USA, 2010. ACM.

[12] R. J. K. Jacob. The use of eye movements in human-computer interaction techniques: what you look at is what you get. *ACM Transactions on Information Systems*, 9(2):152–169, 1991.

[13] M. A. Just and P. A. Carpenter. Eye fixations and cognitive processes. *Cognitive Psychology*, 8:441–480, 1976.

[14] M. Kandemir, V.-M. Saarinen, and S. Kaski. Inferring object relevance from gaze in dynamic scenes. In *Proceedings of ACM Symposium on Eye Tracking Research & Applications (ETRA), Austin, TX, USA*, pages 105–108, New York, NY, 2010. ACM.

[15] L. Kozma, A. Klami, and S. Kaski. GaZIR: Gaze-based zooming interface for image retrieval. In *Proceedings of the International Conference on Multimodal Interfaces (ICMI)*, pages 305–312, New York, NY, USA, 2009. ACM.

[16] M. Kumar and T. Winograd. Gaze-enhanced scrolling techniques. In *Proceedings of the Symposium on User Interface Software and Technology (UIST)*, pages 213–216, New York, NY, USA, 2007. ACM.

[17] J.-Y. Lee, H.-M. Park, S.-H. Lee, T.-E. Kim, and J.-S. Choi. Design and implementation of an augmented reality system using gaze interaction. In *Proceedings of the International Conference on Information Science and Applications (ICISA)*, pages 1 -8. IEEE, 2011.

[18] S. Nilsson, T. Gustafsson, and P. Carleberg. Hands free interaction with virtual information in a real environment. In *Proceedings of The Conference on Communications by Gaze Interaction (COGAIN)*, pages 53–57, 2007.

[19] K. O'Hara, M. Tuffield, and N. Shadbolt. Lifelogging: Privacy and empowerment with memories for life. *Identity in the Information Society*, 1:155–172, 2008.

[20] O. Oyekoya and F. Stentiford. Perceptual image retrieval

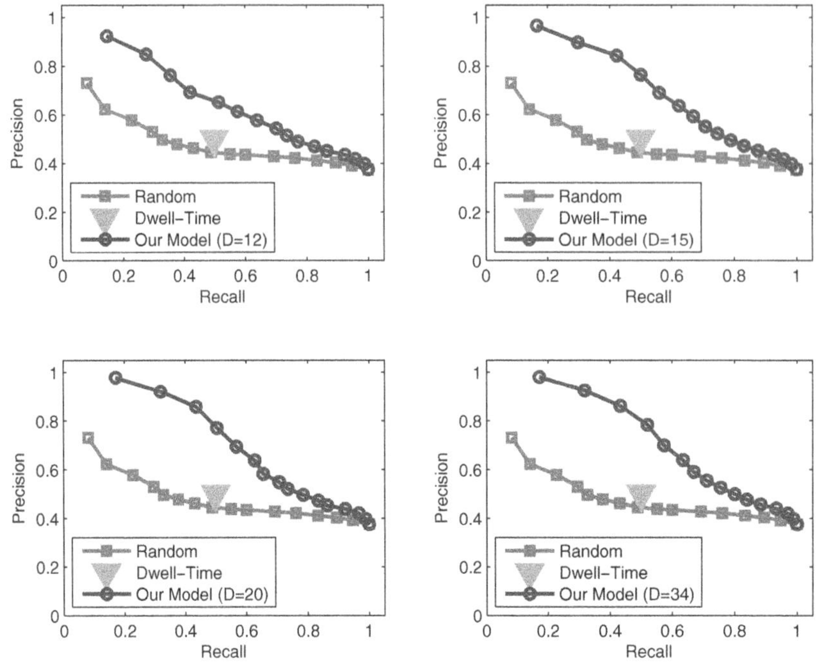

Figure 7: Retrieval performance of our model is better than the baselines for medium and longer delays (D=12,15,20,34). Precision-recall curves of our model (in blue circles), dwell-time thresholding (in green triangles), and random guessing by class ratio (in red squares) are given for 12, 15, 20, and 34 seconds of delay (D).

using eye movements. *International Journal of Computer Mathematics*, 84(9):1379–1391, sep 2007.

[21] H. M. Park, S. H. Lee, and J. S. Choi. Wearable augmented reality system using gaze interaction. In *Proceedings of the International Symposium on Mixed and Augmented Reality (ISMAR)*, pages 175–176, Washington, DC, USA, 2008. IEEE.

[22] P. Qvarfordt and S. Zhai. Conversing with the user based on eye-gaze patterns. In *Proceedings of the SIGCHI Conference on Human Factors in Computing Systems (CHI)*, pages 221–230, New York, NY, USA, 2005. ACM.

[23] C. E. Rasmussen and H. Nickisch. GPML: Gaussian processes for machine learning toolbox, 2010. `http://mloss.org/software/view/263/`.

[24] C. E. Rasmussen and C. K. I. Williams. *Gaussian Processes for Machine Learning (Adaptive Computation and Machine Learning)*. MIT Press, 2005.

[25] D. Schmalstieg and G. Reitmayr. The world as a user interface: Augmented reality for ubiquitous computing. In *Location Based Services and TeleCartography*, Lecture Notes in Geoinformation and Cartography, pages 369–391. Springer Berlin Heidelberg, 2007.

[26] H. Shimodaira, K. Noma, M. Nakai, and S. Sagayama. Dynamic time-alignment kernel in support vector machine. In *Proceedings of the Advances in Neural Information Processing Systems 14 (NIPS)*, pages 921–928, Cambridge, MA, USA, 2001. MIT Press.

[27] T. Starner, S. Mann, B. Rhodes, J. Levine, J. Healey, D. Kirsch, R. W. Picard, and A. Pentland. Augmented reality through wearable computing. *Presence: Teleoperators and Virtual Environments*, 6(4):452–460, 1997.

[28] S. Stellmach and R. Dachselt. Investigating gaze-supported multimodal pan and zoom. In *Proceedings of the Symposium on Eye Tracking Research and Applications (ETRA)*, pages 357–360, New York, NY, USA, 2012. ACM.

[29] S. Stellmach, L. Nacke, and R. Dachselt. Advanced gaze visualizations for three-dimensional virtual environments. In *Proceedings of the Symposium on Eye-Tracking Research & Applications (ETRA)*, pages 109–112, New York, NY, USA, 2010. ACM.

[30] D. Tennenhouse. Proactive computing. *Communications of ACM*, 43(5):43–50, 2000.

[31] V. N. Vapnik. *The nature of statistical learning theory*. Springer-Verlag New York, Inc., New York, NY, USA, 1995.

[32] D. J. Ward and D. J. C. Mackay. Fast Hands-free writing by Gaze Direction. *Nature*, 418(6900), 2002.

[33] C. Ware and H. H. Mikaelian. An evaluation of an eye tracker as a device for computer input. In *Proceedings of the SIGCHI/GI Conference on Human Factors in Computing Systems and Graphics Interface (CHI)*, pages 183–188, New York, NY, USA, 1987. ACM.

[34] C. K. I. Williams and D. Barber. Bayesian classification with Gaussian processes. *IEEE Transactions on Pattern Analysis and Machine Intelligence*, 20:1342–1351, 1998.

[35] J. Wobbrock, J. Rubinstein, M. Sawyer, and A. Duchowski. Not typing but writing: Eye-based text entry using letter-like gestures. In *Proceedings of The Conference on Communications by Gaze Interaction (COGAIN)*, pages 61–64, 2007.

[36] A. L. Yarbus. Eye Movements and Vision. *Vision Science: Photons to Phenomenology*, 1967.

Fishing or a Z?: Investigating the Effects of Error on Mimetic and Alphabet Device-based Gesture Interaction

Abdallah El Ali
ISLA, University of Amsterdam
Amsterdam, The Netherlands
a.elali@uva.nl

Johan Kildal
Nokia Research Center
Helsinki, Finland
johan.kildal@nokia.com

Vuokko Lantz
Nokia Research Center
Helsinki, Finland
vuokko.lantz@nokia.com

ABSTRACT

While gesture taxonomies provide a classification of device-based gestures in terms of communicative intent, little work has addressed the usability differences in manually performing these gestures. In this primarily qualitative study, we investigate how two sets of iconic gestures that vary in familiarity, mimetic and alphabetic, are affected under varying failed recognition error rates (0-20%, 20-40%, 40-60%). Drawing on experiment logs, video observations, subjects' feedback, and a subjective workload assessment questionnaire, results revealed two main findings: a) mimetic gestures tend to evolve into diverse variations (within the activities they mimic) under high error rates, while alphabet gestures tend to become more rigid and structured and b) mimetic gestures were tolerated under recognition error rates of up to 40%, while alphabet gestures incur significant overall workload with up to only 20% error rates. Thus, while alphabet gestures are more robust to recognition errors in keeping their signature, mimetic gestures are more robust to recognition errors from a usability and user experience standpoint, and thus better suited for inclusion into mainstream device-based gesture interaction with mobile phones.

Categories and Subject Descriptors

H.5.2 [**User Interfaces**]: Input Devices and Strategies

General Terms

Experimentation, Design, Human Factors

Keywords

Device-based gesture interaction, mimetic gestures, alphabet gestures, errors, workload, usability

1. INTRODUCTION & MOTIVATION

Whether we like it or not, errors and failures are an inevitable part of interaction with technology. Device-based gestures (gesturing by moving a device in 3-dimensional space), used in research settings, home environments, or as part of everyday mobile interactions, are gaining potential in becoming a suitable alternative to keyboard or touchscreen-based input, especially when users are encumbered (e.g., manual multitasking [12]). Yet whether a gesture fails due to poor system design or due to the user's actions, errors impede smooth (multimodal) interaction, as well as the adoption of these novel gesture-based interaction methods. This is critical if gesture-based interaction is included in consumer mobile phones.

These device-based gestures (or motion gestures [20])[1] are to be distinguished from surface 'touchscreen' gestures [22]), which typically involve two-dimensional gesture interaction on a surface, such as a tabletop or mobile touchscreen. In contrast, device-based gestures typically make use of accelerometer and gyroscope sensors to allow users to rotate the device in the air for performing gestures in three-dimensional space. While there has been extensive taxonomy-driven work on classifying gestures by referential function into classes [20, 19] and recently identifying usable sets of gestures as defined by users [20, 18, 10], it is still an open question which set of gestures are most robust to errors in gesture-based interaction from a performance-centered standpoint.

In this paper, we look closely at device-based gesture performance using two iconic gesture sets, mimetic (e.g., mimicking a handshaking behavior while holding a mobile device) and alphabet gestures (e.g., drawing the letter 'N' in the air using a mobile phone as a brush), and investigate how their referent-independent performance is affected by varying failed recognition rates.

1.1 Research Questions

Our main research question is: how do mimetic and alphabet gesture sets evolve in the course of interaction when the performed gesture is not recognized under varying error rates? Specifically, we investigate how users react when they are less or more familiar with the ideal shape of a gesture, under varying error conditions. Our hypothesis is that since mimetic gestures are less familiar than alphabets, we expect participants to call on their own real-world sensorimotor experience (on how they perform certain activities in daily life) to perform a gesture. We expect the performance of a mimetic gesture to be influenced by this experience, thus morphing the iconic gesture into that previously learned gesture. For example, while a 'fishing' gesture might be designed in a particular way to perform some system function (e.g., hold device flat on palm, tilt towards you, and place device back on palm), given unfamiliarity with its designed ideal form, we suspect that this same gesture is more likely to morph into a more natural, learned fishing gesture upon failed recognition attempts. Given the many ways to fish (where variations could be due to cultural or individual differ-

[1]We use the term 'device-based gestures' and not 'motion gestures' to emphasize that these gestures require holding a device, and not solely about motion as in vision-based gesture recognition such as interacting with a Microsoft Kinect©.

ICMI'12, October 22–26, 2012, Santa Monica, California, USA.

ences), we expect the evolved gesture to exhibit more variation in the face of increasing error, especially since subjects do not know the ideal shape of the mimetic gesture. Complementarily, this variation arises due to the higher degrees of freedom permitted in performing that gesture.

By contrast, we expect alphabet gestures to exhibit much less variation, instead becoming more rigid and structured after repeated failed recognition attempts – this is because alphabet gestures not only have lower degrees of freedom (namely, 2df), but the set of ideal visual shapes is more familiar to users. Similar to work in speech and handwriting recognition, we expect a hyperarticulation [16, 14] of gestures as subjects begin to gesture more carefully to arrive at the ideal shape required by the recognizer. This we hypothesize will negatively impact the user experience (UX)[2] of performing these gestures.

Investigating the usability differences in a primarily qualitative manner between mimetic and alphabet gestures here yields two main research contributions: first, it aids gesture designers in selecting which gesture set (mimetic or alphabet) is more robust to errors, and hence better suited for inclusion into accelerometer and/or gyroscope equipped mobile devices. This is achieved by providing a deeper understanding of whether some gestures are intrinsically more tolerant to recognition errors than others (e.g., by showing that mimetic gestures, in lacking an ideal shape, can foster more variation in gesture-based interaction). Second, it equips gesture designers with the knowledge of which gesture sets overall induce a lower subjective workload to perform, especially under conditions of high recognition failure.

Additionally, we provide initial results on how errors can be an impeding factor in performing gestures in public, as well as use-cases for the tested gestures subjects reported on. The rest of the paper is structured as follows: first we provide a review of related work, then we present our study design and methods, give our results and discuss them, and finally conclude and hint at future work.

2. RELATED WORK

2.1 Gesture-based Interaction

Recent work has looked into the user preferences of certain gestures given a task (e.g., call answering), where the goal was to arrive at a taxonomy of gesture-task pairs that can aid device-based gesture design [20]. Relatedly, a recent study [5] has investigated the naturalness and intuitiveness of gestures, where the goal was to understand how users' mental models are aligned to certain gestures. Another line of research has focused on the social acceptability of produced gestures under different settings (e.g., at home, at the pub, etc.) [18]. The goal here was to equip gesture designers with knowledge of which gestures are socially appropriate under which settings and situations. While much research has focused on the naturalness, intuitiveness, and the social consequences of performing certain (surface and device-based) gestures, little research has addressed how issues of failed recognition can transform a produced device-based gesture in the course of interaction.

2.2 Dealing with Recognition Errors Across Modalities

Human factors research in multimodal interaction concerned with recognition errors [11] is a well researched topic in multimodal interfaces [2, 13, 15], where investigations were typically concerned with error handling strategies devised by users in the face of recognition errors (e.g., modality switching to a 'familiar', more efficient modality). In speech-based interfaces, a common finding is that the most intuitive and instinctive way for correcting errors in speech is to repeat the spoken utterance [21] and hyperarticulate it [14]. For multimodal systems, a common error-correction strategy is to repeat a modal action at least once prior to switching to another modality [15]. In [15], they observed a repetition count (called 'spiral depth') of depth 6, before users would switch to another modality. In a follow-up study by [6], they tested 3 commercial Automatic Speech Recognition (ASR) systems where they found that a little over 50% of the time, subjects would continue to repeat the utterance to a spiral depth of level 3.

However, while recognition errors have been well studied in domains such as speech-based interfaces [2, 14], handwriting recognition [16, 17], and multimodal interfaces [13], less attention has been given to usability issues surrounding device-based gesture interaction. An exception is the study by [8], where they investigated user tolerance for errors in touch-less computer vision-enabled gesture interaction under both desktop (keyboard readily available in front of subjects) and ubiquitous computing settings (keyboard not readily available). In this Wizard-of-Oz study, they found that the interaction context played a significant role in how tolerant users were to errors. Specifically, they found that in the ubiquitous computing scenario, users are much more tolerant to errors than in the desktop condition (where recognition error rates can potentially reach 40%) before users will abandon gesture based interaction in favor of traditional, keyboard-based input.

While the results of the study by [8] are relevant to the current work, our work differs in three main ways: first, their goal was to investigate whether and to what extent subjects would switch modalities when confronted with recognition errors, and not study how gestures evolve in response to error. Second, they were concerned with a single gesture, and not different gesture sets and their respective performance by users under different recognition error rates. Finally, their concern was with computer vision-enabled interaction, and not device-based gesture interaction.

2.3 Gesture Taxonomies

In [19], they distinguish between symbolic gestures and pantomimic gestures. Symbolic gestures are gestures that have come to take up a single, culturally-specific meaning. Examples include American Sign Language (ASL) gestures and natural language alphabets (e.g., letter 'C'). Pantomimic gestures on the other hand, are used for showing (through mimicry) the use of movement of some invisible tool or object in the speaker's hand. For example, when a speaker says "I turned the steering wheel hard to the left", while mimicking the action of turning a wheel with both hands, they are performing a pantomimic gesture. Here, we are not concerned with the external gesture referent, only its iconic movement in space.

In [20], in order to study user-defined motion gestures, they devised an initial taxonomy by which to classify gestures. Here, they distinguished between metaphor gestures (metaphor of acting on a physical object other than the phone), physical gestures (direct manipulation), symbolic gestures (visually depicting a symbol by e.g., drawing with the phone), and abstract (gesture-activity mapping is completely arbitrary). In the foregoing taxonomies, the classifications are based on the communicative intent behind performing the gesture (i.e., its representational aspect), and not on the usability and user experience (UX) of manually performing the gesture.

[2]UX here is based on ISO 9241-210 [1] definition: "A person's perceptions and responses that result from the use or anticipated use of a product, system or service."

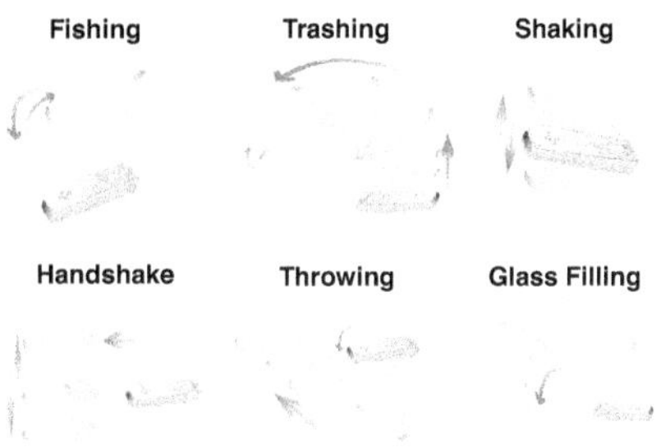

(a) Mimetic gestures.

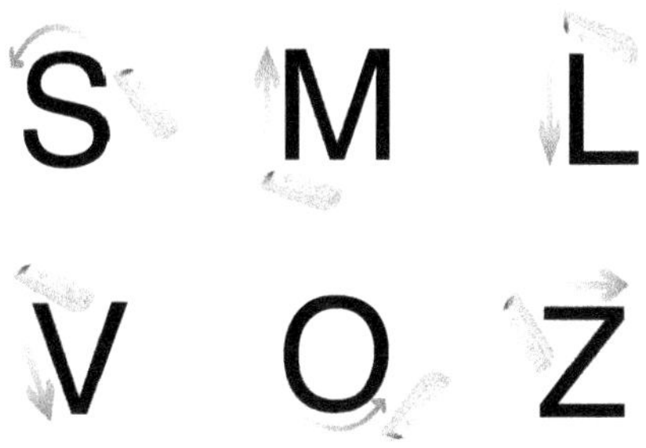

(b) Alphabet gestures.

Figure 1: The designed gesture sets for (a) mimetic gestures and (b) alphabet gestures.

3. METHODS

3.1 Study Design

In this study, we do not to test the communicative intentions of subjects while performing gestures (i.e., no referential aspect), but only the manual 'performance' of the iconic gesture itself. Under this performance-centric view, the mimetic gestures are iconic movements of real-world actions and the alphabet gestures are iconic movements of writing letters.

Mimetic gestures were chosen as they provide a natural means of interaction, making them good candidates for inclusion into mobile technology. Similarly, alphabets can be produced by any literate person, and hence suitable for comparison. Other symbols (e.g., salute or high-five gesture) were not tested to avoid undue cultural bias. Furthermore, like mimetic gestures, alphabets can also be easily learned and recalled, and have practical potential for use in mobile technology (e.g., mid-air writing for user authentication [9]). Given these design considerations, we designed 12 gestures (6 mimetic, 6 alphabetic). Mimetic gestures are: Fishing, Trashing, Shaking, Handshake, Throwing, Glass Filling. These specific gestures were chosen because they represent familiar yet different activities, where all have more than 2 degrees of freedom. Alphabet gestures we chose are English letters (given our subject pools' language), varied by difficulty (e.g., 2 strokes or 3 to draw the letter). Only 6 different gestures for each set was chosen to avoid participant fatigue, given the high number of trials (200 total) each participant entered. Nevertheless, we believe the chosen gesture samples provide sufficient variation to characterize each gesture set with respect to varying failed recognition rates. Both gesture sets, and their movement in space, are shown in Fig. 1.

To investigate how different types of performed gestures respond to varied recognition errors, we used an automated Wizard-of-Oz method [4] where we simulated each of three failed recognition error rate conditions: low (0-20%) error rate, medium error rate (20-40%), high error rate (40-60%). Subjects were told that real gesture recognition engines were being tested, where each of the algorithms differs in terms of how sensitive it is to the user's gesture interaction style. When subjects performed a gesture, the automated wizard would draw for each gesture block an error rate randomly from the assigned error rate range specific to the condition. When a gesture is performed, the subject receives coarse feedback (recognized / not recognized) on whether or not the performed gesture was successfully recognized.

For this study, testing real recognizers is irrelevant as we are only interested in the usability and user experience (UX) of gesture performance under the chosen error rates. This is both in line with previous work [8], and conveniently allows testing our research questions without the unpredictability of real recognizers. Importantly, here we study gesture performance, not how different feedback improves gesture learnability. Additionally, we tested task-independent gestures for two reasons: first, it allows us to understand the differences between the two gesture sets (mimetic and alphabet) independent of task type. This would eliminate potential subject bias in both workload and expected gesture evolution under error conditions due to the mapping of a given gesture to a task. Second, following [10], it allows subjects to freely speculate about the applied real-world use of these two gesture types.

The conducted experiment was a mixed between- and within-subject factorial (2 x 3) design. A between-subjects design between the two gesture sets was chosen for two reasons: first, to disallow any transfer effects between the two gesture sets thereby avoiding any contamination between the gesture mental models formed in subjects. Second, testing all gestures in one session would excessively lengthen the duration of the experiment, and pose a risk of participant fatigue. There are two independent variables (IVs): gesture type (2 levels: mimetic vs. alphabet) and recognition errors (3 levels: low (0-20%) vs. medium error (20-40%) vs. high error (40-60%), where gesture-type was a between-subjects factor and error rate a within-subjects factor. Each between-subject condition tested 6 gestures (12 total), randomized across subjects. Each gesture occurred in all within-subject conditions (counterbalanced across subjects), in addition to two practice blocks, which resulted in 20 gesture blocks per experimental session. Each block consisted of 10 trials. In a block, subjects were asked to perform a given gesture using a Wii Remote® 10 different times (once per trial), where the error rates are randomly distributed within the corresponding recognition error level. In the practice blocks however, the error rate was always low. In total, each subject entered 200 trials (20 practice, 180 test).

The experiment was coded using NBS Presentation®[3], an experimental control and stimulus delivery software. Interaction and syncing with the Wii Remote was done using GlovePie[4], a programmable input emulator. Four data sources were collected: modified NASA-TLX workload data [3, 7], experiment logs, gesture video recordings, and post-experiment interviews. The modified NASA-TLX questionnaire assessed participants' subjective workload quantitatively ([0,20] response range) through the index's constituent categories: Mental Workload, Physical Workload, Time Pressure, Effort Expended, Performance Level Achieved and Frustration Experienced [7], plus the additional categories of Annoyance and Overall Preference [3]. Given no time pressure imposed on subjects in the study, we did not use this category. Additionally,

[3]http://www.neurobs.com/; last retrieved: 15-08-2012
[4]http://sites.google.com/site/carlkenner/glovepie; last retrieved: 15-08-2012

as the Annoyance category is specific to audio interfaces, we only made the additional use of the Overall Preference category.

3.2 Subjects

24 subjects (16 male, 8 female) aged between 22-41 (M_{age}= 29.6; SD_{age}= 4.5) were recruited. Our subject sample spanned 8 different nationalities, where all but one were right-handed (23/24). Many subjects (17/24) had a technical background, and most (19/24) were familiar with gaming consoles that use some form of gesture recognition technology (e.g., Nintendo Wii© or Microsoft Kinect©).

3.3 Setup & Procedure

The experiment was carried out at the usability lab at XYZ center. Each experimental session took approximately 1 hour to complete. Subjects were seated in front of a monitor, where a tripod-mounted camera was aimed at their gesture interaction space. They were allowed to define their own interaction space to ensure their comfort during the session, so long as it was still within the camera's view. Prior to the experiment, each subject filled a background information form, signed an informed consent form, and read through detailed instructions for performing the task. After reading the instructions, a tutorial was given on how to perform each gesture. The tutorial involved the experimenter performing each gesture (using the Wii Remote) right next to the subject.

The first two blocks were practice blocks, set always at a low error rate. Before each block, a video of how the gesture to be performed in the next trials was shown on the screen. The performance of the gestures in the videos was identical to how they were performed by the experimenter in the tutorial. The videos were shown to eliminate any failed memory recall effects, where subjects' (multimodal) interaction requires a visual input (videos watched) and a translation to somatosensory output (performed gesture). In a trial, the subject would be instructed on screen in text to perform the gesture for that block (e.g., "Perform Fishing gesture."). A subject would have to press and hold the A button on the Wii Remote to start recording the gesture, and release it after completing the gesture. After performing the instructed gesture, if the subject falls into a successful gesture recognition trial, a green checkmark image is flashed on the screen, while in a failed recognition trial, a red image with the word "FAIL" is flashed on the screen. After each block, subjects were asked to fill in the modified NASA-TLX questionnaire, where they were provided with an optional 2 min. break after completing it. Subjects were allowed to change their responses on the questionnaire at the end of each block, so that their responses per block can be truly relative to one another. After completing the experiment, subjects were interviewed for around 10 min. about their experience with the experiment. Afterward, they were thanked for participating, and offered a movie theatre ticket.

4. RESULTS

4.1 Subjective Workload

The modified NASA-TLX responses were analyzed within groups, per type of gesture. For each modified NASA-TLX category, one-way ANOVA repeated measures tests were conducted comparing results from all error rates. A mixed between- and within-subjects ANOVA revealed no significant differences between the two gesture sets, and therefore not reported. Descriptive statistics (means, standard deviations, 95% confidence intervals, p-values, partial eta squared) of within-subject results for the mimetic and alphabet gestures are shown in Table 1 and Table 2, respectively. Means and confidence intervals for each category under mimetic and alphabet gesture conditions are shown in Fig. 2 and Fig. 3, respectively.

Post-hoc pairwise comparisons (with Bonferroni correction[5]) between error conditions (Low-Medium, Low-High, Medium-High) were conducted in every case. Where significant, they are represented in the graphs as bars between low and medium error rate conditions, and as brackets between low and high error rates, with the corresponding significance levels (**, $p < 0.01$; *, $p < 0.05$).

Mimetic Gestures

Category	Error	M	SD	95% CI	P-value	η^2_p
Mental	Low	5.3	3	[3.6, 7]	p= .098	
	Med	5.8	3.3	[4, 7.7]	F(2,22) = 2.6	.2
	High	7.2	3.5	[5.3, 9.2]		
Physical	Low	8	4.9	[5.3, 10.8]	p = .365	
	Med	7.7	4.5	[5.1, 10.2]	F(2,22) = 1	.1
	High	8.4	5	[5.6, 11.3]		
Effort	Low	7.5	4.7	[4.8, 10.2]	p=.119	
	Med	7.7	4.4	[5.2, 10.3]	F(2,22) = 2.3	.2
	High	8.9	4.5	[6.4, 11.5]		
Perform.	Low	15.6	2.6	[14.1, 17.1]	**p<.05**	
	Med	13.7	1.9	[12.6, 14.7]	F(1.4,15.1) = 11.2	.5
	High	10.3	4.4	[7.8, 12.8]	(corr. G-G ϵ= .68)	
Frust.	Low	5.5	3.1	[3.7, 7.3]	**p<.001**	
	Med	7.7	3.6	[5.7, 9.7]	F(2,22) = 23.2	.7
	High	10.7	4.3	[8.3, 13.2]		
Pref.	Low	13.3	2.7	[11.8, 14.9]	**p<.05**	
	Med	11	2.6	[9.5, 12.5]	F(2,22) = 5.1	.3
	High	9.7	4	[7.5, 12]		
Workload	Low	5.1	2.1	[3.9, 6.3]	**p<.001**	
	Med	5.9	2.2	[4.6, 7.2]	F(2,28) = 13.2	.5
	High	7.5	2.8	[6, 9.1]		

Table 1: Descriptive statistics for mimetic gestures (N=12) under different error rates (Low, Medium, High).

Alphabet Gestures

Category	Error	M	SD	95% CI	P-value	η^2_p
Mental	Low	5.8	3.1	[4, 7.6]	p=.872	
	Med	5.5	2.7	[3.9, 7.1]	F(2,22) = .1	.01
	High	6	2.2	[4.8, 7.2]		
Physical	Low	10.2	3.4	[8.3, 12.1]	p = .403	
	Med	9.2	3.4	[7.3, 11.2]	F(1.3,14.1) = .9	.08
	High	10.8	3.2	[9, 12.7]	(corr. G-G ϵ= .69)	
Effort	Low	7.4	2.4	[6, 8.8]	**p<.05**	
	Med	8.8	2.9	[7.1, 10.4]	F(2,22) = 6.8	.4
	High	9.9	3.5	[7.9, 11.9]		
Perform.	Low	15.5	2.2	[14.2, 16.8]	**p<.001**	
	Med	12.3	2.4	[11, 13.7]	F(1.2,13.5) = 23.5	.7
	High	8.7	4.7	[6.1, 11.4]	(corr. G-G ϵ= .61)	
Frust.	Low	4.2	2.5	[2.8, 5.7]	**p<.001**	
	Med	6.3	3.2	[4.5, 8.2]	F(1.1,12.6) = 11	.5
	High	9.6	5.6	[6.4, 12.8]	(corr. G-G ϵ= .57)	
Pref.	Low	13.3	2.5	[11.9, 14.8]	**p<.05**	
	Med	11.2	2.8	[9.7, 12.8]	F(1.3,14.3) = 23.6	.7
	High	8.3	3	[6.6, 10]	(corr. G-G ϵ= .65)	
Workload	Low	5.4	1.1	[4.7, 6]	**p<.001**	
	Med	6.2	1	[5.7, 6.8]	F(2,22) = 16.5	.6
	High	7.9	2.1	[6.7, 9.1]		

Table 2: Descriptive statistics for alphabet gestures (N=12) under different error rates (Low, Medium, High).

Since there were no significant differences between the two gesture sets, it appears to be that experimentally our wizard-of-Oz recognizer for both gesture conditions had a similar effect on participants, where statistically the two independent groups did not treat the gesture sets differently. However, there were differences between gesture sets with respect to the differences in error conditions. Based on the within-subjects ANOVA results and post-

[5]Backward-corrected SPSS© Bonferroni adjusted p-values are reported.

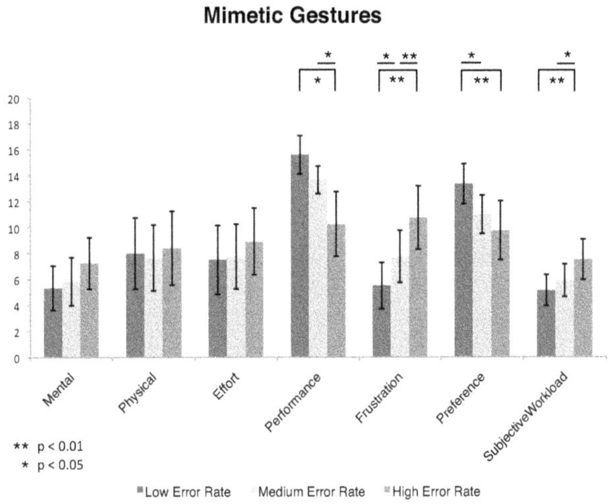

Figure 2: Modified NASA-TLX workload measurements for mimetic gestures. Capped error bars represent a 95% confidence interval.

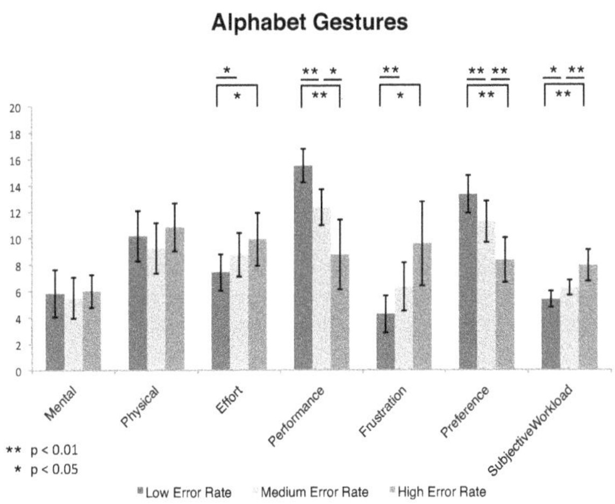

Figure 3: Modified NASA-TLX workload measurements for alphabet gestures. Capped error bars represent a 95% confidence interval.

hoc pairwise comparisons on the modified NASA-TLX scores for mimetic gestures (Table 1; Fig 2) and alphabet gestures (Table 2; Fig 3), we summarize our findings.

Results showed that while subjects in the alphabet gesture condition had to place significantly more effort (Effort Expended) between the low error rate and the medium and low and high error rate conditions, this was not so for the mimetic gestures. Additionally, for the mimetic gestures, Performance Level Achieved between the low and medium error rates was not significant, while it was significant across all error rates for the alphabet gestures. In the mimetic condition, Frustration Experienced was significant across error conditions, however in alphabet gestures, Frustration was significant only between Low-Medium and Low-High. This shows that for alphabet gestures, frustration is more or less consistently experienced beyond 20% error rates. Interestingly, Overall Preference in the mimetic gesture condition fell significantly only between the low and high error rates and between low and medium, while it significantly dropped for each error rate in the alphabet gesture condition. This hints at a feeling of helplessness in the face of errors for alphabet gestures, possibly because fewer parameters can vary for this gesture set when subjects repeatedly try to recover from these errors and still fail.

Finally, Subjective Workload for subjects in the mimetic gesture condition significantly differed only between low and high error rate conditions, and between the medium and high error rate conditions, while there were significant workload increases across all error rates for subjects in the alphabet gesture condition. Together, these findings suggest that mimetic gestures are better tolerated under error rates of up to 40% (cf., [8]), compared with error rates of up to only 20% for alphabet gestures. From a usability perspective, our workload results indicate that mimetic gestures are more robust to recognition failure than alphabet gestures, likely due to the higher design space available for users to experiment with given their unfamiliarity with the ideal shape of the designed gesture.

4.2 Video Analysis

Observation of subjects' behavior from the videos provided early findings on how mimetic and alphabet gestures evolve under varying error conditions.

Mimetic vs. Alphabet Gesture Evolution. While evolution in gesture performance for both sets was observed in as few as 2 successive error trials (i.e., spiral depth of 2), less variation in gesture performance was observed in the alphabet gesture condition. In both conditions however, we observed that the continued successful recognition of a gesture served as a continuos reinforcer for repeating a gesture in the same manner, irrespective of gesturing style. If however a subject chose to experiment with a variation during those success trials, then the variation was repeated on grounds that it will work on a subsequent trial. We call this repeated gesture variation the 'canonical variation'. As shown below, these observations are corroborated by subjects' feedback during the interviews.

We observed the following canonical variations of mimetic gestures under high error: S4's Handshake canonical variant was extending his arm straight and swinging the Wii Remote up and down as if it is a real hand he is reaching out to. S8 exhibited a variation in the Trashing gesture, where the speed of the gesture increased drastically and the end position was raised higher than shown in the video. S10 arrived at the canonical variation of the Glass Filling gesture, which required a slow, calculated twisting of the wrist while the Wii Remote was in the pouring position. S12 exhibited variations on both Fishing and Trashing gestures: Fishing gesture resembled real-world fishing, which involved lightly pulling the Wii Remote diagonally upwards and then with slight force throwing the Wii Remote back as if into an imaginary water pool. The Trashing variation was a trashing gesture that was both small in breadth and with almost no movement of the arm and shoulders.

For alphabet gestures, apart from brief intermittent experimentation with breadth, speed, position, completeness and direction of gestures, the main systematic variations observed were attempts to draw the letter symbol more precisely under high error conditions (cf., [17]). However, there was one subject who appeared to have arrived at a canonical variation: the letter Z was drawn very quickly with the last stroke (bottom line of a 'Z') more slanted.

Persistence vs. Evolution. When do recognition failures cause subjects to persist in repeating the same gesture, and when to push them to explore new gestures? From our observations, certain patterns emerged: first, it seems that if a subject performs a gesture quickly, and it fails, he will experiment with a slower version. If he first performs it slowly, then he will experiment with a faster version. Second, after repeated success trials, the speed of the gesture is the first parameter to vary while the other parameters mostly remain constant, irrespective of gesture class. Usually, though not always, only after failure does exploration take place, where variations come into play. Third, if in a block subjects experience a series of successes (4-5), they will be more likely to repeat the same gesture even in the face of repeated errors later in the block, irrespective of gesture class. This successive positive reinforcement suggests that subjects have figured out what the recognizer wants in that block. Additionally, if a gesture succeeds too many times in succession ($\geq$4), people seem to apply the principle of least effort and perform incomplete gestures (as witnessed by a downsized version of the Throwing gesture by S6 in the low error condition). This was observed mainly in the alphabet gesture condition, where two subjects later mentioned in the interviews that they did not need to complete the gesture for recognition to take place.

4.3 Users' Subjective Feedback

Perceived Canonical Variations. Many subjects (18/24) across both gesture sets reported that in the face of repeated errors, they would start experimenting with different variations of the gesture, and when feedback was positive, they replicated that variation. This suggests that positive reinforcement after repeated error trials was the driving force behind the step-wise evolution of a given gesture, or put differently, survival of the fittest gesture variation. Supporting our observations, subjects reported much less variation in how they performed gestures under high error rate conditions in the alphabet gesture condition than in the mimetic condition. For mimetic gestures, subjects reported many novel strategies for how and when a given gesture was recognized (*S9: "The shaking, that was the hardest one because you couldn't just shake freely [gestures in hand], it had to be more precise shaking [swing to the left, swing to the right]... so not just any sort of shaking [shakes hand in many dimensions]"; S11: "What I noticed was that the fishing for example, it was just a rotation [small upward wrist rotation], and when you did it as if you were really fishing, then it didn't work.*").

In line with our hypothesis, the variations under the alphabet gesture condition were perceived to involve a more precise and well structured gesture for recognition to be successful (*S17:"I think within certain blocks I got the pattern of what was working. It was more apparent in the third one [high error rate condition], you have to do it better.*"). There were exceptions to this, mainly the drawing of the letter O, which can easily vary (in addition to breadth and speed) along the direction and the start/end position parameters (*S16: "I didn't really change the way I did them [the gestures], except for the O, to see different ways it can be written.*"). However, while variations that involved more rigid gesturing of letters was both observed and reported by subjects, some subjects explicitly expressed arriving at the canonical variations of some letters (*S22: "In Z or S, I made them more rounded, and then it worked better this way.*").

Individual and Cultural Differences. For the mimetic gestures, subjects found the Throwing and Glass Filling gestures the most problematic (4 reports each). Throwing in particular appeared not to be as intuitive as the other gestures, possibly because of the many ways people can throw (*S7: "I would have done the throwing gesture differently [shows experimenter how different people throw]*") The mapping to real-world behaviors was evident when explaining why the Glass Filling gesture is difficult (*S10: "For the glass filling, there are many ways to do it. Sometimes very fast, sometimes slow like beer.*") Interestingly, the Shaking gesture, which is already an input technique in some smart phones (e.g., Apple's iPhone 4®[6]), was not taken favorably by at least one subject: *S4: "Shaking was hard... how long should you shake? I tried here, and it was enough to do two movements... and you have to use your wrist, which can be a problem.*").

Two subjects noted that the Fishing gesture was quite easy to perform, however the naturalness of the gesture backfired (*S10: "In the fishing gesture, I was just guessing how to do it. Because I have never done it practically. I cannot really see myself performing well, just simulating it.*") Likewise for the Trashing gesture: (*S10: "I was trying to emulate how I would normally do it. For example trashing, sometimes you're not in the mood, and you do it like this [trashes imaginary object downward softly], very quietly.*") Together, these reports support our hypothesis that mimetic gesture evolve into their real-world counterparts, especially when under high error conditions. Due to the importance of cultural differences in performing certain mimetic gestures, it would be interesting to see whether these cultural forms are the first gestures subjects recourse back to under error conditions.

For the alphabet gestures, the O and M alphabet gestures were perceived to be the most difficult (6 and 5 votes, respectively). The O gesture was perceived to be difficult on grounds that there are many ways to write/draw an O (*S17: "The O was a bit funny, because naturally I start from the top, not the bottom.*"). This was likely a fault of how the videos in the experiment showed the gesturing of the O, which began from bottom to top. However, the other reason for finding the O difficult was due to the completeness and position parameters (*S13: "For the O, I noticed that if I start here [points in space] and I end here, and there is a gap, then it wouldn't be recognized.*"). There were no clear reasons given for why the M gesture was difficult, other than hinting at the number of strokes required (*S14: "The M is more articulated, so you have to spend more time on it.*"). V was perceived to be the easiest letter to gesture, due to the ease by which it can be drawn. This was so despite that V, like the O, varied along the direction parameter.

Perceived Performance. In general, subjects reported they were pleased with their overall performance in both mimetic (7/12) and alphabet (7/12) gesture conditions. Surprisingly, while all subjects noticed the difference in difficulty across blocks, some subjects in the mimetic gesture condition (6/12) and some in the alphabet gesture condition (7/12) seemed to treat their performance on the low error rate and the medium error rate conditions as more or less the same (*S18: "Between the first and second blocks [low and medium error rate conditions], it was the same... 10-15%*"), while attributing very poor performance to the high error rate condition. The reason for this was likely due to the extremely high error rate range (40-60%). This relates to the question of how poor can performance of gesture recognition technology get before the technology is abandoned in favor of well-established methods such as keyboard-based input (cf., the 40% error threshold set by [8]).

Additionally, subjects showed an incredible ability to justify their performance. If subjects fell into the high error rate condition first, they attributed their poor performance to the fact that they are still learning how to perform the gestures (*S22: "In the beginning, it was less because I was still learning.*"). By contrast, if the high error condition comes later in the block, they attribute their poor performance later due to not putting the kind of effort and attention they did on the first block, which supposedly explains their better performance earlier (*S7: "For the third block [high error rate condition]...I had done many already, I was like I'll just do it and see what happens.*"). This is in line with our video observations, where

[6] http://www.apple.com/iphone/; last retrieved: 15-08-2012

gesture performance was different in high error conditions where gestures tended to evolve more for mimetic gestures (poor observed performance) and get more rigid for alphabet gestures (acceptable observed performance if canonical variation is right).

Use of Gestures on Mobile Phones. For mimetic gestures, when asked whether they saw any real-world use of the tested gestures on mobile phones, most subjects (10/12) reported at least one use-case. For the Throwing gesture, a mapping to sending a message was identified as a reasonable interaction method. Another example of Throwing was mobile payment, where one could throw money to a cashier. Similarly for the Handshake gesture, where the handshake could be a form of digital content transaction or a form of business e-card exchange. Trashing was implicated in hanging up a call, deleting content, or what subjects did not favor, to turn off an alarm clock by turning over the device. Subjects reported that shaking was already available in some mobile phones used for switching to the next song. However, some subjects expressed that some of the gestures simply had no use (*S4: "Trashing at a conference is quite natural to turn off a call, but handshake, I can't think of a use.*").

When asked about using alphabet gestures on mobile phones (e.g., gesturing 'S' for sending a message), only half of subjects said they would use such gestures (6/12) (*S24: "If there was a phone with this, I would really like that!*"), and some thought it depended on the situation (3/12) (*S19: "If you're on your bike, you could do that.*"). From those who would use such gestures, they explicitly mentioned that they have to necessarily be free of error (*S20: "Yeah [I would use such a gesture], if it's really fool-proof.*";). Reported use cases included gesturing P to pause a game, C for calling or checking a calendar, or most reported, for traversing an interface's menu structure (*S18: "If you need to access a feature that is hidden away in the menu, like starting to write an SMS, then gesture S*"). Some subjects mentioned that the gestures need to be explicitly different (*S22: "Those gestures need to be so different so you cannot do wrong gestures...V is part of M.*") and others required a distinct gesture-to-task mapping for each application on your device ("*S23: "The applications should not clash for the same gesture.*"). Finally, one subject remarked that while these alphabet gestures might work for the roman alphabet, it would be radically different for chinese characters.

Social Acceptability. For both the mimetic and alphabet gestures, some subjects (8/24) expressed concern over performing these gestures in public. This is in line with previous work, which explicitly addressed the question of what kinds of gestures people would perform while in public [18]. It was surprising to find that there were very few concerns about performing mimetic gestures in public (2/12) (*S9: "I'm not sure [about Fishing], because I'm not fishing myself, why am I doing this?*"), as opposed to performing alphabet gestures (6/12) (*S13: "If I am not in a public place, then yes. Otherwise, you would think I'm a Harry Potter in disguise!*").

While recognition errors play a clear role in preventing gesturing in public settings (*S16: "When it doesn't take your C, you keep doing it, and it looks ridiculous.*"), the breadth of a gesture was also perceived as an important factor (*S18: "Maybe if I do it small, if I don't look very freaky, then it's okay.*"). Still, others thought it fun to try novel things in public (*S14: "I never thought about that [alphabet gestures], but why not? I would not find it embarrassing.*").

5. DISCUSSION

5.1 Limitations

There are three potential limitations to the present study: first, since our study was conducted in a laboratory, it had less ecological validity. While subjects explicitly stated that they would not be comfortable performing some gestures (especially alphabet gestures) in public, from the videos it was evident that all subjects performed all the instructed gestures freely and without hesitation. It is interesting to consider here whether the desire to perform all gestures successfully in each block could have overruled whatever embarrassment might come about from merely performing the gesture to execute some device function. At least one subject explicitly mentioned the importance of performance (*S9: "I eventually got the hang of it, and yeah, I really, really wanted to improve my performance!*"). Additionally, gesture performance under failed recognition rates may not reflect performance when a user is mobile (e.g., walking or in public transport).

Second, while testing how task-independent gestures are affected under varying error rates was an explicit design choice, it could be that a gesture to task mapping is necessary for unraveling the usability of a given gesture. While we agree that the task being performed is an important variable in gesture-based interaction, we nevertheless argue that there are differences between individual gestures and importantly between gesture sets that can be unraveled only by leaving out the task. This is to eliminate any potential bias that the task might evoke. For example, calling someone might be considered more urgent in some situations than skipping to the next song, and that might influence the performance and workload required from a gesture. Finally, our design choice in simulating a gesture recognition engine as realistically as possible meant that the errors had to be randomly distributed in each block. In future work, experimentation with different error distributions would better help understand different types of gesture evolution. Additionally, with a real recognition engine, the precise evolution of the gesturing behavior may differ than what was observed in this study.

5.2 Implications for Gesture Recognition

Our observations and subject reports showed that mimetic gestures and alphabet gestures do indeed differ under increasing recognition error conditions. While our observations and subject reports showed mimetic gestures tend to vary more into their real-world counterparts when they are repeatedly not recognized, alphabet gestures tend to become more rigid and well structured. This is in line with work on other modalities like speech and handwriting recognition [16, 14]. This suggests that for gesture-based interaction to be accepted in the consumer market, accurate recognition from the first attempt appears to be quite important for mimetic gestures. If a gesture is not recognized from the first instance, there is a risk that the subsequent gesture differs radically from the first, which would be beyond the scope of the recognition algorithm. This is in contrast to alphabet gestures, which in having lower degrees of freedom vary in fewer parameters (mainly speed, breadth, and start/end position) under error conditions. This suggests that recognition engines (in uni- or multimodal systems) can more easily deal with post-failure recognition when this set of gestures is used.

Additionally, subjects had no real means to understand the cause of the errors, to avoid errors, or to improve recognition rates. However, they came up with interesting explanations (e.g., canonical variations) why there were more errors in different blocks and what might have caused them (e.g., fatigue). Nevertheless, we observed that they were also active in adapting their gesturing behavior in order to improve recognition errors and to understand the workings of the recognition engine. This seems to suggest that transparency in the gesture recognizer may better support users in their error handling strategies during situations of failed recognition.

5.3 Implications for Gesture-based Interaction

It was evident from our results (modified NASA-TLX workload data, video observations as well as subjects' feedback) that not only do mimetic gestures vary differently than alphabet gestures under error conditions, but also there were differences between individual gestures under each class. We found that while mimetic gestures yield significant increases in overall subjective workload between low and high error rates, and between medium and high error rates, overall workload for alphabet gestures significantly increased across all error rate conditions. This indicates that mimetic gestures are better tolerated under error rates of up to 40%, while alphabet gestures incur significant overall workload with up to only 20% error rates. This is in line with previous work on computer vision-based gesture interaction [8], where our workload results suggested user error tolerance of up to 40% for the mimetic gestures only.

The two gesture sets also differed in potential use and social acceptability. For mimetic gestures, interesting use cases (e.g., handshake for digital content exchange, throwing for mobile payment) were given, while limited use cases (e.g., interface menu structure traversal) were offered for alphabet gestures. Moreover, alphabet gestures were seen as more embarrassing to perform in public, especially if they are not recognized. From a usability perspective, these findings suggest that mimetic gestures are more promising than alphabet gestures for use during device-based gesture interaction, even under conditions of medium recognition error.

6. FUTURE WORK & CONCLUSIONS

A follow-up quantitative study is required to unravel exactly how many errors in succession are required before a given gesture evolves into its canonical variant. While we have presented a qualitative analysis of gesture evolution, quantitative models of the precise evolution behavior would help identify the exact parameter changes across error conditions. Future work will also address how errors influence gesture performance of other gesture sets (e.g., metaphoric and manipulative gestures), and for different device form factors.

In this paper, we described the results of an automated Wizard-of-Oz study to qualitatively investigate how mimetic and alphabet gestures are affected under varying recognition error rates. In line with our hypothesis, it was shown that mimetic gestures, which have a less familiar ideal shape, tend to evolve into diverse real-world variations under high error conditions, while alphabet gestures tend to become more rigid and structured. Furthermore, we showed that mimetic gestures seem to be tolerated under error rates of up to 40% (cf., [8]), while alphabet gestures incur significant overall workload with up to only 20% error rates. From this, we drew usability implications showing the importance of immediate accurate recognition of mimetic gestures (as a way of taming the tendency of these gestures to evolve) and suggested they are better suited than alphabet gestures for inclusion into mainstream device-based gesture interaction with mobile phones.

7. ACKNOWLEDGEMENTS

Authors thank Eurostar (E5262) SmartInside Project for its support.

8. REFERENCES

[1] *ISO 9241-210:2009. Ergonomics of human system interaction - Human-centred design for interactive systems.*

[2] M.-L. Bourguet. Towards a taxonomy of error-handling strategies in recognition-based multi-modal human-computer interfaces. *Signal Process.*, 86:3625–3643, 2006.

[3] S. Brewster. *Providing a structured method for integrating non-speech audio into human-computer interfaces.* PhD thesis, University of York, 1994.

[4] G. D. Fabbrizio, G. Tur, and D. Hakkani-Tur. Automated wizard-of-oz for spoken dialogue systems. In *Proc. INTERSPEECH 2005*, pages 1857–1860, 2005.

[5] S. A. Grandhi, G. Joue, and I. Mittelberg. Understanding naturalness and intuitiveness in gesture production: insights for touchless gestural interfaces. In *Proc. CHI '11*, pages 821–824, NY, USA, 2011. ACM.

[6] C. Halverson, D. Horn, C. Karat, and J. Karat. The beauty of errors: patterns of error correction in desktop speech systems. In *INTERACT '99*, pages 133–140. IOS, 1999.

[7] S. Hart and C. Wickens. *Manprint: an Approach to Systems Integration*, chapter Workload Assessment and Prediction, pages 257–292. Van Nostrand Reinhold, 1990.

[8] M. Karam and M. C. Schraefel. Investigating user tolerance for errors in vision-enabled gesture-based interactions. In *Proc. AVI '06*, pages 225–232, NY, USA, 2006. ACM.

[9] H. Ketabdar, K. A. Yuksel, A. JahanBekam, M. Roshandel, and D. Skripko. Magisign: User identification/authentication based on 3d around device magnetic signatures. In *Proc. UBICOMM '10*, 2010.

[10] C. Kray, D. Nesbitt, J. Dawson, and M. Rohs. User-defined gestures for connecting mobile phones, public displays, and tabletops. In *Proc. MobileHCI '10*, pages 239–248, NY, USA, 2010. ACM.

[11] J. Mankoff and G. D. Abowd. Error correction techniques for handwriting, speech, and other ambiguous or error prone systems. Technical report, GIT-GVU, 1999.

[12] A. Oulasvirta and J. Bergstrom-Lehtovirta. Ease of juggling: studying the effects of manual multitasking. In *Proc. CHI '11*, pages 3103–3112, NY, USA, 2011. ACM.

[13] S. Oviatt. Taming recognition errors with a multimodal interface. *Commun. ACM*, 43:45–51, 2000.

[14] S. Oviatt, M. Maceachern, and G. anne Levow. Predicting hyperarticulate speech during human-computer error resolution. *Speech Communication*, 24:87–110, 1998.

[15] S. Oviatt and R. VanGent. Error resolution during multimodal human-computer interaction. In *Proc. ICSLP '96*, volume 1, pages 204–207, oct 1996.

[16] J. C. Read, S. MacFarlane, and C. Casey. Oops! silly me! errors in a handwriting recognition-based text entry interface for children. In *NordiCHI'02*, pages 35–40, NY, 2002. ACM.

[17] W. R.G. and N. M. An interface-oriented approach to character recognition based on a dynamic model. *Pattern Recognition*, 31(2):193–203, 1998.

[18] J. Rico and S. Brewster. Usable gestures for mobile interfaces: evaluating social acceptability. In *Proc. CHI '10*, pages 887–896, NY, USA, 2010. ACM.

[19] B. Rime and L. Schiaratura. *Fundamentals of Nonverbal Behavior*, chapter Gesture and speech, pages 239–281. Cambridge University Press, 1991.

[20] J. Ruiz, Y. Li, and E. Lank. User-defined motion gestures for mobile interaction. In *Proc. CHI '11*, pages 197–206, NY, USA, 2011. ACM.

[21] B. Suhm, B. Myers, and A. Waibel. Multimodal error correction for speech user interfaces. *ACM Trans. Comput.-Hum. Interact.*, 8:60–98, 2001.

[22] J. O. Wobbrock, M. R. Morris, and A. D. Wilson. User-defined gestures for surface computing. In *Proc. CHI '09*, pages 1083–1092, NY, USA, 2009. ACM.

Structural and Temporal Inference Search (STIS): Pattern Identification in Multimodal Data

Chreston Miller
Center for HCI, Virginia Tech
2202 Kraft Drive,
Blacksburg,Va. 24060, USA
chmille3@vt.edu

Louis-Philippe Morency
Institute for Creative Technologies, USC
Los Angeles, CA 90094, USA
morency@ict.usc.edu

Francis Quek
Center for HCI, Virginia Tech
2202 Kraft Drive,
Blacksburg,Va. 24060, USA
quek@vt.edu

ABSTRACT

There are a multitude of annotated behavior corpora (manual and automatic annotations) available as research expands in multimodal analysis of human behavior. Despite the rich representations within these datasets, search strategies are limited with respect to the advanced representations and complex structures describing human interaction sequences. The relationships amongst human interactions are structural in nature. Hence, we present Structural and Temporal Inference Search (STIS) to support search for relevant patterns within a multimodal corpus based on the structural and temporal nature of human interactions. The user defines the structure of a behavior of interest driving a search focused on the characteristics of the structure. Occurrences of the structure are returned. We compare against two pattern mining algorithms purposed for pattern identification amongst sequences of symbolic data (e.g., sequence of events such as behavior interactions). The results are promising as STIS performs well with several datasets.

Categories and Subject Descriptors

I.2.4 [**Artificial Intelligence**]: Knowledge Representation Formalisms and Methods—*relation systems, temporal logic*

General Terms

Algorithms

Keywords

Structural Search, Multimodal Data, Event Data, Temporal Behavior Models

1. INTRODUCTION

There is a multitude of annotated behavior corpora (manual and automatic annotations) available as research expands in multimodal analysis of human behavior. Many of these corpora and supporting visualization tools store, organize, and display multimodal data based on the structural nature of behavior. By structure we mean discrete events that hold ordered relations in time that may vary between occurrences. For example, the visualization tools MacVisSTA [30], ANVIL [11], and EXMarALDa [34] display multimodal data as interval events with support for continuous signal data. The input formats of these tools are based on discrete interval events (multivariate symbolic data). This organization strategy is also seen in domains where frequent episode mining [25, 26, 31] is applied (e.g., medical records, neural spike data,...). Frequent episode mining is normally based on identifying a sequence of atoms (e.g., symbols or descriptions) and identification of "relevant" patterns is based on frequency and/or statistical modeling. However, for analysis of multimodal data, a pattern's value to an expert may not be based on frequency or statistical significance but on subjective relevance. Hence, a search strategy designed for an expert's interest in multimodal behavior data is motivated.

We present Structural and Temporal Inference Search (STIS), a pattern search strategy for multimodal data built upon the structural nature of human behavior. A pattern defines a sequence of behaviors. Behaviors are encoded as annotated event intervals with temporal order being implicitly or explicitly defined. An example is a greeting among two individuals with the possible formulation: <A walks up to B>[within 1 second]<A shakes B's hand> and <A says "Hello">. We base STIS upon this representation using contextualized information. This is done through viewing a pattern that is of interest to an expert (i.e., a relevant pattern) as not only the focus point of analysis but also defining the search criteria. A pattern is deemed relevant by an expert dependent on the expert's interest in the behavior described by the pattern. Identification of a relevant pattern within a dataset (i.e., search) results in occurrences of the pattern.

The expert's definition of a relevant pattern incorporates his or her knowledge into the search criteria as opposed to relying on statistical modeling to bring to the surface a pattern that may or may not be of interest. Statistical models used to extract frequent and/or statistically significant patterns (episodes) [14, 26] do not address cases where a pattern may only occur a handful of times. As discussed in [21], an algorithm's results based on some automated metric (such as frequent episode mining) would require some form of explicit pattern search anyway. This motivates our interest in identifying pattern occurrences of interest to the expert.

ICMI'12, October 22–26, 2012, Santa Monica, California, USA.

The rest of our paper is organized as followed. In section §2 we present related work of multimodal corpora, analysis tools, visualizations, and temporal pattern mining approaches. The details of STIS are discussed in §3. §4 discusses our experiment methodology, implementation details, the datasets used, the baseline algorithms, the patterns tested, our results, and discussion. Conclusions and future work close our paper in §5.

2. RELATED WORK

Our data domain is multimodal. There has been a strong trend toward creation and analysis of multimodal corpora. This is no surprise as the authors of [29] argue the value and deeper understanding multi-modality adds to analysis of human behavior. Many multimodal corpora have been created in response to this observation which predominantly consist of sequences of descriptive events (behavior patterns). The VACE/AFIT [5] multimodal meeting corpus is a detailed recording of multiple sessions of Airforce officers partaking in war gaming scenarios in a meeting setting. The Semaine corpus [16] is a collection of emotionally colored conversations. The Rapport and Face-to-Face corpora [8, 24] are sets of speaker-listener interactions. One of the largest to date is the AMI corpus [3] which contains 100 hours of recorded meetings. Mörchen created a series of datasets of varying degrees of modalities [23]. These mentioned corpora and datasets are highlights of a growing community of such data.

With the increasing number of multimodal datasets, tools are needed to visualize the data for analysis. These tools have been developed to visualize multi-channel annotation information coupled with varying degrees of multi-channel support of audio and video. Well known examples of these tools are MacVisSTA [30], ANVIL [11], Theme [35], EXMARaLDA [32, 6], ELAN [38], C-BAS[1], Transformer, and VCode [9]. The AMI corpus uses a different approach through use of the Nite XML toolkit which provides extensive support for complex annotation representation and supportive interface. Nite XML toolkit visualization is centered around transcription text (e.g., dialogue) of a corpus being annotated and is linked to supportive media, e.g., audio or video.

It is common for behavior interactions to be described as a sequential sequence of observed events. Many experts in the field of behavior analysis express behaviors of interest in this fashion [3, 5, 11, 12, 16, 17, 19, 33, 36]. This is no surprise as such descriptions capture the sequence of events that define the behavior. Many large corpora have been produced to identify and understand behavior among humans interacting within a small group setting (e.g., [3, 5, 16]) One focus of the analysis of these corpora is identifying the structure of behavior patterns. However, there is limited support for searching based on the structure.

Currently, there are a few search strategies in this data domain. Some visualization tools such as Nite XML toolkit has a supportive query language for searching the annotations. Such an approach can be powerful but construction of queries can be complex and cumbersome. ANVIL supports searching amongst the text of annotated event labels. This can be useful when looking for a specific event. However, identifying a sequence of labels does not seem to be supported. Some tools, such as VCode, can export annotated events to a text file where search outside of the application can be performed. MacVisSTA has the ability to save an observation (notebook) and play it back but not find other occurrences of the observation. EXMARaLDA performs search using a tool created by the EXMARaLDA authors called EXAKT. Their search is modeled after KWIC (keyword in context) and has powerful support for regular expressions in text search (search transcription text, annotations, and descriptions). ELAN has similar search support to EXMARaLDA but has the added ability to add temporal relation constraints (Allen's constraints between two intervals [1]). Transformer is purposed for transforming data files for use in one tool to another. They do support text search in which different corpus files can be specified to search.

The search we are interested in is symbolic temporal pattern mining where the focus is discovering "interesting" patterns among *symbolic* time series data (not numerical) [13, 22]. There are a few approaches related to this aspect of STIS. The first is T-patterns developed by Magnusson [15] where a sequence of events will occur within certain time windows, e.g., $A_1 \xrightarrow{T_1} A_2 \xrightarrow{T_2} A_3$ for time intervals T_1 and T_2. T-patterns are used as the basis of pattern representation in Theme [35] where each T is set through various statistical methods. Time interval windows are used in the second related approach, Frequent Episode Mining (FEM) algorithms of [26, 31]. The FEM algorithms use one of two approaches: conditional probability or a frequency threshold, both on defined timing windows.

3. STIS METHOD

Structural and Temporal Inference Search (STIS) is founded on creating a formalism of a pattern based on structure, timing, and ordered relationships. We operate on a pattern at the semi-interval level (start or end of an interval). This representation was first introduced by Freksa in [7] and later revisited by Mörchen and Fradkin in [23]. Semi-intervals allows a flexible representation where partial or incomplete knowledge can be handled since operation is on parts of an interval and not the whole. In this section we discuss how we use semi-intervals to describe a pattern and build a structured search based on the pattern to identify occurrences within a dataset. An overview of our method can be seen in Figure 1. Given a set of event annotations (e.g., from ELAN or MacVisSTA), create a semi-interval set which is organized in a database of definitions and instances. This is done offline. Then the expert provides an event sequence that is converted into a *pattern* which contains implicit search criteria. This is given to STIS which performs structural analysis on the *pattern*, uses the results of the analysis to form search criteria, searches to identify occurrences based on the criteria and returns a set of occurrences. We will discuss the details of what occurs offline and online in turn.

Offline: Event annotations from a multimodal dataset are transformed into a set of semi-interval annotations. We define an event as:

Definition 1. An *event* is an interval $[r_i, r_j]$ with semi-intervals r_i and r_j, $i, j > 0$, representing the start and end points of the event, respectively.

Our representation of an event does not associate with a particular occurrence time of the event, i.e., r_i and r_j are not the times of the start and end points. This is necessary as many occurrences of the same event can occur.

[1]Developed at Arizona State, http://www.cmi.arizona.edu/, but the url for C-BAS is broken.

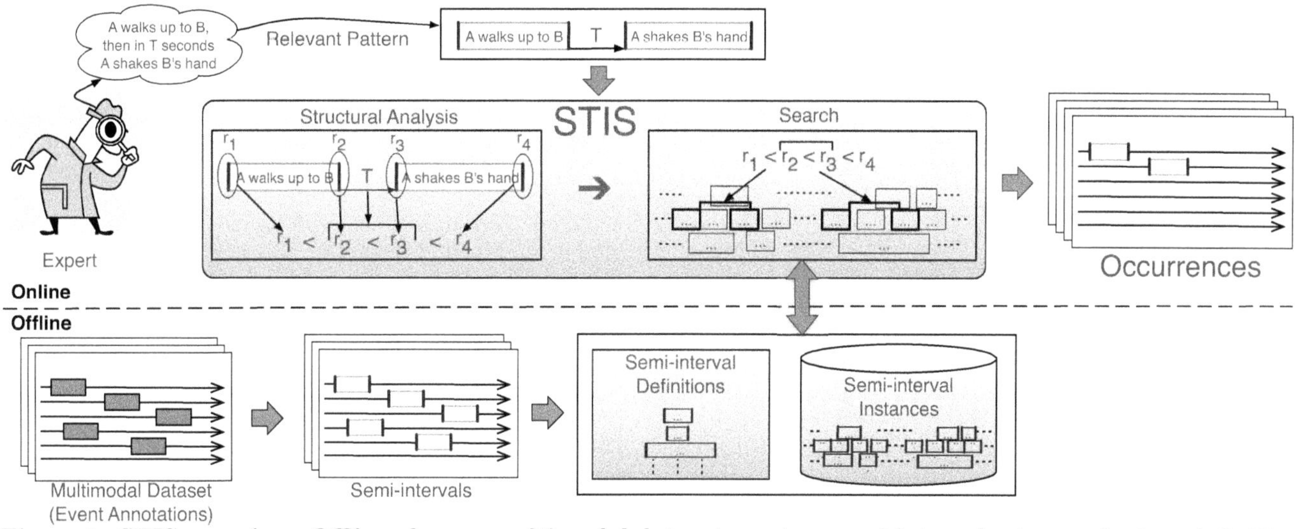

Figure 1: STIS overview: Offline, from a multimodal dataset create a semi-interval set organized as *definition* and *instance* tables. Online, an expert provides an event sequence that is converted into a *pattern* containing implicit search criteria. STIS performs structural analysis on the *pattern*, uses the results of the analysis to form search criteria, searches to identify occurrences based on the criteria and returns a set of occurrences.

Identification with a particular occurrence time is discussed later. For organizing events, two look-up tables are used. The first, a *definition table*, stores semi-interval *definitions*. A *definition* stores characteristics of the event from which it originated. These characteristics consist of a textual description, the actor involved (or source of the event), the type of event, e.g. modality, and whether it is a start or end semi-interval. These descriptive characteristics are a subset of event aspects in [37], except for start/end. Such characteristics have been used as focal aspects during analysis of event-based multimodal data [5, 17, 23]. The *definitions* are used to store descriptive information for each semi-interval without repetition (i.e., look-up table of unique *definitions*). The second look-up table, an *instance table*, stores of all semi-intervals in the dataset organized by temporal order. Each semi-interval in this table links to its *definition* in the first table. The *definitions* in the first table allows querying semi-intervals based on characteristics while the second table allows querying of events based on temporal criteria. Currently, our organization of event information is purposed to store and represent interval and semi-interval data. Point data can also be stored in which case a single semi-interval with no matching semi-interval is stored.

Online: An expert provides an event sequence to identify. The sequence is mapped to a *pattern* representation:

Definition 2. A *pattern* is a sequence S of semi-intervals r_i, $i \in \{1, ..., |S|\}$, such that for each $r_i \in S$, $\exists\ r_j$ such that r_i occurs before or is equal to r_j $\forall\ i \leq j$; $i, j \in \{1, ..., |S|\}$. Each r_i and r_j has an associated *temporal constraint* $\hat{t}_i$ which is a time window between r_i and r_j such that r_j occurs within $\hat{t}_i$ time of r_i where r_i's time $(t_i) \leq r_j$'s time (t_j), i.e., $t_i \leq t_j \leq t_i + \hat{t}_i$.

An example *pattern* can be seen in Figure 2A which represents one rendition of the greeting between two individuals from Section 1. The *temporal constraint* T expresses r_3 and r_4 to occur within T time units of r_2. This is useful as one may only be interested when A shakes B's hand and says "Hello" within a certain time to A approaching B. If no constraint is given, then matches that are not temporally close will be found but do not represent the desired greeting occurrence, i.e., ten minutes passes after A approaching B, then A shakes B's hand, etc., which does not represent the desired greeting structure.

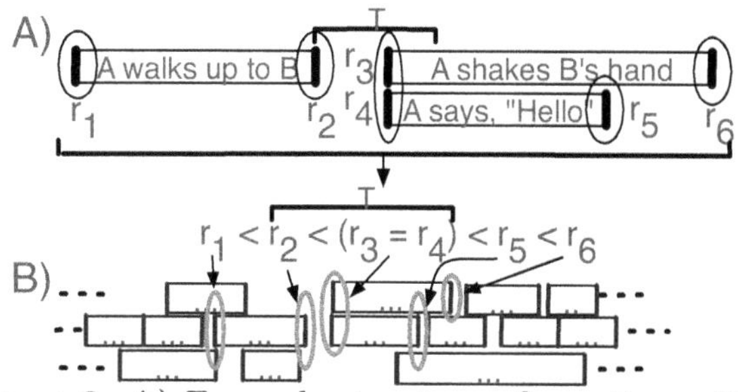

Figure 2: A) Example structure of a *pattern*. Note the temporal constraint between r_2, r_3, and r_4. B) Segmentation into *pockets* of equality.

Following from this, a *pattern* can be viewed in one of two ways: a complete *pattern* or key-parts of the *pattern*. A complete *pattern* contains complete intervals (i.e., matched semi-intervals). The key-parts represent relevant semi-intervals of the pattern that are key to identification of occurrences of the *pattern*, which could include complete intervals. For example, the *pattern* in Figure 2A is a complete *pattern* whereas r_2, r_3, and r_4 within time T represent the key-parts of the *pattern*. Note that the key-parts and the complete *pattern* could be the same and the key-parts need not be unique but their temporal constraints and relational order are relevant to identifying the *pattern*.

The expert's *pattern* is given to STIS as input. STIS then performs two steps: structural analysis and search. The structural analysis step consists of "dissecting" the *pattern* and extract ordered and temporal information. In this step, *temporal constraints* are stored and the *pattern* is segmented into *pockets* of equality. We define a *pocket* as

Definition 3. A *pocket* p of *pattern* R is a set of semi-intervals $r_i \in p$ such that $\forall i, j \in$ indices(p), $0 \leq |t_i - t_j| \leq \varepsilon$ where indices(p) is the set of semi-interval indices within p, e.g., i and j.

This use of *pockets* follows from the observation that at the semi-interval level, semi-intervals in a sequence are either equal (within a certain small time window) or not (outside the time window). Hence, semi-intervals can be grouped

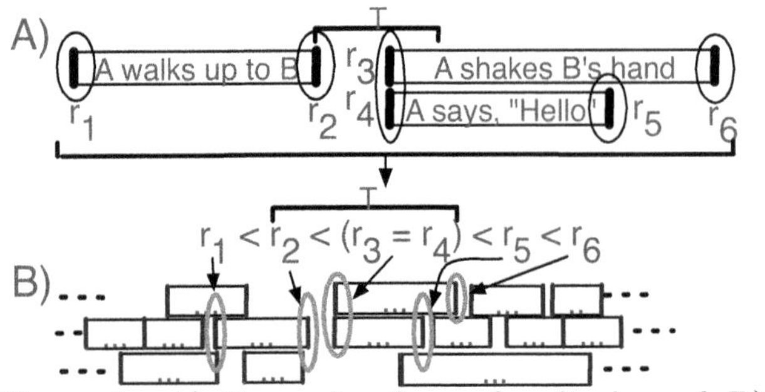

Figure 3: A) Example of search criteria and B) search within the semi-interval instances.

accordingly into *pockets* of equality. All semi-intervals that are within an ε of each other are deemed equal and grouped in a *pocket*. These groups are separated by temporal order (inequality). The segmentation into *pockets* allows a simple method with which to implicitly store ordered relational information, i.e., using the structure to provide relational information. As can be seen in Figure 2, we can see the implicit (ordered) relationships amongst the r_i's. For example, there is no need to explicitly store (remember) that r_3 and r_4 are equal or that r_2 occurs before r_6.

After structural analysis, STIS creates a set of search criteria applied to the *instance table* in which instances are identified. The search criteria contain ordered relationships among the semi-intervals and any defined temporal constraints. An example of search criteria can be seen in Figure 3A, where the greeting *pattern* from Section 1 is revisited. Here, the ordered relational information and a temporal constraint are extracted from the *pattern* and a set of search criteria are created. Then in Figure 3B, these criteria are used to identify occurrences within the semi-interval instances (*instance table*). As can be seen, the search criteria collected from the *pattern* reflect the *pattern's* structure. STIS uses this criteria to scan all semi-interval instances finding occurrence matches and returning a set of matches. The situated context of each occurrence is preserved as is important for multimodal analysis. This is accomplished through storing the occurrences' times and the semi-intervals within a certain defined time window for each occurrence. This process is based on the work of [20].

4. EXPERIMENTS

For multimodal data organized as multi-channel temporal events, we pose the following question: Can search based on a defined *pattern* structure identify occurrences of the *pattern* with greater accuracy than search based on conditional probability thresholds? We first outline our methodology for experimentation followed by a description of the implementations of the search strategies used. After which we describe the datasets used and the behavior categories our experimentation focuses on. The baselines are then discussed. Then we present our results and provide discussion.

4.1 Methodology

Since behavior analysis has many variables to consider, testing our search strategy must be done in a controlled environment. To accomplish this, we introduce occurrences of *patterns* with variation into several datasets at known locations, apply the search techniques, then see if the *patterns* can be identified. This is also necessary as exact known ground truth instances for the datasets used is limited. The techniques used are STIS, FEM frequency, and FEM conditional probability. We chose 5 categories of *patterns* in a meeting room setting deemed important by experts, i.e., relevant *patterns*. These categories come from analysis reported in [5, 17]. We then apply the same search techniques to unaltered real datasets with known ground truth.

We experiment with three datasets from the domain of behavior analysis in a meeting room setting. The first is a generated (synthetic) dataset that is created based on the parameters of real datasets similar to bootstrap aggregating (bagging) [2]. The other two datasets are real datasets consisting of two sessions within a corpora (details in §4.3).

We introduce into each dataset occurrences of relevant *patterns* with variation based on the 5 behavior categories. Each *pattern* is based on relational structures observed by experts. For each *pattern*, we introduce 10 instances into its own copy of each dataset, i.e., there is no interference between the *patterns* of different behavior categories. We also ensure that none of the 10 overlap. Then we search each dataset copy for its respectively inserted *patterns*. The results are compared to the known inserted locations for accuracy. Power/penalty analysis is used as a metric (described in §4.6). We then take the two real datasets unaltered and search for occurrences of known ground truth. We conduct these searches using two versions of each *pattern*: the complete *pattern* and key-parts. This allows a comparison between using complete knowledge of a *pattern* and the relevant pieces according to the expert (sometimes complete knowledge is not needed or unattainable).

Since one of our datasets is generated, there is some concern that the *pattern* instances introduced already exist due to random generation. However, the probability that the generated dataset has many relevant *pattern* instances present is very low. This probability was explored in [21].

4.2 Implementation

STIS is implemented in C++ using Qt 4.7 [27] for the user interface and a SQLite database for the datasets. The current interface of our system is not shown as it is not the focus of this paper. The FEM frequency algorithm (*FEM1*) is implemented in C++ and the FEM conditional probability algorithm (*FEM2*) is implemented in Java. Both FEM algorithms are part of TDMiner (http://people.cs.vt.edu/patnaik/software). In deciding the appropriate *temporal constraints*, the choice depends on the events involved, what events mean to an expert, and the kind of data. Ultimately, it is up to the one performing the search. For our experiments we chose to use a global 3 second window as a *temporal constraint* between each consecutive semi-interval being matched. The timeframe of behavior patterns is normally temporally tight (on the order of milliseconds up to seconds). Using a 3 second window allows the identification of instances that are temporally tight and those a little longer without a flood of results with many potentially being irrelevant. However, this window can be user set.

4.3 Datasets

Here we describe the datasets used for our experiments. Our experiments were conducted using the VACE/AFIT multimodal meeting room corpus [5, 17].

VACE/AFIT: This dataset consists of several meeting sessions of Airforce Officers from the Airforce Insitute of Technology (AFIT) partaking in war-gaming scenarios. We

Table 1: Datasets' Contents.

Data-set	Length (min)	# Semi-interval	# Unique Semi-intervals	Speech Length (secs)			Gaze Length (secs)			Gesture Length (secs)			# Gaze	# Speech	# Gesture
				Ave	Min	Max	Ave	Min	Max	Ave	Min	Max			
Generated	~45	25590	240	1.3	0.06	5	1.27	0.1	5	1.29	0.1	5	10626	7438	7526
										Nodding, Phrase					Nodding, Phrase
AFIT 1	~45	7802	342	1.59	0.1	64.46	2.16	0.1	158.86	0.99, 0.84	0.23, 0.3	10.71, 11.68	4704	1414	1018, 666
AFIT 2	~42	13362	226	2.28	0.03	124.62	1.09	0.07	58.22	0.89, 1.0	0.27, 0.27	13.78, 9.21	11456	1126	610, 170

focus on two sessions (*AFIT 1* and *AFIT 2*). Each session is a scenario in which five officers (C, D, E, F, and G) are given a problem to discuss and resolve. The room where the sessions took place was instrumented for multi-channel audio and video along with motion capture of the officers (details of instrumentation in [5]). The officers in *AFIT 1* are discussing potential candidates for a scholarship. The scenario is that C, D, F, and G are department heads meeting with the institute commandant E to select three scholarship award recipients. The officers in *AFIT 2* are discussing options for exploiting an enemy missile that has been discovered. Each session is approximately 45 minutes with manual and automated annotations for speech, gaze fixations, F-formations, and several gestural forms (including gesture phrases) for each officer. F-Formations, or focus formations, were first identified by Adam Kendon to be units of topical cohesion marked by gaze cohesion of participants to common objects or spaces [10]. Gesture phrases are atomic gestural motions marking a single motion trajectory that typically coincide with atomic speech phrases [18]. These annotations are events that were extracted from the audio, video, and motion capture data and describe the officers' interactions. The sum of the annotations is a dataset consisting of multiple channels (21 for *AFIT 1*, 19 for *AFIT 2*) of overlapping event data extracted from various synched media streams. The sequences of behavior described by the annotations are rich and descriptive. Each dataset is summarized in Table 1. For our experiments, *A1* and *A2* are altered versions (i.e., *patterns* introduced) of *AFIT 1* and *AFIT 2*, respectively, and *A3* and *A4* are unaltered versions (i.e., original) of *AFIT 1* and *AFIT 2*, respectively.

Generated: We generated a dataset based on the parameters of the VACE data. For five fictitious people, we randomly generate 45 minutes of annotations for parallel channels of speech, gaze fixations, and gesture phrases. For each person and each channel, we generate a timeline of events with varying lengths and gaps between them totaling 15 parallel channels. This is fewer channels but much denser as can be seen in Table 1 with significantly more semi-intervals. We label this dataset as *G*.

4.4 Relevant Patterns

Here we describe the general *patterns* that were deemed interesting by experts and introduced into *G*, *A1*, and *A2*, plus the ground truth *patterns*. The *pattern* structures used can be seen in Figure 4. The outlined semi-intervals represent the key-parts of the *pattern*. The actors used for the *patterns* introduced into *A1* and *A2* were chosen so that they did not match the original actors reported by experts in [4, 17]. For example, if a *pattern* we want to introduce was reported involving C gazing at F, then we did not use C and F but instead G and D. This was done to prevent interference from the actual *patterns* observed by the experts.

Mutual Gaze (MG): In the AFIT sessions, different participants controlled the floor at different times (i.e., leading the discussion for the moment). When the control passed from one participant to the next, there was a mutual gaze exchange between the current holder of the floor to the next.

Gaze Coalition (GC): It was discovered in *AFIT 1* that the social interaction amongst the participants had as much to do with the outcome of the meeting as the specific merits of the scholarship candidates being discussed. The participants dynamically formed coalitions to support each-other's candidates through a process of mutual gaze fixations and back-channel expressions of support during discussions [19].

A coalition to support a proposed idea is initialized when the proposer seeks to make eye-contact with other participants while he is presenting the idea. Participants who supported the idea would return the eye-contact, while those who disagreed would avert gaze. When a return gaze was attained, the presenter's gaze moved to another member.

Floor Control (FC): During a session, a participant would gain floor control through a hand movement (gesture) and start speaking. This was deemed 'floor capturing' in [4].

Turn Taking (TT): As detailed above, each session had a meeting manager who normally was the dominant participant and facilitated the meeting. When a participant sought to take a turn speaking, the participant might look at the meeting manager while the current floor controller spoke. Once the current floor controller finished speaking, the participant seeking a turn would then begin speaking.

F-formation (Ff): F-formations were observed throughout the sessions. The defining behavior for F-formations observed were concurrent focus on the same person (or object).

Ground Truth: In *A3* a GC model was known to exist from unpublished analysis. In *A4*, a TT and Ff model were reported in [17]. These represent the only occurrences of a known ground truth *pattern* in which the exact timing within the datasets can be verified (3 in total). The ground truth *patterns* consisted entirely of semi-interval key-parts.

4.5 Baselines

We compare STIS against two Frequent Episode Mining (FEM) algorithms [26, 31]. The motivation behind the particular kind of FEM algorithms (*FEM1* and *FEM2*) we use is the discovery of pattern sequences within temporal event data. The authors of *FEM1* and *FEM2* applied their algorithms to neural spike data (i.e., firing patterns of neurons in the brain). The patterns represented by this data have many similarities to our data domain: a sequence of firing times of neurons in sequence, i.e., a sequence of discrete events governed by temporal constraints.

Since FEM algorithms are meant for mining and not searching, we compromise by tuning them similarly to STIS's parameters, and then search their results for relevant *patterns*. This is necessary as there are no other approach like STIS for comparison. The closest is *FEM1* (discussed shortly). In a FEM algorithm, there are several methods for specifying whether a pattern occurrence is deemed important. The two approaches most pertinent to our problem is frequency (*FEM1*) and statistical significance (*FEM2*). *FEM1* sets a frequency threshold reporting a *pattern* if seen at least as many times as the threshold. *FEM2* is based on the conditional probability of one event given another within a time window. In other words, if interested in A following B within 2 seconds, we would look for $Pr(B|A) \geq \alpha$ where B is within 2 seconds of A and α is a significance (connection strength) threshold. For more details see [31].

Interestingly enough, *FEM1* supports search by *pattern* definition where occurrences of a specified *pattern* are counted

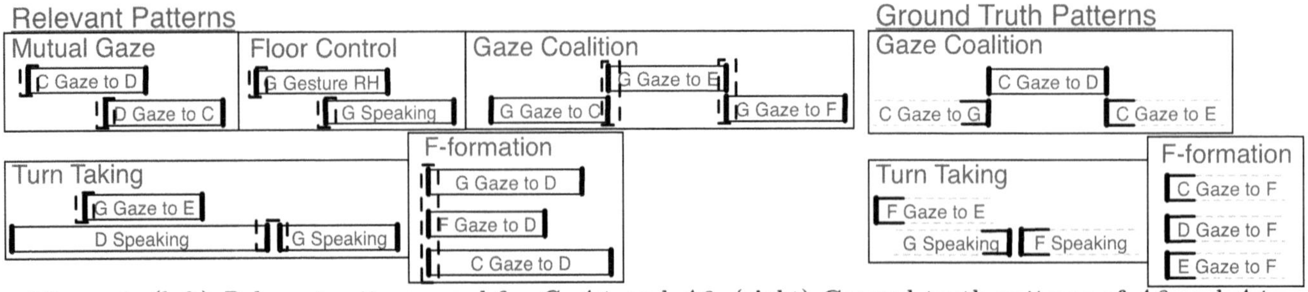

Figure 4: (left) ***Relevant patterns*** **used for** ***G, A1,*** **and** ***A2.*** **(right) Ground truth** ***patterns*** **of** ***A3*** **and** ***A4.***

Table 2: Overall Power/Penalty Analysis

	Complete	Key-Part	Ground Truth
Misses			
STIS	1	0	0
FEM1	9	17	2
FEM2	22	2*	3
Mean Power			
STIS	99.33	100	100
FEM1	94	88.67	33.33
FEM2	85.33	76*	0
Mean Penalty			
STIS	18.67	36.3	75.56
FEM1	19.68	39.87	91.67
FEM2	40.22	23*	100

without using a frequency threshold. This is analogous to an expert defining a *pattern* to search. The results of this kind of search in *FEM1* would be the same if using *FEM1* to search by *pattern* frequency. The main difference is that using frequency results in a long list of *patterns* to sift through for an exact *pattern* (plus choosing an appropriate threshold) whereas defining a *pattern* to count is focused on the exact *pattern* of interest. Definition of a *pattern* in *FEM1* for counting is closely related to how STIS operates, hence, this approach of *FEM1* is used for comparison.

For *FEM2* , the conditional probability threshold ranged from 0.03 to 0.1 depending on the size of the dataset and the *pattern*. We noticed for smaller datasets, in general, a larger threshold could be used. We use the same 3 second window between semi-intervals for *FEM1* and *FEM2*. *FEM1* functioned on all the datasets in semi-interval form. However, *FEM2* had some limitations requiring the use of interval datasets in most cases. With an interval dataset, *FEM2* performs operations with respect to an interval's start.

4.6 Results

The performance of STIS is tested through *power/penatly* analysis of [28]. This is done for datasets *G*, *A1*, and *A2*. We then look at the results for the three ground truth *patterns* also with power/penalty analysis. In total, STIS was run on 33 *patterns*, *FEM1* on 33, and *FEM2* on 30; in total 96 *pattern* searches were performed. For simplicity, we use the naming scheme *X_Y* to reference each *pattern* where *X* is the dataset and *Y* is the *pattern* abbreviation. For example, *A1_MG* is mutual gaze *pattern* from *A1*.

For describing the results, we use power/penalty analysis which reports a power and penalty percentage. The idea behind power/penalty analysis is that if there are x known instances of a phenomenon in a dataset, y instances identified by a method or algorithm, and z number of instances common amongst the known and identified, $z \leq x$, then the power percentage is $z/x*100$. For example, if $x = 10$, $y = 18$ and $z = 7$, then the power is $7/10 * 100 = 70\%$, i.e., the method's power is 70% in identifying the relevant instances. The other 11 identified instances are part of the penalty. These are extra instances the expert must go through and, in turn, are an extra cost. The penalty $= (y - z)/y * 100$, in our example, penalty $= (18 - 7)/18 * 100 = 61.11\%$.

A precision/recall approach is not applied as such approach provides how accurate your model is in identifying an instance. However, in our case, we not only want to accurately identify an instance, but whether that instance represents a specific behavior of interest. For example, one can create a detection system for hand waving. However, an expert may not only be interested in hand waving, but when A waves at B. What is detected will either be related to the behavior of interest (power) or not (penalty).

Table 2 presents the overall power/penalty analysis results. STIS was able to identify nearly all the occurrences (99.33% - only 1 missed). FEM1 and FEM2 missed a number more (94% and 85.33%, respectively). STIS had a higher mean power and a lower mean penalty for the complete *pattern* case. STIS also performed better than *FEM1* for the key-part case. The '*' for *FEM2*'s key-part results signify that these are only partial results. We were only able to run *FEM2* on key-part *patterns* for *A1* due to some limitations of *FEM2* (discussed later). Hence, the results presented in Table 2 are for this case. The corresponding sub-set of results for STIS and *FEM1* are 0, 100, 26.46 and 5, 90, 27.61 for misses, mean power, and mean penalty, respectively. For this case, *FEM2* had a lower mean penalty.

For the ground truth, STIS was the only approach that was able to identify all 3 known ground truth occurrences. We would like to emphasize for the ground truth identification STIS's ability to search for a *pattern* and one of the results be a ground truth occurrence. The high penalty is due to verifying the identification of only one occurrence for each *pattern*. STIS returned at max 5 occurrences for the ground truth *patterns* whereas *FEM1* and *FEM2* returned up to 22 occurrences and for some, did not return any.

In Figure 5 we can see the details of the penalty for the complete *pattern*, key-part *pattern*, and ground truth *pattern* cases. As can be seen, STIS and *FEM1* have competing results. The limitations of *FEM2* caused it to struggle with the ground truth case. Not surprisingly, all approaches had their worst performance for the generated data. There is a noticeable difference between the complete and key-part *pattern* cases. The penalty increased for key-part. The reason for this is most likely because the key-part *patterns* contain mostly semi-intervals (not intervals) leading to a greater chance of having more matching occurrences. This is one of the characteristics of the semi-interval representation as a pattern defined using semi-intervals can match a greater number of *patterns* than an interval representation [23].

Comparing the penalty trends across datasets and *pattern* types, we see that STIS has a similar penalty trend between complete and key-part cases for each dataset. STIS seems to be least affected between the datasets but suffers from the same errors between them also. STIS and *FEM1* display

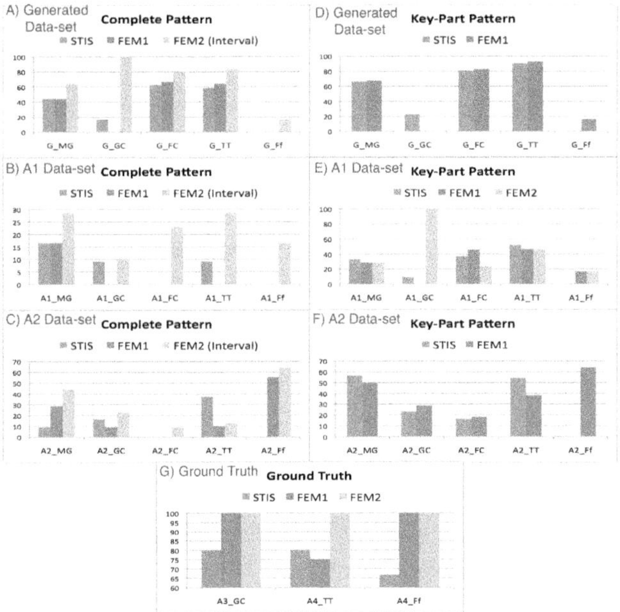

Figure 5: Penalty for *G*, *A1*, *A2*, and ground truth.

similar trends for *G*, *A1* key-part, and *A2* key-part. This suggests that they may have similar strengths and weaknesses. *FEM1* and *FEM2* had strongly correlated trends for *G* and *A2* complete but not for the other cases. Overall, the penalty trends suggest that there are commonalities in the algorithms that aid in identification but also shared pitfalls that hinder. Potential pitfall causes are the necessity to tune the *temporal constraints* and *pocket* size based on characteristics of the dataset and/or the kind of *pattern*, and making sure semi-intervals that are matched to an occurrence actually make sense, e.g., a start and end are matched to the same event occurrence and not two different occurrences of the same kind of event. Current measures in STIS to minimize this is to verify through the *instance table* that the semi-interval occurrences are matched appropriately. Further work in this area is needed to provide more robust matching. For ground truth, there was no trend seen other than STIS had the lowest penalty overall.

4.7 Discussion

In answer to the question posed previously, the results of STIS and *FEM1* confirmed that search based on event structure can identify *patterns* with high-accuracy, and search for *patterns* in multimodal data organized as multi-channel temporal events can benefit from expert input and specification as opposed to a conditional probability method (*FEM2*).

During our experimentation, we observed some limitations in the different algorithms. For *FEM1*, the ground truth *patterns GC* and *FF* could not be found as some semi-intervals of the *patterns* occur at the exact same time. *FEM1* does not handle this case, which was also observed in [21]. For *FEM2*, significant effort was required to obtains results as we had to continually try different conditional probability thresholds (some as low as 3%). This challenge came from the frequency of the *patterns* being searched for. Compared to the size of the data set, 10 occurrences (or 1 for each ground truth *pattern*) is very small. Hence, why search based on event structure with expert input and specification performed well. The *FEM2* implementation had an inherent limit in the number of reported *patterns* that could be outputted for verification (~50K). When this limit was exceeded, verification could not be performed as results could not be outputted. The larger the dataset, the greater the number of reported *patterns*, hence, the use of the interval versions of the datasets as they were half the size of their semi-interval counterparts. However, *FEM2* using intervals suffered since the algorithm would only match according to start times and not (seemingly) use the end times. This left *FEM2* operating as if only start semi-intervals were specified leaving a greater possibility for more matches.

For STIS, we encountered an initial identification error with ground truth *Ff*. Our default size of a *pocket* was temporally very tight as the original analysis of the behavior within *A3* and *A4* was focused at a small time scale (milliseconds). One of the gaze events of the *Ff pattern* was outside of our *pocket* size. Hence, we had to slightly change the structure of the *pattern* used to search in order to identify the ground truth *pattern*. This highlights the necessity for greater flexibility when searching using a structural approach, which is an observation we were aware of and this situation confirms such. Another observation is that *FEM1* had less identified patterns than STIS but still high power. We believe this is because *FEM1* returns non-overlapping *patterns*, i.e., *patterns* that do not overlap each other. STIS does not filter for non-overlapping *patterns* as such *patterns* may contain variations of potential interest to the expert.

FEM2's search strategy is based on identifying *patterns* using defined parameters. We are interested in identifying *patterns* that match parameters *and* also match specific content. By content we mean what the events involved in the *pattern* mean. For example, the structure of the ground truth models (Figure 4) can match any number of *patterns* in the data. It is the provided content along with the structure that allows an expert to pinpoint occurrences of interest. This kind of search is supported by STIS and *FEM1* and despite the limitations observed, they performed well. Overall, STIS outperformed *FEM1* and *FEM2* and poses to be a beneficial search approach in multimodal analysis tools.

The pattern structures investigated in this paper are the beginning of our research into creation of a set of temporal relationship principles for describing interaction patterns in multimodal corpora. A subset was used in this paper but expansion is underway into representing more complex patterns. This expansion includes negation, pre- and post-conditions, interrupts, and many renditions of repetition of specific events. However, the creation of more complex *patterns* may result in very few matches, which may or may not aid the current analysis (flexible vs. rigid *pattern* definition). Another potential venue of pursuit is using STIS to search partially annotated corpora. Some events are easier to annotate than others (e.g., when someone is speaking, or a person's position in the scene), hence, searching partial annotations can provide likely probable occurrences of events not yet annotated. This would identify focal areas where efforts can be applied for more detailed annotation creation.

5. CONCLUSIONS AND FUTURE WORK

In this paper we presented a search strategy for multimodal data based on the structural and temporal aspects of human behavior. We were able to show that a search strategy based on these principles performs well. STIS demonstrated the ability to accurately identify occurrences of *patterns* with an expert defined structure with some (or all) the occurrences identified being ones sought after. *FEM1* was a tough competitor which motivates future investigations of potential incorporation of *FEM1* aspects into STIS. An example being support for non-overlapping events if desired by the expert. Another focus of future work is supporting flexible timing windows (for *pockets* and temporal constraints). Support for such is merely a question of implementation.

6. ACKNOWLEDGMENTS

We would like to thank Debprakash Patnaik for his help in using FEM and Christa Miller for invaluable input as an outside observer and editor. This research was partially funded by FODAVA grant CCF-0937133, NSF IIS-1053039, and NSF IIS-1118018.

7. REFERENCES

[1] J. F. Allen. Maintaining knowledge about temporal intervals. *Commun. ACM*, 26(11):832–843, 1983.

[2] L. Breiman. Bagging predictors. *Machine Learning*, 24:123–140, 1996.

[3] J. Carletta et al. The ami meeting corpus: A pre-announcement. In *MLMI*, volume 3869 of *LNCS*, pages 28–39. Springer Berlin / Heidelberg, 2006.

[4] L. Chen et al. A multimodal analysis of floor control in meetings. In *MLMI'06*, pages 36–49.

[5] L. Chen et al. Vace multimodal meeting corpus. *MLMI '06*, pages 40–51.

[6] EXMARaLDA. *http://www.exmaralda.org*, Last Checked: May, 2012.

[7] C. Freksa. Temporal reasoning based on semi-intervals. *Artificial Intelligence*, 54(1-2):199 – 227, 1992.

[8] J. Gratch et al. Creating rapport with virtual agents. In *Intelligent Virtual Agents*, volume 4722 of *LNCS*, pages 125–138. Springer Berlin / Heidelberg, 2007.

[9] J. Hagedorn, J. Hailpern, and K. G. Karahalios. Vcode and vdata: illustrating a new framework for supporting the video annotation workflow. In *AVI '08*, pages 317–321. ACM.

[10] A. Kendon. *Conducting Interaction: Patterns of Behavior in Focused Encounters*. Cambridge: Cambridge University Press, 1990.

[11] M. Kipp. Anvil - a generic annotation tool for multimodal dialogue. In *Eurospeech*, 2001.

[12] M. Kipp. Spatiotemporal coding in anvil. In *LREC*, 2008.

[13] S. Laxman and P. Sastry. A survey of temporal data mining. *Sadhana*, 31(2):173–198, 04 2006.

[14] S. Laxman, P. Sastry, and K. Unnikrishnan. Discovering frequent episodes and learning hidden markov models: a formal connection. *TKDE*, 17(11):1505 – 1517, Nov. 2005.

[15] M. Magnusson. Discovering hidden time patterns in behavior: T-patterns and their detection. *Behavior Research Methods*, 32:93–110, 2000.

[16] G. McKeown et al. The semaine corpus of emotionally coloured character interactions. In *ICME '10*, pages 1079 –1084.

[17] D. McNeill. Gesture, gaze, and ground. In *MLMI'06*, volume 3869 of *LNCS*, pages 1–14.

[18] D. McNeill. *Hand and Mind: What gestures reveal about thought*. Chicago: U. of Chicago Press, 1992.

[19] D. McNeill et al. Mind-merging. In *Expressing oneself / expressing one's self: Communication, language, cognition, and identity*, 2007.

[20] C. Miller and F. Quek. Toward multimodal situated analysis. In *ICMI '11*.

[21] C. Miller and F. Quek. Interactive data-driven discovery of temporal behavior models from events in media streams. In *ACM MM*, 2012.

[22] F. Mörchen. Unsupervised pattern mining from symbolic temporal data. *SIGKDD Explor. Newsl.*, 9(1):41–55, 2007.

[23] F. Mörchen and D. Fradkin. Robust mining of time intervals with semi-interval partial order patterns. In *SIAM Conference on Data Mining (SDM)*, 2010.

[24] L.-P. Morency, I. de Kok, and J. Gratch. Context-based recognition during human interactions: automatic feature selection and encoding dictionary. In *ICMI '08*, pages 181–188. ACM.

[25] D. Patnaik et al. Experiences with mining temporal event sequences from electronic medical records: initial successes and some challenges. In *KDD '11*, pages 360–368. ACM.

[26] D. Patnaik, P. S. Sastry, and K. P. Unnikrishnan. Inferring neuronal network connectivity from spike data: A temporal data mining approach. *Scientific Programming*, 16(1):49–77, January 2007.

[27] Qt. *http://qt.nokia.com/*, Last Checked: Mar., 2012.

[28] F. Quek. The catchment feature model: a device for multimodal fusion and a bridge between signal and sense. *EURASIP J. Appl. Signal Process.*, 2004:1619–1636, Jan. 2004.

[29] F. Quek, T. Rose, and D. McNeill. Multimodal meeting analysis. In *IA*, 2005.

[30] R. T. Rose, F. Quek, and Y. Shi. Macvissta: a system for multimodal analysis. In *ICMI '04*, pages 259–264.

[31] P. S. Sastry and K. P. Unnikrishnan. Conditional probability based significance tests for sequential patterns in multi-neuronal spike trains. 2008.

[32] T. Schmidt. The transcription system exmaralda: An application of the annotation graph formalism as the basis of a database of multilingual spoken discourse. In *Proceedings of the IRCS Workshop On Linguistic Databases*, pages 219–227, 2001.

[33] T. Schmidt et al. An exchange format for multimodal annotations. In *Multimodal corpora*, pages 207–221. Springer-Verlag, Berlin, Heidelberg, 2009.

[34] T. Schmidt and K. Wörner. Exmaralda – creating, analysing and sharing spoken language corpora for pragmatic research. *Pragmatics*, 19, 2009.

[35] Theme. http://www.noldus.com/human-behavior-research/products/theme.

[36] M. Voit and R. Stiefelhagen. 3d user-perspective, voxel-based estimation of visual focus of attention in dynamic meeting scenarios. In *ICMI-MLMI '10*, pages 51:1–51:8. ACM, 2010.

[37] U. Westermann and R. Jain. Toward a common event model for multimedia applications. *IEEE MultiMedia*, 14:19–29, January 2007.

[38] P. Wittenburg et al. Elan: a professional framework for multimodality research. In *LREC*, 2006.

Integrating Word Acquisition and Referential Grounding towards Physical World Interaction

Rui Fang, Changsong Liu, Joyce Y. Chai
Department of Computer Science and Engineering
Michigan State University
East Lansing, MI 48824, USA
{fangrui, cliu, jchai}@cse.msu.edu

ABSTRACT

In language-based interaction between a human and an artificial agent (e.g., robot) in a physical world, because the human and the agent have different knowledge and capabilities in perceiving the shared environment, referential grounding is very difficult. To facilitate such interaction, it is important for the agent to continuously learn and acquire knowledge about the environment through interactions with humans and incorporate the learned knowledge in grounding references from human utterances. To address this issue, this paper presents a graph-based approach for referential grounding and examines how referential grounding and word acquisition influence each other in physical world interaction. Our empirical results have shown that for most words, automated word acquisition through interaction improves referential grounding performance. However, this is not the case for words describing object types, where human supervision is important. Nevertheless, better referential grounding enables more accurate acquisition of word meanings, which in turn further improves grounding performance for references in subsequent utterances.

Categories and Subject Descriptors

H.5.2 [**User Interface**]: Natural language

General Terms

Algorithms, Experimentation

Keywords

referential grounding, word acquisition, graph matching, human robot interaction

1. INTRODUCTION

Naturally interacting with robots in a physical world using human languages has become increasingly important. This type of interaction often involves objects and their identities in the environment. One critical problem is *referential grounding* - a process to establish mutual understanding between conversation partners about intended references [6]. Robots need to identify referents in the environment that are specified by their human partners. Referential grounding in a physical world, although similar to exphoric reference resolution in a virtual world [12, 3, 18, 17], is significantly more challenging. In virtual world applications, since the world itself is internally generated, it is known to the agent and can be represented symbolically at the design time. Furthermore, unexpected changes do not usually happen in the virtual world (e.g., it is not likely a known object in the virtual environment suddenly becomes unknown to the system). Therefore, in a virtual world, referential grounding mainly involves linguistic processing and concerns less about the environment such as unknown or uncertain objects.

In physical world interaction, the situation becomes much more complex. The agent needs to sense and make inference about the objects and their relations in the environment. This process is often full of uncertainty and error prone. An object may be known to the agent at one moment, but may become unrecognizable at another moment(e.g., due to change of location or lighting condition). Thus a complete symbolic representation of the physical environment is very difficult to acquire. Referential grounding, therefore, will have to go beyond linguistic processing (which assumes the underlying connections between words and symbolic representations of the world), and actively seeks the connection between language and lower level, non-symbolic representation of the world.

To address these challenges, many previous works have focused on either referential grounding [9, 22, 14] or word acquisition [21, 19, 24]. Referential grounding addresses identification of objects in the environment as referents to linguistic referring expressions. Word acquisition focuses on acquiring the meaning of a word in terms of the low level physical properties of the environment, for example, learning an RGB distribution to represent the meaning of the word *red* [19]. However, referential grounding and word acquisition are inter-related and should be integrated together. Better acquiring the physical meaning of a word will allow better grounding of referring expressions to physical entities in the environment. On the other hand, the grounded entities and their linguistic expressions provide a basis to further refine and acquire the physical meaning of a word. This is particularly important in human robot interaction. Since humans and robots have mismatched capabilities in perceiving the shared environment. What a human sees and knows about the environment often is not available to a robot. Integrating referential grounding and word acquisition can potentially allow the robot to continuously learn and acquire knowledge about the environment via grounded objects. To address this issue, this paper presents a graph-based approach for referential grounding and further studies how referential grounding and word acquisition may influence each other in a physical world. Our empirical

ICMI'12, October 22–26, 2012, Santa Monica, California, USA.

results have shown that for most words, automated word acquisition through interaction improves referential grounding performance. However, this is not the case for words describing object types, where human supervision is important. Nevertheless, better referential grounding enables more accurate acquisition of word meanings, which in turn further improves grounding performance for references in subsequent utterances.

In the following sections, we first introduce a graph-based approach for referential grounding and simple online learning for word acquisition. We then describe our experiments that interleave referential grounding and word acquisition, followed by empirical evaluations and results.

Figure 1: An example scene

2. RELATED WORK

Referential grounding in a physical world is a very challenging problem. Different approaches have been developed. Gorniak and Roy present an approach that grounds referring expressions to visual objects through semantic decomposition, using context free grammar that connects linguistic structures with underlying visual properties [9]. Recently, they have extended this work by including action-affordances [10]. To incorporate situational awareness, incremental approaches have been developed to prune interpretations which do not have corresponding visual referents in the environment [22, 2]. A recent work applies a bidirectional approach to integrate bottom-up incremental language processing with top-down constraints on possible interpretation of referents [14].

Automated word acquisition also received an increasing attention. In [21], given speech inputs paired with object images, mutual information was used to acquire words by associating acoustic phone sequences with visual properties (e.g., color, shape) of the objects. In [24], an embodied multi-modal learning interface for word acquisition was proposed and a translation model was used to acquire the meaning of words. However, the focus of this work explores embodied multi-modal learning (e.g., through body movement) for word acquisition without explicit modeling of meanings of words.

In contrast to these previous works, here we aim to examine an integration of word acquisition and referential grounding. In particular, we intend to address physical world interactions where a human and an artificial agent do not have same kind of knowledge or perceptual capabilities of the environment.

3. THE OVERALL FRAMEWORK

To facilitate language-based interaction in a physical world, the agent needs to make sense of the environment based on its own perception. The environment could be represented symbolically if the agent has a superb perceptual capability and sufficient world knowledge. In this case, linguistic processing will be sufficient to connect language to the symbolic representation of the environment. However, the environment itself is not constant and is difficult for the agent to perceive due to its limited capabilities. Thus a complete symbolic representation of the environment is often impossible.

For example, Figure 1 shows an example scene. The agent is able to recognize most objects, but not the white ball (i.e., *unknown* is marked next to the bounding box). The agent cannot recognize it is a *ball* and may not have the knowledge that the color of the ball is actually called *white*. In this case, the agent may not be able to identify the referent of the phrase "the white ball". However, an unknown object often has certain relations with a known object. An expression referring to an unknown object is often expressed in relation to a known object, for example, "the white ball to the right of the red ball". If the agent knows the object *red ball* and the spatial relation *right*, then there is sufficient evidence to infer that the object (which the agent does not recognize) is *the white ball*. Once this connection is made, the agent may acquire additional knowledge about what a ball may look like and what color term *white* stands for. This is exactly the scenario we address in this paper. Because natural language expressions often describe relations between objects in the environment. These relationships will help ground expressions to unknown objects (i.e., objects that are not recognized based on the agent's perceptual capability). Once the grounding to these unknown objects is made, additional knowledge about the environment and the meaning of the relevant words can be acquired. This newly acquired knowledge will further help ground subsequent referring expressions.

In fact, similar type of word acquisition through known words has been previously explored in child language acquisition [11]. Here in this paper, we mainly focus on computational models of this process and aim to examine whether and how it can be applied in physical world interaction. We define *referential grounding* as a process that grounds referring expressions (e.g., "the white ball") to the intended objects in the environment; and *word acquisition* as a process that updates meanings of words in the system's lexicon by acquiring additional knowledge from the environment and interaction. In particular, a graph-based approach is applied to address the referential grounding and a simple learning approach is applied to address word acquisition.

3.1 Lexicons with Grounded Semantic Functions

As mentioned earlier, it is impossible for the agent to come up with a complete and truthful symbolic representation of the physical world. Therefore, to facilitate language-based interaction, it is important to go beyond traditional representation of meanings of words and provide a mechanism that will connect language to the environment. We address this issue by attaching grounded semantic functions to each word in the lexicon.

Grounded semantic functions represent meanings of words by grounding them to the physical properties of the environment. Words that describe different aspects of the environment may have different forms of grounded semantic functions. In previous work, Roy and colleagues [19, 20] treated the meaning of words as random variables and modeled them using Gaussian functions. The parameters of Gaussian models were estimated using the observations of visual features that co-occurred with the words. For example, the meaning of the color term *red* is defined as a multivariate Gaussian distribution in terms of R, G, B color component in RGB color space. The parameters of the Gaussian model are estimated based on the observations that co-occur with the word *red*. In this paper we follow the same idea and model most of our grounded semantic

Lexicon Type	Words	Extracted Visual Features	Grounded Semantic Function	Seed Knowledge
Object Type	apple, etc.	object ID	$S = \{..\}$	$S = \{ID_1, ID_3\}$
Color	red, etc.	R,G,B color component	$N(\mu, \sum)$	μ : RGB value, e.g,[255, 0, 0] for red $\sum$: diagonal matrix with 100 in diagonal
Size	big small	Area of object bounding box: A	$N(\mu, \sigma^2)$	type dependent, not in seed knowledge
Relative Size	bigger smaller	Difference in A	$N(\mu, \sigma^2)$	μ : 300 for bigger, -300 for smaller σ^2 : 100
Position	left_1 right_1	X, Y coordinates	$N(\mu, \sum)$	μ : [150, 150] for left, [250, 150] for right $\sum$: diagonal matrix with 100 in diagonal
Relative Position	left_2 right_2	Difference in X, Y	$N(\mu, \sum)$	μ : [-100, 0] for left,[100, 0] for right $\sum$: diagonal matrix with 100 in diagonal

Table 1: Context dependent words with grounded semantic functions

functions as Gaussian functions. Table 1 shows different types of words (describing the semantic type of objects and the size, color, and position attributes) and their corresponding grounded semantic functions. For example, words describing *size* information are type dependent. means that for each size word, there is a type dependent mean and variance. "big" for the type "car" and "big" for the type "apple" means differently. In our future work, we will take into account more contexts as suggested in [7]. For the words that describe the object's type, the meaning of the word is represented by a set of known objects of that particular type (e.g., the ID of the visual object of apples ID_1 and ID_3 are attached to the word *apple*).

Note that in Table 1, a column under the heading *seed knowledge* provides some examples of reasonable parameter instantiations based on our domain. The specific values here are not important. This could represent any kind of seed knowledge an agent may have in their initial lexicon. This seed knowledge can be updated continuously through interaction by interleaving referential grounding and word acquisition and become more tailored to the current context. Our goal in this paper is to examine this effect.

3.2 Referential Grounding via Graph Matching

Referential grounding is a process that identifies intended referents in the physical environment which are referred in linguistic utterances. From an artificial agent's point of view, it receives two types of information. One type is the utterance from its human partner. This utterance may contain various referring expressions and their semantic relations. The other type of information is the perception from the visual world. Referential grounding in the physical world is in fact mapping linguistic information onto the perception of the visual world. Graph-based representations and graph-matching algorithms are natural solutions to this problem. We can represent the language perception as a *language graph* and the visual perception as a *vision graph*. Then the referential grounding becomes finding the best match from the language graph to the vision graph.

3.2.1 Graph-based Representation

Graph-based approaches have been applied previously in reference resolution [5, 4] and referring expression generation [13]. Here, we use Attribute relational graphs(ARGs) [23] to capture language perception and visual perception.

Language Graph
A language graph encodes the information about the referential expressions and their relations as expressed in an utterance. In the language graph, each node represents a referring expression and captures semantic information extracted from the referring expression such as the intended object's semantic type, color, size and position in the scene. Each edge represents relations between the referring expressions, which captures the relationship between intended referents such as their relative size and relative spatial position in the scene. The language graph is created solely based on linguistic utterances (without considering visual scenes). To extract semantic information and relations from utterances, a grammar-based natural language parser [16] is used. Figure 2(a) shows an example of a language graph for the utterance *the red ball is bigger than the white ball to its right.*

Note that, in this language graph, the semantic information is attached with its corresponding grounded semantic functions (see Section 3.1). For example, in the node representing "white ball", the grounded semantics for the word "white" is unknown (meaning, the parameter for this color term is not known). The grounded semantics for the type "ball" is the set of objects that are known to the agent as *ball*, in this case, the object ID of the red ball in the scene. These grounded semantic attachments provide a bridge to map the language graph to the vision graph.

Vision Graph
A vision graph encodes the information about the perceived objects in the visual scene. Each node represents a detected object and captures the object's visual attributes such as size, color, and position. Each edge represents the relations such as relative size and position between objects in the scene. The attributes and relations in the vision graph are often real values. e.g., the color attribute takes value in the RGB color space; the size attribute takes the detected size of the object's bounding box as its value (e.g.,691 pixels in the bounding box); the relative size relation takes the difference between two objects' bounding boxes as its value. We applied the Template Matching algorithm [1] in OpenCV to detect the objects in the scene. Figure 1 shows an example scene after applying the template matching algorithm. Based on the recognition results, every object's attributes (size, etc.) and relations(relative size, etc.) to all other objects are extracted to build a vision graph as shown in Figure 2(b).

3.2.2 Graph Matching

Graph matching has been applied to reference resolution in a conversational interface [5] and most recently in mediating shared perceptual basis in situated dialogue [15]. In contrast to [15] where beam search is applied to find a solution, here our implementation is a direct extension of [5]. The difference between our application here compared to [5] is that we aim at physical world interaction where the agent does not have a complete knowledge of its environment. Because of the agent's limited perceptual capability, the

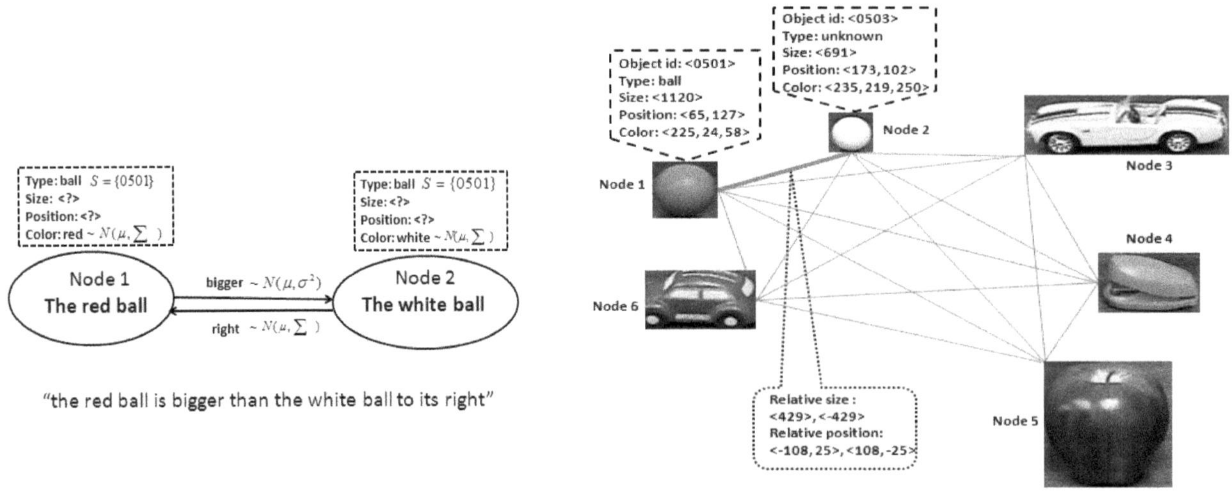

(a) Language graph for the utterance

(b) Vision graph for the scene shown in Figure 1

Figure 2: An example of a language graph and a vision graph

vision graph only captures low level representations and potentially error prone symbolic information.

Let $G_l =< \{n_i\}, \{e_{ij}\} >$ represent a language graph, where $\{n_i\}$ is the node set and $\{e_{i,j}\}$ is the edge set. Let $G_v =< \{\eta_x\}, \{\xi_{x,y}\} >$ be a vision graph where $\{\eta_x\}$ are nodes and $\{\xi_{x,y}\}$ are edges. The goal is to find the best match from the language graph to the vision graph which maximizes the following objective function:

$$Q(G_l, G_v) = \sum_i \sum_j P(n_i, \eta_j) NodeCom(n_i, \eta_j) + \sum_i \sum_j \sum_x \sum_y P(n_i, \eta_x) P(n_j, \eta_y) EdgeCom(e_{i,j}, \xi_{x,y}) \tag{1}$$

where $Q(G_l, G_v)$ measures the overall compatibility between the language graph and the vision graph. $P(n_i, \eta_x)$ is the matching probability between a node in the language graph n_i and a node in the vision graph η_x. $NodeCom$ measures the compatibility between nodes and $EdgeCom$ measures compatibility between edges.

As mentioned earlier, information captured in each node and each edge is different between the language graph and the vision graph. More specifically, the language graph only has symbolic representations and the vision graph has lower level numerical information of the environment. One significant difference between this work and [5] is that, in [5], the compatibility functions can be easily defined because the world itself is encoded symbolically. Here we introduce grounded semantic functions attached to lexicons(see Section 3.1) to implement the node compatibility function (i.e., *NodeCom*) and the edge compatibility function (i.e., *EdgeCom*). These grounded semantic functions bridge the gap between the symbolic representations from linguistic processing and the low level visual representations of the world.

Each node encodes a set of node attributes. Node compatibility is defined as a weighted sum of the compatibility between these attributes ($NodeAttrCom$). For example, to measure the attribute *color* between a node in the language graph and a node in the vision graph, we can simply plug in the numerical values to the grounded semantic functions. Suppose n_1 represents *Node 1 "the red ball"* in the language graph and η_2 represents the *Node 2 (the white ball)* in the vision graph as in Figure 2, the following equation measures their color compatibility:

$$NodeAttrCom(color, n_1, \eta_2) = N([235, 219, 250] | (\mu, \sum) \sim red) \tag{2}$$

This type of attribute comparison is applied to other attributes such as *size, position*, etc. Although currently the weights are set equally, they can be used to represent different contributions from those attributes in the future.

Similarly, each edge encodes a set of edge attributes. Edge compatibility is defined as a weighted sum of the compatibility between edge attributes ($EdgeAttrCom$). For example, as shown in Figure 2, the actual numerical values for relative size and relative position will be plugged in the grounded semantic functions (i.e., Gaussian models) attached to "bigger" and "right".

To find the solution to Equation 1, an graduated assignment algorithm for graph-matching [8] is applied. This algorithm reduces the complexity by searching for sub-optimal solutions. It yields $O(lm)$, where l and m are the number of links in each graph respectively. When the algorithm converges, $P(n_i, \eta_x)$ gives the matching probability between the language node n_i and the vision node η_x that maximizes the overall compatibility function. Given this matrix, we are able to assign each referring expression (in the language graph) the most probable entities in the vision graph.

3.3 Word Acquisition

As described in Section 3.1, each word is attached with a grounded semantic function. Grounded semantic functions are in fact model templates that come with parameters. Given these templates, word acquisition is a process that automatically estimates or updates the parameters in these models based on continuous interaction with the user. Sometimes, the system may not have any knowledge about a particular word to start with. Therefore, the parameters to the grounded semantic function associated with that word will only be acquired through online interaction. Some other times, the system may have seed knowledge to start with. The seed knowledge may be acquired from previous experience. Since many words in the lexicon could be context or scene dependent such as the *color* words, these seed knowledge may need to be updated by revising the values of the parameters to those most suitable for the current

Example utterances with one referring expression:
- a small yellow pear on the left.
- a green pepper on the right.

Example utterances with two referring expressions:
- the small yellow pear on the left is bigger than the red apple.
- the big black stapler is to the left of the green pepper.

Example utterances with three referring expressions:
- the yellow pear to the left of the red apple is smaller than the car
- the black stapler bigger than the yellow pear is to the left of the green pepper.

Figure 3: An example scene with corresponding example utterances

situation. Therefore, automated word acquisition is very important for physical world interactions.

In our current investigation, for the words describing object types (e.g., *apple*, *ball*, etc.), their grounded semantic functions are represented by a set of known objects with that particular type. During word acquisition, when a new object of the same type is grounded, the new object will be added to the set. In other words, updating *type* words are not based on Gaussian distribution. We are simply adding the object as an instance to a particular type, i.e., labeling the object with type label. When the same object is perceived again, its semantic type would likely to be recognized. Although we intend to investigate different forms of semantic functions for different types of words in the future, most of our functions are currently based on Gaussian models as shown in Table 1. In the word acquisition process, the mean and variance of those models are sequentially updated each time as new observation arrives. The specific updating is a combination of previous mean and variance and the value from the new observation. For example, the current mean at nth observation is updated as:

$$\widehat{\mu}^{n}_{MLE} = \frac{1}{n}x_n + (1 - \frac{1}{n})\widehat{\mu}^{n-1}_{MLE} \qquad (3)$$

4. EMPIRICAL EVALUATION

To evaluate the graph-based approach in physical interaction and examine inter-relations between word acquisition and referential grounding, we conducted a series of experiments. A total of 12 scenes are created where each scene contains six objects. For each scene, a set of utterances are provided by an experimenter that describe objects and their relations in the scene. We started with this simplified setting to focus our scope. Because the underlying linguistic structures for utterances can be completely covered by our grammar, this will allow us to focus on the inter-relation between word acquisition and referential grounding, as well as how they might influence each other with respect to an imperfect visual world.

An example scene and corresponding example utterances are shown in Figure 3. In total, we have 385 utterances. Among these utterances, 66 of them only have one referring expression and refer to one object in the scene; 245 of them have two referring expressions and describe two objects and their relations; and 74 of them describe three objects and their relations. Note that language graphs built for these utterances with different number of referring expressions have different number of nodes in the graph.

In the following sections, we first evaluate how well the graph-based approach relies on the semantic relations to known objects to ground unknown objects in the environment. We then examine the role of word acquisition in referential grounding and vice versa. In all these evaluations, we report *accuracy* of referential grounding performance, which is the percentage of referring expressions that are correctly grounded to objects in the environment.

4.1 Results: Referential Grounding for Unknown Objects

Given a scene, human partners may have a perfect perception and be able to describe the scene with objects and their relations (as shown in Figure 3. However, the artificial agent may not have a complete knowledge and perception about this scene. Some objects in the scene may be unknown (i.e., unrecognizable) to the agent. Our first evaluation is to assess how well the graph-based approach can be used to ground those unknown objects when they are mentioned in the utterances. If an object is unknown to an agent, it means the following: (1) the object is detectable, but the agent is not clear what it is. Thus in the agent's vision graph of the scene, that object's semantic type information is unknown (since it is not recognized). However, the other types of lower level numerical information about the object (e.g., size, position, etc) can still be obtained by the computer vision algorithms. (2) In the agent's lexicon, the agent does not have that particular object associated with the type word. Thus, that object (i.e., ID) is not included in the grounded semantic function for any type words. Therefore, in our evaluation, we can simulate different unknown objects by (1) removing the object's semantic type information from the agent's vision graph; (2) remove the object's id from grounded semantic functions of all type words. Based on this strategy, we can randomly simulate any unknown objects from a scene at different degrees. Note that although our current evaluation only included unrecognized/unknown objects rather than misrecognized objects, the graph-matching approach is intended to be general and can support other types of computer vision errors such as misrecognized objects and missing objects due to incorrect background segmentation.

Figure 4 shows the average grounding performance of unknown objects from 1000 trials. In each trial, we randomly select 30% (2 objects) or 70% (4 objects) of objects as unknown from each scene. We apply the graph-matching algorithm on the same set of utterances associated with each scene. We only use the subset of utterances which contain expressions referring to unknown objects in this evaluation. The language graphs automatically created for these utterances contain different number of nodes because these utterances contain different number of referring expressions. We report the grounding performance by grouping the results based on the number of nodes in language graphs. Since any subset of nodes in a language graph could refer to unknown objects, we further group the results based on how many unknown objects are referred to in the utterances. Figure 4 reports when 30% or 70% of unknown objects in the vision graph, how well our approach resolves expressions referring to those unknown objects when the expressions occur in a language graph with one node, two nodes, and three nodes respectively.

As can be seen from Figure 4(a), when one unknown object is referred to in each utterance, the more context there is, the better grounding performance is achieved. For example, in the case of 70% unknown objects in the scene, the performance based on one-node language graph is 40.8%, two-node graph is 63.4%, and three-node graph is 70.5%. All the differences are statistically significant

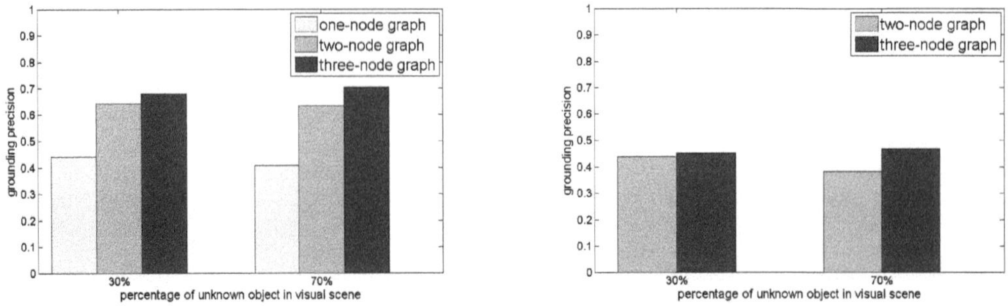

(a) **one node in language graph referring to an unknown object** (b) **two nodes in language graph referring to two unknown objects**

Figure 4: Performance for grounding to one and two unknown objects in the scene

(Paired t-test) based on the 1000 runs ($p < 0.001$). The same results apply to the case of 30% unknown objects in the scene. When two unknown objects are referred to in each utterance, we also observe a similar trend in Figure 4(b): performance from three-node language graph is better than the performance from two-node language graph ($p < 0.001$). These results demonstrate that, the more relations with known objects can be captured by the graphs, the better performance can be obtained to ground referring expressions to those unknown objects. This observation has interesting implications in physical world interaction. For example, an agent can be designed to express what it knows about the environment and encourage human partners to use those known objects as references in order to learn about unknown objects.

4.2 Results: Between Word Acquisition and Referential Grounding

Our assumption is that through continuous interactions with its human partners, the agent should acquire better representations of word meanings, which in turn should improve referential grounding. To validate this hypothesis, we simulate different amount of knowledge in the lexicon at three levels: (1) with a complete seed knowledge (specified in Table 1) where parameters to the grounded semantic functions are initialized; (2) with 50% of seed knowledge (i.e., only 50% of grounded semantic functions have initialized parameters and the other 50% with unknown parameters); and (3) with 0% seed knowledge (i.e., all the parameters are unknown and everything has to be learned from the beginning). These different levels aim to simulate different amount of initial knowledge an agent may have when it enters a novel environment. We further separate the entire data set (385 utterances) into two sets: a training set (with 193 utterances) which is used to update meaning representation (i.e., the parameters in the grounded semantic functions as described in Section 3.3) and a testing set (with 192 utterances) which is used to evaluate referential grounding performance as a result of automated word acquisition from the training data.

In order to reduce the effect of other confounding factors (e.g., the order of training examples, the type of seed knowledge, etc), we ran 500 trials. In each trial, we randomly picked the seed knowledge (in the 50% case) and randomly ordered the utterances used in the training data. To evaluate the role of word acquisition on referential grounding and vice versa, we conducted the experiment in the following three conditions:

- Static knowledge base: use initial lexicon, no word acquisition (i.e., no updating parameters). This condition serves as the baseline.
- Dynamic knowledge base: the initial lexicon is used by the graph-matching approach to ground references for utterances in the training set. The grounded referents are used to update parameters in the lexicon. This condition corresponds to our proposed investigation that iteratively updates the knowledge base by interleaving word acquisition and referential grounding.
- Dynamic knowledge base with ground truth: the initial lexicon is updated by the annotated ground truth for referential grounding in the training set. This condition shows the upper-bound performance.

For each of these conditions, we record referential grounding accuracy on the testing data after incrementally processing each utterance in the training data. The average performance on referential grounding for the testing data over 500 trials based on the above three conditions is reported in Figure 5.

These results indicate that, within our expectation, the performance of grounding strongly correlates with the amount of knowledge in the initial lexicon. Grounding performance is continuously improving when word acquisition is applied. Even in the condition where the initial lexicon has all the seed knowledge, continuously updating the parameters for grounded semantic functions further improve grounding performance for the testing data. These results indicate that, when encountering a new environment, to facilitate better grounding performance, the meanings of words need to be updated in favor of the new environment.

In addition, as shown in Figure 5, the performance under the condition of *dynamic knowledge base with ground truth* always outperforms the performance under the condition of *dynamic knowledge base* based on automated grounding. This further confirms our assumption that better referential grounding leads to more accurate acquisition of word meanings, which in turn leads to better grounding of subsequent references.

We are also interested in seeing how the acquisition of different types of words may affect the referential grounding performance. Similar to the experiment set-up described above, here we remove a particular type of words from our initial lexicon (i.e., the corresponding parameters in the grounded semantic functions are not initialized). We report the similar grounding performance on the testing data over 500 trials in Figure 6. These results indicate that the *position* words and the *color* words can be reliably acquired during continuous interaction. The *type* words are very critical for grounding. As shown in the figure, the baseline without knowledge of *type* words performs very poorly. The meanings of *type* words are also very difficult to acquire if no object in the environment is

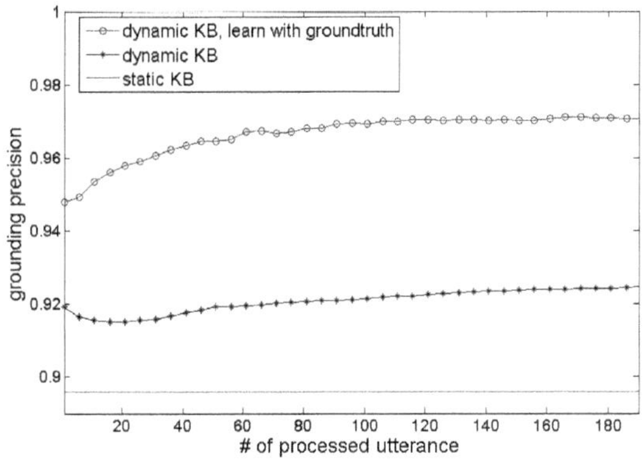

(a) Initial lexicon with 100% seed knowledge

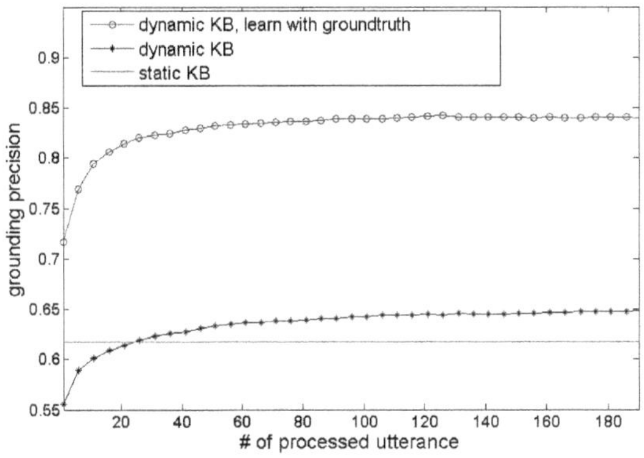

(b) Initial lexicon with 50% seed knowledge

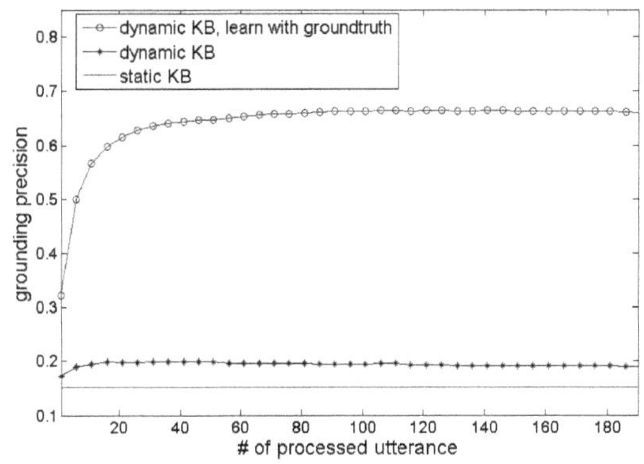

(c) Initial lexicon with 0% seed knowledge

Figure 5: Referential grounding accuracy based on different amount of seed knowledge in the initial lexicon and with (or without) incorporation of word acquisition

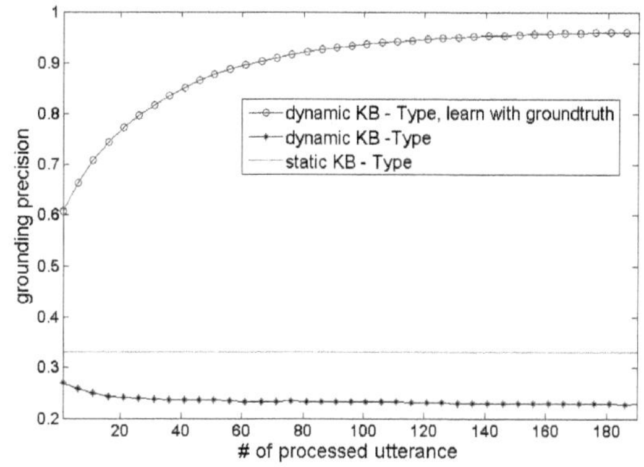

(a) Initial lexicon without seed knowledge of type words

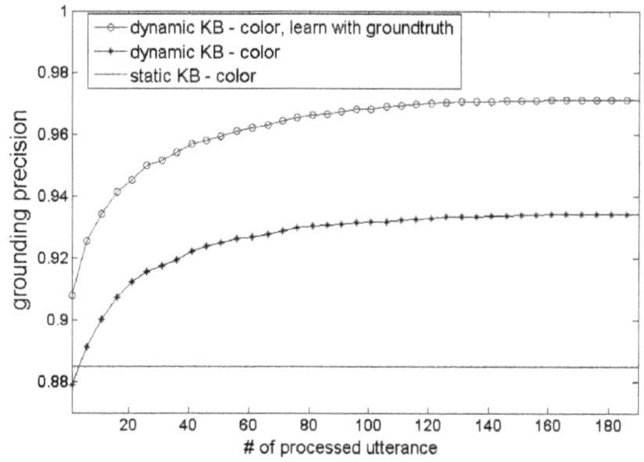

(b) Initial lexicon without seed knowledge of color words

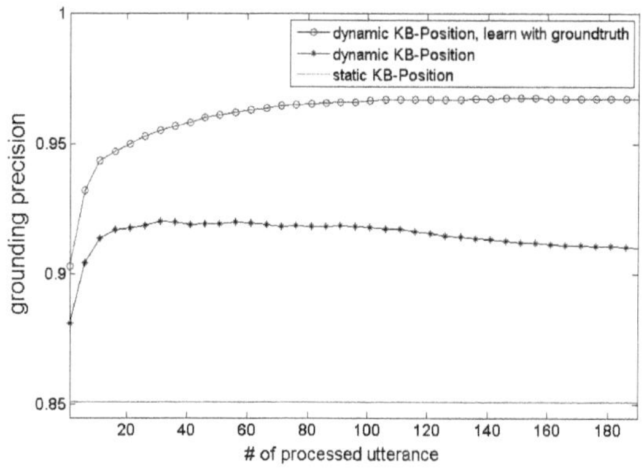

(c) Initial lexicon without seed knowledge of position and relative position words

Figure 6: Referential grounding accuracy based on different type of seed knowledge in the initial lexicon and with (or without) incorporation of word acquisition

known (i.e., the semantic type of the object can be correctly recognized). As shown in Figure 6(a), when meanings of all *type* words are not available, referential grounding based on all other words are not sufficient. It even performs worse than the baseline. However, any supervision, as demonstrated by the results from the third condition where ground truth grounding for the training data is applied, can significantly improve grounding performance for the testing data. This indicates that when the environment is completely unknown (i.e. every object is new and cannot be correctly recognized), any feedback on automated grounding can provide valuable information for learning about the environment and the words. This points to the important role of dialogue in physical world interaction.

5. CONCLUSION AND FUTURE WORK

This paper describes an investigation on integrating word acquisition and referential grounding for physical world interaction where an agent/robot does not have perfect knowledge and perception of the shared environment. In particular, we have applied a graph-based approach for referential grounding. Our empirical results have shown that by capturing rich information from both the context of language and surroundings of the shared physical environment, this approach can potentially ground unknown objects in the environment. Our results further demonstrate that continuously acquiring meanings of words that are tailored to an environment can potentially improve referential grounding performance. In addition, better referential grounding will allow acquiring more accurate meanings of words, which can further improve referential grounding. These results have important implications in designing artificial agents that can engage in language based interaction with humans in a physical world.

Our future work includes three directions. First, our current grounded semantic functions are mostly Gaussian models with simple sequential updating rules. Exploring appropriate representations for different types of words can be beneficial. Second, the current graph-matching algorithm also has limitations. For example, it cannot adequately represent group of objects and grouping information which could occur in real-world interaction. An augmented representation and matching strategy will be pursued. Lastly, our current work only focuses on information from one side, i.e., humans provide sequences of utterances without any feedback from the agent. However, referential grounding should be considered as an interactive process. Our future work will explore how to combine the graph-based approach with dialogue management for efficient grounding.

6. ACKNOWLEDGMENT

This work was supported by IIS-1050004 and CNS-0957039 from National Science Foundation and N00014-11-1-0410 from Office of Naval Research. We also thank anonymous reviewers for their valuable comments and suggestions.

7. REFERENCES

[1] G. Bradski and A. Kaehler. *Learning OpenCV*. O'Reilly Media, 2008.

[2] T. Brick and M. Scheutz. Incremental natural language processing for hri. In *Proceedings of the ACM/IEEE international conference on Human-robot interaction*, HRI '07, pages 263–270, New York, NY, USA, 2007. ACM.

[3] D. Byron, T. Mampilly, V. Sharma, and T. Xu. Utilizing visual attention for cross-modal coreference interpretation. In *In Proceedings of Fifth International and Interdisciplinary Conference on Modeling and Using Context (CONTEXT-05*, pages 83–96. Spring, 2005.

[4] J. Y. Chai, P. Hong, and M. Zhou. A probabilistic approach for reference resolution in multimodal user interfaces. *Proceedings of the 9th ACM International Conference on Intelligent User Interfaces(IUI)*, pages 70–77, 2004.

[5] J. Y. Chai, P. Hong, M. X. Zhou, and Z. Prasov. Optimization in multimodal interpretation. In *Proceedings of the 42nd Annual Meeting on Association for Computational Linguistics*, ACL '04, Stroudsburg, PA, USA, 2004.

[6] H. H. Clark and D. Wilkes-Gibbs. Referring as a collaborative process. *Cognition*, 22:1–39, 1986.

[7] K. S. Ebeling and S. A. Gelman. Children's use of context in interpreting big and little. *Child Development*, 65:1178–1192, 1994.

[8] S. Gold and A. Rangarajan. A graduated assignment algorithm for graph-matching. *IEEE Transactions on Pattern Analysis and Machine Intelligence*, 18:377 - 388, 1996.

[9] P. Gorniak and D. Roy. Grounded semantic composition for visual scenes. *Journal of Artificial Intelligence Research*, 21:429–470, 2004.

[10] P. Gorniak and D. Roy. Situated language under-standing as filtering perceived affordances. *Cognitive Science*, 31:197–231, 2007.

[11] T. T. Hills, J. Maouene, B. Riordan, and L. B. Smith. The associative structure of language: Contextual diversity in early word learning. *Journal of Memory and Language*, 63:259–273, 2010.

[12] J. Kelleher and J. van Genabith. Visual salience and reference resolution in simulated 3-d environments. *Artificial Intelligence Review*, 21:253–267, 2004.

[13] E. Krahmer, S. Erk, and A. Verleg. Graph-based generation of referring expressions. *Computational Linguistics*, 29:53–72, 2003.

[14] G.-J. M. Kruijff, P. Lison, T. Benjamin, H. Jacobsson, and N. Hawes. Incremental, multi-level processing for comprehending situated dialogue in human-robot interaction. In *Symposium on Language and Robots*, 2007.

[15] C. Liu, R. Fang, and J. Y. Chai. Towards mediating shared perceptual basis in situated dialogue. *The 13th Annual SIGDIAL Meeting on Discourse and Dialogue*, pages 140–149, 2012.

[16] E. Loper and S. Bird. Nltk: The natural language toolkit. In *Proceedings of the ACL Workshop on Effective Tools and Methodologies for Teaching Natural Language Processing and Computational Linguistics*, 2002.

[17] Z. Prasov and J. Y. Chai. What's in a gaze? the role of eye-gaze in reference resolution in multimodal conversational interfaces. In *Proceedings of the 13th international conference on Intelligent user interfaces*, IUI '08, pages 20–29, New York, NY, USA, 2008.

[18] Z. Prasov and J. Y. Chai. Fusing eye gaze with speech recognition hypotheses to resolve exophoric references in situated dialogue. In *Proceedings of the 2010 Conference on Empirical Methods in Natural Language Processing*, EMNLP '10, pages 471–481, Stroudsburg, PA, USA, 2010.

[19] D. Roy. Learning visually grounded words and syntax of natural spoken language. *Evolution of Communication*, 4, 2002.

[20] D. Roy, K.-Y. Hsiao, and N. Mavridis. Mental imagery for a conversational robot. *IEEE Transactions on Systems, Man, and Cybernetics, Part B*, 34, 2004.

[21] D. Roy and A. Pentland. Learning words from sights and sounds: A computational model. *Cognitive Science*, 26:113–146, 2001.

[22] M. Scheutz, P. Schermerhorn, J. Kramer, and D. Anderson. First steps toward natural human-like HRI. *Autonomous Robots*, 22:411–42, 2007.

[23] W. Tsai and K. Fu. Error-correcting isomorphism of attributed relational graphs for pattern analysis. *IEEE Transactions on System, Man and Cybernetics*, 9:757–768, 1979.

[24] C. Yu and D. H. Ballard. A multimodal learning interface for grounding spoken language in sensorimotor experience. *ACM Transactions on Applied Perception*, 1, 2004.

Effects of Modality on Virtual Button Motion and Performance

Adam Faeth
Iowa State University
1620 Howe Hall
Ames, Iowa, USA
adfaeth@iastate.edu

Chris Harding
Iowa State University
1620 Howe Hall
Ames, Iowa, USA
charding@iastate.edu

ABSTRACT

The simple action of pressing a button is a multimodal interaction with an interesting depth of complexity. As the development of computer interfaces supporting 3D tasks progresses, there is a need to understand how users will interact with virtual buttons that generate multimodal feedback. Using a phone number dialing task on a virtual keypad, this study examined the effects of visual, auditory, and haptic feedback combinations on task performance and on the motion of individual button presses. The results suggest that the resistance of haptic feedback alone was not enough to prevent participants from pressing the button farther than necessary. Reinforcing haptic feedback with visual or auditory feedback shortened the depth of the presses significantly. However, the shallower presses that occurred with trimodal feedback may have led participants to release some buttons too early, which may explain an unexpected increase in mistakes where the participant missed digits from the phone number.

Categories and Subject Descriptors

H.5.2 [**Information Interfaces and Presentation**]: User Interfaces—*haptic I/O*

General Terms

Human Factors, Experimentation, Design

Keywords

Virtual buttons, multimodal feedback, haptic force-feedback, evaluation, performance

1. INTRODUCTION

Individuals' everyday familiarity with pressing mechanical buttons covers an interesting depth of complexity in what appears to be a simple multimodal interaction. When the user presses a button, the key travels a short distance before closing the electrical circuit to actuate the button. During this travel, the user can feel the resistance of the button and the click sensation, see the key traveling, and hear an actuation sound. This experience forms the expectations that users have when interacting with virtual buttons.

A virtual button has at least some of the feedback generated, rather than produced by inherent mechanical components. This means the designer can control the feedback experience, even though it may be informed by experience with mechanical buttons.

In both three-dimensional and touchscreen interactions, there is an increase in the prevalence of virtual buttons. Virtual buttons used in interfaces are developed to support 3D tasks from medicine, manufacturing, geoscience, and engineering. Gestural interfaces and direct manipulation are more appropriate than buttons for some interactions such as scrolling through a large area. However, buttons retain advantages of discoverability and perceived affordance which make them integral components in an interface.

Compared to mechanical buttons, virtual buttons do not always provide the same feedback modalities and fidelity. It is not well understood whether design tradeoffs, such as omitting modalities, violates expectations users have when interacting with virtual buttons. This study examined the effect on task performance when some feedback modalities were deliberately omitted from a 3D interaction context.

2. RELATED WORK

Pressing a physical button is a multimodal experience that provides visual, audio, and haptic feedback. This study builds upon research in multimodal feedback, keyboard ergonomics, and studies of bimodal and trimodal feedback.

Keyboards are a rich source for virtual button inspiration because the buttons are designed to provide clear feedback for presses in quick succession. The ideal characteristics of shape, size, travel, and force required to actuate a keyboard button are detailed in the literature [3, 14].

The combination of tactile and kinesthetic sensory input make up the haptic system [15]. Touch is an exploratory sense, which requires the active exploration of objects to discover their properties [16]. This also applies to the use of force-feedback haptic devices to render haptic properties of virtual objects.

A desirable characteristic of a button is the haptic click sensation, a gentle rise in force as the button travels, and a sharp drop in force near the actuation point [21]. Typing on a flat surface, where they keys do not travel, decreased performance [4, 29]. This negative effect may be reduced

ICMI'12, October 22–26, 2012, Santa Monica, California, USA.

by adding audio feedback or tactile features to the flat surface [30, 27, 19].

A delay between the press and feedback from the press also hampers the use of keyboard buttons, and an irregular lag in feedback can even cause problems for skilled typists [22]. Humans are more sensitive to a visual or haptic signal that lags behind an audio signal [1, 17].

Many users prefer multimodal interactions, and multimodal feedback can reduce errors and completion times [28]. Users also react faster to multimodal signals than to unimodal signals [10, 12]. Multiple resource theory provides one explanation for how humans process signals from multiple sensory modalities. According to the 4-dimensional multiple resources model, tasks which engage different modalities are less likely to interfere with each other [36].

The addition of either audio or haptic feedback improved completion times and performance scores over visual feedback alone [2]. The addition of vibrotactile feedback can also reduce mental workload [33]. Participants in another study better remained within the walls of a maze when using bimodal and trimodal feedback compared to visual feedback alone [6].

However, when multiple modalities of feedback are combined, the effect is not always straightforward. In the McGurk effect, a strong visual cue changes the auditory perception of spoken syllables [24]. When presenting audio and visual cues together simultaneously, a user is more likely to miss the audio cue than the visual cue [5]. Similarly, one is more likely to miss a haptic cue presented with a visual cue, but this dominance diminishes when trimodal cues are provided [9].

Haptic rendering often employs an illusion where the graphical representation of the stylus remains on the surface of an object, even when the haptic device cannot render enough stiffness to prevent the users hand from penetrating the object. The strong visual cue makes the surface appear stiffer to the user than the haptic device can render [32]. Similarly, the visual displacement of a spring can influence the perceived stiffness of the spring [18]. An audio cue may also reinforce haptic sensation, but the effect may be weaker without carefully selected sounds [7, 26]. However, the dominance of vision is not absolute, the task requirements and user's attention impact the reliance on one modality over another [11, 31].

The congruence between visual, audio, and haptic properties of a button may also affect interaction. Users performed tasks faster when the haptic size of a button key matched the pitch of an audio cue [35]. Users also preferred buttons where the visual appearance matched the vibrotactile feedback of the button [13].

Although there are many studies of bimodal feedback, there are a limited number of studies which examined trimodal feedback. Of the studies that examined trimodal feedback, even fewer investigated multimodal feedback in the context of three-dimensional interaction. To help fill this gap, this study examined the effect of visual, audio, and haptic feedback from virtual buttons on the 3D motion of the button press and on task performance.

3. METHODS

The purpose of the study was to investigate the effect feedback modalities provided by a virtual button have on the motion of button press strokes, and on the task performance of the user. We designed the study to inform the following research questions:

1. How does the combination of feedback modalities affect the motion of the 3D button press?
2. Compared to trimodal feedback, how does reducing the number of feedback modalities affect task accuracy and completion time?
3. When users press a button, are they focusing on a particular type of feedback such as a visual cue?

3.1 Task

To assess the performance of virtual buttons with different feedback modalities, we asked the participants to dial random seven-digit phone numbers. Lewis et al. suggested a wider audience of participants would be more comfortable with a phone number task than a calculator task [21].

The phone numbers used in each task were calculated randomly. The algorithm first picked a random starting digit, then chose a random adjacent digit until completing the seven-digit phone number. This maintained a similar distance between the buttons for all tasks.

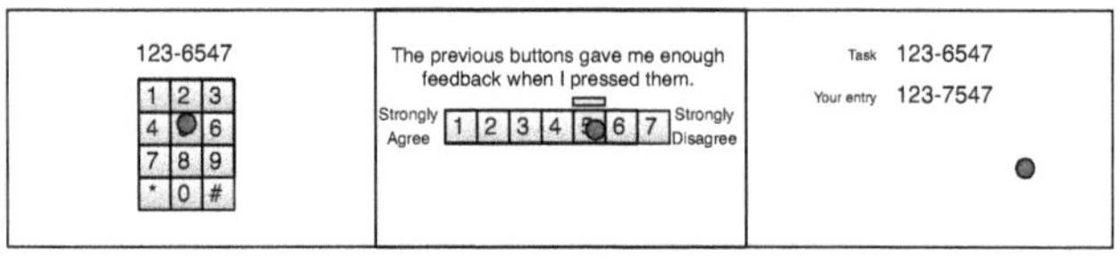

Figure 1: Phone number dialing task

The study divided the task into three parts, shown in Figure 1. The first part displayed the phone number to dial and the keypad, but did not show the digits dialed by the participant. Participants were instructed to dial the phone numbers quickly while maintaining accuracy. The participant could not see a partially dialed number on the screen, ensuring that the only feedback the participant received while dialing came from the virtual buttons.

After the participant dialed the number, the second part displayed a prompt to rate the feedback of the previous keypad, along with another set of virtual buttons for the response. The final part displayed the phone number assigned and the digits dialed by the participant.

We gave the participant feedback on the number dialed after the end of the task because in this experiment, it would lead to a mistake if the participant did not press the button far enough. Although participants had an opportunity to learn the feedback for a successful activation during training, it was possible that their average depth of a press would change over time. If we did not give the participants a realistic opportunity to make a correction during the tasks, this could lead to an inflation of errors.

3.2 Equipment

The setup of the study (Figure 2) used a PHANToM Omni to serve as a 3D input device and to generate haptic force-feedback from the buttons [23]. The PHANToM Omni has a stylus attached to a mechanical arm, and as the participant moves the stylus through the 3D reach of the arm, the device renders forces that push back against the participant's movement, creating an illusion of touching virtual objects.

Figure 2: Pressing virtual buttons

The buttons were shown on a computer monitor, providing the participant with a means of targeting the buttons and any visual feedback from the buttons. The participant wore a pair of headphones to listen for auditory feedback from the buttons. Participants were instructed to hold the Phantom in their dominant hand to press the virtual buttons, and to rest their non-dominant hand on the keyboard spacebar to advance between the three parts of each task, similar to how one might write with their dominant hand and advance the paper with their non-dominant hand [8].

3.3 Button Design

The entry keypad consisted of twelve virtual buttons arranged in a telephone layout. The buttons on the screen measured 2.5 cm square by 2.5 mm thick with a 2.0 cm travel. We chose the travel distance because participants in the pilot study reported that the haptic feedback felt too abrupt with a shorter travel. A longer travel allowed more time between the start of the feedback and reaching the bottom of the button.

The entry keypad did not have a bezel that surrounds the button keys on a physical keypad; this meant that if the participant missed the button key, the stylus would keep moving past the keypad surface. However, it would be confusing to have haptic feedback from a bezel when the buttons did not provide haptic feedback, or to have haptic feedback from a bezel only when the buttons provided haptic feedback.

Each virtual button used in the study had identical geometry and feedback characteristics. The only difference between the conditions was the presence or absence of the feedback modalities.

3.4 Button Feedback

Virtual buttons used in the study generated visual, auditory, and haptic feedback. The virtual buttons provided continuous haptic feedback to generate the feeling of a button click: a continuous rise in force, with a sharp drop at the actuation point, followed by another increasing force to cushion the bottom of the button (Figure 3). The bottom of the button travel was rendered as a solid haptic surface. When the participant touched a button with haptic feedback, the button also rendered four solid, invisible surfaces around the shaft of the button to prevent the stylus from inadvertently slipping off the button surface.

Auditory feedback from the button press played at three

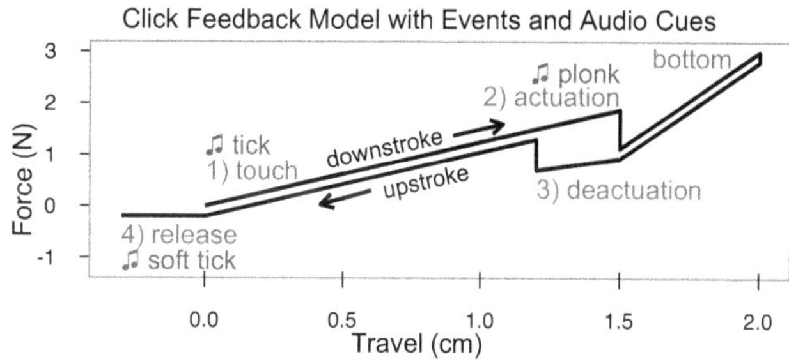

Figure 3: Force/travel for the haptic click

events during the button travel: a *tick* sound when the participant touched the button, a *plonk* sound at the actuation point, and a shorter, quieter *tick* sound when the participant released the button.

Visual feedback incorporated two components: the visible travel of the button, and a color change. As the button was pressed, the participant saw the button key recede relative to the rest of the keypad. The effect was visible without the aid of a stereoscopic display. As the button traveled to the actuation point, the color changed from gray to yellow using a linear interpolation.

Although we excluded visual feedback from some conditions, visual perception was still important for targeting virtual buttons. The participant used the keypad's graphic display and virtual stylus to target the next button to press. Once the stylus contacted the virtual button, it was important to control any visual feedback from that button.

When visual feedback was disabled, the virtual stylus appeared to stop at the button's surface while the participant's hand continued to move through the button's travel. This technique allowed virtual buttons to render haptic or auditory feedback from its travel when visual feedback was disabled. Participants were unaware of this effect and continued to press the button after the stylus appeared to stop on the button's surface.

3.5 Study Design

The study varied the presence or absence of visual, auditory, and haptic modalities to create the seven condition groups listed in Table 1. The characteristics of each modality's feedback were constant between conditions incorporating that modality.

Table 1: Experiment conditions

Condition	Abbreviation
Visual	V
Auditory	A
Haptic	H
Visual + Auditory	VA
Visual + Haptic	VH
Auditory + Haptic	AH
Visual + Auditory + Haptic	VAH

The study used a within-subjects design; each participant performed five repetitions of the task for each condition. The order of conditions were randomly assigned to each participant to control for learning and higher-order effects. To minimize the effect of participant fatigue, the study was designed to require no more than 30 minutes per participant, with a break provided between the training tasks and data collection.

3.6 Procedure

The same investigator conducted the study for all of the participants, and read from a script to aid in the consistency of the experience for each participant. After greeting the participant and explaining the study, the investigator asked participants to complete a short background questionnaire. Each participant then completed three training repetitions of the task for each of the conditions. After a short break, participants completed the five condition repetitions, and data was collected. After completing the tasks, the participants filled-out an exit survey.

3.7 Measures

For each task, we recorded the task duration, the number of errors in the dialed number, and the participant's subjective rating of the button feedback. We measured the completion time for each task between the time a participant initially touched a button after receiving the task, and the release of the last button pressed. The participant signaled completion of the task by pressing the spacebar of a physical keyboard with their non-dominant hand.

During each task, we counted the number of times a participant touched a button and then released it before the button traveled far enough to actuate the button (Figure 3). We called this measurement the number of unactuated presses during each task.

For each task, we calculated the number of digits that the participant inserted, deleted, or replaced from the assigned seven-digit phone number using the Wagner-Fisher algorithm [34]. For example, to change the sequence 123-6547 into 123-564 requires a two-digit replacement of 65 with 56, and deleting the digit 7. We also calculated the total number of insert, delete, and replacement operations, which we called total errors. This is also called the *Levenshtein distance* between the two sequences of phone numbers [20].

3.8 Subjective Rating

After dialing each phone number, but before seeing the phone number recorded by the virtual buttons, we asked the participant to rate the feedback on a 7-point Likert scale. The study prompted the participant with the statement: *"The previous buttons gave me enough feedback when I pressed them."* We used another virtual keypad with seven buttons arranged in a single line, and used the same feedback modalities from the task's condition. We chose to record the Likert feedback using another virtual keypad so that the participant could maintain one hand on the PHANToM and one hand advancing the task.

3.9 Measuring the Motion of Presses

During each button press, we also recorded the position of the stylus and any force rendered by the button click over the elapsed time of the press. Since humans can perceive variations in haptic feedback over very short periods of time, haptic rendering tries to achieve a minimum rate of 1000 Hz. To accurately capture the participant's haptic experience during each button press, we used a sub-millisecond precision timer [25]. Since the haptic rendering was not performed by a real-time system, we observed that between 1500 and 2500 samples from the haptic thread were collected every second.

3.10 Participants

Twenty participants (9 female and 11 male) volunteered to participate in the study; their ages ranged between 19 and 42 years old (median 29). One participant reported color blindness, but reported being able to distinguish between the gray and yellow colors used in the visual feedback. The remaining participants did not report conditions that might impair their ability to see, feel, or hear the button feedback.

Two of the participants reported their arm started to feel fatigued from holding their hand in the air to interact with the haptic device. These two participants opted not to take the break offered between training and recorded trials.

Seven of the participants reported previous experience with haptic devices such as the PHANToM, and three reported using a haptic device at least weekly. Five of the participants reported using a device with a stylus at least once a week. All of the participants used a cell phone several times throughout the day, and fifteen reported their cell phone had a touchscreen.

4. RESULTS

We manipulated the presence or absence of three feedback modalities while participants dialed a phone number on a virtual keypad, resulting in one independent variable with seven combinations of feedback modalities. During each task, we measured the number of errors, the number of unactuated presses, the time on task, and the participant's subjective rating of the feedback. We also measured the motion of the stylus during presses and calculated the maximum depth and mean velocity for individual presses.

4.1 Errors

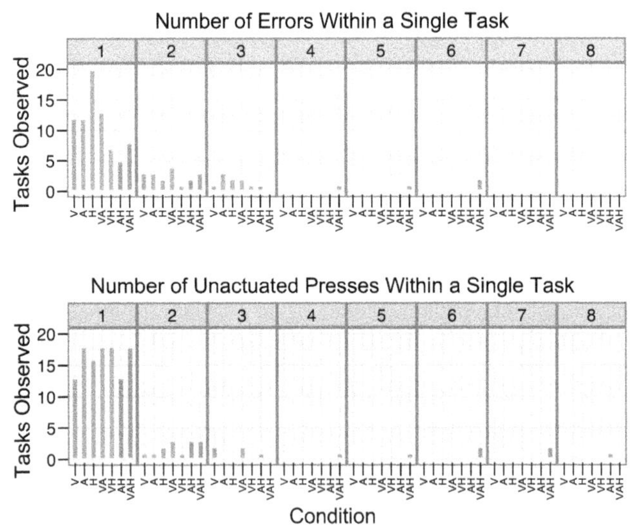

Figure 4: Errors and unactuated presses

Total errors for the conditions are summarized in Figure 4. A repeated-measures ANOVA revealed no significant effect of condition on total errors ($F_{6,114}$=1.289, p=0.268). Similarly, the effect of the condition on the insert and replace errors was not significant. However, a repeated-measures ANOVA did reveal a significant effect of the condition on the number of delete errors, when the participant missed a phone number digit ($F_{6,114}$=3.141, p=0.007). A post hoc

Tukey HSD test with a Holm adjustment revealed a significant increase in the delete errors between the trimodal feedback condition and each other condition, but no other significant differences between pairs of conditions ($\alpha = 0.05$).

This suggests that participants missed phone number digits more frequently when the buttons presented trimodal feedback than in any other condition (Figure 5). A Pearson's R test showed a significant correlation between deletion errors occurring during the trimodal condition and unactuated presses (R=0.69, $p<0.001$). The correlation between deletion errors and unactuated presses across all conditions was lower (R=0.55, $p<0.001$). The results suggest many of the deletion errors that occurred in the trimodal condition were unactuated presses and not simply errors where the participant skipped the digit completely.

4.2 Time on Task

The time on task for conditions is summarized in Figure 5. A repeated-measures ANOVA revealed a significant effect of the condition on completion time of the task ($F_{6,114}=5.097$, $p<0.001$). A post hoc Tukey HSD with a Holm adjustment test showed time on task was shorter for VH compared to V and H; shorter for AH compared to V; and shorter for VAH compared to V and H ($\alpha = 0.05$). There were no significant differences between the other conditions.

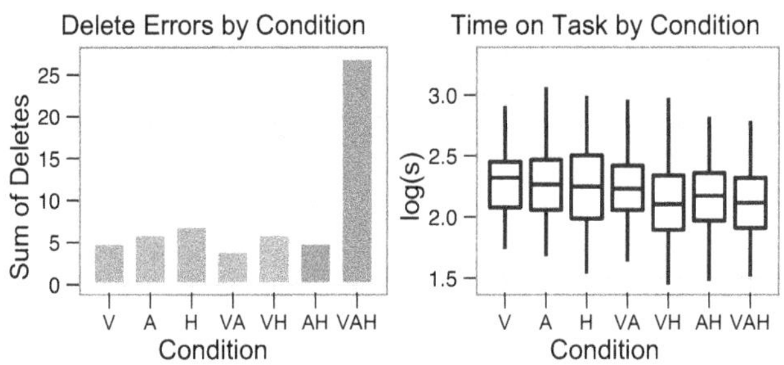

Figure 5: Left: Sum of delete errors in each condition. **Right:** Time on Task for each condition.

The bimodal combination of VH feedback reduced time on task compared to both unimodal V and H conditions. The trimodal condition also showed faster completion times than either unimodal V or A feedback. The bimodal combination of AH feedback also reduced completion time compared to the unimodal V condition.

This suggests that although haptic feedback alone did not improve completion time, bimodal and trimodal conditions including haptic feedback did improve completion times over visual feedback alone. One possible reason is that the haptic feedback paired with other modalities helped to stop the participant's hand at the bottom of the button press, allowing them to move on to the next button quickly.

4.3 Subjective Rating

After each task, we asked participants to rate the feedback provided by the virtual buttons; a summary of their responses appears in Figure 6. A repeated-measures ANOVA revealed a significant effect of the condition on the participant's subjective rating ($F_{6,114}=23.525$, $p<0.001$). A post hoc Tukey HSD test with a Holm adjustment revealed a significant preference for the bimodal and trimodal conditions shown in Table 2. Condition pairs that are not listed in table Table 2 were not significantly different ($\alpha = 0.05$).

Table 2: Subjective preferences

Preference		Over Conditions
VAH	>	{ V, A, H, VA, AH }
VH	>	{ V, A, H, VA }
VA	>	{ V, A }
AH	>	{ V, A, H }

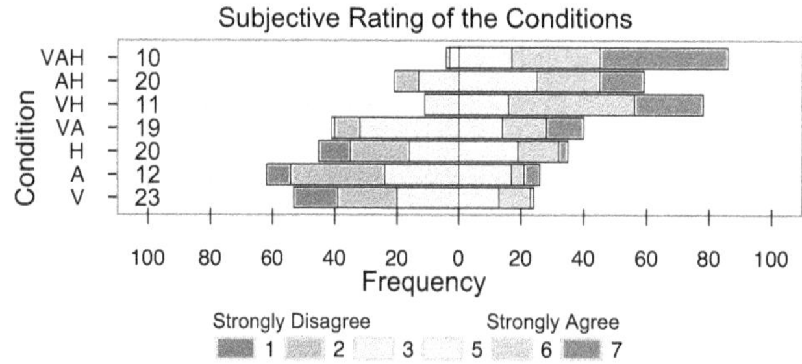

Figure 6: Subjective rating of the conditions. The numbers on the left show the frequency of neutral ratings.

4.4 Effect of Modalities on Task Success

The study also investigated whether a participant's focus on a particular modality affected the successful completion of a task. Past research suggests that attention has an effect on a user's reliance on one modality [31]. We did not ask participants about attention directly, but five participants commented they were paying attention to one modality when provided an opportunity to comment on the tasks.

"I think that visual is more effective for me. When I see the color change, I know I have pressed the button I meant to press" (P14).

"I liked having the visual feedback—the ones that didn't do that, I was concerned whether I pressed it, or I had slipped onto a different button" (P19).

"Visual seemed to be the only 'definitive' feedback" (P2).

"In the haptic-only ones, I wasn't sure how hard to press because there was no visual cue that you'd pressed the button" (P12).

"Midway through [the tasks], I figured out how far I needed to press the button using the audio and visual cues as a clarification" (P4). In this case, the participant reported paying attention to proprioception and using the audio and visual cues for reinforcement.

Despite these statements, the data for these participants shows no clear difference in task success between modalities (Figure 7). To investigate whether any of the participants were more successful with a single modality, we performed a logistic regression for each one. The logistic regression model used the presence of the modalities during the task's condition to predict task success. We performed a Chi-squared test on the logistic regression model for each participant, and rejected any model that failed to meet an α of 0.05.

We only found two incidences where the presented modalities predicted whether the participant would successfully complete the tasks (Table 3). P3 was more likely to succeed when haptic feedback was present than when either auditory or visual feedback occurred. The difference between visual-audio feedback was not significant. P15 was more likely to succeed when visual feedback was present than when haptic

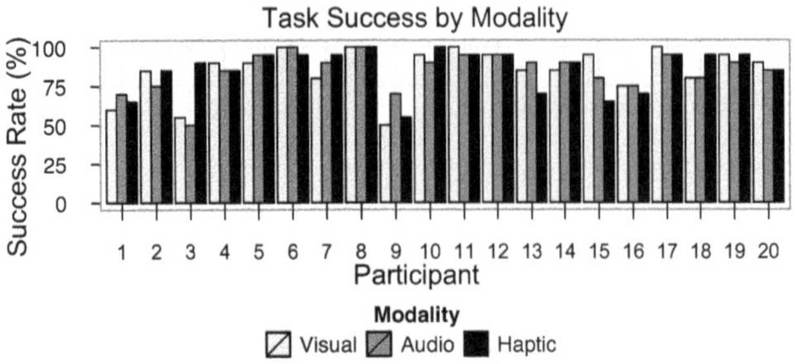

Figure 7: Success rates for each participant

Table 3: Predicting success with modalities

	Modality	Est.	*SE*	Z	*p*
P3[1]	Haptic	2.197	0.745	2.948	0.003
	Visual	-1.997	0.870	-2.294	0.022
	Auditory	-2.197	0.869	-2.528	0.012
P15[2]	Visual	2.944	1.026	2.870	0.004
	Auditory	-1.558	1.168	-1.334	0.182
	Haptic	-2.325	1.128	-2.062	0.039

[1] χ^2(2, N=60)=9.44, p=0.009. Log Lik. -34.13 df=3.
[2] χ^2(2, N=60)=6.19, p=0.045. Log Lik. -26.93 df=3.

feedback was present. The difference between visual-audio and audio-haptic modalities was not significant for P15.

4.5 Press Motion Characteristics

We recorded the position and force of the stylus during a total of 5,015 button presses as the participants each dialed 35 phone numbers. From the motion of the stylus, we calculated the maximum depth the button traveled and the mean absolute velocity of the button press motion.

4.5.1 *Maximum Press Depth*

A summary of maximum press depth is shown in Figure 8. A repeated-measures ANOVA showed a significant effect of the condition on the maximum depth of the press ($F_{6,114}$=11.066, p<0.001). A post hoc Tukey HSD test with a Holm adjustment showed significant differences between the VH, AH, and VAH conditions (Table 4). The remaining condition pairs did not have significant differences (α=0.05).

Table 4: Press depth comparison

Shallower Press		Deeper Press
VAH	<	{ V, A, H, VA, AH }
VH	<	{ V, A, H, VA }
AH	<	{ H }

Although the resistance of haptic feedback did not appear to constrain the depth of the button travel alone, the addition of visual feedback significantly shortened the maximum depth in both the VH and VAH conditions. The effect was also significant for auditory feedback in the AH and VAH conditions.

Even though maximum travel of the button was 2.0 cm, participants continued to press some buttons past 5.0 cm. In conditions where haptic feedback was present, the participants felt the bottom surface of the button at 2.0 cm. Since the haptic device cannot render perfect stiffness, it was possible for the stylus to to sink into the bottom surface of the button, or for the participant to overpower the PHANToM and break through the bottom of the button.

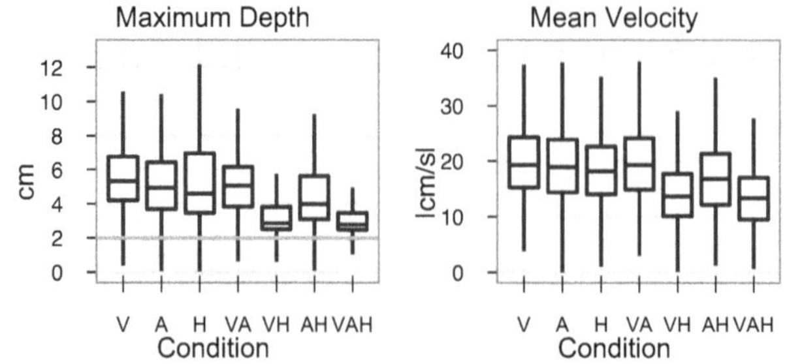

Figure 8: Press motion characteristics

4.5.2 *Mean Press Velocity*

The summary of the mean absolute velocity appears in Figure 8. A repeated-measures ANOVA showed a significant effect of the condition on the press velocity ($F_{6,114}$=20.492, p<0.001). A post hoc Tukey HSD test with a Holm adjustment revealed the significant differences between conditions shown in Table 5. The remaining pairs of conditions were not significantly different from each other ($\alpha = 0.05$).

Table 5: Press Velocity Comparison

Lower Velocity		Higher Velocity
VAH	<	{ V, A, H, VA, AH }
VH	<	{ V, A, H, VA, AH }
AH	<	{ V, A, VA }

Similar to the press depth, the results show a lower mean velocity in the VH and VAH conditions compared to the other conditions. If the press broke through the button bottom, the velocity of the stylus would increase when the resistance dropped away. Since the depth of presses during the H and AH conditions were higher than in the VH and VAH conditions, it is likely this break-through caused the higher mean velocity in the H and AH conditions.

5. DISCUSSION

Participants expressed a significant preference for bimodal and trimodal feedback from virtual buttons. The following will examine how the results from press motion characteristics, task performance, and specific modalities fit into the following research questions.

5.1 Effect of Condition on Press Motion

How does the combination of feedback modalities affect the motion of the 3D button press?

We expected the presence of haptic feedback would shorten the distance the user pressed the button past the bottom because the user would feel resistance. However, it was unexpected that haptic feedback alone did not significantly reduce the maximum depth of button presses. The addition of visual feedback significantly shortened button presses in both VH and VAH conditions. Auditory feedback also demonstrated a significant effect in shortening the button presses in AH and VAH conditions.

Visual and auditory feedback reinforce the subjective haptic perception of stiffness [7, 18, 26, 32]. However we would expect this effect to shorten the presses in the H condition where the button did not appear to travel, rather than in the VH and VAH conditions where the button did appear to travel. Díaz et al. observed a similar effect where participants stayed within the lines of a maze more often when haptic or auditory feedback reinforced visual feedback, but their study did not observe unimodal haptic or auditory feedback [6].

We found anecdotal evidence that some of our participants may have perceived a stronger haptic feedback when visual or auditory feedback was also present. Two participants commented that they thought the force-feedback presented to them changed between keypads, although it was kept constant throughout the study. *"I didn't expect you to change up the forces"* (P12). *"The pressure [force] changed a lot"* (P16). These comments may simply reference conditions without haptic feedback, however, in the context of the previous studies, participants may have perceived a change in force between keypads with identical haptic feedback.

5.2 Accuracy and Time on Task

Compared to trimodal feedback, how does reducing the number of feedback modalities affect task accuracy and completion time?

The feedback condition did have a significant effect on time on task and on the number of delete errors occurring during the task, however it did not have a significant effect on the total number of errors. The results showed a decrease in time on task for the VH, AH, and VAH conditions, the same conditions under which we observed a decrease in the depth of the presses. This is consistent with past studies demonstrating that users react faster to multimodal feedback, because part of the task is reacting to the feedback from the buttons.

However, the results also showed a significant delete error increase in the trimodal condition, which was not consistent with past research showing decreased multimodal feedback errors. One explanation might be that the feedback from one of the modalities was poorly designed, or that lag between two modalities caused participants to make more errors in the trimodal condition. If that were true, we would expect to see increased errors in all conditions where one modality was present, or in bimodal conditions where the lagging modality was present. Instead, the results showed a significant increase in deletion errors in the trimodal condition, compared to the other conditions.

Another explanation might be that the participant never touched the button corresponding to the missing digit. However, we would then not expect to find the significant correlation between unactuated presses and delete errors in the trimodal condition.

The results therefore suggest that the participant released the button early in the trimodal condition and was able to perceive the feedback from all three modalities. This is consistent with multiple resource theory because there was no evidence of contention for a single resource in processing the feedback from multiple modalities.

5.3 Attention to a Particular Modality

When users press a button, are they focusing on a particular type of feedback such as a visual cue?

Only two participants showed a significant increase in task success when a particular modality was present, perhaps indicating they focused on cues from a particular modality while other participants shifted focus between cues from multiple modalities as they performed the tasks. Another explanation might be that the cues from the modality that improved the odds of success for those two participants were simply more salient to them.

Although five participants reported feeling more successful when a particular modality was present, the results do not show that a single modality, such as vision, was necessary to complete the task. Instead, bimodal and trimodal conditions reduced time on task and shortened the depth of presses.

6. CONCLUSIONS AND FUTURE WORK

The results showed that haptic feedback alone was not enough to constrain the button presses to the travel of the virtual button. Reinforcing the haptic feedback with visual or auditory feedback was effective in reducing the distance users pressed a button past the bottom. However, the shallower presses also suggest that participants released some buttons early in the trimodal condition. This may have led participants to make more errors by missing digits.

Some participants demonstrated more success with one particular modality. A future longitudinal study could better determine if the effect observed in this study changes over time for each participant. Another future area of study might investigate whether the color changes used with the buttons in this study have a similar effect on perceived haptic stiffness observed in other studies manipulating the visual displacement of springs and surfaces.

We expect the results of this study will apply to scenarios where users interact with buttons in a 3DUI at a single point instead of with their hand. Klatzky and Lederman documented differences between interacting with a stylus and a whole hand [16], however, it is not clear how those differences affect button presses. The exploratory procedure of applying pressure plays a large role in interaction with buttons, and this procedure is possible with a force-feedback stylus. However, the availability of other exploratory procedures using the hand could change the experience of interacting with a button.

As virtual buttons become more prevalent in supporting 3D tasks, users will seek out the multimodal feedback they prefer. In this study, a difference in the way trimodal feedback was perceived caused users to make more errors. A better understanding of multimodal feedback will help improve future interactions with virtual interfaces.

7. REFERENCES

[1] E. M. Altinsoy. Perceptual aspects of auditory-tactile asynchrony. In *Proc. ICSV 10*, pages 3831–3838, 2003.

[2] J. L. Burke, M. S. Prewett, A. A. Gray, L. Yang, F. R. B. Stilson, M. D. Coovert, L. R. Elliot, and E. Redden. Comparing the effects of visual-auditory and visual-tactile feedback on user performance: a meta-analysis. In *Proc. ICMI '06*, pages 108–117. ACM, Nov. 2006.

[3] C. Clare. Human factors: A most important ingredient in keyboard designs. *EDN Magazine*, 21(8):99–102, 1976.

[4] K. M. Cohen. Membrane keyboards and human performance. *Human Factors and Ergonomics Society Annual Meeting Proceedings*, 26:424–424, 1982.
[5] F. Colavita. Human sensory dominance. *Perception and Psycophysics*, 16(2):409–412, 1974.
[6] I. n. Díaz, J. Hernantes, I. Mansa, A. Lozano, D. Borro, J. J. Gil, and E. Sánchez. Influence of multisensory feedback on haptic accessibility tasks. *Virtual Reality*, 10(1):31–40, May 2006.
[7] D. E. DiFranco, G. L. Beauregard, and M. A. Srinivasan. The effect of auditory cues on the haptic perception of stiffness in virtual environments. In *ASME Dynamic Systems and Control Division*, volume 61, pages 17–22. ASME, 1997.
[8] Y. Guiard. Asymmetric division of labor in human skilled bimanual action: The kinematic chain as a model. *Journal of Motor Behavior*, 19:486–517, 1987.
[9] D. Hecht and M. Reiner. Sensory dominance in combinations of audio, visual and haptic stimuli. *Experimental brain research*, 193:307–314, Jan 2009.
[10] D. Hecht, M. Reiner, and A. Karni. Enhancement of response times to bi- and tri-modal sensory stimuli during active movements. *Experimental brain research*, 185(4):655–665, Mar. 2008.
[11] M. A. Heller, J. A. Calcaterra, S. L. Green, and L. Brown. Intersensory conflict between vision and touch: the response modality dominates when precise, attention-riveting judgments are required. *Perception & psychophysics*, 61(7):1384–1398, Oct. 1999.
[12] M. Hershenson. Reaction time as a measure of intersensory facilitation. *Journal of experimental psychology*, 63:289–293, Mar. 1962.
[13] E. Hoggan, T. Kaaresoja, P. Laitinen, and S. Brewster. Crossmodal congruence: the look, feel and sound of touchscreen widgets. *Proc. IMCI '08*, pages 157–164, Oct. 2008.
[14] R. Kinkead and B. Gonzalez. Human factors design recommendations for touch-operated keyboards — final report. Technical Report 12091-FR, Honeywell, Inc., March 1969.
[15] R. Klatzky and S. J. Lederman. Touch. In I. B. Weiner, editor, *Handbook of Psychology*, pages 147–176. Wiley, Hoboken, NJ, USA, 2003.
[16] R. Klatzky and S. J. Lederman. Object Recognition by Touch. In *Blindness and Brain Plasticity in Navigation and Object Perception*, pages 185–207. 2008.
[17] A. Kohlrausch and S. van de Par. Auditory-visual interaction: from fundamental research in cognitive psychology to (possible) applications. In *Proc. SPIE*, pages 34–44, 1999.
[18] A. Lécuyer, J.-M. Burkhardt, S. Coquillart, and P. Coiffet. "boundary of illusion:" an experiment of sensory integration with a pseudo-haptic system. In *Proc. VR'01*, VR '01, pages 115–122, Washington, DC, USA, 2001. IEEE Computer Society.
[19] S. Lee and S. Zhai. The performance of touch screen soft buttons. In *ACM CHI '09*, pages 309–318, 2009.
[20] V. Levenshtein. Binary codes capable of correcting deletions, insertions, and reversals. *Problems in Information Transmission*, pages 8–17, 1965.
[21] J. R. Lewis, K. M. Potosnak, and R. L. Magyar. *Keys and Keyboards*, chapter 54, pages 1285–1315. Elsevier, Amsterdam, 1997.
[22] J. Long. Effects of delayed irregular feedback on unskilled and skilled keying performance. *Ergonomics*, 19(2):183–202, 1976.
[23] T. H. Massie and J. K. Salisbury. The phantom haptic interface: A device for probing virtual objects. In *ASME Winter Annual Meeting*, 1994.
[24] H. McGurk and J. MacDonald. Hearing lips and seeing voices. *Nature*, 264(5588):746–748, Dec. 1976.
[25] Microsoft. QueryPerformanceCounter. `http://msdn.microsoft.com/en-us/library/windows/desktop/ms644904`, March 2012.
[26] N. Miner, B. Gillespie, and T. Caudell. Examining the influence of audio and visual stimuli on a haptic display. In *Proc. IMAGE '96*, 1996.
[27] A. Nashel and S. Razzaque. Tactile virtual buttons for mobile devices. In *ACM CHI '03*, pages 854–855, 2003.
[28] S. Oviatt. *Multimodal Interfaces*, chapter 21, pages 413–432. CRC Press, 2007.
[29] D. Pollard and M. Cooper. The effect of feedback on keying performance. *Applied Ergonomics*, 10(4):194–200, 1979.
[30] C. J. Roe, W. H. Muto, and T. Blake. Feedback and key discrimination on membrane keypads. *Human Factors and Ergonomics Society Annual Meeting*, 28:277–281, 1984.
[31] C. Spence, F. Pavani, and J. Driver. Crossmodal links between vision and touch in covert endogenous spatial attention. *J. of Experimental Psychology: Human Perception and Performance*, 26(4):1298–1319, 2000.
[32] M. A. Srinivasan, G. L. Beauregard, and D. L. Brock. The impact of visual information on the haptic perception of stiffness in virtual environments. In *ASME Winter Annual Meeting*, volume 58, pages 555–559, 1996.
[33] H. S. Vitense, J. A. Jacko, and V. K. Emery. Multimodal feedback: an assessment of performance and mental workload. *Ergonomics*, 46(1-3):68–87, 2003.
[34] R. A. Wagner and M. J. Fischer. The String-to-String Correction Problem. *Journal of the ACM*, 21(1):168–173, 1974.
[35] P. Walker and S. Smith. Stroop interference based on the multimodal correlates of haptic size and auditory pitch. *Perception*, 14(6):729–736, 1985.
[36] C. D. Wickens. Multiple resources and performance prediction. *Theoretical Issues in Ergonomics Science*, 3(2):159–177, 2002.

Modeling Multimodal Integration with Event Logic Charts

Gregor Mehlmann
Human Centered Multimedia
Augsburg University
Universitätsstraße 6a
86159 Augsburg, Germany
mehlmann@hcm-lab.de

Elisabeth André
Human Centered Multimedia
Augsburg University
Universitätsstraße 6a
86159 Augsburg, Germany
andre@hcm-lab.de

ABSTRACT

In this paper we present a novel approach to the combined modeling of multimodal fusion and interaction management. The approach is based on a declarative multimodal event logic that allows the integration of inputs distributed over multiple modalities in accordance to spatial, temporal and semantic constraints. In conjunction with a visual state chart language, our approach supports the incremental parsing and fusion of inputs and a tight coupling with interaction management. The incremental and parallel parsing approach allows us to cope with concurrent continuous and discrete interactions and fusion on different levels of abstraction. The high-level visual and declarative modeling methods support rapid prototyping and iterative development of multimodal systems.

Categories and Subject Descriptors

D.1.0 [**PROGRAMMING TECHNIQUES**]: General

Keywords

Multimodal Fusion, Interaction Modeling, Event Logic Chart

1. INTRODUCTION

During the last decades, researchers explored ways of enhancing human-computer interaction by developing multimodal dialogue systems. These systems overcome the shortcomings of unimodal dialogue systems that provide only a restricted set of communication modes and devices. They exploit the major characteristics of human interaction which is the coordinated use of multiple modalities such as speech, gestures, gaze, facial expressions and body postures. In the course of this research, it has been demonstrated that users often prefer multimodal interfaces over conventional graphical or unimodal user interfaces, because multimodal interfaces offer a more natural and effective interaction and better flexibility, adaptability and reliability [18, 19].

ICMI'12, October 22–26, 2012, Santa Monica, California, USA.

A critical challenge in the development of robust multimodal dialogue systems is the interpretation of the users' intention by integrating and understanding inputs distributed over multiple modalities. The key function of the modality fusion is the reduction of uncertainty and the mutual disambiguation of the various analysis results by combining partial semantic information provided by each modality [14].

Due to recent technical progress, today there is a new generation of devices on the market that are available and affordable for a large number of users and can be integrated more and more into our daily life. Such devices support features, such as markerless full body motion sensing [1], mobile eyetracking [2] and mobile biosignal capturing for affective interfaces [3]. These devices are boosting the evolution towards an unrestricted natural interaction through multimodal dialogue systems.

However, the recent technical development also poses new conceptual and technical challenges to the capabilities of multimodal fusion engines that have to be overcome to exploit the full potential of multimodal interaction. These are challenges such as the concurrent processing of discrete and continuous interaction forms, the contemporary and incremental parsing and fusion of user input as well as the regression analysis of input data for disambigation, reduction of confounding factors and a more precise decision making. Many state-of-the-art fusion engines do not address these challenges or are just able to cope with a part of these in very specific settings while lacking to present a uniform formalism or representation language for multimodal integration. In this paper we present a novel approach to a unified formalism for multimodal integration and interaction management that tackles these challenges.

2. THE CHALLENGES

In this section we present some major challenges for multimodal fusion engines and present an overview of terms and concepts of our solution approach.

2.1 Problem Description

Many multimodal fusion engines are restricted to a special combination of modalities or require some kind of primary modality. However, in a reusable and flexible formalism for multimodal fusion, all modalities should be treated equally, so that there exist no restrictions for the combinations of

[1]http://www.xbox.com/kinect
[2]http://www.smivision.com
[3]http://www.alivetec.com

different modalities and devices. For example, for the interpretation of sign-language, a primary speech modality obviously makes no sense, but it is important to capture the complex synergy between the various nonverbal signals.

Another shortcoming of many multimodal fusion engines is that they exclusively focus on discrete interaction in form of gestures or spoken commands that are processed after being completed. For example, pointing gestures are used to resolve deictic references in speech after information from both modalities has been received. However, in order to directly manipulate objects in the user interface with continuous movements, it is necessary to contemporarily process dynamic data and to directly forward it to the application while still allowing the concurrent interpretation of discrete interaction.

In order to gain user acceptance and to avoid annoying situations, the system's response times to the user's actions must be reasonably small and feedback needs to be continuously provided. For example, if the system takes too long to react to a command, the user may assume that the command was wrong or not understood. The user could repeat the command and would be confused when the command then gets carried out twice. Providing early feedback to the user creates better transparency and comprehension of the interaction. It also allows an early error recovery in the case of device recognition errors or demands of the system for refinement of user input and explicit ambiguity resolution. For this reason, user input needs to be parsed, fused and processed contemporarily and incrementally by the system.

Sometimes it is not sufficient to analyse only the user's last action and the momentary situation. For example, when regarding continuously provided data from modalities such as gaze, emotions or biological signals, the inspection of the data's time course can reduce the influence of device recognition errors or momentarily recognized unusual behavior of the user and, thus, resolve ambiguities and allow more precise decisions. For this reason, a fusion engine needs to be able to fall back on information about the user's past interaction and to infer generalized and fuzzy knowledge about the interaction history.

Finally, multimodal fusion can be realized during various processing stages [20]. Apart from a few exceptions, most fusion engines operate on only one of those abstraction levels for multimodal fusion. Offering fusion support across different levels of abstractions can help exploit the power of multimodal interactions.

2.2 Solution Approach

Our solution approach to these challenges pursues most widely declarative and visual modeling paradigms and exploits uniform representation languages. Multimodal fusion mechanisms are modeled with declarative specifications in a *multimodal event logic*. This event logic handles all modalities equally and allows us to express a diversity of temporal, spatial and semantic relations between events. It allows us to express structural and functional constraints for the unification of partial information distributed over events from multiple devices and modalities.

Context knowledge is modeled in a *knowledge base* in the form of semantic networks and type hierarchies. This knowledge is directly translated to predicates of the multimodal event logic, so that logic inference enables us to resolve references and to infer semantic relations between entities of the application context or the semantic content of events. The knowledge base enfolds an *event history* recording incoming events in a short-term memory. Together with generalized and fuzzy quantifier predicates of the event logic this creates an intuitive mechanism for ambiguity resolution and regression analysis.

The incremental step-wise multimodal parsing and fusion as well as the behavioral aspects of interaction management are modeled with a parallel and hierarchical *state chart language*. Transitions of the state chart model can be annotated with event logic constraints and are taken whenever such a formula is satisfied. It also allows the modeling of parallel fusion processes on different levels of abstraction and the simultaneous processing of discrete and continuous interactions through synchronized automata.

In the remainder of this paper we first discuss related work in Section 3 and investigate how existing approaches address the above mentioned challenges. In Section 4 we introduce the theoretical background and conceptual framework of our approach and present some illustrative examples that give a good idea of how the approach can be applied for the development of multimodal applications. In Section 5 we explain how the conceptual framework has been realized in a technical framework and which advantages it offers to designers of multimodal applications. Finally, in Section 6, we discuss the conceptual and technical contributions of our work and give a view on potential future directions.

3. RELATED WORK

Since the seminal work of Bolt [2], there have been researched various approaches to multimodal fusion engines [12]. In early work [17, 5] multimodal integration was essentially a procedural extension of an existing speech understanding or text understanding engine. These systems did not allow incremental or parallel parsing of input and, thus, did not allow continuous interaction or multiple parallel interpreation processes.

The first uniform representation formats were introduced by Koons et. al. [11] and Voo et. al. [22], where parallel unimodal parsers translated information from individual modalities to a common *frame-based* representation format. Multimodal fusion was reached by merging those semantic frames together in order to produce the combined interpretation. A more declarative approach was developed by Johnston [10] where multimodal integration was modeled as unification of *typed feature structures* [4]. However, this approach only handeled simple interactions with a single gesture in combination with speech and was therefore extended [7] utilizing techniques from natural language processing, such as *unification-based multimodal grammars* and chart parsing to enable handling of inputs with more than one gesture and more flexible and declarative encoding of temporal and spatial constraints. This approach was the first that allowed incremental parsing and the generic use of arbitrary modalities in contrast to earlier mainly speech-driven approaches. However, it did not address the challenge of the concurrent use of continuous and discrete interaction and had no concept for an event history.

While these unification- and frame-based approaches separate the parsing of the individual modalities and multimodal integration into separate processing steps, Johnston and Bangalore [9] described a highly efficient approach to multimodal understanding with *finite-state automata* in which a single multimodal grammar specifies the integration and understanding of multimodal language. However this approach lacked the specification of complex temporal, spatial and semantic constraints and did not allow continuous and incremental parsing.

Other approaches take a more process-oriented approach to model the dynamics and behavioral aspects of multimodal interaction with *Petri nets* [16] or *temporally augmented state-transition networks* [13]. Issues such as parallelism, sequencing or synchronization of actions can be described by these models. These approaches are also able to cope with discrete and continuous interaction and allow incremental parsing, but they do not enable fusion on different levels of abstraction.

While the above mentioned works are exclusively concerned with multimodal fusion on the decision-level, recent work by Hoste et al. [6] introduces for the first time an approach that deals with the parallel fusion on different levels of abstraction. This approach is based on a declarative *rule-based* language operating over a common fact base. However, this approach does not address incremental parsing and interaction management.

The above investigated approaches have proven to be well suited for certain applications, but each of them misses to meet some of the requirements described in Section 2. The approach described in this paper goes beyond the current state-of-the-art since it enhances well proven concepts of the previous approaches and introduces new concepts to tackle the mentioned challenges. In the next section, we describe the details of the theoretical background and the conceptual framework of our approach.

4. CONCEPTUAL FRAMEWORK

In this section we present some major concepts of our multimodal event logic and show how it can be used in conjunction with state charts for incremental parsing and fusion of multimodal user input.

4.1 The Multimodal Event History

Multimodal events are represented as feature records that can carry a variety of information from different levels of abstraction. They can carry low-level data such as the coordinates describing the position of the user's gaze, but, also high-level information such as the semantic content of a speech act, the referenced object of a pointing gesture or information about the types, phases and the spatial extent of gestures. For illustration purposes, but without limiting the generality, in the following we assume a basic set of the most general features for a multimodal event as shown in Definition 1. This notion of an event can easily be adapted to existing standards [8] or to application specific requirements.

Definition 1. Let Σ be an alphabeth then a multimodal event is defined as a record $\langle n, m, s, e, d, c\rangle$ so that $n \in \Sigma^+$ is the identifier, $m \in \Sigma^+$ is the modality, $s, e \in \mathbb{N}_0^+$ are the start- and end times, $d \in \Sigma^*$ is the semantic content and $c \in]0,1] \subset \mathbb{R}$ is the confidence value of the event.

Due to varying modality specific recognition times and device response times, the fusion engine receives events from different recognition modules with different delays. To handle those events in a sequence, which corresponds to the real chronological sequence, the fusion engine records them to an *event history*. The definition of a well-formed event history is presented in Definition 2.

Definition 2. A finite set $KB \subset \{\langle n, m, s, e, d, c\rangle : n, m \in \Sigma^+, d \in \Sigma^*, s, e \in \mathbb{N}_0^+, c \in]0,1]\}$ is a well-formed event history if and only if each event in the event history has a unique identifier.

Logic inference on the event history allows to answer a diversity of queries concerning its content, such as the existence of events with specific attributes or temporal, spatial and semantic relations between events. The event history enfolds a *short-term memory* mechanism, which deletes events that have reached a certain age so that they are not considered anymore by the inference engine.

$$event(sevt_{23}, speech, 1050, 1450, put, 0.85)$$
$$event(sevt_{24}, speech, 1650, 2050, that, 0.85)$$
$$event(sevt_{25}, speech, 2250, 2750, there, 0.80)$$
$$event(gevt_{354}, gesture, 1750, 1850, ball_3, 0.95)$$
$$event(gevt_{355}, gesture, 2300, 2400, table_2, 0.95)$$
$$event(gevt_{356}, gesture, 2450, 2550, table_2, 0.85)$$
$$event(gevt_{357}, gesture, 2600, 2700, floor_1, 0.90)$$

Figure 1: Exemplary events of an event history.

Figure 1 shows an extract of a well-formed event history containing simple time-stamped event records with semantic contents and confidence values obtained by the modality specific recognition modules. This event history describes a scenario in which the user's voice and full body motions are observed in an environment containing the objects $table_2$, $ball_3$ and $floor_1$. The user gives the spoken command *put that there* and points to the ball and then to the table. During the spoken word *that* the system recognizes a pointing to $ball_3$, however, due to the user's hastily and imprecise movements the system recognizes ambiguous pointings to $table_2$ and $floor_1$ during the word *there*. This could also be caused by the recognition mechanism of the tracking device, since, in contrast to i.e. pen-based devices, in full body tracking, it is not always clear when a gesture starts and when it begins, so that some devices deliver continuous tracking samples. How our approach resolves this ambiguity with the help of generalized quantifiers of our event logic is explained in the next section.

4.2 The Event Logic Predicates

Our multimodal event logic includes a variety of first-order predicates to infer and compare attributes of events and to resolve temporal, spatial and semantic relations between individual events. Additionally, it enfolds higher-order generalized and fuzzy quantifiers to make statements about sets of events that share certain features.

4.2.1 Basic Feature Predicates

Basic features of an event record can be referred to with the *feature predicates* that are defined over the domain of event identifiers. These predicates are the foundation of our event logic and allow to infer the features of an event, such as its identifier, the description of its modality, the timestamps of its start- and end time, information about the semantic content and the corresponding confidence value. They are used to define a variety of *comparison predicates* that allow to compare different events to each other with respect to their basic properties. For example, Definition 3 shows the definition of the comparison predicate *equal_mode* which tests whether two event identifiers n_i and n_j refer to two different events in the event history *KB* and whether their modality descriptions m_i and m_j are equal.

Definition 3. Let *KB* be a well-formed event history and let $n_i, n_j \in \Sigma^+$ then we define *equal_mode* as:

$$equal\_mode_{KB}(n_i, n_j) :\Leftrightarrow \exists m_i, m_j \in \Sigma^+. \left(\begin{array}{l} name_{KB}(n_i) \wedge name_{KB}(n_j) \wedge n_i \neq n_j \wedge \\ mode_{KB}(n_i, m_i) \wedge mode_{KB}(n_j, m_j) \wedge m_i = m_j \end{array} \right)$$

4.2.2 Temporal Event Relations

Time is a key concepts to be represented in order to combine several events received from multiple modalities. Quantitative time allows to represent temporal evolutions related to a given amount of time or at a precise moment in time whereas qualitative time addresses temporal relations between events and the ordering of event such as precedence, succession and simultaneity. To define *qualitative temporal predicates* we refer back to Allen's time intervals [1] as shown in Definition 4.

Definition 4. Let *KB* be a well-formed event history and let $\langle n_i, m_i, s_i, e_i, d_i, c_i \rangle, \langle n_j, m_j, s_j, e_j, d_j, c_j \rangle \in KB$ then we define the quantitative temporal predicates:

$$\begin{array}{lll} before_{KB}(n_i, n_j) & :\Leftrightarrow & s_j > e_i \\ meets_{KB}(n_i, n_j) & :\Leftrightarrow & e_i = s_j \\ concurrent_{KB}(n_i, n_j) & :\Leftrightarrow & s_i = s_j \wedge e_i = e_j \\ during_{KB}(n_i, n_j) & :\Leftrightarrow & s_j < s_i \wedge e_i < e_j \\ starts_{KB}(n_i, n_j) & :\Leftrightarrow & s_i = s_j \wedge e_i < e_j \\ finishes_{KB}(n_i, n_j) & :\Leftrightarrow & e_i = e_j \wedge s_j < s_i \\ overlaps_{KB}(n_i, n_j) & :\Leftrightarrow & s_i < s_j \wedge s_j < e_i \wedge e_i < e_j \end{array}$$

We define *quantitative temporal predicates* to make statements about the temporal distance between different events or between events and fixed points in time. Definition 5 shows the definitions of some of our predicates that infer the distance between two events of a lineary ordered set.

Definition 5. Let *KB* be a well-formed event history and let $\langle n_i, m_i, s_i, e_i, d_i, c_i \rangle, \langle n_j, m_j, s_j, e_j, d_j, c_j \rangle \in KB$ with $n_i \neq n_j$ and $t \in \mathbb{N}^+$ then we define the quantitative temporal predicates:

$$\begin{array}{l} dist\_exactly_{KB}(n_i, n_j, t) :\Leftrightarrow e_i < s_j \wedge s_j - e_i = t \\ dist\_more\_than_{KB}(n_i, n_j, t) :\Leftrightarrow e_i < s_j \wedge s_j - e_i > t \\ dist\_less\_than_{KB}(n_i, n_j, t) :\Leftrightarrow e_i < s_j \wedge s_j - e_i < t \end{array}$$

4.2.3 Event Ordering Relations

Events of the same modality, user and device or multiple events that satisfy a certain constraint can be lineary ordered. In this case, we might be interested in the oldest, latest or just a random event from such a set of events. Additionally, we want to make statements about the ordering of these events, such as determining followers and ancestors or to express neighbourly relations between them. Our multimodal event logic enfolds various *linear ordering predicates* to express these relations. Definition 6 shows the denotational semantics of different overloadings for some of these predicates.

Definition 6. Let *KB* be a well-formed event history and let $\langle n_i, m_i, s_i, e_i, d_i, c_i \rangle, \langle n_j, m_j, s_j, e_j, d_j, c_j \rangle \in KB$ with $n_i \neq n_j$. Let $N \subseteq \{n : \exists \langle n, m, s, e, d, c \rangle \in KB\}$, $n \in N, m \notin N$ and ϕ be a well-formed formula of our event logic with the free variable $\sigma \in \Sigma^+$, then we define the ordering predicates:

$$\begin{array}{l} oldest_{KB}(n, N) :\Leftrightarrow n \in N \wedge \forall n' \in N.(n \neq n' \Rightarrow before_{KB}(n, n')) \\ oldest_{KB}(n, \sigma, \phi) :\Leftrightarrow oldest(n, \{n' \in \Sigma^+ : [n'/\sigma]\phi_{KB}\}) \\ follows_{KB}(n_i, n_j) :\Leftrightarrow equal\_mode_{KB}(n_i, n_j) \wedge after_{KB}(n_i, n_j) \\ follows_{KB}(N, m) :\Leftrightarrow N = \{n' \in \Sigma^+ : follows_{KB}(n', m)\} \\ nextto_{KB}(n_i, n_j) :\Leftrightarrow follows_{KB}(N, n_j) \wedge oldest_{KB}(n_j, N) \end{array}$$

4.2.4 Types and Sematic Relations

Logic and semantic networks are compatible and supplementing formalisms. Semantic networks are an extension to predicate logic because they can be used to encode static and dynamic aspects of semantic knowledge about the domain, the task, the user as well as the types and attributes of events in the system. They constitute a clearly arranged graphical representation of semantic relations and can easily be maintained with graphical editors.

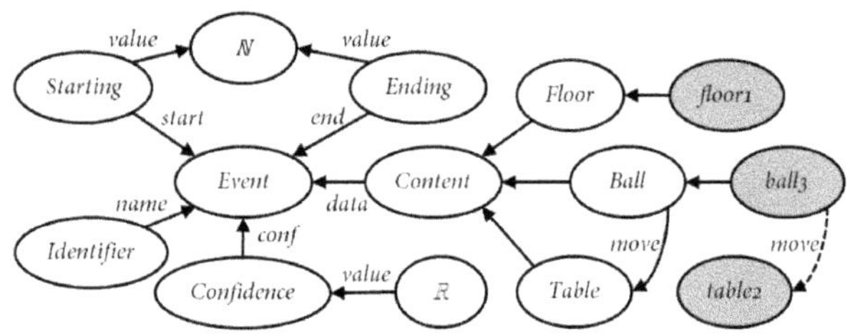

Figure 2: A semantic network describing event features and the *move* relation from balls to tables.

The semantic relations represented by a semantic networks can automatically be translated into entities and predicates of our event logic and be considered by the inference mechanism. Figure 2 shows a simple semantic network as it could be used as part of our knowledge base. It describes the basic features of a multimodal event as well as the semantic relation *move* between tables, balls and the floor.

4.2.5 Generalized and Fuzzy Quantifiers

In addition to infer relations between individual events in the event history, it is very helpful to make statemants about sets of events. For that purpose, we provide a variety of *generalized quantifiers* and *fuzzy quantifiers* for the multimodal event logic. Definition 7 presents the denotational semantics of some of the quantifiers that our event logic provides.

Definition 7. Let *KB* be a well-formed event history and let ϕ and ψ be well-formed formulas of the previously defined predicates with the free variable $\sigma \in \Sigma^+$. Furthermore, let $x \in \mathbb{N}_0^+$ and $y \in [0, 1]$, then we define the following generalized quantifiers:

$$forsome_{KB}(\sigma, \phi, \psi) \quad :\Leftrightarrow$$
$$\{n \in \Sigma^+ : [n/\sigma]\phi_{KB}\} \cap \{n \in \Sigma^+ : [n/\sigma]\psi_{KB}\} \neq \emptyset$$
$$forevery_{KB}(\sigma, \phi, \psi) \quad :\Leftrightarrow$$
$$\{n \in \Sigma^+ : [n/\sigma]\phi_{KB}\} \subseteq \{n \in \Sigma^+ : [n/\sigma]\psi_{KB}\}$$
$$formorethan_{KB}(x, \sigma, \phi, \psi) \quad :\Leftrightarrow$$
$$\left|\{n \in \Sigma^+ : [n/\sigma]\phi_{KB} \wedge [n/\sigma]\psi_{KB}\}\right| > x$$

The major advantage of those quantifiers is that they allow a very intuitive and elegant way of formalizing quantified and fuzzy statements about event sets. This mechanism can be exploited for regression analysis, disambiguation and to reduce the influence of negligible recognition errors.

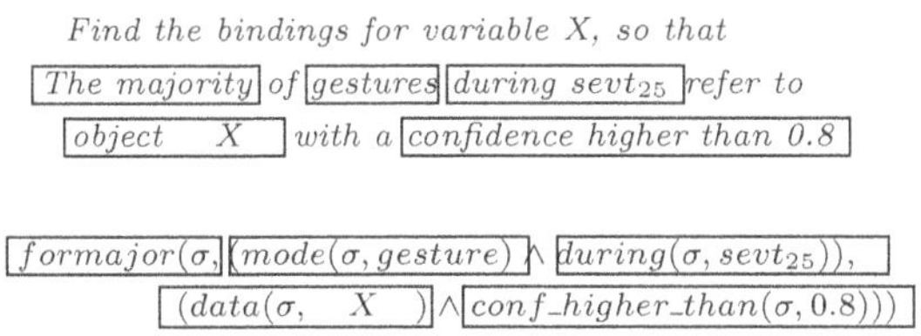

Figure 3: Resolving ambiguities from the example in Figure 1 with the generalized *formajor* quantifier.

Figure 3 illustrates the use of the quantifier *formajor* with the unbound variable X. It shows how a natural language query can be translated straightforward to such a quantifier formula. The logic inference mechanism finds events in the knowledge base that unify with this expression and returns possible bindings for the unbound variable X under which the formula is satisfied. This specific formula describes how the ambiguities of the event history from the example in Figure 1 can be resolved after we have infered that the speech event *there* has identifier $sevt_{25}$. This formula regards only the majority of pointings during the speech event $sevt_{25}$ that refer to the same object with confidence higher 0.8 while neglecting the fact that there has also been a pointing gesture to another object. Therefore, we decide for the object $table_2$ that has been refered to by the majority of pointings during *there* and put object $ball_3$ onto $table_2$.

4.3 The Event Logic State Charts

Beside their general application in the specification of reactive and interactive system behavior, various state chart dialects have been shown to be a suitable method for modeling dialogue and interaction [3, 21]. In the following, we illustrate the integration of our event logic with a state chart language that is used for the incremental parsing and fusion of user input and the parallel management of continuous and discrete interaction.

4.3.1 *Integrating State Charts with Event Logic*

In this work we use a state chart language that was extended with features to facilitate dialogue and interaction management, such as local variable scoping and the parameterization of hierarchical components. Transitions of our state charts can be annotated with variable assignments and logic formulas of our event logic. Outgoing transitions of a state are taken whenever the logic formula on the transition is satisfied with respect to the current state of the event history. Initially unsatisfied formulas may become satisfyable whenever the event history is enriched with new events, context knowlede has changed or some timeout has been reached. States and superstates contain local variable definitions that can correspond to unbound variables in the logic constraints of a transition. If such a constraint can be satisfied, unification is done, which means that the interpreter binds that variable to the infered value so that the variable is instantiated in consecutive computation steps. When using a variable in its uninstantiated form, the variable is annotated with an upward directed arrow index ($X_\uparrow$). After it has been instantiated it is indicated with a downward directed arrow index within a logic formula ($X_\downarrow$).

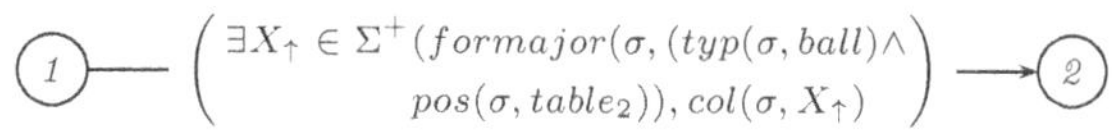

Figure 4: A constraint with an unbound variable.

Figure 4 shows an example of a transition labeled with a constraint containing the unbound variable X. This constraint is satisfied if the majority of objects with type *ball* lying on table $table_2$ have the same color which is then bound to variable X and can be used in the next parsing steps.

4.3.2 *Incremental Parsing and Fusion*

The mechanism of the step-wise evaluation of logic constraints and the consecutive use of the infered knowledge is exploited for the incremental parsing and fusion. It allows to continuously react to user input by executing system commands in the states of the state chart. Such commands can be used to give early feedback to the user, for example by highlighting entities of the user interface or directly executing parts of the user command. The user can be asked as soon as possible to refine a command if the information was not precise or complete, contains ambiguous statements or stands in contradiction with the current application state.

The example in Figure 5 illustrates the incremental parsing and fusion of multimodal input during the execution of a state chart whose transitions are labeled with logic formulas that need to unify with the content of the event history. It shows the specification of a state chart model which can be used to accept the well-known *"put-that-there"* input pattern [2]. It shows a subautomaton which is able to accept the speech part of that utterance accompanied by pointing gestures to two objects in the environment. We now explain the individual steps in more detail whereby we assume that the incoming events successively combine to the event history shown in Figure 1 and that the context knowledge enfolds the semantic relations encoded in the semantic network from Figure 2.

Initially, the automaton is parameterized from the calling process with the last speech event ℓ that has been processed by the calling process. In state ① the interpreter waits until the event history contains the oldest speech event after ℓ which carries the content *put*. When the event history re-

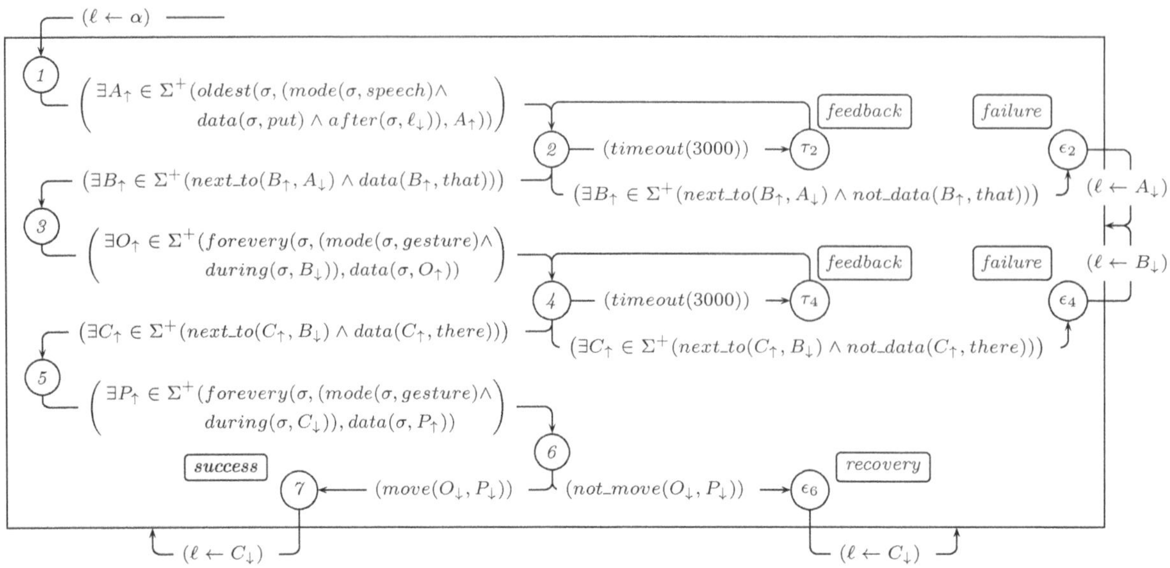

Figure 5: Incremental parsing of Bolt's [2] classical "put-that-there" with state charts and the event logic.

ceives or already contains such an event, then the transition ①→② is taken and the variable A is bound to the identifier of this event. In state ② the interpreter waits until the event history contains a direct successor of the event whose name is now bound to variable A. When the event history receives or already contains such an event, then the transition ②→③ is taken and the variable B is bound to the identifier of the second speech event. In state ③ the interpreter checks if all gesture events during the last speech event carry the same semantic content. In this case, the transition ③→④ is taken and the semantic content of those gesture events is bound to variable O. The transitions ④→⑤ and ⑤→⑥ are evaluated analogue to the transitions ②→③ and ③→④. If the execution reaches state ⑥, then the content of the first set of gestures nas been bound to variable O and the semantic content of the second set of gestures has been bound to variable P. Finally, in state ⑥ the interpreter checks if these semantic contents satisfy the constraint on transition ⑥→⑦ by inspecting the semantic network. This constraint is satisfied if the first set of gestures refer to a movable object (i.e. $ball_3$) and the second set of gestures refer to a valid target position for that object (i.e. $table_3$). Afterwards, the automaton is restarted with the last speech event $C_\downarrow$. The states τ_2 and τ_4 are reached whenever the user waits too long between two words and are used to ask the user for continuation. The states ϵ_2, ϵ_4 and ϵ_6 are reached whenever a constraint can not be satisfied due to a wrong word or the selection of invalid objects.

4.3.3 Continuous and Discrete Interaction

The incremental and parallel parsing and fusion approach using state charts has further major advantages. We are now able to model parallel and synchronized automata that allow us to cope with the concurrent appearance of discrete and continuous interaction forms.

Figure 6 shows an example in which two parallel automata are synchronized in order to switch from a discrete interaction to a continuous interaction and back. During the continuous interaction the automaton that is parsing the discrete interaction pattern remains continuously active. The example describes a scenario in which the user may use the speech commands *drag* and *drop* to take objects and move them around with the help of eye movements using an eye-tracker device. The left parallel automaton is modeling the recognition of the *drag* or *drop* commands. In state ① the interpreter waits until there exists an oldest speech event after ℓ which carries the words *drag* or *drop*. When the event history receives or already contains such an event, then the transition ①→② is taken and the variable X is bound to the identifier of this event. In state ② the interpreter checks if at least 80% of the gaze events during this speech event refer to the same object. The threshold of 80% is choosen here, since eye movements are usually very fast and can be easily distracted, so that there can be a considerable proportion of false measurements that we want to ignore. If the transition ②→③ is taken then the identifier of the focused object is bound to variable Y. Finally, in transition ③→④ the interpreter updates the knowledge base with a new command which contains the triggering speech event and the reference to the focused object.

The automaton on the right side is running in parallel to the left automaton in a concurrent process, waiting for relevant commands. In state ⑤ the interpreter is inspecting the knowledge base for the latest command. If there exists such a command then the transition ⑤→⑥ is taken and the identifier of the event that triggered the command is bound to variable X while the content of this command is bound to variable Y. In state ⑥ the interpreter checks the content of the triggering event and proceeds with transition ⑥→⑦ if the command was a request to drop an object. If the command was a request to drag an object, then the interpreter enters the transition loop ⑥→⑧→⑤→⑥. Within this loop, the interpreter inspects the event history for the latest gaze event and binds the content of the gaze event, which is the position or the object the user is looking at, to the variable P. Afterwards the interpreter checks if the

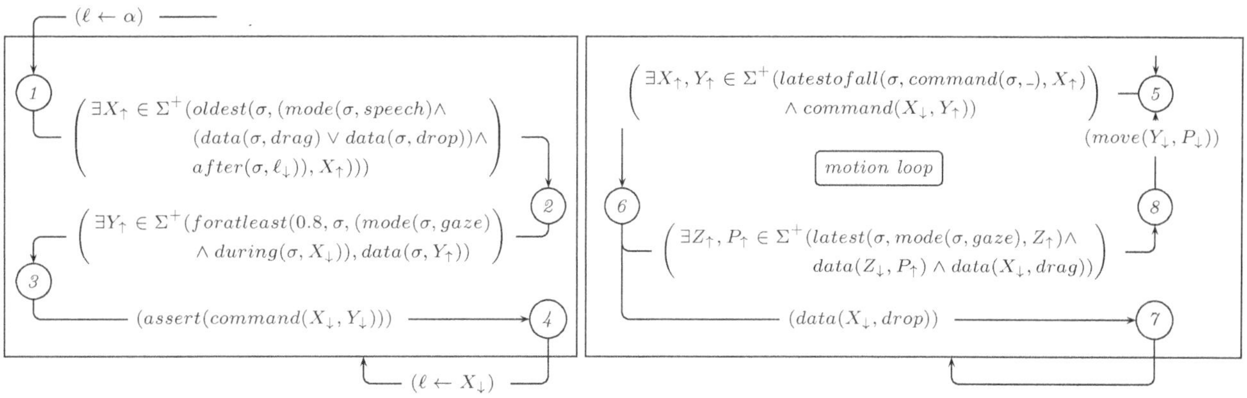

Figure 6: Using parallel processes for the concurrent processing of continuous and discrete interaction.

object reference in Y is movable to position P by inspecting the semantic network, before it looks for the latest command again. A system command within the loop can be used to update the position of the object in the user interface following the user's gaze until the user gives the command to drop the object.

5. TECHNICAL FRAMEWORK

We implemented our multimodal event logic, described in Section 4, and the functionality for the construction and modification of the event history in the logic programming language *Prolog* using the development environment and inference engine of *SWI-Prolog* [24]. The implementation of the event history as part of a Prolog knowledge base and the various Prolog predicates was straightforward. For example, Figure 7 shows the implementation of the *formajor* quantifier in SWI-Prolog.

$$
\begin{aligned}
&formajor(Template, Generator, Condition) :- \\
&\quad bagof(Template, Generator, Range) \\
&\quad bagof(Template, (Generator, Condition), Scope) \\
&\quad length(Range, R), length(Scope, S), S/R > 0.5.
\end{aligned}
$$

Figure 7: The *formajor* predicate in SWI-Prolog.

We used the modeling framework *SceneMaker* [15] for the integration of the event logic with state charts. SceneMaker's plug-in mechanism allowed us to integrate the Prolog inference engine with minimal effort. SceneMaker was very well suited for the rapid realization of our approach since its state chart language allows the *hierarchical refinement* of the model in order to reuse and easily extend already modeled components. *Parallel decomposition* can be used to specify parallel parsing and interaction management in concurrent processes. SceneMaker is implemented in Java and relies on an interpreter approach for the execution of the state charts. Java *reflect invocation* was used to call system commands for feedback and error recovery. SceneMaker's IDE enfolds a *visual state chart editor* and a *runtime visualization* mechanism which facilitates rapid prototyping and testing.

Figure 8 shows parts of the implementation of the example

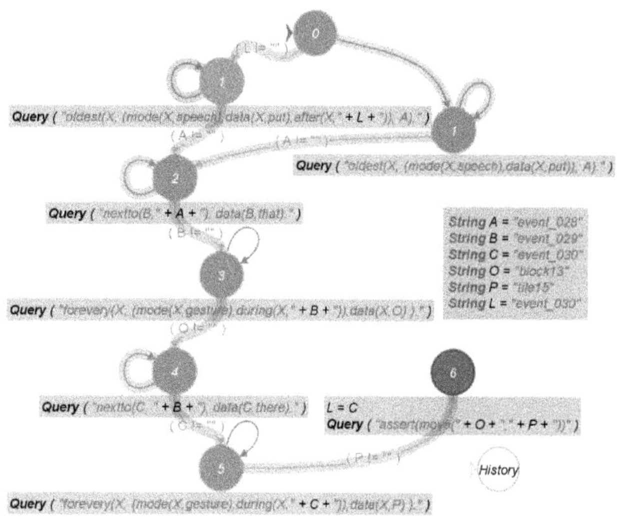

Figure 8: Incremental parsing variant of Bolt's [2] "put-that-there" with SceneMaker and Prolog.

from Figure 5 with SceneMaker. The runtime visualization mechanism is used to highlight states and transitions that are executed during the single parsing steps.

6. CONCLUSION AND FUTURE WORK

In this work we presented a novel approach to the modeling of modality fusion and dialogue management exploiting widely declarative and visual representation languages. The generic and extendable notion of multimodal events avoids restrictions for the combination of different modalities and devices. The event logic defines a variety of functional, temporal and spatial predicates and we use semantic networks for modeling semantic relations and context knowledge. The event history in combination with generalized and fuzzy quantifiers can be used for regression analysis and disambiguation. Our approach allows the contemporary and incremetal parsing and fusion of user input. This is used to realize an early error recovery and feedback delivery to the user. Since we pursue an incremental and parallel parsing approach, we are able to realize the simultaneous processing of discrete and continuous interactions. Our approach also allows the modeling of parallel fusion processes on different levels of abstraction.

This paper describes only a part of our approach's potential which has additional advantages that will be addresses in future work. We are currently exploring the potential of our approach in processing parallel processes. Processing the same interaction with parallel interpreters allows for the concurrent creation of different interpretations providing different confidence values und, thus, being selected with different probabilities for dialogue management. In collaborative or cooperative settings where the actions of the different users need to occur temporally and spatially aligned to each other, parallel processes can be used to parse the interactions of each user in isolation and synchronization can be used to express the various constraints. We will explore this idea by means of a multi-touch table where multiple users plan a travel together by manipulating multiple objects in parallel using speech and gestures.

In addition to that we are currently working on the development of an integrated framework that unifies the data- and feature-level fusion pipeline of the *SSI* framework [23] with our approach. This will provide application designers with a powerful and flexible processing pipeline from the low-level sensor access over various feature-level fusion and machine learning strategies to high-level fusion, dialogue management and application context maintenance.

7. ACKNOWLEDGMENTS

The work described in this paper is funded by the EU under research grant CEEDS (FP7-ICT-2009-5).

8. REFERENCES

[1] J. F. Allen and G. Ferguson. Actions and events in interval temporal logic. *Journal of Logic and Computation*, 4:531–579, 1994.

[2] R. A. Bolt. Put-that-there : Voice and gesture at the graphics interface. In *Proceedings of SIGGRAPH '80*, pages 262–270. ACM, New York, NY, 1980.

[3] J. Brusk, T. Lager, A. Hjalmarsson, and P. Wik. Deal: Dialogue management in scxml for believable game characters. In *Proceedings of Future Play '07*, pages 137–144. ACM, New York, NY, 2007.

[4] B. Carpenter and F. Pereira. *Computational Linguistics*, volume 19, chapter The Logic of Typed Feature Structures. Cambridge University Press, Cambridge, England, 1992.

[5] P. Cohen. Integrated interfaces for decision support with simulation. In *Proceedings of WSC '91*, pages 1066–1072. IEEE Computer Society Washington, DC, USA, 1991.

[6] L. Hoste, B. Dumas, and B. Signer. Mudra: A unified multimodal interaction framework. In *Proceedings of ICMI' 11*, pages 97–104. ACM, New York, NY, USA, 2011.

[7] M. Johnston. Multimodal language processing. In *Proc. of the Int. Conf. on Spoken Language Processing*, 1998.

[8] M. Johnston. Building multimodal applications with emma. In *Proceedings of ICMI-MLMI '09*, 2009.

[9] M. Johnston and S. Bangalore. Finite-state multimodal integration and understanding. *Journal of Natural Language Engineering*, 11:159–187, 2005.

[10] M. Johnston, P. R. Cohen, D. McGee, S. L. Oviatt, J. A. Pittman, and I. Smith. Unification-based multimodal integration. In *Proc. of the Association of Computational Linguistice*, 1997.

[11] D. B. Koons, C. Sparrel, and K. R. Thorisson. *Intelligent Multimedia Interfaces*, chapter Integrating simultaneous input from spech, gaze and hand gestures, pages 257–276. AAAI, Menlo Park, CA, 1993.

[12] D. Lalanne, L. Nigay, P. Palanque, P. Robinson, J. Vanderdonckt, and J. F. Ladry. Fusion engines for multimodal input: A survey. In *Proceedings of ICMI' 09*, pages 153–160. ACM, New York, NY, USA, 2009.

[13] M. E. Latoschik. Designing transition networks for multimodal vr-interactions using a markup language. In *Proceedings of ICMI' 02*, pages 411–416, 2002.

[14] J. C. Martin. *TYCOON: Theoretical framework and software tools for multimodal interfaces.* AAAI Press, 1998.

[15] G. Mehlmann, B. Endraß, and E. André. Modeling parallel state charts for multithreaded multimodal dialogues. In *Proceedings of ICMI' 11*, pages 385–392. ACM,New York, NY, USA, 2011.

[16] D. Navarre, P. Palanque, R. Bastide, A. Schyn, M. A. Winckler, L. Nedel, and C. Freitas. A formal description of multimodal interaction techniques for immersive virtual reality applications. In *Proceedings of INTERACT '05*, volume 3585 of *LNCS*, pages 170–185. Springer-Verlag, 2005.

[17] J. Neal and S. Shapiro. *Intelligent Unser Interfaces*, chapter Intelligent Multi-Media Interface Technology, pages 45–68. Addison Wesley, New York, 1991.

[18] S. Oviatt. Advances in robust multimodal interface design. *IEEE Comput. Graph. Appl.*, 23(5):62–68, September 2003.

[19] S. Oviatt. *The Human-Computer Interaction Handbook*, chapter Multimodal Interfaces, pages 413–432. Mahwah, NJ: Lawrence Erlbaum and Associates, 2008.

[20] R. Sharma, V. I. Pavlovi, and T. S. Huang. Toward multimodal human-computer interface. *Proceedings of the IEEE, Special Issue on Multimodal Signal Processing*, 86:853–860, 1998.

[21] D. Traum, A. Leuski, A. Roque, S. Gandhe, D. DeVault, J. Gerten, S. Robinson, and B. Martinovski. Natural language dialogue architectures for tactical questioning characters. In *Army Science Conference*, 2008.

[22] M. T. Voo and C. Wood. Building an application framework for speech and pen input integration in multimodal learning interfaces. In *Proc. of the Int. Conf. on Acoustics, Speech and Signal Processing*, 1996.

[23] J. Wagner, F. Lingenfelser, and E. André. The social signal interpretation framework (ssi) for real time signal processing and recognition. In *Proceedings of INTERSPEECH' 11*, pages 3245–3248, 2011.

[24] J. Wielemaker, T. Schrijvers, M. Triska, and T. Lager. Swi-prolog. *CoRR*, abs/1011.5332, 2010.

Multimodal Motion Guidance: Techniques for Adaptive and Dynamic Feedback

Christian Schönauer[1,2]
schoenauer@ims.tuwien.ac.at

Kenichiro Fukushi[1,3]
fukushi@isl.titech.ac.jp

Alex Olwal[1]
olwal@media.mit.edu

Hannes Kaufmann[2]
kaufmann@ims.tuwien.ac.at

Ramesh Raskar[1]
raskar@media.mit.edu

MIT Media Lab[1]
Vienna University of Technology[2]
Tokyo Institute of Technology[3]

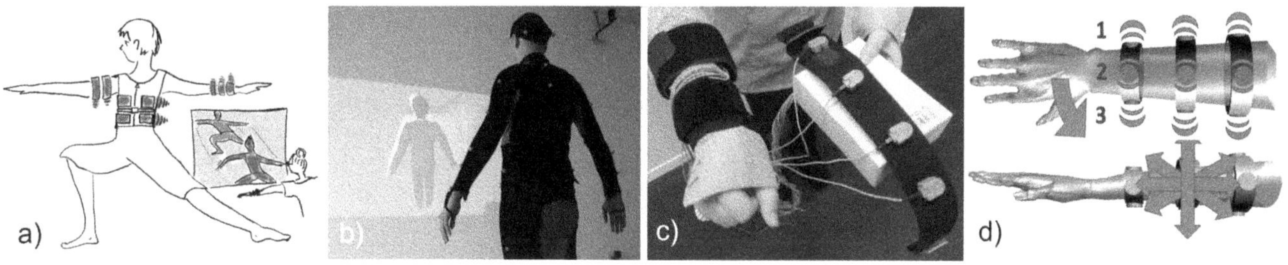

Figure 1: a) Multimodal feedback guides a user to follow directed motion from a remote teacher. b) Motion capture allows full-body feedback. c) Vibrotactor hardware d) for continuous feedback on speed and direction.

ABSTRACT

The ability to guide human motion through automatically generated feedback has significant potential for applications in areas, such as motor learning, human-computer interaction, telepresence, and augmented reality.

This paper focuses on the design and development of such systems from a human cognition and perception perspective. We analyze the dimensions of the design space for motion guidance systems, spanned by technologies and human information processing, and identify opportunities for new feedback techniques.

We present a novel motion guidance system, that was implemented based on these insights to enable feedback for position, direction and continuous velocities. It uses motion capture to track a user in space and guides using visual, vibrotactile and pneumatic actuation. Our system also introduces motion retargeting through time warping, motion dynamics and prediction, to allow more flexibility and adaptability to user performance.

Categories and Subject Descriptors

H.5.2 [**Information interfaces and presentation**]: User Interfaces - Input devices and strategies

ICMI'12, October 22–26, 2012, Santa Monica, California, USA.

Keywords

Multimodal feedback, motion guidance, tactile feedback

1. INTRODUCTION

The development and training of motor skills can greatly benefit from efficient interaction techniques and multimodal feedback. While a teacher manually guides a student's movement in a classical learning scenario, technical systems have the potential to substitute and enhance this process, e.g., in Tai Chi [16]. One of the most important aspects in these systems, as well as for motor learning in general, is real-time motion feedback with respect to a target motion [12]. This naturally extends to other human-computer interaction (HCI) scenarios where feedback is critical for interacting with virtual content. An augmented movie set, for example, could have actors and director interact with computer-generated graphics using different modalities, as illustrated in Figure 1a and 2.

In this work, we distinguish between motor learning and motion guidance. While one of our overall goals is to teach new skills to a user, a technical system specifically designed for motor learning has to take many aspects into account, such as the different stages in the learning process [6] and attention in various phases [22]. We, instead, focus on multimodal feedback for motion guidance, which is an important aspect of acquiring new skills.

We propose a framework for manifold motion guidance and feedback through a motion guidance system (MGS), which includes interfaces for mixed reality scenarios and telepresence applications. Our modular framework, allows reuse and combination of feedback modalities and concepts for different applications. We analyse the design space for motion guidance and discuss the implementation of our framework, which uses full body tracking data and generates real-

Figure 2: An augmented movie set. The director (right) gives tactile feedback through a GUI to an actor (left) that interacts with a virtual object.

time visual, vibrotactile and pneumatic feedback to guide an individual's movement towards a desired motion.

Our **contributions** include:

- Analysis of the **design space** for motion guidance.
- Implementation of **multiple modules** for full-body 3D feedback that combines motion capture with tactile and visual stimuli.
- Dynamically adapting feedback based on a user's motion through **motion retargeting**, employing *time warping, motion dynamics, speed indication* and *movement prediction* for precise timing of feedback.

2. DESIGN SPACE

This section discusses the design space of multimodal feedback for motion guidance and how it relates to the human perceptual system, psychophysiological factors and information processing in the brain.

2.1 Human Information Processing

Human information processing is executed in three phases:

Stimulus identification describes the process of perceiving information. In the context of multimodal interaction, it is important to consider that perception varies under physical or cognitive workload [2] and that the perception of a feedback modality can be influenced by a parallel stimuli.

Response selection is the cognitive mechanism that converts the stimulus (perception) to a response (action). The human body provides a vast amount of possible responses to a stimulus (body movements) with its many degrees-of-freedom (DOFs). A large number of possible responses increases the response time, however, due to the associated cognitive process. Therefore, when considering stimulus-response (S-R) translations, it is often necessary to limit the set of responses and take into account S-R compatibility (e.g., spatial proximity between feedback and action).

Response programming, or "motor execution", executes the action and is affected by factors such as S-R frequency, movement direction, or sequence length. Furthermore, an action can alter the user's focus of attention and perception process.

Attention ([10] p33) and motor centers are tightly linked in the human brain and attention is crucial for motion guidance feedback, as it can lead to more effective motor performance and learning [22]. Selective attention preserves processing capabilites and processes only a subset of information.

2.2 Feedback Modalities

We perceive our environment with multiple senses simultaneously, as real-world feedback is multimodal. To simulate this in a virtual system, different feedback modalities and actuators have to be employed. We provide a brief overview of modalities and attributes relevant for motion guidance. Emphasis is placed on haptics, as an in-depth discussion of all modalities is beyond the scope of this paper.

Visual feedback is often considered the dominant form of feedback [10] (p112) and can provide users with objective observation of their motion (errors), augmented awareness for correction (e.g., emphasized body parts indication), superimposed target trajectories, or scores [3, 15].

Usability and user experience depends on the display hardware and properties, including latency, update rate, size, resolution, mobility and stereoscopy [18, 15].

Spatial Audio can be used to communicate 3D positions or direction. Dozza et al., for example, encode information using sinusoids with variable frequency and loudness [4].

Haptic feedback is composed of skin sensation and proprioception [10] (p194). **Skin sensation** is perceived by sensory receptors that enable us to localize and recognize individual tactile cues. Tactile displays can often indicate body part positions more intuitively than visual or audio feedback [20, 12]. Robustness and low weight has made vibration motors popular for tactile actuation.

Baek et al. [1] present a training system for fencing and dancing, and Rosenthal et al. explore foot step navigation in dance [17]. Spelmezan et al. [20] study spontaneous reactions to tactile patterns, while TIKL [12] gives a user visual information and vibrotactile feedback on the deviation of arm posture. McDaniel et al. [14] propose a framework for mapping vibrotactile patterns to motion.

Pneumatic pressure could potentially provide well localizable high-intensity stimuli, but is less popular due to size and tubing complexity of the required compressor.

Skin stretching with customized actuators may work well for indicating directions as pin-based actuators enable fine-grained feedback to the human skin [10] (p198). Constructions are, however, often bulky.

Feedback affecting **proprioception** (i.e., the sense of body parts' positions) has been shown, for example, using mechanical configurations with exoskeletons and electrogalvanic stimulation [10] (p194). In this work, we focus on modalities that do not directly alter the user's posture as active user engagement and minimal interference with the user's motion is preferred in typical motor learning scenarios [19].

2.3 Feedback vs. Support

Stimuli that are provided for motion guidance can be classified into feedback and support [14]. Feedback observes and takes into account user performance through real-time measurements in a feedback loop. Support is provided based on a predefined sequence regardless of user actions. Continuity of the feedback coupling to the user's performance varies with systems and modalities. Visual feedback, for example, can be used for continuous quantitative feedback on the deviation from desired pose using arrows drawn for each limb [18] or a target pose and qualitative verbal feedback [3].

2.4 Type of Feedback

Various options exist to encode information within the feedback modalities. The **user state** can, e.g., be visually represented by a mirrored virtual avatar in the user's pose [16]. The presentation of **intended pose** through, e.g., a teacher or ghost avatar [1], can be considered either support or feedback, e.g., if the teacher adapts to user performance.

Intended movement encodes how a user is supposed to move, while **motion dynamics** can communicate motion speed, for example. **Timing** and **performance** (e.g., the deviation from an intended pose) can be quantified and encoded in more abstract notions using audio [3]. Finally, the **state of virtual objects or other users** can be incorporated, such as collision with virtual objects in augmented reality or telepresence applications.

2.5 Level of Abstraction

The level of abstraction with which the stimuli are presented to the user has a large impact on the response selection phase in human information processing. Preattentive processing handles stimuli in a highly parallel manner without focused attention, for example, when extracting simple visual features and primitives. Therefore, a lower level of abstraction might trigger a quicker response even without training [22], while abstract feedback requires more cognitive processing to select the appropriate response.

Portillo-Rodriguez et al. [16] provide direct feedback using a push/pull metaphor where two vibration motors on the left and right hand indicate hand distance by varying vibration intensity. McDaniel et al. [14] explore temporal and spatial factors in vibrotactile patterns to encode direction, rotation or timing. They exploit the Sensory Saltation tactile illusion [8], where a series of sequentially activated vibrotactile motors can provide the perception of an interpolated, continuously moving linear stimulus, rather than one that appears and disappears in discrete locations. Israr et al. [9] equip a chair with twelve vibration motors to let users experience the illusion of moving touches on their back. This spatio-temporal pattern display technique enables more informative indication. In contrast, symbolic feedback with a learned meaning, such as Braille or pin-based displays [10] are highly abstract and require significant cognitive processing and training. Many examples of different levels of abstraction for visual and audio feedback can be found throughout HCI. For motion guidance, we can consider, e.g., a virtual hand to follow vs. a symbolic arrow, or a sinusoid played back in stereo headphones vs. a spoken command, to indicate direction.

Level of abstraction can also be viewed from the perspective of shift in attention [10] (p34) [22]. The sudden appearance or disappearence of a stimulus causes an exogeneous, automatic shift in attention. Symbolic cues (e.g., words or signs), on the other hand, cause an endogeneous (performer-driven) shift of attention and will in general require more processing capabilities, reaction time and training. A shift in attention also depends on the perceptual expectation of the user [10]. Therefore, training affects the S-R phase in information processing as well as the stimulus identification. However, generalizing attributes for low/high levels of abstraction is difficult, due to limitations of human cognition and potential interference between modalities and actuators.

2.6 Complexity

Complexity, or the amount of cognitive effort on the user, is not only affected by the level of abstraction, but also by a number of other factors. **The size of the response set**, or the number of movements conveyed through the feedback, should be kept to a minimum or be reduced by combining triggered movements into sequences. **The length of a movement sequence** does, on the other hand, also increase response selection time. An increased **S-R frequency** can, however, be exploited to decrease response selection time, for example, in training. Each application thus needs to find an optimal trade-off between these factors, based on its specific requirements.

2.7 Spatial Locality

Spatial compatibility [6] between a stimulus and response is crucial for an effective feedback system. There are usually advantages in applying a stimulus in spatial proximity to the limbs participating in the intended movement. More recently, this has been explained with a shift in attention [10] (p36) towards the designated region. If a (trained) response set exists, it usually causes an action, an effect also called precuing [10] (p15), which works better with decreasing complexity. Spatial locality is crucial for haptic feedback, but applies also to other modalities, e.g., for visual feedback on the side of the screen that affects that side of the user's body.

Spatial locality for positioning a display for visual feedback is also an important factor. If the user is expected to move around in the physical space, then the display can, for example, be worn (e.g., HMD [18]) or follow the user (e.g., robotic display [15]).

Psychophysichal interference between actuators, such as spatial masking effects for vibrotactors [5], has also to be taken into account. The spatial location of potential distractors thus has to be considered in a trade-off between spatial compatibility and interference.

2.8 Synchronicity & Timeliness

Synchronicity is relevant between user performance and intended pose/movement, as well as, between different modalities. While timing and speed is important for many motion guidance applications, systems often accept the delay between intended and user movement. Feedback could, however, be given ahead of time using **movement prediction** in certain situations, to compensate for system delay and user reaction. Furthermore, the feedback loop usually only compares the state of a user's movement with that of a teacher, which may result in unintended fast or intense corrective motions by the user. To our knowledge, no feedback system takes into account body dynamics. Techniques for prediction and interpolation exist in motion animation [21], but these have not been applied to motion guidance.

Furthermore, while a system should provide stimuli from different modalities synchronously, it needs to take into account that close temporal proximity may cause stimuli to interfere [5].

2.9 Quantification of Performance

The difference between intended and actual movement has to be evaluated to calculate deviation or error for the feedback in a motion guidance system. How this is done, depends on application and the feedback's abstraction level. It can be based on the state or the dynamics of a motion's basic parameters, considering spatial and temporal attributes.

Dynamic real-time feedback is constantly adapted in a closed loop [16], as opposed to offline feedback or pure sup-

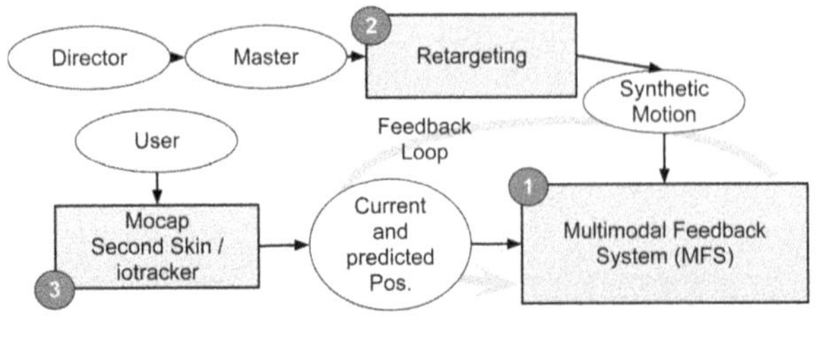

Figure 3: Our multimodal guidance system is based on (1) multimodal feedback, (2) dynamic motion retargeting, and (3) motion capture.

port systems. Motion capture is often used to acquire and compare a user's posture to a prerecorded representation. Visual, haptic or audio feedback can be given for the current state (e.g., virtual avatar [1]) or angular state-differences to a teacher position [12]. However, current systems don't consider dynamics and timing in their feedback loop.

A user will be able to follow feedback better, if it is not opposed to his current body dynamics. **Motion retargeting** has been used for animations to generate physically plausible motions e.g., [21, 13]. However, limitations on processing time are inherently different in real-time MGSs.

Quantitative performance can be measured based on angular joint errors [12], target positions [17] or paths, intra-body constraints, body volume [3] or derived parameters like speed, smoothness and energy efficiency.

Dynamic time warping through scaling in the time domain can provide an error measurement for an offline feedback process after the trial [1], where extreme positions in joint angles are used for alignment. While motions can be represented as a sequence of states [16], we are interested in using the timing information based on motion trajectories to improve student/teacher synchronizity, just as a human coach would adapt to the skill and speed of a student.

3. MOTION GUIDANCE SYSTEM

We have designed and implemented a Motion Guidance System (MGS) based on visual and tactile feedback, with a number of modules that form a subset of the described design space. The components in our system can be flexibly combined into new applications thanks to their modular nature.

Our implemented system consists of three classes of components, as illustrated in Figure 3:

- Motion tracking. We use motion capture systems to track the user's pose, such that appropriate feedback can be generated based on limb or body position and orientation.

- Dynamic motion retargeting. We provide automatically generated feedback based on current and predicted user motion, which can be merged with interactive manual control from an experimenter or director.

  Motion retargeting techniques (detailed in 3.3 and 3.4) enable our system to generate target motion adapting to user motion and state. In order to generate dynamic feedback we don't solely rely on the user's pose at a given time, but are using methods usually applied in motion retargeting for animation to predict future postures based on body dynamics. The user's required effort is minimized by finding the optimal point in time, where user and target trajectories can be matched and aligned.

- Multimodal feedback. Our modules generate visual, vibrotactile and pneumatic feedback for generic use with arbitrary limbs, or for specific tasks like arm movement or navigation (See Figure 4 for an overview).

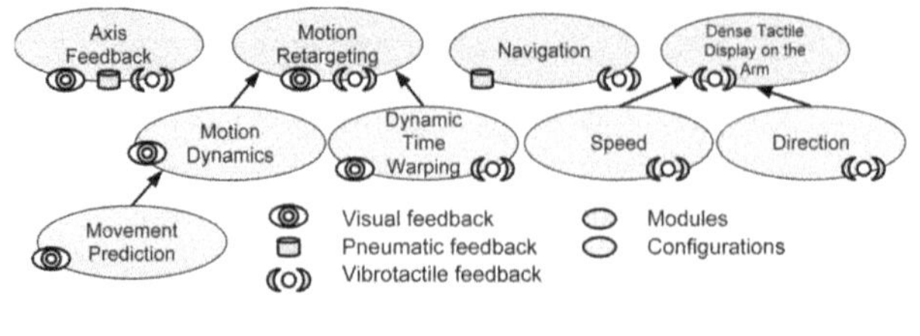

Figure 4: Overview of the implemented modules, their configurations and available modalities

3.1 Position and Direction

As previously discussed, it is often important to provide continuous feedback with a low abstraction level, for quick response selection by the user, as well as having an emphasis on high spatial locality. The rotation of a joint in the human skeleton has a maximum of three DOFs and in a low-level, bottom-up approach, we could consider giving feedback on these three DOFs to each limb in a similar and flexible manner.

The basic concept is to use two tactors to indicate rotation around one axis by activating a tactor on one side to push or pull the limb in a direction [12, 11].

Our implemented module is used to guide a user's limb into a predefined, or interactively specified, posture using two actuators per DOF, to indicate directional movement, as illustrated in Figure 5.

An error function calculates the feedback strength and direction based on current and target rotation, and a director can adjust the feedback, or add/remove DOFs for different limbs through our GUI (Figure 6).

Besides the primary vibrotactile feedback for this module, we also support pneumatic actuation, which provides a stronger tactile sensation. More complex mechanical configuration, however, limits its scalability to a larger number of DOFs.

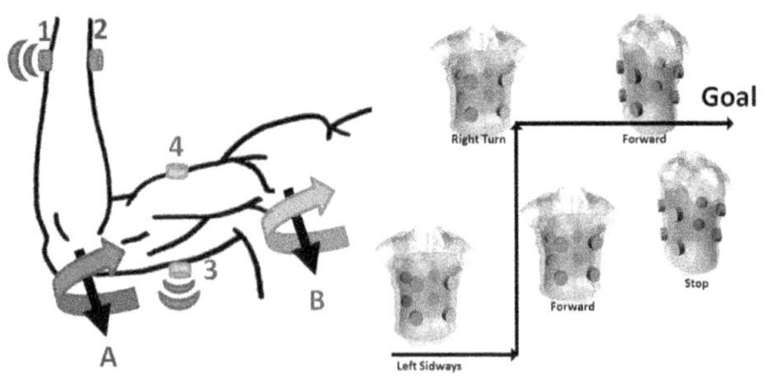

Figure 5: (Left) Vibrotactors 1-2 and 3-4, indicate rotations around axes A and B, respectively. (Right) Activation patterns for navigation with pneumatic feedback vest (active tactors = red).

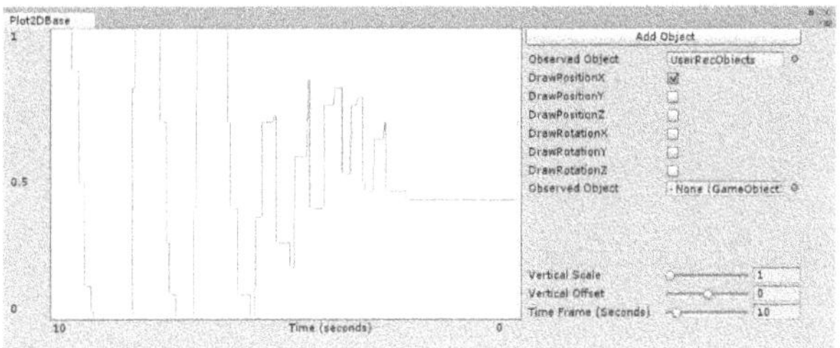

Figure 6: Our GUI provides straightforward access for controlling and adjusting tactile feedback.

These approaches provide high spatial locality and a low level of abstraction. However, they also generate a vast amount of information for multiple limbs, dramatically increasing complexity and cognitive processing time, which might cause psychophysiolocial interference.

Visually, axis feedback can be implemented as arrows drawn over the virtual representation of a user to indicate movement directions for certain limbs.

Similarly to [18], our implemented visual arrows show deviation from intended pose on the user's avatar compared to the teacher avatar (See Figure 7, left). The added arrows increase the level of abstraction, since they need to be interpreted by the user. Nevertheless, they should improve performance when it is difficult to identify small pose differences.

We also support prerecorded target movements, where the feedback dynamically adapts to the user's motion and the current state of the played back sequence.

The position of the end effector (e.g., hand [11]) can be sufficient for many applications, which allows a reduction of the response set, as suggested in Section 2.6. If a larger number of DOFs need to be taken into account (e.g., [12]), then spatial locality and possible resulting interferences become an important factor.

3.2 Continuous Feedback and Velocity

Interaction in many applications is focused on either hands or arms, and it is therefore useful to encode more information in these areas. This is challenging with the low abstraction level from the previously described two-tactor approach for position and direction, due to the limited area and resulting spatial and temporal interference.

Vibrotactors are, however, robust, relatively small and lightweight, consume little power, and can be used wirelessly and in spatial locality. Controllability of frequency and amplitude with quick actuation allows for implementations of different levels of abstraction and information encoding. This has made them popular for many applications, including our implementation of a dense tactile display for an arm.

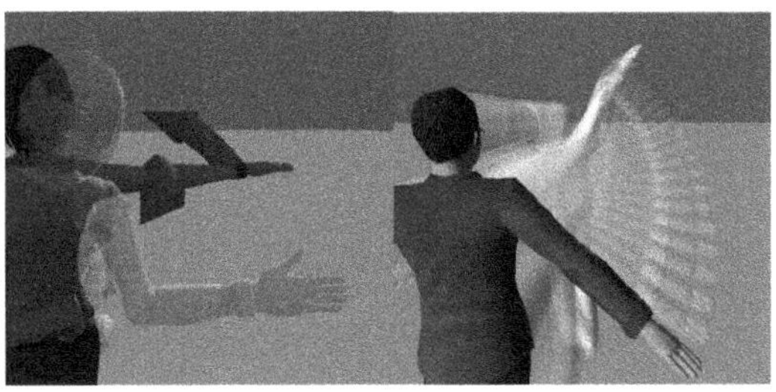

Figure 7: (Left) Motion guidance using ghost avatar and directional arrows. (Right) Motion sequence with transparent avatars, where the red avatar indicate a compulsory pose.

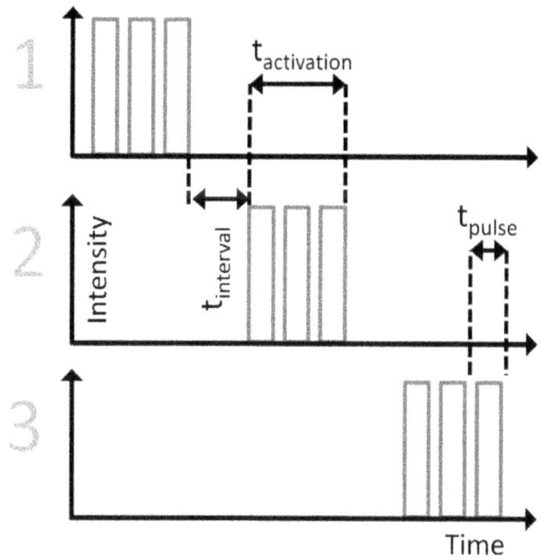

Figure 8: Sequential pulsing of three vibrotactors to indicate directional speed.

The sensory saltation effect can also be employed to add information like vectors or speed of intended movement. While the saltation effect has already been used to indicate rotations of the arm [12] or direction and rotation in a planar setting [9], indication of a vector in three dimensions on the arm, and especially speed, have been less explored.

Our implemented module is designed to provide movement speed sensation in three directions by employing a dense tactile display, where speed is indicated by triggering the vibrotactors in sequence, as shown in Figure 8.

By controlling burst durations and onset times, perceived stroking movements can be generated at a desired target speed. The actuators are turned on for a pulse duration (t_{pulse}) of 20-200 ms, where 20 ms was chosen as the minimum speed which subjects could perceive as a moving tactile stroke in a pilot study. With a t_{pulse} of 200 ms, a single loop of indication would take approximately two seconds, which was chosen as a practical maximum for our applications. $t_{activation}$ is the sum of pulses of a single tactor. The actuation intervals are calculated from user anatomy (i.e., arm length) and target velocity (v_{target}) using the equations:

$$t_{interval} = \frac{\frac{armlength}{v_{target}} - (3 * t_{activation})}{2} \tag{1}$$

$$t_{interval,calibrated} = t_{interval} * factor_{calib} \tag{2}$$

Preliminary experiments with five study participants on perceived absolute speed, indicate individual differences that can be corrected with a calibration factor ($factor_{calib}$), which we plan to explore further in future work.

Directional speed can only be triggered serially as shown in Figure 10, through sequential tactor activation, and depends on a presented prerecorded teacher movement. In the current implementation the sequences are independent of the user's performance and can be considered support rather than feedback.

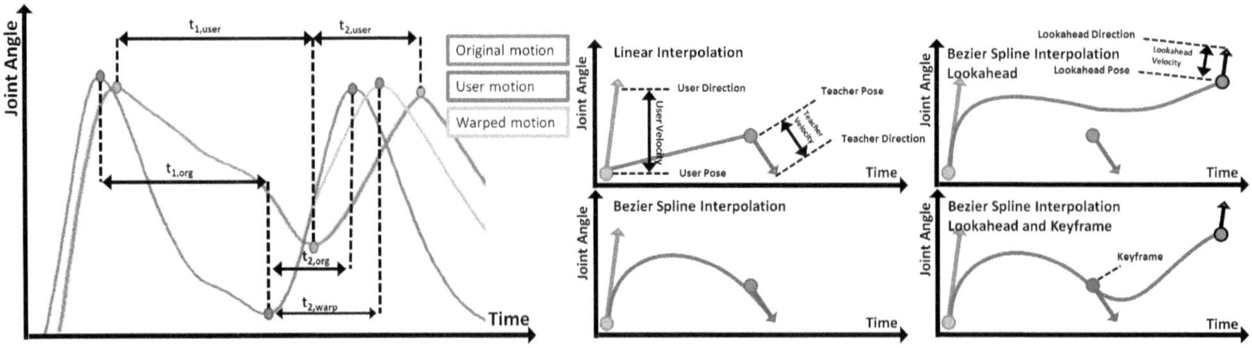

Figure 9: Dynamic Motion Retargeting. (Left) Target motion is time warped to user performance. (Middle) Path interpolation: Linear vs Bezier spline. (Right) Lookahead and keyframe indication.

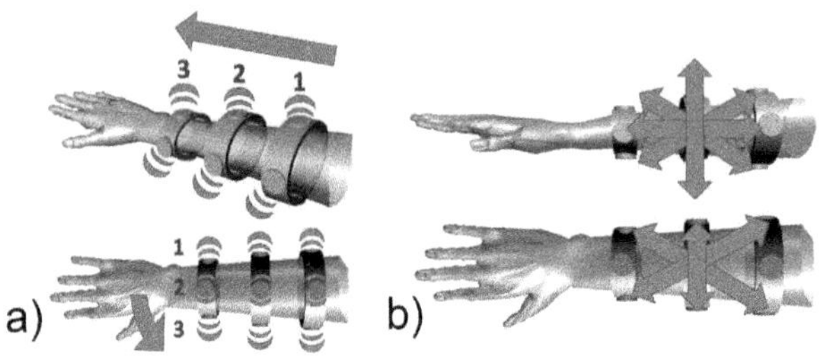

Figure 10: Sequential triggering of vibrotactors can be used to indicate a) speed and b) direction vectors.

The module implementing the rich vibrotactile display can also be configured to present translational forearm-directions through sequentially triggered tactors in seven different directions (See Figure 10). It allows the guidance towards target poses, where target speed can be chosen according to factors such as desired loop time or optimal user perception.

3.3 Dynamic Time Warping

In some situations, where complex feedback prevents a user from reacting in a timely manner, it might be a viable alternative to adapt the timing. When the quantification of performance is based purely on the user's state (e.g., joint angles) and the error needs to be minimized, the intended movement's speed can be matched with the user's movements.

We implemented dynamic time warping for non time-critical sequences, to adjust the teacher's speed and target pose to user performance, using two different approaches.

First, we extend Lieberman and Breazeal's work [12], where an error function is used for evaluation, and apply it to real-time feedback. The error function is calculated for each frame based on joints' angular (and velocity) differences and increases with deviating user motion, such as when user lags behind or performs an incorrect movement. When the error reaches a configurable threshold, the teacher is continuously slowed down towards a static posture or a defined minimal velocity, to allow the user to catch up or correct the motion. Once the error function estimates that the user is acceptably close to the target posture, speed is gradually increased until original velocity is reached.

Our second approach analyzes and searches for minima and maxima for target and user's joint angles' curves, as shown in Figure 9. The curves are matched for each joint axis and the time duration between a number of recent extreme points is measured. Figure 9 shows a warping example where the original motion is slowed down by the factor $t_{1,user}/t_{1,org}$.

An average speed-adjustment factor is calculated based on matches and factors of multiple joints and DOFs to match the teacher and student motion in time. The procedure is repeated as soon as a new local extreme point is discovered in the user's motion for any DOF. The algorithm requires careful parameterization and works only with a limited number of DOFs. The main challenges are correct detection and matching of extreme points over multiple DOFs and a combination of the resulting factors to single warp factor.

In future work, we plan to extend our approach by using subgestures to determine the timing differences between states [16].

3.4 Motion Dynamics and Prediction

Prediction or extrapolation of the user's movement, and consideration of future states of the intended movement, can be used to guide the user towards smoother and more natural movements. The prediction of a user's motion can be based on the movement speed and direction.

Motion dynamics are used to interpolate between user motion and intended movement for feedback on the required corrective path to produce smooth and natural user movement. Bezier spline interpolation is applied between user and teacher joint angles, taking into account rotational speed for each limb, as illustrated in Figure 9. The user's current movement dynamics are also compared to the teacher's future motions. If a teacher pose and velocity is found in the (parameterizable) near future that better matches the user's state than the current target state, then the user may be redirected towards that motion instead. The future state and its velocity is then added as an additional control point and parameterization in the Bezier interpolation.

It might sometimes be necessary to direct the user's selective attention to specific poses or movements. The intended pose might even be more important than the intended movement in certain choreographies, requiring a mechanism to deal with these situations. We have therefore implemented the option for a posture to be interactively marked as a keyframe by an experimenter/director.

Keyframes inform users of important poses that need to be executed and cannot be skipped due to deviating user motion (Figure 9). These keyframes are also emphasized when calculating trajectories by changing the weight of the control points in the Bezier spline. This enables a trade-off between accurate and smooth motion. If less keyframes are annotated beforehand, the system suggests overall movement. More keyframes, on the other hand, require accurate and detailed motion.

Figure 9 shows the possible configurations for the motion dynamics module in a one-dimensional example. Linear and Bezier spline interpolations are used to calculate movement paths with and without taking velocities into account. It also illustrates how a future (lookahead) pose and movement velocity can affect the movement path shown to the user.

When feedback has to be given on more complex movements, visual feedback works well [1, 16]. Presenting a ghost or teacher avatar to show the intended pose and another avatar animated with the current state of the user, is a well-established method. While the representation has a higher level of abstraction, the complexity can be handled because following and imitating the movements of others is a natural learning concept.

Currently, we use visual feedback through ghost target (teacher) and user avatars for motion dynamics and prediction. The avatars consist of a flexible number of animated body parts, which can be aligned and presented for optimal spatial locality based on the scenario (e.g., mirrored or watched from behind).

Furthermore, we have implemented motion guidance paths for feedback on movement dynamics. Instead of a single teacher state (e.g., [16, 18]), we incorporate a movement sequence (e.g., up to a few seconds) into our feedback loop. The visualization consists of multiple transparent avatars in different postures, rendered behind each other to visualize not only a single state of the teacher, but a whole motion sequence (See Figure 7, right). Keyframes are visualized as avatars colored in red and move towards the user during the interpolation.

3.5 Haptic Feedback

Multimodal feedback can also be given to communicate the state of objects in a virtual scene. From visual feedback alone, interaction with virtual objects is often difficult, since depth is hard to judge even with stereoscopic displays, when the sense of touch is missing.

In a movie set, for example, where virtual content is to be merged with video material in a green room environment, actors are usually not aware of their exact position relative to the virtual objects. Current systems deliver visual feedback on the mixed reality configuration, but require the actors to look at screens mounted around the set. Our system could provide tactile feedback as the primary modality, which could be embedded in the actor's clothing. Multiple tasks are useful in this scenario, including feedback on pose, path, reaching [11] or multiple DOFs tasks for one or multiple actors.

Our implemented module augments interactions with virtual objects by using physics simulations to detect collisions with the user's body and generates 3 DOF directional tactile feedback. Our GUI (See Figure 11) makes it straightforward to visually map the feedback to different limbs of a virtual avatar and to arbitrary feedback axes on the body. This module calculates direction and intensity of the feedback and activates the corresponding tactor, which can be used flexibly for different body parts and objects due to its low level of abstraction and complexity.

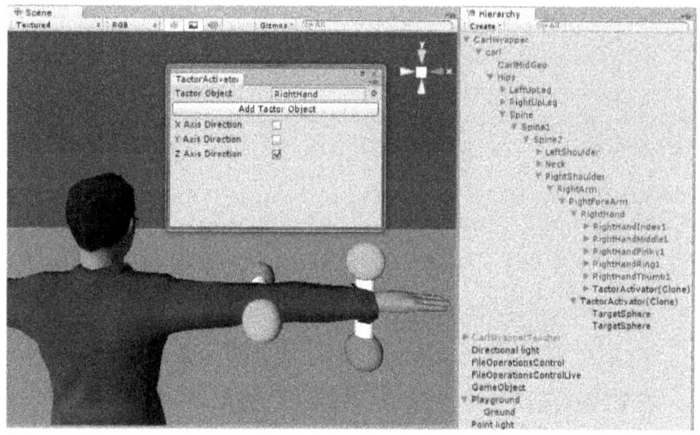

Figure 11: Our graphical interface allows direct editing of haptic feedback on an avatar in a virtual 3D environment.

3.6 Guided Navigation

Feedback on intended movement (path) or pose (target position) of the user in space is important for spatial navigation. Most scenarios primarily deal with a user moving in a plane and we therefore consider only the 2D position and orientation of the user in this plane. For tactile feedback, the torso provides a relatively large input area and interference between tactors is limited. Although providing feedback for navigation to the torso isn't spatially local to the legs, multiple studies show promising results (e.g., [14]).

We steer tracked users towards a target position through generated tactile feedback, as shown in Figure 5, right . Our feedback patterns control 3 DOFs; forward/backward translation, sideways translation, and rotation around the up-axis. Our implementation uses pneumatic feedback since vibrotactile and rotational patterns are less clearly perceived during physically and cognitively demanding tasks [20]. We have, however, also implemented vibrotactile feedback to allow comparisons in a future evaluation.

Directions of translation and rotation are presented sequentially to avoid temporal interference, and preliminary experiments with multiple activation patterns indicate that pulsing at approximately 3 Hz gives clear feedback for our pneumatic actuators. We plan additional experiments to investigate this further.

3.7 Implementation

Our current applications employ the iotracker [19] or Second Skin [7] motion capture systems to track the user's 6 DOFs pose.

Vibrotactile feedback is provided using tactors from Audioacoustics Engineering. Our dense tactile display uses twelve vibrotactors on the arm, as shown in Figure 1 c). Our custom control board drives the tactors at 250 Hz, the recommended frequency for human skin perception [5], and communicates wirelessly with the host PC using bluetooth. We use pulsed vibrations, instead of continuous, as it is better for perception, as shown in related work [2] and confirmed in our early experiments. We have experimented with different activation patterns and tactor configurations. Figure 10 shows the positions where vibrotactile stimuli are applied for our dense tactile display.

Pneumatic feedback is provided using a 3RD Space Vest from TN Games, which applies pressure using four actuators on the chest and four on the back, as shown in Figure 5.

The modules and feedback loop are implemented in C# with the Unity 3.5 game engine. The visual feedback and virtual world is generated with Unity's renderer, while our C/C++ plugins control the tactile feedback modules, and interface with the motion capture systems using the Opentracker middleware. The system and tracking server run on a single PC (Intel i7-2600K, 16 GB RAM).

4. CONCLUSION & FUTURE WORK

In this paper, we discussed the design space, challenges and solutions, potential scenarios, and our implementation of a multimodal motion guidance system. Our system integrates multiple modules that generate feedback based on a user's performance and intended movement. We have integrated a number of different feedback modalities (vibrotactile, pneumatic, and visual) and shown their application for different scenarios and use cases.

Due to the vast nature of feedback options and complexity of human cognition and motor system, we restricted this work to 3D motor movements that are tracked by a motion capture system, and implemented a set of feedback modules, which appeared most promising and generic, after an analysis of the design space.

We are currently extending our real-time authoring framework to better support prototyping, as well as scientific evaluation of motion guidance applications. We also plan to present results from our ongoing evaluation of individual feedback modalities and their combinations.

It would be interesting to explore adding modules for finer feedback granularity (e.g., feedback on finger movement) and integrate other technologies in the system (e.g., HMD for augmented reality, or heat feedback). Finally, we will extend our work from motion guidance to motor learning, focusing on cognitive aspects and processes that are relevant in motion feedback.

5. ACKNOWLEDGEMENTS

This work was funded in part by the European Union within the PROFITEX project (FP7-NMP2-SE-2009-228855). Alex Olwal was supported by a Swedish Research Council Fellowship and a Blanceflor Foundation Scholarship.

6. REFERENCES

[1] S. Baek, S. Lee, and G. J. Kim. Motion retargeting and evaluation for VR-based training of free motions. *Science And Technology*, 2003.

[2] W. Borchers, J. and Prinz. *Design and Recognition of Tactile Feedback Patterns for Snowboarding.* PhD thesis, RWTH Aachen University, 2008.

[3] E. Charbonneau, A. Miller, and J. J. LaViola. Teach me to dance: exploring player experience and performance in full body dance games. In *Proceedings of the 8th International Conference on Advances in Computer Entertainment Technology - ACE '11*, pages 43:1–43:8, Nov. 2011.

[4] M. Dozza, F. B. Horak, and L. Chiari. Auditory biofeedback substitutes for loss of sensory information in maintaining stance. *Experimental brain research*, 178(1):37–48, Mar. 2007.

[5] J. B. F. V. Erp, H. a. H. C. V. Veen, C. Jansen, and T. Dobbins. Waypoint navigation with a vibrotactile waist belt. In *ACM Transactions on Applied Perception*, volume 2, pages 106–117, 2005.

[6] P. Fitts and M. Posner. *Human performance.* Brooks/Cole., Oxford, England, 1967.

[7] K. Fukushi, J. Zizka, and R. Raskar. Second Skin: Motion Capture with Actuated Feedback for Motor Learning. In *ACM SIGGRAPH 2011*, page 4503, 2011.

[8] F. A. Geldard. *Sensory Saltation: Metastability in the Perceptual World.* John Wiley & Sons Inc, 1975.

[9] A. Israr and I. Poupyrev. Tactile brush: Drawing on Skin with a Tactile Grid Display. In *Proceedings of the 2011 annual conference on Human factors in computing systems - CHI '11*, page 2019. ACM Press, May 2011.

[10] J. A. Jacko. *The Human Computer Interaction Handbook.* CRC Press, third edition, 2012.

[11] M. Klapdohr, B. Wöldecke, D. Marinos, J. Herder, C. Geiger, and W. Vonolfen. Vibrotactile Pitfalls: Arm Guidance for Moderators in Virtual TV Studios. *Information Systems*, pages 72–80, Dec. 2010.

[12] J. Lieberman and C. Breazeal. TIKL: Development of a Wearable Vibrotactile Feedback Suit for Improved Human Motor Learning. *IEEE Transactions on Robotics*, 23(5):919–926, Oct. 2007.

[13] C. K. Liu and Z. Popovic. Synthesis of Complex Dynamic Character Motion from Simple Animations. *ACM Trans. Graph.*, 21(3):408–416, 2002.

[14] T. McDaniel, D. Villanueva, S. Krishna, and S. Panchanathan. MOVeMENT: A framework for systematically mapping vibrotactile stimulations to fundamental body movements. In *Haptic Audio-Visual Environments and Games (HAVE), 2010 IEEE International Symposium on*, pages 1–6, 2010.

[15] A. Nakamura, S. Tabata, T. Ueda, S. Kiyofuji, and Y. Kuno. Dance training system with active vibro-devices and a mobile image display. In *Intelligent Robots and Systems, 2005.(IROS 2005). 2005 IEEE/RSJ International Conference on*, pages 3075–3080. IEEE, 2005.

[16] O. Portillo-Rodriguez, O. O. Sandoval-Gonzalez, E. Ruffaldi, R. Leonardi, C. A. Avizzano, and M. Bergamasco. Real-Time Gesture Recognition, Evaluation and Feed-Forward Correction of a Multimodal Tai-Chi Platform. *Haptic and Audio Interaction Design*, 5270:30–39, 2008.

[17] J. Rosenthal, N. Edwards, D. Villanueva, S. Krishna, T. McDaniel, and S. Panchanathan. Design, Implementation, and Case Study of a Pragmatic Vibrotactile Belt. *IEEE Trans. on Instrumentation and Measurement*, 60(1):114–125, 2011.

[18] Y. Ryota Sakamoto, Yuke Yoshimura, Tokuhiro Sugiura and Nomura. A motion instruction system using head tracking back perspective. *World Automation Congress*, 2010.

[19] C. Schönauer, T. Pintaric, and H. Kaufmann. Full Body Interaction for Serious Games in Motor Rehabilitation. In *ACM Augmented Human International Conference*, 2011.

[20] D. Spelmezan, M. Jacobs, A. Hilgers, and J. Borchers. Tactile motion instructions for physical activities. In *Proceedings of the 27th international conference on Human factors in computing systems - CHI '09*, page 2243, New York, USA, Apr. 2009.

[21] S. Tak and K. Hyeong-Seok. A Physically-Based Motion Retargeting Filter. *ACM Transactions on Graphics (TOG)*, 24(1):98–117, 2005.

[22] G. Wulf. *Attention and motor skill learning.* Human Kinetics, 2007.

Multimodal Detection of Salient Behaviors of Approach-Avoidance in Dyadic Interactions

Bo Xiao†, Panayiotis G. Georgiou†, Brian Baucom‡, Shrikanth S. Narayanan†,‡
† Department of Electrical Engineering, ‡ Department of Psychology
University of Southern California, Los Angeles, CA 90089
boxiao@usc.edu, georgiou@sipi.usc.edu, baucom@usc.edu, shri@sipi.usc.edu

ABSTRACT

Approach-Avoidance (AA) coding is a measure of involvement and immediacy in human dyadic interactions. We focus on analyzing the salient events in interactions that trigger change points in AA code in time, as perceived by domain experts. We employ coarse level visual cues associated with body parts, as well as vocal energy features. Motion vector extraction and body pose estimation techniques are used for extracting visual cues. Functionals of these cues are used as features for SVM based machine learning experiments. We found that the coder's judgments on salient events are related to the short time interval preceding the labeling. We also show that visual cues are the main information source for decision making on salient AA events, and that considering the information from a subset of body parts provides the same information as considering the full set. The mean of absolute value and standard deviation of motion streams are the most effective functionals as feature. We achieve an F-score of 0.55 in detecting salient events using cross-validation with a one-subject-out approach.

Categories and Subject Descriptors

J.4 [**Social And Behavioral Sciences**]: Psychology

General Terms

Algorithms

Keywords

Approach-Avoidance, salience, pose estimation, motion vector, multimodal feature

1. INTRODUCTION

The computational analysis of human interactions opens up new challenges and opportunities for signal processing [1]. As one of the common interaction forms, dyadic interactions take place in everyday life as well as in particular application scenarios such as psychotherapy and diagnosis, doctor-patient interviews, and customer care. Psychologists have been studying human behavior including notably in research and clinical settings and developed various coding methods, e.g. [2], as instruments to quantitatively describe behavior in domain-specific dimensions. The ability to model the relation between multimodal observations and expert-derived codes is valuable for both the fields of engineering and psychology, in terms of offering processing efficiency and scalability as well as enabling new tools for seeking insights for the domain experts.

There are mainly two levels of behavior coding. High level codes are often given to entire interaction sessions which are more abstract and summative of constituent behavior details. For example, Black *et al.* [3] and Georgiou *et al.* [4] demonstrated automatic classification of couples' behavior in therapy sessions. In a 96-hour corpus, coders assigned various high level codes to each spouse, such as "acceptance", "blame", *etc.* By using a combination of automatically-derived lexical information and speech features, they demonstrated prediction of the behavior codes with accuracy exceeding 80%.

On the other hand, intermediate level codes are often specified moment by moment, and capture dynamic aspects of the behavior. Oertel *et al.* studied involvement in a group conversation [5]. Two 30 min segments with 4 or 5 subjects were used in their analysis. A one dimensional code along the time axis was assigned to all the participants as an average degree of involvement. Using multimodal features including prosodic and visual cues such as gaze and blinking, they achieved an accuracy of 68% in classification of three involvement levels with a SVM.

Approach-Avoidance (AA) [6] is another intermediate level behavior related to involvement and immediacy that has been studied extensively. It is typically assigned on an individual basis continuously in time using a numerical rating, e.g., on a 9-point likert scale from -4 to 4. The AA code is associated with subject behaviors that can be directly observed such as head, hand and body pose, movement, gaze, facial expression, speech fluency and latency, *etc*, hence suggesting that the use of signal processing is an appropriate tool for its estimation. Rozgić *et al.* [7] studied the problem of estimating the AA code in an Ordinal Logistic Regression (OLR) framework. Acoustic features and motion features derived from a Vicon Motion Capture system were considered. The functionals of these features in time domain were used as input for OLR. By combining OLR with an HMM model to capture dynamics, the algorithm could estimate the AA code with accuracy of 75%. In addition,

ICMI'12, October 22–26, 2012, Santa Monica, California, USA.

their results showed that the AA behavior was more robustly estimated using the visual cues.

While the past work has focused on estimating the code value, not much has been done in predicting the dynamics of AA code change. In fact, over the course of an interaction, the information encoded and conveyed typifying certain behavior patterns are not continuously and uniformly manifested over time. There are salient events which "highlight" specific behavior patterns. Psychologists also refer to the phenomenon of "thresholding" negative influence from the other interlocutor in conversations [8], where people would typically show behaviors whenever the negative influence exceeds a certain tolerance, rather than react to the influence immediately. The moment that the subject makes some substantial change in his/her behavior in response is considered salient. Therefore, computationally modeling these salient phenomena of human behavior is also important. In addition, human-agreement on absolute degree of a behavior code is often arguably lower than agreement on the relative salience.

In this paper, we investigate temporal changes in the AA code, that may indicate a salient event in the interaction. We focus on the coarse level body movements as they are the most prominent observable phenomena. Pixel-wise motion vectors are computed per frame and associated with estimated body parts, which is then summed over blocks and used as the visual cue. Voice energy is employed as an acoustic cue. For a given time point, we analyze a short time interval preceding that point. Functionals of the visual and acoustic cues are adopted as features for classification and detection of salient events. We introduce the data set in Sec. 2, explain the feature extraction procedure in Sec. 3, report experimental results in Sec. 4 and conclude the work in Sec. 5.

2. DATA SET

For the experiments in this paper, we used the multimodal dyadic interaction database presented in [9]. The sessions in this corpus were dyadic interactions based on unscripted role-playing on conflictual topics, such as cheating in relationship, arguing over a drinking problem, *etc.* In order to get interactions that are as realistic as possible, participants were provided with the topics a few days before the recording. At the time of collection, participants were allowed several minutes to prepare for a topic, where they could exchange ideas and make up a story. During the collection, the two subjects took seats on a couch side by side.

The corpus provides near-field frontal view video data for each subject in resolution of 1024×768 and 30 frames per second. Audio data were collected from close-talking lapel microphones. One psychologist annotated eight subjects involved in 32 sessions with respect to individual subject. The total length of the recording is about 135 minutes. The psychologist gave an Approach-Avoidance (AA) code that is discrete in value from -4 to 4, and continuous in time. During annotating the psychologist followed the "three seconds rule", which means a change of AA code is in general based on the observation of the last three seconds. The perceptually salient events are identified by a change of AA code whenever a new code value is assigned along time. When the code value remains stationary, we call that period as perceptually non-salient. In total we found 659 cases of salient events. The details of the data are shown in Table 1.

Table 1: Summary of data from each subject

Subject	1	2	3	4	5
No. session	4	2	6	6	4
Total length (min)	24	5	21	21	13
No. salient events	73	24	118	112	69

Subject	6	7	8	Total
No. session	4	3	3	32
Total length (min)	13	19	19	135
No. salient events	43	124	96	659

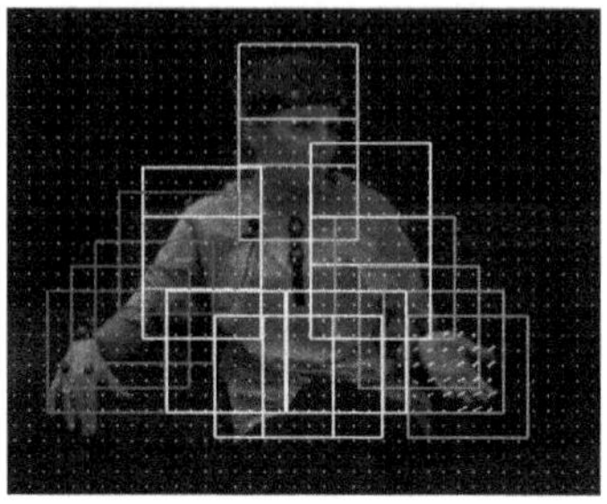

Figure 1: Body pose and motion vector estimation

3. MULTIMODAL FEATURE EXTRACTION

3.1 Motion vector and body pose

We extract the pixel-wise motion vector using Farnebäck's algorithm [10] that is implemented in OpenCV library on a frame basis. However, irrelevant motion may appear in the background. More importantly, the raw motion vectors lack the association with the parts of human body. To address this problem, we use the state of the art body pose estimation approach introduced in [11]. This approach captures orientation with a mixture of templates for each body part, and contextual co-occurrence relations as well as standard spring model encoded spatial relations between parts. When these relations are in a tree structure, the model can be efficiently optimized with dynamic programming.

In our work, we apply an extensively trained upper body model developed by the authors of the tool on each video frame, which returns 18 square blocks over the corresponding position, including 2 blocks for head, 4 blocks each for left and right arms, and 8 blocks for torso. As the two subjects were seated side by side, they talked to counter directions, which may lead to a swapped pattern of left and right arm behaviors. So for the interlocutor seated on the right, we swap the order of the left arm and torso blocks with the right ones to get features aligned for all subjects.

The original estimation procedure adopted an iterative optimization on the block size, which may vary among frames and deviate from the reasonable size. Since in our scenario, the subjects remain seated during the interaction, the block size did not vary significantly. Thus we decided to fix the block size by empirically evaluating the pose estimation using different sizes, and choosing the size that best fits the data. In Figure 1 we show an example of body pose and motion vector estimation.

3.2 Feature design

Let the time index of a video frame in a session be t. Let the row and column indexes of a pixel be i and j. The motion vector of a pixel (i, j) at time t is represented as

$(dx, dy) = f(i, j, t)$. Let $B(k, t)$ be the k-th block of body part at time t, and $M(k, t) = \sum_{(i,j) \in B(k,t)} f(i, j, t)$ be the corresponding raw motion stream. As a result, we obtain a 2-dimension motion stream for each body part, considering horizontal and vertical axes separately. In order to align acoustic and visual cues, we sample the energy of speech signal using the same frequency as video, i.e. 30 frames per second with no overlap. We obtain the vocal energy stream $V(t)$ as the last dimension of raw features.

In light of the "three seconds rule", we define a look-back window (LBW) of length W ending at a given time point t. We extract functionals of the raw feature streams as the final features. Functionals computed include mean of absolute value, standard deviation, absolute value of skewness, and kurtosis of the raw features. We also compute the second moment of the feature in the first and last third of the window, and take the larger of either their ratio or its reciprocal, in order to capture any temporal change of the feature stream. In addition, we compute the entropy of each feature stream. First, the raw feature stream is Z-normalized along the entire session, and then quantized to 8 bins with fixed boundaries. For each LBW the histogram of the quantized feature is used to compute the entropy. The functionals for all raw features are aggregated to get the final feature vector.

4. EXPERIMENTS

4.1 Experiment design

We sample one LBW per second in each session, with length W being 1, 2, 3 or 4 seconds. Normalization of feature value is applied to each subject to account for interpersonal behavior variability. The samples nearest to the salient events in time are labeled as in the salient class. The two closest neighboring samples of the salient sample are also considered as salient, in order to tolerate inaccuracy in coding as well as to cope with the time span of salient event. All other samples are labeled as in the non-salient class.

We found that direct modeling of salient and non-salient classes using all the samples did not yield good results. One reason might be that the salience property is not binary in nature, but thresholded by the coder at the time of perceiving the interaction. In addition the salient event might not be exact in time, but span a short period. Therefore the negative samples are contaminated by some partial salience. To overcome the problem, we use a balanced training design. Assume there are N coder-specified salient samples, then we select N non-salient samples that are at least 4 seconds away from each other as well as those coder-specified salient samples. This set is named as the balanced set. The linear SVM model is cross-validated by leaving one subject for testing at a time, and taking all other subjects for training.

We then apply the models derived with the balanced set to the entire sessions of the corresponding left-out subjects. In practice the size of non-salient class highly exceeds that of the salient class. To address this mismatch, we optimize the F-score of detecting salient events by tuning the threshold on the raw SVM output in making classification decision. Therefore we need a second layer of cross-validation, i.e. we leave one session of the subject for testing at a time, and take all other sessions as development set to carry out the optimization.

For evaluation, we report the accuracy on the balanced set, the precision, recall and F-score of detection on the entire dataset, as well as the Kappa value of agreement between the coder and our result, averaged with weighting on the sample size of each subject.

Table 2: Results of different LBW length

W (sec)	Acc.	Pre.	Rec.	F-score	Kappa
1	0.62	0.34	0.70	0.45	0.15
2	0.68	0.38	0.71	0.50	0.24
3	0.70	0.41	0.70	0.52	0.27
4	0.70	0.42	0.75	0.54	0.31

Table 3: Results by using different functionals

Functional	Acc.	Pre.	Rec.	F-score	Kappa
Mean abs.	0.68	0.42	0.76	0.54	0.31
Standard dev.	0.70	0.43	0.75	0.55	0.32
Skewness	0.60	0.31	0.82	0.45	0.10
Kurtosis	0.61	0.31	0.85	0.46	0.11
2nd moment ratio	0.57	0.32	0.76	0.44	0.12
Entropy	0.70	0.40	0.72	0.51	0.27

4.2 Experiment results

The results of different LBW length W are reported in Table 2. Note that the chance level for the "Acc" column is 0.5 as applied to the balanced set, while the chance level of F-score is 0.42, when claiming all samples as salient. Higher accuracy is obtained with longer LBW length. This suggests that the coder's perception of salience is dependent on a not too short period before the marked time point.

The performance of different functionals are reported in Table 3. W is set to 4 seconds in all of the following experiments. The most effective feature functionals are standard deviation and mean of absolute value. The entropy feature is close to the previous two. The higher order statistics and the second moment ratio do not result in good performance.

The results of using different multimodal cues are reported in Table 4, where all the functionals are incorporated. Here the row of a body part represents only using the motion cues of that part. The last row of "HSH" stands for a combination of upper head, two shoulders and two hands. The results show that using only the audio information does not effectively predict the salient events. The performance when using only some of the motion features does comparably with employing all the motion features. One reason might be that the movements of individual body parts are highly dependent due to the body's articulation. The other cause might be the body pose estimation. As shown in Figure 1, the blocks have a moderate degree of overlap, hence the motion of one body part is leaked to nearby parts. A finer and tighter body part estimation technique that can also resolve occlusion is therefore desired.

Based on the experiments above, we test the performance of selected functionals and cues, as shown in Table 5. MSE stands for mean of absolute value, standard deviation and entropy, while MS stands for the first two. V stands for selected visual features as the "HSH" row in Table 4, while A stands for acoustic features. We see that with only these features we achieve about the same performance as using all cues and functionals. Incorporating the entropy feature does not improve the result.

In Figure 2 we show one example of the precision-recall curve in the development phase, as well as the correspond-

Table 4: Results by using different multimodal cues

Cues	Acc.	Pre.	Rec.	F-score	Kappa
Audio	0.62	0.30	0.81	0.44	0.08
Motion	0.71	0.41	0.72	0.53	0.29
Head	0.69	0.40	0.78	0.53	0.27
Shoulder	0.67	0.39	0.78	0.52	0.26
Torso	0.68	0.40	0.70	0.51	0.26
Arm	0.69	0.43	0.69	0.53	0.31
Hand	0.69	0.42	0.68	0.52	0.29
HSH	0.72	0.42	0.77	0.54	0.31

Table 5: Results by using selective multimodal cues

Cues	Acc.	Pre.	Rec.	F-score	Kappa
MSE_AV	0.70	0.42	0.75	0.54	0.30
MS_AV	0.71	0.43	0.75	0.55	0.32

ing detection result on the left-out session. In general our approach suffers from low precision. This might be due to the limitation of coarse level motion and functionals. For example, not all motions are equally salient. Specific gestures and movements may bear more relevant behavioral meaning that is perceived as salient. Although the F-score is not very high in value, it is much higher than chance level. As a first attempt on the problem, the result shows the feasibility of using multimodal signal processing and machine learning approaches to infer salience in human dyadic interaction. We would also like to study human agreement as an upper bound when data with multiple annotation is available.

5. CONCLUSIONS

In this paper we focused on analyzing the salient events that trigger change points of the AA code, using coarse level visual cues and vocal energy features. State of the art motion vector extraction and body pose estimation were used for extracting visual cues. Functionals of visual and vocal cues were used as features in SVM based machine learning experiments. We found that the coder's perception of salient event is related to the short time interval preceding the change point of code. Visual cues are more informative in predicting salient events, while the subset of head, shoulder and hand yields similar results as the full feature set. The mean of absolute value and standard deviation of the motion streams are the most effective functionals. The best result of detecting salient events has an F-score of 0.55 using models learned on a balanced set and applied to entire sessions in a one-subject-out cross validation.

In the future we will pursue further work to improve the analysis and results with ongoing data collection. For example, better body part estimation techniques are desired. In terms of visual cues, one would like to incorporate finer details such as gaze and facial expressions. In order to separate meaning bearing gestures from casual movement, one needs to analyze the motion with a more complex time sequence model. Moreover, the salient events have their own properties such as the degree and direction of AA code change and we plan on modeling these properties.

6. ACKNOWLEDGMENTS

The research is supported in part by NSF, NIH, and DARPA.

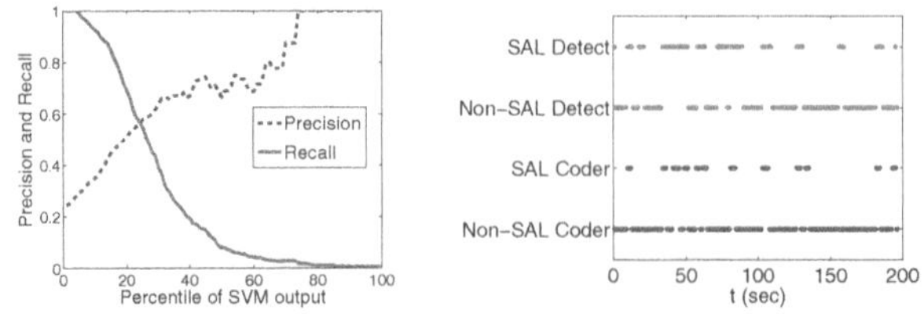

(a) Precision and recall

(b) detection result

Figure 2: Example of detection result

7. REFERENCES

[1] A. Vinciarelli, H. Salamin, and M. Pantic. Social Signal Processing: Understanding social interactions through nonverbal behavior analysis. In *Proc. CVPR Workshops*, pages 42–49, 2009.

[2] C. Heavey, D. Gill, and A. Christensen. *Couples interaction rating system 2*. University of California, Los Angeles, 2002.

[3] M. Black, A. Katsamanis, C.C. Lee, A. Lammert, B. Baucom, A. Christensen, P. Georgiou, and S. Narayanan. Automatic classification of married couples' behavior using audio features. In *Proc. InterSpeech*, 2010.

[4] P. Georgiou, M. Black, A. Lammert, B. Baucom, and S. Narayanan. "that's aggravating, very aggravating": Is it possible to classify behaviors in couple interactions using automatically derived lexical features? In *Proc. ACII*, 2011.

[5] C. Oertel, S. Scherer, and N. Campbell. On the use of multimodal cues for the prediction of degrees of involvement in spontaneous conversation. In *Proc. Interspeech*, 2011.

[6] L.K. Guerrero. Observer ratings of nonverbal involvement and immediacy. *The sourcebook of nonverbal measures: Going beyond words*, pages 221–235, 2004.

[7] V. Rozgic, B. Xiao, A. Katsamanis, B. Baucom, P. Georgiou, and S. Narayanan. Estimation of ordinal approach-avoidance labels in dyadic interactions: ordinal logistic regression approach. In *Proc. ICASSP*, 2011.

[8] J. Gottman, C. Swanson, and J. Murray. The mathematics of marital conflict: Dynamic mathematical nonlinear modeling of newlywed marital interaction. *Journal of Family Psychology*, 13(1):3–19, 1999.

[9] V. Rozgic, B. Xiao, A. Katsamanis, B. Baucom, P. Georgiou, and S. Narayanan. A new multichannel multimodal dyadic interaction database. In *Proc. InterSpeech*, 2010.

[10] G. Farnebäck. Two-frame motion estimation based on polynomial expansion. *Image Analysis*, pages 363–370, 2003.

[11] Y. Yang and D. Ramanan. Articulated pose estimation using flexible mixtures of parts. In *Proc. CVPR*, 2011.

Multimodal Analysis of the Implicit Affective Channel in Computer-Mediated Textual Communication

Joseph F. Grafsgaard[1], Robert M. Fulton[2], Kristy Elizabeth Boyer[1], Eric N. Wiebe[3], James C. Lester[1]

[1]Department of Computer Science [2]Department of Psychology

[3]Department of Science, Technology, Engineering, and Mathematics Education

North Carolina State University, Raleigh, NC, USA

{jfgrafsg, rmfulton, keboyer, wiebe, lester}@ncsu.edu

ABSTRACT

Computer-mediated textual communication has become ubiquitous in recent years. Compared to face-to-face interactions, there is decreased bandwidth in affective information, yet studies show that interactions in this medium still produce rich and fulfilling affective outcomes. While overt communication (e.g., emoticons or explicit discussion of emotion) can explain some aspects of affect conveyed through textual dialogue, there may also be an underlying implicit affective channel through which participants perceive additional emotional information. To investigate this phenomenon, computer-mediated tutoring sessions were recorded with Kinect video and depth images and processed with novel tracking techniques for posture and hand-to-face gestures. Analyses demonstrated that tutors implicitly perceived students' focused attention, physical demand, and frustration. Additionally, bodily expressions of posture and gesture correlated with student cognitive-affective states that were perceived by tutors through the implicit affective channel. Finally, posture and gesture complement each other in multimodal predictive models of student cognitive-affective states, explaining greater variance than either modality alone. This approach of empirically studying the implicit affective channel may identify details of human behavior that can inform the design of future textual dialogue systems modeled on naturalistic interaction.

Categories and Subject Descriptors

I.5.4 [**Vision and Scene Understanding**]: 3D/stereo scene analysis; H.1.2 [**User/Machine Systems**]: Human factors, human information processing; J.4 [**Social and Behavioral Sciences**]: Psychology

General Terms

Algorithms, Experimentation, Human Factors, Measurement.

Keywords

Affect, computer-mediated communication, depth images, Kinect, gesture, posture, textual dialogue.

1. INTRODUCTION

Computer-mediated textual communication has become ubiquitous in recent years with pervasive use of numerous online communication channels [4]. Textual communication also plays an important role in the development of intelligent systems, mitigating challenges associated with automatic speech recognition [25] and providing a record of the interactions, which is particularly useful for tasks such as tutoring [6]. Textual communication is characterized by a limited bandwidth through which multimodal expressions of affect (e.g., facial expressions, posture, and gesture) cannot be carried. Despite this limited bandwidth, it is known that users experience a similar variety of emotional states when interacting in a textual medium [4]. Underlying the overt textual channel may be an implicit affective channel, through which participants interpret each other's cognitive-affective states [4, 14, 22].

This implicit affective channel has received little attention in affective computing, but may be the most "human" component of computer-mediated communication [21]. Understanding the implicit affective channel for computer-based systems is therefore key to providing naturalistic interaction. Achieving this goal requires empirically investigating the implicit communication of affect in a textual medium. These empirical investigations will complement affective research that focuses on the explicit affective content of textual communication [4, 10], such as work that includes emoticons, common Internet phrasing, or textual style [17, 19].

While affective content can be communicated by overt textual dialogue components, many aspects of social, cognitive, and affective information are implicitly conveyed. For example, the ways in which individuals pause or edit their messages may serve as implicit affective signals in social information processing [27]. Due in part to such affective signals, some evidence suggests that computer-mediated textual dialogue can lead to equally fulfilling interpersonal interactions as face-to-face communication [4, 22, 26]. In fact, textual communication has demonstrated utility in emotionally intensive interactions such as couples therapy [22], instant messaging chat [14], and textual communication via websites [4, 10, 26].

Although studies of the implicit affective channel in computer-mediated textual communication have identified some underlying implicit cues, nonverbal phenomena that occur beyond the computer screen have been the subject of limited study [14]. Nonverbal displays, such as facial expression [2, 15, 29], posture [2, 9, 24], and gesture [1, 12, 13] have been empirically studied in other domains and may represent an element of ground truth for cognitive-affective states. However, their roles in computer-mediated textual communication have yet to be investigated. The study of these nonverbal displays is key to empirically understanding the implicit affective channel.

ICMI'12, October 22-26, 2012, Santa Monica, California, USA.

This paper investigates the extent to which some dimensions of affect are implicitly expressed through computer-mediated textual dialogue, and further, how the perceptions of one participant correspond to the posture and gesture expressed by the other participant, even when those multimodal features were not observable through the textual dialogue channel. The focus is on two empirical questions within computer-mediated textual dialogue: 1) Does the affective interpretation by one participant coincide with reported affective states of the other participant?, and 2) Do one participant's bodily expressions coincide with reported affect of either participant?

The investigation was conducted with depth video recordings of human body position from a tutoring study carried out through computer-mediated textual dialogue. To extract posture and gesture automatically from the depth images, novel tracking techniques were designed and applied to the data set. In addition to the extracted posture and gesture data, information regarding cognitive and affective experience was collected from both tutors and students through surveys. The findings suggest that *focused attention*, *physical demand*, and *frustration* were communicated through the hypothesized implicit affective channel that accompanies textual dialogue. Moreover, postural and gestural behaviors were found to co-occur with these cognitive-affective reports, even when posture and gesture were not explicitly communicated to the other participant. These results present empirical evidence to support the notion that an implicit affective channel is at work within computer-mediated textual dialogue, and that bodily displays of posture and gesture correspond to components of this implicit affective communication. This approach yields empirical evidence of human behavior that may be used to aid in developing future naturalistic systems that engage in textual dialogue.

2. RELATED WORK

Over the past three decades, computer-mediated communication has been increasingly studied [4, 10]. Most studies of computer-mediated communication have focused on the explicit act of communication itself [4, 26]. An example of this line of investigation is a system that automatically detects emotional expression from computer-mediated textual dialogue [17]. This system analyzes affective content of messages at the level of both words and statements, and interprets emoticons and common expressions used in internet-based communication.

While studying textual communication of affect is useful, there also appears to be an implicit affective channel in computer-mediated communication. It may be necessary to investigate nonverbal affective phenomena in order to understand the human processes behind implicit affective interpretation. However, research into the relationship between nonverbal behavior and implicit interpretation of affect is scarce. A recent study examined instant messaging interactions while also recording the nonverbal behaviors unseen by the participants [14]. The participants exhibited nonverbal behaviors indicative of cognitive and affective states (postural leaning, facial expressions, gestures), even though these bodily movements were not transmitted to the recipient of the textual dialogue. A limitation of that study is that it did not use surveys or self-reports to gauge affective experience of either participant. The present study builds on that prior work by investigating posture and gesture of participants in computer-mediated textual dialogue through post-interaction surveys to gain a better understanding of specific nonverbal behaviors and participants' implicit communication of affect through a textual medium.

Both posture and gesture have been investigated in recent years for their relationship to cognitive and affective states. The relation of posture has been vigorously studied, with initial investigations utilizing pressure-sensitive chairs to identify shifting of weight [5, 9, 28]. For instance, in two studies involving intelligent tutoring systems [5, 28], boredom was associated with increased postural movement, while inconsistent postural patterns were reported across the two studies for high-arousal positive and negative affective events. In more recent posture analysis work, computer vision-based techniques have been introduced, instead of pressure-sensitive seats. In chess-playing interactions with a robot, computer vision techniques were used to identify quantity of motion, body lean angle, slouch factor, and contraction index as measurements of a child's posture as seen from a side view [24]. Quantity of motion was found to be most informative in diagnosing a child's level of engagement. In the present study, a tracking algorithm was designed to estimate posture from depth images in a frontal view, and quantity of motion was associated with cognitive-affective states such as reduced attention.

In addition to posture, gesture has long been investigated as a medium of communication [16]. Some studies have tracked gestural movements in order to visualize their co-occurrence with speech in face-to-face communication [23]. However, some gestures do not co-occur with explicit communication behavior; instead, they may coincide with cognitive and affective phenomena that occur outside the context of communication. Gesture as a cognitive-affective display was briefly touched upon in a study of nonverbal behavior during interactions with an intelligent tutoring system [28]. In that study, the gesture of a student leaning on one hand coincided with positive affective states such as joy. More recently, a broad investigation of hand-over-face gestures suggests that these gestures co-occur with cognitive-affective states such as thinking, confusion, or boredom [12, 13]. In the current study, an algorithm was developed to detect one-hand-to-face and two-hands-to-face gestures, which were found to coincide with reduced frustration or focus, respectively.

From a theoretical perspective, the functions of nonverbal expression in computer-mediated textual dialogue differ significantly from those in face-to-face interaction. Nonverbal signals in general may express *affective/attitudinal states* (what a person feels), *manipulators* (interaction with objects in the environment, including self or others), *emblems* (culture-specific signals), *illustrators* (accompanying or depicting spoken concepts) or *regulators* (signals to control flow of conversation) [21]. In textual dialogue, the bodily expressions of *emblems*, *illustrators*, and *regulators* are rare or absent [4, 10, 14, 26]. However, textual substitutes for these bodily expressions may be present (e.g., emoticons) [18]. The rarity of *emblems*, *illustrators* and *regulators* aside, nonverbal behavior of participants in computer-mediated textual dialogue contains expressions of *affective/attitudinal states* and *manipulators* [14]. In the case of the present study, bodily expressions of posture display *affective/attitudinal states* and hand-to-face gestures are *manipulators*.

3. DATA COLLECTION

The data consist of computer-mediated textual interactions in the domain of introductory computer science tutoring. Students (N=42) and tutors interacted through a web-based interface that provided learning tasks, an interface for computer programming, and textual dialogue. Each interaction was limited to forty minutes in duration. Each student interacted with a specific tutor across six sessions on different days. Depth images (approximately 8 frames per second from a Kinect depth camera) were collected. Webcam video and skin conductance response were also recorded, but were not used in the present analyses. The student workstation configuration is shown in Figure 1 and the tutoring interface is shown in Figure 2.

Before each session, students completed a content-based pretest. After each session, students answered a post-session survey and posttest (identical to the pretest). The post-session survey items were designed to measure several aspects of engagement and cognitive load. The survey was composed of a modified User Engagement Survey [20] with Focused Attention, Endurability, and Involvement subscales, and the NASA-TLX scale for cognitive load [8], which consisted of response items for Mental Demand, Physical Demand, Temporal Demand, Performance, Effort, and Frustration Level. Students were intentionally not asked about a wider set of emotions in order to avoid biasing their future interactions. Selected student survey items are shown in Figure 3. Additionally, tutors also reported on cognitive and affective phenomena at the end of each session. The tutor post-session survey items are shown in Figure 4.

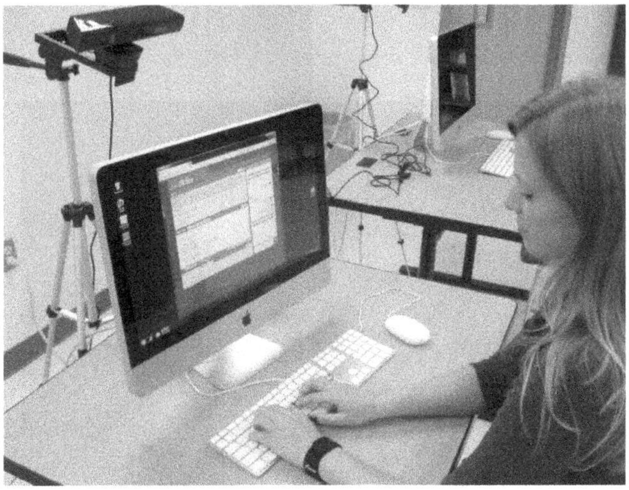

Figure 1. Student workstation with depth camera, skin conductance bracelet, and computer with webcam

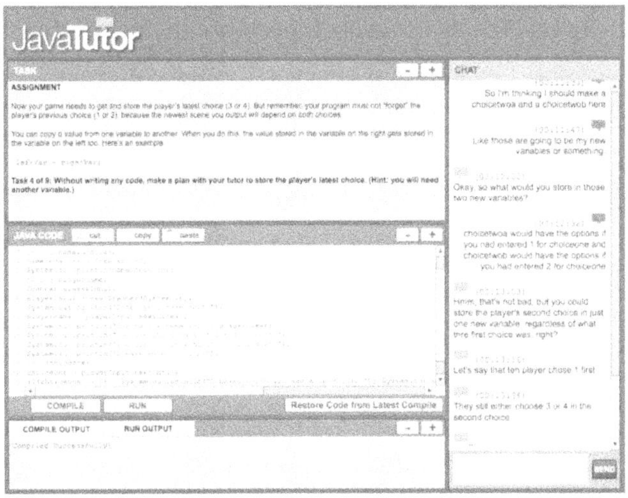

Figure 2. Screenshot of the tutoring interface

Student Post-Session Survey (from UES and NASA-TLX)

Focused Attention:
I lost myself in this learning experience.
I was so involved in my learning task that I lost track of time.
I blocked out things around me when I was working.
When I was working, I lost track of the world around me.
The time I spent working just slipped away.
I was absorbed in my task.
During this learning experience I let myself go.

Physical Demand:
How physically demanding was the task?

Frustration Level:
How insecure, discouraged, irritated, stressed, and annoyed were you?

Figure 3. Selected student post-session survey items

Tutor Post-Session Survey (reported using a 5-point scale)

Rate your agreement with the following statements:
1: Overall, the session was successful.
2: I felt like I provided cognitive support this session.
3: I helped the student finish the programming exercises more quickly than they would have on their own.
4: I helped the student master the most important concepts better than they would have on their own.
5: I was able to help the student finish the session with less effort than they would have on their own.
6: I felt like I provided emotional support this session.
7: I felt like my student was in the flow of the task.
8: I felt like my student thought the task was worthwhile.
9: I felt like my student found the task fun.
10: The student understood the computational thinking concepts.
11: The student understood the written task instructions.
12: The student understood my directions.

The student experienced the following during the lesson:
13: Anxiety (worried or uneasy about the lesson)
14: Boredom (not interested in the lesson or learning programming concepts)
15: Confusion (uncertain about some aspect of the lesson)
16: Contempt (scornful of the tutor, the lesson, or him/herself)
17: Excitement (enthusiastic or eager about the lesson)
18: Frustration (annoyed at difficulties with the tutor, the lesson, or him/herself)
19: Joy (happy about the tutor, the lesson, or him/herself)

I experienced the following during the lesson:
20-26: [tutor experience of emotion terms from items 13-19]
27: Open-ended response.

Figure 4. Tutor post-session survey of student performance and student and tutor affective experiences

4. TRACKING POSTURE AND GESTURE

In order to automatically recognize posture and gesture from the recorded interactions, tracking algorithms were designed to estimate posture and detect certain gestures from depth images. These algorithms were designed to leverage regularities in the depth recordings (e.g., student in center, frontal view). This section describes the algorithms, their output, and evaluation.

4.1 Posture Estimation

A posture estimation algorithm was designed to compute posture for a given frame as a triple, (*headDepth*, *midTorsoDepth*, *lowerTorsoDepth*), as shown in Figure 5. Prior to applying the algorithm, extraneous background pixels were discarded using a distance threshold. An overview of the posture estimation algorithm is given in Algorithm 1 below. The algorithm computes bounding regions for head, mid torso and lower torso based on the height of the top depth pixel. Then, a single point is selected from each bounding region to estimate posture. For the head, the nearest pixel is selected. For the torso points, the farthest pixel in the bounding regions is selected, as the torso was often behind the desk and arms. Distances for each posture estimation point were normalized using standard deviations from the median position for each student workstation in order to account for different camera angles. This overall approach is robust to seated postures that are occluded by a desk, a distinct advantage over the alternative of Kinect skeletal tracking.

The output of the posture estimation algorithm was evaluated manually. The performance metric was the percent of the frames in which the detected points (*headDepth*, *midTorsoDepth*, *lowerTorsoDepth*) coincided with the head, mid torso, and lower torso/waist. Two human judges individually examined images corresponding to one frame per minute of recorded video. The judges had moderate agreement on error instances with Cohen's κ=0.57. To provide a conservative measure of accuracy, the algorithm output was classified as erroneous if either judge found that any of the posture tracking points did not coincide with the target region (i.e., union of errors). Thus, the resulting accuracy was 92.4% over 1,175 depth images. Error conditions occurred primarily when students shifted their head or torso out of frame or covered their torso or waist with their arms and hands.

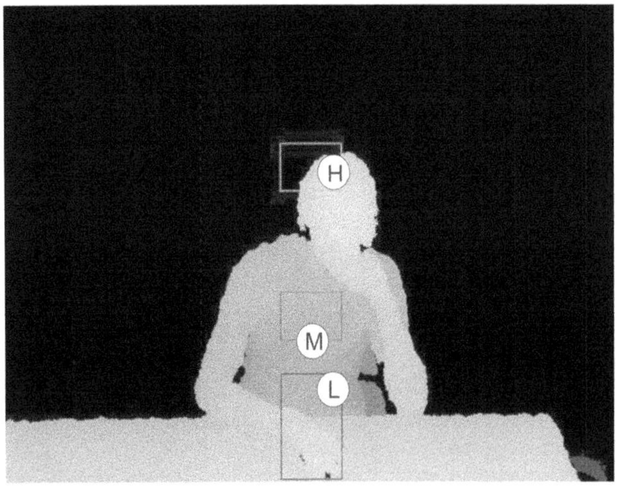

Figure 5. Detected posture points (H = *headDepth*, M = *midTorsoDepth*, L = *lowerTorsoDepth*). Bounding regions for posture point selection are also shown.

4.2 Hand-to-Face Gesture Detection

A second algorithm was developed to detect hand-to-face gestures, which have been shown to co-occur with cognitive-affective states [13]. The algorithm uses surface propagation to avoid issues of occlusion and hand deformation that pose problems for standard hand tracking techniques. Two variants of hand-to-face gestures were detected: one hand to the student's face and two hands to the student's face. Examples of detected hand-to-face gestures are shown in Figure 6. An overview of the hand-to-face gesture detection algorithm is shown in Algorithm 2.

Algorithm 1: POSTUREESTIMATION(*I*)

input : a depth image *I*
output : a triple of posture estimation points
width ← width of depth image *I*;
height ← height of depth image *I*;
bottomRow ← *height* – 1;
center ← *width* / 2;
headRow ← row of first depth pixel in center column;
midRow ← (*bottomRow* + *headRow*) / 2;
lowRow ← *midRow* + (*bottomRow* – *headRow*) / 2;
sideBound ← columns at ± (5% of *width*) from *center*;
headBound ← rows at ± (5% of *height*) from *headRow*;
midBound ← rows at ± (5% of *height*) from *midRow*;
lowBottom ← *lowRow* + (*bottomRow* – *headRow*) / 4;
lowTop ← *lowRow* – (5% of *height*);
headDepth ← closest pixel in [*sideBound*, *headBound*];
midTorsoDepth ← farthest pixel in [*sideBound*, *midBound*];
lowerTorsoDepth ← farthest pixel in [*sideBound*, *lowTop* and *lowBottom*];
return (*headDepth*, *midTorsoDepth*, *lowerTorsoDepth*);

Figure 6. Detected hand-to-face gestures: one-hand-to-face (top left) and two-hands-to-face (top right). Color image frames for the detected gestures are also shown (bottom row).

The breadth-first surface propagation mentioned on line 5 of Algorithm 2 adds pixels to the set of "surface pixels" through a between-neighbors comparison of an empirically-determined surface gradient threshold. Thus, the "head surface" propagates outward from the *headPixel* (the pixel from which propagation began). If a hand-to-face gesture was detected during surface propagation (as determined by difference between mean and median distances of surface pixels from *headPixel* on line 10), then the later-propagated surface pixels were considered "hand pixels."

To evaluate the algorithm, two human judges individually examined images corresponding to one-minute snapshots of the interactions and identified one-hand-to-face and two-hands-to-face gestures. The algorithm output was compared against all instances where the judges agreed (Cohen's κ=0.96 for one-hand-to-face and κ=0.87 for two-hands-to-face). For those agreed-on instances, the accuracy of the algorithm was 92.6% across 1,170 depth images. Error cases typically involved such things as the surface propagation algorithm misidentifying clothing or hair as a hand.

Algorithm 2: HANDTOFACEGESTUREDETECTOR(*I*)

```
input  : a depth image I
output : a value indicating gesture presence or absence
headCenter ← median center column selected from top 10%
               of rows containing non-zero depth values;
headRow ← lowest row in top 10% of rows containing non-
               zero depth values;
headPixel ← pixel location at (headCenter, headRow);
gestureDetected ← false;
while performing breadth-first surface propagation do
    medianXDistance ← median of horizontal distances of
                          surface pixels from headPixel;
    meanXDistance ← mean of horizontal distances of
                          surface pixels from headPixel;
    medianYDistance ← median of vertical distances of
                          surface pixels from headPixel;
    meanYDistance ← mean of vertical distances of surface
                          pixels from headPixel;
    if |mean – median| ≥ 2.5% of mean or median do
            gestureDetected ← true;
if gestureDetected do
    handPixels ← surface pixels propagated after hand-to-
                      face gesture was detected;
    if ≥33% of handPixels to upper right of headPixel do
        return NOGESTURE;
    else if ≥33% of handPixels to upper left of headPixel do
        return NOGESTURE;
    else if ≥33% of handPixels to lower left of headPixel and
            ≥33% of handPixels to lower right of headPixel do
        return TWOHANDSTOFACE;
    else if ≥33% of handPixels to lower left of headPixel or
            ≥33% of handPixels to lower right of headPixel do
        return ONEHANDTOFACE;
    else return NOGESTURE;
else return NOGESTURE;
```

5. SURVEY-BASED ANALYSES

An underlying notion of the implicit affective channel hypothesis is that tutors may have been able to identify student cognitive-affective states to some extent even when bodily movements associated with those affective states were not communicated to the tutor. To examine this, tutor perceptions of student affect were compared against student self-reports using correlational analyses in a two-step process designed to mitigate the potential for false positives (Type I error). In the first step, significant correlations were identified on a test data set drawn from the second of six tutoring sessions in which each tutor/student pair engaged (N=42). Tutor perceptions of student affect were compared against learning outcomes (posttest minus pretest) and student affect self-reports. Student affect self-reports were in turn compared against tutor reports of cognitive variables, tutor reports of student affect, and learning outcomes. Forty-three significant correlations were identified in this first step, and in the second step analyses were conducted to identify which of these significant correlations also held in a different data set, the first tutoring session, which is the main focus of the present study (N=42).[1] The two-phase analysis identified eight statistically reliable correlations, shown in Table 1.

Table 1. Significant correlations (T=tutor report; S=student report)

First Variable	Second Variable	r	p
Focused Attention^{S}	Helped Speed^{T} (Figure 4, item 3)	-0.42	0.019
	Helped Mastery^{T} (Figure 4, item 4)	-0.48	<0.01
	Student Confusion^{T} (Figure 4, item 15)	-0.39	0.029
Physical Demand^{S}	Student Frustration^{T} (Figure 4, item 18)	0.44	0.014
	Tutor Frustration^{T} (Figure 4, item 25)	0.42	0.019
Frustration Level^{S}	Student Confusion^{T}	0.53	<0.01
Student Confusion^{T}	Student Frustration^{T}	0.59	<0.01
Posttest Score	Student Confusion^{T}	-0.38	0.038

The significant correlations highlight three student cognitive-affective states: focused attention, physical demand, and frustration. Students' report of focused attention correlated with tutors' belief that they were less helpful, and tutors' belief that students were less confused. Tutors may have perceived that students who focused on the programming tasks did not need as much help to complete the tasks within the time allotted or to understand the related concepts. This result is compatible with the theory of optimal experience [3], which posits an optimally productive state of *flow* in which a student is learning well and it is often desirable not to interrupt his or her progress. Additionally, tutors may have perceived focused students as having less confusion throughout the session.

In addition to negatively correlating with students' reports of focused attention, tutor reports of student confusion were positively correlated with student self-reports of frustration. The relationship between frustration and confusion during learning may be a complex one. Specifically, frustration is typically considered to be a negative affective state, with persistent frustration referred to as a *state of stuck* [9], in which performance on the task at hand is negatively impacted. However, confusion has been theorized to be a cognitive-affective state with either positive or negative outcomes, depending on its resolution. In the theory of *cognitive disequilibrium* [7], confusion occurs with partial understanding of new knowledge, which may lead to learning when new knowledge is understood. However, it may lead to frustration when the confusion is not resolved. In the current study, positive resolutions of confusion may not have been as memorable for tutors, which could leave the tutor to report lingering confusion that may have led to student frustration. The

[1] This two-step process was used to identify correlations within one data set that generalize to another. The goal is analogous to that of statistical corrections for multiple tests (e.g., Bonferroni) but the two-step approach can be conceived of as confirming the significance of correlations that emerged under an exploratory analysis.

negative correlation between tutor reports of student confusion and posttest scores supports this interpretation, as frustration is known to negatively impact learning [11].

Tutor reports of their own frustration, and of student frustration, correlated with student-reported physical demand. That is, the more physically demanding the student felt the task was, the more frustrated the tutor felt and believed the student felt as well. The student rating of physical demand was measured with an item phrased, "How physically demanding was the task?" At first glance, it is unclear whether the students were rating discomfort related to movement/sitting or physiological stress, since (as will be described in Section 6) student report of physical demand did not correlate with measures of posture and gesture. The significant correlation with this report of physical demand may indicate a co-occurring pattern of negative interaction in which the tutor was frustrated and the student was stressed.

It is also worth exploring the cognitive dimensions of the tutors' reporting. The tutors' reports of helping the student complete the task more swiftly and helping the student better master the subject material were both negatively correlated with focused attention, as described above. However, none of the other tutor cognitive reports noted in Figure 4 correlated across the two-phase analysis. Additionally, student performance, as measured by test performance and learning gains, yielded a single correlation between posttest score and tutor report of student confusion. This may indicate that the phenomena evidenced here are related more to implicit perception of cognitive-affective phenomena than to purely cognitive or task-related phenomena. However, the interplay of cognition and affect in task-oriented domains merits further study.

6. MULTIMODAL ANALYSES

The results in the previous section suggest that cognitive-affective states are implicitly communicated in textual dialogue. Examining bodily expressions such as posture and gesture may reveal aspects of affective ground truth related to the implicit affective channel.

Two aspects of posture were used as features in the models reported here. First, variance of the tracked posture points was used as a measure of quantity of motion. Second, the average postural position across a session was used to capture the predominant body position of the student. In addition to these, gesture features include relative frequencies of one-hand-to-face and two-hands-to-face gestures. The set of posture and gesture features is shown in Table 2. The *H*, *M*, and *L* prefixes correspond to the three posture estimation points (Figure 5), while the *All* prefix indicates the sum of all three points. After removing sessions with errorful depth recordings, thirty-one sessions were included in the multimodal analyses.[2]

[2] Four sessions did not have depth recordings due to human error, as recordings were manually initiated. Three sessions were discarded due to extreme postural positions, such as a student leaning far to the side for the majority of the session. Four sessions were discarded due to dark and/or wavy hair that produced persistent noise in the infrared signal, or wearing a baseball cap.

Table 2. Posture and gesture features used in analyses

Feature Set	Feature Names
Averages of posture points	*HAvg, MAvg, LAvg, AllAvg*
Variances of posture points	*HVar, MVar, LVar, AllVar*
Relative frequencies of hand-to-face gestures	*NoGestRFreq, OneHandRFreq, TwoHandsRFreq*

6.1 Correlational Analyses

The first analysis goal was to determine whether the cognitive-affective dimensions investigated earlier also correspond to bodily movements. To accomplish this, correlational analyses were performed between posture/gesture and variables that were involved in significant correlations reported in Section 5. The posture and gesture features in Table 2 were paired with the survey variables in Table 1, and the resulting statistically significant correlations are shown in Table 3 (N=31).

Posture and gesture primarily correlate with survey variables for three cognitive-affective phenomena: student self-report of focused attention, tutor report of student confusion, and tutor report of both student and tutor frustration. Students' report of increased focused attention corresponded to less movement in the lower torso (*LVar*), and to a lower frequency of two-hands-to-face gestures (*TwoHandsRFreq*). These correlations may highlight instances of students leaning forward onto both hands while also moving about the lower torso. Additionally, *LVar* negatively correlated with posttest score, which may illustrate a trend related to lower focused attention.

Table 3. Posture and gesture correlations with survey variables (T=tutor report; S=student report)

First Variable	Second Variable	r	p
Focused Attention[S]	*LVar*	-0.37	0.040
	TwoHandsRFreq	-0.39	0.031
Student Confusion[T] (Figure 4, item 15)	*HAvg*	-0.44	0.012
	MAvg	-0.47	<0.01
	LAvg	-0.40	0.026
	AllAvg	-0.48	<0.01
Student Frustration[T] (Figure 4, item 18)	*MAvg*	-0.38	0.035
	LVar	-0.37	0.043
	OneHandRFreq	-0.43	0.017
Tutor Frustration[T] (Figure 4, item 25)	*HVar*	0.44	0.013
	NoGestRFreq	0.37	0.043
	OneHandRFreq	-0.39	0.029
Posttest Score	*LVar*	-0.40	0.026

Tutor reports of student confusion negatively correlated with average student postural distance. Thus, higher tutor reports of student confusion co-occurred with a more forward student body position. Conversely, farther postural distances co-occurred with lesser tutor reports of student confusion. Similarly, farther mid torso distances co-occurred with tutor reports of student frustration. Taken as a whole, these correlations appear to suggest that forward-leaning postures occur with negative cognitive-affective experience (as perceived by the tutor). Conversely, average postural configurations closer to a straight sitting posture co-occurred with more positive cognitive-affective experience.

Tutor reports of student and tutor frustration both negatively correlated with relative frequency of one-hand-to-face gestures. This is in contrast with the two-hands-to-face gesture, which co-occurred with lower student focused attention. It may be that one-hand-to-face gestures tend to express a positive or thoughtful state, as noted in related literature [13].

6.2 Predictive Models

The correlations presented in Section 6.1 suggest ways in which posture and gesture are associated with student and tutor perceptions of cognitive-affective experience. To further elucidate these relationships, multivariate regression models were built with the significantly correlated variables as predictors. The three survey variables for student focused attention, confusion, and frustration were modeled as outcome variables. Each stepwise linear regression used a conservative 0.05 significance threshold for addition of features.

The regression model for focused attention, shown in Table 4, incorporates two-hands-to-face gestures with variance and average postural position of the lower torso. The model R^2 shows that a moderate amount of the variance in focused attention is explained. Both two-hands-to-face gestures and lower torso variance were negative predictors of focused attention. However, lower torso average distance explains further variance of focused attention as a positive predictor. This model augments the results of the correlational analyses by showing that posture and gesture together combine to predict student focused attention.

Table 4. Stepwise linear regression model for student-reported Focused Attention. Partial R^2 shows the contribution of each feature, while model R^2 shows cumulative model effect.

Focused Attention =	Partial R^2	Model R^2	p
-40.90 * *TwoHandsRF*	0.150	0.150	0.031
-2.90 * *LVar*	0.143	0.293	0.025
0.99 * *LAvg*	0.103	0.396	0.041
23.66 (intercept)	**RMSE** = 10% of variable's range		

The stepwise linear regression model for tutor-reported student confusion, displayed in Table 5, contains a single posture feature that explains a small amount of variance. The absence of additional features shows that the other posture features correlated with student confusion in Table 3 were redundant.

Table 5. Stepwise linear regression model for tutor-reported student confusion.

Confusion =	Partial R^2	Model R^2	p
-0.16 * *AllAvg*	0.231	0.231	<0.01
4.24 (intercept)	**RMSE** = 20.4% of variable's range		

The stepwise linear regression model for tutor-reported student frustration, shown in Table 6, includes relative frequency of one-hand-to-face gestures and lower torso variance as negative predictors. Contrary to the correlational analyses in Table 3, head variance and absence of hand-to-face gestures did not meet the threshold of significance. This model underscores the interplay of posture and gesture, as the addition of lower torso nearly doubles the explained variance.

The regression analyses revealed cumulative effects when posture and gesture were integrated into linear regression models. The model for focused attention incorporated two-hands-to-face gestures and lower torso variance and average distance. Either posture or gesture alone would have explained a small amount of variance, so this demonstrates that the combination of multimodal features such as posture and gesture can improve a predictive model.

Table 6. Stepwise linear regression model for tutor-reported student frustration.

Frustration =	Partial R^2	Model R^2	p
-2.96 * *OneHandRF*	0.182	0.182	0.017
-0.16 * *LVar*	0.155	0.337	0.016
2.86 (intercept)	**RMSE** = 16.2% of variable's range		

The regression model for student confusion did not include gesture, with a small amount of variance explained. However, the regression model built for student frustration included one-hand-to-face gestures and lower torso variance features, resulting in greater explained variance. The root mean squared error of the model for student frustration was less than that of the model for student confusion, as would be expected of the model that explains more variance.

7. CONCLUSION

Although textual communication has limited bandwidth, interactions through the medium still retain high cognitive and affective complexity. If the textual content itself is emotionally sparse, the participants may rely on implicit interpretation of affect. The information relevant to this interpretation may be conceived of as being transmitted through an implicit affective channel. Understanding this implicit affective channel may hold great benefit for systems that aim to interact in naturalistic ways with humans. Toward this end, this paper has presented an empirical study to investigate two aspects of implicit affective communication in textual dialogue: 1) The extent to which the participants converge on shared perceptions of affect, and 2) The ways in which affective ground truth, as captured by depth recordings of gesture and posture, correlates with those affective perceptions even when the bodily movements were not transmitted to the other participant.

This paper has introduced novel posture and gesture recognition algorithms that are robust to occlusions such as desks as a first step toward developing more sophisticated techniques. The automatically recognized posture and gesture features were explored within models that indicate *focused attention*, *physical demand*, and *frustration* were perceived through the hypothesized implicit affective channel accompanying textual dialogue. These results support the notion that an implicit affective channel is at work within computer-mediated textual communication, and that bodily displays of posture and gesture co-occurred with implicit affective communication.

Future investigations of the hypothesized implicit affective channel should seek to identify specific processes through which individuals are able to interpret affect in computer-mediated textual dialogue. For instance, analyses based on fine-grained temporal features of computer-mediated textual dialogue may reveal relationships between perceived affect and how participants construct messages. Additionally, bodily expressions that correlate with aggregate cognitive-affective measures may be explored within discrete time windows to provide a more dynamic view of affective phenomena that occur during textual dialogue. Machine learning techniques may also be applied to identify complex patterns of interaction that may shed light on underlying human processes. Such investigations may lead to future textual dialogue systems that leverage the implicit affective channel.

ACKNOWLEDGEMENTS

This work is supported in part by the North Carolina State University Department of Computer Science along with the National Science Foundation through Grant DRL-1007962 and the STARS Alliance Grant CNS-1042468. Any opinions, findings, conclusions, or recommendations expressed in this report are those of the participants, and do not necessarily represent the official views, opinions, or policy of the National Science Foundation.

REFERENCES

[1] Baltrusaitis, T. et al. 2011. Real-Time Inference of Mental States from Facial Expressions and Upper Body Gestures. *Proceedings of the IEEE International Conference on Automatic Face and Gesture Recognition*, 909-914.

[2] Calvo, R.A. and D'Mello, S.K. 2010. Affect Detection: An Interdisciplinary Review of Models, Methods, and Their Applications. *IEEE Transactions on Affective Computing*. 1, 1, 18-37.

[3] Csikszentmihalyi, M. 1990. *Flow: The Psychology of Optimal Experience*. Harper-Row.

[4] Derks, D. et al. 2008. The Role of Emotion in Computer-Mediated Communication: A Review. *Computers in Human Behavior*. 24, 3, 766-785.

[5] D'Mello, S.K. and Graesser, A.C. 2010. Mining Bodily Patterns of Affective Experience during Learning. *Proceedings of the International Conference on Educational Data Mining*, 31-40.

[6] Forbes-Riley, K. and Litman, D. 2011. Benefits and Challenges of Real-Time Uncertainty Detection and Adaptation in a Spoken Dialogue Computer Tutor. *Speech Communication*. 53, 9-10, 1115-1136.

[7] Graesser, A.C. and Olde, B.A. 2003. How Does One Know Whether a Person Understands a Device? The Quality of the Questions the Person Asks When the Device Breaks Down. *Journal of Educational Psychology*. 95, 3, 524-536.

[8] Hart, S.G. and Staveland, L.E. 1988. Development of NASA-TLX (Task Load Index): Results of Empirical and Theoretical Research. *Human Mental Workload*. P.A. Hancock and N. Meshkati, eds. Elsevier Science. 139-183.

[9] Kapoor, A. et al. 2007. Automatic Prediction of Frustration. *International Journal of Human-Computer Studies*. 65, 8, 724-736.

[10] Kiesler, S. et al. 1984. Social Psychological Aspects of Computer-Mediated Communication. *American Psychologist*. 39, 10, 1123-1134.

[11] Kort, B. et al. 2001. An Affective Model of Interplay between Emotions and Learning: Reengineering Educational Pedagogy-Building a Learning Companion. *Proceedings of the IEEE International Conference on Advanced Learning Technologies*, 43-46.

[12] Mahmoud, M. et al. 2011. 3D Corpus of Spontaneous Complex Mental States. *Proceedings of the International Conference on Affective Computing and Intelligent Interaction*, 205-214.

[13] Mahmoud, M. and Robinson, P. 2011. Interpreting Hand-Over-Face Gestures. *Proceedings of the International Conference on Affective Computing and Intelligent Interaction*, 248-255.

[14] Marcoccia, M. and Atifi, H. 2008. Text-Centered Versus Multimodal Analysis of Instant Messaging Conversation. *Language@Internet*. 5.

[15] McDuff, D. et al. 2011. Crowdsourced Data Collection of Facial Responses. *Proceedings of the 13th International Conference on Multimodal Interfaces*, 11-18.

[16] McNeill, D. 2005. *Gesture & Thought*. The University of Chicago Press.

[17] Neviarouskaya, A. et al. 2011. Affect Analysis Model: Novel Rule-Based Approach to Affect Sensing from Text. *Natural Language Engineering*. 17, 01, 95-135.

[18] Neviarouskaya, A. et al. 2007. Analysis of Affect Expressed through the Evolving Language of Online Communication. *Proceedings of the 12th International Conference on Intelligent User Interfaces*, 278-281.

[19] Neviarouskaya, A. et al. 2007. Textual Affect Sensing for Sociable and Expressive. *Proceedings of the International Conference on Affective Computing and Intelligent Interaction*, 220-231.

[20] O'Brien, H.L. and Toms, E.G. 2010. The Development and Evaluation of a Survey to Measure User Engagement. *Journal of the American Society for Information Science and Technology*. 61, 1, 50-69.

[21] Pantic, M. et al. 2006. Human Computing and Machine Understanding of Human Behavior: A Survey. *Proceedings of the 8th International Conference on Multimodal Interaction*, 239-248.

[22] Perry, M.S. and Werner-Wilson, R.J. 2011. Couples and Computer-Mediated Communication: A Closer Look at the Affordances and Use of the Channel. *Family and Consumer Sciences Research Journal*. 40, 2, 120-134.

[23] Quek, F. et al. 2002. Multimodal Human Discourse : Gesture and Speech. *ACM Transactions on Computer-Human Interaction*. 9, 3, 171-193.

[24] Sanghvi, J. et al. 2011. Automatic Analysis of Affective Postures and Body Motion to Detect Engagement with a Game Companion. *Proceedings of the ACM/IEEE International Conference on Human-Robot Interaction*, 305-311.

[25] Schuller, B. et al. 2011. Recognising Realistic Emotions and Affect in Speech: State of the Art and Lessons Learnt from the First Challenge. *Speech Communication*. 53, 9-10, 1062-1087.

[26] Walther, J.B. 1992. Interpersonal Effects in Computer-Mediated Interaction: A Relational Perspective. *Communication Research*. 19, 1, 52-90.

[27] Walther, J.B. 2007. Selective Self-Presentation in Computer-Mediated Communication: Hyperpersonal Dimensions of Technology, Language, and Cognition. *Computers in Human Behavior*. 23, 5, 2538-2557.

[28] Woolf, B.P. et al. 2009. Affect-Aware Tutors: Recognising and Responding to Student Affect. *International Journal of Learning Technology*. 4, 3-4, 129-164.

[29] Zeng, Z. et al. 2009. A Survey of Affect Recognition Methods: Audio, Visual, and Spontaneous Expressions. *IEEE Transactions on Pattern Analysis and Machine Intelligence*. 31, 1, 39-58.

Towards Sensing the Influence of Visual Narratives on Human Affect

Mihai Burzo*
Mechanical and Energy Engineering
University of North Texas
Mihai.Burzo@unt.edu

Daniel McDuff
Media Lab
Massachusetts Institute of Technology
djmcduff@mit.edu

Rada Mihalcea
Computer Science and Engineering
University of North Texas
rada@cs.unt.edu

Louis-Philippe Morency
Institute for Creative Technologies
University of Southern California
morency@ict.usc.edu

Alexis Narvaez
Mechanical and Energy Engineering
University of North Texas
AlexisNarvaez@my.unt.edu

Verónica Pérez-Rosas
Computer Science and Engineering
University of North Texas
veronica.perezrosas@gmail.com

ABSTRACT

In this paper, we explore a multimodal approach to sensing affective state during exposure to visual narratives. Using four different modalities, consisting of visual facial behaviors, thermal imaging, heart rate measurements, and verbal descriptions, we show that we can effectively predict changes in human affect. Our experiments show that these modalities complement each other, and illustrate the role played by each of the four modalities in detecting human affect.

Categories and Subject Descriptors

I.2.7 [**Artificial Intelligence**]: Natural Language Processing—*Discourse*

General Terms

Algorithms, Experimentation

Keywords

Multimodal signal processing, Multimodal sensing, Affective Behavior

1. INTRODUCTION

Narratives are a constant presence in our everyday lives, and can have significant influence on one's thoughts and actions. Narratives are often designed to explicitly appeal to the emotions of the reader or listener, and act as an "emotional prime" [11, 16]. Once an affective state has been induced, it can also lead to changes in cognition and action, in agreement with the large body of previous research on emotions [15].

A specific type of narrative that is becoming extremely popular with the Internet age is the visual narrative. With more than 10,000 new videos posted online every day, social websites such as YouTube and Facebook are an almost infinite source of visual narrative. People are posting videos to express their opinion and sentiment about different topics, products and events. To better understand how these online videos are influencing individuals and eventually the society at large, it is imperative that we develop automatic techniques to analyze human reactions to visual narrative.

In this paper, we propose a non-invasive multimodal approach to sense and interpret human reaction while watching online videos. This is a first important milestone toward a deeper understanding of visual narrative influence on human affective states. Our approach senses changes in human affect through four different modalities: visual facial behaviors, physiological measurements, thermal imaging, and verbal descriptions. The first three modalities are recorded live during the narrative interaction while the verbal descriptions are acquired during a post-study interview. We evaluate our multimodal approach on a new corpus of 70 narrative interactions. Figure 1 shows the overall flow of our approach.

The following section summarizes related work in visual, physiological, and linguistic analysis of human affective state. Section 3 presents our experimental methodology to create this new visual narrative corpus. Section 4 presents a detailed description of the multimodal features automatically extracted. Section 5 presents experimental results comparing the performance of our multimodal predictive models. Section 6 discusses our results and shows an analysis of the multimodal features and their effectiveness to predict human affective state. Section 7 presents our conclusions and future directions.

*The order of the authors is alphabetical, as all the authors have equally contributed to this work.

ICMI'12, October 22–26, 2012, Santa Monica, California, USA.

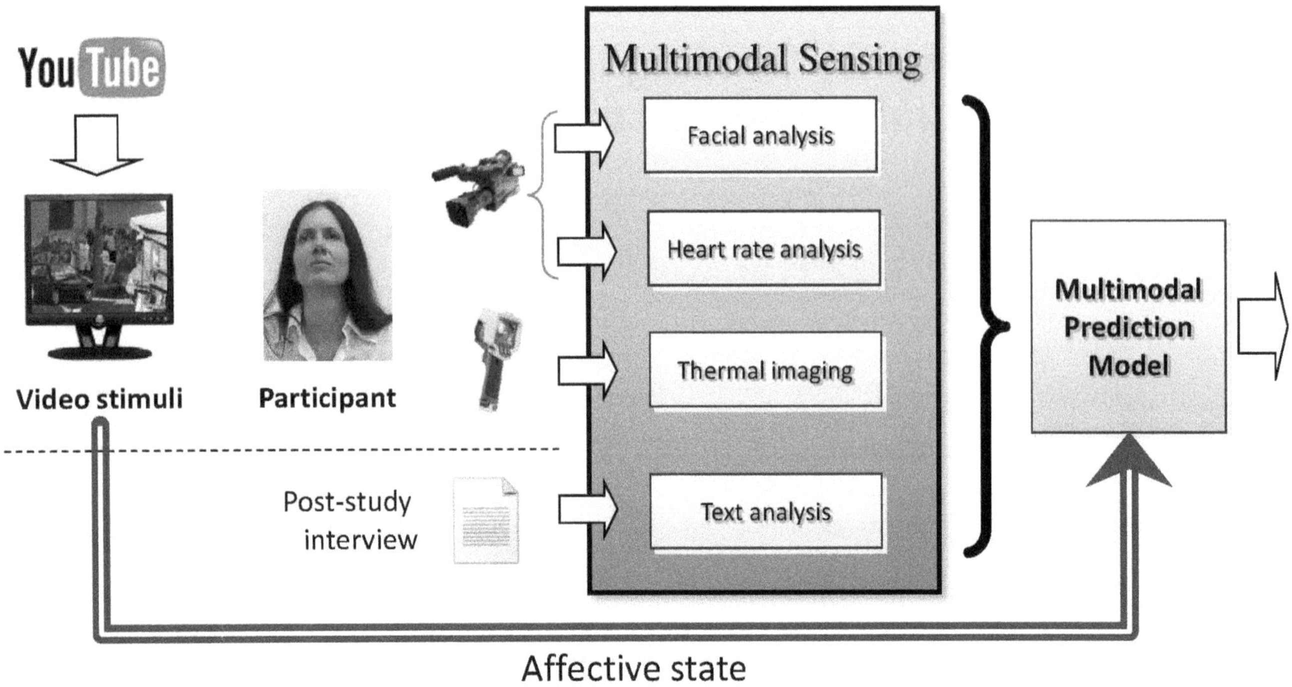

Figure 1: Overview of our multimodal approach for sensing affective state.

2. RELATED WORK

Influence models have been widely used to detect and predict human behavior, including game theory [5], statistical Bayesian models [26], and Markov models [18]. In our work, we build upon our own previous experience and related work in several research areas, including natural language processing, computer vision, and computational physiology.

2.1 Affect Recognition in Text

There has been growing interest in the recognition of affect in text, focusing on the automatic identification of private states, such as opinions, emotions, sentiments, evaluations, beliefs, and speculations. Most of the work in this area has addressed the analysis of the affective property (positive, negative, or neutral), where affective properties are associated with words [43, 39], phrases [45], sentences [33, 35], or entire documents [27, 19].

Finer-grained affect recognition has also been addressed, where emotions (e.g., anger, disgust, fear, joy, sadness, surprise) are automatically identified in text [37, 2, 35, 20, 36].

2.2 Physiological Sensing

Previously proposed solutions for non-contact measurement of vital signs, such as heart rate (HR) and respiratory rate (RR), include laser Doppler [40], microwave Doppler radar [13], variations in transmitted or reflected light [1], and thermal imaging [12, 10]. In particular, skin temperature detected from thermal images was found to be correlated with changes in affect [17], deceptive behavior [29], and stress [31].

2.3 Visual Sensing

There have been numerous approaches to track and analyse facial feature points from single images or image sequences [28, 48]. Approaches that can be considered model based are Active Shape Models [8], Active Appearance Models [7], 3D Morphable Models [3], and Constrained Local Models [9]. There exist also many techniques for estimating head pose [23, 22]. Research work in this area has also shown that visual features can be effectively used for dimensional and categorical affect recognition [48, 14, 46, 24, 25].

2.4 Multimodal Analysis of Affect

Also related to our work is the research done on multimodal emotion analysis [4, 34, 49]. For instance, a novel algorithm is defined in [47], based on a combination of audio-visual features for emotion recognition. The features used by these novel algorithms are usually basic and low level like tracking points for collecting visual data. An engineering approach is then applied to this large set of data points, in order to extract the ones that would be useful for the actual analysis. It is also worth noting the recent work on multimodal sentiment analysis, where textual, visual, and audio sensing is combined in order to determine the polarity orientation of statements expressed in YouTube videos [21]. Finally, somehow related is also the research reported in [32], where speech and text have been analyzed jointly for the purpose of opinion identification.

To the best of our knowledge, our paper is the first to integrate these four modalities (visual, thermal, physiologic and linguistic) to predict affective response to visual narrative.

3. METHODOLOGY

Our goal is to identify cues that are indicative of people's reactions when exposed to visual narratives. Specifically, in this first set of experiments, we target the identification of affective states (as compared to neutral states), and furthermore we also aim to classify the valence of the affect experienced by a person (positive or negative).

We first selected four video stimuli from the YouTube website, all of them in English, two of them with negative content (one showing the effects of a tsunami, 153s; and one showing an accident, 145s), and two of them with positive content (one about the Coca-Cola happiness truck in Brazil, 152s; and one about an amusing incident during a wedding, 143s). These videos were selected based on popularity and the positive/negative comments written on YouTube. Several videos were considered as candidates, and the four final videos are the ones for which two of the authors of the paper agreed on their affective properties.

The participants consisted of fourteen subjects, three women and eleven men, all of them within the age range of 25-45, and all of them living in the United States although coming from different backgrounds (Asian, African-American, Caucasian, Hispanic). Each participant was first recorded during a "neutral" state while simply looking at the recording station and/or the lab were the recording took place. The four video stimuli were then played in random order, and the participant was recorded while watching the videos.

The recordings were done with two cameras. A regular Logitec Web camera, with a resolution of 980x720 and a frame rate of 15 frames per second, and a FLIR ThermoVision A40 thermal camera with a resolution of 340x240 and a frame rate of 60 frames per second.

After each recording, the participants were asked to write 2-4 sentences reflecting how they felt about the video they just saw.

Figures 2 and 3 show sample frames from the visual and the thermal camera recordings. Table 1 shows sample textual statements provided by the participants.

It is important to note that in these experiments we use the prior classification of the videos (as either positive or negative) as our approximation of the induced affective state. We thus assume that a positive video induces a positive affective state, while a negative video induces a negative affective state. In the future, we plan to use the PANAS-X survey [42] to capture the actual affective state experienced by a person during exposure to the visual narratives.

Figure 2: Sample snapshots taken by the Web camera showing participants exposed to positive and negative video narratives.

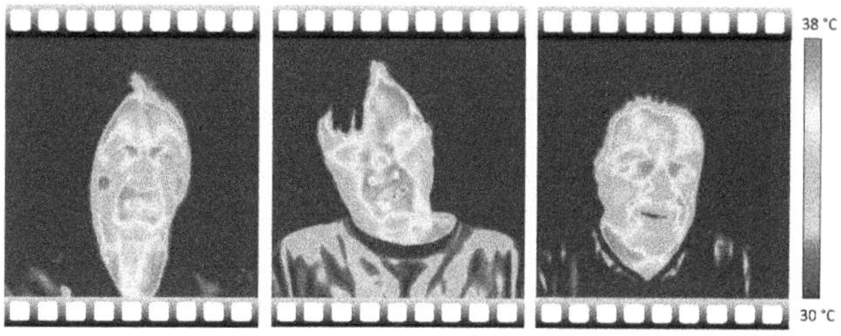

Figure 3: Sample snapshots taken by the thermal camera.

4. SENSING AFFECTIVE RESPONSE TO VISUAL NARRATIVES

We are sensing changes in human affect through four different modalities: (1) facial expressions obtained by processing the visual recording of the participants; physiological features, including (2) thermal features obtained from the thermal recording, and (3) heart rate measurements obtained from the visual recording; and (4) linguistic descriptions of the participants' state after exposure to the stimuli.

We describe below each of these modalities in detail, along with the features obtained from each of them.

4.1 Facial Expressions

The visual features are automatically extracted from the video sequences. Since only one person is present in each video clip and they are all the time facing the camera, current technology for facial tracking can efficiently be applied to our dataset. We use a commercial software called OKAO Vision that detects at each frame the face, it extracts the facial features, and extrapolates some basic facial expressions as well as eye gaze direction. The main facial expression being recognized is smile. This is a well-established technology that can be found in many digital cameras. For each frame, the vision software returns a smile intensity (0-100) and the gaze direction, using both horizontal and vertical angles expressed in degrees. The sampling rate is the same as the video framerate: 15Hz.

An important aspect when generating visual features is the quality of the video, and correspondingly the quality of the visual processing that can be automatically performed on the video. OKAO provides a confidence level for each processed frame in the range 0-1000. We discounted all the frames with a confidence level below 700.

For each video in our dataset, we define three series of summary features, which were used in previous work on affect analysis [21]:

- **Smile duration:** Given all the frames in a video, how many frames are identified as "smile." In our experiments, we use three different variants of this feature with different intensity thresholds: 25, 50, 75.
- **Look-away duration:** Given all the frames in a video,

Positive	Negative
I like it when people have fun even during the more "official" moments of their life. This seems like a joyful couple, I hope they will have many years together. The priest was a bit disheartened at first (or so it seemed), but then he managed to joke himself about the whole situation. I am sure this made for an even more memorable event for all those present.	This is so distressing! It may have to do with the fact that I have a small daughter myself, or with the innocence of the child who suffered in this video, but I found it extremely sad. It is so unfair how we always depend on other people's decisions - like in this video, one's rush brought an end to somebody else's life. It almost makes you think that life before the technology age was better and safer.
Nice to see people feel happy at an unexpected moment during their regular daily routine. I felt it was a very creative way of making people smile. Feels relaxing when you watch happy stuff.	Interesting to get to view natural disasters and its effects on structures and other things around it. Its sad to think of how people who live in places which are hit by natural calamities suffer and recover from something like that. The video was interesting.

Table 1: Sample textual statements made by the participants after watching the videos.

in how many frames is the speaker looking at the camera. The horizontal and vertical angular thresholds were experimentally set to 10 degrees.

- **Eye gaze direction:** Given all the frames in a video, in how many frames is the speaker looking to the left with an angle higher than N degrees, where N can be 10, 20, or 30. Variants of these features were also created for eye gaze to the right, eye gaze up, and eye gaze down.

All the visual features are normalized by the total number of frames in the video. Thus, if the person is smiling half the time, then the smile feature will be equal to 0.5 (or 50%).

4.2 Thermal Analysis of the Face

Another major sensorial input is the skin temperature, which relies on thermal features drawn from images captured with the thermal camera.

Using the thermal recordings, we infer several features that reflect the temperature of the face and the overall temperature (including face, neck, and shoulders). Starting with a map of pixel-level temperature measurements obtained from each frame in the recording, we collect the following features:

- **Face temperature features:** Using the temperature measured on the face, we calculate: average temperature; overall minimum and overall maximum temperature; average of the minimum and maximum temperature observed in each frame; standard deviation; standard deviation for the minimum and maximum temperature observed in each frame; difference between the minimum and the maximum temperature.

- **Overall temperature features:** We also calculate the same features listed above, but using the entire frame as input, which includes the face, neck, and shoulders of the subject (as well as a static white background, which did not contribute to changes in temperature).

4.3 Heart Rate

In addition to the physiological signals captured through thermal imaging, we also measure the heart rate using the recording made with the video camera. In order to calculate the heart rate from the video sequences we used an adapted version of the method presented by Poh et al. [30]. We performed analysis on a sliding window of 30s length (15fps x 30s = 450 frames) with a 1s (15 frame) time increment.

For each video frame within a particular time window the face was segmented using the Open Computer Vision library (OpenCV) face detector [41]. The facial region of interest (ROI) was determined as the full height and central 60% of the width of the face box as determined by OpenCV. The ROI was separated into the three RGB (red, green and blue) channels and a spatial average of the resulting image components calculated. This was performed for every frame to yield the raw time varying signals r(t), g(t) and b(t). The raw traces were detrended using a procedure based on a smoothness priors approach [38] with a smoothing parameter $\lambda=10$. The channels were each normalized by subtracting their mean and then dividing by their standard deviation. The normalized signals were decomposed into the three independent source signals using the JADE implementation of Independent Component Analysis (ICA) [6].

Each of the source signals were band-pass filtered with normalized low and high 3dB frequency cut-offs of 0.08 and 0.2 respectively. The power spectrum of each of the resulting source signals was then calculated. The source channel containing the BVP was selected as the signal with the greatest frequency peak within the frequency range of interest: 0.08 to 2. For the first window the frequency with the maximum power within the range was selected as the heart rate frequency. Artifacts due to motion of the subject, ambient lighting changes or other noise can be problematic. Therefore for the remaining windows historical estimations of the pulse frequency were performed to reject artifacts by fixing a threshold for maximum change in pulse rate between successive measurements (taken 1s apart). If the difference between the current pulse estimation and the previously computed value exceeded the threshold (threshold = 10% of previously computed value) the algorithm rejected it. The frequency range was searched again for the second highest peak, this was repeated until the conditions were satisfied. If no frequency peaks met the criteria the previous pulse frequency estimation was maintained.

Using the extracted heart rate vectors, we calculate the following features:

- **Average, minimum, and maximum heart rate:** We calculate statistics over the entire vector, reflecting the average heart rate, as well as the minimum and the maximum heart rate.

- **Total heart rate changes:** Given the heart rate vector for a video, we determine the total absolute changes in heart rate over time, normalized with the duration of the video.

4.4 Verbal Descriptions

After each recording, the participants were asked to make a verbal statement describing how they felt about the video they just saw. We use a bag-of-words representation of these textual statements to derive unigram counts, which are then used as input features. First, we build a vocabulary consisting of all the words, including stopwords, occurring in the transcriptions of the training set. We then remove those words that have a frequency below three (value determined empirically on a small development set). The remaining words represent the unigram features, which are then associated with a value corresponding to the frequency of the unigram inside each transcription. These simple weighted unigram features have been successfully used in the past to build sentiment classifiers on text [27, 19]. The remaining words represent the unigram features, which are then associated with a value corresponding to the frequency of the unigram inside each line.

We also derive and use coarse textual features, by using mappings between words and semantic classes. Specifically, we use the OpinionFinder lexicon [44] to derive coarse textual features. The OpinionFinder lexicon was compiled from manually developed resources augmented with entries learned from corpora. It contains 6,856 unique entries, which are labeled as strong or weak clues of subjectivity, and also annotated for their polarity. In our classification, we use the *positive* and *negative* classes, and disregard the strength annotations. We thus derive two main types of linguistic features:

- **Unigrams:** For each of the unigrams selected as part of the vocabulary, we create a vector of features reflecting the frequency of the unigram.

- **Affective lexicon classes:** For each of the positive and negative affective classes obtained from the OpinionFinder lexicon, we infer a feature indicating the number of words in the verbal description belonging to that class.

5. PREDICTION OF AFFECTIVE RESPONSE

Our goal is to explore the changes in human affect during exposure to visual narratives. We formulate the task as a prediction problem, and use the features obtained from the four modalities described above in order to infer changes in affect and to classify them as either positive, negative, or neutral.

We run three main experiments. First, we run an experiment where we try to predict whether a person is being exposed to a stimulus that induces an affective state (either positive or negative), or is in a neutral state. Second, we also experiment with a three-way classification, where we differentiate in a single classifier between positive affect, negative affect, and a neutral state. Finally, we also run an experiment where we try to predict the valence of the affective state experienced by a person, and classify it as either positive or negative.

In all the experiments, we use the Ada Boost classifier with decision stumps as the classification algorithm,[2] and we run ten-fold cross validation experiments, meaning that we repeatedly train on a subset of the data and test on a separate subset. Thus, we do not use the entire data set for training, and the validation is independent.

5.1 Affective State versus Neutral State

We first build classifiers that attempt to determine if a person is in a positively or negatively valenced affective state, regardless of the valence of the affect she experiences. Since no linguistic descriptions have been collected from the participants during the neutral state, these classifiers are build using the non-verbal features, namely the facial expression features, thermal features, and heart rate. For these classifiers, we use all 70 videos that we collected, which include 56 videos recorded when the subjects were exposed to positive or negative stimuli, and 14 videos recorded when the subjects were in a neutral state.

Table 2 shows the results obtained with individual classifiers based on one modality at a time, and a combined classifier that makes use of all the non-verbal modalities. The figures in the table represent the percentage of times the classifiers have correctly identified the correct state (i.e., the percentage of times the classifiers have correctly labeled the state as either affective or neutral). The baseline for these classifiers is 80%, which corresponds to selecting by default an affective state (the majority class in this dataset).

Modality	Accuracy
Baseline	80.00%
Facial expressions	81.42%
Thermal features	90.00%
Heart rate features	88.57%
All modalities	**92.85%**

Table 2: Automatic classification performances to differentiate between an affective and a neutral state for three different non-verbal models: facial expressions, thermal features, and heart rate features. The integration of the three models provides the best results.

5.2 Three-way Classification: Positive, Negative, or Neutral

The second set of classifiers is concerned with the identification of the presence of affect, as well as the valence of the affect (positive or negative). As in the previous set of experiments, since no linguistic descriptions are available for the neutral state, we only use the features obtained from the non-verbal sensing.

Table 3 shows the results obtained by this three-way classification, using one non-verbal modality at a time, and all three modalities combined. Note that these classifiers use all 70 videos, and have a baseline of 40%, which corresponds to selecting by default a positive (or negative) affective state.

5.3 Positive State versus Negative State

Finally, we also build classifiers that try to determine the valence of the affect experienced by a person, by differentiating between a positive affect and a negative affect. Here,

[2]We use the implementation available in the Weka package www.cs.waikato.ac.nz/ml/weka/

Modality	Accuracy
Baseline	40.00%
Facial expressions	51.42%
Thermal features	54.28%
Heart rate features	**57.14%**
All modalities	55.71%

Table 3: Automatic classification performances for three-way classifiers that differentiate between a positive state, a negative state, and a neutral state for three different models: facial expressions, thermal features, and heart rate features.

we build individual classifiers for all verbal and non-verbal modalities, and also a combined classifier that includes all four modalities. For these experiments, we only use the videos recorded during exposure to positive or negative stimuli. We thus use features extracted from 56 videos, including 28 positive videos and 28 negative videos.

Table 4 shows the results obtained with individual classifiers based on one modality at a time, and a combined classifier that makes use of all the modalities. The baseline for these classifiers is 50%, which corresponds to selecting by default a positive (or negative) affective state.

Modality	Accuracy
Baseline	50.00%
Facial expressions	61.02%
Thermal features	50.00%
Heart rate features	53.57%
Linguistic features	67.51%
All modalities	**73.21%**

Table 4: Automatic classification performances to differentiate between a positive and a negative affective state for four different models: facial expressions, thermal features, heart rate features, and linguistic features. The integration of the four models provides the best results.

6. DISCUSSION

These initial experiments reveal interesting findings about the influence of visual narratives on affect, and how that can be captured through four different modalities.

The first experiment on differentiating between an affective and a neutral state clearly shows that physiological modalities, such as heart rate and changes in skin temperature, are more effective than a visual modality that relies primarily on facial expressions. This is probably explained by the fact that a state of excitement, which typically corresponds to an affective state, induces changes in our physiological functions that are very well captured by thermal recordings and measurements of heart rate. On the other side, it appears that the facial expressions made during a neutral state are not very different from those that are made in an affective state, as a neutral state may also include occasional smiles or look aways that can confuse a classifier that relies primarily on visual clues. The joint use of all non-verbal modalities provides the best result, representing a relative error rate reduction of 64% compared to the baseline.

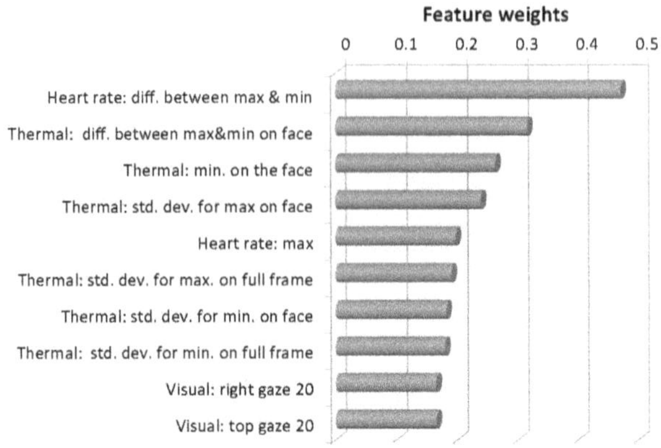

Figure 4: Top ten non-verbal features selected by the affective state classifier.

The second experiment shows a similar trend, where the physiological measures provide the best results. An analysis of the confusion matrix produced by these classifiers shows that once again these measures are doing very well in separating an affective state from a neutral state. Unlike the previous experiments, the visual features are also effective when compared to the baseline, which can be explained by their ability to differentiate positive and negative excitement (as also shown by the third experiment).

Finally, the last experiment shows the effectiveness of the facial expressions to distinguish between different types of affect (positive and negative). The thermal features and the heart rate features are significantly less effective here. This is probably due to the fact that the excitement experienced in an affective state induces changes in heart rate and skin temperature regardless of the valence of the affect (e.g., our heart beats faster when we are sad and it also beats faster when we are happy). In this experiment, we were also able to add the linguistic modality, which is the most effective overall. This suggests that when present, verbal communication can be a very useful clue for the prediction of affective state. The combination of all four modalities provides the best results, with a relative error rate reduction of 46% compared to the baseline.

To gain further understanding into the role played by the non-verbal features in predicting the changes in affective state, we compare the information gain assigned by the learning algorithm to each of these features. Figure 4 shows the top ten non-verbal features selected by the classification algorithm, obtained during the experiment that differentiates between affective and neutral states.

In line with the observations above, the physiological measures are the most useful when making a distinction between affective and neutral states. Among these, the difference between the maximum and minimum heart rate and the difference between the maximum and minimum temperature on the face seem to be the most useful features, followed by several other physiological features that reflect the minimum temperature, the standard deviation for the minimum and the maximum temperature, the maximum heart beat, and others. Among the visual features, the gaze to the right and gaze to the top appear to be the features that matter most for this classification.

For the distinction between positive and negative affect, the only significant features identified by the classifier are two smile features (number of smiles with intensity of 50 and 75 respectively), followed by the gaze to the right and gaze to the top features. None of the physiological features appear to be strong indicators of the valence of the affective state.

7. CONCLUSIONS AND FUTURE WORK

In this paper, we explored a non-invasive multimodal approach to sense changes in human affect when exposed to emotionally loaded videos. We experimented with four different modalities: visual facial behaviors, physiological measurements - including thermal imaging and heart rate measurements, and verbal descriptions. The first three modalities are non-verbal and are recorded during the narrative interaction, while the fourth modality is acquired in a post-study interview. Our experiments show that these modalities complement each other in detecting human affect. Specifically, our initial findings seem to suggest that physiological measures are most effective in identifying the presence of an affective state (as compared to a neutral state), whereas facial behaviors and verbal descriptions are most effective at differentiating between positive and negative states.

To our knowledge, this is the first attempt to integrate these four modalities (visual, thermal, heart rate, and linguistic) to predict human affective response to visual narratives. In future work, we plan to perform a more fine-grained temporal analysis of the multimodal features as they align with the content of the visual stimuli, to reach a better understanding of when and why do changes in affect take place, and how they can be effectively sensed and predicted.

Acknowledgments

We are grateful to Prof. Bill Buckles from the University of North Texas for allowing us to use the thermal camera. This material is based in part upon work supported by National Science Foundation awards #0917170 and #0917321. Any opinions, findings, and conclusions or recommendations expressed in this material are those of the authors and do not necessarily reflect the views of the National Science Foundation.

8. REFERENCES

[1] J. Allen. Photoplethysmography and its application in clinical physiological measurement. *Physiological measurement*, 28:R1, 2007.

[2] C. Alm, D. Roth, and R. Sproat. Emotions from text: Machine learning for text-based emotion prediction. In *Proceedings of the Conference on Empirical Methods in Natural Language Processing*, pages 347–354, Vancouver, Canada, 2005.

[3] V. Blanz and T. Vetter. A morphable model for the synthesis of 3d faces. In *SIGGRAPH '99: Proceedings of the 26th annual conference on Computer graphics and interactive techniques*, pages 187–194, New York, NY, USA, 1999. ACM Press/Addison-Wesley Publishing Co.

[4] C. Busso and S. Narayanan. Interrelation between speech and facial gestures in emotional utterances: a single subject study. *IEEE Transactions on Audio, Speech and Language Processing*, 15(8):2331–2347, November 2007.

[5] C. Camerer. *Behavioral Game Theory: Predicting Human Behavior in Strategic Situations*. Princeton University Press, 2004.

[6] J. Cardoso. High-order contrasts for independent component analysis. *Neural computation*, 11(1):157–192, 1999.

[7] T. Cootes, G. Edwards, and C. Taylor. Active appearance models. *Pattern Analysis and Machine Intelligence, IEEE Transactions on*, 23(6):681–685, Jun 2001.

[8] T. F. Cootes and C. J. Taylor. Active shape models - 'smart snakes'. In *Proceedings of the British Machine Vision Conference*, 1992.

[9] D. Cristinacce and T. Cootes. Feature detection and tracking with constrained local models. In *Brittish Machine Vision Conference*, 2006.

[10] J. Fei and I. Pavlidis. Thermistor at a distance: Unobtrusive measurement of breathing. *Biomedical Engineering, IEEE Transactions on*, 57(4):988–998, 2010.

[11] G. Fine. *The Storied Group: Social Movements as "Bundles of Narratives"*. SUNY Press, 2002.

[12] M. Garbey, N. Sun, A. Merla, and I. Pavlidis. Contact-free measurement of cardiac pulse based on the analysis of thermal imagery. *Biomedical Engineering, IEEE Transactions on*, 54(8):1418–1426, 2007.

[13] E. Greneker. Radar sensing of heartbeat and respiration at a distance with applications of the technology. In *Radar 97 (Conf. Publ. No. 449)*, pages 150–154. IET, 1997.

[14] H. Gunes and M. Pantic. Automatic, dimensional and continuous emotion recognition. *Int'l Journal of Synthetic Emotion*, 1(1):68–99, 2010.

[15] C. Izard. Emotion theory. *Annual Review of Psychology*, 60(1), 2009.

[16] A. Kane. *Finding Emotion in Social Movement Processes: Irish Land Movement Metaphors and Narratives*. University of Chicago Press, 2001.

[17] M. Khan, R. Ward, and M. Ingleby. Classifying pretended and evoked facial expressions of positive and negative affective states using infrared measurement of skin temperature. *ACM Transactions on Applied Perception*, 6(1), 2009.

[18] A. Liu and D. Salvucci. Modeling and prediction of human driver behavior. In *Proceedings of the International Conference on Human-Computer Interaction*, 2001.

[19] A. Maas, R. Daly, P. Pham, D. Huang, A. Ng, and C. Potts. Learning word vectors for sentiment analysis. In *Proceedings of the Association for Computational Linguistics (ACL 2011)*, Portland, OR, 2011.

[20] G. Mishne. Experiments with mood classification in

blog posts. In *Proceedings of the 1st Workshop on Stylistic Analysis Of Text For Information Access (Style 2005)*, Brazile, 2005.

[21] L. Morency, R. Mihalcea, and P. Doshi. Towards multimodal sentiment analysis: Harvesting opinions from the web. In *Proceedings of the International Conference on Multimodal Computing*, Alicante, Spain, 2011.

[22] L. Morency, J. Whitehill, and J. Movellan. Generalized adaptive view-based appearance model: Integrated framework for monocular head pose estimation. In *Automatic Face and Gesture Recognition*, pages 1–8, 2008.

[23] E. Murphy-Chutorian and M. Trivedi. Head pose estimation in computer vision: A survey. *IEEE Transactions on Pattern Analysis and Machine Intelligence*, 31:607–626, 2009.

[24] M. Nicolaou, H. Gunes, and M. Pantic. Audio-visual classification and fusion of spontaneous affective data in likelihood space. In *ICPR*, 2010.

[25] M. Nicolaou, H. Gunes, and M. Pantic. Output-associative rvm regression for dimensional and continuous emotion prediction. In *IEEE FG'11*, 2011.

[26] N. Oliver, B. Rosario, and A. Pentland. A Bayesian computer vision system for modeling human interactions. *IEEE Transactions on Pattern Analysis and Machine Intelligence*, 22(8), 2000.

[27] B. Pang and L. Lee. A sentimental education: Sentiment analysis using subjectivity summarization based on minimum cuts. In *Proceedings of the 42nd Meeting of the Association for Computational Linguistics*, Barcelona, Spain, July 2004.

[28] M. Pantic and M. S. Bartlett. Machine analysis of facial expressions. In K. Delac and M. Grgic, editors, *Face Recognition*, pages 377–416. I-Tech Education and Publishing, Vienna, Austria, July 2007.

[29] I. Pavlidis and J. Levine. Thermal image analysis for polygraph testing. *IEEE Engineering in Medicine and Biology Magazine*, 21(6), 2002.

[30] M. Poh, D. McDuff, and R. Picard. Non-contact, automated cardiac pulse measurements using video imaging and blind source separation. *Optical Society of America*, 2010.

[31] C. Puri, L. Olson, I. Pavlidis, J. Levine, , and J. Starren. Stresscam: non-contact measurement of users' emotional states through thermal imaging. In *Proceedings of the 2005 ACM Conference on Human Factors in Computing Systems (CHI)*, 2005.

[32] S. Raaijmakers, K. Truong, and T. Wilson. Multimodal subjectivity analysis of multiparty conversation. In *Proceedings of the Conference on Empirical Methods in Natural Language Processing*, pages 466–474, Honolulu, Hawaii, 2008.

[33] E. Riloff and J. Wiebe. Learning extraction patterns for subjective expressions. In *Conference on Empirical Methods in Natural Language Processing (EMNLP-03)*, pages 105–112, 2003.

[34] N. Sebe, I. Cohen, T. Gevers, and T. Huang. Emotion recognition based on joint visual and audio cues. In *ICPR*, 2006.

[35] C. Strapparava and R. Mihalcea. Semeval-2007 task 14: Affective text. In *Proceedings of the 4th International Workshop on the Semantic Evaluations (SemEval 2007)*, Prague, Czech Republic, 2007.

[36] C. Strapparava and R. Mihalcea. Learning to identify emotions in text. In *Proceedings of the ACM Conference on Applied Computing ACM-SAC 2008*, Fortaleza, Brazile, 2008.

[37] C. Strapparava and A. Valitutti. Wordnet-affect: an affective extension of wordnet. In *Proceedings of the 4th International Conference on Language Resources and Evaluation*, Lisbon, 2004.

[38] M. Tarvainen, P. Ranta-Aho, and P. Karjalainen. An advanced detrending method with application to hrv analysis. *Biomedical Engineering, IEEE Transactions on*, 49(2):172–175, 2002.

[39] P. Turney. Thumbs up or thumbs down? semantic orientation applied to unsupervised classification of reviews. In *Proceedings of the 40th Annual Meeting of the Association for Computational Linguistics (ACL 2002)*, pages 417–424, Philadelphia, 2002.

[40] S. Ulyanov and V. Tuchin. Pulse-wave monitoring by means of focused laser beams scattered by skin surface and membranes. In *Proceedings of SPIE*, 1993.

[41] P. Viola and M. Jones. Rapid object detection using a boosted cascade of simple features. In *Computer Vision and Pattern Recognition, 2001. CVPR 2001. Proceedings of the 2001 IEEE Computer Society Conference on*, volume 1, pages I–511. IEEE, 2001.

[42] D. Watson and L. Clark. *THE PANAS-X Manual for the Positive and Negative Affect Schedule - Expanded Form.* University of Iowa.

[43] J. Wiebe. Learning subjective adjectives from corpora. In *Proceedings of the American Association for Artificial Intelligence (AAAI 2000)*, pages 735–740, Austin, Texas, 2000.

[44] J. Wiebe, T. Wilson, and C. Cardie. Annotating expressions of opinions and emotions in language. *Language Resources and Evaluation*, 39(2-3):165–210, 2005.

[45] T. Wilson, J. Wiebe, and P. Hoffmann. Recognizing contextual polarity in phrase-level sentiment analysis. In *Proceedings of Human Language Technologies Conference/Conference on Empirical Methods in Natural Language Processing (HLT/EMNLP 2005)*, Vancouver, Canada, 2005.

[46] M. Wöllmer, F. Eyben, S. Reiter, B. Schuller, C. Cox, E. Douglas-Cowie, and R. Cowie. Abandoning emotion classes - towards continuous emotion recognition with modelling of long-range dependencies. In *INTERSPEECH*. ISCA, 2008.

[47] M. Wollmer, B. Schuller, F. Eyben, and G. Rigoll. Combining long short-term memory and dynamic bayesian networks for incremental emotion-sensitive artificial listening. *IEEE Journal of Selected Topics in Signal Processing*, 4(5), October 2010.

[48] Z. Zeng, M. Pantic, G. I. Roisman, and T. S. Huang. A survey of affect recognition methods: Audio, visual, and spontaneous expressions. *IEEE Transactions on Pattern Analysis and Machine Intelligence*, 31(1):39–58, 2009.

[49] Z. Zhihong, M. P. G. Roisman, and T. Huang. A survey of affect recognition methods: Audio, visual, and spontaneous expressions. *PAMI*, 31(1), 2009.

Integrating Video and Accelerometer Signals for Nocturnal Epileptic Seizure Detection

Kris Cuppens
Bart Vanrumste
MOBILAB/K.H.Kempen - KU Leuven, ESAT-SCD/IBBT, Belgium
kris.cuppens@khk.be

Chih-Wei Chen
Kevin Bing-Yung Wong
Hamid Aghajan
AIRLab, Department of Electrical Engineering, Stanford University, California USA

Tinne Tuytelaars
KU Leuven, ESAT-PSI and IBBT Future Health Department, Belgium

Anouk Van de Vel
Berten Ceulemans
University Hospital of Antwerp, Child neurology, Belgium

Lieven Lagae
University Hospital Leuven, Paediatrics, Belgium

Sabine Van Huffel
KU Leuven, ESAT-SCD-SISTA/IBBT Future Health Department, Belgium

ABSTRACT

Epileptic seizure detection is traditionally done using video/electroencephalogram (EEG) monitoring, which is not applicable in a home situation. In recent years, attempts have been made to detect the seizures using other modalities. In this paper we investigate if a combined usage of accelerometers attached to the limbs and video data would increase the performance compared to a single modality approach. Therefore, we used two existing approaches for seizure detection in accelerometers and video and combined them using a linear discriminant analysis (LDA) classifier. The results for a combined detection have a better positive predictive value (PPV) of 95.00% compared to the single modality detection and reached a sensitivity of 83.33%.

Categories and Subject Descriptors

J.3 [**Computer Applications**]: Life & Medical Sciences—*Health, Medical information systems*

General Terms

Algorithms, Performance

Keywords

Accelerometry, Epilepsy, Video

1. INTRODUCTION

Traditionally, epileptic seizures are detected by using video/EEG-monitoring. Although this technique is the most reliable way for seizure detection in terms of sensitivity and specificity, as the actual brain activity can be investigated, it is not practically usable outside the hospital environment. This is due to the impractical way of attaching the electrodes to the scalp which is time consuming for the nursing staff, and it hampers the patient. Therefore, researchers have increasingly been investigating the detection of seizures based on other modalities during the last decade. In previous research, we have focused on the detection of seizures based on the usage of only video recordings and only accelerometers. In this paper we want to integrate both modalities to investigate if a better performance is feasible when using a multi-modal approach. Indeed, although the two modalities both express the same measure, i.e. the movement of the patient, we believe that they are complementary to some extent. The accelerometers are directly attached to the body, and can record accurately (both in amplitude and time) the acceleration of each individual limb even when covered, but the video data has a better global view of the patient and can register, in contrast to the accelerometers, movement of the head and torso. That is why a combined approach could show in improvement of the performance. In the approach using only accelerometers, normal activity was modeled and based on the distribution of this normal activity, outliers were classified as seizures [4]. The detection based on video recordings [3] is based on the spatio-temporal interest point (STIP) method proposed by Laptev [7], which was originally proposed for detecting realistic actions in movies, but is now also used by different research groups for different settings in human action recognition.

Other research groups also already investigated the detection of epileptic seizures based on video or accelerometers. Lockman [8] validated the SmartWatch which is a watch-like sensor with an integrated accelerometer that patients can wear to detect large epileptic seizures. Nijsen et al. [10] used multiple accelerometers instead of one attached to a wristwatch. Most of the video detection algorithms for seizure detection make use of markers [1]. In the work of Karayiannis et al. [6] the limbs could be tracked as they were visible in the video because the neonatal patients were

ICMI'12, October 22–26, 2012, Santa Monica, California, USA.

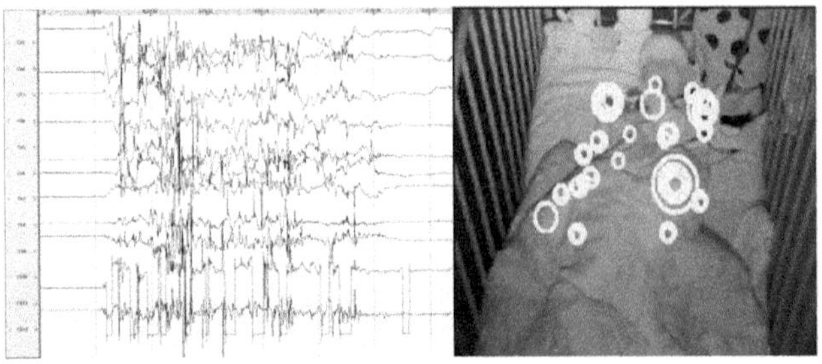

Figure 1: Visualization of the accelerometer signals during a seizure (left) and the detected STIPs in one video frame (right)

monitored in the neonatal intensive care unit. Seizure detection based on other modalities combining EMG, acceleration and angular velocity [2] or EEG and ECG [5] can also be found in literature. In their work an early integration (combining features from both modalities or *feature fusion*) and late integration (combining output from classifiers on both modalities or *decision fusion*) are considered. In our study we also perform a late integration of the data. Although fusion at a late stage in the processing stream naturally incurs performance loss, it is a feasible solution when fusion at a lower level is not practical [12].

2. METHOD

To test our method we used the data including hypermotor seizures and normal nocturnal movements. The data is acquired at the Pulderbos rehabilitation center for children and youth where epileptic children are monitored and treated. Hypermotor seizures are marked by intense and random movement in the arms and legs, which can last from a few to tens of seconds. Due to the violent nature of this type of seizures and its resistance to treatment, it is important to detect them and alarm parents or caregivers.

Figure 1 shows both modalities. The raw acceleration signals on the left, and a frame of the video data with the spatio-temporal interest points (STIPs) that are detected on the right. The processing of this data and the detection of these STIPs is further discussed in the next sections. The video and acceleration data used in this study is simultaneously acquired with other modalities such as EEG, ECG and EMG. The EEG is only used for the ground truth labeling. In a first step the movement epochs in the data are detected based on the calculation of the standard deviation within a sliding window on the acceleration data. A simulation dataset was recorded to quantify the smallest movements we want to detect. Based on this dataset, thresholds were defined for movement detection. After the movement detection step, the data is segmented in epochs containing normal or epileptic movement.

To be able to objectively compare both approaches, based on acceleration and on video, we use the same segmentation of the data for both modalities. This means that the segmentation of the data, both accelerometer and video, is based on the movements in the accelerometer signals. The training and testing is done in a 10-fold randomization. This means that we randomly select a number of normal and epileptic movements for the training and test set and perform the modeling and validation 10 times using a different combination of movements, and average out the obtained results. This makes the results less dependent on the division of the data in a training and test set. We use two thirds of the data as the training set, and one third as test set. The same randomizations are used in both approaches and for the acceleration/video integration.

2.1 Accelerometer detection

For the detection of seizures based on acceleration, four 3 dimensional accelerometers were attached to the wrists and ankles of the patient. This method is already discussed in [4]. From the epochs detected in the first step, as described in the previous section, multiple time and frequency domain features are derived, more specific: mean amplitude, standard deviation, max amplitude of resultant, correlation, kurtosis, rms, skewness, peak frequency, energy, spectral edge frequency (80%, 90%, 95%), power in sub-bands (1-3Hz, 4-8Hz, 9-13Hz, 14-20Hz) and the normalized power in the sub-bands. These features were calculated for each channel individually and also the mean and standard deviation over all the channels was calculated. Based on the Kruzkal-Wallis test, the features with the best discriminating power are determined and used in the rest of the detection algorithm. The selected features are the the maximum of resultant over both arms (Equation 1), the mean standard deviation (std) over all channels (Equation 2), the length of the epoch n, the mean root mean square (rms) over all the channels (Equation 3) and the minimal power in the frequency band 1-3 Hz over all the channels (Equation 4), where i is the index of the 12 different channels, n is the length of the epoch in samples, t represents the time index of the epoch in samples and PSD is the power spectral density.

$$\max_t \left(\|x_{1-3}(t)\|, \|x_{4-6}(t)\|\right) \tag{1}$$

$$\frac{1}{12}\sum_{i=1}^{12}\sqrt{\frac{1}{n-1}\sum_{t=1}^{n}(x_i(t)-\bar{x_i})^2} \tag{2}$$

$$\frac{1}{12}\sum_{i=1}^{12}\sqrt{\frac{1}{n}\sum_{t=1}^{n}x_i(t)^2} \tag{3}$$

$$\min_i(PSD_{1-3Hz}(x_i)) \tag{4}$$

For the classification of seizures, normal movement was modeled based on the probability density function (pdf) using these best features. The movements that are outliers in the test phase with respect to the pdf, are considered as epileptic movement. The pdf is determined by using the non-parametric Parzen window approach. The bandwidth that is needed for this approach is determined in a group specific way as used in [4]. In that research, the optimal bandwidth was determined on 6 patients and used on the 7th patient in a leave-one-out approach. The best performing bandwidth for the patient in this study is chosen based on that previous study. The threshold for discriminating between normal and epileptic movement is set at the 95% probability boundary on the pdf. This means that the 5% movements with the lowest probability are classified as epileptic.

2.2 Video detection

The video detection is based on the STIP method proposed by Laptev [7], and we applied this method on epileptic data in a previous study [3]. First, spatio-temporal interest

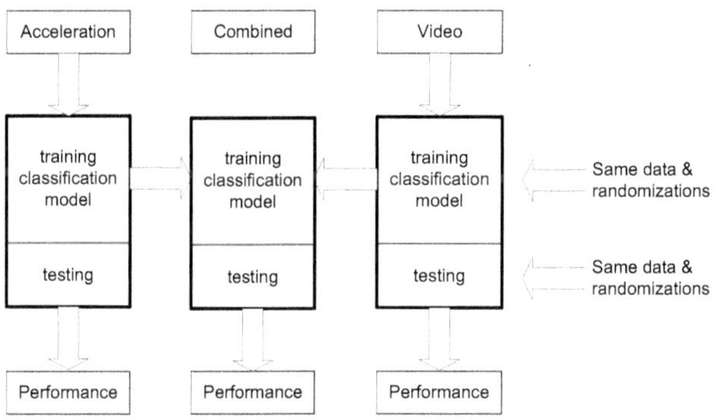

Figure 2: Overview of the integration of both modalities. The high level classifier makes use of the outputs of both the video detection and the accelerometer detection algorithm.

points are found in the video, on multiple spatio-temporal scales. The detection of these interest points is based on the Harris corner detection, but extended to three dimensions (two spatial and one temporal dimension). The neighborhood of each detected interest point is then divided into multiple spatio-temporal cuboids. In our approach we use a division of 3 in each spatial direction, and 2 in the temporal direction. In a second step, features are extracted from these cuboids that describe the appearance and the movement in the video, namely the histograms of gradients (HoG) and the histograms of the optical flow (HoF). In our approach we only use the flow features, which describe the movement, because the appearance of the patient's limbs can change from sequence to sequence (e.g. when they are covered with a blanket). The motion can also change because of the occluded part, but in practice the motion vectors are similar. In the last step, video sequences are classified using a bag-of-features approach. In our initial approach [3], the movement epochs were split up into video sequences of 1, 2, 5 or 10 seconds. But in this study, the full length of the movement is used to have the same data as those used in the accelerometer approach. From these sequences, all the STIPs and the according features are calculated. The STIPs are assigned to the cluster prototypes that are found using k-means clustering in the training phase. A histogram is constructed with each bin representing one cluster. The histograms of the video sequences are used as input in a support vector machine (SVM) classifier, considering every bin as one feature with the number of STIPs assigned to the cluster as the according feature value. The SVM parameters are optimized using a three-fold cross validation in the training set, and a cost function, stating that a missed seizure has a cost that is 5 times higher than a false detection, as we want to reduce the number of missed seizures. The output value of the classifier gives a probability of the video sequence belonging to the epileptic seizure class, as we use the LIBSVM[1] implementation for extending SVM to give probability estimates based on Wu et al. [14].

2.3 Multi-modal detection

To integrate the accelerometer and video detection, first we made sure that the data to process is exactly the same.

[1]http://www.csie.ntu.edu.tw/~cjlin/libsvm/

Table 1: Results of the single and multi-modal approach, in terms of sensitivity, positive predictive value and specificity.

	sens	std	PPV	std	spec	std
acc	100.00	0.00	36.49	11.78	95.28	2.26
video	70.00	36.68	94.44	11.02	99.84	0.33
combi	**83.33**	28.33	**95.00**	10.54	**99.84**	0.33

In the training and test sets, the same randomization of both modalities is used and the video data is not cut into smaller windows, the entire movements are classified as one event.

The outputs of the two detection algorithms are used as an input in a new LDA classifier. The LDA classifier [9] finds a linear transformation that maximizes the inter-class variance and minimizes intra-class variance to get the best separation between the classes. The probability value of an event on the pdf of the accelerometer detection, and the probability that a movement belongs to the seizure class in the video approach are used as features in the integrated approach. The model is trained based on these new features making use of the training data. In the test phase, the movement events are first classified by the accelerometer and video detection algorithms, and their outputs are again used for the LDA classifier, which produces the final classification. An overview of the working method is shown in Figure 2.

3. RESULTS

Table 1 shows an overview of the results for the uni-modal and multi-modal detection. We see that the result for the detection based on the accelerometers has the highest sensitivity, 100.00% is reached. The PPV is low (36.49%), as almost 2 in 3 detections are false detections. The video detection scores better in terms of PPV, with 94.44% but the sensitivity is lower (70.00%).

The specificity of 95.28% using the accelerometer approach can be explained by the 95% threshold we have set in the algorithm. We expect this value to be situated between 95% and 100%, as (more or less) 5% of the movement events are classified as seizures.

The multi-modal approach gives the best result in terms of the PPV (95.00%). The sensitivity is situated between the results of the single modality approaches (83.33%). In general we can say that the multimodal approach performs better than the video detection alone. Compared to the accelerometer detection, the sensitivity is lower but the PPV is much higher. The approach that gives the best performance is a subjective interpretation and depends on which factor is most important in the application. And although in our application it is more important to have a high sensitivity as we do not want to miss too many seizures, we believe the combined approach to give the best results as the accelerometer detection generates too many false positives to be of practical use.

4. DISCUSSION

Using the different approaches for both modalities makes a comparison more difficult. Due to the nature of the approach based on the accelerometer data, the obtained result has a higher sensitivity compared to the lower PPV as we chose our threshold to be conservative by detecting all the seizures and allowing more false detections. The video approach is optimized using a cost function, stating that the cost for a missed seizure is five time higher than for a false detection. This generates a different result in terms of sensitivity and PPV. The combined approach is obtained using a linear discriminant analysis, but applying a different thresholding on the accelerometer results could already give an improvement of the PPV. But as said before, this threshold is chosen in a conservative way without explicitly not making use of prior knowledge in this accelerometer detection.

The test is now performed on an initial dataset to see whether an integrated approach would give better results. A total of 7 seizures and 381 normal movements were used in the study. Seizures lasted from 3 to 6 minutes but they are often merged with post-ictal movement. The normal movements lasted from 1 second to 35 minutes. The seizures do not occur very frequently in our patient database, which makes it harder to gather a larger number of seizure data. Although the first indications are promising, this approach should be tested on a larger group of patients and seizures.

Now we have integrated accelerometer and video signals, but in the future, it would be interesting to also integrate other modalities. The datasets we have collected also contain ECG, EMG, EEG, electrooculogram (EOG) and audio data. Combining multiple modalities can improve the performance. However, we have to keep in mind that adding more sensors makes the recording of the data more cumbersome, which is contrary to the research goals of making the monitoring easier and more comfortable for the patient.

There are also other ways to combine the input from different classifiers. For example voting methods, Bayesian fusion methods on the soft outputs of the classifiers (as available in our approach) or using Fuzzy integrals or Fuzzy templates [11]. If we have a dataset with more positives examples, we can integrate both modalities based on the stacked generalization [13]. This would be a logic extension of our current approach. Up till now, we used only one training set for learning the high level model, instead of the separate training sets for the low level and high level modeling in the stacked generalization. Another possibility is the fusion on the feature level. In this respect, it would be interesting to also apply a bag-of-features approach on the 12 channel accelerometer data. This is feasible by detecting spikes in the signals and derive features around them or simply by taking the raw input data around each spike. This would make it easier to integrate both modalities. Other ways that the multi-modality can be used is for example performing the training on the multi-modal data (in our case e.g. video and accelerometers) and test it on unimodal data (e.g. only video). In this way, the different modalities can provide extra information to train a better modal, but once the detection algorithm is employed in a real setting, fewer modalities have to be registered which makes the detection system easier and more comfortable to use.

5. ACKNOWLEDGMENTS

Research supported by Research Council KUL:GOA-MANET, IWT: TBM070713-Accelero, Belgian Federal Science Policy Office IUAP P6/04 (DYSCO, Dynamical systems, control and optimization, 2007 - 2011); EU: Neuromath (COST-BM0601). Kris Cuppens is supported by a PhD grant of the Agency for Innovation by Science and Technology in Flanders (IWT).

6. REFERENCES

[1] L. Chen, X. Yang, Y. Liu, D. Zeng, Y. Tang, B. Yan, X. Lin, L. Liu, H. Xu, and D. Zhou. Quantitative and trajectory analysis of movement trajectories in supplementary motor area seizures of frontal lobe epilepsy. *Epilepsy & Behavior*, 14(2):344–353, 2009.

[2] I. Conradsen, S. Beniczky, P. Wolf, J. Henriksen, T. Sams, and H. B. D. Sorensen. Seizure onset detection based on a uni- or multi-modal intelligent seizure acquisition (UISA/MISA) system. *2010 32nd Annual International Conference of the IEEE Engineering in Medicine and Biology Society (EMBC 2010)*, pages 3269–72, 2010.

[3] K. Cuppens, C.-W. Chen, K. Wong, A. Van de Vel, L. Lagae, B. Ceulemans, T. Tuytelaars, S. Van Huffel, B. Vanrumste, and H. Aghajan. Using spatio-temporal interest points (STIP) for myoclonic jerk detection in nocturnal video. *EMBC: 2012 Annual International Conference of the IEEE Engineering in Medicine and Biology Society, submitted*, 2012.

[4] K. Cuppens, P. Karsmakers, A. Van de Vel, S. Luca, B. Bonroy, M. Milosevic, B. Ceulemans, L. Lagae, S. Van Huffel, and B. Vanrumste. Accelerometer based home monitoring for detection of nocturnal hypermotor seizures with estimation of probability density function. *Internal report*, 2012.

[5] B. Greene, G. Boylan, R. Reilly, P. de Chazal, and C. S. Combination of EEG and ECG for improved automatic neonatal seizure detection. *Clin Neurophysiol*, 118(6):1348–59, 2007.

[6] N. B. Karayiannis, G. Z. Tao, J. D. Frost, M. S. Wise, R. A. Hrachovy, and E. M. Mizrahi. Automated detection of videotaped neonatal seizures based on motion segmentation methods. *Clinical Neurophysiology*, 117(7):1585–1594, 2006.

[7] I. Laptev. On space-time interest points. *International Journal of Computer Vision*, 64(2-3):107–123, 2005.

[8] J. Lockman, R. S. Fisher, and D. M. Olson. Detection of seizure-like movements using a wrist accelerometer. *Epilepsy & Behavior*, 20(4):638–641, 2011.

[9] G. J. McLachlan. *Discriminant analysis and statistical pattern recognition*. Wiley Series in Probability and Mathematical Statistics, 1992.

[10] T. M. E. Nijsen, R. M. Aarts, P. J. M. Cluitmans, and P. A. M. Griep. Time-frequency analysis of accelerometry data for detection of myoclonic seizures. *IEEE Transactions on Information Technology in Biomedicine*, 14(5):1197–1203, 2010.

[11] D. Ruta and B. Gabrys. An overview of classifier fusion methods. *Computing and Information Systems*, (7):1–10, 2000.

[12] P. Varshney. Multisensor data fusion. *Electronics and Communications Engineering Journal*, 9:245–253, 1997.

[13] D. Wolpert. Stacked generalization. *Neural Networks*, pages 241–259, 1992.

[14] T.-F. Wu, C.-J. Lin, and R. C. Weng. Probability estimates for multi-class classification by pairwise coupling. *Journal of Machine Learning Research*, 5:975–1005, 2004.

GeoGazemarks: Providing Gaze History for the Orientation on Small Display Maps

Ioannis Giannopoulos
Institute of Cartography and Geoinformation
ETH Zurich
Wolfgang-Pauli-Str. 15
CH-8093 Zurich, Switzerland
igiannopoulos@ethz.ch

Peter Kiefer
Institute of Cartography and Geoinformation
ETH Zurich
Wolfgang-Pauli-Str. 15
CH-8093 Zurich, Switzerland
pekiefer@ethz.ch

Martin Raubal
Institute of Cartography and Geoinformation
ETH Zurich
Wolfgang-Pauli-Str. 15
CH-8093 Zurich, Switzerland
mraubal@ethz.ch

ABSTRACT

Orientation on small display maps is often difficult because the visible spatial context is restricted. This paper proposes to provide the history of a user's visual attention on a map as visual clue to facilitate orientation. Visual attention on the map is recorded with eye tracking, clustered geo-spatially, and visualized when the user zooms out. This implicit gaze-interaction concept, called *GeoGazemarks*, has been evaluated in an experiment with 40 participants. The study demonstrates a significant increase in efficiency and an increase in effectiveness for a map search task, compared to standard panning and zooming.

Categories and Subject Descriptors

H.5.2 [**Information Interfaces and Presentation**]: User Interfaces—*Interaction styles, Input devices and strategies*

General Terms

Human Factors, Experimentation, Performance

Keywords

Gaze Interaction, Eye Tracking, Mobile Applications, Map History, Orientation, GeoGazemarks

1. INTRODUCTION

Map services on small display devices are restricted by the spatial area that can be apprehended at one time [5]. Orientation on these maps can thus be challenging. For instance, it may be difficult to switch the view coordinates back to places one has already interacted with, but not explicitly tagged. Information needs, such as 'show me again that nice place by the river I saw five minutes ago', are hard to satisfy with current interaction concepts. With classical panning and zooming the user has to rely on her cognitive map [11, 18], which contains inaccuracies. It is well known that humans are typically bad at estimating the cardinal direction back to a previously visited position (path integration, [19]). Zooming out, however, will only highlight the places regarded as relevant by the labeling algorithm, not necessarily those that support orientation.

The objective of this paper is to mark those places on high zoom levels the user has previously paid visual attention to. Our hypothesis is that these *GeoGazemarks* will support orientation on the map because these places have become part of the user's cognitive map.

We measure visual attention with eye tracking, a methodology commonly used in HCI research, especially in multimodal interaction. The visual context switches between, say, a mobile and a projected screen [6], or the road and in-vehicle instruments [31], are critical for the usability and safety of such systems. Head-mounted (mobile) eye trackers allow us to measure visual attention also for large-scale spaces, such as outdoor urban settings [16] where small display maps are prevalent. Current trends in smartphone hardware development[1] indicate that eye tracking through the front-facing cameras of standard smartphones might soon become a reality, which facilitates (and calls for) new interaction concepts, such as the one presented here.

In this paper we introduce *GeoGazemarks*, a novel interaction concept for small display maps that uses gaze history to provide orientational clues. Although its name is inspired by the Gazemarks approach introduced in [15], our GeoGazemarks are conceptually different as only one display is used, because the focus is on small displays, and because the marks are attached to geospatial coordinates (latitude, longitude), not to screen coordinates. We have implemented GeoGazemarks in a smartphone application that accesses data from a mobile eye tracker. A user study with 40 participants has demonstrated a significant increase in efficiency and an increase in effectiveness for a map search task with GeoGazemarks, compared to standard map interaction.

The rest of this paper is structured as follows: we continue with related work in section 2, and introduce the GeoGazemarks interaction concept in section 3. Our implementation of GeoGazemarks is described in section 4. The user study

[1]Refer to Apple's patent application number 20120036433, `http://www.freepatentsonline.com/y2012/0036433.html`, and Samsung's announcements on Galaxy S III, `http://www.technewsworld.com/story/75033.html`, retrieved August 27, 2012

(section 5) and its results (section 6) are followed by a discussion of the results in section 7. Section 8 provides directions for future research.

2. RELATED WORK

2.1 Eye tracking in HCI

Eye trackers capture a person's eye movements [8]. Most state-of-the-art devices, including the one used in this research, work with infrared corneal reflection, combined with image processing and a mathematical model of the eye. They output the point of gaze, which in our case comes as an overlay to a video of the environment captured with a head-mounted camera.

Eye trackers can be used as input media in computer systems for easy, natural, and fast ways of interacting by using gaze as input [14, 30]. Several novel interaction concepts based on eye tracking have been proposed recently, using both, explicit and implicit interactions. According to Schmidt [26], explicit interaction refers to the intentional direct manipulation of a computer system by the user, whereas implicit interaction is defined as an action that is not primarily intended to be an interaction, but is registered by the system as such. Examples for explicit interaction include, among many others, eye-typing [20] and steering a virtual character [28].

In contrast to these approaches, our paper focuses on implicit interaction. An interface aware of its user's gaze can support user interaction with extended context based information, such as translations of foreign words currently read [4], or with eye-driven cursors that behave differently depending on the context [21]. Another example is *eyeBook* [3], an application that uses augmented text to respond with real-time effects according to the current reading position.

The *Gazemarks* approach mentioned in section 1 is another example for implicit gaze interaction [15]: fixations were used as digital placeholders in order to assist users during attention switches when working with two (large) screens, independent of the screen content. Conceptually different is our GeoGazemarks approach, which is designed for interaction with geographic information shown on a single small sized screen. It also solves a different problem: that of orientation on maps.

2.2 Interaction with small display maps

Devices with small displays, such as smartphones, have become ubiquitous. Location-based services (LBS) running on these devices support users during mobile decision-making. They are sensitive to the location of a mobile person (through GPS and other positioning technologies) and relate the person's location to the surrounding environment via a geographic information system (GIS) database. This in turn allows the system to provide location-based information in the form of written instructions or cartographic maps that facilitate the successful completion of spatio-temporal tasks. Different media can be utilized for communicating location-based information. Maps have been the most prominent medium and researchers working in the area of *mobile cartography* have been investigating the particularities of mobile map design and use [10].

Several issues arise when using maps on smartphones. Mobile displays are limited in size and resolution compared to larger screens, which makes map reading more difficult for the average user [7]. Mobile map adaptation based on the user's preferences, task, and location, among other context parameters, can help reduce both user interaction with the device and cognitive load for the user. For example, when the user reaches a decision point during a navigation task, the service can automatically zoom in to local detail [23]. Maps are traditionally aligned on the display with north facing up. Just as users of traditional analog maps often turn the map as their travel direction changes, users of mobile devices typically prefer digital maps to maintain 'track-up' alignment [2]. Sensor-based information can be used to determine a user's direction of movement and automatically provide track-up oriented maps on mobile devices.

An implication of limited screen size this paper mainly focuses on is that the spatial area visible at one time is restricted, unless the user zooms out at the price of loosing map details. Rohs et al. [25] investigated map navigation with mobile devices with regards to virtual versus physical movement and in combination with large static maps. They implemented a magic lens approach that tracks the device above a high resolution paper map (which provides an overview of the larger spatial area in the user's visual periphery) in real time and provides augmented reality overlays with dynamic geospatial data. In a user study the advantage of dynamic over static peephole interaction was demonstrated both regarding search time and degree of exploration of the search space. The paper map used by Rohs et al. puts the currently inspected map area into a larger spatial context. This allows the user to interpret the information with respect to landmarks of the larger surroundings she already knows. GeoGazemarks also put spatial information into the context of previously acquired spatial knowledge, but are more individualized using the visual attention during knowledge acquisition.

2.3 Spatial knowledge and Wayfinding

Spatial knowledge is assumed to be represented in a cognitive map [9, 22], which is a mental representation that corresponds to people's perception of the real world, although other metaphors, such as cognitive collages and spatial mental models, have also been proposed [29]. Studies have suggested that cognitive maps are structured hierarchically [12]. One consequence of hierarchies in cognitive maps is that they may have an influence on wayfinding performance, e.g., bias in spatial judgments such as distance estimates [13]. Researchers from various disciplines have thoroughly investigated the role cognitive maps play in spatial behavior, spatial problem solving, acquisition, and learning [17].

People employ different means to solve their wayfinding tasks, such as piloting and path integration [1]. During *piloting* wayfinders follow a sequence of landmarks while maintaining and updating their position information in relation to a single or multiple landmarks. *Path integration* consists of velocity- and acceleration-based wayfinding. It relies on information regarding one's heading and bearing relative to a point of origin [19]. During wayfinding, people usually take advantage of both methods rather than relying on only one of them. Path integration is relevant not only for physical navigation, but also for navigating information spaces such as 2D maps. In this paper we will use a path integration task that consists in finding the point of origin after having navigated along a given vector sequence on a mobile map.

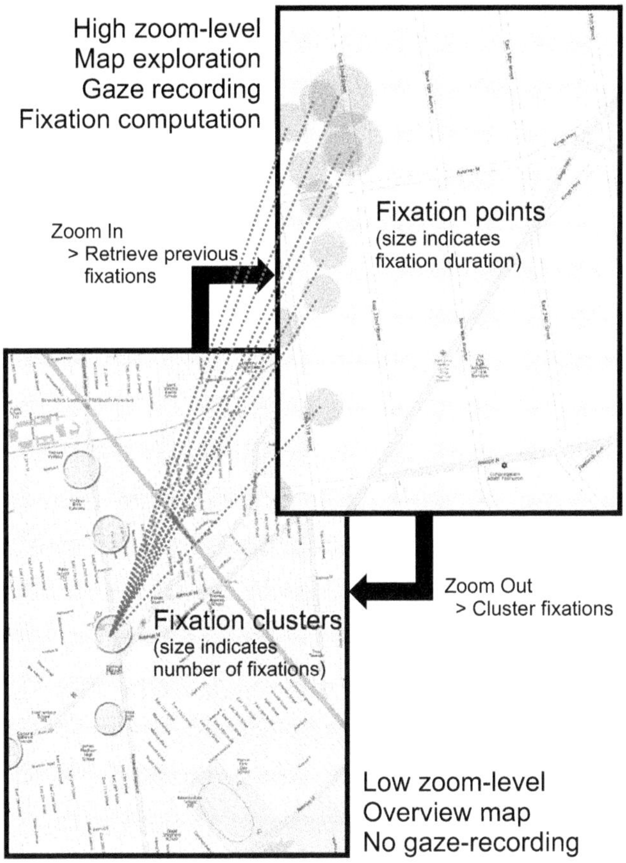

Figure 1: The GeoGazemarks interaction concept.

3. GEOGAZEMARKS

3.1 Disorientation on small display maps

The GeoGazemarks concept approaches the problem that orientation on small display maps is often difficult due to the absence of information on map usage history. Consider the following example scenario:

Alice has just arrived in X-town, a city she has never visited before. She starts a map application on her smartphone. The screen, sized 4 inches, shows a satellite image of the area at a high zoom level, centered at the train station. Alice has no firm plans yet, so she starts exploring the map. By swiping her finger across the screen she pans to the North, East, South-East, and finally a few swipes South-West. She then decides that the small antique shop, which she noticed during the 'East' swipe, might be a good start for her visit.

The example describes a typical scenario for current standard mobile map applications. Users are not supported in information requests that relate to the map usage history, such as 'show me the place I saw two minutes ago, approx. North West of the current screen'. Finding one's way back via text search is relatively time consuming and often ambiguous. It does also not help for non-indexed places (e.g., 'this nice place by the river where I saw the big oak trees'). Thus, the user has to rely on standard map interaction, i.e., panning and zooming:

Version 1: *Alice suspects the store to be somewhere North-North-West of the current screen position. She pans into that direction, but unfortunately misses her goal.*

Panning often fails on small display maps because of the *path integration problem*, which consists of summing up inverted movement vectors to get the exact direction that needs to be traveled to return to the origin. Humans are known to be generally bad path integrators [19]. The further away the goal, the harder it becomes to keep the exact direction while panning.

Version 2: *Alice zooms out to get an overview of the area. The antique shop is too small to be labeled on that zoom level. Alice remembers the store being located close to a park. She zooms to a green spot, but picks the wrong park.*

Zooming does not help if the searched place is not labeled on higher zoom levels. An individual marker has typically not been set because the place did not seem sufficiently relevant at the time of the first interaction.

3.2 The GeoGazemarks interaction concept

GeoGazemarks builds on the assumption that the user's map usage history, recorded as gaze information with an eye tracker, can be used to provide orientational cues that support the retrieval of places on a small display map. GeoGazemarks serves as an augmentation – it does not replace existing interaction possibilities, such as panning by swiping and two-finger zooming.

The GeoGazemarks interaction concept consists of two phases, the *recording* and the *retrieval phase*, which are switched depending on the zoom level of the map.

3.2.1 Recording gaze history

The recording phase is activated when the user interacts with the map on a high zoom level. The user's gaze on the map is recorded and aggregated to fixations[2]. Fixations are stored with the geospatial coordinates (latitude, longitude) the user has fixated. We restrain from automatically snapping fixations to the closest point of interest (or other geo feature) as this would not account for places of interest that are not explicitly labeled on the map (such as, 'the nice place by the river').

Fixations that were logged during previous recording phases are shown as icons. This helps the user to recall which places in a particular area she had been interested in. Figure 1 (top) shows an example of our implementation of the recording phase (red dots: previous fixations). Note that fixations are *not* visualized instantly in real time during recording to avoid distraction from the map task. Fixations on this zoom level will only appear after the user has changed into the retrieval mode, and back to the recording phase.

3.2.2 Place retrieval with gaze history

The retrieval phase is activated when the user zooms out below a certain zoom level threshold[3]. No gaze is recorded in this phase. All previously recorded fixations that fall into the current view of the map are clustered and visualized.

[2]See implementation section for one possible fixation algorithm.

[3]The zoom level threshold depends on the implementation.

A standard cartographic generalization approach is used to cluster fixations that are in spatial proximity[4].

Figure 1 (bottom) shows our implementation of the retrieval phase. In order to see all the fixation points on the map, that are aggregated by a given cluster, one can zoom into this region. When the zoom-in interaction crosses the zoom threshold, it leads back to the recording phase where previous fixations are shown unaggregated (as described above).

The multimodality of GeoGazemarks strongly couples the gaze based and zoom/pan interactions, since the zoom level (de)acticvates the recording and retrieval phase, and the panning influences the geo-location of the gaze fixations.

4. IMPLEMENTATION

We implemented a prototype of the GeoGazemarks interaction concept that was used in the experiment described in section 5.

4.1 Hardware

Our hardware consisted of the Ergoneers Dikablis mobile eye tracker[5] with a gaze capture rate of 50Hz. The data was transmitted to a laptop via a coaxial cable. The laptop forwarded the data to a Samsung Galaxy Nexus smartphone where the prototype application was running. The connection between laptop and smartphone was established over WiFi in a closed network with a data rate of 25 Hz.

4.2 Software

4.2.1 Calibration and Recording (Laptop)

The Dikablis mobile eye tracking system comes with a series of software modules. We used the Dikablis Live Recorder software which allowed us to calibrate the users, as well as to start and stop the recording sessions. The software also provides real-time visual marker detection, returning marker dependent coordinates with respect to a marker attached to the smartphone screen. These marker dependent coordinates were transmitted over UDP to the smartphone.

4.2.2 GeoGazemarks Application (Smartphone)

The GeoGazemarks concept was realized as an Android application (Android 4.0). The graphical user interface is based on an OpenStreetMaps[6] map service that includes standard panning and zooming functionality. The application implements implicit gaze interaction by computing fixations and visualizing them on the map.

From raw gaze data to fixations

The marker dependent coordinates received over UDP were first transformed into pixel coordinates with respect to the smartphone screen. As the human eyes are constantly moving, not all of these screen gazes imply perception: the gaze data need to be pre-processed by a fixation detection algorithm.

A fixation occurs when the eyes remain relatively still over some time. In the eye tracking literature it is generally assumed that information is only perceived during these fixations [24]. A fixation has a spatial ('relatively still') and a temporal component ('over some time'). The mean fixation duration necessary in order to obtain information is task specific [24]. For instance, the mean fixation duration during scene perception is about 330 ms. After a preliminary test, we implemented our fixation algorithm with a radius of 30 pixels and a duration of 380 ms. In other words, if all gazes during a time span of 380 ms were within a radius of 30 pixels, they would form a fixation. If they were within this radius for 760 ms they would form a fixation with double duration, and so on.

Finally, the application transforms the fixation screen coordinates to respective geospatial map coordinates (latitude, longitude) using a method provided by the map service.

Cartographic visualization and clustering

The map service is enhanced by two overlays. One overlay is used for the visualization of the items that are only visible on the highest zoom level (i.e., fixation icons and points of interest), and the other overlay serves for the visualization of the fixation clusters which are visible on all other zoom levels. The fixation points computed in the previous step are used to set the fixation icons (See Figure 1, top).

The fixation clusters are computed by a grid clusterer. The grids are based on the screen density of the device, thus making the GeoGazemarks application also device independent. The clusters are formed according to the existing gaze fixations on the map. We used three sizes to visualize the clusters. The smallest cluster visualization was used for up to 3 fixations, the middle one for up to 8, and the largest one for more than 8 fixations. We selected a semi-transparent orange color their visualization, allowing the user to recognize the map characteristics underneath.

The proportions of the clusters as well as the proportions of the fixation icons were determined by a process known as perceptual scaling, with the following formula ([27], p. 308):

$$r_i = \left(\frac{v_i}{v_L}\right)^{0.57} \times r_L$$

r_i = *radius of the circle to be drawn*
r_L = *radius of the largest circle on the map*
v_i = *data value for the circle to be drawn*
v_L = *data value associated with the largest circle*

The fixation intervals for the clusters as well as the color selection for them were decided by a pilot user study and expert interviews (See 5.4).

5. EXPERIMENT

We used the implementation described in section 4 and conducted a user study in order to compare two conditions: a search task on a mobile phone screen using GeoGazemarks (Ggz), and the same task without (Std). The hypothesis we tested was that participants would be able to find a previously seen place on a smartphone map faster in the Ggz condition, i.e., when a gaze history visualization is present. The research hypothesis is stated accordingly (with respect to task completion times):

$$H_0 : \mu_{Ggz} = \mu_{Std}$$
$$(H_1 : \mu_{Ggz} < \mu_{Std})$$

[4]Refer to the implementation section for technical details.
[5]`http://www.ergoneers.com/`
[6]`http://www.openstreetmap.org/`

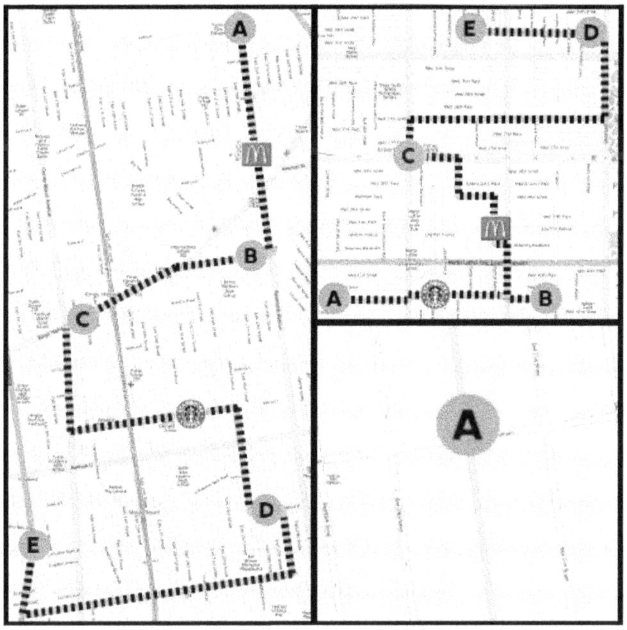

Figure 2: Point configurations for maps of New York (left) and Los Angeles (top right). The dotted line was not visible during the experiment. At most one point was visible at the same time on the screen (bottom right).

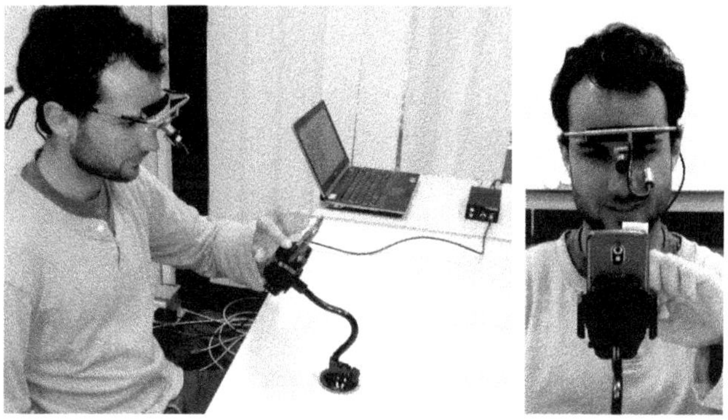

Figure 3: Experiment setup.

		Cases			
		I	II	III	IV
Order	1st	NY, Std	LA, Std	NY, Ggz	LA, Ggz
	2nd	LA, Ggz	NY, Ggz	LA, Std	NY, Std

Ggz = with GeoGazemarks, Std = without GeoGazemarks

NY = map of New York, LA = map of Los Angeles

Table 1: Four test cases of the experiment.

5.1 Setup

Participants were placed in front of a smartphone with a screen size of 4.6", fixed to an office desk using a car mobile phone holder (See Figure 3). They were told to choose the distance to the device naturally and keep this distance as constant as possible during the experiment.

Directly before the part of the experiment that requires eye tracking, the mobile eye tracker was mounted on the participant's head and calibrated to the distance of the device using the eye tracker's calibration software. In the parts of the experiment that did not require eye tracking, the participants did not wear the mobile eye tracker.

5.2 Design

A within subjects design was employed. Each participant had to perform the same search task in both conditions (with GeoGazemarks = Ggz; only standard map interaction = Std) with two different map areas. We chose one map section of New York, NY, USA (NY), and another map section of Los Angeles, CA, USA (LA). NY and LA were counterbalanced among the two test conditions. The reason we prepared two maps with distinct urban characteristics was to avoid confounding among variables. For the same reason we also switched the order (first/second) in which GeoGazemarks was tested. This yields the four cases listed in Table 1. Ten participants were tested for each case.

We placed seven point objects on each of the two maps: five of them were blue circles labeled from 'A' to 'E', two were famous logos of a restaurant chain and a coffeehouse chain (one McDonald's^{TM}, one Starbucks^{TM}). The five blue circles determined a vector sequence the participants had to traverse (A $\rightarrow$ B $\rightarrow$ C $\rightarrow$ D $\rightarrow$ E). The vector sequences for LA and NY were chosen to be different, and to cover all cardinal directions at least once. The two logo point objects were each placed in a way that one had to stumble upon them while traversing the vector sequences. The point layouts for LA and NY are displayed in Figure 2. The seven point objects were only visible on the highest zoom level – just as regular mobile map services would hide away unimportant points of interest when zooming out.

During each trial we logged all explicit user interactions with the phone (i.e., zooming, panning). In those trials with the Ggz condition we also collected implicit interactions (gaze).

5.3 Procedure

Each trial was composed of four steps. In the first step, the participants had to provide their demographic information as well as to state their experience level in using mobile maps. Steps 2 and 3 were the actual trials, with test condition and map depending on the test case (See Table 1).

Each trial started with a map of the respective city, centered at point 'A' on the highest zoom level. The participant was told to follow the navigation instructions given by a researcher. These instructions lead her along the vector sequence until she reached 'E'. Instructions included cardinal directions and linear features, such as *'Continue on Normandie Avenue heading west until you reach point B'*. These instructions were unambiguous and easy to follow. Up to this point, participants were not informed about the two logo points (McDonald's^{TM}and Starbucks^{TM}) – they just stumbled upon them.

At point 'E' participants were asked to tap on the 'E' point, and then find their way back to McDonald's^{TM}(for NY), or Starbucks^{TM}(for LA), as fast as they could. In the Std test condition they were allowed to use standard interaction, i.e., panning by swiping and two-finger zooming. In the Ggz test condition they could additionally see the GeoGazemarks history. Task completion time was recorded as the time between the 'E' tapping and a tap on the goal.

Participants could decide to give up on the task if they got totally lost on the map.

Just before the Ggz condition was tested, participants could try out the GeoGazemarks concept on a map of a European city (max. 3 minutes) in order to get used to it and to see at least once how the visualizations look.

In the last step, participants filled in another questionnaire and rated the GeoGazemarks concept in terms of usability. The overall duration of the experiment was between 20 to 30 minutes per participant.

5.4 Pilot Study

To optimize the test procedure and the visualization of our GeoGazemarks we conducted a small pilot study with 8 participants (5 male, 3 female) that had a professional background in Cartography and Geomatics. These users participated only in the pilot study.

The pilot followed the same procedure as described in section 5.3. In this version of the study, however, instructions included only cardinal directions, such as *'Swipe to the South-West until you find B'*. The participants had severe problems in keeping these diagonal directions during swiping, probably because mobile screens are not quadratic. As we did not want participants to get lost in the instructions phase, we modified the instructions for the final study to refer to linear features, such as roads (See section 5.3).

The gaze clusters in the retrieval phase were initially not semi-transparent. The pilot study revealed that this was hiding too much of the map, so we determined a good transparency level through testing. Our expert participants also suggested surrounding the gaze clusters with a distinctive border to increase their visibility (refer to Figure 1, bottom).

In the pilot study only two participants could solve the search task in the Std condition. This gave us a first indication that our assumption that people would be much faster with GeoGazemarks might actually be true.

5.5 Participants

40 participants took part in the main study and were compensated with 15 CHF for their efforts. The mean age was 27.9 years, with 13 females and 27 males. They had different cultural and professional backgrounds. Half of the participants (20) had a professional background in Geomatics, GIScience, or Cartography. The participants rated their expertise on mobile maps on a scale ranging between 1 (no experience) and 7 (very experienced) with 3.73 (SD = 2.063). None of the participants had ever been to NY or LA, and none had any other previous knowledge about the two areas.

6. RESULTS

We analyzed the data collected during the user study in order to compare the differences in task effectiveness and efficiency for the standard interaction (Std) and GeoGazemarks (Ggz) conditions.

6.1 Effectiveness

Task effectiveness was analyzed by comparing the number of participants who completed the task successfully, and the number of participants who gave up: in the Std condition, 25 participants (62.5%) completed the task. With GeoGazemarks (Ggz condition) all 40 participants completed the task successfully.

6.2 Efficiency

Two efficiency measures were chosen for the analysis: task completion time and interaction sequence length. Both measures in the two conditions were compared using the non-parametric Wilcoxon signed-rank test.

6.2.1 *Task completion time*

As described in the procedure section, the task completion time was defined as the time difference between the tap on the 'E' point and the tap on the goal. For those 15 participants (37.5%) who gave up, the time difference between the 'E' tap and the give-up time was considered.

As predicted, participants could complete the search task significantly faster using GeoGazemarks than without (See Table 2).

	Task Competition Time	
	Median	Standard Deviation
Ggz	50.7965 sec.	24.01 sec.
Std	124.098 sec.	85.36 sec.

Ggz = with GeoGazemarks, Std = without GeoGazemarks
$p < 0.001$, $Z = -5.027$

Table 2: Task Completion Time. The search task was completed significantly faster using GeoGazemarks.

6.2.2 *Interaction sequence length*

Interaction sequence length was defined as the number of interactions needed to complete the search task. For instance, if a participant completed the search task by performing the following interaction sequence *"Swipe North - Swipe West - Zoom in"*, this was considered as an interaction sequence of length three. Again, the interaction sequence of those 15 participants who gave up was considered as finished at the time they gave up.

The findings for task completion time were reflected in the analysis of interaction sequences. The interaction sequences were significantly shorter using GeoGazemarks than without(See Table 3).

	Interaction Sequence Length	
	Median	Standard Deviation
Ggz	25.5	17.17
Std	75	52.6

Ggz = with GeoGazemarks, Std = without GeoGazemarks
$p < 0.001$, $Z = -4.799$

Table 3: Interaction Sequence Length. The interaction sequences were significantly shorter using GeoGazemarks.

6.2.3 *Group differences*

We were interested in whether task efficiency would differ significantly depending on user groups. We first looked at the group of expert users: we considered those participants as experts that have a professional background in Geomatics, GIScience, or Cartography (20 participants, see section 5.5), and all other participants as non-experts (20 participants). We suspected that people working with geoinformation on a daily basis might have superior cognitive mapping strategies. To separate professional background from experience with mobile maps, we compared the participants' self-estimation on mobile map usage expertise (See section 5.5) for expert and non-expert users: non-expert users rated their expertise with 3.40 (SD = 2.010), expert users with 4.05 (SD = 2.114). A non-parametric Wilcoxon rank sum test revealed that the difference in their expertise is not significant ($p > 0.05$, $Z = -1.013$).

A non-parametric Wilcoxon rank sum test of the tracked data revealed that there is no significant difference in the task completion times between expert and non-expert users with GeoGazemarks ($p > 0.05$, $Z = -1.082$), as well as for task completion time in the Std condition ($p > 0.05$, $Z = -0.784$). The same holds also for interaction sequence lengths, once with GeoGazemarks ($p > 0.05$, $Z = -0.515$) and once without ($p > 0.05$, $Z = -0.595$).

We also did not find any significant differences between female and male participants, neither for the search condition with GeoGazemarks ($p > 0.05$, $Z = -1.314$) nor for the condition without ($p > 0.05$, $Z = -0.967$). The same is also reflected in interaction sequences (Ggz: $p > 0.05$, $Z = -1.099$, Std: $p > 0.05$, $Z = -0.838$).

6.3 Analysis of questionnaires

On a questionnaire participants were asked to rate GeoGazemarks. The rating scale ranged between 1 (strongly disagree) and 7 (strongly agree). The results showed that the visualization of clusters on the map was perceived as helpful: the relation between cluster size and the number of fixations aggregated by them was rated as helpful with a mean of 6.37 (SD = 1.005). The cluster visibility on the map was rated with a mean of 6.68 (SD = 0.730).

The mean of the overall rating for the GeoGazemarks concept (*'do you like the GeoGazemarks approach?'*) was 6.60 (SD = 0.591), and the task-dependent question (*'was the GeoGazemark approach helpful for performing the task?'*) resulted in a rating with a mean of 6.52 (SD = 0.847). Asked for their preference for GeoGazemarks over standard map interaction, participants showed a high preference (Mean = 6.53, SD = 0.877) for GeoGazemarks when dealing with situations such as the one in the experiment.

7. DISCUSSION AND CONCLUSION

In this paper we have introduced GeoGazemarks, an implicit gaze interaction concept for small display maps. It is based on the assumption that places on a map the user has spent visual attention to have become part of her cognitive map, and can thus be used as orientational cues on overview zoom-levels. This is relevant for any map task that requires the user to search for previously seen places. By highlighting places she has looked at before, GeoGazemarks prevent the map user from getting lost when zooming out, which is often the case for standard map interaction.

An analogy to the 'browsing history' of web browsers seems obvious: our system silently records the map usage history in the background, even though the user does not yet know at recording time whether the recording will be needed later. Intentionally setting a waypoint, on the other hand, can be compared to bookmarking a website. Still, GeoGazemarks are different because our visualization addresses spatial memory, not sequential memory (like the plain list in a browser history).

In our experiment we focused on a path integration task in which participants had to find back to a point of interest they had stumbled upon before. The paths they had to follow were predefined for each of the two city maps to make experimental conditions comparable between participants. We expect that GeoGazemarks will also be beneficial for free map exploration tasks in which the user is free to choose her own path (such as Alice in the example in section 3.1), as this can also be reduced to path integration.

We chose two different cities and two different vector sequences to avoid confounding between variables. One might argue that this does not cover other geographic areas with completely different characteristics, such as the Sahara desert. However, as LBS are mostly used in cities, we believe that urban settings are the most relevant ones. Participants also told us that they did not focus much on city landmarks when GeoGazemarks were present. It is intuitive that the length and complexity of the vector sequence influence the performance of path integration. However, detailed research on this is out of the scope of this paper. We tried to choose sequences of realistic length and complexity for ordinary map search tasks. Two unfamiliar cities were selected in order to not give anyone the advantage of previous spatial overview knowledge. If the GeoGazemarks principle was applied to an area the user already has a cognitive map of, we still expect that the visual attention history would help to reduce the search space, although the efficiency advantage of GeoGazemarks might be a bit smaller.

Using monocular head-mounted eye trackers for small distances requires the participant to keep the distance to the device relatively constant. We instructed participants accordingly and observed an accuracy of approx. 5mm. These slight inaccuracies were smoothed out by the clustering. The eye camera (See Figure 3, right) has no serious impact on the field of view since after a few minutes, it is no longer perceived (recall that we had the training phase). With less intrusive hardware we would expect the GeoGazemarks concept to perform at least as good as in our current experiment.

8. OUTLOOK

An interesting aspect for future work where GeoGazemarks could be valuable, is to get a better understanding of people's information needs when interacting with maps by analyzing their browsing behavior. One question for future research is how mid- or long-term usage of GeoGazemarks will change the way participants use gaze. We might expect that they will use GeoGazemarks for explicit interaction, 'bookmarking' places by intentionally staring at them to create long fixations. An open question is also how to deal with multiple GeoGazemarks sessions in the same map region: can we just aggregate GeoGazemarks from different sessions? How helpful or confusing is gaze history recorded several days or weeks earlier?

Some participants suggested adding sequential information by connecting GeoGazemarks with lines. Future research will show whether such information could make GeoGazemarks even more efficient. However, it is yet unclear which visualization will prevent visual clutter due to frequently self-intersecting gaze tracks (on a high zoom-level) and self-intersecting map usage paths (on a low zoom-level).

9. REFERENCES

[1] G. L. Allen. Spatial Abilities, Cognitive Maps and Wayfinding - Bases for Individual Differences in

Spatial Cognition and Behavior. In R. Golledge, editor, *Wayfinding Behavior - Cognitive Mapping and Other Spatial Processes*, pages 46–80. Johns Hopkins University Press, 1999.

[2] A. Aretz and C. Wickens. The Mental Rotation of Map Displays. *Human Performance*, 5:303–328, 1992.

[3] R. Biedert, G. Buscher, and A. Dengel. The eyebook - using eye tracking to enhance the reading experience. *Informatik-Spektrum*, 33(3):272–281, June 2010.

[4] R. Biedert, G. Buscher, S. Schwarz, J. Hees, and A. Dengel. Text 2.0. In *CHI extended abstracts on human factors in computing systems*, pages 4003–4008, New York, NY, USA, 2010. ACM.

[5] S. Burigat, L. Chittaro, and S. Gabrielli. Navigation techniques for small-screen devices: An evaluation on maps and web pages. *International Journal of Human-Computer Studies*, 66(2):78–97, 2008.

[6] J. R. Cauchard, M. Löchtefeld, P. Irani, J. Schöning, A. Krüger, M. Fraser, and S. Subramanian. Visual separation in mobile multi-display environments. In *24nd annual ACM symposium on User interface software and technology (UIST)*, pages 451–460, New York, NY, USA, 2011. ACM.

[7] J. Dillemuth. Map Design Evaluation for Mobile Display. *Cartography and Geographic Information Science*, 32(4):285–301, 2005.

[8] A. T. Duchowski. *Eye Tracking Methodology: Theory and Practice.* Springer, London, 2nd edition, 2007.

[9] T. Gärling, A. Böök, and E. Lindberg. Cognitive mapping of large-scale environments: The interrelationship of action plans, acquisition, and orientation. *Environment And Behavior*, 16(1):3–34, 1984.

[10] G. Gartner, D. A. Bennett, and T. Morita. Towards ubiquitous cartography. *Cartography and Geographic Information Science*, 34(4):247–257, 2007.

[11] R. Golledge. Human wayfinding and cognitive maps. In R. Golledge, editor, *Wayfinding behavior: Cognitive mapping and other spatial processes*, pages 5–45. Johns Hopkins University Press, Baltimore, MA, 1999.

[12] S. C. Hirtle and P. B. Heidorn. The structure of cognitive maps: Representations and processes. In T. Gärling and R. Golledge, editors, *Behavior and Environment: Psychological and Geographical Approaches*, pages 170–192. Elsevier, 1993.

[13] S. C. Hirtle and J. Jonides. Evidence of Hierarchies in Cognitive Maps. *Memory & Cognition*, 13(3):208–217, 1985.

[14] R. J. K. Jacob. The use of eye movements in human-computer interaction techniques: What you look at is what you get. *ACM Trans. Inf. Syst.*, 9(2):152–169, 1991.

[15] D. Kern, P. Marshall, and A. Schmidt. Gazemarks: gaze-based visual placeholders to ease attention switching. In *Proc. of the International Conference on Human Factors in Computing Systems (CHI)*, pages 2093–2102. ACM, 2010.

[16] P. Kiefer, F. Straub, and M. Raubal. Towards location-aware mobile eye tracking. In *Symp. on Eye-Tracking Research and Applications (ETRA)*, pages 313–316, New York, 2012. ACM.

[17] R. M. Kitchin. Cognitive maps: What are they and why study them? *Journal of Environmental Psychology*, 14(1):1–19, 1994.

[18] B. Kuipers. The "Map in the Head" Metaphor. *Environment and Behavior*, 14(2):202–220, 1982.

[19] J. M. Loomis, R. L. Klatzky, R. G. Golledge, and J. W. Philbeck. Human navigation by path integration. In R. G. Golledge, editor, *Wayfinding Behavior: Cognitive Mapping and Other Spatial Processes*, pages 125–151. The John Hopkins University Press, Baltimore, Maryland, USA, 1999.

[20] P. Majaranta, U. K. Ahola, and O. Spakov. Fast gaze typing with an adjustable dwell time. In *Proc. of the International Conf. on Human Factors in Computing Systems (CHI)*, pages 357–360. ACM, 2009.

[21] M. Porta, A. Ravarelli, and G. Spagnoli. *ceCursor*, a contextual eye cursor for general pointing in windows environments. In *Symp. on Eye-Tracking Research and Applications (ETRA)*, pages 331–337. ACM, 2010.

[22] J. Portugali. The construction of cognitive maps. In J. Portugali, editor, *GeoJournal library*, volume 32, pages 321–344. Kluwer Academic Publishers, 1996.

[23] M. Raubal and I. Panov. A Formal Model for Mobile Map Adaptation. *Location Based Services and TeleCartography II*, pages 11–34, 2009.

[24] K. Rayner. Eye movements in reading and information processing: 20 years of research. *Psychological bulletin*, 124(3):372–422, 1998.

[25] M. Rohs, J. Schöning, M. Raubal, G. Essl, and A. Krüger. Map navigation with mobile devices: virtual versus physical movement with and without visual context. In *Proc. of the International Conference on Multimodal Interfaces (ICMI)*, pages 146–153. ACM, 2007.

[26] A. Schmidt. Implicit human computer interaction through context. *Personal and Ubiquitous Computing*, 4(2/3):191–199, 2000.

[27] T. A. Slocum, R. B. Mcmaster, F. C. Kessler, and H. H. Howard. *Thematic Cartography and Geovisualization (3rd Edition)*. Prentice Hall Series in Geographic Information Science. Prentice Hall, 3 edition, 2008.

[28] S. Stellmach and R. Dachselt. Designing gaze-based user interfaces for steering in virtual environments. In *Symp. on Eye-Tracking Research and Applications (ETRA)*, pages 131–138, New York, NY, USA, 2012. ACM.

[29] B. Tversky. Cognitive maps, cognitive collages, and spatial mental models. *Spatial Information Theory: Theoretical Basis for GIS*, 716:14–24, 1993.

[30] T. Vildan and R. J. K. Jacob. Interacting with eye movements in virtual environments. In *Proc. of the SIGCHI conference on Human factors in computing systems (CHI)*, pages 265–272, New York, NY, USA, 2000. ACM.

[31] G. Weinberg, B. Harsham, C. Forlines, and Z. Medenica. Contextual push-to-talk: shortening voice dialogs to improve driving performance. In *Proc. of the 12th Conference on Human-Computer Interaction with Mobile Devices and Services (MobileHCI)*, pages 113–122, New York, NY, USA, 2010. ACM.

Lost in Navigation: Evaluating a Mobile Map App for a Fair

Anders Bouwer
Intelligent Systems Lab Amsterdam
Faculty of Science
University of Amsterdam
The Netherlands
andersbouwer@uva.nl

Frank Nack
Intelligent Systems Lab Amsterdam
Faculty of Science
University of Amsterdam
The Netherlands
nack@uva.nl

Abdallah El Ali
Intelligent Systems Lab Amsterdam
Faculty of Science
University of Amsterdam
The Netherlands
a.elali@uva.nl

ABSTRACT
This paper describes a field study evaluating a mobile map application for the Paris Air Show. The aim of the study was to investigate how well users can navigate (to static and moving targets) and orient themselves in a fair (an unknown environment posing realistic challenges for wayfinding) with a mobile map system. The study involved 14 fair visitors who carried out three navigation tasks, which required them to switch between map navigation and deciding upon their orientation in the physical environment. Our results indicate that navigation and orientation are not as tightly coupled as described in the traditional wayfinding literature and may require different modality approaches to optimally support users. Based on this, we draw design implications on how to balance supporting the user in navigation and orientation with mobile systems without diminishing users' awareness of their surroundings.

Categories and Subject Descriptors
H5.2. Information interfaces and presentation (e.g., HCI): Ergonomics; D.m. Miscellaneous: Software psychology.

Keywords
Mobile maps, pedestrian wayfinding, navigational aids, location-based services, friend finding, indoor localization.

1. INTRODUCTION
Wayfinding in large indoor environments is known to be difficult for various reasons, including low visibility of destinations beyond the direct surroundings [17], a lack of clear landmarks to aid navigation [1], loss of orientation when moving from one buiding or floor to another [6], and stimuli in the environment drawing attention [20]. Besides architectural features, various types of aids have traditionally been used to support people in navigating buildings, such as signs, route directions, and maps [1]. Research on wall-mounted and standing maps lists several features as important for a map's usefulness, including visible landmarks, a You-Are-Here symbol indicating the user's position, and alignment of the map with the user's orientation [8,16].

Map use triggers interaction in multiple modalities. For example, a study on the use of standing maps at a large fair showed that people often point and talk while interacting with the map, in order to make sense of the map, discuss and select potential destinations, and plan routes [2]. In order to support wayfinding, it is also important to realize that this is a multi-dimensional process, with multiple goals, which may conflict with each other. For example, improving wayfinding performance may be at the expense of the acquisition of an accurate cognitive map [3]. In many cases however, visitors of complex indoor environments, such as a fair, hospital, or airport, are not interested in acquiring an accurate cognitive map as much as getting to specific destinations without trouble. In this paper, we focus on the difference between *orientation*, which we define as the process of understanding one's own location and the direction of nearby destinations in relation to one's current location, and *navigation*, which we define as the process of moving to a destination.

In this paper, we present the results of a field study with a mobile map app developed specifically for a large international fair. A fair provides a suitable test-bed to investigate the relationship between navigation aids, navigation and orientation, as it poses real wayfinding challenges to visitors, due to unfamiliarity with the fair layout, the number of exhibits, and crowdedness.

The research questions addressed in this study are the following: To what extent does the mobile map app (which is state-of-the-art in publicly available mobile map apps) support orientation and navigation at the fair? What kinds of problems occur while using the app, in terms of wayfinding and usability?

The rest of the paper is structured as follows: first we provide a review of related work, followed by our study design and methods. We then describe and evaluate our results and conclude with design guidelines for mobile map-based navigation applications based on the self-localization paradigm as used in large, complex indoor environments.

2. RELATED WORK
2.1 Maps and Orientation
Orientation in the sense of understanding one's location in relation to the environment has traditionally been considered essential for wayfinding [7, 8]. When using a map, one needs to compare features (cues) of the surroundings with features (other cues) of the map [22]. To accurately determine one's own location, a single matching cue is not enough. Since direction is also a factor, at least two corresponding points have to be established to complete spatial localization [8]. Here, the map needs to be aligned (mentally or physically) with one's physical orientation in space, which is not straightforward [18]. For example, in maps for outdoor environments there is a strong convention of displaying North as up, but maps for indoor environments may follow different conventions, such as aligning the map with the main building axis. Car navigation systems often follow the convention of displaying the car's orientation as up, and this option has been implemented in systems for pedestrian navigation too (e.g., see [18], and Google Maps Navigation [5]).

2.2 Indoor Navigation Systems

Research on mobile indoor navigation has so far focused on problems related to spatial orientation, resulting in work on cognitively adequate presentation of maps [14], facilitating localization and navigation via visual or audible landmarks [11], personalized navigation support [24], or supporting collaborative interaction [2, 4]. The underlying assumption of these works has been that localization, i.e. the system knows about and displays the position of the user and target destinations, supports orientation, and therefore aids wayfinding.

Recently this correlation between localization, orientation and navigation has been challenged for mobile maps. Willis et al. [23] demonstrated that a mobile map affects the user's attention and hinders learning of spatial knowledge. They compared two groups that should learn the topography of a given space. One group had learned the environment from a map and the other from a mobile map. The mobile map group needed significantly longer time for this task because they had to simultaneously perform two effortful tasks that required conscious attention, i.e., learning the topography of the environment as well as observing the map during their exploration of the space.

Puikkonen et al. [14] argued that instead of incorporating automated positioning information, mobile support for indoor use should incorporate more landmark information. This information can be easily mapped from a mobile application to the physical surroundings. This is in line with observations made by Cosley et al. [4], who found that learning a spatial environment is hindered when the participant experiences it in a passive mode. Ramirez et al. [15] showed for the case of fire fighters, that it is more useful to support their spatial cognition and navigation practices rather than guiding them through predefined paths based on precise location information.

It is important to note that most of this work has been done on research prototypes. There are systems available for general use (e.g., Google Indoor Maps for selected locations in the US and Japan), but because indoor location-aware technology still requires mapping (or fingerprinting) of signals to locations onto a map of a specific building, and floor plans of buildings are often proprietary and not as standardized as road maps, many sites currently develop their own localization services and mobile map support for their own buildings.

3. METHODS

To answer our research question of whether self-localization indeed helps in such large, complex indoor environments, we tested a mobile application designed for the Paris Air Show at Le Bourget Airport, France. The Paris Air Show is a typical example of a complex environment for mainly in- as well as outdoor navigation. Reasons are the unfamiliarity of many visitors with the fair layout, the large number of exhibits (~2000 exhibitors), the large area covered (130,000 m2 of rented space), the need to move between multiple buildings, and crowdedness (~47,000 visitors per day).

A mobile application was developed specifically for the Paris Air Show by Insiteo, a company specialized in indoor navigation solutions. The functionality included an overview map of all halls and outdoor spaces (see Figure 1), several hall-specific maps of the fair (see Figure 2), a graphical visualization of the user's current position, graphical visualizations of the current locations of people who share their position with the application (the

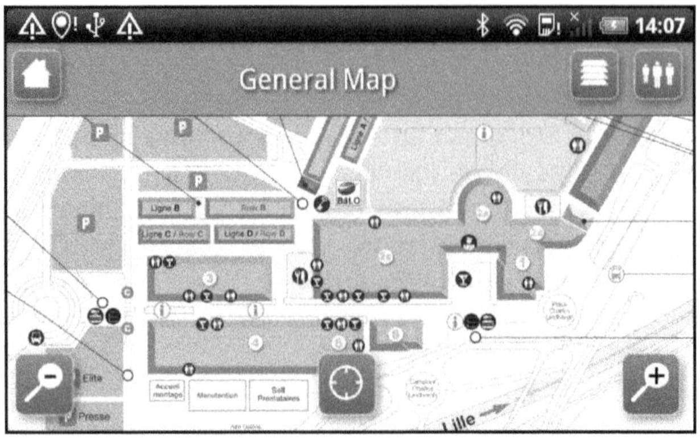

Figure 1. The general map, zoomed in 2x to display the fair's main halls.

MeetMe feature), services such as route planning to a selected destination, and information about exhibitors at the fair.

The visualization of cues, i.e. the position of the user, the position of the destination in form of a pin, and the presentation of stand IDs follows state-of-the-art methods in mobile indoor navigation systems [19]. The application runs on HTC Desire (HD) Android 2.3 smartphones. The localization was done by matching the signal strengths of WiFi beacons measured by the phone to previously recorded 'fingerprint' data.

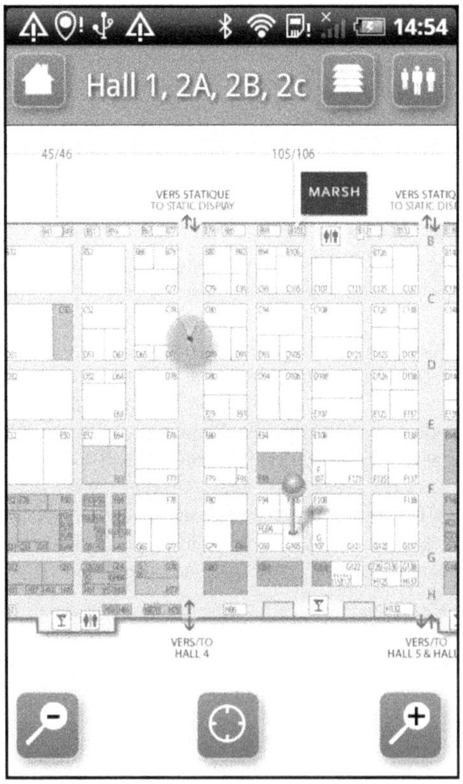

Figure 2. Screenshot displaying the map for hall 2B, with a pin marking the destination. The blue dot and compass symbol mark the user's location and orientation (going north).

3.1 Study Task Design

The study took place in Hall 2B, with one of the destinations located in hall 3. Figure 2 shows a screenshot of the map of Hall 2B, zoomed in on the area that participants used most frequently.

Participants were asked to perform 3 different tasks, where each task was composed of a number of subtasks. The tasks were designed to determine to what extent the system helped users to orient themselves, understand location information, and navigate through the fair. The tasks and subtasks were as follows:

Task 1: Find a stand within the hall

a) find information about the stand on the app
b) point to the stand from your current position
c) navigate to the stand

Task 2: Find and meet another person

a) locate and meet the person using the MeetMe feature
b) after you meet the person, take the provided paper map and put a mark where you think you are

Task 3: Find a stand in another hall

a) find information about the stand on the app
b) point to the stand from your current position
c) on the paper map, put a mark where you think the stand is located

For Task 1, the experimenter selected the destination stands, where it was made sure that the location was not already known to the participant and that all participants had to face a similar set of parameters with respect to distance and navigation complexity. For Task 2, participants had to find a member of the research team that they had already met during the introduction phase. For Task 3, the experimenter again selected the destination stand, ensuring that the participant had not already visited the location.

Task 2b and 3c explored to what extent people were able to apply knowledge gained from the mobile map to a paper map, which was provided by the fair organizer to all visitors. Because the paper map contained very little detail, and displayed the buildings at a different angle than the mobile map, these tasks were considered to be non-trivial.

3.2 Procedure

The participants were informed about the goal of the study. Each participant also got a short introduction on the features of the application to be used. Participants were informed that they were videotaped during the study. Each participant signed a consent form about the use of the collected data for scientific purposes and publication. Participants then filled in a pre-questionnaire with 20 questions about general personal information, their reasons for visiting the fair, their experience of navigating the fair, and their self-reported navigation skills.

Next, participants were provided with a phone, a HTC Desire HD (selected because of its large 4.3 inch touch screen), and asked to carry out the three tasks described earlier. All participants except one (who refused to be recorded) were captured on video during the study.

After completing the tasks, each participant filled in a questionnaire to evaluate the app in terms of usability and perceived usefulness, comparison of the app with other navigational aids, acceptance, and suggestions for improvements. Participants were rewarded with €15 for taking part in the study.

3.3 Participants

14 fair visitors (9 male, 5 female), aged between 20-54 (M=34.8, SD=12.6), were recruited for participation on site. The participants varied in nationality: 8 were French, 2 Dutch (of which 1 also half Italian), 1 Chinese, 1 Senegalese, 1 Moroccan, and 1 Indian. They had different professions, including 5 engineers/technicians, 5 students, 1 secretary, 1 budget coordinator, 1 project manager, and 1 unknown. All participants had received some form of higher education: bachelor's degree (9x), master's degree (3x), or professional education (2x). Three participants had little experience with smartphones, five had more than 12 months of experience, and five reported something in between. All participants indicated that they were familiar with Google Maps©, some also with other mobile map or location-based applications or automotive GPS systems.

4. RESULTS

In this section we present the quantitative and qualitative results gathered during the study. For each subtask we measured task duration and for the tasks that allowed for different levels of performance (Task 1b, 2b, 3b, and 3c), also the performance accuracy. We collected qualitative data in the form of the video recordings, and transcribed spoken comments. Finally, the questionnaire responses were collected from participants upon completion of all three tasks. We first present the quantitative data and then describe the different qualitative data sets in detail.

4.1 Technical Issues

Despite pre-tests on site, during which the system worked smoothly, we experienced technical problems during the study that affected the precision and timeliness of location updates. This caused temporary inaccurate positioning, temporary disappearance, or jumpiness of the localization symbol (as expressed by participant P7: *"It jumps too much ... I'm sure I didn't jump!"*). The problems were found to be due to the crowdedness on both the WiFi and telecom networks during specific times of day (around lunch time). Those problems had an influence on the usability of the collected data (see the section on Task Timing and Performance below). However, in accordance with the findings of [8, 16], participants were easily able to correct potential misalignments between the cue(s) on the map and their mental map representation.

4.2 Task Timing and Performance

We timed each of the tasks manually with a stopwatch. We scored participants' performance on the subtasks *1b, 2b, 3b,* and *3c.* This was done by two observers who studied the video recordings of position, map app, and paper map, and agreed on a score between 1 and 5. Scoring was achieved according to the scheme shown in Table 1.

Table 1. Scoring scheme for accuracy of participants' actions.

5: very high accuracy	Pointing in the correct direction (within a 10 degree angle); drawing in the right location on the map (correct building and correct subquadrant, i.e., quadrant of a quadrant within that building).
4: high accuracy	Pointing at a 10-30 degree angle from the correct direction; drawing on the map in the right building, but neighboring subquadrant.
3: medium accuracy	Pointing at an angle of 30-60 degrees; drawing in the right building but neighboring quadrant.

2: low accuracy	Pointing at an angle of 60-120 degrees; drawing in the right building but in the opposite quadrant.
1: very low accuracy	Pointing at an angle of 120-180 degrees; drawing a location in a wrong hall on the map.

The resulting durations and participant performance scores are shown in Table 2. Some values of N in Table 2 are lower than 14 because one participant (P12) did not do the last two tasks because of delays during the first task and another (P7) could not perform Task 1c because the self-localization point did not show at that time. Technical issues, as already mentioned, prevented the performance of Task 2a in 5 cases.

Table 2. Duration (in m:s) and scores for the different tasks.

		Duration				Score			
Task	N	Min	Max	Mean	SD	Min	Max	Mean	SD
1a	14	0:10	3:48	1:08	1:09				
1b	14	0:01	4:00	0:58	1:05	1.0	5.0	2.57	1.22
1c	13	1:16	8:03	2:45	1:49				
2a	9	0:37	3:49	1:51	1:16				
2b	13	0:10	4:00	1:10	1:02	1.0	5.0	3.64	1.32
3a	13	0:20	1:35	0:47	0:22				
3b	13	0:02	2:50	1:02	0:57	1.0	5.0	3.46	1.51
3c	13	0:05	1:30	0:41	0:23	2.5	5.0	4.23	0.88

The task durations show remarkable variation, with some participants completing a task in just a few seconds, and others taking several minutes for the same task. Also in performance, strong variations were found. For task 1b (point to stand), all levels from 1 to 5 occurred at least once. In other words, participants aiming at the same destination actually pointed in many different directions, as illustrated by Figure 3. 11 participants scored 3 or lower, of which seven scored 2 or lower, indicating that this exercise was quite difficult for the majority of participants.

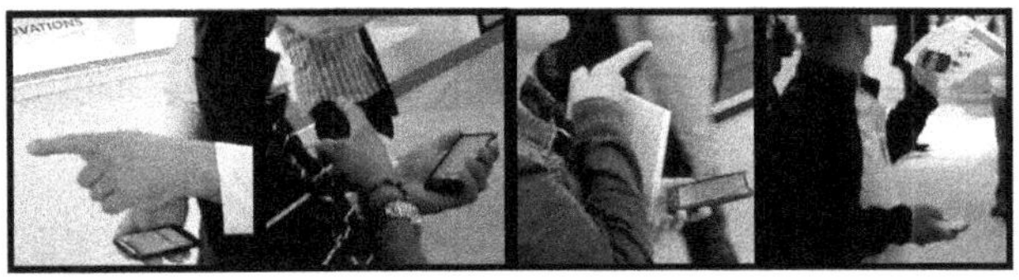

Figure 3. Four participants pointing during task 1b.

For task 2b (drawing own location on a paper map), two participants scored only 1. Three scored a 3. Nine scored a 4 or higher, of which three received the maximum score of 5. In short, a lot of variation, but on average higher scores for this exercise than the previous one.

For task 3b (point to stand in other hall), again, performance variation was observed, with five participants scoring 2 or less, three participants scoring between 3 and 4, and five participants scoring the maximum score of 5.

The last exercise, task 3c (on the paper map, put a mark where you think the stand is located) was performed best. Nobody scored less than 2.5, five scored between 4 and 4.5, and five scored the maximum score of 5. A participant performing this exercise is shown in Figure 4.

Figure 4. A participant performing exercise 3c, drawing the location of a stand in another hall on the paper map.

Considering individual differences, one participant (P10) consistently scored highly on all tasks, with a mean score of 4.75. Four participants scored quite low, with P9 scoring the lowest average score of 2.13. This indicates that there was a large gap between poor and optimal (but nearly attainable) performance.

4.3 Questionnaire Results

The post-study questionnaire contained 34 questions in total, related to evaluation of the navigation app in terms of usability, perceived usefulness of functionality, comparison with other navigational aids, acceptance, and suggestions for improvements.

General impression

Three questions asked about participants' general impression towards the system, its usefulness and helpfulness for navigating around the fair. Table 3 shows Median and Interquartile ranges for these Likert-scale questions (1-Very negative; 5-Very positive).

Table 3. Medians (MD) and inter-quartile ranges (IQR) for questions on the users' general impressions of the system.

Question	MD	IQR
1. Overall attitude towards the system	4	4-4
2. The system is very useful to me	4	3-4
3. The system helped me to navigate better around the fair	4	3.25-5

Most participants (11/14) had a positive attitude towards the system, where the rest were were neutral. Nine participants found the system useful, and ten participants found that the system helped them to navigate at the fair. Three people were slightly critical of the system's usefulness, and two were slightly critical of the system's helpfulness.

Functionality

Five questions asked about functionality and features of the system. Table 4 shows Median and Interquartile ranges for these Likert-scale questions (1-Not useful at all; 5-Very useful).

Table 4. Medians (MD) and inter-quartile ranges (IQR) for questions on system functionality and features.

Question	MD	IQR
4. Seeing your own location on the map	5	4.25-5
5. Finding the location of POIs	4.5	4-5
6. Finding other info about POIs	4.5	4-5
7. Planning a route to a POI	5	4-5
8. Finding another person's location (MeetMe)	4.5	4-5

All offered functionalities were regarded as useful by most participants (13/14). Few scores were lower than 4. Judging from the highest scores, the self-localization feature on the map was considered most useful, followed by planning a route to a Point-of-Interest (POI), finding the location of POIs and another person's location (Meet Me).

Comparison with Navigational Aids

We asked participants to rate different ways of gathering information for navigation on a usefulness Likert-scale (as described above). Their scores were then transformed to ranks. 10 participants rated the system as most useful, followed by the physical signs in the environment (9x), the large standing maps (6x), the paper map (4x), and talking to people face to face (3x). Talking to people on the phone was rated as least useful to find out where to go. If people preferred other navigational aids than the system, they either preferred a paper map or using no navigation aid *(P13: "Habit of finding one's way without help. My generation wasn't born with mannerist aids.").*

Task Difficulty

Three questions asked participants about the difficulty of the given tasks. Median and Interquartile ranges for these Likert-scale questions (1-Very difficult; 5-Very easy) are shown in Table 5.

Table 5. Medians (MD) and inter-quartile ranges (IQR) for task difficulty.

Question	MD	IQR
12. Difficulty finding own location	4	4-4
14. Difficulty finding destinations	4	4-4.75
16. Difficulty finding other people	4	3.5-5

Finding destinations (14/14) and one's own location (12/14) is considered relatively easy by most participants, although two found the latter reasonably difficult. Finding other people was judged very differently by the various participants, with some (8/14) scoring 4 or 5, and others (3/14) scoring 3 or lower.

Task Problems Encountered

Participants were asked whether they experienced any problems during the given tasks. For the task of finding out one's own location on the map using the system (Q13), participants mentioned that the localization pin on the map was changing (3x), that localization lacks precision (2x), the map does not rotate (1x), the orientation of the compass was not working (1x), the text on screen hindered orientation (1x), and that the current location was not always timely updated (1x). For the task of finding destinations using the system (Q15), one additional issue was reported, which is that the position of the localization pin disappeared sporadically. For the task of finding other people using the system (Q17), participants reported that self-localization on the map did not work correctly (3x), and that the position of the pin changes too fast sometimes, which is confusing (1x). One participant however was quite positive; P9: *"It was good and easy and user friendly... I could correct my direction easily."*

Interface Usability

Nine questions asked about the usability of the user interface, specifically focusing on the ease of use. Median and Interquartile ranges for these Likert-scale questions (1-Very difficult; 5-Very easy) are shown in Table 6.

The zoom feature was overall considered the easiest to use (14/14). The map of the fair area was mostly perceived as reasonably easy to use (9/14). Route planning was found to be relatively difficult to use by two people, and the Meet Me feature only by one. The interface was mostly perceived to be relatively easy to use (7/14), or very easy (6/14). Q25 asked about the need for help when using the system (see Table 6). This resulted in much variation, where some participants found they needed help to use the system (4/14), and others not at all (3/14). For perceived system response speed, most participants found it to be sufficiently responsive (11/14).

Table 6. Median (MD) and Inter-quartile ranges (IQR) for system usability, with a focus on ease of use.

Question	MD	IQR
18. Map of the fair area	4	3.25-4
19. Zoom in and out	5	4-5
20. Route planning	4	4-5
21. Info about POIs	4	4-5
22. Searchable index	5	4-5
23. Meet Me	4.75	4-5
24. Interface in general	4	4-5
25. System can be used without help	4	3.25-4.75
26. Perceived system response speed	4	4-4
27. Overall interface design (appearance)	4	4-4
28. System acceptance	4	3-5

User Suggestions

When participants were asked what they liked about the system (Q30), their responses included: interface ease of use (4x), overall interface (3x), application utility (3x), Meet Me feature for finding friends (2x), storing favorite locations (1x), application responsiveness (2x), similarity to existing systems (2x), learnability (1x), and enjoyable user experience (1x). However, participants found the following problematic: Imprecise localization (4x), problems with the Meet Me feature (2x), localization functionality failing (1x), system responsiveness (1x), touch screen sensitivity (1x), and map orientation (1x).

When asked for suggestions to improve the system (Q32), responses included: precision improvement (4x), speed/frequency improvement (2x), inclusion of a tutorial or guide with explanations (2x), showing complete map layout when moving to a specific hall (1x), better advertising of the app on site (1x), finding back favorited locations (1x), and improving map orientation (1x).

4.4 Video Transcript Case Analysis

The video recordings were transcribed, in terms of actions and spoken dialogue. Below we present dialogue and video examples for participant P9 (female, reasonable experience with smartphones, new to the fair). The examples outline a number of suboptimal navigation actions, insightful dialogue, and also interesting behavior during her interaction with the mobile phone, while she performed task 1b and 1c. The actual walking route and pointing actions are displayed in Figure 5.

She started off task 1b by pointing almost immediately (t=0:05) in the direction of the corridor (score = 3 out of 5, see arrow at location 0 in Figure 5, and Figure 6). At t=0:58, she said, while pointing at the pin on the map, *"If I'm facing this way, this is where they are situated, right? Ok. So what I'm saying is I should be walking this way (points straight). And this pinpoint, in my head, it should be in front of me, right, because it's in front of me."* Next, she focused on the screen rather than the environment. At t=2:10, she turned the phone around several times (180 degrees, 0 degrees, 90 degrees, 180 degrees, 90 degrees), commenting: *"I'm playing around, just changing it. I just wanted to see how it would situate me if I turned the phone. Because I don't necessarily have to hold it this way to tell me where I am. So if I turn it anyway, it should still tell me where I'm situated."*

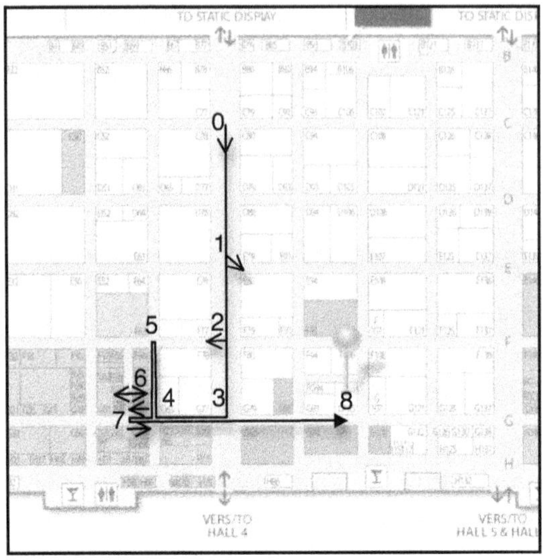

Figure 5. Walking route taken by participant P9, from start (0) to destination (8). Open arrows depict pointing actions.

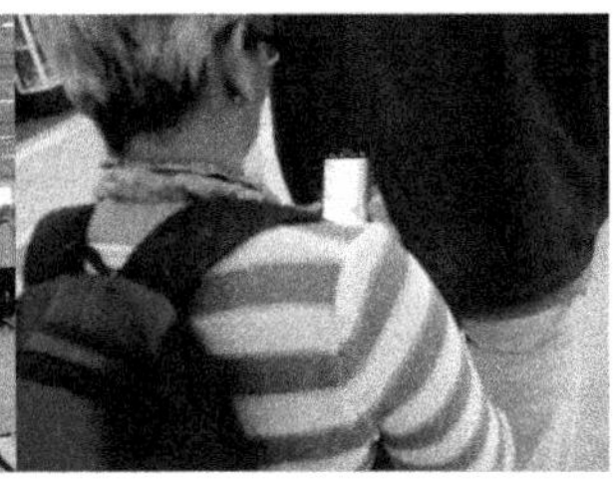

Figure 6. Pointing (task 1b). **Figure 7. Almost bumping.**

While walking (see Figure 5, location 1), she spontaneously pointed in the correct direction to the destination stand (about 45 degrees to the left). At point 2, a little further, she stopped and pointed 90 degrees to the right, however. She almost bumped into somebody at t=2:27, but kept looking at the phone (see Figure 7). Not until t=3:03, she looked up again from the phone. At point 3, she said: *"I'm at G, so it's on my right, is what I'm saying"* (which is 180 degrees wrong).

At t=3:40 and 3:52, while looking at the phone, she bumped into two different people, one of whom was reading a paper map. At point 4, she said *"I should be going this way"*, turning right (still going away from the target). At point 5, she stopped and looked around the corner to the right, saying: *"It doesn't make sense"*. At point 6, she turned around, stopped for a while, and went back again. She pointed to the left and right along the G-aisle, saying *"It said it was in G, so it should be somewhere here"*. She pointed to the right, then turned right and started walking, towards point 7 (again, 180 degrees wrong). At point 7, she said: *"No, I'm going too far"*. She turned around, and pointed the right way, towards point 8, saying, *"I think I'm going away from it"*. From then on, she walked straight along the G-aisle, laughing and saying *"You might be walking around with me for the rest of the morning"*. Approaching the destination she suddenly looked up and stated, *"There it is"*, finally reaching the stand at t=6:06.

4.5 Behavior Analysis and Observations

From our observations and subsequent analysis of the video recordings, like the one described above, we found that the participants encountered several types of problems:

- Misinterpreting a destination's location on the mobile map in relation to the environment, exemplified by pointing the wrong way (see Table 1, task 1b and 3b);
- Difficulties in self-localization, evident when drawing on a paper map (task 2b);
- Wrong turns (12x in total, during task 1 and 2), e.g., turning right when it should be left, often followed by a self-correcting turn of 180 degrees (14x);
- Almost (9x) or actually (2x) bumping into other people, during task 1 and 2;
- Missing a turn (4x in total), or turning too soon (3x), leading to a suboptimal route (1x even leaving the hall);
- Although all participants were afterwards generally positive about the system and the study, 6 of them seemed very insecure while performing the tasks.

Furthermore, users displayed very different strategies in orientation, planning and path finding. 6 out of 14 participants transformed their navigation process into a game-like process where moving the self-localization dot to the destination pin on the phone's screen was the winning target. They were looking almost continuously at the phone's screen, and 3 of these 6 participants did not spot the destination stand until they had reached it. On the other hand, the remaining 8 participants were able to avoid this tendency, and alternated much more between looking at the environment, and at the phone. They either seemed to use a strategy of planning (and verbalizing) a route (3x), or making use of signs on the floor and ceiling (4x). Relatively more women (3/5) adopted the screen-fixating strategy than men (3/9), suggesting a possible gender effect, as found in other studies [7].

Considering the problems mentioned earlier (wrong turns, near and actual collisions, missing turns, turning too soon), the 6 participants with the strategy of fixating mostly on the mobile screen were more likely to experience problems than the other 8 (on average, 5.3 vs 1.7 problems per person, |2=16.85, df=2, $p<0.005$). The other 8 also reached their goal faster, as was shown for task 1c.

Two of the problems mentioned above were related to the current interface design of the system used:

- The current compass symbol (see Figure 2) led to misinterpretations by some participants with respect to their own position, causing them to point or walk in the opposite direction of their destination. This clearly indicates that a localization icon that also provides information about the user's orientation needs to be carefully designed. More importantly, it also indicates that the fixation and reliance on the virtual map representation of the fair space hinders an active construction of the actual physical environment.
- Several participants mentioned they would like the map to rotate when they change direction (similar to Google Maps Navigation [5]), so that their orientation is always facing up on the display. Some participants expressed a strong preference for static maps with the North facing up, however.

As this clearly influences the ability of users not only to navigate but also orient themselves, a mobile map system needs to be able to adapt to the user's preferences.

5. DISCUSSION

If one looks only at whether people find their destination and whether they are content with the system, one gets very positive results, as the questionnaire results indicate. However, upon closer inspection, people encounter several kinds of problems during the various tasks, including mistakes during navigation, and in particular during the initial orientation phase. There is a large variation in performance between individual cases, despite that all participants were given our system as a navigational aid.

The misinterpretation of the compass symbol and the lack of orientation-up display may be part of the reason for some of the navigation failures. These issues should be addressed in future versions of the interface by redesigning the compass symbol in a way that is not ambiguous, and allowing both automatic rotation and north-up display of the map. Seager and Fraser [18] found that physically rotating a phone displaying a steady map works better (in terms of navigation errors and mental workload) than automatic rotation of the map on the phone. In our study, only five participants were physically rotating the phone occasionally. Perhaps participants were afraid of dropping it (as in Seager and Fraser's study), or the phone's dimensions made it difficult to rotate it.

Overall, it appears that many of the observed navigational errors stem from a general failure of associating one's own view of the map with the perception of one's immediate environment. The provided map reduced the environment to a simple set of shapes and only provided letter-number combinations as identifiers for stands, which may have made it hard to relate the contents of the map to the surroundings. This difficulty is further amplified by the hectic fair environment that depletes users' already limited attentional and memory resources [20]. This may be partially alleviated by adding pictures or pictographic icons of landmarks in the nearby surroundings to the map in order to support orientation. Puikkonen et al. [14] suggest that part of the design of the digital map should be done in situ in order to achieve better consistency between the map and the environment in terms of basic features such as colors, shapes and materials. However, this is difficult to achieve in large indoor exhibition centers, as they often do not have many large architectural landmarks as reference points. Also, there is only a short time for development once the fair layout is determined for a particular fair, which makes thorough preparation for in situ design difficult. Nevertheless, some markers at fairs do exist, and more attention should be given to ensuring a general consistency between not just the mobile map and the environment, but also between provided paper maps, large standing maps, and signs within the building [19].

The current interface design seems to stimulate users to focus mostly on the movement of the self-localization dot on the screen representing their own location (and that of the person to meet). This was highlighted by one of the participants (P9: *"I realized that you don't need to think much when using navigation systems. You just avoid going in the opposite direction")*. Although participants were able to reach their goals due to this feature and were generally positive about the system, we believe the current system demonstrates two general shortcomings of the dominant visual paradigm of self-localization on a mobile map.

First, although people are capable of finding both static as moving destinations, their scores vary widely on orientation tasks, i.e., pointing to their destination, or indicating where they have ended up after using the system. This indicates that navigation aids do not necessarily support the orientation phase preceding or following actual navigation, and that these phases may need different means of support. Schmid et al. [17] show that reducing the level of representational detail on a map can achieve better orientation, but they focus on outdoor rather than indoor applications. Futher experiments are needed to test whether varying the representational detail on a map (i.e., number of landmark symbols) could also support orientation in large, complex indoor environments.

Second, we noticed many instances of inattentional blindness [9], where several people focused so much on the screen to the point of diminished awareness of their surroundings. In these cases, participants spotted their destination only shortly before they reached it, and occasionally (almost) collided with other people. One participant expressed this concern explicitly (P11: *"You risk having your eyes on the phone all the time. You then benefit less from the surroundings!")*. Related work focusing on bumping into things while *talking* on a mobile phone could not confirm that this increases the likelihood of collisions [21], but our results suggest more research is needed on the detrimental effects of *looking* at a phone while carrying out other tasks. A mobile map with automated position information seems able to draw so much attention away from the environment that users can get 'lost in navigation'. For tasks where orientation plays an important role, this tendency towards screen fixation needs to be limited somehow. This could for example be done by providing the bare minimum route information, such as directions to the next landmark that is within visual reach.

Our results suggest that navigation and orientation are not as tightly coupled as described in the traditional wayfinding literature [1, 22], and furthermore may require different forms of mobile support. Different wayfinding tasks may be served by other modalities such as audio [10] or haptic feedback [13], instead of, or in combination with visual maps.

In order to guide navigation from point A to B, information in the visual modality seemed to suffice for our users. Since the system was found to decrease awareness of the fair's surroundings, information supporting navigation (such as directions, or distance information) might be presented in other modalities, in particular haptics [13]. Field studies of haptic systems will be necessary to determine if they indeed support navigation in complex indoor environments, whether they are accepted by the general public, and to what extent they allow more attention to be spent on the surroundings.

In order to support orientation and route planning however, the visual modality currently remains the best option. Since orientation still provides problems for current visual map interfaces, it remains an open question how to support orientation with audio or haptic information, alone, or in combination with visual information. We imagine that future support for wayfinding might combine information in different modalities for different wayfinding tasks, e.g., use visual information to convey information about points of interests and support (collaborative) route planning, use auditory information (speech or sonification [10]) to convey locations or directions when these do not interfere with other auditory information in the environment, and use tactile information (e.g., a haptic belt) to aid orientation to support body alignment with the map, or give navigational directions when visual and auditory channels are busy elsewhere [12]. How to integrate and balance these resources depends on the demands of specific settings, and personal navigation strategies.

6. CONCLUSIONS & FUTURE WORK

To evaluate a mobile indoor map-based support system we have carried out a field study with 14 visitors at the Paris Air Show.

The results of the questionnaire were generally positive for all functionalities of the system, including self-localization, finding the location of points of interest, route planning, finding extra information, and finding another person's location. However, findings from the study indicated that users encountered serious difficulties during the various orientation and navigation tasks. Most importantly, they had trouble identifying the correct direction from consulting the mobile map, which indicated that the current paradigm of self-localization on a map is insufficient for supporting users in acquiring a sense of orientation in large indoor environments. In six of the 14 cases, much attention was allocated to the mobile screen, resulting in diminished awareness of the participants' surroundings, and more navigation mistakes. To address this, care should be taken on giving the right amount of representational detail on a map, the role of the mobile phone's form factor for map rotation, and the possibility of providing eyes-free interaction to maintain awareness of surroundings.

In future work, we will address the shortcomings of the current system by (1) improving on technical issues such as localization imprecision, (2) improving support for the orientation phase by experimenting with varying representational detail on a map, and (3) investigate eyes-free interaction methods, in particular, haptics, for the navigation phase, and in combination with visual maps, for the orientation phase. By disentangling the needs related to the processes of orientation and navigation, we aim to ultimately provide a better mapping between needs and presentation modes to establish adequate support for wayfinding in large, complex indoor environments.

7. ACKNOWLEDGMENTS

This work is supported by the European Union as part of the Eurostars Program, project SmartINSIDE (E! 5262). We would also like to thank all participants for taking part in our study.

8. REFERENCES

[1] Arthur, P., and Passini, R. (1992). Wayfinding: People, signs and architecture. McGrawHill, New York.

[2] Bouwer, A. J., Nack, F., and Evers, V. (2011). Towards Support for Collaborative Navigation in Complex Indoor Environments. In Proc. of CSCW 2011, ACM, 601–604.

[3] Chen, J., and Stanney, K. (1999). A theoretical model of wayfinding in virtual environments: proposed strategies for navigational aiding. Presence, 8(6), 671–685.

[4] Cosley, D., Baxter, J., Lee, S., Alson, B., Nomura, S., Adams, P., Sarabu, S., and Gay, G. (2009). A tag in the hand: supporting semantic, social, and spatial navigation in museums. In Proc. of CHI '09. ACM, 1953–1962.

[5] Google Maps Navigation. Retrieved on 20 Aug. 2012 from: http://www.google.com/mobile/navigation/.

[6] Hölscher, C., Büchner, S. J., Meilinger, T., and Strube, G. (2009). Adaptivity of wayfinding strategies in a multi-building ensemble: The effects of spatial structure, task requirements and metric information. Journal of Environmental Psychology, 29, 208–219.

[7] Lawton, C. A. (1996). Strategies for indoor wayfinding: The role of orientation. Journal of Environmental Psychology, 16, 137–145.

[8] Levine, M. (1982). You-are-here maps: psychological considerations. Environment and Behavior, 14, 221– 237.

[9] Mack, A., and Rock, I. (1998). Inattentional Blindness. MIT Press, Cambridge, Massachusetts.

[10] McGookin, D., Brewster, S., and Priego, P. (2009). Audio Bubbles: Employing Non-speech Audio to Support Tourist Wayfinding. In Altinsoy, M., Jekosch, U., and Brewster, S. (eds.), Haptic and Audio Interaction Design, Lecture Notes in Computer Science, Vol. 5763, 41-50, Springer, Berlin.

[11] Nurmi, P., Salovaara, A., Bhattacharya, S., Pulkkinen, T., and Kahl. G. (2011). Influence of landmark-based navigation instructions on user attention in indoor smart spaces. In Proc. of IUI '11. ACM, 33–42.

[12] Pielot, M., and Boll, S. (2010). Tactile Wayfinder: Comparison of tactile waypoint navigation with commercial pedestrian navigation systems. In Floréen, P., Krüger, A., and Spasojevic, M. (eds.), Pervasive computing. Springer, Berlin, 76–93.

[13] Pielot, M., Poppinga, B., and Boll, S. (2010). Pocket-Navigator: vibro-tactile waypoint navigation for everyday mobile devices. In Proc. of MobileHCI '10. ACM, New York, 423-426.

[14] Puikkonen, A., Sarjanoja, A., Haveri, M., Huhtala, J., and Häkkilä, J. (2009). Towards designing better maps for indoor navigation: experiences from a case study. In Proc. of Mobile and Ubiquitous Multimedia (MUM '09), ACM.

[15] Ramirez, L., Denef, S., and Dyrks, T. (2009). Towards human-centered support for indoor navigation. In Proc. of CHI '09. ACM. 1279–1282.

[16] Rossano, M. J., and Warren, D. H. (1989). Misaligned maps lead to predictable errors. Perception, 18, 215– 229.

[17] Schmid, F., Kuntzsch, C., Winter, S., Kazerani, A. and Preisig, B. (2010). Situated local and global orientation in mobile you-are-here maps. In Proc. of MobileHCI '10, ACM, New York, 83-92.

[18] Seager, W. and Fraser, D. S. (2007). Comparing physical, automatic and manual map rotation for pedestrian navigation. In Proc. of CHI '07. ACM, New York, 767-776.

[19] Taher, F. and Cheverst, K. (2011). Exploring user preferences for indoor navigation support through a combination of mobile and fixed displays. In Proc. of MobileHCI '11. ACM, New York, 201-210.

[20] Thorndyke, P. W., and Hayes-Roth, B. (1982). Difference in spatial knowledge acquired from maps and navigation. Cognitive Psychology, 14, 560–589.

[21] Tractinsky, N. and Shinar, D. (2008). Do we bump into things more while speaking on a cell phone? In Proc. of CHI '08 Extended Abstracts, Alt CHI. ACM, New York, 2433-2442.

[22] Warren, D.H. (1994). Self-Localization on Plan and Oblique Maps, Environment and Behavior, 26:1, 71-98.

[23] Willis, K. S., Hölscher, C., Wilbertz, G., and Li, C. (2009). A comparison of spatial knowledge acquisition with maps and mobile maps. Computers, Environment and Urban Systems, 2009: 100–110.

[24] Yao, X. (2007). Pedestrian navigation systems: a showcase for deep personalization theory. In Proc. of MobileHCI '07, vol. 309. ACM, New York, NY, 174-177.

An Evaluation of Game Controllers and Tablets as Controllers for Interactive TV Applications

Dale Cox, Justin Wolford, Carlos Jensen, Dedrie Beardsley
Oregon State University
Department of Computer Science
Corvallis, OR 97331
{cox, wolfordj, cjensen, beardsld}@eecs.oregonstate.edu

ABSTRACT
There is a growing interest in bringing online and streaming content to the television. Gaming platforms such as the PS3, Xbox 360 and Wii are at the center of this digital convergence; platforms for accessing new media services. This presents a number of interface challenges, as controllers designed for gaming have to be adapted to accessing online content. This paper presents a user study examining the limitations and affordances of novel game controllers in an interactive TV (iTV) context and compares them to "second display" approaches using tablets. We look at task completion times, accuracy and user satisfaction across a number of tasks and find that the Wiimote is most liked and performed best in almost all tasks. Participants found the Kinect difficult to use, which led to slow performance and high error rates. We discuss challenges and opportunities for the future convergence of game consoles and iTV.

Categories and Subject Descriptors
H.5.2Information Interfaces and Presentation (e.g., HCI): User Interfaces – Graphical User Interfaces, Input Devices and Strategies, Interaction Styles.

General Terms
Performance, Reliability, Human Factors.

Keywords
Digital convergence, interactive television, iTV, game controller, text entry, navigation, natural user interfaces.

1. INTRODUCTION
Interactive television promises viewers more flexibility and control over their viewing experience, while enriching it with Internet accessible content. By giving viewers a communication channel back to service providers, viewers can access new services and shape their viewing experience in unprecedented ways. As a result, services have emerged like video on demand (Netflix, Hulu, etc.), internet content accessibility on TV screens (YouTube & Flickr channels on Apple TV, etc.) and social networking (see Boxee.tv) allowing for content ratings, or contextual searching.

ICMI'12, October 22-26, 2012, Santa Monica, CA, USA.

For trivial tasks like navigating a simple movie rental UI, or controlling streaming video content, a traditional remote control is often sufficient. However services have become more complex, requiring finer levels of control or interaction – such as navigating web page or GUI, drag and drop tasks, or extensive text entry for search or socialization. For this more sophisticated input devices may be required. Some of these tasks overlap with those integral to the modern gaming experience. Video game consoles, with dedicated game controllers, due to their pervasiveness, connectivity and processing power are often at the center of this digital convergence of TV and Internet content. It is therefore important to examine how suitable current systems are for bridging this gap.

The last generation of game consoles have each introduced some device capable of spatial gestures allowing the possibility for a natural user interface (NUI), and which could be especially helpful for navigating complex UIs. Microsoft released the Kinect for the Xbox 360 in 2010, a camera based system that tracks players' movement to allow for complex and natural interactions without holding any kind of controller. Nintendo released the Wii in 2006, which introduced the Wii Remote (nicknamed Wiimote), a wireless controller that tracks spatial movement through accelerometers and infrared sensors. Sony has a similar system for the Playstation 3.

These game consoles and their controllers have sparked the development of tools and solutions beyond those in traditional gaming. The motion-driven Nintendo Wiimote was the first to attract the attention of the hacker community outside the console market. The Bluetooth interface of the Nintendo Wiimote made it a simple and accessible device to "hack" and adopt for various uses. Soon after the Kinect was released, the open source community reverse engineered the device and released a driver package allowing others to develop systems that took advantage of its capabilities. Its USB interface makes it ideal for use with a PC. Today, several different open source SDKs exist, as well as an official Microsoft Kinect SDK for Windows.

In addition, tablets continue to evolve and increase in popularity. Some proposed game controllers are exploring the use of such touch interfaces (most notably the upcoming Wii U). Tablets are also being considered as companions to both gaming devices and iTV services (often referred to as second screen navigation). According to a recent Pew study [13], tablet ownership nearly doubled over just the 2011 holiday season. There are a number of applications currently available that allow a tablet to serve as an input device for another computer such as IntoNow (http://www.intonow.com) that detects which show or movie you're watching and provides additional media content and social networking capabilities. These applications allow the tablet to function like a touch screen display or a track pad found on most laptops and would serve as a suitable baseline.

This paper explores the challenges and opportunities of using game-related control technologies to control interactive television applications through the study of a hypothetical, but representative set of navigation, selection, and control tasks for an iTV application. We examine learnability and ease of use, as well as accuracy and error rates.

The rest of this paper is laid out as follows. First we discuss related work looking at the control of interactive television applications as well as gaming systems. We then discuss our user experiment and the design considerations we took into account. Finally, we present our findings, and a discussion of future work.

2. RELATED WORK

Much innovation has taken place in the design of new interaction techniques and devices for gaming devices. The research community is still catching up with the necessary evaluation of the potential, effectiveness and usability of these novel game input devices, both within their targeted use domain as well as in other environments like PC or interactive television.

Looking to the modern interactive TV interface, we see that it combines many types of user interaction. The areas we chose to focus on cover the core functionality of pointing, navigation, and text entry. Pointing is perhaps the more novel and difficult task with todays' hardware, but is a prerequisite for many of the more sophisticated types of applications and use cases. Individually, each of these topics has an established body of research, but in the context of a media center or iTV there is very little. We feel our work contributes in this area in a practical way by combining choosing an itv-like interface and a living room environment. We also present the recent adoption rate history of streaming services, which are at the center of modern interactive television systems.

2.1 Growing Popularity of Streaming Services

With the spread of broadband internet access throughout North America, high bandwidth services like high definition on-demand streaming video, previously limited in either quality or duration, have become commonplace. Between 2001 and 2009, broadband Internet use increased seven-fold, covering from 9% to 64% of American households [17]. A 2011 Nielsen study found that from 2008 to 2011 there was a 22% increase in the number of users watching video on the Internet, and an 80% increase in the average viewing time [15].

One of the key players in the Internet-based video-on-demand area has been Netflix. Netflix debuted as a DVD-by-mail service in 1997, and has since introduced and popularized a broadly available Internet streaming service. By the end of 2011, Netflix had over 21 million paying streaming subscribers [14]. In a Fall 2010 report by Sandvine, Netflix was shown to account for 20.6% of all downstream prime-time Internet traffic in North America [19]. Just 7 months later, Netflix users were consuming 29.7% of all downstream prime-time Internet traffic in North America [19].

Other online video services such as Hulu, Amazon Instant Video and YouTube (though the latter still mostly offers shorter clips, it has branched into feature content delivery as well) have also grown in popularity. Internationally, over 4 billion videos are viewed on YouTube each day [22]. Hulu just passed 1.5 million paying subscribers of its paid Plus service [7].

In part this success is driven by the growth of systems that help these users bridge the gap between the computer and the TV experience. This includes a plethora of streaming devices like the Roku and Apple TV, a new generation of connected TV's and DVD/Blue-ray players, and last but not least game consoles. Each of the three leading game consoles have added mechanisms for viewing streaming Netflix content on their devices. Services like Netflix and Hulu that began as a PC experiences, can now be accessed from a number of different devices and platforms. This has made enabled these services to go from a niche technophile market to appealing to the average consumer. In a 2011 Nielsen study, 50% of all Netflix users were found to watch Netflix content through a gaming console [16]. In the same study, Nielsen found 162 million Americans own a game console. This means that these platforms are natural ways to deliver these experiences.

The need to manage users' media viewing experience has led to the development of media center applications like the Xbox Media Center (XBMC) and Windows Media Center. Internet-enabled set-top devices like Boxee and AppleTV have also appeared allowing easy streaming video viewing from a normal TV. These allow users to consolidate their media consumption, as well as manage their local library. Due to the interactive and highly customizable experience allowed by these services, the need for robust input methods will continue to gain importance.

2.2 Pointing and Navigation Using Novel UI Devices

Over the last few years there has been a growing trend to develop and evaluate what are being referred to as Natural User Interfaces (NUI's). These interfaces extend the basic direct manipulation paradigm by allowing users to interact with the computer with motions more closely resembling those we'd use in real life. Among the leading platforms for such interfaces we find game consoles. These techniques could help bridge the complexity gap between the new interactive TV applications and the interactions afforded by conventional remote controls. Because of space limitations we will only review some of the most directly applicable research to our study.

Starting with camera and motion based techniques, Cheng and Takatsuka [12] introduced dTouch, a finger pointing technique for large displays that uses an off-the-shelf webcam. Using the concept of a "virtual touchscreen", dTouch enables users to manipulate onscreen objects in an absolute coordinate system. They performed a user study comparing dTouch to a method using the EyeToy camera, used on the PlayStation console. Results indicated the two methods were comparable with users preferring dTouch.

Lee [10] described a cursor technique using the Wiimote that enabled finger-tracking through the use of reflective tags taped to the fingers of users. Rather than holding the Wiimote in the hand, they used the IR camera built into the Wiimote with an IR LED array to allow almost bare-hand operation. Lin et al. [11] demonstrated a technique similar to Lee's, but using a second Wiimote for additional functionality.

Using more traditional controllers, Natapov et al. [4] performed a comparative study evaluating the Wiimote and traditional gamepad for pointing and selecting tasks. Although the error rate was higher, 14 out of 15 participants said they preferred the Wiimote in a home entertainment environment. They found that the Wiimote had a 75% performance increase over the traditional gamepad when comparing speed and accuracy.

Finally, turning to smart phones and tablets, McCallum et al. [5] developed a hybrid system called ARC-Pad, which combined absolute and relative positioning techniques for use with large displays. A smart phone screen was used like a touchpad. ARC-Pad was compared against a traditional touchpad style interface, which employed cursor acceleration. ARC-Pad performed slightly better (166ms faster) than the relative in completion time. The results suggested as pixel distance increased beyond what was studied, ARC-Pad performance would change minimally while the relative touchpad would continue to worsen.

2.3 Text Entry With Keyboard Alternatives

Over the last two decades, the need for text entry without a traditional mechanical keyboard has increased. With the introduction of PDAs and smart phones, text entry presents a challenge due to a limited input area. Most interactive TV systems attempt to minimize the necessity of text entry through the use of various widgets and interface choices. Though the need may be reduced, it is difficult to completely do away with text entry for applications such as search or social media.

This has led TV manufacturers like Samsung to market 2-sided remote controls; one side having normal remote control functions and the reverse a full keyboard, or Sony to merge a PlayStation controller and a full keyboard in their Google TV products. While such solutions may provide speed advantages, they lead to cumbersome and intimidating user experiences. We examined alternatives to keyboard text entry, focusing on touchscreens, game controllers and freehand gesture techniques.

The Graffiti pen-based gesture alphabet made popular by Palm in the late 90s, allowed users to quickly input text using a proprietary alphabet. MacKenzie and Zhang [9] analyzed the learnability and accuracy of Graffiti. Participants were given practice time using a reference chart showing the gesture alphabet. After practice they repeated the entire alphabet 5 times without having a reference available and again 1 week later. The results showed a nearly 97% character accuracy rate after 5 minutes of practice.

Ni, et al. [21] adapted the Graffiti alphabet to a freehand gesture-based text entry system called AirStroke. They compared two AirStroke implementations, one with word completion and one without. Airstroke with word completion averaged 11 wpm while no word completion was at 6.5 wpm. The error rate with word completion averaged 6.6% compared to 11.8% without. Some participants reported arm fatigue, which lessened as their proficiency increased.

Several techniques have been developed enabling text input using a traditional gamepad. Költringer et al. [20] designed and evaluated TwoStick, a novel text entry system using both analog joysticks on an Xbox 360 controller. TwoStick was compared to a traditional selection keyboard. Initially, users typed slower and had a higher error rate using TwoStick, but after 15 sessions TwoStick averaged 14.87 wpm while the selection keyboard had a mean of 12.9 wpm. Wilson and Agrawala [1] also created a dual joystick QWERTY method, which showed modest improvement upon the traditional single stick selection keyboard.

Shoemaker et al. [6] compared 3 techniques for mid-air text input. A circle keyboard, QWERTY keyboard and cube keyboard all used a Wiimote as an input method. The QWERTY method performed best in accuracy and performance; this method is similar to our Wiimote text entry task. A questionnaire taken after the study revealed users preferred the QWERTY method overall.

Castellucci and MacKenzie [18] presented an alternative to an on-screen keyboard using the Wiimote called UniGest. UniGest is a technique that takes advantage of the motion-sensing capabilities of the controller to capture movement and rotation. A gesture alphabet is proposed which maps the gestures to character input. Their results predict an upper-bound of 27.9 wpm using the UniGest technique.

3. METHODOLOGY

This section describes a user study designed to measure the effectiveness of video game and tablet input methods in a iTV context. We used 4 input methods: the Microsoft Kinect, Nintendo Wiimote and 2 methods using an Android tablet; a condition where subjects had to scroll (relative coordinate condition), and one using an absolute coordinate space (mirror condition). The idea was that in the relative condition subjects would have to scroll around like when using a mouse pad, and in the absolute coordinate condition, the whole TV image would be represented on tablet at once. Participants completed pre and post-experiment questionnaires and also a post-experiment interview. All sessions were recorded using a video camera and screen capturing software.

Participants were recruited in pairs from a college campus and surrounding community. Examining pairs offered a realistic social context in the living room. There were 33 male and 29 female participants with ages ranging from 18 to 57 years. The mean age was 24.5 and all but 4 were right-handed. Demographic data and media viewing frequency were gathered prior to the study. Two devices were randomly assigned to each pair.

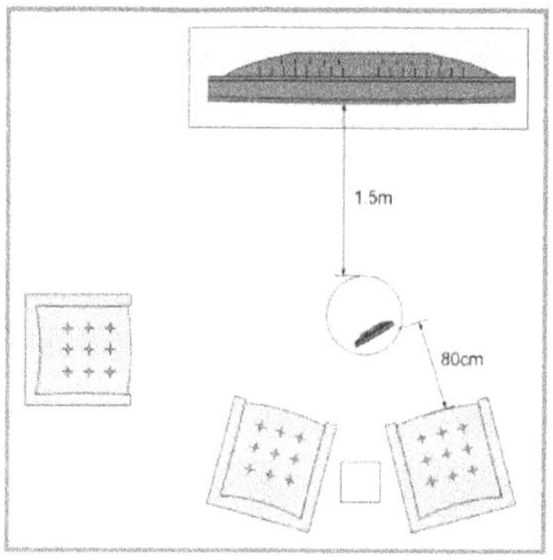

Figure 1: Room configuration used during the experiment.

The system ran on a PC hooked up to a 55" HDTV, in a mock living room environment (see room layout in Figure 1). The subjects sat in the two center seats, while the experimenter sat off to the side. The center table was only purposed as a platform for the Kinect sensor. A small table (15x15cm surface area) placed between the two chairs, was large enough to hold a drink or a plate, but not both at the same time.

A Nintendo wireless sensor bar was used in combination with a standard Nintendo Wii Remote for relevant conditions. A Microsoft Kinect sensor was used for the Kinect tasks, and a 10.1" tablet running Android 2.3 was used for the tablet tasks. A windows application called GlovePIE was used to control the cursor using the Wiimote. A GlovePIE script enabled the IR camera in the Wiimote to control the mouse cursor and the 'A' button to control the left mouse click.

A custom application was created to allow the Kinect to control the mouse cursor and left button. The application was written in C# using the OpenNI framework. To move the cursor, participants moved their right hand, which positioned the cursor similar to a traditional mouse. To initiate a drag, participants moved their left hand forward to cross the threshold of a virtual plane 30-40cm in front of them. This action is equivalent to a left mouse down event. To initiate a drop, participants would simply pull their arm back and break the plane in the opposite direction. This action is equivalent to a left mouse up event. To initiate a left click, participants move their left hand quickly through the plane and back out in one fluid motion.

The software used in the relative tablet condition was an open source Android application called RemoteDroid. This application turns the entire tablet into one large touchpad similar to what is found on most laptop computers (see Figure 2). This is application was paired with an application that runs on the host computer.

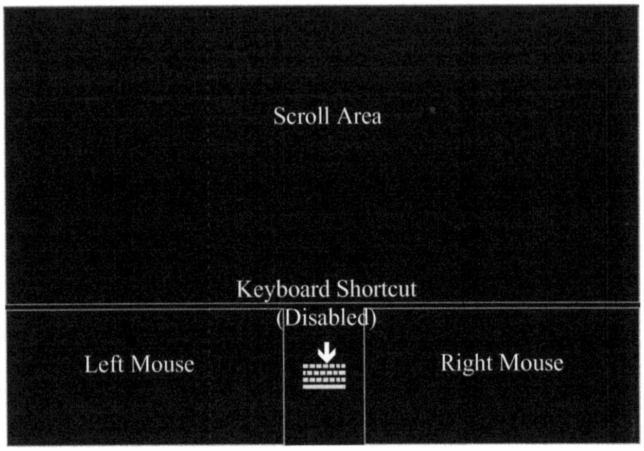

Figure 2: The configuration of the relative tablet app.

The mirrored condition used a modified version of the RemoteDroid application. It continually updates the tablet display with a screenshot of the TV. Instead of using a relative coordinate system where the cursor movement corresponds to relative changes in cursor position, an absolute coordinate system is used. By using an absolute coordinate system, a user can click on any location of the mirrored display and have it mapped to the equivalent location on the PC display.

Subjects were trained on the devices they were going to use and given time to practice on a screen that allowed dragging and dropping an object and clicking a button. When they felt comfortable with the device they began the drag-and-drop task.

The only actions allowed in the drag and drop task were dragging and dropping a widget into a target box (see Figure 3). If the widget was dropped fully within the boundary of a target presented at a random point on the screen, then a hit was recorded, and the subject would be presented with a new, slightly smaller target. A miss was recorded if the user missed the widget when attempting to select it, or if they released the widget outside of the target box. They were able to keep trying until they ran out of time for the trial. If the user was unable to place the widget in the target within 16 seconds, the box and widget were moved to random locations on the screen and the target box got bigger. If the user hit the target, then both the widget and target were randomly moved and the target shrank, with the minimum size for the target being 3 pixels wider and taller than the widget.

Figure 3: Sample screen for drag and drop task.

After completing the drag-and-drop accuracy task, we asked subjects to complete a number of navigation tasks on an iTV environment, simulated using the popular XBMC media center.

The navigation tasks included 3 different activities in XBMC. The first required the subject to navigate from the main menu to the weather settings screen and change the city name. This may have been the most challenging task due to the text entry requirement. Next, subjects would go to the weather screen and change the city currently displayed. This was difficult at times because it required clicking on a very small button. After changing the city, the subject would navigate to the movie selection screen and select a movie using a scrollbar. Finally, after the movie started, a slider was used to adjust movie volume. In all navigation tasks, an error was recorded if a subject clicked on a non-interactive item or if they clicked on the wrong UI widget.

We measured users' time to complete tasks and their error rates. Additionally we collected qualitative data in a post experiment interview and survey. Finally we used screen capture software and a video camera to record subjects. Subjects performed the experiment in pairs, taking turns with each device (subject A would try device 1, then subject B would use the same device. Next Subject A would try device 2, and then Subject B would do the same). Pairs were randomly assigned two input methods.

Because of previous research showing the importance of studying the effectiveness of UI techniques under similar manual loads [2], and the oft-informal nature of TV viewing, we decided to give each subject a slice of pizza and a drink to hold and consume during the course of the experimental tasks. Subjects were not allowed to place the food items on the floor or on the larger central table, but had to balance them on their seat or lap.

After both subjects completed all tasks using the first device assigned to them, they were introduced to the second device, and the process started anew, from the training period onward. After both subjects completed both conditions, they were asked to complete a short survey asking them about learnability, ease of use and practicality of the devices they had been assigned. All questions were on a 5-point Likert scale, 1 meaning strongly agree and 5 meaning strongly disagree.

Finally, they were interviewed to get a deeper understanding of their experience. We were interested in their satisfaction with the various input devices. This included the ease with which the subjects could use the device along with their enjoyment of using the device. Additionally we asked about their comfort level using the device in a social context where others were observing them.

4. RESULTS

4.1 Drag and Drop Task

The main task we used to measure the efficiency of a UI technique for manipulation was the timed drag and drop task, as it combined selection, movement, as well as accuracy. The more drops a subject managed within the time allotted, the more accurate their manipulation of the widgets on the screen. The highest mean number of targets hit was with the mirror tablet, where subjects hit an average of 14.09 targets (see Figure 4). Subjects using the Wiimote and relative tablet scored 12.97 and 11.90 hits respectively. Those using the Kinect averaged a score of 7.37 hits. The Kinect did significantly worse than all other devices (One-way ANOVA $F(3,19)=54.5$, $P<0.001$ with Tukey's HSD for Post Hoc analysis). The relative tablet also did significantly worse than the Wiimote and mirror tablet ($P<0.05$). There was no significant difference between the Wiimote and mirror devices.

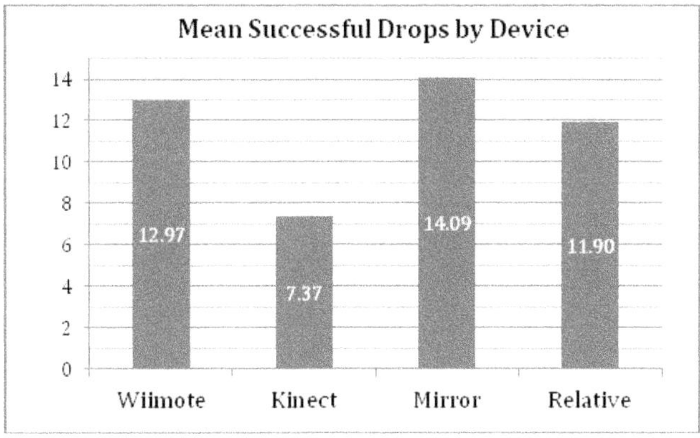

Figure 4: More drops show that the user was quicker and more accurate than users with fewer successful drops.

There is of course a direct relation between accuracy and speed in this task. The quicker the manipulation, the more likely you are to be able to complete the task, and even try multiple times in case of failure. Therefore an inaccurate but very quick technique could lead to misleading results. To investigate this we decided to look at the average target size for the last 5 targets subjects successfully hit. This allowed us to give subjects some additional practice time, and allowed subjects' performance to plateau. The results are shown in figure 5.

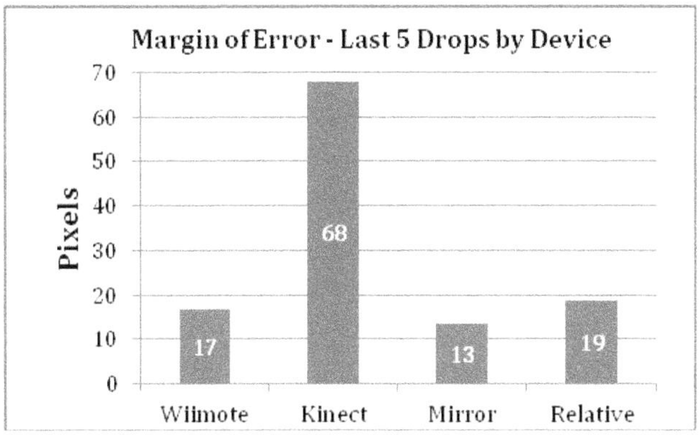

Figure 5: Average final margin of error in pixels by condition

Users were much less accurate with the Kinect than with any other device. Users of the mirror, relative and Wiimote conditions averaged a 13 to 19-pixel difference between the widget dimensions and the target dimensions. With the widget being 152px square, this meant a margin of error of less than ±9-12% of the widget size, or ±1-2% of the total screen real estate (1920x1080). For the Kinect the margin of error was ±45% of the widget, and ±6% of the total screen real estate. There were significant differences (One-way ANOVA $F(3,120)=13.77$, $P<0.001$ with Tukey's HSD for Post Hoc analysis) between the Kinect and all the other devices ($P<0.001$). Other differences were not significant.

During the experiment and in the post experiment interview, several subjects mentioned that the sensitivity for the relative tablet was low and that they would have to slide their finger across the device more than once to get the cursor to traverse from one side of the screen to the other. Users needed to swipe 3 times to go from one side of the screen to the other. No enhancements such as cursor acceleration were implemented; this could potentially improve performance of the relative condition. This may in part explain why the relative tablet scored worse than the mirror and Wiimote. However, because speed and accuracy are often traded off against each other, it is not a given that acceleration would lead to better results. This is something that should be investigated more in-depth. Users were not able to move the cursor rapidly enough to hit the same number of targets.

The issues with using the Kinect were more pronounced and deep-rooted. Subjects were observed having a difficult time both beginning a drag (selecting and dragging the target) and dropping the widget into the target (widget would often be dropped prematurely and unintentionally). A less common but also real problem was that in order to establish a difference between a click event and a drag event users had to press forward and hold for 0.5 seconds before beginning the drag. It was common to see users attempt to drag before the drag event had been registered. They were told about this in the training but as the user began the trial and were trying to rush through the task, they would often not pause long enough. Some visual indicator to let them know that the event had been registered could have made a difference.

The more fundamental problem with the Kinect condition was the 2-handed operations. Subjects usually had little trouble placing a cursor over a target using one hand, though fatigue was mentioned as a concern in some trials. However, the action of bringing or removing the second hand from the camera plane often caused subjects to inadvertently rotate their bodies to retain balance, even while seated. This of course would make their targeting hand move, resulting in a missed target. This same phenomenon was observed time and again across tasks and subjects. The only effective remedy we saw was for subjects to plant their elbows in the seat, and use this to counter the natural body rotation action. Though effective, this led to a very restrictive seating position.

4.2 Nudging

There is a tradeoff between speed and accuracy, and with a sufficiently fast UI, users can home in on the target effectively. We referred to this behavior as "nudging". In our experiment, this turned out to be a relatively common strategy; if a subject failed to hit the target on the first try, they would rethink their strategy (a longer pause) and then pick up the widget and home in through a series of rapid follow-up moves. This was especially common with the smaller targets, where the margin for error was low. The majority of times subject were able to hit the target in one or two attempts. However, sometimes it took longer.

Figure 6 shows how subjects using the Wiimote employed this strategy. Wiimote users were among the most successful and accurate, and the technique allowed for quick and easy nudging, or homing in on the target. As we can see, after a longer rethink following an initial miss, subjects engaged in a lot of rapid moves aimed at trying to hit the target. Subjects in this condition were still among the most accurate and successful. We see a very similar behavior among subjects using the mirror tablet application, though there is less of a long-tail (see Figure 7).

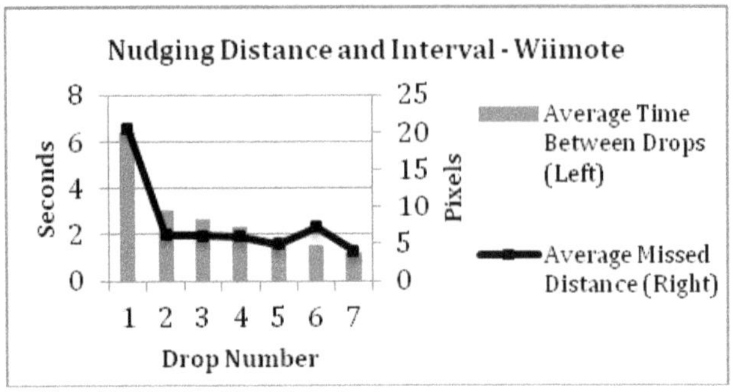

Figure 6: Nudging interval (left axis, blue columns, in seconds) and distance (black line, right axis, in pixels) over number of tries to hit one target – Wiimote.

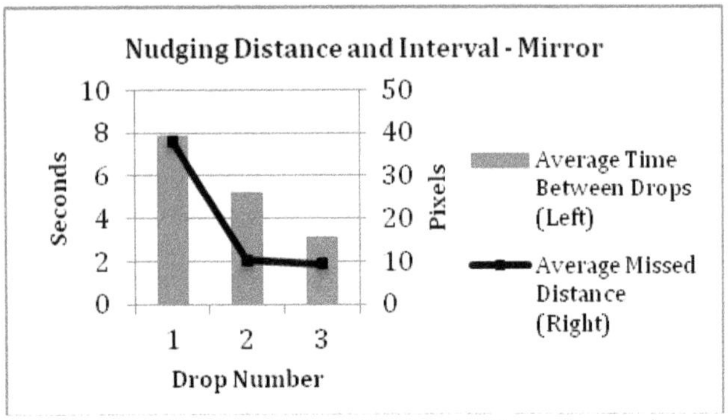

Figure 7: Nudging interval (left axis, blue columns, in seconds) and distance (black line, right axis, in pixels) over number of tries to hit one target – Mirror Tablet.

This strategy however seemed to be less successful, even counterproductive in the other two conditions (see Figure 8 and Figure 9). In the case of the Kinect condition, accuracy was an enormous issue, and though subjects were more successful with repeated tries, they did not home in on the target, but rather hit random new points. In the case of the relative tablet application, the nudging strategy appears to be counterproductive. Subjects would after the second try engage in very rapid moves that rather than take them closer to the target would distance them more. To us this is an important distinction between these two groups of techniques. Our subjects naturally gravitated to this strategy, and therefore it should be supported.

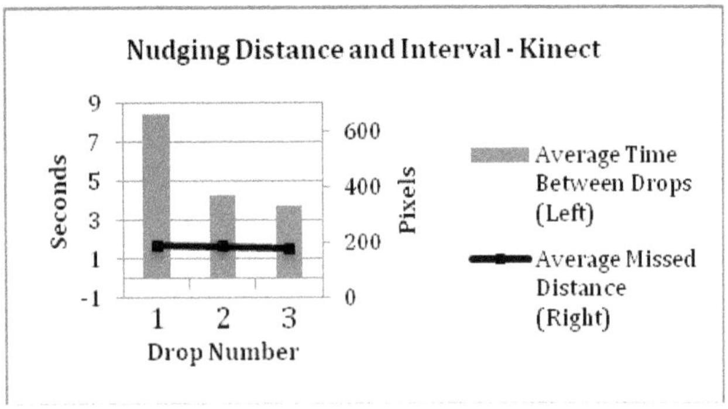

Figure 8: Nudging interval (left axis, blue columns, in seconds) and distance (black line, right axis, in pixels) over number of tries to hit one target – Kinect.

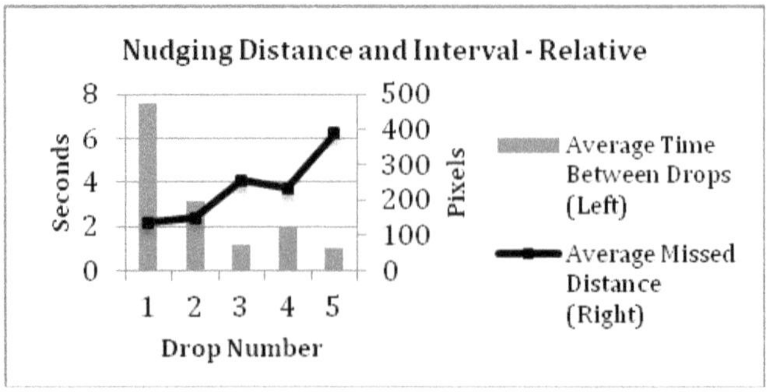

Figure 9: Nudging interval (left axis, blue columns, in seconds) and distance (black line, right axis, in pixels) over number of tries to hit one target – Relative Tablet.

4.3 Text Entry

An important task for iTV applications is text entry, as it allows more rapid customization, search, etc. We chose to examine two factors, the number of clicks that landed off of the intended target (key) and the time it took users to input the text string (a 9 character string).

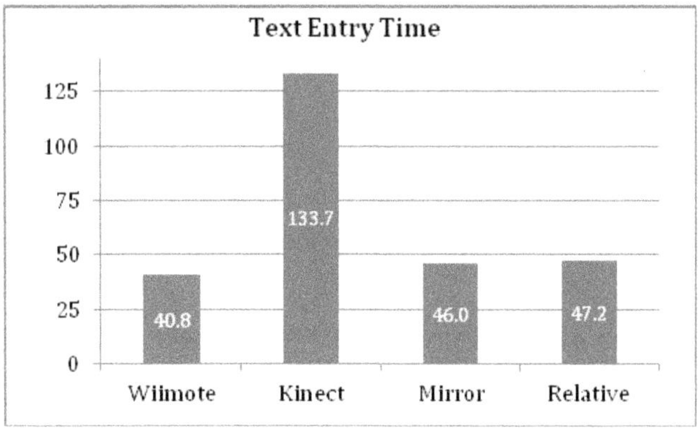

Figure 10: Average text entry time in seconds

As we see in Figure 10, text entry was significantly slower with the Kinect when compared to the other devices (One-way ANOVA $F(3,115)=19.53$ $P<0.001$ with Tukey's HSD for Post Hoc analysis). The Kinect was significantly slower than all other devices ($P<0.001$). There were no other significant differences.

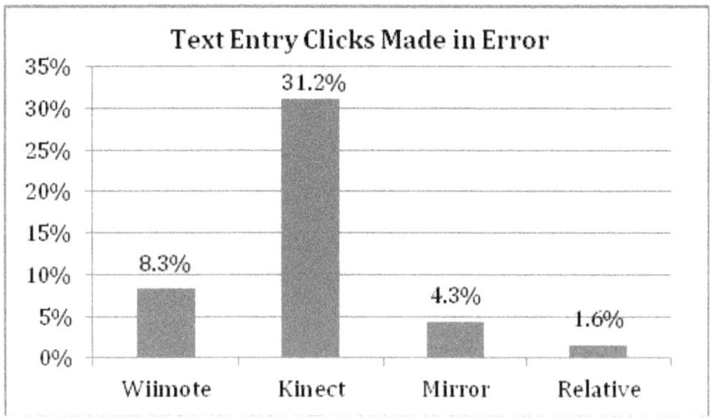

Figure 11: Text entry mistakes using virtual keyboard

Again, because a lack of accuracy can lead to slower task completion, we chose to look at how many mistakes subject made. A mistake in this case could be a subject hitting the wrong letter, or trying to click on something other than a letter on the on-screen virtual keyboard. As in just about every task in our experiment, the Kinect fared most poorly with 31.2% of clicks missing their target. This is significantly worse than the other three devices (One-way ANOVA $F(3,116)=19.14$ $P<0.01$ with Tukey's HSD for Post Hoc analysis).

Of the remaining devices the Wiimote fared the worst with an error rate of 8.3%, though this did not affect completion time. The mirror app came next, with an error rate of 4.3%, likely caused by the small size of the keys when shown on the tablet. The error rate for the relative app was a surprisingly low 1.6%. The difference between these devices was not significant.

4.4 Effects of Prior Experience

Prior experience can have a significant impact on performance, especially when dealing with the novel. Subjects were asked to rate their prior experience with devices similar to those used in our study. A linear regression was used to compare the number of successful drops in the drag and drop task and the speed of text entry versus their prior experience (see Table 1).

Table 1: Slope of linear models. Steeper slopes indicate stronger experience effect.

	Hits vs. Experience	Text Entry vs. Experience
Wiimote	0.61	0.33
Kinect	0.51	-5.42
Relative	0.39	-0.79
Mirror	0.25	-7.85

We see that the prior experience played the largest role in the Wiimote case. Despite being seen as universally easy to use, subjects were able to effectively leverage prior experience to improve further. The same was the case in the Kinect condition, though here, novices really suffered, and even experts performed marginally. There may have been a floor effect here as fewer subjects had experience with Kinect compared to other devices, and those that did have experience tended to have less experience than with the Kinect than with other devices.

More surprising, there was only a relatively mild learning effect for the two tablet solutions. While experience did help, it seems that these two techniques were so universally well-known and intuitive that all subject were able to use them effectively regardless of experience level.

5. DISCUSSION

In our post experiment interviews we focused on understanding the limitations and advantages of the different approaches. One thing we stumbled on were issues related to the sensitivity, or lack thereof for some of our conditions. 76% of users of the relative tablet mentioned that sensitivity was an issue (it took too long to scroll from one side of the display to the other). 43% of Wiimote subjects complained about the device being too sensitive, reacting to slight hand tremors.

Despite the negative results, 13% of Kinect subjects commented positively about its usefulness. This was obviously surprising, but shows that people like the concept of this technique, if not the implementation. We also found that 40% of those who used the mirror tablet and 47% of those who used the Wiimote commented positively about these. Surprisingly only 13% of the relative tablet users commented positively about it despite the high performance.

When asked if the input method could be learned quickly, the Wiimote won out, and it was also rated as the least awkward to use. Subjects liked the simplicity of the Wiimote, both in interface navigation and physically. One participant said, "It was simple. Just point and click. You just aim at it and it's right there." One of the most common answers about what people liked about the Wiimote input method was that it had only 1 button. People also liked the familiarity with holding the Wiimote, that it felt like a remote control and had a physical button.

By far, the least liked device was the Kinect. The most frequent negative comments had to do with physical fatigue and issues with sensor range and sensitivity. Having to hold their right arm up to position the cursor and left arm for click control resulted in almost all Kinect users complaining of arm fatigue. Finding a one-handed method for controlling the system could result in a significant improvement, as indicated by 60% of Kinect users. 60% also complained about the sensor range or sensitivity. To limit interference, the sensor was placed 80cm away from the subject. As a consequence, subjects felt they were unable to move their hands as far to the left and right as they would like. Although most comments focused on why the Kinect was not effective, several participants liked how it did not require them to hold a physical device. One participant talked about how nice it would be to have no remotes and control everything with gestures. Most subjects however indicated that they would be embarrassed to use this technique in front of friends and family.

The two tablet techniques achieved roughly the same ratings, which were generally good. 30% of mirror application users commented positively on being able to directly manipulate the interface. One person said "I really liked being able to click on exactly what I can see on the screen." Others disagreed, saying how they prefer to only have one screen to interact with. One participant commented "Occasionally I found myself not knowing which screen to look at."

A side-effect of our implementation of the mirror app was noticeable "lag" between the TV and the tablet images of between 0.25 and 0.5 seconds. This delay was often mentioned as an annoyance. Likewise, nearly everyone who used the relative tablet app disliked its low sensitivity and the lack of acceleration techniques. With appropriate tweaking, both of these techniques would have likely scored higher on both likability and effectiveness.

6. FUTURE WORK

This was meant as an exploratory study examining the relative merits of a number of gaming-related UI methods, and their usefulness in an iTV setting. Looking forward, there are several improvements worth exploring based both on user feedback and our findings. As mentioned in the results and discussion sections, implementing motion smoothing for the Wiimote, acceleration for the relative tablet app, and reducing the lag for the mirror app are natural next steps. We believe all of these could drastically improve the user experience.

In implementing smoothing for the Wiimote, a slight delay will be introduced. Pavlovych and Stuerzlinger [3] studied the relationship between jitter and latency and their results could help inform an appropriate balance.

A more tricky problem was the noisiness and occasional false positive for hands for the Kinect. We were unable to use the Kinect API's native skeleton tracking because only the upper half of the users' body was visible to the sensor. Instead, we used a hand tracking method and filtered based on depth field data. Even with these precautions, a knee or other object could register as a hand. This led to a very frustrating user experience. In future revisions, we would look for a more robust tracking solution. We did not use the official Kinect SDK as it was not available in time.

When asked what they would change about the Kinect method, several people said they would prefer a one-handed solution. We think this would substantially decrease the physical fatigue and provide a more intuitive experience. Due to the Kinect's 640x480 resolution depth camera, robust finger tracking was difficult. Perhaps with a different library or algorithm, a more feasible approach could be found. One option might be the work of Oikonomidis et al. [8], who have demonstrated complex finger articulation, though not in real-time.

We chose not to investigate the use of voice commands in our experiment, in part because it would be difficult to filter noise and could be socially awkward. As the introduction of the Siri system on the iPhone, and the flurry of interest this has caused, these assumptions and prejudices may need to be revisited in future work.

7. CONCLUSIONS

With the growing availability of broadband Internet access, highly extensible game consoles, and the increasing popularity of social and streaming online entertainment services, their convergence is presenting a number of new challenges for HCI researchers. To the best of the authors' knowledge, there has been very little research on the adoption and use of novel game controller technology in a media center or iTV context. While our research was largely exploratory, we hope it will serve as a base for future work in this area.

Looking at the results we see that devices designed for gaming have the potential to be effective input devices for a typical iTV interface. We also see that some devices are better suited to this task than others. The Wiimote was effective, well liked, and very easy to learn. At the same time, it offered ample room for improvement as users gain experience. On the other hand, it is potentially limiting UI-wise, as all information has to be displayed on the primary display. The tablet systems were both well liked and effective as well, though they potentially offer more flexibility and exploration, albeit at a much higher hardware cost.

The Kinect, though appealing to many subjects due to its novelty and the promise of device-free interaction, proved to be too unreliable and cumbersome to use for any extended period of time. While it may be refined with better hardware and algorithms, its suitability and desirability for a social lean-back viewing experience may be limited. Fear of ridicule as much as physical fatigue and the problem of interference from others' movement are serious problems that need to be overcome.

REFERENCES

[1] A. D. Wilson and M. Agrawala. "Text entry using a dual joystick game controller." In Proc. of the SIGCHI conf. on Human Factors in computing systems (CHI '06), ACM, New York, NY, USA, 475-478.

[2] A. Oulasvirta and J. Bergstrom-Lehtovirta. "Ease of juggling: studying the effects of manual multitasking." In Proc. of the 2011 annual conf. on Human factors in computing systems (CHI '11). ACM, New York, NY, USA, 3103-3112.

[3] A. Pavlovych & W. Stuerzlinger. "The tradeoff between spatial jitter and latency in pointing tasks." In Proc. of the 1st ACM SIGCHI symposium on Engineering interactive computing systems (EICS '09). ACM, New York, NY, USA, 187-196.

[4] D. Natapov, S.J. Castellucci, and I.S. MacKenzie. "ISO 9241-9 evaluation of video game controllers." In Proc. of Graphics Interface 2009 (GI '09). Canadian Information Processing Society, Toronto, Ont., Canada, Canada, 223-230.

[5] D.C. McCallum and P. Irani. "ARC-Pad: absolute+relative cursor positioning for large displays with a mobile touchscreen." In Proc. of the 22nd annual ACM symposium on User interface software and technology (UIST '09). ACM, New York, NY, USA, 153-156.

[6] G. Shoemaker, L. Findlater, J.Q. Dawson, and K.S. Booth. "Mid-air text input techniques for very large wall displays" In Proc. of Graphics Interface 2009 (GI '09). pp. 231-238.

[7] Hulu, 2012. "Hulu Financial Results:" http://blog.hulu.com/2012/01/12/2011-2012-and-beyond/

[8] I. Oikonomidis, N. Kyriazis, and A. Argyros. "Efficient model-based 3d tracking of hand articulations using kinect." Procs. of BMVC, Dundee, UK, pages 1-11, 2011.

[9] I.S. MacKenzie and S.X. Zhang. "The immediate usability of graffiti." In Proc. of the conf. on Graphics interface '97, Toronto, Ont., Canada, Canada, 129-137.

[10] J. C. Lee. Hacking the Nintendo Wii Remote. IEEE Pervasive Computing, 7(3):39-45, July 2008.

[11] J. Lin, H. Nishino, T. Kagawa, and K. Utsumiya. "Free hand interface for controlling applications based on Wii remote IR sensor." In Proc. of the 9th ACM SIGGRAPH Conf. on Virtual-Reality Continuum and its Applications in Industry (VRCAI '10). ACM, New York, NY, USA, 139-142.

[12] K. Cheng and M. Takatsuka. "Initial evaluation of a bare-hand interaction technique for large displays using a webcam" In Proc. of the 1st ACM SIGCHI symposium on Engineering interactive computing systems (EICS '09). ACM, New York, NY, USA, 291-296.

[13] L. Rainie. "Tablet and E-book reader Ownership Nearly Double Over the Holiday Gift-Giving Period" Pew Internet. 2012.

[14] Netflix, "Netflix Q4 2011 Letter to Shareholders." http://goo.gl/4vgP1

[15] Nielsen, 2011. "Nielsen: The Cross-Platform Report." http://goo.gl/JxEpn

[16] Nielsen. "State of the Media: Consumer Usage Report," 2011. http://goo.gl/PzAzc

[17] NTIA, 2010. "Exploring the Digital Nation: Home Broadband Adoption in the United States." http://goo.gl/ErsnS

[18] S.J. Castellucci and I.S. MacKenzie. "Unigest: text entry using three degrees of motion" In extended abstracts of the 2008 Conf on Human factors in computing systems; CHI '08. ACM, New York, NY, USA, 3549-3554.

[19] Sandvine, 2011. "Sandvine. Global Internet Phenomena Spotlight: Netflix Rising." http://goo.gl/dbkPz

[20] T. Költringer, P. Isokoski, and T. Grechenig. "TwoStick: writing with a game controller." In Proc. of Graphics Interface 2007 (GI '07). ACM, New York, NY, USA, 103-110.

[21] T. Ni, D. Bowman, and C. North. "AirStroke: bringing unistroke text entry to freehand gesture interfaces." In Proc. of the 2011 annual conference on Human factors in computing systems (CHI '11). ACM, New York, NY, USA, 2473-2476.

[22] YouTube, 2012. YouTube Press Statistics: http://www.youtube.com/t/press_statistics

Towards Multimodal Deception Detection – Step 1: Building a Collection of Deceptive Videos

Rada Mihalcea
Computer Science and Engineering
University of North Texas
rada@cs.unt.edu

Mihai Burzo
Mechanical and Energy Engineering
University of North Texas
Mihai.Burzo@unt.edu

ABSTRACT

In this paper, we introduce a novel crowdsourced dataset of deceptive videos. We describe the collection process and the characteristics of the dataset, and we validate it through initial experiments in the recognition of deceptive language. The collection, consisting of 140 truthful and deceptive videos, will enable future experiments in multimodal deceptive detection.

Categories and Subject Descriptors

I.2.7 [**Artificial Intelligence**]: Natural Language Processing—*Discourse*

General Terms

Algorithms, Experimentation

Keywords

Deception detection, Corpus construction

1. INTRODUCTION

Work on deception has received significant attention from several fields of study, ranging from psychology to sociology, linguistics, and computer vision. While a number of studies have been carried out in the past for the automatic detection of deception, most of this previous work has primarily targeted one modality at a time. There is very little work that has considered the simultaneous exploitation of multiple modalities for the purpose of lie detection.

In this paper, we take a first step toward addressing this gap, and introduce a novel dataset consisting of deceptive and truthful videos. The dataset, collected using crowdsourcing, contains 140 videos that can enable data-driven exploration of multimodal methods for lie detection.

As a validation of the dataset, we perform a proof of concept experiment using the language modality, and show that we can distinguish between truthful and deceptive statements with an accuracy significantly higher than the baseline. This suggests that the dataset is useful for the identification of deceit, and the performance obtained by using language alone is likely to be improved in future experiments when the visual and audio modalities will be also exploited.

This paper makes two main contributions. First, we introduce a novel dataset of deceptive videos, and show that crowdsourcing can be successfully used to collect such video datasets. Second, we validate the dataset by conducting an initial experiment on the linguistic modality, and show that truthful and lying statements are separable. An analysis of the salient features in the dataset also reveals interesting findings concerning the language of deceit.

2. RELATED WORK

Lie detection has been studied in several fields, including psychology, sociology, linguistics, and computer vision.

In psychology, it is worthwhile mentioning the study reported in [4], where more than 100 cues to deception are mentioned. Many of these cues involve speaker's behavior, including facial expressions and eye shifts, but linguistic cues such as word and phrase repetitions are also included. Pennebaker and colleagues [13] report on a psycholinguistic study, where they conduct a qualitative analysis of true and false stories by using word counting tools. Studies have also been made in neuroscience, such as the one reported in [11], where EEG signals are used to predict deceit.

Computational work applied to language includes the studies described in [26, 18], which included linguistic cues for deception detection in text-based and face-to-face communication. Deception in speech was also addressed in [7, 21], where the main focus was on acoustic and prosodic features. In more recent work, larger scale experiments were performed with the help of data collected through crowdsourcing. Mihalcea and Strapparava [10] proposed a method for the collection of linguistic deceptive datasets using crowdsourcing, and they showed through classification experiments that the data was indeed useful for this task. Similar to this, a review dataset was collected and used in experiments reported in [15], with the goal of identifying spam reviews.

There is also a significant amount of work carried out on the recognition of deception through visual clues. Some of the earliest work is due to Ekman [5], who studied how deception is expressed on the face and the body. Following his work, a corpus of deceptive videos was compiled [6]. More recently, a number of studies have been made on the use of thermal imaging for deception detection, focusing primar-

ICMI'12, October 22–26, 2012, Santa Monica, California, USA.

ily on the identification of thermal signatures for specific areas of the face [27, 22]. Deceptive expressions have also been studied through computer vision methods, which can separate between expressions of genuine and posed pain [9], facial expressions [25], brow movements [24], and smile [3, 23].

3. CROWDSOURCING A COLLECTION OF DECEPTIVE VIDEOS

Since our main research goal is to explore multimodal aspects of deception, the first step is to compile a corpus of deceptive videos. To this end, we used the Amazon Mechanical Turk service, which is a crowdsourcing platform provided by Amazon.com. While the platform has been heavily used in the past for tasks such as linguistic annotations [19], image labeling [8], and translation evaluations [1], we are not aware of previous work that used this service to build collections of video recordings. In fact, at the time when the collection was built, there was only one other task that required a video recording, and even that was asking for video reviews for a commercial site.

A HIT (Human Intelligence Task) was set up on Mechanical Turk, in which workers were provided specific instructions about how to record and upload both deceptive and truthful videos. We provided concrete information about the quality of the videos they were to record, as well as about the task to perform. First, regarding the video, they were asked to use one of the standard containers to record the video, i.e., avi, mp4, mov, or wmv. The video had to have a resolution of at least 640x480, and the entire head and shoulders had to be included in the recording with the head representing ideally about 1/4-1/8 of each frame. They were asked to look into the camera when recording the video, and speak clearly. They were also asked to avoid background noise and music, and had a clearly lit setting so that their face could be seen clearly. Finally, the length of the recording had to be between 1.5 - 3 minutes.

The workers had to produce and upload two videos. For the first video, the guidelines asked the contributor to think about their best friend, and record a video of them talking about the best friend. The video could include a description of their friendship, mentioning the reasons for which they were such good friends, including anecdotes or anything that seemed relevant to their relationship and what kept them together. Thus, the first video consisted of a truthful recording about a best friend.

Next, for the second video, the workers were asked to think about a person they could not stand, and record a video of them talking about this person and describing her as though she were their best friend. Therefore, in this video they recorded a deceptive description of a (fake) best friend.

One of the main challenges associated with the use of crowdsourcing for data collection is the large amount of spam that often occurs on these public platforms. In line with this observation, we also had many spam contributions for the task, partly motivated by the reward of $3/contribution, which was at the higher end of the payments typically made on Amazon Mechanical Turk. While previous work has considered a number of spam detection techniques, such as check points inserted in the data and agreement between contributors, in our case we were able to use a filter that removed most of the spam, followed by manual verification of the recordings. The filter consisted of removing contributions where no files were uploaded or where the file type was different from the required file formats. A large number of spam contributions did not upload a video, or attempted to upload other file formats (e.g., jpg or txt), and thus they could be easily detected and rejected. For the remaining contributions, we manually verified them to make sure they indeed contained recordings about the speaker's best friend, and to rule out random recordings (there a few such videos uploaded for our task).

The final collection consists of 140 videos, out of which 70 include deceptive recordings, and 70 contain truthful recordings. The recordings were made by: 33 women and 37 men; 6 teenagers, 62 adults between 18-60 years of age, 2 adults over 60 years old; 51 Whites, 5 African Americans, 4 Hispanics, 10 Asians.

Another time consuming aspect related to the construction and use of video collections is the transcription of the speech. To perform this task, we once again used the Amazon Mechanical Turk service, and collected transcriptions for the videos in the dataset. The guidelines specifically asked for complete, correctly spelled sentences, with punctuation included as needed. The workers were also asked to use filler words, such as "um," "like," "you know." Unlike the first task, we received significantly less spam in the transcription task, perhaps due to the fact that this is a widespread task type, and there is a skilled workforce on Mechanical Turk. Nonetheless, the transcriptions were manually verified for correctness. Table 1 shows sample transcriptions for segments of a truthful and a deceptive video.

Overall, the dataset contains a total of 38,326 words. Interestingly, the deceptive videos have an average of 254 words per video, which is significantly less than the average of 292 words per video in the truthful videos. This difference may reflect the ease with which people can talk about their true best friend, as compared to the cases when facts and attributes about a person have to be made up.

4. PROOF OF CONCEPT

The main goal of this paper is to describe the corpus of deceptive videos that we collected through crowdsourcing, and thus experiments making full use of this corpus are beyond the scope of the paper. Nonetheless, in order to validate the usefulness of this corpus for deception detection, we ran a proof of concept study that makes use of one modality (language) in order to differentiate between truthful and deceptive statements.

For this initial study, we are using the transcripts associated with the videos in the corpus. From these, we are extracting features that were successfully used in the past for deception detection. Specifically, we use: (1) unigram features obtained from a bag-of-words representation, which are the features typically used by corpus-based methods; and (2) lexicon features, indicating the appartenance of a word to a semantic class defined in manually crafted lexicons, which are often used by knowledge-based methods.

Unigrams. We use a bag-of-words representation of the transcripts to derive unigram counts, which are then used as input features. First, we build a vocabulary consisting of all the words, including stopwords, occurring in the transcripts of the training set. We then remove those words that have a frequency below 10 (value determined empirically on a

Truth	Lie
I'm going to describe my friend, Mike. I have known him for approximately 15 years, we [um], met in St. Paul, Minnesota and then moved to [umm] Madison, Wisconsin at the same time. So I that that kind of [um] solidified our friendship. And then coincidently, actually also moved back to St. Paul [um] at approximately the same time later on, so [um], for about 10 years, like I said, we've been friends. [Um], we originally went to high school together, [um], here in St. Paul. [Um], we did have a job together. [Um], mostly we've been friends [umm] just outside of work and everything like that.	Hi there. Now I'm going to describe my friend, my good friend, Archie. [Um] Archie and I have been friends for [errr] quite a long time, I've known him since I was probably six or seven years old. [Um] We always had a great time during childhood. [Um] When we were growing up, playing games, having fun. Since then, him and I have really [um] gotten to know each other really well and we.. we have maintained this [um] this strong bond, that I really feel [um] I really feel that he's.. you know.. one of my better friends. He's such a [um].. such a interesting person, nice, kind, smart.

Table 1: Transcriptions of sample true and deceptive videos

Feature	Info Gain	Deceptive	Truthful
Semantic Classes			
SELF (our, myself, mine, ours)	0.13	3.75	4.91
WE (we, use, our, ours)	0.12	1.22	1.85
I (I, me, mine, my)	0.07	2.52	3.05
PAST (ago, became, had, made)	0.07	4.51	6.71
PREPS (about, above, in, if)	0.06	9.88	11.52
OPTIM (ready, hope, accept, super)	0.05	2.41	2.44
POSEMO (agree, best, care, cheer)	0.04	5.28	5.57
Unigrams			
years	0.12	0.32	1.07
me	0.09	1.78	3.51
we	0.07	5.74	9.72
best	0.07	1.31	2.17
my	0.07	2.28	3.94
sister	0.07	0.00	0.24
been	0.06	0.42	1.18

Table 2: Top dominant features in the classification of deceptive language.

small development set). The remaining words represent the unigram features, which are then associated with a value corresponding to the frequency of the unigram inside each video transcription. This bag-of-word representation was successfully used for lie detection in text by [10] and more recently by [15].

Semantic Classes. We also derive and use coarse textual features, by using mappings between words and semantic classes. Specifically, we use the Linguistic Inquiry and Word Count (LIWC) and WordNet Affect (WA) to derive coarse textual features. LIWC was developed as a resource for psycholinguistic analysis [16, 17]. The 2001 version of LIWC includes about 2,200 words and word stems grouped into about 70 broad categories relevant to psychological processes (e.g., emotion, cognition). WA [20] is a resource that was created starting with WordNet, by annotating synsets with several emotions. It uses several resources for affective information, including the emotion classification of Ortony [14]. From WA, we extract the words corresponding to the six basic emotions used in our experiments. For each semantic class, we infer a feature indicating the number of words in a video transcription belonging to that class.

Using these linguistic features, we use an Ada Boost classifier with a decision stump and run a ten-fold cross-validation on the entire set of transcripts.[1] The baseline for these experiments is 50%, corresponding to assigning one class (truth or deceit) by default. The classifier leads to an accuracy of 68.57%, which represents a significant improvement over the baseline. This indicates that the deceptive and truthful videos in our corpus can be indeed differentiated using automatic learning techniques.

In order to gain a better understanding of the characteristics of the deceptive language in our collection, we perform an analysis of the weight of the features as used by the classifier. Table 2 shows the top seven unigram and semantic class features that have the highest information gain, along with their normalized frequency in deceptive and truthful videos.

Interestingly, for both the unigrams and the semantic class features, several of the top dominant features are related to humans. In particular, the use of words closely connected to the self (I, WE, SELF, *me*, *we*, *my*) seem to be good indicators of truthful statements, where the speaker is comfortable with identifying herself with the statements she makes. Also interesting is the importance of temporal expressions in the classification. This may be an observation specific to the dataset that we constructed, where the speakers talk about their best friend, and where a true best friend is associated with the PAST with a relationship that spans many *years*.

5. CONCLUSIONS AND FUTURE WORK

In this paper, we described our work to create a novel dataset of 140 deceptive and truthful videos, which is the first step required to enable explorations in multimodal deception detection. We showed that crowdsourcing can be successfully used to build such video collections, and also to collect the corresponding manual transcriptions for the speech in the videos.

We also performed a proof of concept experiment to test the validity of the dataset. Through machine learning eval-

[1] We use the implementation available in the Weka package www.cs.waikato.ac.nz/ml/weka/

uations run on the linguistic modality in the collection, we showed that the deceptive and truthful statements can be separated with an accuracy of 68%.

In line with previous work on multimodal models for human behavior analysis [12, 2], we expect that the addition of features learned from the other modalities available in this corpus (audio and visual features) will significantly improve this performance.

6. REFERENCES

[1] M. Bloodgood and C. Callison-Burch. Using Mechanical Turk to build machine translation evaluation sets. In *Proceedings of the NAACL HLT 2010 Workshop on Creating Speech and Language Data with Amazon's Mechanical Turk*, 2010.

[2] O. Brdiczka09, M. Langet, J. Maisonnasse, and J. Crowley. Detecting human behavior models from multimodal observation in a smart home. *IEEE Transactions on Automation Science and Engineering*, 6(4), 2009.

[3] J. F. Cohn and K. L. Schmidt. The timing of facial motion in posed and spontaneous smiles. *International Journal of Wavelets, Multiresolution and Information Processing*, 2, 2004.

[4] B. DePaulo, J. Lindsay, B. Malone, L. Muhlenbruck, K. Charlton, and H. Cooper. Cues to deception. *Psychological Bulletin*, 129(1):74—118, 2003.

[5] P. Ekman. Detecting deception from the body or face. *Journal of Personality and Social Psychology*, 29(3), 1974.

[6] M. Frank, J. Movellan, M. Bartlett, and G. Littleworth. RU-FACS-1 database, Machine Perception Laboratory, U.C. San Diego, 2012.

[7] J. Hirschberg, S. Benus, J. Brenier, F. Enos, S. Friedman, S. Gilman, C. Girand, M. Graciarena, A. Kathol, L. Michaelis, B. Pellom, E. Shriberg, and A. Stolcke. Distinguishing deceptive from non-deceptive speech. In *Proceedings of INTERSPEECH-2005*, Lisbon, Portugal, 2005.

[8] C. Leong, R. Mihalcea, and S. Hassan. Text mining for automatic image tagging. In *International Conference on Computational Linguistics*, pages 647–655, Beijing, China, August 2010.

[9] G. Littlewort, M. Bartlett, and K. Lee. Faces of pain: automated measurement of spontaneous all facial expressions of genuine and posed pain. In *Proceedings of the International Conference on Multimodal Interaction*, 2007.

[10] R. Mihalcea and C. Strapparava. The lie detector: Explorations in the automatic recognition of deceptive language. In *Proceedings of the Association for Computational Linguistics (ACL 2009)*, Singapore, 2009.

[11] A. Mohammadian, V. Abootalebi, M. H. Moradi, and M. A. Khalilzadeh. Multimodal detection of deception using fusion of reaction time and p300 component. In *Biomedical Engineering Conference*, 2008.

[12] L. Morency, R. Mihalcea, and P. Doshi. Towards multimodal sentiment analysis: Harvesting opinions from the web. In *Proceedings of the International Conference on Multimodal Computing*, Alicante, Spain, 2011.

[13] M. Newman, J. Pennebaker, D. Berry, and J. Richards. Lying words: Predicting deception from linguistic styles. *Personality and Social Psychology Bulletin*, 29:665–675, 2003.

[14] A. Ortony, G. L. Clore, and M. A. Foss. The referential structure of the affective lexicon. *Cognitive Science*, (11), 1987.

[15] M. Ott, Y. Choi, C. Cardie, and J. Hancock. Finding deceptive opinion spam by any stretch of the imagination. In *Association for Computational Linguistics (ACL)*, 2011.

[16] J. Pennebaker and M. Francis. Linguistic inquiry and word count: LIWC, 1999. Erlbaum Publishers.

[17] J. Pennebaker and L. King. Linguistic styles: Language use as an individual difference. *Journal of Personality and Social Psychology*, (77), 1999.

[18] T. Qin, J. K. Burgoon, J. P. Blair, and J. F. Nunamaker. Modality effects in deception detection and applications in automatic deception-detection. In *Proceedings of the 38th Hawaii International Conference on System Sciences*, 2005.

[19] R. Snow, B. O'Connor, D. Jurafsky, and A. Ng. Cheap and fast – but is it good? evaluating non-expert annotations for natural language tasks. In *Proceedings of the Conference on Empirical Methods in Natural Language Processing*, Honolulu, Hawaii, 2008.

[20] C. Strapparava and A. Valitutti. Wordnet-affect: an affective extension of wordnet. In *Proceedings of the 4th International Conference on Language Resources and Evaluation*, Lisbon, 2004.

[21] J. F. Torres, E. Moore, and E. Bryant. A study of Glottal waveform features for deceptive speech classification. In *International Conference on Acoustics, Speech, and Signal Processing*, 2008.

[22] P. Tsiamyrtzis, J. Dowdall, D. Shastri, I. Pavlidis, M. Frank, and P. Ekman. Imaging facial physiology for the detection of deceit. *International Journal of Computer Vision*, 71(2), 2006.

[23] M. Valstar, H. Gunes, and M. Pantic. How to distinguish posed from spontaneous smiles using geometric features. In *Proceedings of the ACM International Conference on Multimodal Interfaces*, 2007.

[24] M. Valstar, M. Pantic, Z. Ambadar, and J. Cohn. Spontaneous vs. posed facial behavior: automatic analysis of brow actions. In *Proceedings of the ACM International Conference on Multimodal Interfaces*, 2006.

[25] Z. Zhang, V. Singh, T. E. Slowe, S. Tulyakov, and V. Govindaraju. Real-time automatic deceit detection from involuntary facial expressions. In *Conference on Computer Vision and Pattern Recognition*, 2007.

[26] L. Zhou, J. Burgoon, J. Nunamaker, and D. Twitchell. Automating linguistics-based cues for detecting deception in text-based asynchronous computer-mediated communication. *Group Decision and Negotiation*, 13:81–106, 2004.

[27] Z. Zhu, P. Tsiamyrtzis, and I. Pavlidis. Forehead thermal signature extraction in lie detection. In *Proceedings of the 29th Annual International Conference of the IEEE Engineering in Medicine and Biology Society*, Lyon, France, 2007.

A Portable Audio/Video Recorder for Longitudinal Study of Child Development

Soroush Vosoughi
MIT Media Lab
75 Amherst St, E14-574K
Cambridge, MA 02139
soroush@mit.edu

Matthew S. Goodwin
Northeastern University
312E RB, 360 Huntington Ave
Boston, MA 02115
m.goodwin@neu.edu

Bill Washabaugh
Hypersonic Engineering and Design
33 Flatbush Avenue, 7th Floor
Brooklyn, NY 11217
bill@hypersoniced.com

Deb Roy
MIT Media Lab
75 Amherst St, E14-574G
Cambridge, MA 02139
dkroy@media.mit.edu

ABSTRACT

Collection and analysis of ultra-dense, longitudinal observational data of child behavior in natural, ecologically valid, non-laboratory settings holds significant promise for advancing the understanding of child development and developmental disorders such as autism. To this end, we created the Speechome Recorder - a portable version of the embedded audio/video recording technology originally developed for the Human Speechome Project - to facilitate swift, cost-effective deployment in home environments. Recording child behavior daily in these settings will enable detailed study of developmental trajectories in children from infancy through early childhood, as well as typical and atypical dynamics of communication and social interaction as they evolve over time. Its portability makes possible potentially large-scale comparative study of developmental milestones in both neurotypical and developmentally delayed children. In brief, the Speechome Recorder was designed to reduce cost, complexity, invasiveness and privacy issues associated with naturalistic, longitudinal recordings of child development.

Categories and Subject Descriptors

H.5.2 [**User Interfaces**]: Graphical user interfaces(GUI); H.5.1 [**Multimedia Information Systems**]: miscellaneous; J.4 [**Social and behavioral sciences**]: psychology

General Terms

Human Factors, Design, Reliability

Keywords

multimedia recording, longitudinal recording, naturalistic recording, video annotation, speech annotation, privacy management, video recorder, audio recorder, child development

1. INTRODUCTION

Collection and analysis of ultra-dense, longitudinal observational data of child behavior in natural, ecologically valid, non-laboratory settings holds significant promise for advancing the understanding of both typical and atypical child development. To that end, we developed the *Speechome Recorder (SR)*(Figure 1), a portable version of the Speechome audio/video recording technology developed for the Human Speechome Project (HSP)[22]. Launched in 2005, the goal of the HSP was to study early language development through collection and analysis of longitudinal, ultra-dense and naturalistic recordings daily in the home of a family with a young child. A total of 14 microphones and 11 omni-directional cameras were installed throughout the house. Video was recorded with 1 megapixel resolution at 15 frames per second using cameras with fisheye lenses embedded in the ceiling. Audio was recorded at 16-bit resolution with a 48 KHz sampling rate using ceiling mounted boundary-layer microphones. Due to the unique acoustic properties of the boundary layer microphones, most speech throughout the house was captured with sufficient clarity to enable reliable transcription. Overall 230,000 hours of high fidelity, synchronized audio-video was recorded continuously for the first three years of the child's life[21], wherein approximately 2.5 million utterances have been manually transcribed to date.

The HSP captured one child's development in tremendous depth. While this corpus is illuminating in a myriad of ways, it focuses on one child of typical development, limiting tests of generalizability with other typically developing children and/or children with developmental delays. The original audio/video recording technology used in the HSP had several issues that did not lend itself to installation in other households. First, the original recording system was too expensive and complex with cameras and microphones recording every room of the house - requiring a total of 11 cameras,

14 microphones and many terabytes of storage. Second, the recording system required that modifications be made to the home, with holes cut into ceilings for installing the cameras and microphones, and over 3,000 feet of wiring. Third, the recording system was not portable as it was integrated into the house. Finally, since the recording system was installed in the house of the principal investigator, it was relatively easy to manage privacy and there was little need for remote control and upkeep of the system since engineers were free to come and go into the house to fix and replace components. The SR is our attempt at a portable version of the HSP audio/video recording technology designed to address these limitations and be suitable for remote deployment, while still allowing for naturalistic and longitudinal recordings of the same quality. As reviewed in greater detail in this paper, the SR enables swift, cost-effective, and easy-to-use deployment in multiple home settings, and is organized in the following way. The first section describes our motivation and deployment scenario for the SR. The second section reviews the SR design. The third section covers SR hardware architecture, followed by on-board software in section four. The fifth and sixth sections review privacy and data management features, respectively. The final section presents our conclusions of this work and promising future directions.

2. MOTIVATION & DEPLOYMENT

2.1 Motivation

Autism Spectrum Disorders (ASD) include autism, Asperger syndrome, and atypical autism (otherwise referred to as Pervasive Developmental Disorder Not-Otherwise-Specified)[3], and affects 1 in 88 children in the United States[4]. Criteria for diagnosing ASD rely on behavioral features since reliable biological markers have yet to be established.

Currently, ASD is not diagnosed until 3-5 years of age[10], despite a growing body of literature suggesting that behavioral abnormalities are evident in the first two years of life. While a few case studies have been carried out (e.g., [8]), parents' retrospective reports (e.g., [17]) and analyses of home videos of children later diagnosed with ASD (e.g., [2]) are the primary methods used to identify behavioral features of ASD before 24 months.

When asked about initial concerns regarding their child with ASD, at least 30-50% of parents recall abnormalities dating back to the first year, including poor eye contact[11, 12, 25], lack of response to the parents' voices or attempts to play and interact[11, 12, 17, 25], and extremes of temperament and behavior ranging from alarming passivity to marked irritability[11, 12]. Similarly, several studies of early home videos have revealed behaviors indicative of ASD in children later diagnosed compared to those of typically developing children[2, 5, 15, 18]. During the first year of life, children with ASD are distinguished by a failure to orient to name[18, 15], decreased orienting to faces[18, 15], reduced social interaction[2], absence of social smiling[2], lack of spontaneous imitation[15], lack of facial expression[2], lack of pointing/showing[18, 15], and abnormal muscle tone, posture, and movement patterns (e.g., inactive or disorganized)[2]. Taken together, these findings indicate that disruptions in social, communicative, affective, regulatory, and motor domains are evident early in autistic children's development.

Although parents' retrospective reports and home video analyses clearly point to early abnormalities in an autistic child's development, this body of research is potentially limited by a host of methodological problems (as reviewed in [28]). First, a parent's incidental observations regarding subtle social and communicative differences may be limited compared to systematic assessments by trained clinicians[23]. Second, parents' tendency to use compensatory strategies to elicit their child's best behaviors (with or without awareness) may affect their behavioral descriptions[5]. Retrospective parental reports may also suffer from distortions of recall, especially when parents are asked to remember behaviors that occurred many years earlier. For instance, having already received a diagnosis of ASD for their child, parents may over-report behaviors that are consistent with the diagnosis. Retrospective reports are also likely to include significant inaccuracies with respect to the description and perceived timing of early behavioral signs. Finally, environmental manipulations and systematic presses for specific behaviors cannot be controlled in retrospective studies.

Home video analysis has significant strengths over retrospective parental reports as it allows the observation of behaviors as they occur in familiar and natural settings, and enable objective rating of behavior by unbiased observers. However, this methodology also has potential limitations. The primary shortcoming is that parents typically record videotapes to preserve family memories rather than document their child's behavior over time. As a result, tapes from different families vary as a function of the length of time the child is visible, the activities that were recorded, and the quality of the recording. Moreover, if children do not behave as expected or desired, parents may re-record taped segments until they obtain a more favorable response. Observations from home videos also vary considerably between children and depend on the particular contexts selected for taping. Another potential problem relates to the sampling contexts of home videotapes in so much as they may not have provided sufficient opportunity for social communicative behaviors.

Innovative audio/video systems that can easily be deployed in home settings are needed to better capture, quantify, and communicate early behavioral manifestations of ASD in order to refine early detection methods, elucidate developmental trajectories and neurodevelopmental mechanisms associated with the disorder, and refer children on the spectrum to early intervention programs during critical periods of development.

2.2 Deployment

From January of 2011 to July of 2011, a total of four SRs were deployed in households in Massachusetts, Rhode Island, and Connecticut. Of the four households, three had typically developing children and one had a child diagnosed with ASD, all 2yrs of age. The purpose of the deployment was to supplement a longitudinal NIH-funded study of language development in children with ASD led by researchers at the University of Connecticut to assess language comprehension; investigate the relationships between ASD children's early language development and their later language/cognitive outcomes; and determine how more detailed measures of on-line efficiency in language comprehension might predict ASD children's individual variation. Use of the SRs in this research was undertaken to provide an ecologically-valid, densely sampled (2-3 hours per day), and extremely efficiently analyzed audio-visual corpus of each child's speech and home environment. This project is in line with recent studies of young typically developing children's motor[1] and language[16] development, which reveal that such dense sampling vastly increases sensitivity to the occurrence and non-occurrence of words/motor behaviors, thus rendering more accurately the patterns of development involved in their use. The audio from three of the households has been fully transcribed and preliminary results were presented at the International Meeting for Autism Research (IMFAR) in May of 2012[7].

In future deployments we envision deploying one SR per household. Its location will vary depending on the aims of any given study. Our current focus has been on the study of child development. For this purpose an SR is typically placed in a child's playroom, where the greatest amount of social interaction with other people can be repeatedly observed.

3. DESIGN

Given our motivation and deployment scenario, requirements for the SR design necessitated an observation system that was easy to transport, setup, install, and use without the requirement for home modifications (i.e., reduce invasiveness). The system also had to be inconspicuous and unobtrusive, without looking like a piece of "lab equipment." It was also designed to contain all necessary hardware in a modern furniture-like form factor easily adjustable for many room configurations.

Design inspiration drew from modern furniture lighting including overhead and cantilevered overhead lamps. A central base unit was chosen to house all electronics, hard drives, audio processing equipment, horizontal view camera, and touch screen controller in a secure and easy-to-access custom shelving system. A brushed stainless steel vertical boom extended from the base unit, curving slightly to meet a stainless steel curved horizontal boom that housed a vertical view camera near the middle of a room ceiling. Because of the large overhanging vertical camera boom, the system had a tendency to be unstable. As a solution, the vertical boom was designed to adjust through a manual crank system whereby one can brace the SR "head" against the ceiling, with additional adjustability for angled ceilings. The SR can be moved easily and installed in approximately 30 minutes, and once in place is very stable.

Initial designs for the SR included automated leaf-style lens cover systems to shield camera lenses during times when not recording, and a curved fiberglass base enclosure. However, to simplify the unit and cut costs, we replaced this design with a painted sheet metal cover and coverless camera lens system with an LED light indicating whether the device was recording or not. Over the course of the project, nine units were manufactured in Brooklyn, NY with custom designed parts fabricated at factories in Florida, Oregon, and New York.

4. HARDWARE ARCHITECTURE

The SR has a dual camera system, one overhead facing down and the other frontal facing horizontally. The cameras used in the recorders are "Lumenera Le165c" that transmits data over Ethernet. Both cameras are outfitted with "Fujinon FE185C057HA-1" lenses that have a 185-degree angle-of-view. This allows the overhead camera to capture most of the room from the top. The cameras are configured to record at 15 frames per second at a resolution of 960 by 960 pixels. Figure 2 shows sample downsized frames taken from the overhead and frontal cameras from one of the SRs. The resolution of the video is sufficient to identify human participants and surrounding objects. The audio sensors used in the recorders are "AKG C562CM" boundary layer microphones that use the surface in which they are embedded as a pickup. This allows a microphone placed in the head of the recorder to pick up speech in any corner of the room.

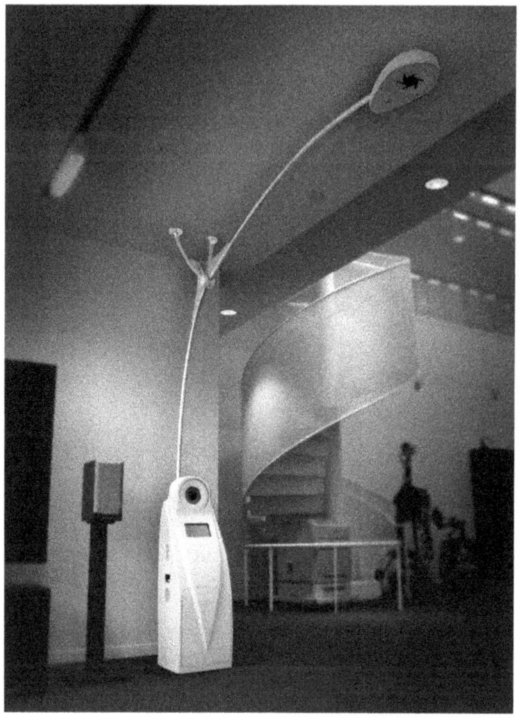

Figure 1: *The Speechome Recorder. Photo by Rony Kubat.*

To further reduce cost and invasiveness, and increase usability, the SR was designed to run for months without maintenance or technical support. The recorders were outfitted with a voltage regulator, cooling fans and UPS battery backup (allowing the recorder to run for up to 30 minutes without power). Additionally, we included an IP-Addressable power supply that allowed us to remotely turn power to any of the hardware components in the recorders on or off. Moreover, the recorders have on-board computers for data compression, and a touch display controller. Finally, the recorders have 4TB of disk storage, sufficient to hold about 60 days of continuous recordings (however, as noted in the section below, we can record continuously for much longer than 60 consecutive days using periodic remote data uploads).

5. ON-BOARD SOFTWARE

The SR employs both on-board and server-side software. For video/audio encoding we used tools developed for the HSP[9]. Other than the encoding tools, the on-board software can be divided into two categories: *Remote Upkeep* and

Figure 2: *Sample frames from the overhead and frontal cameras. Faces have been blurred in order to maintain privacy.*

User Interface.

5.1 Remote Upkeep

To enable the SR to run for months without the need for on-site visits, we wrote a comprehensive diagnostic software suite that runs on the recorders. This software automatically checks the operational status of all hardware components in a recorder and sends hourly reports to our off-site server. This, along with the ability to remotely control power with the IP-Addressable power supply, helps address possible issues at their outset (e.g., if the temperature inside a recorder is rising we can remotely shut the system down to cool it). The UPS battery backup allows the recorder to run for 30 minutes in the event of a power outage. During that 30 minutes, all data is backed up, a report is sent to our off-site server, and the recorder prepares for a clean shutdown by closing all applications and turning of non-essential hardware components. When the power comes back on, the recorder automatically starts itself and becomes fully operational in a matter of minutes.

To eliminate the need for swapping hard drives, data is transmitted over Internet to our servers during periods of inactivity (i.e., when the recorder is not being used). In this way, new data can be recorded over old data, ensuring that the 4TB disk storage in the recorders never get full, thus removing the need for manual drive replacement. Additionally, since data is transmitted daily to our server, researchers with appropriate permissions can access newly acquired data with only a few days delay.

5.2 User Interface

Figure 3 shows the user interface on the SR. The user interface on the touch screen controller was designed to be very simple, containing the following:

- *On/Off*: The top red button, marked with a camera icon, is the video-audio recording *"on/off"* button. It allows the user to turn recording on or off (the device itself is always on). The button turns green when recording and red when not recording.

- *Consent*: The left most button at the bottom, marked with a check mark, is the *"consent"* button. This button uses the front facing camera to take a picture of the person who is consenting to be recorded. The picture is sent to our off-site server and then used by an auditing officer to verify that only people who have consented have been recorded. This data auditing process is explained in detail in the *Privacy Management* section below.

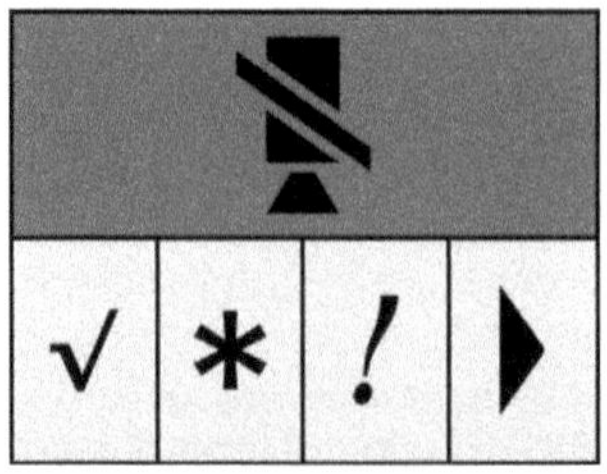

Figure 3: *User Interface of the Speechome Recorder.*

- *Ooh*: The second button from the left, marked with a star, is the *"ooh"* button. This button allows the user to event mark (i.e., create a time stamp in the video and audio record) recently recorded material, thus enabling researchers and/or the family to easily access interesting footage/data.

- *Oops*: The third button from the left, marked with an exclamation mark, is the *"oops"* button. This button allows the user to mark any recently recorded segment for deletion(e.g., in case something embarrassing was mistakenly recorded). Any segment marked in this way is automatically deleted without being seen by anyone else.

- *Playback*: The last button, marked with a play icon, is the *"playback"* button. This button allows the user to playback and review any recorded data using the recorder's screen. Figure 4 shows the playback interface. The calendar on the right highlights days when data was recorded. Once a day is selected, the user can playback clips from that day using the movie player on the left. The user can also switch between overhead and frontal cameras. If the user wishes to share any of the clips with others they grant permission, they can select the "Share this clip" button to mark the clip. As we will describe in the *Data Management* section, users have access to a website that allows them to view and download their clips.

6. PRIVACY MANAGEMENT

Privacy management was a very important factor in our design of the SR. With the HSP, the principal investigator and his family was the focus of recording, this is not true of SRs. The "oops" button on the recorders described earlier was borrowed from the HSP to allow for local control of the data by the users. The button opens a dialog box that allows users to specify any number of minutes of recorded data and retroactively and permanently delete it from disk (both local and server-side).

More importantly however, we needed to make sure not to record anyone who did not consent to be recorded. When a recorder was installed, parents signed consent forms for themselves and their children. Moreover, consent was also obtained from frequently visiting grandparents, therapists, and friends. Using the "consent" button on the recorders,

Figure 4: *The playback interface of the Speechome Recorder. Faces have been blurred in order to maintain privacy.*

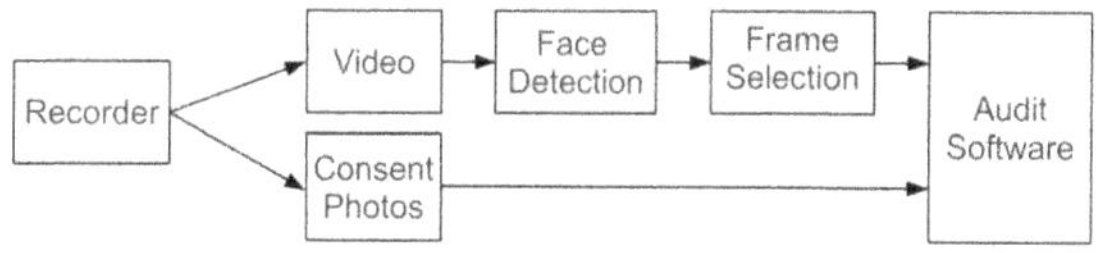

Figure 5: *Data processing pipeline for the auditing software.*

Figure 6: *Data auditing software for the Speechome Recorder. Faces have been blurred in order to maintain privacy.*

pictures were taken of all consented participants. In order to make sure no unconsented individuals were recorded, an independent *data-auditor* was hired to review captured data on a weekly basis. The job of the data-auditor was to go over all data recorded that week for each of the households and check people in the video against pictures of consented individuals in that household.

However, due to the large amount of data recorded every week, it was impractical to have the data-auditor manually inspect all videos in full. To overcome this problem we developed a semi-automated auditing system that allowed the data-auditor to efficiently review collected data.

Figure 5 shows the processing pipeline of our semi-automated auditing system. The system works by first running the video data through an automatic face detection algorithm, using frontal camera video. This face detection system uses OpenCV's[6] automatic face detection algorithm and is trained on sample faces from different angles (front, profile, etc). The algorithm detects frames in which there is at least one human face. Our system then randomly picks one of these frames for every 15 seconds of recorded video, with the assumption that the recording of any one person would be at least 15 seconds in length. These frames, along with the consent pictures, were then passed to our auditing software to be used by the data-auditor.

Figure 6 shows the auditing software. The numbered buttons on the top allow the data-auditor to select between SRs in different households. Once a recorder is selected, frames detected by our automated system are shown (the left image in Figure 6) alongside a list of pictures of consented people from that household (the image scroll-panel on the right side in Figure 6). The data-auditor can then compare the faces in the frames to the consent pictures. If a face is not found in the consent pictures, the auditor can use the giant red "X" button to mark that picture. When completed, a report is sent to the researchers about all marked images. If a non-consented person was identified, we could either try to get the person's consent or, if that fails, delete all recorded data where that person is present. These audits were performed once a week on all data. Over our six months of deployment recording, auditing revealed no instances of errors in which recordings were made of unconsented individuals.

7. DATA MANAGEMENT

A SR generates a large database of multimedia content. In this section we describe how we manage and process this massive dataset. As mentioned earlier, when the recorders are inactive (i.e., not being used) data is transmitted over Internet to our servers. The data transmitted is lossless compressed video and raw audio, both time stamped and time-aligned. Once the data reaches our servers it is immediately backed up on multiple drives. After that, the raw data goes through various pipelines described below.

7.1 Data Processing

Before any data processing is undertaken it goes through the auditing process described earlier. After privacy auditing, the audio is processed and transcribed. Figure 7 shows the complete audio processing pipeline. The audio is first passed through a noise reduction filter using the "Audacity" speech processing toolkit[24]. Next, the audio is passed to an automated speech detection system (which uses a boosted decision tree classifier[20]) that categorizes the audio into speech and non-speech segments. The speech segments are then passed through an automated speaker identification system[20] (trained on the dataset) to identify the speakers in each speech segment. The speech segments are also passed to a state-of-the-art, semi-automatic transcription

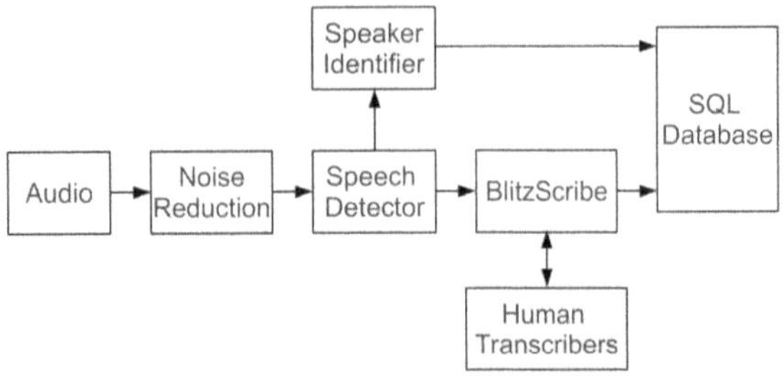

Figure 7: *Audio processing pipeline.*

Figure 9: *The Speechome Recorder movie player. The player shows the video feed from the top and front cameras. Users can search for and play videos from specific dates and times. Faces have been blurred in order to maintain privacy.*

tool called *BlitzScribe*[1][20] prior to manual transcription. The transcriptions along with the speaker identifiers and time-stamps are saved in a central SQL database.

Next, the raw data from the three channels (audio, front-view video, top-view video) are time aligned and converted to a standard mpeg movie format (keeping the raw data). The movie is then time-aligned with the transcriptions. Since data collected by an SR are recorded using the same technology as the HSP, many of the visualization tools developed for that project, such as *TotalRecall*[2][13] can also be used for SR recorded data.

7.2 Data Access

Three primary groups of people access data captured by a SR: engineers who maintain the system; families who have recorders installed in their homes; and scientists who analyze collected data. In order to facilitate data access to these parties we created a secure, password protected website that serves as a front-end user tool. Figure 8 shows a simplified overview of the data pipeline from the recorders all the way to the end users: the families, engineers, and scientists. Below we describe what type of data each of these groups accessed.

7.2.1 Families

One of the motivations for families to participate in this project was to have access to all data they recorded with the SR. In order to facilitate that, all the raw audio and video collected was converted to an mpeg movie format and uploaded to a movie player on our secure website for family access. Figure 9 shows a screenshot of the movie player. The player comes with an interface that allows families to lookup videos based on days and times they were recorded. All the recordings, including clips selected for sharing, could be viewed using this movie player. The families also had the option of saving any of the video segments to their local drives.

7.2.2 Engineers

The engineers involved in this project needed to have access to data to maintain the recorders and servers. The video player described above allowed the engineers to review the quality of audio and video feeds (e.g., to see if lenses are focused) and make sure they are time-aligned. Moreover, the engineers received nightly reports from the recorders on their operational state (as described earlier in the *Remote Upkeep* section). These reports included information on different operational aspects of the recorders, such as the amount of data recorded that day, the average temperature of the recorders, the status of different hardware parts in the recorders, and more.

7.2.3 Scientists

As mentioned previously, the main goal of the SR project was to record longitudinal and naturalistic data to study child language development and developmental disorders. Other than being able to watch the recordings using the movie player, researchers analyzing the data could read the transcripts associated with the video they were viewing (Figure 10). The transcripts were displayed in a format compatible with CLAN[14], a standard analysis tool used by child language researchers. Moreover, the researchers could automatically divide the recordings into continuous segments of recorded data showing one or more activities (e.g. play time, therapy sessions, etc). In addition to being able to search the recordings by date and time, the researchers could also search for clips containing particular words or phrases (e.g. all instances of the word "water").

Additionally, researchers had access to weekly transcription reports to assess transcript progress and generate various language statistics. Moreover, the researchers had access to usage data reports (Figure 11) that allowed them to monitor the use of the recorders and, if needed, to encourage families to use the recorders more or differently, and to address any questions. It is also worth noting that due to our mostly automated processing pipeline, it took on average two days for any recorded data to go through the pipeline and for all information to be available on the website (excluding transcriptions) for viewing.

8. CONCLUSIONS

The main contributions of the SR are addressing privacy management issues and reducing cost, complexity, and invasiveness of naturalistic longitudinal recordings to facilitate swift, cost-effective deployment in home settings. With

[1]BlitzScribe is a tool for manual speech transcription that is up to six times faster than other available transcription methods[20].

[2]TotalRecall is an audio-video browser and annotation system. It provides a global view of the corpus indicating when and where recordings were made. The system also supports limited types of speech transcription and video annotation.

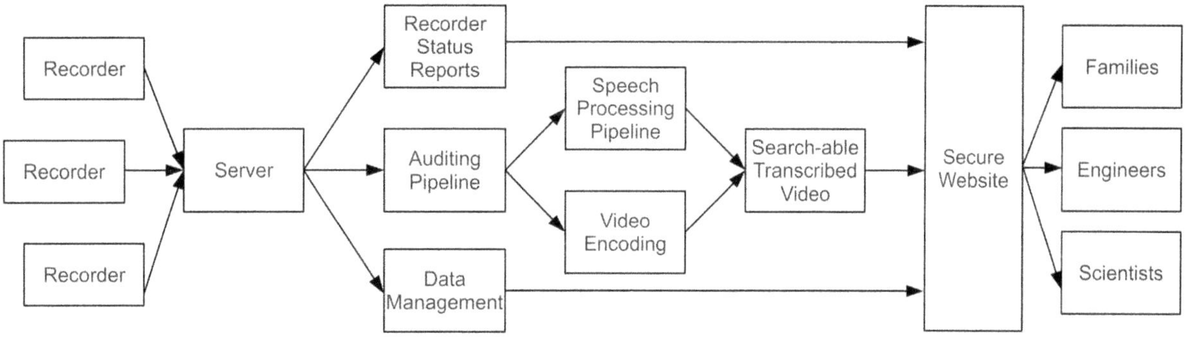

Figure 8: *A simplified overview of the data pipeline from the "field"(households) all the way to the end users: families, engineers and scientists.*

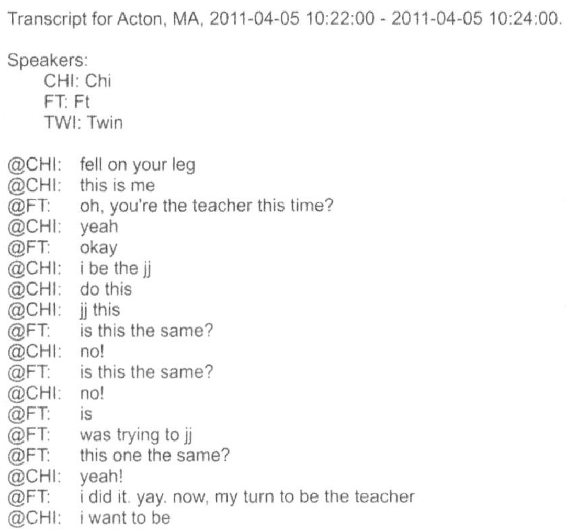
Transcript for Acton, MA, 2011-04-05 10:22:00 - 2011-04-05 10:24:00.

Speakers:
CHI: Chi
FT: Ft
TWI: Twin

@CHI: fell on your leg
@CHI: this is me
@FT: oh, you're the teacher this time?
@CHI: yeah
@FT: okay
@CHI: i be the jj
@CHI: do this
@CHI: jj this
@FT: is this the same?
@CHI: no!
@FT: is this the same?
@CHI: no!
@FT: is
@FT: was trying to jj
@FT: this one the same?
@CHI: yeah!
@FT: i did it. yay. now, my turn to be the teacher
@CHI: i want to be

Figure 10: *Sample transcribed session. Some information has been modified in order to maintain privacy.*

Figure 11: *Sample data report from one recorder. Each row represents a month and each column represent a day in the month. Green blocks mark the times when the Speechome Recorder was being used.*

the help of the SR, ultra-dense, longitudinal studies of child development can now be scaled to include multiple households and participants, allowing for generalization of findings between multiple children and developmental comparisons across clinical and non-clinical populations. Moreover, the recording, processing, and visualization pipelines enabled by this technology allow for data to be transferred from the "field" (i.e., households) and processed and analyzed by researchers with unprecedented speed.

With rapid advancements in video capture, processing, and storage capabilities currently underway, the SR can be further enhanced to reduce size, cost, and complexity. Also, in the future, the SR could be modified to receive additional data streams from wireless, wearable physiological sensors that may shed light on internal biological processes involved in speech and behavioral development observed in audio and video channels. Finally, future work could explore the use of the SR to facilitate real-time tele-consultation applications, bridging families in the home with allied health professionals at a distance.

On a final note, building the SR commenced a few years ago. The focus of the project was to develop engineering, privacy, and data access management methods for making ultra-dense, longitudinal recordings in multiple home settings. However, with rapid advancements in technology, any such recording technology will not be practical from an engineering point of view for more than a few years. Future recording technologies will likely be as small as a light bulb, require little to no installation and cost very little. However, the scientific practicality of this project is independent of its engineering practicality. The scientific approach employed in this project opens a new door of data analytics on a scale not seen before, and is already producing interesting research results using similarly obtained datasets[27, 19, 26].

9. ACKNOWLEDGMENTS

We would like to thank all the families who participated in this work. We also thank Joe Wood for help installing the recorders; Philip DeCamp, Rony Kubat, Matt Miller, Brandon Roy, and George Shaw for help with various technical aspects of the project; and Prof. Letitia Naigles and Devin Rubin for help recruiting families to be recorded.

This work was generously funded by grants from NIH (R01 2DC007428) and the Nancy Lurie Marks Family Foundation.

10. REFERENCES

[1] K. E. Adolph. *Encyclopedia of Infant and Early Childhood Development*, chapter Motor/Physical Development: Locomotion. San Diego, CA: Academic Press., 2008.

[2] J. L. Adrien, C. Bathelemy, A. Perrot, S. Roux, P. Lenoir, L. Hameury, and D. Sauvage. Validity and reliability of the infant behavioral summarized evaluation (IBSE): A rating scale for the assessment of young children with autism and developmental disorders. *Journal of Autism and Developmental Disorders*, 22:375–395, 1992.

[3] A. P. Association. *Diagnostic and statistical manual of mental disorders (4th ed.)*. Washington, D.C: APA, 1994.

[4] J. Baio. Prevalence of autism spectrum disorders: autism and developmental disabilities monitoring network, 14 sites, United States, 2008. *Surveillance Summaries*, 61 (SS03):1–19, 2012.

[5] G. Baranek. Autism during infancy: A retrospective video analysis of sensory-motor and social behaviors at 9-12 months of age. *Journal of Autism and Developmental Disorders*, 29:213–224, 1999.

[6] G. Bradski. The OpenCV Library. *Dr. Dobb's Journal of Software Tools*, 2000.

[7] I. Chin, D. Rubin, A. Tovar, S. Vosoughi, M. Cheng, E. Potrzeba, M. Goodwin, D. Roy, and L. Naigle. Dense recordings of naturalistic interactions reveal both typical and atypical speech in one child with asd. In *Proceedings of the International Meeting for Autism Research*, Toronto, Canada, (2012, in press).

[8] G. Dawson, J. Osterling, A. N. Meltzoff, and P. Kuhl. Case study of the development of an infant with autism from birth to two years of age. *Journal of Applied Developmental Psychology*, 21:299–313, 2000.

[9] P. DeCamp. Headlock: Wide-range head pose estimation for low resolution video. MIT M.Sc. thesis, 2007.

[10] P. Filipek, P. Accardo, G. Baranek, E. Cook, G. Dawson, B. Gordon, J. Gravel, C. Johnson, R. Kallen, S. Levy, N. Minshew, B. Prizant, I. Rapin, S. Rogers, W. Stone, S. Teplin, R. Tuchman, and F. Volkmar. The screening and diagnosis of autistic spectrum disorders. *Journal of Autism and Developmental Disorders*, 29:439–484, 1999.

[11] C. Gillberg, S. Ehlers, H. Schaumann, G. Jakobsson, S. O. Dahlgren, R. Lindblom, A. Bagenholm, T. Tjuus, and E. Blinder. Autism under age 3 years: A clinical study of 28 cases referred for autistic symptoms in infancy. *Journal of Child Psychology and Psychiatry*, 31:921–934, 1990.

[12] Y. Hoshino, M. Kaneko, Y. Yashima, H. Kumashiro, F. R. Volkmar, and D. J. Cohen. Clinical features of autistic children with setback course in their infancy. *Japanese Journal of Psychiatry & Neurology*, 41:237–245, 1987.

[13] R. Kubat, P. DeCamp, B. Roy, and D. Roy. Totalrecall: Visualization and semi-automatic annotation of very large audio-visual corpora. In *Ninth International Conference on Multimodal Interfaces*, 2007.

[14] B. MacWhinney. The childes project: Tools for analyzing talk. Lawrence Erlbaum Associates, Mahwah, NJ, 3rd edition, 2000.

[15] A. E. Mars, J. E. Mauk, and P. W. Dowrick. Symptoms of pervasive developmental disorders as observed in prediagnostic home videos of infants and toddlers. *Journal of Pediatrics*, 132:500–504, 1998.

[16] L. R. Naigles, E. Hoff, and D. Vear. Flexibility in early verb use: Evidence from a multiple-n diary study. *Monographs for the Society for Research in Child Development*, 74, 2009.

[17] M. Ohta, Y. Nagai, H. Hara, and M. Sasaki. Parental perception of behavioral symptoms in Japanese autistic children. *Journal of Autism and Developmental Disorders*, 17:549–563, 1987.

[18] J. Osterling and G. Dawson. Early recognition of children with autism: A study of the first birthday home videotapes. *Journal of Autism and Developmental Disorders*, 24:247–257, 1994.

[19] B. C. Roy, M. C. Frank, and D. Roy. Relating activity contexts to early word learning in dense longitudinal data. In *Proceedings of the 34th Annual Cognitive Science Conference*, 2012.

[20] B. C. Roy and D. Roy. Fast transcription of unstructured audio recordings. In *Proceedings of Interspeech*, Brighton, England, 2009.

[21] D. Roy. New Horizons in the Study of Child Language Acquisition. In *Proceedings of Interspeech 2009*, Brighton, England, 2009.

[22] D. Roy, R. Patel, P. DeCamp, R. Kubat, M. Fleischman, B. Roy, N. Mavridis, S. Tellex, A. Salata, J. Guinness, M. Levit, and P. Gorniak. The Human Speechome Project. In *Proceedings of the 28th Annual Cognitive Science Conference*, pages 2059–2064, Mahwah, NJ, 2006. Lawrence Earlbaum.

[23] W. L. Stone, E. L. Hoffman, S. E. Lewis, and O. Y. Ousley. Early recognition of autism: Parental reports vs. *clinical observation. Archives of Pediatrics and Adolescent Medicine*, 148:174–179, 1994.

[24] A. Team. Audacity (version 1.3.4-beta) [computer program]. http://audacity.sourceforge.net/, 2008.

[25] F. R. Volkmar, D. M. Stier, and D. J. Cohen. Age of recognition of pervasive developmental disorder. *American Journal of Psychiatry*, 142:1450–1452, 1985.

[26] S. Vosoughi. Interactions of caregiver speech and early word learning in the speechome corpus: Computational explorations. MIT M.Sc. thesis, 2010.

[27] S. Vosoughi, B. C. Roy, M. C. Frank, and D. Roy. Contributions of Prosodic and Distributional Features of Caregivers' Speech in Early Word Learning. In *Proceedings of the 32nd Annual Cognitive Science Conference*, 2010.

[28] L. Zwaigenbaum, A. Thurm, W. Stone, G. Baranek, S. Bryson, J. Iverson, A. Kau, A. Klin, C. Lord., R. Landa, S. Rogers, and M. Sigman. Studying the emergence of autism spectrum disorders in high-risk infants: Methodological and practical issues. *Journal of Autism and Developmental Disorders*, 37:466–480, 2007.

Integrating PAMOCAT in the Research Cycle: Linking Motion Capturing and Conversation Analysis

Bernhard Brüning
CITEC Central Lab
University of Bielefeld
Germany 33615 Bielefeld
+49 521 106-67258
bbruening@uni-bielefeld.de

Christian Schnier
Applied Informatics Group
University of Bielefeld
Germany 33615 Bielefeld
+49 521 106-12230
cschnier@uni-bielefeld.de

Karola Pitsch
Applied Informatics Group
University of Bielefeld
Germany 33615 Bielefeld
+49 521 106-12240
karola.pitsch@uni-bielefeld.de

Sven Wachsmuth
CITEC Central Lab
University of Bielefeld
Germany 33615 Bielefeld
+49 521 106-2937
swachsmu@techfak.uni-bielefeld.de

ABSTRACT

In order to understand and model the non-verbal communicative conduct of humans, it seems fruitful to combine qualitative (Conversation Analysis [6] [10] [11]) and quantitative analytical (motion capturing) methods. Tools for data visualization and annotation are important as they constitute a central interface between different research approaches and methodologies. With this aim we have developed the pre-annotation tool "PAMOCAT – Pre Annotation Motion Capture Analysis Tool" that detects different phenomena. These phenomena are in the category single person and person overlapping phenomena. Included are functions for the analysis of head focused objects, hand activities, single DOF- degree of freedom activity, posture detection and intrusions into the co-participant's space. These detected phenomena related to the frames will be displayed in an overview. The phenomena can be chosen to search for a specific constellation between these different phenomena. A sophisticated user interface easily allows the annotating person to find correlations between different joints and phenomena, to analyze the corresponding 3D pose in a reconstructed virtual environment, and to export combined qualitative and quantitative annotations to standard annotation tools. Using this technique we are able to examine complex setups with three participants engaged in conversation. In this paper we propose how PAMOCAT can be integrated in the research cycle by showing a concrete PAMOCAT-based micro-analysis of a multimodal phenomenon, which deals with kinetic procedures to claim the floor.

Categories and Subject Descriptors

Multimodal Corpora Analysis Tool

General Terms: Human Factors, Languages, Theory, Verification.

Keywords: Motion Capturing, annotation, motion analysis.

1. INTRODUCTION

Despite important progress in the field of human-robot and human-agent interaction, robotic communication skills are still far from the smoothness of the social behavior of humans in natural conversation. In order to build more appropriate interaction models both – human-human and human-robot interaction scenarios – it is necessary to be analyzed and understood in detail, so that results can be fed back into the model. To do so, researchers began to link qualitative sequential analysis of videotaped interaction data with quantitative approaches based on Motion Capture data. Then an in-depth understanding of interactional procedures could be combined with quantifiable three-dimensional measures of body motions [1]. In order to carry out such combined analyzes, not only conceptual issues need to be discussed but also novel tools for supporting the visualization and analysis of the different types of data are required. Existing annotation software, such as ELAN [2] or Anvil [3], has recently started to integrate facilities for displaying time series data. These tools allow linking text annotations with segments of digital media files. ELAN is specialized on Audio and Video media data and provides forms of automatic annotation, especially for audio signals. Anvil is additionally able to display the motion capture data of a single person. It has an axes plot for the position, velocity, and acceleration. Besides this last, it has advanced trajectory visualization, via the color of related annotations and an illustration of the speed. However, Anvil, in the current version, lacks the ability to handle data from multiple participants and it only offers limited support for motion analysis. Our pre-annotation tool PAMOCAT [7] addresses these gaps: It is able to deal with data from multiple participants to show their skeletons and corresponding motion and to highlight different kinds of single person and person overlapping phenomena. Based on research that has shown the importance of body movements for turn-taking [6] [5] [12] [13] and, in particular, for the precise localization of pre-initial turn pointing gestures in the local environment [4], we investigate in this paper a first attempt to find such interactional relevant body postures and phenomena (single DOF, global activity, gazing at, oriented at each other, intruding into others user space). With the included search mechanisms you get the possibility to find all specific situations, when different phenomena and the combination of them occur, faster. In particular, it allows both to visualize and analyze Motion Capture data, and to export automatically generated annotations to annotation software such as ELAN. In the first part we will introduce PAMOCAT and in the second we will show the direct integration of PAMOCAT into the research cycle.

ICMI'12, October 22–26, 2012, Santa Monica, California, USA.

2. PAMOCAT

PAMOCAT was developed for the analysis of the so called "Obersee" [1] corpus. The main features and benefits are:

2.1 Visualization of data

The main visualization features of PAMOCAT include "free viewing position", "multiple skeleton visualization in relation to each other", "skeleton to marker", "trajectories with speed", "synchronous inspection of all recorded videos", "plot of angle, speed, and acceleration", "single DOF activity", and "motion in relation to a virtual environment".

2.2 Analysis of data

The most important features are in the field of motion analysis and represent different phenomena; these can be combined to a search for constellations of phenomena. First we will take a look at the single person phenomena and later at the person overlapping phenomena.

2.2.1 Single DOF motion activity analysis

It is useful to inspect the point in time when activity at a specific DOF of the skeleton occurs. First of all we will show how key-intervals can be calculated from motion capture data. These key-intervals represent the motion activity for each DOF and could be calculated through motion decomposition. The motion capture data coming from the tracking system with global position and orientation were transformed into a local skeleton representation. This local motion of the entire skeleton gets decomposed into key-intervals (joint activity intervals). A key interval belongs to one single DOF of a joint. It consists of a starting time, a length, a starting angle, and an ending angle. In the case of the upper body, the skeleton has 24 DOF (full body 41 DOF). Each single DOF is individually analyzed, with regard to speed and acceleration, to reduce the values that have to be compared by the motion analysis (for example, not all values of a shoulder joint with 3 DOF have to be compared when only one DOF is an active key-interval). Behind the concept of key-interval is the idea that in case there is a similar speed over a number of frames, the angle information could be stored in a single key-interval only once. The figure 1 shows an arm movement from a starting to an ending time during an angle change. The movement of the

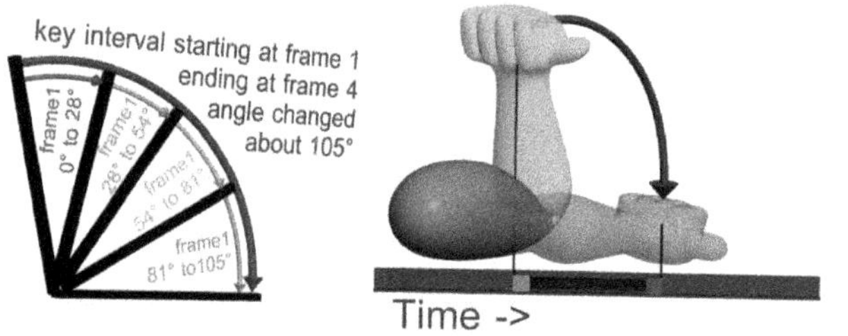

Figure 1 (a) A key-interval saves the same information of four frames when the speed is similar, (b) key intervals activity

arm in the figure can be decomposed to one single key-interval. Normally, the speed at the beginning rises slowly, reaches a maximum, and then decreases again. These maximums are interesting information for the annotator, so that the human motion can be decomposed into more than only one key-interval. These motions are then saved as the key animation often used in animation movies. The result is a compressed motion, which means that the important and interesting information of the motion have been extracted. In the case that the annotator is searching for activity at, e.g., a single joint, he can easily select the particular joint. The selected joint gets highlighted through a blue transparent line (cf. figure 2a: the line goes from the left to the right) and it is possible to scroll with the time shift slider or a next button, swiftly, to all the frames with activity. The annotator then can swiftly find the key-interval of interest containing the relevant information of activity for each joint. The key-intervals represent joint activity to an extrema in the speed (cf. figure 2b), and from an extrema to no joint activity. Back to the example of the head orientation, it changes from the basic position and moves to the right side, and the software decomposes the motion into two key-intervals (one to the extrema and one to the end). For a detailed analysis of performed gestures (e.g. a pointing gesture), the tool shows the sequences of each DOF enabling the understanding of the activity of every joint of the entire skeleton. There is a detailed view of the time when certain DOF is active, maybe, in combination with other DOF. It could be seen as a hierarchical (skeleton) description of the whole movement decomposed into sub movements down to the level of single DOFs.

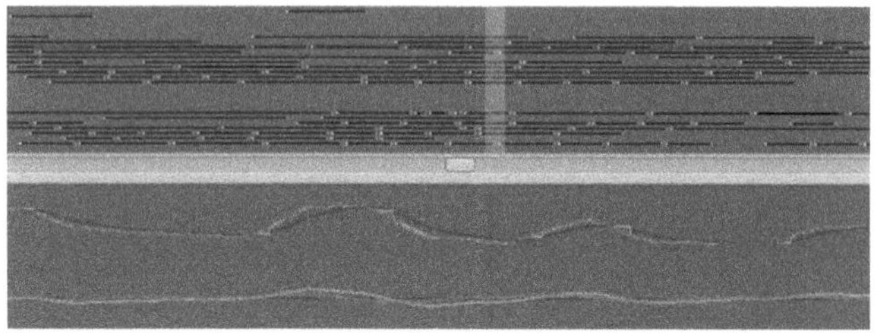

Figure 2 (a) Key-interval overview with the DOF vertical and the time horizontal (b) below this is the additional plot of the selected joint with angle, speed and acceleration.

2.2.2 Posture learning and retrieval

Posture retrieval is a frequent operation in data annotation and analysis. By looking at points in time where a posture reappears, it can be examined in which situations a gesture or posture is used, how many participants reacted with the same gesture, or what different meanings special gestures could have. This procedure builds an enormously advantage for the analytical work of Conversation Analysts: (i) The operation saves a lot of time so that it is easier to verify findings on a broader corpus. (ii) The detection of one particular posture is more precise because the integrated search mechanisms of PAMOCAT allow fixing the key characteristics of one particular posture. Therefore, the user marks a specific posture in the corpus data and automatically retrieves other points in time with similar postures that get highlighted with separated colors [7] (cf. figure 2). Therefore, in an annotation area, there are different annotation lines: each posture has, for each person, a different annotation line which gets highlighted when it is detected (RightArmPointingPerson1 ...).

2.2.3 Global activity

Sometimes it is not of interest which DOF is active and moves a bit; but only what kind of effect it has on a limb in the global environment. For example, two or more DOF of the complete arm could be pure compensation-remains of the hand´s movement. Another case of minor priority could be that the hand moves only a little bit around a particular position. The detection of global activity is an observation from a variable; if it reaches a speed limit it will label it as global activity. Depending on the participants, it would be difficult to detect a pointing gesture based only on a static (single moment) posture. In analysis of the records of our corpus, "Obersee" [1], we found out, that some participants rested their hand very close on the table after a pointing gesture. The result was that the posture detector recognized a pointing gesture in the case in which human beings see that there is no action. A solution to distinguish between these two cases is to use additionally a dynamic algorithm in part represented through the global activity. In a pointing gesture the hand does not move during pointing for a short time before it has retracted. We use two parameters for the calculation of the activity. The first is the minimum speed of the activity and the second is the break time during which a gesture with the hand maybe kept still before it continues.

2.2.4 Home positions

The home positions are the positions in which the hands are when they rest. A hand can have different home position during a record. In the case a limb is not in global activity, it will be at one of his home positions. The calculation of the home positions is very close to the global activity, we use three parameters. The first two are both to calculate the global activity. The third one is the interaction radius. In the case that a new position is "not global active" (labeled at a time point) and is close to an already existing home position, it will be integrated in the mean value calculation of this home position. If it is not close at an existing h. position, a new home position would be found.

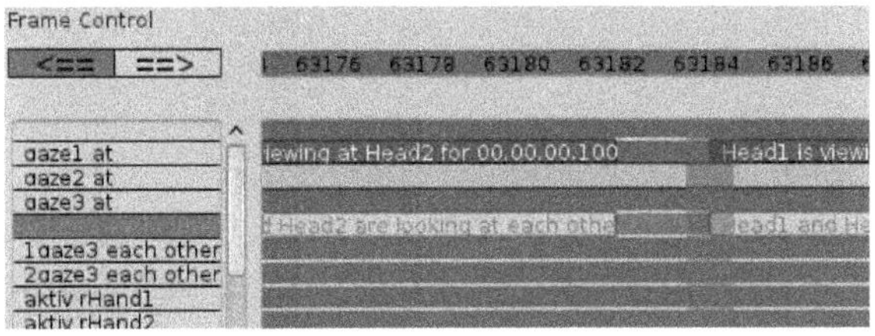

Figure 3 Searching for special phenomena constellations.

2.2.5 Intrusion into the personal space

During a conversation, one procedure to take the floor is by pointing to the user space of another participant. To detect this, we need, to calculate the user space of each participant, the fore we use a cylindrical volume with a height equal to the human body height. The radius of it is the length from the user´s body center to the hand (center to shoulder, shoulder to elbow and elbow to hand distance added together). To make the user space more sensible or inure to intrusion of other users, the radius can be manually changed afterwards. The calculation of detection of the intrusion into the personal space of another participant is a calculation of distance from all persons center to all other hand positions.

2.2.6 Participants oriented to

With the combination of the virtually represented skeletons and the virtually added environment, we are able to automatically annotate who is oriented at which object. This could be a part of the body or a part of the environment. Then we can automatically annotate the information related with at what time and for how long the participants were orientated at the objects. In the motion capture view with the virtual environment, the viewing direction of each participant is visualized by a ray with an offset to the head rigid body (pattern of 5 single markers [1]). The geometrical intersection object with this ray (or in the view of the participants) gets highlighted through a box of the same color as the gazing participant. Alternatively, the detection could be done with the cone but because of variations in the view area of the eyes (additionally there are vertical and horizontal angles variants), it seems to be more realistic and easy to use a ray. To analyze the conversation in detail it is important to know when the participants orient to each other. For example – only based on the motion capture data – we can be sure that in the case when two of three participants are oriented at the third, the third person is the active person. In the case where two participants are oriented to each other, they are, probably, having a close and deep conversation. In multi user conversations, the participants are not only focusing their heads on each other, they are, additionally using their eyes. To have a greater potential to highlight these situations, we add a virtual sphere (user can adjust the radius) around the heads of the tracked participants. This sphere represents a much bigger volume of the head, with which the view ray of another participant could intersect. The variation of the head size makes the algorithms more or less sensible, as it is wanted. Of course, there is some kind of error introduced into the results when the head is made bigger as it was, but for this analysis it is enormously helpful to search for possible situations where they were "oriented at each other". This can easily be checked through a short look at the automatically annotated time point "is oriented at" in the synchronized motion capture data and the multi video visualization.

2.2.7 Constellations of different phenomena

The annotation area is separated into several annotation lines that have different meanings in each analysis mode. The first mode is the key-interval annotation mode with the overview of all single degrees of freedom of the skeleton. It is concentrated in the time when the joints are active in relation to other joints. The second mode is the phenomenon annotation overview (cf. figure 3), in which different phenomena like "postures of the skeleton", "oriented at", "oriented at each other", "hand activity", "intrusion into other user space", "all gazing at table" can be arranged as constellations. These phenomena could be categorized into single participant, participants overlapping, static, or dynamic. In order to easily search for constellations of these phenomena, we can select different phenomena for the constellation of interest, browse through all the found ones, and watch them near in detail on all visualization widgets (multiple video view, motion capture view, angle plots, skeleton activity overview, and phenomena/annotation overview).

2.3 GUI Overview

These features from the previous section are combined in the Graphical User Interface - GUI. The main window shows the 3D visualization from the recorded participants (cf. figure 4d) with additionally loaded 3D objects defining reference points for the recorded interactions. In this way, the motion can be analyzed in relation to the virtual environment with free control of the viewing position. The key-interval-over-view-widget (figure 4b) gives an overview of all DOF from all joints of a selected person, which shows the motion activity for each joint separately. One key-interval is represented by a horizontal line with a green point at the beginning and a red point at its end (cf. figure 4b). Below this widget there is an optional plot (if this option is selected) of the corresponding angle, speed, and acceleration (go back to figure 2). With a plot and a decimal display of the angle, speed, and acceleration all related information's become available for the selected joints. A synchronized view of all recorded videos completes the screen (figure 4a). At the bottom is a slider that allows the user to scroll in time (figure 4h) and the annotation widget (figure 4f) allows manually adding information or editing the automatically generated or previously added information.

2.4 Support and exchange of data

The idea of this development was to create a tool that could be helpful to as many researchers as possible. We directed the development of the tool to be widely flexible for exchange of data. PAMOCAT, as we already said, is a **pre** annotation tool

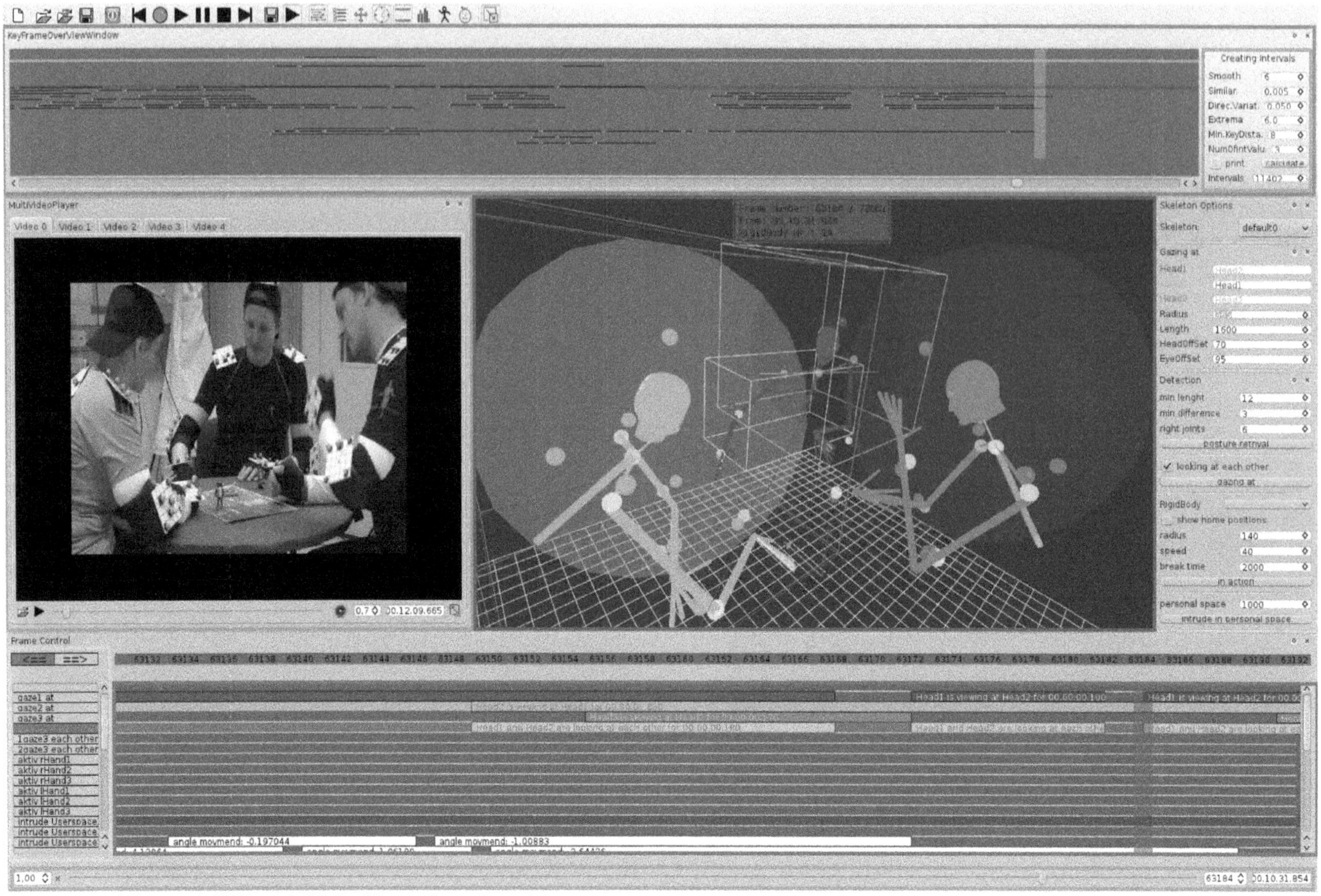

Figure 4 GUI with VideoPlayerFunctions (a), KeyIntervalOverViewWidget (b), MoCapView (d), Annotation Widget (e), KeyIntervalCalculationParameters (f), Time Slider (h), SearchSurfWidgets (i).

with many abilities on the field of motion capturing analysis but in contrast to ANVIL and ELAN, it has not so many abilities on video and audio signal analysis. This is why it has an import and export functionality to ELAN.

2.5 Comparison to common annotation tools

We compare the features of PAMOCAT with the common annotation tools. The symbols have the meaning "x" = included, "-" = not and "/" = separator.

Table 1 Comparison with ANVIL and ELAN

Features description	PAMOCAT	ANVIL	ELAN
Motion Capture visual-ization/ multiperson	x/x	x/-	-/-
Manual Annotation area	simple	x	x
Functionality for automatic audio annotation	-	-	x
Multi-video annotation/ Multi-camera synchro.	x/x	x/x	x/-
auto. motion detection/ posture/ oriented to/ orien. to each other/ activity body part /intrude into other userspace	x/x/ x/x/ x/x	-/-/ -/-/ -/-	-/-/ -/-/ -/-
constellation of phenomena	x	-	-

3. FROM VIDEO ANALYSIS TO MOTION CAPTURING

In order to motivate our approach and the development of our tool, we begin with a short fragment of human-human interaction. We will reveal, on the one hand, analytical issues that arise when carrying out in-depth manual analysis of the participants' interactional practices and show on the other hand the limitations of a video-based approach and how a corpus of combined video and motion capture data could help to overcome these limits. Let us consider the following short fragment, in which three participants in a semi-experimental setup are seated around a table and were asked to jointly plan a local recreation area while manipulating a range of objects [1] [4]. Here, our analytical interest focuses on one particular aspect of the interactional organization: multimodal aspects of turn-taking and kinetic procedures about how to take the floor in multiparty conversations. Empirical investigation of similar situations has revealed that participants systematically use pointing gestures to objects in the local environment in order to announce and establish themselves as possible next speaker. Mondada [5] states that „[...] pointing gestures are precisely timed, being synchronized with the moment-by-moment organization of talk-in-interaction, with recipient oriented talk and bodily conducts, with appropriate arrangements of bodies and objects [...]". Participants, who attempt to take the turn and position themselves as next speaker tend to bodily claim the floor before even starting to talk, and use as a systematic procedure „pre-initial turn pointing"[5]. Taking these findings further, we have been able to show that the precise localization of such pointing gestures in the interaction space matters [4]. The following fragment sheds some light on this phenomenon and reveals that a precise knowledge about hand positions, arm positions and body alignment of the participants is of particular importance:

Fragment1:

```
01 A:      |JA dann würden sie das ja noch verSCHLIMMERN|
                (YES then you would even worsen it)
   B-act:                                         |pG(RH)|
   A-gaz: |......................@C....................|
   C-gaz: |......................@A....................|
   A-C:   |..............aligned posture...............|
                                                      *1
  02 B-act: |......................pG(RH)..................|
     B:               |dann bauen wa=n !HIER! hin........|
                         (then we build up it !HERE!)
     C-gaz: |...~B(RH)...............|.....@map..........|
     A-act: |...~C..................|.......~B(RH)........|
                   *2a+b                 *3
03 C:      |JA:- das wär auch ne option;|
            (YES:- that would be an option;)
   C-gaz: |...........@map.............|
```

*1

*2a

*2b

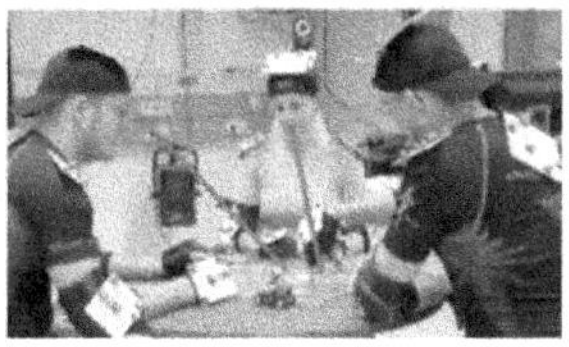

*3

Prior to this fragment, participants A and C enter into a stable two-party conversation for a longer period of time. Their body posture is aligned and they are mutually oriented to each other (cf. *1). At this point in time, participant B assumes a status as observer. Then, in line 01 participant B projects to enter again the discussion and to take the floor by a pre-initial turn pointing (shaded gray "pG-RH" (pointing Gesture Right-Hand)). As pointing practices and turn-taking practices are deeply intertwined, it can be shown that his pointing orients to a transition relevance place (TRPs mark places in the current turn where turn exchanges occur because of a completeness of multimodal cues [6]) at the end of A´s turn. What are the interactional consequences of B's pointing action? Our analysis reveals that the structural order of the ongoing course of interaction is affected by the localization of the pointing gesture. In this case B´s pointing takes place in a shared space of action between him and his co-participant C. Taking an existing concept, motivated by a notion of neuroscience for the relationship between body and space, our analysis suggest that B´s pointing is located in the "peripersonal space" [8] of participant C. Thereby the "peripersonal space" is defined by the maximal arm-length of a participant (stretched arm) and surrounds the body in a circular shape [8]. We determinate the peripersonal space by a video-based measurement of the participants´ arm-length. In doing so it should be mentioned that video-based artefacts like distortions of the lens restricts the precision of our results, which are based only on manual annotation. However, after B´s pointing, C reacts to B's action by interrupting his dialogue with A and orients to the new attention focus represented by B´s right-hand pointing gesture (cf. 02 shaded green "B(RH)", *2a+b). Afterwards participant A treats C´s digressing view as a relevant orienting device to change her own focus of attention and also to follow B´s pointing gesture (cf. *3). We observe that the precise timing and spatial placement of the pointing gesture seems to be consequential for the question "which participant will comment on the pointer´s action?". If the pointer does not simultaneously address its turn to a specific co-participant, that participant will tend to react to whom firstly re-orientates to the new attention focus (cf. 03). Using only the video data, we overlayed a position mask over the video data (cf. 2b) and manually annotated the hand positions of each participant at any point in time. This allowed us, for single cases, to specify pointing gestures with regard to their local occurrence. However, if we want to use such findings for interactional modeling in e.g. human-robot-interaction, we would need to describe the different aspects of this interactional practice in greater detail and to examine them over a large corpus basis:

1. What are typical interaction spaces for joint action, in which participants e.g. point to objects or collaboratively manipulate objects?
2. To which extent does the speed and precise trajectory of the hand movements matter in the described set of practices?
3. What are the participants' home positions of the hands? When do they leave them and return to them? Are different home positions used over time?
4. Where the participants are oriented to? When do they are oriented to each other?
5. Once we have singled out a specific phenomenon/ action pattern via qualitative analysis, can we find similar occurences over the corpus using motion capture data? In which situations do these phenomena occur?
6. More generally, can we automatically find interactional relevant movement and activity? Could we use such information to pre-structure a corpus?

To answer these questions, we can recur to motion capture data because it can describe the kinetic aspects with greater precision and is able to provide measures for their speed, acceleration and posture. An automated motion analysis would allow detecting certain types of gestures or activities over a larger corpus basis. These 6 points are a promising advantage for the analytical investigation of interactional phenomena.

4. PAMOCAT IN THE ANALYSIS OF INTERACTION

How can PAMOCAT be integrated into the research cycle? How can it support annotation and empirical analysis considering both qualitative and quantitative research? – In what follows we will give a short overview of the ways in which PAMOCAT is useful both for (i) visualizing data and (ii) analyzing data. Thereby we will take up the analytical example – pre-initial turn pointing – detailed in section 3, and show the benefits of integrating PAMOCAT into our analysis. Our presentation includes both traditional Conversation Analytic forms of transcription and snapshots from PAMOCAT focusing on the visual aspects of the phenomenon.

4.1 A second instance of the phenomenon

The following fragment – another instance of the phenomenon revealed in section 3 – stems from a different group of participants. Similar to the analysis of fragment 1, we enter the interaction when two participants (A and B) have established a focused two-party conversation while the third person (C) is not involved and thus assumes a status as observer. While in fragment 1, the third person successfully manages to claim the floor, fragment 2 presents a more elaborated case: Participant B, who is challenged as current speaker in the focused two-party conversation, reacts immediately via a particular gestural activity and is able to maintain the floor. The fine-grained micro-coordination of gestural activities within the presented case points to the need of an analytical support with higher accuracy than manual annotation in order to detect the phenomenon in its holistic character.

Fragment2:

just before the fragment:
focused two-party conversation between A and B

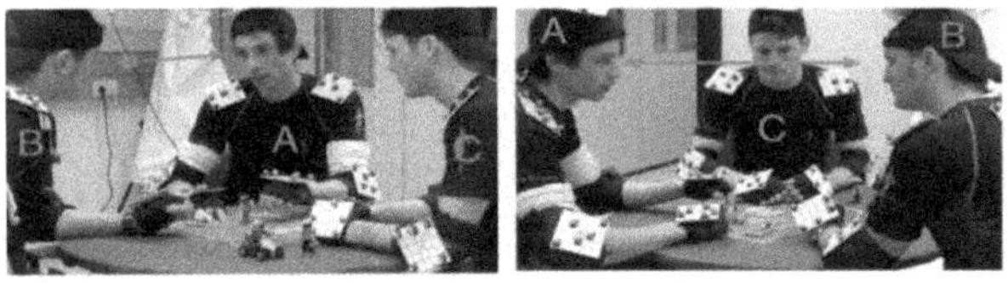

img. 1a: 14:09.84 img. 1b: 14:09.84

```
VP-group-03: 14:19.48-14:26.48

01 A:       |wie wollen denn die TAUcher|
               (how should the divers)
   A-act:  |pG~map..............♠......|
   B-act:  |pG@map.....................|
   A-B:    |aligned posture............|

02 A:       |wäh:rend der:|
              (du:ring the:)
   C:                     |°hh NA |SCHAUN sie|
                            (well  |TAKE A LOOK)
   C-act:  |pG(RH)~map.♠.|pG(LH)~map........
   A-B:      .............|
   A-gaz:                |~C ....|@C........|
   B-act:                        |pG~map....|

03 C:      |es=ist   |
            (it=is)
   B:      |^!NA!JA |es=es DU kannst sie ja auch|
            (oh well |it=it YOU can bring them out
   C-act:   ..X.....|pG(BH)~HP..................|
   A-gaz:  |~pG(B)..|@pG(B)....................

04 B:       ((...)) mit den BOOten herausbringen;|
                     with BOATS as well)
   A-gaz:   ....................................|
   A-B     |aligned posture.....................|
```

4.2 Accessing the corpus

In a first step, we were interested in using PAMOCAT to help us access the corpus. Could we find similar occurrences of our phenomenon on the basis of the motion capture data? – To do so, we need to specify the salient characteristics of the phenomenon and abstract its relevant features. Ideally, in our research project we would specify the constellation of the phenomenon as (i) two participants are mutually oriented with regard to their head orientation and (ii) the third person makes a pointing gesture in the interaction space between the three co-participants. For our search operation we take the PAMOCAT function of mutual head orientation detection (2.2.6), which automatically detects those situations where co-participants orient to each other. This allows a pre-structuring of the corpus and helps to create a collection of cases.

4.3 Revealing zones of activity: Interaction space

In what follows we use particular PAMOCAT functions, which automatically detect relevant cues for a focused two-party conversation between A and B. As we have shown in section 3 one indication for this focused two-party conversation consists in a mutually aligned head orientation, which can be automatically detected (cf. 2.2.6). At that point in time participant C assumes a status as listener/observer, which is displayed through his downwards oriented posture (cf. img. 1a and 1b). In addition to the head and posture orientation, the PAMOCAT function of recording motion trajectories of specific joints allows us to reveal an additional layer of description of the situation: Using the 3D trajectories of the participants' hands in this time interval (cf. fig. 6), we can also describe how the participants make different use of the space on the table between them. A basic evidence for the stable dyadic constellation at the beginning consists in the consideration of the most frequent hand activities within the duration of the sequence. When we compare T1 and T2 we are

trajectories: 13:47.841-14:26.665

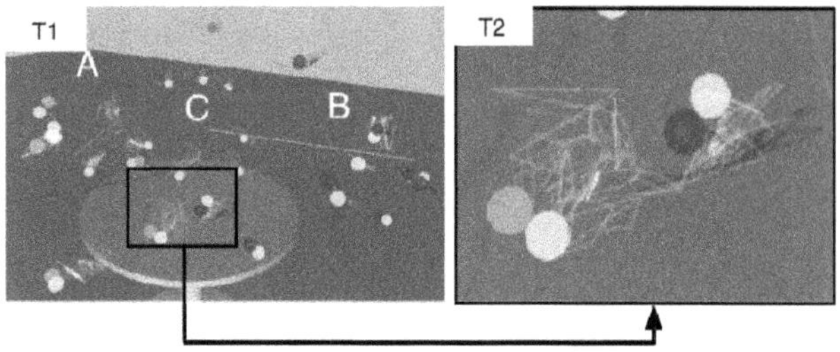

Figure 6: Trajectories in spaces of joint action

able to reveal that the particular place where participants A and B collaboratively manipulate objects and point to the map is the shared place of joint action with the most frequently trajectories (green marker ball = A´s right hand; blue marker ball = B´s left hand). Accordingly the trajectory data shows how these two participants constitute a common interactional space for joint activity in which participant C has no authority for action and is thus excluded as potential co-participant. This gives us a precise representation of the dimensional expansion of shared spaces of interaction where participants cooperatively manipulate objects.

4.4 Interactional micro-coordination: Home position & hand movements

The next step of the described procedure shows how C comes into action in 14:20.16. Thereby, three basic PAMOCAT functions reveal helpful cues for describing and analyzing the procedure the observer uses to claim the floor. In this way the precise micro-coordination of his bodily and gestural activities becomes particularly well visible. In a first step, taking the PAMOCAT function of calculating homepositions (cf. 2.2.4), we analyze the onset position of his forthcoming pre-initial turn pointing. Considering figure 7 it becomes visible (cf. right hand marker (red point in black circle) with homeposition (yellow point in black circle)) that the starting point of the pre-initial turn pointing is inherent in a frequently used location of his hands – what we call home position (automatically calculated homepositions are marked with yellow points). First analyzes of similar cases on the broader corpus reveal that the described procedure often starts in such locations. We observe that resting positions in frequently used locations have only rarely an interactive relevance and

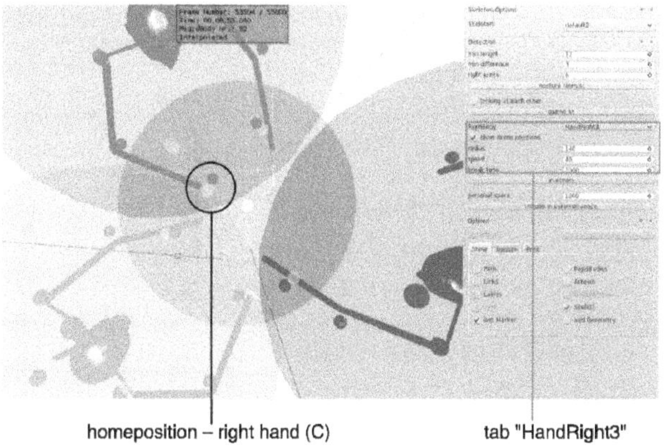

Figure 7: homepositions of participant C (yellow points)

thereby do not constitute a point of attraction for the focused two-party conversation. Out of his home position participant C passes his right hand to a particular point of the map in front of participant A (cf. line 02, transcript). Taking the PAMOCAT function of key-interval detection (2.2.1) even the small-sized movements in the onset of the ongoing turn pointing becomes detectable (cf. fig. 8). In the video-data this would be hardly

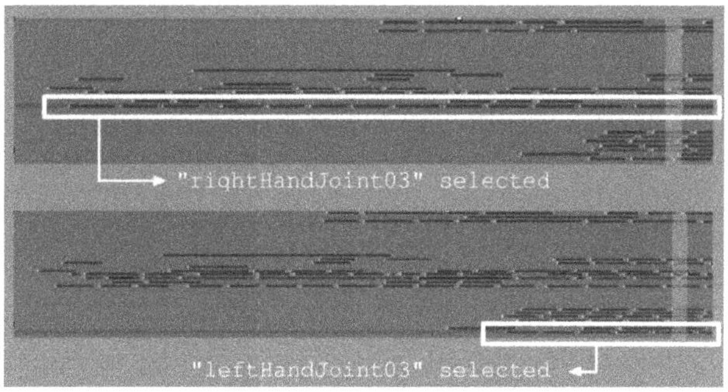

Figure 8: keyframes of the single joint "right hand" (above) and "left hand" (below), participant C

detectable because of distortions in perspective. The figure shows precisely the starting point of his right-hand pre-initial turn pointing (above) and the following left-hand gesture for visualizing his argument on the map (below). If we consider the trajectories for this single hand movement, it becomes visible – through the precise direction of the red trajectories (participant C) to the co-participant A (green marker) – that his pointing is characterized by both a hand-movement and a posture shift in direction to participant A (cf. fig. 9).

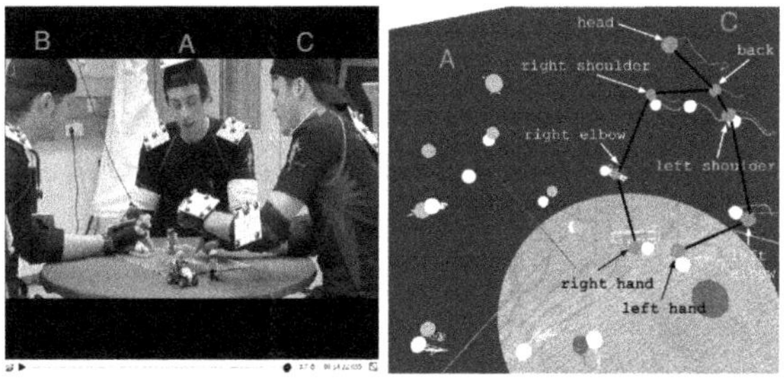

Figure 9: trajectories for the pre-initial turn pointing of participant C (trajectories in red)

4.5 Highlighting and annotation support: Peripersonal Space

The precise localization of his pointing shows that C's hand enters into A´s peripersonal space (cf. PAMOCAT section 2.2.5) which was already revealed as relevant interactive space within the described phenomenon in fragment 1. However, C´s pointing (HEAD 3) takes place in a shared space of action between him and his co-participant A (HEAD 2) (cf. fig. 10). We have implemented in PAMOCAT a function that calculates and highlights the participants' peripersonal spaces. This allows us to immediately see whether C's action is actually placed in A's peripersonal space. In comparison, for the analysis presented in section 3 using video-data only, we had to manually measure for each point in time the distance of the stretched arms via a measurement scale tool on the video data. Thereby, measuring on video data is because of video-based distortions not as accurate as a MOCAP-based calculation (we will compare the accuracy of the two approaches in a future paper). A reacts to C's action by interrupting his dialogue with B (cf. line 02, transcript) and orients to the new attention focus represented by C´s right-hand pointing gesture. Taking the PAMOCAT function "detect orientated to" this procedure is automatically annotated (cf. fig. 10). The green annotation bar shows the attention shift from participant A (HEAD 2) which leads to a mutual orientation of participant A and C (HEAD 2 and 3, yellow annotation bar). Interestingly the pre-initial turn pointer C uses a two-step procedure: Firstly he engenders A´s attention via the right hand pointing gesture. As this hand takes the task of attention getting,

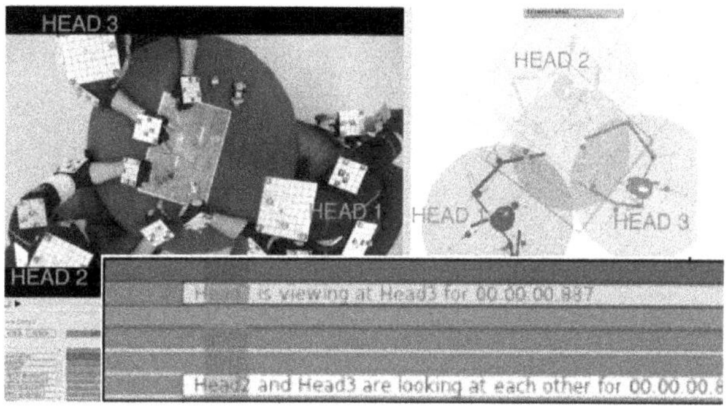

Figure 10: pre-initial turn pointing in the peripersonal space of participant A & participant A (head 2) orients to the new attention focus

he additionally uses the second hand (left one) in order to orient the addressee to a particular part of the map (cf. line 02, transcript). That means that he uses a task sharing regarding the modalities "left" and "right" hand in order to attempt as active co-participant again. In its basic version of the phenomenon, the sequence is completed when the pre-initial turn pointer becomes the co-participant of the addressee. However, this case is different because the participant (B) who is pushed out of the focused two-party conversation reacts to the easing dyad not via a gaze shift to the new attention focus. Instead the "pushed out participant" B reacts via an "initial turn pointing" (simultaneous pointing and speaking [6]) and interrupts in this way C´s attempt to claim the floor (cf. line 03, transcript). The 3D PAMOCAT scene (fig. 11) shows that B´s "intial turn pointing" is done in the peripersonal space of his so far dyadic co-participant A. We observe that only his hand movement of the initial turn pointing regains the attention focus of participant A (cf. fig.11), line 03+04, transcript) and leads to a stable dyad between participant A and B again.

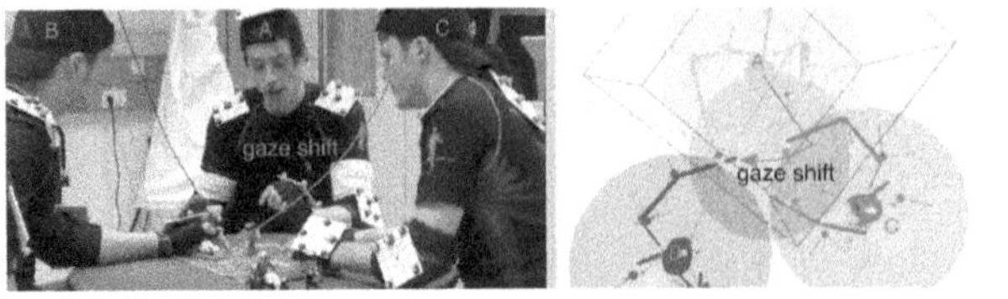

Figure 11: the initial turn pointing regains the attention focus of participant A

To sum up, the basic advantage of the used PAMOCAT functions within our second example consists in the precise automatic detection of micro-coordinative procedures, which would be very time-consuming in pure manual CA-driven analyzes. Nevertheless, only the combination of quantitative data-driven methods for pre-structuring the corpus with qualitative CA-driven methods for analyzing the prepared data leads to precise insights in interactional phenomena.

5. CONCLUSION

PAMOCAT is a **pre** annotation tool specialized on motion capture data, and based on these kinds of data, it can detect different phenomena. These phenomena are in the areas "single person", "person overlapping", "static" and "dynamic". PAMOCAT includes a search engine to choose and sift through different phenomena constellations. It allows looking fast through the synchronized motion capture data, multiple videos, and different phenomena constellation highlighted elements. With this functionality POMOCAT can be well integrated into the research cycle. The benefit of this tool is that it saves a lot of time and makes it possible to combine quantitative with qualitative analyzes. With regard to our analysis in section 4 we showed how a PAMOCAT-based analysis could reveal a particular phenomenon – in this case: the kinetic turn taking procedure of pre-initial turn pointing and initial turn pointing – with higher accuracy and in greater detail (so that even the precise micro-coordination of the phenomenon becomes transparent). Thereby, PAMOCAT provides additional cues like the automatically calculation of homepositions, displaying trajectories for a chosen time interval or displaying of how participants intrude in peripersonal spaces of their co-participants. All these procedures would be hardly recognizable in only video-based analyzes tools like ELAN or ANVILE, which points to the need of a tool for micro-analytical conversation-research based on motion capture data. The next steps will be to add the important functionality of the common motion capture data format, "bvh", to integrate more phenomena like facial expression, finger tracking, person based audio segmentation and to add a more complex logical combinations of these phenomena.

6. ACKNOWLEDGMENTS

This research is supported by the Center of Excellence 'Cognitive Interaction Technology' (CITEC, EC277), the project C5 'Alignment in AR-based cooperation' in the SFB/CRC 673 and the Volkswagenstiftung/Dilthey Fellowship 'Interaction & Space'.

7. REFERENCES

[1] Pitsch, K., Brüning, B., Schnier, C. and Wachmuth, S., 2010. *Linking Conversation Analysis and Motion* Capturing: *"How to robustly track multiple participants?"*. In Proceedings Workshop on Multimodal Corpora, LREC.

[2] Auer, E., Russel, A. Sloetjes, H., Witternurg, P., Schreer, O., Masneri, S., Schneider, D. & Toepel, S., 2010. *ELAN as flexible annotation framework for sound and image processing detectors*. Proceedings of LREC

[3] Heloir, A., Neff, M., Kipp, M., 2010, *Exploiting Motion Capture for Virtual Human Animation: Data Collection and Annotation Visualization.* In Proceedings of LREC Workshop on "Multimodal Corpora", ELDA.

[4] Schnier, C., 2010. Turn-Taking: *Interaktive Projektionsleistungen über Kinesische Displays*. Masterarbeit Universität Bielefeld, p. 93.

[5] Mondada, L., 2007. *Multimodal resources for turn-taking: pointing and the emergence of possible next speakers*. In Discourse Studies, 9, 2, pp. 194-225.

[6] Sacks, H., Schegloff, E. A. and Jefferson G., 1974. *A Simplest Systematics for the Organization of Turn Taking for Conversation.* In: *Language*, 50, pp. 696–735.

[7] Brüning, B., Schnier, C., Pitsch, K., Wachsmuth, S., 2012, *PAMOCAT: Automatic retrieval of specified postures,* In Proceedings Workshop on Multimodal Corpora, LREC 2012

[9] Chilton, P., 2009, *Get and the grasp schema.* In: Evans, V. & Pourcel, S. (Hrsg.). *New Directions in Cognitive Linguistics.* (333-337). Amsterdam, Philadelphia: John Benjamins Publishing Company.

[10] Sacks, H., 1992. *Lectures on conversation.* Malden; Oxford: Blackwell

[11] ten Have, P., 1999. *Doing conversation analysis. A practical guide.* London: Sage.

[12] Duncan, S., 1972. *Some signals and rules for taking speaking turns in conversations.* Journal of Personality and Social Psychology, 1972, 23, (2), (pp. 283-292).

[13] Goodwin, C., 1981. *Conversational Organization: Interaction between Hearers and Speakers.* New York, NY: Academic Press.

8. APPENDIX

`A,B,C-gaz` = A, B, C looks
`A,B,C-act` = A, B, C acts bodily
pG(RH/LH/BH) = pointing gesture of the (right hand/ left hand/ both hands)
~ = "XY" in movement
@ = "XY" at an object
♠ = peak of a pointing gesture
X = interruption of a pointing gesture
HP = homeposition
~pG(B) = gaze shift to pointing gesture of participant B
| = beginning/end of simultaneous activities
`-, ;, .` = pitch movement at the end of units : from "constant" to "falling deeply"
`:, ::, :::` = lengthening (depends on duration)

Motion Retrieval Based on Kinetic Features in Large Motion Database

Tianyu Huang
School of Software
Beijing Institute of Technology
Haidian, Beijing, China, 100081
huangtianyu@bit.edu.cn

Haiying Liu
School of Software
Beijing Institute of Technology
Haidian, Beijing, China, 100081
liuhaiying@bit.edu.cn

Gangyi Ding
School of Software
Beijing Institute of Technology
Haidian, Beijing, China, 100081
dgy@bit.edu.cn

ABSTRACT

Considering the increasing collections of motion capture data, motion retrieval in large motion databases is gaining in importance. In this paper, we introduce kinetic interval features describing the movement trend of motions. In our approach, motion files are decomposed into kinetic intervals. For each joint in a kinetic interval, we define the kinetic interval features as the parameters of parametric arc equations computed by fitting joints trajectories. By extracting these features, we are able to lower the dimensionality and reconstruct the motions. Multilayer index tree is used to accelerate the searching process and a candidate list of motion data is generated for matching. To find both logically and numerically similar motions, we propose a two-level similarity matching based on kinetic interval features, which can also speed up the matching process. Experiments are performed on several variants of HDM05 and CMU motion databases proving that the approach can achieve accurate and fast motion retrieval in large motion databases.

Categories and Subject Descriptors

I.3.7 [Computer Graphics]: Three-Dimensional Graphics and Realism – *animation*; H.3.3 [Information Storage and Retrieval]: Information Search and Retrieval – *retrieval models.*

General Terms

Algorithms, Management, Performance, Experimentation.

Keywords

Motion capture data, motion retrieval, kinetic interval, multilayer indexing.

1. INTRODUCTION

Motion capture technology has been widely used for capturing character motions in many applications such as performance animation, virtual reality, video games and so on [1, 2]. An increasingly large amount of motion capture data has been recorded, and some large motion databases [3, 4] have emerged in the past few years. In order to reuse the recorded data better, an efficient approach of motion retrieval in large motion databases is still a challenge problem.

Several factors impact motion retrieval efficiency: motion expression, matching algorithm, indexing structure, search space and more. Motion expression is an important basis of constructing motion databases. Usually we abstract motion features to represent the characteristics of a motion sequence. However, using overly abstract descriptions of motion speeds up the searching procedure at the expense of information loss in retrieval results. By providing properly representative features of motion content and a multi-resolution searching mechanism in this paper, we can achieve better efficiency and accuracy in retrieval results for large-scale motion databases.

Some prior works have shown potentially effective retrieval methods. One popular method of motion expression is the numerical method [2], but it is inefficient on large motion databases because of the high-dimensional motion data. Researchers have proposed various dimension reduction methods, like principal component analysis (PCA) [5] and singular value decomposition (SVD) [6], to decrease the dimensionality of motion data which usually causes feature information loss. Some other researchers focus on content-based motion expression [7]. However, this technique requires user interaction to specify the content-based features of the query for each retrieval.

In this paper, we introduce a kinetic interval feature of motion data. A kinetic interval is a set of kinetic features describing the movement trend of a motion sequence. For each joint of a continuous motion interval, we compute the parametric arc equations by fitting joint trajectories in the same movement trends. The kinetic interval features are defined as the parameters of these parametric equations. Using kinetic intervals, high-dimensional motion capture data can be decomposed as low-dimensional kinetic features. The original motion data is easily reconstructed from this low-dimensional form.

To speed up retrievals in the large-scale motion database, matching and indexing method are also considered in this paper. A two-level matching method based on kinetic interval features is adopted. We get a rough result by Derivative Dynamic Time Warping (DDTW)[21] algorithm with mean values of kinetic intervals in the first level of the algorithm. Then matching results will be refined by interpolating re-sampled the kinetic interval features in the second level. Indexing structure and search space are also major aspects of fast motion retrievals. A k-means based iterative method is used to construct the multilayer clustered index

ICMI '12, October 22–26, 2012, Santa Monica, California, USA.

tree. We find that constructing index trees with kinetic intervals is too time consuming as the scale of motion database increases. To solve this problem, a Gaussian-based method is used to roughly segment motion sequences. After constructing the index tree with segments, we can locate the query in a coarse range of motion files by pruning of the index tree nodes. Then, we use the kinetic intervals for precise matching.

Our contributions can be summarized as follows:

1) We propose a method to interpret motion features as kinetic interval features to lower the data dimensionality and it is re-constructible.

2) A two-level similarity matching based on kinetic interval features is introduced to speed up the matching process. Similarity can be matched both numerically and logically.

3) We propose a pipeline of motion retrieval for large motion databases.

The rest of this paper is organized as follows. Section 2 summarizes the related work on motion retrieval. In Section 3, we introduce the kinetic interval method to represent high-dimensional motion data in a lower dimensional way. In Section 4, similarity matching based on kinetic intervals is presented. Section 5 gives the pre-computing and indexing of the motion database construction. The whole process of motion retrieval pipeline is described in Section 6. Section 7 offers a experiment results of our methods, and we make a conclusion in Section 8.

2. RELATED WORK

Motion preprocessing and retrieval are key issues of motion synthesis and reuse in applications, which have been studied for over a decade. Most solutions are based on the framework proposed by Faloutsos et al. [8]. The main idea of the framework is about efficient pruning of searching space and the low dimensional approximation extraction. However, their framework cannot work well with logically similar motions. In recent years, many researchers have improved this framework or even proposed new methods, such as semantics-based motion retrieval [7, 9] and example-based human motion retrieval [10].

Various ways have been pursued to transform original high-dimensional human motion data to a lower expression. Chuanjun Li et al. [6] proposed a method which can extract the motion features by exploiting the SVD, but it fails in finding similar sub-body motions in varied whole-body motions. Wang et al. [11] reduced the high-dimensional motion data by a curve simplification algorithm. They devise an EigenDis distance measure, use k-means to cluster motions, and then apply APP method to compress the motion database in a lossless manner. Forbes et al. [5] proposed a weighted PCA method to extract motion features, but as a result the non-linear motion data cannot be well-represented. Chuan Sun et al. [12] used a low-rank subspace decomposition method to reduce motion dimensions.

Several index methods have been proposed to organize the motion database efficiently. Yasuhiko Sakamoto et al. [13] used the method of motion map based on SOM, but it fails in distinguishing and retrieving motions containing the same movements at different velocities. Muller et al. [9] transformed the motion retrieval problem into a binary matching problem by proposing an efficient semantics-based motion retrieval method. However, the retrieval results rely on the quality of the geometry feature relationship in the query motion. Huang et al. [14] presented a geometric feature coding method to build index of the database. Deng et al. [10] decomposed motions into body parts and extracted common motion patterns for each part. A motion clip can be represented as a string of pattern indices, and so motion retrieval becomes simple string matching. Björn Krüger et al. [15] proposed a method for local and global similarity searches by kd-tree based local neighborhood searches. Yi Lin [16] segmented and clustered geometric features automatically into an index tree, and this method can find logically similar motions.

There are also several works about matching method used to automatically search for similar motions to the query. Since the motion data is kind of signal, researchers usually use DTW [5, 17] or uniform scaling [18] for motion matching. Keogh et al. [19] presented an indexing method based on lower bounding for retrieving in large motion database. Kovar et al. [20] proposed the pre-computing "match webs" to describe potential matches for each motion segment in the data set, but while dealing with large motion databases, building the "match webs" for every possible pair of motions may not work. Muller et al. [7] introduced a fault-tolerant retrieval method based on fuzzy hits and mismatches.

Two main similarity measures are numerical similarity and logical similarity. Numerical similarity methods like Böhm et al. [2] determined similarity through direct numerical comparison by comparing a computed distance against a user-supplied threshold. Logical similarity methods like Muller et al. [9] identified the logical similar motions by the binary geometric features and the "motion templates".

In summary, prior works in motion expression are not effective enough in reconstructing motion data after dimension reduction or compression. If the compression procedure is not lossless, additional error will be introduced. We solve this problem by presenting a kinetic interval method to compress and reconstruct the motion data while maintaining the lossless property. Both similarity match methods mentioned above have their strengths and weaknesses. In our approach, we combine the two similarity matching methods. A numerical DDTW-based method is used for rough similarity matching, and then a logical kinetic interval-based method is used to refine the matching results. The efficiency of matching is also improved by this strategy.

3. KINETIC INTERVAL FEATURES

In this section, we introduce a method to compress high-dimensional motion capture data into low-dimensional sequences by using kinetic intervals. A kinetic interval feature f_{KI} is defined as a set of parameters of parametric equations which describe the motion trajectories of a joint.

In the human skeleton, a limb between each joint and its parent joint is a lever. The parent joint is the fulcrum, and the joint moves around an axis that passes through the center of its parent joint. So we can say the range of motion (ROM) of each joint satisfies the sphere constraint. The movement trajectories of each joint can be represented as several arcs along the sphere surface in its parent joint's coordinate. In such a coordinate, the joint moves around a sphere S where the center is the parent joint and the radius is the length of the limb. Since an arc is the intersection of a sphere and a plane, the arc trajectory of a joint can be computed by the parameters of the sphere and the plane. We assume the joint moves along different arcs if it behaves movements with different semantic. The expression of joints' movement arcs, shown in figure1, is a kind of geometric representations, which guarantees numerical-logical similarity while matching in motion database.

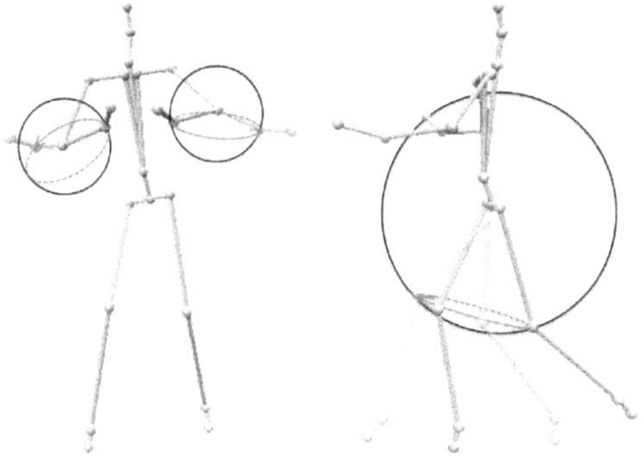

Figure 1. Joints' movement arcs of human motion data.

Assume that the position of the j-th joint in the i-th frame which is in the parent's coordinate is $p_{i,j}=[x_{i,j},y_{i,j},z_{i,j}]$ and $p_{i,j}$ satisfies the constraint of equation (1) where r_j is the radius:

$$S(x_{i,j},y_{i,j},z_{i,j})=x_{i,j}^2+y_{i,j}^2+z_{i,j}^2-r_j^2=0 \quad (1)$$

A joint moves along an arc under consistent force action in its parent's coordinate. This arc is the intersection of a plane and a sphere. The joints' positions in a consecutive sequence of frames with the same semantics lie on the same plane, so $p_{i,j}$ satisfies the constraint of (2) as well.

$$P(p_{i,j})=\hat{n}\cdot(p_{i,j}-q)=0 \quad (2)$$

Here, $\hat{n}$ denotes the normal of the plane, and q is an arbitrary point on this plane. Then, we can fit the plane and its normal $\hat{n}$ to all those $p_{i,j}$ of the kinetic interval by using the Levenberg Marquardt method.

Assume that the plane P can be represented as $Ax+By+Cz+D=0$, $\hat{n}=[A,B,C]$ denotes the normal of the plane P, the basis vectors of P are $\hat{u}=[B,-A,0]$ and $\hat{v}=\hat{n}\times\hat{u}$. The center c of the arc is the intersection of plane P and a line $L(c)$:

$$L(c)=O+\lambda\hat{n} \quad (3)$$

where $O=[0,0,0]$ and λ is an arbitrary value. The radius R of the arc can be computed as $R=\sqrt{r_j^2-|c|^2}$ where r_j is the radius of the sphere S of the j-th joint. And the arc can be represented as:

$$f_{KI}(t)=c+R(\hat{u}\cos t+\hat{v}\sin t) \quad t\in(0,2\pi] \quad (4)$$

Assume p_{start} and p_{end} denote the position of the beginning and the end frames of the kinetic interval. Now, we get all the elements of kinetic interval feature $f_{KI}=\{u,v,c,R,p_{start},p_{end}\}$.

Figure 2 illustrates the wrist joint trajectory represented by a kinetic interval feature. In this figure, the wrist joint moves from J_{wrist} to J'_{wrist} along the green dashed line in the joint space of its parent J_{elbow}. The parametric equation of the kinetic interval can be obtained by fitting the trajectory, and $\hat{u}$, $\hat{v}$, c and R are variables of the parametric equation.

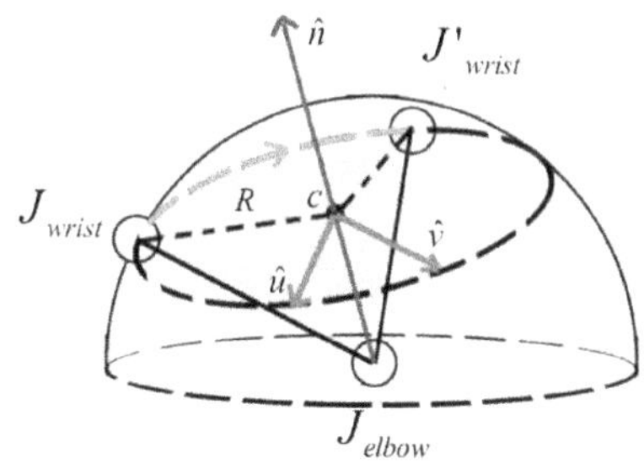

Figure 2. Illustration of wrist joint trajectory represented by kinetic interval feature.

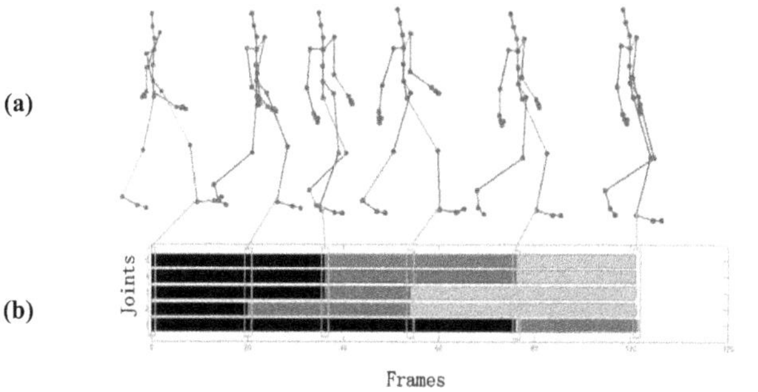

Figure 3. Walking motion decomposed by kinetic interval method. (a): Poses of a motion at frame position 0, 20, 37, 56, 78 and 100(30Hz). (b): Feature matrix of the walking motion used in (a). The gray gradient means the alteration of different planes of joints. The green blocks depict the kinetic interval segmentation.

The start and the end of the arc can be computed by fitting a period of the trajectory to a plane P using least square method. The fitting error $E(p,P)$ can be computed as:

$$E(p,P)=\left(\sum_{i=start}^{N}\frac{|A\cdot x_{i,j}+B\cdot y_{i,j}+C\cdot z_{i,j}+D|}{\sqrt{A^2+B^2+C^2}}\right)\Big/N \quad (5)$$

where N is the number of points from the start point to the current point. When $E(p,P)<\tau$, where τ is a threshold, the current point belongs to the arc; When $E(p,P)\geq\tau$, we take the current point as the start point of the next arc. All the f_{KI} s in a kinetic interval should have the same frames. When a kinetic interval is segmented from the motion sequences, we resize all the f_{KI} s as long as the shortest one and computing the next arc for all joints with the same start frame. The process is shown in figure 3.

4. SIMILARITY MATCHING BASED ON KINETIC FEATURES

To speed up the matching process, we propose a two-level matching method based on the kinetic interval features. In the first level, we match each kinetic interval of the two motion files to get rough results by using DDTW algorithm. Unlike DTW, DDTW considers the first derivative of the sequences instead of the data points' values and works well when features in one sequence are slightly higher or lower than their corresponding features in another sequence. The matching results will be refined in the second level by interpolation between kinetic intervals based on kinetic interval features. The two-level matching method can improve the matching speed with a time requirement of $O(m/K*n/L)$, where K is the average length of kinetic intervals of an m-frame motion file, and L is the average length of kinetic intervals of an n-frame motion file.

Assume that $M=[Mean_1, \mathrm{L}, Mean_m]$ is the mean set of a motion file with m kinetic intervals, and $Mean_i$ denotes the mean of motion data in the i-th kinetic interval. While using DDTW, the distance D can be computed as:

$$D_x[Mean_i] = \left((Mean_i - Mean_{i-1}) + (Mean_{i+1} - Mean_{i-1})/2\right)/2 \quad 1<i<m \tag{6}$$

$$D = \left(D_x[Mean_i] - D_x[Mean_i']\right)^2 \quad 1<i<m, 1<j<n \tag{7}$$

where $D_x[Mean_i]$ is the derivative of $Mean_i$.

In the second level, we introduce the refining process with interpolation based on kinetic interval feature. First, the variable of kinetic interval features f_{KI_i} varies from $\Omega_i = [f_{KI}^{-1}(p_{start}), f_{KI}^{-1}(p_{end})]$. And the inverse function of (5) $f_{KI}^{-1}(p)$ can be represented as:

$$f_{KI}^{-1}(p) = \left(\hat{u}(p-c) \pm \hat{v}\sqrt{R^2-(p-c)^2}\right)/R \tag{8}$$

Assume that there are M and N frames in the two matched kinetic intervals KI_i and KI_j. We take $\min(N,M)$ as the grain size of the resampling. The sample set S_i can be obtained by uniformly sampling the range of $f(t), t\in\Omega_i$. We can get the sample set S_j of f_{KIj} from the other kinetic interval KI_j in the same way.

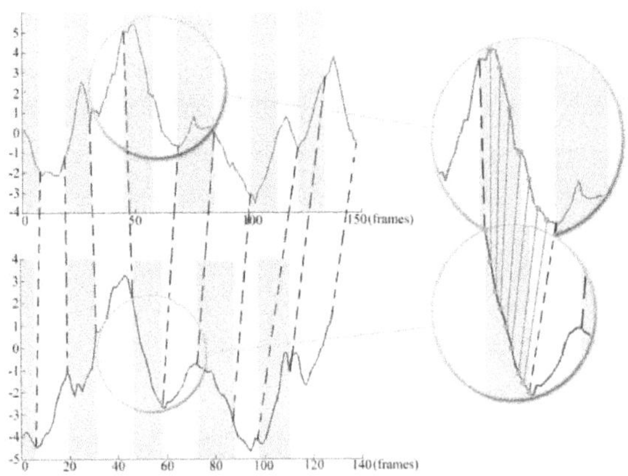

(a) **(b)**

Figure 4. Running exercise motion matching by kinetic interval method. (a) shows the matching result of two kinetic intervals sequences. (b) indicates the process of the interpolation between two kinetic intervals.

We then interpolate the samples in S_i and S_j one-by-one using weighted Euclidean distance with a user defined ω for the joint. Considering the different speeds of motion sequences, we use the ratio of N and M to show the differences between the speeds.

Finally, we modify the matching result by

$$Sim' = Sim \cdot w_d + w_i \cdot \frac{N}{M} \cdot \sum_{s=1}^{J^n} \sum_{t=1}^{m} \left((S_i - S_j)\cdot\omega_s\right) \tag{9}$$

Sim is the roughly matching result we calculated in the first level; w_d and w_i are user-defined parameters, ω_s is the weight of the s-th joint, N and M are the length of kinetic intervals and $m=\min(N,M)$, and J^n is the number of joints.

One example of matching by by kinetic interval method is shown in figure 4. Figure 4(a) shows the matching result of two kinetic intervals sequences. Figure 4(b) indicates the process of the interpolation between two kinetic intervals.

5. MOTION DATBASE CONSTRUCTION

There are two procedures in constructing motion database, pre-computing and indexing. In the pre-computing process, we use Gaussian-based segmentation method to decompose motion sequences. In indexing, an iterative procedure is used for constructing the multilayer clustered index tree from the segments. This structure can generate a candidate list of a coarse range of motion files by pruning of the index tree nodes.

Gaussian model can describe characteristics of human motion. In pre-computing process, we use Gaussian-based method to segment the motion sequences. The centroid of human body C_i at the i-th frame can be computed by

$$C_i = \left(\sum_{j=0}^{J^n}(x_{i,j}+y_{i,j}+z_{i,j})\right)/J^n \tag{10}$$

For each frame, where $p_{i,j}=[x_{i,j}, y_{i,j}, z_{i,j}]$ denotes the position of each joint in each frame, and J^n denotes the number of the joints. The mean μ of the motion sequence and standard deviation σ of motion sequence can be computed as:

$$\mu = \sum_{i=f_{begin}}^{f_{end}} (C_i) \Big/ (f_{end} - f_{begin}) \tag{11}$$

$$\sigma = \sqrt{\sum_{i=f_{begin}}^{f_{end}} (C_i - \mu)^2} \tag{12}$$

where f_{end} denotes the number of the processing frame and f_{begin} denotes the starting frame number of the current motion sequence segment. the $(f_{end}+1)$ -th frame satisfies the current Gaussian model, if the following inequality holds.

$$C_{f_{end}+1} - \mu < range\ \sigma \tag{13}$$

where $C_{f_{end}+1}$ denotes $(f_{end}+1)$-th frame motion data, $range$ is a user parameter which means the deviations from μ.

If $f_{end} - f_{begin} < \varepsilon$, for some value epsilon, we combine the current segment with the previous segment because it contains less information to express a simple action. The time requirement of this method is $O(n)$. Our experiments show that when ε is 30, the result of segmentation is desirable for retrieval.

In Indexing, multilayer clustered index tree is applied. We cluster μ of all the motion segments into several clusters. Then if there are more than k elements in this cluster we cluster again until there are less than k elements. Finally, we construct an index tree for all the motion segments. Each node of the index tree denotes a category of motion. As the layer goes deeper, the precision of classification is higher. The time requirement of the whole process is $O(n*k*t)$ where k is the number of desired clusters and t is the number of iterations.

6. PIPELINE AND RETRIEVAL

Figure 5 visualizes the pipeline of our motion retrieval approach. Preprocessing motion data and constructing the index tree are offline procedures. Step 1-3 is offline processes, and Step 4-7 is real-time retrieval processes.

Given a human motion repository,

Step 1: Decompose the motion files into kinetic interval features.

Step 2: Segment motion files by Gaussian-based method for the indexing process.

Step 3: Cluster the segments iteratively to build up an index tree.

Given a query motion file,

Step 4: Decompose the query file into kinetic intervals and segments.

Step 5: Retrieve similar segments from the index tree.

Step 6: Generate a candidate list of similar motion files.

Step 7: Compute the similarity of the kinetic intervals between these candidate motion files and the query, and get the matching results.

Given a query motion file, we first decompose it into segments $S = \{seg_1, seg_2, seg_3, ..., seg_n\}$ by using the method in Section 5. For

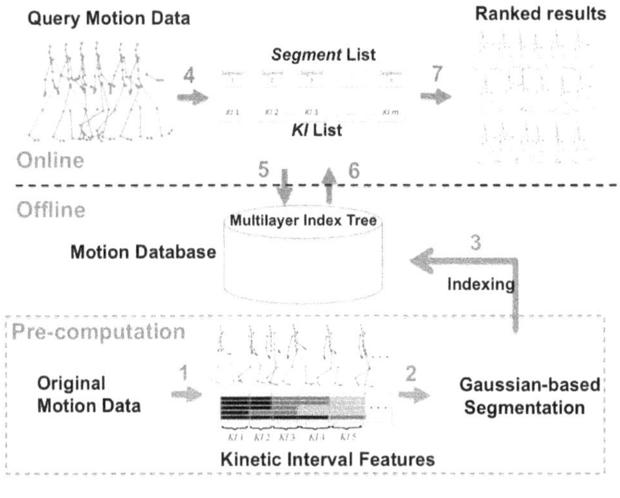

Figure 5. Pipeline of motion retrieval based on kinetic features and multilayer index tree. Step 1-3 is offline processes. Step 4-7 is real-time retrieval processes.

each segment seg_i, $i \in [1,n]$, we can get a set of segments S_{result} by searching in the index tree. The motion files containing S_{result} will be added to a candidate list. Then, in order to match the file precisely, we decompose the query motion file by using kinetic interval method and extract the kinetic interval features. We match each interval of the query motion file with every interval of the motion files in candidate list by using the two-level matching method mentioned in Section 4. Also, we adopt the feature sets F_E^{15}, F_E^{30}, F_E^{39} devised by Björn Krüger et. in [15] to discuss whether they can help us to reduce time overhead.

7. RESULTS AND DISCUSSION

To prove the applicability of the proposed method, we conducted several experiments. The presented algorithm has been implemented in Matlab. All experiments were executed on a computer with an Intel Core T7500 and 2GB of RAM.

7.1 Performance of Matching Method Based on Kinetic Features

We evaluate the proposed method on the HDM05 database by analyzing the performances on five pairs of motion files of various lengths. The comparisons are made between our proposed method $(DD_{msm} + I_{msi})$, $DD_{msm} + DD_{msi}$ and DDTW. DD_{msm} denotes the method of matching $M = [Mean_1, \ldots, Mean_m]$ and $M' = [Mean_1', \ldots, Mean_m']$ by DDTW algorithm. I_{msi} denotes the method of linear interpolation between two resampled kinetic intervals. DD_{msi} denotes the method of matching two kinetic intervals by DDTW[21] algorithm. The time requirement of all those DDTW methods are $O(m*n)$. The matching time results are shown in Table 1.

Comparing the results between $DD_{msm} + DD_{msi}$ and DDTW, we can see that the time cost is lower after segmenting the motion file into kinetic intervals. Linear interpolation between resampled motion data can improve the performance by comparing the results between $DD_{msm} + I_{msi}$ and $DD_{msm} + DD_{msi}$. Therefore, $DD_{msm} + I_{msi}$ performs well in our motion matching tasks.

7.2 Performance Analysis on Motion Retrieval

To evaluate the performance of our motion retrieval method, we run the experiments on several variations of CMU [3] motion database of different scales with different segmentation methods.

Table 2 shows the pre-computing time, matching time, indexing time, searching time of $M_{KI} + M_{GS}$, M_{GS} and M_{KI}. $M_{KI} + M_{GS}$ is our proposed method. M_{GS} is segmenting the motion sequences only using the Gaussian-based motion sequence segmentation method and M_{KI} is segmenting the motion sequences only using kinetic interval method, and visualized in Figure 6. The query is an 800-frame length motion file. From the experiment results, we can see that the $M_{KI} + M_{GS}$ can significantly reduce the retrieval time, so our method can meet the performance on real-time applications. The reduction is even more significant when the size of the database is large. Unlike the retrieval time, we do not have to be strict with the offline preprocessing time for segmenting and indexing; 2036 seconds is tolerable for such a huge database.

Table 1. **Matching time (in seconds) for five pairs of motion files (in frames) with different methods.**

Motion file pairs	$DD_{msm} + I_{msi}$	$DD_{msm} + DD_{msi}$	DDTW
Pair (500 ,500)	0.0692	0.2394	8.6635
Pair (500 ,1000)	0.1456	0.4505	16.3010
Pair (1000,1000)	0.2371	0.6988	28.3173
Pair (1000,2000)	0.4617	1.4352	54.0013
Pair (2000,2000)	0.9360	2.7331	205.7091

Table 2. The detailed time (in seconds) of retrieval, indexing and segmenting in different databases (in frames).

DB Size	Time	$M_{KI} + M_{GS}$	M_{GS}	M_{KI}
5762	Pre-computing Time	7.72	0.03	7.69
	Indexing Time	0.10	0.10	1.69
	Retrieval Time	0.04	0.14	2.42
25125	Pre-computing Time	32.40	0.20	32.21
	Indexing Time	0.30	0.30	3.16
	Retrieval Time	0.17	0.78	2.52
100190	Pre-computing Time	131.02	0.68	130.34
	Indexing Time	0.54	0.54	16.30
	Retrieval Time	0.25	2.86	2.60
1273227	Pre-computing Time	2036.11	12.85	2023.26
	Indexing Time	8.14	8.14	890.44
	Retrieval Time	0.59	10.39	2.84

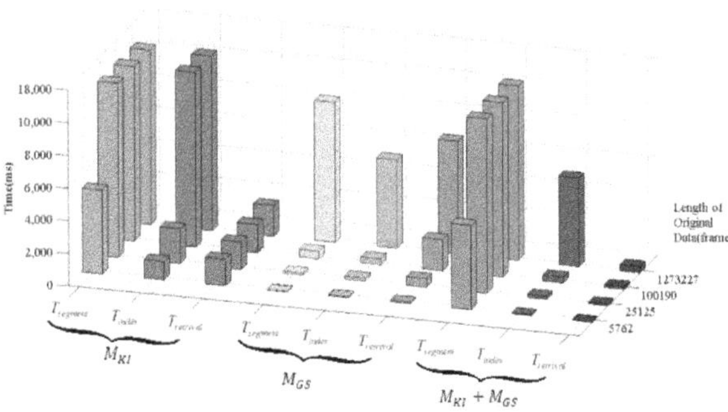

Figure 6. The cost in retrieval, indexing and segmenting of our proposed method compared to the other two in four motion databases with different sizes.

Kinetic interval feature is not only a low-dimension expression of original motion data, but also a kind of compression representation. It records time-space information of motion data. In retrieval experiments, the matching results are similar numerically and logically. The motion categories do not affect the retrieval accuracy.

7.3 Performance on Different Feature Sets

We conducted this experiment to evaluate performance on different feature sets. The feature sets are defined by Björn Krüger et al. [15], F_E^{15} consists of the positions of 4 end-effectors and head; F_E^{30} consists positions of 4 end-effectors and head, as well as the 5 positions of the elbows, knees and one chest joint (30 dimensions); F_E^{39} has all features of F_E^{30} and adds position of the shoulders and one lower-back joint (39 dimensions). The efficiency and usability of F_E^{15}, F_E^{30} and F_E^{39} has already been proved, especially for F_E^{15}. We use these feature sets and full feature set F_E^{all} consisting all the joints to compute the segmenting, indexing, and matching time on databases with different sizes to speed up the offline procedure and evaluate their performances on our approach. In Table 3, segmenting time is the sum of kinetic interval segmenting time and Gaussian-based segmenting time, indexing time is the time for constructing the index tree, and matching time is the sum of time for matching processes between query motion file and all the motion files in the candidate list. In addition, there are more than 20000 frames in the candidate list and 1273227 frames in the entire database.

Table 3. Average computation times (in seconds) for segmenting, indexing, matching using various feature sets on motion of four CMU databases (in frames) with different sizes

DB Size	Feature Sets	Pre-computing Time	Indexing Time	Matching Time
5762	F_E^{15}	2.6520	0.1092	0.0208
	F_E^{30}	4.5084	0.1092	0.0210
	F_E^{39}	5.6940	0.1248	0.0215
	F_E^{all}	7.7237	0.1092	0.0225
25125	F_E^{15}	10.9045	0.3432	0.0936
	F_E^{30}	18.7513	0.1560	0.0960
	F_E^{39}	23.7746	0.1716	0.0998
	F_E^{all}	32.4042	0.2028	0.1009
100190	F_E^{15}	41.9487	0.6084	0.3533
	F_E^{30}	76.0349	0.6552	0.3550
	F_E^{39}	96.5334	0.6396	0.3571
	F_E^{all}	131.0273	1.0920	0.3581
1273227	F_E^{15}	514.0723	9.1261	2.8584
	F_E^{30}	1044.1354	45.1467	2.8721
	F_E^{39}	1394.7034	66.6124	2.8891
	F_E^{all}	2036.1132	89.8878	2.8972

In Table 3, the computation times shows that as the number of features gets smaller, the segmenting and indexing process can be more efficient, especially for F_E^{15}.

Whereas lower dimensional feature sets make an improvement on offline procedure efficiency, we still need to keep the accuracy of the motion retrieval. We synthesize motion sequence by using the parameter equation of kinetic interval with different feature sets. Qualitative comparison between original motion sequence and calculated motion sequence has been made with the aims of experimenting variations of movement trend in different feature sets.

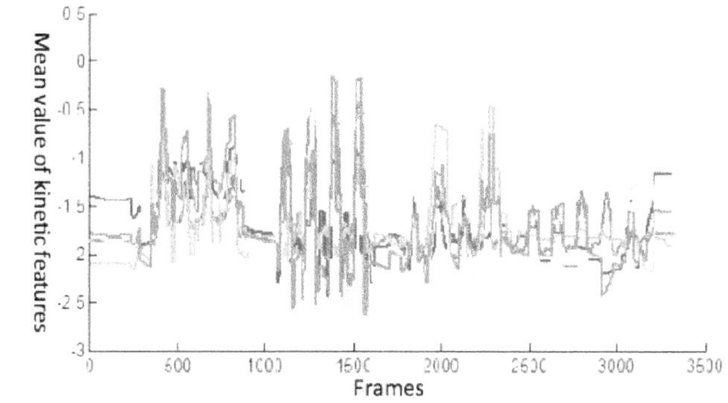

(a)

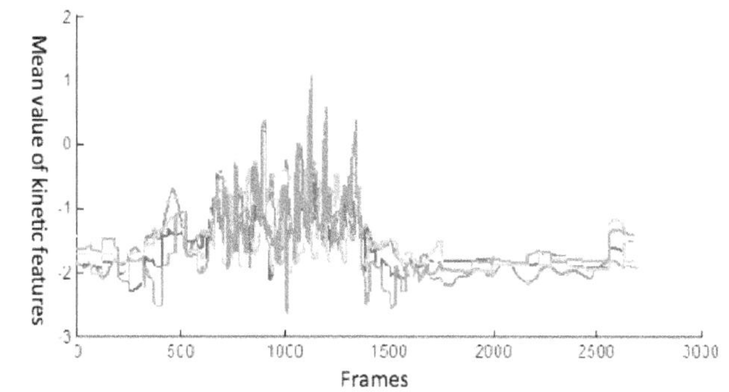

(b)

Figure 7. Kinetic intervals of different motion categories, (a) stylized walking motion, (b) dancing motion. The horizontal axis is frames of motion file, and the longitudinal axis is mean value of kinetic interval features. The red curves are the raw motion data, the blue ones are F_E^{all} ,the light blue ones are F_E^{15} ,the yellow ones are F_E^{39} ,the purple ones are F_E^{all} .

In Figure 7, the curves with low-dimensional feature sets can keep the feature of the original motion well. As Table 3 has already proved the efficiency of low-dimensional feature sets, it is reasonable to use low-dimensional feature sets while the accuracy requirement is not very strict.

8. CONCLUSION

In this paper, we proposed kinetic interval features which transform the motion expression from geometric space to a kinetic parameter space, at the same time they speed up the matching process. We use multi-layer clustered index tree to organize the motion databases. Given a query motion, The numerical and logical similar results can then be efficiently computed by two-level matching method. A numerical DDTW-based method is used for rough similarity matching, and then a logical kinetic interval-based method is used to refine the matching results. To evaluate the performance and usability of our approach, we tested our approach in a series of databases with different sizes. By analyzing the results, we found that the kinetic interval method has a significant improvement in the performance of matching process, and also has potential for applications of reconstructing motion from relatively few markers.

The current approach does not consider data compression for the repeated motion data or cycle data. If make such improvement for repeated and cycle motion data, the database construction and retrieval could be much more efficient. Also user study can be applied for retrieval results, which could gradually improve the accuracy for a motion database.

9. ACKNOWLEDGMENTS

Our thanks to HDM Stuttgart and CMU motion lab for sharing their motion data files. We also thank all anonymous references for constructive and valuable comments.

This research is supported by National Natural Science Foundation of China (61202243) and Doctoral Fund of Ministry of Education of China (20091101120032).

10. REFERENCES

[1] Rosenhahn B., Klette R., and Metaxas D. 2007. *Human Motion Understanding, Modeling, Capture, and Animation. Springer-Verlag Press*, Rio de Janeiro, Brazil.

[2] Christian B., Stefan B. and Daniel A. K. 2001. Searching in High-dimensional Spaces Index Structures for Improving the Performance of Multimedia Databases. *ACM Computing Surveys* 33, 3 (September 2001), 322–373. DOI= http://doi.acm.org/10.1145/502807.502809.

[3] CMU. Carnegie-Mellon Mocap Database. http://mocap.cs.cmu.edu.

[4] HDM05. Hochschule der Medien Database. http://www.mpi-inf.mpg.de/resources/HDM05/.

[5] Forbes K. and Fiume E. 2005. An Efficient Search Algorithm for Motion Data Using weighted PCA. In *Proceedings of the 2005 ACM SIGGRAPH/Eurographics* (Los Angeles, CA, USA, July,2005). SCA '05. ACM, New York, NY, 67-76. DOI= http://doi.acm.org/10.1145/1073368.1073377.

[6] Chuanjun L., Gaurav P., Siqing Z. and Prabhakaran B. 2004. Indexing of variable length multi-attribute motion data. In *Proceedings of the 2nd ACM international workshop on Multimedia databases* (Washington D.C., USA, November 8 - 13, 2004). MMDB '04. ACM, New York, NY, 75-84. DOI= http://doi.acm.org/10.1145/1032604.1032617.

[7] Meinard M., Tido R. and Michael C. 2005. Efficient Content-Based Retrieval of Motion Capture Data. *ACM Trans.on Graphics* 24, 3 (July 2005), 677–685. DOI= http://doi.acm.org/10.1145/1073204.1073247.

[8] Christos F., Ranganathan M. and Yannis M. 1994. Fast Subsequence Matching in Time-Seies Databases. In *Proceedings of the 1994 ACM SIGMOD international* (Minneapolis, Minnesota, USA, May 24 - 27, 1994). SIGMOD '94. ACM, New York, NY, 419-429. DOI= http://doi.acm.org/10.1145/191839.191925.

[9] Meinard M. and Tido R. 2006. Motion Templates for Automatic Classification and Retrieval of Motion Capture Data. In *Proceedings of the 2006 ACM SIGGRAPH/ Eurographics symposium on Computer animation* (Vienna, Austria, September 2 - 4, 2006). SCA '06. ACM, New York, NY, 137-146.

[10] Zhigang D., Qin G. and Qing L. 2009. Perceptually Consiste nt Example-based Human Motion Retrieval. In *Proceedings of the 2009 symposium on Interactive 3D graphics and games* (Boston, MA, USA, February 27 - March 1, 2009).

I3D '09. ACM, New York, NY, 191-198. DOI= http://doi.acm.org/10.1145/1507149.1507181.

[11] Pengjie W., Rynson W.H., Mingmin Z., Jiang W., Haiyu S. and Zhigeng P. 2011. A real-time database architecture for motion capture data. In *Proceedings of the 19th ACM international conference on Multimedia* (Scottsdale, Arizona, USA, Nov. 28 - Dec. 1, 2011). MM '11. ACM, New York, NY, 1337-1340. DOI= http://doi.acm.org/10.1145/2072298.2072008.

[12] Chuan S., Imran J. and Hassan F. 2011. Motion Retrieval Using Low-Rank Subspace Decomposition of Motion Volume. *Computer Graphics Forum*, 30,7 (September 2011), 1953-1962.

[13] Yasuhiko S., Shigeru K. and Toyohisa K. 2004. Motion Map: Image-based Retrieval and Segmentation of Motion Data. In *Proceedings of the 2004 ACM SIGGRAPH/Eurographics symposium on Computer animation* (Grenoble, France, August 27 - 29, 2004). SCA '04. ACM, New York, NY, 259-266. DOI= http://doi.acm.org/10.1145/1028523.1028557.

[14] Tianyu H., Feng-xia L., Shouyi Z. and Xiangchen L. Motion Retrieval Method Based on Geometric Feature Coding. *Journal of System Simulation*, 18, 10 (Oct. 2006), 2767-2773.

[15] Bjorn K., Jochen T., Andreas W. and Arno Z. 2010. Fast Local and Global Similarity Searches in Large Motion Capture Databases. In *Proceedings of the 2010 ACM SIGGRAPH/Eurographics Symposium on Computer Animation* (Madrid, Spain, July 02 - 04, 2010). SCA '10. ACM, New York, NY, 1-10.

[16] Yi L.. 2006. Efficient Human Motion Retrieval in Large Databases. In *Proceedings of the 4th international conference on Computer graphics and interactive techniques in Australasia and Southeast Asia* (Kuala Lumpur, Malaysia, November 28 - December 02, 2006). GRAPHITE '06. ACM, New York, NY, 31-37. DOI= http://doi.acm.org/10.1145/1174429.1174434.

[17] Chihyi C., Shihpi C., Mingyang W., Shinine Y. and Hsinchih L. 2008. Content-Based Retrieval for Human Motion Data. *Journal of Visual Communication and Image Representation*, 15, 3 (September, 2004), 446-466. DOI= http://dx.doi.org/10.1016/j.jvcir.2004.04.004.

[18] Eamonn K., Themistoklis P., Victor B. Z., Dimitrios G. and Marc C. 2004. Indexing Large Human-Motion Databases. In *Proceedings of the Thirtieth international conference on Very Large Data Bases* (Toronto, Canada, August 31 - September 3 2004). VLDB '04. Morgan Kaufmann Publishers, San Fransisco, CA, 780-791.

[19] Eamonn K. 2002. Exact indexing of dynamic time warping. In *Proceedings of the 28th international conference on Very Large Data Bases* (Hong Kong, China, August 20 - 23, 2002). VLDB '02. Morgan Kaufmann Publishers, San Fransisco, CA, 406-417.

[20] Kovar, L. and Gleicher, M. 2004. Automated extraction and parameterization of motions in large data sets. *ACM Trans.on Graphics* 23, 3 (August 2004), 559–568. DOI= http://doi.acm.org/10.1145/1015706.1015760.

[21] Eamonn J. K. and Michael J. P. 2001. Derivative Dynamic Time Warping. In *Proceedings of the First SIAM International Conference on Data Mining* (Chicago, IL, USA, April 5 - 7 2001).

Vision-Based Handwriting Recognition for Unrestricted Text Input in Mid-Air

Alexander Schick* Daniel Morlock*,† Christoph Amma†
Tanja Schultz† Rainer Stiefelhagen*,†
*Fraunhofer IOSB
Karlsruhe, Germany
alexander.schick@iosb.fraunhofer.de, daniel.morlock@gmail.com
†Karlsruhe Institute of Technology
Karlsruhe, Germany
{christoph.amma, tanja.schultz, rainer.stiefelhagen}@kit.edu

ABSTRACT

We propose a vision-based system that recognizes handwriting in mid-air. The system does not depend on sensors or markers attached to the users and allows unrestricted character and word input from any position. It is the result of combining handwriting recognition based on Hidden Markov Models with multi-camera 3D hand tracking. We evaluated the system for both quantitative and qualitative aspects. The system achieves recognition rates of 86.15% for character and 97.54% for small-vocabulary isolated word recognition. Limitations are due to slow and low-resolution cameras or physical strain. Overall, the proposed handwriting recognition system provides an easy-to-use and accurate text input modality without placing restrictions on the users.

Categories and Subject Descriptors

H.5.2 [**User Interfaces**]: Input devices and strategies

Keywords

Handwriting recognition, 3D hand tracking

1. INTRODUCTION

With current advances in technology, we see a rapidly increasing availability, but also demand, for intuitive human-machine interaction. Devices are not only controlled by mouse and keyboard anymore, but we are now using gesture-controlled devices in public areas and at our homes. Distant hand gestures in particular removed the restriction to operate a device directly; we can now interact freely with machines while moving around. In this work, we are interested in human-machine interaction that does not force users to touch a specific device or to wear special sensors, but that allows for unrestricted use.

While there is a great variety of human-computer interaction techniques to interact with distant virtual objects, *e.g.* to select menu entries, there is still a lack for intuitive and unrestricted text input. Although there are ways to input text by using a virtual keyboard on a display [11] or by speech recognition, there are situations where both are not suitable: the first requires interaction with a display and occupies space on it and for the latter, users must speak which is not always possible depending on the surroundings. With this work, we extend the available text input modalities by introducing an intuitive handwriting recognition system.

In the remainder of this work, we present a system that combines vision-based 3D hand tracking with 3D handwriting recognition. It allows users to write characters and words in mid-air. This extends the use of 3D hand gestures to allow for convenient and unrestricted text input. In Section 2, we discuss related work before introducing the proposed system in Section 3. In Section 4, we present the experimental evaluation before concluding in Section 5.

ICMI'12, October 22–26, 2012, Santa Monica, California, USA.

2. RELATED WORK

We will first discuss established approaches for handwriting recognition before focusing on approaches that are closest to the proposed system.

A comprehensive review of handwriting recognition can be found in Plamondon *et al.* [8]. In our work, we recognize handwriting while the text is written which is called an online handwriting recognition task. Following [8], online handwriting recognition can be classified into structural or rule-based approaches where the trajectory is analyzed by rules and grammars and into statistical methods based on linear discriminant analysis, principal component analysis, neural networks, or Hidden Markov Models (HMM) [9]. In particular, Hidden Markov Models are widely used to model motion trajectories. They can be considered a state-of-the-art technique and are also used in the proposed system.

Handwriting recognition is not limited to paper or digital surfaces, but has also been extended to the third dimension. Amma *et al.* introduced a wearable text input system based on a motion sensor attached to a glove [1]. Acceleration and angular rate are measured and processed in a left-to-right

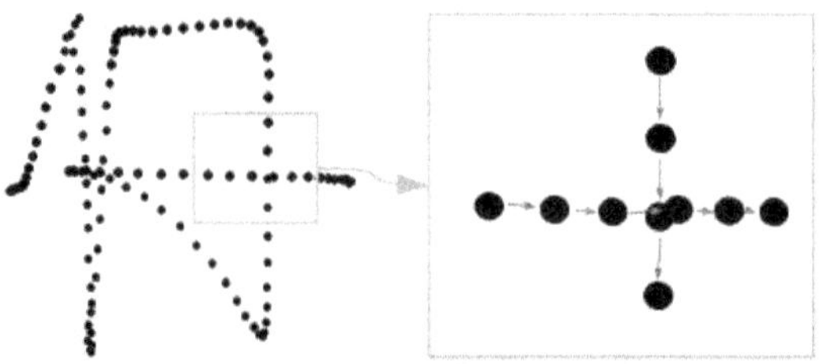

Figure 1: **Features. The connecting vectors between sampled points of the trajectory serve as features for the handwriting recognition system.**

(a) (b)

Figure 2: Handwriting recognition. The images show a) handwriting in front of a videowall and b) different trajectories when writing the letter *E*.

HMM for recognition of whole sentences. This system is most similar to our system, but since it is intended for mobile applications it requires the user to wear a glove, which is not desireable in stationary use. Other approaches include Zhou *et al.* [13] and Kim *et al.* [4] with the same restrictions introduced by requiring to use handheld or wearable devices. Text input for large displays was also investigated by Shoemaker *et al.* [11], but for the Wiimote and without handwriting recognition. In contrast, our system has no such requirements and allows unrestricted text input.

In sign language recognition, hand gestures are interpreted as symbols and words. A recent overview can be found in [3]. Depending on the system, we have some techniques in common, in particular the use of computer vision in combination with HMM-based gesture recognition [12]. However, our targeted problem domain differs as in our case, we focus on recognizing continuously written words.

Hand tracking systems are of much interest in computer vision because they are a prerequisite for many forms of human-machine interaction. Examples of vision-based tracking of hands and arms in 3D were given by Azarbayejani and Pentland [2] and Nickel and Stiefelhagen [7], to name just a few. A survey for vision-based gesture recognition can be found in [6]. Gesture-based handwriting recognition with a head-mounted camera was shown by Liu *et al.* [5], but only for the Graffiti 2 alphabet and only for single characters. In our work, we will combine a vision-based hand tracking system with handwriting recognition to provide a text input modality that does not require additional devices. To the best of our knowledge, we are unaware of vision-based handwriting recognition of whole words based on concatenated individual character models.

3. VISION-BASED HANDWRITING RECOGNITION

The proposed handwriting recognition system consists of three modules: vision-based data aquisition, feature extraction, and handwriting recognition that will now be introduced in more detail.

3.1 Data aquisition

The proposed system recognizes characters and words that are written in mid-air with the hand acting as the pen. Therefore, the 3D trajectory of the hand is of interest. To compute this trajectory, we use a voxel carving approach to reconstruct users in 3D [10]. Based on the user's pose, we extract the arm and track the 3D trajectory of the hand. There are also other ways to aquire this data, e.g. with sensors based on structured light like the Microsoft Kinect. But a vision-based system has the advantage that there is a much broader variety of sensors to chose from with varying resolutions and framerates which can be important for the overall performance (Section 4.3). To deal with sensor noise and occasional misclassifications, we applied a Kalman filter to smooth the trajectory. The system setup is described in Section 4.

3.2 Feature extraction

Due to the discrete capturing process of cameras, the trajectory is formed by an ordered set of points. The features used in our system are based on the connecting vectors between each of these consecutive pairs of trajectory points. These connecting vectors are position invariant. To account for variations in writing size, we normalize the connecting vectors which makes them also scale invariant.

When writing in mid-air, users tend to write on a virtual plane in front of themselves. We exploit this by projecting the 3D trajectory of the writing hand on a 2D plane in front of the users which has the advantage that it reduces the feature space. The beginning and ending of handwriting can be easily detected because users usually move their hands forward or backward, respectively. We found that there were no pen-up and pen-down movements while writing as is the case in traditional handwriting. This leads to ligatures being part of the trajectory because we get one continuous stroke instead of alternating pen-up and pen-down movements. Figure 1 shows an example of the extracted 2D features and Figure 2b of trajectories with ligatures.

3.3 Handwriting recognition

Character and word recognition are both based on Hidden Markov Models which is an established technique in handwriting recognition [8]. Specifically, the system is based on left-to-right HMMs. First, for each character, a separate HMM is trained with training data of multiple people (see Section 4 for more details) with the extracted features described above as observations. Then, words can be modeled as a concatenation of character HMMs, i.e. for any given arbitrary word, an HMM can be constructed. A vocabulary defines the set of words that can be actually recognized. The number of words in the vocabulary equals the number of possible classes and, therefore, a larger vocabulary results in a more difficult recognition problem.

We examine two recognition tasks, the recognition of single characters and the recognition of words. Our system

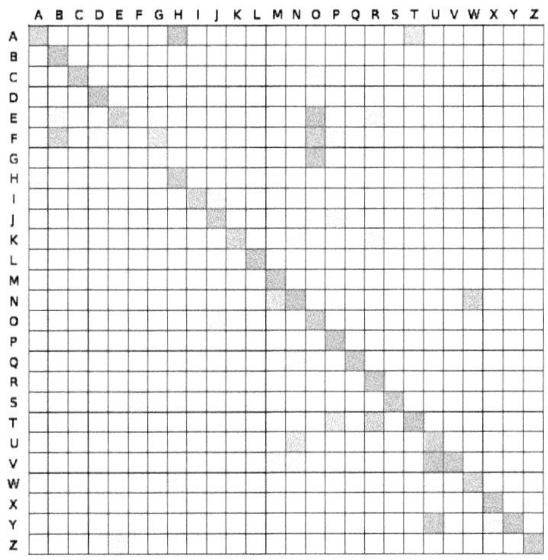

Figure 3: Confusion matrix for character recognition.

allows the continuous input of isolated words, that means no artificial pauses or segmentation between characters is necessary. Words contain not only a sequence of characters but also the motion between the characters. For word recognition, we therefore perform an additional EM-training on word data to refine the beginning and end of character models in order to model the transitional motion between consecutive characters without introducing additional states.

The proposed system recognizes handwriting in mid-air based on the 3D trajectory of the writing hand. We want to note that it can also be used for general purpose gesture recognition if the gesture is based on a continuous hand trajectory.

4. EXPERIMENTS

We will first discuss the technical evaluation of the proposed system before discussing qualitative feedback that we received during data aquisition. To record the hand's trajectory, a two-camera setup [10] was used in all experiments. The cameras captured 30 frames per second with a resolution of $640x480$ pixels. While the hand tracking system is able to run with $50fps$, it was limited by the cameras to $30fps$.

We asked users to stand in front of a videowall in a distance of about $1.5m$ (see Figure 2a). We instructed users to write large, block capital letters. The trajectory of the writing hand was displayed in front of the users on the videowall as visual feedback. The beginning and ending of each word was recognized by moving the hand forward or backward, respectively. Before we started collecting the data, we let users familiarize themselves with the system first. The data collection was part of a larger study; however, in this paper we focus on the handwriting recognition as it is our contribution. Details of the full experiment will be made available.

4.1 Technical evaluation

We evaluated both the accuracy of recognizing single characters and words. All evaluation was done in a person-independent manner. We asked five users to write each letter of the alphabet five times. These samples build the character recognition dataset D_C. For the word recognition, we selected 40 words from a list of frequent english words [1]. The length of the words were equally distributed between 2 and 11 characters, e.g. *to*, *about*, *support*, and *performance*. We asked 16 users to write each word one time. These samples were collected in the word recognition dataset D_W. The datasets are shown in Table 1.

Figure 4: Similar trajectories. The images show similar trajectories for characters E and G. Ligatures are highlighted in red.

Name	Type	Users	Samples	Total samples
D_C	characters	5	5×26	650
D_W	words	16	40	640

Table 1: Evaluation datasets.

For character recognition, we used a leave-one-out cross-validation. The best performance with 86.15% recognition rate was achieved by a system with 24 states per HMM with 10 GMMs per state with diagonal covariances. We further used silence states to model no-motion at the beginning and end of each HMM. We explain the rather high number of Gaussians by two factors. First, the handwriting styles varied for each person even for block capital letters (see Figure 2b). Second, the low number of sample points for each trajectory due to limited framerates of the cameras can lead to varying trajectories even for the same writing style. The low sample rate will also be discussed in Section 4.3. Figure 3 shows the confusion matrix for character recognition. While recognition is generally good, we observe typical confusions between N and W, and A and H which have also been observed for a glove based system [1]. Specific to our system is the confusion of letters *E*, *F*, and *G* with *O*. This can be explained by the continuous writing style of characters together with the position independence of the features: when writing each of these letters, one starts on the left and moves to the top, makes a clock-wise circle before moving the hand to the right again; hence the confusion. Figure 4 gives a visual example.

For word recognition, the HMMs were build by concatenating the character HMMs and refining them based on word examples (see Section 3.3). The character models were based on D_C. To evaluate the word recognition accuracy, the dataset D_W was used. As mentioned in Section 3.3, the word models were build by concatenating the individual character models and additionally trained on word data of the training set to refine the transitions between characters. The training and evaluation was done in a leave-one-out cross-validation setting. For the D_W dataset, the system achieved average recognition rates of 97.54%. This

[1]http://wortschatz.uni-leipzig.de/html/wliste.html

high recognition rate is due to the relatively low number of words and the high number of varying writing styles in the training set which lead to a good generalization. We expect this rate to drop with less samples and a higher number of words. However, when evaluating the same models trained with the 40 words of the D_W dataset against an increased vocabulary of 99 words, the recognition rates were still 86.60% even though the number of classes to recognize was more than doubled.

4.2 User feedback

While recording the D_W dataset, we also gathered user feedback about the system. Handwriting in mid-air was generally perceived as intuitive and easy to understand. Users almost immediately understood the system and quickly felt comfortable using it. However, they criticised the low input speed and the physical strain. The low input speed was also confirmed by our measurements: it took on average about three seconds per character which can be explained by the hand tracking system (see Section 4.3). Low input speed leads to longer writing times which ultimately is responsible for increased physical strain.

Surprisingly, visual feedback was generally perceived as disturbing. While we first expected it to help users to see what they were writing, the continuous trajectory was generally perceived as confusing. Because our system does in no respect depend on the visual feedback, this source of disturbance can easily be avoided. Further, it would also be possible to display machine-written single characters on-the-fly when they are recognized.

4.3 Improvements

We will now discuss the major shortcommings and possible improvements. While the recognition rates were good for both character and word recognition, the system was criticized for taking too much time and being physically too straining. These problems can be explained by the hand tracking system, specifically the camera framerates of $30fps$ and resolutions of $640x480$ pixels. While $30fps$ is generally considered real-time in computer vision, it turns out that this is not sufficient for the proposed handwriting recognition system. When writing quickly, only few points of the trajectory are sampled. (In comparison, wearable handwriting recognition devices have sample rates of over 800 samples per second [1].) These sparse samples are not sufficient to robustly recognize handwriting with the proposed system when writing quickly and, therefore, users had to write rather slowly. Further, due to the low resolution, small hand movements were not clearly visible thus forcing users to write larger letters. Both problems can be addressed by using cameras with higher framerates and higher resolutions to allow for higher writing speeds and smaller characters. While the current system is well suited to input small amounts of text, we recommend using higher framerates in future vision-based handwriting recognition systems.

5. CONCLUSION

We presented a vision-based handwriting recognition system for person-independent single character and word recognition in mid-air. The system achieved recognition rates of 86.15% for character recognition and 97.54% for word recognition. The only requirement of the system is that users are visible for the cameras. Apart from that, neither a display nor wearable sensors are required, thus offering users an intuitive way to insert text anywhere in a given area. This enables us to use natural text input in the fast-growing field of gesture-based interactive systems. In future work, we want to experiment with faster cameras and higher resolutions to allow for increased input speeds, smaller characters, and less physical strain.

6. ACKNOWLEDGMENTS

This work was partially supported by the FhG Internal Programs under Grant No. 692026.

7. REFERENCES

[1] C. Amma, M. Georgi, and T. Schultz. Airwriting: Hands-Free Mobile Text Input by Spotting and Continuous Recognition of 3d-Space Handwriting with Inertial Sensors. In *Proc. International Symposium on Wearable Computers*, pages 52–59, 2012.

[2] A. Azarbayejani and A. Pentland. Real-time self-calibrating stereo person tracking using 3-D shape estimation from blob features. In *Proc. International Conference on Pattern Recognition*, 1996.

[3] H. Cooper, B. Holt, and R. Bowden. Sign Language Recognition. In *Visual Analysis of Humans*, pages 539–562. 2011.

[4] D. Kim, H. Choi, and J. Kim. 3D Space Handwriting Recognition with Ligature Model. In *Proc. Ubiquitous Computing Systems*, 2006.

[5] Y. Liu, X. Liu, and Y. Jia. Hand-Gesture Based Text Input for Wearable Computers. In *Proc. Computer Vision Systems*, 2006.

[6] S. Mitra and T. Acharya. Gesture Recognition: A Survey. *IEEE Transactions on Systems, Man, and Cybernetics, Part C: Applications and Reviews*, 37(3):311 –324, 2007.

[7] K. Nickel and R. Stiefelhagen. Pointing Gesture Recognition based on 3D-Tracking of Face, Hands and Head Orientation. In *Proc. International Conference on Multimodal Interfaces*, 2003.

[8] R. Plamondon and S. N. Srihari. On-Line and Off-Line Handwriting Recognition: A Comprehensive Survey. *Transactions on Pattern Analysis*, 22(1):63–83, 2000.

[9] L. Rabiner. A tutorial on hidden Markov models and selected applications in speech recognition. *Proceedings of the IEEE*, 77(2):257–286, 1989.

[10] A. Schick, F. van de Camp, J. Ijsselmuiden, and R. Stiefelhagen. Extending Touch: Towards Interaction with Large-Scale Surfaces. In *Proc. Interactive Tabletops and Surfaces*, pages 117–124, 2009.

[11] G. Shoemaker, L. Findlater, J. Q. Dawson, and K. S. Booth. Mid-air text input techniques for very large wall displays. In *Proc. Graphics Interface*, pages 231–238, 2009.

[12] Z. Zafrulla, H. Brashear, T. Starner, H. Hamilton, and P. Presti. American Sign Language Recognition with the Kinect. In *Proc. International Conference on Multimodal Interfaces*, pages 279–286, 2011.

[13] S. Zhou, Z. Dong, W. Li, and C. P. Kwong. Hand-written character recognition using MEMS motion sensing technology. In *Proc. Advanced Intelligent Mechatronics*, pages 1418 –1423, 2008.

Investigating the Midline Effect for Visual Focus of Attention Recognition

Samira Sheikhi
Idiap Research Institute and EPFL, Switzerland
samira.sheikhi@idiap.ch

Jean-Marc Odobez
Idiap Research Institute and EPFL, Switzerland
odobez@idiap.ch

ABSTRACT

This paper addresses the recognition of people's visual focus of attention (VFOA), the discrete version of gaze indicating who is looking at whom or what. In absence of high definition images, we rely on people's head pose to recognize the VFOA. To the contrary of most previous works that assumed a fixed mapping between head pose directions and gaze target directions, we investigate novel gaze models documented in psychovision that produce a dynamic (temporal) mapping between them. This mapping accounts for two important factors affecting the head and gaze relationship: the shoulder orientation defining the gaze midline of a person varies over time; and gaze shifts from frontal to the side involve different head rotations than the reverse. Evaluated on a public dataset and on data recorded with the humanoid robot Nao, the method exhibit better adaptivity often producing better performance than state-of-the-art approach.

Categories and Subject Descriptors

I.2.9 [**Artifical Intelligence**]: Robotics- *Operator Interfaces*

Keywords

Gaze, visual focus of attention, HRI, HCI

1. INTRODUCTION

As a good indicator of people's interest and due to its major role in non-verbal communication, VFOA is an key cue for human interaction analysis and in Human-Computer/Robot interactions (HCI, HRI) design [3].

Sensor based methodologies can be used to estimate people gaze. They are accurate but quite invasive and restrictive. Computer vision techniques relying on perceived information from gaze or head has also made good progresses, but still usually restrict subject mobility considering the need for cameras with narrow field-of-views for looking at the eyes.

As an alternative, researchers have considered the use of head pose as a clue for gaze [7, 9, 1, 10, 4]. Head poses, however, are ambiguous: in realistic scenarios, the same head pose can be used to look at different targets, depending on the situation. To address this issue, researchers have proposed to exploit other cues: speaker information or conversational regimes [7] that can be exended with contextual knowledge from the group activity [1].

While context is important, a central issue is how to set the expected head pose of an observer that looks at a given target? in other words, how to define a mapping from the gaze target direction to the corresponding head pose. This is essential to set the parameters of recognizers like Hidden Markov Models (HMM) and decode the sequence of VFOA targets given the head pose sequence. Methods often rely on manual setting, potentially followed by adaptation [7].

One of the few work addressing this problem is [1]. Exploiting results on human gazing behavior and head-eye dynamics involved in saccadic gaze shifts [6, 5], they introduced a linear gaze model relating the head pose, gaze direction, and head reference (coined gaze midline in [5]) as illustrated in Fig. 1(a). While the method worked when applied to meetings, it suffers from two drawbacks: the reference direction, which corresponds to the direction perpendicular to the shoulder, was assumed to be fixed and set according to the setup. This approach might not be feasible in more dynamic settings, like in HRI with multiple people where the robot is not always the main focus, and more generally in scenarios involving people free to move and re-orient themselves, as illustrated in Fig. 2. The second drawback, pointed out in several psychovisual works, is that the mapping not only depends on the the gaze direction and midline reference, but also on the head or gaze direction before the shift, resulting in different head poses for looking at different targets even for the same head reference direction.

In this paper, we investigate both problems. In absence of shoulder orientation measures, we introduce an implicit estimation of the midline direction, and propose two approaches inspired by [5] to improve gaze-to-head mapping and gaze shift models. Experiments on meeting benchmark data and on data recorded by a robot (Nao) shows the benefit of several modeling components. To our knowledge, this has not been done before. The work in [9] is the closest to ours. In a dynamic scenario authors proposes to use a discrete set of head-to-gaze ratios and estimate the most likely based on gaze prediction and differential head pose indicators. However, the reference direction setting was not addressed, and their approach is quite different from our proposition that compensates the models' limitation relying on models inspired from human behaviors [5].

ICMI'12, October 22–26, 2012, Santa Monica, California, USA.

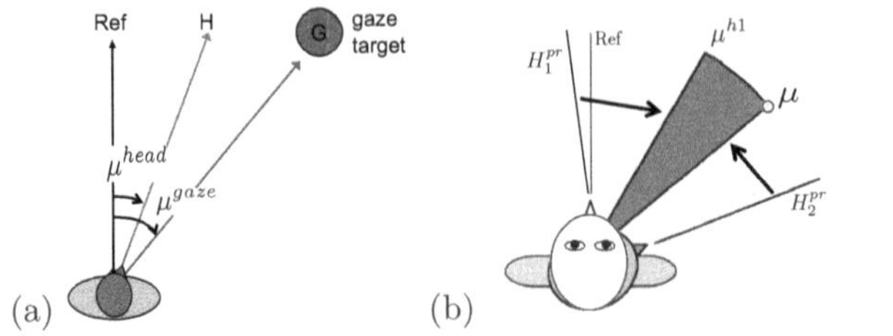

Figure 1: Gaze models. (a) Geometrical model. The person is assumed to be looking at the reference direction, or midline (grossly, the body orientation). Then, looking at a gaze target is accomplished by rotating both the eyes and head, with the head part being a fixed fraction of the full gaze rotation. (b) Midline effect [5]. The interval of head positions $[\mu^{h1}, \mu]$ corresponding to the target at position μ. When the gaze is moved to μ from initial position H_1^{pr}, the head is moved to μ^{h1} according the geometrical model. When the gaze shift is centripetal from H_1^{pr} to μ, the head is moved to μ. For initial head positions between μ^{h1} and μ, an eye-only saccade to μ is made (the head position remains the same).

2. VFOA RECOGNITION MODEL

2.1 VFOA recognition using a HMM model

In this model, the distribution of head poses associated to a given VFOA target is represented by a distribution (a Gaussian) with different parameters, whereas transitions between VFOA targets is represented by a transition matrix A. More specifically, let H_t and F_t indicate head pose and focus values at time t, and $\mu^h \in (\mathbb{R}^2)^K$ and $\Sigma_H \in (\mathbb{R}^4)^K$ denote the means and covariances of each of the K Gaussians associated with the targets. The HMM equations can be written as follows:

$$P(H_t|F_t = n) = \mathcal{N}(H_t|\mu^h(n), \Sigma_H(n)) \quad (1)$$

$$P(F_t = m|F_{t-1} = n) = A_{nm} \quad (2)$$

Parameter setting. This is a major issue. Following previous work, the covariance of each target can be set according to its size and head pose estimation variability. In absence of other prior, the transition matrix A can also reasonably be set to satisfy our expectation of preserving the VFOA continuity in the sequence.

However, although they play the most important role in the model, setting the means of the Gaussians μ^h is not possible in an easy way. Using training data is not really an option, since VFOA annotation is difficult, time consuming, and data needs to be gathered and annotated for each configuration of the observer, targets and settings. This is especially problematic if people are free to move.

A solution to the above difficulty is to use **gaze models** derived from gazing behavior [6, 5]. Accordingly, gazing at a target is accomplished by rotating both the eyes ('eye-in-head' rotation) and the head as illustrated in Fig. 1. More precisely, as a first approximation, the means of the Gaussians can be set as a fixed linear combination of the gaze and *head reference* directions. For a gaze target n, we have:

$$\mu^{hb}(n) - R = \alpha\ (\mu(n) - R) \Rightarrow \mu^{hb}(n) = \alpha\ \mu(n) + (1-\alpha)R \quad (3)$$

where $R \in \mathbb{R}^2$ denotes the reference direction and $\mu \in (\mathbb{R}^2)^K$ the target directions. The coefficient α is usually set between 0.5 and 0.7 for pan and between 0.3 and 0.5 for the tilt angle. Eq. 3 can be used to set the Gaussian mean corresponding to target n in our HMM model. Our baseline will consist of the above model with the reference R set to a constant value as done in most previous works.

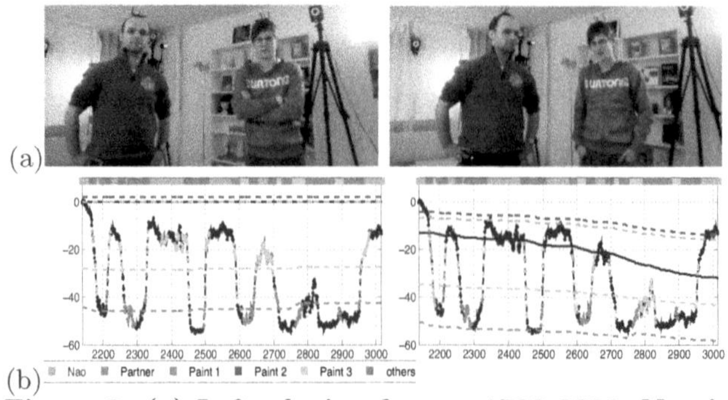

Figure 2: (a) Left: during frames 1700-2200, Nao is the main speaker, participants tend to look straight at him. Right: afterwards (quiz part) participants alternatively look at the robot and the second person (amongst others). Their reference direction is thus different, and so are the pose for looking at Nao. (b) head pose (pan angle) of the person on the right in image (a). The ground truth VFOA is displayed in the top bar, with color codes below. The head pose data is displayed in black when the recognition is correct, and in the color of the wrongly recognized VFOA otherwise. Dashed lines indicate the pan pose mean for looking at each target for the baseline (left), or the proposed model (right). In this later case, the black line shows the head reference. With the dynamic reference, head poses for looking at each of the target are better predicted, like for looking at Nao (despite its high variability: pan near 0 at frame 2150, near -17 at frame 2550).

2.2 Model G1: Dynamical Head References and the Midline Effect

Reference setting. Setting the Gaussians means using the above model requires the knowledge of R and of the target directions. Eq. 3 shows the importance of the reference: using a wrong value for R shifts mean values for all targets $\mu^h(n)$ simultaneously, which can have dramatic effects.

This importance of knowing the head reference is also illustrated in Fig. 2. Unless the reference direction (shoulder orientation) is constrained by the setting (eg when people are seated) using a constant reference can be problematic. General interactions will result in more variations and shifts in the reference as people are free to move, motivating the need for setting the reference dynamically.

Midline effect. As documented in [5], and illustrated in Fig. 1, the gaze model defined by Eq. 3 is only valid if the gaze shift goes from the reference to a given target. Indeed, in [5] shows that how much of a gaze shift is accomplished by the head or by the eye depends on the position of the head (which is not aligned with the reference in general) at the start of the gaze, and whether the shift goes through the reference or not, hence the term 'midline effect' used in [5][1]. From the analysis of the psychovision literature, the

[1]In [5], the reference is called midline.

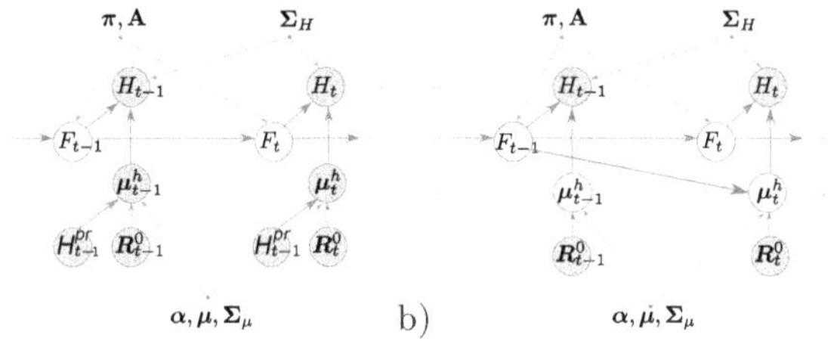

a) b)

Figure 3: Graphical models. (a) Model G1. The head reference direction and the mean head pose of the Gaussians are now variables over time, and the recent head pose can be exploited. (b) model G2. The mean head pose for looking at a target depends on the gaze target at the previous time step.

authors derived a gaze model which is illustrated in Fig. 1b, and that we have investigated in our research.

First model G1. Our goal is to derive a gaze model that accounts both for a dynamically estimated reference, and for the midline effect. To address the first point, we relied on the following intuition. A person tends to orient himself towards the set of gaze targets he/she spends time looking at. Such a body position makes it more comfortable and less energy consuming to rotate his head towards different gaze targets. As a corollary, this means that his average head pose over time is a good indicator of his reference direction, and can be used as reference estimate. Therefore we set the reference value at frame R_t^0 as the head pose average over a previous time window:

$$R_t^0 = \sum_{i=t-w}^{t} H_i / w$$

To investigate the midline effect, we need to know what was the value of the head pose before the gaze shift occurs. To this end, we introduced the variable H^{pr} defining the previous head pose and used as estimate of this variable the average of the head poses computed over a window of size w^p separated by a gap δ^p from the current instant:

$$H_t^{pr} = \frac{1}{w^p} \sum_{i=t-w^p-\delta^p}^{t-\delta^p} H_i \quad (4)$$

Finally, the G1 gaze model was implemented by setting the head pose mean $\mu_t^{hg1}(n)$ of the nth target at time t using the rules (for $\mu(n) > 0$ and omitting (n) for simplicity):

$$\mu_t^{h1} = \alpha\mu + (1-\alpha)R_t^0 \quad (5)$$

$$\text{if } H_t^{pr} < \mu \text{ then } \mu_t^{hg1} = \mu_t^{h1} \quad (6)$$

$$\text{otherwise } \mu_t^{hg1} = Min\left(\mu, \mu_t^{h1} + \alpha_H(H_t^{pr} - \mu_t^{h1})\right) \quad (7)$$

The above equations can be adapted for $\mu(n) \leq 0$. The factor α_H indicates how much we take into account the previous head pose in the estimate. When $\alpha_H = 0$, we always have $\mu_t^{hg1} = \mu_t^{h1}$, which means that the head pose means are set using the standard geometric model, but using a dynamically set reference. When $\alpha_H = 1$, the implemented model is exactly the one proposed by [5].

2.3 Model G2: implementing gaze shifts

When implementing the midline effect, the previous model has one drawback: at each time step, a gaze shift is assumed. In other words, even if the person is focusing on target i, the previous head pose H_t^{pr}, estimated through recursion over a short window, evolves and introduces an evolution of what the head pose mean of the target i itself should be.

Figure 4: Settings. Left. Meeting, with VFOA targets for the person on the right. Middle. Nao D1. Right. Nao D2, from vernissage recordings, with the VFOA targets for one of the 2 participants.

As alternative to the G1 model, we define the gaze situation prior to the gaze shift by the gaze at the previous instant. In this case, the head pose mean to look at target n at time t, given the previous focus F_{t-1}, is given by:

$$\mu_t^{hg2}(n) = \alpha_1\mu(n) + \alpha_2\mu(F_{t-1}) + (1-\alpha_1-\alpha_2)R_t^0 \quad (8)$$

Thus, in absence of gaze shift ($F_{t-1} = n$), the head pose mean is simply given by the geometrical model with $\alpha = \alpha_1 + \alpha_2$, while in case of a gaze shift $F_{t-1} \neq n$, the head pose is not only affected by the reference and new gaze direction $\mu(n)$, but also by the previous gaze (the head should be closer to the previous gaze than what would be predicted by the geometrical model).

Fig. 3(b) shows the G2 graphical model. The link between the hidden states F_{t-1} and μ_t^h renders the inference more complex than in a standard HMM. In practice, we conducted the inference sequentially, using the estimated focus at time $t-1$ to estimate the optimal focus at time t.

3. EXPERIMENTAL RESULTS.

3.1 Data Sets and Experimental Protocol

We used three datasets for experiments, with setup illustrated in Fig. 4. The **Meeting dataset** was taken from [2]. It has 8 meeting sessions (1 hour of data), and provides the ground truth head poses for the two persons in front of the camera. Each person has 5 possible gaze targets: the 3 other persons (the one on his side, two on the other table side), the slide screen and the table.

The two other datasets were recorded with the humanoid robot Nao and in both cases, head poses were extracted with an automatic algorithm [8]. In the first dataset, **D1**, two participants were seating in front of Nao and discussing about Nao's features. At one point, one of the person leaves and a third person comes in. The session lasts 22 minutes (min). Each person has 3 visual targets: the other participant, Nao and a booklet which they refer to during the recording. The 3rd dataset **D2**, involves two participants standing in front of Nao and free to walk around and look at different objects. In a first part, Nao explains three paintings to them; in a second part, Nao makes them a quizz where the participants can discuss before giving their answer. VFOA annotations are available for 3 recordings, for a total of around 22:30min per side, ie 45min in total. As shown in Fig.4, the VFOA labels were Robot (NAO), Partner, Painting1, Painting2, Painting3, and in addition, Others, that we used when people were looking elsewhere.

Performance Measure: We uses the Frame based Recognition Rate (FRR), that is, the percentage of frames where the VFOA has been correctly recognized.

Algorithms: For each datasets, 3 models were tested. The baseline is the HMM model with a fixed reference value. G1 uses the head pose average R_t^0 as reference, and sets the

Table 1: Performance on the Meeting data

Person	Training	Baseline	Model G1	Model G2
Person on left	same seat	64.7	65.7	**68.4**
Person on left	other seat	64.5	66.7	**69.3**
Person on right	same seat	57.0	**58.7**	58.5
Person on right	other seat	43.9	**59.0**	57.8

head pose using the new formula to account for the midline effect. G2, in addition to using R_t^0, implements gaze shifts by using the previous gaze.

3.2 Parameter Setting

Meeting Data. We set the gaze target directions from the physical setting and the Gaussians variances as in [2]. The reference direction for the baseline was set as the middle between VFOA gaze target as in [2]. The remaining parameters were adjusted by cross-validation for each model, by considering two different set-ups: cross validation using training data either from the same seat, or from the other seat. The second case is useful to see whether our model is sensitive to a specific setting or it is more general.

Nao Data. For **D1 and D2** the gaze directions were defined from the geometrical setting. The reference direction for the baseline was set as looking at Nao, which is a reasonable choice in an HRI scenario. Standard deviations of Gaussian were set to 10 and 8 for pan and tilt. Other parameters were adjusted by leave-one-out cross validation on the three participants in D1, and on the 6 sequences (2 participants in 3 recordings) for D2.

3.3 Results

Meeting data. Table 1 shows the results of the three models. The first model outperforms the baseline, particularly in more mismatched conditions, when parameters are learned from the other seat, exhibiting therefore a better adaptation capacity. The main (mismatched) parameters leading to the degradation is the parameter α of the gaze model (see Eq. 3) that directly impact the prediction of the head poses: for PL, the optimal parameters is around 0.8, whereas for PR, it is around 0.5. The different values of α_{pan} obtained from two different seats could be due to the fixed choice of the reference which leads to different values for these two settings. This effect does not exist for the first model G1 and the chosen parameters through cross-validation are completely consistent with an optimal value for both seats around 0.7 for α_{pan}. On the other hand, we can see that G2 performs better than the G1 in most cases. We observed that the improvement happened mainly during consecutive gaze shifts involving stable head pose changes, and was also observed in the Nao case.

Nao Data. For **D1** the results are summarized in Table 2. Despite the quite different setting, the conclusions are similar to the meeting data. However, model G1 outperforms the baseline with a larger difference. This is particularly true for the first person, who, being more dynamic during the interaction, shifted her body orientation towards both the robot and the other participants, wheras the two other people remained more firmly seated in the sofa and oriented towards Nao, which better matches the looking at Nao assumption of the baseline. Also, model G2 performs better than model G1 for all of the sequences. Table 3 contains the results for **D2**. The same conclusion than with D1 can be drawn: G1 outperforms the baseline with a noticable difference and G2 is performing slightly better than G1.

Table 2: Performance First Nao Data (D1)

Person	Baseline	Model G1	Model G2
Person1	49.78	64.36	**65.32**
Person2	91.52	93.73	**95.45**
Person3	67.83	66.12	**68.01**

Table 3: Performance on Second Nao Data (D2)

Person	Baseline	Model G1	Model G2
Person on right	54.4	59.0	**59.2**
Person on left	55.9	59.1	**60.9**

When looking at the parameters selected by cross-validation on the 3 datasets for model G1, most of the time the value of α_H was 0: the main improvement with G1 was thus due to the use of an adaptive reference, rather than to the midline effect illustrated in Fig. 1b.

4. CONCLUSION.

We investigated two drawbacks of the previous work for mapping vfoa targets to head pose values. To overcome the problem with the fix reference (midline) we provided an implicit estimate of it. To account for the dependency of the gaze-to-head mapping to the previous head or gaze before the shift we proposed two approaches inspired from human behaviors [5]. Experiments on meeting benchmark data and on two datasets recorded by a humanoid robot shows the benefit of several modeling components.

As future work, using image-based gaze directions [4] would be beneficial, and can be combined with our approach. However, this is true only if they can be extracted sufficiently reliably from the available images.

Acknowledgments. This work was supported by the European Community's Seventh Framework Programme through the HUMAVIPS project (Theme Cognitive Systems and Robotics, Grant agreement no. 247525).

5. REFERENCES

[1] S. Ba and J. Odobez. Multi-party focus of attention recognition in meetings from head pose and multimodal contextual cues. In *ICASSP*, 2008.

[2] S. O. Ba and J.-M. Odobez. Recognizing visual focus of attention from head pose in natural meetings. *Trans. Sys. Man Cyber. Part B*, 39:16–33, February 2009.

[3] D. Bohus and E. Horvitz. Facilitating multiparty dialog with gaze, gesture and speech. In *ICMI*, 2010.

[4] S. Gorga and K. Otsuka. Conversation scene analysis based on dynamic bayesian network and image-based gaze detection. In *ICMI*, 2010.

[5] D. A. Hanes and G. McCollum. Variables contributing to the coordination of rapid eye/head gaze shifts. *Biol. Cybern.*, 94:300–324, March 2006.

[6] S. R. Langton, R. J. Watt, and I. Bruce. Do the eyes have it? cues to the direction of social attention. *Trends Cogn Sci*, 4(2):50–59, feb 2000.

[7] K. Otsuka, Y. Takemae, J. Yamato, and H. Murase. A probabilistic inference of multiparty-conversation structure based on markov-switching models of gaze patterns, head directions, and utterances. In *ICMI*, 2005.

[8] E. Ricci and J.-M. Odobez. Learning large margin likelihoods for realtime head pose tracking. In *ICIP*, 2009.

[9] M. Voit and R. Stiefelhagen. Deducing the visual focus of attention from head pose estimation in dynamic multi-view meeting scenarios. In *ICMI*, Oct. 2008.

[10] Z. Yücel and A. Salah. Resolution of focus of attention using gaze direction estimation and saliency computation. In *Int. Conf. on Affective Computing and Intelligent Interfaces*, 2009.

Let's Have Dinner Together: Evaluate the Mediated Co-dining Experience

Jun Wei
Keio-NUS CUTE Center, NGS
National University of Singapore
weijun24@nus.edu.sg

Adrian David Cheok
Keio Graduate School of Media Design
Keio University, Japan
adriancheok@gmail.com

Ryohei Nakatsu
Keio-NUS CUTE Center, NGS
National University of Singapore
elenr@nus.edu.sg

ABSTRACT

Having dinner together is undoubtedly a kind of pleasurable experience, which involves various channels for mutual interactions, not only audio, vision and touch, but also smell and taste. With the aim to extend this rich experience to remote situations, we developed the Co-dining system to support a range of mealtime interactions to enhance the feeling of social togetherness. This paper describes the preliminary study with this interactive multisensory system. It aims to investigate the actual effectiveness of the working prototype on enhancing the social presence and engagement during telepresent dining, and also to get a comprehensive understanding about users' perception. This evaluation focused on three main aspects: the overall Co-dining feeling, cultural awareness, and engagement. The study results revealed that this system positively achieved the sense of "being together" among users, through the interactive activities touching upon tableware, tablecloth and real edible food, and each interaction module contributed differently to the overall experience. In this paper, we report the evaluation process, present and interpret the data, and discuss the initial insights to enhance the sense of co-presence through multi-channel interactions.

Categories and Subject Descriptors

H.5.2 [**Information Interfaces and Presentation (e.g. HCI)**]: User Interface, Evaluation/methodology

Keywords

Co-dining experience, multimodal interaction, mediated co-presence, multisensory communication, user study

1. INTRODUCTION

The speedy pace of modern life has decreased the opportunities for families to have meals together, especially dual-income families and those who live away from their parents.

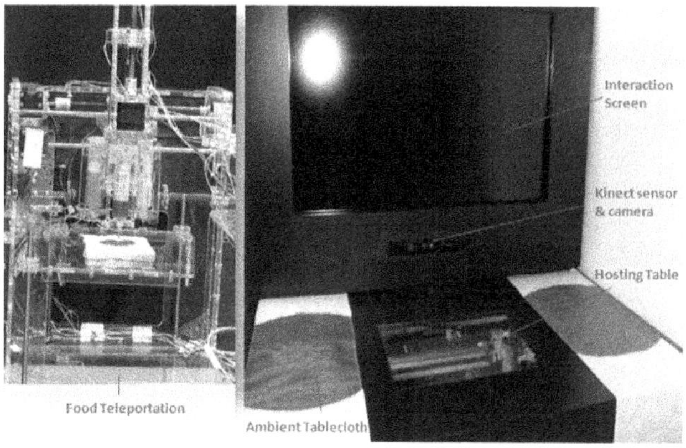

Figure 1: Overview of the Co-dining system.

The Co-dining system was developed to provide a new solution for family bonding, which is a dining table embedded with interactive subsystems that augment and transport the experience of communal family dining. As shown in figure 1, this system consists of four modules: (1) an Interaction Screen that enables gesture-based control; (2) a Hosting Table that can move the partner's dishes remotely to serve food, showing respect and care; (3) an Ambient Tablecloth that displays animated message on fabric, expressing love and warmth physically; and (4) Food Teleportation to transmit digital messages and self-designed gifts by reproducing them using edible food materials at the remote location [2].

The system connects partners through interactive dining activities. In the Co-dining scenario, remote partners can enjoy dinner together in front of the connected tables in physically-apart households. A list of dining activities is represented by several icons on the screen. To initiate, users move hands to choose icons, confirmed by a push gesture towards the icon. The system tracks the user's hand and transmits the icon chosen via the Internet to the paired table, triggering the corresponding module of the system on the other side to serve food, to display pattern on tablecloth, or create edible food messages. For example, "rice" icon activates serving rice bowl to remote partner using Hosting Table, "smiley" icon means sending and displaying the smiley on partner's tablecloth through animated color-changing on fabric, and selecting "LOVE" icon allows the remote partner to receive this message with the printed out edible food. Through these communicative activities over dinner, this system aims to reconstruct the dining experience in the new

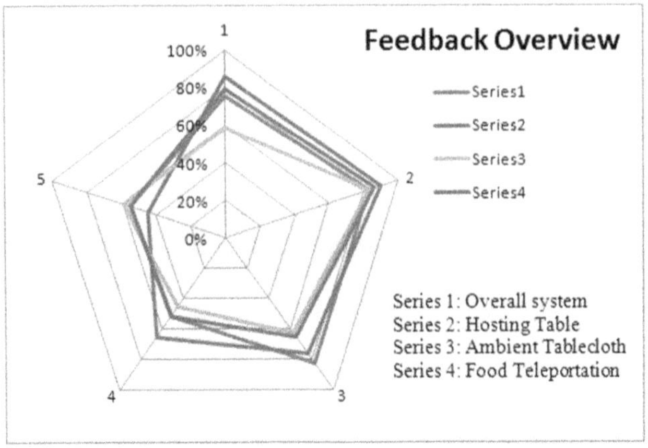

Figure 2: Radar chart of the overall feedback (percentage shown is the sum of rate "4" (Agree) and "5" (Strongly Agree) in the questionnaire.

context, enriching the communication with multiple interaction channels. The intention is to create a sense of co-presence while dining remotely (defined as "Co-dining").

Although research has been done on social co-presence in connected virtual environments, little has focused on the family dinner context. In this paper, we explored how the use of multiple interactive channels during mealtime can affect the co-present dining experience. We conducted the preliminary study to test the system's performance, know how it was received, and how it would influence users' dining experience through these shared mealtime interactions.

2. STUDY OVERVIEW

We recruited 29 volunteers (17 male and 12 female) from the public, aged from 20 to 40 years old. They are from different countries, like China, India, Japan, Sri Lanka, Korea, and Spain. We believe the varieties of users' backgrounds can help to access the cultural aspect of the system. After explaining the general concept and how to use the system, we asked each user to try it for about 15 minutes. In this initial study, we did not apply the paired setting, users can try all the modules and experience the corresponding output directly. It was easier for them to understand how the system works and obtain clearer impression to tell their perceptual feelings, helping us to assess users' overall feedback about these interaction modalities and the system's potential effectiveness in paired setting. Then we use the post-study questionnaire to elicit their responses about what they think and feel about what have been designed, in terms of usability, engagement, and the emotional experience it evoked.

Besides demographic data, the questionnaire includes two parts. The first is about their life experience of family dinner, like how frequently they have dinner with families previously and currently, and the importance of family dinner to them, etc. The second part is for their feedback on the prototype, both the integral system as a whole and each module individually. We use the Likert Scales [1], a series of statement to which the respondents rate their level of agreement on a 5-point scale. The rankings from 1 to 5 indicate from "Strongly Disagree" to "Strongly Agree". What's more, in order to avoid the "social desirability bias" [1], we collect the post-test data in such a way that the evaluator did not see the responses until the participant has left, and we made the survey itself anonymous to elicit more honest reactions.

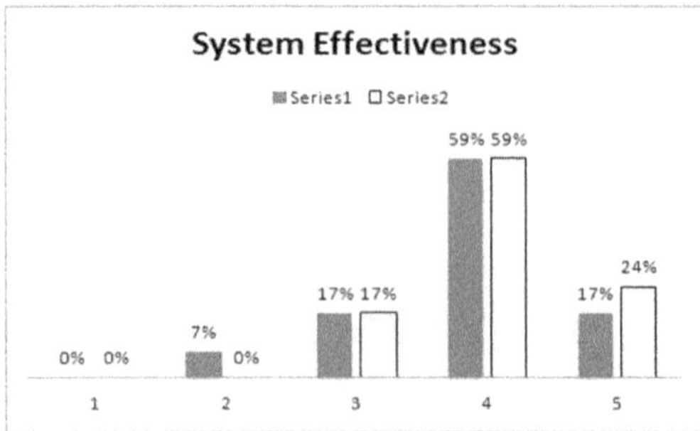

Figure 3: Effectiveness of the integrated system. Series 1: It provides the feeling of Co-dining; Series 2: Tangible interactions can enhance the sense of "being together".

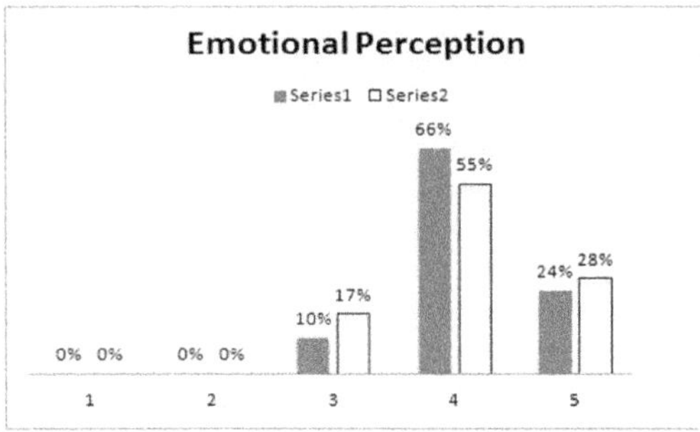

Figure 4: Users' emotional perception. Series 1: It can increase family bonding when people are away from each other; Series 2: It enhances the engagement between co-diners.

3. STUDY RESULTS AND DISCUSSIONS

From the demographic data, we noticed most of the users are foreigners, either study or work here, thus live away from their families. The unavailability to have dinner together with their families regularly and their strong desire to do so made them suitable to be the potential users for this system.

3.1 User responses overview

The purpose of this study is to evaluate how the system can support remote dinner through multiple interactive dining activities, and how it can influence people's emotional feelings. In the questionnaire, we focused on 5 main attributes: 1. It provides the feeling of Co-dining; 2. It enhances the engagement between Co-diners; 3. Tangible interactions can enhance the sense of "being together"; 4. It supports the cultural awareness of family dining; 5. It provides natural interactions over dinner. Each user should rate their agreement on these 5 statements towards the integral system, and also regarding each subsystem individually.

Generally, as shown in Figure 2, users rated higher for the first three statements than the last two. From this feedback, we can tell that both the integrated system as a whole

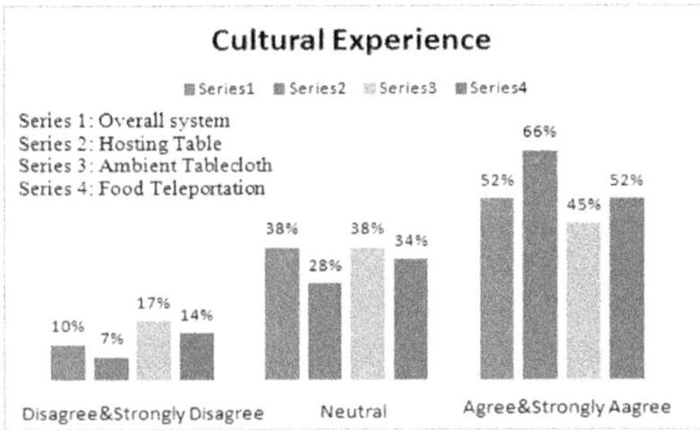

Figure 5: Cultural awareness of family dinner.

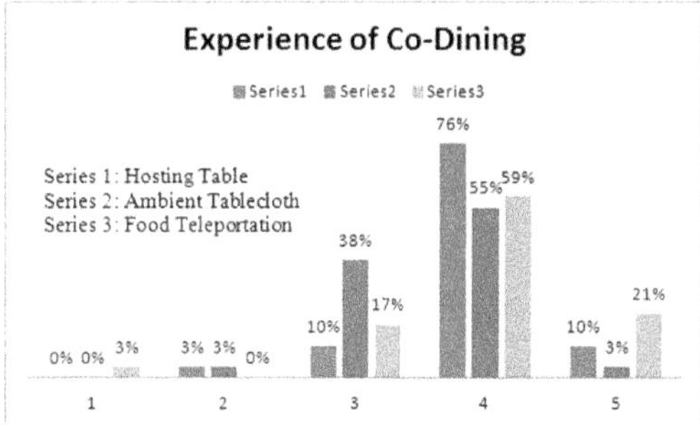

Figure 6: Feedback of each interaction module towards co-dining feeling.

and the three subsystems individually achieve to provide the co-dining feeling for the users, as well as the increased engagement and sense of "being together"(around 80%), but did not achieve the expected cultural awareness and natural interaction so well(50%-60%). Respectively, 76% of the users reported positive ratings (Strongly Agree & Agree) for the Co-dining feeling, increased engagement and enhanced sense of "being together" through tangible interactions, while only 52% indicated the sense of cultural awareness. Among the three activity modules, the Hosting Table module got the most confirmation regarding the Co-dining feeling, the engagement, the sense of "being together" and the cultural awareness, except the natural interaction aspect. Compared with the Hosting Table and the Food Teleportation, the Ambient Tablecloth generally did not obtain as high ratings, but appeared to be quite natural interaction for the users.

3.2 Effectiveness of the Integrated System

The purpose of the first two statements is to evaluate the effectiveness of triggering Co-dining feeling, as well as the contribution of tangible interactions to the feeling. Reviewing the data in Figure 3, we got very positive ratings regarding both aspects. A majority of users agreed on the fostered Co-dining feeling and the sense of "being together" physically provided by the multifaceted interactions.

Post-study questionnaire is an important method to collect self-reported data. At the emotional level, self-reported data can also tell something about how the users feel about the system [1]. Therefore, we also included statements to obtain users' emotional perception while using the system. Shown in Figure 4, none of the users disagreed with the statements about increased family bonding and engagement experience from the Co-dining system, 66% agree and 24% strongly agree that the system would help to reconnect the remote family members, 55% agree and 28% strongly agree on the enhanced engagement while dining.

3.3 Cultural Awareness

Family dinner is a social event correlated closely with culture, interwoven with and represented by the ritual and habitual manners people conduct during family dinner. The intention of the exploration is to recreate the experience of family dinner, not only the emotional sense of being together, but also to trigger the underlying cultural awareness.

Cultures of family dinner varies according to the regional, religious, historical and ritual traditions, including the dinner manners and the varieties of food ingredients. Although this test only provided a snapshot into the specific aspect of family dinner culture, it is helpful to indicate and enlighten the potential role of mediated interaction channels in influencing people's cultural feelings. From Figure 5, the system actually supported the cultural feeling in a certain degree, with 52% users rated positively for the integrated system. Compared among the three modules, the Hosting Table achieves the highest ratings (66%), followed by the Food Teleportation with 52% agreement, but the Tablecloth only got 45%. These results generally support our assumption that remote tangible interaction achieved by the Hosting Table actually recalls the traditional dining etiquette of serving food even if people fail to share the same dining table, which is considered as an important social dining activity with symbolic cultural meanings especially in Asia.

3.4 Effectiveness of each interaction module

In the questionnaire, we also ask users to assess the effectiveness of each interaction module individually, to acquire their different influences to different aspects. We assumed that each interaction model designed in the system contributed differently to the overall interaction experience; therefore, analysing this feedback from the users would be more targeted for us to improve the design; probably different combinations of these interaction modals can achieve higher level of Co-dining experience for the users.

3.4.1 Statement 1: It provides the feeling of Co-dining.

As mentioned, the main purpose of this system is to provide the "Co-dining" feeling, defined as the sense of "being together" physically. In Figure 6, we can tell the different opinions users had regarding these three modules. In comparison, we would infer users did not feel so obviously the Co-dining feeling through the Ambient Tablecloth, since quite a lot rated "Neutral" and only a small amount rated "Strongly Agree". The possible reason for this phenomenon can be: from the users' perspective, instant responses at remote side are more effective to trigger the sense of "being together", and the slow-rate animation on tablecloth did not achieve that so successfully. Interestingly, although a very large portion (86%) agreed on the contribution of the Hosting Table to the Co-dining feeling, most rated "Agree" rather than "Strongly Agree", while slightly more users rated "Strongly Agree" on the Food Teleportation.

3.4.2 Statement 2: It enhances the engagement.

Regarding the contribution to engagement experience, the results for each module did not vary too much (Figure 7).

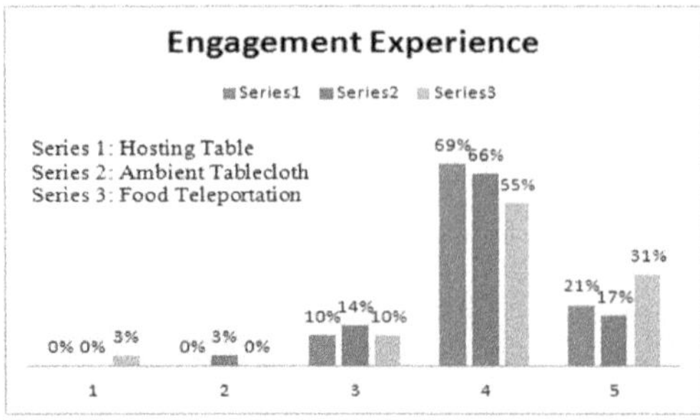

Figure 7: Feedback of each interaction module towards the increased engagement.

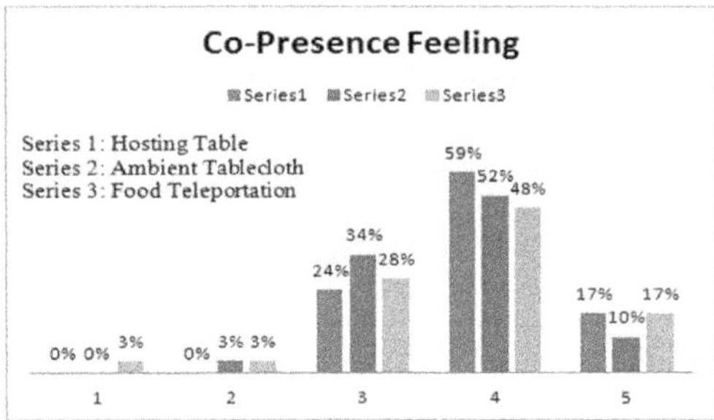

Figure 8: Feedback of each module towards the sense of "being together" via tangible interactions.

It seemed that most of the users admitted that compared with purely video or audio communications, these interactive dinner activities provided by this system would enhance the engagement during remote family dinners.

3.4.3 Statement 3: Tangible interactions can enhance the sense of "being together".

During the design, one of our main focuses is to highlight the tangible interactions with the normal dinner wares (e.g. bowls, tablecloth, and food), augmenting them as embodiments for remote communication. The intention of this is to enhance the sense of "being together" even if users fail to share the same physical space. We hypothesized that compared with virtual interactions through only digital graphics, the tangible interactions involving diversified sensory channels would foster intensified feeling about the presence of remote people. The data in Figure 8 verifies our hypothesis, about 65% rated "Strongly Agree" and "Agree", but still some users were not so confident about this feeling.

3.5 Interaction Screen

These three interaction modules are connected with and controlled by the Interaction Screen, which uses the Kinect to achieve the gesture-based icon selection. Users move hand towards the screen to choose different icons on the screen to initiate corresponding interaction module on the other side. We assumed gesture selection can be more intuitive, convenient, and also increase the playfulness during dinner.

From the feedback, a large portion of the users would accept this natural interaction mode (45% rated "Agree" and 24% rated "Strongly Agree"). For the rest, the potential reason would be their failures to activate the system after a few trials, since they did not follow strictly the directions for the appropriate gesture. To select one icon on the screen, user needs to push straightly towards the Kinect, so if they just push freely, the icon can't be selected. Noticing this, we think it is necessary to refine the Kinect tracking method, making it more flexible. As for the playfulness, 52% rated "Agree" and 38% rated "Strongly Agree", with no users indicated as "Disagree", indicating the increased playfulness and engagement experience through this gesture interaction.

3.6 Open-ended question

Besides rating, we also include open-ended question at the end to ask for suggestions on how to improve the system design from users' personal perspectives. Users gave many valuable suggestions. For instance, one user mentioned the role of smell during dinner, so it would be good to have smell generators within the system, to enable share the aroma of dishes. Another user suggested using part of the screen for movie or TV program, because watching TV together while dining is also a dinner routine for most families, and there should be more ubiquitous integration with traditional dinner tables. User also proposed to add background music to provide a pleasant time and bring back the family memories while eating. All these would be very helpful for the next design to improve the Co-dining experience, triggering more emotional connection and cultural recollection.

3.7 Limitations

This study acts as an initial test of the Co-dining system, providing referential information for further evaluation and development. Although we did not apply the remote and paired setting, we think it is very necessary to test the real experience, involving two remote users, and in a real dinner environment. Family dinner is a very casual event and the environmental atmosphere can also have significant effect on people's emotional feelings. There are many more points to be explored with the mediated Co-dining issue.

4. CONCLUSIONS

Through this preliminary study, we acquired valuable feedback about the system effectiveness, and how users feel about the dining experience through the interactions. Positively, the results justified our main assumption in the system design, which is to enrich the social and cultural experience of remote family dinner, through multiple interactive dinner activities, going beyond information transmission to enriched experience, via interactions through various models.

5. ACKNOWLEDGMENTS

This research is supported by the Singapore NRF under its International Research Centre @ Singapore Funding Initiative and administered by the IDM Programme Office.

6. REFERENCES

[1] T. Tullis and B. Albert. Chapter 6 - Self-Reported Metrics. In *Measuring the User Experience*, pages 123–166. Morgan Kaufmann, San Francisco, 2008.

[2] J. Wei, X. Wang, R. L. Peiris, Y. Choi, X. R. Martinez, R. Tache, J. Koh, V. Halupka, and A. D. Cheok. Codine: an interactive multi-sensory system for remote dining. In *Proc of UbiComp ' 11*, pages 21–30. ACM, 2011.

Infusing the Physical World into User Interfaces

Ivan Poupyrev
Disney Research Pittsburgh
4720 Forbes Avenue, Suite 110
Pittsburgh, PA 15213 USA
+1-412-6887406
ivan.poupyrev@disneyresearch.com
http://ivanpoupyrev.com
@ipoupyrev

ABSTRACT

Advances in new materials and manufacturing techniques are rapidly blending the computational and physical worlds. With every new turn in technology development -- e.g., discovering a novel "smart" material, inventing a more efficient manufacturing process or designing a faster microprocessor -- there are new and exciting ways to take user interfaces away from the screen and blend them into our living spaces and everyday objects, making them more responsive, intelligent and adaptive. As the world around us becomes increasingly infused with technology, the user interfaces and computers themselves will disappear into the background, blending into the physical world around us. Thus, the old tried-and-true paradigms for designing interaction and interfaces must be re-evaluated, re-designed and, in some cases, even discarded to take advantage of the new possibilities that these cutting-edge technologies provide. While the challenges and opportunities are distinct, the fundamental goal remains the same: to provide for the effortless and effective consumption, control and transmission of information at any time and in any place, while delivering a unique experience that is only possible with these emerging technologies.

In this talk I will present work produced by myself and the research group that I have been directing at Disney Research Pittsburgh. We are addressing these exciting challenges. This talk will cover projects investigating tactile and haptics interfaces, deformable computing devices, augmented reality interfaces and novel touch sensing techniques, as well as biologically-inspired interfaces, among others. The presentation will cover both projects conducted while at Sony Corporation and more recent research efforts in the Interaction Group at Walt Disney Research, Pittsburgh.

Categories and Subject Descriptors

H.5 [**Information Interfaces and Presentation**]: User interfaces – Haptic I/O, Input devices and strategies, Prototyping, Interaction styles.

General Terms

Measurement, Performance, Design, Human Factors, Theory.

Keywords

Physical interfaces, haptics, tactile interfaces, deformable computers, biological computers, augmented reality

ICMI'12, October 22–26, 2012, Santa Monica, California, USA.
ACM 978-1-4503-1467-1/12/10.

ABOUT THE SPEAKER

Dr. Ivan Poupyrev directs an Interaction Technology group in Disney Research's Pittsburgh Lab, a unit of Walt Disney Imagineering, tasked with dreaming up and developing future technologies for Disney parks, resorts, and cruises.

Dr. Poupyrev and his group focus on inventing new interactive technologies for the seamless blending of digital and physical properties in devices, everyday objects, and living environments, a direction he broadly refers to as physical computing. His interests, however, span a broad range of research fields including haptic user interfaces, tangible interfaces, shape-changing and flexible computers, augmented and virtual reality, as well as spatial 3D interaction. His research has been broadly published and has received awards at prestigious academic conferences, exhibited world-wide, widely reported in popular media, and released on the market in various consumer products and applications.

Prior to Disney, Ivan worked as a researcher at Sony Computer Science Laboratories in Tokyo, Japan. He also did a stint at the Human Interface Technology Laboratory at the University of Washington as a Visiting Scientist while working on his Ph.D. dissertation at Hiroshima University, Japan.

Child-Computer Interaction: ICMI 2012 Special Session

Anton Nijholt
University of Twente
PO Box 217, 7500 AE Enschede, The Netherlands
anijholt@cs.utwente.nl

ABSTRACT
This is a short introduction to the special session on child computer interaction at the International Conference on Multimodal Interaction 2012 (ICMI 2012). In human-computer interaction users have become participants in the design process. This is not different for child computer interaction applications. However, technological advances have also led to developments where children not only have the role of future consumers of an application (a game, maybe an educational game), but also design and create the application, where designing and creating is both fun and serving educational purposes. In this special session the different aspects of child computer interaction (design, usability, learning, fun, creating, collaboration) are investigated and illustrated. In addition we pay attention to the efforts to create a child-computer interaction research community.

Author Keywords
Children; Interaction Design; Child Computer Interaction; Constructivism, Tangible Interfaces, Games, Virtual reality.

ACM Classification Keywords
H.5.2 [Information Interfaces and Presentation]: User Interfaces - Interaction styles.

General Terms
Human Factors; Design; Measurement.

INTRODUCTION
While in the late 1940s, early 1950s there were discussions about how many computers the world needed, now, sixty years later we are talking about computers everywhere, not only as one of the many personal computers in our home, but also embedded in our home environment, our personal devices, our clothes and in our social media and entertainment applications. Children have grown up with internet, the world wide web and mobile devices that give access to role-playing games and entertainment, news, and education, but most of all, communication using social media and games with friends and others that have similar interests. Many of them play games many hours a day. Mostly this is done using mouse, joystick, keyboard and screen. New interaction technologies become available. These new technologies process speech, gestures, facial expressions, body movements, and physiological information, including brain-computer interfacing.

In child-computer interaction (CCI) research children are the user group for which we want to design interfaces that take into account the special characteristics of this user group. Moreover, we want to take into account special applications, in particular applications that have educational goals, applications that aim at fun, and applications that combine fun and education..

FROM LOGO TO TANGIBLES
The development of Logo in the late 1960s by Seymour Papert and others [1] as a child-friendly programming language is often mentioned as a start of the interest in using the computer for educational purposes for children. Logo was designed as a tool for learning. In early Logo virtual and physical (including touch sensors) 'turtles' could be programmed to move and draw shapes and pictures ('turtle graphics'). Underlying the design of Logo was the (cognitive) constructivist educational philosophy, advocated by Jean Piaget: learners must construct their own knowledge through experience. Only with the advent of personal computers Logo got more widespread, various Logo environments were created for different teaching purposes and Logo projects were introduced at schools. Many interesting developments followed, for example LEGO Logo could be used to control machines built from LEGO blocks, with sensors, motors and light, while LEGO 'Programmable Bricks' (later called LEGO Mindstorms) could run programs autonomously. In later years, up until now, Logo programming environments have been extended to allow designing interactive stories, animations and music and art applications, and to interface with micro controller boards (e.g. Arduino) that allow reading sensors and controlling motors and other actuators, hence, integrating a constructivist view on programming with sensor-equipped environments and interactive objects, such as tangibles.

TECHNOLOGICAL ADVANCES AND HCI
Clearly, other 'historical' viewpoints can be mentioned as well. Independently of thoughts about constructionist learning and ways to implement them in educational software there have been technological advances that made it possible to have access to all kinds of information, to communicate with fellow-learners and teachers, and, in particular, to communicate with fellow-students. Hence, there is more than the typical HCI view, where now slowly it is understood that there is more than efficiency and

ICMI '12, October 22–26, 2012, Santa Monica, California, USA.
ACM 978-1-4503-1467-1/12/10..

control when talking about computer applications and when talking about personal preferences.

It has become common to have an ambient intelligence view, where the assumption is that we have sensor equipped environments, the sensors have intelligence, the environment knows about its inhabitants, how they communicate with each other and how they interact with the environment. And it assumes that the environment can act pro-actively, that is, can anticipate the activities of its users. These technological developments have, probably more than the previously mentioned developments with the Logo environments, made it possible that applications that address children make use of tangible and multi-touch interfaces, include interaction with robotic and mobile devices, and can include interaction with sensors embedded in the environment and its inhabitants.

A CCI RESEARCH COMMUNITY

CCI has become a well-established research area. Its main conference is Interaction Design and Children (IDC), first organized in 2002 in Eindhoven (the Netherlands), and since then yearly in various countries. The main global objectives that have been put forward are "*to understand children's needs and how to design for them, by presenting and discussing the most innovative research in the field of interaction design for children, by exhibiting the most recent developments in design and design methodologies, and by gathering the leading minds in the field of interaction design for children*". Each year a conference can have different theme, reflecting research progress and technological advances. In 2009 the aim was "*to foster an investigation of technological and methodological issues related not only to learning and play, but also to social awareness of young people in relationship to environment, cultural heritage, cultural roots of minorities, local identity vs. wider community identity*", in 2010 the main theme was "*Full-body interaction for children: to enhance physical, mental and social well-being of children.*"

There are now many conferences and workshops, special sessions, and special issues of journals where research on child computer interaction can be published. We should mention the Workshops on CCI (WoCCI) held in conjunction with ICMI 2008, ICMI 2009, and Interspeech 2012. Growing interest has led to the establishment in 2012 of a journal: International Journal of Child-Computer Interaction (IJCCI), with the aim to serve as a forum to communicate research in CCI.

SUMMARY OF THE CONTRIBUTIONS

In this special session of ICMI 2012 we have five papers by distinguished researchers in the field. Some papers are along the lines of a recent review paper [2]. There are many claimed benefits of tangible user interfaces for children, but there is little theoretical or empirical work that supports these claims. Alissa Antle targets hands-on problem solving in spatial domains and discusses three theoretical mechanisms that may explain benefits two-handed and inter-hemispheric interaction, complementary actions that couple cognitive resources with external, physical elements, and manipulating the spatial structure of the environment to modify ideas.

Janet Read's paper is concerned with metrics and experience. She describes the main tools of the Fun Toolkit, a toolkit to collect opinions from children about interactive technology. These tools are the Smileyometer (faces that are meant to elicit opinions), a Fun-Sorter (a tool to rank activities), and the 'Again-Again' tool, meant to measure the willingness to repeat a certain activity. In this paper the results of various studies using the Smileyometer for measuring experience are reported.

Betsy van Dijk and co-authors present a study on the use of a multi-touch table in an educational museum environment. The study is part of a European project on constructing information services for children. This study aims at investigating how collaborative interaction with a multi-touch table can make children's visits more engaging and enjoyable. Results of a comparative study (with and without multi-touch table use) are presented. The Smileyometer was used as one of the measures for enjoyment.

In the paper by Paulo Blikstein the concept of bifocal modeling is introduced. A technological platform is offered that allows students to build - and with the use of sensors relate in real time - physical and virtual models to do .physics-oriented experiments. The paper addresses how students appreciate a linking of physical world activities with a computer simulation of these activities.

Casual science games can be played by children in Whyville, a free virtual world. In the final paper of this session by Kafai and Fields the learning and communication behavior of children in this virtual world is investigated using detailed log file data, interviews and observations. The main aim of this paper is to show different approaches to analyzing log file data and data obtained from other observations qualitatively.

Together these five papers give a good coverage of the current issues in state-of-the-art research in Child Computer Interaction

REFERENCES

1. Papert, S. Mindstorms: Children, *Computers, And Powerful Ideas.* Basic Books, 1980.
2. Zaman, B., Vanden Abeele, V., Markopoulos, P. and Marshall, P. Editorial: the evolving field of tangible interaction for children: the challenge of empirical validation. *Personal and Ubiquitous Computing*, 16, 4 (2012), 367-37.

Knowledge Gaps in Hands-on Tangible Interaction Research

Alissa N. Antle
Interactive Arts + Technology
Simon Fraser University
250 -13450 102 Avenue, Surrey, B.C., Canada
aantle@sfu.ca

ABSTRACT

Multimodal interfaces including tablets, touch tables, and tangibles are beginning to receive much attention in the child-computer interaction community. Such interfaces enable interaction through actions, gestures, touch, and other modalities not tapped into by traditional desktop computing. Researchers have suggested that multimodal interfaces, such as tangibles, have great potential to support children's learning and problem solving in spatial domains due to the hands-on physical and spatial properties of this interaction style. Despite a long history of hands-on learning with physical and computational materials, there is little theoretical or empirical work that identifies specific causes for many of the claimed benefits. Neither is there empirically validated design guidance as to what design choices might be expected to have significant impacts. In this paper I suggest several avenues of investigation, based on my own research interests, which would address this knowledge gap. I provide summaries of theoretical mechanisms that may explain claimed benefits, outline how the specific features of tangible interfaces might support or enhance these mechanisms, and describe current and future investigations that address current gaps of knowledge.

Categories and Subject Descriptors

H5.2. Information interfaces and presentation: User interfaces. K.3.m Computers and education: Miscellaneous.

General Terms

Design, Theory.

Keywords

Multi-modal user interfaces, tangible user interfaces, touch interfaces, child-computer interaction, digital manipulatives, hands-on interaction, hands-on learning, research agenda.

1. INTRODUCTION

Multimodal interfaces involving hands-on actions, gestures, and touch are becoming increasingly available with the commercialization of touch interfaces and growth of tangible computing research. Children as young as two-year-olds are using tangible prototypes and touch-based tablets to interact with digital media. Far predating such technical development is a long history of pedagogical approaches that facilitate hands-on learning with physical materials. In Europe and North America, this tradition can be formally traced to Froebel and Dewey [9, 14], but surely children's playful learning through interaction with natural and crafted physical materials predates written history.

Recent technical advancements combined with a rich history of hands-on learning result in a unique and timely research opportunity to better understand how hybrid digital-physical materials may be designed to support, enhance, and perhaps change children's lives. Multimodal interfaces, such as tangibles user interfaces and touch tabletops, have achieved much attention in both the human-computer interaction and learning science communities (e.g. [35, 46]). These new forms of technologies may change everything from the way children do written work in the classroom to how they interact with their grandparents at home. It is critical that technology development is grounded in research that investigates what makes effective interaction – how we think with our hands, how we express ourselves through gestures, and how movement is formative in human thought. Research is necessary to understand and enable the real benefits of these increasingly popular technologies. In a special issue of *Personal and Ubiquitous Computing* on Tangibles and Children, the editors emphasize the need for "... research on tangibility that transcends system descriptions, focusing on empirical investigations to inform theory and generate design guidance"[46]. Providing such a theoretically grounded research base for innovative technical development has great potential to provide design guidance for multimodal interfaces and positively influence children's digital experiences with these new forms of technology.

One area that may be revolutionized by tangible and touch technologies is hands-on problem solving in spatial domains. Focusing on theorizing and empirically validating design guidelines for spatial domains is novel and likely to be fruitful due to the physical and spatial affordances of tangibles, and to a more limited degree, touch interfaces. Research is needed in order to better understand the motor-cognitive mechanisms that underlie spatial problem solving, design computational supports for these mechanisms, and evaluate putative benefits [4, 46]. This research area is important not only because a variety of real world challenges require spatial thinking (e.g. molecular biology, environmental planning, object oriented programming), but also because an embodied account of cognition suggests that spatial reasoning forms the basis for the development of all abstract thought [16].

In this paper, I lay out a (partial) research agenda for understanding how tangible user interfaces may support and augment children's spatial problem solving. These areas are primarily influenced by my own research interests. I focus primarily on tangibles because they offer unique opportunities to support multimodal interaction through touch, vision, and audition; as well as offer physical and spatial properties not available with desktop systems. I discuss spatial problems that are content-free (e.g. jigsaw puzzles), as well as problems that require learning about domain-specific concepts (e.g. sustainable land use planning problems). Through content-free spatial problems, children may learn strategies and skills that enable spatial reasoning. Through domain-specific problems, children may apply spatial reasoning and develop an understanding of domain-specific concepts. There is a rich body of research about children's problem solving and conceptual learning in spatial domains. Due to lack of space, I will not mention more than a few key references. Instead, I focus on three threads of inquiry into how tangibles may support specific aspects of problem solving in order to illustrate typical approaches to child-computer interaction research in this space.

My intention is to provide inspiration, insight, and ideas for researchers eager to move forward with rigorous work in this field. Thus, this paper can be viewed as both an educational piece for other researchers and a call to action for research that I think will substantially impact our understanding of how to design tangible interfaces to support children's spatial problem solving.

2. HANDS-ON INTERACTION

Intelligent behavior develops not by thinking, but through acting physically in the world [37]. An embodied account of development suggests that Piaget underestimated children's cognitive abilities, and that through facilitated interaction with the physical world, children can learn and solve concrete problems in specific domains long before they can solve them symbolically or express related concepts verbally[18]. Central to this claim is the view that sensory-motor activity is critical to cognitive development [17]. This stance is reflected in the pedagogical "hands-on" traditions of Dewey, Froebel, Montessori, and more recently Papert, in which it is claimed that children develop cognitively from physical engagement in reasoning with materials in real world settings [9, 14, 34, 36]. Such claims are not accepted uncritically. For example, Uttal and others point out that successful learning outcomes associated with manipulatives typically require extensive teacher support, and that children must be able to see the relationship between concrete and abstract relations for knowledge transfer to occur [13, 44].

2.1 Hands-on Interfaces

One form of hands-on interface is a tangible user interface. Unlike physical manipulatives, tangibles involve using real physical objects that are linked to digital representations [40]. They involve input objects that have physical and spatial properties linked to computational models, in contrast to keyboard or mouse that act only as input devices. By linking physical materials with digital (abstract) representations, tangibles may address Uttal and other's criticisms by enabling children to explicitly see the relationship between concrete and abstract representations. Another form of hands-on interface is a multitouch interface. Touch interfaces, such as tablets and touch tables, enable hands-on interaction with screen-based digital representations. Hybrid tangible and touch systems are also becoming available (e.g. Microsoft Surface table).

Various researchers have suggested that digital learning materials in the form of tangibles, and to a lesser degree multitouch interfaces, might benefit children's learning in a variety of domains (e.g. [1, 29, 38]). However, little research exists that investigates the benefits of these claims [4, 30, 46]. A comprehensive review of early research focusing on children's learning and tangible user interfaces describes theoretical foundations and summarizes case studies, but none of these studies provides linkages between theory and interface designs, or outline empirically validated evidence of benefits [35]. Most current work in the field still invokes high level theories to explain possible learning effects without empirical validation [4]. There continues to be a lack of theoretically grounded guidance for designers as to what design choices might be expected to have significant impacts.

2.2 Spatial Problem Solving

Problem solving is a complex skill that, depending on the nature of the problem, involves different cognitive processes including divergent thinking, convergent thinking, visual search, spatial reasoning, mental visualization and justification; as well as metacognitive processes and non-cognitive variables (e.g. motivation, affective state) [42]. For domain-specific problems, it also involves conceptual reasoning. Spatial problem solving involves problems in which spatial characteristics of the problem are integral to successful solutions. Characteristics of space that may be important to the problem include object location, position, orientation, shape, size, proximity, grouping, or other spatial relationships. Examples of spatial problems that may be encountered by children include puzzles; mazes; simplified geographic, urban, ecological, or biological planning problems (e.g. creating a toy town, farm, or park); architectural, engineering, or transportation structural problems (e.g. making a building from blocks, laying down toy train tracks); geometric modeling (e.g. shape sorting); and organizing one's bedroom!

Research is needed to understand the role of hands-on interaction in spatial problem solving, what kinds of behaviours are most productive, and how to design interfaces that support these behaviours.

3. THEORETICAL GROUNDING

Exploring this research space requires theoretical grounding followed by empirical work. In the next subsections, I suggest three theoretical areas that I think deserve attention. For each, I provide a summary of the theory, links to further readings, and an explanation of how the theory articulates mechanisms by which tangible interface features might be designed to support and augment hands-on spatial problem solving with computational materials. There may be additional theoretical avenues worthy of exploration, but these three are good starting points.

3.1 Two-Handed Inter-Hemispheric Interaction

Interaction with tangibles and some touch surfaces is often two-handed. Evidence from cognitive neuroscience suggests that the actual handling of objects is important in creative tasks such as problem solving [21]. The right brain hemisphere is associated with the production of ideas or problem solutions. The left brain hemisphere is largely responsible for logic and selecting from this vast set of choices presented by the right hemisphere. Communication between the two spheres is enabled by the corpus callosum. Inter-hemispheric interaction (IHI) is the interaction of the right and left brain hemispheres through the connecting brain tissue of the corpus callosum. Creative problem solving requires this back and forth communication between the two spheres. Researchers have shown that mental and physical operations that require IHI have been linked with enhanced performance on divergent thinking tasks [19, 21, 28, 41].

One way that IHI has been enhanced in lab experiments is through bilateral eye movement exercises in which participants scan their eyes back and forth. Other bilateral movements may have a similar effect. From here I suggest that handling objects with two hands – in particular, moving objects from one hand to the other – may stimulate IHI. This may in turn improve the creative problem solving ability of those using both hands to manipulate physical or digital objects as part of a problem solving task.

What is not known is whether these ideas hold and if so the magnitude of their effects. We do know that tangibles can be designed to encourage this kind of two-handed interaction with everyday objects. This idea has been explored in an unpublished M.Sc. thesis (described below) [8]. Future research with children is necessary. I summarize this knowledge gap with the following high level research question: *Does facilitating two handed interaction improve children's divergent thinking in spatial problem solving?*

3.2 Complementary Actions: Coupling Internal and External Resources

Studies have shown that humans, and children in particular, rely on being embedded in an environment to help develop and coordinate their use of internal cognitive resources with external tools and representations required to solve problems [10, 43]. One of the ways they do this is by using actions to improve their cognitive purposes. Complementary actions are actions that recruit external elements to reduce cognitive loads [25]. Another way to say this is that certain gestures or actions on objects may offload some aspect of a mental process to actions in the world. The result of such an action may aid memory, improve perception, or simplify mental computation needed to solve a problem. In a jigsaw puzzle task children may use complementary actions for all three of these purposes, although they are largely unaware of these benefits. For example, children can improve memory by using space to organize piles of pieces. They can simplify perception by rotating rotate pieces to see how the pieces look in different orientations rather than moving themselves or trying to mentally visualizing the piece in a different orientation. These two strategies are complementary and epistemic because the act of moving pieces changes the world in order to simplify (and change) the task. Through the development and use of complementary actions, a child may be able to solve a problem that is otherwise too difficult.

Tangibles have similar characteristics as physical objects and thus may facilitate complementary actions through two-handed manipulation of objects, digital feedback, tactile feedback, and the use of structural aspects of 3D space. Touch interfaces also enable direct manipulation of objects. However, unlike physical objects, these objects can be manipulated in two dimensions of physical space or three dimensions of virtual space. For these reasons, tangibles, and possibly touch interfaces, may enable more effective and efficient spatial problem solving than physical or mouse-based interfaces [4]. What is not known is how to design specific interface features to facilitate complementary epistemic actions for a particular problem. We also do not know if using complementary actions in problem solving improves conceptual learning associated with that problem. Future research is necessary. I summarize these knowledge gaps with the following high level research questions: *What kinds of tangible and touch interface features support complementary actions for particular types of problems? Do these features enable children to solve harder problems than they might without such support? Does more this type of problem solving improve conceptual learning related to the problem's content domain?*

3.3 Learning Through Co-Evolution of Ideas and the Environment

The theory of mutual adaptation explains how children's ideas and actions change in an environment where they can modify their ideas over time through modifying the spatial structure of the world in some way [32]. In spatial problem solving, this may involve complementary actions that simplify the task, but manipulating the environment also leads to changes in the understanding of the ideas represented through the environment. In the context of solving a problem, the ideas may be about the underlying domain concepts.

This theory can be demonstrated through the example described in [39]. When children solve simple arithmetic problems with physical math manipulatives, they are using spatial problem solving skills and developing an understanding of concepts related to arithmetic (e.g. division). This approach may enable children to both the change the way they group the manipulatives in space and change their ideas about number concepts. In an experiment, children with a nascent understanding of division were asked to share a bag of candy with four friends. Children were allowed to restructure the environment by organizing piles of candies into various groups until a satisfactory solution was reached (i.e. four equal groups). A second group of children solved the problem using a graphical representation (i.e. drawing pictures of the candies to be shared). Children who learned through spatial reconfiguration of the actual candies were later better able to transfer their understanding of spatial groupings to symbolic representations of division problems in arithmetic.

Tangible or touch interfaces can be designed to enable dynamic spatial reconfiguration of the problem space [4]. Unlike physical manipulatives, the digital component of a tangible or touch system can result in feedback in the form of graphical or symbolic representations about the laws governing the problem. It may also enable feedback about the history of interaction. The combination of spatial and digital features and a dynamic system (rather than static materials) may enable children to adapt their understanding of such laws, which in turn, may be transferred to new problems and potentially to new domains.

What is not known is whether tangible or touch manipulatives for arithmetic problem solving are more effective than virtual manipulatives used in [39]. Studies of mutual adaptation have so far focused on learning arithmetic, not spatial problem solving. It is unknown whether the findings will apply to spatial tasks. Studies of groups of children mutually adapting their ideas are also needed. I summarize these knowledge gaps with the following high level research questions: *Are tangible or touch manipulatives effective for spatial problem solving? Does learning how to solve a specific spatial problem transfer to similar problems? Do tangibles or touch tools that enable mutual adaptation and improve spatial problem solving in one domain enable such understanding to transfer to other spatial domains? What features best enable social mutual adaptation?*

4. STUDIES: PAST AND FUTURE

In this section, I provide summaries of research I have been involved in that begins to address some of the knowledge gaps identified above. Rather than present the full details of studies here, I provide a concise overview of the work and provide pointers to the original publications. I follow this with ideas for future work that builds on or extends current work through study design variations, improvements, or replications with different audiences. In this way, I hope to open up this research space to other researchers interested in understanding how children's hands-on interaction supports spatial problem solving performance and skills development in a variety of contexts.

4.1 Comparative Studies: Two-Hands

One thread of investigation suggested by the research questions above is to understand how enabling children to use both their hands to manipulate tangible objects may enhance inter-hemispheric interaction (IHI), which in turn may improve problem solving outcomes.

One way to approach this is to conduct comparative studies of children using single and two-handed multimodal interfaces for a problem solving task involving divergent thinking. The goal would be to compare how children perform with single and two-handed interaction, and to determine if two-handed interaction can boost the number, type or quality of solutions.

4.1.1 Past Work

One area that we have explored involves an investigation through a comparison of two-handed and single-hand touch, and mouse-based interaction focusing on divergent thinking performance with adults [8]. The goal was to determine if two-handed interaction as afforded by a desktop-sized touch screen affects divergent thinking, which is a key aspect of many spatial problem solving tasks. We conducted a between-groups evaluation of 65 adults using one of three interface styles. Divergent thinking was measured using a computerized version of an assessment tool called the alternate uses task (AUT). Participants were asked to interact with 3D models of a series of everyday objects (e.g. shoe, brick, socks) and generate new uses for each (see Figure 1). Verbal data describing uses was analyzed to compare divergent thinking outcomes. Measures from the AUT included expert ratings of fluency, originality, level of detail, categorical distinctiveness, and usefulness. The study rests on the assumption that the three interface styles differ in their influence on divergent thinking primarily in terms of the IHI enabled by two-handed interaction with AUT objects.

Preliminary results of this unpublished Master's thesis found no significant differences in divergent thinking performance that could be attributed to interface style. It is possible that two-handed interaction does not boost IMI to the degree that it affects divergent thinking as measured by the AUT. However, we suggest that display size, which may have enabled eye-movement-based IHI for all the participants, may have contributed to this result. Other issues including oral language proficiency may have masked expected effects. We also suggest that the lack of significance may be because the AUT is not sensitive enough to capture differences between groups resulting from two-handed interaction.

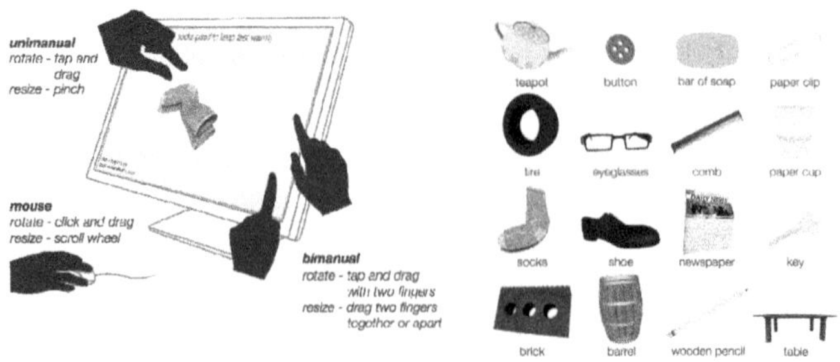

Figure 1. Computerized AUT (left); AUT objects (right).

4.1.2 Future Work

One avenue for future work would be to conduct a similar study with different age groups of children who are pre-screened for language proficiency. Some groups could be constrained to single-handed interaction while others would be encouraged to use two-handed interaction. One consideration when conducting this type of study with children would be the age at which children develop functional fixedness. Functional fixedness occurs when a child is hindered in reaching the solution to a problem by their knowledge of an object's conventional function [12]. It occurs at about the age that children enter school.

Since it is possible the computerized AUT might vary from the original paper test in terms of representational cues (e.g. 3D objects). We suggest that there may be value in investigating of the effects of representation modality as well as interaction mode on divergent thinking by comparing performance between paper, computerized, and physical object based versions of the AUT.

4.2 Comparative Studies: Spatial Puzzles

Another thread of investigation suggested by the research questions above is to investigate how specific affordances of tangible interfaces enable successful behavioral and cognitive strategies that support content-free spatial puzzle solving. Content-free puzzles are those that do not require domain knowledge for successful completion, such as jigsaw puzzles, tangrams, and 3D building puzzles (e.g. Equilibrio).

One way to approach is this is to conduct comparative studies of children using traditional and multimodal interfaces for the same spatial problem solving task. The goal would be to compare how the properties of physical and digital interfaces involved in the task affect patterns of hands-on actions, problem solving strategies, and outcomes. Another approach would be to compare different forms of tangible interaction. Another approach would be to compare tangible and touch with other forms of interaction. Comparative studies have the potential to provide evidence regarding the relation between interface features and problem solving outcomes. However, consideration must be given to both creating comparable designs (e.g. control functions, feedback salience) and creating designs that take advantage of the affordances each style of interaction provides [46].

4.2.1 Past Work

One area that we have explored involves an investigation of how complementary actions were affected by interface style for a spatial puzzle task. We conducted a study comparing children's performance using mouse-based, tangible and cardboard jigsaw puzzles (see Figure 2). A jigsaw puzzle is a prototypical activity that requires complementary actions to successfully solve it. We identified and coded three main classes of hands actions depending on the role they served in cognition (see [2, 3] for more details). One class is non-complementary actions, which are used when a child manipulates a piece simply to move it into its correct position. Another class is complementary pragmatic actions, which are used when a child manipulates a piece to determine its placement and correctly places it. A third class is complementary epistemic actions, which are used when a child manipulates a piece in order to simplify the problem space. For example, a child may organize puzzle pieces into groups, which simplifies the puzzle solving task by offloading memory to spatial location.

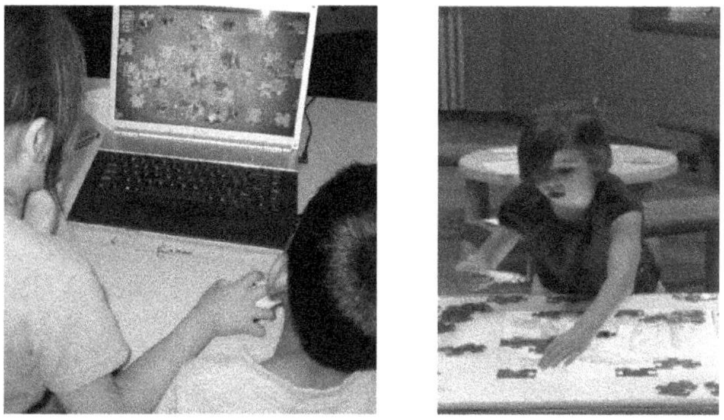

Figure 2. Comparative study: mouse-based (left) and tangible (right) jigsaw puzzles.

Data analysis focused on analysis of hand actions types including a temporal analysis. Briefly, we found that the spatial features of the tangible puzzle (e.g. 3D interaction space, table edges) provided opportunities for epistemic actions that resulted in the highest completion rates with a slight time cost [2, 3]. Analysis of the temporal sequences of events in successful pairs reveals a shared pattern of interleaved sequences of communication, epistemic actions, and direct placements. Analysis also revealed a positive correlation between higher number of actions on pieces and successful puzzle completion. Based on further analysis we suggested that an optimal strategy does not involve the minimum number of actions to complete the puzzle, but rather 'extra' actions that serve epistemic functions. Epistemic actions involved making piles of pieces, using one hand to push a pile of pieces around and the other to select (i.e. bimanual asymmetric interaction), moving around the table to get a different perspective, and connecting pieces off the table with two hands (bi-manual interaction).

In a later jigsaw puzzle study with adults, we compared how tangible versus touch interaction affected complementary actions and performance [45]. Using a within-subjects design, sixteen adults completed two comparable puzzles (see Figure 3). The goal of this exploratory study was to better understand the differences in strategies, sequences of hands-action types, and performance between interactions with virtual puzzle pieces (touch) and physical pieces (tangible). We found that players used more, shorter, complementary actions in the tangible condition, and finished puzzles faster (at the $p < 0.01$ level). In particular, we noted how players used the edges of the tabletop to organize and store pieces, offloading memory and reducing the number of steps in puzzle solving. Although a virtual "edge" area was available in the touch puzzle, players rarely used it. We found that bimanual interaction was observed in both interaction styles. However, in the touch group they were mostly symmetric (e.g. using one finger of each hand to rotate a piece). In the tangible group bimanual actions were more varied and asymmetric, which may better support IHI.

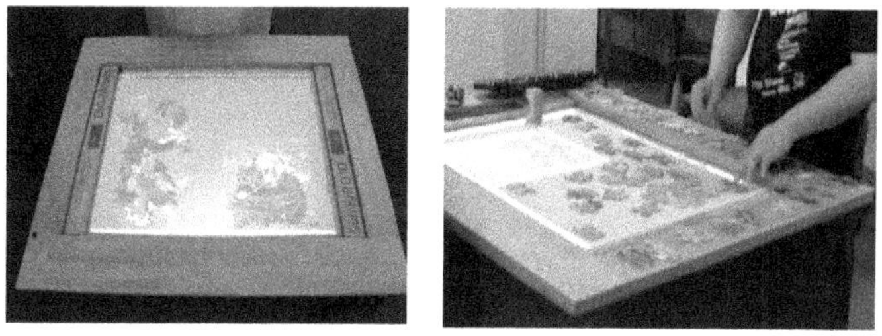

Figure 3. Comparative study: touch and tangible puzzles.

4.2.2 Future Work

Our early work suggests that table edges, offline space, and 3D manipulation space are all important factors in supporting complementary actions. One avenue for future work would be to compare graphical, tangible, and touch interfaces for other spatial puzzles (e.g. tangrams, 3D building). See [15] for some recent work in this area. Another avenue for future work would be to conduct a study using touch and tangible tabletop jigsaw puzzles for children of different age groups. Since children are still developing problem solving skills, it would be useful to compare results to the adult study. It may also be informative to compare different ages in order to look for a trajectory of developing skills and determine what design features may support younger children to succeed. One improvement to early data analysis methods would be to account for individual differences such as ability, gender, and age, by correlating these with performance measures (e.g. time to solution) in order to clarify if individual differences affect performance and strategy.

4.3 Case and Comparative Studies: Contextualized, Problem Solving

To fully explore this research space, it is important to move past content-free tasks, such as puzzles, and study interfaces and materials to support children in solving contextualized, ill-structured problems. In these tasks a spatial problem is situated in a domain-specific context (e.g. sustainable land use planning) with opposing or contradictory evidence and opinions, and there is not a single, correct solution [26]. To succeed children must both solve spatial problems (e.g. where to position resources) as well as learn domain-specific concepts (e.g. the pros and cons of hydro-electric versus natural gas for generating energy). These kinds of ill-structured spatial problems are a suitable test bed for tangibles research because their successful solution requires 1. Consideration of the physical and spatial elements of the problem that can be represented with physical objects; 2. Iterative problem framing and reframing that is enabled through computational models; 3. Integration of subject-matter content that is enabled by digital media.

One way to approach this research is to use findings from content-free puzzle studies to design interfaces for specific content domains. Exploratory single case studies can be used to determine if previous findings hold and to reveal new issues for investigation. Later comparative studies can be used to understand the tradeoffs between interaction, interface, and learning designs.

4.3.1 Past Work

One area that we have explored was a case study of primary school children's interactions and learning with a tangible tabletop system for land use planning. The system was designed to facilitate learning about key concepts in sustainable land use planning (described in [5]). The case study was comprised of theoretical underpinnings that informed design choices, a detailed description of the system (called Towards Utopia, shown in Figure 4), a design analysis and rationale, and a summary of a pre-test and post-test clinical style learning evaluation with 30 individual children. One key design requirement was that the system should enable dynamic, spatial reconfiguration of its components to support mutual adaptation and knowledge transfer.

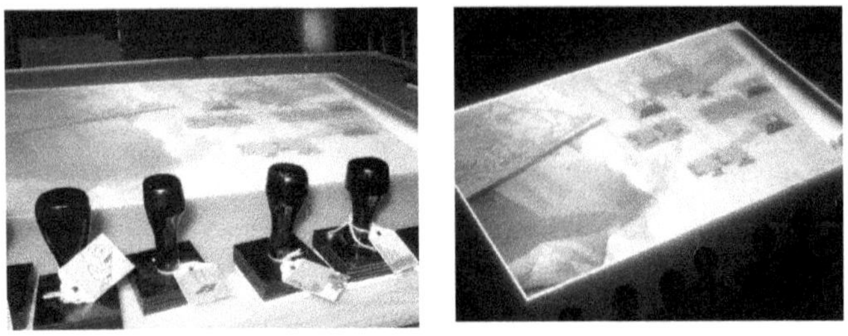

Figure 4. Tangible sustainable land use planning activity.

We observed that all children were able to quickly learn how to use the "stamps" to designate land use types on the tabletop map, check the results, and change land uses until a successful solution was found. We observed children using two hands asymmetrically to organize and use stamps, using table edges to store and organize stamps (epistemic actions), and using a trial and error approach consistent with dynamic spatial reconfiguration. Learning results from clinical style interview showed an increase in post-test scores compared to pre-test scores. The average learning gain score was a 22% increase, which was significant at the $p<0.001$ level (non-parametric statistics). The standard deviations for pre-test and post-test are relatively small, indicating that participant scores were fairly tightly clustered around the mean scores.

While these results provide evidence of short term learning benefit, we do not have a control group or a comparison with other learning approaches or materials. Thus, we cannot say that children learned better or differently with our system compared to another. However, it is clear that students significantly increased their scores after using the system. In future designs, a follow-up activity assessing knowledge transfer would enable stronger claims to be made. In addition, in this study it is not possible to isolate one feature of the prototype (e.g. dynamic re-configuration) from others (e.g. 3D interaction space).

4.3.2 Future Work

One avenue for future work is to explore if results from single case studies are generalizable. To do this requires creating different ill-structured spatial problems using the same interface strategies identified in previous research. Another avenue for future work that we have currently begun involves comparing different approaches for supporting collaborative mutual adaptation with pairs of children. We are redesigning the Towards Utopia system to enable collaborative activity that may support mutual adaptation. To support collaboration it is important that children have a shared focus around which negotiation can occur [11]. In addition, children need to have a reason to negotiate with each other. True collaborative tasks create positive interdependence, requiring the coordinated activity of multiple children for success [27]. One way this is often instantiated in CSCL is through variations on the "jigsaw" script [6] in which each child only has access to part of the solution [33].

In a tangible system, access points enable multiple children to participate as a group and interact with the system. In Towards Utopia, access points are enabled by 13 land use stamps. However, previous non-tangibles research has shown that multiple access points may result in a non-collaborative situation of parallel play [24]. One option is to design a constrained input system that has limited number of access points. This approach requires sharing and coordination [22] since a limited number of access point can also lead to competitive behaviors [31]. Another approach is to design co-dependent inputs; that is, while they are sensed individually, the system responds to them collectively. Each child needs to take a specific action in order for the system to respond in the desired way.

Research is needed to determine how a constrained versus a co-dependent approach influences children's co-evolving interactions and ideas. Our new design of Towards Utopia supports pairs of children to adapt their ideas by trying out different spatial configurations (as in [5]) and also triggers opportunities for discussion during spatial reconfiguration. We will compare how constrained versus co-dependent access points support children in productively negotiating with each other during the land use planning task, and if such interactions provide benefits for conceptual learning.

4.4 Designer Studies: Making Knowledge Accessible and Usable in Design Practice

Another pressing problem associated with child-computer interaction research that is often neglected, is determining how to get resulting design knowledge into design practitioners' hands. Design cards are a method that has been suggested for making research-based design knowledge into a form that is accessible and usable for designers [7, 23].

4.4.1 Future Work

We are currently working on a set of design cards for tangible learning. The goal of the project is to take information in the form of design guidelines from research papers and distill and illustrate the guidelines on design cards. For example, we have taken guidelines from [4], including guidelines related to complementary actions and mutual adaptation, and created preliminary cards, called the Tango set (see Figure 5). Future plans are to run a design-in-use study to evaluate if the cards present design knowledge in ways that are useable and accessible to researchers and designers of tangibles for children.

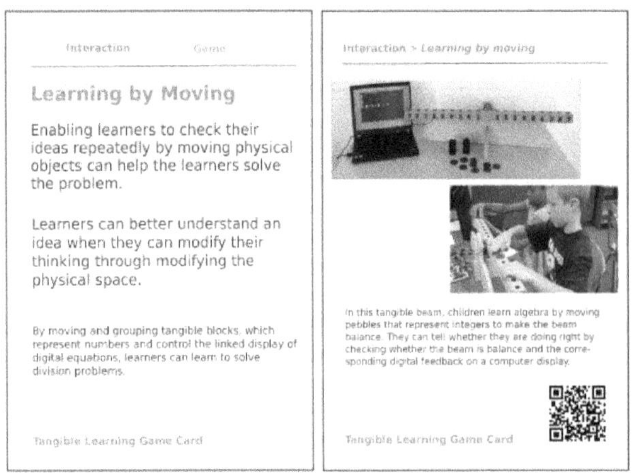

Figure 5. Tango card for mutual adaptation (draft).

5. SUMMARY

In this paper I have identified three threads of research, provided summaries of some of my work in each area, and made suggestions for future work. I encourage interested readers to read my original papers in order to understand the details of each piece of research, and follow links in these papers to read works of other researchers working in this space. By focusing on research questions derived from theory, I hope to provide a grounded research agenda that will enable other researchers to move forward with rigorous empirical work. Without such work, the HCI and educational technology communities interested in children's hands on interaction may remain focused on performance, observation of behaviors and experiential measures, and neglect important details about how manipulating objects in space helps, changes or limits children's ability to think with and through those objects. Of course translating theory to empirical study designs is difficult and each methodology has its limitations. Single case studies are often not generalizable. Comparative studies often have multiple factors that vary between interfaces. No single approach is right to address all questions. However, taken together, a body of research can be undertaken that contributes to better understanding of how and why tangibles might support the development of children's spatial problem solving skills.

Research outcomes in this space will make important contributions to communities including learning sciences, educational technology, educational psychology, computer-supported collaborative learning (CSCL), interaction design for children, child-computer interaction, and cognitive development. Knowledge transfer to other researchers, undergraduate and graduate students, and industry practitioners may enable the design of effective tangible and touch interfaces for numerous educational and professional domains that include spatial problems solving in science, art, engineering, and design; and may be transferable to other user groups including teens and college students.

6. ACKNOWLEDGMENTS

I gratefully acknowledge funding from GRAND NCE, SSHRC and NSERC RTI for this work.

7. REFERENCES

[1] Antle, A.N. The CTI framework: Informing the design of tangible systems for children. In *Proc. Conference on Tangible and Embedded Interaction*, ACM Press, (2007) 195-202.

[2] Antle, A.N. Exploring how children use their hands to think: An embodied interactional analysis. *Behaviour and Information Technology*, in press, available at http://dx.doi.org/10.1080/0144929X.2011.630415

[3] Antle, A.N., Droumeva, M. and Ha, D. Hands on what? Comparing children's mouse-based and tangible-based interaction. In *Proc. Conference on Interaction Design and Children*, ACM Press, (2009) 80-88.

[4] Antle, A.N. and Wise, A.F. Getting down to details: Using learning theory to inform tangibles research and design for children. *Interacting with Computers*, accepted, draft available at www.antle.iat.sfu.ca/publications

[5] Antle, A.N., Wise, A.F. and Nielsen, K. Towards Utopia: Designing tangibles for learning. In *Proc. Conference on Interaction Design for Children*, ACM Press, (2011) 11-20.

[6] Aronson, E., Blaney, N., Stephan, C., Sikes, J. and Snapp, M. *The Jigsaw Classroom*. Sage Publications, Beverly Hills, CA, 1978.

[7] Bekker, M.M. and Antle, A.N. Developmentally Situated Design (DSD): A design tool for child-computer interaction. In *Proc. Conference on Human Factors in Computing Systems*, ACM Press, (2011) 2531-2540.

[8] Bevans, A. *Investigating the Effects of Bimanual Multitouch Interaction on Creativity*. Thesis, Interactive Arts + Technology, Simon Fraser University, Supervisor: Antle, A.N. (2011) 101 pages.

[9] Brosterman, N. *Inventing Kindergarten*. Harry Abrams Inc., New York, NY, USA, 1997.

[10] Clark, A. *Being There: Putting Brain, Body and World Together Again*. Bradford Books, MIT Press, Cambridge, MA, USA, 1997.

[11] Clark, H.H. and Brennan, S.E. Grounding in communication. In Resnick, L.B., Levine, J.M. and Teasley, S.D. eds. *Perspectives on Socially Shared Cognition*, American Psychological Association, Washington, DC, 1991, 127-149.

[12] Defeyter, M. and German, T. Acquiring an understanding of design: evidence from children's insight problem solving. *Cognition 89*, 2, (2003) 133-155.

[13] DeLoache, J.S. Dual representations and young children's use of scale models. *Child Development 71*, 2, (2000) 329-338.

[14] Dewey, J. *Logic: The Theory of Inquiry*. Holt and Co., New York, 1938.

[15] Evans, M. and Wilkins, J.L.M. Social interactions and instructional Artifacts: Emergent socio-technical affordances and constraints for children's geometric thinking. *Journal of Educational Computing Research 44*, 22, (2011) 141 - 171.

[16] Gattis, M. Space as a basis for abstract thought. In *Spatial Schemas and Abstract Thought*, Bradford Books, 2001, 1-14.

[17] Gibbs, R.W. *Embodiement and Cognitive Science*. Cambridge University Press, Cambridge, USA, 2005.

[18] Goldin-Meadow, S. *Hearing Gesture: How Our Hands Help Us Think*. First Harvard University Press, Cambridge, MA, USA, 2005.

[19] Heilman, K.M., Nadeau, S.E. and Beversdorf, D.O. Creative innovation: Possible brain mechanisms. *Neurocase 9*, 5, (2003) 369–379.

[20] Hernik, M. and Gergely Csibra, G. Functional understanding facilitates learning about tools in human children. *Current Opinion in Neurobiology 19*, 1, (2009) 34-38.

[21] Hoppe, K.D. Hemispheric specialization and creativity. *The Psychiatric Clinics of North America 11*, 3, (1988) 303-315.

[22] Hornecker, E. A design theme for tangible interaction: Embodied facilitation. In *Proc. Conference on Computer-Supported Cooperative Work*, Springer, (2005) 23-44.

[23] Hornecker, E. and Creative idea exploration within the structure of a guiding framework: the card brainstorming game. In *Proc. Conference on Tangible, Embedded, and Embodied Interaction* ACM Press, (2010) 101-108.

[24] Inkpen, K., Ho-Ching, W., Kuederle, O., Scott, S. and Shoemaker, G. This is fun! we're all best friends and we're all playing: supporting children's synchronous collaboration. In *Proc. Conference on Computer Support for Collaborative Learning*, International Society of the Learning Sciences, (1999) 1-12.

[25] Kirsh, D. Complementary strategies: Why we use our hands when we think. In *Proc. Conference of the Cognitive Science Society*, (1995) 212-217.

[26] Kitchner, K.S. Cognition, metacognition, and epistemic cognition:A three-level model of cognitive processing. *Human Development 26*, (1983) 222-232.

[27] Kreijns, K., Kirschner, P.A. and Jochems, W. Identifying the pitfalls for social interaction in computer-supported collaborative learning environments: A review of the research. *Computers in Human Behavior 19*, 3, (2003) 335-353.

[28] Lewis, R.T. Organic signs, creativity, and personality characteristics of patients following cerebral commissurotomy. *Clinical Neuropsychology 1*, (1979) 29-33.

[29] Marshall, P. Do tangible interfaces enhance learning? In *Proc. Conference on Tangible and Embedded Interaction*, ACM Press, (2007) 163-170.

[30] Marshall, P., Cheng, P.C.H. and Luckin, R. Tangibles in the balance: a discovery learning task with physical or graphical materials. In *Proc. Conference on Tangible, Embedded, and Embodied Interaction*, ACM Press, (2010) 153-160.

[31] Marshall, P., Fleck, R., Harris, A., Rick, J., Hornecker, E., Rogers, Y., Yuill, N. and Dalton, N.S. Fighting for control: Children's embodied interactions when using physical and digital representations. In *Proc. Conference on Human Factors in Computing Systems*, ACM press, (2009) 2149-2152.

[32] Martin, T. A theory of physically distributed learning: How external environments and internal states interact in mathematics learning. *Child Development Perspectives 3*, 3, (2009) 140-144.

[33] Miyake, N., Masukawa, H. and Shirouzou, H. The complex jigsaw as an enhancer of collaborative knowledge building in undergraduate introductory science courses. In *Proc. European Conference on Computer-Supported Collaborative Learning*, Maastricht University, (2001) 454-461.

[34] Montessori, M. *The Secret of Childhood*. Ballantine Books, New York, NY, USA, 1966.

[35] O'Malley, C. and Stanton-Fraser, D. Literature review in learning with tangible technologies (2004) http://archive.futurelab.org.uk/resources/documents/lit_reviews/Tangible_Review.pdf (accessed Aug 17 2012).

[36] Papert, S. *Mindstorms: Children, Computers, And Powerful Ideas*. Basic Books, New York, NY, USA, 1993.

[37] Piaget, J. *The Origins of Intelligence in Children*. University Press, New York, NY, USA, 1952.

[38] Resnick, M. Computer as paintbrush: Technology, play, and the creative society. In Singer, D., Golinkoff, R.M. and Hirsh-Pasek, K. eds. *Play = Learning*, Oxford University Press, 2006.

[39] Schwartz, D.L. and Martin, T. Distributed learning and mutual adaptation. *Pragmatics & Cognition 14*, 2, (2006) 313-332.

[40] Shaer, O. and Hornecker, E. Tangible User Interfaces: Past, Present and Future Directions. *Foundations and Trends in Human-Computer Interaction 3*, 1-2, (2010) 1-137.

[41] Shobe, E.R., Ross, N.M. and Fleck, J.I. Influence of handedness and bilateral eye movements on creativity. *Brain and Cognition 71*, 3, (2009) 204-214.

[42] Sinnott, J.D. A model for solution of ill-structured problems: Implications for everyday and abstract problem solving. In Sinnott, J.D. ed. *Everyday problem solving: Theory and applications*, Praeger, New York, 1989, 72-99.

[43] Thelen, E. and Smith, L., B *A dynamic systems approach to the development of cognition and action*. MIT Press, Cambridge, MA, USA, 1996.

[44] Uttal, D. On the relation between play and symbolic thought: The case of mathematics manipulatives. In *Contemporary Perspectives in Early Childhood*, Information Age Press, 2003, 97-114.

[45] Wang, S. *Comparing tangible and multitouch interfaces for a spatial problem solving task.* Thesis, Interactive Arts + Technology, Simon Fraser University, Supervisor: Antle, A.N. (2010) 94 pages.

[46] Zaman, B., Van den Abeele, V., Markopoulos, P. and Marshall, P. Editorial: the evolving field of tangible interaction for children: the challenge of empirical validation. *Personal and Ubiquitous Computing 16*, 4, (2012) 367-378.

Evaluating Artefacts with Children: Age and Technology Effects in the Reporting of Expected and Experienced Fun

Janet C Read
ChiCI group
University of Central Lancashire
Preston, UK
+44(0) 1772 893285
jcread@uclan.ac.uk

ABSTRACT

In interaction design, there are several metrics used to gather user experience data. A common approach is to use surveys with the usual method being to ask users after they have experienced a product as to their opinion and satisfaction. This paper describes the use of the Smileyometer (a product from the Fun Toolkit) to test for user experience with children by asking for opinions in relation to expected as well as experienced fun.

Two studies looked at the ratings that children, from two different age groups and in two different contexts, gave to a set of varied age-appropriate interactive technology installations. The ratings given before use (expectations) are compared with ratings given after use (experience) across the age groups and across installations.

The studies show that different ratings were given for the different installations and that there were age-related differences in the use of the Smileyometer to rate user experience; these firstly evidence that children can, and do, discriminate between different experiences and that children do reflect on user experience after using technologies. In most cases, across both age groups, children expected a lot from the technologies and their after use (experienced) rating confirmed that this was what they had got.

The paper concludes by considering the implications of the collective findings for the design and evaluation of technologies with children

Categories and Subject Descriptors

H.5.2 [**User Interfaces**]: Evaluation / Methodologies

General Terms

Design, Human Factors

Keywords

Fun Toolkit, Children, Evaluation Methods, User Experience

1. INTRODUCTION

Asking users about technologies is a commonly used method for understanding user experience and for evaluating products – especially in 'competitive (as, for example, when product A is compared with product B)' ways. Asking children about user experience is a relatively recent idea and for that purpose several new methods and innovative approaches have been developed. These include the laddering technique [1], the This and That method [2], and the problem identification picture card method [3]. Determining what children think about technologies can give insights into software appeal and can provide a designer or developer with feedback as well as with a very useful endorsement of a product. In addition, many academic papers, especially design papers, use the opinions of end users as an indication of value or worth.

Collecting children's opinions is not always straightforward and there are several known hurdles that need to be overcome if the opinions that are gathered are to have value. Where opinions are elicited by questioning, an area of concern is the degree to which the child understands the question being asked. Answering questions is complex as not only does the child need to understand and interpret the question being asked, he or she then has to retrieve the relevant information from memory, and then integrate this information into a summarised judgment. In many instances, the child then has to code the answer in some way, typically using rating scales. Researchers often discuss the importance of the question-answer process in determining the reliability of responses provided by children in surveys [4].

Factors that impact on question-answering include developmental effects (the child may be too young to understand), language (the child may not have the words needed), reading age (the child might be unable to read the question), motor abilities (the child may be unable to write neatly enough), and temperamental effects including confidence, self-belief and the desire to please. Another factor, especially evident in surveys where respondents are being asked to pass attitudinal judgments [5], is the degree to which the respondent either optimises, satisfices, or guesses, his or her answers.

For validity in a survey, of these three methods, optimising is the preferred process. Optimising occurs when a survey respondent goes thoughtfully and carefully through each of the three or four stages of the question and answer sequence. Thus, the respondent will ensure that he or she understands what the question is really about, will take care to retrieve an appropriate answer, will think about how the response should be articulated in order to make it clear what he or she is thinking, and, where there is a rating to apply, will carefully consider where on the rating scale each answer should be placed.

Satisficing is a midway approach (less good than optimising but better than guessing!) and occurs when a respondent gives more or less superficial responses that generally appear reasonable or acceptable, but without having so carefully gone through all the steps involved in the question-answer process. Satisficing is not to do with guessing answers or choosing random responses, it is to do with picking a suitable answer. The degree or level of satisficing is known to be related to the motivation of the respondent, the difficulties of the task, and the cognitive abilities of the respondent [6].

Especially because of having high motivation but also cognitive immaturity, it is the case that children are prone to satisficing - they find survey participation difficult and often lack the abilities to articulate answers or to fully understand the questions.

As well as there being concerns, in the interaction design community, with children's responses to questions given at a moment in time, there are also concerns about the stability of these responses over time; both of these concerns affect the reliability of self-reported data from children. It is generally considered that all that can be elicited from a survey is a general feel for a product or a concept with a particular group of children at a particular time, e.g. [7]. This is not especially good news for researchers hoping to evaluate user experience with children, but there is some comfort in that, in most user experience work, the reliability of responses is generally not critical (as could be the case, for example, where a child is being interviewed as part of a criminal investigation).

Given the general difficulties of surveying children, there are several useful approaches that can be taken to make the process more valuable and at least satisfactory for all the parties. One of these is to use specially designed tools that fit the task of evaluating user experience for children [8], [9]. Such tools may be easy to use but because they are relatively novel, they may be unreliable and may be applied inappropriately. The remainder of this paper describes one suite of such tools, the Fun Toolkit [10], and then looks at one tool in particular, the Smileyometer, before describing two studies that used the Smileyometer and shed light on its efficacy.

2. THE FUN TOOLKIT

The Fun Toolkit is a selection of tools that have been designed to gather opinions from children about interactive technology. They use only essential language and lend themselves well to the use of pictures to convey information with options for gluing and sticking for input. They are fun and attractive to use, and they reduce some of the effects of satisficing.

2.1 The Three Main Tools

The Fun Toolkit was originally described with four tools but has since been tested and evaluated with the result that it is now considered to be sufficient to have three main tools for use. The three tools, and their advised use, are briefly described here.

The Smileyometer (shown in Figure 1) is a discrete visual analogue scale (VAS). Research has shown that children aged from seven and over can use VAS effectively and so, for the Fun Toolkit, this was an obvious choice of tool to consider [11]. In validations of the Smileyometer, studies by the authors and others have shown VAS to be useful for considerably younger children than was previously reported, but it should also be noted that when these scales are used to elicit opinions about software or hardware products, younger children are inclined to almost always indicate the highest score on the scale [12].

During use children are asked to tick one face. This makes it a very easy tool for the children, note that it also includes textual information to improve the validity. The Smileyometer can be easily coded; it is common to apportion scores of 1 to 5 for the different faces; if used in this way.

Figure 1 - The Smileyometer

The Smileyometer has been used by the Interaction Design and Children community in many studies to rate experienced but also anticipated (expected) fun; in the latter case the child is asked, before an experience, to tick a face according to 'How much fun will it be?' This is an important facet of the Smileyometer that will be returned to later in this paper.

In many evaluation studies, the desire is not to carry out an isolated evaluation but to rank a series of connected or competing activities or technologies. These comparative evaluations can help the evaluator determine which may be more appealing or which may be least fun. Repeated instances of the Smileyometer can be used (and are used in the study in this current paper) but it is worth describing the Fun-Sorter, a variation on a repertory grid test [13], as it can be useful in this context. The Fun-Sorter (shown in Figure 2) has one or more constructs (rows) and a divided line (or table – columns) that has as many spaces in it as there are activities to be compared. The children either write the names of the competing activities in the spaces, or for younger children, picture cards can be made and placed on the empty grid.

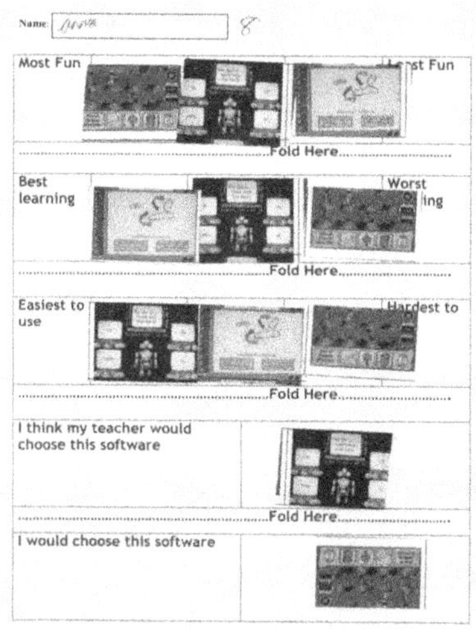

Figure 2 - The Fun Sorter

The attractiveness of the Fun-Sorter, over repeated use of the Smileyometer is that it forces the children to rank the items or activities in order. Where the Smileyometer has been used for comparative studies, the tendency of children to give maximum ratings to products can makes it difficult to see which item, from a set of four, is the least fun. This facet of the Smileyometer is studied in this paper. The Fun-Sorter is recommended to be used one row at a time so children do not 'copy' one row down to another.

The 'Again–Again' tool (see Figure 3) can also be used to compare activities / events. This table lists some activities or instances on the left hand side, and has three columns headed Yes, Maybe, and No.

Would you like to do it Again?

	Yes	Maybe	No
Visit U Boat	✓		
Puppet show		✓	

Figure 3 - Part of an Again-Again table

The child ticks either yes, maybe or no for each activity, having in each case considered the question 'Would you like to do this again?' The rationale to this is that, for most children, a fun activity would be one that the child would want to repeat.

2.2 Tests of the Validity of the Fun Toolkit Instruments

The Fun Toolkit has been around for quite some time now and has been evaluated in several studies. The major findings to date have been that;

- With the Smileyometer, children almost always pick 5 for everything, this is more the case the younger the children [14] , [10] – Either, everything children see is great, or, children see everything as great!
- Children tend to report their experience as being the same as, or slightly better than, their expectation [15] – This suggests that what is seen at the beginning is very important
- The Smileyometer is measuring Fun rather than Usability [16]
- The tools, when used together, give similar results [10] – This suggests that the tools are fundamentally not flawed and that children know what they are doing when they use them.

Of these findings, there are several research questions that merit further study, especially in the case of the Smileyometer. In the work that reported that children 'got what they expected', the technologies being evaluated were all quite 'even' in their attractiveness and we all perceived to be products that children would enjoy using. Whether this result would hold with less attractive technology was worth investigating as it was hoped, but not known, that children might actually be quite discriminating and it would be the technology, rather than the tool, that had limited their possibility to show this. It was also worth looking at the tendency for most children to pick 5 (brilliant) – this was thought to be partially age-related but this had not been well tested. A third question was around the reliability of the scales, especially the Smileyometer. Could it be shown that the Smileyometer was being completed thoughtfully by children, i.e. was there more satisficing than guessing and more optimising than satisficing? These three questions prompted the studies reported in this paper.

3. THE STUDIES

In the studies, two different groups of children, of different ages, were given the Smileyometer to each rate three age-appropriate different technology experiences. There were three hypotheses:

1. All children would give overall experienced (after fun) ratings that would roughly align with the predicted experiences of different technology installations
1. The younger children would generally rate all technologies highly, especially in terms of anticipated fun, with 5 being a common score; older children would have lower scores on average.
2. Some of the younger children, and most of the older children, would demonstrate discriminatory behaviour according to their reporting of expected and experienced fun that would align with the predictions (associated with the technologies being evaluated) of the adult research team.

3.1 Method

The method was the same for both studies. Children met three interfaces and in each case rated their expected fun and then their experienced fun using a pair of Smileyometer grids. In both cases the interfaces were different, in order to account for age appropriateness, but for both studies three interfaces were specifically chosen that looked good and were good, looked good and weren't great and looked ordinary but were actually quite fun.

3.1.1 Study 1

The first study, with younger children, took place at a Mess day [17] at the University of Central Lancashire in the UK. 24 children aged 6 and 7 (9 girls, 15 boys) came to the lab and each child took part in 10-minute activities on the three technologies in question. The technologies were intended to offer different user experiences as follows.

- Interface A1 was a tangible block game that was entirely novel to the children, it looked fun, was very easy to play, and it was expected that all the children would enjoy playing it. The prediction for this was that it would score mostly 5's in expected and mostly 5s in experienced fun.
- Interface B1 was a PDA application that was probably new to most of the children, it looked interesting, it was not especially easy to use (due to the size of the stylus), and the children were expected to find it rather dull as they were carrying out a writing activity. The prediction was that children would expect this to be better than it would be experienced.
- Interface C1 was a laptop PC with paint installed on it. This was not especially novel but was expected to be greeted with enthusiasm by the children. However, there was a catch as the interface was relatively difficult to work due to there being no mouse attached to the computer and so children had to draw using the touch pad. Thus, it was expected that most children would find this hard, but would still enjoy it, and that this might result in an average expected score being followed by possibly a slightly lower than average experienced score.

3.1.2 *Study 2*

The second study, with older children, took place at a science day at the University campus in Cumbria, Forty eight children aged 13 and 14 each took part in a 10-minute activity on each of the three technologies in question. The technologies were intended to offer different user experiences as follows.

- Interface A2 was an iPad game that was (at that time) entirely novel to the children, it looked fun, was very easy to play, and it was expected that all the children would enjoy playing it. Like A1, the assumption was for the scores to be high before and high after.
- Interface B2 was a digital pen application that was probably new to almost all of the children, it looked interesting, it was easy enough to use but the children were expected to find it rather dull as they were simply carrying out a writing activity. This, like B1 was expected to start high (expected) but actually end up being downgraded (experienced).
- Interface C2 was an ordinary PC with a web based Flash game on it with paint installed on it. This was not especially novel but was expected to be greeted with some enthusiasm by the children. The interface was a bit clunky so there was an expectation that children might be a bit disappointed with this activity. Like C3, the scores were expected to be about average across both ratings.

3.1.3 *Predicted Results for the Six Interfaces*

interface	Anticipated scores	interface	Anticipated scores
A1	High, high	A2	High, high
B1	High, med	B2	High, med
C1	Med, med	C2	Med, med

Table 1 - Predictions of the Paired Expected and Experienced Fun Scores for each Interface

Table 1 shows the expected ratings for each interface. Note that no numerical value is given to the ratings as high for the younger children was also hypothesized to be 'higher' than high for the older children. This is revisited in the results.

3.2 Procedure

In both studies, children moved around the activities in a predetermined order. Each child moved from A to B to C but this was in a cyclic order and so some began with C (then moved on to A and B), others started with B (and moved to C then A). A couple of children in each groups failed to properly complete the Smileyometer or were called away for one of the installations – this accounts for the missing data in the results. Despite the problems, every participating child filled in Smileyometers for at least two installations and most (91%) filled in Smileyometers for all three. Comparisons are not being made in this paper across individual children's scores and so this was not considered to be detrimental to the research being undertaken.

On arriving at an activity, the activity was briefly described, the children were told what they were going to do and shown the technology (but it was not demonstrated), then each child completed a 'Before Smileyometer' to indicate how much fun they thought it was going to be (expected fun). Having completed the activity, the child then completed an 'After Smileyometer' (the before version was hidden from view at this point) to indicate how much fun the activity had been (experienced fun).

The scores from the children were coded as follows: Brilliant = 5, Really good = 4, Good = 3, Not very good = 2, Awful = 1. Note that in some of the analysis in this paper arithmetic averages have been taken of these scores in order to show differences. This can be argued to be an incorrect use of the data as the Smileyometer has not been proved to be an interval scale. This is justified in this paper simply to show the relative strength of opinion towards one or more installation(s) and the reader should interpret this treatment with appropriate caution.

At the end of the activity the children were thanked for their assistance and given certificates to take home.

3.3 Results

The results are presented in two sections, section 1 looks at the younger children's responses, section 2 at the older children's responses. Within each section the results are presented firstly in terms of the technologies and then, considering all the technologies in one analysis and looking at the variations and data patterns of the participating children.

3.3.1 *Study 1*

In this study, in total, 59 pairs of ratings were gathered. 16 of these related to Interface A1, 21 related to Interface B1, and 22 related to Interface C1.

The average before and after ratings for the three interfaces are shown in Table 2:

	Interface A1	Interface B1	Interface C1
Before	4.75	3.71	4.36
After	4.75	3.52	3.64
Number rating	16	21	22

Table 2 - Average ratings, before and after

For Interface A1, all but two of the children gave a 5 rating for expected (before) fun and all but two children (a different two), gave a 5 for experienced (after) fun.

For Interface B1, 10 children gave it 5 before playing and 9 gave it 5 after playing with the other children rating it from 1 – 4 for expected and experienced fun.

Interface C1 was rated at 5 by 14 children before it was played and by 9 after playing. The other children rated it at 3 or 4 before playing and between 1 and 4 after playing.

Across the interfaces there were some trends in respect of individual children, six of the twenty-four, in every single instance gave the same ratings before they used the technology as they did after use. Another six never changed their ratings by more than one from before use to after use, whereas half the children, on at least one occasion made a shift of two or more. Table 3 shows the frequency and spread of the different scores, the row indicates the after score, the column the before score.

25	3	3	1		**5 after**
3	3	3	1		**4 after**
5	2	1	1		**3 after**
5					**2 after**
1		1		1	**1 after**
5 before	**4 before**	**3 before**	**2 before**	**1 before**	

Table 3 - The 59 results from the younger children

This table shows that out of the 59 pairs, 25 (42%) were rated (5,5) – it also shows that only one interface was rated as 'awful' before use (this was B1), and only three rated as awful after use (B1 and C1). Across all the paired scores, the average change between the before and after score was 0.95. For this age of children, the average score across all the children and all the interfaces was 4.24 as a before (expected) rating and 3.90 as an after (experienced) rating.

3.3.2 Study 2

In this study, with the older children, in total, 132 pairs of ratings were gathered. 45 of these related to Interface A2, 46 related to Interface B2, and 41 related to Interface C2.

The average before and after ratings for the three interfaces are shown in Table 4:

	Interface A2	**Interface B2**	**Interface C2**
Before	4.33	3.91	3.30
After	4.55	4.00	3.43
Number rating	45	46	41

Table 4 - Average ratings, before and after

For Interface A2, over half of the children gave a 5 rating for expected (before) fun and all but twelve children, gave a 5 for experienced (after) fun. Only 4 children changed their expected score of 5 to a lower score (and these all recorded 5,4)

For Interface B2, the modal score before playing was 4 (with 43% choosing this) and this was also the modal score after playing (with 39%).

Interface C2 was rated at 5 before play by just 4 children, this rose to 7 after play. The modal scores before and after for this interface were 3 with 54% before and 44% after choosing this score.

As with the younger children, for this age group, overall the score of 5 before and 5 after was the most popular choice (22%) but other paired scores were also very popular with this age group, as was the score of 4 before and 5 after. Table 5 shows the frequency and spread of the different scores, the row indicates the after score, the column the before score.

29	20	6			**5 after**
6	18	9		1	**4 after**
3	6	21	2	1	**3 after**
	1	9			**2 after**
					1 after
5 before	**4 before**	**3 before**	**2 before**	**1 before**	

Table 5 - The 132 results from the older children

The average change in score across all the older children and all the interfaces was 0.48 (which is half as much as the average for the younger children) with the average score for expected fun (before) being 3.86 and the average score for experienced fun being 4.02.

4. DISCUSSION

The discussion here is in two sections, the first section looks at the results reported here and offers some explanations for them; the second section looks at the broader area of expected and experienced usability and discusses the findings of this work against the backdrop of Hassenzahl et al.'s model of hedonic and ergonomic usability and the impacts of both on user experience [18].

4.1 General Discussion of Findings

The first hypothesis for these studies was that children would be discriminating and that their ratings for experienced fun would match the predicted ratings for the six interfaces. The prediction was that the A interfaces would score highly in terms of experienced fun and the B and C interfaces would score more lowly. For interface A this was very much the case across both age groups. Interface C showed an average score that was 1 point less than interface A in both age groups – this was in line, therefore, with the prediction that it would be lower. Interface B was a bit surprising, the B1 interface (the PDA which then was a bit hopeless) rated similarly with C1 and this met the hypothesis but the B2 interface (the digital pens that did very little) scored quite well on experienced fun with an average half a point below that of interface A2. There are two explanations for this – one is that interface B2 was 'better' than we predicted in terms of user experience, the second is that interface C2 was worse than we anticipated given that overall, the spread of scores for the older children was less broad. This second explanation may be closer to the reality. Looking at the spread of scores across the two ages for experienced fun (see Figure 4), the younger children do appear to have more spread but this could be by chance and could be associated with the choices of interface

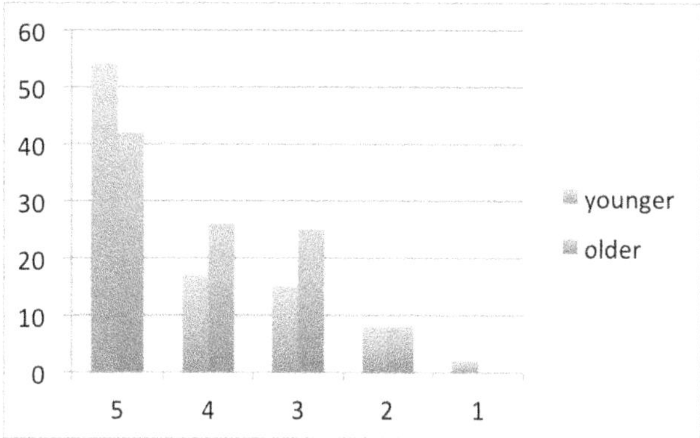

Figure 4 - Spread of scores (shown as percentages) for experienced (after) fun across the two ages

The second hypothesis being investigated was that younger children would more often choose 5 and would, by and large, rate the interfaces higher than the older children. The averages across the two ages are as follows:

	Younger	Older
Average expected rating	4.24	3.86
Average experienced rating	3.90	4.02
% of 5s given 'before' use	66	29
% of 5s given 'after' use	54	42
% of 5,5 scores	42	22

Table 6 - Comparison between the ages

It can be seen that overall a much higher percentage of younger than older children chose the 5,5 score and also that both before and after they gave more 5 scores. However, the averages tell an interesting story with the older children actually rating, over all instances, experienced fun higher than the younger children. It is worth referring back to Table 3 at this stage and noting that 5 of the younger children went from a 5 before to a 2 after, for instance. Overall the younger children gave a pro rata higher number of low scores to interfaces than the older children did and this brought down the averages. Thus, this hypothesis, that younger children give more 5s, is actually supported across the two uses of the Smileyometer (before and after) but in terms of experienced fun there does not appear to be any difference across the ages.

The third hypothesis was that children would discriminate across the interfaces by changing their scores from their expected to experienced fun, especially the older children aligning more to the predicted results (as shown in Table 1) than the younger children. The two interfaces that were expected to give high scores for both expected and experienced fun both delivered across both age groups. Interface A1, and interface A2 had the highest expected and highest experienced rating in each study with A1 getting 4.75 before and 4.75 after and A2 getting 4.33 before and 4.55 after. The two B interfaces were predicted to begin with high ratings that would then fall. This marginally held for interface B1 but not for B2 but in each case the average ratings were lower, in both instances, than for interface A. The fall in interface B1 was very small and would probably not be significant could this to be tested. The C interface fell from quite high scores to relatively low scores with the younger children but also held up, like B, with the older children. Explanations for this align with those for the first hypothesis, it could be that the older children were better at predicting the expected fun of an interface and thus their scores were closer, an alternative is that there was a difference across the interfaces that accounted for this finding. To unpick this, a count was made of the 'size of the changes; across both ages where children changed their mind. The assumption was that if this were simply about a single interface being significantly different across the two instances, then when all was balanced out this effect would be much less noticeable. Figure 5 below shows the frequency of 'changed move' across the two age groups.

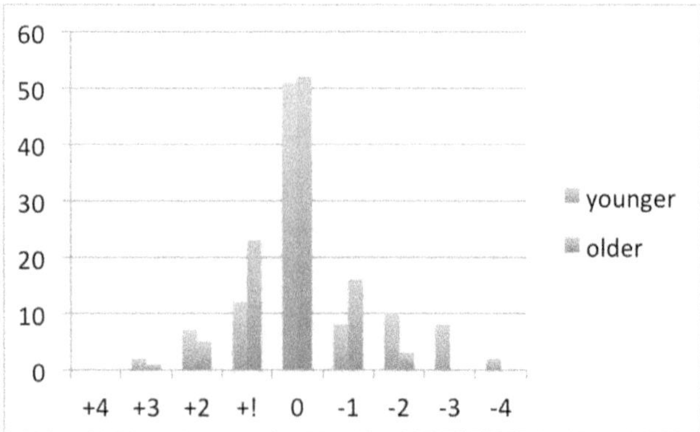

Figure 5 - Percentages of differences from Before and After Fun Scores across both age groups

This chart shows a bigger spread among the younger children in terms of 'mind changing; which may support the explanation that younger children are less able to estimate the fun they expect and that older children are better at this activity.

4.2 Applying the Findings to User Experience Evaluations with Children

The findings from this work may shed some light on design for children and on the approaches needed in usability evaluations. The APPEAL of software was mapped out by Hassenzahl et al. [18] in a model that separates out the 'intended' quality of products from their 'perceived' quality as shown in Figure 6. Perceived quality in this instance can be mapped onto what the user experiences, whilst intended might be what was designed in. In this model it is shown that pleasure and attractiveness (hedonic qualities) are an essential part of user experience. The work by Hassenzahl et al. demonstrated several key aspects including that the balance between the hedonic and the ergonomic aspects might shift but the two behave in tandem. In [19] the authors postulated that expected appeal was more about hedonic aspects that ergonomic aspects and that experienced appeal was more of a balance of the two. Certainly the findings in our study suggest that in the cases of the B interfaces, especially the one with the younger children, the overall judgments went down as the lack of functionality was shown.

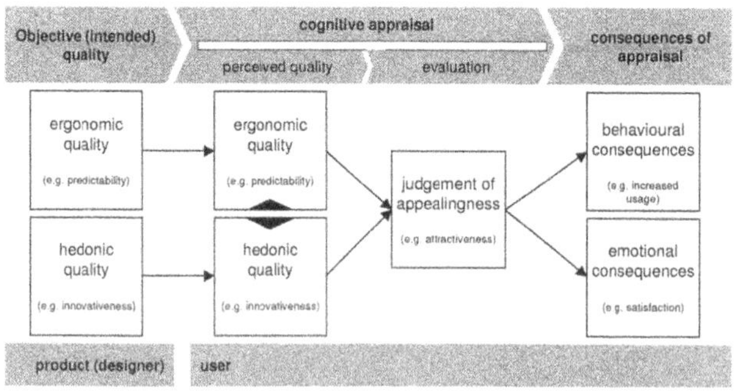

Figure 6 - Hassenzahls's model of APPEAL

When using the Smileyometer before and after technology use it therefore seems reasonable to suggest that researchers and evaluators need to take account of the limitations of this approach in terms of what it might be measuring. For the younger children, the scale was possibly very 'fun' related and thus, when the interfaces failed to deliver what they promised, the scores plummeted. The use of the Fun Sorter with the Smileyometer, with a construct like 'Easy to Use', may be needed in order to get a better judgement of overall appeal.

Using the Smileyometer after use seems to be a reasonably appropriate way of gauging user experience, especially as, with both age groups, it delivered the results that were expected in most cases. It may not be reasonable to compare Smileyometer scores across age groups as older children may be much better at predicting the fun of a technology and therefore, having more reasonable expectations, may be much less likely to give extreme low marks to items.

5. CONCLUSION

This work adds to the knowledge on measuring the experience of children with technology. It also adds to the already published work on the use of the Fun Toolkit and, specifically, the Smileyometer. The work has shown that children of all ages can be discriminatory and can use the Smileyometer. The work has also highlighted some of the differences in the way children of different ages use this tool.

Where good, fun, technology is being evaluated, the children will, by and large, rate it very highly and the expected and experienced fun will hardly vary. Where the technology is familiar but difficult to use, expectations will be quite high but children will adjust their ratings based on the experience with the product. Technology that appears uninteresting will be rated lower before use than technology that appears interesting.

The limitations of this work include the differences between the technoloies and the assumptions made in terms of allowing reporting of results as averages. In defence of the different technologies, the two ages considered in these studies are quite different and even had there been a technology installation that suited both, the expectations and understanding of that technology would still have had an impact. In terms of the use of averages, these have only been used in collective senses where they serve to compare across like reports (same children, same technologies). No attempt to interpret these data beyond descriptive statistics has been made and the standard deviation has not been used. Where possible, modal values have been referenced.

Further work will explore the use of the other Fun Toolkit metrics with 'less attractive' and 'less functional' technologies and will test the ideas developed in this study with a larger cohort of children and across a more diverse set of technologies. Some of the questions raised in this study will inform the production of a set of guidelines for the use of the Fun Toolkit with children of different ages.

6. ACKNOWLEDGEMENTS

Thanks to the researchers of the ChiCI group at UCLan and the children of both of the schools for their assistance in this study.

7. REFERENCES

[1] Zaman, B. and V.V. Abeele. Laddering with young children in User eXperience evaluations: theoretical groundings and a practical case. in IDC '10. 2010. ACM Press.

[2] Zaman, B. Introducing a Pairwise Comparison Scale for UX Evaluations with Preschoolers. in Interact 2009. 2009. IFIP.

[3] Barendregt, W., M.M. Bekker, and E. Baauw, Development and evaluation of the problem identification picture cards method. . Cognition Technology and Work (10) pp.95-105., 2008. 10: p. 95 - 105.

[4] Borgers, N., J. Hox, and D. Sikkel, Response Effects in Surveys on Children and Adolescents: The Effect of Number of Response Options, Negative Wording, and Neutral Mid-Point. Quality and Quantity, 2004. 38(1): p. 17 - 33.

[5] Krosnick, J.A., Response Strategies for coping with the Cognitive demands of attitude measures in surveys. Applied Cognitive Psychology, 1991. 5: p. 213 - 236.

[6] Borgers, N. and J. Hox, Item Non response in Questionnaire Research with Children. Journal of Official Statistics, 2001. 17(2): p. 321 - 335.

[7] Vaillancourt, P.M., Stability of children's survey responses. Public opinion quarterly, 1973. 37: p. 373 - 387.

[8] Airey, S., et al. Rating Children's Enjoyment of Toys, Games and Media. in 3rd World Congress of International Toy Research on Toys, Games and Media. 2002. London.

[9] Hanna, L., K. Risden, and K. Alexander, J, Guidelines for usability testing with children. Interactions, 1997. 1997(5): p. 9-14.

[10] Read, J.C. and S.J. MacFarlane. Using the Fun Toolkit and Other Survey Methods to Gather Opinions in Child Computer Interaction. in Interaction Design and Children, IDC2006. 2006. Tampere, Finland: ACM Press.

[11] Shields, B.J., et al., Predictors of a child's ability to use a visual analogue scale. Child: Care, Health and Development, 2003. 29(4): p. 281 - 290.

[12] Read, J.C., et al. An Investigation of Participatory Design with Children - Informant, Balanced and Facilitated Design. in Interaction Design and Children. 2002. Eindhoven: Shaker Publishing.

[13] Fransella, F. and D. Bannister, A manual for repertory grid technique1977, London: Academic Press.

[14] MacFarlane, S.J., G. Sim, and M. Horton. Assessing Usability and Fun in Educational Software. in IDC2005. 2005. Boulder, Co: ACM Press.

[15] Metaxas, G., et al. SCORPIODROME: An exploration in Mixed Reality Social Gaming for Children. in ACE 2005. 2005. Valencia, Spain: ACM Press.

[16] Read, J.C., Validating the Fun Toolkit: an instrument for measuring children's opinions of technology. Cognition Technology and Work, 2007.

[17] Read, J.C. and E. Mazzone, MESS days. Interfaces, 2008. 71.

[18] Hassenzahl, M. and N. Tractinsky, User experience: A research agenda. Behaviour and IT, 2006. 25(2): p. 91 - 97.

[19] Hassenzahl, M., et al. Hedonic and Ergonomic Quality Aspects Determine a Software's Appeal. in CHI2000. 2000. The Hague, Amsterdam: ACM Press.

Measuring Enjoyment of an Interactive Museum Experience

Elisabeth M.A.G. van Dijk
University of Twente
Human Media Interaction
PO Box 217, 7500 AE Enschede
The Netherlands
0031 53 489 3781
e.m.a.g.vandijk@utwente.nl

Andreas Lingnau
University of Strathclyde
Dept. of Computer & Information sciences
Glasgow
UK
lingnau@ieee.org

Hub Kockelkorn
Museon
Stadhouderslaan 37
2517 HV The Hague
The Netherlands
0031 70 33 81 338
hkockelkorn@museon.nl

ABSTRACT

Museums are increasingly being equipped with interactive technology. The main goal of using technology is to improve the museum-going experience of visitors. In this paper, we present the results of a study with an electronic quest through a museum aimed at children in the age of 10-12. We wanted to find out whether personalization of the quest effects enjoyment. For this purpose we involved an interactive multi-touch table in the experiment, which also offered the opportunity to add the element of collaboration. We compared a group that did the original non-personalized quest with a group that did the personalized quest. This last group interacted with the multi-touch table to personalize the quest before they started on it. No significant differences were found between the experimental groups. We did find many differences between the children of age 10-11 and those of age 11-12, on almost all measurements. On this aspect we present some methodical results about measuring enjoyment and intrinsic motivation with children of 10-12 years old.

Categories and Subject Descriptors

H5.2. Information interfaces and presentation: User interfaces. K.3.m Computers and education: Miscellaneous.

Keywords

Personalization, multi-touch interaction, child-computer interaction, enjoyment, intrinsic motivation.

1. INTRODUCTION

The role of museums has been shifting from mainly conserving, collecting, research, exhibiting and educational institutions to institutions that are competitive and popular as well [12]. Nowadays museums have to compete more and more with other activities and cultural centers that focus both on education and entertainment [7]. One way for museums to deal with these challenges is to improve the museum-going experience for children by making children's visits more dynamic, engaging and enjoyable.

ICMI'12, October 22-26, 2012, Santa Monica, CA, USA.

To help achieve this, museums are increasingly being equipped with interactive technology. Museums have started to offer handheld devices that provide supplementary information on the spot and that additionally allow visitors to specify exhibits for which they would like to retrieve related information later. For instance Hsi [10] conducted a study in a museum with such an electronic guide. One of the main findings from this study was that the technology isolated the visitors from their surroundings because they wore headsets and that they tended to focus on the device, instead of on the rest of the museum. However, social interaction is an important part of learning [5]. Therefore museums have a growing interest in the use of novel technologies that support collaborative interaction between children [24]. Lately, the use of interactive multi-touch tables in museums receives considerable interest because they facilitate collaborative interactions: they provide space and give access to multiple co-located visitors [9]. In the study reported in [23] the use of technology by young children in the context of a museum visit added a social dimension to the museum visit because it supported and invoked interaction and collaboration. Klopfer et al. [11] introduced an interactive game that aimed to engage visitors more deeply and broadly in museum exhibits and that encouraged collaboration between visitors. Hall and Bannon [7] articulated design guidelines for novel technology to enhance children's educational experience in museums, including collaboration, engagement and active participation and interpretation.

This paper presents findings from a study in Museon[1], an educational museum with a permanent exhibition 'Your World, My World' about humans and their relation with nature, culture, society, science and technology. The study was part of the European project PuppyIR that had as a main objective to help children search the internet in a safe and child-friendly way and to develop new interaction paradigms that allow children to interact with information in an intuitive way.

In Museon children can choose to do an electronic quest. In this study, we wanted to find out whether personalization of the quest would have an effect on the children's enjoyment. Hence half of the participants of the study used a multi-touch table at the beginning of their museum visit, to personalize the quest. Three or four children simultaneously interacted with the multi-touch table where they chose topics of interest from the exhibition. The choice of the children was used to automatically generate the electronic quest for their visit. The other half of the children received a non-personalized quest, like the ones that are normally

[1] http://www.museon.nl

used in Museon. They were also grouped in groups of three or four but they started with the quest immediately. At the table and during the quest children were allowed to collaborate but they did not get instructions to do so. The main goal of the study was to find out whether personalization of the quest actually did enhance enjoyment but we were also interested in whether there was an effect on collaboration as well. Since touch tables are known to facilitate collaborative interactions [9], the interaction with the touch table might have influenced collaboration during the quest as well.

In the next section we will present related work on touch table interaction, interest and personalization. Section 3 will present the context in which the experiment took place. In section 4 we will describe the setup of the experiment and we will motivate the way we measured enjoyment and intrinsic motivation with results from a former pilot study. The results of the experiment will be presented in section 5, followed by a discussion and conclusions in section 6.

2. RELATED WORK

The educational benefits of touch table interaction for children have been investigated before. For instance Sluis et al. [21] used an augmented tabletop application that supported children in learning to read. Africano et al. [1] investigated a more general application that has been tested with exercises in reading, writing and mathematical skills.

Touch table interfaces were found to be suitable for multi-user simultaneous interaction [8], to promote group interaction and discussion [25] and to facilitate collaboration [19, 9, 2]. Moreover, tabletop interfaces were found to be engaging [25] and to allow for playful interaction and an enjoyable user experience [14] while keeping the technology in the background [6]. Enjoyment and fun have been found to support and deepen learning and to facilitate engagement and motivation [15].

In the museum context Zancanaro et al. [24] developed Story Table, a multi-touch table application for collaborative storytelling. It was designed as a tool that helps children reflect on their experience in the museum. Story Table gives children an active role in re-elaborating the material and creating new material collaboratively.

Correia et al. [4] designed and evaluated a multi-touch interactive tabletop application for a contemporary art exhibition with many visitors. One of their main findings was that most visitors engaged in further virtual exploration of the exhibition in order to obtain more information and provide feedback.

The importance of the concept of interest for learning was pointed out by Schiefele [x] who proposed to do future research on interest and motivation. In a follow-up study, Krapp [x] reviewed studies that showed that the concept of interest is positively related to, amongst others, allocation of attention, the use of learning strategies, and quality of experience.

According to Reeve [x], interest and enjoyment both contribute to intrinsic motivation in a different way. From his experiments he concluded that interest motivates individuals towards exploration and investigation while the motivational effects of enjoyment are the willingness to continue and persist in the activity.

Cordova and Lepper [x] examined the effects of personalization of an educational activity on the learning process of children. They personalized several features in the learning context in order to associate the learning activities with characters and objects of interest to the child. They showed that personalization increased, amongst others, children's motivation and depth of engagement in learning.

3. CONTEXT OF THE EXPERIMENT

The museum where we did the experiment (Museon in the Hague, the Netherlands) is an educational museum that is visited by children with their parents or grandparents and by school classes. Museon has the aim of educating people, in particular children, in such a way that they also enjoy themselves.

Museon has an electronic quest that children can choose to do during their visit. The quest makes use of many terminals, about 120, with touch input and a bar code scanner. These terminals are available all over the exhibition area. Figure 1 shows children answering a question at a terminal. The admission tickets have a bar code on the back that can be scanned at a terminal. The first time a ticket is used with one of the terminals the visitor is asked to register his or her name. Then a quest is generated with 12 questions about different topics in the exhibition area. When the admission ticket is scanned at any one of the terminals, the next question appears. If the visitor has to move to another area in the exhibition to find the answer, he or she can use an available terminal in that area and the question will re-appear. Once the question is answered the visitor gets immediate feedback whether or not the answer is correct and why this is the case. The question re-appears until the correct answer is given or after a fixed number of attempts, in which case the correct answer is given and a new question is displayed. To avoid that the children just find the right answer by trial and error, every wrong answer is counted and decreases the overall performance value that is presented on the screen.

Figure 1. Children answer a question at a terminal.

In the experiment we used this existing infrastructure and enhanced it with a multi-touch table that was placed in the museum's entrance area (see Figure 2). The table can identify fiducial markers. Physical objects with a marker can be placed on top of the table and be identified by the system through a unique identifier.

These fiducial markers were used in the experiment with the museum's admission tickets. Each participant received a ticket with a fiducial marker at one side and a bar code at the other side. Hence the ticket could be used as an identifier at the table and at the terminals in the exhibition area.

Up to four users could use the table simultaneously. They registered themselves by placing the admission ticket at the table. Once four users registered themselves (or if fewer users were available after a certain period of time) the initial game started with a small introduction.

Figure 2. Multi-touch table in the entrance hall of Museon.

The purpose of the game was to let the players choose 12 topics that are part of exhibits in the permanent exhibition. The topics were represented by pictures and a title and were placed in a slowly rotating circle. When touched and/or dragged they grew in size and showed some more text to inform the user about the represented topic. To be accessible from each side of the table the pictures automatically changed their orientation by rotating towards the user's position. Figure 3 presents a snapshot of participants in the experiment playing the initial game.

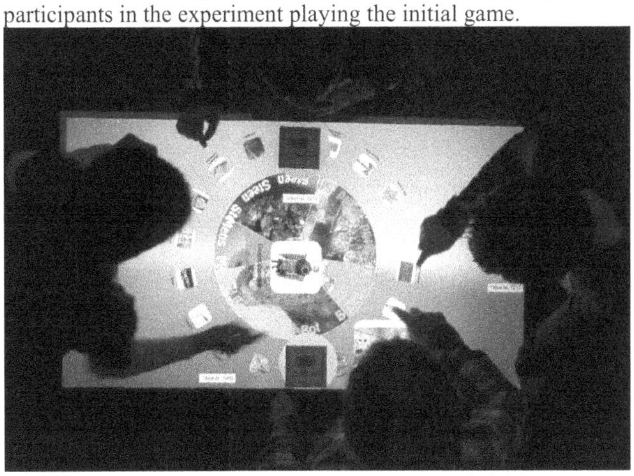

Figure 3. Snapshot of children playing the initial game.

The children could move the pictures around the table and pass them on to each other. When a picture was not touched for a while it disappeared back into the circle but could be dragged outside again at any time.

If a child was interested in a certain exhibit or topic the picture could be dropped into the middle of the circle. Up to 12 different pictures could be selected and thereby the topics that were used to create the electronic quest were selected. The group did not have to choose only topics everybody was interested in. Instead, the initial game at the table offered the possibility to either individually or collaboratively explore the topics that were available in the museum exhibition. When 12 pictures had been chosen, the topics were automatically stored in a central database and for each child a personal quest with 12 questions about the 12 chosen topics was generated. After that the children took their admission tickets and went to the exhibition room where they used the bar code side of the ticket to access the questions of their quest at the terminals

After all the children of a group had answered all 12 questions of the quest in the exhibition area they went to the multi-touch table as a group, to play the final game. They had to register themselves using their tickets after which the final game started immediately. The final game at the table had an interface that resembled the interface of the initial game. The slowly rotating circle with pictures of topics appeared again in the middle but this time the pictures displayed were related to the topics from the questions the children answered. Analogous to the initial game children could drag pictures out of the circle to view further information (now more extended) or show them to each other at the table. Instead of choosing topics and dragging them into a common circle in the middle, now the pictures could be dropped into a private circle that appeared in one of the corners of the table. See Figure 4 for a snapshot of participants in the experiment playing the final game.

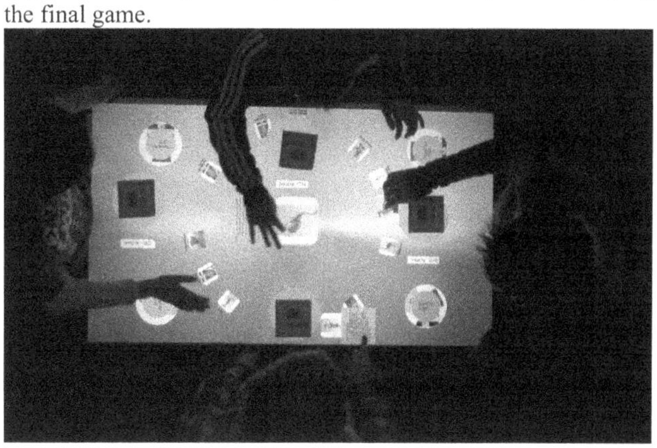

Figure 4. Snapshot of children playing the final game.

The main idea behind the final game was to give the children the opportunity to create their own, personalized virtual museum catalogue. It is common practice that museums offer catalogues with information and photos of exhibits. The final game aimed to offer children an intuitive way of creating such a catalogue by collecting topics and exhibits they liked during their tour. With the unique identification on the admission ticket it will be possible for the children to access the information after the visit from outside the museum, for instance at home or at school, allowing an extended search for related data.

4. SETUP OF THE EXPERIMENT

An experiment was conducted in Museon as to find an answer to the question whether personalization of the interactive quest enhanced the fun experience of doing the quest. The quest was personalized by the participants by playing a game at a multi-touch table. In addition, we evaluated whether the combination of the interaction at the table and the personalization of the quest supported and invoked collaboration between the participants of the experiment.

4.1 Experimental conditions

The experimental setup consisted of two conditions, a condition with a personalized quest and a control condition with a non-personalized quest. In the condition with the personalized quest the children started the museum visit at the multi-touch table, where they selected topics they were interested in by choosing images that represented these topics. The chosen topics were parts of the exhibition and were used to determine a route through the exhibition room of the museum. Based on the results of the initial game, the children received a personalized quest of twelve questions to be answered at twelve different exhibits. In the control condition, the children did a non-personalized electronic quest, similar to the quest children can normally choose to do when they visit Museon. Hence in this condition the children started the museum visit with the quest and they did not play the initial game at the table.

4.2 Participants

The experiment took place at Museon in the Hague in the Netherlands. Two classes from a Dutch primary school in the Hague (Nutsschool M.M. Boldingh), a school located close to Museon, participated in the study. In total there were 48 children who participated, 21 children aged 11-12 years old that were in their final year of primary education and 27 children of 10-11 years old from the pre-final year.

4.3 Procedure

The teachers formed groups of four children (sometimes three if necessary) before the museum visit. The children of the pre-final year were divided into seven groups and the children of the final year were divided into six groups. In total seven groups (four from the pre-final year and three from final year, in total 26 children) were assigned to the condition with the personalized quest and six groups (three groups from both the pre-final and the final year, in total 22 children) were assigned to the control condition with the non-personalized quest.

The groups were given an explanation about the procedure of the experiment. They were also told that they could ask for help if something was not clear. Then the groups started with either the initial game or the quest, depending on the condition they were assigned to. After all members of a group had finished the quest, they went to the multi-touch table to play the final game. All teams played the final game, also the teams that did not start at the table. While playing the final game the children could get further information about the exhibits they had visited and they could choose topics/exhibits they were most interested in. Their choices were used later at school, using a web application also developed for the PuppyIR project. This paper does not include the evaluation of that web application.

After the final game the children handed in their tickets and they filled in a paper questionnaire that they gave to their teacher afterwards.

4.4 Measures

A questionnaire was used to measure the constructs enjoyment and collaboration. Subscales for the constructs were inserted in the questionnaire. The complete questionnaire can be found in the user evaluation toolkit on the PuppyIR site[2]. the questionnaire.

[2] http://www.puppyir.eu/results/user-evaluation-toolkit

4.4.1 Enjoyment and intrinsic motivation

We measured enjoyment in three different ways that each focus on a different aspect of enjoyment. The first measure used is the Smileyometer taken from the Fun Toolkit for children by Read and MacFarlane [16].

The Smileyometer was especially designed for children. It is based on a 5-point Likert scale and uses five smileys. See Figure 5 for an example. For each of the three parts of the museum visit (initial game, quest, final game) the children used the Smileyometer to answer the question "How much fun was it to do that part?"

Figure 5. The Smileyometer.

The answers on the Smileyometer were re-coded from 1 (for awful) to 5 (for brilliant). According to Read and MacFarlane [17], the Smileyometer is not very useful for young children. They did a study in which almost half of the children aged between 7 and 9 used the highest score and they found a significant difference in the mean score of these young children and the mean score of an older age group (ages 12 and 13).

The results of our first pilot study in Museon, in which 36 children took part, confirmed this difference between age groups [22]. The data indicated that younger children had a higher tendency to select the highest ratings, but did select non-extreme scores as well. Hence we argued that the Smileyometer is probably a useful tool for children of 10-12 years old and decided to use it in this study again.

The second enjoyment related measure we used is the Again-Again table (see Figure 6), also from the Fun Toolkit [16]. The Again-Again table measures engagement. The children were asked whether they would like to do the activities (initial game, quest, final game) again. This measure is based on the knowledge that people like to do fun things again.

Read and MacFarlane [17] did another study where they investigated the relation between results obtained using the Smileyometer and results obtained using the Again – Again table. They found very strong correlations and concluded that both tools measure the same construct.

Would you like to do it Again?

	Yes	Maybe	No
Museon quest	✓		

Figure 6. The Again–Again table.

In our first pilot study in Museon we used both the Smileyometer and the Again-Again table. Hence we could easily investigate the relation between the results as well by carrying out non-parametric correlations. We also found strong correlations between the results of the Smileyometer and the Again-Again table, for all measurements. The results are presented in Table 1.

Table 1. Correlations between the scores on the Smileyometer and the Again-Again table in the first pilot study

Activities	N	Spearman's rho	Significance
Initial game	36	0.447	$p < 0.01$
Quest	35	0.620	$p < 0.0005$
Final game	35	0.562	$p < 0.0005$

These results seem to support the conclusion of Read and MacFarlane [17]. However, when we looked at age differences again we found that these correlations varied for different age groups. For the older children (above 10 years old) the correlations were weaker and for two of the three activities not even significant. These older children rated the Smileyometer questions (if they liked it) very high but still sometimes answered 'maybe' or 'no' on the questions if they wanted to do it again. Hence we decided to use both measures again because the difference in emphasis of the evaluation (judging the software versus giving your own opinion on what you would like to do again) might have influence in some cases.

The third measure we used to measure enjoyment in the experiment was the Children IMI interest/enjoyment scale. This scale was derived from the Intrinsic Motivation Inventory (IMI), a multidimensional measurement device which can be modified to fit specific activities (University of Rochester, retrieved 2012[3]). The interest/enjoyment subscale we used is considered to be the self-report measure of intrinsic motivation and was developed for use by adults. Although this scale basically also measures fun, like the tools of the Fun Toolkit, this scale measures interest as well. If we manage to get a reliable scale for children here, the constructs enjoyment and interest are coupled to get a measure of intrinsic motivation, a very important factor for learning.

The IMI consists of seven statements:

- I enjoyed doing this activity very much.
- This activity was fun to do.
- I thought this was a boring activity.(R)
- This activity did not hold my attention at all.(R)
- I would describe this activity as very interesting.
- I thought this activity was quite enjoyable.
- While I was doing this activity, I was thinking about how much I enjoyed it.

All these statements are rated on a 7-point Likert scale where 1 represents 'not at all true', 4 represents 'somewhat true' and 7 represents 'very true'.

We adapted the IMI interest/enjoyment scale to make it more suitable for children. We reversed the two negatively formulated statements. Hence the third and fourth statements were changed into:

- I thought this was an exciting activity
- This activity held my attention very well

In addition, we used a 5-point scale with 'Totally disagree' at the negative end and 'Totally agree' at the positive end and we used the smileys from the Smileyometer. See Figure 7.

Figure 7. Answer categories of the Children IMI interest/enjoyment scale.

The new Children IMI interest/enjoyment scale was used to measure enjoyment during the quest. It is part of the User Evaluation Toolkit on the PuppyIR site[4]

4.4.2 Collaboration

To measure perceived collaboration, we added three items to the questionnaire:

- I tried very hard to support others in doing the quest
- I collaborated with my classmates a lot
- I liked supporting others during the quest

We also observed the children while they did the quest but it was very difficult to keep track of the many things that happened because many groups did the quest almost simultaneously. Hence no systematic observation results could be obtained.

5. RESULTS

5.1 Enjoyment and intrinsic motivation

Table 2 presents the results of Enjoyment for the three main parts (initial game, quest, final game), as measured with the Smileyometer on a 5-point Likert scale.

Using the Mann-Whitney test no significant differences were found between the two experimental groups on enjoyment of the quest and the final game.

We found significant differences between the pre-final and the final year of primary education. Table 3 shows the descriptive statistics per age group. Even though the difference in age is only one year, for the quest the scores measured with the Smileyometer were significantly higher for children from the pre-final year of primary education than for children from the final year (Mann-Whitney U=121.0, p (two-tailed) < 0.0005).

[3] http://www.selfdeterminationtheory.org/questionnaires/10-questionnaires/50

[4] See http://www.puppyir.eu/results/user-evaluation-toolkit

Table 2. Enjoyment measured with the Smileyometer for the three main parts

Activities	N	Personalized quest	Non-personalized quest
Enjoyment initial game	26	Mean=3.77, SD=0.77	-
Enjoyment quest	48	Mean=3.50, SD=0.95	Mean=3.00, SD=1.27
Enjoyment final game	48	Mean=3.54, SD=0.86	Mean=3.95, SD=1.09

For the initial game the differences between the scores of the pre-final and the final year were marginally significant (Mann-Whitney U=47.0, *p* (two-tailed)= 0.061). No significant difference was found for the final part.

Table 3. Difference in enjoyment between age groups as measured with the Smileyometer.

Activities	Age group	N	Mean	SD	Signific.
Enjoyment initial game	Pre-final	16	4.00	0.82	p=0.061
	Final year	10	3.40	0.52	
Enjoyment quest	Pre-final	27	3.78	1.05	p<0.0005
	Final year	21	2.62	0.87	
Enjoyment final game	Pre-final	27	3.74	0.90	p=0.948
	Final year	21	3.71	1.10	

The results for enjoyment as measured by the Again-Again table are shown in Table 4. Chi-square tests showed that there was no significant difference between the two conditions for the quest part of the visit. For the final game there was a significant difference: children who already used the multi-touch table at the start of the visit were more positive to use the table again than children who used the table for the first time in the final game (chi-square=6.06, df=2, p=0.048).

Table 4. Enjoyment measured with the Again-Again table for the three main parts.

Activities	Answer	Table at start	No Table at start	Total
Again-Again table initial game	No	0	-	
	Maybe	10	-	
	Yes	16	-	
Again-Again table quest	No	5	6	11
	Maybe	9	7	16
	Yes	12	8	20
Again-Again table final game	No	2	5	7
	Maybe	7	10	17
	Yes	16	6	22

We investigated the relation between the results on the Smileyometer and the Again-Again table by carrying out non-parametric correlations. We again found strong correlations between the results of the Smileyometer and the Again-Again table, for all measurements. The results are presented in Table 5.

Table 5. Correlations between the scores on the Smileyometer and the Again-Again table.

Activities	N	Spearman's rho	Significance
Initial game	26	0.613	$p < 0.001$
Quest	47	0.703	$p < 0.0005$
Final game	46	0.456	$p < 0.001$

When we looked at age differences again we found that these correlations varied for different age groups. For the children of the pre-final year the correlations for all activities were strong (for the initial game p=0.004, for the quest p<0.0005 and for the final game p<0.0005). For the children of the final year only the results for the quest were correlated but the correlation was much weaker (p=0.025). For the initial game and the final game no significant correlations were found between the results on the Smileyometer and the results on the Again-Again table.

Enjoyment/Intrinsic motivation was measured by the Children IMI interest/enjoyment scale. This adapted scale appeared to be very reliable for the children who participated in our study (Cronbach alpha= 0.923). Hence we used the mean score on this enjoyment/motivation scale in our analyses.

The mean score on this Enjoyment scale was 3.54 (SD=1.01) on a 5-point scale which is quite high but not extremely high and variability seems to be high enough, indicating that the scale is useful for children of 10-12 years old. We used the Mann-Whitney test to check whether there was a significant difference between the scores of the two experimental conditions on this enjoyment/motivation scale. No significant difference was found for enjoyment/motivation doing the quest. We did find significant differences between the results of the class in the pre-final year of primary education (10-11 years old) and the class in the final year (11-12 years old). The mean enjoyment/motivation score of younger age group was 3.96 (SD=0.88) and the mean score of older age group was 3.003 (SD=0.94). This mean score was significantly higher for the younger children as compared to the older children (Mann-Whitney U=123.5, p=0.001).

5.2 Collaboration

We tested the three items of the questionnaire that measured perceived collaboration on reliability. The Cronbach's alpha for the three questions was 0.649 which was not really high enough (we used a threshold of 0.7). By deleting the question "I collaborated with my classmates a lot" we got a 2 item scale with a Cronbach's alpha of 0.763. Hence we analyzed this scale about supporting others and the question about perceived collaboration separately.

The mean score on the supporting others scale was 3.73 (SD=0.87) for the children in the condition with the personalized quest and 3.52 (SD=1.13) for the children in the control condition. According to the Mann-Whitney test there was no significant difference between the two experimental groups. For perceived collaboration the mean scores of the experimental groups were

3.77 (SD=0.95) for the personalized condition and 3.55 (SD=1.10) for the control condition. Again the Mann-Whitney test showed the difference in means was not significant. Using the Mann-Whitney test we did not find any significant differences between the children of the two age groups on perceived collaboration and on the supporting others scale.

6. DISCUSSION AND CONCLUSIONS

We presented the results of a study in an educational museum. Children of 10-12 years old followed a tour with an electronic quest through the permanent exhibition of the museum. The children were assigned to two experimental conditions. One condition reflected the normal situation in the museum: children did a non-personalized quest that was generated with randomly chosen topics from the exhibition. The other group used a multi-touch table at the start to personalize the quest.

No significant differences were found between the two experimental conditions on enjoyment as measured by the Smileyometer and the Children IMI interest/enjoyment scale. Moreover we did not find any significant differences between the experimental conditions on collaboration. We did find one significant difference between the conditions: on the Again-Again table measure there was a significant difference for the final game. Children who already used the multi-touch table at the start of the visit were more positive to use the table again than children who only used the table for the final game. The only explanation we can think of is that the children did not fully understand the purpose of the final game. Either this was more the case for the children that did not have experience with the multi-touch table yet or this was equally true for the children that played the initial game but this last group still remembered the positive experience of playing the initial game and that was reflected in their opinion. However, the results of the other enjoyment measure on the final game were similar for the two experimental conditions hence no conclusive explanation can be given.

Getting back to our main research question: we did not find evidence that personalization of the quest by addition of an initial game at the multi-touch table enriched the children's fun experience during the quest. The results on the enjoyment scales were quite high for all children but not so high that we think a ceiling effect will have caused the lack of evidence for positive effects of personalization. In addition, we did not find any evidence that the combination of the two differences between the conditions - the extra interaction with the multi-touch table and the resulting personalization of the quest - enhanced collaboration between the participants of the experiment. Of course as an extra attraction, interaction with the multi-touch table will have a value of its own.

Although this was originally not the focus of our study, we found significant differences between age groups: children from the pre-final year of primary education scored higher than children from final year on enjoyment of the quest and initial game as measured by the Smileyometer. In addition the overall mean score on the Children IMI interest/enjoyment scale was significantly higher for children from the pre-final year than for children from the final year.

We found strong correlations between the results of the Smileyometer and the Again-Again table, for all measurements. When we looked at age differences we found that these correlations varied for different age groups. For younger children the correlations for all measurements were strong, for older children (above 10 years of age) the correlations were much weaker or absent. From this we conclude that the Again-Again table is valuable to use alongside the Smileyometer, especially for children above 10 years old. When judging the software the older children seem to over-score to be polite, while when giving their opinion on what they would like to do again they express their doubts.

Probably the most important result of this evaluation is the fact that we adapted the IMI scale for adults to get a reliable scale to measure intrinsic motivation of children of 10-12 years old. It would be interesting to validate this Children IMI interest/enjoyment scale in a larger experiment and with different age groups.

7. ACKNOWLEDGMENTS

The research leading to these results has received funding from the European Community's Seventh Framework Programme FP7/2007-2013 under grant agreement n° 231507.

8. REFERENCES

[1] Africano, D., Berg, S., Lindbergh, K., Lundholm, P., Nilbrink, F., and Persson, A. 2004. Designing tangible interfaces for children's collaboration. In *CHI '04 Extended Abstracts on Human Factors in Computing Systems.* ACM, New York, NY, 853-868.

[2] Buisine,S., Besacier, G., Aoussat,A. and Vernier,F. 2012. How do interactive tabletop systems influence collaboration? In *Computers in Human Behavior.* 28, 1, 49-59.

[3] Cordova, D.L. and Lepper M.R. 1996. Intrinsic motivation and the process of learning: Beneficial effects of contextualization, personalization, and choice. In *Journal of Educational Psychology*, 88, 4, 715-730.

[4] Correia, N. Mota, T, Nóbrega, R., Silva, L. and Almeida, A. 2010. A multi-touch tabletop for robust multimedia interaction in museums. In *ACM International Conference on Interactive Tabletops and Surfaces.* ITS '10. ACM, New York, NY, 117-120.

[5] Gage, N.L. and Berliner, D. 1998. *Educational Psychology.* 6th edition,. Wadsworth Publishing.

[6] Geller, T. 2006. Interactive Tabletop Exhibits in Museums and Galleries. *IEEE Computer Graphics and Applications.* 26, 5, 6-11.

[7] Hall, T. and Bannon, L. 2005. Designing ubiquitous computing to enhance children's interaction in museums. In *Proceedings of the 2005 conference on Interaction Design and Children* (Boulder, Colorado). IDC'05. ACM, New York, NY, 62–69.

[8] Hinrichs, U., Hancock, M., Carpendale, S., and Collins, C. 2007. Examination of Text-Entry Methods for Tabletop Displays. In *2nd IEEE International Workshop on Horizontal Interactive Human-Computer Systems.* TABLETOP '07. 105-112.

[9] Hornecker, E. 2008, "I don't understand it either, but it is cool" - Visitor interactions with a multi-touch table in a museum. In *3rd IEEE International Workshop on Horizontal Human-Computer Systems.* TABLETOP '08. 113-120.

[10] Hsi, S. 2003. A study of user experiences mediated by nomadic web content in a museum. In *Journal of Computer Assisted Learning.* 19, 3, 308-319.

[11] Klopfer, E., Perry, J., Squire, K., Jan, M.F. and Steinkuehler, C. 2005. Mystery at the museum: a collaborative game for museum education. In *Proceedings of the 2005 conference on Computer-Supported Collaborative Learning : learning 2005: the next 10 years!* CSCL '05. 316-320.

[12] Kotler, N. and Kotler, P. 2000. Can museums be all things to all people?: Missions, goals, and marketing's role. *Museum Management and Curatorship.* 18, 3, 271–287.

[13] Krapp, A. 1999. Interest, motivation and learning: An educational-psychological perspective. In *European Journal of Psychology of Education*, XIV, 1, 23-40.

[14] Mahmud, A., Mubin, O., Renny Octavia, J., Shahid, S., Yeo, L., Markopoulos, P., Martens, J.-B, and Aliakseyeu, D. 2007. Affective Tabletop Game: A New Gaming Experience for Children. In 2nd *IEEE International Workshop on Horizontal Interactive Human-Computer Systems.* TABLETOP'07. 44-51.

[15] Price S., Rogers, Y., Scaife, M., Stanton, D. and Neale, H. 2003. Using 'tangibles' to promote novel forms of playful learning. In *Interacting with Computers*, 15, 2, 169-185.

[16] Read, J.C. and MacFarlane, S. 2002. Endurability, engagement and expectations: Measuring children's fun. In *Proceedings of the 2002 Conference on Interaction Design and Children.* IDC'02. ACM, New York, NY, 1–23.

[17] Read, J.C. and MacFarlane, S. 2006. Using the Fun Toolkit and other survey methods to gather opinions in Child Computer Interaction. In *Proceedings of the 5th International Conference on Interaction Design and Children.* IDC'06. ACM, New York, NY, 81-88.

[18] Reeve, J. 1989. The interest-enjoyment distinction in intrinsic motivation. In *Motivation and Emotion*, 13, 2, 83-103.

[19] Rogers, Y. and Lindley, S. 2004. Collaborating around vertical and horizontal large interactive displays: which way is best? In *Interacting with Computers*, 16, 6, 1133-1152.

[20] Schiefele, U. 1991. Interest, learning, and motivation. In *Educational Psychologist*, 26, 3 and 4, 299-323.

[21] Sluis, R., Weevers, I., and Van Schijndel, C. 2004. Read-It: five-to-seven-year-old children learn to read in a tabletop environment. In *Proceedings of the 2004 Conference on Interaction Design and Children.* IDC'04. ACM, New York NY, 73-80.

[22] Van der Sluis, F., Van Dijk, E.M.A.G. and Perloy, B. 2012. Measuring fun and enjoyment of children in a museum: Evaluating the Smileyometer. In *Measuring Engagement: Affective and Social Cues in Interactive Art and Media.* Special session at Measuring Behavior 2012. Accepted, to appear.

[23] Yiannoutsou, N. , Papadimitriou, I., Komis, V. and Avouris, N. 2009. Playing with Museum Exhibits: Designing Educational Games Mediated by Mobile Technology. In *Proceedings of the 8th International Conference on Interaction Design and Children.* IDC '09. ACM, New York, NY, 6–9.

[24] Zancanaro, M., Pianesi, F., Stock, O., Venuti, P., Cappelletti, A., Iandolo, G., Prete, M., & Rossi, F. (2007). Children in the museum: an environment for collaborative storytelling. *PEACH-Intelligent Interfaces for Museum Visits.* 165-184.

[25] Zuckerman, O., Arida, S., and Resnick, M. 2005. Extending tangible interfaces for education: digital montessori-inspired manipulatives. In *Proceedings of the SIGCHI conference on Human Factors in computing systems.* CHI'05. ACM, New York, NY, 859-868.

Bifocal Modeling: A Study on the Learning Outcomes of Comparing Physical and Computational Models Linked in Real Time

Paulo Blikstein
Stanford University
520 Galvez Mall
CERAS 232
+1 (847) 571 4538
paulob@stanford.edu

ABSTRACT

Computer modeling has been successfully used in a large number of distinct scientific fields, transforming scientists' practice. Educational researchers have come to realize its potential for learning. Studies have suggested that students are able to understand concepts above their expected grade level after interacting with curricula that employ multi-agent simulation. However, most simulations are 'on-screen', without connection to the physical world. Therefore, real-time model validation is challenging with extant modeling platforms. I have designed a technological platform to enable students to connect computer models and sensors in real time, to validate and refine their models using real-world data. In this paper, I will focus on both technical and pedagogical aspects, describing pilot studies that suggest a real-to-virtual reciprocity catalyzing further inquiry toward deeper understanding of scientific phenomena.

Categories and Subject Descriptors

K.3.1 [Computers and Education]: Computers Uses in Education

General Terms

Design, Experimentation.

Keywords

Computer modeling, sensing, constructivism, physical computing, bifocal modeling.

1. INTRODUCTION

Fifteen years ago, few would have predicted that children would be doing advanced robotics in middle-school. Indeed, since the seminal work by Papert, Martin, and Resnick [16, 19], the creation of the Lego Mindstorms platform, and the appearance of robotics competitions across the country, robotics has become a common activity in public and private schools. However, one crucial component of the revolution predicted by its proponents is still far away – its integration with the normal school curriculum. Robotics activities are often too focused on competitions and prescribed, standardized "challenges," and ended up being segregated to after school programs. In most schools, robotics teachers conduct activities regardless of what happens in science or math classrooms.

At the same time, science classrooms and laboratories are not well suited to support students for authentic scientific inquiry, developing and investigating their own scientific hypotheses and projects. For example, a student examining an acid-base reaction in a laboratory might identify the chemical elements involved and even hypothesize as to their proportions and concentrations, but the investigation cannot dive deep into chemical mechanisms. Later, in the classroom, he will learn about chemical equations and theories which bear little resemblance, in terms of scale and mechanism, to the phenomenon observed in the laboratory. Bifocal Modeling [1, 2, 5, 6] is a framework to link these disconnected types of activities and environments (computational manipulatives/sensors, science laboratories, and theoretical content in science), providing continuity between observation, physical construction of artifacts, and model-building. As this modeling platform enables seamless integration of the theoretical/computational models and the physical world, allowing modelers to focus simultaneously on their 'on-' and 'off-screen' models, I termed it *bifocal modeling*.

When building a bifocal model, students have three main tasks. First, they build a computer model of the phenomenon using various computer modeling platforms (in particular, I use NetLogo [22] in my studies). This model should encapsulate students' hypotheses about a given scientific phenomenon. Second, students use electronic sensors and low-cost analog-to-digital interfaces, such as the GoGo Board [21], to build their own sensor-equipped "science lab" to collect data about the phenomenon. Finally, students run both systems connected in real time to validate, refine, and debug their hypotheses using real-world data. The computer screen becomes a display for the computer model, which is a proceduralization, through programming, of equations, text, or other representations of scientific content, and the actual phenomenon, which is discretized and measured by means of sensors and other laboratory apparatus (see Figures 1-3, for models of an acid-base reaction, Gas Laws, and heat transfer). Because the computer models are carefully constructed to imitate the phenomenon's visual language, the bifocal methodology minimizes interpretive challenges. That is, the seen and the hypothesized are displayed such that their perceptual differences are backgrounded and, therefore, their procedural differences are more likely to be revealed. By thus utilizing the power of computation and representation, bifocal modeling constitutes a multi-disciplinary research tool that offloads aspects of both the interpretive and menial burden of scientific practice, freeing cognitive, discursive, and material resources that can thus be allocated toward validation of the hypotheses.

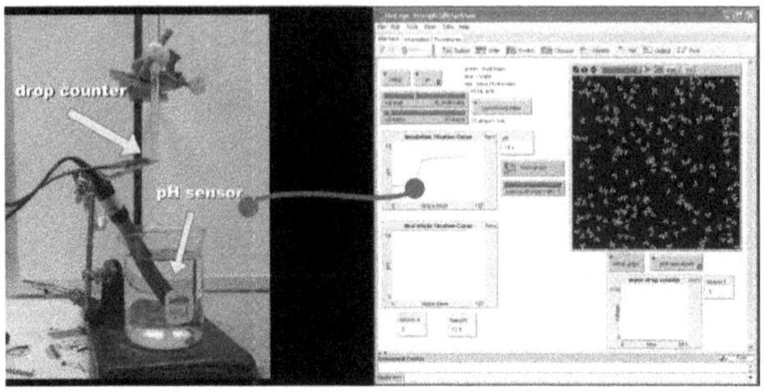

Figure 1. A model of an acid-base reaction, with the physical apparatus (left) and the computer model (right), which compares the pH 'measured' in the two models and exhibits the values in real-time for easy comparison.

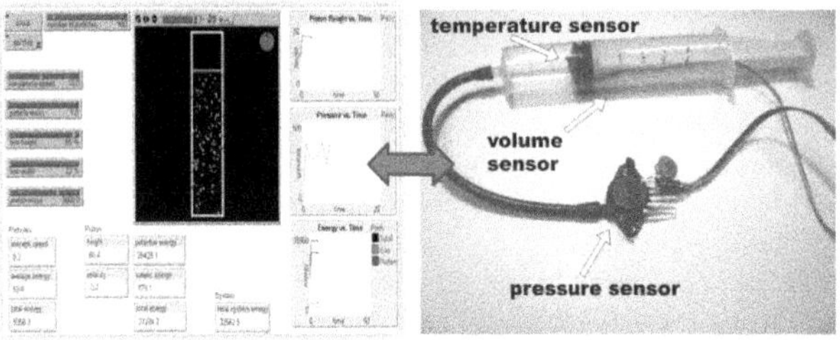

Figure 2. A model of a gas laws model, with the physical sensor-enabled syringe (right) and the computer model (left). When students press the physical syringe, the virtual syringe moves accordingly, and the students can compare the pressure measured in both.

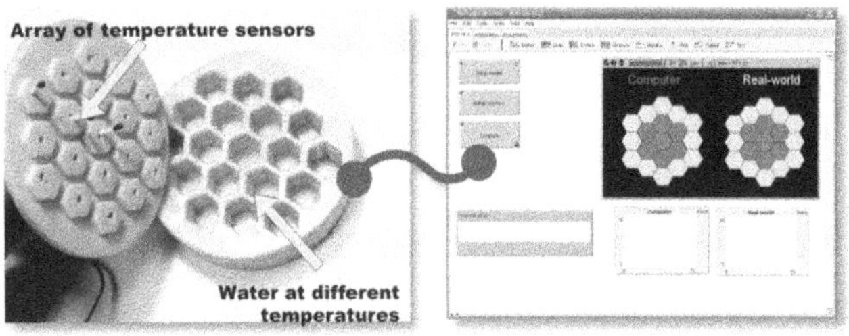

Figure 3. A model of heat transfer, with the physical model with multiple temperature sensors and hexagonal water receptacles (left), and the computer interface showing a side-by-side real-time visualization of the physical and the computer data (right).

Investigating novel ways to use computational representations and tools is timely because the use of computational models of scientific phenomena has become an increasingly viable option for classroom science learning as technology and accessibility improve. There is a large body of literature on the use of virtual models to display data, simulate complex phenomena, and permit student experimentation in domains that might be costly, impractical, or dangerous [9, 11, 12, 17, 18]. The potential of a combination of virtual and physical models to aid science learning has been documented for a wide range of ages and domains. For instance, Liu and collaborators [14] explored high school students' understanding of chemistry concepts. They found that the combination of a virtual model and hands-on lab activity was more effective than either alone, balanced for time-on-task, in promoting students' conceptual understanding of the gas laws. Recent studies have also investigated the importance of the sequencing of physical and virtual model activities on student learning, with the general result that better learning resulted from the virtual experiment following a physical one [10, 20].

However, there are two under researched areas. First, the literature has focused almost entirely on pre-designed physical and computer models. Pre-designed models can scaffold and direct students to attend to relevant problem information, but they fail to give students opportunities to evaluate the assumptions and limitations of the models themselves [16]. Creating and critically evaluating models is an important part of scientific practice, and is being increasingly recognized as a valued educational goal [3, 4, 10]. Second, the literature has also under-explored the potential for deeper support of student comparison between the physical and virtual models. Smith and collaborators [20] noted that scaffolds in the virtual model, or direct data-sharing between virtual and physical, could help students to see the similarities and differences between model and reality. However, there has been no work studying physical and computer models connected in real-time.

In this paper, I present pilot studies that demonstrate a pedagogical framework to augment the comparison between real and ideal systems as an avenue to deeper understanding of scientific phenomena. In the first study, high school students built virtual and physical models of bacterial growth in order to learn content knowledge, computational thinking, and critical meta-modeling skills. Our main research questions were: (1) how do students' understand the mismatch between idealized virtual and physical models?, and (2) how do they decide which variables and phenomenal factors are necessary to include in their own theoretical models to match the real-world data? In the second set of studies, I examined different models of implementation of bifocal modeling in classrooms, from more open-ended themes to more constricted tasks. I investigated many different formats of implementation in which I varied the topic (Biology or Physics) and the amount of model construction (students building their own models versus students being presented with ready-made models).

2. RESEARCH SETTING

In Bifocal Modeling (BM) activities, the most common software to implement virtual experiments has been NetLogo [22], a free and open-source environment for agent-based modeling. A NetLogo model typically consists of a set of autonomous agents (such as gas particles or people at a party) moving through a world and interacting to produce emergent outcomes. Students define the variables held by the agents and the world and specify a set of rules for agent-level behavior, such as "if two gas particles collide, they exchange energy and bounce off each other." Their goal is to build a model whose behavior matches the data they collected. This challenge encourages students to refine their content knowledge as they iteratively improve their virtual models, and to question the validity of their own representational choices. A student, for instance, trying to match a computer model of Newtonian motion and a real experiment may be forced to confront the existence of a missing friction coefficient, to determine how to measure motion using a given set of sensors, or even whether to model an object as a single unit or as a collection of atomic particles. In this way, BM can serve as a method to learn scientific content, modeling skills, and scientific research methods.

As a BM activity comprises many different tools, techniques, and classroom facilitation, there are multiple possible formats and phases for its implementation. These are the four major components of a BM activity, which could be present or ordered in different ways:

A. Research - In each study, students were encouraged to use external learning resources, such as the web or books, to gather initial information about the phenomenon. The format of this phase was dependent on the context of the study and students' previous knowledge about the phenomenon. The general goal of this phase was to give students baseline information about the normative representations of the phenomenon under scrutiny.

B. Design - Within a guiding theme (e.g., gas laws), students select variables that they want to explore, make hypotheses about what they will observe, and design physical and virtual models that can potentially answer those hypotheses. In designing the virtual model, students typically define the possible variables, and conceptualize micro-rules or equations to describe the phenomenon.

C. Build (program or develop)- Students construct physical models (e.g. a ball and ramp, a Petri dish filled with agar and bacteria, a system with interconnected beakers with different substances) and virtual models (e.g. a physics model of gravity and friction, an agent-based model of bacteria growth, or a computer model of diffusion) that will capture the phenomena under study.

D. Interact - Students interact with their physical models by direct observation and collecting data using embedded sensors. Similarly, they interact with the virtual model by changing parameters, running the model, observing the results, and recording data.

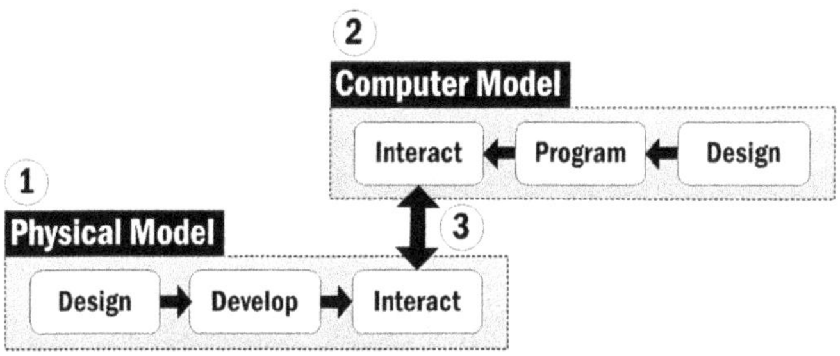

Figure 4. Components of a Bifocal Model and activity: (1) The physical model, (2) the computer model, (3) the comparison phase.

3. METHODS

In this paper I will present four BM studies conducted in our lab. I will describe the first study (Biology) in detail, and discuss in much more brief terms three other implementations of Bifocal Modeling activities (Physics, Chemistry, Open-ended). We generally employed a design-based research framework in which implementation and redesign are closely coupled [7, 8]. The four modes of BM implementation are visually summarized in Figure 5. The rectangles in black indicate the design elements used. (Note that the "Research" element was not included in the figure, but all of the activities began with students engaging in research.)

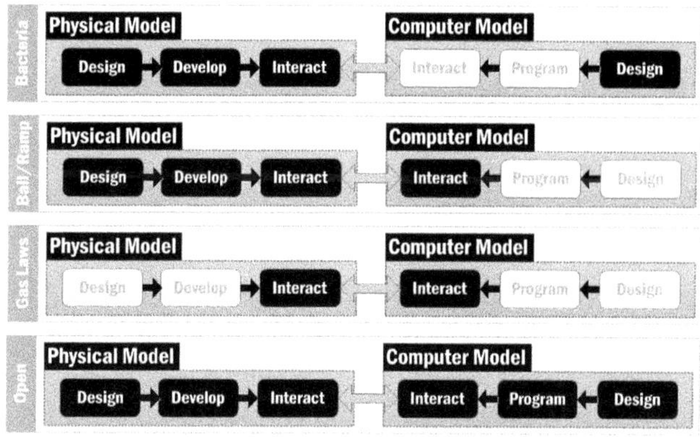

Figure 5. A visual summary of the different Bifocal Modeling activities, showing the blocks I used in the four studies (in black).

3.1 First Study: Biology

The first study was conducted with four female high school students. The topic of the workshop was bacterial growth. The study lasted for a total of about five hours, split across three afternoon sessions. Students' first task was to grow real bacteria using supplied tools. They were also shown a short video about bacteria growth in a petri dish. Then, the students in groups of two did internet research on the bacterial growth curve. For the final assignment, the authors conducted a variation of "paper modeling" [3, 4] session in which students collectively designed an agent-based model of bacterial growth on a whiteboard (Figure 6 and 7). In the paper modeling activity, students in small groups create a detailed block diagram of all aspects of a computer model and simulate a few runs (without a computer). For example, students define all the needed variables for the model, all the agents and their properties/rules, all possible interactions between agents, etc. The facilitator helps students translate their ideas into the proper "code blocks," but once students understand the general idea, the role of the facilitator transitions to becoming more of a documenter of students' ideas. Paper modeling offers some advantages over full-fledged modeling. Namely, students only need a short introduction to the programming language, and the time is spent almost entirely on conceptual programming rather than on the minutiae of writing code. Evidently it is not equivalent to programming, but in previous work [4] I have shown that it is possible to map ideas and concepts from paper modeling to what students would accomplish when doing full-fledge coding.

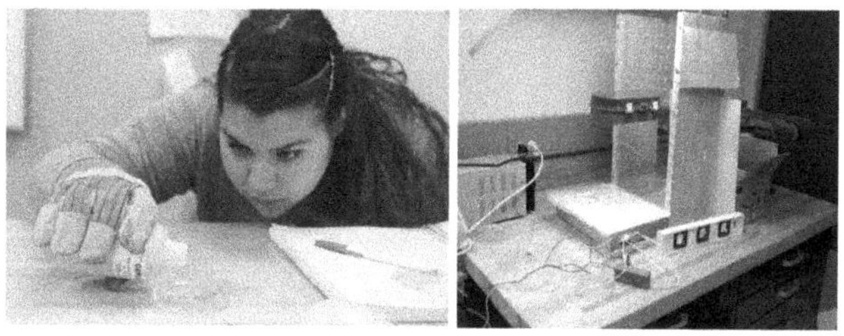

Figure 6. Students preparing their petri dishes to grow bacteria (left), and the time-lapse camera apparatus (right).

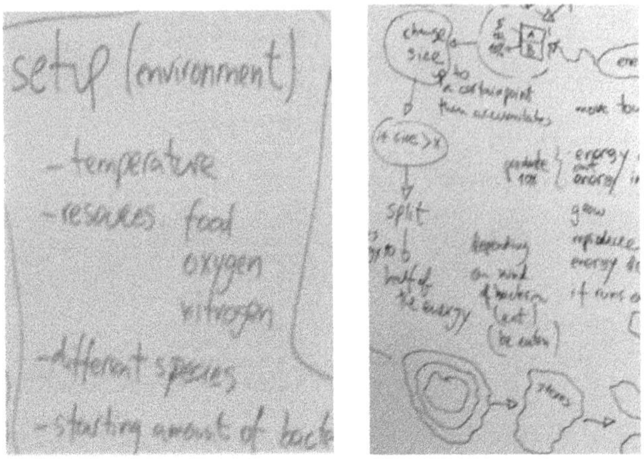

Figure 7. Some small snapshots of the "paper modeling" activity, in which students collaboratively created a flowchart of an agent-based model of bacterial growth.

3.2 Second study: Physics

In the second study, 11 high school students (4 females and 7 males) studied Newton's laws by investigating the time it takes for a ball to travel down a ramp. The study lasted for 6 hours. Students were first asked to build a physical model to investigate the variables affecting the time it took for a ball to roll down a ramp. In groups of two or three, they built ramps and attached light and infrared sensors to detect the position of the balls. For this pilot study, I shortened the activity of designing a virtual model and let students investigate and interact with a pre-made NetLogo model. It enabled students to simulate a ball rolling down a ramp and vary parameters such as ball mass and ramp angle without them having to program the model from scratch. Finally, the staff led the students in comparing the behavior of the virtual and real models – particularly, to observe that the virtual model predicted that ball's mass had no effect, while the empirical data suggested otherwise.

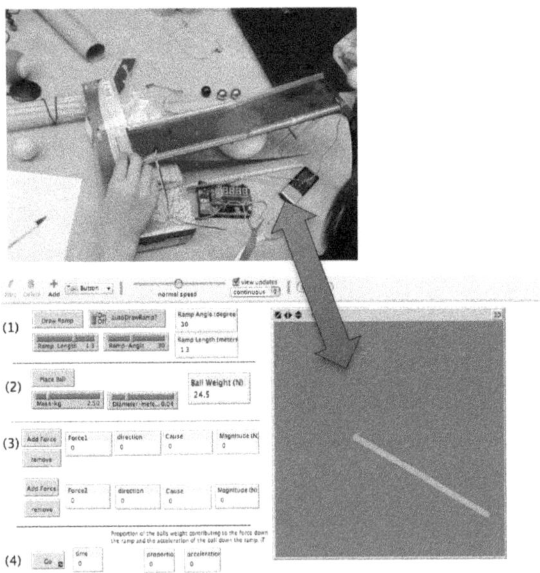

Figure 8: One of the projects in the "ball and ramp" study, in which students had a kit of parts to build their ramp (above) and then compared it with a computer model programmed in NetLogo in which students could change several parameters.

3.3 Chemistry

In the third study, students investigated the relationship between gas volume and pressure in a closed system. This study was conducted with the same group of school students as the previous study, and for the same amount of time (6 hours). Students were asked to interact with a pre-built syringe system with pressure sensors, and collected data about the relationship between pressure and volume. Next, I provided a NetLogo computer model of the gas laws, with which students could interact and see the behavior of gas particles in a container with a moving piston. As the volume of the physical syringe changed, the computer model varied accordingly, and the students compared the match between the pressure sensor values and the results supplied by their virtual model.

3.4 Open-ended

In this study, students could freely choose their topic of interest. The group had 12 freshmen high school students (11 male, one female), and was conducted as an after school program in a school in Moscow, Russia. Over three days (24 hours total), they were supposed to build a physical model, a computer model in NetLogo, and write a report about the comparison about them.

Figure 9 shows one typical project, a model investigating liquid diffusion, with the physical model on the left and the computer model on the right.

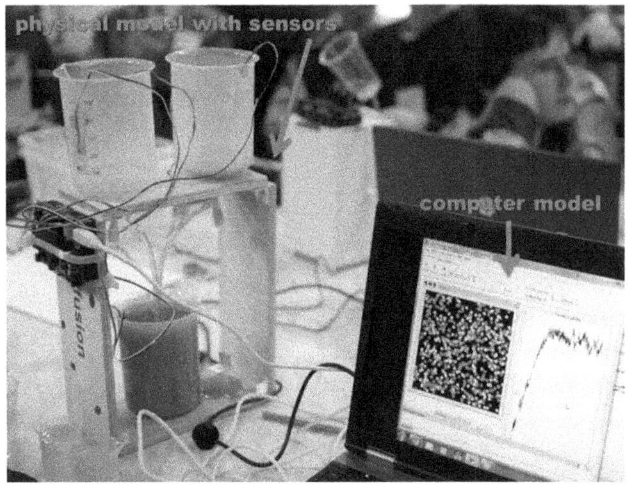

Figure 9: One of the projects in the 'open-ended' workshop. Note the physical model of diffusion on the left, with sensors, and the computer model in NetLogo on the right, connected in real time. The colored dots represent particles of two different liquids mixing, and the graph shows the change over time in a "mixing index".

4. DATA AND DISCUSSION

In the discussion, I will mainly focus on the first study. I will also discuss one dimension of the data and its presence within the four studies

I will start with a commented narrative of several classroom episodes centered on the perceived and hypothesized affordances of BM in the first study- the bacterial growth: (a) resolving model mismatch, (b) converging on appropriate variables, (c) critically evaluating the assumptions of models, and (d) translating between micro and macro perspectives.

4.1 Iteratively improving the virtual model to resolve mismatch

Overall, the group's method was to "run" their whiteboard virtual model in order to see how the bacteria grew, to compare the results to their goal of the growth curve from the physical data, and to resolve the perceived differences between the two by adding rules and variables to the virtual model. They repeated this process a total of four times in the 1.5 hours of the session, developing an increasingly accurate model in the process (figure 3).

- add bacteria, food, moisture, temperature
- add rule: bacteria move around randomly
- RUN MODEL: results were a flat growth curve
- add food rule: bacteria absorb food and moisture
- add waste rule: bacteria release waste
- add reproduction
- RUN MODEL: results are exponential growth and no death
- add death rule: if bacteria don't get food/moisture, they die
- RUN MODEL: results were exponential growth and then death
- add lag phase rule: first generation takes longer to multiply

Figure 10: A chronological list of the additions the students made to the model, and the instances in which they ran it. The results of each run prompted a subsequent rule addition that made the model more accurate.

For example, a student observed at one point after "running" the virtual model that their growth curve was increasing exponentially from the start. She noted that this was not correct, because the real growth curve had an initial flat "lag phase" before beginning to grow. After a moment's reflection, she remembered that this was because real bacteria have an initial phase of settling into a new environment before multiplying. She said "We need to make a rule that it takes time before the bacteria grow." Another student chimed in, saying that this would have to be different from a maturation period for individual bacteria, because it would apply only to the first bacteria on the dish. After more discussion about how to code the lag phase in their system, they came up with the following rule: "If a bacterium is in the first generation, it has to wait two time steps before reproducing." Upon running the model again, students could see from the resulting curve that they had successfully created the lag phase. The students went through a similar process to add all of the variables in their model.

4.2 Converging on appropriate variables

When the students were searching the web for information about bacteria, they collected and wrote down a great deal of information that was not necessary for the modeling task they were given. For example, some students noted that bacteria are prokaryotes, eat many types of human food, and live in a range of conditions. However, during the whiteboard virtual modeling session, the students only included variables that were necessary to define the shape of the growth curve - food/moisture, waste, and bacteria health. Global variables like temperature and oxygen affect bacterial growth, but the dynamics of the curve assume that these global variables are constant or the variations are too small. The fact that the students left these variables out without prompting suggests that they implicitly understood this instance of a controlled variable.

Students also made decisions regarding the granularity with which to describe variables. One student noted multiple types of bacteria nutrients in her web research, but went along with the group in representing food as a single variable of just one type. When asked about this issue, she replied that "I don't need to be that specific for this model."

4.3 Critically evaluating the assumptions of models

In addition to learning about the relevant variables for modeling bacterial growth, the students in the Bifocal Modeling workshop, also, reflected on the underlying assumptions of their models themselves - in this case, their representations of space and time. Space is represented in NetLogo as a grid of square "patches", units of space that can possess variables like location or food concentration. This patchwork representation of space was explained to the students at the start of the whiteboard modeling session, but at the time of introduction it was only relevant as a way to explain how to represent environmental variables such as food. However, as the session progressed, the students noticed that their bacteria were scattered randomly across the surface in their model, and filled the entire surface uniformly as they multiplied. In contrast, the real bacteria that they grew formed small circular spots. In order to explain the difference, students engaged in a discussion about how far bacteria can move, which quickly led to the question of the size of whole square grid itself. As one student put it, "This square could be a whole dish, or it could be just a tiny spot in the real Petri dish… if we were looking through a microscope, zooming in, they [the bacteria] will move much more. " At the end of their discussion, they decided that it was up to them to define the size of the virtual world they designed, if they kept thing in proportion. In previous work [2] I have observed students reconsidering space in their computer models and engaging in sophisticated discussions about sampling, relative size of the molecules in relation to containers, and similarity concluding that the arbitrary sizes of the model "seemed" unrealistic but were still useful modeling abstraction for their projects.

Time in NetLogo and in the whiteboard model was represented as a series of discrete steps called "ticks." While discussing the proper time delay for the lag phase, one student realized that they had no agreed conversion between ticks and real time. She asked, "Do bacteria get food and moisture each minute? Each hour? Each day? Right now we are just doing this with ticks... how can we translate the tick into real time?" At the end of another discussion about the time scale of bacteria growth in the real world and in NetLogo program, the students decided that if bacteria can multiply every 20 minutes, they will agree that one tick in the virtual world equaled 20 minutes in the physical world. Though they did not entirely resolve their questions about representing time and space in their model, the students were asking the "right" questions; that is, they were asking about the assumptions that models make about the world, which are at the heart of scientific critical thinking, and again understanding that even seemingly unrealistic assumptions or abstractions can be "good enough" for their modeling purposes.

4.4 Translating between micro and macro perspectives

A final theme that arose during the modeling session was the continual switching of perspectives, from the rules for an individual bacterium to the emergent behavior of its entire colony. The literature on complex systems education suggests that people find it difficult to move in either direction between macro and micro perspectives -- either inferring the emergent result of a micro-level change to a system, or predicting the micro level changes that could cause a given macro-level result [23, 24]. Complex system dynamics are also typically taught only in highly advanced math and science settings. However, the literature also suggests that properly designed activities can help people to grasp complex systems concepts much more easily. The iterative process of modeling that students went through can be seen as a process of writing rules at the level of the individual bacterium in order to create emergent outcomes at the level of the colony. With no prior academic knowledge of agent-based modeling or complex systems, the students in this study managed to describe and manipulate a complex system at both levels, micro and macroscopic. While BM is not inherently bound to a complex-systems framework, the data suggests that the process of modeling a phenomenon was an effective way to intellectually engage students with the dynamics of complex systems.

4.5 Various approaches toward resolving mismatches

Results from these four pilot studies suggest that adjustment in a BM activity would change students' approach toward resolving mismatches between the real and virtual models, within the main goal of evaluating the different implementation models (see Figure 5). In this section, instead on analyzing particular aspects of the bacteria growth study, I change our focus to comparing different implementation models, in order to investigate how the presence of each of the components of a bifocal modeling changes students' engagement and learning. For example, I was interested in finding out how the presence of a longer model building phase would influence how students conducted the model comparison.

In the first study (bacterial growth), I designed the activities so that I mostly had students focused on creating a conceptual agent-based model to match the imagined emergent behaviors to the real time-lapse video data. Students were actively constructing a model on the whiteboard, even though they were *not* writing the code. Overall, the group's method was to "run" a few steps of their whiteboard virtual model in order to see how the bacteria grew, and compare the results to their goal – the growth curve calculated from the physical model. Then, they would resolve the perceived differences between the two by adding rules and variables to the virtual model. In general, as I will discuss in the following paragraphs, I observed that due to the intense model building activity, students in this study were more engaged in investigating the behavior of the phenomenon.

In the second study about the "ball on a ramp" model, I made different design decisions, given the size of the group (11) and the available time (6 hours total). Students partially designed and developed their own physical model, but the virtual model was given to them, so the emphasis was just on interacting with the pre-made virtual model. Interestingly, as students proceeded in the activity, they became more critical about their own observations rather than questioning the pre-made model and its assumptions. For example, in their physical experiment, heavier balls appeared to roll down faster, possibly due to air resistance, slipping, and friction. When the virtual model appeared to refute the idea that heavier balls would roll faster (as they experienced in their physical experiment), students were surprised, and ended up trusting the given computer model more than their own observations. For example when asked about which model would better represent the scientific phenomenon, one student said that it would be "...the virtual model! It is computerized and can calculate the time, it is a computer so we trust it!" In general, students never questioned if the computer model could possibly be wrong, and just assumed that if since they were (supposedly) created by experts, they would be "right."

In the "Gas Laws" study, again, the emphasis was on interacting with pre-made models rather than creating them. In this case, students did not build any of the two models: they were given both a physical and a virtual model. Students were tasked with collecting real-time data from the pressure sensor, and comparing with the "ideal" data generated by the pre-made virtual model. Students critically evaluated the scientific experiment with sensors and offered many ideas about how to improve it, trying to make sense of the discrepancies between the two datasets. For example, when asked about the discrepancies between the P-V graph which resulted from their own physical measurement, compared to the one demonstrated by the virtual model, the causes that students mentioned were the accuracy of the sensor and data-logging software. Again, they never mentioned that the virtual models could have been wrong. For example, when trying to critique their physical model, students only looked for technical issues such as limitations of the sensors, or the limits of compressibility of the air inside the syringe. Again, judging by their utterances during the activity, similarly to the previous study, students did not even consider that the computer models could have been wrong or imperfect. They took their accuracy for granted and simply critiqued their own data, even after having repeated the experience many time with similar results.

In the last study, students had not only to come up with their own idea for a project, but design both the physical and virtual models from scratch. During the construction itself of the physical model, many dissimilarities were foregrounded. For example, one group decided to build a bridge to investigate how much vibration it would withstand, together with the accompanying computer model (Figure 11).

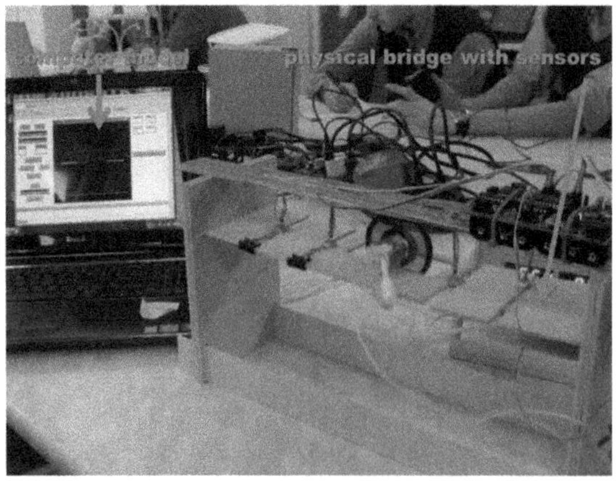

Figure 11: A Bifocal Model for bridge harmonics, with the NetLogo model of a bridge (left), and physical bridge with sensors and a vibrating motor (right).

During the construction of the bridge, the facilitators encouraged students to run systematic experiments with different frequencies of vibration, comparing them with the canonical formula. Even though they were able to construct a plot that approximated the canonical formula, it was evidently not a perfect match since there is intrinsic error in the empirical measures. At first, students felt that their model was wrong since it was not fitting the theoretical curve perfectly – a big disappointment for the group. However, through multiple cycles of measurement and rebuilding the system, students realized that they were always getting "messy" results, and that their initial goal of a perfect fit was not just a matter of "getting it perfect," but an impossibility. They tried to carefully control the voltage source (which controlled the vibration frequency), the location of the sensors, and the magnetic pieces, but finally realized that even after multiple changes to both the computer model and the physical mode they could make the models match.

In this case, I hypothesize that by constructing both the computer and the physical models, and glass boxing the entire process, students had a much more comprehensive set of tools to make sense of the differences and mismatches, as evidenced by the sophistication of their attempts to make both systems match. However, further research needs to be done to evaluate if the extra time invested in learning the programming language and all the digital fabrication machines was advantageous in terms of the further insight into the models and the learning activity.

One last example from this implementation model sheds some light into the usefulness of the full-fledged Bifocal Modeling activity, in which students build both the physical and computer models. A group of three students got interested in building a model to explain how an ice cube would melt (Figure 12). They froze temperature sensors inside an ice cube and placed it on top of a heat source (a toaster oven) and also instrumented it with the same type of sensors. They carefully tracked the temperature of the surface of the heat source and of the ice cube, and carefully examined the two plots to generate a tentative equation and plot relating them (see top right plots in Figure 12). However, after some hours, they realized that their equation was not a mechanistic model of what was happening with the ice cube – it was merely a descriptive relationship. Even after several refinements, the students were unease about their project because they wanted to dive deeper into the mechanism of melting and really understand why the ice was melting, and not only how fast it was happening. They embarked then in a much more ambitious project: create a NetLogo model to describe what was happening microscopically "inside" the ice cube. They programmed an atomic-level agent-based model (see bottom right of Figure 12) in which the atoms were connected by springs and allowed to vibrate and eventually break off, and "heat waves" (represented by small triangles at the bottom) would collide with the atoms and increase their vibrational energy. Therefore, students arrived at a remarkably complex and accurate mechanistic model of melting by going through several iterations of model building and comparison. Ultimately, they realized that the equations they were given at school (which they were using as a reference pattern for the initial part of their project) were not exposing the mechanism of the phenomenon, which was ultimately their goal for the project. The Bifocal Modeling activity, I hypothesize, gave them the technological tools and activities that highlighted imperfections in the models, and led them to increasingly complex endeavors: their goal went from generating hypotheses about "blackboxed" numerical relationships to deep insight into mechanisms behind them.

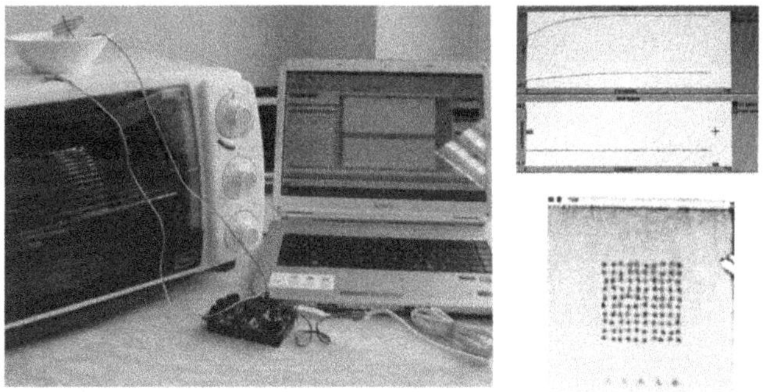

Figure 12: A Bifocal Model for a melting ice cube. The kitchen oven melts the ice (left), and NetLogo both models the phenomena from a differential equations perspective (top right) and agent-based perspective (bottom right).

6. CONCLUSION

Our goal in this paper was to offer initial data on the comparison of many different implementation models for Bifocal Modeling. The first study was a proof of concept that established the feasibility and some of the learning gains of students engaging in Bifocal Modeling. Next, I intended to compare several models of implementation of BM. From the four studies, I observed at least one overall pattern across different implementations: resources that are given to students have a different perceived value compared to the ones that are constructed by the student. "Given" resources are always trusted more. Thus, the only way for a constructed resource to achieve the same validity as a given one would be for it to perfectly match the latter. Therefore, it seems like this asymmetry could be counterproductive for students, especially when the given model is the theoretical model.

A second pattern was that in the studies in which there was no virtual model-building (gas laws and ball/ramp), students' level of sophistication in comparing real and virtual models was lower, and their epistemological stance was even more radical: they would critique their work and their own observations but rarely question the computational models that were given to them.

I also observed that the benefits of model-building appear even if students are not coding, but creating "paper models" models, but only if they use the paper or the whiteboard as a 'computational surface' that can enact the imagined agent-rules. Within this context, the use of the physical model as a reference pattern for the creation and refinement of the virtual model was generally effective. When students were instructed to design a virtual model that recreated the bacterial growth curve, they used their previously-learned knowledge about the curve and the physical appearance of the bacteria as a reference patterns for what their model should generate. When the model data did not match the observed data, they went back and made changes.

One key conclusion from these four implementations is that the full model building experience (both physical and virtual) was indeed a richer learning experience, especially considering students who build several versions and types of computer models. However, with the proper facilitation and a careful choice of which modeling phase to abbreviate (e.g., bacteria study), relatively rich learning outcomes can be achieved in a dramatically reduced time-frame. *However, these studies have shown that model-building, rather than simply having access to sensors and tangible learning tools, was the determinant factor in generating deep engagement with the phenomenon.* Further research is needed to determine the degree to which model building can be abbreviated without significant decrease in learning gains and engagement.

7. ACKNOWLEDGEMES

Thanks to Daniel Greene, Tamar Furhmann, and Shima Salehi for their work in the research and revisions. This work is funded by the NSF CAREER Award #1055130.

8. REFERENCES

[1] Blikstein, P., & Wilensky, U. (2006). "Hybrid modeling:" Advanced scientific investigation linking computer models and real-world sensing. *Proceedings of the International Conference of the Learning Sciences, Bloomington, USA, pp. 890-891*

[2] Blikstein, P. & Wilensky, U. (2007). *Bifocal modeling: a framework for combining computer modeling, robotics and real-world sensing.* Paper presented at the Annual meeting of the American Research Education Association, Chicago, IL.

[3] Blikstein, P. (2009). *An Atom is Known by the Company it Keeps: Content, Representation and Pedagogy Within the Epistemic Revolution of the Complexity Sciences.* PhD. dissertation, Northwestern University, Evanston, IL.

[4] Blikstein, P., & Wilensky, U. (2010). MaterialSim: A constructionist agent-based modelling approach to engineering education. In M. J. Jacobson & P. Reimann, (Eds.), *Designs for learning environments of the future: International perspectives from the learning sciences.* New York: Springer, pp. 17-60.

[5] Blikstein, P. (2010). Connecting the science classroom and tangible interfaces: the bifocal modeling framework. *Proceedings of the 9th International Conference of the Learning Sciences,* Chicago, Illinois, pp. 128-130.

[6] Blikstein, P., Fuhrmann, T., Greene, D. & Salehi, S. (2012). Bifocal Modeling: Mixing Real and Virtual Labs for Advanced Science Learning. *Proceedings of Interaction Design and Children (IDC)*, Bremen, Germany, pp. 296-299.

[7] Confrey, J. (2005). The evolution of design studies as methodology. *The Cambridge handbook of the learning sciences*, 135-151

[8] Edelson, D. C. (2002). Design research: What we learn when we engage in design. *The Journal of the Learning Sciences*, 11(1), 105-121.

[9] Finkelstein, N. D., Adams, W. K., Keller, C. J., Kohl, P. B., Perkins, K. K., Podolefsky, N. S. Reid, S. and LeMaster, R. (2005). When learning about the real world is better done virtually: A study of substituting computer simulations for laboratory equipment," *Physical Review Special Topics - Physics Education Research*, vol. 1, pp. 10103-10110.

[10] Gire, E., Carmichael, A., Chini, J., Rebello, S., & Puntambekar, S. (2010). The Effects of Physical and Virtual Manipulatives on Students' Conceptual Learning About Pulleys. *Proceedings of the 9th International Conference of the Learning Sciences.* Chicago, IL, pp. 937-943.

[11] Jaakkola, T., & Nurmi, S. (2008). Fostering elementary school students' understanding of simple electricity by combining simulation and laboratory activities. *Journal of Computer Assisted Learning*, 24(4), 271-283.

[12] Klahr, D., Triona, L. M., & Williams, C. (2007). Hands on what? The relative effectiveness of physical versus virtual materials in an engineering design project by middle school children. *Journal of Research in Science Teaching,* 44(1), 183-203.

[13] Levy, S. T., & Wilensky, U. (2008). Inventing a "mid-level" to make ends meet: Reasoning through the levels of complexity. *Cognition and Instruction*, 26(1), 1-47.

[14] Liu, X. (2006). Effects of combined hands-on laboratory and computer modeling on student learning of gas laws: A quasi-experimental study. *Journal of Science Education and Technology*, vol. 15, pp. 89-100.

[15] Martin, F. and M. Resnick (1993). *Lego/Logo and electronic bricks: Creating a scienceland for children.* Advanced educational technologies for mathematics and science. D. L. Ferguson. Berlin, Heidelberg, Springer-Verlag.

[16] Papert, S. (1980). *Mindstorms: children, computers, and powerful ideas.* New York: Basic Books.

[17] PhET: Free Online Physics, Chemistry, Biology, *Earth Science and Math Simulations.* Web. 09 Nov. 2011. <http://phet.colorado.edu/>.

[18] Resnick, M., & Wilensky, U. (1998). Diving into Complexity: Developing Probabilistic Decentralized Thinking Through Role-Playing Activities. *Journal of the Learning Sciences*, 7(2), pp. 153-171.

[19] Resnick, M., Ocko, S., & Papert, S. (1991). *Lego/Logo: Learning through and about design,* in Constructionism, I. Harel, Papert, S., Editor 1991, Ablex: Norwood, NJ.

[20] Smith, G., Gnesdilow, D., & Puntambekar, S. (2010). Examining the Combination of Physical and Virtual Experiments in an Inquiry Science Classroom. *Computer Based Learning Science Conference Proceedings.*

[21] Sipitakiat, A., Blikstein, P, & Cavallo, D. (2004). GoGo Board: Augmenting Programmable Bricks for Economically Challenged Audiences. *Proceedings of the 5th International Conference of the Learning Sciences,* Los Angeles, USA, pp. 481-488.

[22] Wilensky, U. (1999). NetLogo [computer software]. *Center for Connected Learning and Computer-Based Modeling,* Northwestern University, Evanston, IL.

[23] Wilensky, U. & Reisman, K. *Thinking like a Wolf, a Sheep or a Firefly: Learning Biology through Constructing and Testing Computational Theories.* Cognition & Instruction, 2006. 24(2), 171-209.

[24] Wilkerson-Jerde, M. & Wilensky, U. (2010). Restructuring change, interpreting changes: The deltatick modeling and analysis toolkit. *Proceedings of Constructionism 2010*, Paris, France.

Connecting Play: Understanding Multimodal Participation in Virtual Worlds

Yasmin B. Kafai
University of Pennsylvania
3700 Walnut Street
Philadelphia, PA 19106
001-215-746-3468
kafai@upenn.edu

Deborah A. Fields
Utah State University
2800 Old Main Hill
Logan, UT 84322
001-435-797-1437
deborah.fields@usu.edu

ABSTRACT

In this paper we propose a multimodal approach to log file data analysis to develop a better understanding of player participation and practices in virtual worlds. To deal with the massive amounts of data collected via log files researchers traditionally have employed quantitative reduction techniques for revealing trends and patterns. We contend that certain qualitative analysis techniques can reveal particular play practices across online and offline spaces and aspects of individual players' participation invisible through other methods. We present examples from our research in the tween virtual world Whyville.net that illustrate the uses of these new techniques. In the discussion we address the benefits and limitations of our approach.

Categories and Subject Descriptors

H.5.3 Group and Organization Interfaces

General Terms

Measurement, Design, Human Factors

Keywords

Virtual worlds, log file analyses, case studies, connected learning

1. INTRODUCTION

Virtual worlds, like other settings, prove to be complex environments, perhaps even more so because they are designed not only by the companies that host them but also by the players who contribute content to them. Researchers who study players and practices have faced two challenges given the particular nature of virtual worlds: capturing player participation across multiple spaces within these virtual worlds and capturing player participation between online and offline interactions. These challenges make clear that player engagement within virtual worlds is not confined to the screen alone but needs to be understood within the context of a larger play culture. A common problem for researchers has been tracking and making sense of players' navigation and interactions across the hundreds of public and private places that constitute virtual worlds. This is not simply an issue in online environments. Previous sociological traditions had teams of researchers follow a child through different settings throughout the course of a day (see [1]) or conduct extensive ethnographies in virtual worlds [2, 26]. Access to server level data where tracking data captures time stamps of locations and chat interactions can alleviate some of the labor of following people across spaces but is often not available to researchers because companies consider these data to be of a proprietary nature.

A second, equally important challenge concerns the distinction that has been drawn between online and offline interactions. Researchers have begun to argue that the boundaries between play in the virtual and the real are not as distinct as some have made them out to be, and both need to be considered as integrated aspects of play in virtual communities [5, 16, 17, 23]. Experiences in cyberspace have become a part of the everyday activities and meaning-making of many players [22]. Indeed, thinking of either physical/offline/real or digital/online/virtual as self-contained denies their flexibility and the ways that people negotiate performance, meaning, and embodiment within them: "Only when we really acknowledge these spaces as legitimate and powerful sites of production, and acknowledge the diverse agents involved in their creation, can we begin to address the challenges facing them progressively" [26].

In this paper, we address these challenges by illustrating different approaches to analyzing log file data both quantitatively and qualitatively. First, we chose a traditional approach aggregating the log file data across activities and players. We then present a case study of a tween player called Zoe/bluwave that we built by sampling her log file records and supplementing this data with what we know about her from observations and post-study interviews. Following one person provided us with an in-depth view of how she became a player in Whyville and revealed some unexpected facets and disparities of her time on Whyville not captured otherwise. Finally, we chose a secret gaming practice, called teleporting, and examined how it was learned not just within the virtual world but also across the club and other settings. Collectively, the multimodal approach to data collection and analyses allowed us to understand better how players came to participate and perform in the virtual world.

2. BACKGROUND

Different methodologies and data sources have been used to address these challenges ranging from in-depth observations and interviews to collection of log files and large-scale surveys, alongside participation in virtual and local spaces by the researchers themselves. Some researchers have begun to acknowledge that the dividing lines between the quantitative and qualitative methodologies create a false dichotomy because each

ICMI'12, October 22–26, 2012, Santa Monica, CA, USA.

perspective contributes to our understanding of what, when, and why players engage in these worlds (see [27]). Furthermore, the complexity of virtual worlds indicates that not any one data source alone but the triangulation of many may do better justice in understanding player practices, purposes, and psychology (e.g., [3]). Yet we still find that particular data sources such as log files are associated with quantitative analysis for generalization purposes. For instance, Williams, Yee, and Caplan [28] suggested using log file analyses for identifying general patterns across players while using interviews for more individualized assessments. While such approaches promote data integration and triangulation, they also limit our possibilities in harnessing new ways to meet the challenges of researching virtual worlds.

We decided to approach the log file data with two different perspectives: in one, the *person* perspective, we wanted to build case studies of players thus recreating their participation over time, while in the other, the *practice* perspective, we wanted to develop an account of how a particular gaming practice was adopted over time. In both cases we used log file data to capture the "who, when, how and where" but supplemented this with information available from field notes, video records, and interviews. Making sense of log files qualitatively, especially longitudinally following one person or one practice over several months, is challenging and unusual and represents one of the contributions of this paper. Some researchers have used logfiles selectively over a short period of time, for instance two girls over a few days [4] or a small group during a few class periods [6]. Others have done extensive quantitative analysis of log files (e.g., [28]) or analyses of social networks [7] or combined multiple data sources [8]. Perhaps the most common *qualitative* use of log files is to collect and analyze chat [24] but collection of chat has generally been limited to whatever place the researcher virtually inhabits at a given time.

One particular issue we faced was the overwhelming amount of data and detail collected in field notes, survey answers, and log files of 681 consenting participants aged 10-13 years over 6 months in the virtual world of Whyville. In particular, the log files recorded every word of chat typed in Whyville as well as click-level data, i.e., records of every click that were stamped with time, location, and where applicable, chat text, over a six-month time period. Though this might suggest comprehensive coverage of tweens' participation, initial analyses of chat counts, location visits, or other trends (see [14]) left us wishing for a better understanding of how players manage to navigate these virtual worlds and learn about different norms and practices from others. This was particularly important since we researched a tween virtual world and thus our own adult play experiences were most likely not comparable in many aspects.

With only a few exceptions, previous studies of online and offline gaming have focused on older teenagers or adults, in general, the intended audiences of the most popular massively multiplayer online games and the general populace of cybercafés. To date, children and tweens' increasing activity in popular virtual worlds such as Club Penguin, Neopets, Habbo Hotel, Webkinz, and Whyville has largely been ignored [15]. Before we delve into the different examples of using log file data to understand multimodal participation in virtual worlds, we will provide some background on Whyville.net, the virtual world we studied, and on the design of our data collection.

3. VIRTUAL WORLD

Whyville.net is a massive, free virtual world (in 2005, at the time of our study, it had over 1.2 million registered players; now in 2012, it has over 5.6 millions registered players) that encourages youth ages 8-16 (with an average of 12.3 years) to play casual science games in order to earn a virtual salary (in "clams"), which they can then spend on buying and designing parts for their avatars (virtual characters), projectiles to throw at other players, and other goods such as cars and plots of land. The general consensus among Whyvillians (the citizens of Whyville.net) is that earning a good salary and thus procuring a large number of clams to spend on face parts or other goods is essential for fully participating in Whyville [21]. Looks also demonstrate a player's tenure on Whyville and relative experience level; new players have fewer clams, and their looks generally show this because cheaper face parts are perceived as less attractive [20].

When Whyvillians enter the site, they immediately arrive at the Welcome Page with links to events for the week, *The Whyville Times* newspaper articles, survival tips, and FAQs. Upon arrival, users can also check their personal email, status on their Whyville salary, and their latest bank statement. From the Welcome Page Whyvillians may head straight to the Sunroof, Pool Party, and other locales to chat with friends and other users on topics related to school, friendships, and appearance. They may also engage in a number of other community-related activities. Whyville has an active community life that elects its own mayor, organizes annual virtual proms, and posts many public petitions that campaign to include or change features of Whyville. Places such as the Trading Post allow Whyvillians to exchange goods.

4. DATA COLLECTION

We collected data across three different spaces. The first space was the online community of Whyville where we tracked 681 consenting participants. We recorded every time each player went to a different place in Whyville–in other words every time the screen changed–with a marking of the virtual location and time stamp as well as everything each child typed in public chat or private whisper (private chat from one individual to another in the same virtual location/screen). In addition, we set up an after-school club where 21 tweens (9-12 years old) came to play on Whyville for an hour most days after school. While the club began as a quiet place, it quickly became loud and lively as participants learned about the site and began to shout advice to each other, arrange virtual parties, chat, throw digital projectiles at one another, and critique each other's avatars [10,17]. Most of the tweens were new to Whyville, so learning to participate in the site was a common (if tacit) goal. Club members eagerly displayed their knowledge of the site by offering advice and answering questions, such as how to create a good look or throw a projectile. The third space where students played on Whyville included the two sixth grade classes at the school. In this classroom setting, students' activities on Whyville were structured primarily to facilitate their learning about the root and spread of infectious diseases [19].

We collected several kinds of data during the study. For all 681 participants, we collected log file data. For the 88 children who were members of the club and/or the classes alone, log files included over 950,000 lines. In addition, ethnographic field notes were recorded daily to capture the overall activity of the club. Two video cameras focused on small groups of youth clustered at tables with two to three computers over the nine weeks in which the club took place during the winter of 2005. Club participants were interviewed individually at the end of the club.

5. CONNECTING PLAYERS ACROSS ACTIVITIES

The most common approach to analyzing massive log files is to aggregate the data of players across activities and understand the overall difference in players' participation in Whyville. In a first step, we took every click players made and every word of chat they typed and performed a few different analyses to unpack what they did (for more detail on this statistical approach, see [14]). We divided all of the activities in Whyville into 13 categories and used these to look for similarities and differences in players' activities (see Table 1).

Table 1. Frequency of player participation in Whyville activities by gender

	Overall		Girls (N = 462)		Boys (N = 219)		
Categories	Mean	SD	Mean	SD	Mean	SD	t-test
chat	6209.85	11822.87	6670.59	11993.56	6913.64	12679.61	-0.48
face	3714.41	5359.62	4074.40	4798.74	3851.47	6638.31	0.42
ymail	3159.89	4502.16	3581.21	4875.54	2958.65	3757.85	1.49
social	1609.06	2332.00	1702.85	2246.88	1796.82	2625.32	-0.79
misc	679.53	2344.28	718.67	2515.26	763.40	2283.26	-0.18
economic	670.25	991.49	649.63	815.30	877.11	1327.27	-3.15**
whisper	574.65	1277.84	597.89	1170.97	693.56	1600.27	-0.73
game	548.06	649.32	518.47	561.66	728.25	777.62	3.45***
bbs	373.98	1733.01	460.87	2044.27	298.73	1162.17	1.04
info_com	370.75	857.97	400.35	869.22	400.45	933.73	0.11
multigam	182.41	621.77	136.13	391.84	318.69	976.98	-3.55***
house	155.01	256.98	155.09	221.82	187.11	326.99	-1.3
whypox	38.02	37.92	36.68	28.66	47.21	50.80	-2.89**

Note: **p<.01, ***p<.001. Results were based on independent sample t-tests and were replicated using negative binomial regression.

We first looked for differences in gender and found there were very few significant differences between girls' and boys' participation on Whyville; both girls and boys played the same activities with roughly the same frequency. Both boys and girls spent the same amount of time customizing their avatars through shopping, dressing, and trading face parts – in fact, on average all Whyvillians spent nearly 1/3 of their clicks on their avatars' appearance [8]! Only in a few minor activities did relatively small differences reveal themselves. On average, boys tended to play more multiplayer games or do economic things (e.g., looking at their bank accounts) more often, but these differences were still quite slim.

Next, we conducted cluster analyses to see if there were any players who had similar patterns of activity. We found the only major difference involved frequency of activity – about 7% of Whyvillians we studied were the most heavily involved on Whyville. We call this tier of players "Core." A much larger set of players (34%) fill the second tier, what we call the "Semi-Core" players. Finally, most players on Whyville form the third and largest tier, what we call the "Peripheral" players because they played less frequently than the other tiers of players. Figure 1 shows a breakdown of the activities of each player tier and the relative frequency of engagement in 13 different types of activities.

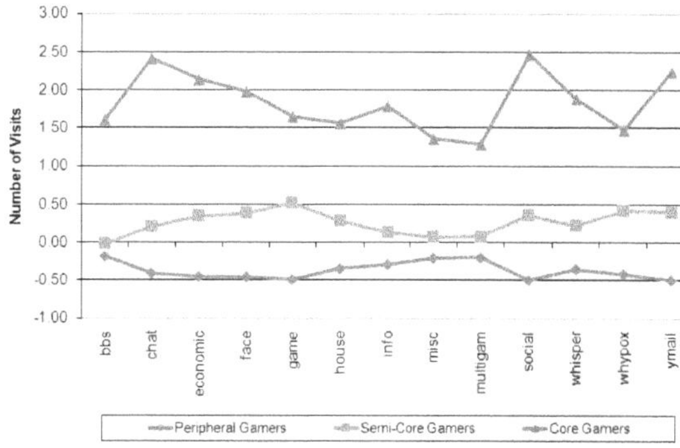

Figure 1. Player profiles by type of activity

The "Core" players spent by far the most time on Whyville, and perhaps not surprisingly this group spent much more time socializing, chatting, ymailing, and customizing avatars than any other group. "Semi-Core" players took part in far fewer activities than the Core tier, but they also engaged in more economic activities like salary-raising games ("game") and checking bank statements ("economic") as well as going to more social spots ("social") and ymailing ("ymail") than the "Peripheral" players. Across our 681 participants in the larger study, representative of the population of Whyville as a whole, Zoe/bluwave was in the top group of players, the group that participated most regularly and intensely on the site. Her case study is presented next.

6. CONNECTING A PLAYER ACROSS ACTIVITES

We choose one female club member, Zoe (bluwave), an African-American girl who was a sixth grader (12 years old) at the time of the study. In the club she was one of the first members to learn inside gaming practices on Whyville such as teleporting and throwing projectiles [9, 10], and she often taught others how to do things on Whyville, such as trading face parts. In fact, what she said that she most liked about Whyville in an interview three months into her life on the site was the social opportunity to hang out with friends and the financial side of life: "almost like a real everyday life, because you get a salary... and you can raise it by playing games or selling parts." Zoe/bluwave was not only one of the quicker learners of the club, she was also one of the core 7% of participants on Whyville.

Our log files, identified with usernames, contain every click and word of chat and whisper of the 681 participating individuals in our larger study. We isolated Zoe's/bluwave's log files and by going click by click through the data, we first created minute-by-minute summaries of her Whyville activities and then condensed these into short daily narratives that noted patterns and innovations in participation. Each line of her log files contained her username (bluwave), a time stamp (year-month-day-hour-minute-second), her location in Whyville, and if applicable, chat or whisper text. In all there were over 54,000 lines of text in bluwave's log files. To create the minute-by-minute summaries, we sampled the days she was on Whyville, selecting the first seven days and then alternating every five or six days to ensure breadth of days of the week in our sample. In all we analyzed 35 days during her first two months on Whyville from January to June 2005. In the final interpretation of Zoe's activities, we also took into account video, field notes, and interview data from the club (for more detail, see [12]).

Early on bluwave took up what is probably a very familiar pattern of Whyville participation: logging on to Whyville, checking ymail messages (Whyville's e-mail system), checking her bank statement, adjusting her look (using a feature called "Pick Your Nose"), and then alternating between socializing and earning clams, perhaps with a shopping break at Akbar's Face Mall (where you can use clams to buy face parts for your avatar). Earning clams is accomplished by playing science games, trading face parts (for a profit), or designing and selling face parts – the latter of which is more difficult than meets the eye and is usually only taken up after several weeks of participation [20]. Bluwave gradually built up her salary by finishing several levels of science games, going through periods of heavier and lighter play of these games – she played salary-raising games more regularly during weeks 1-3 and 6-8, with a dip in participation during weeks 4-5. In creating her avatar, she began with donated parts from Grandma's – Whyville's charity – supplemented with parts from trading at the Trading Post or shopping at Akbar's Face Mall. After her first two weeks, she completely left off going to Grandma's and relied solely on shopping and trading. This in itself was a move toward higher competence in Whyville – what might be considered an important move toward a socially acceptable look since parts from Grandma's are generally held in ill-esteem by other Whyville players (*ibid).*

While this summary describes time spent on Whyville that is fairly typical of other Whyville players, there were a few aspects that were not captured in our field notes or video records from the club. Only through digging through the log files were we able to identify the scope of bluwave's search for racial representation (wanting to be African-American on Whyville), her period of heavy flirting, and a short time of scamming others in the Trading Post (for more detail on these activities, see [12]). Here we will focus on one of the places where bluwave spent extensive amounts of time in Whyville – the Trading Post. In the after school club, Zoe was one of the first members to teach others how to trade on Whyville, and she often solicited others to go to the Trading Post and trade with her. In her final interview, she said that one of her favorite parts about Whyville was trading as it related to the financial exploration she enjoyed. But how did she figure out how to trade well and what did her time at the Trading Post consist of?

Bluwave first went to the Trading Post on her second day in Whyville. In total during her first seven days, bluwave spent over 20 hours on Whyville and 38% of those (or almost 8 hours) were at the Trading Post, where she quickly learned to trade parts. There was a significant learning curve as within that first week she dramatically changed the way she negotiated trades. At first she spoke in long phrases such as "does anyone want a head?" or "okay, ill trade the pokadot hair pin for the clams." But by the end of her first week she had adapted to a shortened, more precise language that fit her trading interests. Consider the differences between the two different trading exchanges on Day 3 and Day 6 in Table 2. These two trade negotiations are indicative of bluwave's trading conversations in the first three days and in the last two days of her first week. In contrast to the early part of her first week, by Day 6 she started with a shorter invitation to trade, having put up a barrette for trade (probably the same polka dot hair pin discussed on Day 3 as it is a common newbie part): "u lik." She had a sales pitch, "a barrette for your hair." Instead of saying that she wanted clams, something she had realized was more versatile than face parts, she simply listed a price ("25??") and followed quickly with a markdown, "how about 20." She also used shortened spellings and language more commonly used in Whyville, "u" for you, "lik" for like, "Kk" for okay.

Table 2: Bluwave's Changed Discourse of Trading

Day 3	Day 6
you have anything else?	u lik
let me see!!	a barrette for your hair
some clams	HI!
okay, ill trade the pokadot	25??
hair pin for the clams	Kk
ill trade the clamz for the hair	how about 20
do you hav any oter hair?	
let me see!	
yes..the first one looks cool!!!!	
wanta trade	

The change in discourse shown in Table 2 demonstrates part of bluwave's new ability to negotiate trades. She also changed her pattern of participating at the Trading Post from having longer conversations with Whyvillians in a given room in the Post to cycling from room to room saying, "u lik?" or "got any clamz?" and quickly moving on to another room if she did not like the answers. This probably made better use of her time, allowing her to see more people in a shorter amount of time and quickly gather whether others had clams or if they were interested in anything she had. The log files were essential for observing this kind of shift in discourse because these kind of changes were not captured in video records or field notes.

On February 21, six weeks into her life in Whyville, bluwave began using the Trading Post in a new way – to scam or fraud other Whyvillians out of their clams. It began when she herself was scammed. In the main lobby of the Trading Post, where Whyvillians mill around trying to identify people to trade with before moving on to a specific Trade Room, some Whyvillians broadly solicited people who wanted their "clams doubled." Bluwave expressed interest in this and followed them to the designated Trade Room (#48), but on finding out the details, she initially expressed skepticism (see the conversation quoted below). After pressing with questions, "r u a scammer?? TELL THE TRUTH," she agreed to their methods, which consisted of one person (bluwave, the victim) putting all her clams up in a one-sided trade while the others put nothing up for trade. After the other party left their seat (giving the illusion of the trade ending and pretending there was a fake software glitch), bluwave was told to press "agree" to complete the trade, thus giving all of her money to the scammers. Bluwave's side of the conversation appears below:

2:53 p.m.	Trade Room 48
	O SRRY
2:54 p.m.	i don't beleive u!!!!
	WAIT
	r u just gonnin on his side>>>>>
2:55 p.m.	fine
	r u a scammer?? TELL THE TRUTH
2:56 p.m.	fine ill do it

get back in the chair ill do it
soo what am i supposed 2 do?

After following the instructions, bluwave checked her bank statement and realized that all of her money was gone. Then she went immediately back to the Trading Post where she begged time and again for people to donate 5 clams to her (the amount charged for each trade) – she was so bereft that she could not even trade face parts! She actually found the culprits who tricked her, confronted them with their actions, and briefly followed them to their Trade Room to try to stop the next victim from falling prey to their scam. Shortly after this she gave up on trying to disrupt their scam and after finally succeeding in getting someone to give her 5 clams unconditionally, she began to try the same scam on others.

Over the next two weeks, bluwave consistently tried to get unsuspecting Whyvillians to fall for the "clam doubling" scam as it is known among the Whyville designers. This involved going to densely populated areas on Whyville like the Beach and the Trading Post Lobby and asking people "do u want ur clamz doubled?" If someone expressed interest, she directed them to a specific trading room and told them, "put up all of ur clamz plz," then instructed them, "ok when i get out of the chair press the agree." From a chat frequency count, we know that she used the word "doubled" over 200 times, demonstrating persistency in her scamming activity, though it did not continue past two weeks. In a single day (February 25), she actually recruited for her scam 30 times in 90 minutes and got six people to go to a trading room. We know that she completed her scam at least once and probably enough times to keep her continuing at it for a time. Below is the account of when she successfully completed her scam:

11:44am	The Moon
	do u want ur clamz doubled?
11:45am	rm 49 at the trading post kk
	Foyer, TradeRoom 49
	...
	put up ur clamz plz
11:48am	ok when i get out of the chair press agree
	the typ all clear?
11:49am	leave
	Index, tradeResult, oneMail, delete, records, userDetails
11:50am	records, userDetails, index 2x, bankStatement

In this conversation, bluwave began by recruiting a victim for her scam on the Moon with her typical solicitation, "do u want ur clamz doubled?" When the person responded positively, bluwave directed the person to Trade Room 49, then went there herself. A couple minutes later the person arrived and bluwave directed the Whyvillian to put all of his/her clams up for trade "put up ur clamz plz" then said to press "agree" when she left her chair. Bluwave then left her chair ("leave") and immediately went to check the result of the trade ("tradeResult"), checked her ymail and looked at someone's profile on City Records (perhaps her victim's?), then checked her bank statement. Because there was a trade result, we know the trade went through. That bluwave checked her bank statement afterward is another confirmation that she successfully obtained the Whyvillian's clams. She continued for a few more days and then all scamming stopped.

Scams are not infrequent on Whyville, though they are strongly discouraged and warned against by both the designers and local citizens. Along the range of cheating practices in Whyville, from making guides for science games to identity theft (stealing people's passwords and accounts), scams are on the unethical and fraudulent side and certainly not publicly condoned (Fields & Kafai, 2010b). There are regular ymail warnings against giving out one's password and newspaper articles alerting citizens to the latest clever innovations in scamming. In some ways, Zoe's scamming could be seen as part of her efforts to be an insider on Whyville and in one sense it demonstrates her growing expertise in Whyville. She was a victim and then became a perpetrator; she imitated the practices of others in an effort to become rich (a common value in Whyville). It is also one other way that her Whyville life was tied to her frequenting of the Trading Post and her interests in the financial opportunities in Whyville.

Not surprisingly, it is not something she discussed in her interview at the end of the after-school club. She did acknowledge in the interview that she had a few other Whyville accounts – a common way to earn more clams on Whyville (the second author even did this to earn enough for her first Whyville car), though she did not describe the way that she persistently begged people to give her accounts that already had high salaries – an activity she carried out about the same time that she began scamming people. Both of these activities – seeking multiple Whyville accounts and scamming others – are indications of bluwave's move toward being a Whyville insider, building up experiences with practices that were common on the site, including scamming. But her adoption of the questionable practice of scamming was also temporary, lasting only two weeks within our six-months time period of observation. With help of the log files we were able to capture these hidden aspects of her online participation.

7. CONNECTING ACTIVITIES ACROSS SPACES

There are two reasons why we chose to study the teleporting practice. First, it was a secret, insider practice important to socializing on Whyville that could only be learned from another player. This meant that we could study the spread of teleporting as a form of socially shared knowledge, as a way to observe kids helping other kids learn to be a part of Whyville. At the time of our study, most places in Whyville were easy to access by means of the "Destination Menu" which citizens pull down, scroll through, then click on a specific location (such as the Beach). However, some of the more popular places in which to socialize were not visible to players in the menus available on the site: Earth, Moon, Mars, Jupiter, and Saturn. Because these sites were not listed in any written records on Whyville, the only way to discover them was from other people. The only exception to this can be found on some cheat sites where instructions on teleporting are included on "tips" for newbies [9]. Therefore, these teleporting destinations came to represent insider status and many players prized them as social hangouts because they were not overcrowded or overpopulated by "newbies," or players new to Whyville. Second, because teleporting is accomplished by typing a specific command, "teleport moon" (or "teleport [place]"), each teleport action is visible in the chat records that are part of the log files we collected. We can easily search for the occasions when the word "teleport" was typed and find each time a participant teleported.

Once we identified teleporting as a practice to study (a process that involved significant immersion in the data), we conducted different kinds of analyses. After an initial coding of the field notes and logging of the video data, we combed both types of data for any mention of teleporting or the places to which one can teleport. Whenever teleporting was mentioned in either source it was highlighted and/or transcribed. Similarly, the online tracking data was searched for the first time players teleported, and the first time they teleported to Saturn, since that place was not commonly known early in the club. This was done by selecting out club members' chat data from the larger database and searching for those times they typed "teleport" in their chat. This data allowed us to identify the first time each player teleported, even if they were logged on to Whyville from home, and whether they sought any online help. After these incidents of teleporting were identified from all of the data, we organized them into a timeline to coordinate when and how players learned to teleport. We then further analyzed both the online log files and the video data to flesh out the context(s) in which players discovered that teleporting existed and was an option for them. Through this process we were able to compile a more complete picture of how and where club members learned to teleport than if we had not had access to these multiple data sources.

Teleporting may be the least obvious insider knowledge since one cannot observe it in others' chat (the typed command "teleport moon" is not visible to others) unless people are publicly discussing the command option during a social gathering. Out of 39,673 lines of chat data from club members, 2372 (5.98%) were instances when the word "teleport" was used. By searching through this online chat data, we were able to determine when each club member first teleported (see Table 3). This formed the basis of further investigations into from whom, how, and where participants learned to teleport.

Table 3: First Teleports

Username	Name	Date	Time	Whyville	Physical
fairi60	Kaitlyn	Jan 3	1:41:32 p.m.	Nutrition Counter	Home
whskr29	Briana	Jan 7	1:29:37 p.m.	Whyville Square	Class
WOW4	Gabe	Jan 10	8:20:11 a.m.	Leila Patio	Class
bluwave	Zoe	Jan 13	3:25:41 p.m.	Sector Y	Club
sharky404	Kyle	Jan 14	10:44:30 a.m.	Beach	Class
masher47	Aidan	Jan 19	11:56:52 a.m.	Warp Tarmac	Class
raybeams	Blake	Jan 24	7:20:28 p.m.	Bazaar	Home
stngray09	Trevor	Jan 24	3:57:33 p.m.	Beach	Club
zink	Bryce	Jan 25	4:08:34 p.m.	Taxi	Club
leo95	Cole	Jan 28	3:45:44 p.m.	Courtyard	Home
ivy06	Isabel	Jan 31	4:01:32 p.m.	Beach	Club
betelguice	Paolo	Feb 1	3:43:18 p.m.	Spin Geek	Club
vulcan61	Brad	Feb 2	9:24:44 p.m.	Beach	Home
sirius	Scott	Feb 2	3:38:06 p.m.	LeilaPatio	Club
amarylys	Jill	Feb 3	3:30:12 p.m.	Mall Fountain	Club
Peachy5	Leslie	Feb 3	4:54:22 p.m.	Beach	Home
funster	Paul	Feb 8	3:58:41 p.m.	Checkers	Club
Lucky7	Marissa	Feb 16	3:59:54 p.m.	Main Page	Club
violet5	Ulani	Feb 16	4:08:03 p.m.	Main Page	Club
BluSwirls 93	Molly	Mar 3	3:50:35 p.m.	Beach	Club
bloofer	Paige		*never teleported*		

The broad trends of teleporting activity reported in Table 3 reveal two interesting things. First, Table 3 maps out the most basic order in which club members first teleported – and that all but one of the club members (named "bloofers") did learn to teleport, a finding that should not be dismissed. Second, it begins to take into account the multiple spaces that tweens occupied in the club and Whyville. We can already see from this table that learning to teleport took place in a range of locations and differed between the club members. Indeed, the table points to the need to expand beyond the club and Whyville to take into account both the sixth-grade classes where some club members played on Whyville and implied home space.

However, when we refocus our research lens to look at individual trajectories of learning to teleport, we will see that this table is vastly oversimplified. Learning to teleport did not take place at a single second in time, though it may have been recorded that way in chat data. Further, the word-search capability of tracking data does not even begin to make use of the potential of information embedded in those logs. This identification of time points of first teleports for the club members was an essential beginning step in tracing individual trajectories of learning this insider practice (for more detail see [9]). As a case in point, Isabel, a fourth-grade club participant (9 years old) provides yet another initial context for the start of a trajectory to learning the insider practice of teleporting, this time in the after-school club. From Table 1, we can see that Isabel first teleported on Monday, January 31, while in the club. Or did she? When we took into account the combined field notes, video, and logfiles surrounding the time of her teleporting, we came to a different conclusion.

On Jan. 31, the video data show that Blake yelled across the room to Cole, telling him to meet him at the Moon. While it is apparent from the field notes that Cole was in the room with Isabel and logged on to her computer not long after Blake's call, the online tracking data show that Isabel (ivy06) teleported to the moon directly after Blake called to Cole, then gossiped to someone on Whyville that Cole (leo95) was "hot." The table below is a shortened version of the event that shows what we were able to glean about the incident from the three primary types of data (see Table 4).

Table 4: Connecting Data Sources for January 31

FIELD NOTES	VIDEO DATA	ONLINE CHAT RECORDS	ANNOTATION
~3:45pm Cole visits with Isabel, telling her about a girl who sent him a ymail. He types the girl's username on Isabel's computer so she knows what the girl looks like.	Blake: Cole! Meet me at the Moon!" Cole: Hang on! *((far away))*:		*Cole is at Isabel's computer showing her a girl he had flirted with.* *Blake urgently tells Cole to go to the Moon,*
		4:01:32pm ivy06 teleport moon	*Cole types in "teleport moon" on Isabel's computer.*
~4:00pm Cole asks Isabel to log off so he can use the computer			*Isabel sees the girl Cole pointed out earlier and whispers to her.*
		4:02:38pm ivy06 leo95 says that u are hott	*Isabel logs off and Cole logs on to her computer*

This incident explains Isabel's effort to learn how to teleport on the following day. It seems apparent that Cole either gave her direct instructions or typed "teleport moon" on her computer while she was logged on because the next day during club she tried to teleport but did it incorrectly a number of times and asked Whyvillians several times how to get to the Moon:

3:13 p.m.	ivy06	Beach	go to moon
	ivy06	Beach	do u now how to go to the moon?
3:14 p.m.	ivy06	Beach	how?
	ivy06	Beach	teleport mars
3:15 p.m.	ivy06	Mars	teleoport moon
3:16 p.m.	ivy06	Mars	teleoport moon
...			
3:17 p.m.	ivy06	Beach	no how to go to moon?
3:24 p.m.	ivy06	Beach	how do u go to the moon?

Isabel eventually learned how to teleport consistently to Mars and the Moon, because on the following dates her tracking data show a typical club member pattern of teleporting from one location to the next in rapid succession (teleport Mars, teleport Moon, teleport Earth) while on Whyville. Interestingly, while Isabel saw the Moon and chatted with someone there on Jan. 31, in her interview she said that she learned how to teleport from people at Whyville. Other members of the club received mixed instruction on teleporting from youth physically present in the club and from club members virtually present on Whyville.

8. Discussion

The purpose of our paper was to illustrate additional approaches to analyzing log file data beyond the traditional quantitative summaries of pages viewed or sites visited and to go beyond traditional ethnographic observation. We did some of the traditional data aggregations too in order to illustrate how these additional analyses can provide new insights into player participation. Most commercial games or virtual worlds do not lend themselves to large log file or chat data gathering by independent researchers, and the companies who develop them regard any large database of virtual activities as proprietary information, making such data difficult to access. Our study is an exception to this rule, as the creators of the virtual world of our study, Whyville.net, allowed us access to the entire body of log file data for participating tweens who gave signed permission.

Arguably, our analyses of a practice and a person were conducted through both direct and indirect means. Strategic choices allowed us to leverage the record-keeping facility of log files to focus our multimodal analysis on particular time points. This analytic technique responded to growing concerns to understand participants' learning across multiple spaces and practices. The analyses clearly demonstrated that a focus solely on the after-school club space and on any one data source would have limited our understanding of when and how players came to learn about teleporting or how Zoe/bluwave engaged in very different trading/scamming practices in the Trading Post. One contribution provided by our study is to showcase how the integration or connection of multiple data sources in our analysis allowed for a "thicker description", to use Geertz's term [13], of how young players learned a particular practice and ways of being in a virtual world.

While documenting and analyzing club members' learning of teleporting and Zoe/bluwave's trading practices in this way illuminated many aspects of players' participation in ways that were hidden to us before, our approach to the qualitative analyses of log file data is far from omniscient. First, reading the logs was often like listening to a one-sided telephone conversation because only consenting players' log files and chat were recorded and available for our analysis. We are left to guess at what others were saying, and when they switched from talking from one person to another. Occasionally if we thought they were with someone else participating in the study from school, we would look at that specific moment in time and sort by usernames from school participants, isolating the people in the same virtual room with them and documenting a fuller conversation. However this was rare.

Second, we do not have all of the club members' online data. For instance we do not have screenshots or spatial records of their movements within particular spaces on Whyville. As one might imagine, avatars move around in Whyville, and much can be signified by relative proximity. Many people move next to each other when whispering on Whyville, embodying the closeness of a private conversation. We also did not collect ymails (the email in Whyville) because these were deemed to be more personal than live chat. This means that we cannot document who they might have ymailed, how often they ymailed specific individuals, or the content of ymails. While we know how much time they spent ymailing and can often guess who they ymailed based on the order of activities (talking to someone, saying they would ymail him/her, and going immediately to ymail), we have very limited knowledge of this practice that leant itself to more enduring relationships (ymail is generally used to keep in touch with already established friends – it does not depend on finding someone live on Whyville).

Finally, these were analyses of one particular practice and one particular girl player in a particular virtual world for a limited amount of time (six months) at a certain period of time in the development of that virtual world. We chose two different perspectives, practice and person, in our analyses of logfiles for an additional view on their developments. In future steps, we're planning to examine other practices and more cases to validate this qualitative approach to logfile analysis. We have already taken first steps into this direction by choosing a more complex practice such as projectile throwing [10] for analysis. Projectile throwing is also traceable in chat but is more complex because it involves multiple actions such as purchasing and selecting projectiles and different ways and contexts of using them. We also created five other case studies to get a better sense of individuals' different trajectories in virtual worlds [25]. In addition, we have analyzed the log files to capture social practices such as flirting and dating that are not tied to particular commands (as teleporting and projectile throwing are) but to a different discourse in chat and whisper [14]. These further applications will provide us with a better understanding of how fruitful this type of log file analysis can be. In the end, we understand that even adding more data sources will not solve a fundamental conundrum of all research – to account as fully as possible about events, activities, and players in communities. But we advocate considering multiple data sources and even considering different ways of how to analyze them. As we demonstrated in this paper, there is more than one way to look at log files.

9. ACKNOWLEDGMENTS

The data collection for this case study was supported by a grant of the National Science Foundation (NSF-0411814) and the analyses and writings in part by a grant of the MacArthur Foundation to the first author. The views expressed are those of the authors and do not necessarily represent the views of National Science Foundation, the MacArthur Foundation, the University of Pennsylvania, Utah State University or Numedeon. Numedeon, Inc., the company that owns and hosts Whyville.net, had no control over the publication of the results. The authors have no financial interest or any other official relationship with Numedeon, Inc. We appreciated Numedeon's willingness to cooperate in the research studies and to provide access to their log file data. Special thanks also to Michael Giang who taught us how to use SPSS to sort through log files and Cameron Aroz, Tina Tom, and Kristin Searle who assisted in reducing the clicks and chat to first minute-by-minute and finally daily summaries.

10. REFERENCES

[1] Barker, R. G. & Wright, H. F. (1951). *One Boy's Day*. New York: Harper.

[2] Boellstorff, T. (2008). Coming of age in second life: An anthropologist explores the virtually human. Princeton, NJ: Princeton University Press.

[3] Bruckman, A. (2006). Analysis of Log File Data to Understand Behavior and Learning in an Online Community. In Joel Weiss, Jason Nolan, Jeremy Hunsinger, and Peter Trifonas (Eds.), *International Handbook of Virtual Learning Environments* (pp.1449-1465). New York: Springer

[4] Bruckman, A. (2000). Situated support for learning: Storm's weekend with Rachael. *Journal of the Learning Sciences, 9*(3), 329-372.

[5] Castronova, E. (2005). *Synthetic worlds: The business and pleasure of gaming*. Chicago: Chicago University Press.

[6] Clarke, J. & Dede, C. (2007). MUVEs as a powerful means to study situated learning. In C. Chinn, G. Erkins, and S. Puntambekar (Eds.), *The proceedings of CSCL 2007: Of mice, minds and society*. New Brunswick, NJ, USA.

[7] Ducheneaut, N., Yee, N., Nickell, E., Moore, R. (2006). Building an MMO with Mass Appeal: A Look at Gameplay in World of Warcraft. *Games and Culture*, 1, 281-317.

[8] Feldon, D. F., & Kafai, Y.B. (2008). Mixed methods for mixed reality: Overcoming methodological challenges to understand user activity in a massive multi-user virtual environment. *Educational Technology Research and Development*, *56*(5&6), 575-593.

[9] Fields, D. A. & Kafai, Y. B. (2009). A connective ethnography of peer knowledge sharing and diffusion in a tween virtual world. *International Journal of Computer Supported Collaborative Learning* , *4*(1), 47-68.

[10] Fields, D. A. & Kafai, Y. B. (2010a). Knowing and throwing mudballs, hearts, pies, and flowers: A connective ethnography of gaming practices. *Games and Culture,* (Special Issue), 5(1), 88-115.

[11] Fields, D. A. & Kafai, Y. B. (2010b). Stealing from Grandma or generating knowledge? Contestations and effects of cheating in Whyville. *Games and Culture,* (Special Issue), 5(1), 64-87.

[12] Fields, D. A. & Kafai, Y. B. (2012). Navigating life as an avatar: The shifting identities-in-practice of a girl player in a tween virtual world. In C. C. Ching & B. Foley (Eds.), *Constructing identity in a digital world*, Cambridge, UK: Cambridge University Press, 222-250.

[13] Geertz, C. (1973). The interpretation of cultures: Selected essays. New York: Basic Books.

[14] Giang, M. T., Kafai, Y. B., Fields, D. A., & Searle, K. A. (2012). Social interactions in virtual worlds: Patterns and participation of tween relationship play. In Johannes Fromme & Alexander Unger (Eds.), *Computer games/player/game cultures: A handbook on the state and perspectives of digital games studies (pp. 543-556).* New York: Springer Verlag.

[15] Grimes, S. & Fields, D. (2012). *Kids online: A new research agenda for understanding social networking forums.* New York. The Joan Ganz Cooney Center at Sesame Workshop.

[16] Jenkins, H. (2006). *Convergence culture: Where old and new media collide.* New York and London: New York University Press.

[17] Kafai, Y. B. (2008). Gender play in a tween gaming club. In Y. B. Kafai, C. Heeter, J. Denner & J. Sun (Eds.), *Beyond Barbie and Mortal Kombat*. Cambridge, MA: MIT Press.

[18] Kafai, Y. B., Cook, M. S., & Fields, D. A. (2010). "Blacks deserve bodies too!" Design and discussion about diversity and race in a tween virtual world. *Games and Culture*, 5(1), 43-63.

[19] Kafai, Y., Feldon, D., Fields, D. A., Giang, M., & Quintero, M. (2007). *Life in the time of Whypox: A virtual epidemic as a community event.* In C. Steinfeld, B. Pentland, M. Ackerman, & N. Contractor (Eds.) *Communities and Technologies* (pp. 171-190). Berlin: Spring Verlag.

[20] Kafai, Y. B., Fields, D. A., & Cook, M. S. (2007). Your second selves: Avatar designs and identity play. *Games and Culture,* 5(1), 23-42.

[21] Kafai, Y. B. & Giang, M. (2007). Virtual playgrounds. In T. Willoughby & E. Wood (Eds.), *Children's Learning in a Digital World* (pp. 196-217). Oxford: Blackwell Publishing.

[22] Leander, K. M., & McKim, K. K. (2003). Tracing the everyday 'sitings' of adolescents on the internet: A strategic adaptation of ethnography across online and offline spaces. *Education, Communication, Information, 3*(2), 211-240.

[23] Leander, K. M., Phillips, N., C. & Taylor, K. H. (2010). The changing social spaces of learning: Mapping new mobilities. *Review of Research in Education*, 34, 329-394.

[24] Nardi, B. A., Ly, S., & Harris, J. (2007). Learning conversation in World of Warcraft. *Proceedings, HICSS.*

[25] Searle, K. A. & Kafai, Y. B. (in press). Beyond freedom of movement: Boys play in a tween virtual world. *Games & Culture.*

[26] Taylor, T. L. (2006). *Play between worlds*. Cambridge: MIT Press.

[27] Williams, D. (2005). Bridging the methodological divide in game research. *Simulation & Gaming, 36*(4), 1-17.

[28] Williams, D., N. Yee & S. Caplan (2008). Who plays, how much, and why? Debunking the stereotypical gamer profile. *Journal of Computer Mediated Communication, 13*(4), 993-1028.

Gestures as Point Clouds: A $P Recognizer for User Interface Prototypes

Radu-Daniel Vatavu
University Stefan cel Mare of Suceava
Suceava 720229, Romania
vatavu@eed.usv.ro

Lisa Anthony
UMBC Information Systems
1000 Hilltop Circle
Baltimore MD 21250
lanthony@umbc.edu

Jacob O. Wobbrock
Information School | DUB Group
University of Washington
Seattle, WA 98195-2840 USA
wobbrock@uw.edu

ABSTRACT

Rapid prototyping of gesture interaction for emerging touch platforms requires that developers have access to fast, simple, and accurate gesture recognition approaches. The $-family of recognizers ($1, $N) addresses this need, but the current most advanced of these, $N-Protractor, has significant memory and execution costs due to its combinatoric gesture representation approach. We present $P, a new member of the $-family, that remedies this limitation by considering gestures as clouds of points. $P performs similarly to $1 on unistrokes and is superior to $N on multistrokes. Specifically, $P delivers >99% accuracy in user-dependent testing with 5+ training samples per gesture type and stays above 99% for user-independent tests when using data from 10 participants. We provide a pseudocode listing of $P to assist developers in porting it to their specific platform and a "cheat sheet" to aid developers in selecting the best member of the $-family for their specific application needs.

Categories and Subject Descriptors

H.5.2 [**Information Interfaces and Presentation**]: User Interfaces—*Input devices and strategies*; I.5.2 [**Pattern Recognition**]: Design Methodology—*Classifier design and evaluation*

General Terms

Algorithms, Experimentation, Performance

Keywords

Gesture recognition, point clouds, comparing classifiers, multistrokes, Euclidean, Hausdorff, Hungarian, $P, $1, $N.

1. INTRODUCTION

The currently increasing mainstream use and adoption of touch input devices like the iPad, iPhone, and Microsoft Surface, along with the surge in touch-based app development, fosters a rising need for tools to support development for such platforms. New applications may require gesture recognition tailored to new gestures that are simply not built into existing software.

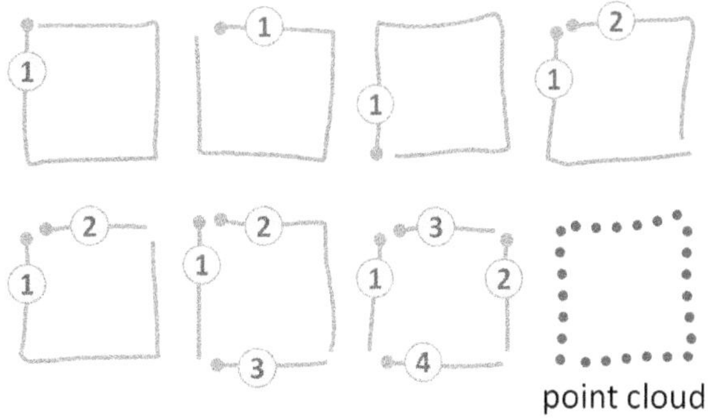

Figure 1: Even a simple square can be drawn using 1, 2, 3, or 4 strokes which can vary in order and direction (with a total of 442 possible cases). However, all the articulation details are ignored when looking at the square as a time-free cloud of points.

State-of-the-art gesture recognition techniques, such as Hidden Markov Models [19], feature-based statistical classifiers [17, 22], or mixture of classifiers [12], typically require significant technical knowledge to understand and develop them for new platforms, or knowledge from other fields such as graph theory [11]. Therefore, our growing body of work has been tackling this problem by proposing low-cost, easy to understand and implement, yet high performing, gesture recognition approaches [2, 3, 23]. These approaches, which we will call the $-family of techniques, involve only simple geometric computations and straightforward internal representations. Furthermore, the algorithms are highly accessible through the publication of pseudocode which developers may use for their own platforms. Indeed, both $1 and $N have experienced swift uptake with implementations available in JavaScript, C#, and Objective-C by third-party developers[1].

Yet the $-family approaches each have limitations. For example, $1 and Protractor only handle unistroke gestures [14, 23]. $N and $N-Protractor have focused on remedying this limitation, adding support for multistrokes [2, 3]. The $N approaches do so by treating multistrokes as unistrokes obtained by connecting individual strokes "in the air" [2], which enables them to use the same matching algorithm as $1. However, as stroke order and direction may differ among users drawing the same symbol (Figure 1), $N needs to generate all possible permutations of a given multistroke [2, 3], which causes an explosion in both memory and execution

[1] See "$1 implementations by others" at $1 homepage, http://depts.washington.edu/aimgroup/proj/dollar/

time for \$N and even for \$N-Protractor, albeit to a lesser extent. For example, a 2-stroke gesture such as an "X" has 8 permutations to represent, and a 4-stroke gesture such as a square has $4! \times 2^4 = 384$ different permutations. To support a cube, a symbol typically drawn with 9 strokes[2], the system must represent $9! \times 2^9 = 185{,}794{,}560$ permutations. This exceedingly high number poses a challenge for modern desktops, let alone mobile platforms. Although \$N uses run-time optimizations that reduce the number of comparisons to stored permutations [2], the cost of storing these permutations is currently its main limiting factor [3].

To address the aforementioned problems, we present our new approach, the \$P recognizer, which avoids the storage complexity of \$N by representing gestures as "clouds of Points" and thus ignoring variable user behavior in terms of stroke order and direction. Just like its predecessors \$1 [23] and \$N [2, 3], \$P yields high accuracy, low complexity, and low barriers to adoption (only 70 lines of code, 50% reusing \$1 code [23]). Experiments showed an average accuracy of 98% for \$P, which outperformed \$N in both user-dependent and user-independent testing[3]. Also, \$P delivered >99% accuracy in user-dependent testing with 5+ training samples per gesture and stayed above 99% for user-independent tests when using data from 10 participants.

The contributions of our work include: (1) a straightforward algorithm called \$P that represents and recognizes stroke gestures as point clouds; (2) an evaluation of \$P showing that it is more accurate and needs considerably less memory than \$N-Protractor [3]; and (3) a pseudocode listing for \$P to enable rapid uptake of this new member of the \$-family of stroke recognizers for user interface prototypes. Finally, to assist developers in selecting the most suitable classifier for their needs (\$1, \$N, \$P), we contribute a "cheat sheet" for the \$-family of recognizers highlighting the main similarities and differences among the family members.

2. RECOGNIZING POINT CLOUDS

Most limitations of the \$N recognizer come from reasoning about gestures in terms of a chronological order of drawn points, which enforces a predefined order for strokes and points within each stroke. In consequence, to retain user independence, \$N needs to permute and store gestures by stroke order and direction, which considerably affects the size of the training set [2, 3] and negatively impacts memory usage and system performance. However, such complications no longer apply when reasoning *outside* the gesture timeline. Discarding the timeline makes gestures appear as simple sets without any particular order associated to strokes or points: $\{p_i = (x_i, y_i) \mid i = 1..n\}$. Point p_i does not necessarily follow p_{i-1}, nor does it necessarily precede p_{i+1}. Point p_1 does not mark the starting point of the gesture nor is p_n its endpoint. Instead, gestures are seen as unordered sets, or what we call *clouds*, grouping points together. By adopting this time-free view of gestures, aspects such as the number of strokes, stroke ordering, and stroke direction become irrelevant. To make an analogy, such a diminished representation resembles the input of off-line optical character recognition systems that only use bitmaps delivered by an optical scanner [16].

[2]See http://embedded.eecs.berkeley.edu/research/hhreco/

[3]For conciseness, we use the term \$N to refer to the state of the art \$N, which is \$N-Protractor [3], an improved version over [2].

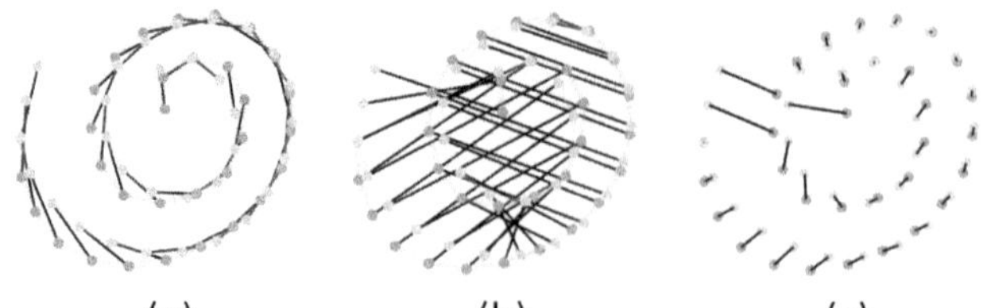

Figure 2: Point alignments for two *spiral* gestures. The time-ordered alignment performed by \$1 and \$N (a) fails when one of the *spirals* is simply drawn backwards (b) which is why \$N creates permutations of all stroke orders and directions in its training set. The time-free alignment of point clouds (c) ignores such execution details.

In order to better highlight the advantages of discarding the execution timeline, Figure 1 illustrates some of the many ways to draw a square. Drawing a square could be done via 1, 2, 3, or 4-stroke gestures with many variations for the individual strokes in terms of ordering and direction. Instead, when looking at the same gesture as a simple cloud of points with no time labels, all such execution details are hidden away into the final result. Indeed, just by looking at the point cloud of Figure 1, the reader cannot tell whether this is a unistroke or a multistroke gesture; whether it is composed of 2 or 3 strokes; or what the order and direction of strokes might be. We argue that the answers to these questions are not essential for recognizing the gesture, and in many cases they even complicate the structure of the recognizer [2] rather than helping with classification.

Once the gesture execution timeline has been discarded, the number of strokes, stroke ordering, and stroke direction become irrelevant. The task of the recognizer remains to match the point cloud of the candidate gesture (C) to the point cloud of each template (T) in the training set and compute a matching distance. In the tradition of the Nearest-Neighbor approach, the template located at the smallest distance from C delivers the classification result.

We define the matching between two point clouds C and T as a function $\mathcal{M}$ that associates each point $C_i \in C$ with exactly one point $T_j \in T$, $T_j = \mathcal{M}(C_i)$. If C and T have been both resampled[4] into the same number of points n, then the matching will also consist of exactly n pairs of points. Inspired by the Euclidean sum of \$1 [23] and the Proportional Shape Distance of SHARK[2] [13], we define the goodness of matching $\mathcal{M}$ as the sum of Euclidean distances for all the pairs of points from $\mathcal{M}$:

$$\sum_{i=1}^{n} \|C_i - T_j\| = \sum_{i=1}^{n} \sqrt{(C_i.x - T_j.x)^2 + (C_i.y - T_j.y)^2} \quad (1)$$

In this equation, j depends on i but, for ease of notation, we only iterate on i and discard additional notation formalisms by simply considering that point C_i from the first cloud was matched to point T_j from the second cloud by some matching algorithm implementing $\mathcal{M}$. Note that when j equals i (i.e., $\mathcal{M} = \{(C_i, T_i) \mid i = 1..n\}$), the formula becomes the Euclidean sum of the \$1 recognizer. Figure 2 illustrates the difference between time-ordered (a and b) and time-free point alignments (c).

[4]Resampling is a common practice in gesture preprocessing [2, 14, 20, 23] in order to uniformize input data for classifiers.

2.1 The Hungarian Gesture Recognizer

With these considerations, a point cloud recognizer needs to search for the minimum matching distance ("goodness") between C and T from all the $n!$ possible alignments. Actually, this represents a well-known problem in combinatorial optimization which is called the *Assignment Problem* [6]:

> There are n men and n jobs for which we know the cost of assigning man i to job j. Assign all men to jobs so that each man gets only one job and the total cost of assignments is minimum (p. 5).

The Assignment Problem is one that has been solved in graph theory [9]. Our matching problem can be easily translated into the formalism of graphs by constructing an undirected graph with $2n$ vertexes corresponding to the points of C and T and edges weighted by the Euclidean distances between these points. With this correspondence, the recognizer simply needs to solve the assignment problem on this constructed graph. In fact, the graph is a special case in which vertices are split into two sets so that edges only exist *between* and not *inside* the sets, which is known as a bipartite graph [7] (p. 1083). If we were to adhere strictly to graph theory, we would refer to our problem as finding the Minimum Weighted Matching in a bipartite graph, which is classically solved using the Hungarian algorithm [15].

Now that we have established that the problem of finding the best match between two point clouds can be represented as a problem from graph theory, we investigate the success of this approach in recognizing multistrokes. As we will show, the Hungarian algorithm delivers the ideal minimum-cost matching performance, but at a high time complexity ($O(n^3)$). We discuss approximation methods to reduce complexity of this approach, selecting the best one as our $P recognizer. For the rest of the paper, we refer to the Hungarian algorithm within the Nearest-Neighbor classification approach as the HUNGARIAN recognizer. As we only use the Hungarian algorithm as a reference for our $P recognizer, we refer the reader to [15] (p. 248) for more details.

2.2 Analysis of the Hungarian Recognizer

We first conducted a recognition experiment in order to understand the performance of the HUNGARIAN recognizer and to compare it with its main competitor, $N [2, 3]. Also, as the Euclidean [13], angular cosine (e.g., Protractor) [14], and dynamic time warping (DTW) [23] distances have been successfully used for gesture recognition before, we included these metrics into our experiment as well. The experiment was conducted in accordance with the practices of the domain [2, 14, 20, 23]. We ran all 5 recognizers on the $N multistroke set [2] which contains a total of 3,200 samples = 16 (gestures) × 20 (participants) × 10 (repetitions)[5].

Our experiment extends previous studies [2, 23] by reporting both user-dependent and user-independent recognition results. For the **user-dependent scenario**, recognition rates were computed individually for each participant. For each gesture type, T samples were randomly selected for training and 1 extra sample was additionally chosen for testing. This process was repeated 100 times for each value of T and results were averaged into a recognition rate per participant. The number of training samples per gesture T varied from 1 to 9. In the **user-independent scenario**, data from P participants was used for training while 1 additional participant

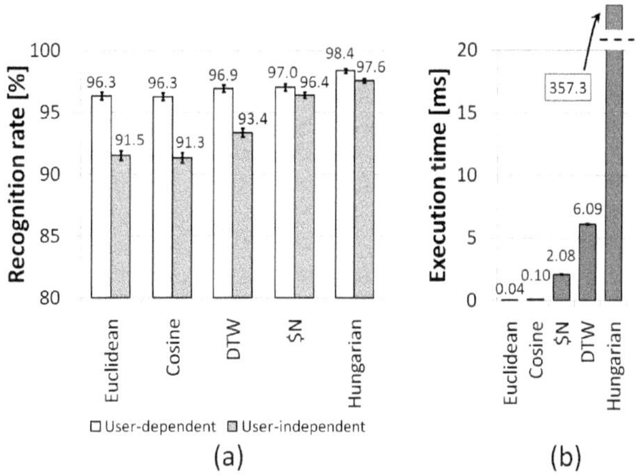

Figure 3: Performance of the Hungarian vs. competitor recognizers: (a) recognition rate; (b) execution time (for a training set of 16 gestures × 3 samples). Error bars show 95% CI.

User-dependent	User-independent
	19 values for P ×
20 participants ×	100 repetitions for each P[a]×
9 values for T[b] ×	9 values for T ×
100 repetitions for each T ×	100 repetitions for each T ×
5 recognizers ×	5 recognizers ×
16 gestures	16 gestures
≈ 1.5×10^6 recognition tests	≈ 1.4×10^8 recognition tests

[a] P represents the number of training participants (only applies to the user-independent scenario).
[b] T is the number of training samples per gesture type.

Table 1: Controlled variables for the Hungarian recognition experiment.

was randomly selected for testing. T samples were randomly selected for each gesture type from each training participant. One sample for each gesture type was selected from the testing participant and submitted for classification. The process was repeated 100 times for each P and 100 times for each T with $100 \times 100 = 10{,}000$ classification results averaging into a recognition rate depending on P and T. P varied from 1 to 19 and T from 1 to 9. As $N uses $n = 96$ sampling points [3], all recognizers used this resolution. We report recognition results from 1.5 $\times 10^6$ recognition tests for the user-dependent and 1.4 $\times 10^8$ tests for the user-independent scenario (see Table 1).

The HUNGARIAN recognizer delivered the best average recognition performance[6] for both user-dependent (98.4%) and user-independent (97.6%) testing. $N came next with 97.7% and 96.4% accuracy, followed by DTW with 96.9% and 93.4% for the two testing scenarios (Figure 3a). A Friedman test [10] showed a significant difference between the performance of all 5 recognizers for both user-dependent ($\chi^2(4) = 342.879$, $p < .001$) and user-indepedent testing ($\chi^2(4) = 3478.055$, $p < .001$). Post-hoc Wilcoxon signed-rank tests showed the HUNGARIAN recognizer outperforming $N significantly ($Z = -11.367$, $p < .001$) for both testing scenarios (with effect sizes $r < .15$).

[5] http://depts.washington.edu/aimgroup/proj/dollar/ndollar.html

[6] Averaged across all $T = 1..9$ and $P = 1..19$.

3. IN SEARCH OF A $-LIKE RECOGNIZER FOR POINT CLOUDS

Despite its very good performance on the multistroke gesture set, the HUNGARIAN recognizer hardly fits into the $-family paradigm of delivering simple and easy-to-use recognition tools for user interface prototypers. Quite the opposite of a $-like recognizer [2, 23], the HUNGARIAN algorithm employs advanced concepts such as feasible labelings, equality graphs, alternating paths, and alternating trees [15] (p. 248), along with graph representation and traversal techniques [7]. Even more, its $O(n^3)$ complexity is one order higher than DTW's $O(n^2)$ and two orders higher than the complexity of EUCLIDEAN and COSINE recognizers (both running in $O(n)$ time). As a result, running the HUNGARIAN algorithm to classify a candidate gesture against the multistroke set (16 gestures × 3 samples loaded) took 357 ms to complete (see Figure 3b) on an Intel® Core™ i5 2.27 GHz processor. This was 60 times slower than DTW (6.1 ms) and 3000 times slower than COSINE and EUCLIDEAN (both under 0.1 ms). Even the non-optimized $N-Protractor took only 2.0 ms to execute (due to the fast COSINE it employs [3, 14] and the number of permutations being low for this set). Therefore, a low-cost alternative to the HUNGARIAN algorithm is necessary for qualifying the point cloud matching approach as a $-recognizer.

Luckily, because the assignment problem is an important one with many implications [6], many approximation algorithms exist. They either rely on complex data structures [1] or on the use of greedy heuristics [4]. The fastest approximation for the Euclidean space is currently an algorithm from Agarwal and Varadarajan [1] with near linear time $O(n^{1+\epsilon})$ with $\epsilon \in (0, 1)$. However, in terms of trying to optimize conceptual complexity, the algorithm is even farther away from the $-paradigm than is the HUNGARIAN recognizer, as it relies on advanced data structures and tight upper bounds, hardly to be understood without considerable effort outside the algorithms research community. Another option is to use simple heuristics [4] that do not provide optimal alignment but are extremely simple to understand and implement. Therefore, such heuristics seem to be more in accordance with the $-paradigm of delivering simple recognizers.

Inspired by Avis [4] and the HUNGARIAN algorithm's inner workings, we implemented the following heuristics for matching clouds (which we named GREEDY-X with X=1..5):

❶ GREEDY-1. All the Euclidean distances between the n points of cloud C and the n points of cloud T are computed and sorted in ascending order. The first n pairs of points that can form a valid match are selected (each point is only used once). The complexity is $O(n^2 \times log(n))$ as the list needs to be sorted (using the quick sort algorithm).

❷ GREEDY-2. For each point in the first cloud (C_i), find the closest point from the second cloud that hasn't been matched yet. Once point C_i is matched, continue with C_{i+1} until all points from C are matched ($i = 1..n-1$). The complexity is $O(n^2)$ as for every point from C a linear search needs to be performed in T.

After having implemented this heuristic, we observed that the result varies with the order in which points C_i are selected from the first cloud. Therefore, we decided to run the algorithm multiple times with different starting points and return the minimum matching of all runs. If C_k is the starting point then:

$$\sum_i^n \|C_i - T_j\| = \sum_{i=k}^{n} \|C_i - T_j\| + \sum_{i=1}^{k-1} \|C_i - T_j\| \quad (2)$$

where i goes circularly through all points in C. We introduce a parameter ϵ to control the number of runs. If $\epsilon = 0$, GREEDY-2 runs once (for points $C_1, C_2, \ldots C_n$ in this order). If $\epsilon = 1$, the algorithm runs n times (with each point C_i getting the first chance to pair up). If $\epsilon < 1$ the algorithm runs for $n^\epsilon < n$ times. Using this formalism, the complexity of GREEDY-2 is easy to express as $O(n^{2+\epsilon})$ and lies between $O(n^2)$ and $O(n^3)$. As the HUNGARIAN delivers the result in $O(n^3)$, there is no point working with $\epsilon > 1$.

❸ GREEDY-3. Similar to GREEDY-2, except that the order in which points C_i are matched is randomized at each run. GREEDY-3 also needs $O(n^{2+\epsilon})$ time.

❹ GREEDY-4. Presumably difficult points from cloud C are matched first: a point C_i is more difficult to match if its sum of Euclidean distances to all the points in T is larger. This heuristic sorts the points from C in descending order by their total distance to T. Each point in C is then assigned the closest point from T similar to GREEDY-2. GREEDY-4 runs in $O(n^2)$.

❺ GREEDY-5. Similar to GREEDY-2, except the sum of Euclidean distances (eq. 2) contains weights:

$$\sum_i w_i \cdot \|C_i - T_j\| \quad (3)$$

Weights w_i encode the confidence in each pair (C_i, T_j) computed during the greedy run. The first match is weighted with $w_1 = 1.0$ (meaning high confidence) because we trust it: the first point has all the data in order to make a decision for its closest match. As the algorithm progresses, few options remain for the rest of the points from the first cloud when searching their closest pair into the second. Therefore, we can't trust these matches completely so we weight them with confidence values in [0..1]. For example, the last point to be matched has only one option (the last point from the second cloud that has been left unmatched) so the confidence in this alignment should also be small. We adopted a linear weighting scheme in which:

$$w_i = 1 - \frac{i-1}{n} \quad (4)$$

where $i = 1..n$ encodes the current step of the algorithm. GREEDY-5 also runs in $O(n^{2+\epsilon})$ time.

The results of GREEDY-X depend on the direction of matching (e.g., whether cloud C is matched to T or vice versa) so their implementations must return:

$$\min(\text{GREEDY-X}(C, T), \text{GREEDY-X}(T, C)) \quad (5)$$

This change affects the heuristics execution time but not their algorithmic complexities as discussed above.

Besides these heuristics, we note that Hausdorff distance [18] can also be interpreted as an approximation of the matching of two sets of points. Hausdorff computes the minimum Euclidean distance for each point from the first cloud to all the points in the second cloud and returns the maximum of these minimum distances. The distance is heavily used in computer vision for matching templates [18], and it has also been applied for recognizing hand sketches [12]. However, studies have expressed concerns on Hausdorff being

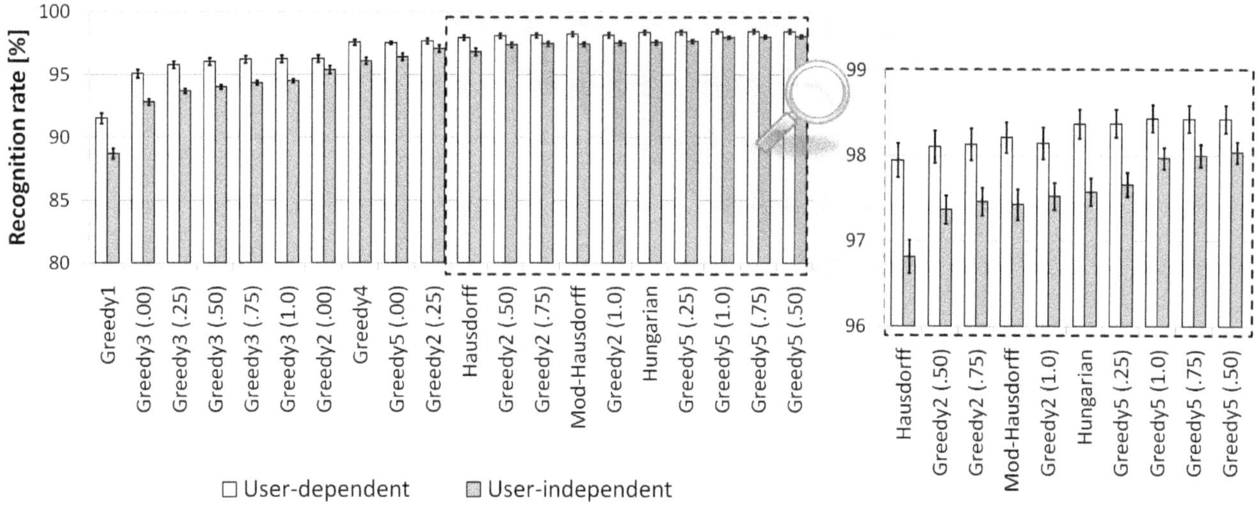

Figure 4: Recognition performance of greedy heuristics vs. the Hungarian. Note: recognizers are ordered on the horizontal axis by their average recognition performance. Error bars represent 95% CI.

too sensitive to outliers [18], which led to a variant called the Modified Hausdorff distance [8]. Due to the relevance of this previous work, we added both Hausdorff and the modified version to our list of heuristics:

❻ HAUSDORFF. Returns the maximum value of the minimum Euclidean distances computed for each point in C and every point from T [18]:

$$\max_{i=1..n} \min_{j=1..n} \|C_i - T_j\| \tag{6}$$

❼ MODIFIED-HAUSDORFF. Returns the average value of the minimum Euclidean distances computed for each point in C and every point from T [8]:

$$\frac{1}{n}\sum_{i=1}^{n} \min_{j=1..n} \|C_i - T_j\| \tag{7}$$

Both HAUSDORFFs are directional in the forms presented, so their implementations also need to consider both matching directions (C is matched to T and vice-versa). HAUSDORFFs are computed with $O(n^2)$ complexity.

3.1 Performance Analysis of Greedy-X

A second experiment was conducted in order to compare the recognition performance of the proposed heuristics. The goal of the experiment was to discover a good $-like recognizer candidate that would come as close as possible to the performance of the HUNGARIAN algorithm which implements the ideal behavior of the cloud point matching technique. We used the same gesture corpus and experiment design as in the first study. GREEDY-2, GREEDY-3, and GREEDY-5 were tested with $\epsilon \in \{0.00, 0.25, 0.50, 0.75, 1.0\}$ resulting in $5 + 5 + 5 = 15$ different recognizers. HAUSDORFF and MODIFIED-HAUSDORFF were also included in the experiment for comparison purposes. In total, we tested 19 heuristic recognizers (17 GREEDY-X and 2 HAUSDORFFs) and report results from 4.3×10^6 recognition tests for user-dependent and 4.1×10^8 tests for user-independent testing. Again, all gestures were resampled into $n = 96$ points. Figure 4 shows the recognition performance of all the 20 recognizers (the HUNGARIAN included for comparison).

User-dependent results. GREEDY-1 delivered the poorest performance with only 91.6% accuracy. It was followed by GREEDY-3 (all ϵ-versions) with the highest accuracy being 96.3% for $\epsilon = 1.0$. GREEDY-4 achieved 97.6% while almost all GREEDY-2 versions (except $\epsilon = .00$) stayed above 98%. Both HAUSDORFFs performed well with 98.0% accuracy. GREEDY-5 performed the best, staying above the HUNGARIAN (which delivered 98.4%). A Friedman test showed a significant difference between the recognition rates of all 20 recognizers ($\chi^2(19) = 10991.741$, $p < .001$).

GREEDY-2 (98.1% for $\epsilon = 0.5$, 0.75, and 1.0), MODIFIED-HAUSDORFF (98.2%), and GREEDY-5 (98.4% for ϵ=0.25, 0.5, 0.75, and 1.0) were the recognizers that came closest to the performance of HUNGARIAN (98.4%). Figure 4 shows a close up view for these heuristics. Follow-up Wilcoxon signed-rank tests were used to test differences between all these 8 recognizers and the HUNGARIAN (a Bonferroni correction was applied and effects are reported at $0.05/8 = 0.0063$ level of significance). The performance of HUNGARIAN was significantly different from that of GREEDY-2 and MODIFIED-HAUSDORFF (the effect size r stayed below .20). However, there was no significant difference in recognition between HUNGARIAN and the GREEDY-5 metrics ($\epsilon \geq .25$).

User-independent results. Results were similar for the user-independent testing. Again, GREEDY-1 had the worst performance with only 88.8% accuracy and it was followed by GREEDY-3 (<95%). GREEDY-4 achieved 96.1% while GREEDY-2 stayed above 97.1% for $\epsilon > 0$. The HAUSDORFF metrics delivered 96.8% and 97.4% accuracies. GREEDY-5 recognizers (98.4% for $\epsilon \geq 0.25$) stayed above the performance of the HUNGARIAN (which was 97.6%). A Friedman test confirmed a significant difference between all 20 recognizers ($\chi^2(19) = 32709.094$, $p < .001$). The same recognizers that performed well in user-dependent testing were also the ones that came closest to the performance of the HUNGARIAN for the user-independent scenario. GREEDY-2 achieved 97.4% for $\epsilon \geq 0.5$. MODIFIED-HAUSDORFF delivered 97.4%. GREEDY-5 managed to achieve 98% for $\epsilon = 1.0$. Post-hoc Wilcoxon signed-rank tests showed significant differences between all these 8 metrics and the HUNGARIAN (effect sizes r stayed below .20).

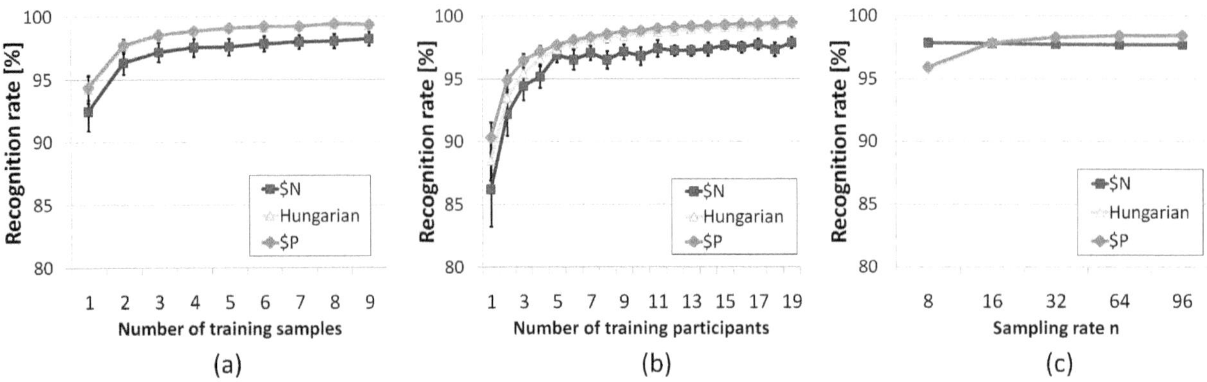

Figure 5: Recognition performance of $P vs. $N [2, 3] and Hungarian [15].

4. THE $P RECOGNIZER

Results obtained place GREEDY-5 as the best candidate for the $P recognizer. Recognition performance of GREEDY-5 running with $\epsilon \geq 0.50$ was not significantly different from that of HUNGARIAN for user-dependent tests (as confirmed by Wilcoxon tests). However, significant differences were detected between the two recognizers for user-independent testing, with GREEDY-5 exhibiting better performance. As the highest accuracy was found for $\epsilon = 0.50$, we denote GREEDY-5 (0.50) as the $P recognizer. Pseudocode for $P is listed in the appendix ($\approx$ 70 lines of code, out of which 50% reuse $1 code). We continue to analyze $P against its two main competitors: $N and HUNGARIAN.

Effect of number of training samples. Figure 5a shows the influence of the amount of training samples on $P's performance for user-dependent testing. $P reached 98.5% accuracy with $T = 3$ training samples per gesture type and stayed above 99% for $T \geq 5$ (with a maximum of 99.4%). The performance of HUNGARIAN was almost identical (the two lines practically overlap in the graph). $N delivered 97.8% performance with $T = 3$ samples and attained a maximum accuracy of 98.7% for $T = 9$.

Effect of number of training participants. For user-independent testing, we are interested in how many participants need to provide data samples for recognizers to deliver high performance for new users. $P achieved 90% recognition with data from just 1 training participant while $N delivered 86% and the HUNGARIAN 88% in the same conditions (see Figure 5b). Again, the performance of $P and HUNGARIAN were closely related, with $P showing slightly yet significantly higher rates. $P reached 97% with data from 4 participants only and stayed above 99% with 10 participants (with a maximum of 99.5%). $N needed data from 7 participants to reach 97% and stayed under 98% even when data from 19 participants was available for training.

Execution time. Recall that, aside from being a complex algorithm, the drawback of HUNGARIAN is large execution times (see Figure 3b). $P has $O(n^{2.5})$ complexity, and classifies a candidate gesture in just 32 ms, under the same conditions of Figure 3b[7]. This is 10 times faster than HUNGARIAN but still 15 times slower than $N. However, these times were measured for a sampling rate of $n = 96$ points as needed by $N to run optimally [2]. Recent work has shown the benefits of downsampling to speed-up execution time and reduce memory constraints [20, 21]. We suspected $P would exhibit similar behavior, and therefore we investigated its performance under various sampling rates. Figure 5c shows results obtained for sampling rate $n \in \{8, 16, 32, 64, 96\}$. $N delivered the same performance under all sampling rates (around 97.7%). $P and HUNGARIAN had a worse start with 96% for $n = 8$ points but delivered 98.3% starting with $n = 32$ points. Wilcoxon tests showed a significant but extremely small effect size $r = .04$ between $n = 32$ and $n = 96$ for $P. Changing n from 96 to 32 reduced the execution time of $P down to 5.5 ms from 32.0 ms.

[7]Classification of a candidate against a training set of 16 gestures with 3 loaded templates per gesture type.

5. DISCUSSION AND FUTURE WORK

What does the $P name mean? We decided to name our new recognizer $P for two reasons. First, we wanted to keep the $ in the name as it has come to denote a low-cost, easy to understand and implement recognizer, while the "P" comes from "Point clouds." Therefore, $P is a point-based recognizer instead of a stroke-based one, as are $1 (one stroke) and $N (N strokes). The second reason is motivated by a simple pun. $P was introduced as a low cost memory alternative to $N. As $N generates all permutations, it relates to NP class problems from complexity theory [7](p. 984). And by removing N from NP (as $P does not use the N strokes at all), we end with a single P in the name and achieve polynomial time complexity.

Performance on single-stroke gestures. Although $P was designed to alleviate $N's dependency on stroke permutations, it is not specific to multistrokes. $P can be run on unistroke gestures as well. Therefore, we tested $P on the 16 gestures of the $1 set [23]. This time, EUCLIDEAN ($1) would be its main competitor. $P achieved 99.3% for user-dependent and 96.6% for user-independent testing, similar to EUCLIDEAN's 99.5% and 97.1% performance.

Memory for storing the training set. As $P does not require permutations, the memory it needs to represent the training set T is linear with the size of the set, $O(T)$. This is similar to $1 and Protractor [14, 23]. In contrast, $N needs $O(T \times S! \times 2^S)$ memory where S represents the number of strokes in a multistroke. As shown in the introduction, the memory required by $N becomes quickly impractical (e.g., 185 million records for storing a 9-stroke cube).

Direction invariance. Due to its point cloud representation, $P is invariant to direction. This delivers freedom to designers and users but also means that clockwise and counterclockwise circles can't be discriminated. Future work can address this by reasoning on direction invariant stroke features derived from curvature [22] (p. 3310).

Criteria	\$1	Protractor	\$N	\$P
❶ Gesture types				
recognizes single strokes	✓	✓	✓	✓
recognizes multistrokes	×	×	✓	✓
is scale-invariant	✓	✓	✓	✓
is rotation-invariant	✓	can be	can be	×
is direction-invariant	×	×	✓	✓
❷ Performance				
user-dependent accuracy (single/multi-strokes)	99.5% / ×	99.4% / ×	98.0% / 97.7%	99.3% / 98.4%
user-independent accuracy (single/multi-strokes)	97.1% / ×	95.9% / ×	95.2% / 96.4%	96.6% / 98.0%
algorithmic complexity	$O(n \cdot T \cdot R)$	$O(n \cdot T)$	$O(n \cdot S! \cdot 2^S \cdot T)$	$O(n^{2.5} \cdot T)$
memory to store the training set	$O(n \cdot T)$	$O(n \cdot T)$	$O(n \cdot S! \cdot 2^S \cdot T)$	$O(n \cdot T)$
❸ Code writing				
needs rotation search (GSS)	yes ✍	no	no	no
needs writing filters to speed-up matching	no	no	yes ✍	no
approx. # of lines of code	100 ✍	50	200 ✍	70

[1] n is the number of sampled points; T = the number of training samples per gesture type; R = the number of iterations required by the Golden Section Search (GSS) algorithm used by \$1 (experimentally set to 10 [23]); S = the number of strokes in a multistroke; $S! \cdot 2^S$ = the number of different permutations of stroke ordering and direction needed by \$N [2].

[2] A ✍ symbol means more coding is required (e.g. GSS, filters, or simply more lines of code).

Table 2: Cheat sheet for the \$-family: \$1 [23], Protractor [14], \$N [2, 3], and \$P.

User behavior in producing multistrokes. An interesting finding was revealed while running the recognition tests on the EUCLIDEAN metric (see Figure 3a). EUCLIDEAN works by performing 1-to-1 associations between points ordered by their timeline. Therefore, users producing multistrokes in many different ways would confuse such a simple recognizer, which should exhibit low accuracy. However, the recognition rate of EUCLIDEAN was 96.3% on user-dependent and 91.5% on user-independent testing. The first value suggests that users are consistent in the way they input multistroke gestures (same order and direction of strokes). The user-independent result suggests that a high degree of consensus may exist between different users for the same gesture. We note for now the interesting aspect of this finding and leave the investigation of such user behaviour for future work.

Faster than $O(n^{2.5})$. In its current form which adheres to the simple implementation requirements of \$-recognizers, \$P needs $O(n^{2.5})$ time to produce a classification result. Although execution times are more than reasonable for a 2 GHz processor (as shown in the previous section), practitioners porting \$P to low resource devices may want faster versions. For such extreme cases, developers can opt for space partitioning structures such as k-d trees which deliver $O(n \times log(n))$ performance, similar to the accelerated Iterative Closest Point (ICP) registration technique [5].

Extension to 3D gestures. Due to its straightforward internal representation of gestures as point clouds, \$P can be easily extended to recognize 3D gestures simply by adding the z dimension. Future work will compare \$P against today's state-of-the-art 3D gesture recognizers.

Multistroke segmentation. Point cloud representations could be exploited to address the multistroke segmentation problem by formulating it as a cost minimization task usually solved with dynamic programming [7] (p. 323).

The designer's \$-family cheat sheet. \$P extends the \$-family [2, 3, 14, 23] by addressing existing limitations. Therefore, we provide practitioners a cheat sheet to inform which recognizer to use in their prototypes. Table 2 compares \$1, Protractor, \$N, and \$P on 3 criteria: gesture types, performance, and amount of code writing required.

6. CONCLUSION

We have demonstrated in this work that point clouds can be useful in reducing the time and space complexity of the \$N recognizer while still retaining a simple algorithm implementable in about 70 lines of code. Our resultant recognizer, \$P, extends the \$-family of recognizers with a low-cost, fast, accurate recognizer for rapidly prototyping interfaces requiring unistroke and multi-stroke recognition. \$P performs similarly to the \$1 recognizer on unistrokes and is superior to the \$N recognizer on multistrokes. It is our hope that \$P will be embraced as \$1 and \$N have been, and will aid in advancing the quality and speed of next-generation user interface prototypes.

7. ACKNOWLEDGMENTS

The authors would like to thank Isaac Simmons for implementation assistance on \$N testing procedures.

8. REFERENCES

[1] Agarwal, P., and Varadarajan, K. A near-linear constant-factor approximation for euclidean bipartite matching? In *SCG '04* (2004), 247–252.

[2] Anthony, L., and Wobbrock, J. O. A lightweight multistroke recognizer for user interface prototypes. In *GI '10* (2010), 245–252.

[3] Anthony, L., and Wobbrock, J. O. \$N-Protractor: A fast and accurate multistroke recognizer. In *GI'2012* (2012), 117–120.

[4] Avis, D. A survey of heuristics for the weighted matching problem. *Networks 13* (1983), 475–493.

[5] Besl, P. J., and McKay, N. D. A method for registration of 3-d shapes. *IEEE TPAMI 14*, 2 (Feb. 1992), 239–256.

[6] Burkard, R., Dell'Amico, M., and Martello, S. *Assignment Problems*. Society for Industrial and Applied Mathematics, Philadelphia, PA, USA, 2009.

[7] Cormen, T. H., Leiserson, C. E., Rivest, R. L., and Stein, C. *Introduction to algorithms*. MIT Press, Cambridge, MA, USA, 2001.

[8] Dubuisson, M.-P., and Jain, A. A modified Hausdorff distance for object matching. In *IAPR'94* (1994), 566–568.

[9] Edmonds, J. Paths, trees, and flowers. *Canad. J. Math. 17* (1965), 449–467.

[10] Friedman, M. The use of ranks to avoid the assumption of normality implicit in the analysis of variance. *J. Am. Statist. Assoc. 32*, 200 (1937), 675–701.

[11] Hammond, T., and Paulson, B. Recognizing sketched multistroke primitives. *ACM TIIS 1*, 1 (2011), 4:1–4:34.

[12] Kara, L. B., and Stahovich, T. F. Hierarchical parsing and recognition of hand-sketched diagrams. In *UIST '04* (2004), 13–22.

[13] Kristensson, P.-O., and Zhai, S. SHARK^2: a large vocabulary shorthand writing system for pen-based computers. In *UIST '04* (2004), 43–52.

[14] Li, Y. Protractor: a fast and accurate gesture recognizer. In *CHI '10* (2010), 2169–2172.

[15] Papadimitriou, C. H., and Steiglitz, K. *Combinatorial optimization: algorithms and complexity.* Dover Publications, Mineola, New York, USA, 1998.

[16] Plamondon, R., and Srihari, S. N. On-line and off-line handwriting recognition: A comprehensive survey. *IEEE TPAMI 22*, 1 (Jan. 2000), 63–84.

[17] Rubine, D. Specifying gestures by example. In *SIGGRAPH '91* (1991), 329–337.

[18] Rucklidge, W. *Efficient Visual Recognition Using the Hausdorff Distance.* Springer-Verlag New York, 1996.

[19] Sezgin, T. M., and Davis, R. HMM-based efficient sketch recognition. In *IUI '05* (2005), 281–283.

[20] Vatavu, R.-D. The effect of sampling rate on the performance of template-based gesture recognizers. In *ICMI '11* (2011), 271–278.

[21] Vatavu, R.-D. Small gestures go a long way: how many bits per gesture do recognizers actually need? In *DIS '12* (2012), 328–337.

[22] Willems, D., Niels, R., Gerven, M. v., and Vuurpijl, L. Iconic and multi-stroke gesture recognition. *Pattern Recognition 42*, 12, 3303–3312.

[23] Wobbrock, J. O., Wilson, A. D., and Li, Y. Gestures without libraries, toolkits or training: a $1 recognizer for user interface prototypes. In *UIST '07* (2007), 159–168.

APPENDIX

We provide complete pseudocode for $P. POINT is a structure that exposes x, y, and *strokeId* properties. *strokeId* is the stroke index a point belongs to (1, 2, ...) and is filled by counting pen down/up events. POINTS is a list of points and TEMPLATES a list of POINTS with gesture class data.

```
$P-RECOGNIZER (POINTS points, TEMPLATES templates)
n ← 32
NORMALIZE(points, n)
score ← ∞
for each template in templates do
    NORMALIZE(template, n) // should be pre-processed
    d ← GREEDY-CLOUD-MATCH(points, template, n)
    if score > d then
        score ← d
        result ← template
return ⟨result, score⟩
```

```
GREEDY-CLOUD-MATCH (POINTS points, POINTS template, int n)
ε ← .50
step ← ⌊n^(1−ε)⌋
min ← ∞
for i = 0 to n − 1 step step do
    d1 ← CLOUD-DISTANCE(points, template, n, i)
    d2 ← CLOUD-DISTANCE(template, points, n, i)
    min ← MIN(min, d1, d2)
return min
```

```
CLOUD-DISTANCE (POINTS points, POINTS tmpl, int n, int start)
matched ← new bool[n]
sum ← 0
i ← start // start matching with points_i
do
    min ← ∞
    for each j such that not matched[j] do
        d ← EUCLIDEAN-DISTANCE(points_i, tmpl_j)
        if d < min then
            min ← d
            index ← j
    matched[index] ← true
    weight ← 1 − ((i − start + n) MOD n)/n
    sum ← sum + weight · min
    i ← (i + 1) MOD n
until i == start // all points are processed
return sum
```

```
NORMALIZE (POINTS points, int n)
points ← RESAMPLE(points, n)
SCALE(points)
TRANSLATE-TO-ORIGIN(points, n)
```

The following pseudocode addresses gesture preprocessing (or normalization) which includes resampling, scaling with shape preservation, and translation to origin. The code is similar to $1 [23] and $N [2, 3] and we repeat it here for completeness. We highlight two minor changes only.

```
RESAMPLE (POINTS points, int n)
I ← PATH-LENGTH(points) / (n − 1)
D ← 0
newPoints ← points_0
for each p_i in points such that i ≥ 1 do
    if p_i.strokeId == p_{i−1}.strokeId then
        d ← EUCLIDEAN-DISTANCE(p_{i−1}, p_i)
        if (D + d) ≥ I then
            q.x ← p_{i−1}.x + ((I − D)/d) · (p_i.x - p_{i−1}.x)
            q.y ← p_{i−1}.y + ((I − D)/d) · (p_i.y - p_{i−1}.y)
            APPEND(newPoints, q)
            INSERT(points, i, q) // q will be the next p_i
            D ← 0
        else D ← D + d
return newPoints
```

```
PATH-LENGTH (POINTS points)
d ← 0
for each p_i in points such that i ≥ 1 do
    if p_i.strokeId == p_{i−1}.strokeId then
        d ← d + EUCLIDEAN-DISTANCE(p_{i−1}, p_i)
return d
```

```
SCALE (POINTS points)
x_min ← ∞, x_max ← 0, y_min ← ∞, y_max ← 0
for each p in points do
    x_min ← MIN(x_min, p.x)
    y_min ← MIN(y_min, p.y)
    x_max ← MAX(x_max, p.x)
    y_max ← MAX(y_max, p.y)
scale ← MAX(x_max − x_min, y_max − y_min)
for each p in points do
    p ← ((p.x − x_min)/scale, (p.y − y_min)/scale)
```

```
TRANSLATE-TO-ORIGIN (POINTS points, int n)
c ← (0, 0) // will contain centroid
for each p in points do
    c ← (c.x + p.x, c.y + p.y)
c ← (c.x/n, c.y/n)
for each p in points do
    p ← (p.x - c.x, p.y - c.y)
```

Influencing Gestural Representation of Eventualities: Insights from Ontology

Magdalena Lis
Centre for Language Technology
University of Copenhagen
Njalsgade 140, 2300 Copenhagen, Denmark
magdalena@hum.ku.dk

ABSTRACT

In the present paper we report results of a pilot study on the verbal and gestural representation of eventualities. We investigate the relationship between eventuality characteristics, as reflected in linguistic categorizations of verbs denoting the eventuality referred to, and physical form of co-speech gesture. Most importantly we look at whether referent's ontological type, information about which we derive from plWordNet 1.5, correlates to the viewpoint adopted in co-occuring gesture. Our results indicate a strong correlation between eventuality type and gestural viewpoint and are the first step towards a model of gestural behaviour planning driven by referents' types as reflected in speech and categorized in linguistic ontologies.

Categories and Subject Descriptors

E.m [**Data**]: Miscellaneous

General Terms

Human Factors

Keywords

Gesture, Speech, Reference, Ontology

1. MOTIVATION

People spontaneously gesture when they speak. Co-speech gestures are meaningful body movements which are temporally, pragmatically and semantically tightly integrated with concurrent speech [11, 19]. The multimodal speech-gesture ensembles together express one underlying concept; however, each modality has its affordances and limitations and so conveys aspects of the common meaning in its own way [19, 20]. Those co-speech gestures the form of which corresponds to physical characteristics of the referent are called iconic gestures [20]. Although iconic mapping is their primary motivation, it is not enough to on itself fully explain the gesture's form. Every representation is by its nature partial and from the whole concept to be conveyed it can within one unit (a sentence, a gesture, etc.) represent only some aspects of that referent [4]; metonymy has been found to be one of the main driving forces for meaning creation in gesture [21]. One and the same referent can be in gesture represented in various ways, by referring to its different aspects or presenting it from different perspectives. For instance, to refer to a cup of tea the gesturer can draw its shape in the air, point to the cup's location or mime an action of holding or drinking, to refer to an eventuality of e.g. climbing, he can draw the path of an upward movement or alternatingly flap his hands showing the manner of the motion. Which aspects are chosen to be depicted in gesture and how is a referent eventually represented - determines gesture's form. The issue why gestures take the particular form they do, is one of the most salient but still open questions in gesture research [14]. Finding the factors that influence gestural representation will not only enable us to better understand human communication patterns but is a prerequisite for building theoretical models of multimodal behaviour production. Such models are, in turn, needed for gesture generation for believable Embodied Conversational Agents (ECAs). Computational approaches to synthesizing multimodal communicative behaviour for ECAs can be modelled as two consecutive steps: planning (what and how to convey) and surface realization (conveying) [13]. Our work is concerned with the planning stage. In the present study, we investigate the issue of what influences gestural representation by focusing on reference to eventualities and examining eventuality characteristics as potential candidates. By eventualities we understand 'abstract entities with constitutive participants and with a constitutive relation to the temporal dimension' [25], that is entities like events, states, processes, etc. In language such state of affairs are denoted with verbs and in non-verbal behaviours they are represented by means of iconic gestures. Thus, on the level of speech our study focuses on verbs and on the level of bodily behaviours - on iconic gestures.

The theoretical framework for our work is given in the remaining part of this section. In section 2, we present our primary and secondary data. We report the results of our study in section 3 and discuss them in the following section, where directions for future research are also described. Finally, we conclude in the final section.

ICMI'12, October 22–26, 2012, Santa Monica, California, USA.

1.1 Previous research

Co-speech gestures are dependent on concurrent speech and a body of research has shown that gestural representation is strongly influenced by different aspects of co-occuring verbal utterance. However, recent studies have demonstrated how properties of the referent itself also determine gestural depiction. In a number of studies, Kopp and colleagues [13] examined non-verbal reference to landmarks in a direction-giving task. They have found that the way a landmark was portrayed gesturally was influenced by its spatial properties like number of sub-parts and symmetry axes. Recently, Poggi [24] has suggested that one of the steps in predicting gestural representation is not only to take into account perceivable features of the referent but also its "ontological type, that is, the type of semantic entity it constitutes." She has distinguished four types: artefacts, animates, natural objects and eventualities and claimed that different features of the referent are being chosen to be depicted in gesture depending on the referent's type. In her experiment, participants were asked to gesturally depict a number of lexemes. To represent an eventuality, all the participants mimed the behaviour described by the lexeme in question. However, it has been shown that to refer to an eventuality in a natural discourse, speakers use various representational formats by adopting different viewpoints. An eventuality can be presented in gesture from different perspectives, which reflect the distance the speaker adopts towards the eventuality: whether he takes on the perspective of an agent or of an observer. McNeill [2] distinguishes three viewpoints in iconic gestures:

- Character viewpoint (C_vpt) – an eventuality is shown from the perspective of the agent, gesturer re-enacts the behaviour of the agent, his hands stand for the agent's hands and mime his movements. The gesturer is inside the story
- Observer viewpoint (O_vpt) – the narrator looks at the story from a distance. He is not involved. He sees the eventuality as an observer. His hand stands for the agent himself as a whole
- Dual viewpoint (D_vpt) – gesturer presents the eventuality from two perspectives simultaneously, both Character and Observer one at the same time.

Parrill [22] claims that one of the factors influencing the choice of viewpoint is eventualities' structure. She argues that while linguistic and discursive factors also play a role in viewpoint selection, first eventuality properties should be taken into account. She proposes that eventualities which have trajectory as the more salient element - elicit O_vpt gesture, while eventualities in which handling is more prominent - tend to evoke C_vpt gestures. Moreover, for eventualities also a number of other phenomena were analyzed with relation to the form of the gesture. Duncan has studied the relationship between handedness and aspect of the verb [7]. Handedness regards which hand(s) performs the movement and, in case of bi-handed gestures, whether they mirror each other. Aspect concerns the eventualities' relation to time. Duncan's results indicate that symmetrical bi-handed gesture more often occur with perfective verbs than with imperfective ones; the latter are mostly accompanied by two handed non-symmetrical gestures. Aktionsart is a notion similar to, but discernible from, aspect. It refers to Vendler's [27] classification of eventualities into: States, Activities, Accomplishments and Achievements. A study on the relation between Aktionsart and gestural representation has been performed by Becker and colleagues [3]. They suggest that gestures which go with Achievement and Accomplishment verbs are completed, or repeated, on the goal of the verb. In case of gestures which accompany Activity verbs, the stroke coincides with the verb itself.

1.2 The present study

Our work rests upon the above-mentioned findings, combines and extends them. As Kopp and colleagues [13] we examine the relationship between gestural representation and referent's characteristics but while their work covered landmark descriptions, we focus on eventualities. The characteristics of the referent that we investigate is their ontological type, as suggested by Poggi [24]. We extend her findings by distinguishing different types among eventualities. In our classification of those types we adopt Parrill's [22] insights regarding eventuality structure, largely overlapping the two concepts. We formalize those insights by employing plWordNet1.5 [2] as an external source of information about eventualities' properties. Our work is focused on the analysis of the influence of eventuality type (as expressed in verbs classification in plWordNet) on gestural viewpoint. Moreover, we also analyse verbal and gestural features like verb class, handedness and iteration, following Duncan [7], Parrill and colleagues [23] and Becker and colleagues' [3] observations.

2. THE DATASET

2.1 The corpus

Our study was conducted on an enriched version of PCNC corpus. The corpus has been created by the DiaGest research group at the Adam Mickiewicz University [5]. It consists of audio-video recordings of 10 subjects performing a narration task. All subjects are adults and native Polish speakers and there is an even distribution between the sexes (5 man, 5 women). The data has been collected following the well-established McNeill's [19, 20] methodology - subjects were presented with a 6,5 minute long 'Canary Row' cartoon and asked to retell its content to an addressee they do not know. The cartoon shows unsuccessful attempts of the cat Sylvester to seize the bird Tweety. It abounds in eventualities and has proved to elicit rich verbal and bodily representation of them and as such it is perfectly suited for our purpose.

2.2 The annotation

DiaGest research group has transcribed and coded speech and gesture for various attributes. Those of DiaGest's annotations that we employ in our work include orthographic transcript of speech (with word time-stamps), annotation of gestures' internal structure (phrases and phases) and their dominating semiotic type (iconic, metaphoric, deictic and beat). DiaGest's coding of bodily behaviours has been carried out in ELAN [28] following McNeill and Duncan's scheme [19, 20]. For the purpose of our study, we enriched the corpus with further annotations. We imported ELAN transcripts into ANVIL [12], where our scheme was implemented and tested. In the paper we present a slightly modified version of our scheme described in more detail in [16].

2.2.1 *Speech*

Annotation was performed on the orthographic transcript. Since the focus was on representation of eventualities, the annotation concerned verbs.

2.2.1.1 *Wordnet.*

Ontology has to do with the symbolic representation of knowledge - it is 'a formal specification of a shared conceptualization' [10]. Wordnet is an example of a linguistic ontology. It views lexicon in terms of 'semantic fields that contain lexicalized concepts of conceptual fields' [1]. It is a large taxonomy, in which entities are classified into domains (fields) and relationships between them are described. This is achieved by grouping lexemes into sets of synonyms (synsets) and encoding conceptual-semantic and lexical relations between them [8]. Polish WordNet [2] is, as most of existing wordnets, largely based on the structure of the WordNet developed at Princeton University [1]. Non-lexical synsets (NLSs) in its upper-level hierarchies define semantic domains. A domain denotes a segment of reality symbolized by a set of related lexemes, which all have a common semantic property [5]. PlWordnet's set of domains is a data driven modification of lexicographer files' domains of Princeton's WordNet, the distinctions introduced in which are well-grounded in psycholinguistic studies [1]. Semantic domains are related to the notion of hyponymy, which is one of the fundamental relations wordnets encode. Hyponymy defines a lexeme in terms of relation of a subclass to class. The NLSs, thus, define a general domain reflecting the characteristic shared by all the entities described by the subordinated words. As such, we perceive hyponymical encodings in plWordNet as a proper tool for classification of ontological types. There are twelve main semantic domains for verbs in plWordNet [17]:

- ABS_REL - abstract relations (*adresować* 'address', *wyróżniać* 'distinguish')
- MEN_EMO - mental or emotional reactions (*zastanawiać się* 'wonder', *płakać* 'cry')
- MON_SPAT_REL - motion and spatial relations (*biegać* 'run', *rzucać* 'throw')
- NAT_PHEN - natural phenomena/physical world (*świecić* 'shine', *palić się* 'burn')
- PER_COG - perception and cognition (*patrzeć* 'look', *doświadczać* 'experience')
- PHYS_CON - physical contact (*bić* 'beat', *łapać* 'catch')
- PHYS_REA - physical (re)actions (*śnieżyć* 'snow', *chrapać* 'snor')
- POSS - possession (*dawać* 'give', *brać* 'take')
- PROD - producing (*budować* 'build', *gotować* 'cook')
- SOC_REL - social relationships (*dziękować* 'thank', *żartować* 'joke')
- TEMP_SEQ_CAUS - temporal sequence and causation (*wynikać* 'result', *powtarzać się* 'recur')
- STA - states (*być* 'be', *pozostawać* 'remain')

Few of the main fields contain further two domains due to incorporating alterational and causative variant of the the basic sense. For 'motion and spatial relations' the domains are:

- LOC_SPAT_REL - location or spatial relations (*spadać* 'fall', *zderzać się* 'collide')
- ALT_LOC_SPAT_REL - change of location or spatial relations change (*biegać* 'run', *skakać* 'jump')
- CAUS_ALT_LOC_SPAT_REL causing change of location or causing spatial relations change (*rzucać* 'throw', *otwierać* 'open')

Apart from the domains, hyponymy-hyperonymy relations encoding of verbs in plWordNet provides also information about class and aspect [18]. Classes are an adaptation of Vendler's Aktionsart categorisation to features typical for Polish language and were introduced by Laskowski [15]. According to properties of eventualities the verbs denote, Vendler [12] distinguishes States, Activities, Accomplishments and Achievements. Laskowski categorizes verbs along the dimensions of dynamicity, telicity, punctuality and intentionality, and distinguishes the following classes:

- States
- Acts
- Activities
- Accidents
- Events
- Actions
- Processes

Aspect has to do with eventualities' relation to time and is 'a different way of viewing the internal temporal constituency of a situation' [13]. With regard to aspectuality, Polish verbs can be divided into:

- perfective
- imperfective

Perfective verbs draw focus to the completeness of an action, while imperfectives to its duration.[1]

All the values for speech annotation (aspect, class, type) were obtained from NLSs in hyponymy relations in plWordNet 1.5. Inspired by Parrill's distinction between eventualities with a more prominent trajectory element and those more concerned with handling, we extended and generalized it by distinguishing between eventualities in which (trans) location or spatial relations ((trans)loc_spat_rel) are more salient and those in which body internal motion is (bod_int _mot). Parrill's Trajectory eventualities fall under the former group, while Handling is included in the latter. Due to our interest in that distinction, our corpus contained mostly verbs from the domains 'MOT_SPAT_REL', 'POSS' and 'PHYS_CON.' Verbs of 'LOC _SPAT_REL' and its alterational counterpart were subsumed under the type (Trans)loc

[1] Although instances of bi-aspectual verbs occur in Polish, they are rare [14].

Table 1: Attributes and values for speech annotation.

Attribute	Value
Aspect	Perfective
	Imperfective
Class	State
	Act
	Accident
	Action
	Process
	Activity
	Event
Type	(Trans)loc_spat_rel
	Bod_int_mot
	Other

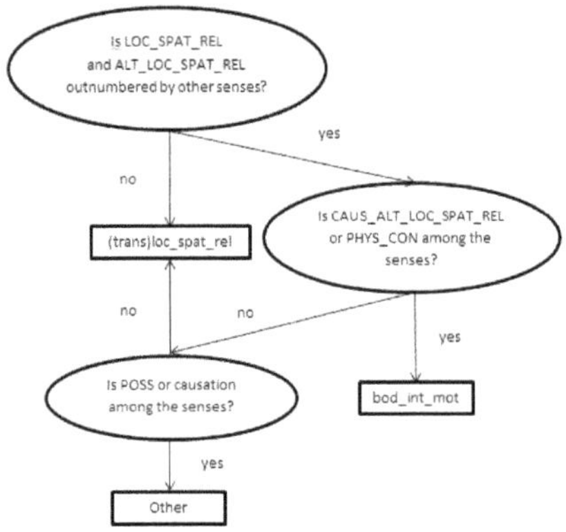

Figure 1: Decision tree for ambiguous verbs.

_spat_rel, while verbs denoting 'ALT_LOC_SPAT_REL', 'POSS' and 'PHYS_CON' were grouped under the type 'body internal motion' - Bod_int_mot. The remaining verbs, of which less than 15% of all verb tokens were found in our data, were collected under the umbrella term 'Other.' Tags used for annotation of the verbs are presented in Table 1.

2.2.1.2 Verb polysemy.

Often verbs are polysemous and express more than one sense. This is reflected in the structure of plWordNet where frequently multiple NLSs, and as a consequence various domains, are assigned to a single verb. A heuristics was created to enable unequivocal choice of the value for the Type attribute, which is based on the domains. The limited number of distinctions we are interested in in our study, enabled creating a simple decision tree (Figure 1). We took LOC_SPAT_REL' and its alerational counterpart as a starting point; the former is a prototypical sense for the whole group 'MOT_SPAT_REL' and the sense of both the former and the latter is included in the senses of all the remaining domains under investigation. The tree lead to correct assignment of the domain in 97 % of the cases in our data, which is a promising result for automatisation of the process of tagging verbs according to our scheme with the use of plWordNet.

Table 2: Attributes and values for gesture annotation.

Attribute	Value
Handedness	Right_Hand
	Left_Hand
	Symmetric_Hands
	Non-symmetric_Hands
Handshape	Claw
	Fist
	Index
	Open
	Purse
	Ring
	Other
Viewpoint	O_vpt
	C_vpt
	D_vpt
Iteration	Single
	Repeated
	Hold

2.2.2 Gesture

Since we focus on non-verbal representation of eventualities, only iconic gestures referring to eventualities are taken into account. Those gestures were identified based on DiaGest's annotation of semiotic types. Our tagging was performed on the gesture phase annotation created by the DiaGest group. We tagged strokes - the meaning-bearing part of gestures. The attribute Handedness reflects which hand performs a stroke. Handshape refers to the configuration of palm and fingers of the gesturing hand(s). Iteration indicates whether a particular movement pattern within a stroke occurs once or multiple times, or whether the stroke consists of a hand frozen in a static configuration. The attribute Viewpoint is more extensively discussed in the introductory section of this paper. Each stroke was associated with the corresponding verb by means of a MultiLink option in Anvil. MultiLink marks relations between elements on different tracks. It enables annotator to select and link any elements from the tracks. The verb temporally closest to the gesture was chosen unless the two clearly did not refer to the same eventuality. All attributes and the corresponding values for gesture annotation are listed in Table 3.

3. THE RESULTS

3.1 Inter-coder agreement

After all the data was annotated by a first coder, two out of the ten videos were used for inter-coder agreement experiment. The videos come from one male and one female speaker and include examples of all the values available in the scheme for all attributes besides Handshape and Class (some of which do not occur in our entire corpus at all). Agreement, measured in terms of Cohen's Kappa [6], was calculated automatically in ANVIL. The videos were independently annotated by a second coder - an inexperienced one without any prior training in the annotation scheme - and the agreement was measured between second and first coders' annotations. The agreement values ranged between 0.57 and 0.97 with the exception of Handshape, where agree-

Table 3: Inter-coder agreement scores for gesture annotation

Annotation attribute	κ
Handshape	0.7
Viewpoint	0.86
Iteration	0.87
Handedness	0.95

ment was below 0.5.[2] The file that posed more problems to the second annotator was independently annotated by a third coder - an expert after initial training. The agreement with first coder's annotation was again calculated. The obtained scores are given in Table 5. According to Rietveld and van Hout's scale [26], the results of the inter-coder test range from fair to almost perfect agreement, with an average of slightly substantial agreement, for the inexperienced coder without training and improve for the expert coder after initial training - with substantial agreement for one attribute and almost perfect agreement for all the remaining attributes. It needs to be noted that to ensure stability of the scores, the number of annotation elements needs to be higher. But the first inter-coder tests suggest high reliability of the annotation in our study.

3.2 The corpus analysis

Annotation from the orthographic and gesture phase track in ANVIL were extracted. The relation between the two is indicated by the MultiLink which joins the annotated attributes on the two tracks.

The material contains 234 verbs relevant to our study. The analysis of occurrences of particular values shows that the speakers used more imperfective than perfective verbs (141/ 93), but that both categories are well represented in our data. As for the Class, instances of all the values besides Processes are found in our material. However only very few examples of Accidents (8) and States (2) occur, while the most popular verb Class is Activity (96). There are almost as many verbs in the combined groups of the types 'Bod_int_mot' and 'Other' (113) as for the type '(Trans)loc_spat_rel' (121). For the purpose of our study, we combined the two former groups - this is due to a small amount of tokens in the group 'Other' and because we expected (trans)locational and spatial element to be the strongest predictor of viewpoint (see the next section). Table 5 lists number of occurrences for each value in the speech annotation in the corpus.

The corpus contains 330 gestures coded by DiaGest group as iconic. 269 gestures were relevant to our study, i.e. those were iconic gestures referring to an eventuality from to stimulus and co-occuring with a verb denoting the eventuality.[3] The mean is 26.9 gestures per speaker with SD=15.8. Analysis of the annotations created in our study reveals that the speakers produced 145 O_vpt, 95 C_vpt and 29 D_vpt gestures altogether. Distribution of different viewpoint values varies per speaker, seven out of ten speakers produced more O_vpt gestures than C_vpt ones, while for the remaining

[2]For discussion on the score of Handshape annotation, cf. [16].

[3]Note that more than one gesture could be linked to one verb, thus the number of verbs in the tables is smaller than the number of gestures.

Table 4: Verbal features occurrences for all 10 speakers.

Attribute	Value	No.
Aspect	Imperfective	141
	Perfective	93
Class	Activity	96
	Act	61
	Action	41
	Event	26
	Accident	8
	State	2
	Process	0
Type	(Trans)loc_spat_rel	121
	Bod_int_mot + Other	113

Table 5: Gestural features occurrences for all 10 speakers.

Attribute	Value	No.
Handness	Right_Hand	118
	Symmetric_Hands	79
	Left_Hand	40
	Non-symmetric_Hands	32
Handshape	Claw	55
	Fist	68
	Index	14
	Open	76
	Purse	25
	Ring	17
	Other	14
Viewpoint	O_vpt	145
	C_vpt	95
	D_vpt	29
Iteration	Single	200
	Repeated	63
	Hold	6

three this proportion was reverse. There are much more single than repeated strokes and only very few holds referring to eventualities. The small amount of holds seem justified considering that the stimulus cartoon was abundant in motion eventualities and in speech only very few 'State' verbs occurred. Nine out of ten speakers in the study were right handed and gestures performed with right hand strongly outnumber those made with the left one (118/40). Gestures where two hands mirror each other come more often than non-symmetric ones (79/32). This is in line with recent findings of van Gijn, Kita and van der Hulst [20], who argue that the Symmetry Condition found in two-handed signs in sign languages holds also for spontaneous gestures of hearing subjects.

To sum up, both verbal and non-verbal reference to eventualities is well represented in our data. The material should provide sufficient grounds for a pilot investigation of the relationship between eventuality characteristics and gestural representation.

3.3 Correlation

We computed the occurrences of gestural viewpoint and the types of eventualities. The results show that (Trans)loc _spat_rel verbs in our data tend to be accompanied by O_vpt gestures, while C_vpt gestures are likely to co-occur with the verbs of Bod_int_mot. The relationship is highly significant ($p<.0001$, $\chi=126.272$, df=1). D_vpt occurred in very few instances in our data (29 out of 269) and did not provide clear-cut results. Since D_vpt was also the most problematic value for the annotators, we plan to discard it in future research (cf. [16]). We have also tested the relation between Aspect on the one hand and Handedness and Iteration on the other but the results were not statistically significant. Nor did Class give any conclusive results. We also looked at the relationship between gesture's physical form and bodily representation, and our results indicate that C_vpt gestures are more likely to be bi-handed symmetrical ones, while O_vpt gestures are single handed ($p<.0001$, $\chi=19.336$, df=1). Claw and Fist are the handshapes likely to occur with C_vpt in our data, while Open hand and Index finger are more likely to be the handshapes of O_vpt gestures ($p<.0001$, $\chi=17.782$, df=1).

4. DISCUSSION AND FUTURE RESEARCH

Our results support the hypothesis that the choice of gestural viewpoint may depend on the ontological type of the entity referred to. The results may furthermore be a step towards a model of gestural behaviour planning. They provide preference rules for determining gesture's physical form based on automatically annotated speech content. Gestural representation, conceived in terms of viewpoint, serves as a link between gestural morphological features (like handedness and handshape) and plWordNet's classification of speech data, taken to reflect referent's ontological type. Our data enable testing to which extent verb classification in plWordNet can be used to predict gestural viewpoint. The annotation extracted from the corpus can be used as training data for machine learning experiments and annotation scheme can be used for classification tasks. Models stemming from the findings from such basic research are applicable in multimodal systems. They can be used for gesture generation in ECAs. We perceive entities' type as only one of the elements defining gestural representation. As shown by among others Kopp and colleagues [13], a number of other factors like information structure and communicative intent also influence non-verbal behaviours. We hypothesize the entities' type to be the first step in predicting gesture's form (the reason being restrictions that entities' type pose on bodily articulators) on top of which discursive and linguistic factors exert further influence.

A popular approach to modelling multimodal communication is utilizing predefined lexicons of words and associated gestures. The model based on correlation between the type and viewpoint would be a more open and productive one. New data could be accounted for to the degree to which appropriate lexemes are present in wordnet. Furthermore, our results suggest semantic categorization to benefit research on non-verbal behaviours. While machine-readable ontologies have been proven a valuable tool for studying and processing language data, we suggest fruitfulness of applying them to research on multimodality. We claim that existing linguistic ontologies can be used for the investigation of co-speech gesture - as exemplified by employment of plWordNet in our study which provided formalization and automatisation for the annotation schemes proposed by Poggi [24] and Parrill [22]. While our annotation scheme for non-verbal behaviours is language independent, the scheme for verbs was tested on, and the results come from, the Polish data. We, however, hypothesize that they can be extended to other languages by utilising local ontologies. There exist numerous wordnets for various languages and many of them are based on the same source as plWordNet (i.e. on Princeton WordNet).

In future research we plan to incorporate Framenet. It is a database founded on the concept of semantic frame: a description of a type of eventuality, relation, or object and the participants in it [9]. We expect that the ontological type of the object involved in the eventuality may contribute further constraints on the viewpoint choice rules. Furthermore, in the second part of the project and within the same framework as presented in the paper, we plan to examine remaining types of entities (e.g., garment, body part, manipulable vs. non-manipulable objects) and their relationship to gestural representation. Also, future research needs to look at verbs subsumed in our study under the category 'Other.' Further insights into eventualities' representation can be obtained by investigating the distinctions possible to be drawn within that category. We hypothesize that some of them can be accounted for by investigating representation in gestures performed by other articulators than hands (e.g., emotional reactions might be primarily represented by re-enacting associated facial expressions). Future developments of our research aim at taking more holistic approach to non-verbal behaviours by incorporating gestures produced by the remaining articulators.

Finally, the restricted character of our data needs to be acknowledged. Due to the popularity of the data collection method adopted, the chosen corpus makes possible cross-linguistic and cross-cultural comparisons, as numerous comparable corpora for various languages and cultures exist. Also, our choice of the corpus enables us to primarily focus on one of the most productive areas for gestural representation, i.e. motion eventualities. However, as the result of this choice, our scheme and findings are applicable to instances of those types of eventualities only and may not be able to account for other types. The hypothesis presented in the paper need to be further examined and tested on a variety of other data.

5. CONCLUSIONS

The paper presents a pilot study on the relationship between verbal and non-verbal representation of eventualities. The results indicate that there is a strong correlation between eventuality type, as reflected in the categorization of verbs in plWordNet 1.5, and gestural viewpoint. We hope that at a later stage, the results will allow us to examine to which extent plWordNet's verb taxonomy can be used to automatically predict gestural viewpoint.

6. ACKNOWLEDGMENTS

This research has been sponsored by the European Commission's 7th Framework Program (grant agreement no. 238405 - CLARA). We are grateful to DiaGest research group, especially Maciej Karpiński and Ewa Jarmołowicz-Nowikow, for making their corpus available for our study. Special thanks to Costanza Navarretta for her guidance.

7. REFERENCES

[1] *WordNet: An Electronic Lexical Database.* MIT Press, Cambridge, MA, fellbaum, ch. edition, 1998.

[2] Polish wordnet, plwordnet1.5., http://plwordnet.pwr.wroc.pl/wordnet/.

[3] R. Becker, A. Cienki, A. Bennett, C. Cudina, C. Debras, Z. Fleischer, M. Haaheim, T. Mueller, K. Stec, and A. Zarcone. Aktionsarten, speech and gesture. In *Gesture and Speech in Interaction '11*, 2011.

[4] F. Boas. *Introduction to the Handbook of American Indian languages.* Government Printing Office, Washington DC, 1911.

[5] L. Brinton. The structure of modern english: A linguistic introduction. 2000.

[6] J. Carletta. Assessing agreement on classification tasks: The kappa statistic. *Computational Linguistics*, 22(2):249–254, 1996.

[7] S. Duncan. Gesture, verb aspect, and the nature of iconic imagery in natural discourse. *Gesture*, 2(2):183–206, 2002.

[8] C. Fellbaum, editor. *WordNet: An Electronic Lexical Database.* MIT Press, Cambridge, MA, 1998.

[9] C. J. Fillmore and C. Baker. *A Frames Approach to Semantic Analysis.* Oxford University Press, Oxford, 2010.

[10] T. Gruber. A translation approach to portable ontologies. *Knowledge Acquisition*, 5(2):199–220, 1993.

[11] A. Kendon. Gesture. *Annual Review of Anthropology*, 26:109–128, 1997.

[12] M. Kipp. *Gesture Generation by Imitation - From Human Behavior to Computer Character Animation.* Boca Raton, Florida, 2004.

[13] S. Kopp, K. Bergmann, and W. Ipke. Multimodal communication from multimodal thinking - towards an integrated model of speech and gesture production. *Semantic Computing*, 2(1):115–136, 2008.

[14] R. M. Kraus, Y. Chen, and R. F. Gottesman. *Lexical Gestures and Lexical Access. A Process Model*, pages 261–283. Cambridge University Press, New York, 2000.

[15] R. Laskowski. *Kategorie morfologiczne języka polskiego — charakterystyka funkcjonalna.* PWN, Warszawa, 1998.

[16] M. Lis. Annotation scheme for multimodal communication: Employing plwordnet 1.5. In *Proceedings of the Formal and Computational Approaches to Multimodal Communication Workshop. 24th European Summer School in Logic, Language and Information (ESSLLI 2012).*

[17] M. Maziarz. Non-lexical verb synsets in upper-hierarchy levels of polish wordnet 2.0. Technical report, Wrocław University of Technology, 2012.

[18] M. Maziarz, M. Piasecki, S. Szpakowicz, J. Rabiega-Wiśniewksa, and B. Hojka. Semantic relations between verbs in polish wordnet 2.0. *Cognitive Studies*, (11):183–200, 2011.

[19] D. McNeill. *Hand and Mind: What Gestures Reveal About Thought.* University of Chicago Press, Chicago, 1992.

[20] D. McNeill. *Gesture and Thought.* University of Chicago Press, Chicago, 2005.

[21] I. Mittelberg. Metaphor and metonymy in language and gesture: Discourse evidence for multimodal models of grammar. 2006.

[22] F. Parrill. Viewpoint in speech–gesture integration: Linguistic structure, discourse structure, and event structure. *Language and Cognitive Processes*, 25(5):650–668, 2010.

[23] F. Parrill, B. Bergen, and P. Lichtenstein. Grammatical aspect in multimodal language production: Using gesture to reveal event representations. In *Conceptual Structure, Discourse, and Language*, in press.

[24] I. Poggi. Iconicity in different types of gestures. *Gesture*, 8(1):45–61, 2008.

[25] G. Ramchard. Post-davidsionianism. *Theoretical Linguistics*, 31(3):359–373, 2005.

[26] T. Rietveld and R. v. Hout. *Statistical Techniques for the Study of Language and Language Behavior.* Mouton De Gruyter, Berlin, 1993.

[27] Z. Vendler. *Linguistics in Philosophy.* Cornell University Press, Ithaca, NY, 1967.

[28] P. Wittenburg, H. Brugman, A. Russel, A. Klassmann, and H. Sloetjes. Elan: a professional framework for multimodality research. In *LREC 2006, Fifth International Conference on Language Resources and Evaluation*, 2006.

Using Self-Context for Multimodal Detection of Head Nods in Face-to-Face Interactions

Laurent Nguyen
Idiap Research Institute
EPFL
Switzerland
lnguyen@idiap.ch

Jean-Marc Odobez
Idiap Research Institute
EPFL
Switzerland
odobez@idiap.ch

Daniel Gatica-Perez
Idiap Research Institute
EPFL
Switzerland
gatica@idiap.ch

ABSTRACT

Head nods occur in virtually every face-to-face discussion. As part of the backchannel domain, they are not only used to express a 'yes', but also to display interest or enhance communicative attention. Detecting head nods in natural interactions is a challenging task as head nods can be subtle, both in amplitude and duration. In this study, we make use of findings in psychology establishing that the dynamics of head gestures are conditioned on the person's speaking status. We develop a multimodal method using audio-based self-context to detect head nods in natural settings. We demonstrate that our multimodal approach using the speaking status of the person under analysis significantly improved the detection rate over a visual-only approach.

Categories and Subject Descriptors

I.4.m [**Computing Methodologies**]: Image Processing and Computer Vision—*Miscellaneous*

Keywords

Social computing, head nods, face-to-face interaction, self-context, multimodal processing

1. INTRODUCTION

In face-to-face interactions, head nods occur in every discussion. In most cases, people producing the head nods are not even aware of the social signal they emit: head nods are often the result of automatic processes. Independently of their function or meaning, head nods can be defined as vertical up-and-down movements of the head, rhythmically raised and lowered [5].

The social psychology community was the first to examine the functions of head nods during face-to-face interactions. Apart from the obvious function of signaling a 'yes', head nods are used *inter alia* to display interest, enhance communicative attention by occurring in synchrony with the other's speech, or anticipate an attempt to capture the floor (*i.e.*, signaling a turn claim) [5, 1]. Head nods form a major mode of communication in *backchannelling*, that is, during listener turns [5, 1]. Additionally, head nods can be used during speaker turns to elicit feedback from the listener [1]. The psychology literature suggests that the frequency of head nod events in face-to-face interactions can reveal personal characteristics or even predict outcomes. For instance, job applicants producing more head nods in employment interviews have been reported to be often perceived as more employable than applicants who do not [3, 7]. In this sense, the ability to automatically detect head nods could be useful to build automatic inference methods of high-level social constructs.

Most methods for automatically detecting head nods have been developed in the context of human-computer interaction (HCI). The primary goal of these studies was to enable a machine to detect a 'yes' signaled by a head nod. Within this context, some studies proposed to track interest points of the face [6, 13] and use state-based approaches such as finite state machines [2] and hidden Markov models [10, 13] to detect nodding. These approaches show good performance in restricted contexts where the head motions are explicit. However, these methods do not allow to detect subtle head movements that occur quite often in natural human face-to-face interaction.

Nodding does not occur in a void. It is known that the speaking status of people influences the dynamics of the displayed head gestures [5]. When a person is speaking, the motion of his head has typically greater amplitude, larger frequency range, and follows a close to random pattern [5]. On the other hand, when the person is listening, his head tends to be more static as a result of both attention to the speaker and the fact of being silent. In this sense, head gestures are multimodal: the dynamics are conditioned on the speaking status of the actor.

The contextual nature of nodding has been used in the recent past. Work addressing the prediction of backchannel feedback makes use of these findings. The goal of this line of research is to enable robots or conversational agents to produce natural backchannels. In this type of setting, the contextual information such as lexical information or prosodic cues are used to predict head nods [9].

Furthermore, communicative contextual audio-based features have been used to improve the detection of head nods in dyadic scenarios [10, 8]. In [10], the scenario consists of a human interacting with an embodied conversational agent; hence, head nods produced by the participant are not entirely natural. In [8], automatically and manually extracted

Figure 1: (a) Snapshot of the recording room. (b-c) Frame extracted from the video data for two protagonists in a dyad.

contextual cues (prosodic and lexical features) related to the speaker were used to improve the detection of the listener's head nods. In this constrained dyadic scenario, only one person spoke while the other person was asked to listen silently.

While the value of using audio-based context from the perspective of the speaker to improve the detection of listener head nods has been established, one aspect that to our knowledge has not been studied in detail is the effect of the audio-based self-context on head nod detection. This study develops a multimodal method using the self-context to detect head nods in fully natural conversations where both protagonists freely interact. We create an annotated dataset of natural dyadic interactions in order to benchmark our method. This paper is structured as follows. In Section 2, we present the dataset on which our method was trained and tested. In Section 3, we explain our method to automatically detect natural head nods. We discuss our results in Section 4 and conclude in Section 5.

2. NATURAL HEAD NOD DATASET

In order to benchmark head nod detection methods, we collected a dataset of 8 natural interactions (16 videos treated individually). Pairs of participants were asked to sit at both sides of a table and have a relaxed conversation on a topic of their choice. Dyads were acquainted before taking part to the experiment. In total, there were 9 different people (one person was in all conversations).

Video was recorded during the natural interactions. Illustrations of the experimental setup and the recorded data are displayed in Figure 1. Two 1280x960 monocular cameras were used, recording both protagonists of the dyad at 26.6 frames per second. Camera views were quasi-frontal, filming the upper part of the body. In addition to the images, the timestamps for each video frame were also recorded with a resolution of $1\mu s$. In total, the dataset comprises approximately 160 minutes of recording ($\sim$260'000 frames). Average video duration was 10 minutes.

In order to train and test the algorithm, annotations were performed on the dataset. Depending on the amplitude and duration of the up-and-down oscillatory movements, head nods can be difficult to code; two classes of head nods were therefore defined: *obvious* and *subtle*. Head nods were annotated by one of the authors, thus well acquainted with the concept of nodding, who noted the onset and offset time of an event, and qualitatively decided the nod class based on nod amplitude and duration. Speaking status was also manually annotated, marking the beginning and the end of a speaking segment. In total, nodding occurred during 858 seconds (22'812 frames), of which 92% occurred when the person under analysis was silent. Average head nod duration was 1.2 seconds. On average, speaking and silent times were split equally for each speaker in the dataset.

3. MULTIMODAL HEAD NOD DETECTION

As stated in the introduction, head nods are defined as vertical up-and-down movements of the head rhythmically raised and lowered. This implies an oscillatory pattern in the vertical axis, while the motion in the horizontal axis is limited. In order to encode this effect, we constructed features based on fine-grain motion detection and transformation into the frequency domain. The extraction of the features to characterize head nods follows a similar spirit than [10], but relies directly on the motion estimates derived from the video sequence rather than on the output state of a head tracker, which might not be so sensitive to subtle movements of the head. A binary classifier is then used to assign frames to one of two classes, *nodding* and *not nodding*.

3.1 Motion Estimation

Given the bounding box output of a face tracker (using the method described in [12]), the goal is to detect the motion in the horizontal and vertical directions. To perform this task, we used a parametric motion model which estimates the best set of parameters between the previous and current frames, using the face bounding box region.

We used the affine motion model defined in Equation 1, where (x_i, y_i) denotes a point in the image, $V(x_i, y_i)$ the flow vector modeled at point (x_i, y_i). Visual motion estimation over the whole face region provides an accurate estimation of head movements and therefore allows to capture subtle patterns using a multiresolution robust estimation method [11]. Parameters t_x, t_y, $a_{1:4}$ were estimated using least-mean-squares, implemented by the software package Motion2D[1].

$$V(x_i, y_i) = \begin{bmatrix} v_x(x_i, y_i) \\ v_y(x_i, y_i) \end{bmatrix} = \begin{bmatrix} t_x + a_1 x_i + a_2 y_i \\ t_y + a_3 x_i + a_4 y_i \end{bmatrix} \qquad (1)$$

We then computed the velocity at three arbitrarily defined points (see Figure 2) inside the bounding box, using the parameters of the optical flow model (Equation 1), providing the horizontal and vertical components of the motion at these three points. Roughly speaking, these points are around the mouth and eyes of the participant. Typical motion time-series for speaking, nodding while silent, and not nodding while silent are illustrated in Figure 2. The figure illustrates that head nod activity does present differences depending on the self-speaking status, and that building nodding models separately for the speaking and silent cases could reduce the confusion between, for instance, a head nod and a quasi-random head gesture displayed during a speaking turn.

3.2 Frequency Domain Analysis

Given the head motion in the horizontal and vertical directions, the goal is to capture the oscillatory characteristics

[1]http://www.irisa.fr/vista/Motion2D/

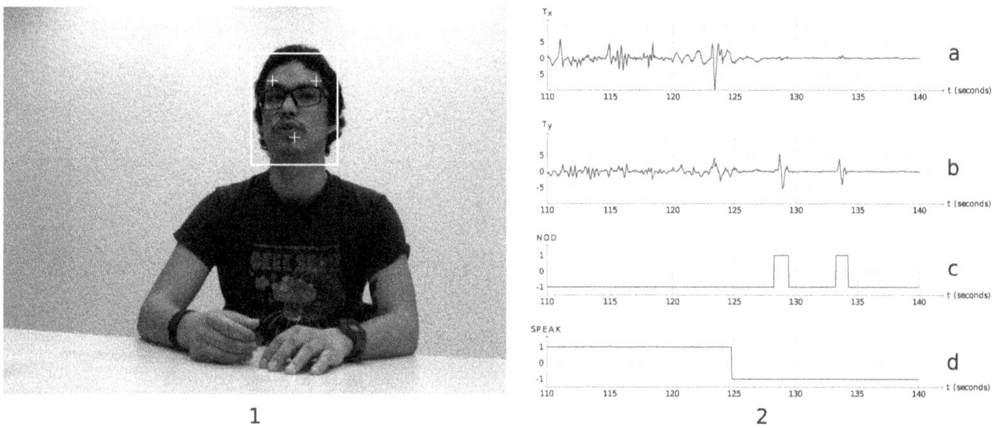

Figure 2: Illustration of the motion estimation step. In (1), the white rectangle is the face bounding box provided by the face tracker; the three white crosses are the pre-defined points where the motion is computed using the parametric model of Equation 1. A 30-second sequence of the motion is displayed in (2); (a) and (b) are the estimated motion in the horizontal and vertical directions, respectively; (c) shows the sequence of annotated nods (1 = *nod*, -1 = *non-nod*); (d) shows the speaking status of the participant (1 = *speaking*, -1 = *silent*).

of a head nod. In order to perform this task, we applied a Fourier transform (with Gaussian temporal window) to the velocity vectors $(v_x(x_i, y_i), v_y(x_i, y_i))^T$ of the pre-defined points, considering each vector component as an independent time-series. Although this independence assumption does not strictly hold, the computation is greatly simplified. Finally, the feature vectors are constructed by concatenating the Fourier transform outputs. Typical Fourier features for speaking, nodding while silent, and not nodding while silent are illustrated in Figure 3.

3.3 Classification

The goal is now to assign each feature vector to either of these two classes, *nodding* or *not nodding*. For each of the speaking status values, we trained a separate linear support vector machine (SVM) to perform the classification. This multimodal approach directly takes into account the switching dynamics of head movements, depending on the speaking status of the person under observation, as suggested by previous work in psychology [4].

The training set was defined as follows. The positive set was composed of all frames labeled as *obvious nods*. The negative set was selected randomly from the set of frames labeled as *non-nod*. Frames labeled as *subtle nods* were not used for training because they can be too similar to *not nodding* features. In addition to this, transitional frames were discarded to attenuate the dependence to time-related annotation inaccuracy. The training set was balanced, *i.e.* the number of positive and negative examples was equal. Approximately 5000 training examples were used for each class. We then further segmented the data into *speaking* and *silent*, training each separate model on its own training set.

To validate our hypothesis that self-context in terms of speaking status improves nodding detection, we implemented a baseline method using the visual modality only. For the visual-only method, we used a single SVM trained on the full training set (*i.e.* not separating it into *speaking* and *silent*).

4. RESULTS

The evaluation of the head nod detection method was conducted at the frame level. Leave-one-out cross validation was performed at the sequence level: the algorithm was trained on all except one sequence and tested on the remaining one. The binary output of the SVM classifier was compared to the annotated ground truth (including *obvious* and *subtle* nods).

In Figure 4, we display the receiver-operating characteristic (ROC) curve for both the visual-only and the multimodal approaches. The F_1 score, defined by the harmonic mean of precision and recall, was also computed. The multimodal method significantly outperforms the visual-only one: $F_1^{visual} = 0.559$, $F_1^{multi} = 0.6283$. These results show that using the self-speaking status of a person improves the detection rate, highlighting the difference in dynamics of head gestures between *speaking* and *silent* suggested in the psychology literature [5]. This result confirms previous findings [10, 8] that have shown the advantage of using audio-based contextual cues for this task, with the novel angle that using self-context (as opposed to interaction partner-based context) is also advantageous. Moreover, independently of the approach (multimodal or visual-only), the method we developed to extract head nods in natural settings yields competitive results on this dataset.

Head nods of small amplitude and duration are in general accurately detected by the proposed method. Additionally, because of the switching dynamics conditioned on the speaking status, the number of false positives is kept low. In other words, *speaking* can be seen as an attenuation factor of the head nod detector.

5. CONCLUSIONS

In this study, we developed and evaluated a multimodal method to detect natural head nods in face-to-face interactions. Our work brings the novel angle of examining in detail the effect of the speaking self-context on head nod detection. Two nodding models were trained, depending on the speaking status of the person under analysis. Compared to the baseline vision-only method, results demon-

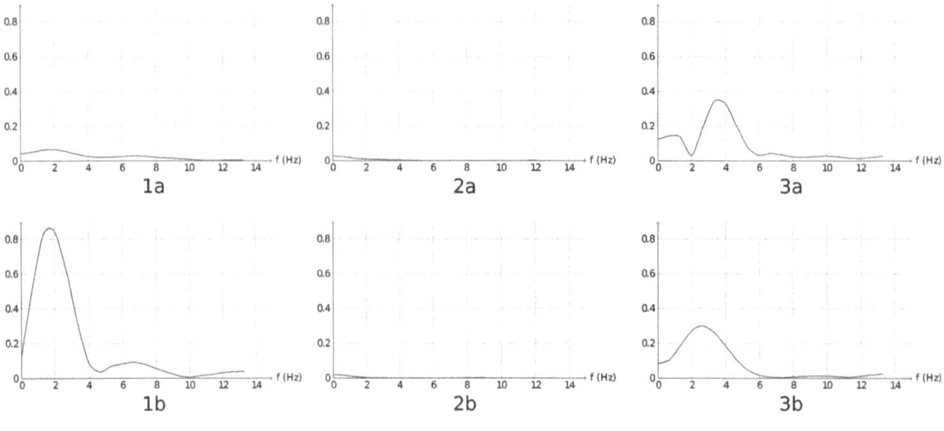

Figure 3: Examples of typical Fourier transform outputs. (a) and (b) are the Fourier outputs taken on the temporal motion sequence in the horizontal and vertical direction, respectively. Referring to Figure 2, (1) is a Fourier sample taken at $t = 128.8s$ (*nod, non-speaking*); (2) is sampled at $t = 131.4s$ (*non-nod, silent*); (3) is taken at $t = 116.2s$ (*non-nod, speaking*).

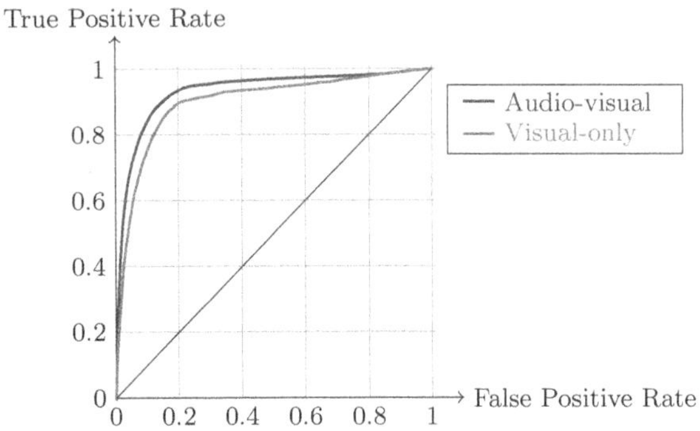

Figure 4: Receiver-operating characteristic curve (ROC) for the two head nod detection approaches. In red: visual-only method. In blue: audio-visual approach.

strated that audio-based self-context improved the detection of head nods, underlining the difference of head gesture dynamics conditioned on the speaking status of the person, as suggested by previous work in psychology. The developed method yielded competitive results on this dataset, allowing to detect subtle nods while keeping the number of false positive low.

The method presented in this paper could be extended for the detection of head shakes by using the same frequency domain motion features. Other possible avenues for future work would be to use more detailed audio context, *e.g.* taking into account the prosody or lexical information of both protagonists in the interaction. The presented method could also be seen as a first step towards the classification of head nods defined by their communicative functions; we hypothesize that context from both protagonists in the form of visual, prosodic, and lexical features would have to be used for this task.

Acknowledgments

This research was funded by SNSF SONVB project and the EC HUMAVIPS project. We thank Denise Frauendorfer (Université de Neuchâtel) for the support with data collection.

References

[1] J. Allwood and L. Cerrato. A study of gestural feedback expressions. In *Proc. First Nordic Symposium on Multimodal Communication*, 2003.

[2] L. Dong, Y. Jin, L. Tao, and G. Xu. Recognition of multi-pose head gestures in human conversations. In *Proc. Int. Conf. on Image and Graphics (ICIG)*, Aug. 2007.

[3] R. Gifford, C. F. Ng, and M. Wilkinson. Nonverbal cues in the employment interview: Links between applicant qualities and interviewer judgments. *Applied Psychology*, 70(4):729–736, 1985.

[4] U. Hadar, T. Steiner, E. Grant, and F. Rose. Kinematics of head movements accompanying speech during conversation. *Human Movement Science*, 2(1-2):35–46, June 1983.

[5] U. Hadar, T. J. Steiner, and F. Clifford Rose. Head movement during listening turns in conversation. *Nonverbal Behavior*, 9(4):214–228, 1985.

[6] A. Kapoor and R. W. Picard. A real-time head nod and shake detector. In *Proc. Workshop on Perceptive User Interfaces (ICMI-PUI)*, number 544, 2001.

[7] T. V. McGovern, B. W. Jones, and S. E. Morris. Comparison of professional versus student ratings of job interviewee behavior. *Counseling Psychology*, 26(2):176–179, 1979.

[8] L. Morency, I. de Kok, and J. Gratch. Context-based recognition during human interactions: automatic feature selection and encoding dictionary. In *Proceedings of the 10th international conference on Multimodal interfaces*, pages 181–188. ACM, 2008.

[9] L. Morency and I. D. Kok. Predicting Listener Backchannels: A Probabilistic Multimodal Approach. *Journal of Autonomous Agents and Multi-Agent Systems*, pages 1–14, 2008.

[10] L.-P. Morency, C. Sidner, C. Lee, and T. Darrell. Contextual recognition of head gestures. In *Proc. Int. Conf. on Multimodal Interfaces (ICMI)*, 2005.

[11] J. Odobez and P. Bouthemy. Robust multiresolution estimation of parametric motion models. *Visual Communication and Image Representation*, 6(4):348–365, 1995.

[12] E. Ricci and J. Odobez. Learning large margin likelihoods for realtime head pose tracking. In *Proc. Int. Conf. on Image Processing (ICIP)*, Nov. 2009.

[13] W. Tan and G. Rong. A real-time head nod and shake detector using HMMs. *Expert Systems with Applications*, 25(3):461–466, Oct. 2003.

Multimodal Multiparty Social Interaction with the Furhat Head

Samer Al Moubayed, Gabriel Skantze, Jonas Beskow, Kalin Stefanov, Joakim Gustafson
Department of Speech, Music and Hearing
KTH Royal Institute of Technology
Lindstedtsv. 24, 10044 Stockholm, Sweden
{sameram, skantze, beskow, kalins, jocke}@kth.se

ABSTRACT

We will show in this demonstrator an advanced multimodal and multiparty spoken conversational system using Furhat, a robot head based on projected facial animation. Furhat is a human-like interface that utilizes facial animation for physical robot heads using back-projection. In the system, multimodality is enabled using speech and rich visual input signals such as multi-person real-time face tracking and microphone tracking. The demonstrator will showcase a system that is able to carry out social dialogue with multiple interlocutors simultaneously with rich output signals such as eye and head coordination, lips synchronized speech synthesis, and non-verbal facial gestures used to regulate fluent and expressive multiparty conversations.

Categories and Subject Descriptors

H.5.2 [**Information Interfaces and Presentation**]: User Interfaces – Natural Language; D.2.2 [**Software Engineering**] Design Tools and Techniques – State diagrams; D.2.11 [**Software Engineering**] Software Architectures – Languages

Keywords

Multiparty interaction, Gaze, Gesture, Speech, Spoken dialog, Multimodal systems, Facial animation, Robot head, Furhat, Microphone Tracking

General Terms

Design

1. The Furhat Head

Furhat [1] is a robot head that deploys a back-projected animated face that is realistic and human-like in anatomy. Furhat relies on a state-of-the-art facial animation architecture allowing accurate synchronized lip movements with speech, and the control and generation of non-verbal gestures, eye movements and facial expressions.

Furhat is built to study, implement and validate patterns and models of human-human and human-machine situated and multi-party multimodal communication, a study that demands the co-presence of the talking head in the interaction environment, something that cannot be achieved using virtual avatars displayed on flat screens [2,3]. In Furhat, the animated face is back-projected on a translucent mask that is a printout of the animated model. The mask is then rigged on a 2DOF neck to allow for the control of head movements. Figure 1 shows snapshots of Furhat in different contexts.

ICMI'12, October 22–26, 2012, Santa Monica, California, USA.
ACM 978-1-4503-1467-1/12/10.

Figure 1. Snapshots of Furhat[1] in close-up and in interaction

2. Multimodal Input

For speech recognition, we used the Windows 7 ASR, running in two separate modules, one for each microphone. This allowed the system to process simultaneous speech in both microphones.

In addition to the speech signal from several microphones, the system uses the SHORE™ 2 real-time, robust and multi-person face tracking developed by Fraunhofer [4]. The tracker provides the system with information about the location and the pose of the different visible faces. The tracker also provides non-verbal information about the faces such as estimates of the age, gender, and facial expressions. Such information is utilized by the dialogue system: estimates of the facial expressions are used for example to establish facial mimicry between Furhat and the interlocutor.

To enable the system to engage in multi-party dialogue, it must be able to detect the speaker in the set of possible speakers in front of Furhat. To establish this, two microphones were rigged with two different patterns of Infra-Red reflective markers, and an Infra-Red camera is used in combination with the video camera to detect and track the microphones and align them to the faces. Figure 2 shows the setup of the microphones and the cameras, and Figure 3 shows the face and microphone trackers in action.

[1] For more info on Furhat, see http://www.speech.kth.se/furhat
[2] Fraunhofer SHORE™
http://www.iis.fraunhofer.de/en/bf/bsy/fue/isyst

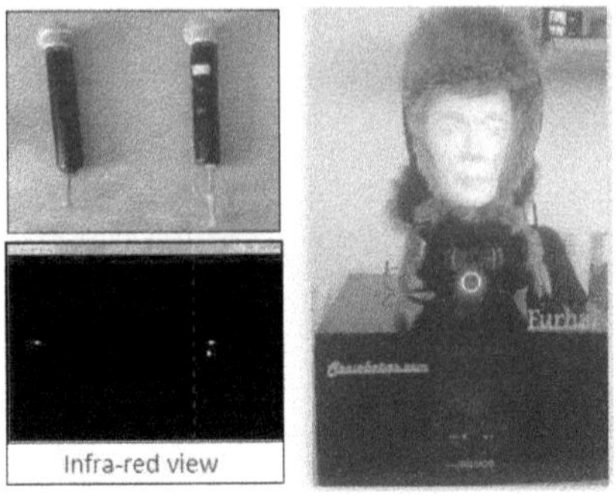

Figure 2. Left top: a snapshot showing two microphones rigged with Infra-Red markers. Left bottom: A screen capture showing a processed Infra-Red view of the microphones. Right: Furhat rigged with the Infra-Red and video cameras.

Figure 3. A snapshot of the face tracker and the microphone tracker in action.

3. Multiparty Dialogue

For every microphone, an ASR engine is used. Each ASR engine used two parallel language models, one context-free grammar with semantic tags (SRGS3), tailored for the domain, and one open dictation model. To interpret the dictation results, we have implemented a robust parser that uses the SRGS grammar to find islands of matching fragments.

The multi-modal dialog system is implemented using a newly developed framework based on the notion of statecharts [5] which is a powerful formalism for complex, reactive, event-driven systems. Using multimodal input events such as speech input, entry and movements of interlocutors, the demonstrator will show a social dialogue system that supports mixed initiatives (the system and the user can alternate the initiatives in asking questions). The dialogue is designed to account for multiparty properties, such as interruptions and overlaps, posing open questions to all interlocutors, and context and memory of previous questions and addressees during the dialogue.

4. Multimodal Output

The speech synthesis used is CereVoice developed by CereProc4. The speech output is automatically synced with accurate lips movements using the visual speech synthesis architecture used in Furhat [6]. In addition to speech, head and eyes coordinated movements are used by an attention control module to regulate attentive multiparty interaction in a highly human-like fashion, such movements serve to the following and alternating between the interlocutors, and used to model cognitive states such as "idle" and "thinking". In addition to that, gestures are used as non-verbal facial signals to feedback, mimicry, attentiveness, and interest.

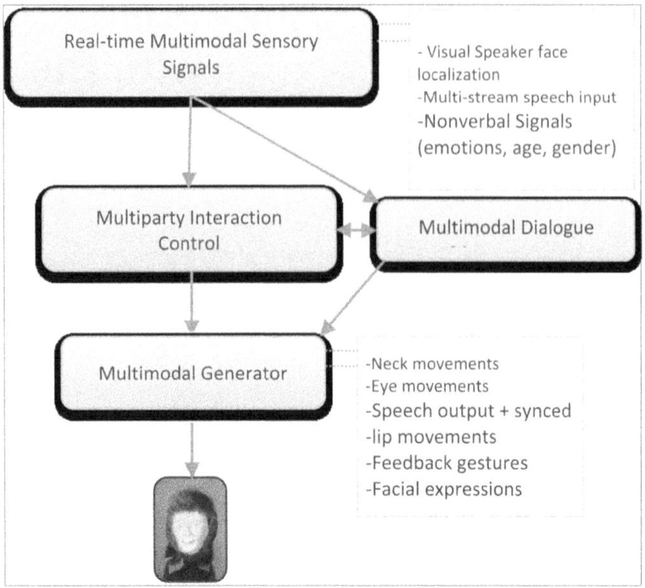

Figure 4. A simplified diagram of the architecture of the system.

Figure 4 shows a simplified scheme diagram of the architecture of the system.

5. ACKNOWLEDGMENTS

This work has been partly funded by the EU project IURO (Interactive Urban Robot) No. 248314, and the SAVIR project (Situated Audio-Visual Interaction with Robots) funded by the Swedish Government (strategic research areas).

6. REFERENCES

[1] Al Moubayed, S., Beskow, J., Skantze, G., & Granström, B. 2012. Furhat: A Back-projected Human-like Robot Head for Multiparty Human-Machine Interaction. In Esposito et al. (Eds.), Cognitive Behavioural Systems. Lecture Notes in Computer Science. Springer.

[2] Al Moubayed, S., Edlund, J., & Beskow, J. 2012. Taming Mona Lisa: communicating gaze faithfully in 2D and 3D facial projections. *ACM Transactions on Interactive Intelligent Systems, 1(2), 25.*

[3] Al Moubayed, S., & Skantze, G. 2011. Turn-taking Control Using Gaze in Multiparty Human-Computer Dialog: Effects of 2D and 3D Displays. *In Proceedings of AVSP.* Florence, Italy.

[4] Kueblbeck, C. and Ernst, A. 2006. Face detection and tracking in video sequences using the modified census transformation. *Journal on Image and Vision Computing*, vol. 24, issue 6, pp. 564-572, 2006, ISSN 0262-8856

[5] Skantze, G. and Al Moubayed, S. 2012. IrisTK: a statechart-based toolkit for multi-party face-to-face interaction. *Proc. of the 14th ACM International Conference on Multimodal Interaction ICMI.* Santa Monica, CA, USA.

[6] Beskow, J. 1997. Animation of talking agents. In Benoit, C., & Campbel, R. (Eds.), *Proc of ESCA Workshop on Audio-Visual Speech Processing* (pp. 149-152). Rhodes, Greece.

[3] http://www.w3.org/TR/speech-grammar/

[4] CereProc ltd: http://www.cereproc.com/

An Avatar-based Help System for a Grid Computing Web Portal

Helmut Lang
Institute of Communications Engineering
Ulm University, Germany
helmut.lang@uni-ulm.de

Florian Nothdurft
Institute of Communications Engineering
Ulm University, Germany
wolfgang.minker@uni-ulm.de

ABSTRACT

We developed a help system that employs an avatar to cover various aspects of user assistance. In addition to assisting users with the completion of specific goals by means of dynamically generated step-by-step guides, the system is also able to provide information concerning elements of the user interface. Furthermore it answers follow-up questions entered by the user. Compared to other systems, our system is able to present help directly on the page the user is currently visiting. It also interacts with the content to help the user in finding pages and interface elements relevant to complete given tasks. According to the user's preference, help is either provided in a textual form or by speech output.

Categories and Subject Descriptors

H.5.2 [**Information Interfaces and Presentation**]: User Interfaces—*Training, help, and documentation*

Keywords

HCI, Computer Assisted Learning, User Support

1. MOTIVATION

To spare users from using command line interfaces to access the grid computing facilities of the bwGRiD [1], a web portal was implemented. Due to the complexity of the concepts related to grid computing – especially security constraints – we observed a lot of frustration with users working with the portal. A first approach using traditional hyperlinked text pages in a dedicated help section to assist those users revealed the following drawbacks:

- All changes to the quite volatile portal layout had to be reflected in the documentation. For example, all references to a tab in the navigational area had to be updated when the name of that tab was altered.
- Users felt lost trying to find those parts in the provided help texts that where relevant to solve their problem.
- Users permanently had to switch their focus of attention from the help text to the content they were editing.

ICMI'12, October 22–26, 2012, Santa Monica, California, USA.
ACM 978-1-4503-1467-1/12/10.

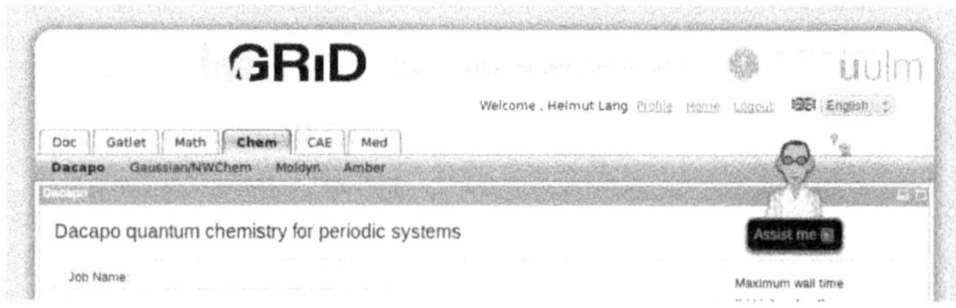

Figure 1: The avatar in idle state.

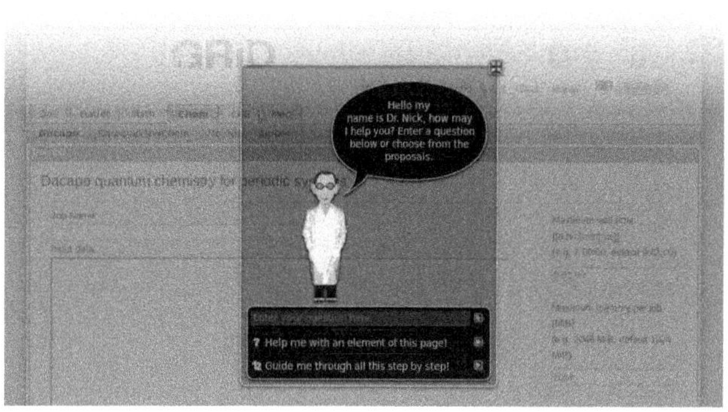

Figure 2: The avatar after clicking "Assist me".

Due to these reasons we abandoned the traditional approach and implemented an avatar based solution. The system is similar to the one proposed by [5], but offers additional capabilities.

The following section will elucidate the features of this help system.

2. FEATURES

In idle state, the avatar is displayed as a small icon along with an "Assist me" button. To keep the avatar from concealing other elements on the page, it is possible to drag the icon to a different location. The current location is stored and retained between page reloads. Thus the avatar consistently remains where he was placed by the user.

A click on the "Assist me" button activates the avatar. In this state the actual content of the page is shaded, the avatar speaks a short introductory message and different options for further actions are presented in an interactive area below the avatar (see Figure 2). If the user disables the speech output of the avatar, messages are displayed as text in the avatar's speech balloon.

2.1 Step-by-Step Guidance

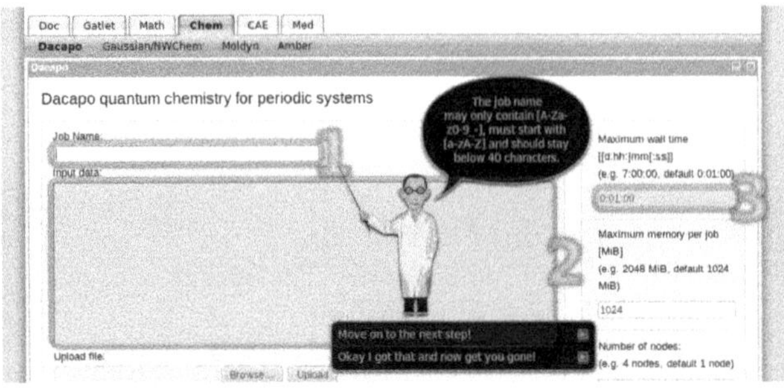

Figure 3: The avatar in step-by-step mode.

When the user clicks on the "Guide me through all this step by step!" option of Figure 2, a step-by-step guide is started and the avatar directs the user to the elements that need to be edited to complete the given task (see Figure 3). In case not all elements needed for task completion are available on one page of the portal, the avatar also assists the user to navigate to the pages containing relevant elements by pointing at the corresponding items in the navigational menu.

2.2 Element Explanation

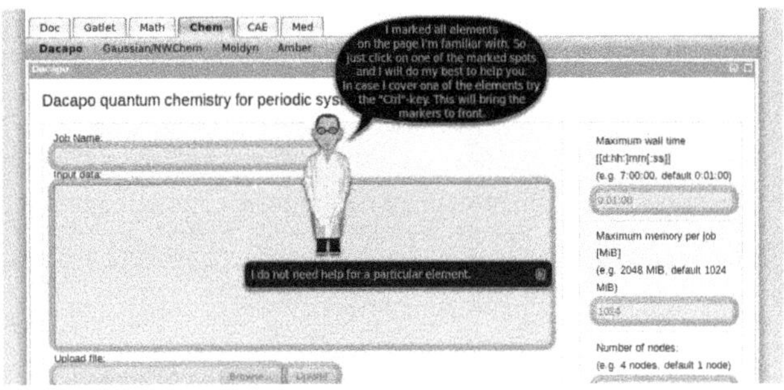

Figure 4: The avatar offering help for elements on the page.

In order to provide further information on elements of the user interface, the user may choose "Help me with an element of this page!" at the greeting dialogue (see Figure 2). After this all elements the avatar is able to explain are distinctively marked (see Figure 4). A click on one of the markers causes the avatar to point at it and provide additional information. The flexible design of this system allows the addition of extra information to virtually every part of the interface. It is possible to address groups of input fields as well as bits of text like table headers. During explanation, the current input field remains editable. It is also possible to define example data for input fields. This example input is pasted into the field when the user chooses the corresponding option in the interactive area below the avatar.

2.3 Related Information

An input field directly below the image of the avatar (see Figure 2) allows to enter questions covering related topics. The input is sent to the server, scanned for keywords and a list containing the seven best matching answers is returned to the client. Those answers are proposed to the user. When the user clicks on one of the proposals, the answer is presented in a slide-show like manner, where the avatar makes remarks on certain elements. Next to this rather sophisticated way of presentation, it is also possible to just display some text in the speech balloon, depending on the complexity of the answer.

Furthermore it is possible for developers to suggest context dependent questions, displayed as options in the greeting dialogue. That way users get an idea on how to formulate questions for the avatar and which kind of questions the avatar might be able to answer.

Keeping logs of questions asked on certain pages can be used to determine frequently asked questions and make appropriate suggestions.

3. TECHNICAL REALIZATION

As a web portal constitutes the user interface of the given system, the avatar was also developed using web technologies. Hence the client side part of the implementation is completely JavaScript based and thus compatible to the majority of contemporary browsers without additional plugins or addons. On the server side, the avatar is integrated into an existing web portal. A servlet is used to find answers for user questions and to dynamically generate step-by-step guides according to the current layout of the portal.

Files containing answers as well as the step-by-step guides are tagged with keywords. When the user asks a question, the text of this question is compared to those keywords by means of their Levenshtein distance [3]. The list of best answers is generated considering the number of words in the query that appear in the set of keywords of a particular answer along with a ranking based on the overall number of appearances of a certain keyword. This means for example that a match of a quite common word like "How", that appears in the keyword list of most step-by-step guides, has less influence on the ranking than a rather exotic word like "credential".

To facilitate the avatar's speech output, a text-to-speech engine is used and audio files are generated according to the text messages the avatar is supposed to speak.

4. CONCLUSION

Despite the fact that our system was developed for a quite explicit use case, its flexible design and its dependency on standard web technologies nevertheless allow to easily port it to different domains and systems. We have already developed versions of the system for Liferay [4] and GridSphere [2].

5. REFERENCES

[1] bwGRiD portal project. `http://www.bw-grid.de/`.

[2] GridSphere Portal Framework. `http://www.gridsphere.org/`.

[3] W. I. Levenshtein. Binary Codes Capable of Correcting Deletions, Insertions and Reversals. *Soviet Physics Doklady*, 10:707, 1966.

[4] Liferay.com. `http://www.liferay.com/`.

[5] T. Rist, E. André, and J. Müller. Adding animated presentation agents to the interface. *Proceedings of the 2nd international conference on Intelligent User Interfaces*, pages 79–86, 1997.

GamEMO: How Physiological Signals Show your Emotions and Enhance your Game Experience

Chanel Guillaume
Swiss Center for Affective Sciences
University of Geneva
Rue des Battoirs 7
1205 Geneva, Switzerland
+41 22 379 98 11
guillaume.chanel@unige.ch

Kalogianni Konstantina
Computer Science Department
University of Geneva
Rte de Drize 7
1227 Carouge, Switzerland
+41 22 379 01 83
kkalogia@gmail.com

Pun Thierry
Computer Science Department
University of Geneva
Rte de Drize 7
1227 Carouge, Switzerland
+41 22 379 01 53
thierry.pun@unige.ch

ABSTRACT
The proposed demonstration is an automatic emotion assessment installation used for game's dynamic difficulty adjustment. The goal of the system is to maintain the player of the game in a state of entertainment and engagement where his/her skills match the difficulty level of the game. The player's physiological signals are recorded while playing a Tetris game and signal processing, feature extraction and classification techniques are applied to the signals in order to detect when the player is anxious or bored. The level of the Tetris game is then adjusted according to the player's detected emotional state. The demonstration will also serve as an experimental protocol to test the player's experience through their interaction with the proposed platform.

Categories and Subject Descriptors
D.3.3 [Programming Languages]: Python, I.5.4 [Applications]: Signal processing, K.8.0 [General]: Games

Keywords
Affective Computing, Games, Emotion Assessment, Physiological Signal Processing, Pattern Recognition, Classification.

1. INTRODUCTION
Computer game experience can be described as joyful and entertaining, though it can sometimes produce negative feelings as anxiety or boredom. Certainly, it elicitates various feelings to players that can be taken into consideration in order to enhance the gaming experience. For instance it seems that different game difficulty levels correspond to distinguishable emotions [1]. According to emotion and flow theories [3], [4] strong involvement in a task occurs when the skills of an individual meet the challenge of a task (Fig. 1). Too much challenge would raise anxiety and not enough would induce boredom. Affective computing [7] along with multimodal interaction has opened a new path in human-computer interaction (HCI) where machine's behavior is adjusted dynamically to user's affective cues. It follows that entertainment and engagement of players, as being the main goals of a game, can be achieved through automatic adjustment of a game's level according to user's emotional feedback: the difficulty of the game should be lowered when the player is anxious and increased when the player is bored.

According to [6], a dynamic difficulty adjustment affective computer game can enhance the gaming experience by making it less stressful and more challenging.

ICMI '12, October 22–26, 2012, Santa Monica, California, USA.
ACM 978-1-4503-1467-1/12/10.

Emotions can be detected through measurements of the peripheral nervous system activity (e.g., heart rate, electrodermal activity-EDA, Blood Volume Pulse- BVP). Evidence for emotion's detection through peripheral signals and its use in affective computing can be given from several studies in the literature [1], [2], [5], [6], [7], [8]. The challenge is to compute and then classify multimodal physiological features into given emotional states with a sufficient accuracy.

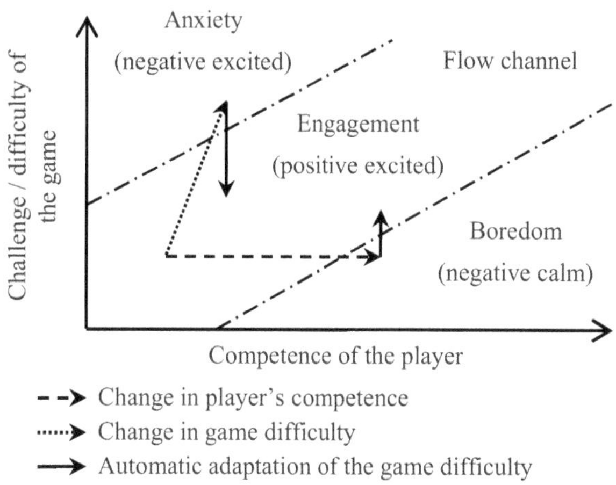

Figure 1: Flow chart and the suggested automatic adaptation to emotional reactions [1].

In the current study, automatic emotion assessment through several peripheral signals is implemented in order to provide emotional feedback to the computer game (Tetris) and adapt the difficulty level of the game (speed of the falling blocks). In this way the considered emotional states, anxiety and boredom are used to automatically adjust the Tetris level to the player's skills.

2. SYSTEM
2.1 System's Description
2.1.1 Game Player (P)
The player (P) is seated in front of the computer G (Fig. 2). In his disposal there are a keyboard and a screen that are used to play the Tetris game. While interacting with the game, P's peripheral physiological signals (ElectroDermal Activity - EDA, Blood Volume Pulse - BVP, Skin Temperature and Chest Cavity Expansion) are continuously recorded from his non-dominant hand and his chest. P is thus able to play Tetris with his dominant hand using the keyboard.

2.1.2 Amplifier Box (B) & Data Acquisition Computer (A)

The peripheral electrodes are connected to the ActiveTwo AD-box from Biosemi™ (B) (Fig. 2). B is used to convert the analog recorded signals to digital signals and to send the data, via an optical fiber, guaranteeing player's galvanic isolation, to the data acquisition computer (A) (Fig. 2). The signal acquisition program (Actiview™) is installed on computer A and is used for displaying the physiological signals and sending the physiological data via TCP/IP connection to the main computer (G) (Fig. 2).

2.1.3 Gaming and Processing Computer (G)

This computer is situated in front of P and is used in the current installation for the following reasons:

- interaction of the player with the game;
- multimodal signals processing;
- classification of player's emotional state;
- adjustment of Tetris difficulty level according to the detected emotion.

The Tetris game is an adapted installation of DotNETris implementing 25 difficulty levels modulated by the speed of the falling blocks (one block going down a line every 0.54 s at level 1 and every 0.003 s for level 25). The game is played by using the arrows of the keyboard.

The signal's processing and the classification are implemented with modules written in Python. Before starting the processing and the classification, the system need to be calibrated by recording a one minute baseline with the player staying relaxed. Once the baseline is recorded the signal processing and classification systems are executed together with the game. The system always uses the last minute of recorded physiological activity to infer the emotional state of the player. In consequence the first estimation can only be given after one minute of playing after which the system gives an estimate every 30 seconds.

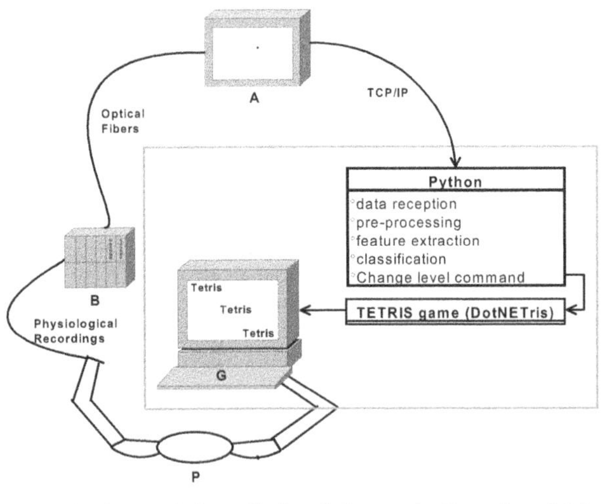

Figure 2: System's Installation Schema: A: Data Acquisition Computer, B: Amplifier G: Main computer, P: Game Player

The first processing step is the data reception through TCP/IP connection and buffering in a one minute data buffer. Then all physiological data are pre-processed through filtering and referencing. Heart rate is computed from the BVP signal. Feature extraction is then required to characterize player's physiological states. Six features were chosen based on our previous study [1]: average temperature, average heart rate, average EDA, the duration of decreasing EDA over the recording period, the number of peaks in the EDA signal and chest expansion standard deviation. A Linear Discriminant Analysis (LDA) classifier is trained on the data collected in [1] and is then applied to the on-line extracted features in order to determine the current emotional state of the player among boredom and anxiety. The last step is to adjust game's level to player's current state. Detection of anxiety leads to the decrease of one game level and detection of boredom to an increase of one game level.

3. TESTING PROTOCOL

In order to test the present installation, participants will be asked to sit in front of the demonstration computer. They will be equipped with 5 recording electrodes at their non-dominant hand for referencing, EDA and temperature measurements. A BVP sensor will be clipped around the thumb of the same hand and one respiration belt will be tied around their abdomen. They will be asked to stay calm and relaxed for at least 1 min in order to record the baseline activity and then they will start playing the game. The game will be adjusted by the experimenter and some of the participants will start with the high difficulty level and some other from the low difficulty level. Affective game experience will be evaluated at the end of the demo session with a questionnaire.

4. REFERENCES

[1] Chanel, G., Rebetez, C., Bétrancourt, M., and Pun, T. 2011. Emotion Assesment From Physiological Signals for Adaptation of Game Difficulty. IEEE Transactions on Systems, Man ans Cybernetics. Vol. 41.no. 6.

[2] Chanel, G., Kierkels, J. J. M., Soleymani, M. and Pun, T. 2009. Short-term emotion assessment in a recall paradigm. Int. J. Human-Comput. Stud.. Vol. 67. no. 8. pp. 607-627.

[3] Cowie, R Cowie, R., Douglas-Cowie, E., Tsapatsoulis, N., Votsis, G. and Kollias, S. 2001. Emotion recognition in human-computer. interaction IEEE Signal Process. Mag. vol. 18. pp. 32-80.

[4] Csikszentmihalyi, M. Flow: The Psychology of Optimal Experience. New York : Harper Collins, 1991.

[5] Lisetti, C. L. and Nasoz, F. 2004. Using noninvasive wearable computers to recognize human emotions from physiological signals. J. Appl. Signal. Process. no. 11. pp. 1672-1687.

[6] Liu, C., Agrawal, P., Sarkar, N. and Chen. S., 2009 . Dynamic Difficulty Adjustment in Computer Games Throughh Real Anxiety-Based Affective Feedback. Intil. Journal Of Human–Computer Interaction. vol. 25. pp. 506-529.

[7] Picard, R.W. 1997. Affective Computing. Cambridge: MIT Press

[8] Rani, P., Liu, C., Sarkar, N. and Vanman, E. 2006. An empirical study of machine learning techniques for affect recognition in human-robot interaction. Pattern Anal. Appl. vol. 9. pp. 58-69.

Multimodal Collaboration for Crime Scene Investigation in Mediated Reality

Dragoş Datcu
Delft University of Technology
Faculty of Technology, Policy and Management
Jaffalaan 5, 2628BX Delft, The Netherlands
D.Datcu@tudelft.nl

Thomas Swart
Delft University of Technology
Faculty of Industrial Design Engineering
Landbergstraat 15
2628CE Delft
The Netherlands

Stephan Lukosch
Delft University of Technology
Faculty of Technology, Policy and Management
Jaffalaan 5, 2628BX Delft, The Netherlands
S.G.Lukosch@tudelft.nl

Zoltan Rusak
Delft University of Technology
Faculty of Industrial Design Engineering
Landbergstraat 15
2628CE Delft,
The Netherlands
Z.Rusak@tudelft.nl

ABSTRACT
In this paper, we present an innovative mediated reality-oriented, real-time software system designed to support multimodal collaboration among remote CSI experts and forensic investigators at the crime scene. Our prototype integrates state-of-the art technologies for stereo navigation, 3D digital mapping and adaptive hand gesture-based user interface for natural interaction. The multimodal interface accepts mouse inputs, audio and hand gestures possibly while interacting with a purposively designed physical object. The evaluation done by a panel of international CSI practitioners [5] using an adapted Burkhardt et al. method [1], shows that our prototype system genuinely fits into the common practice of forensic investigation while clearly boosting the quality of collaboration. At the moment, the system is under consideration for routinely being adopted as part of special procedures by The Forensic Institute in The Hague, The Netherlands [6].

Categories and Subject Descriptors
H.1.2 **[User/Machine Systems]**: Human factors

General Terms
Human Factors, Measurement, Documentation, Design, Security.

Keywords
Collaborative systems, Mediated reality, Multimodal interfaces, Hand-gesture interaction, Marker-less tracking and mapping.

1. INTRODUCTION
Heavy crime cases that are typically handled by the Netherlands Forensics Institute commonly require complex procedures with regard to the technology capabilities, personnel instruction, promptness of reaction, diligence, time-constrains and collaboration among personnel. Starting from the first moment of the forensic procedure, the forensic investigators have to swiftly discover, track and secure the decaying evidence and to formulate, collect and store information for later processing. All these procedural steps present a rather high workload associated to the human factor. In this work context, the use of a wearable head mounted device combined with the mediated reality technology [4] and with support for multimodal interaction can prove its appropriateness due to the ability to add extra visual information to and to enhance the perception of direct visual observation with the goal of easing the forensic undertaking. As partner of the Netherlands Forensic Institute in the CSI The Hague project [6], the Delft University of Technology has developed a mediated reality system that supports the joint work of forensic personnel, laymen as well as remote forensic experts. Figure 1 shows a typical work scenario involving a forensic investigator at the crime scene. By using a lightweight head mounted device, the investigator accesses the mediated reality oriented system and digitizes the physical scene, places virtual tags, loads 3D models, computes bullet trajectories, places restricted virtual area ribbons and collaborates with the remote experts.

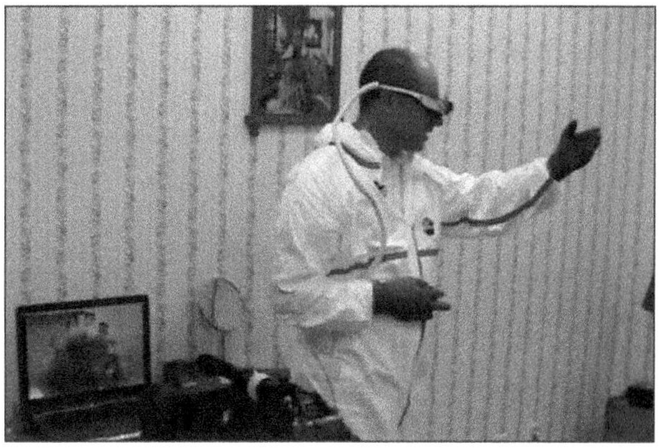

Figure 1. Typical work scenario depicting the forensic investigator at the crime scene. The lightweight head mounted device provides access to the mediated reality-based multimodal interface.

The system graphically renders an overlay on the real scene, showing virtual scene with a dense map as well as virtual artifacts placed during the collaborative work session, a user interface and a tool set. The graphical rendering is done by OGRE 3D game engine [2]. Users benefit from the hand gesture interaction to access the icon-based interface, possibly in combination with using physical objects. To design the system, we followed a clear set of requirements and suggestions given by five international forensic experts during a series of structured interviews held at the beginning of the project.

2. MEDIATED REALITY SYSTEM
The demo of the multimodal CSI The Hague system implies the collaborative work of two or more people, laymen, forensic

ICMI '12, October 22–26, 2012, Santa Monica, California, USA.
ACM 978-1-4503-1467-1/12/10.

investigators and experts. The system provides different ways of interaction, according to the location and type of user. The user at the crime scene uses a head mounted device taking the form of a modified Carl Zeiss Cinemizer OLED having attached in front two disassembled Microsoft HD-5000 webcams. The cameras provide a full stereoscopic 30Hz, 720p resolution pipeline. The assembly weighs about 170 grams and complies with the requirement for a lightweight head mounted device. The user wearing a head mounted display has a lightweight backpack containing a laptop, and operates according to the standard CSI procedure. While the user walks around at the crime scene, our software system processes the video data from the camera rig in real-time and automatically computes the 3D pose information, generates and extends the 3D maps of the physical scene. The implementation for stereo video processing is based on an adapted stereo vision model of Parallel Tracking and Mapping – PTAM algorithm [2][3]. The 3D pose estimation relies on the detection and tracking of natural 2D visual features on both left and right video channels. In this way, visual markers need not be physically placed in the scene so as to make the system operational. The mechanism is highly robust to visual occlusions. The multimodal interface for the user at the crime scene is reactive to hand gestures and supports the interaction with the virtual objects and menu items in mediated reality, possibly in combination with specific physical objects (Figure 2). Our real-time hand gesture recognition system is able to distinguish between three types of gestures. To trigger the activation or deactivation of the on-screen menu, the user proceeds with the left thumb-up or the left thumb-down gestures. Once activated, the interface renders the graphical menu in form of a set of icons surrounding the left hand. Then the menu is spatially locked.

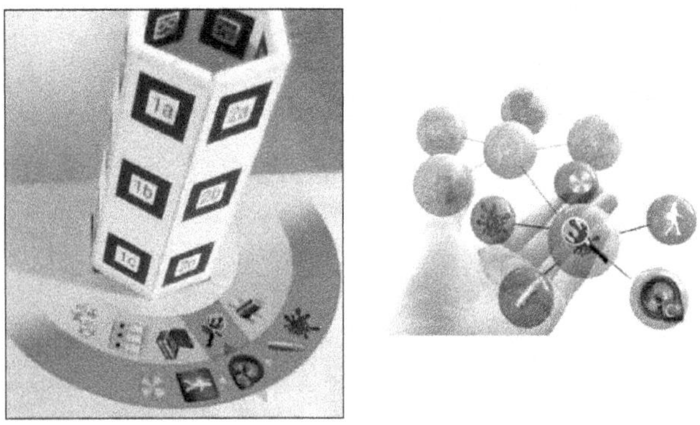

Figure 2. Mediated view illustrating the multimodal interface with menu icons around a physical object or hand.

The user triggers the menu selection event by moving the left or the right hand forward quickly and moving it again more than halfway backwards along the path. This mechanism ensures that both small and large hand gestures for selections are detected correctly. Apart for the menu interface, the user uses the right hand also as a 3D pointing device and for selecting virtual objects in the scene. The automatic detection of hands employs an adaptive mechanism to determine whether to rely on using the previously generated disparity maps, on skin color segmentation or on both, depending on the lighting conditions. The automatic gesture recognition efficiently fulfills the forensic experts' requirement for bare hand gesture interface. As a separate type of multimodal interaction, the user can hold and manipulate a physical object with the left hand and use the right hand to access the interface menu items which are available in the mediated reality (Figure 2, left). The system can be used either by one forensic user at the crime scene or by multiple users during collaborative remote work sessions, possibly involving experts at the distance. In the multiuser scenario, the collaboration follows a turn-based approach, the functions to alter the common 3D work space being accessible to only one user at the time. The multimodal system interface enables users to use also audio communication. Remote experts benefit also of other types of interfaces including big screens, tablet devices and mouse device interaction. Our prototype for mediated reality enhanced collaboration was measured in specific experimental scenarios involving remote cooperation between a forensic expert and a layman. The evaluation based on a model on seven dimensions extended from Burkhardt et al.[1], indicated that the system is suitably ready for being used by actual teams in real forensic investigation scenarios [5].

3. CONCLUSIONS AND FUTURE WORK

One of the goals of the CSI The Hague project is the introduction of new technologies to support collaboration of forensic investigators with remote experts using multimodal interaction and mediated reality. In our demonstration, we will show our prototype for collaborative and multimodal interaction in mediated reality for forensic investigation. As future work we plan to adapt the system for a modular and multiplatform architecture, to build a software version for handheld devices, to investigate the use of inertia trackers, to improve the accuracy of depth maps and to explore the potential of automatic face analysis technology with a special focus on face recognition models. In addition we will prospect the possibility to extend the use of existing physical objects to turn them into active components for multimodal user interaction in mediated reality.

4. ACKNOWLEDGMENTS

This project is funded by Pieken in de Delta, Provincie Zuid-Holland, Gemeente Den Haag.

5. REFERENCES

[1] Burkhardt, J., Détienne, F., Hébert, A., Perron, L., Safin, S., Leclercq, P. 2009. An approach to assess the quality of collaboration in technology-mediated design situation, *European Conference on Cognitive Ergonomics: Designing beyond the Product - Understanding Activity and User Experience in Ubiquitous Environments*, 1-9.

[2] Kerger, F. 2010. OGRE 3D 1.7 Beginner's Guide, Packt Publishing.

[3] Klein,G., and Murray, D. 2007. Parallel Tracking and Mapping for Small AR Workspaces, In *Proceedings of the International Symposium on Mixed and Augmented Reality*, 225-234.

[4] Mann, S., Barfield, W. 2003. Introduction to mediated reality, *International Journal of Human-Computer Interaction*, 205-208.

[5] Poelman, R., Akman, O., Lukosch, S., and Jonker, P. 2012. As if being there: mediated reality for crime scene investigation. In *Proceedings of the ACM 2012 Conference on Computer Supported Cooperative Work*. CSCW'12. ACM, New York, NY, 1267-1276.

[6] http://www.csithehague.com/.

PAMOCAT: Linking Motion Capturing and Conversation Analysis

Bernhard Brüning
CITEC Central Lab
University of Bielefeld
Germany 33615 Bielefeld
+49 521 106-67258
bbruening@uni-bielefeld.de

Christian Schnier
Applied Informatics Group
University of Bielefeld
Germany 33615 Bielefeld
+49 521 106-12230
cschnier@uni-bielefeld.de

ABSTRACT
In order to model the non-verbal communicative conduct of humans, it is needed to be understood in detail. Therefore it is fruitful to combine qualitative (Conversation Analysis) and quantitative analytical (Motion Capturing) methods. Tools for data visualization and annotation are important since they constitute a central interface between different research approaches and methodologies. With this aim we have developed the pre-annotation tool "PAMOCAT– Pre Annotation Motion Capture Analysis Tool" [2]. This has a sophisticated user interface that easily allows the annotating person to find correlations between different joints and/or phenomena, to analyze the corresponding 3D pose in a reconstructed virtual environment, and to export combined qualitative and quantitative annotations to standard annotation tools. The tool has the functionality to easily search for distinct constellations of different phenomena and display frames in which these could be found in an annotation overview.

Categories and Subject Descriptors
Multimodal Corpora Analysis Tool

General Terms
Human Factors, Languages, Theory, Verification.

Keywords
Motion Capturing, annotation, motion analysis.

1. INTRODUCTION
Despite important progress in the field of human-robot and human-agent interaction, communication skills are still far away from the smoothness of the social behavior of human natural conversation. In order to build up more appropriate interaction models both – human-human and human-robot interaction scenarios – it is necessary to be analyzed and understood in detail. So when new behaviors are discovered, these results can be fed back into the model. To do so, researchers began to link qualitative sequential analysis of videotaped interaction data with quantitative approaches based on Motion Capture data. Then an in-depth understanding of interactional procedures could be combined with quantifiable three-dimensional measures of body motions. In order to carry out such combined analyzes, novel tools for supporting the visualization and analysis of the different types of data are required. Existing annotation software, such as ELAN or Anvil, has recently started to integrate facilities for displaying time series data. The current software lacks the ability to handle data from multiple participants and it offers only limited support for motion analysis. ELAN [3] has no Motion Capture view ability and ANVILE [4] has a limited single person motion capture view, but no automatically motion analysis abilities). Our tool PAMOCAT addresses these gaps. We will show how PAMOCAT can be used for annotation support in a case were three participants are recorded with a motion tracking system and 4 HD cameras [1].

ICMI '12, October 22–26, 2012, Santa Monica, California, USA.
ACM 978-1-4503-1467-1/12/10.

2. PAMOCAT FEATURES

2.1 Visualization of data
The main visualization features of PAMOCAT include "free position of view", "multiple skeleton visualization", "trajectories", "synchronic inspection of all data", and "analysis of the recorded motion in relation to a virtual environment".

2.2 Analysis of data
The most important features are in the field of motion analysis and represent different phenomena, which can be combined to search for individual situations of interest in the corpus. These phenomena include:

2.2.1 Single Person Phenomena
- At which time does global motion activity occur? The automatic identification of motion activity allows faster detection of relevant segments in larger corpus.
- When local activity does occur at a particular joint?

  Specific activity at some particular DOF - degree of freedom, for example: head orientation changes.
- Where are the home positions?
- When will occur one of the learned postures?

2.2.2 Person overlapping Phenomena
- When does an intrusion occur into co-participant´s peripersonal space?
- Where are the participants oriented at?

  With the represented skeletons and the virtually added environment we are able to calculate if a participant is oriented at one of these objects or limbs.

2.2.3 Constellations of different phenomena
The annotation area has two analysis modes with several annotation lines. The first mode is the key interval annotation with an overview of all single DOFs of the skeleton (each DOF is an annotation line). This mode focuses on the time relations of the active joints. The second mode is the annotation overview

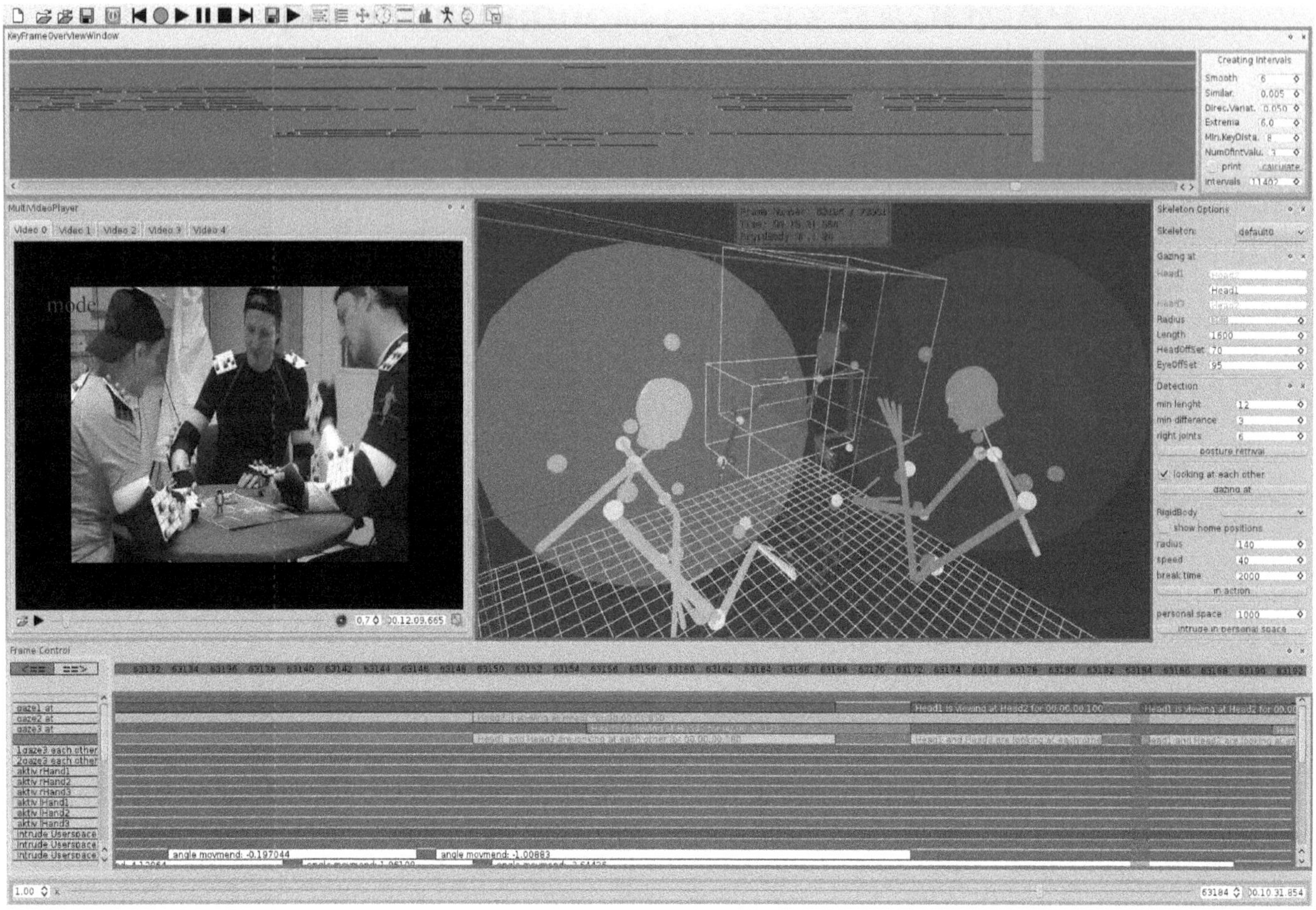

Figure 1 GUI with VideoPlayerFunctions (a), KeyIntervalOverViewWidget (b), MoCapView (d), Annotation Widget (e), KeyInterval-Calculation-Parameters (f), Time Slider (h), SearchSurfWidgets (i).

phenomenon (cf. figure 1i, similar color marked area), in which different phenomena like "postures", "oriented at", "oriented at each other", "hand activity", "intrude into other user space", "all gazing at table" of each person and person overlapping are arranged (each line is for a different phenomenon). In order to search for constellations of these phenomena, we select these phenomena and, finally, browse through the results. The results are moments in time when each constellation phenomenon starts. At each of these moments, it can be made a detailed analysis of all the synchronic views of the data. Besides this, each DOF can be used as additional phenomena for the constellations search.

2.3 GUI OVERVIEW

The main window shows the 3D visualization from the recorded participants (cf. figure 1d) with 3D objects additionally loaded. These define reference points are represented for the recorded interactions with the skeletons, so that the motion can be analyzed in relation to them. Above the motion capture view is a widget (figure 1b) which displays an overview of all DOF from all the joints of a selected person. The display shows the motion activity for each joint separately. Below this widget there is an optional plot (must be selected in an option widget) for the corresponding angle, speed, and acceleration. Additionally, there is always a synchronized view of all the recorded videos with the rest of the data (figure 1a). At the bottom of the window is a slider that allows the user to scroll the time (figure 1h). The annotation widget (figure 1f) allows to add information manually or to edit the automatically generated or previously added information. Finally, these annotations can be exported into the ELAN file format to make the concluding annotations.

3. REFERENCES

[1] Pitsch, K., Brüning, B., Schnier, C. and Wachmuth, S., 2010. *Linking Conversation Analysis and Motion Capturing: "How to robustly track multiple participants?"*. In Proceedings Workshop on Multimodal Corpora, LREC.

[2] Brüning, B., Schnier, C., Pitsch, K., Wachsmuth, S., 2012, *PAMOCAT: Automatic retrieval of specified postures,* In Proceedings Workshop on Multimodal Corpora, LREC

[3] Auer, E., Russel, A. Sloetjes, H., Witternurg, P., Schreer, O., Masneri, S., Schneider, D. & Toepel, S., 2010. *ELAN as flexible annotation framework for sound and image processing detectors*. Proceedings LREC

[4] Heloir, A., Neff, M., Kipp, M., 2010, *Exploiting Motion Capture for Virtual Human Animation: Data Collection and Annotation Visualization.* In Proceedings of LREC Workshop on "Multimodal Corpora", ELDA.

Multimodal Dialogue in Mobile Local Search

Patrick Ehlen
AT&T
525 Market Street
San Francisco, CA 94105
ehlen@research.att.com

Michael Johnston
AT&T Labs Research
180 Park Ave
Florham Park, NJ 07932
johnston@research.att.com

ABSTRACT

Speak4it[SM] is a multimodal, mobile search application that provides information about local businesses. Users can combine speech and touch input simultaneously to make search queries or commands to the application. For example, a user might say, "gas stations," while simultaneously tracing a route on a touchscreen. In this demonstration, we describe the extension of our multimodal semantic processing architecture and application from a one-shot query system to a multimodal dialogue system that tracks dialogue state over multiple turns. We illustrate the capabilities and limitations of an information-state-based approach to multimodal interpretation. We provide interactive demonstrations of Speak4it on a tablet and a smartphone, and explain the challenges of supporting true multimodal interaction in a deployed mobile service.

Categories and Subject Descriptors

H.5.2 [**Information Interfaces and Presentation (e.g. HCI)**]: User Interfaces—input devices and strategies (e.g. mouse, touchscreen), natural language

General Terms

Algorithms, Design

Keywords

Multimodal, Dialog, Search

1 INTRODUCTION

Speak4it is a commercially-available, multimodal mobile search application that allows users to find information on local businesses. Using a smartphone or tablet device, a user can issue commands that integrate simultaneous inputs from speech and touchscreen gestures traced with the finger on a dynamic map. For example, a user might say "gas stations" while tracing a route on which to search for gas stations, or, "Are there any nail salons in this area?" while circling a particular region.

Speak4it performs simultaneous recognition of user speech and deictic touch gestures. Speech, gesture, and context data are streamed to a server-based Multimodal Semantic Interpretation System (MSIS) [8], which fuses speech and gesture recognition results into a single semantic representation [1], and then interprets that representation in context, hopefully producing a search query that conforms to what the user intended.

ICMI '12, October 22–26, 2012, Santa Monica, California, USA.
ACM 978-1-4503-1467-1/12/10.

While Speak4it has been widely available as a multimodal search application [11], until recently it performed traditional "one-shot" search, where each new query is presumed to be independent of information from earlier queries. There was one exception to this "stateless" basis of interaction. The application keeps track of the user's last spoken location, and also map manipulations, in order to determine the intended search location from among four possible options: The user's current GPS location, the location now displayed on the map, the location mentioned in a prior utterance, or the location indicated with some touch gesture [4]. The process that disambiguates which location the user intended to use was informed by discourse theory—in particular the theory of grounding [3]—and leveraged some state data about the discourse context (time of last map movement, last spoken location, etc.) that was passed back with each new query. In this sense, Speak4it functioned as a fairly rudimentary dialogue system.

Figure 1. Speak4it[SM] interaction

As our system collected query data over time, we witnessed users attempting to say more sophisticated, dialogue-oriented things, such as making corrections or revisions to prior queries. To properly handle these types of dialogue moves, we required a more sophisticated dialogue handler, and implemented an information-state-based multimodal dialogue system—in the spirit of some other multimodal dialogue prototypes [cf. 6, 7, 9, 10]—that is the subject of this demonstration.

2 MULTIMODAL DIALOGUE

Speak4it handles four types of dialogue actions: *Search*, such as "coffee shops around here"; *Command*, such as "Call this place"; *Revision*, such as "Is there a 7-Eleven in this area?…How about a Quiznos?"; and *Correction*, such as "I said *Pita* House, not Pizza House." Speech recognition and high-level parsing are performed by a Hierarchical Language Model that comprises several deterministic models used for identifying commands and carrier phrases, and a deep stochastic model to perform business and location recognition [2]. The deterministic models provide semantic labels for some phrase segments, and other segments that are recognized in the stochastic model are parsed by a statistical parser [5]. These semantic labels, in combination with semantic labels from touch gestures, are then used to determine which dialogue action to associate with a multimodal utterance.

The information state tracks the conversational salience of two types of entities: locations, and search topics. A separate stack is maintained for each. When new entities of either type appear in the dialogue parse, a binding function attempts to integrate them with the top entity in the corresponding stack. If the two entities cannot bind, the top entity in the stack is pushed down, with the new entity replacing it as the salient entity. For example, consider the following:

User: Are there any Japanese restaurants around here?

[System returns some results near user's current location]

User: How about Korean?

In this example, the word "Korean" is parsed as a potential search topic, though the word "Korean" by itself is not an adequate replacement of the search topic. This would cause a search for other types of non-restaurant businesses that contain the word, though intuitively we know the intended search topic is "restaurants," with "Korean" as a constraining adjective. So when the prior search topic can be bound to the new adjective, either by replacement or refinement, then the result of that operation becomes the new search topic. Otherwise, if no binding can occur, the prior entity is pushed down and the new entity placed at the top of the stack.

Similar operations work on locations, as in this Correction example:

User: chiropractors in Glendale

[System returns chiropractors in Glendale, California]

User: I meant Arizona

[System returns chiropractors in Glendale, Arizona]

In this case, the second query results in a parse with "Arizona" as a location, of type *state*, which binds to the entity on the salient location stack to replace the *state* slot with a new value. Deictic gestures can also serve as location entities, so the user above might then say:

User: What about here? [circles an area]

[System zooms in to the circled region and returns chiropractors there]

This would result in the area gesture attaching to the top entity in the location stack and refining the salient location. Note that, because deictic gestures are made on a dynamic map whose state is always the result of the prior operation that produced the top entity in the salient locations stack, a gesture will always bind to the prior entity and serve as a refinement that constrains the last location entity.

3 DEMONSTRATION

We demonstrate the Speak4it dialogue capability on a tablet and a smartphone, and explain, in as much detail as time allows, our approach, and similarities to and differences from other multimodal dialogue systems. The only equipment required is a decent wireless connection over WiFi.

4 REFERENCES

[1] Bangalore, S. and Johnston, M. 2009. Robust Understanding in Multimodal Interfaces. *Computational Linguistics* 35:3, 345-397.

[2] Bocchieri, E., Caseiro, D., and Dimitriadis, D. 2011. Speech Recognition Modeling Advances For Mobile Voice Search. In *Proceedings of the 2011 International Conference On Acoustics, Speech and Signal Processing (ICASSP'11),* 4888-4891

[3] Clark, H.H. 1996. *Using Language*. Cambridge: Cambridge University Press.

[4] Ehlen, P. and Johnston, M. 2010. Location Grounding in Multimodal Local Search. In *Proceedings of ICMI-MLMI 2010.*

[5] Feng, J., Bangalore, S., and Gilbert, M. 2009. Role of Natural Language Understanding in Voice Local Search. In *Proceedings of Interspeech 2009*, 1859-1862.

[6] Gustafson J., L. Bell, J. Beskow, J. Boye, R. Carlson, J. Edlund, B. Granström, D. House D., and M. Wirén. 2000. AdApt—A Multimodal Conversational Dialogue system in an Apartment Domain. In *Proceedings of ICSLP 2000*, 134-137.

[7] Johnston, M., Bangalore, S., Vasireddy, G., Stent, A., Ehlen, P., Walker, M., Whittaker, S., and Maloor, P. 2002. MATCH: An Architecture for Multimodal Dialogue Systems. In *Proceedings of ACL 2002*, 376-383.

[8] Johnston, M. and P. Ehlen. 2011. Speak4it and the Multimodal Semantic Interpretation System. In *Proceedings of Interspeech 2011*, Florence, Italy, 3333-3334.

[9] Lemon, O., Bracy, A., Gruenstein, A., and Peters, S. 2001. Information States in a Multi-modal Dialogue System for Human-Robot Conversation. In *Proceedings of the 5th Workshop on Formal Semantics and Pragmatics of Dialogue (Bi-Dialog 2001)*, 57-67.

[10] Wahlster, W. 2006 *SmartKom: Foundations of Multimodal Dialogue Systems (Cognitive Technologies)*. Springer-Verlag New York, Inc.

[11] http://speak4it.com/

Toward an Argumentation-based Dialogue Framework for Human-Robot Collaboration

Mohammad Q. Azhar
Computer Science
Graduate Center, CUNY
New York, New York
mqazhar@gmail.com

ABSTRACT

The research on human-robot dialogue to support fluent human robot interaction is still in its early stages. Current issues in the human-robot dialogue domain could be divided into two major categories, which are described in this proposal as the "what to say" problem and the "how to say it" problem. The "what to say" problem addresses ways to determine the content of plausible dialogue during human robot interaction, whereas the "how to say it" problem addresses the best ways for a robot to deliver that content (e.g., using text, gestures, speech or different modalities). Dialogue within the robotics domain also needs to address the "when to say it" problem that considers the timing of dialogue delivery (e.g., turn taking).

Human-robot collaboration may fail for many reasons. This research focuses on conflicts and robot errors during human-robot collaboration. Conflicting beliefs occur when participating collaborators have two different views of the physical world due to inaccessible or non-static information. Intuitively, collaborators need to persuade each other to agree on the same beliefs about the state of the world in order to complete collaborative tasks successfully. Robot errors may happen due to miscommunication or simply lack of communication. Moreover, lack of dialogue support for a human to query a robot makes it even more difficult for error recovery. This may lead to failure of a collaborative plan or shared goal. Dialogue is the natural way to resolve errors due to miscommunication. This research explores the notion of an argumentation-based dialogue method for human-robot interaction (HRI). The proposed research aims to design and implement a logic-based dialogue framework grounded on argumentation theory to address the "what to say" problem of human robot communication during a collaborative task.

Categories and Subject Descriptors

I.2.9 [**Robotics**]: Miscellaneous; H.1.2 [**Models and Principles**]: User/Machine Systems—*Human factors*

ICMI'12, October 22–26, 2012, Santa Monica, California, USA.

General Terms

Design, Human Factors, Theory

Keywords

Dialogue Modeling, Argumentation, Human-Robot Collaboration, Human Robot Interaction

1. MOTIVATION

The research on human-robot dialogue to support fluent human robot interaction is still in its early stages[14, 18]. The current issues in the human-robot dialogue domain could be divided into two major categories, which are described in this proposal as the "what to say" problem and the "how to say it" problem. The "what to say" problem addresses ways to determine the *content* of plausible dialogue during human robot interaction, whereas the "how to say it" problem addresses the best way for a robot to *deliver* (e.g., using text, speech or different modality) that content. Dialogue within the robotics domain also needs to address the "when to say it" problem that considers the timing of dialogue delivery (e.g., turn taking). This research concentrates on the design and implementation of a logic-based dialogue framework grounded on argumentation theory to address the "what to say" problem of human robot communication during a collaborative task.

2. BACKGROUND

According to Goodrich and Schultz [8], "The HRI problem is to understand and shape the interaction between human and robot". Due to the dynamic physical nature of this interaction, HRI has many challenging aspects that are yet to be explored and investigated and providing support for human-robot dialogue is a daunting task.

Dialogue is a communication process between two or more parties. Humans naturally use dialogue to communicate with other humans. Thus, dialogue has been considered as a natural means of communication for humans to interact with robots. As with two humans, *human-robot dialogue* requires sharing of information (e.g., data, symbols, and context) and control. The style of dialogue varies based on the task and the environment. Typically, a *dialogue management* module provides the basic functionality to translate human language to machine language and provides feedback that the human uses. A *user model* represents the system's knowledge about users (e.g., novice, expert) with whom the system interacts [7].

The research on embodied cues for dialogue with robots delves into the delivery of human-robot dialogue which is referred to in this proposal as the "how to say it" problem [14, 22]. Thomaz and Chao [26] explored the turn-taking aspects of human-robot communication. Turn-taking is the challenge of figuring out which partner has the floor to speak or act during conversation and could be categorized as the "when to say it" problem. Tellex et al. [25] proposed a framework that addresses the challenge of mapping between human language (e.g., here, there) and the robot's external world (e.g, room1, room3). TeamTalk [13] is a multimodal human-robot interface that focuses on interpreting spoken dialogue interactions (as well as mouse clicks and pen gestures) between humans and robots to perform tasks associated with hunting for treasure.

Recently, researchers have looked into generating dialogue for robots (e.g., chef-robot [28], HRI-OS [7]) based on a user's level of experience (e.g, novice, expert). In addition, natural language processing (NLP) models have also been integrated into a robot dialogue module [4]. Many existing HRI systems use scripted dialogue management modules (e.g., museum robot [27], robot receptionist [10]). However, a scripted dialogue model does not scale for robots (e.g., rescue robot, team robot) that operate in a highly dynamic and changing environment (e.g, rescue arena) where human and robot work together to achieve a common goal. Scheutz et al. [21] demonstrated the challenges faced by natural language parsers for robotics systems. The authors categorized six properties for NLP for robots namely: real-time, parallel, spoken, embodied, situated and dialogue-based. One of the challenges of NLP parsers for robotics is that a large amount of corpus data is required to train the system, which is lacking in the domain of human-robot collaboration. Although a natural language dialogue model is a plausible approach in some contexts, it does not yet address many problems of human-robot dialogue due to lack of feasible NLP solutions.

Fischer [12] studies how robot dialogue could be designed to reduce uncertainty about the capabilities of the robot and the joint task. However, the author uses a Wizard-of-Oz study and does not show how this effective dialogue could be generated. A dialogue framework that can generate effective dialogue incorporating participants' beliefs, plans and goals will go a long way.

Rich et al. [19] proposes an application-independent collaboration manager that supports the user's problem-solving process based on a *shared plan theory* [9] of discourse that might be useful for effective human-robot dialogue generation. In the agent-oriented software engineering community, researchers have developed a plan-based dialogue model using a belief, desire and intention (BDI) architecture. A logic-based argumentation approach could be incorporated into BDI architecture [20].

Logic-based argumentation has been proposed for both reasoning and for modeling dialogues between *agents*. *Argumentation theory* [15] can be used to evaluate the acceptability of argument, update or persuade participating collaborator's beliefs and resolve conflicts [15]. An argumentation-based model has been used as a mechanism for conflict resolution in the software-agent paradigm [1] by providing support for dialogue. The notion of an argumentation-based dialogue framework stems from natural human-human dialogue and has been applied to software-based agent-agent dialogue [3]. According to Walton and Krabbe [29], there are six primary types of human dialogue based on participants' knowledge, individual and shared goals. Argumentation-based dialogue has not yet been applied to the human-robot domain, but could be employed to provide effective support to help with diagnosis of robot errors from hardware or software, or conflicts due to changes in the environment. The research described here proposes to apply logic-based argumentation to model three types of dialogues between human and robot.

3. PROBLEM DOMAIN AND PROPOSAL

Generating effective robot dialogue during human-robot collaboration is a daunting task. Both human and robot have to constantly deal with uncertain and conflicting information while collaborating in the dynamic physical world [30], which can lead to *conflicting beliefs*. *Information-seeking*, *inquiry* and *persuasion* dialogues are human communication techniques for conflict resolution during collaboration [16]. At the same time, *robot errors* may happen due to conflicting information, miscommunication or simply lack of communication. Inquiry and information-seeking dialogues could be employed to resolve robot errors due to miscommunication [11].

My research proposes an *argumentation-based HRI dialogue framework* that can provide an effective mechanism of support for generating dialogues to resolve conflicts (i.e., conflicting beliefs, plans and goals) and diagnose robot errors during human-robot collaboration. My approach centers around generating the content of effective dialogue based on reasoning using logical argumentation (e.g., [2]). In my framework, a robot will have models of its world and of its human dialogue partner that will get updated in real time. Using these two models, the robot will reason about the world and be able to generate plausible task-based dialogue that will aid towards fluent and meaningful human-robot communication resolving conflicting beliefs and explaining robot errors. The proposed research is motivated by the following research hypotheses:

- *Hypothesis 1:* Dialogue can provide support for conflict resolution during human-robot collaboration.

- *Hypothesis 2:* Dialogue can provide support for human understanding of why plan/action(s) failed and determining how to recover.

4. APPROACH AND METHODOLOGY

My argumentation-based human-robot interaction system, *ArgHRI*, is comprised of several components: an **ontology** that describes the robot's environment and capabilities, a **memory system** for the robot to maintain its beliefs, an **argumentation engine** that supports the robot's internal decision-making, and a **dialogue system** for interacting with a human.

A critical component of this system is the application of an argumentation engine that the robot can use to reason about how a goal might be achieved, or to resolve conflicts found in the components of its memory. The argumentation engine that will be adapted is called *ArgTrust* and is a partial implementation of the formal system from [24].

My contribution to the ArgHRI framework is a dialogue system for discussing the robot's beliefs with the human.

Three types of dialogues from argumentation theory are relevant here: *information-seeking*, *inquiry* and *persuasion*. A dialogue can be modeled as a two-player game, where each player has a set of "moves" she can make, and the rules of the game dictate which moves are allowed under which conditions.

The dialogue game and associated rules for HRI are applied here by identifying four basic needs for human-robot dialogues: (1) the human could ask the robot to do something for her: *persuasion*; (2) the robot could ask the human for information that the robot does not have and believes that the human has, and vice versa: *information-seeking*; (3) the robot discovers information that the human does not know or that contradicts something the human knows: *persuasion*; and (4) the robot and human together agree to find an answer to something neither of them knows: *inquiry*.

An argumentation-based dialogue manager for human-robot collaboration will be implemented, as illustrated in Figure 1, and integrated into the *HRTeam* framework [23]. HRTeam is designed to support experimentation with mixed-initiative human/multi-robot teams. The current HRTeam system does not contain a dialogue manager. Thus, my proposed argumentation-based dialogue manager will contribute to the existing HRTeam framework.

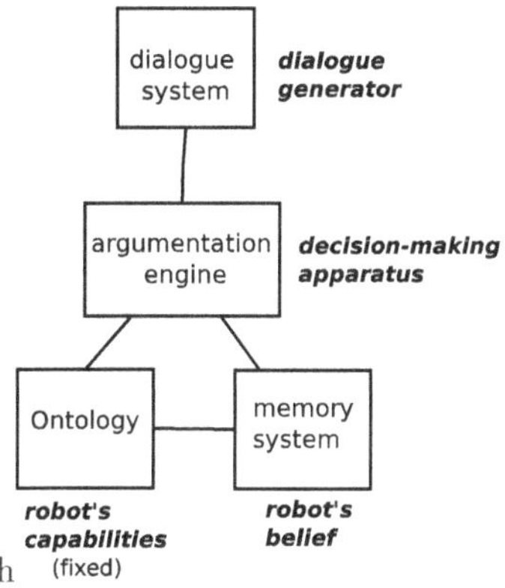

widthwidth

Figure 1: ArgHRI Dialogue Manager

The ArgHRI framework supports human collaboration with only *one* robot and it does not support natural language processing. The human participant provides the robot with an abstract action plan (e.g., go to room 1) for a given goal (or sub goals). This framework allows the human and robot to engage in a dialogue in which they share premises and can exchange the reasons for the beliefs that they hold to resolve conflicts or diagnose errors. The rules for each type of dialogue (e.g., persuasion dialogue) define the allowable set of responses for each opening and subsequent move. The rules followed here are outlined in [17] and illustrated in Figure 2.

For the evaluation of the proposed approach, the *Treasure Hunt* domain [5] will be adapted. The human participant does not have continuous visibility access of the environment and must communicate through dialogues as in a real-world rescue scenario ([6]). The shared *goal* for both human and robot is that the robot needs to find a number of treasures hidden in an arena, within a limited amount of time, while collaborating with the human. All physical experiments will be conducted in the HRTeam arena [23].

Two different studies will be conducted to examine each

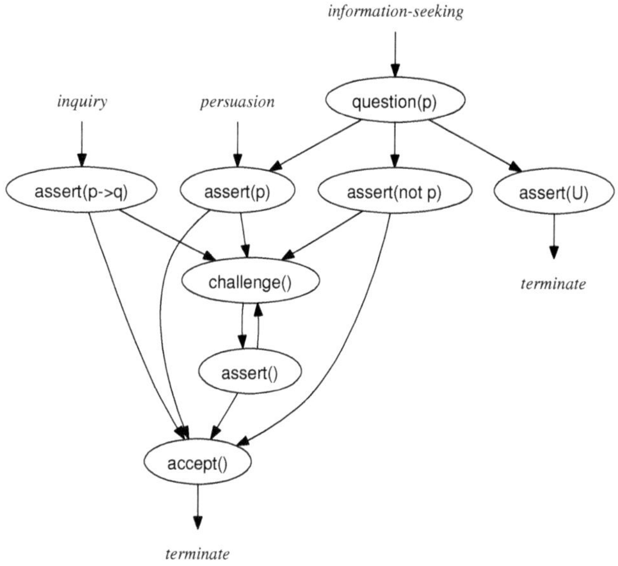

Figure 2: Basic rules of Dialogue Game

hypothesis. The first study will compare the ArgHRI dialogue system that supports *persuasion dialogue* with a system that does not provide support for such dialogue. My hypothesis is that the human and robot will have a higher task-completion rate and the ArgHRI dialogue framework will demonstrate the effectiveness of persuasion dialogue for resolving conflicting plans, goals and beliefs. The second study will compare the ArgHRI dialogue system that supports *information-seeking* and *inquiry* dialogues with a system that does not provide support for such dialogues. My hypothesis is that the human and robot will have higher a task-completion rate and the ArgHRI dialogue framework will demonstrate the effectiveness of information-seeking and inquiry dialogues for recovering from robot errors.

5. RESEARCH PLAN

My research plan is described below:

Complete development of ArgHRI framework	Sep 2012
Complete user studies	Nov 2012
Complete analysis of user studies	Feb 2013
Complete thesis write up	Oct 2013
Defense	Nov 2013

6. CONTRIBUTION

This research will contribute to both the human-robot interaction and argumentation communities: first by bringing into HRI a structured method for a robot to maintain its beliefs, to reason using those beliefs, and to interact with a human via dialogue to resolve conflicts and diagnose errors; and second, by demonstrating a practical implementation in which argumentation is successfully applied in a real-time domain.

7. ACKNOWLEDGEMENTS

I would like to thank my mentor Dr. Elizabeth Sklar for her support and encouragement.

8. REFERENCES

[1] L. Amgoud, S. Belabbes, and H. Prade. Towards a formal framework for the search of a consensus between autonomous agents. In *Workshop on Argumentation in Multi-agent Systems (ArgMAS)*, 2005.

[2] L. Amgoud, N. Maudet, and S. Parsons. Modelling dialogues using argumentation. In *Fourth Conference on Multi-Agent Systems*, Boston, 2000.

[3] E. Black. *A Generative Framework for Argumentation-Based Inquiry Dialogues*. PhD thesis, University of London, 2006.

[4] D. Bohus, A. Raux, T. K. Harris, M. Eskenazi, and A. I. Rudnicky. Olympus: an open-source framework for conversational spoken language interface research. In *HLT-NAACL Workshop on Bridging the Gap: Academic and Industrial Research in Dialog Technology*, 2007.

[5] M. B. Dias, B. Kannan, B. Browning, E. Jones, B. Argall, M. F. Dias, M. B. Zinck, M. Veloso, and A. Stentz. Sliding autonomy for peer-to-peer human-robot teams. Technical report, Robotics Institute, Carnegie Mellon University, 2008.

[6] K. Eberhard, H. Nicholson, S. Kuebler, S. Gundersen, and M. Scheutz. The indiana Cooperative Remote Search Task (CReST) corpus. In *Seventh International Conference on Language Resources and Evaluation (LREC)*, 2010.

[7] T. W. Fong, C. Thorpe, and C. Baur. Collaboration, dialogue, and human-robot interaction. In *Tenth International Symposium of Robotics Research*, 2001.

[8] M. A. Goodrich and A. C. Schultz. Human-robot interaction: a survey. *Foundations and Trends in Human-Computer Interaction*, 1(3), 2007.

[9] B. Grosz and S. Kraus. The evolution of SharedPlans. In *Foundations and Theories of Rational Agency*, 1999.

[10] R. Kirby, F. Broz, J. Forlizzi, M. P. Michalowski, A. Mundell, S. Rosenthal, B. P. Sellner, R. Simmons, K. Snipes, A. Schultz, and J. Wang. Designing robots for long-term social interaction. In *Intl Conf on Intelligent Robots and Systems (IROS)*, 2005.

[11] T. Koulouri and S. Lauria. Exploring miscommunication and collaborative behaviour in human-robot interaction. In *Tenth Annual Meeting of the Special Interest Group on Discourse and Dialogue (SIGDIAL)*, 2009.

[12] F. Krestin. How people talk with robots: Designing dialogue to reduce user uncertainty. *AI Magazine*, 32(4), 2011.

[13] M. R. Marge, A. K. Pappu, B. Frisch, T. K. Harris, and A. I. Rudnicky. Exploring spoken dialog interaction in human-robot teams. In *Workshop on Robots, Games, and Research: Success stories in USARSim*, 2009.

[14] B. Mutlu. Designing embodied cues for dialog with robots. *AI Magazine*, 32(4), 2011.

[15] S. H. Nielsen and S. Parsons. A generalization of Dung's Abstract Framework for Argumentation: Arguing with sets of attacking arguments. In *Workshop on Argumentation in Multi-agent Systems (ArgMAS)*, 2006.

[16] S. Parsons and P. McBurney. Argumentation-based dialogues for agent co-ordination. *Group Decision and Negotiation*, 12(5), 2003.

[17] S. Parsons, P. McBurney, and M. Wooldridge. The mechanics of some formal inter-agent dialogue. In *Advances in Agent Comm.* Springer-Verlag, 2004.

[18] J. Peltason and B. Wrede. The curious robot as a case-study for comparing dialog systems. *AI Magazine*, 32(4), 2011.

[19] C. Rich and C. L. Sidner. Collagen: A collaboration manager for software interface agents. *User Modeling and User-Adapted Interaction*, 8(3-4), 1998.

[20] N. D. Rotstein, A. J. García, and G. R. Simari. Defeasible argumentation support for an extended BDI architecture. In *Workshop on Argumentation in Multi-agent Systems (ArgMAS)*, 2008.

[21] M. Scheutz, R. Cantrell, and P. Schermerhorn. Toward humanlike task-based dialogue processing for human robot interaction. *AI Magazine*, 32(4), 2011.

[22] R. Simmons, M. Makatchev, R. Kirby, M. K. Lee, I. Fanaswala, B. Browning, J. Forlizzi, and M. Sakr. Believable robot characters. *AI Magazine*, 32(4), 2011.

[23] E. Sklar, A. T. Ozgelen, J. P. Munoz, J. Gonzalez, M. Manashirov, S. L. Epstein, and S. Parsons. Designing the HRTeam Framework: Lessons learned from a rough-and-ready human/multi-robot team. In *Workshop on Autonomous Robots and Multirobot Systems (ARMS)*, 2011.

[24] Y. Tang, K. Cai, P. McBurney, E. Sklar, and S. Parsons. Using argumentation to reason about trust and belief. *Journal of Logic and Computation, Special Issue on Agreement Technologies*, 2012 (to appear).

[25] S. Tellex, T. Kollar, S. Dickerson, M. R. Walter, A. G. Banerjee, S. Teller, and N. Roy. Approaching the symbol grounding problem with probabilistic graphical models. *AI Magazine*, 32(4), 2011.

[26] A. Thomaz and C. Chao. Turn taking based on information flow for fluent human-robot interaction. *AI Magazine*, 32(4), 2011.

[27] S. Thrun, M. Beetz, M. Bennewitz, W. Burgard, A. B. Cremers, F. Dellaert, D. Fox, D. Hähnel, C. Rosenberg, N. Roy, J. Schulte, and D. Schulz. Probabilistic algorithms and the interactive museum tour-guide robot minerva. *International Journal of Robotics Research*, 19(11), 2000.

[28] C. Torrey, A. Powers, M. Marge, S. R. Fussell, and S. Kiesler. Effects of adaptive robot dialogue on information exchange and social relations. In *Intl Conf on Human-Robot Interaction (HRI)*, 2006.

[29] D. N. Walton and E. C. W. Krabbe. *Commitment in Dialogue: Basic Concepts of Interpersonal Reasoning.* State University of New York Press, 1995.

[30] H. Yanco, M. Baker, R. Casey, B. Keyes, P. Thoren, J. Drury, D. Few, C. Nielsen, and D. Bruemmer. Analysis of Human-Robot Interaction for Urban Search and Rescue. In *IEEE International Workshop on Safety, Security and Rescue Robotics (PERMIS)*, 2006.

Timing Multimodal Turn-Taking for Human-Robot Cooperation

Crystal Chao
School of Interactive Computing
Georgia Institute of Technology
801 Atlantic Drive, Atlanta, Georgia, USA
cchao@gatech.edu

ABSTRACT

In human cooperation, the concurrent usage of multiple social modalities such as speech, gesture, and gaze results in robust and efficient communicative acts. Such multimodality in combination with reciprocal intentions supports fluent turn-taking. I hypothesize that human-robot turn-taking can be made more fluent through appropriate timing of multimodal actions. Managing timing includes understanding the impact that timing can have on interactions as well as having a control system that supports the manipulation of such timing. To this end, I propose to develop a computational turn-taking model of the timing and information flow of reciprocal interactions. I also propose to develop an architecture based on the timed Petri net (TPN) for the generation of coordinated multimodal behavior, inside of which the turn-taking model will regulate turn timing and action initiation and interruption in order to seize and yield control. Through user studies in multiple domains, I intend to demonstrate the system's generality and evaluate the system on balance of control, fluency, and task effectiveness.

Categories and Subject Descriptors

H.1.2 [**Models and Principles**]: User/Machine Systems; H.5.2 [**Information Interfaces and Presentation**]: User Interfaces—*Natural language*; I.2.9 [**Artificial Intelligence**]: Robotics—*Operator interfaces*

Keywords

Turn-taking, engagement, reciprocity, multimodality, dialogue, human-robot teamwork, human-robot interaction

1. INTRODUCTION

1.1 Motivation

The foundation of human cooperation is *reciprocal interaction* — the implicit notion that, in order to maintain cooperation, each participant in the interaction owes something to the other. Humans have expectations about when to expect actions or information, and they resolve their misunderstandings when their expectations are not met. Human communication is also *multimodal*. People communicate through speech and eye contact while performing instrumental actions with their bodies. This concurrency and multimodal coordination allows for the dynamic adaptation of modalities to different situations and the reinforcement of communicative intent through redundancy. The result of multimodal reciprocal behavior is interaction *fluency*, the seamless and efficient manner by which humans adapt to each other's timing and decisions when interacting to achieve their goals.

To cooperate with the same fluency, a robot needs a sense of when to relinquish and seize control in turn-taking interactions with humans. This includes a sense of obligation of when to take a turn, and knowledge of when to expect responses from the human. I intend to approach the problem of understanding and achieving fluency through the *timing* of multimodal actions. Timing is a factor of great importance to any domain where task efficiency is a concern, but timing can also have a significant impact on interaction fluency. Imbalances in the amount of time taken by each interaction partner lead to perceptions of power or loss of control. This can affect the decisions that people make in a social situation, which in turn can affect the outcome of a task.

Existing robotic systems focus on achieving appropriate semantics and performing actions in the correct order. A robot can make sequential plans and attempt to select the correct response in a dialogue. Independently of domain-specific task execution semantics, I would additionally like for robots to be able to manage how they time their actions. Managing timing means having an understanding of the impact that timing changes can have on interactions, as well as having a control system that allows the manipulation of timing changes with enough flexibility.

1.2 Proposed contributions

The work described in the next few sections supports the following hypothesis:

> The ability to control the timing of multimodal reciprocal behavior enables robots to cooperate more fluently and effectively with humans.

Specifically, I propose to make the following contributions:

- Develop a computational model and controller for the timing of reciprocal turn-taking interactions.
- Develop an architecture to support multimodal reciprocal behavior generation.

- Demonstrate an autonomous robotic system that cooperates with humans using multiple social modalities.
- Evaluate the benefits of the system on cooperative task completion and user experience with respect to balance of control, fluency, and task effectiveness.

2. BACKGROUND

Because the innate skills for reciprocal interaction and cooperation are so deeply embedded in humans since infancy, they are easy to take for granted. Research from developmental psychology on infant preverbal interactions has indicated that turn-taking emerges early on in mother-infant dyads. For example, Tronick defined dyadic phases of social interaction consisting of initiation, mutual-orientation, greeting, play-dialogue (turn-taking), and disengagement [17].

Much literature also exists on the phenomenon of turn-taking in verbal communicative acts. The seminal work of Sacks et al. [15] describes a turn-constructional component, describing the syntactical units that can form turns, and a turn-allocational component, describing how participants select subsequent speakers during discourse. In contrast to approaching turn-taking in terms of the linguistic content of the dialogue, other discourse analysts have focused on the role of nonverbal cues. [8] and [13] describe the presence and distributions of gaze shift, gesticulation, body motion, and paralinguistic cues that form signals that convey intentions to yield, hold, seize, and avoid the floor. In addition, gaze and gestures play roles in progressively conveying semantic understanding so as to repair miscommunications as early as possible [7]. The diversity of these cues demonstrates the highly multimodal nature of the turn-taking process.

Implementations of turn-taking behavior have included virtual conversational agents that coordinate nonverbal cues [4]. More recent work on engagement in virtual agents uses more elaborate turn-taking models and supports multiparty conversation [2]. Turn-taking models have also been developed for improving single-modality spoken dialog systems [14]. In robots, [10] described connection events, which were interaction patterns found in analysis of human-human interaction data, and showed how a robot could generate connection events to maintain engagement. Robot gaze has also been shown to have a role in designating speaker or listener roles in multiparty settings [12].

The idea of fluency is important to this research. Fluency in teamwork s often framed as achieving minimal task completion time or idle time [9]. [11] supposes that fluent turn-taking emerges automatically from reactive behavior, but this view does not explain the effort that humans spend on repair due to overlapping and misunderstanding that occurs in human interactions [16]. An architecture designed for turn-taking should be able to handle these situations, both perceptually and behaviorally.

3. RESEARCH PLAN

This section gives an overview of the scope of the proposed computational model and architecture of reciprocal interactions, as well as the evaluation thereof. Descriptions of previously conducted research are injected where relevant.

3.1 Hardware and software infrastructure

The robot used for this research is the upper-torso humanoid robot Simon, depicted in Figure 1. Simon has two

(a) Simon Says. (b) Towers of Hanoi.

Figure 1: Dyadic domains previously investigated. Simon Says is an imitation game, and Towers of Hanoi is a cooperative manipulation task.

7-DOF arms, 4-DOF hands, and a socially expressive head and neck. The arms and hands are compliant for safe operation alongside a human. Simon has two speakers near the base of his torso for communication through text-to-speech. Perceptually, Simon has access to two eye cameras, an overhead camera, and an externally positioned structured light depth sensor (Microsoft Kinect) for human skeleton tracking. Simon typically perceives human participant speech through a microphone worn on the participant. Software development occurs within the Creatures 6 (C6) cognitive architecture, a framework in Java that has a pipeline for triggering robot actuations from sensory inputs [1].

3.2 Computational model development

An expected contribution is the formalization of a computational model of the structure and timing of reciprocal interactions. The model should serve as a tool for interaction analysis as well as a way to define estimation of timing parameters. It should also be used to control the robot's role in turn-taking dynamics. The model is intended to apply for dyadic interactions.

The model should have an expectation of human response delays to robot turns. The time humans take to respond is influenced by time required for cognitively processing the robot's turn and selecting a response. It also depends on the structure of the robot's turn. In previous work in the domain of the imitation game "Simon Says" (Figure 1(a)), I found that human turn timing depended on the point at which the *minimum necessary information (MNI)* to respond had been conveyed during a robot turn [5]. Context (e.g. power structures) and priming (e.g. from repetitive practice) can also affect human response delays. In addition, turn-taking behavior varies across individual users, and the robot should be able to adapt to the user's parameters.

It is intended that the result of this work be a generic turn-taking module that interacts with a domain-dependent context model. The context model is primarily responsible for generating semantically appropriate communicative acts, and the turn-taking module for orchestrating the timing of those acts. Examples of turn-taking parameters could be turn durations, wait times between turns, and whether to interrupt self or others' turns.

3.3 Architecture design and implementation

Collaborative tasks are often multimodal in nature. The concurrency offered by employing multiple channels for communication allows humans to collaborate efficiently and fluently. To achieve this in human-robot cooperative activity, the robot's action architecture should support the precise production of coordinated actions across multiple modalities. Ideally, action implementation should also transfer easily between domains.

Common control mechanisms for robots are finite state machines (FSMs) and partially observable Markov decision processes (POMDPs). These "state-space" automata are effective for single-modality control, such as in spoken dialog systems [14], but can be unwieldy in multimodal interactions because modalities must be coupled together to form states. Domain-specific information is also coupled into states, making the development effort ungeneralizable to novel domains. Parallelizing single-modality machines in an attempt to generalize behavior does not provide an explicit way to synchronize across modalities.

To achieve finer-grained and more generalizable control of multimodal interactions, I use a timed Petri net (TPN). A Petri net, or Place/Transition (P/T) net, is a bipartite multigraph comprising two finite disjoint sets of nodes, places P and transitions T. A multiset of arcs $A : (P \times T) \cup (T \times P)$ connects the node types in alternating fashion. Places can contain a nonnegative integer number of tokens, which are a metaphor for any kind of resource, e.g. a queue of parameters to be processed, a discrete variable, or a shared tool. The state of the system is implicitly represented through the marking $M : P \rightarrow \mathbb{N}$, the number of tokens in each place, preventing combinatorial explosion. The presence of tokens in a place triggers output transitions from that place; when transitions fire, they transmit tokens between places. The addition of inhibitor arcs, which allow firing only when the source place is empty, makes Petri nets Turing complete. A timed Petri net (TPN) includes management of timing by placing a stochastic timer in each place; transitions do not fire until the timer runs down to 0. A more detailed specification of my TPN system can be found in [6]. Petri nets without timing have also been used for realizing Behavior Markup Language (BML) on robots [10].

My system integrates Petri net modeling techniques that support the control of multimodal reciprocal human-robot interactions. The intent is to create a turn-taking model in TPN form, such that the firing timing distributions of the transitions is controllable and learnable. This format for specifying time durations is more intuitive than transition matrices in POMDPs, where time passed in a given state is determined through self-transition probabilities repeatedly applied over fixed time steps.

Part of the research will involve developing reusable structural patterns for interaction modeling. An example from my previous research is an interruptible communicative action template (Figure 2) [6]. Interactions can be more fluent when communicative actions are interruptible. The implication of an agent continuing a communicative action is that it holds the belief that the listener has not yet received the information; interrupts can prevent information bottlenecking. In addition, interrupts can alter the balance of control (Section 3.4.1). Future work will include the development of more such structures.

3.4 Evaluation methodology

First, there must be a system demonstration showing that the robot can behave autonomously using the model and architecture as described. Then, some evaluation will be necessary to demonstrate the advantages of multimodal reciprocal robot behavior, and to show that the proposed system is successful in achieving it.

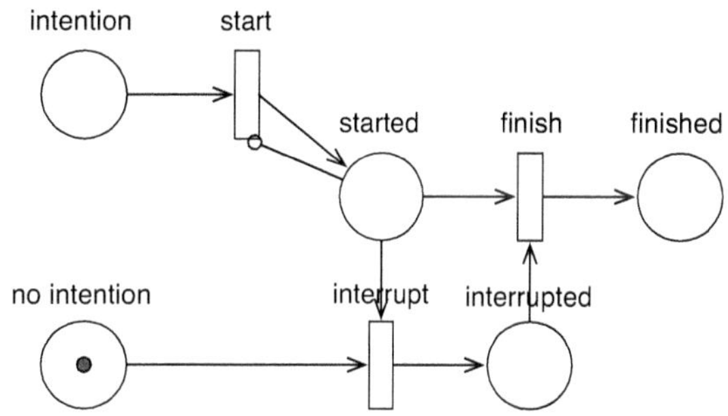

Figure 2: A template for an interruptible communicative action.

The primary mechanism proposed for evaluation will be user studies. These may be supplemented by studies in which subjects view videos of others interacting with the robot. This style of evaluation may be useful when a larger amount of subjective data is required, as in the analysis of multiple confounding factors.

In addition, I presented a novel system evaluation technique using TPN simulations in [6], in which the user is modeled as a TPN graph connected to the robot's TPN controller. The user graph generates inputs according to parameters of the task that are hypothesized to be important. One can then simulate large numbers of interactions by uniformly sampling over the parameter space, and then measure the effects on relevant outcome variables. This technique can be used to determine what parameter values would be required to achieve significant differences in the outcome variables.

The metrics are expected to be taken from subjective questionnaires as well as measures of the performance of the robot and of the human, either coded from video or derived from logged interaction data. My previous research shows potential for improving balance of control, fluency, and task effectiveness in collaboration. Thus, my aim is to shape the evaluation around these dimensions.

3.4.1 Balance of control

Any human-machine interaction should allow the human to maintain a clear cognitive model of the task as well as control over the outcome. It is possible for robots behave in a way that humans lose ability or motivation to form a good mental model of the task. This can occur when robots seize the floor too often or hold the floor for too long. From my previous research using active learning on a robot to learn from a human teacher, teachers lost track of mental models of teaching when the robot queried more frequently [3].

In another study I conducted, subjects collaborated with Simon on a manipulation-based puzzle, the Towers of Hanoi (Figure 1(b)), and afterwards were asked about their mental and physical contributions to the task [6]. Participants were statistically more likely to state that their mental contribution was equal to or higher than the robot's when the robot interrupted its actions to relinquish control as compared to the baseline condition without interrupts, $\chi^2(2, N = 8) = 6.17, p = .05$. Subsequent analysis of action sequences revealed that users took increased initiative in solving the task when the robot interrupted its actions.

3.4.2 Fluency

Fluency is not necessarily straightforward to evaluate. One way to characterize fluency is the absence of awkwardness or frustration. In the Towers of Hanoi study previously mentioned, one of the survey questions asked participants to rate their agreement or disagreement, on a 7-point Likert scale, with the following statement: *"There were awkward moments in the interaction."* When the robot interrupted its actions, people were less likely to agree that there were awkward moments in the interaction ($M = 3.75$, $SD = 1.71$) as compared with participants in the baseline condition ($M = 5.50$, $SD = 1.71$), $t(7) = 2.64$, $p = .03$.

More metrics for fluency will need to be explored. [9] outlines several promising subjective ones relating to trust and teamwork. In addition, a longer, more repetitive interaction may be needed to induce practice effects, as these are the cases where fluency in human collaboration is most salient.

3.4.3 Task effectiveness

The effectiveness of task execution is not a primary objective of this research but is still a consideration. Usually task metrics are domain-specific, and the turn-taking model aims to be generalizable across domains. However, for the domains instantiating the model, our goal is for turn-taking decisions to help and not hinder task execution. Examples of common task metrics are efficiency and optimality.

Although the precise effects of reciprocal behavior on team communication are still to be decided, improvement in the overall efficiency or optimality of the task as an indirect effect can be measured. In the Towers of Hanoi study, when the robot interrupted its actions to allow humans more control of the workspace, the dyad completed the task in fewer minutes ($M = 3.43$, $SD = 0.69$) compared to baseline ($M = 4.56$, $SD = 1.55$), $t(7) = -1.90$, $p = .05$. Even though the robots planned actions to minimize the action sequence length, humans moved faster, so increasing human control increased efficiency.

4. CONCLUSION

My research goal is to enable a robot to engage in fluent multimodal reciprocal behavior when cooperating with humans, and specifically time its actions in socially appropriate ways. The proposed approach is to develop a computational model of the timing of reciprocal interactions; implement an architecture supporting coordinated behaviors across the social modalities of speech, gesture, and gaze; and evaluate benefits of the approach, including improved balance of control, fluency, and task effectiveness.

5. ACKNOWLEDGMENTS

Crystal Chao is advised by Dr. Andrea L. Thomaz.

6. REFERENCES

[1] B. Blumberg, M. Downie, Y. Ivanov, M. Berlin, M. Johnson, and B. Tomlinson. Integrated learning for interactive synthetic characters. In *Annual Conference on Computer Graphics and Interactive Techniques (SIGGRAPH)*, pages 417–426, 2002.

[2] D. Bohus and E. Horvitz. Facilitating multiparty dialog with gaze, gesture, and speech. In *Proceedings of the 12th International Conference on Multimodal Interfaces (ICMI)*, 2010.

[3] M. Cakmak, C. Chao, and A. L. Thomaz. Designing interactions for robot active learners. *IEEE Transactions on Autonomous Mental Development*, 2(2):108–118, June 2010.

[4] J. Cassell, T. Bickmore, L. Campbell, K. Chang, H. Vilhjálmsson, and H. Yan. Requirements for an architecture for embodied conversational characters. In *Computer Animation and Simulation*, pages 109–120. Springer Verlag, 1999.

[5] C. Chao, J. H. Lee, M. Begum, and A. Thomaz. Simon plays Simon says: The timing of turn-taking in an imitation game. In *IEEE International Symposium on Robot and Human Interactive Communication (RO-MAN)*, 2011.

[6] C. Chao and A. Thomaz. Timing in multimodal reciprocal interactions: Control and analysis using timed Petri nets. *Journal of Human-Robot Interaction*, 1(1):46–67, 2012.

[7] H. H. Clark and M. A. Krych. Speaking while monitoring addressees for understanding. *Journal of Memory and Language*, 50(1):62–81, 2004.

[8] S. Duncan. On the structure of speaker-auditor interaction during speaking turns. *Language in Society*, 3(2):161–180, 1974.

[9] G. Hoffman and C. Breazeal. Effects of anticipatory action on human-robot teamwork: Efficiency, fluency, and perception of team. In *Proceedings of the 3rd ACM/IEEE Conference on Human-Robot Interaction (HRI)*, 2007.

[10] A. G. Holroyd. Generating engagement behaviors in human-robot interaction. Master's thesis, Worcester Polytechnic Institute, 2011.

[11] H. Kose-Bagci, K. Dautenhan, and C. L. Nehaniv. Emergent dynamics of turn-taking interaction in drumming games with a humanoid robot. In *Proceedings of the 17th IEEE International Symposium on Robot and Human Interactive Communication*, pages 346–353, 2008.

[12] B. Mutlu, T. Shiwa, T. K. H. Ishiguro, and N. Hagita. Footing in human-robot conversations: How robots might shape participant roles using gaze cues. In *Proceedings of the 4th ACM/IEEE Conference on Human-Robot Interaction (HRI)*, 2009.

[13] B. Orestrom. *Turn-taking in English conversation.* CWK Gleerup, 1983.

[14] A. Raux and M. Eskenazi. A finite-state turn-taking model for spoken dialog systems. In *Proceedings of the Human Language Technologies (HLT)*, 2009.

[15] H. Sacks, E. Schegloff, and G. Jefferson. A simplest systematics for the organization of turn-taking for conversation. *Language*, 50:696–735, 1974.

[16] E. Schegloff. Overlapping talk and the organization of turn-taking for conversation. *Language in Society*, 29(1):1–63, 2000.

[17] E. Tronick, H. Als, and L. Adamson. Structure of early face-to-face communicative interactions. In M. Bullowa, editor, *Before Speech: The Beginning of Interpersonal Communication*, pages 349–374. Cambridge University Press, Cambridge, 1979.

My Automated Conversation Helper (MACH): Helping People Improve Social Skills

Mohammed (Ehsan) Hoque
MIT Media Lab
70 Amherst Street,
Cambridge, MA 02139
mehoque@media.mit.edu

ABSTRACT

Ever been in a situation where you didn't get that job despite being the deserving candidate? What went wrong? Psychology literature suggests that the most important skill towards making an impression during interviews is your interpersonal/social skills. Is it possible for people to improve their social skills (e.g., vary the voice intonation, and pauses appropriately; use social smiles, when appropriate; and maintain eye contact) through a computerized intervention? In this thesis, I propose to develop an autonomous and *Automated Conversation Helper* (3D virtual character) that can play the role of the interviewer, allowing participants to practice their social skills in context of job interviews. The *Automated Conversation Helper* is being developed with the ability to "see" (facial expression processing), "hear" (speech recognition and prosody analysis) and "respond" (speech and behavior synthesis) in real-time and provide live feedback on participant's non-verbal behavior.

Categories and Subject Descriptors

J.4 [**Social and Behavioral Sciences**]: *Psychology*

General Terms: Algorithms, Measurement, Performance, Design, Experimentation, Human Factors, Standardization.

Keywords: Training conversation helper, speech processing, facial expressions processing, prosody analysis, feedback.

1. INTRODUCTION

Let us consider John, a junior undergraduate student at MIT - technically gifted and would be a great fit for any technical company. However, despite being the deserving candidate, John has not had any luck in getting an internship of his preference during his junior year. John is disappointed; however, he is also determined to improve his interview skills so that he has better luck for his senior year. John seeks help at the MIT career services and sets up a mock interview with a counselor. After a 15-minute session, the career counselor gives John specific recommendations. These may include maintaining eye contact with the interviewer when necessary. Starting and ending the interview with a social smile, to appear friendly. Varying voice intonation and loudness to express enthusiasm about the position. John returns to his dorm with an understanding of the socially accepted behaviors that he should exhibit during interviews. Yet, he wishes it was possible for him to practice the interview scenarios a few more times and obtain feedback, as he continues to reflect on the advice that he received from the career services. However, John is unwilling to ask his peers for feedback because they are extremely busy, and to some extent, he fears social stigma. Is it possible to help John and many others like him to improve their interview skills by using an *Automated Conversation Helper*?

In this thesis, I propose to develop an *Automated Conversation Helper*, a new technology that is best described as a virtual agent - an animated and embodied computer generated character that is capable of interacting with its human users (shown in Figure 1). The *Automated Conversation Helper* is being developed with the ability to not only automatically recognize its user's nonverbal behaviors (e.g., facial expressions, body movements, spoken words, and paralinguistic cues), but also synthesize behaviors within a defined scenario. With the ability to see, hear and react, the helper will able to play the role of a conversational partner, carry on a conversation and provide feedback to its user's nonverbal cues in real-time.

Figure 1. Automated Conversation Helpers, John and Mary

2. BACKGROUND RESEARCH

Even though interaction during interviews are often short and limited, a handful of studies [1][2][3] has provided evidence that interviewers often use that short interaction to predict job performance. Given the limited interaction, interviewers focus on applicant's nonverbal cues to get an understanding of the applicant's personality, social skills and knowledge to determine applicant's suitability. Along with nonverbal cues, there are also knowledge and skills, mental capability, traits, social skills, organizational fit, and preference that are considered towards hiring an applicant. Among other things, Huffcut et al. [1], based on an intensive literature review, have identified that personality traits and social skills were the most frequently rated constructs, followed by mental capability and job knowledge and skills. Some of those social skills include eye contact, frequent smiles, and modulation of speech [4]. For example, as described in [4], an interviewee could appears direct, and honest by maintaining eye contact, or be perceived as more sociable and extroverted by smiling more frequently and varying their voice intonation. Exhibiting the appropriate nonverbal behavior helps to establish rapport with the interviewer, which, according to [5], is the heart

ICMI'12, October 22–26, 2012, Santa Monica, California, USA.

of the interview process. Is it possible to develop an *Automated Conversation Helper* that can play the role of the interviewer and can establish rapport with the interviewee through simple contingent nonverbal behavior?

3. PROPOSED RESEARCH

Development of autonomous *Automated Conversation Helper* introduces two unique challenges. First, pushing the boundary of facial expression processing, and speech processing to automatically recognize and understand the nonverbal cues in face to face interactions. Secondly, finding the right medium for the *Automated Conversation Helper* to provide feedback back to the user. The conversation helper could directly provide the feedback through its nonverbal channels (e.g., look disinterested if the interview is not going very well). Another possibility is to provide verbal feedback at the end of the interview similar to standard mock interviews. However, feedback sessions during mock interviews are often very interactive and spontaneous where the interviewee and interviewer engage in somewhat open ended natural conversations. Supporting that level of open ended interactions with an autonomous agent still remains an open problem. Therefore, in this thesis, I have proposed to develop a system that can provide feedback to its users using two different visual formats – immediate and with a time line. In the immediate feedback scenario, participants get to view bird's eye data of a few selective nonverbal behaviors, as shown in **Figure 2**. In the upper half of the screen, user gets to view the smile track of his/her interaction across different interview sessions. At the bottom half of the screen, user gets to see comparative analysis of features such as average duration of pauses, speaking rate and amount of weak language (e.g., "like", "basically", "I guess" etc.) being used in each session. As a second step, users are given the option to also view the time line format of their interaction as shown in Figure 3. In mock interviews, interviewees often get video-taped and then as part of the feedback process, the counselor and the interviewee watch the video together. To simulate such feature, in time line, interviewees watch their own video along with their entire interaction being visualized through embedded emotional overtones. Some of the emotional overtones include prosodic interpretation of the recognized text. A preliminary diagram is demonstrated in Figure 3, where the vertical displacement between words are presented by pitch, the size of the blobs containing the words represent loudness (bigger the size of the blob, the louder the word was), the colors of the blobs symbolizes smiles (green = really smiling, yellow = might be smiling, red = not smiling).

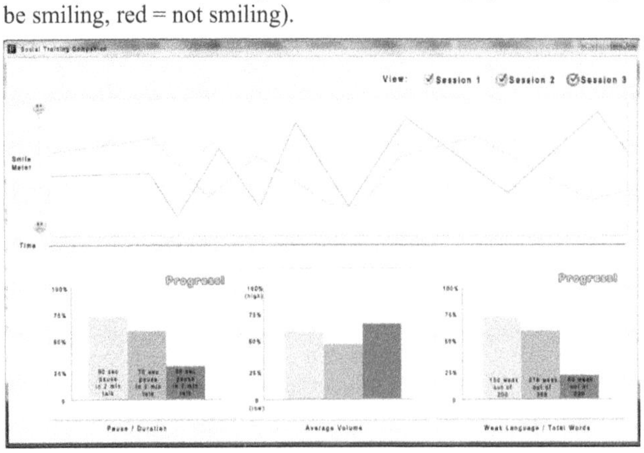

Figure 2: An example of how someone's nonverbal behavior could be happed to show overall performance

4. HYPOTHESIS

This thesis will primarily investigate whether it is possible to help people improve their interview skills through an *Automated Conversation Helper*. Below are the two hypotheses that will be evaluated in this thesis.

H1: Interaction with an Automated Conversation Helper and then watching his/her own interview video improves interview skills, over self-directed learning of the interview techniques.

H2: Interaction with an Automated Conversation Helper and then watching his/her own video along with a time line view of the nonverbal improves interview skills, over just interaction with the helper and watching one's own video.

Figure 3. A preliminary example of how an interaction could be automatically transcribed and then visualized according to its non-verbal properties, in real-time.

5. RESEARCH PLAN

The entire study takes place in two phases: study 1 and study 2.

5.1 Study 1

This phase contains job interview scenarios between two individuals – an MIT undergraduate student and an MIT career counselor. Study 1 is more of an exploratory analysis on developing predictive relationships between nonverbal behaviors and job interview skills based on the ratings produced by the counselors as the gold standard. The data generated from Study 1 will be used towards developing models that will drive the interaction between human participants and *Automated Conversation Helper* in study 2. It will also allow for comparison and evaluation of the modeled predictive relationships between nonverbal behaviors and job interview skills with what has been reported in the psychology literature so far. A few possible exploratory research questions that are going to be explored in study 1 are:

- What social behaviors are correlated with interview skills?
- Is it possible to rank social behaviors in order of importance especially in context of job interviews?
- Are there gender effects in interview patterns?

5.1.1 Participants

The interviewers are 4 MIT professional career counselors (3 women and 1 man), who have an average of over 5 years of professional experience as career counselors at MIT and have advanced graduate degrees in professional career counseling.

Interviewees are 28 MIT undergraduates (16 female and 12 male). All participants are MIT undergraduate students in their junior year, and native speakers of English.

5.1.2 Experimental Setup

The experiment was conducted in a room equipped with a desk, two chairs, and two cameras mounted on the wall (Figure 4). Camera 2 was used to record the interviewer and camera 1 to record the interviewee, as shown in Figure 4.

Figure 4: Experimental Setup between the interviewer and the interviewee. Camera 1 is recording the facial expressions and audio of interviewee, whereas Camera 2 is recording the facial expressions and audio of interviewer.

Figure 5: Experiment control room where the experimenter controls the camera to zoom into the participants. The interviewee will be oblivious of the existence of this room.

5.1.3 Procedures

MIT junior students were recruited through flyers and emails in this study. They were told that they would have the opportunity to practice mock interviews with a professional career counselor at MIT and they would get $10 for just participating. In addition, they were also informed that as part of regular mock interview practice, their interview would be recorded. Each male participant was paired with the male counselor and all the female participants were paired up with the female career counselors. This was done to control for possible gender effects. After the interview, they were informed of the objective of the study and were given the choice to sign the consent form to share their data for research.

5.1.4 Interaction

We spoke to the 4 MIT career counselors and asked them to provide us with 15 questions that are more likely to be asked in any job interview situations, regardless of the position. The 5 questions generated below were the common ones in their list. Below is the exact sequence of the interaction between the MIT career counselor and the participants during study 1.

Counselor: So how are you doing today?(or any question of that sort to initiate the interview)

Participant answers.

Q1. Counselor: (Generic acknowledgement of the answer provided) So, please tell me about yourself?

Participant answers.

Q2. (Generic acknowledgement of the answer provided) Tell me about a time when you demonstrated leadership.

Participant answers.

Q3. (Generic acknowledgement of the answer provided) Tell me about a time when you were working on a team and faced with a challenge, how did you solve that problem?

Participant answers.

Q4. Counselor: (Generic acknowledgement of the answer provided) What is your weakness and how do you plan to overcome it?

Participant answers.

Q5. Counselor: (Generic acknowledgement of the answer provided) Now why do you think we should hire you?

Participant answers.

5.1.5 Debriefing

After the interview ends, the counselor spends a couple of minutes providing feedback to the participant. Then, the counselor walks the participant to the debrief room to the experimenter. The experimenter asks the participant to fill out a questionnaire. In the questionnaire, the participant self-evaluates (on a scale of 1-7) on how well s/he did maintaining eye-contact with the interviewer, how relevant was his/her answers, and how engaging was his/her voice tone, as well as how well s/he did overall in the interview. The interviewer, on the other hand, fills out a similar questionnaire rating the interviewee on speech content, vocal characteristics, and social smiles as well as their individual answers on those 5 questions on a scale of 1 to 7.

5.1.6 Data coding

In study 1, the audio and video files of the participants (i.e., interviewer and interviewee) are being coded. In particular, the facial expressions (different kinds of smiles), vocal characteristics (pitch range, speaking rate, pauses), speech content (structure, qualifications, directness, relevance), speaker presence (enthusiasm, qualifications, directness, relevance), body postures (immediacy cues – orientation, leaning forward, nodding, rocking, fidgeting, mirroring/following gaze, power poses) are now being coded. The coded data will be utilized to develop predictive relationships between nonverbal behaviors and job interview skills.

5.2 Study 2

The purpose of the study 2 will be to evaluate whether social skills can be improved through interactions with Automated Conversation Helper (i.e., validating the hypotheses from Section 4).

5.2.1 Participants

90 Participants, who were not part of study 1, will be recruited for study 2. 90 participants will be randomly divided into 3 groups.

There are three phases to study 2: a) Baseline evaluation; b) Intervention; c) Post-intervention evaluation.

5.2.2 Baseline evaluation

The 4 counselors from study 1 will also participate in study 2 and will play the role of interviewers. The interaction between the interviewer and the interviewee and the questionnaire that they would have to fill out will be identical to study 1.

5.2.3 Intervention

Participants will be randomly assigned into 3 groups with equal gender representation. Group 1, consisting of 30 participants, are the control group. After the base line interaction, they are given a standard handout on general tips on how to become successful in interviews. The handout is identical to what MIT students get from the career services after their mock interviews. Group 2 and 3 will consist of 30 participants in each group, who will be part of the conversation helper intervention. As part of their intervention, they will come to the lab and interact with the *Automated Conversation Helper* in an empty room. Participants from Group 2 will get to interact with the Automated Conversation Helper who will engage with the participants and at the end will only show the video of the participant as part of the feedback. With participants from Group 3, the *Automated Conversation Helper* will engage with the participants and at the end will display the video of the interaction as well as the nonverbal behavior as part of a time line.

5.2.4 Post-Intervention evaluation

The interaction in post-evaluation section will be identical to the baseline evaluation. The interviewees will get paired up with the same counselor for mock interviews. The counselor, however, remains oblivious of the fact of whether participant has gone through which part of the intervention. Interviewers will ask the same set of questions. But the questions will be framed differently. It is done to see whether the knowledge learned would generalize when asked the same questions differently.

6. DATA ANALYSIS

Expert assessment: During the baseline, and post-intervention evaluations, we will have measures on how well the participants did according to the ratings of the counselor. The counselor will rate participant's overall performance on eye contacts, engagement in voice tone, relevancy in answers, and being able to smile when necessary. Additionally, the counselor is also going to rate the quality of answer provided for each question.

Self-assessment: During the baseline and post-intervention, the participants are going to rate themselves on the nonverbal cues such as eye-contact, voice tone, relevancy in answers, and being able to smile when necessary. They are also going to rate themselves on their overall performance during the interview.

Third Party assessment: The answers from baseline and post-intervention assessment will be evaluated in random order by others using amazon's Mechanical Turk service. Based on the analysis a set of behavioral variables will be identified for automated analysis. Those behavioral variables, which are indicative of performance in job interviews, will be analyzed and compared before, during and at the end of the intervention.

Automated Behavioral assessment: Based on the findings from study 1 on the predictive relationships between nonverbal Anova analysis will be performed through objective, subjective and behavioral data to investigate changes in performance through the intervention. Other statistical framework, e.g., PARAdigm for Dialogue System Evaluation (PARADISE) [6] will also be explored.

7. CONCLUSION

Findings from this thesis could potentially unravel the possibility of using Automated Conversational Helper to improve people's public speaking skills, assist people diagnosed with Asperger's syndrome to improve their social skills, or even automate some aspects of psychotherapy.

8. ACKNOWLEDGEMENT

The author would like to acknowledge Rosalind Picard, Jeffrey Cohn, Bilge Mutlu, and Louis-Philippe Morency, Amy Cuddy and Maarten Bos for providing feedback towards the design of this study. The conversation helper in this thesis is being developed on the existing Multimodal Affective Reactive Characters (MARC) platform developed by Matthieu Courgeon, and Jean-Claude Martin of LIMSI-CNRS. Angela Zhang, Nicole Pan and Anji Ren helped with the data collection.

9. REFERENCES

[1] A. I. Huffcutt, J. M. Conway, P. L. Roth, and N. J. Stone, "Identification and meta-analytic assessment of psychological constructs measured in employment interviews.," *Journal of Applied Psychology*, vol. 86, no. 5, pp. 897-913, 2001.

[2] M. A. McDaniel, D. L. Whetzel, F. L. Schmidt, and S. D. Maurer, "The validity of employment interviews: A comprehensive review and meta-analysis.," *Journal of Applied Psychology*, vol. 79, no. 4, pp. 599-616, 1994.

[3] P. M. Wright, P. A. Lichtenfels, and E. D. Pursell, "The structured interview: Additional studies and a metaanalysis," *Journal of Occupational Psychology*, vol. 62, pp. 191-199, 1989.

[4] T. DeGroot and J. Gooty, "Can Nonverbal Cues be Used to Make Meaningful Personality Attributions in Employment Interviews?," *Journal of Business and Psychology*, vol. 24, no. 2, pp. 179-192, 2009.

[5] J. W. Cogger, "Are you a skilled interviewer?," *The Personnel journal*, vol. 61, no. 11, pp. 840-843, 1982.

[6] M. A. Walker, D. J. Litman, C. A. Kamm, and A. Abella, "PARADISE: A Framework for Evaluating Spoken Dialogue Agents," *Proceedings of the eighth conference on European chapter of the Association for Computational Linguistics*, p. 10, 1997.

A Touch of Affect: Mediated Social Touch and Affect

Gijs Huisman
University of Twente, Human Media Interaction Group
Drienerlolaan 5, PO Box 217, 7500 AE, Enschede, The Netherlands
gijs.huisman@utwente.nl

ABSTRACT

This position paper outlines the first stages in an ongoing PhD project on mediated social touch, and the effects mediated touch can have on someone's affective state. It is argued that touch is a profound communication channel for humans, and that communication through touch can, to some extent, occur through mediation. Furthermore, touch can be used to communicate emotions, as well as have immediate affective consequences. The design of an input device, consisting of twelve force-sensitive resistors, to study the communication of emotions through mediated touch is presented. A pilot study indicated that participants used duration of touch and force applied as ways to distinguish between different emotions. This paper will conclude by discussing possible improvements for the input device, how the pilot study fits with the overall PhD project, as well as future directions for the PhD project in general.

Categories and Subject Descriptors

H.5.2 [**User Interfaces:**]: Haptic I/O; Theory and Methods.

Keywords

Mediated social touch; haptic interfaces; affect; emotion.

1. INTRODUCTION

Look around your office and ask a random colleague to hold hands with you. If said person complies, close your eyes for ten seconds and try to determine what you feel. Most likely, you will feel the warm, soft, perhaps slightly sweaty hand of your colleague. But more importantly, you are feeling the hand of a *person*.

Touch pertains not only to tactile sensations through which we can determine the shape, size, texture, and temperature of an object (i.e. discriminative touch), but also has a very strong social, and emotional component too [10, 23]. Most likely your request was met with puzzled looks from your colleague, and a sense of unease upon first contact. Such feelings do not only depend on the tactile sensation itself, but are strongly influenced by your relationship with your colleague, as well as your gender, and culture [10].

HCI research investigating touch focusses mostly on discriminative touch, for instance in interaction with touch screens [19], tangible interfaces [20], and haptic feedback [28]. However, recent efforts have recognized the importance of social touch [12, 30], and have investigated how mediated social touch (i.e. communicative touch between at least two people through input and output devices) is perceived, and can influence someone's affective state [31]. The ongoing PhD work outlined in this position paper builds on this last line of research. Two main research questions guide the PhD project, namely: to what extent can interpersonal touch occur through mediation? And, to what extent does mediated touch influence people's affective state?

2. RELATED WORK

2.1 What is touch?

The touch sense can be divided into two separate systems, namely: the cutaneous and kinesthetic systems. Haptic perception refers to touch sensations involving both the cutaneous and the kinesthetic system [12]. One's awareness of the position of one's limbs in time and space is made possible by the kinesthetic system, which draws on information from mechanoreceptors in the muscles, skin, and joints, as well as from motor-commands executed in the brain [12]. The kinesthetic system can, for instance, provide information about the size and weight of an object. The cutaneous system pertains to sensations that are a result of stimulation of different receptors in the skin. The human skin contains thermoreceptors that sense temperature, nociceptors that sense pain, and mechanoreceptors that sense deformations of the skin [12, 21]. Recent evidence suggests that the hairy skin contains a type of receptive afferent (i.e. nerve carrying information to the central nervous system), called CT afferent, which is not found in the glabrous (i.e. hairless) skin. These CT afferents respond particularly strongly to slow stroking motions, for example when applied to the forearm, while being insensitive to stimulations typically associated with discriminative touch [25]. This has lead researchers to propose the social touch hypothesis, which states that CT afferents have a potential to elicit pleasant subjective experiences, which are highly relevant for interpersonal social touch [25]. Considering mediated social touch, this finding is important in that it

ICMI'12, October 22–26, 2012, Santa Monica, California, USA.

highlights the social nature of touch, as well as that it provides insights into which actuators might best be used to produce tactile sensations reminiscent of social touch.

2.2 Interpersonal touch

Touch is considered as one of the earliest types of communication for humans [22], and it is a powerful mode of communication too: studies have shown that interpersonal physical contact is essential in the development of cognitive and socio-emotional skills in infants [1], can increase compliance to requests (i.e. the 'Midas touch' effect) [10], and can have stress-reducing effects [9]. Touch can have strong immediate affective consequences [30, 31]. For example in romantic couples, being touched by one's partner is typically considered pleasant, whereas being touched by a coworker can be considered unpleasant [10]. In these examples touch is either positively, or negatively valenced. Moreover, touch is considered to be an intensifier of emotional displays from other modalities. However, recent evidence suggests that touch can also be used to communicate specific emotions [16, 18]. In a series of experiments, Hertenstein et al. [18] found that three basic emotions, and three pro-social emotions were recognized at above chance levels when they were communicated solely through touching of the arm and hand of the decoder. Accuracy ratings of the decoded emotions were very similar to accuracy ratings obtained from studies into facial, and vocal expressions of emotion. Moreover, in a follow-up study, Hertenstein et al. [16] found that when participants were allowed to touch each other on the whole body, two additional emotions were decoded at above chance level. However, many of the effects of social touch depend on the interpersonal relationship [5, 29], and the gender of the individuals applying, and receiving the touch [6, 17] as well as their cultural background [9], and the body location to which the touch is applied [16]. Such factors need to be taken into consideration when designing devices and experiments for mediated social touch (see for instance [11]).

2.3 Mediated touch

Numerous devices have been designed and built that allow people to communicate a touch over a distance. For example devices that communicate a sense of presence of another person through a shared object [4], devices that add tactile input and output as an additional communication channel [8], and devices that aim to provide more intimate communication over a distance through touch [15, 24]. While this work provides valuable insights into, for instance, possible designs for mediated touch devices, some argue [12, 30, 31], that there is a lack of empirical research into the underlying mechanisms of mediated touch. Some studies that are a noticeable exception to this, have for instance found that the Midas touch effect occurs to some extent after mediated touch [13], that body location effects are similar between real and mediated touch conditions [11], that mediated touch can, to some extent, affect a person's emotional experience of a story when combined with the auditory channel [31], and that touch can help communicate empathy during interaction with a virtual agent [3]. Similar to Hertenstein et al.'s [16, 18] approach, some studies have also found indications that people can successfully communicate emotions through mediated touch. In one study, participants were asked to encode seven basic emotions using a force-feedback joystick. The encoded emotions were played back to different participants, who were tasked with decoding the emotions from the joysticks movements. Results showed that all emotions were recognized at above chance level [2]. In another study, participants used a turning-knob in two metaphorical tasks (i.e. a Ping Pong game, and stroking each other's hand), during which they communicated four different emotions. Overall the four emotions were decoded at above chance level [27].

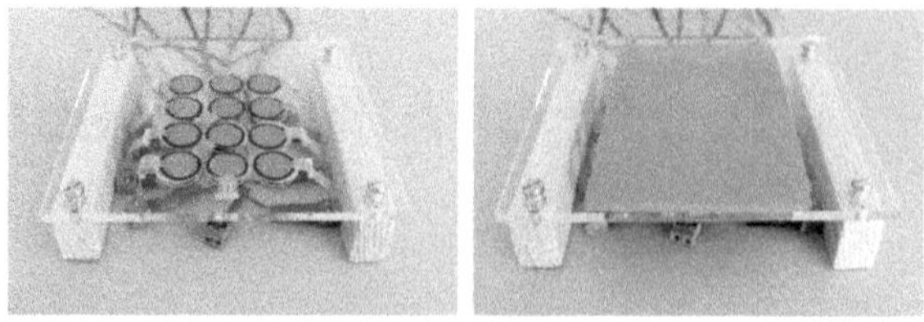

Figure 1: Prototype of the input device containing twelve force sensitive resistors.

Wang et al. [30, 31] state that most studies into mediated touch use some form of symbolic tactile communication. The authors argue that touch is a much richer communication channel and that in using touch for symbolic communication, it is reduced to a low bit rate tool [31]. However, the immediate affective consequences of remote touch are a result of a sense of presence [14, 26] (i.e. the feeling of being touched by another person). Therefore symbolic tactile communication can also have immediate affective consequences when a strong sense of presence is present in the communication. One way to study the level of presence is to compare emotional responses between 'real' and mediated conditions [26]. Similar emotional responses can be considered an indication of a felt sense of presence. This approach is considered an important element of the research outlined in this position paper.

3. MEDIATED TOUCH AND AFFECT

The aim of the current ongoing PhD work is to build on experimental studies into mediated touch. In the first stages of the PhD project, devices, such as depicted in Figure 1, will be used as tools to simulate human touch. Through the design of these devices, specific manipulations can be introduced in the experiments (e.g. cutaneous or kinesthetic stimulation). The main interest of the PhD project described here is perception and elicitation of affect in mediated touch [3, 18, 30]. In later stages of the project, psychophysiological measurements of emotion, such as facial electromyography, electrodermal activity, and heart rate [7] will be applied to assess similarities between real and mediated touch, as well as the extent to which a sense of presence is elicited by the mediated touch [26]. The next section will outline the design of a mediated touch device (Figure 1), and describe a first pilot study as an initial investigation of the communication of emotions through mediated touch.

3.1 Communicating emotions

An I/O device was conceived in order to partially replicate Hertenstein et al.'s [18] experiments. The output side consists of a grid of 4x3 eccentric-mass vibration motors

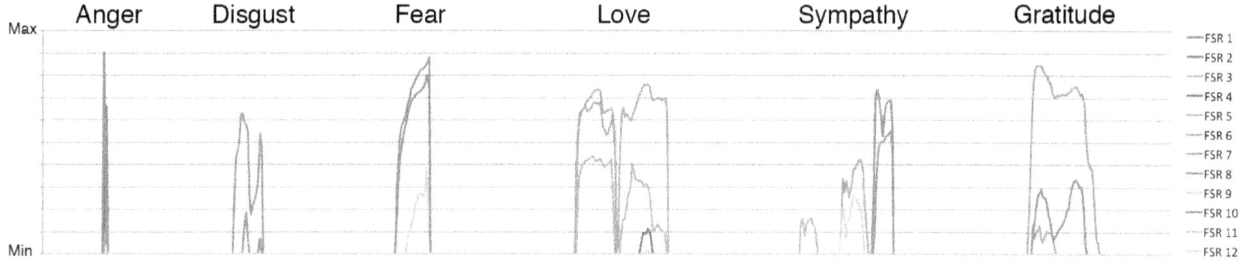

Figure 2: All six emotions as encoded by one participant. For each emotions the colored lines indicate activation of individual FSRs.

inside a sleeve that is worn on the forearm. The intensity of vibration of the motors will be controlled by the input device, which consists of a grid of 4x3 force-sensitive resistors (FSR) mounted on a plain surface, and covered by a foam sheet (Figure 1). Data from the FSRs will be logged in order to identify patterns in the expression of emotion using the device (Figure 2). Compared to other studies that investigated the communication of emotions through mediated touch using force-feedback devices [2, 27], the experiment proposed here focusses on cutaneous perception (i.e. vibrations applied to the skin surface) instead of kinesthetic perception.

3.2 Pilot study

The goal of the pilot study was to see if participants could encode a number of emotions using the input device. It was hypothesized that participants would use force, duration, and location of touch as ways to encode emotions using the device. Five participants (four male, one female), all graduate students, were asked to encode six emotions (anger, disgust, fear, love, sympathy, and gratitude) that have been found to be recognizable through touch of the forearm [18]. In addition to video recordings, data from all twelve FSRs was recorded.

It was explained to participants that it was their task to communicate six different emotions by touching the foam sheet, which they were told, represented the forearm of another person. Participants were told that the data from the sensors would be recorded and played back to another

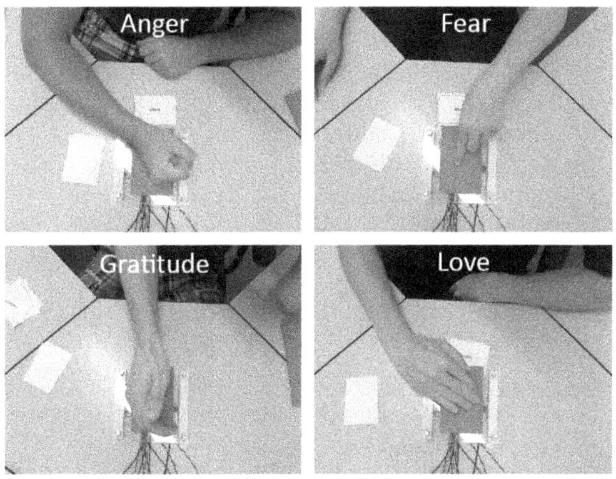

Figure 3: Examples of participants encoding emotions using the input device.

person through a grid of vibration motors, after which the other person would have to decode the emotion from the vibrations.

It was observed (Figure 3) that participants mostly used brief, and forceful touches for the negative emotions (two participants used more prolonged touches for disgust), whereas for the positive emotions they used more prolonged touches covering more sensors. To some extent these observations were corroborated by data from the FSRs. Figure 2 shows the sensor data for all six emotions encoded by a single participant. For both positive and negative emotions, participants mostly used expressive touch (e.g. hitting in the case of anger). One participant used more symbolic touches, for example in the case of gratitude in which this participant simulated a handshake (Figure 3). Participants made a number of comments in regard to the input device. First, it was mentioned that considerable force was required to activate the sensors. This was mainly due to the thickness of the foam covering the FSRs. It is plausible that the expressions of some emotions may only differ in the force applied during touch (e.g. love and sympathy). These subtleties were not captured in the pilot study. Replacing the foam with a thinner material may improve on this issue. Second, one participant mentioned that the active area was a rather small, flat surface, not representative of a human arm. Indeed, expanding the active surface as well as using a curved surface might make for a more realistic input device and allow participants to more accurately encode emotions as if they were making contact with the forearm of another person.

4. CONCLUSIONS

The goal of the PhD project outlined in this position paper is to provide insights into how people experience mediated touch. Paradigms from psychology research (e.g. [18]) can guide the design of experiments using mediated touch. This approach should provide insights into the underlying elements of mediated touch, such as the influence of other modalities, cultural factors, interpersonal relationships, gender, and effects of body site [11, 17, 16, 29]. It has to be noted here that mediated touch is in itself somewhat of a paradox, since touching someone requires two people to be in each others personal space. Therefore, investigating the felt sense of presence of another person [14, 26] as well as emotional responses to this sense of presence will be of vital importance to the current PhD project. Furthermore, experiments, such as the pilot study, can inform the design of new mediated touch devices to be used in other experiments during the PhD project. Moreover, results can guide implementation of tactile communication into existing devices. The results from the pilot study could for instance be translated to vibration patterns of a mobile phone. While such an approach is a strong simplification of human touch, and even of mediated touch, it might be a viable starting point for introducing mediated social touch into our daily mediated communication with others.

5. ACKNOWLEDGMENTS

This publication was supported by the Dutch national program COMMIT. Special thanks to Dirk Heylen and Betsy van Dijk for their contribution to this work.

6. REFERENCES

[1] P. A. Andersen and L. K. Guerrero. Haptic behavior in social interaction. In M. Grunwald, editor, *Human Haptic Perception: Basics and Applications*, pages 155–163. Birkhäuser Basel, 2008.

[2] J. Bailenson, N. Yee, S. Brave, D. Merget, and D. Koslow. Virtual interpersonal touch: Expressing and recognizing emotions through haptic devices. *Human-Computer Interaction*, 22(3):325–353, 2007.

[3] T. W. Bickmore, R. Fernando, L. Ring, and D. Schulman. Empathic Touch by Relational Agents. *IEEE Transactions on Affective Computing*, 1(1):60–71, 2010.

[4] S. Brave and A. Dahley. inTouch: a medium for haptic interpersonal communication. In *Proceedings of CHI '97*, pages 363–364. ACM, 1997.

[5] J. K. Burgoon. Relational message interpretations of touch, conversational distance, and posture. *Journal of Nonverbal Behavior*, 15(4):233–259, 1991.

[6] J. K. Burgoon, J. B. Walther, and E. J. Baesler. Interpretations, Evaluations, and Consequences of Interpersonal Touch. *Human Communication Research*, 19(2):237–263, 1992.

[7] J. Cacioppo, G. Bernston, J. Larsen, K. Poehlman, and T. Ito. The psychophysiology of emotion. In M. Lewis and J. Haviland-Jones, editors, *Handbook of Emotions*, pages 173–191. The Guilford Press, 2000.

[8] A. Chang, S. O'Modhrain, R. Jacob, E. Gunther, and H. Ishii. Comtouch: design of a vibrotactile communication device. In *Proceedings of DIS '02*, pages 312–320. ACM, 2002.

[9] T. Field. Touch for socioemotional and physical well-being: A review. *Developmental Review*, 30(4):367–383, 2010.

[10] A. Gallace and C. Spence. The science of interpersonal touch: an overview. *Neuroscience and Biobehavioral Reviews*, 34(2):246–59, 2010.

[11] A. Haans, C. de Nood, and W. A. IJsselsteijn. Investigating response similarities between real and mediated social touch: a first test. In *Proceedings of CHI '07*, pages 2405–2410. ACM, 2007.

[12] A. Haans and W. IJsselsteijn. Mediated social touch: a review of current research and future directions. *Virtual Reality*, 9(2-3):149–159, 2006.

[13] A. Haans and W. A. IJsselsteijn. The Virtual Midas Touch: Helping Behavior After a Mediated Social Touch. *IEEE Transactions on Haptics*, 2(3):136–140, 2009.

[14] A. Haans and W. A. IJsselsteijn. Embodiment and Telepresence: Toward a Comprehensive Theoretical Framework. *Interacting with Computers*, In Press.

[15] R. Hansson and T. Skog. The lovebomb: encouraging the communication of emotions in public spaces. In *Proceedings of CHI '01*, pages 433–434. ACM, 2001.

[16] M. J. Hertenstein, R. Holmes, M. McCullough, and D. Keltner. The communication of emotion via touch. *Emotion*, 9(4):566–573, 2009.

[17] M. J. Hertenstein and D. Keltner. Gender and the Communication of Emotion Via Touch. *Sex roles*, 64(1-2):70–80, 2011.

[18] M. J. Hertenstein, D. Keltner, B. App, B. a. Bulleit, and A. R. Jaskolka. Touch communicates distinct emotions. *Emotion*, 6(3):528–33, 2006.

[19] C. Holz and P. Baudisch. Understanding touch. In *Proceedings of CHI '11*, pages 2501–2510. ACM, 2011.

[20] H. Ishii. Tangible Bits: Beyond Pixels. In *Proceedings of TEI '08*, pages 15–25. ACM, 2008.

[21] K. O. Johnson. The roles and functions of cutaneous mechanoreceptors. *Current Opinion in Neurobiology*, 11(4):455–61, 2001.

[22] E. McDaniel and P. A. Andersen. International patterns of interpersonal tactile communication: A field study. *Journal of Nonverbal Behavior*, 22:59–75, 1998.

[23] F. McGlone, A. B. Vallbo, H. Olausson, L. Loken, and J. Wessberg. Discriminative touch and emotional touch. *Canadian Journal of Experimental Psychology*, 61(3):173–183, 2007.

[24] F. F. Mueller, F. Vetere, M. R. Gibbs, J. Kjeldskov, S. Pedell, and S. Howard. Hug over a distance. In *Proceedings of CHI '05*, pages 1673–1676. ACM, 2005.

[25] H. k. Olausson, J. Wessberg, I. Morrison, F. McGlone, and A. Vallbo. The neurophysiology of unmyelinated tactile afferents. *Neuroscience and Biobehavioral Reviews*, 34(2):185–91, 2010.

[26] M. Slater. Presence and Emotions. *Cyberpsychology & Behavior*, 7(1):121–121, 2004.

[27] J. Smith and K. MacLean. Communicating emotion through a haptic link: Design space and methodology. *International Journal of Human-Computer Studies*, 65(4):376–387, 2007.

[28] R. Stone. Haptic feedback: a brief history from telepresence to virtual reality. In S. Brewster and R. Murray-Smith, editors, *Haptic Human-Computer Interaction*, volume 2058 of *Lecture Notes in Computer Science*, pages 1–16. Springer Berlin / Heidelberg, 2001.

[29] E. H. Thompson and J. a. Hampton. The effect of relationship status on communicating emotions through touch. *Cognition & Emotion*, 25(2):295–306, 2011.

[30] R. Wang and F. Quek. Touch & talk: contextualizing remote touch for affective interaction. In *Proceedings of TEI '10*, pages 13–20. ACM, 2010.

[31] R. Wang, F. Quek, D. Tatar, K. S. Teh, and A. Cheok. Keep in touch: channel, expectation and experience. In *Proceedings of CHI '12*, pages 139–148. ACM, 2012.

Depression Analysis: A Multimodal Approach

Jyoti Joshi
Faculty of Information Sciences and Engineering
University of Canberra, ACT 2601, Australia
Jyoti.Joshi@canberra.edu.au

ABSTRACT

Depression is a severe mental health disorder causing high societal costs. Current clinical practice depends almost exclusively on self report and clinical opinion, risking a range of subjective biases. It is therefore useful to design a diagnostic aid to assist clinicians. This project aims at developing a novel multimodal framework for depression analysis. In this PhD work, it is hypothesized that a multimodal affective sensing system can better capture what characterises a person's affective state than single modality systems. The project will explore facial dynamics, head movements, upper body gestures, EEG measures and speech characteristics related to affect, in subjects with major depressive disorders. Integrating the individual sensing modalities, a multimodal approach that show improved performance characteristics over single modality approaches will be developed.

Categories and Subject Descriptors

I.5 [**PATTERN RECOGNITION**]; I.5.4 [**Pattern Recognition**]: Applications; I.4.9 [**Image Processing and Computer Vision**]: Applications

General Terms

Design, Human Factors, Experimentation

Keywords

Affective Computing; Depression Analysis; Multimodal framework

1. OBJECTIVE

This PhD project aims to solve the fundamental affective computing problem of developing robust non-invasive approaches for sensing a person's affective state with a mental health disorder such as depression and for further improving the robustness of such approaches through multimodal fusion. The focus of this research is (a) to investigate and develop multimodal affective sensing technology in general and (b) to validate the utility of such technology on the real-world example of detecting and monitoring mental health disorders, such as depression in particular. The proposed multimodal approach is aimed at underpinning a new generation of objective laboratory-style markers of illness expression. The central hypothesis is that a multimodal affective sensing system can better capture what characterises a person's affective state than single modality systems.

Depression and other mood disorders are common disabling disorders. Their impact on individuals and families is pro-found. The landmark WHO Global Burden of Disease (GBD) report by Mathers *et al.* [8] quantified depression as the leading cause of disability world-wide. Despite the high prevalence, current clinical practice depends almost exclusively on self-report and clinical opinion, risking a range of subjective biases. There currently exist no laboratory-based measures of illness expression, course and recovery, and no objective markers of end-points for interventions in both clinical and research settings. This compromises optimal patient care, compounding the burden of disability. As health care costs increases, the provision of effective health monitoring systems and diagnostic aides is highly important. With the advancement in affective sensing technology and machine learning, computer aided diagnosis can play a major role in providing an objective assessment. Thus, the aim is to develop robust multimodal affective sensing technology that gives clinicians additional tools for depression diagnosis and monitoring.

2. MOTIVATION & BACKGROUND

Depression is a severe psychiatric disorder that has a major impact on society and the workforce. The 1997 Australian Survey of Mental Health and Well-Being reported a 12-month prevalence rate of 6.3% for major depression [1]. The GBD report [8] quantified depression as the leading cause of disability in (10% of all years of life lost due to disability) and projected it to be the second-leading cause of disease burden by 2020. Disturbances in the expression of emotion reflect changes in mood and interpersonal style, and are arguably a key index of a current depressive episode. This leads directly to impairments in interpersonal functioning, causing a range of interpersonal disabilities including intimate relationships (and their loss), functioning in the workforce and difficulties with a range of everyday tasks (such as shopping). While these are a constant source of distress in affected subjects, they have arguably received insufficient research attention.

ICMI'12, October 22–26, 2012, Santa Monica, California, USA.

Affective state recognition has been an active field of research over a decade but with a limited attention towards applicability of these techniques for depression analysis. Researchers have also explored various multimodal approaches for better affect recognition. Zeng *et al.* [18] presented a thorough survey on all the existing approaches and outlined some of the challenges.

In one of the first works for automatic depression analysis, Cohn *et al.* [3] explored the relationship between FACS-based facial features, vocal features and clinical depression detection. They trained subject-dependent Active Appearance Models (AAM) [16] to automatically track facial features. The shape and appearance features after AAM fitting are further used to compute parameters such as the occurrence of action units (associated with depression), mean duration, ratio of onset to total duration and ratio of offset to onset phase. Vocal behaviour analysis was performed by pitch extraction and the results from two different modalities were compared. The audio and video features were not fused in this work.

According to the hypothesis proposed by Ellgring [5], depression leads to a remarkable drop in facial activity, while with the improvement of subjective well-being facial activity increases. Considering Ellgring's hypothesis as a starting point, McIntyre *et al.* [10] analysed the facial response of the subjects when shown a short video clip. Like Cohn *et al.* [3], subject-specific AAMs were trained and shape features were computed from every fifth video frame. The shape features were combined and classified at the frame level by the means of Support Vector Machine (SVM). However, this work just analysed the static features where as facial activity is quite dynamic in nature. It has been shown in the literature that temporal facial dynamics provides more information than using static information alone [2]. A limitation of both [3] and [10] is their use of subject-specific AAM models. For a new subject, a new AAM model needs to be trained, which is both complex and time consuming.

Speech analysis has also been used for depression analysis [12]. Research into possible indicators of affective disorders, such as depression, has explored subtle changes in speech characteristics. Depression patterns of speech have been recognised for many years, finding differences in the pitch, loudness, speaking rate, and articulation [12]. It has been found that depressed subjects have a lower dynamic range for the fundamental frequency than normal subjects, which increases after treatment [14]. Moreover, it has been found that depressives have a slower rate of speech and a relatively monotone delivery when compared to normal speaking patterns as well as lacking in significant expression [11]. Also, there is convincing evidence that sadness and depression are associated with a decrease in loudness [17]. In addition, mel-frequency cepstral coefficients (MFCC) were investigated [4] and their classification results were significant for detecting depression.

Researchers have been using physiological measures such as EEG [15], MRI [6] *etc.* to analyse the affective state of a person. It is evident from the literature that EEG [15] and other psychophysiological signals [9] can effectively help in analysing someone's affective state. But so far, to the best of our knowledge, there has not been any attempt to integrate these individual modality techniques to establish profound multimodal approaches for depression analysis.

3. CHALLENGES

Data Collection - Collecting relevant data is one of the biggest challenges involved in this project. The project is in collaboration with the Black Dog institute [1], a medical research institute in Sydney, where a mood/affect induction experimental setup is used to collect data. During the session, the participant's facial and vocal expressions are recorded while they watch a video, a set of images and are interviewed with a set of questions to elicit a certain emotion. A common problem is the limited number of the participants. Depressed participants are selected who are diagnosed with depression but no other mental disorders and medical conditions. Control subjects are carefully selected to have no history of mental illness and to match the depressed subjects in age and gender. This is an ongoing study and the number of participants is expected to further grow. Due to the sensitive nature of data and privacy issues, one cannot share and expect other research groups working in similar area to share the data. To analyse subjective well-being and improvement/worsening of participants over time, it is also required to have multiple sessions with the same participants, which again is not an easy task. Furthermore, this data is spontaneous in nature as opposed to current main stream facial dynamics research data, which is typically acted.

Feature Selection - Choosing the right features, which capture the expression information and have high discriminative power, is very important for robust affect analysis and a non-trivial task. For vision based facial expression analysis, features such as the Scale-Invariant Feature Transform (SIFT) and the Pyramid of Histogram of Oriented Gradients (PHOG) have been used recently and have been found to give promising results. In this project, the associated temporal information for the facial expressions, head pose/movements and shoulder movements will also be explored. In that case, the feature vectors should be able to capture the spatio-temporal variation. For audio based affect analysis, both linguistic and paralinguistic cues are taken into account. However, finding an optimal feature set that can best describe depression in the audio modality is quite a challenging task.

Curse of Dimensionality - Extensive long interviews, which are initially aimed at capturing different emotions from the participant, result in very long feature vectors. Dimensionality reduction methods such as Principal Component Analysis (PCA), Latent Discriminant Analysis (LDA), Fixed Component Analysis (FCA), or Kernel PCA (KPCA) need to be applied to the extracted features so as to use the highly discriminating features and omitting the non-contributing features.

Robust Face Tracking - Robust face tracking is a very well researched problem. It has met with success but there is a scope of extending the current state of the art AAM [16] to 3D for achieving pose and illumination invariance. 3D morphable model exist but are computationally very expensive. For vision based depression diagnosis while analysing facial expressions, robust face tracking plays a key role.

Person Independent Model - Being able to create a person-independent face model, which can generically fit to any unseen data, is another very crucial point involved in this research. The biggest problem posed by working with

[1] `http://www.blackdoginstitute.org.au/`

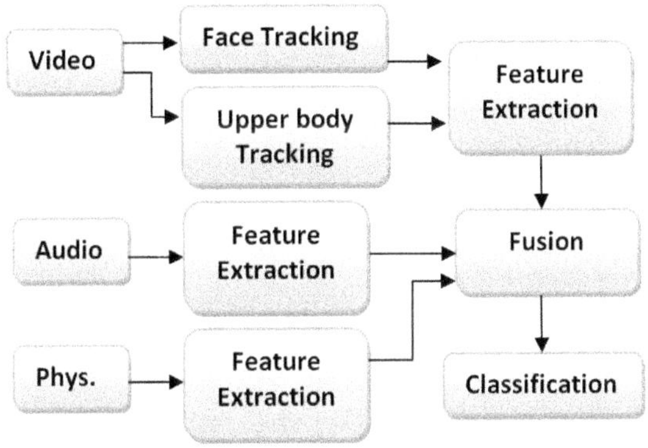

Figure 1: Flow of the proposed system.

person-dependent models is that for every new participant, one needs to train the system, which is highly time consuming and computationally expensive. One possible way of addressing this issue is to be able to train the algorithms on a large amount of data (which is also challenging to obtain). Moreover, new machine learning methods of using unlabelled data for learning robust system will be explored.

4. APPROACH & METHODOLOGY

The objective is to first investigate various uni-modal techniques for depression analysis. Depression analysis methods can be broadly classified into four main categories: a) Vision based, b) Audio based, c) Physiological measures based, and d) Fusion based methods. Initially, individual channels will be analysed for their discriminative ability and later various fusion methods will be experimented on for finding the most discriminative combination of the three different channels. Figure 1 outlines the proposed framework.

4.1 Vision Based

As vision based expression analysis is a well studied problem, various facial expression analysis methods and their aptness for depression analysis will be explored. Studies by psychologists have shown that depressed people show fewer facial movements and also display reluctance to participate in social activities. This can be analysed through head pose/movements and body gestures. Integration of these different behavioural cues seems to be of particular importance when judging such complex affective states.

Facial Expression Analysis - Facial expressions are dynamic in nature and convey a lot about the affective state of a person. So far, virtually all research in automatic facial expression recognition (FER) has been on static, single images. This completely leaves the temporal aspect of facial expressions consisting of onset, apex and offset aside, yet for human observers, this is an important clue in correctly judging someone's facial expression. In recent years, the Local Binary Patterns (LBP) [19] and Local Phase Quantisation (LPQ) [13] classes of visual descriptors have been widely employed for FER. Local Binary Pattern - Three Orthogonal Planes (LBP-TOP) [19] considers patterns in three orthogonal planes: XY, XT and YT, and concatenates the pattern co-occurrences in these three directions. The LBP-TOP descriptor assigns binary labels to pixels by thresholding the neighbourhood pixels with the central value assuming that the XY plane is always near to the apex of expression. Problematic is that this assumption does not always hold true, particularly in the case of spontaneous expression analysis over 30 – 40min long video recordings. LBP-TOP will be extended by addressing this key issue.

Head Pose/Movements - It is worthwhile to investigate features such as optical flow and features based on Space Time Interest Points (STIP) [7], which have found much attention in temporal video analysis recently to analyse head pose and movements.

Upper Body Gesture Analysis - Pose estimation is a classic problem in computer vision. Analysing the pose and upper body movements of subjects can provide useful information. Pose estimation based on pictorial structures and similar methods will be explored. Further, pose dynamics will be fused with face information.

4.2 Audio Based

In the audio modality, the focus is on prosodic patterns in the speech signal. To this end, existing freely available software tools, such as Praat[2] will be employed to analyse range, mean, median, and variability of the pitch, pitch contour, intensity / energy of the speech signal, speech rate and duration, and lag in responding to stimuli and questions. Initially, the approach will be based on the most basic conceivable emotion / mental state recognition system, with design choices in accordance with simple baseline systems of this kind commonly found in the literature.

4.3 Physiological Measures Based

Human electroencephalography (EEG) measures electrical activity generated by the brain. The use of EEG has enabled researchers to study regional brain activity and brain function, in particular various human cognitive and emotional processes. Recently, EEG information has also been recorded as part of data collection and will be explored for depression detection.

4.4 Integration of Uni-Modal Techniques

The primary objective is to validate the proposed affective sensing approaches by characterising the visual, audio and physiological data as a function of severity and the presence or absence of melancholic features to better understand disturbances in major depression. The individual sensing modalities will be integrated to develop multimodal approaches with improved performance characteristics over uni-modal approaches. This will be achieved by understanding the co-variation between the affective data and the behavioural, disability and neuro-cognitive data using standard multi-variate techniques, such as logistic regression and partial least squares.

5. PROGRESS TO DATE

In one of the initial work, visual cues for depression analysis have been investigated. A holistic model for upper body movements and facial dynamics is explored. STIP are computed for the videos for analysing the upper body move-

[2]http://www.fon.hum.uva.nl/praat/

ments and a temporal visual words dictionary is learned from it. Intra-facial muscle movement is captured by computing LBP-TOP on the aligned face. Due to a large number of interest points, the size of the feature vector grows very quickly. This problem is addressed by defining multiple spatio-temporal grids in a bag of visual words approach inspired by [7] for LBP-TOP and STIP separately.

Initial experiments in the direction of multimodal depression analysis are also performed by exploring visual and audio cues and fusing them to improve the performance of the system. For the video data analysis, intra-facial muscle movements and the movements of the head and shoulders are analysed by computing STIP. In addition, various audio features are computed. Next, a bag of visual features and a bag of audio features are generated. Fusion methods at feature level, score level and decision level have been compared.

As part of ongoing research, the work of McIntyre *et al.* [10] is being extended by scaling it to a larger dataset, investigating use of temporal features and using person independent AAM tracking in the existing framework.

6. RESEARCH TIMELINE

First six months are for survey of existing technologies and performing initial experiments looking at the visual cues mainly facial dynamics for depression analysis. In later half of first year, the plan is to explore temporal information at both feature extraction and classification level. In second year, contribution of other visual cues such as body pose and head movements in depression analysis will be investigated. Other modalities viz. audio and physiological measures will be analysed and different fusion methods will be explored in the final year.

7. ACKNOWLEDGEMENTS

I would like to thank Dr. Roland Goecke, primary supervisor and panel chair, and Prof. Michael Wagner for their invaluable guidance and support. I would also like to thank collaborators at Australian National University and Queensland Institute of Medical Research, Australia. This PhD project is funded by Australian Research Council discovery project grant DP110103767.

8. REFERENCES

[1] Mental health and wellbeing: Profile of adults. Technical report, Australian Bureau of Statistics, Australia, 1997.

[2] Z. Ambadar, J. Schooler, and J. Cohn. Deciphering the enigmatic face: The importance of facial dynamics to interpreting subtle facial expressions. *Psychological Science*, 16(5):403–410, May 2005.

[3] J. F. Cohn, T. S. Kreuz, I. Matthews, Y. Yang, M. H. Nguyen, M. T. Padilla, F. Zhou, and F. De la Torre. Detecting Depression from Facial Actions and Vocal Prosody. In *Proc. Affective Computing and Intelligent Interaction (ACII2009)*, pages 1–7, 2009.

[4] N. Cummins, J. Epps, M. Breakspear, and R. Goecke. An Investigation of Depressed Speech Detection: Features and Normalization. In *Proc. Interspeech*, 2011.

[5] H. Ellgring. *Nonverbal communication in depression.* Cambridge University Press, 2008.

[6] K. Krishnan, J. Hays, and D. Blazer. MRI-defined vascular depression. *American Journal of Psychiatry*, 154(4):497–501, Apr. 1997.

[7] I. Laptev, M. Marszałek, C. Schmid, and B. Rozenfeld. Learning Realistic Human Actions from Movies. In *Proc. IEEE Conference on Computer Vision and Pattern Recognition (CVPR2008)*, 2008. DOI: 10.1109/CVPR.2008.4587756.

[8] C. Mathers, T. Boerma, and D. M. Fat. The global burden of disease: 2004 update. Technical report, WHO Press, Switzerland, 2004.

[9] M. Mauri, V. Magagnin, P. Cipresso, L. Mainardi, E. N. Brown, S. Cerutti, M. Villamira, and R. Barbieri. Psychophysiological signals associated with affective states. In *32nd Annual International Conference of the IEEE, Engineering in Medicine and Biology Society*, pages 3563–3566, 2010.

[10] G. McIntyre, R. Goecke, M. Hyett, M. Green, and M. Breakspear. An Approach for Automatically Measuring Facial Activity in Depressed Subjects. In *Proc. ACII2009*, pages 223–230, Sept. 2009.

[11] E. Moore, M. Clements, J. Peifer, and L. Weisser. Critical analysis of the impact of glottal features in the classification of clinical depression in speech. In *IEEE Transactions on Biomedical Engineering*, volume 55, pages 96–107, 2008.

[12] J. C. Mundt, P. J. Snyder, M. S. Cannizzaro, K. Chappie, and D. S. Geralts. Voice acoustic measures of depression severity and treatment response collected via interactive voice response technology. *Journal of Neurolinguistics*, 20(1):50–64, 2007.

[13] V. Ojansivu and J. Heikkilä. Blur Insensitive Texture Classification Using Local Phase Quantization. In *Proc. 3rd International Conference on Image and Signal Processing*, Lecture Notes in Computer Science, pages 236–243. 2008.

[14] A. Ozdas, R. Shiavi, S. Silverman, M. Silverman, and D. Wilkes. Analysis of fundamental frequency for near term suicidal risk assessment. In *Proc. IEEE International Conference on Systems Man and Cybernetics*, 2000.

[15] H. Peng, B. Hu, Q. Liu, Q. Dong, Q. Zhao, and P. Moore. User-centered depression prevention: An EEG approach to pervasive healthcare. In *Proc. PervasiveHealth*, pages 325–330. IEEE, May 2011.

[16] J. Saragih and R. Goecke. Learning AAM fitting through simulation. *Pattern Recognition*, 42(11):2628–2636, 2009.

[17] K. R. Scherer. *Vocal assessment of affective disorders*, pages 57–82. Lawrence Erlbaum Associates, 1987.

[18] Z. Zeng, M. Pantic, G. Roisman, and T. Huang. A Survey of Affect Recognition Methods: Audio, Visual and Spontaneous Expressions. *IEEE Trans. Pattern Analysis and Machine Intelligence*, 31(1):39–58, Jan. 2009.

[19] G. Zhao and M. Pietikäinen. Dynamic texture recognition using local binary patterns with an application to facial expressions. *IEEE Trans. Pattern Analysis and Machine Intelligence*, 29(6):915–928, 2007.

Design Space for Finger Gestures with Hand-held Tablets

Katrin Wolf
TU Berlin
Telekom Innovation Laboratories
Ernst-Reuter-Platz 7, 10587 Berlin
Germany
katrin.wolf@acm.org

ABSTRACT

This paper presents research how a finger-gesture design space for interacting with hand-held tablets may be defined. The parameters that limit or extend this space, such as anatomy-dependent gesture feasibility, grasp requirement, gesture occlusion or complexity, are discussed based on initial explorative expert interviews and following user studies. The goal of this research is defining parameters that have to be taken into account for developing a finger-gesture UI model for hand-held tablets. Although this model has a strong user-centric design approach, rather than being technology driven, technical solutions for detecting finger gestures are also considered. A model design is presented and research questions for investigating this model in greater detail are outlined.

Categories and Subject Descriptors

H.5.2 [Information inter-faces and presentation]: User Interfaces - Ergonomics; Haptic I/O.

Keywords

Gestures; back-of-device; feedback; occlusion.

1. INTRODUCTION

Since human-computer interaction has become mobile and is no longer limited to mouse and keyboard, there are now many possibilities for interacting with computers, e.g. through free-hand gestures, touch, speech, device-gestures, gaze. The interactions with desktop computers are – compared to mobile devices – well investigated and paradigms for designing desktop interactions, such as WIMP, direct touch, and instrumental interactions [3] have been established. Current mobile interfaces mostly rely on the established paradigms mentioned above or on some modification of them with respect to a mobile scenario and different device form factors. For instance, the UIs on mobile phones usually make use of icons and menus but in a different appearance, such as icon groups on the iPhone. The greatest difference between mobile UIs and desktop computers is probably having a single device with far fewer physical buttons and which has a screen, which has replaced the mouse and touchpad by being able to detect finger-touches directly screen positions of icons. The thumb, with respect to mobility, is replacing mouse and cursor, but can also lead to problems, such as content occlusion and the "fat finger" problem.

In recent years researchers have developed interfaces that avoid occlusion and that allow access to the back of a hand-held device for input, such as pointing from the rear at content that is displayed at the user-facing screen [2,16]. Widgor *et al.* [16] describe how a hovering finger may be sensed with an external camera and Baudisch and Chu [2] use a back-of-device touch-pad for input. Moreover, the first game controller with a rear touch-pad was recently released by Sony. In a similar manner to the research projects mentioned above, this device uses back-of-device touch events for absolute pointing at graphical elements at the front screen. Devices that are larger than Apple's Nano Touch device [2] or the Sony Vita console, such as pad devices or tablets, are often held in such a way so that the fingers are already touching the rear surface. This can result in input errors through unintentionally released touch events. This phenomenon is known as the "Midas touch" problem [7], and is already known to cause problems with gaze input [8] through misinterpreted eye movements.

Back-of-device interactions address the problem of content occlusion caused by the fingers pointing directly at the displayed content. However, such an approach requires the ability to distinguish between intentional and unintentional touch-event releases. In addition, it might be the case that areas in the middle of a tablet screen may not be easily reachable from the device rear and therefore direct pointing may not be the best solution for back-of-device interactions. In order to address these problems as well as designing interaction techniques with respect to ergonomics, error resistance and mobility, this paper describes an approach for developing a mobile UI model that strongly focuses on capitalizing on the grasp and fingers that already hold the device.

2. RELATED WORK

2.1 Interacting while grasping

As Wimmer and Boring [17] suggest, detecting how users hold their devices could serve as a means for designing new implicit and explicit interactions as well as a way to enhance existing mobile interfaces. Researchers have already developed interfaces that rely on releasing grasping fingers or on re-adjusting the grasping hand. Kratz et al. [9] and Wigdor et al. [16] detect finger movements around grasped devices, and Baudisch [2] interpret back-of-device touch events as pointing commands. These projects mainly focus on specific interaction techniques that have become possible through novel interfaces. So far no research has been carried out that summarizes existing back- and around-device interaction techniques or that investigates UI requirements

ICMI '12, October 22–26, 2012, Santa Monica, California, USA.

with respect to a user-centric and ergonomic design. Moreover, the problem of content occlusion might be solved through back-of-device interactions; however, this may lead to the problem of gesture occlusion by the device itself. If visual information is not available, humans tend to rely more on other modalities. Usually in HCI, other system modalities, such as audio is provided if vision in not available. So far the potential for humans' internal feedback modalities, such as touch and kinesthetics have not been investigated. Therefore, in addition to ergonomics, internal modalities for gestural motor control are also relevant aspects that ought to be taken into account when modeling a gestural mobile UI for hand-held devices in general and for tablets specifically.

2.2 Ergonomic studies

The goal of ergonomic design approaches is to develop products, machines and working environments that are suited to human body size, and in such a manner that the user does not incur a physical or psychological penalty even over a long period of usage. Therefore handles are designed to fit in user's hand. For human-computer interaction design that relies on back-of-device finger movements, an ergonomic design could rely on hand sizes and finger lengths. Ergonomic studies for designing ergonomic physical products have been carried out. Lange [10] and Tilley [13] collected human's body sizes as well as degrees of freedom for flexing, bending and moving body parts, such as hands and arms. And Otl Aicher [1] described the ergonomics of grasping regarding the design of handles and hand-held tools. The ergonomics of human-computer interactions is a much younger discipline and therefore a lot of work remains to be carried out in order to understand how ergonomic hand-movement based interactions should be designed. Some lessons can be learned from research driven by prosthesis design. For instance, Feix *et al.* [5] merged several grasp taxonomies and presented an overview of the three main grasp types and their variations according to different grasp functions as well as form factors of the grasped objects.

2.3 Motor control modalities

In HCI research, feedback is a central issue regarding good interaction design. However usually system feedback of the computer is meant, and humans' internal feedback modalities have so far not been investigated with respect to their potential for supporting interaction design. The benefit in investigating human feedback modalities is to keep systems simple. Moreover in mobile scenarios there is a lot of audio and visual noise that may overlay or distract from system feedback. During the last ten years in cognitive science a lot work has been done in investigating internal feedback modalities for motor control: The Sensorimotor Adaption Model [14] is based on information of multiple sensory modalities that serve to monitor physical movement. For instance, vision and proprioception both provide information about hand movements. Vision had been thought to dominate this process [15], but studies, such as [14] have shown that the sensorimotor system weights modalities based on their information quality. If a modality loses information, such as when poor lighting reduces vision, proprioceptive information is given more weighting, becoming the dominant feedback control modality. Taking Sensorimotor Adaption Theory as inspiration, it can be suggested that proprioception can serve as an internal feedback modality when the gestures are occluded without decreasing back-of-device interaction performances, such as pointing or scrolling.

3. DESIGNINING A GRASP-BASED UI

3.1 Research questions

The general question that underlies the development of a fingergesture based UI is: to what extent can users interact with hand-held tablets through tiny microgestures that are performed while grasping? As there are several interaction design aspects to be taken into account, three sub-questions are leading the research for the model design:

Q1: Which finger movements are feasible while grasping?

Q2: Which touch positions and finger movements should be excluded from the design space to avoid the Midas touch problem?

Q3: What are the appropriate microgetures to use for common tasks such as pointing, selecting, and sliding?

Q4: How should microgestures be supported through guidance and end-of-gesture feedback?

The methods for answering these questions are interviews with experts in anatomy and human physiology as well as evaluations of interactive prototypes.

3.2 Feasibility based design space

3.2.1 Gestural atoms

In expert interviews [18] we asked physiotherapists and sport scientists, which gestures were easily feasible while holding objects in three main grasp types [5]. For all grasp types, just touching or sliding on the grasped objects using the thumb, index and middle fingers, were identified by the experts as being easily feasible without decreasing the stability of the grasp.. Actually these two movements can be slightly modified or combined and then a lot of potential gestures can be designed using these gestural "atoms". Any further gesture design will basically be built out of active touches and slides. Just by modifying the intensity, speed or acceleration of touches and slide movements means that taps, press events, flip gestures, and slide movements of several shapes, such as lines or circles, are added to the design space.

3.2.2 Touchable surface regions

Depending on the type of device, the grasp, and the finger lengths of the user, some regions of the device surface are already touched when the device is held, while others would be still easy to reach through releasing and readjusting single fingers or one of the two grasping hands (while still maintaining a loose grip on device with this hand). However, some surface regions might be harder or impossible to reach without risking dropping the held device or it slipping towards the floor. In a user study (see Fig. 1) we

Figure 1. Participants were asked to touch with every finger and the thumb all possible device regions through drawing on the touch screen.

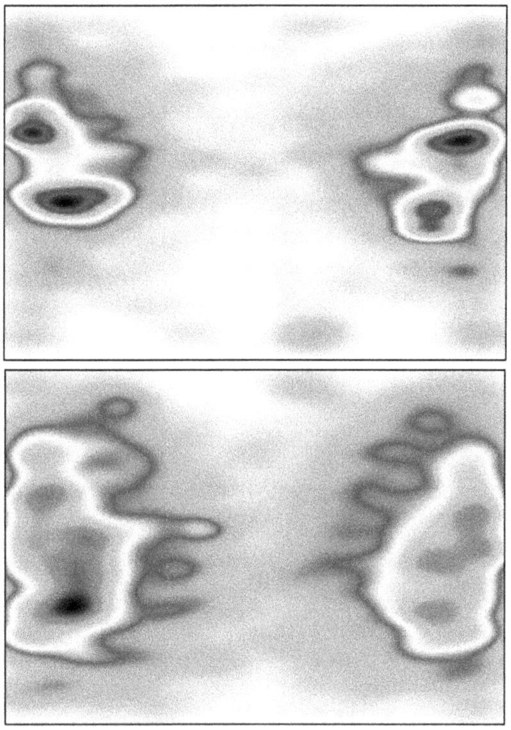

Figure 2. The touched areas at the hand-held tablet's front (top) and rear (bottom) are presented through heatmaps. The locations that are touched while grasping are displayed in dark orange, red, and brown.

investigated the touchable regions on the front and on the rear of held tablets (see Fig. 2). One fact that restricts UI design a lot is the unpredictability of the grasp and unintentional touch events; based on how different people hold devices. Therefore touchable regions can serve for placing touch-based interactions, but because the finger touches that are necessary for holding the device and those that indent interactions are located in the same area, these interactions have to be labeled for been differentiated from the natural grasp touches. Gesture combinations or touch releases could potentially provoke fewer errors. Also gestural trigger events that label gestures, similar to push-to-gesture or end-of-gesture events can help to design error resistant interactions.

3.2.3 Guidance feedback

Back-of-device interactions, such as finger movements and touches at the device's rear are occluded by the held device. The section on related work outlined how missing visual information is substituted with the hand behind the device [16] or fingers that are touching the device [2] are visually simulated on screens at the user facing device side. In many mobile scenarios a user's visual attention might be needed for other issues, rather than being directed to the display of a mobile device. Much work has already been done on designing non-visual displays [12], progress information [4] and end-of-gesture design [11]. Inspired by the Sensorimotor Adaption Model [14] we investigated whether widgets that are displayed on the screen of a mobile device can be pointed to from its rear without either system feedback or displayed touch positions. We discovered that users do not feel confident with absolute pointing from the back of the device, but that their performance without additional visual system guidance is as good as when it is present, provided that they point relatively from their current finger position [19].

3.3 Technology

Even though the presented work has a user-centric approach, many human-computer interfaces are rather technology-driven developed than designed focusing on human skills and needs With respect to mobility and changing environments any camera-based approach would cause too much noise as well as limiting mobility, (and therefore scalability to a large number of use cases). For any touch-based gestures on the device surface, we often used common touch screens. For gestures that might be hard to detect with that technology, we used inertia sensors that are worn on the fingers, which perform the gestures (see Fig. 3). Therefore it becomes possible to classify gestures that would not easily be distinguished from simple touch and slide gestures with common capacitive sensors, such as pitch or rapid releases that serve as end-of-gesture event. This aspect actually points to a big challenge in grasp-based interfaces: the Midas touch problem that describes unintentional movements that are interpreted by computers as commands.

3.4 Conceptual mismatches

Midas touch problems and many other input errors usually cause gesture classification errors because of certain differences between humans and computers that can be summarized as conceptual mismatches. These errors include instances where natural movements are misunderstood by the computer as gesture, as well as instances where intentional gestures performed by the user are either not recognized by the system or else wrongly classified. Even the simple touch gesture that is positioned by users at a certain point is not exactly measured by common capacitive screens at the same position [6]. However in this case the error is small enough that it does not cause completely wrong and unexpected system reactions.

The raw data of inertia sensors has a completely different structure than those which serve for humans recognize and control body movements. For instance, if a gesture is done without acceleration, in human communication this gesture might still be understood. Computers excuse far fewer modifications in gesture execution. The interactive prototype that is shown in Fig. 3 classifies swipe gestures through accelerations in certain directions.

Figure 3. Inertia sensors (accelerometer and gyroscope) augment fingers for detecting gestures beyond touch and slide.

Because finger worn sensors are used, the gesture can be executed at the rear surface or in the air. To avoid tiny finger movements that release a command, a tap is labeling the swipe gesture. In the displayed interface, the index and the middle finger perform the gesture, and if the index finger is tapping, the middle finger might unintentional tap as well. Therefore having the same gesture for all fingers might be easy to learn but is also very error prone. Alternative gesture triggers could rely on other modalities or also on using two fingers from two hands instead of just one.

3.5 Future work

User studies on exploring the ability to perform gestures with more than one finger at the same time are currently underway, and studies on the performance of absolute and relative pointing as well as the requirements and needs for feedback will be carried out in the future. Moreover, a prediction model for Midas touch error for certain gestures and their trigger events will be developed, because successful handling of the Midas touch problem very much influences the success or failure of a gestural interface. All these findings will lead to the development of a post-WIMP paradigm for hand-held devices that focuses on mobility, ergonomic gesture design, and suitability for tasks that require visual attention or that cannot use audio due to environment noise, or when auditory input and output is not suitable for the scenario.

4. SUMMARY

This paper presents an approach for developing a UI paradigm for finger gestures with hand-held devices using the example of tablets. The work is still in progress and at this stage, parameters that ought to be taken into account are introduced based on the requirements of mobile scenarios and the focus on ergonomic and user-centric design. For designing a scalable model, the parameters are hard to define statically and ad-hoc layouts and dynamic interface component setups seems

to be promising. Also non-visual and non-audio feedback modalities are promising with respect to providing interaction support and feedback. Finally, any gestural design has to be different from natural behavior so as not not provoke Midas touch events. This work will be continued during the next 1.5 years and finally be published as my Ph.D. thesis.

5. ACKNOWLEDGMENTS

I would like to thank Sebastian Möller, Michael Rohs, and Robert Schleicher for their valuable advice and input.

6. REFERENCES

[1] Aicher, O., Kuhn, R. Griffe und Greifen, Köln, 1995.

[2] Baudisch, P., Chu, G. 2009. Back-of-device interaction allows creating very small touch devices. In *Proc. CHI 2009*, 1923-1932.

[3] Beaudouin-Lafon, M. Instrumental interaction: An interaction model for designing post-WIMP user interfaces. In *Proc. CHI 2000*, 446–453.

[4] Brewster, S. and King, A.. 2005. An investigation into the use of tactons to present progress information. In *Proc. INTERACT* 2005, 6-17.

[5] Feix, T. et al. Grasp Taxonomy Comparison Sheet, DOI = http://web.student.tuwien.ac.at/~e0227312/ documents / taxonomy_comparison.pdf.

[6] Holz, C. and Baudisch, P. Understanding Touch, In Proc. *CHI 2011*, 2501-2510.

[7] Istance, H., Bates, R., Hyrskykari., Vickers, S. Snap clutch, a moded approach to solving the Midas touch problem. In *Proc. Symposium on Eye tracking research 2008*, 221-228.

[8] Jacob, R.J. 1990. What You Look at is What You Get: Eye Movement-Based Interaction Techniques, In *Proc. CHI 1990,* 11–18.

[9] Kratz, S., Rohs, M. 2009. Hoverflow: exploring around-device interaction with IR distance sensors. In *Proc. Mobile HCI 2009*, 4 pages.

[10] Lange, W. Kleine Ergonomische Datensammlung, Köln, 1991.

[11] McAdam, C. and Brewster, S.A. *Distal Tactile Feedback for Text Entry on Tabletop Computers*. In Proc. BCS HCI 2009, 504-511.

[12] Sawhney, N. and Schmandt, C.. 2000. Nomadic radio: speech and audio interaction for contextual messaging in nomadic environments. *ACM Trans. Comput.-Hum. Interact.* 7, 3 (September 2000), 353-383.

[13] Tilley, A. R. The Measure of Man and Woman: Human Factors in Design, New York, 1993.

[14] van Beers, R. J., Wolpert, D. M., Haggart, P. 2002. When Feeling Is More Important Than Seeing in Sensory Adaption, *Current Biology*, Vol. 12, May 14, 2002, 834–837.

[15] Welch, R. B., Warren, D. H. 1986. Intersensory interactions. In *Handbook of Perception and Human Performance*, Vol. 1, 1986, 25.1–25.36.

[16] Wigdor, D., Forlines, C., Baudisch, P., Barnwell, J., Shen, C. 2007. LucidTouch: A See-Through Mobile Device, In *Proc. UIST 2007,* 269-278.

[17] Wimmer, R., Boring, S. HandSense - Discriminating Different Ways of Grasping and Holding a Tangible User Interface, In *Proc. TEI 2009*, 359-362.

[18] Wolf, K., Naumann, A., Rohs, M., and Mueller, J. 2011. A Taxonomy of Microinteractions: Defining Microgestures based on Ergonomic and Scenario-dependent Requirements, In *Proc. INTERACT 2011*, Springer-Verlag, Berlin, Heidelberg, 559-575.

[19] Wolf, K., Müller-Tomfelde, C., Cheng, K., and Wechsung, I. 2012. Does proprioception guide back-of-device pointing as well as vision? In *Proc. CHI 2012*, 1739-1744.

Multi-Modal Interfaces for Control of Assistive Robotic Devices

Christopher McMurrough
Department of Computer Science and Engineering
The University of Texas at Arlington
Arlington, Texas
mcmurrough@uta.edu

ABSTRACT

This paper presents an outline of dissertation research activities which aim to advance the use of non-traditional, multimodal interfaces in assistive robotic devices. The data modalities which are of particular interest in the work are perception of the environment using 3D scanning and computer vision, estimation of the user point of gaze, and perception of user intent during interaction with objects of interest. The main goal of this research is to explore the hypothesis that the combination of these data modalities can be used to provide intuitive and effective means of control over existing robotic platforms, such as wheelchairs and manipulators, to users with severe physical impairments.

Categories and Subject Descriptors

H.5.2 [**User Interfaces**]: Input devices and strategies; I.4.8 [**Image Processing and Computer Vision**]: Scene Analysis—*object recognition, range data, sensor fusion*

General Terms

Design; Human Factors; Algorithms; Experimentation

Keywords

Eye tracking; multimodal systems; human-computer interaction; robotics

1. INTRODUCTION

Eye gaze based interaction has many useful applications in human-machine interfaces, assistive technologies, and multimodal systems. Traditional input methods, such as the keyboard and mouse, are not practical in many situations and can be ineffective for some users with physical impairments. Knowledge of the user point of gaze (PoG) can be a powerful data modality in intelligent systems by facilitating intuitive control, perception of user intent, and enhanced interactive experiences.

ICMI'12, October 22–26, 2012, Santa Monica, California, USA.

Gaze tracking devices have proven to be extremely beneficial to impaired users. In the case study presented in [9], 16 amyotrophic lateral sclerosis (ALS) patients with severe motor impairments (loss of mobility, unable to speak, etc.) were introduced to eye tracking devices during a 1-2 week period. The patients were assessed by a psychologist during an initial meeting in order to evaluate their general quality of life. Eye tracking devices and proper training, as well as access to a speech and language therapist and a computer engineer, were provided for the duration of the study. Patients completed questionnaires related to their experiences with the equipment at multiple times during the study. Several patients reported a clear positive impact on their quality of life during the study, resulting from the enhanced communication facilitated by the eye tracking devices over other non-gaze based assistive devices.

2. RELATED WORK

While the utility of gaze interaction in a variety of applications has been demonstrated, the availability of the technology has been a limiting factor in more widespread use. Due to the relatively high monetary cost and proprietary nature associated with commercial eye tracking equipment and software, several low-cost solutions have been developed using inexpensive off-the-shelf components. Many of these designs have been made publicly available through the open source community. The openEyes project [2] presents a low-cost head-mounted eye tracker which uses a pair of inexpensive IEEE-1394 cameras to capture images of both the eye and scene. This hardware device, coupled with the open source Starburst algorithm [13], facilitates estimation of the user PoG in the 2D scene image. A similar open source project, the EyeWriter [3], provides detailed build instructions for creating a head-mounted eye tracker from a modified Playstation Eye USB camera. The project was designed to enable digital drawing by eye gaze control for artists with ALS while using the device with the accompanying open source software. Interestingly, in [11], the effectiveness of a low-cost eye tracker is shown to be comparable to that of commercial devices for target acquisition and eye-typing activities.

The head-mounted eye gaze systems mentioned above facilitate effective interactive experiences with some limiting constraints. In general, these solutions are designed for interaction with fixed computer displays or 2D scene images. These types of systems provide a 2D PoG, which does not directly translate into the 3D world without additional data modalities. An accurate estimate of the 3D user PoG can be especially useful in mobile and ubiquitous applications, human-robot interaction, and in designing intelligent assistive environments. Knowledge of the 3D PoG within an environment can be used to detect user attention and intention to interact [8], leading to multimodal attentive systems able to adapt to the user state.

Some mobile 3D PoG tracking systems have been proposed in literature. In [10], a head-mounted multi-camera system is presented that estimates the 3D PoG by computing the intersection of the optical axis of both eyes. This approach gives the 3D PoG relative to the user's frame of reference, but does not provide a mapping of this point to the environment in which the user is present. A similar stereo camera approach is presented in [12], which also includes a forward facing scene camera for mapping of the 3D PoG to scene coordinates. While multi-camera approaches such as these provide a 3D PoG, their use is limited by increased uncertainty at increasing PoG depths. Another limiting factor is the scene camera, which is generally a standard 2D camera that does not provide any 3D information of the environment itself.

3. HYPOTHESIS

The key hypothesis of this dissertation work is that currently emerging or under-utilized data modalities, such as eye tracking and RGB-D scanning, can be combined with existing robotics platforms in such a way that the resulting system will enable a severly disabled user to perform environmental interaction and object manipulation beyond the capabilities provided by currently existing approaches. It is my belief that this hypothesis is not only true, but can also be realized while meeting an additional criterion: that relatively inexpensive and readily available hardware devices can provide the majority of the necessary human interfacing capabilities for such a solution, particularly by utilizing eye gaze tracking and environmental RGB-D scanning techniques.

4. RESEARCH PLAN

In order to fully investigate the proposed hypothesis, a 4 year research plan has been developed which involves background investigation of the problem domain, development of necessary hardware devices and software modules, and experimental evaluation of the approach in collaboration with volunteers who face severe physical disabilities. An outline of the reserach plan is as follows:

1. First year
   (a) Completion of assigned coursework
   (b) Initial background research of problem domain
2. Second year
   (a) Completion of diagnostic examination
   (b) Development of necessary hardware and software modules
3. Third year
   (a) Completion of comprehensive examination
   (b) Completion of dissertation proposal
   (c) Development of robotic system
4. Fourth year
   (a) Evaluation of system with volunteer subjects
   (b) Completion of research activities
   (c) Completion of dissertation defense

It is the consensus of the Ph.D. candidate and commitee members that the proposed milestones are both realistic and present a significant contribution to the field of human-computer interfaces for assistive devices, particularly assistive robotics. To date, all milestones have been met on time.

5. METHODOLOGY

The underlying goal of this work is to prove the proposed hypothesis by developing a robotic aid which is able to provide environmental navigation and object manipulation capabilties to a physically disabled user to a degree which surpasses any available commercial device. The target user group in this study will be subjects who are affected by physical disabilities such as ALS and tetraplegia, specifically cases where upper and lower limb movement are completely or severely limited but eye movements are unaffected.

The realization of this aid will take the form of an electric wheelchair equipped with a robotic arm for manipulation. The key contribution, the human interface, will take the form of a headset device which will facilitate 3D PoG estimation and other data modalities. Specifically, the following data modalities will be investigated:

- 3D PoG estimation
- blink detection
- voice commands
- mouth and "puff" control
- brain-computer interface

The above will be integrated in such a way that eye tracking will provide the critical input while all other modalities will play a supporting role in perception of the user intent.

6. RESULTS

During the initial stages of forming the dissertation hypothesis, background research was performed in related areas. In [4], a general survey of assistive devices used for cerebral palsy (CP) patients was performed. One of the focus areas of the survey was on robotic devices, both for Robot Mediated Therapy (RMT) and for everyday use as mobility enhancing devices. This work provided key insight to the state of the art in assistive robotic devices and user interfaces, particularly since CP patients face a wide range of physical disabilities and are often not able to use standard computer interfaces.

In [1], a prototype assistive guide robot for visually impaired users was developed and tested. The system is designed to lead the user to a desired location by following pedestrian paths using compter vision, and avoiding obstacles using a LIDAR scanner. The mechanical platform used in the initial prototype was a commercially available iRobot ground vehicle. During experimental testing, the robot was able to lead the user by detecting and aligning to indoor

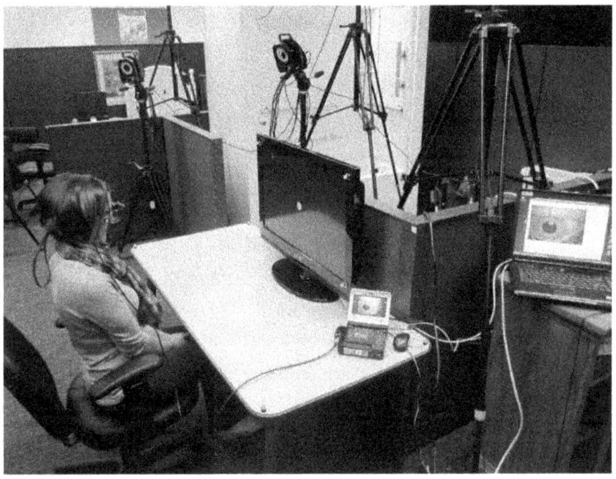

Figure 1: Image of data collection process

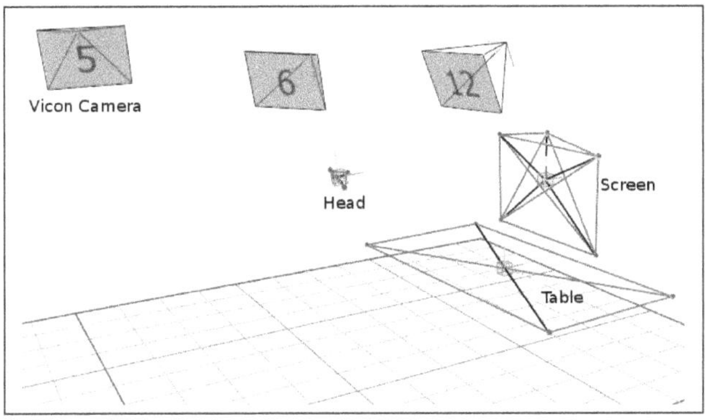

Figure 2: A representation of the 3D space and the tracked objects as perceived by the motion capture system.

hallways and outdoor concrete paths while "tugging" the user along using a handheld leash. While this system was not designed for users with motor impairments, the software and lessons learned during testing provide a foundation for future assistive robots.

Following the previous work on robotic devices, further investigation and development was performed on eye tracking as an interface method for disabled users. During background work, it was realized that current eye tracking devices tend to be expensive and have issues when the head pose is allowed to change or drift over time. It was also realized that attempts by other researchers to address these issues might be limited by the availability of hardware and lab space. For these reasons, a publicly available dataset was created which provides synchronized video streams of user eye motions, on screen video targets, and high fidelity head position and pose data acquired with a high end motion capture system [6]. This dataset involved 20 users performing 6 common eye gaze related scenarios, such as calibration procedures, smooth target tracking, target following while moving the head, etc., while wearing a commercially available head-mounted eye tracker. The aim of this work was to provide eye tracking researchers with a standard set of video and tracking data to evaluate computer vision or calibration algorithms without requiring any special hardware. A subject wearing the headset during the data collection process is shown in Figure 1. Figure 2 visualizes the locations of the head and the computer display in the 3D space as perceived by the motion capture system.

Further work to address the limitations of eye tracking was performed in [5], where a low-cost head mounted eye tracker with 3D head tracking capabilities was developed. In this work, a forward facing infrared stereo camera capable of 6DOF position and orientation tracking was created using a pair of inexpensive, commercially available sensors, while an embedded infrared camera is used to acquire the image of the eye. Figure 3 shows an eye camera image frame while the headset is worn by a user. A detailed discussion of the calibration procedure and the necessary coordinate transformations are provided. Experimental results obtained when comparing the tracking capabilities against a high end motion capture system show that the headset provides promising results. Later, an additional headset system was described in [7]. This system replaces infrared stereo camera component with a forward facing RGB-D camera which provides 3D scanning of the user's field of view. A 3D object segmentation method is also presented, along with mapping of the user's pupil position to physical 3D points in space. The combination of these two modalities, along with a feature based visual recognition approach, allow the resulting system to determine exactly what object is being gazed upon by the user, its 3D structure, and its classification if such an object has been previously identified. The complete headset hardware solution is shown in Figure 4.

Remaining work will focus on combining the headset solutions with other data modalities to control mobile robots and manipulators. Control of an electric wheelchair equipped with a robotic manipulator will be investigated with the goal of enabling a quadriplegic user to successfully navigate and interact with objects in the environment.

7. CONTRIBUTIONS

The key expected contributions of this research will be to provide a functional and useful robotic system for users with severe physical disablities. The hardware devices and software modules developed during this work will be well documented and made publicly available for further use by the community. In addition, evaluation of the resulting systems will be performed with participation of volunteers with phys-

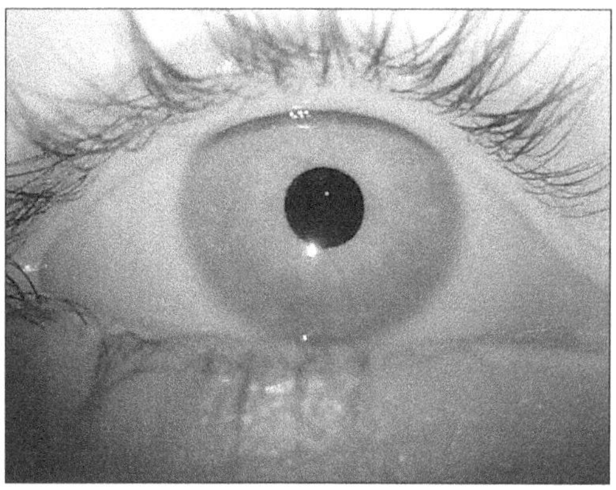

Figure 3: Eye camera image provided by headset

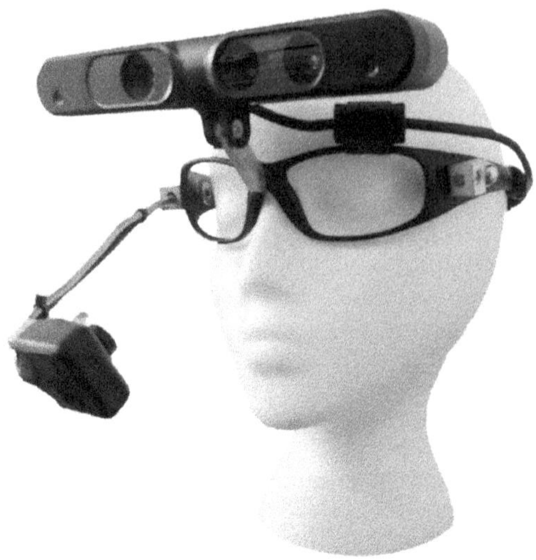

Figure 4: Headset with eye and scene cameras

ical disabilities who could benefit from such devices. This evaluation process will be done during the semester prior to the dissertation defense, and will be held according to the policies and procedures of The University of Texas at Arlington. The pool of volunteer participants will be selected from the local student population, where several qualified persons have already expressed interest. The critical feedback of these volunteers will be a significant part of the overall contribution of this work, as it is imperative that the end user for such systems be included in the earliest stages possible.

8. CONCLUSION

This disseration research aims to further advance the use of multimodal interfaces, particularly eye tracking and RBD-D scanning, in assistive robotic devices. The currently established results have laid the foundation for future efforts in creating advanced interfaces while utilizing inexpensive, readily available components. The individual milestons of the proposed research plan have been meet on-time to date, and the remaining milestones are being vigorously researched and implemented.

9. ACKNOWLEDGMENTS

I would like to thank my advisor, Fillia Makdeon, for her support and encouragement during my PhD studies. I would also like to thank my colleagues who have contributed to the works cited in this paper.

10. REFERENCES

[1] G. Galatas, C. McMurrough, G. L. Mariottini, and F. Makedon. eyeDog. In *Proceedings of the 4th International Conference on PErvasive Technologies Related to Assistive Environments - PETRA '11*, volume 10, New York, New York, USA, 2011. ACM Press.

[2] D. Li, J. Babcock, and D. J. Parkhurst. openEyes: a low-cost head-mounted eye-tracking solution. In *Proceedings of the 2006 symposium on Eye tracking research & applications - ETRA '06*, page 95, New York, New York, USA, 2006. ACM Press.

[3] Z. Lieberman, C. Sugrue, T. Watson, J. Powderly, E. Roth, and T. Quan. The EyeWriter, 2009.

[4] C. Mcmurrough, A. Papangelis, and A. Boisselle. A Survey of Assistive Devices for Cerebral Palsy Patients. In *Proceedings of the 5th International Conference on PErvasive Technologies Related to Assistive Environments - PETRA '12*, 2012.

[5] C. McMurrough, J. Rich, V. Metsis, A. Nguyen, and F. Makedon. Low-cost Head Position Tracking for Gaze Point Estimation. In *Proceedings of the 5th International Conference on PErvasive Technologies Related to Assistive Environments - PETRA '12*, 2012.

[6] C. D. McMurrough, V. Metsis, J. Rich, and F. Makedon. An eye tracking dataset for point of gaze detection. In *Proceedings of the Symposium on Eye Tracking Research and Applications - ETRA '12*, page 305, New York, New York, USA, 2012. ACM Press.

[7] C. D. McMurrough, J. Rich, C. Conly, V. Athitsos, and F. Makedon. Multi-Modal Object of Interest Detection Using Eye Gaze and RGB-D Cameras. 2012.

[8] D. Milner and M. Goodale. *The Visual Brain in Action*. Oxford University Press, Oxford, UK, 2nd edition, 2006.

[9] V. Pasian, F. Corno, I. Signorile, and L. Farinetti. The Impact of Gaze Controlled Technology on Quality of Life. In *Gaze Interaction and Applications of Eye Tracking: Advances in Assistive Technologies*, chapter 6, pages 48–54. IGI Global, 2012.

[10] F. Pirri, M. Pizzoli, and A. Rudi. A general method for the point of regard estimation in 3D space. In *CVPR 2011*, pages 921–928. IEEE, June 2011.

[11] J. San Agustin, H. Skovsgaard, J. P. Hansen, and D. W. Hansen. Low-cost gaze interaction: ready to deliver the promises. In *Proceedings of the 27th international conference extended abstracts on Human factors in computing systems - CHI EA '09*, page 4453, New York, New York, USA, 2009. ACM Press.

[12] K. Takemura, Y. Kohashi, T. Suenaga, J. Takamatsu, and T. Ogasawara. Estimating 3D point-of-regard and visualizing gaze trajectories under natural head movements. In *Proceedings of the 2010 Symposium on Eye-Tracking Research & Applications - ETRA '10*, volume 1, page 157, New York, New York, USA, 2010. ACM Press.

[13] D. Winfield and D. Parkhurst. Starburst: A hybrid algorithm for video-based eye tracking combining feature-based and model-based approaches. In *2005 IEEE Computer Society Conference on Computer Vision and Pattern Recognition (CVPR'05) - Workshops*, volume 3, pages 79–79. IEEE.

Space, Speech, and Gesture in Human-Robot Interaction

Ross Mead
Interaction Lab
University of Southern California
Los Angeles, CA 90089-0781
+1 213 740-6245
rossmead@usc.edu

ABSTRACT

To enable natural and productive situated human-robot interaction, a robot must both understand and control *proxemics*, the social use of space, in order to employ communication mechanisms analogous to those used by humans: social speech and gesture production and recognition. My research focuses on answering these questions: How do social (auditory and visual) and environmental (noisy and occluding) stimuli influence spatially situated communication between humans and robots, and how should a robot dynamically adjust its communication mechanisms to maximize human perceptions of its social signals in the presence of extrinsic and intrinsic sensory interference?

Categories and Subject Descriptors

I.2.9 [**Artificial Intelligence**]: Robotics – *operator interfaces*.

General Terms

Algorithms; Design; Experimentation; Human Factors; Theory.

Keywords

Human-robot interaction; proxemics; speech; gesture; multimodal.

1. INTRODUCTION

If a person speaks or gestures, and no one is in a position to hear or see, is the person being social?

Proxemics is the study of the interpretation, manipulation, and dynamics of spatial behavior in face-to-face social encounters. These dynamics are governed by sociocultural norms, which determine the overall sensory experience of social stimuli (speech, gesture, etc.) for each interacting participant [1]. Extrinsic and intrinsic sensory interference requires such spatially situated behavior to be dynamic. For example, if one is speaking in a quiet room, listeners do not need to be nearby to hear; however, if one is speaking in a noisy room, listeners must be much closer to hear at the same volume and, thus, perceive the vocal cues contained in the utterance. Similarly, if one is speaking in a small, well-lit, and uncrowded or uncluttered room, observers may view the speaker from a number of different locations; however, if the room is large, poorly lit, or contains visual occlusions, observers must select locations strategically to properly perceive the speech and body language of the speaker.

To facilitate natural and productive situated human-robot interaction (HRI), a robot must often employ multimodal communication mechanisms analogous to those used by humans: speech production (via speakers), speech recognition (via microphones), gesture production (via physical embodiment), and gesture recognition (via cameras). My research focuses on answering the question: How do social (auditory and visual) and environmental (noisy and obstructive) stimuli influence spatially situated communication between humans and robots in social encounters? Within that question there are several others, including: How does the relative pose (position and orientation) between a robot and a person affect speech and gesture recognition for each of them? How can a robot dynamically adjust its communication mechanisms to maximize human perceptions of its social signals in the presence of extrinsic sensory interference (e.g., loud noise or visual occlusions) and intrinsic sensory interference (e.g., hearing or vision impairments)?

2. BACKGROUND

A number of rule-based spatial interaction controllers have been investigated in HRI [2-4]. Interpersonal dynamic models have been evaluated with sociable robots [5, 6]. Contemporary probabilistic modeling techniques have been applied to socially appropriate person-aware robot navigation in dynamic crowded environments [7], to calculate a robot approach trajectory to initiate interaction with a walking person [8], and to recognize the averse and non-averse reactions of children with autism spectrum disorder to a socially assistive robot [9].

My previous work utilized advancements in markerless motion capture (specifically, the Microsoft Kinect) to automatically extract low-level spatial features based on metrics from the social sciences [10]. These features were then used to recognize high-level spatiotemporal interaction behaviors, such as the initiation, acceptance, and termination of an interaction [11]. These investigations offered insights into the development of situated spatial interaction controllers for autonomous sociable robots, suggesting an alternative approach to proxemic behavior that goes beyond simple distance and orientation. Mead & Matarić [12] proposed a probabilistic framework for spatially situated interaction that considered the sensory experience of each agent (human or robot) in a co-present social encounter. This methodology established an elegant connection between previous approaches and illuminated the functional aspects of proxemic behavior in human-robot interaction, specifically, the impact of spacing on speech and gesture behavior recognition and production. My research is now aimed to formally model the relationship between these spatial, speech, and gesture parameters to inform spatially situated autonomous robot controllers for HRI.

3. APPROACH

My work will develop literature-grounded data-driven models of proxemic behavior that will be implemented as autonomous controllers for both telepresence and autonomous robots in HRI. Section 3.1 considers how all represented social agents—the person co-located with the robot ("co-located person"), the teleoperator ("remote person"), and the robot (telepresent or autonomous)—experience a co-present interaction; specifically, this work seeks to model the perception (input) and production (output) of auditory (speech) and visual (gesture) stimuli conditioned on interagent pose (position and orientation) and detected extrinsic interference (from the environment). Section 3.2 discusses a spatially situated autonomous controller for robot social behavior. A situated robot should be capable of generating a goal state (a set of spatial, speech, and gesture parameters) that is optimal for engaging in social interaction based on the estimated sensory experience of all interacting agents. The robot should then produce behaviors based on this goal state; this includes setting its speech and gesture output levels, as well as traversing a trajectory to an estimated goal pose, for which the model makes performance predictions about its speech and gesture recognition systems. Once the goal pose is reached, the robot should maintain the interaction, while responding to any changes in the interaction (as a result of movement, environmental interference, or additional co-located agents joining or leaving).

3.1 Space, Speech, and Gesture Model

The parameters of the model are presented first, then the data that will be used to instantiate the model, noting that the data might not be available in a given interaction and thus should be inferred.

3.1.1 Model Parameters

Social agents *A* and *B* are co-located in a room and would like to interact. Ideally, at any point in time and from any location in the room, *A* should be capable of estimating:

1. **a base pose,** POS_A — a position and orientation representing where it is located with respect to *B*;
2. **a speech output level,** SOL_A — a sound pressure level representing how loudly it should speak for *B* to hear (from POS_A);
3. **a speech input level,** SIL_A — a sound pressure level representing how loudly it will likely perceive speech produced by *B* (from POS_A);
4. **a gesture output level,** GOL_A — a *gesture locus* [14] representing the space in which its gestures should occupy for *B* to see (from POS_A);
5. **a gesture input level,** GIL_A — a *gesture locus* [14] representing the space in which it will likely perceive gestures produced by *B* (from POS_A).

In addition, *A* should be able to estimate how desirable these pose, speech input/output, and gesture input/output values are, based on sensed *extrinsic interference* (*INT*) in the room (e.g., loud noise or visual occlusions) and should be able to estimate these values even if neither agent has spoken or gestured yet in the interaction.

Note that these speech and gesture input/output parameters are not concerned with the *meaning* of the behavior, but, rather, the *manner* with which the behavior is produced.

3.1.2 Data Collection

Mead et al. [10] describes the software and hardware infrastructure developed for data collection and visualization (Figure 1). The Microsoft Kinect will be used to monitor the relative pose between agents (*POS*). Sound pressure levels (*SIL*, *SOL*) will be detected and produced by microphones and speakers, respectively. Mead *et al.* [10] demonstrated the ability to extract 6-DOF pose information from Kinect joint positions, affording the modeling of continuous distributions of *GOL* with respect to an agent frame (e.g., a distribution of hand locations with respect to the agent's base pose); these gesture output levels can serve as parameters for an existing robot gesture generator, described in my previous work [14]. The Kinect field-of-view also allows the extraction of the perceived *GIL* based on the body features (e.g., head, shoulders, arms, torso, hips, stance, etc.) observed by a mobile autonomous robot [12] (Figure 2).

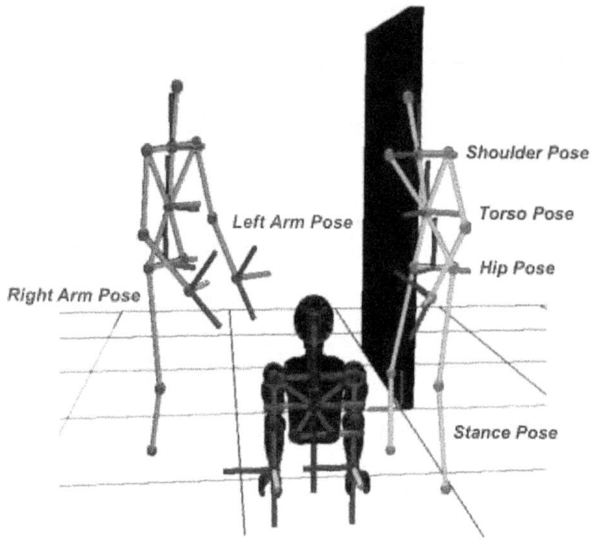

Figure 1: Noisy pose estimates of two humans and a robot interacting in a room with a visual occlusion (physical barrier) in the background. [10]

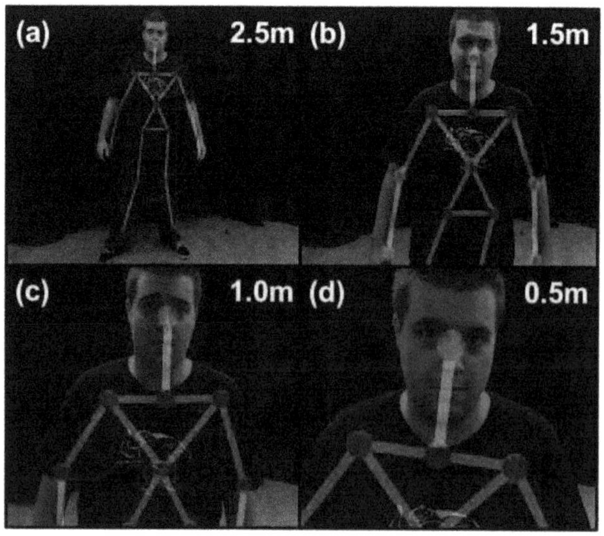

Figure 2: Body features that might fall into the visual field of a camera mounted on a robot, depicted at four distances: (a) 2.5 meters, (b) 1.5m, (c) 1.0m, and (d) 0.5m. [12]

Using the described sensor suites and agents (co-located person, remote person, and robot), a series of large-scale data collection sessions will be performed to expose how: (1) extrinsic interference influences interagent placement, (2) extrinsic interference and interagent placement influence agent speech and gesture production (output), and (3) extrinsic interference and interagent placement influence agent speech and gesture perception (input); formally:

1. $p(POS_A \mid POS_B , INT)$
2. $p(SOL_A , GOL_A \mid SIL_B , GIL_B , POS_A , POS_B , INT)$
3. $p(SIL_A , GIL_A \mid SOL_B , GOL_B , POS_A , POS_B , INT)$

A co-located person will interact with either a telepresence or autonomous robot in simple interactions designed to highlight the discussed sensory factors. The telepresence condition will investigate how the remote person perceives and produces auditory and visual stimuli through a telepresence interface, and how these factors impact the manual positioning of the telepresence robot. The autonomous robot case will analyze how the robot's pose impacts the performance of its speech recognition and gesture recognition. Both scenarios will also collect auditory (from microphones) and visual data (from the Kinect) for estimating the experience of the co-located person. In all conditions, controlled amounts of extrinsic interference (loud noise, visual occlusions) will be introduced to determine their impact on interagent placement and social input/output levels.

It is acknowledged that a comprehensive data collection exercise for the large number of independent variables involved necessitates a large number of interaction scenarios. My work will focus on specific cases of interagent distance (close, medium, and far) and auditory and visual interference (no noise, small, medium, and large amounts of noise), and will motivate future work in adaptive models and controllers for situated HRI.

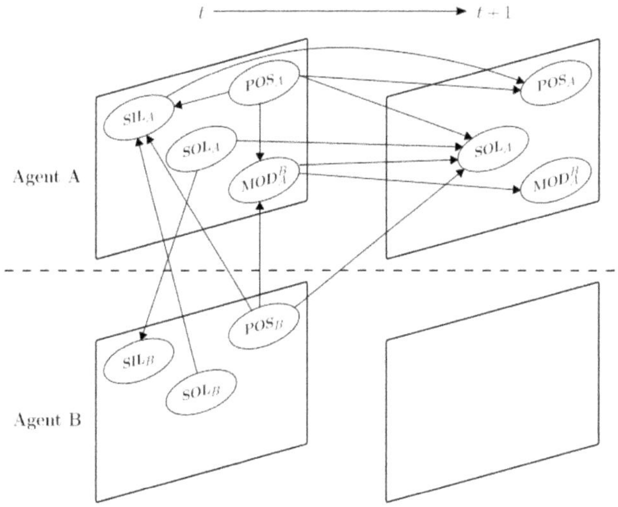

Figure 3: The Dynamic Bayesian Network representation of the estimated perception and production of social stimuli; for clarity, only the base pose (*POS*) and speech input/output levels (*SIL* and *SOL*, respectively) are shown; the gesture input/output levels are modeled in the same way. Note that agent *A* also maintains a model of agent *B* (MOD_A^B).

3.1.3 Probabilistic Graphical Model

Parameters of distributions will be estimated over the collected data conditioned on the variables listed above; an agent *A* will maintain a model for itself (implicit), as well as a model for agent *B* (MOD_A^B). These distributions and their interdependencies will be modeled as a Dynamic Bayesian Network [15] (Figure 3). At this point in the research, a co-located agent (telepresence or autonomous) would be capable of estimating its spatial, speech, and gesture parameters for engaging in a social interaction.

3.2 Space, Speech, and Gesture Controller

Using the Dynamic Bayesian Network (DBN), a spatially situated controller (for both telepresence and autonomous robots) could infer information about unobserved variables (e.g., the perceived speech and gesture input levels of a person) based on sensed data (e.g., interagent distance and environmental interference), and use these inferences to select parameters for robot social behavior (e.g., speech and gesture output levels) from some base pose. The robot will consider possible base poses that it could occupy, estimating how all interacting agents would perceive and produce social stimuli (speech and gesture) if the interaction occurred with the robot at that pose. As a first step, the space will be discretized using a grid-based approach (Figure 4). For each possible grid pose ($POS_{x,y}$), the speech input/output levels ($SIL_{x,y}$, $SOL_{x,y}$) and gesture input/output levels ($GIL_{x,y}$, $GOL_{x,y}$) will be inferred from the DBN as if the interaction were to occur at that grid pose; the pose will then be assigned a weight ($w_{x,y}$) based on the likelihood that an interaction would actually occur with these parameters under the sensed environmental conditions (*INT*). The grid pose and output levels with the maximum weight will be selected as the goal state parameters; conditioning these parameters on the previous state ensures that they will not change drastically between timesteps (Figure 3). For interactions between two agents, this level of inference might be excessive; however, for interactions between three or more agents, such inference is necessary to determine an appropriate set of parameters.

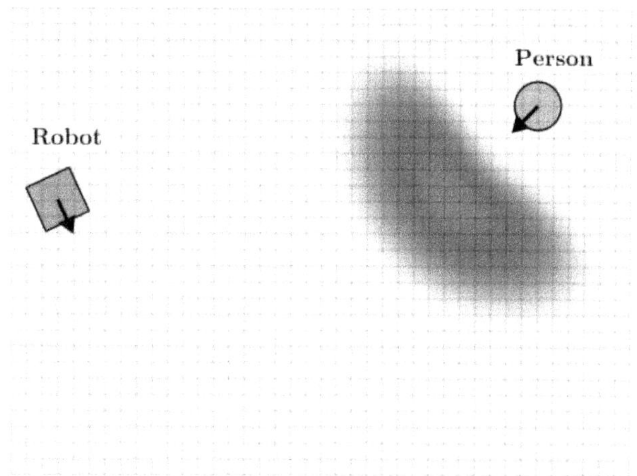

Figure 4: Pose and parameter likelihoods estimated by model.

To traverse to the selected goal pose, the robot could then use a cost-based trajectory planner for safe navigation. Previous work by colleagues in the USC Interaction Lab has demonstrated the feasibility of real-time person-aware trajectory planning by weighting the calculated cost based on its fit to a more socially appropriate model of navigation [9]. The approach could be extended and applied to my research by weighting the trajectory cost by its fit to a model, such as that demonstrated in [11].

4. EVALUATION

To evaluate the developed models and resulting controllers, incremental as well as cumulative evaluation studies will be performed. First, individual models and the controller will be evaluated, then complete robot system implementations with the models in a variety of settings and tasks. To address generality, three different robot testbeds will be used, each capable of both telepresence and fully autonomous operation: the Willow Garage PR2, the Bandit upper-torso humanoid, and the Giraff mobile remote presence robot, all available in the USC Interaction Lab.

4.1 Individual Model/Controller Evaluations

The models of the auditory and visual sensory experiences of the co-located social partner, the remote social partner, and the robot, will each be individually evaluated using cross-validation on collected data. To evaluate the robot controller, two robot embodiments will be used (PR2 and Giraff; between participants), two modes of autonomy (manual and mixed initiative control; within-participants), and four cases of extrinsic interference (none, auditory, visual, and auditory+visual; within-participants). The evaluation studies will be performed at USC, with 40 participants across the adult age-span.

4.2 Complete System Evaluation

In a large multi-session study, 60 older adults from a partner senior living facility will each participate in four experimental sessions. All groups will interact with the Bandit robot platform in the context of seated exercises. In all cases, Bandit will enter the room, guide the participant(s) to the designated exercise chair, position itself in the coach location, and lead an exercise session. The first two of four sessions are one-on-one, the second two sessions are group sessions. To facilitate socialization among facility residents, this work aims to scale up to small groups of four participants, within the technical capabilities of the robot (perception, as well as interaction). Thus, the groups will consist of at least two or as many as four facility residents sitting in chairs arranged in a line and being coached by Bandit. Using group sessions will test the robot's spatially situated behavior, as well as any secondary socializing effects the session might have on the residents (i.e., do they discuss about the shared session?, do they tend to socialize more as a result of it?, etc.). This provides the opportunity to collect data and evaluate outcomes related to controller quality and effectiveness, one-on-one and in group settings, and overall task performance and adherence.

5. CONTRIBUTIONS

This research will contribute to the foundation of HRI, spanning both mobile remote presence and situated robot domains, providing validated, general, and reusable data-driven models and software for use by the robotics community at large. All code will be part of the Social Behavior Library (SBL) in the USC ROS Packages Repository (http://sourceforge.net/projects/usc-ros-pkg).

6. ACKNOWLEDGMENTS

This work is supported in part by an NSF Graduate Research Fellowship, as well as NSF NRI-1208500, IIS-1117279, and CNS-0709296 and ONR MURI N00014-09-1-1031 grants, and the Willow Garage PR2 Beta Program. I thank Maja Matarić (PhD advisor), Leila Takayama, Clifford Nass, Fei Sha, Louis-Philippe Morency, Amin Atrash, David Feil-Seifer, and Edward Kaszubski for their support on this research endeavor.

7. REFERENCES

[1] Hall, E. T. 1974. *Handbook for Proxemic Research*. Society for the Anthropology of Visual Comm., Washington, D.C.

[2] Shi, C., Shimada, M., Kanda, T., Ishiguro, H., and Hagita, N. 2011. Spatial formation model for initiating conversation. *Proc. of Robotics: Science and Systems*, Los Angeles, CA.

[3] Kuzuoka, H., Suzuki, Y., Yamashita, J., and Yamazaki, K. 2010. Reconfiguring spatial formation arrangement by robot body orientation. *Proc. of the 5th ACM/IEEE Int'l. Conf. on Human-Robot Interaction,* Osaka, Japan, 285-292.

[4] Walters, M. L., Dautenhahn, K., Te Boekhorst, R., Koay, K. L., Syrdal, D. S., and Nehaniv, C. L. 2009. An empirical framework for human-robot proxemics. *New Frontiers in Human-Robot Interaction*, 144-149.

[5] Mumm, J. and Mutlu, B. 2011. Human-robot proxemics: physical and psychological distancing in human-robot interaction. *Proc. of the 6th Int'l. Conf. on Human-Robot Interaction*, Lausanne, Switzerland, 331-338.

[6] Takayama, L. and Pantofaru, C. 2009. Influences on proxemic behaviors in human-robot interaction. *Proc. of the IEEE/RSJ Int'l. Conf. on Intelligent Robots and Systems*, St. Louis, MO, 5495-5502.

[7] Trautman, P. and Krause, A. 2010. Unfreezing the robot: navigation in dense, interacting crowds. *Proc. of the IEEE/RSJ Int'l. Conf. on Intelligent Robots and Systems*, Taipei, Taiwan, 797-803.

[8] Satake, S., Kanda, T., Glas, D. F., Imai, M., Ishiguro, H., and Hagita, N. 2009. How to approach humans?: strategies for social robots to initiate interaction. *Proc. of the 4th ACM/IEEE Int'l. Conf. on Human Robot Interaction*, San Diego, CA, 109-116.

[9] Feil-Seifer, D. and Matarić, M. 2011. People-aware navigation for goal-oriented behavior involving a human partner. *Proc. of the IEEE Int'l. Conf. on Development and Learning*, 2, Frankfurt Am Main, 1-6.

[10] Mead, R., Atrash, A., and Matarić, M. J. 2011. Proxemic feature recognition for interactive robots: automating metrics from the social sciences. *Proc. of the 2011 Int'l. Conf. on Social Robotics*, Amsterdam, Netherlands, 52-61.

[11] Mead, R., Atrash, A., and Matarić, M.J. 2011. Recognition of spatial dynamics for predicting social interaction. *Proc. of the 6th ACM/IEEE Int'l. Conf. on Human-Robot Interaction*, Lausanne, Switzerland, 201-202.

[12] Mead, R. and Matarić, M.J. 2012. A probabilistic framework for autonomous proxemic control in situated and mobile human-robot interaction. *Proc. of the 6th ACM/IEEE Int'l. Conf. on Human-Robot Interaction*, Boston, MA, 201-202.

[13] Rossini, N. 2004. The analysis of gesture: establishing a set of parameters. *Gesture-based Comm. in Human-Computer Interaction, LNCS*, 2915, Springer, 463-464.

[14] Mead, R., Wade, E.R., Johnson, P., St. Clair, A., Chen, S., and Matarić, M.J. 2010. An architecture for rehabilitation task practice in socially assistive human-robot interaction. *Proc. of The 19th IEEE Int'l. Symp. in Robot and Human Interactive Communication*, Viareggio, Italy, 404-409.

[15] Koller, D. and Friedman, N. 2009. *Probabilistic Graphical Models*. MIT Press, Cambridge, MA.

Machine Analysis and Recognition of Social Contexts

Maria Francesca O'Connor
Department of Computer Science and Engineering
University of Notre Dame
Notre Dame, IN USA
moconn13@nd.edu

ABSTRACT

As computers move into the social spaces traditionally reserved for humans via mobile and ubiquitous computing, they must develop into socially intelligent machines. Social context information will allow current content-based approaches in the fields of social signal processing and affective computing to be placed in the appropriate setting. Analysis of multimodal data for social context recognition and the application of this information to other problems in the field of social signal processing is the research area discussed here. This paper explains the motivation and background for this research, provide details on some preliminary work, and outlines future plans. It concludes with some expected contributions to the field of social signal processing.

Keywords

Context awareness; social signal processing; machine learning; multimodal processing; social interfaces; scene classification.

Categories and Subject Descriptors

I.2.0 [**Artificial Intelligence**]: General—*Cognitive Simulation*; I.2.10 [**Artificial Intelligence**]: Vision and Scene Understanding; I.5.4. [**Pattern Recognition**]: Applications

1. INTRODUCTION AND MOTIVATION

1.1 What is Social Context?

Social Context is the environment within which a person operates, limited by the person's social role, the social situation, cultural context, and social norms [14]. Studies in psychology, neuroscience, and linguistics have shown that context plays an important role when humans try to remember something relevant, or decide which actions are appropriate to take [12, 2, 5]. This is also true for social contexts. Especially in ambiguous circumstances, humans, as social creatures, leverage information such as social hierarchy, formality, place, time, and event to guide our behaviour [7]. However, why is it of interest in the field of computer science?

ICMI'12, October 22–26, 2012, Santa Monica, California, USA

1.2 Computer Science and Social Context

As computer systems become more ubiquitous in traditionally social areas, they require interfaces which behave intelligently with respect to social interaction. The area of social signal processing is especially concerned with this.

Social signal processing aims to recognise social behaviours such as turn-taking, arguments, politeness, etc [18]. However, by focusing on purely content-based approaches, relational information may be ignored, or inefficiently process many pieces of a scene separately which could be more effectively understood together. In the area of social signal processing, great importance has been placed on the role of context in social situations. SSPnet, the Social Signal Processing network, is a european network of researchers in the field of social signal processing. Their research agenda suggest that as social signals occur in context, context should to be leveraged to provide information not present in the signals themselves. They also suggest, as a long term goal, the use of context-informed multimodal fusion [11]. Fei-Fei et al. [6] have used non-social contextual information to perform classification, annotation and segmentation of still images in one step, leading to increased performance in all tasks.

Social robotics and virtual agent interaction are related areas where social context would provide useful information. When dealing with a socially intelligent machine, it would be beneficial for their actions to be limited to only ones that are contextually appropriate. In order to create machines like this, both the operational context, and the set of associated appropriate actions must be known. For exmaple, the SEMAINE project developed a virtual agent, which aims to interact with a human, sustain the interaction, and react appropriately to non-verbal behaviour in a multimodal dialogue [1]. There have also been attempts to incorporate audio context in this virtual agent with some success [17, 19].

Finally, social context could be applied to creating more intelligent interfaces. Minimal contextual information would allow applications such as phones which do not interrupt a person when talking to a senior colleague or which notify someone of their own inappropriate behaviour while vacationing somewhere with a different cultural context.

All of these areas overlap with multimodal interaction. Social context analysis and recognition is an important area, as social signal processing provides valuable content-related data which require contextual setting to be used effectively.

Figure 1: Some example shots from video clips depicting social scenes. From right to left, starting at the top left they represent: Weddings, Parties, Dinners, Birthday Parties, Classes, Interviews, Nightclubs, and Sports viewing.

2. BACKGROUND AND RELATED WORK

2.1 Context in Humans

In the cognitive science literature, Bar [2] proposed a neurological model of visual context in humans. Within this model, contexts are represented as frames. These frames can be activated by objects, or vice versa; an object may prime a person to expect a particular context, or a brief view of the environment may cause the expectation of some object. Bar suggests that both global scene/context processing and local object-based perception work concurrently to develop a model of context. This idea is applicable to computer modelling, as there is an analogy with feature extraction and machine learning. His work also allows particular sets of objects to activate a contextual frame, taking into account relational information, such as relative position in a scene, or use by a person.

Context is, likewise, an interesting problem in psychology [10]. Psychologists at the University of Notre Dame published work last year which found that walking through doors, and thus changing spatial context, affected memory [12]. This agrees with the idea that context can activate other mental functions, such remebering.

Also in the psychological literature, Lieberman [7] specifically discusses the area of situational context in a social arena from a neurological point of view. He notes that "people look to the social environment and external context to guide their behaviour, particularly when the appropriate course of action is ambiguous or undefined." This provides a connection between context and behaviour which may provide social signals.

2.2 Computer Science Approaches

In computer science there have been calls for both the general use of context and social context over the last decade [3, 14, 11]. The author and her colleagues have already completed some work in this area [13, 9], and presented preliminary findings at the Spanish Association for Pattern Recognition and Image Analysis (AERFAI) Summer School in Spain this year. Our findings are described in Section 5, though here we introduce other approaches to date and compare our approaches to them.

In work by Tankoyeu et al. [16] on personal photograph collection interfaces, global contextual information is used to automatically cluster added images by event. This approach is similar to the author's in that global features are used to discern relatively high-level semantic information, such as an event [8]. Shah [21] has also attempted to classify scenes in this way. However, personal collections work focuses on identifying particular events; a friend's birthday party, a relative's wedding, etc. It also uses other contextual clues like time stamps to help determine this, while the author's work aims to recognise whether video clips, such as those in Figure 1, belong to the class of weddings or parties. Such personal systems are nonetheless a clear example of how to use relatively simple contextual features to help a content-based system, in this case an image viewer, better suit a user's needs.

A more relational approach is taken by the members of Fei-Fei's lab at Stanford. Yao and Fei-Fei have modelled the human-object interactions of athletes and musicians in still images using the probability of an object or pose given the other; this uses a relational model of context [20]. Similarly, Li, Socher and Fei-Fei [6] have attempted total scene understanding using a generative model which captures probabilistic relations between image regions, annotations, objects, and scenes. While the later is not primarilly concerned with context, using Bar's model, it is clear to see that these approaches could be valuable when attempting to relate a contextual frame, rather than a scene type, to the elements which create such a context (objects, actions, textures, etc).

Audio processing researchers working on the SEMAINE Project take a third approach to the problem of context [1]. By using Long Short-Term Memory (LSTM) networks, Wollmer et al. [19] have been able to encode temporal affective contextual audio information. LSTM networks work similarly to other recurrent neural networks, but also contain a short temporal memory, meaning they may be well suited to tasks where actions alter the social context [4]. It is likely that the author will employ LSTM in the future, given their ability to implicitly model temporal context. However, as outlined in Section 4, the inital work will focus on identifying suitable social signals to use for later contextual models.

3. RESEARCH QUESTIONS

The overarching goal of this research into social context is to aid the development of social machines via the provision of contextual information. This yields two kinds of questions: those which concern the definition, sensing and processing of contextual information, and those related to use of that information in applications.

The first application-independent question is; **RQ1:** *How should social context be defined?* This question has been tackled by both social scientists and computer scientists, especially over the past decade [14, 3, 18, 7, 2, 10]. However, it is necessary to consolidate these definitions before beginning any experiments. Once there is a definition in place, the next question will be; **RQ2:** *Which aspects of social context leave behind social signals which can be processed?*

The last two application-independent questions deal with the computer science aspects of the author's dissertation: **RQ3:** *How reliably can these aspects be identified using current computer vision and signal processing techniques?* and **RQ4:** *Of the most reliably sensed aspects, how could they be best modeled?*

After these questions have been addressed, the focus should move to the application of contextual information to affective and social signal processing applications. This brings up questions such as: **RQ5:** *How should social context information be incorporated in affective computing methodologies?*, and, **RQ6:** *What constraints are there for such applications?* Possible constraints may be that context should be processed before or after context, that only a certain level of ambiguity is acceptable, etc.

Finally, in order to make use of social context, the following questions must be addressed: **RQ7:** *Which tasks benefit from the addition of social contextual information?*, and **RQ8:** *How much do these tasks benefit?*

4. RESEARCH PLANS AND METHODS

While RQ1 can be answered by completing a literature review, RQ2; "which aspects of social context have machine-readable social signals?", will require more work. Aspects which come together to create a context will then be listed, and have classification tests performed on them using simple features. These tests will follow the standard machine learning approach of classification and evaluation, and use only quantitative measures for results. While these will not be conclusive for social context recognition, they will help limit the kinds of data to focus on in later experiments, as signals which cannot be processed at all can be ignored. This work will be completed before the end of the first year of this project.

The main work will be to answer the questions related to how well these signals can be processed, and how they should be best modelled (RQ3-4). In order to answer these questions, a large, labelled dataset will need to be obtained. It is likely that some of the AVEC data sets will suffice for this purpose [15], but in the case they they are insufficient, independant collection and crowd-sourcing will be required. Social context data is extremely suitable for crowd-sourced annotations, as it is a subject in which every person is an expert in perception.

Once this data is obtained, the author plans to test which features are most useful for recognition, the benefits of early or late fusion, and which machine learning approaches are best.

Fusion refers to the combination of two or more modalities and is performed at two possible levels. In early fusion the modalities are fused at the feature level while in late fusion modalities which have been processed sepparately are fused at the decision level. Members of SSPnet [11] have proposed contextually informed fusion.

Figure 2 shows a broad outline of the research plan to this point. Note that much of it takes the form of a standard machine learning study. In the later work, there will be more focus on using the knowledge from this step to build up a theory of computational context in use, and validate it by testing it's effect on user evaluations of embodied machines.

Next the author will explore computationally, psychologically, and neurologically inspired models. Computer science has developed many useful algorithms, such as LSTM networks which may yield interesting models [4]. However, the psychological and neurological bodies of work on context analysis are larger, and the models such as those proposed by Bari[2] are worthy of investigation. Because social context is naturally subjective, and because it is so fluid and unlikely to form clear distinctions, evaluation will be both quantitative and qualitative; by having human subjects evaluate the classification results as well as reporting the accuracy, a more representative result will be achieved. This work should take until the end of the second year of the project to complete, and will represent the bulk of the author's dissertation.

In the third year of this research project, focus will shift to possible applications of this contextual information. In order to learn how to incorporate this data, and find which constrains it will have to conform to, the author will collaborate with other researchers in the area to see what sort of improvements could be made to their work. She will also survey those in the field to determine their requirements; these will become the constraints. In addition to these user studies, she will assess the tasks which benefit from contextual information using quantitative methods. For example, in action recognition, she will compare how a given method performs with and without the use of contextual data.

Finally, it will be possible to answer how much tasks benefit from social contextual information. The last experiments will plot the relationship between the amount of contextual information used, and the results obtained for affective or social signal processing tasks such as emotion detection, action recognition, etc.

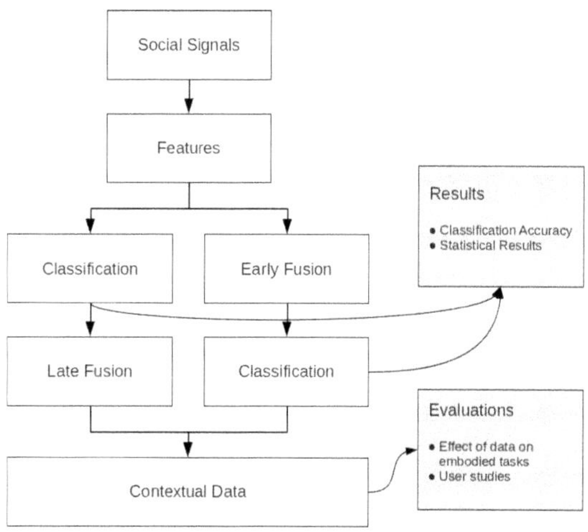

Figure 2: Overview of initial stages of the research plan.

5. PRELIMINARY RESULTS

Thus far, the author and her colleagues have only explored global approaches to context recognition [8, 9]. The first aspects of context investigated were social events (which are related to the situation context of a scene [14, 13]). This involved collecting a data set consisting of YouTube videos which were then annotated labeled using a crowdsourcing game.

The main focus of the author's current work is on establishing the classification accuracy for social events possible when using simple audio visual features and well known learning algorithms. This work uses the dataset collected from YouTube. Example frames from some of the event classes are visible in Figure 1. Currently, using global audio-visual features, the type of social event (party, wedding, sporting event, etc.) can be determined with greater than chance accuracy, however this is a work in progress.

In addition to consolidating definitions of social context, the next steps will be to determine which other aspects of context yield identifiable social signals, followed by the remainder of the research plan outlined in section 4.

6. EXPECTED CONTRIBUTIONS

By the end of this research project the author plans to address all of the aformentioned research questions, which are recounted here:

- How should social context be defined?
- Which aspects of social context leave behind social signals which can be processed?
- How reliably can these aspects be identified using current computer vision and signal processing techniques?
- Of the most reliably sensed aspects, how could they be best modeled?
- How should social context information be incorporated in affective computing methodologies?
- What constraints are there for such applications?
- Which tasks benefit from the addition of social contextual information?
- How much do these tasks benefit?

The process of answering these questions will also yield contributions to the field. In particular, methods for evaluating the impact additional information (eg: contextual data) has on existing systems.

Hopefully, this information will aid the work of researchers in the areas of affective computing, interface design, and social signal processing. This may lead to the development of machines able to leverage social context to better adapt to human behaviour.

7. ACKNOWLEDGEMENTS

The author would like to thank her advisor, Dr. Laurel Riek, who has contributed greatly to this paper as well as supporting her research.

8. REFERENCES

[1] Semaine project. http://www.semaine-project.eu. Accessed: 15 June 2012.

[2] Bar, M. Visual Objects in Context. *Nature Reviews | Neuroscience 5* (2004).

[3] Dey, A. K. Understanding and Using Context. *Personal and Ubiquitous Computing 5* (2001).

[4] Hochreiter, S., and Schmidhuber, J. Long short-term memory. *Neural Computing.* (1997).

[5] Labov, W. *The study of language in its social context.* Cambridge University Press, 2006.

[6] Li, L., Socher, R., and Fei-fei, L. Towards total scene understanding: Classification, annotation and segmentation in an automatic framework. *Computer Vision and Pattern Recognition* (2009).

[7] Lieberman, M. Neural bases of situational context effects on social perception. *Social Cognitive and Affective Neuroscience 1* (2006).

[8] O'Connor, M. F. Understanding social scenes. Master's thesis, University of Cambridge, 2011.

[9] O'Connor, M. F., and Riek, L. D. Social event detection for context recognition. *Under Review.* (2012).

[10] Palmer, E. The effects of contextual scenes on the identification of objects. *Memory and Cognition 3* (1975).

[11] Pantic, M., Cowie, R., D'Errico, F., Heylen, D., Mehu, M., and et al. Social signal processing: The research agenda. In *Visual Analysis of Humans.* 2011.

[12] Radvansky, G. a., Krawietz, S. a., and Tamplin, A. K. Walking through doorways causes forgetting: Further explorations. *Quarterly journal of experimental psychology (2006) 64* (2011).

[13] Riek, L. D., O'Connor, M. F., and Robinson, P. Guess What? A Game for Affective Annotation of Video Using Crowd Sourcing. In *ACII'11 Proceedings of the 4th International Conference on Affective Computing and Intelligent Interaction - Volume Part I* (2011).

[14] Riek, L. D., and Robinson, P. Challenges and Opportunities in Building Socially Intelligent Machines. *Signal Processing Magazine, IEEE 28* (2011).

[15] Schuller, B., Valstar, M., Eyben, F., McKeown, G., Cowie, R., and Pantic, M. Avec 2011-the first international audio/visual emotion challenge. In *Proceedings of the 4th International Conference on Affective Computing and Intelligent Interaction - Volume Part II*, ACII'11 (Berlin, Heidelberg, 2011).

[16] Tankoyeu, I., and Paniagua, J. Event detection and scene attraction by very simple contextual cues. In *Proceedings of the 2011 joint ACM workshop on Modeling and Representing Events* (2011).

[17] ter Maat, M., and Heylen, D. Using context to disambiguate communicative signals. *Multimodal Signals: Cognitive and Algorithmic Issues* (2009).

[18] Vinciarelli, A., Pantic, M., and Bourlard, H. Social signal processing: Survey of an emerging domain. *Image and Vision Computing 27* (2009).

[19] Wollmer, M., Eyben, F., and Graves, A. A Tandem BLSTM-DBN architecture for keyword spotting with enhanced context modeling. *In Proc. NOLISP* (2009).

[20] Yao, B., and Fei-fei, L. Recognizing Human-Object Interactions in Still Images by Modeling the Mutual Context of Objects and Human Poses. *IEEE Transactions on Pattern Analysis and Machine Intelligence 1* (2012).

[21] Zhai, Y., Rasheed, Z., and Shah, M. A framework for semantic classification of scenes using finite state machines. In *Machines," Intl Conf on Image and Video Retrieval* (2004).

Task-Learning Policies for Collaborative Task Solving in Human-Robot Interaction

Hae Won Park
Human-Automation Systems Lab
Georgia Institute of Technology
85 5th st NW, Atlanta GA, 30308
haewon.park@gatech.edu

ABSTRACT

The objective of this doctoral research is to design multimodal task-learning policies for a robotic system that targets the exchange of task rules between humans and robots. This objective is achieved through a collaborative task application during human-robot interaction where the two partners learn a task from each other and accomplish a shared goal. As a first step, a method to model human-action primitives using a pattern-recognition technique is presented. Next, algorithms are developed to generate turn-taking strategies in response to human task behaviors. The contribution of this work is in engaging robots with humans in collaborative play task by modeling statistical patterns of play behaviors and reusing previously learned knowledge to reduce the decision process. Here, results of previous work are presented, and remaining works including deploying a physically embodied agent and developing an evaluation platform are outlined.

Categories and Subject Descriptors

I.2.9 [**Artificial Intelligence**]: Robotics; I.2.6 [**Artificial Intelligence**]: Learning; I.2.10 [**Artificial Intelligence**]: Vision and Scene Understanding

Keywords

Human-robot interaction, Collaborative task learning and solving

1. INTRODUCTION

The need for robots being able to socially interact with humans is becoming greater as more applications emerge that require interactions between human and robot. Robots that interact with humans or other physical agents by following social behaviors and rules attached to their roles are defined as social robots [2]. In 2005, Feil-Seifer and Matarić [3] introduced the term *socially assistive robots* (SAR) that extends on this definition. Traditionally, assistive robots referred to mechanical actuator devices built to assist people with disabilities or help with physical rehabilitations. Compared to these devices, examples of SAR include robots that create cognitive bonding with the user by responding to the user's touch and sound [9]. The focus of this doctoral research is on SAR systems that possess the ability to engage in collaborative activity, which in turn promote a subject's social skills and mediate the process of transferring the subject's learned knowledge for interaction with other people. As a social mediator, the child-like humanoid Kaspar has shown potential in encouraging autistic children to participate in an imitation play [6]. In this work, the child and the therapist take turns imitating Kaspar's expressions. Some subjects, after observing the robot play with a tambourine, start to mimic the action. The authors also mention how robots generate a high degree of motivation and engagement in subjects, including those who were unwilling to interact with human therapists. Their subjects showed positive social behaviors, such as touching, vocalizing, and smiling at the robot. The result of the study promises that repeated exposure to interactive robots can effectively enhance the social ability of the subjects. Compared to this work where the robot was remotely controlled by the therapist, the goal of this research is to develop a robotic system that could observe, understand the subject's play, and autonomously generate its own turn-taking behavior.

In the following sections, the key research questions are posed, followed by discussions on current accomplishments and approaches for the remaining work.

2. RESEARCH QUESTIONS

Endowing robots with learning capability is one of the active research areas in robotics. Learning from demonstration (LfD) can greatly reduce time for computing task constraints or planning manipulation trajectories. In the studies where LfD was coupled with social machines, it was shown that social guidance promotes the robot's learning process [8]. By building on these previous efforts, this doctoral research focuses on implementing a task-learning behavior on a robotic platform where the robot (1) observes and interprets human motions, (2) deduces the underlying objective, (3) generates an appropriate response, and (4) takes turns with the human partner to accomplish a task. Play tasks have been chosen as the application domain in order to evaluate the proposed task-learning system. Specifically, the following questions are posed and answered through this research.

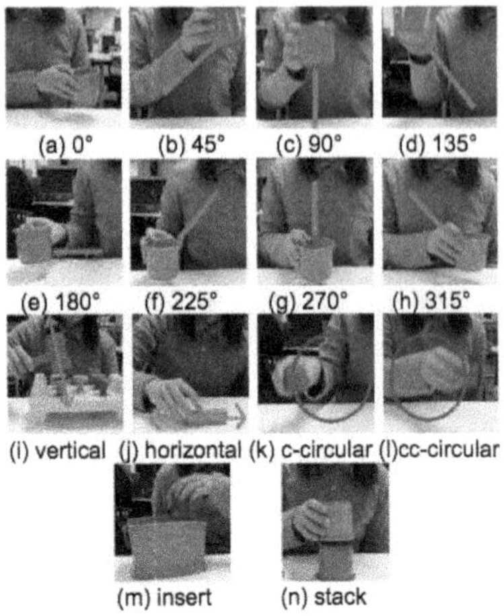

Figure 1: The most frequently observed low-level motions are defined as play-task primitives.

1. Given a task objective, how should a task behavior be effectively modeled and recognized?
2. What are the methods to autonomously select and perceive task-learning cues (TLCs) in a scene?
3. In what way should the TLCs be combined to generate a transferable task-learning policy (TLP)?
4. What metrics should be used to measure learning performance, i.e., task knowledge transfer, of a robotic agent?

The following two sections report the approaches and findings of the research questions 1 and 3. The future work focuses on improving the previous results and providing answers to the remaining questions.

3. TASK-BEHAVIOR MODELING

Baranek *et al.* list in their work a subset of toy manipulations that could be used towards screening a child's developmental stage [1]. Based on the list, a study has been conducted with public sources from the web to identify the kinds of basic motions that form these manipulations when people interact with various types of toys. With regards to a robotic partner, these basic motions are further defined as *play-task primitives*. The fourteen most distinct primitives found from the study are the renditions of the behaviors in the list of Baranek *et al.* (Figure 1).

Much of the prior literature refers to hidden Markov model (HMM) as a very effective gesture pattern-recognition algorithm [7]. The HMM provides a probabilistic framework for modeling a time series of multivariate observations. The power of the algorithm comes from the characteristic that defines a Markov process. In a Markov process, the conditional probability distribution of the future event only depends on the current event and not on the sequence of predecessor events. In modeling play actions, it might not be valid to assume that the entire play sequence has a Markov property. However, the assumption is still useful when considering the constant changes in motion gradients and object appearances that form the play motions. The contribution of this approach is in decomposing a large action to

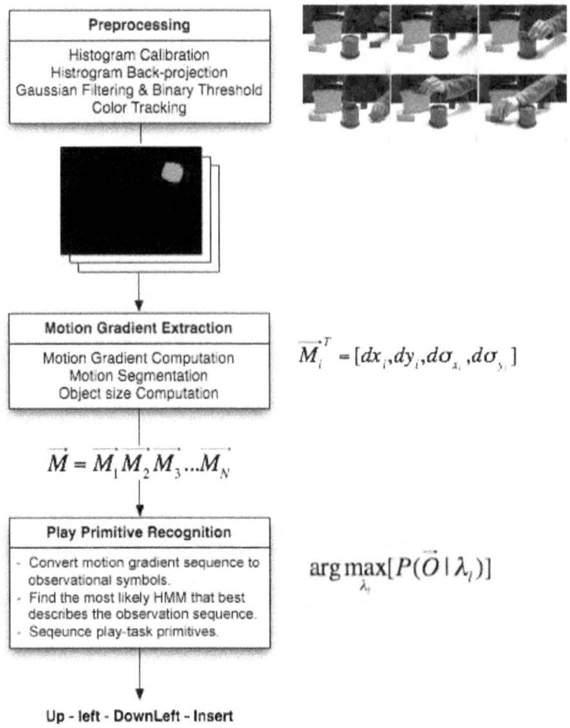

Figure 2: Steps of training the hidden Markov models and recognizing the sequence of play-task primitives.

temporally-sequenced primitives with a first order Markov process, thereby providing recognition of unpredicted behaviors.

The task-primitive recognition algorithm is depicted in Figure 2. The features used to model the primitives are motion gradients and object spreads. What defines the movement of an object is the directional difference in the object's center of mass in adjacent frames. The term motion gradient is used to describe the normalized direction of the task motion. Besides the x and y directional changes of the object movement, the variation in the object size is used to distinguish whether the object has been inserted, stacked, or dropped. Detailed algorithm and results are discussed in [5].

4. GENERATING A TASK TURN

Case-based reasoning (CBR) is a concept that solves new problems based on the solutions of similar past problems. By comparing the current task to some past task cases stored in memory, the best solution is retrieved and adapted to the current task. This process allows the system to bypass a long complicated decision process. One of the issues associated with CBR is that complexity of retrieving a data from a database increases exponentially depending on the size of the database. Therefore, efforts have been made to maintain database size under threshold by re-building the database for each new task and grouping cases by task objectives. Also, low-dimensional feature descriptors have been proposed to reduce data size.

The first phase of CBR is acquiring knowledge, i.e., training the database. During this phase, the system observes a play task performed by the subject and generates a case (problem-solution pair) for each turn which is then saved in the database. In the second phase when a new problem is introduce, the most similar past problem and its solution are retrieved from the database. The distance between the two problems $\mathbf{C_i}$ and $\mathbf{C_j}$ is computed as the sum of weighted distances between each feature descriptor:

$$\begin{aligned}\delta(\mathbf{C}_i, \mathbf{C}_j) = \; & \underbrace{w_1 \cdot \delta(\mathbf{p}_{A_i}, \mathbf{p}_{A_j})}_{\text{primary-object SD distance}} + \underbrace{w_2 \cdot \delta(\mathbf{p}_{B_i}, \mathbf{p}_{B_j})}_{\text{secondary-object SD distance}} \\ & + \underbrace{w_3 \cdot \delta(\rho_i, \rho_j)}_{\text{size ratio distance}} + \underbrace{w_4 \cdot \delta(\gamma_{A_i}, \gamma_{A_j})}_{\text{primary-object color distance}} \\ & + \underbrace{w_5 \cdot \delta(\gamma_{B_i}, \gamma_{B_j})}_{\text{secondary-object color distance}}\end{aligned}$$

The weight coefficients $w_1, \cdots, w_5$ provide factor information of the task objective. For example, if w_1 and w_2, which are the shape descriptors (SD) of the objects, are greater than other weights, the task objective most likely involves shape matching. Next is the reuse step where the retrieved solution is compared to the current task. Using the distance function $\delta(\mathbf{C}_i, \mathbf{C}_j)$, a new solution is generated that adapts to the current scene. During the last phase, the new problem-solution pair is revised and retained in the database. Using double-thresholding variables, the new case is either discarded, saved in the database, or prompted for human input.

The preliminary result of the proposed system in generating a task turn during collaborative play has been published in [4]. The results were compared between the two distance metrics using equally distributed weights and task-adaptive variable weights. An example in Figure 3 shows that when the weights are equally distributed, the system does not cope well in situations when there is no exact match to a retrieved solution in the current scene. The proposed framework was able to deduce a solution within a second with a successful solution rate of 92% using the distance metric with task-adaptive variable weights.

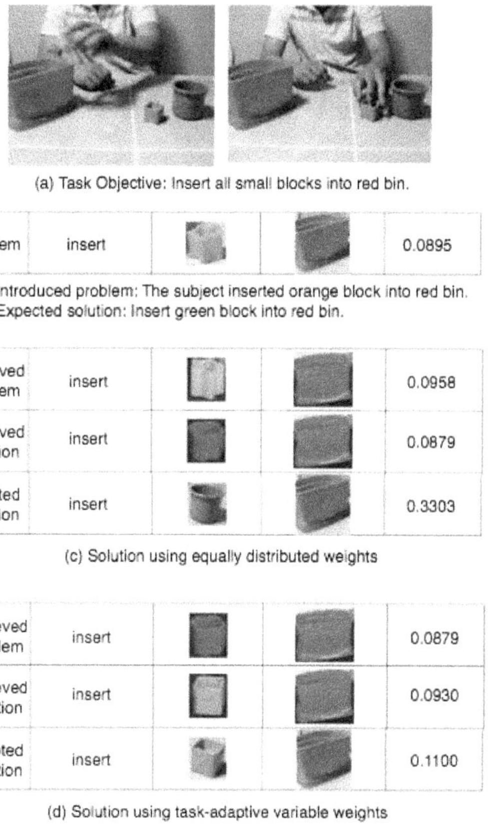

Figure 3: Example result comparing the solutions deduced by using equally distributed weights and task-adaptive variable weights.

5. REMAINING WORK

The remaining work to achieve the aforementioned goals are detailed in the following sections. In each section, the current status is summarized, and the expected approach to complete each goal is proposed.

5.1 Designing a Task-learning Policy

It was discussed in the preliminary research that carefully selected problem descriptors are able to characterize a play task. A new solution was created using the CBR system by retrieving a similar problem and its solution. This approach is capable of generating solutions in a fast pace by reusing the retrieved solutions. However, the current design of the case structure has the following limitations: First, if the problem space in the case-base is sparse, the effectiveness of the retrieval process reduces significantly. Second, the system tends to generate consistent, biased solutions depending on the current case-base. Therefore, the general flow of the task, i.e., the task objective, is difficult to be understood or learned. These limitations will be investigated further and a system that is capable of deducing a task rule will be developed. The previous problem descriptors will serve as task-learning cues (TLC), and the corresponding task-learning policy (TLP) will be deduced in a form of logical equation from observing the patterns of these cues.

5.2 Physically Embodied Interactions

The physically embodied interactions, when compared to telepresence robots or an on-screen simulation, produce deeper engagement for the user [10]. Such engagement provides a better understanding of the robot's capabilities and increases the subject's enjoyment in a task-oriented setting. In the previous work, video sequences were collected for training and evaluating the system. In the proposed work, a robotic platform will be used for the evaluation of the presented algorithms.

5.3 System-evaluation Application

Whether the robotic agent has achieved a successful task learning should be evaluated through the use of interactive applications. The previous evaluation method using video sequences will be modified to engage both humans and robots. An application will be developed on a tablet computer which will function as a shared workspace. TLP will be demonstrated through a touchscreen interface where the subject and the robot take turns interacting with the objects within the application. The tablet application pro-

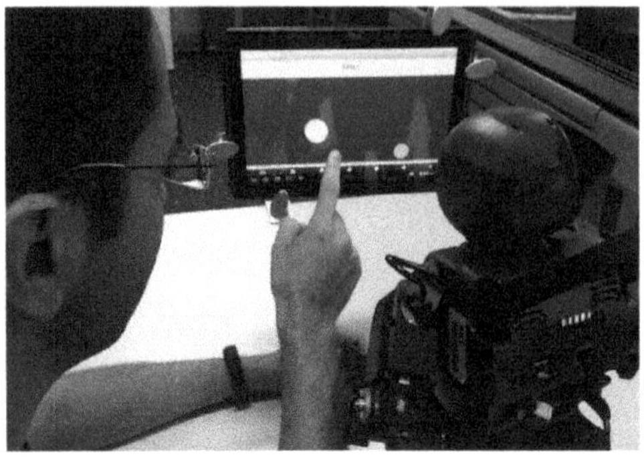

Figure 4: **A touchscreen tablet computer will function as a shared workspace for human-robot collaborative task solving.**

vides versatility in designing different tasks, and using tablet computers reduces expensive kinematic computations of the robot manipulators.

Tablet computers are becoming more available to general populace, and the demand for tablets as assistive-technology platforms is increasing. Therefore, developing a robotic platform that can interact with touchscreen computers provides great potential in deploying robots as companions, therapeutic devices, and playmates.

5.4 Subject Testing and Evaluation

In this section, methods for measuring the effectiveness of a task-policy transfer from human to robot are proposed. First, a study will be conducted with multiple video sequences that demonstrate different tasks. Subjects will be invited to predict what the underlying task rules are for each video sequence. The objective of this study is to identify how humans perceive learning cues in a scene, what kinds of visual cues the subjects focus on, and how the subjects link the cues to understand the task rules. The visual cues used for learning the tasks will be added to the previously defined features. The second evaluation will measure how effective the demonstrated task cases are in transferring task policies. The researcher will provide the same set of demonstrations using the tablet application to the subject and the robot. The task rules predicted by the subject will be compared to the task policy generated by the robot. The final experiment will also be conducted with the tablet application. The subject will first demonstrate a given task and take turns manipulating objects in the application scene with the robot (Figure 4). The task policy generated by the robot will be compared to the one that was originally intended by the human subject. The performance of the robot executing the learned task will be measured, and the subject will be asked to complete a survey that focuses on evaluating the interactiveness of the robot.

6. CONCLUSION

This thesis work focuses on developing an autonomous system that generates collaborative task-solving behavior through understanding a human's task. This work seeks to contribute to defining a general task-learning policy through observed visual task-learning cues. The system is applied to a play-task domain using a tablet application as a shared workspace between human and robot. Additionally, this work anticipates positioning the tablet workspace as a convenient multimodal-interaction research platform in the near future.

7. ACKNOWLEDGMENTS

My most sincere thanks go to my advisor and mentor, Dr. Ayanna Howard. I'd like to also thank my committee members Dr. Aaron Lanterman, Dr. Linda Wills, Dr. Andrea Thomaz, and Dr. Charlie Kemp for their comments on the proposal. This work was supported in part by the National Science Foundation under Award Number IIS-0705130.

8. REFERENCES

[1] G. Baranek, C. Barnett, E. Adams, N. Wolcott, L. Watson, and E. Crais. Object play in infants with autism: Methodological issues in retrospective video analysis. *American Journal of Occupational Therapy*, 59(1):20–30, 2005.

[2] C. Breazeal. *Designing sociable robots*. The MIT Press, 2004.

[3] D. Feil-Seifer and M. Mataric. Defining socially assistive robotics. In *Rehabilitation Robotics, 2005. ICORR 2005. 9th International Conference on*, pages 465–468. IEEE, 2005.

[4] H. W. Park and A. Howard. Case-based reasoning for planning turn-taking strategy with a therapeutic robot playmate. In *Biomedical Robotics and Biomechatronics (BioRob), 2010 3rd IEEE RAS and EMBS International Conference on*, pages 40 –45, Sept. 2010.

[5] H. W. Park, A. Howard, and C. Kemp. Understanding a child's play for robot interaction by sequencing play primitives using hidden markov models. In *Robotics and Automation, 2010. ICRA '10. IEEE International Conference on*, May 2010.

[6] B. Robins, K. Dautenhahn, and P. Dickerson. From isolation to communication: a case study evaluation of robot assisted play for children with autism with a minimally expressive humanoid robot. *Proc. Second Inter. Conf. Advances in CHI, ACHI'09.*, 2009.

[7] T. Starner and A. Pentland. Visual recognition of american sign language using hidden Markov models. In *International Workshop on Automatic Face and Gesture Recognition*, pages 2982–2987, 1995.

[8] A. Thomaz, C. Breazeal, A. Barto, and R. Picard. Socially guided machine learning. *Computer Science Department Faculty Publication Series*, page 183, 2006.

[9] K. Wada, T. Shibata, T. Saito, K. Sakamoto, and K. Tanie. Psychological and social effects of one year robot assisted activity on elderly people at a health service facility for the aged. In *Robotics and Automation, 2005. ICRA 2005. Proceedings of the 2005 IEEE International Conference on*, pages 2785–2790. IEEE, 2005.

[10] J. Wainer, D. Feil-Seifer, D. Shell, and M. Mataric. Embodiment and human-robot interaction: A task-based perspective. In *Robot and Human interactive Communication, 2007. RO-MAN 2007. The 16th IEEE International Symposium on*, pages 872–877. IEEE, 2007.

Simulating Real Danger? Validation of Driving Simulator Test and Psychological Factors in Brake Response Time to Danger

Daniele Ruscio
Università Cattolica del Sacro Cuore
Largo A. Gemelli, 1
Milan - Italy
++39 02 7234 5931
daniele.ruscio@unicatt.it

ABSTRACT
The aim of the present research is to study the role of human factor during the use of driving simulator for a specific driving ability: brake response time. In particular I intend to a) study the influence of interaction with virtual simulation on driving response to hazard, and b) validate a virtual driving test with external data from real life driving. I conducted a study on a real car, measuring the response time for this specific driving task and I want to compare the response to the same conditions on a driving simulator, in order to better understand the psychological factors that can influence the brake time response. Furthermore the data will give some specific information for developing validated virtual simulations that can be used for training and infrastructure design.

Categories and Subject Descriptors
H.5.2 [INFORMATION INTERFACES AND PRESENTATION]: User Interfaces - *Evaluation/methodology, Natural language, Training.*

Keywords
Brake-reaction time; emotions; human factor; road accidents; prevention; driving simulators.

1. INTRODUCTION
Every day hundreds of people are killed or injured on our roads. 1.2 million people die every year in road accidents, and 50 million people will suffer severe injuries after being involved in a road accident [1]. We know that road accidents are caused up to 90% by human factors, e.g. distraction is responsible for the 65% of all the rear ends, and erroneous driving behaviors for the 80-85% of all crashes [2-4].
Within Traffic Psychology the human factor can be studied analyzing the different psychological processes and components that underlie the driver's behavior i.e. attention, perception, individual's dispositional traits, attitudes and cognitive / emotional evaluation of hazards [5].
I focus my research attention on a particular driving behavior in which the human factor is crucial: the reaction time to hazard, that is the few seconds that come before the potential crash when it's still possible to avoid the accident. What happen in these crucial seconds? How long does it take to recognize and react to danger while driving? And how is possible to scientifically study the psychological components of brake reaction time to danger in realistic and yet safe situations?
Previous literature has distinguished among five main components [6] that are involved in the management of the driver's response in front of a potential hazard: 1) orientation of attention in the visual field; 2) sensory and perceptual processing of environmental data [7] [8]; 3) appraisal and recognition of the potential hazardous stimulus [9]; 4) decision making and response selection [10]; 5) visual and motor coordination to execute the programmed behavior.
Each of these components takes part in the brake reaction time. They are influenced by internal factors and external conditions that could speed up or slow down the entire braking response [11].
For example, the emotional system acts as a human alert device in the monitoring process, and it could improve the detection of novel elements and the reaction to them [12], but this system needs to be effectively coordinated in order to be useful for specific driving behaviors [13]. Expectations and knowledge about hazards also play an important role in the reaction times. Experimental studies have shown that these elements can foster a more effective visual exploration and a faster motor response [14-17].
For these reasons it's essential to control the levels of expectations in experimental studies employing laboratory, virtual or controlled road settings [18] [19] in order to study at best the driver's performance in this particular situation.
Several researches have investigated the behaviors of drivers in different way, using for examples driving simulators, controlled road studies, naturalistic observations, time responses to pictures, questionnaires.
Driving simulators are currently the best tools used in traffic psychology research. Modern driving simulators have reached levels of realism, immersion, accuracy and driving dynamics that can give the driver a very accurate experience, and at the same

ICMI '12, October 22–26, 2012, Santa Monica, California, USA.

time they can guarantee to the researcher a precise measurement of driving behaviors in different scenarios and solid internal validity to their data. They are useful tools for training and researches on different driving behaviors (e.g. sleep deprivations, use of Advanced Driver Assistance Systems, study on visual orientation while driving…).
However the remarkable variability of the reaction times found in research results raises several questions about external validity and generalization in real life of results for reaction times coming from driving simulators [20].
It could be questioned if the awareness of the driver, and the protected contest of the driving simulator, could play an important role affecting the reaction times to danger emerging from simulator studies and at what extent they could be generalized to real life.

2. HYPOTHESES

With this research I intend to tackle this specific issue in measuring the brake reaction times, that is how expectations and the experimental setting could impact on brake reaction times.
In particular I want to test whether and to what extent brake reaction times in virtual environment can be compared to real driving conditions.
The main hypothesis is that even if a flow experience and high levels of immersion can be reached by the driving simulators, the reaction times could still be different due to role of expectations and awareness of simulated danger in the driver. Understanding how these variables impact the reaction times will be essential to build a proper driving test.
As first step I conducted a pilot study on a real life car in a controlled road, manipulating the expectations of the drivers and monitoring their emotional responses. Results showed significant differences in the brake response time in function of expectations in specific parts of the reaction process. (see paragraph 4.1 for more details).
I would like to recreate an identical driving task, with different degrees of predictability for the driver, in a driving simulator, in order to compare the performance in the driving simulator of an homogeneous groups of drivers with different levels of driving-experience and age [10] [21] [22] .
Results may be used to built a database of up-to-date brake reaction times in virtual and in real driving contexts to a specific driving task, and obtain some scientific data about external validity of data in brake reaction time.
It could be also important to study the individual differences in brake reaction times in order to better understand the role of emotional alert and appraisal as part of the reaction process to danger.
Furthermore quantify the impact of driving simulators in reaction times could give us some practical outcomes for proper training programs or intelligent alerting device, in a "protected" environment that could be properly transferred into a real driving contest.
At the same time these kind of results could give us some information about the variability of the human factor and the impact of alert and expectations in interaction with vehicle and infrastructure. Thereby they could be useful for modeling and design user friendly road environment, training programs and car equipment that could help the driver to react properly towards potential hazard.

3. METHODOLOGY

The goals of the research will be twofold.
1) On one side, study how human behave during the reaction-time process: (a) What psychological factors are involved during critical response to sudden danger (i.e. studying risk perception and time reaction to danger). (b) How we can improve reactions in order to make them functional and safer during risky driving situations.
2) On the other hand, understand the meanings and factors behind driving in simulators or in controlled road studies: how driving and risk is perceived in those different contest and how can we improve them?
I think that an integrated (real car and driving simulator) approach is the more suitable in order to tackle the complexity of the psychological dynamics that take place while driving. Also is important to work closely with car engineers, driving instructor, and accident analysis and reconstruction engineers, for the technical support, in order to get an interdisciplinary know-how about road accidents and risky behaviors.
A unique set of sensors will be used to precisely monitor the action of drivers on pedals, their facial expression and their visual attention while driving a real car, in a real road. It will be possible to measure the reaction times of drivers in function of experimental manipulation of setting variables and driving conditions (e.g. creating cognitive overload, creating expectations, distractions, mobile phone talking..).
Different levels of danger (in a safe circuit) and expectations will be created by 1) special in-car "traffic light" that could be lighted with-without coherent-incoherent warnings, as well as 2) an external foam rubber object that would suddenly cross the road while the unaware driver would be approaching.
In particular the reaction times will be analyzed in five micro-behaviors, in order to cover the whole reaction process:
A) Perception time: time from the appearance of the stimuli in the environment, to the gaze-shift of the driver towards the object. B) Start of motor execution: Time needed from the gaze shift to the first decrease of pressure on the throttle pedal. C) Release the throttle: Time requested to completely rise the foot from the throttle pedal. D) Movement time: duration of the movement from throttle to brake pedal. E) Brake: Time and pressure on the brake needed to start decreasing car speed after the brake engagement.
It is possible to recreate the same scenario in a driving simulator, in order to statistically compare the results of the reaction times and intensity of the drivers on the car pedals. A virtual driving environment is already available to be tested, but it has to be shaped according to the responses of the subjects.
For these reasons along with the driving behaviors, it will be essential to study: - the non verbal reaction (e.g. human facial expressions analyses using the Facial Action Coding System [23], and the physiological activation of the drivers) - Orientation of attention, using an eyetraking systems, overall behavior using the Behavioral Coding System [24] and drivers feedback about their user-experience with interview and ad hoc questionnaires. Data will be analyzed thought specific software like The Noldus Observer XT, MindWare HRV / EDA and Statistical Package for the Social Sciences IBM SPSS Data Collection.

4. RESEARCH PLAN

4.1 Study 1

I conducted a pilot study on real life car, manipulating the expectations of 30 drivers in order to measure their reaction rime in functions of expectations and emotions. The driving behaviors on car pedals were recorded with a rate 100/Hz. The real driving performance was a reaction-to-danger task with the manipulating of the stimuli type (i.e. in-vehicle lights and foam rubber obstacle) and drivers expectations (i.e. driving instructions), on a sample controlled for age (M= 43.8, SD=15.9), gender, BMI (height M=1.74, SD=0.09; weight M=74.1, SD=13.5) and scoring in BIS-11 and DBQ.

Drivers had to face different kind of potential hazards in their driving task, characterize by different levels of predictability and coherent/incoherent warnings they had to recognize and elaborate.

4.2 Results

Results showed significant differences in the RT phases for different situation and personal variances ($F = 17.530$, $p < .000$, $\eta 2 = .590$). The importance of non verbal behavior is also pointed out as it regularly anticipated the response on the brake.

In particular coherent expectations could faster the reaction times in detecting potential danger, and in the release of the throttle, ($t = -4.224$; $p = .001$) while no statistical differences were found in the movement time from throttle to brake pedal (Figure 1). On the other hand when the signals from the environment were incoherent (signal "no danger" → subsequently followed by signal "danger") or unexpected (i.e. the foam rubber cube) the time in perception was significant longer ($t = -3.775$; $p < .002$), and could be followed by no response on the brake. This didn't mean the drivers were distracted, as the gaze shift was properly oriented toward danger (Figure 2). Rather they needed more time to elaborate the unexpected/incoherent stimuli, lingering in a decision making process, that was longer then the time available to safely avoid the collision.

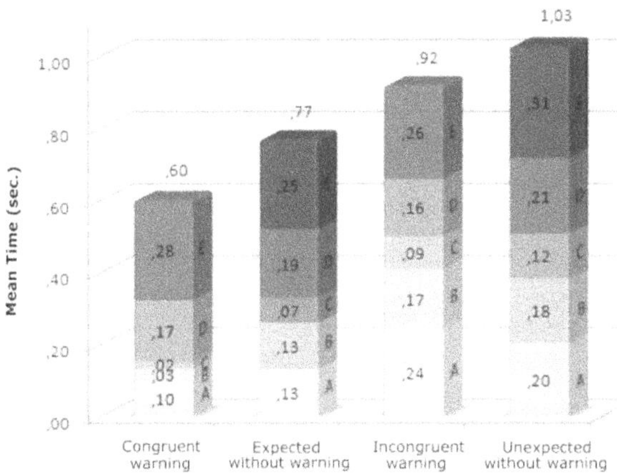

Figure 1. Time reactions in function of expectations and behaviors.

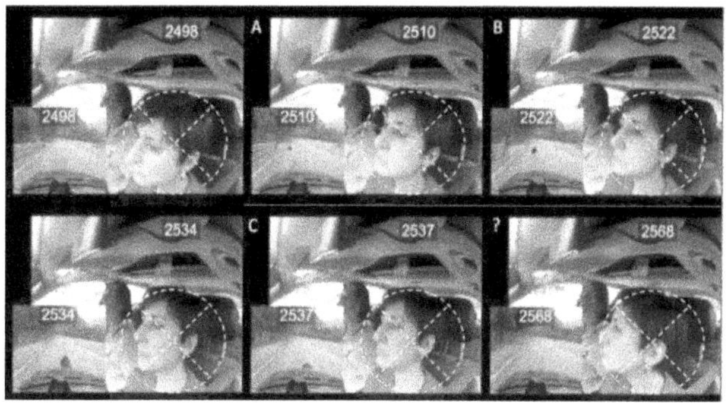

Figure 2. The driver shift her attention towards the unexpected obstacle but does not press the brake.

4.3 Remaining work

Expectations seemed to play an important role in perception and decision making during the brake-reaction time. It's possible to improve the detection time if a correct expectation and awareness is present. Appraisal and decision making are essential in all the brake-reaction phase. Working on these aspects could shorten the overall time of reaction, but they need a proper training in order to became efficient. Also a proper training has to be tested back on the road to be validated.

I would like to improve the sample and compare the results with a similar experimental structure in virtual environment.

I'm currently working on:

1) Create a virtual environment in a driving simulator, with the same features and stimuli characteristic of the Study 1 (i.e. expectations and degree of predictability of the danger for the drivers). A generic virtual environment is available but it must be systematically tested to understand how variations in the virtual setting could create different responses in the driver reaction to danger.

2) Measure the reaction times, facial expressions, and orientation of attention of drivers in virtual simulations.

3) Compare the results with Study 1.: are the behaviors on the pedals the same in all the experimental conditions? Will the times remain statistically similar?

4) Modify the virtual environment and the experimental task in order to train expectations and faster perception and decision making in specific driving reaction, shortening the overall reaction time.

5. CONCLUSIONS

An accurate external validity and the precise recording of a set of behaviors (about man, car, and interaction man-car with the environment) in real driving context compared to reaction times in simulator, is what make this research interest.

The research could obtain some contextualized data that would allow us to better understand and asses the human factor during the virtual driving experiences, in order to make more solid prevention and training systems, study the reaction times in a simulated environment and eventually supply concrete information to decrease the impact of road accidents.

6. ACKNOWLEDGMENTS

I would like to thank my advisor Prof. Dr. Maria Rita Ciceri, Ing. M. Balestra, the researchers at the Laboratory of Communication Psychology and the Research Unit on Traffic Psychology of Università Cattolica del Sacro Cuore - Milan, Italy, TCS and Strade Sicure - Canton Ticino for the support.

7. REFERENCES

[1] M. Peden, R. Scurfield, D. Sleet, D. Mohan, A. Jyder, E. Jarawan, & C. Mathers. World report on road traffic injury prevention.. (Geneva 2004), WorldHealth Organization.

[2] Klauer, S. G., Dingus, T. A., Neale, V.L., Sudweeks, J.D., and Ramsey, D.J. *The Impact of Driver Inattention on Near-Crash/Crash Risk: An Analysis Using the 100-Car Naturalistic Driving Study Data*. No. DOT HS 810 594, National Highway Traffic Safety Administrationo. Document Number, Washington, DC, 2006.

[3] OECD. *Young drivers. The road to safety.* Joint Transport Research Centre, ECMT and OECD, Paris, 2006.

[4] ACI and Istat. *Incidenti Stradali*. 2010.

[5] Groeger, J.A. *Understanding driving: applying cognitive psychology to a complex everyday task*. Psychology Press, Hove, 2001.

[6] Summala, Heikki. Brake Reaction Times and Driver Behavior Analysis. *Transportation Human Factors*, 2, 3 (2000), 217–226.

[7] Groeger, J and Chapman, P.R. Judgment of Traffic Scenes: The role of danger and difficulty. *Applied Cognitive Psychology*, 10 (1996), 349-364.

[8] Chapman, P.R. and Underwood, G. Visual search of driving situations: danger and experience.. *Perception*, 27 (1998), 951-64.

[9] Lamble, D., Kauranen, T., Laakso, M., and Summala, H. Cognitive load and detection thresholds in car following situations: safety implications for using mobile (cellular) telephones while driving. *Accident Analysis and Prevention*, 31, 617-623.

[10] Warshawsky-Livne, L. and Shinar, D. Effects of uncertainty, transmission type, driver age and gender on brake reaction and movement time. *Journal of safety research*, 33, 117-28.

[11] Isler, R.B. and Starkey, N.J. Evaluation of a sudden brake warning system: effect on the response time of the following driver. *Applied Ergonomics*, 41, 569-576.

[12] Damasio, A.R. *Descartes error: Emotion, reason and the human brain*. G.P. Putnam's & Sons., New York, 1994.

[13] Underwood, Goffrey, ed. *Traffic and Transport Psychology. Theory and Application: Proceedings of the ICTTP 2004*. Elsevier Ltd., Oxford, 2005.

[14] Duncan, J., Williams, P., Nimmo-Smith, M.I., and Brown, I. The control of skilled behavior: Learning, intelligence, and distraction. In Meyer, D. and Kornblum, S., eds., *Attention and performance XIV*. MIT Press, Cambridge, MA, 1992.

[15] Olson, P.L. and Sivak, M. Glare from automobile rear-vision mirrors. *Human Factors*, 26 (1989), 269-282.

[16] Martens, M.H. Stimuli fixation and manual response as a function of expectancies. *Human Factors*, 46 (2004), 410-423.

[17] Koustanaï, A., Boloix, E., Van Elslande, P., and Bastien, C. Formation of expectations while driving: Influence of the possibility and the necessity to anticipate on the ability to identify danger. *Transportation Research Part F: Traffic Psychology and Behavior*, 11 (2008), 147-157.

[18] Lee, H.C., Cameron, D.F., and Lee, A.H. Assessing the driving performance of older adult drivers: On-road versus simulated driving. *Accident Analysis and Prevention*, 35 (2003), 797-803.

[19] Kemeny, A. and Panerai, F. Evaluating Perception in driving simulation experiments. *Trends in Cognitive Sciences*, 7, 31-37.

[20] Green, M. 'How long does it take to stop?' methodological analysis of driver perception-brake times. *Transportation Human Factors*, 2 (2000), 195-216.

[21] Martin, Pierre-Luc, Audet, Thérèse, Corriveau, Hélène, Hamel, Mathieu, D'Amours, Monia, and Smeesters, Cécile. Comparison between younger and older drivers of the effect of obstacle direction on the minimum obstacle distance to brake and avoid a motor vehicle accident. *Accident Analysis and Prevention*, 42 (2010), 1144-1150.

[22] Underwood, G., Crundall, D., and Chapman, P. Driving simulator validation with hazard perception. *Transportation Research Part F: Traffic Psychology and Behaviour*, 14, 6 (2001), 435-446.

[23] Ekman, P., Friesen, W.V., and Hager, J.C. *The Facial Action Coding System*. A Human Face, Salt Lake City, UT, 2002.

[24] Ciceri, M.R., Colombo, P., and Balzarotti, S. Proceedings of AISB 2005 Annual Conference, Agents that want and like: emotional and motivational roots of cognition and action. (Hatfield 2005).

Virtual Patients to Teach Cultural Competency

Raghavi Sakpal
University of North Carolina, at Charlotte
rsakpal@uncc.edu

ABSTRACT
Cultural Competence has emerged as an important strategy in addressing issues of racial and ethnic disparities in a diversely populated country like the United States. The challenge for health care providers is to learn how cultural factors influence patients' responses to medial issues such as healing and suffering, as well as doctor-patient relationship. My research investigates a new approach for teaching cultural competency to health care providers – using Embodied Conversational Agents (ECA) that represents different cultures.

Objective: The goal of this project is to develop and test pool of culturally diverse virtual patients (VPs), as a training tool to teach nursing students effective communication technique (display cultural sensitivity) while interacting with patients from different cultures.

Methods: 1) To develop VPs – belonging to diverse culture, age and gender. 2) Develop Agent Architecture for cultural adaptation of the virtual patients. 3) Implement VPs in a clinical setting, as a tool to teach cultural sensitivity and communication skills to medical/nursing students.

Categories and Subject Descriptors
H.5.2 [**Information Systems Applications**]: User Interfaces.

General Terms
Design, Human Factors, Theory.

Keywords
Virtual Patient; Agent Architecture; Healthcare; Cultural Competency.

1. INTRODUCTION
The 2010 United States Census reports that the population of the US continues to grow and become more culturally diverse [10]. According to the census reports, it is estimated that 35% of the population is from a racial/ethnic minority group with 13% of the population being African-American, 16% Hispanic, and 5% Asian/Pacific Islander [11]. The US Bureau of Census has projected that by the year 2035, 40% of the population will be comprised of minorities [12]. Such diversity raises the issue of multiculturalism or what is commonly known as cultural diversity. Catering health care to such a culturally diverse population can be difficult for health care professionals. Sociocultural factors may influence providers' decision-making, which in turn would affect the interaction between patients and the health care delivery system [6].

The field of 'Cultural Competency' in health care has emerged as an important issue to eradicate racial/ethnic disparities and improve the quality of the health care industry. The goal of cultural competence is to create a health care system and workforce that is capable of delivering the highest quality care to every patient regardless of race, ethnicity, culture or language proficiency [5]. A key question I seek to answer is – "How does one become culturally competent?" This can be achieved if medical and nursing schools participate in creating cultural awareness among the students and providing them with actual experience of working with diverse groups [13]. This research proposed using culturally diverse VPs as a pedagogue to help train health care professionals in developing cultural proficiency. I believe that active learning experience with the VPs will enhance ability of health care practitioners to provide quality professional practice in an increasingly diverse society.

2. RELATED WORK
2.1 Existing Virtual Patients
The term Virtual Patient (VP) has been coined to describe interactive computer interfaces or virtual humans used in health care education. VPs allow the learner to take the role of health care professional and develop clinical skills such as making diagnosis and therapeutic decisions [4]. Ben Lok's VP DIANA helps teach medical students history taking and patient-doctor communication skills [1]. Virtual Patients Tutorial Library at Harvard Medical School is an interactive web-based program enabling users to interact with computer-based patients in simulated clinical encounters. The tutorials on clinical skills (neurological exam, breast exam, pelvic exam) are used to instruct students on the physical examination and, by showing the interactions between physician and patient, present role models of physician performance as well [9]. The main focus is to use interactive VPs to teach cultural competency to nursing students at the basic level of their undergraduate education.

2.2 Existing Teaching Techniques for Cultural Competency
This project is collaboration between the Department of Computer Science and the School of Nursing at the University of North Carolina at Charlotte (UNCC). At the School of Nursing awareness regarding cultural competency for undergraduate students is included within the existing nursing curricula. The focus of the curricula is on the development of competency for nursing care management of culturally diverse individuals, families, and populations within the communities with emphasis on the nurse's role in health promotion and maintenance. There is

a lot of emphasis on the impact of cultural beliefs on health and health behaviors. One of its key objectives is:

- **To incorporate diverse cultural beliefs and practices into planning nursing interventions:** The students must identify a patient whose culture is different from their own, interview this person regarding his/her health beliefs and culture, and report their findings in the form of a term paper.

These teaching methods are helpful in creating awareness among the nursing students on how different cultures impact the way patients perceive and react to their environment. But for the overall development of cultural competency, interaction with patients from different ethnic backgrounds is also important [13]. Inclusion of such cultural VPs in the existing curricula will help create a transdisciplinary, transcultural model that will help the nursing students become more sensitive towards the needs of an increasingly diverse society.

3. PROBLEM STATEMENT

I propose the creation of cultural-specific VPs that will serve as tools to train nursing/medical students in cultural competence. My research has two main goals:

1. **Develop VPs belonging to different cultural groups** to help train-nursing students to understand and handle patients of different cultural backgrounds.
2. **Develop an Agent Architecture** that allows for cultural adaptation of the VPs. Creating autonomous agents can help in the development of cultural competency for other sectors (banking, education, social services) as well.

3.1 Research Plan

To achieve the above-mentioned goals, I have identified the following specific tasks:

1. **Task 1:** Develop a full profile (history, present situation, cultural background) of my VP.
2. **Task 2:** Develop a full-bodied VP whose physical characteristics (physical appearance, clothes, voice) are similar to his/her own culture.
3. **Task 3:** Design the Cognitive Behavior of the VP i.e. create an Agent Architecture that will determine the behavior of the patient based on its cultural dimension.
    a. **Subtask 1:** Develop different components of the Agent Architecture- identify how information will be stored/retrieved, goals and intentions of the VP, memory (VPs knowledge repository), set of emotions and gestures portrayed by the VP.
    b. **Subtask 2:** Develop a Knowledge Repository containing all questions asked during the training, and populate with multiple versions of questions & answers, follow up questions & answers, informative commentary, and key items to be used in developing feedback.
    c. **Subtask 3:** Develop a Natural Language interaction between the user and the VP.
4. **Task 4:** Implement the VP in a clinical setting to evaluate the interaction between the students and the patient.

4. CURRENT IMPLEMENTATIONS

4.1 Creating Virtual Patient

Sita is my first VP, created as a tool to train students or medical professionals in developing cultural awareness (see Figure 1). Sita represents a young professional from India residing in the US for the past three years. Sita's heritage will be largely based on cultural dimensions for India [2][3] and her personality will be largely influenced by an online survey I conducted to understand the typical behavior of Indian females. The following section discusses my Culturally Modified Agent Architecture (CMAA) and how results from my survey will tie in with Sita's cultural adaptation in CMAA.

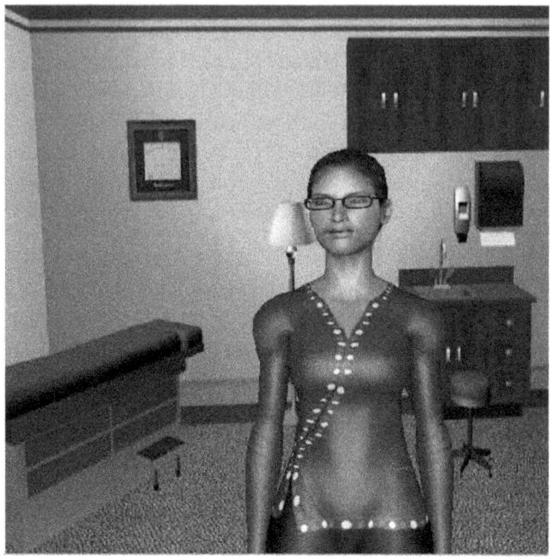

Figure 1. Cultural Patient SITA

4.2 Agent Architecture – CMAA

Culturally Modified Agent Architecture (CMAA) [8] was developed to allow us to create believable agents based on three main categories: emotional expressivity, personality and cultural adaptation (see Figure 2).

Behavior manifested using CMAA is as follows:

1. Agents perceive the outside world based on their Sensors. The perceived events are then passed to Symbol Translation.
2. Cultures perceive similar events differently based on their symbols. The symbol translation captures the specificities of communication in the agent's culture. For example, shaking head in India represents 'yes' as opposed to 'no' in the US.
3. Once the agent has identified the event, the appraisal process is triggered. In the appraisal process the situations are interpreted so as to enable a valence reaction. The appraisal process consist of two main components:
    - Motivational System: Calculates the desirability of the event depending upon the agent's needs and drives. If an event is perceived positive for the agent then the desirability of the event is high and vice-versa. Desirability ties into goals, and also expectations.
    - Cultural Dimensions: Captures the social norms of the culture that the agent is part of,

which includes psychological dimensions, or value constructs, which can be used to describe a specific culture. I utilize the World Values Survey, which dictates that cross-cultural variation can be viewed across two dimensions: 1) Traditional/Secular-Rational values and 2) Survival//Self-Expression. Inglehart determines that these dimensions are robust and allow for any society to be mapped in a two-dimensional map at any time reflecting their relative positions [2][3]. These dimensions incorporate influences in values and beliefs by economic development and the changes in societies from industrial to knowledge/post-industrial societies. .

4. Deliberation Process: Based on the agent's goals, intentions and plans, an emotion is activated producing an update of agent's memory and starting the deliberation process. The OCC model of emotions determines the emotional state of the agent [7].
5. Once the action is chosen, symbol translation is invoked and the agent translates the action, taking into account its symbol. Finally the Effectors perform the translated action.

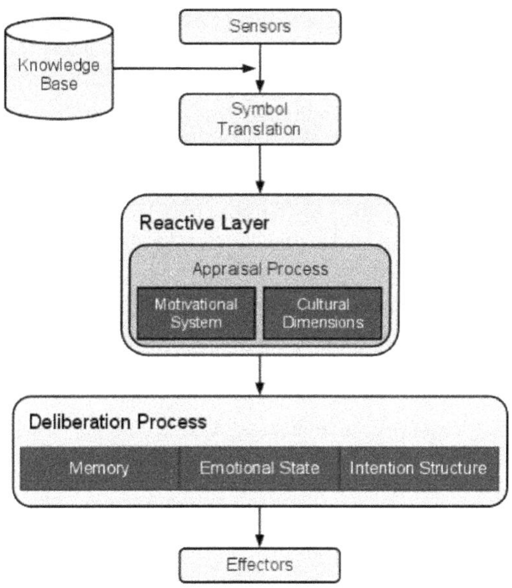

Figure 2. Culturally Modified Agent Architecture (CMAA)

5. PLAN OF STUDY

Students of UNC Charlotte will be recruited to interact with life-sized projections of my VPs. I plan to conduct the following set of studies throughout the project lifetime:

1. **Research survey to understand the culture of he patient:** To design the patient as a true representation of his/her own culture it is necessary for us to understand the behavior of the people the patient is representing. To design the behavior of my first VP Sita, an online survey was conducted to understand the behavior of Indian females based on questions typically asked by a medical examiner. Results from this study are discussed are discussed in the Results section.
2. **Evaluate different emotions and behavior of the VP:** A study will be conducted to evaluate the various emotions and behavior projected by the VP. From the set of animations shown to the users, they will have to guess the appropriate behavior/emotions projected by the patient (uncomfortable, nervous, sad, happy, and so on).
3. **Evaluate VPs based on their cultural traits:** I want to evaluate VPs based on their behavior pertaining to their culture. UNCC students belonging to the patient's cultural group will be recruited to interact with and evaluate the patient. I want to measure students' perception of my patient based on cultural characteristics, including appearance, behavior, voice, personality, facial expressions and gestures.
4. **Evaluate nursing students based on their interaction with the VP:** Once I have evaluated my VPs based on their cultural aspects, they will be integrated as part of NURN 4440: Community Health Nursing syllabus to train undergraduate nursing students in cultural competency. The goal of the students is to receive answers to their list of required questions. The students get to interact with the VP one-on-one. The interaction between the patient and the student will be video recorded and analyzed by a faculty member. The faculty member can annotate the video recording with their comments as they evaluate the students' performance. The student as a learning tool will then use the annotated video.

6. RESULTS

6.1 Research Survey to Understand the Culture of the Patient

I conducted an online research survey to understand the behavioral characteristics of Indian females. Twenty females of Indian origin participated in this study. All participants were between ages 18 and 40 with 10 participants currently residing in India, 8 residing in the US and 2 residing in other countries. The survey consisted of a patient intake questionnaire that was provided to me by the School of Nursing. The survey questionnaire was divided into 7 main categories: Cultural Assessment (to understand the culture of the patient), Medical History, Sexual Orientation & Sexual History, Gynecologic & Obstetric History, Hormones for Gender/Sex Transitioning, Lifestyle & Health Habits, and Substance Use History.

Each participant rated (on a likert scale of 1 to 5 labeled from 'Very Comfortable' to 'Very Uncomfortable') how comfortable they felt answering each questions from the above 7 categories when asked by a male nurse vs. a female nurse. My objectives were to determine: 1) Whether the gender of the medical examiner has any effect on the response of the participant; 2) What effect certain categories have on the response of the participant; 3) Does the country of residence have any effect on the response of the participant. Below are the results of my survey.

1. **Effect of gender of the medical examiner on the response of the participants:** Test of Within Subjects Effect was conducted and a significant difference, ($F=21.812$, $p<.001$), was seen in participants' response towards a male nurse vs. a female nurse. Results show that participants' felt comfortable interacting with the female nurse over the male nurse, thus confirming that

gender plays an important role in patient-provider communication for females of Indian origin.

2. **Effect of the categories on the response of the participants:** Test of Within-Subjects was conducted and a significant difference, *(F=22.831, p<.001)*, was seen in the participants' response towards the different categories. Results show that participants' felt comfortable talking about certain topics, whereas reaction to other categories elicited uncomfortable responses. I can conclude that these categories are of a sensitive nature to the participant.
3. **Effect of gender and category on the response of the participants:** The test results showed significant difference, *(F=5.045, p<.001)*, between the response of the participants' for each category depending upon the gender of the medical examiner. Results show that for sensitive categories, a male nurse elicited more negative response, *(avg. mean = 2.653)*, as compared to the female nurse, *(avg. mean = 3.176)*, whereas for general categories a female nurse elicited a more positive response as compared to the male counterpart.
4. **Effect of country of residence on the response of the participants:** Out of 20 participants', 10 resided in India, 8 resided in the US and 2 in other countries. Though difference in mean value was seen in the response of participants' residing in India vs. outside, no statistically significant difference was noticed. Results may be affected because of the small pool of participants in each category.

7. CONCLUSION

The problem of cultural competency has been present in the health care industry for quite some time now. It has also been included as part of medical curricula to create awareness among students. Existing work in the field of VPs has been done pertaining to clinical diagnosis and improving communication skills (see Related Work). Utilizing VPs as tools for teaching cultural competency to students is yet an unexplored and novel idea.

Proposed research is an amalgamation of information science, computer science and health care system. With this research I am pushing the boundaries of human computing in terms of virtual humans. Currently, virtual humans are designed to have personality and portray emotions, but my proposed framework allows for their cultural adaptation as well. The CMAA framework will enable people to create virtual humans with different personalities within specific cultural boundaries. These culturally specific virtual humans will be helpful tools for developing communication skills in not just the health care industry, but also in other sectors where service providers have to communicate with diverse populations. Creating patients belonging to underrepresented groups in terms of gender and ethnicity will help broaden their participation too. This research aims to create a society free of any discrimination that arises due to cultural diversity.

8. ACKNOWLEDGMENTS

I would like to thank my advisor Dr. Dale-Marie Wilson, Kieran Jordine and Dr. Sonya Hardin for their timely guidance and support.

9. REFERENCES

[1] Amy Stevens, Jonathan Hernandez, Kyle Johnsen, Robert Dickerson, Andrew Raij, Cyrus Harrison, Meredith DiPietro, Bryan Allen, Richard Ferdig, Sebastian Foti, Jonathan Jackson, Min Shin, Juan Cendan, Robert Watson, Margaret Duerson, Benjamin Lok, Marc Cohen, Peggy Wagner, D. Scott Lind, "The use of virtual patients to teach medical students history taking and communication skills", The American Journal of Surgery, Volume 191, Issue 6, June 2006, Pages 806-811, ISSN 0002-9610, 10.1016/j.amjsurg.2006.03.002.

[2] Hofstede G. Hofstede's Cultural Dimensions. Journal of Cross-Cultural Pyschology, 1984; 15, 417-433.

[3] Inglehart, R. (2006) Mapping Global Values. In Comparative Sociology, Vol 5, Iss 2, Pgs 115 – 136. DOI: 10.1163/156913306778667401.

[4] Imison M, Hughes, The virtual patient project: using low fidelity, student generated online case studies in medical education. "in Hello? Where are you in the landscape of educational technology?" Proceedings ascilite Melbourne 2008.

[5] Lavizzo-Mourey R, Mackenzie E, "Cultural Competence: An essential hybrid for delivering high quality care in the 1990's and beyond". Trans Am Clin Climatol Assoc 1996:VII: 226-238.

[6] L. S. Robins et al., "Improving Cultural Awareness and Sensitivity Training in Medical School", Academic Medicine 73 (Supplement 10, 1998): S31, S34.

[7] Ortony A, Clore G, Collins A, "A Cognitive Structure of Emotions". Cambridge University Press, 1988.

[8] Sakpal, R. and Wilson, D.M. "Can Culture Translate to the Virtual World?" HCI INTERNATIONAL 2011 Communications in Computer and Information Science, 2011, Volume 173, Part III, 242-246.

[9] Stevens A, Hernandex J, Johnsen K, et al. "The Use of Virtual Patients to Teach Medical Students Communication Skills". The 2005 Association for Surgical Education Annual Meeting; 2005 April 7, 10; New York, NY.

[10] U.S. Census Bureau, Statistical Abstract of the United States: 2001 (Washington: Census Bureau, 2001), 17, Table 15.

[11] U.S. Census Bureau, Statistical Abstract of the United States: 2011 (130th Edition) Washington, DC, 2010; http://www.census.gov/statab/www/.

[12] U.S. Census Bureau. (2008). U.S. population projections. Retrieved from http://www.census.gov/population/www/projections/summarytables.html.

[13] Wells MI. "Beyond cultural competence: A model for individual and institutional cultural development". Journal of community Health Nursing, 2000; 17, 189-199.

Multimodal Learning Analytics - Enabling the Future of Learning through Multimodal Data Analysis and Interfaces

Marcelo Worsley
Stanford University
520 Galvez Mall
CERAS 102
Stanford, CA 94305
mworsley@stanford.edu

ABSTRACT

Project-based learning has found its way into a range of formal and informal learning environments. However, systematically assessing these environments remains a significant challenge. Traditional assessments, which focus on learning outcomes, seem incongruent with the process-oriented goals of project-based learning. Multimodal interfaces and multimodal learning analytics hold significant promise for assessing learning in open-ended learning environments. With its rich integration of a multitude of data streams and naturalistic interfaces, this area of research may help usher in a new wave of education reform by supporting alternative modes of learning.

Categories and Subject Descriptors

K.3.1 [**Computers and Education**]: Computer Uses in Education – *collaborative learning, computer assisted instruction, computer managed instruction;* I.2.1 [**Artificial Intelligence**]: Applications and Expert Systems – *natural language interface;*. I.2.7 [**Artificial Intelligence**]: Natural Language Processing – *discourse, language parsing and understanding, text analysis;* I.2.10 [**Artificial Intelligence**]: Vision and Scene Understanding – *motion, video analysis;*

Keywords

Constructionism; Probabilistic Modeling; Learning; Data Mining

1. INTRODUCTION

Since the work of Dewey [1][2], Vygotsky [3] and Papert [4] there has been an increased integration of student-designed project-based learning (SPBL) – constructionism [4], inquiry based learning and constructivism, for example - in classrooms and in informal contexts. However, systematically assessing learning in these environments remains a significant challenge and an area of significant importance [5]. Traditional assessments, which are easy to distribute and analyze, may necessarily be incongruent with the objectives of SPBL because most assessments tend to focus on outcomes, whereas SPBL is largely focused on the process. Furthermore, the forms of assessment that may be well suited to the objectives SPBL environments: ethnographies, micro-genetic analysis and portfolio based assessments; are unable to scale to the level that is needed for educators to consistently and reliably turn to SPBL. This creates a conflict that can often times be difficult to resolve, and leave individuals dissatisfied with the lack of measurable changes in learning outcomes in project based learning studies.

In order to develop a more appropriate measure and means for assessing SPBL I want to construct a complete picture of how learning takes place in SPBL environments through the use of multimodal learning interfaces and techniques. To this end, the overarching research question that I have is, 'How do students learn in SPBL environments?' with primary sub-question: 'Can the learning processes in SPBL environments be characterized using a system of continuous, multi-modal monitoring based on a composition of artificial intelligence technologies?' It is my hypothesis that leveraging multimodal data can better allow educators and education researchers to capture a holistic picture of their students. This complete picture will lend to developing a rich and intricate representation of each student's learning. Furthermore, as we are able to better understand and automatically process this data, we will be able usher in the future of learning interfaces.

ICMI '12, October 22 -26, Santa Monica, California, USA.

2. PREVIOUS LITERATURE

My work builds on literature from the learning sciences, cognitive science and learning analytics (or educational data mining). More specifically, previous works describe the importance of student-designed project based learning experiences for promoting learning of STEM (Fortus, Dershimer, Krajcik, Marx, & Mamlok-Naaman 2004; Roth, 1996; 1997; 1998 in [6]); techniques for observing behavioral and developmental changes among students through rich ethnographic studies [7][8][9][10][11]; and using automated techniques for identifying salient markers of learning in a range of modalities [12][13][14]. Furthermore, this research builds on the work that I have done during the past three years which has found that there are meaningful cues in student speech [15][16][17], gaze [18], programming state [19]; epistemological beliefs and identity [20]; and in a combination of modalities [21][22]. It also builds on a number of published and unpublished research tools that enable: object tracking [23]; user localization [24]; and multi-modal data capture of collaborative work [25][26][27]. To this end, my previous research has looked at a variety of modalities in isolation, but as I move forward into my dissertation work I want to begin to better leverage the integration of different data streams in extended analyses of student learning.

3. INITIAL STUDY DESIGN

In order to realize the above considerations and answer my research questions, I will be studying high school and undergraduate students as they participate in engineering design workshops. During these workshops students do bifocal modeling, computational modeling, digital fabrication, robotics and introductory electronics, computer programming, wood working, polymer casting and more. As students interact within this space, I will be using previously developed tools, in conjunction with in process multimodal interfaces, in order to synchronously capture data from a range of modalities. The specific modes of data capture that I am currently considering include:

Digital Design Drawing Data - Using digital pens and paper, I will capture continuous inking streams of student drawings. This will enable me to have the full evolution of their designs in a high precision fashion. These drawings will be aligned with speech data.

Student Gaze Data, Explanations and NetLogo logs – students will be asked to participate in a pair of studies in which they explore STEM phenomena in Netlogo, an agent based modeling environment. I will log their gaze, verbal explanations and Netlogo actions through synchronous data capture.

Student Wifi-based Localization – Using a custom Android application, I will capture student's relative locations at half-second increments as they move around the lab. This information will be useful for studying relative student collaboration, as well as for bootstrapping other data streams.

Student Motivation and Sentiment – This data will come from a mobile phone survey platform. Students will be asked multiple choice, likert scale and free response questions through periodic polling. This information is useful for grounding some of the interpretations that I make from looking at students speech and actions near the time of polling.

Student Dialogue Capture – An array of microphones arrays, lapel and head-mounted microphones will be used to capture student dialogue throughout the lab. I am still trying to find the best solution to do this synchronously, in a relatively large space, and for a large number of users.

Student Location Capture – Using Kinect Sensors and a Teachscape Panoramic Camera, I will capture student location and actions.

4. DATA ANALYSIS

As one can imagine, this dataset represents a large and difficult technological undertaking. As mentioned above, there are significant challenges in building a system that can synchronously capture data from a large number of participants (n=20), for hours at a time, and in a relatively large space (1000 sq ft.). At the moment I am considering extending existing tools. For example, one possibility is to extend the OpenGesture [24][25] platform: an easy to author platform that individuals can use to make speech and gesture-based applications from HTML and Javascript. Furthermore the platform can synchronously capture speech, gestures, audio and the number of people and faces in the vicinity of the user. I am also working on a couple of applications that make use of arrays of Kinect sensors. Beyond the technological tasks associated with synchronously capturing the data, aligning data from different modalities also presents a significant challenge. From previous observation a user's actions and words are often misaligned, with one noticeably lagging behind the other. This will be a challenge when trying to integrate elements from natural language understanding, gesture recognition and action recognition, recalling that the goal is to use these channels to make an accurate prediction about a student's learning.

However, despite the technological challenges, I believe that my previous work has properly positioned me to successfully complete this work. As mentioned in the previous literature section, I have done a number of projects that involve the use of the various modalities. Moreover, some of my published work includes: 1) demonstrated techniques for using linguistic, semantic and syntactic cue; 2) creation of a multimodal interface that use multimodal integration to address the challenges of an open microphone environment; and 3) involved doing rich data capture and analysis of prosodic, spectral and vision based features. In addition to this, I have a number of unpublished works that look at areas of gesture recognition, natural language understanding, domain adaptation for language modeling, object tracking and more.

5. TENTATIVE TIMELINE

This summer I will be refining and testing some of the research tools that I have developed, so that I can iterate on them again during the fall before launching into a focused data capture phase. I will then instrument the Learning Fabrication Lab at Stanford , where I will collect data from the high school and undergraduate students that use the lab. Data collection will likely occur over the course of six months, and will then move me into data preprocessing at the beginning of 2013. Once the data has been preprocessed I will move into a data annotation phase in which I begin to explore ways for automating data analysis. During data annotation I will also be working with human annotators in order to provide validity for the automated techniques that I use.

6. RESEARCH IMPACT

In this short document I have attempted to summarize my initial ideas for dissertation work, which is to study project-based learning techniques through multimodal technologies. The larger goal is to transform the nature and design of the technological tools used for promoting and supporting student learning. Furthermore, this work will help in advancing the use of multimodal interfaces and multimodal learning analytics in both formal and informal learning environments by elucidating techniques that can be used to make the bridge between multimodal interfaces and learning. In addition to this, the work is intended to uncover novel techniques and inferences that can generally improve multimodal interface development. For example, the research has the potential to assist in the areas of scalability, both in terms of number of participants and in terms of the physical space being analyzed. Additionally, I am also interested in advancing the use of open-microphone environments, through multimodal cues, and the community's ability to do speech recognition, and speaker identification in learning environments, which tend to be noisy and unstructured. Lastly, this research should help the future design and implementation of multimodal learning interfaces. While it is nice to know more about how students learn, the ultimate objective is to find useful ways to improve each student's learning by making learning assessments more naturalistic, and create interfaces that enable learners to better understand their own learning.

7. ACKNOWLEDGEMENTS

I would like to thank my advisor, Dr. Paulo Blikstein for his on-going support and guidance in my research. Additionally, I would like to recognize AT&T Labs and the Stanford Vice Provost of Graduate Education DARE Fellowship for supporting this research.

8. REFERENCES

[1] Dewey, J. (1897). My Pedagogic Creed. School Journal 54, 77-80.

[2] Dewey, J. (1913). Interest and effort in education. Cambridge, MA: The Riverside Press.

[3] Vygotsky, L.S. (1978). Mind and society: The development of higher psychological processes. Cambridge, MA: Harvard University Press

[4] Papert, S. (1980). Mindstorms : children, computers, and powerful ideas. New York: Basic Books.

[5] U.S. Department of Education, Office of Educational Technology (2010). Transforming American Education: Learning Powered by Technology. National Education Technology Plan 2010. Washington, DC.

[6] Kelly, T and Copabianco, B. (2012) Think-aloud Protocol Analysis as a Measure of Students' Science Learning through Design Assessment. Paper Presented at National Association for Research in Science Teaching Annual Meeting, March 25-28, 2012, Indianapolis, IN.

[7] Shulman, L. S. (2006). From hermeneutic to homelitic: The professional formation of clergy. Change. March/April, 28-31.

[8] Abrahamson, D. (2009). Orchestrating Semiotic Leaps from Tacit to Cultural Quantitative Reasoning—The Case of Anticipating Experimental Outcomes of a Quasi-Binomial Random Generator. Cognition and Instruction, 27(3), 175-224.

[9] Barron. B. (2006). Interest and self-sustained learning as catalysts of development: A learning ecologies perspective. Human Development, 49, 193-224.

[10] Barron, B. (2004). Learning ecologies for technological fluency: Gender and experience differences. Journal of Educational Computing Research, 31(1), 1-36.

[11] diSessa, A.A. 2002. Why "conceptual ecology" is a good idea. In M.Limón & L.Mason (Eds.), Reconsidering conceptual change: Issues in theory and practice (pp. 29–60). Dordrecht: Kluwer.

[12] Litman, D., Moore, J., Dzikovksa, M. and Farrow, E. (2009). Using Natural Language Processing to Analyze Tutorial Dialogue Corpora Across Domains and Modalities. Proceedings 14th International Conference on Artificial Intelligence in Education (AIED), Brighton, UK, July.

[13] Forbes-Riley, K., Rotaru, M. and Litman, J. (2009). The Relative Impact of Student Affect on Performance Models in a Spoken Dialogue Tutoring System. User Modeling and User-Adapted Interaction (Special Issue on Affective Modeling and Adaptation), 18(1-2), February, 11-43.

[14] Forbes-Riley, K. and Litman, D. 2010. Metacognition and Learning in Spoken Dialogue Computer Tutoring. Proceedings 10th International Conference on Intelligent Tutoring Systems (ITS), Pittsburgh, PA.

[15] Worsley, M. and Blikstein P. (2011). What's an Expert? Using learning analytics to identify emergent markers of expertise through automated speech, sentiment and sketch analysis. In Proceedings for the 4th Annual Conference on Educational Data Mining.

[16] Worsley, M. and Blikstein P. (2010) Towards the Development of Learning Analytics: Student Speech as an Automatic and Natural Form of Assessment. Paper Presented at the Annual Meeting of the American Education Research Association (AERA).

[17] Worsley, M. (2011). Qualifying Paper – What's an Expert? Using learning analytics to identify emergent markers of expertise through automated speech, sentiment and sketch analysis.

[18] Worsley, M. and Blikstein, P. (2012). An Eye For Detail: Techniques For Using Eye Tracker Data to Explore Learning in Computer-Mediated Environments. In the Proceedings of the 2012 International Conference of the Learning Sciences.

[19] Piech, C., Sahami, M., Koller, D., Cooper, S., & Blikstein, P. (2012). Modeling how students learn to program. Paper presented at the 43rd ACM technical symposium on Computer Science Education (SIGCSE '12).

[20] Worsley, M. and Blikstein, P. (2012). A Framework for Characterizing Changes in Student Identity during Constructionist Learning Activities. In the Proceedings of Constructionism 2012.

[21] Worsley, M. and Huang, Z. (2012). Semi-Supervised Object Tracking. (unpublished)

[22] Worsley, M. and Huang, Z (2012). Mining through Mobile: Using Smart Phones to Monitor Student Action, Affect and Interaction In Open-Ended Learning Environments. (unpublished)

[23] Worsley, M. and Johnston, M. (2010). Multimodal Interactive Spaces: MagicTV and MagicMAP. IEEE Workshop on Spoken Language Technology (SLT) Demonstration.

[24] Worsley, M., Johnston, M. and Blikstein P. (2011) OpenGesture: a low cost authoring framework for gesture and speech based application development and learning analytics. In Proceedings for the 10th Annual Conference on Interaction Design and Children.

[25] Worsley, M. and Blikstein P. (2012). OpenGesture: A Low-Cost, Easy-to-Author Application Framework for Collaborative, Gesture-, and Speech-Based Learning Applications. Paper Presented at the Annual Meeting of the American Education Research Association (AERA)

[26] Li, M. Ruiz-Primo, M.A. & Shaveloson, R.J. (2006). Towards a science achievement framework: The case of TIMSS 1999. In S. Howie & T. Plomp (Eds.), Contexts of

learning mathematics and science: Lessons learned from TIMSS (pp. 291–311). London: Routledge

[27] Litman, D., Moore, J., Dzikovksa, M. and Farrow, E. (2009). Using Natural Language Processing to Analyze Tutorial Dialogue Corpora Across Domains and Modalities. Proceedings 14th International Conference on Artificial Intelligence in Education (AIED), Brighton, UK, July.

[28] Worsley, M. and Blikstein P. (2010) Towards the Development of Learning Analytics: Student Speech as an Automatic and Natural Form of Assessment. Paper Presented at the Annual Meeting of the American Education Research Association (AERA).

A Hierarchical Approach to Continuous Gesture Analysis for Natural Multi-modal Interaction

Ying Yin
Massachusetts Institute of Technology
32 Vassar St, Cambridge MA, 02139 USA
yingyin@csail.mit.edu

ABSTRACT

I propose a systematic hierarchical approach to continuous gesture analysis using a unifying framework based on abstract hidden Markov models (AHMMs). With this framework, I will develop a gesture-based interactive interface that allows users to do both manipulative and communicative gestures without artificial restrictions, and hence enabling natural interaction.

Categories and Subject Descriptors

H.5.2 [**Information Interfaces and Presentation**]: User Interfaces—*input devices and strategies, interaction styles*

Keywords

Multi-modal interaction; natural human computer interaction; fingertip tracking; hand tracking

1. INTRODUCTION

Consider the following scenario:

> *An earthquake has hit a populous area. You are the incident commander at the crisis management center coordinating the search and rescue teams working in the field. There is a large tabletop display in front of you, showing the map of the site with live information coming from the field. A report about a big explosion at a chemical plant comes in and you move the map around, zoom in and rotate it to get a good view of the plant. Then you select a group of unmanned vehicles on the map with your hand, and speak to the interface "Go nearer to the explosion site to gather more information," while tracing the route the vehicles should take to avoid obstacles. After that you instruct a rescue team to evacuate the residents in the surrounding buildings by going under a bridge because the surface of the bridge is blocked. You gesture with one hand as the bridge and the other hand moving underneath it to emphasize this.*

The scenario above is an example in the Urban Search and Rescue (USAR) domain. It shows an application of a multimodal interface to a real-world problem. Gestures play an important part in this scenario, providing key information about location, method and timing of movements, and about spatial relationship among the objects being described [13].

Recent trends in user interfaces have brought on a new wave of interaction techniques that depart from the traditional mouse and keyboard. These include multi-touch interfaces such as the iPhone, the iPad and the Microsoft Surface® as well as camera-based systems such as the Microsoft Kinect and the Nintendo® Wii. Most of these devices gained instant popularity among consumers because they make interacting with computation more natural and effortless. Users feel more natural to directly manipulate the virtual objects by hands and/or body gestures as this is how we interact with our environment in everyday life.

My goal is to take this aspiration to the next level by developing an intelligent multi-modal interface for natural interaction. By *natural interaction*, I mean the kind of cognitively transparent, effortless multi-modal communication that can happen between people; I want to make this possible in human-computer interaction such that the computer interface understands what the user is saying and doing, and the user can simply behave.

Gesture plays an important part in multi-modal interaction, especially for conveying spatial information. The focus of my doctoral research is developing a hierarchical approach for continuous gesture analysis that can be easily applied in different domains and applications. Specifically, I focus on gestures made with hands.

I propose to develop a gesture-based interface that allows users to perform manipulative and communicative gestures continuously with no arbitrary restrictions. The key elements of the approach are the hierarchical framework for gestural analysis based on abstract hidden Markov models (AHMMs) and the accurate real-time detection of the onset of natural gestures that convey information intended by the users, while filtering out movements that do not convey information.

2. BACKGROUND

In a computer controlled environment people use hands to mimic both the natural use of the hand as a manipulator, and its use in human-machine communication [8]. Hence, a

ICMI'12, October 22–26, 2012, Santa Monica, California, USA.

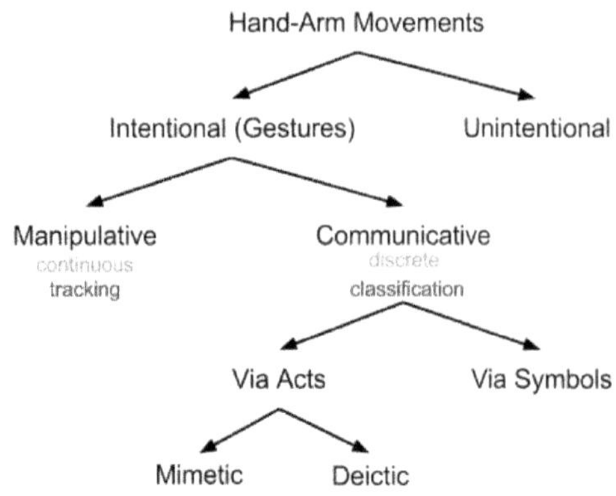

Figure 1: Gesture taxonomy

natural interface should handle both manipulative and communicative gestures.

Gestures originate as a mental concept, and are expressed through the motion of arms and hands [8]. The mental concept represents the intention of the gesturer. In this dimension, hand movements can be divided into different categories, each has its own characteristics and requires different responses from the computer interface. The gesture taxonomy in Figure 1, modified from [8], is the basis of my hierarchical approach to gesture interpretation.

Gestures, as *intentional* movements, should be distinguished from *unintentional* hand movements (like beats). By *unintentional* movements, I mean movements that are not intended to convey information. The distinction is important for a natural interface because there should not be any restriction on how people should place or move their hands when they are not doing any meaningful gestures.

Gestures are then further divided into manipulative and communicative categories. For manipulative gestures, the system needs to respond frame by frame while the user is doing certain direct manipulations. This can be achieved by tracking the hand state in real-time. For communicative gestures, the system needs to respond to the meaning of the gesture when the user finishes the gesture. This part is accomplished by gesture recognition.

3. RESEARCH QUESTIONS & HYPOTHESES

This thesis focuses on several research questions that aim to solve some of the key challenges in developing a multimodal interface with natural gesture input.

- **Fine-grained hand pose estimation.** The hand model for gestural input can range from a very simplistic one (one point) to a very comprehensive one (a 26 degrees of freedom (DOF) skeleton). There is a trade off between the accuracy of the model and computational complexity. The question here is what hand model is sufficient for the HCI tasks for both manipulative and communicative gestures.

  My hypothesis is that a simplified 3-D skeletal hand model with fingertip positions is useful for manipulative gestures because we need to know exactly where the fingertips are. For communicative gestures, we only need to know the meaning of the gesture instead of the exact spatial parameters. Hence example-based template models would be more suitable which also require less computation.

- **Online gesture spotting.** A real-time gesture-driven HCI application requires gesture spotting with minimum delay. The questions are how to accurately determine the start and the end of a gesture in real-time, and how to filter out unintentional hand movement without arbitrary restrictions.

  My hypothesis is that the characteristics in the movement of hands (such as speed, repetitive patterns, and hand poses) and the context of the applications can be used to differentiate gestures from non-gestures, and manipulative gestures from communicative ones.

- **Unified hierarchical model for gestural analysis.** I propose a unified framework based on AHMMs that distinguishes unintentional movements, manipulative gestures and communicative gestures in real-time and provides appropriate responses to the user. The research questions are how to first differentiate the broader categories of gestures, and then further classify the gestures into more specific categories, and whether this improves the recognition accuracy.

  My hypothesis is that by dividing the hand movements into broader categories first, then using different models for different categories can improve the performance of the system because the features that are relevant for each category are different. For manipulative gestures, we need to track the positions and orientation of fingertips and hands so that the position and the orientation of the virtual object being manipulated can be updated. For deictic gestures, we need to know only the general pointing direction. For symbolic gestures, both the static hand poses and the dynamic hand movements need to be considered as features in the models.

4. RELATED WORK

There is a large body of active research on using the hand as an input modality for human-computer interaction.

As [1], I use the Kinect sensor to capture hand movements and configurations. However, in addition to detecting touch-based gestures, I also detect above-surface 3D gestures. Tracking fingertips is usually sufficient for manipulating objects on the 2D surface [8] as exemplified in [7, 1, 4]. I developed my own finger tracking method which makes fewer assumptions about hand positions as compared to [1].

To distinguish meaningful gestures from unintentional movements, i.e., *gesture spotting*, Peng et al. [9] train several nongesture hidden Markov models (HMMs) by identifying nongestures from the training data. But in real life the possible unintentional movements are limitless, and it is not clear how this approach will scale.

For dynamic gesture recognition, HMM is a commonly used technique [11]. Wang et al. [12] introduced hidden conditional random fields (HCRF) for gesture recognition, but they do not handle continuous input. Morency et al. [5] present a latent-dynamic conditional random field (LDCRF) model that is able to perform sequence labeling and segmentation simultaneously for bounded input sequences. There is not much prior work that distinguishes manipulative gestures and communicative gestures. Oka et al. [7]

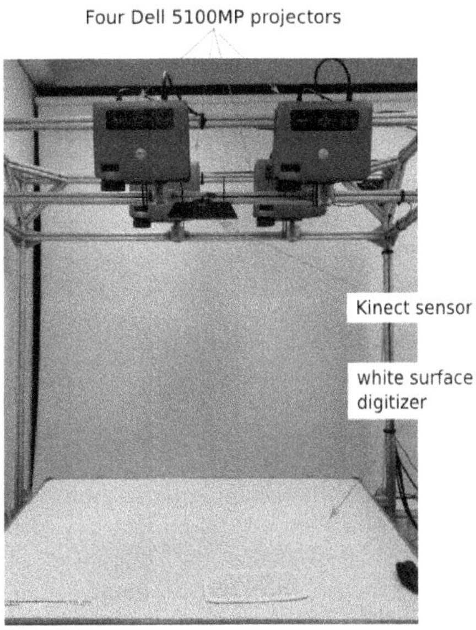

Figure 2: System setup.

developed a system that allows both direct manipulation and symbolic gestures. They regard gestures with an extended thumb as direct manipulation and those with a bent thumb as symbolic gestures. But this seems to be arbitrary and "unnatural".

5. PROPOSED WORK AND PROCEDURE

Our custom tabletop interface includes four 1280×1024 pixel projectors that provide a 2560×2048 pixel resolution display. The display is projected onto a flat white surface digitizer. The projected displays were mechanically aligned to produce a single seamless large display area. One Microsoft Kinect motion sensor is placed above the center of the tabletop among the projectors (Figure 2).

5.1 Hand Tracking

I use the averaging background method for background subtraction, which learns the average and average difference of each pixel in the depth image. Then I use 1 iteration of morphological opening to clear out small pixel noise. I find connected components by finding all contours that are greater than the minimum length of a hand. These components are considered to be the forelimbs and are approximated with convex hulls and bounding boxes. The hand region is at either end of the bounding box depending on the position of the arm relative to the table.

I base the estimation of the hand model on geometric properties of the hand. First, I compute the convexity defects from the convex hull of the forelimb. For an extended finger, it has one convexity defect on each side, and the two adjacent sides of the defects form an acute angle. Then, I iterate through the adjacent convexity defects, and mark the intersection of those sides that form an angle smaller than a threshold value as the potential fingertip. I further refine the fingertip position by searching in the direction of the finger and finding the edge where the gradient of the depth value is greater than 0.05.

5.2 Hierarchical Gestural Analysis

I propose a systematic approach to enabling gestural interaction according to the hierarchical taxonomy of gestures. I will explore the differences between unintentional movements, manipulative gestures and communicative gestures. Unintentional movements, like "beats", tend to be fast, repetitive, and close to the body; manipulative gestures tend to be slower, and have definite hand poses. I can also use the context constraints to narrow down the possibilities of gestures. For example, if the hand is at the position of a movable object, the probability it is a manipulative gesture is higher. I can combine the hand movement features and the context constraints to build a probabilistic model to differentiate the broader categories of the hand movements.

5.2.1 Abstract Hidden Markov Model

I will combine different levels of recognition using the abstract hidden Markov model (AHMM), which is a probabilistic model used to explain the interaction between behaviors at different levels of abstraction [2]. I can map the levels in the gesture taxonomy into the levels of abstraction in an AHMM. The higher abstract levels represent the mental intention of the gesturer. I need to determine what is the optimal number of levels to use in AHMM. One possibility is using the number of levels in the hierarchy of the taxonomy. But the greater the number, the greater the computational complexity. A flatter model may be more reasonable and may not affect accuracy very much. The bottom level in the AHMM consists of observations and states in a typical HMM. An HMM is suitable for modeling sequential data such as time series, and has been used widely for dynamic gesture recognition with reasonable success. Kalman filter model is widely used for tracking objects. It can be viewed as a special case of HMM where state transition probabilities and emission probabilities are all Gaussian. As a result, I propose to combine these two together under a unified framework of AHMM where a Kalman filter is used for tracking hands for manipulative gestures and HMMs are used for dynamic gesture recognition. Static gestures are treated as a special case of dynamic gestures with only one state.

I will start with a simple 1-level AHMMs [6] (Figure 3). G_t represents the mental concept of the gesture that the gesturer currently has. It includes unintentional movements (U), manipulative gestures (M), and various communicative gestures (C_i). S_t is the hidden state of the hand pose and movement, which is essentially a vector quantization of the actual, observed (but noisy) feature vector X_t. F_t^G is a binary indicator variable that is "on" (has value 1) if the lower level HMM at time t has just "finished" (i.e., is about to enter an end state), otherwise it is "off" (has value 0).

AHMM is a generative model. I will use discriminative training methods to further improve the discriminative power of the model.

5.2.2 Gesture Spotting

I will detect the start and the end of a hand movement by the amount of motion. This forms a segment which is a candidate hand movement. Instead of using hard coded threshold values for detecting candidate start and end frame as in [3], I will use machine learning methods to make the result more robust. I propose to use a support vector machine (SVM) to classify each frame into either a candidate start, candidate end or neither. One important question

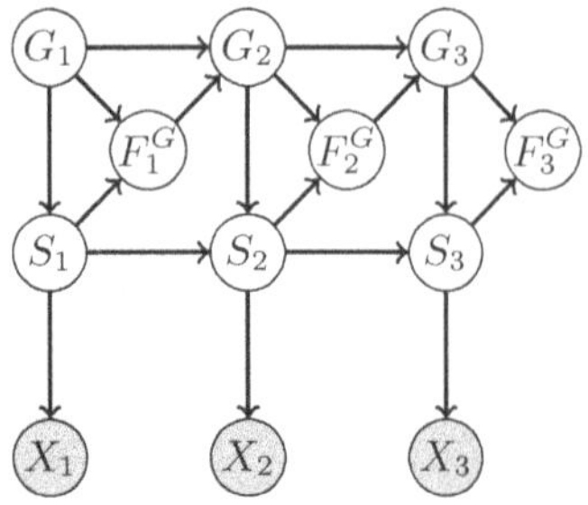

Figure 3: A 1-level AHMM.

here is what features I should use for the feature vector. I will experiment with the criteria used in [3] which are motion energy, static poses, and curvature, and will also explore other possible features such as positions relative to the body or table, and accompanying speech etc.

5.3 Multi-modal Interaction with Speech

I will use an off-the-shelf speech recognizer, and investigate how to combine speech and gesture to make the interaction more natural. I will explore the alignment of speech and gesture, mutual disambiguation of speech and gesture, and how speech and gesture complement each other.

In addition to using deictic gestures to provide spatial information as a complement to speech [10], I will explore the use of speech as a complement to manipulative gestures based on the finding from our user study [15]. I observed that manipulative gestures are at times accompanied by adjectives and adverbs that refine the actions.

5.4 Motivating Application and User Study

I am developing a browser-based game-like application that allows the use of hand gesture for interaction. So far, I have developed the infrastructure that can enable gesture input to a web application. Some of the gestural input functionalities I want to demonstrate are: moving units from one location to another; panning the map; command a unit to build different kinds of buildings; command units to attack the enemies by doing an attack gesture and pointing to the location of attack.

I will bootstrap the system with a set of natural gestures defined based on the user studies done by Yin et al. [15] and Wobbrock et al. [14] on the set of natural gestures people do for surface computing. I will next conduct a user study where the user can perform both manipulative and communicative gestures, aiming to evaluate the accuracy of hand tracking and gesture recognition.

6. CONTRIBUTIONS

To date, I have developed the finger tracking method described in Section 5.1 using a depth sensor. The average fingertip position error (Euclidean distance) is 5.3px, about 10mm on the tabletop. The method is non-obtrusive, easy to setup and relies on fewer assumptions about how users move their hands on the tabletop. I believe our method is general and accurate enough to allow manipulative interaction using hands on a tabletop display.

The expected contribution of this work is a unified framework for continuous gesture input that allows users to perform manipulative and communicative gestures seamlessly with no arbitrary restrictions. Part of the framework also includes a machine learning based probabilistic model for detecting the onset of natural gestures that convey information intended by the users, while filtering out movements that do not convey information.

7. ACKNOWLEDGEMENTS

I would like to thank my advisor Professor Randall Davis for his support and invaluable advice for my thesis work.

8. REFERENCES

[1] C. Harrison, H. Benko, and A. Wilson. Omnitouch: wearable multitouch interaction everywhere. In *UIST'11*, pages 441–450, 2011.

[2] J. Johns and S. Mahadevan. A variational learning algorithm for the abstract hidden markov model. In *Proceedings of the 20th national conference on Artificial intelligence - Volume 1*, pages 9–14, 2005.

[3] H. Kang, C. Woo Lee, and K. Jung. Recognition-based gesture spotting in video games. *Pattern Recognition Letters*, 25(15):1701–1714, 2004.

[4] E. Larson, G. Cohn, S. Gupta, X. Ren, B. Harrison, D. Fox, and S. Patel. Heatwave: thermal imaging for surface user interaction. In *CHI'11*, pages 2565–2574, 2011.

[5] L. Morency, A. Quattoni, and T. Darrell. Latent-dynamic discriminative models for continuous gesture recognition. In *CVPR'07*, pages 1–8, 2007.

[6] K. Murphy. *Dynamic bayesian networks: representation, inference and learning.* PhD thesis, University of California, 2002.

[7] K. Oka, Y. Sato, and H. Koike. Real-time fingertip tracking and gesture recognition. *IEEE Computer Graphics and Applications*, 22(6):64–71, 2002.

[8] V. I. Pavlovic, R. Sharma, and T. S. Huang. Visual interpretation of hand gestures for human-computer interaction: A review. *IEEE Transactions on Pattern Analysis and Machine Intelligence*, 19:677–695, 1997.

[9] B. Peng and G. Qian. Online gesture spotting from visual hull data. *IEEE Trans. Pattern Anal. Mach. Intell.*, 33(6):1175–1188, 2011.

[10] I. Rauschert, P. Agrawal, I. R. Pyush, and R. Sharma. Designing a human-centered, multimodal GIS interface to support emergency management, 2002.

[11] R. Sharma, J. Cai, S. Chakravarthy, I. Poddar, and Y. Sethi. Exploiting speech/gesture co-occurrence for improving continuous gesture recognition in weather narration. In *FG'00*, pages 422–427. IEEE, 2000.

[12] S. Wang, A. Quattoni, L. Morency, D. Demirdjian, and T. Darrell. Hidden conditional random fields for gesture recognition. In *CVPR'06*, volume 2, pages 1521–1527. IEEE, 2006.

[13] A. Wexelblat. *A feature-based approach to continuous-gesture analysis.* PhD thesis, MIT, 1994.

[14] J. Wobbrock, M. Morris, and A. Wilson. User-defined gestures for surface computing. In *CHI'09*, pages 1083–1092, 2009.

[15] Y. Yin and R. Davis. Toward natural interaction in the real world: Real-time gesture recognition. In *ICMI'10*, November 2010.

AVEC 2012 – The Continuous Audio/Visual Emotion Challenge – An Introduction

Björn Schuller
JOANNEUM RESEARCH Forschungsgesellschaft mbH*
Graz, Austria
schuller@tum.de

Michel Valstar
University of Nottingham
Mixed Reality Lab
Nottingham, UK
mfv@cs.nott.ac.uk

Roddy Cowie
Queen's University Belfast
School of Psychology
Belfast, UK
R.Cowie@QUB.AC.UK

Maja Pantic†
Imperial College London
iBUG
London, UK
m.pantic@imperial.ac.uk

ABSTRACT

The second international Audio/Visual Emotion Challenge and Workshop 2012 (AVEC 2012) is introduced shortly. 34 teams from 12 countries signed up for the Challenge. The SEMAINE database serves for prediction of four-dimensional continuous affect in audio and video. For the eligible participants, final scores for the Fully-Continuous Sub-Challenge ranged between a correlation coefficient between gold standard and prediction of 0.174 and 0.456, and for Word-Level Sub-Challenge between 0.113 and 0.280.

Categories and Subject Descriptors

H.4 [**Information Systems Applications**]: Miscellaneous; D.2.8 [**Software Engineering**]: Metrics—*complexity measures, performance measures*

General Terms

Theory

Keywords

Affective Computing, Emotion Recognition, Speech, Facial Expression, Challenge

*The author is further affiliated with Technische Universität München, Munich, Germany

†The author is further affiliated with Twente University, EEMCS, Twente, The Netherlands.

ICMI'12, October 22–26, 2012, Santa Monica, California, USA.

1. INTRODUCTION

The international Audio/Visual Emotion Challenge and Workshop (AVEC 2012) is the second competition event subsequent to AVEC 2011 [6] aimed at comparison of multimedia processing and machine learning methods for automatic audio, visual, and audiovisual emotion analysis, with all participants competing under strictly the same conditions. Where AVEC 2011 had the goal to determine whether at any time the value of an emotional dimension label was above or below the average, for AVEC 2012 the goal was to predict the actual value of the annotated dimension.

The goal of the challenge is to provide a common benchmark test set for individual multimodal information processing and to bring together the audio and video emotion recognition communities, to compare the relative merits of the two approaches to emotion recognition under well-defined and strictly comparable conditions and establish to what extent fusion of the approaches is possible and beneficial.

A second motivation is driven by the need to advance emotion recognition systems to be able to deal with naturalistic behaviour in large volumes of un-segmented, non-prototypical and non-preselected data as this is exactly the type of data that both multimedia retrieval and human-machine/human-robot communication interfaces have to face in the real world. The data used consists of exactly that type of data: natural dyadic interactions, over periods of approximately 15 minutes per subject.

The challenge called for teams to participate in emotion recognition from acoustic audio analysis, linguistic audio analysis, video analysis, or any combination of these. As benchmarking database the SEMAINE database [4] of naturalistic video and audio of human-agent interactions, along with labels for four affect dimensions is used. Emotion needs to be recognised in terms of continuous time, continuous valued dimensional affect [1] in four dimensions: arousal, expectation, power and valence.

In the SEMAINE database, participants speak to one of four emotionally stereotypical characters: Spike, who is always angry and confrontational, Obadiah, who is sombre to the point of being depressed, Poppy who is always happy and

Figure 1: A subject speaking to Spike, one of the SEMAINE characters. Spike is always angry and confrontational.

excited, and Prudence, who takes a very pragmatic matter of fact approach to life. Fig. 1 shows a participant holding a conversation with Spike. The final SEMAINE system [5] resulted in the virtual agents shown in Fig. 1, and many recordings of interactions with the final system are included in the SEMAINE database. But to develop the virtual agents, 24 recordings were made of conversations between participants and human operators pretending to be the virtual agents. It is these recordings which are most heavily annotated in terms of dimensional affect, and it is these recordings that were used in the challenge.

Two sub-challenges are organised: The first involves fully continuous affect recognition, where the level of affect has to be predicted for every moment of the recording. The second sub-challenge requires participants to predict the level of affect at word-level, that is, only when the user is speaking. Different from the previous AVEC challenge, we do not have separate sub-challenges for the audio, video or audio-visual modalities. This was done in the hope that it would encourage participants to try to make optimal use of all modalities, rather than trying to attain the best results for the modality that they are traditionally comfortable using.

Baseline features for Audio [2] and Video [3] modalities were provided, as well as results of an easy to reproduce baseline system.

Besides participation in the Challenge, papers addressing the overall topics of this workshop, in particular works that address the differences between audio and video processing of emotive data, and the issues concerning combined audio-visual emotion recognition were called for.

2. PARTICIPATION AND RESULTS

In total, 34 teams from 12 countries signed up for the challenge and created an account to download the challenge data. This included teams from MIT, University of Cambridge, NASA Ames lab, and the BBC. After the peer review process, the papers of 8 teams were accepted, a condition for being eligible to win the challenge. Of those, 6 teams participated in the Fully-Continuous Sub-Challenge (FCSC), and 5 in the Word-Level Sub-Challenge (WLSC). Note that the winners of the two sub-challenges had the highest scores among all submitted results, including the results of teams whose papers were not accepted.

For the eligible participants, final scores for the FCSC ranged between a correlation coefficient of 0.174 and 0.456, and for WLSC between 0.113 and 0.280. The highest score on a single dimension was attained for the dimension Arousal on the FCSC Sub-Challenge, with a correlation of 0.612.

3. ACKNOWLEDGEMENTS

The research leading to these results has received funding from the European Community's Seventh Framework Programme (FP7/2007- 2013) under grant agreement No. 289021 (ASC-Inclusion). The authors would further like to thank the sponsor of the challenge, the Social Signal Processing Network (SSPNet). The responsibility lies with the authors.

We would further like to particularly thank all 26 members of the Technical Program Committee for their timely and insightful reviews of the submissions: Elisabeth André, Anton Batliner, Felix Burkhardt, Rama Chellappa, Fang Chen, Mohamed Chetouani, Laurence Devillers, Julien Epps, Anna Esposito, Raul Fernandez, Roland Göcke, Hatice Gunes, Julia Hirschberg, Aleix Martinez, Marc Méhu, Marcello Mortillaro, Matti Pietikäinen, Ioannis Pitas, Peter Robinson, Stefan Steidl, Jianhua Tao, Fernando de la Torre, Mohan Trivedi, Matthew Turk, Alessandro Vinciarelli, and Stefanos Zafeiriou, as well as the additional reviewers Florian Eyben, Wenjing Han, Erik Marchi, Felix Weninger, and Martin Wöllmer, and of course all participants.

4. REFERENCES

[1] Cowie, R., Douglas-Cowie, E., Savvidou, S., McMahon, E., Sawey, M., and Schröder, M. Feeltrace: An instrument for recording perceived emotion in real time. In *Proc. ISCA Workshop on Speech and Emotion* (Belfast, UK, 2000), pp. 19–24.

[2] Eyben, F., Wöllmer, M., and Schuller, B. openSMILE – The Munich Versatile and Fast Open-Source Audio Feature Extractor. In *Proc. ACM Multimedia (MM)* (Florence, Italy, 2010), pp. 1459–1462.

[3] Jiang, B., Valstar, M., and Pantic, M. Action unit detection using sparse appearance descriptors in space-time video volumes. In *Proc. IEEE Int. Conf. on Automatic Face and Gesture Recognition* (Santa Barbara, USA, 2011), pp. 314–321.

[4] McKeown, G., Valstar, M., Cowie, R., Pantic, M., and Schroder, M. The semaine database: Annotated multimodal records of emotionally colored conversations between a person and a limited agent. *IEEE Transactions on Affective Computing 3* (2012), 5–17.

[5] Schröder, M., Bevacqua, E., Cowie, R., Eyben, F., Gunes, H., Heylen, D., ter Maat, M., McKeown, G., Pammi, S., Pantic, M., Pelachaud, C., Schuller, B., de Sevin, E., Valstar, M., and Wöllmer, M. Building Autonomous Sensitive Artificial Listeners. *IEEE Transactions on Affective Computing* (2012). 20 pages, to appear.

[6] Schuller, B., Valstar, M., Eyben, F., McKeown, G., Cowie, R., and Pantic, M. AVEC 2011 Ű- The First International Audio/Visual Emotion Challenge. In *Proc. Int'l Audio/Visual Emotion Challenge and Workshop, AVEC 2011, in conjunction with the Int'l Conf. Affective Computing and Intelligent Interaction, 2011*, vol. II. Springer, Memphis, TN, October 2011, pp. 415–424.

ICMI'12 Grand Challenge – Haptic Voice Recognition

Khe Chai Sim
National University of Singapore
13 Computing Drive
Singapore 117417
simkc@comp.nus.edu.sg

Shengdong Zhao
National University of Singapore
13 Computing Drive
Singapore 117417
zhaosd@comp.nus.edu.sg

Kai Yu
Shanghai Jiao Tong University
800 Dongchuan Road
Shanghai 200240
P.R. China
kai.yu@sjtu.edu.cn

Hank Liao
Google
76 Ninth Avenue
New York, NY 10011
hankliao@google.com

ABSTRACT

This paper describes the Haptic Voice Recognition (HVR) Grand Challenge 2012 and its datasets. The HVR Grand Challenge 2012 is a research oriented competition designed to bring together researchers across multiple disciplines to work on novel multimodal text entry methods involving speech and touch inputs. Annotated datasets were collected and released for this grand challenge as well as future research purposes. A simple recipe for building an HVR system using the Hidden Markov Model Toolkit (HTK) was also provided. In this paper, detailed analyses of the datasets will be given. Experimental results obtained using these data will also be presented.

Categories and Subject Descriptors

H.5.2 [**Information Interfaces and Presentation**]: User Interfaces—*Voice I/O, Natural language, User-centered design* ; I.2.7 [**Artificial Intelligence**]: Natural Language Processing—*Speech recognition and synthesis*

Keywords

mobile text input; multimodal interface; haptic voice recognition

1. INTRODUCTION

Haptic Voice Recognition (HVR) Grand Challenge 2012 is a research oriented competition designed to bring together researchers across multiple disciplines to work on Haptic Voice Recognition (HVR) [10], a novel multimodal text entry method for modern mobile devices. HVR combines both voice and touch inputs to achieve better efficiency and robustness. Since modern portable devices are now commonly equipped with both microphones and a touchscreen display, it will be interesting to explore possible ways of enhancing text entry on these devices by combining information obtained from these sensors. The purpose of this grand challenge is to define a set of common challenge tasks for researchers to work on in order to address the challenges faced and to bring the technology to the next frontier. Basic tools and setups are also provided to lower the entry barrier so that research teams can participate in this grand challenge without having to work on all aspects of the system.

The remainder of this paper is organized as follows. Section 2 gives a brief introduction to Haptic Voice Recognition (HVR). Section 3 describes the challenges to be addressed by the grand challenge. Section 4 presents the datasets and the data collection procedures. Section 5 gives a detailed account of the analyses performed on the datasets. Section 6 describe the HVR recipe provided for the challenge. Finally, Section 7 reports some experimental results on the datasets.

ICMI'12, October 22–26, 2012, Santa Monica, California, USA.

2. HAPTIC VOICE RECOGNITION

Haptic Voice Recognition (HVR) is a multimodal interface designed for efficient and robust text entry on modern portable devices. Nowadays, modern portable devices such as the smartphones and tablets are commonly equipped with microphone and touchscreen display. Typing using an on-screen keyboard is the most common way for users to enter text on these portable devices. In many situations, users can only type with one hand, while the other hand is holding the device. Furthermore, typing on smaller devices such as smartphones can be quite challenging. As a result, typing speed on portable devices is significantly slower compared to that on desktop and laptop computers with full-sized keyboard [4]. Voice input offers a hands-free solution for text entry. This is an attractive alternative to typing because voice input completely eliminates the need for typing. However, voice input relies on Automatic Speech Recognition (ASR) technology, which requires high computational resources and is susceptible to performance degradation due to acoustic interference. These are practical issues to be addressed since portable devices typically have limited computation and memory resources to accommodate state-of-the-art ASR system. Moreover, ASR systems have to cope with a wide range of acoustic conditions due to the mobility of these portable devices. In addition, ASR systems often do not work as well for non-native speakers or speakers with a heavy accent. Users often find that voice input is like a black box that listens to the users voice and returns the recognition output without much flexibility for human intervention in case of errors. Certain applications will return multiple recognition hypotheses for the users to choose from. Any remaining unhandled errors are typically corrected manually. Instead of accepting human inputs after the recognition process, it may be more helpful to integrate additional human input into the voice recognition process. This is the basis motivated the development of Haptic Voice Recognition (HVR) [10].

Haptic Voice Recognition (HVR) is a multimodal interface designed to offer users the opportunity to add his or her '*magic touch*' in order to improve the accuracy, efficiency and robustness of voice input. HVR is designed for modern mobile devices equipped with an embedded microphone to capture speech signals and a touchscreen display to receive touch events. The HVR interface aims to combine both speech and touch modalities to enhance speech recognition. When using an HVR interface, users will input text verbally, at the same time provide additional cues in the form of *Partial Lexical Information* (PLI) [11] to guide the recognition search. PLIs are simplified lexical representation of words that should be easy to enter whilst speaking (*e.g.* the prefix and/or suffix letters). Preliminary simulated experiments conducted by [10] show that potential performance improvements both in terms of recognition speed and noise robustness can be achieved using the initial letters as PLIs. For example, to enter the text "*Henry will be in Boston next Friday*", the user will speak the sentence and enter the following letter sequence: 'H', 'W', 'B', 'I', 'B', 'N' and 'F'. These additional letter sequence is simple enough to be entered whilst speaking; and yet they provide crucial information that can significantly improve the efficiency and robustness of speech recognition. For instance, the number of letters entered can be used to constrain the number of words in the recognition output, thereby suppressing spurious insertion and deletion errors, which are commonly observed in noisy environment. Furthermore, the identity of the letters themselves can be used to guide the search process so that partial word sequences in the search graph that do not conform to the PLIs provided by the users can be pruned away.

3. THE HVR CHALLENGES

This section will present a detailed description of the HVR Grand Challenge. The main objective of the HVR Grand Challenge 2012 is to provide a common platform on which competitive research work can be performed easily by researchers across multiple disciplines. The HVR Grand Challenge is set to address two major challenges pertaining to HVR: 1) What kind of *haptic information* can be provided via touch input and how to provide them? and 2) What kind of inference models to be used and how to combine multiple inference models together?

In order to address the above two challenges, the grand challenge consists of two challenge sub-tasks, which correspond to one of the two components of the HVR system, as depicted in Figure 1. The front-end of an HVR system (HVR interface) captures the voice and touch inputs from the user using a microphone and a touchscreen display. The multiple streams of information captured by the front-end component are then processed by the back-end component (HVR recognition) to decipher the user intended input texts. The details of the two challenge subtasks will be described in the following.

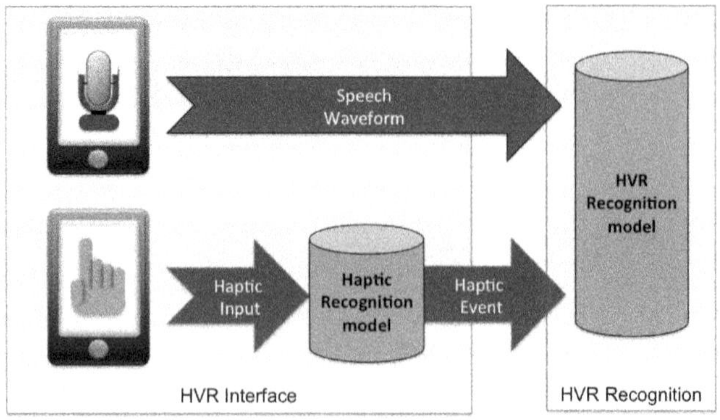

Figure 1: HVR System Architecture.

3.1 T1 – The HVR Interface Challenge

The objective of this challenge subtask was to design innovative user interfaces for HVR. The core of this task was to design appropriate haptic events for HVR and methods for generating these events using touchscreen inputs. The complexity of the haptic event will affect the quality of the realized speech as well as the throughput using the overall HVR interface. For example, the haptic events may represent partial lexical information [11] of the words in the utterance, such as the initial and/or final letter of the words; and these letters may be generated by tapping on the appropriate keys on a soft keyboard or using more complex gesture recognition approaches. Through this challenge subtask, participants were given the freedom to propose innovative haptic events for HVR. For this challenge subtask, a list of text prompts were provided. Participants were asked to use their respective HVR interfaces to generate the corresponding speech data and haptic events. Systems were evaluated in terms of the word accuracy of the final text output from the overall HVR system. Participants in this challenge subtask may not need to build their own back-end recognition systems. A baseline HVR recognition system was provided to the participants to evaluate their HVR interfaces.

3.2 T2 – The HVR Recognition Challenge

This subtask was designed to challenge the research community to propose innovative recognition algorithms for HVR. HVR is essentially an extension to the conventional ASR, where haptic events are augmented as additional input. Participants were encouraged to discover new ways of making use of this additional information to improve the final recognition performance. Previously, haptic pruning was proposed in [10] to incorporate haptic inputs in order to constrain the decoding search space. A more generic probabilistic framework of integrating the haptic inputs based on Weighted Finite State Transducers (WFST) was introduced in [11]. Participants were invited to explore other possibilities, including but not limited to aspects such as acoustic and language model adaptation using the additional haptic events. For this subtask, participants were given a set

Entry Method	HVR Mode	Haptic Input
Method 1	Synchronous	Keyboard
Method 2	Synchronous	Keystroke
Method 3	Asynchronous	Keyboard
Method 4	Asynchronous	Keystroke

Table 2: Four different entry modes for HVR data collection.

of speech utterances along with the corresponding haptic inputs. In HVR Grand Challenge 2012, the initial letter sequences were generated using keyboard and keystroke inputs. Systems were evaluated based on the word accuracy of the final text output.

4. DATASETS

This section will describe the datasets used for the HVR Grand Challenge 2012. Three sets of data were made available to the challenge participants. A summary of these datasets in terms of the number of subjects, number of utterances and the amount of speech data is given in Table 1. The pilot dataset contains data collected from one subject. This subject has used the HVR interface for more than one year and can be regarded as an experienced user. The development and challenge datasets contains data collected from 4 and 15 subjects respectively. These subjects do not have prior experience using the interface. They were given the opportunity to practice with the HVR interface for several sentences before the data collection. These subjects were university students. Most of them were non-native English speakers.

4.1 Data Collection Procedures

The challenge datasets were collected using an HVR interface prototype implemented on iPad. The screenshots of the interface using the *keyboard* and *keystroke* input modes are depicted in Figures 2(a) and 2(b) respectively. Data collection was carried out with the HVR iPad interface operating in the *landscape* mode. For keyboard input, an onscreen soft keyboard with a standard QWERTY keyboard layout was used to enter the initial letters. The size of the keyboard is 352×1024, which is the same size as the standard English QWERTY keyboard provided by iOS. For keystroke input, subjects are required to use a predefined set of single-stroke handwriting gestures to enter the letters. These predefined gestures are given in Figure 3. Most of these letters can be represented by single-stroke gestures using the standard handwritten lowercase form, except for the letters 'F', 'I', 'L', 'T' and 'X', whose keystrokes are slightly modified to be single-stroke. Single-stroke handwriting input simplifies the recognition process since the letter boundaries are explicitly provided. Therefore, the system only needs to handle isolated handwritten letter recognition.

During data collection, each subject will enter a series of prompted texts using the HVR iPad interface. Each sentence was entered four times, each corresponds to a different HVR mode and a different haptic input method, as shown in Table 2. The synchronous HVR mode indicates that the subjects will enter the texts verbally, at the same time provide the corresponding initial letter sequence using either the keyboard or keystroke input method. On the other hand, for asynchronous HVR mode, subjects will read the prompted sentence first and then provide the initial letters afterwards.

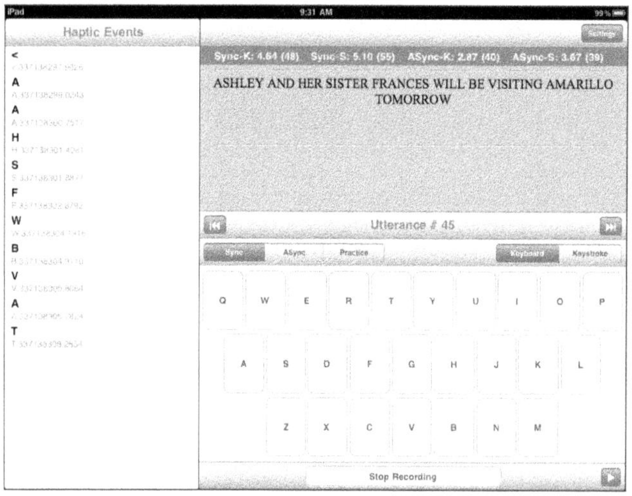

(a) Keyboard Input Mode

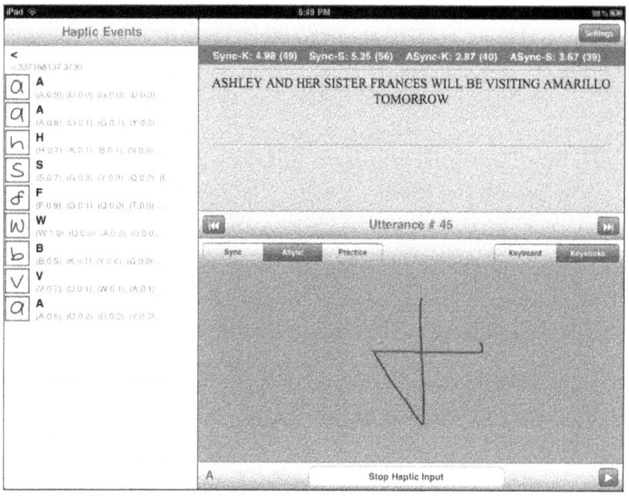

(b) Keystoke Input Mode

Figure 2: Screenshots of HVR iPad interface used for data collection.

For each text entry method, the speech utterances were recorded and stored as single channel 16 bit linear pulse code modulation (PCM) sampled at 16 kHz. For keyboard input, the HVR interface also captured the corresponding letter sequence as the subjects tap on the onscreen keyboard. The timestamps of the key presses relative to the start of the speech recording were also saved. For keystroke inputs, the HVR interface captured a series of 2-dimensional coordinates for each handwriting gesture. Likewise, the start times of the keystrokes relative to the start of the speech recording were also saved.

The data collected was conducted in a research laboratory where the recorded speech may be considered noise free. Noisy speech data were then artificially created by corrupting the clean speech with *additive* noise. The noise samples were collected from a school canteen where the primary noise type is babble noise. Three sets of noisy data were created at signal-to-noise ratios of 20dB, 15dB and 10dB.

Datasets	No. of Subjects	No. of Utterances		Amount of Speech (mins)	
		Train	Test	Train	Test
Pilot	1	164	20	12.0	1.5
Development	4	243	80	25.1	9.3
Challenge	15	977	180	94.3	20.8

Table 1: Number of subjects, number of utterances and amount of speech data in the pilot, development and challenge datasets.

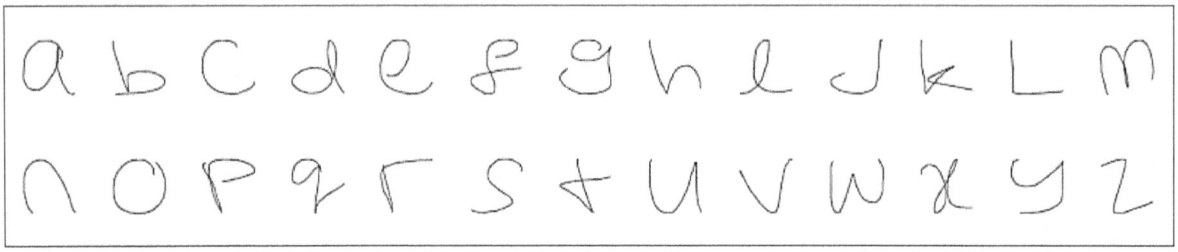

Figure 3: Single-stroke letter keystrokes used for data collection.

5. ANALYSES OF DATASETS

This section gives an account of the characteristics of the datasets in various aspects. First of all, the effects of HVR interface on the speech produced by the subjects were investigated. The durations of the speech and silence segments of the resulting speech collected using the synchronous and asynchronous modes were compared in Figure 4. Forced-alignment [13] was used to obtain the phone boundaries. The speech data produced by the subjects when using HVR in asynchronous mode were considered to be normal speech since their speech was not affected by any concurrent touch inputs. Therefore, the durations of the phones and silences for asynchronous mode were about the same for keyboard and keystroke inputs, as show in Figures 4(b), 4(d) and 4(f). Three types of silences were considered. A leading silence means the portion of silence at the beginning of each utterance. Likewise, a trailing silence denotes the portion of silence at the end of each utterance. Inter-word silences are the gaps in between successive words. These gaps are typically very small for fluent continuous speech.

In general, the average durations of phones and various types of silences are longer for synchronous data compared to asynchronous data. The average duration of the leading silence for synchronous mode is about 1 second for all the datasets. This is consistently longer than the leading silence durations for asynchronous data, which indicates that there is a finite delay for the subjects to locate the key on the soft keyboard or determine the appropriate keystroke for the first letter of the first word of the sentence before he or she began to speak. There seems to be no difference in the leading silence durations between keyboard and keystroke inputs. On the other hand, the trailing silence for the keyboard and keystroke inputs are quite different for synchronous mode. For keyboard input, the trailing silence durations are almost the same for both synchronous and asynchronous cases. However, since the time taken to speak a word may be shorter than the time needed to complete a handwriting gesture for the corresponding initial letter, the trailing silences for synchronous keystroke mode was found to be more than 2 times longer than those for synchronous keyboard mode.

Similarly, the silence durations in between successive words were significantly longer for synchronous data. Beginners (subjects for development and challenge data) were found to spend on average 0.11s – 0.13s longer in between words to locate the right keys for synchronous keyboard input and 0.30s – 0.34s longer to complete the handwriting gestures. An experienced user, on the other hand, spent on average 0.06s and 0.07s longer in between words for keyboard and keystroke inputs. This shows that, with sufficient practice, potential speedup in HVR text entry can be achieved.

Besides, synchronous input also caused the average phone durations to be longer. The average phone duration for beginners increased by 0.02s –0.06s for synchronous keyboard input and 0.04s – 0.10s for synchronous keystroke input. On the other hand, the phones produced by an experienced user lengthened by 0.03s for both keyboard and keystroke inputs.

Next, the characteristics of the touch inputs were analyzed. Table 3 shows the average durations between successive haptic inputs. They were measured as the difference between the timestamps of the successive key presses or the start times of the successive handwriting gestures. The corresponding effective input speeds, measured in the number of words per minute (WPM), were also reported in the same table. For asynchronous mode, beginners' keyboard and keystroke input speeds were 69 – 79 WPM and 44 WPM respectively. An experienced user can achieve much higher input speeds, at 122 WPM and 95 WPM respectively. However, despite the additional cognitive loads, the effective haptic input speeds increased slightly for synchronous inputs. The input speeds for beginners increased to 73 – 87 WPM and 54 – 58 WPM for keyboard and keystroke inputs respectively. The keystroke input speed for an experienced user also increased to 102 WPM. This phenomenon may be due to the fact that the subjects subconsciously increase the haptic input speed to catch up with the faster speaking rate in synchronous mode.

Given the timestamps of the haptic inputs and the time boundaries of the phones obtained using forced-alignment, it will be interesting to analyze the synchrony of these two streams of inputs. Table 4 shows the average deviation of the haptic inputs from the start of the corresponding words.

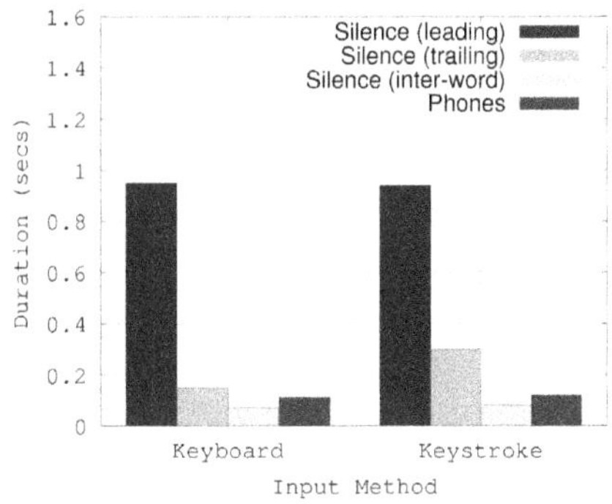

(a) Synchronous – Pilot

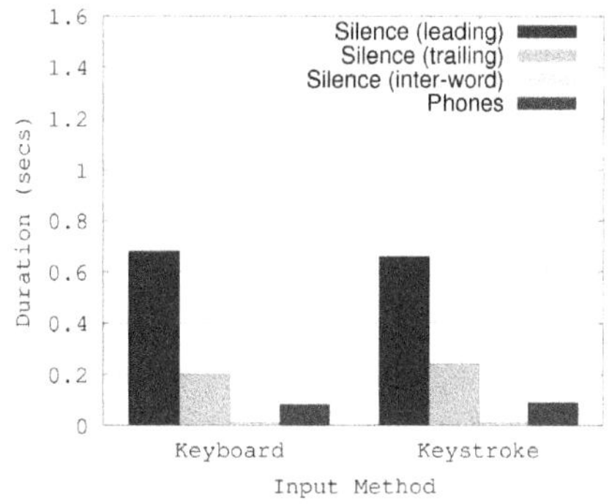

(b) Asynchronous – Pilot

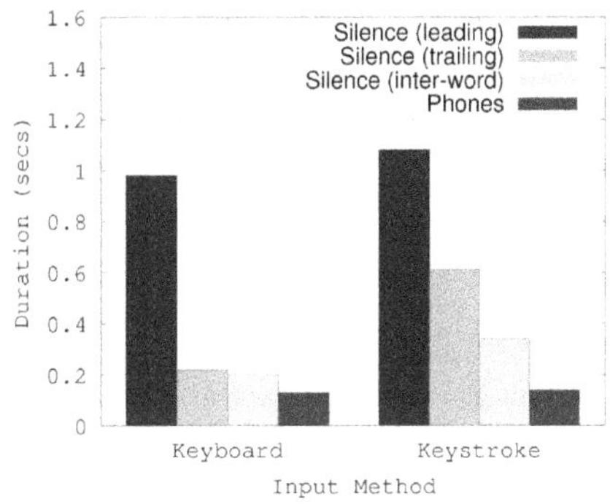

(c) Synchronous – Development

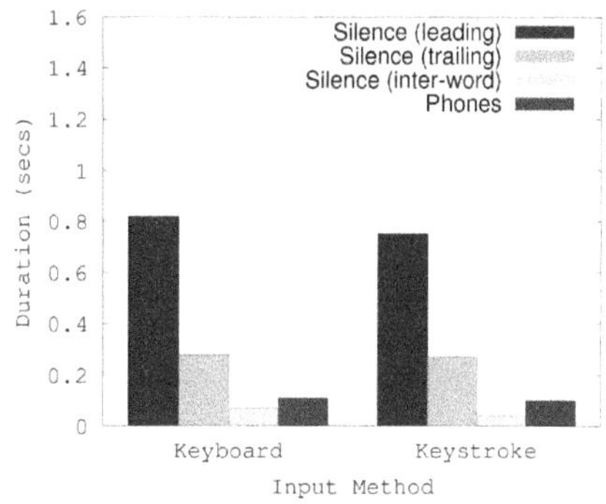

(d) Asynchronous – Developement

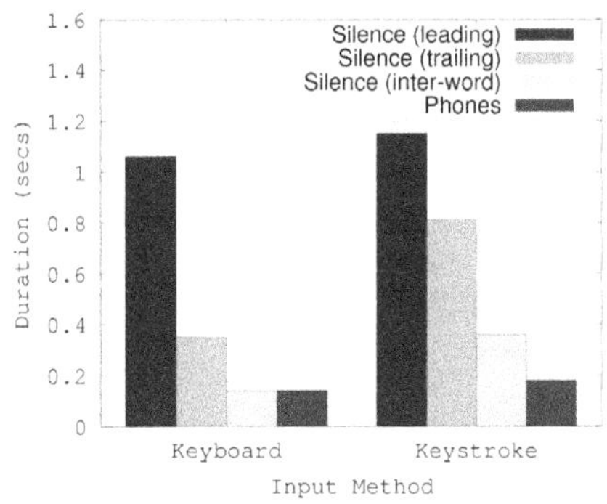

(e) Synchronous – Challenge

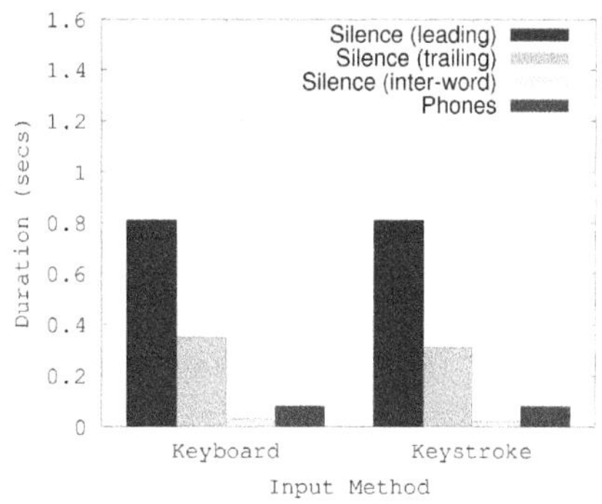

(f) Asynchronous – Challenge

Figure 4: Durations between successive haptic events in the pilot, development and challenge datasets.

Datasets	Average Input Duration (sec)				Effective Input Speed (WPM)			
	Synchronous		Asynchronous		Synchronous		Asynchronous	
	Keyboard	Keystroke	Keyboard	Keystroke	Keyboard	Keystroke	Keyboard	Keystroke
Pilot	0.49	0.59	0.49	0.63	122	102	122	95
Development	0.82	1.04	0.87	1.36	73	58	69	44
Challenge	0.69	1.12	0.76	1.36	87	54	79	44

Table 3: Durations between successive haptic inputs and the effective input speed for the pilot, development and challenge datasets.

Datasets	Average Deviation (sec)	
	Keyboard	Keystroke
Pilot	0.10	0.36
Development	0.44	0.61
Challenge	0.22	0.62

Table 4: Deviation of haptic inputs from the start of the corresponding words for the pilot, development and challenge datasets.

Datasets	Input Method	Occurrence (%)		
		Before	Within	After
Pilot	Keyboard	4	96	0
	Keystroke	1	91	8
Development	Keyboard	8	80	12
	Keystroke	2	83	15
Challenge	Keyboard	11	84	5
	Keystroke	4	85	11

Table 5: Percentage of haptic inputs occurring before, within and after the corresponding words for the pilot, development and challenge datasets.

Only sentences whose length matches the number of corresponding haptic inputs were considered[1]. For beginners, key presses occurred about 0.22s – 0.44s after the start of the corresponding words; keystrokes happened 0.61s – 0.62s after the subjects started speaking the words. However, the deviations for an experienced user were much shorter: 0.10s and 0.36s for keyboard and keystroke inputs respectively. Sometimes, subjects may also enter the haptic inputs before they started speaking the word or after they have finished the word. Table 5 shows the percentage of haptic inputs occurring before, within and after the corresponding words. For beginners, between 80% – 85% of the haptic input occurrences fall within the corresponding words. About 2% – 11% and 5% – 15% of them happened before and after the words respectively. The haptic inputs for an experienced user were more precise. About 91% – 96% of them occurred within the words. Only 1% – 4% were before the words and 8% after the words.

6. HVR RECIPE

As part of this challenge, a simple recipe based on the Hidden Markov Model Toolkit (HTK) [13] was also provided. This recipe adopts an *offline* implementation of HVR where the recognition is performed after all the speech and haptic inputs are captured (*e.g.* at the end of an utterance). This allows the haptic inputs to be incorporated as constraints to restrict the decoding network so that the standard speech recognition algorithm can be used without modification. This implementation uses *regular expressions* to represent the Partial Lexical Information (PLI) for each word. For example, for the sentence "*My name is Peter*", the initial letter sequence 'M', 'N', 'I' and 'P' is represented as

`^M, ^N, ^I, ^P`

Likewise, the final letter sequence 'Y', 'E', 'S' and 'R' is represented as

`Y$, E$, S$, R$`

Combining the above initial and final letter information yields the following PLI representation:

`^M.*Y$, ^N.*E$, ^I.*S$, ^P.*R$`

Given the PLI information, a *lexically constrained* decoding network will be constructed in the form of a confusion network (see Figure 5). Each PLI is expanded into a set of word alternatives by matching its regular expression against all the words in the vocabulary. For example, the regular expression `^M.*Y$` will expand to words including *MACY*, *MANY*, *MAY*, *MY* and so on. This is a very simple implementation of HVR which does not support a tight integration of haptic inputs into the decoding process in an online manner. It also does not support the incorporation of language model scores which are typically used in speech recognition. Furthermore, this implementation also assumes that the PLI information provided are accurate since any haptic input error will lead to the correct words being excluded from the resulting lexically constrained decoding network. A more advanced probabilistic integration framework based on Weighted Finite State Transducer (WFST) has been proposed in [11], which is able to incorporate language model scores and handle uncertainties in haptic inputs.

7. EXPERIMENTAL RESULTS

This section presents the experimental results using the HVR Grand Challenge 2012 datasets described in Section 4. This section is divided into two parts. The first part describes the inference models for different haptic input methods and presents the letter recognition performance of these inference models. The second part describes the HVR recognition systems and their performances.

7.1 Haptic Input Performance

The datasets provided for the HVR Grand Challenge 2012 comprise the speech recording as well as the corresponding initial letter sequences for the words in the utterances. These

[1]There were a small number of sentences where subjects entered more or fewer letters than necessary by mistake.

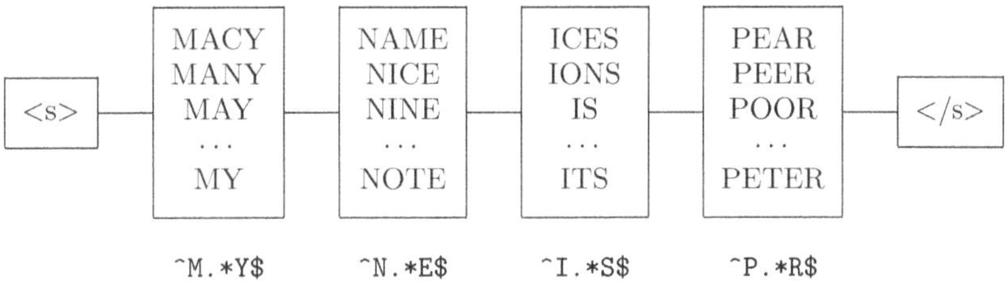

Figure 5: An example lexically-constrained decoding network based on the given initial and final letter Partial Lexical Information (PLI) for the sentence "*My name is Peter*". <s> and </s> denote the start and end of the sentence respectively.

Input Method	HVR Mode	LER (%)		
		Pilot	Dev.	Challenge
Keyboard	Sync	0.0	2.3	0.7
	Async	1.4	0.7	1.3
Keystroke	Sync	0.0	6.8	10.7
	Async	0.0	9.5	11.6

Table 6: Letter error rate performance of haptic inputs for the pilot, development and challenge datasets.

initial letters were entered by users either using an onscreen QWERTY keyboard or handwriting gestures (see Section 4.1 for more details on the data collection procedures). For the keystroke input, a 3-state left-to-right Hidden Markov Model (HMM) [9] was used to model the handwriting gesture for each letter. The emission probability of each state was represented by a Gaussian distribution with a full covariance matrix. The input features were 6-dimensional vectors given by the two-dimensional normalized coordinates of the touch points together with the first and second order differential parameters representing the instantaneous gradient and curvature of the keystroke. These differential parameters were computed using HTK [13], similar to the way the dynamic parameters were generated for speech recognition. Table 6 shows the Letter Error Rate (LER) performance of the haptic inputs provided by the users. For keyboard input, the LER indicates the error rate of the user tapping on the incorrect keys. Likewise, the LER indicates the performance of the underlying handwriting recognition system for keystroke input. One of the difficulties faced by the beginners is getting accustomed to the handwriting gestures shown in Figure 3 for keystroke input. This results in much higher LERs compared to keyboard inputs. Surprisingly, the LERs were lower for synchronous mode despite the additional cognitive loads involved. The LERs for keyboard inputs were 0.7% – 2.3% for synchronous input and 0.7% – 1.3% for asynchronous input. However, subjects in the development set made more errors for synchronous input while those in the challenge set made more errors for the asynchronous mode. So, one can only say that the error patterns are user specific. An experienced user, however, was able to provide a more consistent haptic inputs. There were no errors in inferring the letters in all cases, except for asynchronous keyboard input. They were substitution and deletion errors indicating that the user may have subconsciously replaced or skipped certain words as the sentence was being recalled after it was first spoken.

7.2 HVR Recognition Performance

Finally, we report the performance of the baseline HVR system. The baseline system was provided together with the HVR Grand Challenge 2012 datasets. In this baseline system, triphone acoustic models were represented by 3-state left-to-right Hidden Markov Model (HMM) [9]. Decision tree state clustering [14] was used to control the model complexity such that the final system comprised about 3000 distinct states. The emission probability of each HMM state is represented by a Gaussian distribution. Although more advanced configuration are used in state-of-the-art large vocabulary continuous speech recognition (LVCSR) [12] systems (e.g. Gaussian Mixture Model (GMM) state emission probability [7] and n-gram statistical language model [3]), a much simpler baseline system was chosen for HVR so that it is more practical for mobile devices with limited computation and memory resources. Mel Frequency Cepstral Coefficient (MFCC) [5] features were used for acoustic model training. 12 static coefficients together with the `C0` energy term and the first two differential parameters were used to form a 39 dimensional acoustic feature vector. Maximum likelihood Baum-Welch training [2] was used to estimate the HMM parameters. Maximum Likelihood Linear Regression (MLLR) [8] was used to adapt the Gaussian mean and variance vectors to specific users and noise conditions[2].

Figure 6 summarizes the Word Error Rate (WER) performances of *synchronous* HVR in various noise conditions for the pilot, development and challenge datasets. The ASR performances were obtained using the speech data collected in the *asynchronous* mode. In general, one observes a consistent improvement of HVR (either using keyboard or keystroke inputs) over ASR across different noise conditions. This shows the effectiveness of using additional haptic inputs to enhance the robustness of voice input in noisy environment. Further, the WER results on the pilot dataset were much better than those on the other datasets. This is because the subject in the pilot dataset has a good English proficiency while the subjects in the development and challenge datasets were mostly non-native English speakers. In general, HVR using keyboard input achieved better WER performance compared to using keystroke input. This is expected since the letter recognition error for keystroke input is much higher than keyboard input (see Table 6). Further-

[2]This work adopts MLLR as a simple approach to adapt the acoustic models to different noise conditions since it is readily supported by HTK. More advanced model-based noise compensation techniques, such as Parallel Model Combination (PMC) [6] and Vector Taylor Series (VTS) [1] can also be used.

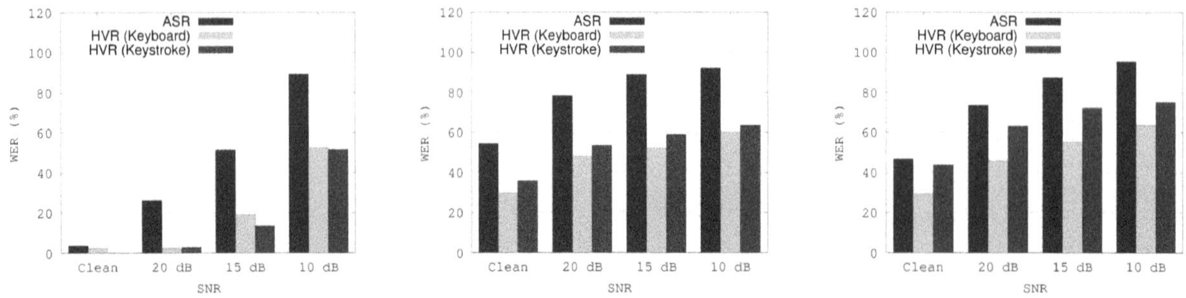

(a) Pilot (b) Development (c) Challenge

Figure 6: Word error rate performance of *synchronous* HVR for the pilot, development and challenge datasets.

more, it was also observed that the WER performance of HVR still degrades significantly as the signal-to-noise ratio (SNR) decreases. This shows that MLLR is not very effective for noise compensation. However, it was found in [11] that the combination of VTS [1] noise compensation and HVR can greatly enhance the noise robustness.

8. CONCLUSIONS

This paper has presented a detailed description of the Haptic Voice recognition (HVR) Grand Challenge 2012 and the datasets collected for this challenge. Various analyses conducted on the datasets showed that synchronous input has the effect of increasing the durations of the phones and gaps in between words. The effect is smaller for a more experienced user. Keyboard inputs were found to be much quicker to input and had much lower inference error compared to keystroke inputs. However, since this study involved only one experienced user, more detailed studies are needed to properly understand the full potential of HVR.

9. REFERENCES

[1] A. Acero, L. Deng, T. Kristjansson, and J. Zhang. HMM adaptation using vector Taylor series for noisy speech recognition. In *Proc. of ICSLP*, volume 3, pages 869–872, 2000.

[2] L. E. Baum and J. A. Eagon. An inequality with applications to statistical estimation for probabilistic functions of Markov processes and to a model for ecology. *Bull. Amer. Math. Soc.*, 73:360–363, 1967.

[3] S. F. Chen and J. Goodman. An empirical study of smoothing techniques for language modeling. In *Proceedings of the 34th annual meeting on Association for Computational Linguistics*, ACL '96, pages 310–318, Stroudsburg, PA, USA, 1996. Association for Computational Linguistics.

[4] E. Clarkson, J. Clawson, K. Lyons, and T. Starner. An empirical study of typing rates on mini-qwerty keyboards. In *CHI '05 extended abstracts on Human factors in computing systems*, CHI EA '05, pages 1288–1291, New York, NY, USA, 2005. ACM.

[5] S. B. Davis and P. Mermelstein. Comparison of parametric representations for monosyllabic word recognition in continuously spoken sentences. *IEEE Transactions on Acoustic, Speech and Signal Processing*, 28(4):357–366, 1980.

[6] M. Gales, S. Young, and S. J. Young. Robust continuous speech recognition using parallel model combination. *IEEE Transactions on Speech and Audio Processing*, 4:352–359, 1996.

[7] X. Huang, A. Acero, H.-W. Hon, and R. Reddy. *Spoken Language Processing: A Guide to Theory, Algorithm and System Development.* Prentice Hall PTR, 1st edition, 2001.

[8] C. J. Leggetter and P. C. Woodland. Maximum likelihood linear regression for speaker adaptation of continuous density hidden markov models. *Computer speech and language*, 9(2):171, 1995.

[9] L. A. Rabiner. A tutorial on hidden Markov models and selective applications in speech recognition. In *Proc. of the IEEE*, volume 77, pages 257–286, February 1989.

[10] K. C. Sim. Haptic voice recognition: Augmenting speech modality with touch events for efficient speech recognition. In *Proc. SLT Workshop*, 2010.

[11] K. C. Sim. Probabilistic integration of partial lexical information for noise robust haptic voice recognition. In *Proceedings of the 50th annual meeting on Association for Computational Linguistics*, ACL '12. Association for Computational Linguistics, 2012.

[12] S. J. Young. Large vocabulary continuous speech recognition: A review. In *Proceedings of the IEEE Workshop on Automatic Speech Recognition and Understanding*, pages 3–28, Snowbird, Utah, December 1995.

[13] S. J. Young et al. *The HTK Book (for HTK version 3.4).* Cambridge University, December 2006.

[14] S. J. Young, J. J. Odell, and P. C. Woodland. Tree-based state tying for high accuracy acoustic modelling. In *Proceedings ARPA Workshop on Human Language Technology*, pages 307–312, 1994.

Audio-Visual Robot Command Recognition

D-META'12 Grand Challenge

Jordi Sanchez-Riera
INRIA Grenoble Rhône-Alpes
Perception Team
665 Avenue de l'Europe
38334, Montbonnot, France
jordi.sanchez-riera@inria.fr

Xavier Alameda-Pineda
INRIA Grenoble Rhône-Alpes
Perception Team
665 Avenue de l'Europe
38334, Montbonnot, France
xavier.alameda-pineda@inria.fr

Radu Horaud
INRIA Grenoble Rhône-Alpes
Perception Team
665 Avenue de l'Europe
38334, Montbonnot, France
radu.horaud@inria.fr

ABSTRACT

This paper addresses the problem of audio-visual command recognition in the framework of the D-META Grand Challenge[1]. Temporal and non-temporal learning models are trained on visual and auditory descriptors. In order to set a proper baseline, the methods are tested on the "Robot Gestures" scenario of the publicly available RAVEL data set, following the leave-one-out cross-validation strategy. The classification-level audio-visual fusion strategy allows for compensating the errors of the unimodal (audio or vision) classifiers. The obtained results (an average audio-visual recognition rate of almost 80%) encourage us to investigate on how to further develop and improve the methodology described in this paper.

Categories and Subject Descriptors

H.4 [**Information Systems**]: Applications

General Terms

Algorithms, Datasets, Evaluation

Keywords

Audio-Visual Categorization, Multimodal Learning

[1]Datasets for Multimodal Evaluation of Tasks and Annotations: `http://d-meta.inrialpes.fr` Organizers: Xavier Alameda-Pineda (PhD candidate at Perception Team, at INRIA Rhône-Alpes), Kristiina Jokinen (adjunct Professor of language technology at the University of Helsinki) Dirk Heylen (Professor at University of Twente), Roman Bednarik (interaction technology researcher at the University of Eastern Finland) and Michal Hradiš (PhD candidate at Faculty of Information Technology, Brno University of Technology)

ICMI'12, October 22–26, 2012, Santa Monica, California, USA.

1. INTRODUCTION

Humans use several sensory modalities to gather information into order to build an internal representation of the real world, e.g, visual, auditory, tactile, or olfactory sensing. Among these modalities, vision and audition are the most suitable to be used by a robot due to the wide availability of associated sensors, namely cameras and microphones. Nevertheless, the data collected by these sensors are often corrupted by occlusions, reverberations, and bad recording conditions such as poor lighting, competing sound sources, background noise, etc. Hence unimodal interpretation leads to ambiguities. It seems natural to investigate how one can obtain a better understanding of a human action if several modalities are used simultaneously. Indeed, the fusion of information coming from different modalities is likely reinforce the true hypothesis. In addition, several challenging questions arise when dealing with different modalities: At which level of abstraction one should fuse the information coming from physical different sensors? How can one build the concept of multimodal features? how can one fuse features representing different aspects (time, position, appearance, spectrum, etc) of the events to be recognized or categorized?

This work is presented in the framework of the D-META ICMI Grand Challenge aiming at setting up the basis for comparison, analysis, and further improvement of multimodal data annotations and multimodal interactive systems. The main goal of D-META is to foster research and development in multimodal communication and to further elaborate algorithms and techniques for building various multimodal applications. Held by two coupled pillars, method benchmarking and annotation evaluation, the D-META challenge envisions a starting point for transparent and publicly available application and annotation evaluation on multimodal data sets. Five tasks were proposed in D-META: **AVRGR**, recognize gestures addressed to the robot by means of vision and the audio, **AVSR**, detect, localize and track multiple speakers using audio-visual information, **CEP**, estimate the level of engagement in a video-mediated communication, **AVCGR**, recognize conversational gestures in first encounter dialogues and **AVFGR**, recognize feedback gestures in first encounter dialogues.

In this paper we set the baseline for the task audio-visual recognition of human commands. The proposed method combines auditory and visual information for recognition using the publicly available RAVEL data set [2], which contains annotated binocular-binaural recordings.

The remainder of the paper is organized as follows. Section 2 describes the previous work done on the topic and the main contributions of the paper. The learning approach as well as the auditory/visual features are described in section 3. In section 4 are explained the different experiments carried out to validate the fusion methods and in section 5 conclusions and directions for future work are briefly presented. Finally, section 6 is devoted to the discussion of some Challenge organizational aspects.

2. RELATED WORK & CONTRIBUTIONS

As mentioned before, a few choices have to be done when combining different sensory modalities for classification. Indeed, the level of abstraction at which the fusion should be done depends on the targeted application. Most of the existing audio-visual categorization methods perform the fusion either at the feature level [5, 9, 10] or at the classification level [7, 14, 17]. The reader is referred to [11] for a study using support vector machines (SVM) that compares feature-level fusion techniques to classification-level fusion techniques.

An example of a feature-level fusion method is [5]. The idea is to track short-term visual features. These features are associated to the auditory signal in order to construct a joint audio-visual codebook. Used to describe a part of a sequence, the codebook feeds a multiple-instance learning (MIL) paradigm, training a semantic concept detector. Another way to perform audiovisual fusion at a feature level is to map both modalities into the same "audio-visual object" space and to perform clustering [6, 1].

The authors in [9] target a speech detection application, and perform the audio-visual fusion at a feature level as well. Principal component analysis (PCA) features are taken from the face images and Mel Frequency Cepstral Coefficients (MFCC) are the auditory features. Both types of features are then projected in a joint subspace using canonical correlation analysis (CCA). A Gaussian mixture model (GMM) is used for classification.

The authors in [10] target general activity recognition. High dimensional features (around 3000) for video and audio are collected and then reduced using the sequential forward floating selection (SFFS) algorithm. The SFFS is a pruning algorithm that selects most relevant features. With this the dimension is reduced (to 40). Finally a kNN algorithm is used as classifier.

Among the classification-level fusion methods we remark [7], in which the authors experiment different combination strategies for object detection. Visual features are based on texture description and entropy-based variable-size patches. Auditory features correspond to the energy of the signal's gammatone filter bank decomposition. Monocular video and monaural audio are used and there is a strong need of uniform visual background.

Object recognition based SVMs is used in [14] where a probabilistic method combining posterior class probability output by each classifier is proposed; Basically this means that each modality is trained separately and then combined. SIFT descriptors are used as visual features and a commercial speech recognizer is used to classify the incoming audio signal.

A different approach from the ones mentioned so far is described [17] which finds sport highlights using a coupled hidden Markov model (CHMM). Several video features are used such as quantization average motion vectors and color. On the auditory side, the authors chose to use MFCC features. Both these features train a CHMM to perform the classification.

In this paper we introduce a method that compares different learning schemes. The first scheme is based on a bag-of-words (BoW) approach while the second one incorporates temporal structure by means of HMMs. Scene-flow [15] and STIPs [8] are used as visual features and MFCC as auditory features. The fusion is done at the classification stage through a modality-weighting scheme, i.e., pooling. Experimental validation is done using a publicly available data set, in which we set the performance baseline.

3. AUDIO-VISUAL CATEGORIZATION

This section is devoted to the proposed audio-visual command learning approach, which performs classification-level fusion. By means of the scene flow from one side and STIPs on the other side, we are able to describe the visual information (see section 3.1). The auditory information is characterized by standard features used in speech recognition (section 3.2). The learning is performed through two different supervised techniques: without any temporal model (section 3.3) and with a temporal model (section 3.4). Finally, the procedure to combine the output of the unimodal classifiers is described (section 3.5).

3.1 The Visual Descriptor

We used two different visual descriptors. The first one was proposed in [15] and it is based on the scene flow, which is the 3D equivalent of the optical flow [16]. The scene flow is represented by the optical flow plus the depth at each image position. Together with the camera calibration, this is equivalent to a vector field of 3D position and associated 3D velocities. This intrinsic representation is potentially less sensitive to changes of texture and illumination than the intensity images. Moreover, the notion of depth allows to focus on the actor, while discarding any activity from the background. We assume that the actor of interest is the person closest to the camera. This is a reasonable assumption, since it holds in most of the human-robot-interaction applications and on movies. The final descriptor consists on the position and disparity relatives to the actor's face plus the optical flow (see Figure 1 for a detailed example).

The second descriptor, STIPs, was proposed in [8]. This descriptor consists on the histogram of gradients concatenated to the histogram of optical flow (HOG-HOF), applied at Harris 3D interest points. Notice that, while the first descriptor uses stereo-vision and has low dimension (five), the second uses monocular vision and is high dimensional (200). Furthermore, while the former has a semi-dense nature, the latter is sparse in the spatiotemporal domain.

3.2 The Speech Descriptor

The auditory stream is represented by the Mel Frequency Cepstral Coefficients (MFCC). Widely used for speech and sound recognition (see [13, 12]), the MFCC are computed following the three steps: (i) perform the short-time Fourier transform (STFT), (ii) map the power spectrum onto the Mel scale and (iii) take the discrete cosine transform of these mapped powers. The are three main parameters associated with MFCC features. First, the frame size defines the length of the STFT (denoted by W). Second, the frame shift (F)

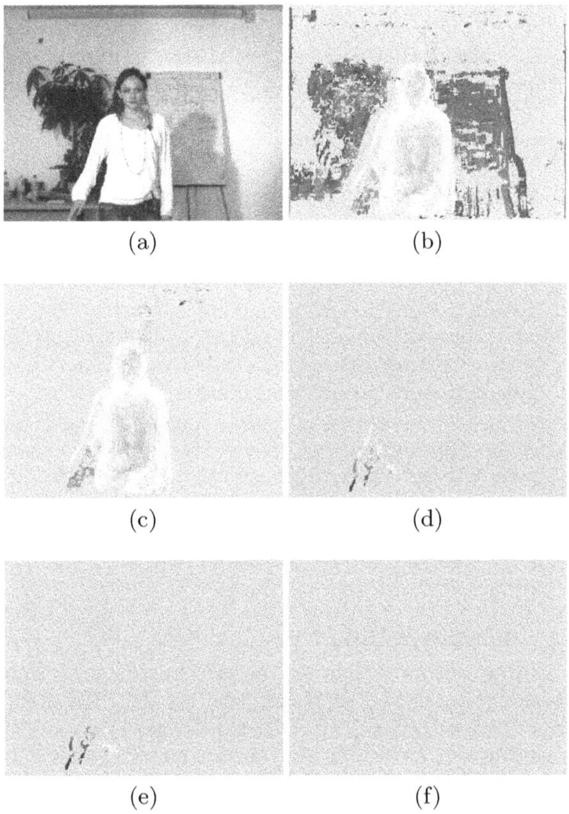

Figure 1: Construction of the proposed descriptor. The actor's face is detected from the left input image (a). The raw disparity map (b) is segmented, such that all pixels having the lower disparity than the actor's face are discarded (c). The descriptor is then computed for all remaining pixels undergoing non-zero motion, such that it consists of the pixel's position relative to the face, it's disparity (d), and horizontal (e) and vertical (f) components of optical flow.

determines the time between two consecutive STFT windows. Third, the amount of cepstral coefficients (D), that sets the dimension of the output MFCC representation.

3.3 Bag-of-Words Gesture Learning

The Bag-of-Words (BoW) paradigm has shown to have very high performance in model learning from low-level features. Following [8], it requires to:

1. Collect a set of local descriptors (possibly associated with interest points) of all training gesture instances.
2. Group these descriptors into K clusters.
3. Quantize all the descriptors assigning the label corresponding to its nearest cluster centroid. This provides for the "words".
4. Represent a gesture instance as a K-bin histogram of the quantized descriptor ("bag of words").
5. Train a classifier with these histograms in order to construct the gesture model.

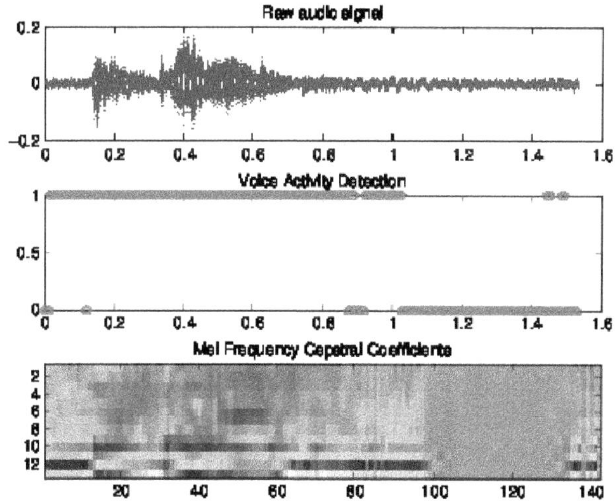

Figure 2: Mel Frequency Cepstral Coefficients for one voice-command instance. From the raw signal (top) the voice activity is detected (middle) and used to mask the extracted MFCC (bottom).

In steps 1–3, the word vocabulary (or the codebook) is constructed. The amount of local descriptors is typically high. Clustering these descriptors allows to represent an instance as a histogram, which in turn provides for a compact representation with fixed (chosen) length K. During steps 4–5, these compact representations together with their annotated labels are used to train a classifier. The BoW representation encodes the relative frequency of occurrences of the quantized descriptors, which discriminates among command classes.

We use the BoW paradigm to build auditory and visual models for each of the commands. Hence we have both a visual and an auditory classifier. When an instance of an unknown command class has to be recognized, the auditory and visual representations are computed and sent to their respective classifiers. The outputs of the two classifiers are fused to perform audio-visual gesture recognition (as explained in section 3.5).

3.4 Temporal Gesture Learning

The standard BoW approach is notoriously lacking a temporal model. Indeed, the order of the extracted features is not taken into account when learning the command model. A powerful statistical learning tool to model time series are hidden Markov models (HMMs). These models assume the existence of a discrete-valued hidden variable that describes the state of the sequence. At each of these states, the model is assumed to generate observations following different probability distributions (called emission distributions).

To fully specify such an HMM, two choices have to be done:

1. The amount of hidden states and the possible transitions among them.
2. The emission probability distributions at each of the states.

An expectation-maximization (EM) algorithm is derived in order to estimate the posterior distributions of the hidden state sequence, the transition probabilities, and the parameters of the emission distributions (see [12, 3] for more details).

3.5 Audio-Visual Command Recognition

Once the auditory and visual classifiers are trained, we are ready to fuse the information coming from both classifiers. Let $a_c(g)$ and $v_c(g)$ denote the score of the command instance g to belong to class c given by the auditory and visual classifiers respectively. In order to combine the information from both classifiers we train a combined classifier consisting on (i) whitening the training data (unimodal classifier scores) and (ii) apply a weighting function.

The whitening procedure consists on computing the mean (μ_a) and the standard deviation (σ_a) of the auditory classification scores $\{a_c(g_n)\}_{n=1,c=1}^{N,C}$, being N the number of command instances. A new auditory score is computed as $\tilde{a}_c(g) = \frac{a_c(g)-\mu_a}{\sigma_a}$. The same procedure is applied to the visual classification scores.

Finally, the combined score is the result of a convex combination of the two whitened scores:

$$m_c^l(g) = l\tilde{v}_c(g) + (1-l)\tilde{a}_c(g).$$

The value of l determines the trust we put on each modality. Actually, some cases deserve a special mention:

$l = 0$ is equivalent to audio-based classification.

$l = 0.5$ the auditory and visual scores stand on equal foot,

$l = 1$ is equivalent to vision-based classification, and

In general, $l > 0.5$ means that we put more trust on the visual classification score, whereas $l < 0.5$ means that we do it with the auditory score. This way of combining the two classifiers allows us to evaluate the relative trust we put on the modalities. The final classification is:

$$c^* = \arg\max_c m_c^l(g).$$

4. EXPERIMENTAL VALIDATION

In this section we describe the experiments done using different classification methods, such as HMMs and SVMs. The details are given below.

4.1 Implementation

The visual descriptors were computed using for STIPs the default vaules given in the binary code [2] and for Sceneflow using a disparity margin around 5 pixels with the intention to include most of the body of the actor and exclude the rest of the scene (see [15] for other details). The parameters to compute the MFCC features were set to the standard ones in speech recognition: $W = 21.3$ ms, $f = W/2$ and $D = 13$.

We tried the two different learning schemes (non-temporal and temporal) with audio and video features.

sSVM The classifier of the histogram of the scene-flow visual descriptors is a SVM. All the visual descriptors are grouped into $K = 500$ clusters. For each command clip, an histogram of centroid occurrences is computed and normalized. This is used to train the SVM.

lSVM We use the same method as before but on features from [8].

[2]http://www.di.ens.fr/ laptev/

aSVM The classifier of the histogram of auditory features is a SVM. We trained the SVM using histograms of size $K = 500$ in that case. Since the speech information is sparse in time, a voice activity detector is needed, we chose to use the state-of-the-art voice activity detector available in VOICEBOX [4].

sHMM The per-frame histogram of visual features train temporal models (HMM). Five states per commands and mixture of five Gaussian components were trained. The size of the histogram was $K = 20$.

aHMM A temporal model is added to the auditory features. In that case eight states per command and Gaussian emission probabilities were trained.

lHMM This options was not explored because of the nature of the descriptor. As explained before, the HOG-HOF descriptor is sparse. Actually there are many image frames without any descriptor. Hence this descriptor is not well suited for a per-frame representation.

4.2 The Ravel Data Set

The experimental validation is performed on the "Robot Gestures" scenario of the Ravel data set [2]. We use the eight sequences proposed for the Challenge, each one containing three instances of nine command categories. The set of voice-and-gesture commands are the followings: (i) *wave* ("Hello!"), (ii) *walk towards the robot* ("I am coming."), (iii) *walk away from the robot* ("Bye!"), (iv) *stop* hand-wave ("Stop!"), (v) *turn around* gesture ("Turn around."), (vi) *come here* gesture ("Come here."), (vii) *point* action ("Look!"), (viii) head motion for *yes* ("Yes") and (ix) head motion for *no* ("No"). In all cases, the human gesture is accompanied by speech corresponding to the gesture, shown above in brackets. Notice that all the actors in the data set are non-native English speakers of five different nationalities, hence there is a large variability in the speech commands.

4.3 Performance Results

In order to properly validate the method, the leave-one-out strategy is applied. This strategy is a cross-validation strategy that consists on selecting one of the sequences as test data and perform the training with the rest. Applying this to all the sequences makes the presented results statistically significant.

Evaluating multicategory classifiers means providing the confusion matrices. The ij-th entry of such matrix contains how many instances of the i-th class have been classified as class j. By averaging the elements of the diagonal, one obtains the average recognition rate (ARR) of the classifier.

4.3.1 Visual Categorization

Figures 3a, 3b and 3c show the confusion matrices for the **sSVM**, the **sHMM** and the **lSVM** classifiers. Notice that **sSVM** performs very well in five out of nine gestures (*Hello*, *I am coming*, *Look*, *No* and *Bye*), well in two gestures (*Yes* and *Come here*) and poorly in two gestures (*Stop* and *Turn around*). However, the **sHMM** classifier performs poorly compared to **sSVM**. Indeed, it gets good results for most of the actions, very good results for just two of them (*Hello* and *Bye*) and poor results in three gestures (*Yes*, *Stop* and *Turn*

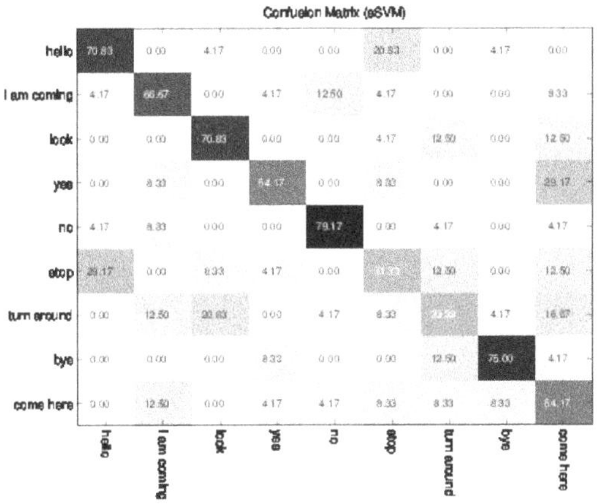

(a) **sSVM**

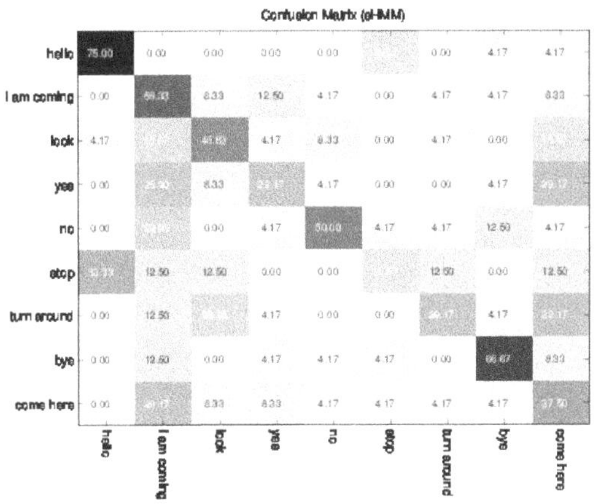

(b) **sHMM**

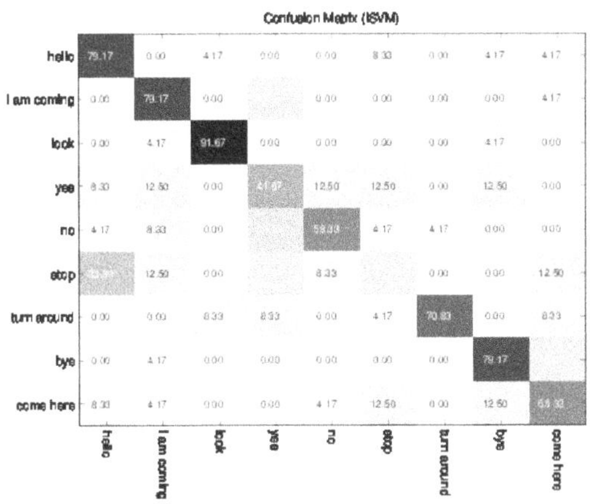

(c) **lSVM**

Figure 3: Confusion matrix of the three visual classifiers: (a) **sSVM**, (b) **sHMM** and (c) **lSVM**.

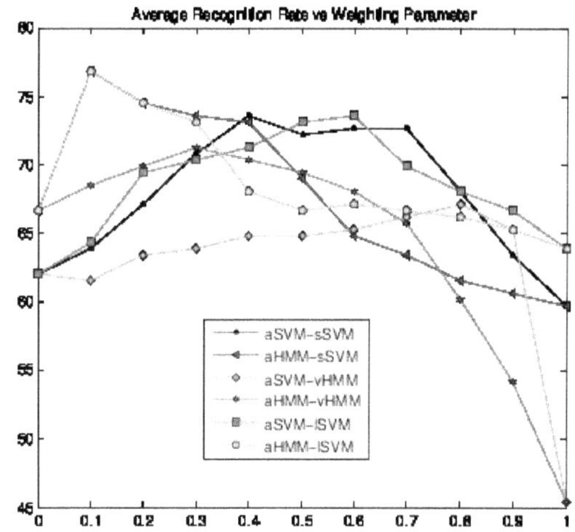

Figure 5: Average Recognition Rate as a function of the multimodal weighting parameter l.

around). Notice also that there is no much difference between the **sSVM** and the **lSVM** classifiers. Actually, they mainly differ in two of the gestures *No* and *Turn around*.

4.3.2 Auditory Categorization

The confusion matrix of **aSVM** and **aHMM** can be seen in figures 4a and 4b respectively. The SVM-based classifier performs very good in six out of nine actions, good in two of them (*Bye* and *Stop*) and poorly just in one command (*Turn around*). However the **aHMM** classifier has very good performance everywhere except for the *Bye* and *Turn around* commands.

4.3.3 Audio-Visual Categorization

It is worth to notice that, for instance, some actions that are difficult to recognize by **sSVM** as *Stop* or *Come here* are easily classified by **aSVM**, and viceversa with the actions *Bye* or *Hello*. This supports the idea that the combined classifier should outperform both unimodal classifiers. Figure 5 show the ARR of the combined classifier as a function of the weighting parameter l. Please remark that when using the same underlying model (curves **aSVM-sSVM**, **aSVM-lSVM** and **aHMM-sHMM**) the maximum performance of the combined classifier is achieved for values of l around 0.5. However, when the temporal classifier is combined with a non-temporal classifier, the maximum performance of the combined tends to shift towards the modality with temporal modeling. Furthermore, the temporally modeled classifier performs much better when some global information (coming from the non-temporal classifier) is taken into account. In that sense, it is worth to notice that, except for one case (left side of **aSVM-sHMM**), the combined classifiers outperform the unimodal ones when a small weight is given to the other modality's classifier.

Finally, Figures 6a-6f show the confusion matrix of all the multimodal classifiers for the optimal weighting parameter l. Generally speaking, we notice that the performance of these combined classifiers improved with respect to the unimodal ones. Most of them obtain outstanding results for some of the commands and very good results for most of the commands. We need to remark that the **aHMM-sSVM** and the **aHMM-lSVM** classifiers achieve an ARR of 77%,

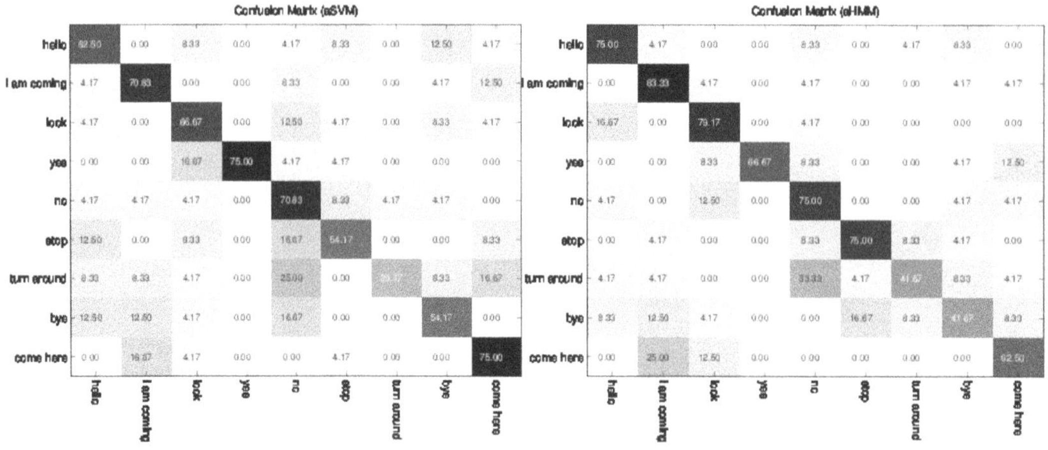

(a) **aSVM** (b) **aHMM**

Figure 4: Confusion matrix of the two auditory classifiers: (a) **aSVM** and (b) **aHMM**.

that represents a considerable increment respect the ARR computed on each modality independently.

5. CONCLUSIONS & FUTURE WORK

In this work we presented a method to recognize human commands from auditory and visual input signals. Based on a high-performance and solid learning technique, the method uses binocular/monocular visual features and monaural auditory features. Audio-visual recognition is performed at a later stage in which the classification scores from audio and video are combined to get the final audio-visual score, yielding to important increasings on the ARR. The method is tested in leaving-one-out fashion on a publicly available data set. Results show the importance of using both modalities for recognition and leave some room for improving.

More tests can be done trying different type of descriptors for visual and auditory data, as well as, try to fuse these data at different stages.

Acknoledgments

This work was supported by the European project HUMAVIPS FP7-ICT-2009-247525, `http://humavips.eu/`

6. CHALLENGE ORGANIZATION

D-META (Data sets for Multimodal Evaluation of Tasks and Annotations) is the answer that a group of researchers gave to the call for Grand Challenges at the International Conference on Multimodal Interaction (ICMI) 2012. The aim of this challenge is to group researchers working in the same multimodal applications and to encourage them to test their algorithms on a common data set. Obviously, this will set a baseline on the quality of the current methods, the usability of such data sets as well as some hints about the quality of the provided data and annotations.

We would like to remark that the spirit of D-META is far from pursuing a standardization or universal agreement on how to process, present or annotate multimodal data. Instead, we would like to have a deep understanding of the underlying problems related to the use of multimodal data targeting different tasks. Where do the algorithms fail? Why? Which algorithm is best suited for each task?

In order to implement those thoughts we selected five different tasks for which we had associated data sets. The tasks were defined by a few researchers working on the field, and they covered a variety of topics: (i) recognition of gestures addressed to the robot by means of the vision and the audio, (ii) detection, localization and tracking of multiple speakers using audio-visual information, (iii) estimate of the level of engagement in a video-mediated communication, (iv) recognition of conversational gestures in first encounter dialogues and (v) recognition of feedback gestures in first encounter dialogues. A call-for-papers was enthusiastically written accordingly to the spirit of the challenge, delineating the proposed tasks and their evaluation procedures, referring to the associated data sets and fitting the quality and logistic criteria of the holding conference, ICMI.

Once the first boost was given and the structure was set, the data set needed to be made public. The data and annotation formats had to be specified too. In addition, the access to this data set had to be free, such that any researcher in the world could participate to the Challenge. Notice that a Golden Standard (the annotation of the Ground Truth) had to be provided for evaluation and transparency purposes.

In parallel, a crucial task for the success of such Challenge needed to be done: the advertising. We informed the community about what we were proposing. This is a difficult task because the communication channels are many and not always easy to find and use. Several mailing lists and the ICMI'12 website were used to make the event visible.

We encountered several problems through the organization of this Challenge. First of all, the process of publishing a data set is very resource- and time-consuming. Lots of efforts were made to set a proper access to the data set and their annotations. Secondly, we had also troubles advertising the Challenge. Even if we used all our communication channels, we had almost no external submissions. We think that several factors may have influenced this sad outcome:

- People are not always willing to test their methods to

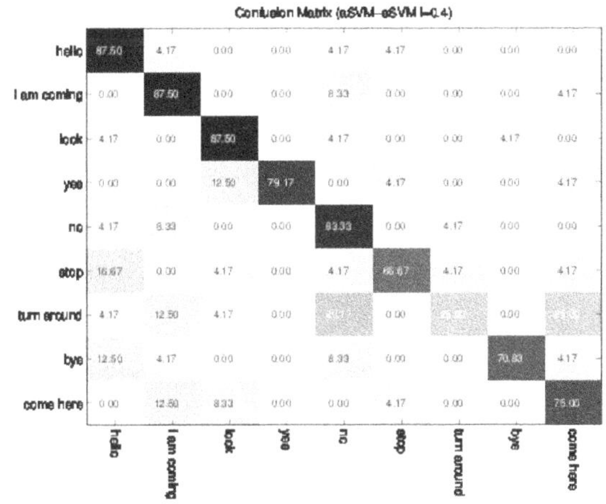

(a) **sSVM-aSVM** ($l = 0.4$)

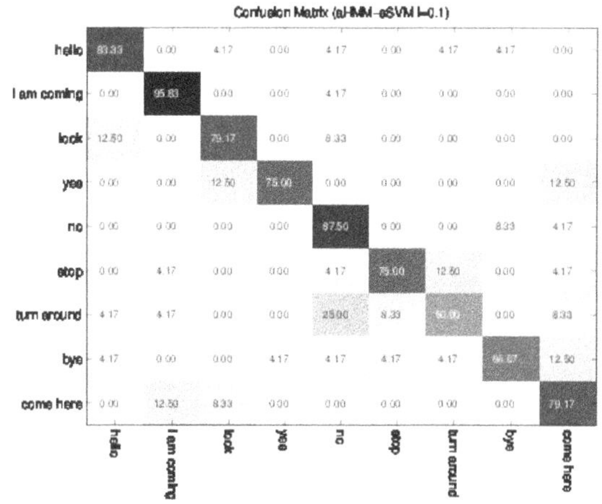

(b) **sSVM-aHMM** ($l = 0.1$)

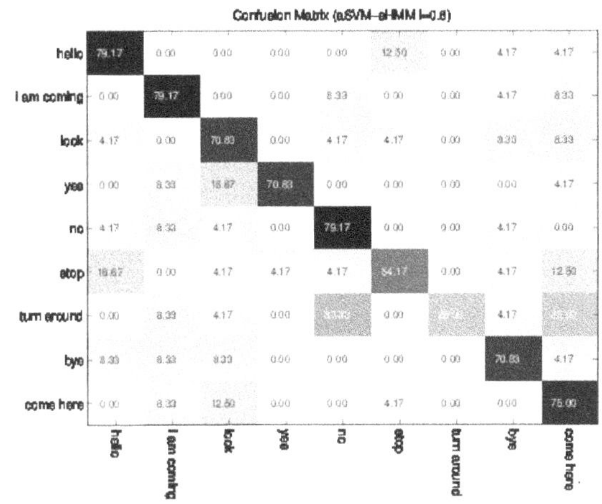

(c) **sHMM-aSVM** ($l = 0.8$)

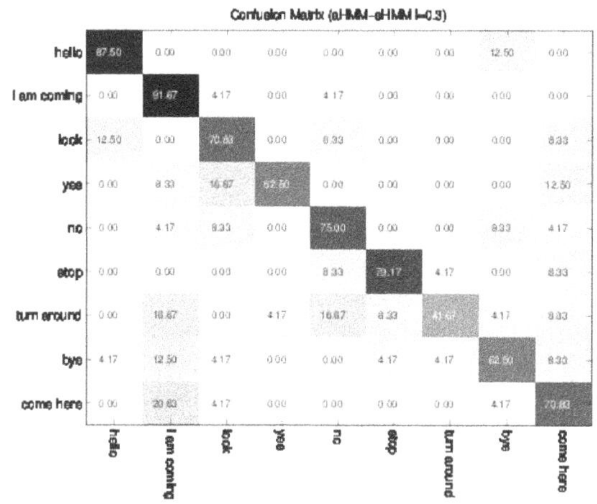

(d) **sHMM-aHMM** ($l = 0.3$)

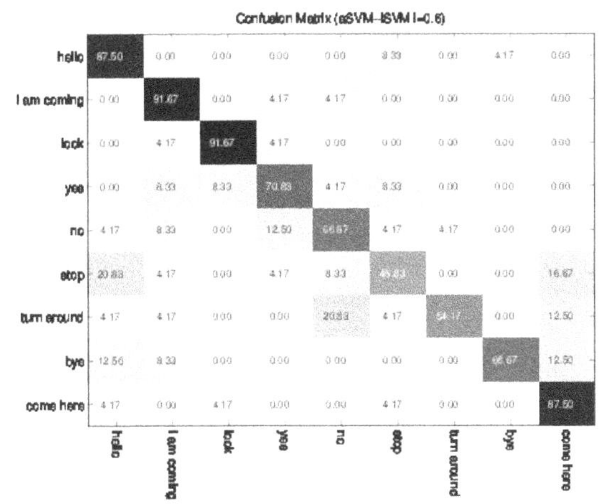

(e) **lSVM-aSVM** ($l = 0.6$)

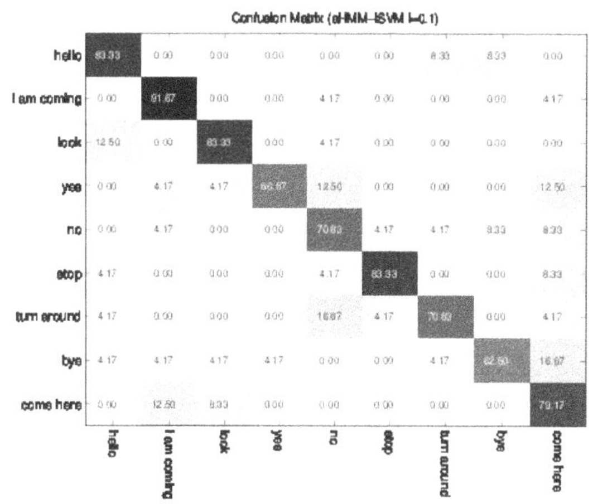

(f) **lSVM-aHMM** ($l = 0.1$)

Figure 6: Confusion matrix of the optimal combined classifiers: (a) **sSVM-aSVM** ($l = 0.4$), (b) **sSVM-aHMM** ($l = 0.1$), (c) **sHMM-aSVM** ($l = 0.8$), (d) **sHMM-aHMM** ($l = 0.3$), (e) **lSVM-aSVM** ($l = 0.6$) and (f) **aHMM,lSVM** ($l = 0.1$).

other data sets/data type without having any guarantees of good performance or a possible award.

- Adapt the software/method to a new data set is not always straightforward, and that may be an obstacle for some researchers.

- Since the Challenge just started (it's its first edition), some people may not find this attractive enough or not even a good way to publish their research, even if we think it is worth.

- We should also consider the possibility that the community is simply not interested in what we propose.

For next editions of the Challenge, we should take into account two important points. On one hand, be aware that the processing and formatting of a data set is a long and tedious task, even for small data sets. The format has to be chosen carefully, since it may constrain the access to the data. On the other hand, take advance on the advertising campaign. The larger the amount of people knows about it, the higher the number of participants and the richer the discussion. We hope to be able to overcome these difficulties for the oncoming editions of D-META.

7. REFERENCES

[1] Xavier Alameda-Pineda, Vasil Khalidov, Radu P. Horaud, and Florence Forbes. Finding audio-visual events in informal social gatherings. In *Proceedings of the 13th International Conference on Multimodal Interfaces*, pages 247–254, Alicante, Spain, November 2011. ACM.

[2] Xavier Alameda-Pineda, Jordi Sanchez-Riera, Vojtech Franc, Johannes Wienke, Jan Čech, Kaustubh Kulkarni, Antoine Deleforge, and Radu P. Horaud. Ravel: An annotated corpus for training robots with audio visual abilities. *Journal of Multimodal User Interfaces*, 2012.

[3] Christopher M. Bishop. *Pattern Recognition and Machine Learning (Information Science and Statistics)*. Springer-Verlag New York, Inc., Secaucus, NJ, USA, 2006.

[4] Mike Brookes. VOICEBOX: Speech processing toolbox for MATLAB. `http://www.ee.ic.ac.uk/hp/staff/dmb/voicebox/voicebox.html`.

[5] Wei Jiang, Courtenay Cotton, Shih-Fu Chang, Dan Ellis, and Alexander Loui. Short-term audio-visual atoms for generic video concept classification. In *Proceedings of the 17th ACM International Conference on Multimedia*, 2009.

[6] Vasil Khalidov, Florence Forbes, and Radu P. Horaud. Conjugate mixture models for clustering multimodal data. *Neural Computation*, 23(2):517–557, February 2011.

[7] L. Lacheze, Y. Guo, R. Benosman, B. Gas, and C. Couverture. Audio/video fusion for objects recognition. In *Proceedings of the IEEE/RSJ International Conference on Intelligent Robots and Systems*, 2009.

[8] I. Laptev. On space-time interest points. *International Journal on Computer Vision*, 64(2-3), 2005.

[9] Ming Liu, Yun Fu, , and Thomas S. Huang. An audio-visual fusion framework with joint dimensionality reduction. In *Proceedings of the IEEE International Conference on Audio Speech and Signal Processing*, 2008.

[10] José Lopes and Sameer Singh. Audio and video feature fusion for activity recognition in unconstrained videos. In *Intelligent Data Engineering and Automated Learning*, 2006.

[11] Jie Luo, Barbara Caputo, Alon Zweig, Jörg-Hendrik Bach, and Jörn Anemüller. Object category detection using audio-visual cues. In *Proceedings of the 6th International Conference on Computer Vision Systems*, 2008.

[12] Lawrence R Rabiner and Ronald W Schafer. *Theory and Applications of Digital Speech Processing*. Pearson, 2011.

[13] V. Ramasubramanian, R. Karthik, S. Thiyagarajan, and Srikanth Cherla. Continuous audio analytics by HMM and viterbi decoding. In *Proceedings of the IEEE International Conference on Audio, Speech and Signal Processing*, pages 2396–2399. IEEE, 2011.

[14] Kate Saenko and Trevor Darrell. Object category recognition using probabilistic fusion of speech and image classifiers. In *Proceedings of the 4th International Conference on Machine Learning for Multimodal Interaction*, 2008.

[15] Jordi Sanchez-Riera, Jan Cech, and Radu Horaud. Action recognition robust to background clutter by using stereo vision. In *In 4th International Workshop on Video Event Categorization, Tagging and Retrieval (VECTaR), in conjunction with IEEE European Conference on Computer Vision*, 2012.

[16] Jan Čech, Jordi Sanchez-Riera, and Radu P. Horaud. Scene flow estimation by growing correspondence seeds. In *Proceedings of the IEEE International Conference on Computer Vision and Pattern Recognition*, 2011.

[17] Ziyou Xiong. Audio-visual sports highlights extraction using coupled hidden markov models. *Pattern Anal. Appl.*, 8(1-2):62–71, 2005.

Brain Computer Interfaces as Intelligent Sensors for Enhancing Human-Computer Interaction

Mannes Poel
Human Media Interaction
University of Twente
Enschede, The Netherlands
m.poel@utwente.nl

Femke Nijboer
Human Media Interaction
University of Twente
Enschede, The Netherlands
femke.nijboer@utwente.nl

Egon L. van den Broek
Media and Network Services
TNO
Delft, The Netherlands
vandenbroek@acm.org

Stephen Fairclough
School of Natural Sciences and Psychology
Liverpool John Moore University
Liverpool, United Kingdom
shfairclough@googlemail.com

Anton Nijholt
Human Media Interaction
University of Twente
Enschede, The Netherlands
a.nijholt@utwente.nl

ABSTRACT

BCIs are traditionally conceived as a way to control apparatus, an interface that allows you to "act on" external devices as a form of input control. We propose an alternative use of BCIs, that of monitoring users as an additional intelligent sensor to enrich traditional means of interaction. This vision is what we consider to be a grand challenge in the field of multimodal interaction. In this article, this challenge is introduced, related to existing work, and illustrated using some best practices and the contributions it has received.

Categories and Subject Descriptors

H.5.2 [**Information Interfaces and Presentation**]: User Interfaces—*Evaluation/Methodology, Input devices and strategies*

General Terms

Algorithms, Measurement, Performance, Design, Reliability, Experimentation, Human Factors

Keywords

Brain-Computer Interface (BCI), Intelligent sensors, Human-Computer Interaction (HCI)

1. INTRODUCTION

A Brain-Computer Interface (BCI) is traditionally conceived as a way to control apparatus, an interface that allows you to "act on" external devices as a form of input control [9, 11, 21]. However, most Brain-Computer Interfaces (BCIs) do not provide a reliable and efficient means of input control and are difficult to learn and use relative to other available modes. We propose to change the conceptual use of "BCI as an actor" (input control) into "BCI as an intelligent sensor" (monitor). This shift of emphasis promotes the capacity of BCI to represent spontaneous changes in the state of the user in order to induce intelligent adaptation at the interface. BCIs can be increasingly used as intelligent sensors which "read" passive signals from the nervous system and infer user states to adapt Human-Computer Interaction (HCI), Human-Robot Interaction (HRI), or Human-Human Interaction (HHI). This perspective on BCIs challenges researchers to understand how information about the user state should support different types of interaction dynamics, from supporting the goals and needs of the user to conveying state information to other users. What adaptation to which user state constitutes opportune support? How does the feedback of the changing HCI, HRI, and HHI affect brain signals? Many research challenges need to be tackled.

This article introduces the grand challenge of BCIs as intelligent sensors for enhancing HCI. The next section will provide the required background and will discuss the challenge of BCIs as intelligent sensors for enhancing HCI, HRI, and HHI. Next, in Section 3 the best practices on BCIs as intelligent sensors will be presented. First three operational BCIs as intelligent sensors will be discussed. Subsequently, a concise discussion on the contributions accepted for this grand challenge will be presented. We conclude this article with a brief conclusion in Section 4.

2. ON BCI AS INTELLIGENT SENSOR

The current grand challenge poses that BCIs can be used as intelligent sensors to enhance HCI, HRI or HHI. However, what does this mean and what does this imply? To answer this question, we define three sub questions:

1. How do BCIs as intelligent sensors relate to conventional BCIs and how do they enhance interaction?
2. What would make these BCIs intelligent? and

ICMI'12, October 22–26, 2012, Santa Monica, California, USA.

3. How could such BCIs be realized?

These three questions will be addressed in the next three subsections and, in parallel, the work presented during the grand challenge will be held against them.

2.1 Types of BCIs and how they can enhance interaction

In 1973, Jacques J. Vidal coined the expression BCI [19]. Let us start with two quotes from his milestone article: "Spectral content and correlation 'have been related to various emotional and behavioral states. ... To provide a direct link between the inductive mental processes used in solving problems and the symbol-manipulating, deductive capabilities of the computer, is, in a sense, the ultimate goal in man-machine communication." (p. 157 and 158). Vidal [19] (more or less) already identified the value of BCI and Zander and Kothe [21] suggested the following distinction in outputs that are directly derived from brain activity:

- *Active BCI* : Independent of external events, for controlling an application.
- *Reactive BCI* : Arising in reaction to external stimulation, which is indirectly modulated by the user for controlling an application.
- *Passive BCI* : Arising without the purpose of voluntary control, for enriching HCI with implicit information on the actual user state.

The current grand challenge addresses BCI as passive BCI, which enhances other (traditional) interaction modalities (e.g., mouse, keyboard, speech and gestures). However, such a combination of modalities was already described by, among others, Nijholt and colleagues [10].

2.2 Towards intelligence!?

In principle, the processing pipeline of BCIs as intelligent sensors is no different from that of active or reactive BCIs up to the phase where the signals are received [7]. From that point on the processing pipeline is, most likely, essentially different. Recently, there has been a vivid discussion on the definition of BCI, which is described in [9]. However, for reasons of brevity, in this article, we adopt the definition of Pfurtscheller and colleagues [11], who determined that a (conventional) BCI should satisfy the following criteria:

1. signals are recorded directly from the brain;
2. at least one recordable brain signal, which the user can intentionally modulate to effect goal-directed behavior;
3. real time processing; and
4. the user must obtain feedback.

BCIs as intelligent sensors, however, need only to satisfy the first and third criteria. The fourth criteria can be satisfied; but, this is not a (strict) requirement. Implicit feedback of which the user is unaware would be in line with the concept of BCIs as intelligent sensors (e.g., a subtle change in the interaction with other (artificial) agents). This leaves us with the second criteria, which excellently marks the difference between conventional BCIs and BCIs as intelligent sensors. In both cases, at least one recordable brain signal is needed. However, in the case of BCIs as intelligent sensors no intentional modulation (i.e., altering brain activity) to achieve a certain goal is needed.

BCIs as intelligent sensors are a type of passive BCI that monitor a person by recording signals directly from the brain and processes them fast, preferably in real time. However, subsequently, no direct (conscious) goal has to be met (e.g., driving a wheelchair). As we will discuss next, this can relieve the true complexities underlying BCIs [5, 17]:

1. the definition of constructs;
2. their operationalization; and, subsequently,
3. their mapping upon the biosignals (e.g., EEG signals or other (peripheral) signals).

The outcome of the processing pipeline could be interpreted in terms of higher cognitive processes (e.g., the amount of attention [8, 20]), unconscious processes [12]), or (even) social processes [1, 15]. With such processes a discretization into a certain number of levels is not needed, the direction the process is going to can already be sufficient [3, 6]. Furthermore, it may even not be necessary to interpret patterns in EEG signals in terms of cognitive processes, a physiologically driven system could also serve the user [15, 18].

2.3 Suggestions for their implementation

Loosening the criteria of intentional modulation (cf. [11]) also introduces additional complexity and requires more intelligence than with conventional BCIs. If there is not a specific goal to be met, what then is the target to aim at? And how does this influence the signal processing and machine learning part of BCIs' processing pipeline? With BCIs as intelligent sensors, an interdisciplinary approach would be advisable; so, this would imply that all signals need to be processed in an integral framework. Recent advances in neuroscience support such an approach, as cognitive processes are distributed and, at best, (some) can only be partly localized [12]. Moreover, such localized approaches often fail in beauty when brought outside the lab into (the noisy) real world practice. Although signal processing and machine learning can rely on a thorough foundation [17], the high complexity introduced by a holistic approach will make it challenging.

Signal processing and machine learning for BCIs as intelligent sensors asks for new paradigms and unconventional approaches (cf. [7]). This grand challenge introduces some of them. Kyrgyzov and Souloumiac [8] present a processing scheme for adaptive artifact rejection from the EEG. Plass Oude-Boss and colleagues [13] propose to improve BCI performance *after* classification. De Sa [3] proposes a method to tackle the traditional problem of non-stationary EEG signals. To enable more robust BCIs as intelligent sensors, they suggest the use of a "control signal that depends intimately on what has already been transmitted, interpreted, and received". Most likely a combination of methods and techniques will be required to enable a successful holistic approach as is needed with BCIs as intelligent sensors.

3. BEST PRACTICES

This section presents the best practices on BCIs as intelligent sensors. In the first subsection, three operational BCIs as intelligent sensors, each originating from another domain, will be discussed as representatives of current state of the art best practices. In the second subsection, a concise discussion is presented on the contributions accepted for this grand challenge.

3.1 The state of the art

Although BCIs are rarely approached as intelligent sensors, there has already been work conducted on this. Here, we present three examples of BCIs as intelligent sensors. The domains of application are art, gaming, and office work, which nicely illustrates the breadth of application of BCIs as intelligent sensors.

An artistic example of the use of BCI as an intelligent sensor is the exposition *Staalhemel*[1] created by Christoph de Boeck. *Staalhemel* is an interactive installation with 80 steel segments suspended over the visitor's head as he walks through the space. Tiny hammers tap rhythmic patterns on the steel plates, activated by the brain waves of the visitor who wears a portable BCI (EEG scanner). Thus, visitors are directly interacting with their surroundings, in this case an artistic installation. Although the visitors have a certain level of control and get a kind of feedback on their user state by variations in the generated sounds, the exact level of control on the generated sounds is not deducible due to the intrinsic variability already present in, and the influence of other visitors on the sounds generated.

In *Alpha-World of Warcraft (alphaWoW)* [14] neural correlates with the mood of players are coupled to their avatars in the immersive game environment. Alpha activity (8-12 Hz rhythms in the EEG) recorded over the parietal lobe is used to control one aspect of the game character, while conventional controls are still used for the rest. A user playing World of Warcraft® can use both conventional controls and brain activity to control her character in the game. How changes in alpha activity are experienced by the user, depends on the location where the activity is measured. According to Cantero et al. [2], high alpha activity measured over the parietal lobe is related to a relaxed alertness. This seems a beneficial state of mind for gaming, especially compared to drowsiness, which is said to be measured frontally.

Transparant is an office window that aims to reduce distractions in the user's environment by varying its opacity based on the user's level of focus [4]. The state of the user (e.g., this focus) is determined by a wireless EEG headset, which communicates the user state to a smart glass module which changes the transparency of the office window accordingly. The opacity of the office window is based on the state of the user and changes accordingly. This serves two goals: i) support to be and remain focussed and ii) a signalling function whether or not the user can be disturbed.

3.2 Contributions to this grand challenge

This subsection takes the article of Fairclough and Gilleade [5] as starting point and adopts their biocybernetic loop as fundamental and generic to all categories of physiological computing system, including BCI. The biocybernetic loop describes the data processing protocol at the heart of all physiological computing systems, including BCI. The loop also encompasses the goals of the system design with respect to the anticipated impact of the adaptation on user behaviour. Par excellence, it supports the positioning of the contributions of the current grand challenge. The article by Ramirez and Vamvakousis [16] is concerned with the use of EEG classification to transform the audio properties of musical performance. In this case, the emotional responses from the performer are translated into a model of emotional states. The authors describe how EEG measures may be interpreted within an activation-valence space to describe emotional responses. The next step would be to translate those emotional responses into appropriate audio transformations, that is, audio manipulations that represent and possibly reinforce the emotional state of the performer.

A number of articles focused on the inherent challenges of stage four when the system must classify the psychophysiological data into specific categories in order to trigger a response. Plass-Oude Bos and colleagues [13] describe simple methods to improve detection accuracy after the incoming brain activity has already been classified, such as gathering additional evidence from other sources of information, for instance context, and transforming the unstable classification results to be more easy to control. They provide an overview of the different techniques, showing where to apply them and comparing the effects.

Kyrgyzov and Souloumiac [8] present an approach to improve system interaction via EEG by refining the process of artifact rejection. The EEG is especially susceptible to the influence of gross movement, such as head movement, as well as the impact of eye movement on frontal sites. This adaptive approach to artifact rejection, which involves pre-calibration of the user and independent component analysis, represents a way of reducing the number of erroneous responses from the system.

The article by de Sa [3] presents the intriguing possibility of categorizing user perceptions of what constitutes an appropriate response into the process of classification. The biocybernetic loop generally represents a mapping of psychophysiological triggers onto commands elicited at the interface, for example move up, move down. These authors argue that EEG activity could be classified into categories of intended and unintended movement; this distinction could be used to guide input control and allow the system to detect erroneous movement.

Physiological computing systems have the potential to increase the efficiency of human information processing as well as providing novel methods for communication. The article by Weiden and colleagues [20] describes how detection of the P300 component may be used to improve the classification of moving images based on rapid presentation. This technique was previously used with still images but the application of this technique to moving images is novel.

The contribution from Pope and Stephens [15] is concerned with the application of biofeedback training across individuals in order to create a collective dynamic, that is, two users collaborating either competitively or as part of a team. This paper describes how physiological responses may be aggregated and modulated on a group basis. This type of system relies heavily on the latter stages of adaptive design and evaluation. The papers presented in the Grand Challenge have focused on improvement of classification and the implementation of novel application domains.

4. CONCLUSION

This paper has focused on what we consider a grand challenge in BCI: the use of a users' physiological signals to automatically adapts HCI. This grand challenge has signif-

[1]http://www.staalhemel.com/

icant implications for BCI, HCI, HRI, HHI, as well as for neuroscience. It asks for a new definition of BCI and a (significant) adaptation of its processing pipeline (cf. [9]). HCI can be enriched in subtle ways and interactions hinting towards intelligence become within reach. Moreover, par excellence, it could provide neuroscience the means to validate its lab research in real world contexts. Hence, BCIs as intelligent sensors can add to basic knowledge on neuroscience, requires rethinking signal processing and machine learning paradigms for BCI, can enrich HCI, and, as such, yields a new landscape of BCI applications orthogonal to many of the existing ones.

If anything, this grand challenge brought, once more, to bear that a true interdisciplinary approach is required in making BCIs as intelligent sensors a success. A prerequisite for this requirement is not only close cooperation between disciplines, which yields multidisciplinary approaches, but true interest in and respect for each others theories, methods and models. Then, and only then, can true interdisciplinary research arise. If this can be achieved, the development of BCIs as intelligent sensors can and will take a leap forward.

5. ACKNOWLEDGMENTS

The authors Nijboer, Nijholt and Poel gratefully acknowledge the support of the BrainGain Smart Mix Programme of the Netherlands Ministry of Economic Affairs and the Netherlands Ministry of Education, Culture and Science.

6. REFERENCES

[1] R. Adolphs. Cognitive neuroscience of human social behaviour. *Nature Reviews – Neuroscience*, 4(3):165–178, 2003.

[2] J. L. Canteroa, M. Atienzaa, C. M. Gómez, and R. M. Salasa. Spectral structure and brain mapping of human alpha activities in different arousal states. *Neuropsychobiology*, 39(2):110–16, 1999.

[3] V. R. de Sa. An interactive control strategy is more robust to non-optimal classification boundaries. In *Proceedings of the 14th international conference on multimodal interfaces*, ICMI '12, 2012.

[4] A. Ducao, T. Tseng, and A. von Kapri. Transparent: Brain computer interface and social architecture. In *Proceedings of the SIGGRAPH 2012*, 2012.

[5] S. Fairclough and K. Gilleade. Construction of the biocybernetic loop: A case study. In *Proceedings of the 14th international conference on multimodal interfaces*, ICMI '12, 2012.

[6] J. H. Janssen, E. L. van den Broek, and J. H. D. M. Westerink. Tune in to your emotions: A robust personalized affective music player. *User Modeling and User-Adapted Interaction*, 22(3):255–279, 2012.

[7] D. J. Krusienski, M. Grosse-Wentrup, F. Galán, D. Coyle, K. J. Miller, E. Forney, and C. W. Anderson. Critical issues in state-of-the-art brain-computer interface signal processing. *Journal of Neural Engineering*, 8(2):025002, 2011.

[8] O. Kyrgyzov and A. Souloumiac. Adaptive EEG artifact rejection for cognitive games. In *Proceedings of the 14th international conference on multimodal interfaces*, ICMI '12, 2012.

[9] F. Nijboer, J. Clausen, B. Z. Allison, and P. Haselager. The asilomar survey: Stakeholders' opinions on ethical issues related to brain-computer interfacing. *Neuroethics*, pages 1–38, 2011.

[10] A. Nijholt, D. P.-O. Bos, and B. Reuderink. Turning shortcomings into challenges: Brain-computer interfaces for games. *Entertainment Computing*, 1(2):85–94, 2009.

[11] G. Pfurtscheller, B. Z. Allison, C. Brunner, G. Bauernfeind, T. Solis-Escalante, R. Scherer, T. O. Zander, G. Mueller-Putz, C. Neuper, and N. Birbaumer. The hybrid BCI. *Frontiers in Neuroscience*, 4:Article No. 30, 2010.

[12] C. L. Philippi, J. S. Feinstein, S. S. Khalsa, A. Damasio, D. Tranel, G. Landini, K. Williford, and D. Rudrauf. Preserved self-awareness following extensive bilateral brain damage to the insula, anterior cingulate, and medial prefrontal cortices. *PLoS ONE*, 7(8):e38413, 2012.

[13] D. Plass Oude-Bos, H. Gürkök, B. Reuderink, and M. Poel. Improving BCI performance after classification. In *Proceedings of the 14th international conference on multimodal interfaces*, ICMI '12, 2012.

[14] D. Plass-Oude Bos, B. Reuderink, B. van de Laar, H. Gürkök, C. Mühl, M. Poel, A. Nijholt, and D. Heylen. Brain-computer interfacing and games. In D. Tan and A. Nijholt, editors, *Brain-Computer Interfaces. Applying our Minds to Human-Computer Interaction*, Human-Computer Interaction Series, pages 149–178. Springer Verlag, London, 2010.

[15] A. Pope and C. Stephens. Interpersonal biocybernetics: Connecting through social psychophysiology. In *Proceedings of the 14th international conference on multimodal interfaces*, ICMI '12, 2012.

[16] R. Ramirez and Z. Vamvakousis. Emotion-based EEG control in music performance. In *Proceedings of the 14th international conference on multimodal interfaces*, ICMI '12, 2012.

[17] E. L. van den Broek. *Affective computing: A reverence for a century of research*, volume 7403 of *Lecture Notes in Computer Science*, pages 434–448. Berlin/Heidelberg, Germany: Springer-Verlag, 2012.

[18] E. L. van den Broek, J. H. Janssen, J. H. D. M. Westerink, and J. A. Healey. Prerequisites for Affective Signal Processing (ASP). In P. Encarnação and A. Veloso, editors, *Biosignals 2009: Proceedings of the International Conference on Bio-Inspired Systems and Signal Processing*, pages 426–433, Porto – Portugal, 2009.

[19] J. J. Vidal. Toward direct brain-computer communication. *Annual Review of Biophysics and Bioengineering*, 2(1):157–180, 1973.

[20] M. Weiden, D. Khosia, and M. Keegan. Electroencephalographic detection of visual saliency of motion towards a practical brain-computer interface for video analysis. In *Proceedings of the 14th international conference on multimodal interfaces*, ICMI '12, 2012.

[21] T. O. Zander and C. Kothe. Towards passive brain-computer interfaces: Applying brain-computer interface technology to human-machine systems in general. *Journal of Neural Engineering*, 8(2):025005, 2011.

Using Psychophysical Techniques to Design and Evaluate Multimodal Interfaces

Roberta L. Klatzky
Carnegie Mellon University
5000 Forbes Ave., Pittsburgh, PA 15217
001-412-268-8026
klatzky@cmu.edu

ABSTRACT

"Psychophysics" is a an approach to evaluating human perception and action capabilities that emphasizes control over the stimulus environment. Virtual environments provide an ideal setting for psychophysical research, as they facilitate not only stimulus control but precise measurement of performance. In my research I have used the psychophysical approach to inform the design and evaluation of multi-modal interfaces that enable action in remote or virtual worlds or that compensate for sensory-motor impairment in the physical environment of the user. This talk will describe such projects, emphasizing the value of behavioral science to interface engineering.

Categories and Subject Descriptors

J.4 [**Social and Behavioral Sciences**]: Psychology – *interface design, psychophysics, human performance.*

General Terms

Performance, Experimentation, Human Factors.

Keywords

Perception, Psychophysics, Virtual Environments, Interface.

1. PSYCHOPHYSICAL TECHNIQUES

The term *psychophysics* refers to a behavioral method in which some dimension of physical variation is submitted to people for judgment, with the goal of characterizing, as a perceptual entity, the dimension, the perceivers, or both. The term can be traced back to the mid-19th century and the work of Gustav Fechner [1]. The "physics" in psychophysics refers to the dimension itself, over which the experimenter is supposed to have tight control. The "psycho" refers to the perceptual system of the perceiver, which constrains and filters the input to further cognition and action.

Classical methods of psychophysics tackle two broad questions about perception: (i) How do perceptual channels operate near the limits of sensation? Several methods exist to measure the smallest quantity of the input that can be detected, called the threshold—or, when it is an increment or decrement that is to be sensed, the just noticeable difference (JND). (ii) At stimulus levels that are clearly above threshold, how do variations in the physical input induce variations in the perceptual outcome?

ICMI '12, October 22–26, 2012, Santa Monica, California, USA.
ACM 978-1-4503-1467-1/12/10.

The answer to this question reflects how the complexities of the perceptual channel filter, analyze, and interpret the physical quantity that is sensed. Both questions have implications not only for the perceptual outcome of stimulation, but for action, which may be directed at physical reality but is mediated by perception.

2. PSYCHOPHSYICS IN VIRTUAL REALITY

Whereas psychophysical techniques were initially developed for purposes of basic understanding of perceptual processes, they have broad utility in applied contexts. The conventional eye examination performed by an optometrist, for example, is an application of threshold measurement techniques. Applications based on virtual reality are particularly well suited to exploit psychophysical methods. Virtual reality allows the power of psychophysics to be expanded, by enabling tight control of simulated dimensions that are input to psychophysical tasks, and also by providing precise and dense behavioral measurements that go well beyond the traditional subjective judgments..

3. EXAMPLES

The combination of psychophysics and VR has considerable utility for guiding interface design and evaluation Examples of this approach can be found in my own research projects, which have addressed questions like the following: When information in one sensory modality is to be substituted for another, what is an effective mapping between the source and substitution dimensions? How do physical dimensions such as stiffness, torque, and damping interact in virtual environments, and can one dimension be used to substitute for another in in perception and action? If we want to induce a person to exert more effort, can we begin with workloads that are judged easily manageable and gradually increase effort with sub-threshold increments? Can people simultaneously process sensed forces for purposes of perceptual judgment and motor control? The practical applications to which these questions are directed include designing navigation aids for the blind, robot tele-manipulation, and rehabilitation of patients with stroke and brain injury.

The first of these questions was addressed some years ago in the Ph.D. work of Anne Murray, who investigated whether vibrotactile stimulation could be used to substitute for force sensing during tle-manipulation [2]. Her tested was a dexterous robot hand equipped with fingertip force sensors, which was controlled by a human operator who wore a data glove and wrist tracker. The positions of the robot arm and fingers were mapped directly from the operator's arm and fingers. The contact forces sensed by the robot, however, initially had no counterpart in this control apparatus. To provide feedback about contact forces at the level of individual fingers, we decided to use vibrotactile stimulators, in the form of small inexpensive speakers. How to convert forces to vibrations was then a major issue. Thus, among our psychophysical efforts were experiments to determine how vibratory amplitude and frequency, independently and together, induced a subjective impression of stimulus magnitude. Further experiments tested whether the subjective magnitude of vibrations could be interpreted as forces and used to control the robot in operations such as pick-and-place and even for direct judgments of weight. This seminal study serves as a model for the application of psychophysics to interface design and evaluation and has inspired other efforts to develop sensory substitution based on vibrotaction.

4. REFERENCES

[1] Fechner, G.T. 1860. *Elemente der Psychophysik.*. Breitkopf und Härtel, Leipzig, Germany.

[2] Murray, A., Klatzky, R. L., and Khosla, P. 2003. Psychophysical characterization and testbed validation of a wearable vibrotactile glove for telemanipulation. *PRESENCE: Teleoperators and Virtual Environments,* 12, 156-182.

Reproducing Materials of Virtual Elements on Touchscreens using Supplemental Thermal Feedback

Hendrik Richter, Doris Hausen, Sven Osterwald, Andreas Butz
HCI Group
University of Munich LMU
Amalienstraße 17, 80333 Munich, Germany
{hendrik.richter, doris.hausen, andreas.butz}@ifi.lmu.de

ABSTRACT

In our everyday life, the perception of thermal cues plays a crucial role for the identification and discrimination of materials. When touching an object, the change of temperature in the skin of our fingertips is characteristic for the touched material and can help to discriminate objects with the same texture or hardness. However, this useful perceptual channel is disregarded for interactive elements on standard touchscreens.

In this paper, we present a study in which we compared the rate of object discrimination for stand-alone thermal stimuli as well as supplemental thermal stimuli characterizing virtual materials on a touchscreen. Our results show that five materials could be discriminated at a stable rate using either stand-alone or supplemental thermal stimuli. They suggest that thermal cues can enable material discrimination on touch surfaces, which gives way for expanded use of thermal stimuli on interactive surfaces.

Categories and Subject Descriptors

H5.2 [**User Interfaces**]: Haptic I/O

General Terms

Experimentation

Keywords

thermal stimuli, material discrimination, remote tactile feedback, interactive surfaces, touch input

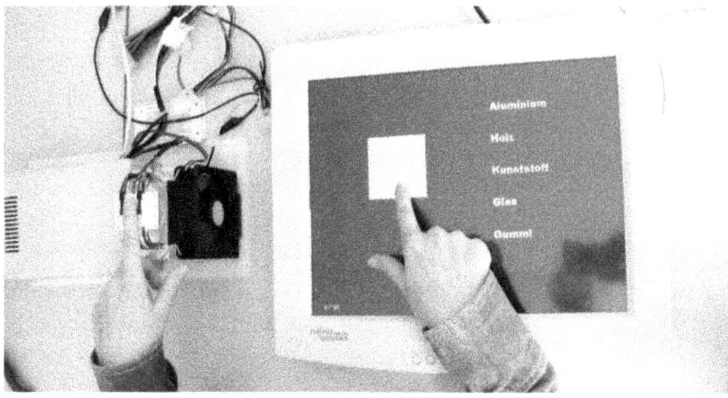

Figure 1: Supplemental thermal cues were given (left hand) to simulate different materials on the touchscreen (right hand).

1. INTRODUCTION

When we rummage in our crammed shoulder bag in order to find the car keys, we hardly use our sense of vision. Instead, we rely on our sense of touch to discriminate objects based on their texture, malleability and temperature. For objects with similar hardness and with a non-textured surface, such as metal and hard-plastics keys, it is primarily the characteristic change of temperature in the skin of our fingertips, which lets us discriminate between them.

Thermal stimulation is a rich and emotive perceptual channel, yet underused in human-computer-interaction. This especially holds true for direct touch surfaces. Touching flat and uniformly tempered screens and interactive surfaces with our fingertips or hands has become the de facto standard for interaction with digital interfaces. From mobile devices to tabletops and interactive walls, direct touch is well established because it is cost-efficient, easy to use, and allows for flexible GUI-design. However, the feedback is almost solely based on visual stimuli. Apart from ambiguous vibrotactile buzzes, no information on form, texture, function or state of the virtual input elements is provided haptically. Therefore, researchers have tried to integrate electromechanical actuators into displays to communicate state, form and function of virtual elements. This approach has shown to be greatly beneficial in terms of objective (total task time, accuracy) and subjective (user experience, naturalness) measures of direct touch interaction [3, 11, 15]. The benefits are particularly evident in dynamic multitasking scenarios such as in-vehicle or mobile touch interactions [18, 26].

However, our perception of temperature and our ability to identify and discriminate objects solely based on their thermal reaction is still underused on direct touch based interfaces. To this day, temperature feedback for the rendering and simulation of materials is not available on touchscreens. In addition to other tactile stimuli such as vibration or movement, thermal stimuli could help to make buttons and elements on touchscreens more diverse and understand-

ICMI'12, October 22–26, 2012, Santa Monica, California, USA.

able. Simulated materials such as wood or metal could be part of a touch interface and the additional thermal cues could help to reduce visual and cognitive load.

In this paper, we present the results of a user study in which we use a purpose-built remote tactile interface to simulate thermal characteristics of virtual elements on a touchscreen (see figure 1). Our results show that participants could discriminate five different materials on touch screens solely by their thermal feedback characteristics.

2. RELATED WORK

2.1 Thermal Perception

In related literature from the fields of physiology, perceptional research or HCI, the term *haptic* refers to all matters related to the sense of touch. In contrast to the *cutaneous sense*, which incorporates the skin itself including sensations of pressure, temperature and pain, the common term *tactile* is mostly used to only describe sensations of pressure [21].

Being classified as a cutaneous sense, perception of thermal cues is produced by either constant (static) or altered (dynamic) skin temperature. For *static temperatures* between 30-36°C, no thermal sensation is noted [29]. This range is called physiological zero or neutral zone, because the observer does not experience any thermal stimuli due to adaption [17]. Below 30°C and above 36°C, we perceive a constant sensation of coldness or warmth, respectively. With *static temperatures* above 45°C or below 18°C, the adaption to thermal cues is not possible and the tactile sensation of temperature is replaced by pain [28]. For *dynamic thermal sensations*, the perceived stimuli differ depending on the range of temperature. Here, for temperature changes outside the neutral zone, the increasing or decreasing skin temperatures are experienced as increasing or decreasing warmth or coolness [17]. Within the neutral zone, we perceive a rapid increase or decrease of skin temperature as static sensations of warm and cold [30]. Our perception of a material's thermal characteristics is based on these dynamic temperature changes inside the neutral zone.

2.2 Material Discrimination

Our skin temperature is ranging from 20°C to 40°C in daily activity, but typically remains between 32°C and 35°C [13]. Consequently, the temperature of our skin is usually higher than the temperature of surrounding objects. When we touch a material's surface, heat is transferred away from our skin. The resulting thermal cues are influenced by the material's temperature and the heat flux that is conducted out of the skin. These characteristics depend on thermal conductivity, heat capacity, and initial temperatures of both skin and material [10]. However, studies show that the rates of change have to be over 0.5°C/minute to be perceived at all and that there have to be large differences in thermal properties of objects for the user to perceive them [13]. For our perception and discrimination of various materials such as wood or aluminum, the perception of thermal cues is only one of many tactile stimuli providing information. Others include texture, hardness or profile [5].

2.3 Thermal Feedback in HCI

In virtual reality or telepresence, thermal feedback has been used in combination with vibration and kinesthetics in order to generate a holistic haptic sensation. Kron et al.[16] combined tactile, kinesthetic, visual and auditory feedback to support a physician's diagnosis on a virtual patient. Caldwell et al.[5] present an instrumented finger, which transmits tactile sensations from a robot to a remote operator. Dionisio [6] constructed an application with multiple forms of thermal feedback using Peltier devices[1], infrared lamps and ventilators. Thus, thermal characteristics of a virtual scenario are communicated to the user. Oohara et al.[22] suggest to use the whole body as area of application for thermal stimuli. In a recent work, Wilson et al.[30] focused on designing structured thermal feedback on mobile devices to assess how well users perceive thermal notifications on hand and forearm.

Other fields of research deal with the human ability to discriminate objects by the decrease of temperature of the human skin when touching colder materials. Caldwell et al.[5] used a purpose-built instrumented finger to sense and communicate tactile cues from a robot device to the operator. Both Ino et al.[12] and Ho et al.[10] developed stand-alone thermal displays using Peltier elements to simulate the heat flux behavior of touched objects. Their results show that materials with similar heat conductivity, such as copper and stainless steel, were often confused. However, there was no significant difference in the performance of the subjects between identifying real and simulated materials. Ino et al.[12] measured the decrease in finger temperature when in contact with the physical materials aluminum, glass, rubber, polyacrylate and wood. Then, they simulated these cues using their device. Subjects could reliably identify aluminum and wood with rates above 80%, but sometimes confused glass, rubber and polyacrylate. This could result from different individual orderings of the materials from cold to warm. We consider these findings in our evaluation (see chapter 3.2).

2.4 Tactile Feedback on Touchscreens

Touch interfaces are ubiquitously used due to their cost-efficiency, flexibility in GUI-design and ease-of-use. Touchscreens form a de facto standard for the interaction with multi-functional systems such as mobile phones or in-vehicle-infotainment systems. Still, the feedback that is coming from a touchscreen is mostly visual. The only non-visual feedback that is provided by touchscreens today mostly is a buzz from a vibrating motor or an audible beep. This reduction of multimodal information flowing from the interface to the user results in increased visual and cognitive load [18] and forms a potentially dangerous source of distraction [26].

Therefore, researchers try to utilize the users' sense of touch as an additional information channel. Tactilely conveyed information can be of very diverse nature: e.g. the form, surface structure, malleability, state, meaning, function or distance of a depicted interactive virtual element. Tactile feedback on mobile touchscreen devices has resulted in significantly more text entered per time, fewer errors made and more corrected errors [3, 11]. Other studies show that tactile feedback reduces visual and cognitive load [21, 18]. This especially holds true for dynamic scenarios entailing noise, movement, distraction, attention shifts or high cogni-

[1]These thermoelectric heat-pumps consist of two dissimilar conductors, of which one is cooling and the other is warming, depending on the direction and amount of the applied current. The effect of cooling is increased, if the heat is actively transferred away, e.g. by using a cooler fan [7].

tive load [4]. In addition, the provision of palpable stimuli on flat touch surfaces also has beneficial effects on the user's subjective impression [3, 23].

However, researchers and designers still struggle with the technical implementation of tactile actuator technology into the touch display [31]. Proposed solutions entail the movement or actuation of the screen as a whole [14, 26, 1], the segmentation of the interactive surface in individually movable actuator elements (i.e. 'tactile pixels') [8, 24] or the use of additional tangible user interfaces atop the touch display [19]. For high resolution tactile feedback, which corresponds to the visual feedback in terms of resolution and scalability, a potentially high number of single actuator elements have to be integrated into the touch device. Most feedback elements only provide one tactile stimulus, which is the same for every touching finger, this hindering from multi-touch tactile feedback. Recent approaches to provide tactile stimuli on arbitrary interactive surfaces are based on separating the area of touch (i.e. fingertip or hand) and resulting tactile stimuli on the user's body. The provision of remote tactile feedback incorporates the use of actuators in the user's direct environment or wearable interfaces. Evaluations indicate positive effects of remote tactile stimuli on user performance and subjective evaluation [20]. The notion of remote tactile feedback can also enable for the simplification of actuator design [25] and the creation of novel tactile modalities by combining different actuators on the user's body [27] . For engineers and designers of touch based interfaces with growing functionality, the incorporation of additional tactile stimuli such as pressure, movement and temperature remains fundamental [31].

However, to our knowledge, thermal cues are still underused on touchscreens as a source of information on the state of the interaction or on virtual elements. Therefore, our goal was to incorporate previous findings on how to simulate materials using defined decreases of temperature [12, 10] and to transfer these findings in order to create discriminable materials on touch-screens. Our approach could help to reduce visual load and to increase user-experience during touch interactions. With the integration of thermal cues as an additional channel of information, the interaction can be greatly enriched.

3. PROTOTYPE

The design of the thermal actuator and the characteristics of the five thermal patterns presented (aluminum, glass, rubber, polyacrylate, wood) are based on values obtained in related research projects [12, 10]. For comparability to related results, we also chose the fingertip as the area of application of the stimuli.

3.1 Thermal Actuator Device

The structure of our thermal feedback system is illustrated in figure 2. The actuator is composed of a Peltier element (29.5 x 29.5 x 4.1 mm), which is attached to a 12V cooler fan[2] with heat conducting film. Two analog temperature sensors[3] are fitted upon the Peltier module next to the touching area to measure the temperature of the heat pump. The Arduino-based[4] control element reglates the intensity and direction of the current, which drives the Peltier element. The maximum speed of cooling is around 6.2°C/s, heating works with 5.5°C/s.

For the evaluation, the thermal stimulus can be given in two ways:

1. The subject rests the index finger of the dominant hand on the Peltier actuator and the temperature decrease is given.
2. The subject touches the virtual interactive element on the touchscreen with the dominant hand, while the associated thermal material information is provided to the non-dominant hand, whose index finger rests on the actuator.

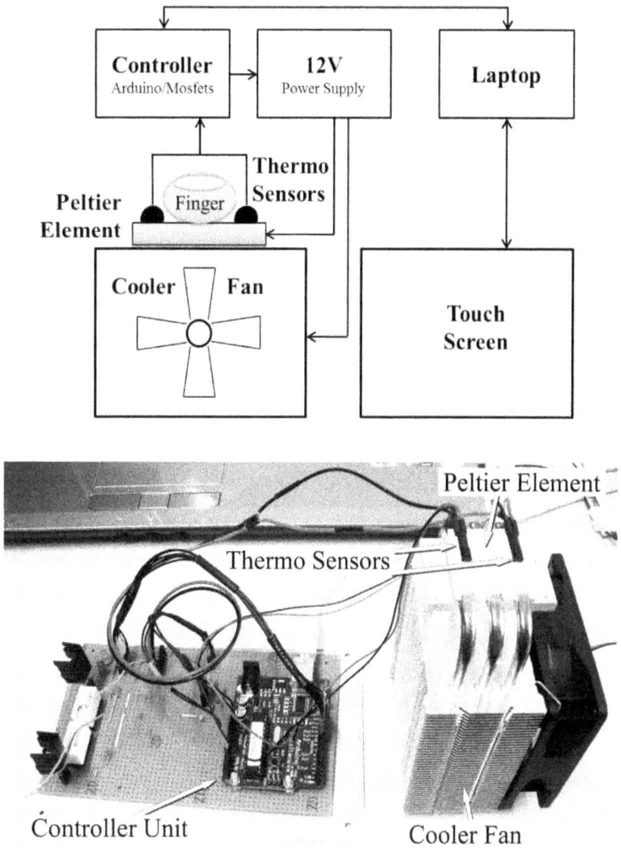

Figure 2: Schematic representation (top) and photo (bottom) of the thermal display prototype.

3.2 Design of Stimuli

The measured temperature characteristics of the finger touching the 5 materials are depicted in figure 3. For wood, a small temperature decrease of 0.1°C is needed and can be provided by our device in 500ms. For aluminum, which is the coldest material, a temperature change of -6.9°C is needed [12]. Our device is able to provide this stimulus in 3200ms when cooling down from the starting temperature of 30°C. For each material, the cooling process was preprogrammed.

[2]RR-910-HTX3-GB
[3]KTY81-210
[4]www.arduino.cc

material	ΔT	cooling time
wood	-0.1°C	500ms
polyacrylate	-1.7°C	600ms
rubber	-2.6°C	1000ms
glass	-3.1°C	1200ms
aluminum	-6.9°C	3200ms

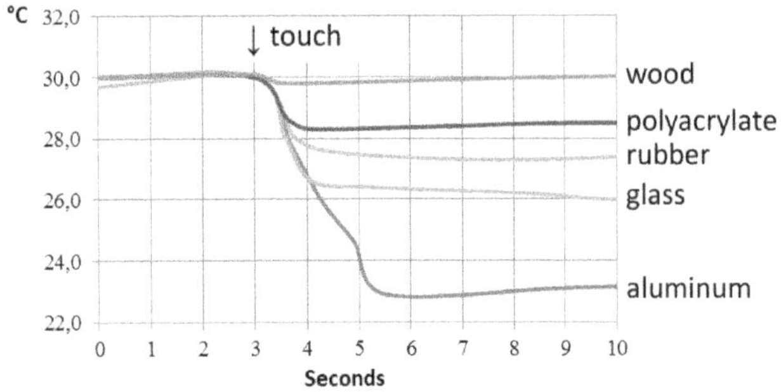

Figure 3: Measured temperature decreases (ΔT) and corresponding cooling times for the five applied temperatures (top). Resulting temperature decreases for the five materials (bottom).

4. EVALUATION

The objective of our evaluation was twofold: First, we wanted to assay whether participants were able to discriminate virtual materials using our stand-alone prototype. Second, we were interested in evaluating the participants' ability to discriminate virtual objects on touchscreens using the prototype as a supplemental tactile feedback device. In both parts of this experiment we evaluated the identification rate for five virtual materials based on predefined thermal cool-down characteristics.

4.1 Measuring Finger Temperature

According to related work, the temperature of the finger remains between 25°C to 36°C[13, 10] and is highly individual. In a preliminary evaluation, we asked 18 participants (13 male) to hold an analog temperature sensor[5] between the thumb and index finger of their dominant hand for 30 seconds (see figure 4). The results show a mean of 30.01°C (SD=2.79) and a median of 30.62°C. Consequently, we used 30.0°C as the resting temperature of the fingertip during the following evaluations.

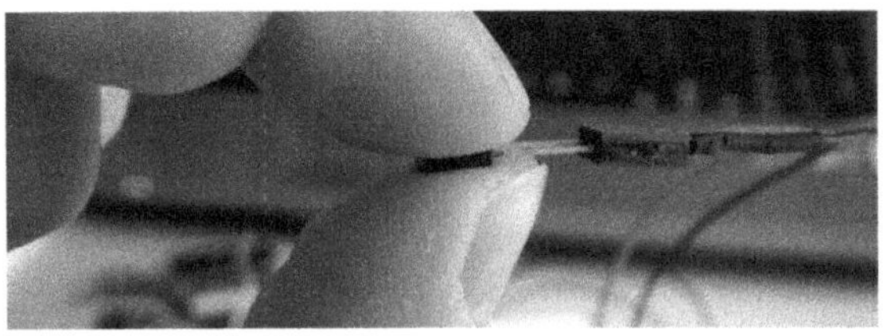

Figure 4: In a prestudy, the skin's temperature of the fingertip was measured.

[5]KTY81-210

4.2 Research Questions and Hypotheses

As stated before, the temperature decreases measured from real materials [12] served as a basis for our evaluation. The thermal feedback device and the thermal stimuli were implemented accordingly. Our main goal is to use the applied thermal stimuli to augment interactive touchscreen-elements with additional tactile information on their materiality. Hence, we formulated the following two hypotheses:

H1: Material identification by thermal cues is possible and scores are not significantly different for stand-alone and supplemental thermal stimuli (feedback on the nondominant hand resulting from a touch interaction with the dominant hand).

H2: Subjective ratings of realism, signal-design and information-transfer of the thermal stimuli are comparable for stand-alone and supplemental thermal stimuli.

4.3 Experimental Design

We used a within-subject/repeated-measures design. The independent variables were feedback location (index finger's tip of dominant hand vs. non-dominant hand) and the applied stimulus (five defined temperature changes (ΔT) for aluminum, glass, rubber, polyacrylate and wood). As the dependent variable we recorded the user's decision for a material.

4.4 Apparatus

As shown in figure 5, we used a thermal feedback device and a touch screen (capacitive single touch) for the study. The set-up was mirrored for left-handed persons. A list of the five materials was presented on the screen and was randomized for every trial.

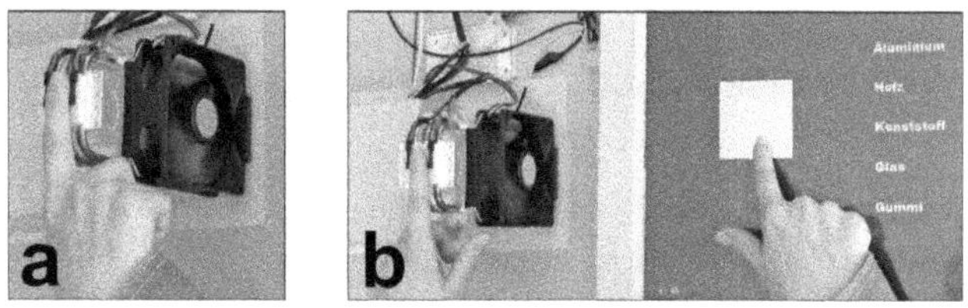

Figure 5: The two uses of the thermal display during the evaluation: (a) the stand-alone thermal display is used to present cues to the dominant hand; (b) the dominant hand interacting on the screen with the supplemental thermal display presenting cues to the non-dominant hand.

For stand-alone thermal feedback, the seated participant's index finger of the dominant hand was rested on the thermal display. Upon touch, the subject was given a thermal cue. Subsequently, the perceived stimulus had to be selected by touching the list on the touchscreen. For supplemental applied stimuli, the participant's index finger of the non-dominant hand was rested on the device and stimuli were given when the user touched the white rectangle on the screen with his dominant hand. When the participants had decided on a material, they selected it from the list. For both parts, the system measured the duration of stimulus presentation and registered the user's selection. Every material was given eleven times in a randomized sequence for every subject. In order to calibrate participants to the task, the first five selections contained each of the five materials. These selections were not measured. The order in which the two tests had to be performed was counterbalanced across subjects. Additionally, we analyzed the participants' subjective evaluation of both types of stimuli using a questionnaire. We measured the evaluation of the signal's realism, signal design and information bandwidth by adapting AttrakDiff, an evaluation method stemming from user experience research [9]. The method is originally used for measuring the user's opinion on pragmatic quality, hedonic quality and attractiveness of a product. In our experiment, participants rated the stimuli on a 7-point scale of semantic differentials, i.e. pairs of opposing adjectives.

4.5 Participants

A total number of 20 subjects (nine female) participated in the user study. They were aged from 20 to 29 (average age 24). Two subjects declared to be left-handed.

4.6 Procedure

At the beginning, the users were asked to fill out a demographic questionnaire on age, sex, handedness, diseases or finger-injury, which could affect the measurement. Next, participants were informed about the five available virtual materials (Aluminum, Glass, Rubber, Polyacrylate and Wood) and were asked to rank them from cold to warm according to their personal experience. For the stand-alone thermal feedback task, the defined temperature decrease was started as soon as the subject touched the Peltier element directly. Participants could take as much time for the decision as they wanted, but were only allowed to touch the element once for each decision. Once the subjects had decided on the material, they lifted their finger from the device and selected the perceived material from the list on the touch-screen. The experimenter made sure that there was a two-second break in order for the element to reheat to the resting temperature of 30°C. For the supplemental thermal feedback task on the touchscreen, the participants interacted on the screen with their dominant hand. Participants were asked to touch the virtual white rectangle on the screen. A synchronized thermal feedback (temperature decrease) was given and the reduced temperature was held as long as the participant touched the material. When they lifted their finger from the square on the touchscreen, the device's temperature was heated back to 30°C. The perceived material had to be selected from the list on the touch-screen. After both tasks, participants were asked to fill out the semantic differential questionnaires about the signal's realism, signal design and information bandwidth. Finally, the participants were asked in a semi-structured interview about other possible locations and uses of thermal feedback.

5. RESULTS

5.1 Material Identification

Figure 6 shows the rates of material discrimination for both stand-alone thermal stimuli and supplemental thermal feedback. For stand-alone thermal feedback, identification rates differ between individual materials. Aluminum (identification rate: 65.5%) was most reliably identified followed by glass (39.0%), polyacrylate (36.5%) and wood (33.0%), which are nearly equally well identified. Rubber was identified in only 14% of all cases. In other words, identification of rubber was worse than the chance level of 20% when selecting one material out of five, while all other materials were

	wood	polyacrylate	rubber	glass	aluminum
stand-alone feedback					
wood	**33.0**	28.5	37.0	1.0	0.5
polyacrylate	31.0	**36.5**	24.0	6.0	2.5
rubber	21.0	36.5	**14.0**	21.0	7.5
glass	16.0	23.0	11.0	**39.0**	11.0
aluminum	0.5	0.5	1.5	32.0	**65.5**

	wood	polyacrylate	rubber	glass	aluminum
supplemental feedback					
wood	**43.5**	30.0	22.5	3.0	1.0
polyacrylate	18.5	**45.5**	17.5	14.0	4.5
rubber	12.5	36.5	**10.0**	33.0	8.0
glass	10.5	21.0	9.0	**45.5**	14.0
aluminum	0.5	2.5	5.0	21.5	**70.5**

Figure 6: Identification scores ("percentage of correct identifications") for both stand-alone and supplemental thermal stimuli.

identified clearly above chance level. Looking at the results for supplemental feedback on the touch screen, aluminum is identified best (70.5%), followed by glass (44.5%), polyacrylate (45.5%) and wood (43.5%). Once again rubber is identified below chance level with 10%. Although identification means are a bit higher for all cases (except rubber), there is no statistical significant difference ($p = 0.060$) between stand-alone and supplemental feedback.

Thus, we can confirm H1.

Our results are comparable to those of Ino et al.[12] (see figure 7). However, they used a small sample of five participants whereas we incorporated 20 subjects. Our observations concerning the order of identification (aluminum was best identified, while rubber was hardly identified) is also visible in Ino's results.

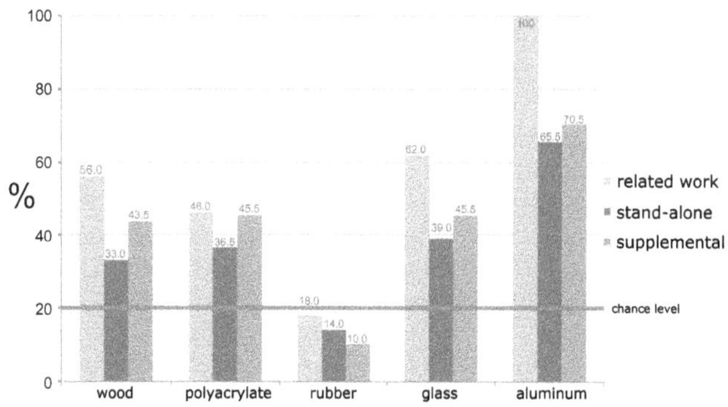

Figure 7: Identification scores in percent by related work (Ino et al.[12]), and using our standalone and supplemental setup.

	stand-alone feedback		
order	used	investigated	individual
wood	33.0	37.0	44.5
polyacrylate	36.5	31.0	40.5
rubber	14.0	36.5	48.0
glass	39.0	39.0	45.0
aluminum	65.5	65.5	78.0
average	**37.6**	**41.8**	**51.2**

	supplemental feedback		
order	used	investigated	individual
wood	43.5	22.5	32.0
polyacrylate	45.5	18.5	33.5
rubber	10.0	36.5	42.5
glass	45.5	45.5	54.5
aluminum	70.5	70.5	78.5
average	**43.0**	**38.7**	**48.2**

Figure 8: Comparison of identification scores for the material order used in the evaluation, for the investigated average order and for individual order for each participant.

In summary, we can state that we achieved stable rates of discrimination for either stand-alone or supplemental thermal feedback. Results show no significant differences between the results for directly applied stimuli and stimuli that were given to the non-interacting hand. In tendency, participants were even better in discriminating materials on touchscreens than with the stand-alone device, even though the touchscreen did not show additional information about the material.

5.2 Effect of ordering

For our analysis, we used the order of materials proposed by Ino et al.[12] (from cold to warm: aluminum, glass, rubber, polyacrylate, wood). Having asked our participants about their personal order of the materials, however, it became obvious that most users expected a different ordering. Looking at all different orders we can observe two groups of materials, generally cold materials (aluminum and glass) and generally warm materials (wood, polyacrylate and rubber). While participants' answers differ in the order of materials in one material group, no participant ordered the materials in a sequence mixing cold and warm materials. Figure 8 shows the identification rates based on the order of Ino et al.[12] we used in our evaluation (depicted by two of our participants), investigated order (averaged order based on all participants from cold to warm: aluminum, glass, polyacrylate, wood, rubber; depicted by five of our participants) and individual order for every participant. With the exception of supplemental feedback in investigated order, all identification rates increase. Our observations show the clearly individual nature of thermal material perception.

5.3 Subjective ratings

Subjects were asked to rate realism, signal design and information bandwidth of both stand-alone and supplemental

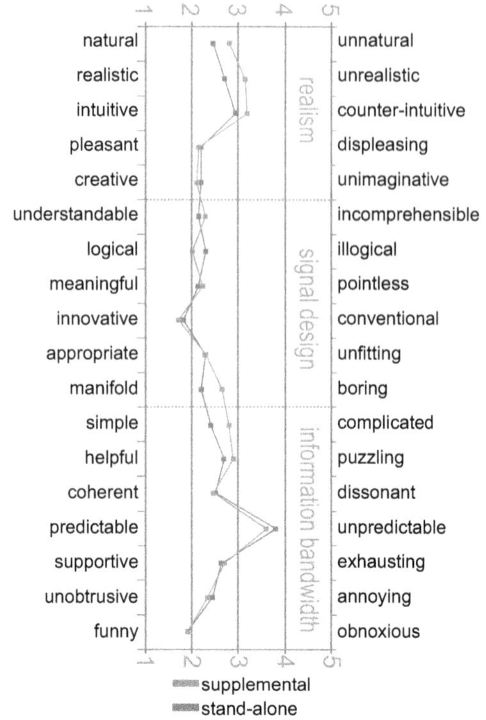

Figure 9: Average results of subjective ratings of stand-alone and supplemental thermal stimuli, positive adjectives left. Discrete values are connected for readability.

thermal stimuli on a five-grade semantic differential. The results are depicted in figure 9. Both stand-alone and supplemental stimuli were perceived as being pleasant and creative (realism); understandable, logical, meaningful and innovative (signal-design) and even fun to use (information). Ratings below 3 for thermal cues were given for being far from reality and difficult to understand (realism). Subjects also described the stimuli as being unpredictable (information). In general, the subjective ratings for both stand-alone and supplemental thermal stimuli showed no difference of more than one grade. Small differences were stated for supplemental stimuli as being less natural (realism), not manifold (signal design) and complicated in comparison to direct stimuli (information). In summary, both types of signal communication obtained similar values, thus affirming H2.

6. FUTURE WORK

We used off-the-shelf materials to implement our actuator system. Consequently, our device has certain limitations, such as the relatively large amount of energy that is needed to generate the thermal stimuli. The size of the actuator currently impedes the implementation on mobile devices. We assume that in future implementations the actuators will be smaller and the cool-down and reheating process will be faster due to improved actuator technology (e.g. higher amperage, enhanced thermal conduction). This could result in improved discrimination rates and would allow for an even greater range of discriminable materials. We will repeat our evaluation with more participants in order to gain more significant and stable results.

7. DISCUSSION

We used a supplemental actuator device to simplify the implementation of thermal cues on touch surfaces; no dedicated thermal display for every single pixel of the interactive surface is needed. Previous work has shown the potential of remote tactile interfaces to create novel haptic stimuli by combining different actuators (e.g. vibrotactile, mechanical, thermal) on the user's body [27].

It was interesting to see that the notion of remote tactile feedback did not have a negative effect on discrimination rates. Discrimination rates were even better for 4 out of 5 materials. The perception of a reference value is a possible explanation for this: When supplemental thermal feedback is given, our finger remained on the prototype, so we perceive both the active cooling and the active heating of the element. The temperature of the finger on the touchscreen did not change, thus a constant reference value was given. The nature of our receptors may have helped to detect the slight temperature changes between the index fingers of both hands [13].

We also discovered a strong effect of the personal ordering of materials in temperatures from cold to warm. When taking the users' personal estimation of object temperatures into account, the rates for detecting materials increased considerably. Some people consider aluminum to be colder than glass, while others thought it was the other way around. This documents the clearly individual nature of tactile perception and should be considered in future implementations on personal touch displays such as on mobile devices or in-car touchscreens. This could help to generate a more life-like impression of the virtual materials.

7.1 Applications

When spatially separating touch input and resulting tactile feedback, we have to incorporate the psychophysics of temperature perception and varying density of thermal receptors in the human skin. Thermal feedback can be given using wearable actuators or by instrumenting the user's environment. Better than mechanical stimuli such as movement or vibration, thermal cues can also be provided 'over a distance', e.g. using warm air jets. We can think of using the forearm, the back or thighs for thermal cues during touch interactions; e.g. by instrumenting the frame of an interactive table, the steering wheel or the driver's seat in the car.

Material Simulation.

First of all, supplemental thermal cues could be used to support the non-visual exploration of an interactive surface. Thermal cues could help to make GUI objects discriminable, thus helping to reduce visual and cognitive load. This could be especially helpful in dynamic scenarios such as mobile device interaction or the driver's interaction with touch based in-vehicle infotainment systems. Here, thermal stimuli should be used *in addition* to other tactile information (e.g. vibration, movement) representing material and surface characteristics to establish a rich and redundant representation of virtual elements.

Additional Information.

Furthermore, thermal cues could also communicate semantic information such as state, function or proximity of a virtual element. Virtual touchscreen buttons could feel hot or cold to inform the user about their important function ("Buy ticket?"). Icons of data files or applications could feel cold when not used for a long time. Being a personal and private channel of information, supplemental thermal cues are appropriate for collaborative and multi-user scenarios involving tabletops or interactive walls. The temperature of data objects could communicate its ownership ("It's hot so it's not mine!"). It is important to consider that with supplemental thermal stimuli (and user identification), an object can have different temperatures for different users. The feedback is interlinked with the user rather than the touch surface.

Thermons.

Finally, thermal cues could also be used without touch interfaces. They could serve as structured, abstract messages communicating information non-visually. Brewster et al. have established the concept of 'Tactons' or tactile icons to support users of desktop interfaces and mobile devices as well as visually impaired users with a variety of tactile information [2]. For thermal cues, a similar principle could be developed. Useful parameters are absolute temperature, rate of temperature change or total temperature difference (see chapter 2.1). We propose the term 'Thermons' for structured thermal messages or 'thermal icons'.

8. CONCLUSIONS

In summary, our results show that virtual touchscreen elements are discriminable based on thermal feedback. To a certain extent, even a simulation of materials is possible. We exemplified an easy and versatile implementation of a supplemental thermal interface. Our results will enable the future exploitation of our perception of temperature to naturalize and enrich the interaction with touch surfaces.

9. REFERENCES

[1] O. Bau, I. Poupyrev, A. Israr, and C. Harrison. TeslaTouch. In *Proceedings of the 23nd annual ACM symposium on User interface software and technology - UIST '10*, page 283. ACM Press, 2010.

[2] S. Brewster and L. M. Brown. Tactons: structured tactile messages for non-visual information display. In *Proceedings of the fifth conference on Australasian user interface - AUIC '04*, pages 15–23, 2004.

[3] S. Brewster, F. Chohan, and L. Brown. Tactile feedback for mobile interactions. In *Proceedings of the SIGCHI conference on Human factors in computing systems - CHI '07*, page 159. ACM Press, 2007.

[4] J. L. Burke, M. S. Prewett, A. A. Gray, L. Yang, F. R. B. Stilson, M. D. Coovert, L. R. Elliot, and E. Redden. Comparing the effects of visual-auditory and visual-tactile feedback on user performance. *Proceedings of the 8th international conference on Multimodal interfaces - ICMI '06*, page 108, 2006.

[5] D. Caldwell. Enhanced tactile feedback (tele-taction) using a multi-functional sensory system. *Robotics and Automation*, pages 955–960, 1993.

[6] J. Dionisio. Virtual hell: A trip through the flames. *IEEE Computer Graphics and Applications*, 17:11–14, 1997.

[7] S. Godfrey. An introduction to thermoelectric coolers. `http://www.electronics-cooling.com/1996/09/`

an-introduction-to-thermoelectric-coolers/, Sept. 1996.

[8] C. Harrison and S. Hudson. Providing dynamically changeable physical buttons on a visual display. In *Proceedings of the 27th international conference on Human factors in computing systems - CHI'2009*, pages 299–308. ACM, 2009.

[9] M. Hassenzahl, M. Burmester, and F. Koller. AttrakDiff: ein Fragebogen zur Messung wahrgenommener hedonischer und pragmatischer Qualität. In *Proceedings of Mensch & Computer 2003: Interaktion in Bewegung*, pages 187–196. B. G. Teubner, 2003.

[10] H. Ho and L. Jones. Material identification using real and simulated thermal cues. *Annual International Conference of the IEEE Engineering in Medicine and Biology Society.*, 4:2462–5, 2004.

[11] E. Hoggan, S. A. Brewster, and J. Johnston. Investigating the effectiveness of tactile feedback for mobile touchscreens. In *Proceeding of the twenty-sixth annual CHI conference on Human factors in computing systems - CHI '08*, page 1573, 2008.

[12] S. Ino, S. Shimizu, T. Odagawa, M. Sato, M. Takahashi, T. Izumi, and T. Ifukube. A tactile display for presenting quality of materials by changing the temperature of skin surface. In *Robot and Human Communication, 1993. Proceedings., 2nd IEEE International Workshop on*, pages 220 -224, 1993.

[13] L. A. Jones and M. Berris. The psychophysics of temperature perception and thermal-interface design. In *Proceedings of the 10th Symposium on Haptic Interfaces for Virtual Environment and Teleoperator Systems*, HAPTICS '02, page 137. IEEE Computer Society, 2002.

[14] T. Kaaresoja and L. Brown. Snap-Crackle-Pop: Tactile feedback for mobile touch screens. volume 6, pages 565–566, 2006.

[15] E. Koskinen, T. Kaaresoja, and P. Laitinen. Feel-good touch: finding the most pleasant tactile feedback for a mobile touch screen button. In *Proceedings of the 10th international conference on Multimodal interfaces*, ICMI '08, pages 297–304. ACM, 2008.

[16] A. Kron and G. Schmidt. Multi-Fingered Tactile Feedback from Virtual and Remote Environments. In *Proceedings of the 11th Symposium on Haptic Interfaces for Virtual Environment and Teleoperator Systems (HAPTICS'03)*, HAPTICS '03, pages 16–. IEEE Computer Society, 2003.

[17] S. Lederman and R. Klatzky. The hand as a perceptual system. *Clinics in Developmental Medicine*, pages 16–35, 1998.

[18] R. Leung, K. MacLean, M. B. Bertelsen, and M. Saubhasik. Evaluation of haptically augmented touchscreen gui elements under cognitive load. In *Proceedings of the ninth international conference on Multimodal interfaces - ICMI '07*, volume 07, page 374. ACM Press, 2007.

[19] N. Marquardt, M. A. Nacenta, J. E. Young, S. Carpendale, S. Greenberg, and E. Sharlin. The haptic tabletop puck: tactile feedback for interactive tabletops. In *Proceedings of the ACM International Conference on Interactive Tabletops and Surfaces*, ITS '09, pages 85–92. ACM, 2009.

[20] C. McAdam and S. Brewster. Distal tactile feedback for text entry on tabletop computers. In *Proceedings of the 2009 British Computer Society Conference on Human-Computer Interaction*, pages 504–511. British Computer Society, 2009.

[21] I. Oakley, M. R. McGee, S. Brewster, and P. Gray. Putting the feel in 'look and feel'. In *Proceedings of the SIGCHI conference on Human factors in computing systems*, CHI '00, pages 415–422. ACM, 2000.

[22] J. Oohara, H. Kato, Y. Hashimoto, and H. Kajimoto. Presentation of positional information by heat phantom sensation. In *Proceedings of the 2010 international conference on Haptics - generating and perceiving tangible sensations: Part II*, EuroHaptics'10, pages 445–450. Springer-Verlag, 2010.

[23] I. Poupyrev, S. Maruyama, and J. Rekimoto. Ambient touch: designing tactile interfaces for handheld devices. In *Proceedings of the 15th annual ACM symposium on User interface software and technology*, UIST '02, pages 51–60. ACM, 2002.

[24] I. Poupyrev, T. Nashida, S. Maruyama, J. Rekimoto, and Y. Yamaji. Lumen: interactive visual and shape display for calm computing. In *ACM SIGGRAPH 2004 Emerging technologies*, SIGGRAPH '04, page 17. ACM, 2004.

[25] H. Richter, B. Blaha, A. Wiethoff, D. Baur, and A. Butz. Tactile feedback without a big fuss: simple actuators for high-resolution phantom sensations. In *Proceedings of the 13th international conference on Ubiquitous computing*, UbiComp '11, pages 85–88. ACM, 2011.

[26] H. Richter, R. Ecker, C. Deisler, and A. Butz. Haptouch and the 2+1 state model: potentials of haptic feedback on touch based in-vehicle information systems. In *Proceedings of the 2nd International Conference on Automotive User Interfaces and Interactive Vehicular Applications*, AutomotiveUI '10, pages 72–79. ACM, 2010.

[27] H. Richter, S. Löhmann, and A. Wiethoff. Hapticarmrest: remote tactile feedback on touch surfaces using combined actuators. In *Proceedings of the Second international conference on Ambient Intelligence*, AmI'11, pages 1–10. Springer-Verlag, 2011.

[28] R. J. Schepers and M. Ringkamp. Thermoreceptors and thermosensitive afferents. *Neuroscience and Biobehavioral Reviews*, pages 177–184, 2010.

[29] R. Verrillo, S. Bolanowski, C. Checkosky, and F. McGlone. Effects of hydration on tactile sensation. *Somatosensory and Motor Research*, pages 93–108, 1998.

[30] G. Wilson, M. Halvey, S. A. Brewster, and S. A. Hughes. Some like it hot: thermal feedback for mobile devices. In *Proceedings of the 2011 annual conference on Human factors in computing systems*, CHI '11, pages 2555–2564. ACM, 2011.

[31] A. Wright. The touchy subject of haptics. *Commun. ACM*, 54(1):20–22, Jan. 2011.

Feeling It: The Roles of Stiffness, Deformation Range and Feedback in the Control of Deformable UI

Johan Kildal
Nokia Research Center
PO Box 407
FI-00045 Nokia Group
johan.kildal@nokia.com

Graham Wilson
Glasgow Interactive Systems Group
School of Computing Science
University of Glasgow
G12 8QQ, UK
gawilson@dcs.gla.ac.uk

ABSTRACT

There has been little discussion on how the materials used to create deformable devices, and the subsequent interactions, might influence user performance and preference. In this paper we evaluated how the stiffness and required deformation extent (bending up and down bimanually) of mobile phone-shaped deformable devices influenced how precisely participants were able to move to and maintain target extents of deformation (bend). Given the inherent haptic feedback available from deforming devices (over rigid devices), we also compared performance with, and without, external visual feedback. User perception and preference regarding the different devices were also elicited. Results show that, while device stiffness did not significantly affect task performance, user comfort and preferences were strongly in favour of softer materials (0.45 N·m/rad) and moderate amounts of deformation. Removing external visual feedback led to less precise user input, but inaccuracy remained low enough to suggest non-visual interaction with deformable devices is feasible.

Categories and Subject Descriptors

H.5.2 [**Information Interfaces and Presentation**]: User Interfaces – *Haptic I/O.*

General Terms

Design, Human Factors.

Keywords

Deformable UI, stiffness, deformation, visual feedback, kinaesthetic feedback.

1. INTRODUCTION

There has been considerable interest in developing flexible and deformable user interfaces over recent years: devices that can be bent/twisted [3, 5, 14, 20, 26, 28], compressed [17] and pressed [4, 11, 26]. However, devices that are too physically difficult or uncomfortable to flex/deform accurately are likely to produce undesirable and inaccurate interfaces. Kildal [12] has shown that increasing stiffness negatively influences preference and performance when bending and twisting a deformable device. However, it is unclear how the required extent of deformation, in isolation as well as in relation to different stiffness, may have an impact. Features such as stiffness, elasticity and deformation extent have a profound effect on our ability to tactually judge the physical characteristics of an object [1, 10, 22], suggesting that more rigid devices provide less haptic feedback concerning user input. Also, when required to apply precise amounts of force, accuracy varies depending on the target force and the way it is applied [8, 18]. In other words, bending harder devices, and having to bend them to a large extent, may result in inaccurate input. However, the effects that different physical characteristics might have on how precisely and comfortably users can deform/interact with flexible devices have not yet been considered. In this paper we focus specifically on device stiffness and the required extent of deformation to fulfill the interaction.

There has been a similar lack of research within psychophysical science on the influence of object deformation on human control of force. To our knowledge, psychophysics has focused solely on isometric force, where the manipulanda are effectively rigid. Within this research, it is apparent that providing the individual with external visual feedback concerning how much force is being applied is necessary for precise application of target forces [6, 7, 18]. While haptic feedback (both kinaesthetic and cutaneous feedback) is of some importance, it is less accurate on it's own [7, 9]. Conversely, when judging the compliance of an object, cutaneous feedback is both sufficient and necessary [1, 10, 22].

Therefore, in this paper we look to contribute to both fields of research by investigating the influences of material stiffness and the extent of device deformation on ability to precisely deform a flexible device. In order to test if the cutaneous and kinaesthetic feedback from deformation provides sufficient information for accurate input, we also compared performance when presented with and without visual feedback. We used three mobile phone-sized flexible devices, which varied only in their stiffness, and tasked users with applying and maintaining target levels of deformation, specifically bending the device up and down (applying torque) with both hands. We measured precision in maintaining target levels of deformation and gained subjective user reports on the comfort and ease of use of each device.

2. BACKGROUND

2.1 Flexible Devices

Researchers have demonstrated many different designs of partially or fully flexible devices, which can be bent, twisted or otherwise deformed due to the use of elastic or malleable materials. These manipulations then frequently recreate facsimile outcomes in digital content. Mimicking and digitizing paper-based interactions (such as folding, leafing, piling *etc.*) are most common, by using physical paper as an input method [3], or paper-like flexible sheets, which can provide facsimile digital input [15, 26]. Other flexible devices have used similar shapes but for different purposes. Gummi [20] provided bending movements to control zooming and level-transition of map and file browsing applications. PaperPhone [14] aimed to show how an entirely flexible mobile phone could be controlled by simply bending the corners, or side, of the device. While these two devices had built-in displays, Cobra [28] used a blank deformable sheet and shoulder-mounted projector for flexible mobile gaming, by bending the sides and corners of the sheet. Twend [5] allowed for similar bending gestures but had no associated display.

All of these examples required users to bend or flex a part of the given device, but the amounts of bend/flex that users are required to perform, in order to produce a recognized input, vary across devices and the materials used to make the devices are also rather different, leading to varying levels of stiffness. For a flexible device to be useable, it must be comfortable to deform, and easy to deform accurately. Lee *et al.* [15] found that users believed a more rigid plastic material would be less preferable for use as an input device, compared to more flexible paper and cloth. This study involved no actual interaction, however, Kildal found that the preferences hold when actively engaged in navigation tasks, specifically using discrete and continuous bend and twist gestures [12]. Gallant *et al.* [3] used highly flexible paper; Twend [5] did not report the limits of available flex, but used foam and thin plastic. PaperPhone [14] used thin plastic and flexible e-ink display. In contrast Wightman *et al.* [26], Tajika *et al.* [24] and Gummi [20] used seemingly stiffer plastic devices, with Gummi in particular requiring relatively high maximum force (100N).

Most of these studies included only perfunctory user testing, and Wightman *et al.* [26] and Kildal [12] are the only examples to test the influence of device flexibility. Kildal found that the stiffest device resulted in the poorest task performance and the lowest user preference. Extent of deformation is also an important variable, one that has not been considered in previous studies. A controlled study that investigates both variables together is necessary to understand the role of stiffness and deformation in performance and preference in controlled input tasks, where accuracy of input is important. Stiffer devices will require more force to produce a given amount of deformation, and requiring more force can be less comfortable and more difficult to do accurately. We hypothesised that stiffer devices, and having to deform a device by a greater extent, will result in less precise deformation, due to being more physically difficult to bend. So we sought to answer the following research questions (RQ):

RQ1: Does device stiffness influence our ability to accurately deform a device?

RQ2: Does the extent of physical deformation influence our ability to accurately deform a device?

RQ3: How do device stiffness and deformation extent influence ease, comfort and enjoyment of use?

2.2 Force Control & Active Touch

Cutaneous tactile feedback from the fingers, particularly the size and rate of contact-area spread, resulting from investigative touching of objects, provides sufficient information for an individual to judge the comparative compliance of an object relative to another [1, 10, 22]. However this is true only if the object surface is at least partly compliant. Otherwise, if the surface is rigid (even if the object itself is compliant) a combination of both cutaneous and kinaesthetic feedback (from the muscles) is required in order to judge the compliance/hardness of an object [9, 22].

While haptic (cutaneous and kinaesthetic) feedback is sufficient to judge object material properties, it is largely insufficient with regards to precisely judging the degree of force being exerted to a rigid device or manipulandum. Removing cutaneous cues degrades accuracy of applied force, which suggests cutaneous feedback is of some importance [9]. However there are marked differences in precision of applied force when comparing cutaneous/kinaesthetic feedback alone to when also presented with external visual feedback [6, 7, 18]. This suggests that, when applying force to a rigid object, we need extra feedback concerning how much force we are applying in order to do so accurately. In fact, when presented with visual feedback we may even become dependent on it, as when presented with contradictory visual and haptic feedback (concerning the stiffness of a spring) responses were biased towards the content of the visual feedback [21]. When relying only on haptic feedback we regularly over-exert (i.e. overshoot) low target forces and under-exert (undershoot) high target forces, with better accuracy at moderate forces [7-9, 18]. What constitutes "low", "moderate" or "high" forces depends on the muscles being used (e.g. pressing with finger, squeezing with hand, pushing with elbow) and the individual's ability.

This dependence on visual feedback has also been shown within HCI interfaces based on isometric force input. Reducing or outright removing visual feedback results in much lower precision of targeting interactions, across a range of devices [16, 19, 23]. Audio feedback can successfully substitute for visual feedback [27], but some external feedback remains necessary. This leads us to the final research question we sought to address:

RQ4: Is haptic feedback from device deformation sufficient to accurately maintain force output or is external feedback necessary?

2.3 Kinetic Deformable Device

Kildal [13] has described the Kinetic Deformable UI Research Prototype (DUI-RP) device (see Figure 1, left), which served as a research platform for the Nokia Kinetic Device[1] (Figure 1, right). It consists of two rigid plastic grips at either end of a central flexible/deformable body, forming a shape similar to that of a smartphone. The device is elastic and so returns to it's original, flat, shape after being deformed. A set of strain gauges within the central body can detect bending and twisting gestures, with 10 bit resolution at 200Hz sample rate. Sensor values were taken over HDMI to a custom microcontroller, which filtered and amplified the values before sending them to the host PC over USB. For the purposes of the current study we limited interaction to only bending up and down (see Figure 2). Input from the device is based on deformation of the central body, and so the interaction language was chosen based on changes in the central body. Therefore pushing the central body up (pointing the ends down) constituted bending up and pushing the central body down (pointing the ends up) constituted bending down.

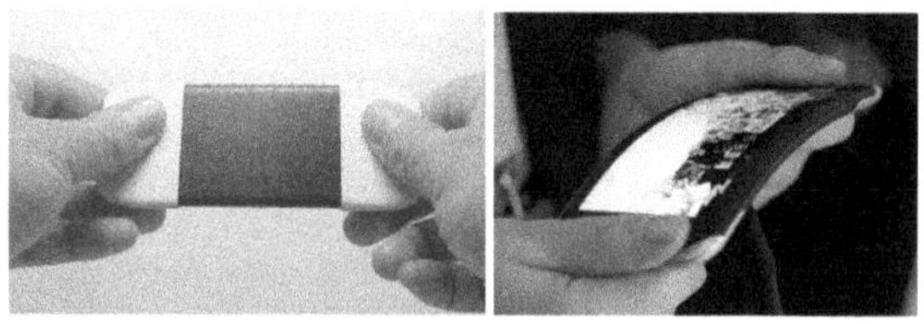

Figure 1: Kinetic DUI-RP (left) and Nokia Kinetic (right).

We used three DUI-RP devices, each aesthetically identical (as in Figure 1, left), but differing in the stiffness of the central body. The three devices, referred to here as *Soft*, *Medium* and *Hard*, had rotational stiffness of 0.45, 1.3 and 2.5 N·m/rad respectively. This

[1] http://research.nokia.com/news/12110

set of devices is equivalent to that used in Kildal [12]. As an illustrative example of the comparative stiffness, bending the *Soft* device might be like bending the sole of a beach flip-flop/sandal with the hands while the *Hard* device might be like bending the sole of a hiking boot.

3. EVALUATION

Lee *et al.* [15] identified bending as a common user-generated gesture for flexible devices, which had a high preference rating, suggesting it is a natural means of interacting with a flexible object. Bending is also a commonly used gesture in other deformable devices [5, 14, 20, 26, 28]. Therefore we also used bending as the primary interaction in our research, specifically one-dimensional, bi-directional bending. As mentioned before, participants held the DUI-RP devices at either end with both hands. Because both bending up and bending down were included in the task, we considered the neutral (flat) resting state as the starting position, with the target torque or deformation extents measured from here, both up and down.

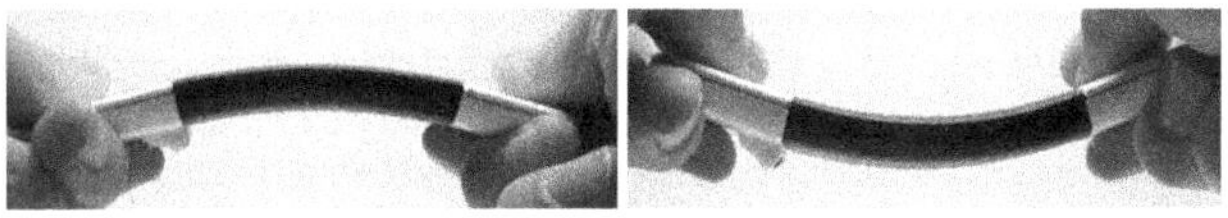

Figure 2: Bend Up Gesture (left) and Bend Down (right)

3.1 Task

A linear targeting/force-matching task was chosen as the means to evaluate the effect of stiffness, deformation extent and feedback on the precision of device deformation. This is a common task in other HCI research [16, 19] and is also very similar to force-matching tasks used in psychophysical science [6, 7, 18]. The task gives an indication as to how precisely users can apply and maintain target levels of force, by measuring the difference between the applied force and the target force (i.e. the error). Here we are applying the same process, only to levels of applied torque, or, more specifically, the extents of deformation resulting from applied torque. In our task we asked participants to maintain the target level of bend for a total of 8 seconds: 4 with visual feedback concerning the extent of bend and 4 without.

3.1.1 Feedback

The visual feedback for the task can be seen in Figure 3. In the middle of the screen is a rectangular 'parking' area indicating the neutral starting position of the device. The lines running vertically above and below parking indicate the size of the interaction space, extending from -10 to +10 in arbitrary distance units. The target bend distance to be acquired and maintained is shown as a short, horizontal line bisecting the vertical line. Bending-up targets were shown above parking and bending-down targets were shown below parking. The current extent of bend was indicated by the position of a circular cursor, which ran along the vertical line.

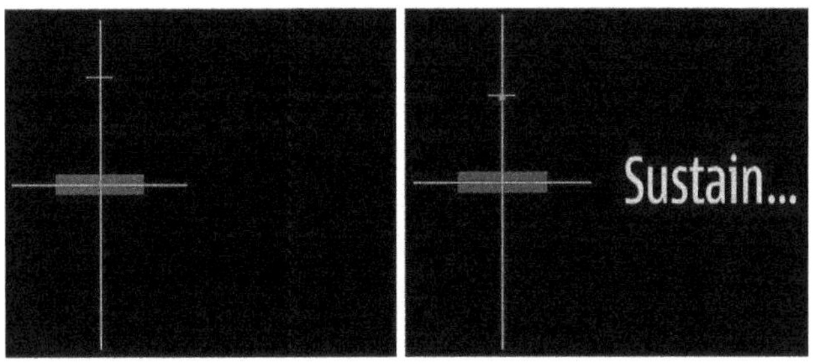

Figure 3: Task interface including cursor dot, central 'parking' area and target distance (short bisecting horizontal line).

Once the device had been bent sufficiently to bring the cursor in proximity of the target (within a distance of 0.49 of the target distance, i.e. 4.9% of the interaction space), the 'sustain' phase began. The sustain phase was split into two 4-second sub-phases: the first *with* visual feedback concerning user input and the second *without* visual feedback. During the first 4 seconds, the screen displayed the word "Sustain", as shown in Figure 3, and the *cursor remained visible*, showing the current user input. After these 4 seconds, *the cursor was made invisible* and only the word "Sustain" remained onscreen for a further 4 seconds, instructing participants to maintain bend without the cursor, until the trial ended and the participant was instructed to return to parking.

3.1.2 Mechanics of Interface Deformation

Most of the research from HCI and psychophysics concerning force input has studied linear forces (measured in Newtons in SI). Examples of this type of input include pressing or squeezing. Bending a device with two hands, however, requires that a torque or momentum (M), and not a linear force, be applied with each hand. The SI unit for a torque is Newton meters (N·m). Thus, when applying a torque in opposite direction on each end of the device, the effect obtained is that one end of the device rotates with respect to the other end. In the case of a Kinetic DUI-RP, the rigid sections on each end, which are parallel to each other in the resting position, will rotate with respect to each other an angle α after the torque is applied (Figure 2). The ratio between the torque applied (M) and the resulting deformation angle (α) is called rotational stiffness (k), which depends on the physical characteristics of the deformable body. This relationship is described by the equation:

$$\frac{M}{\alpha} = k \qquad (1)$$

This is the rotational equivalent of Hooke's Law. To investigate the effect of varying device stiffness (k) on the interaction, we kept either torque (M) or deformation angle (α) constant, and observed how the other variable was affected. Thus, we chose to run two separate studies: one where levels of torque were kept constant across devices with different k (Study 1) and one where angles of deformation were kept constant across devices (Study 2). Given the relationship shown in equation 1, each target distance in study 1 was reached by applying the same torque on each device, which resulted in different deformation extents. Conversely, in study 2, each target distance was reached by producing the same deformation angle on different devices, which required applying different levels of torque.

As mentioned, target distances through the interaction space ranged from 0 to 10 in both directions (bending up and down). 10 target distances were chosen, as other research on force-based input has found that users are able to apply this number of different force levels accurately [27]. The just noticeable difference (JND) of force production is approximately 10% [7-9, 18], so successive force levels must differ by at least 10% to be perceptually different. In the task, each target required 25% more torque than the preceding target, to increase the likelihood of making the targets feel perceptually distinct. The target distances and their expected relative torque or deformation extents (according to equation 1) are shown in Table 1 and Table 2..

3.1.3 Study 1

In the first study, the target distances were defined in terms of the required torque, which were kept constant across devices. They are shown in Table 1, along with the resulting angle of deformation across the three devices. In our measurements, the level of torque required to reach the furthest target with the *Medium* device was 10.06 N·m. In equation 1, this torque would result in a maximum angle of deformation of 7.6°. That same maximum torque value would require deforming an angle of 22.35° with the *Soft* device, but only 4.02° with the *Hard* device. The rest of target distances were also defined taking the torque required by the *Medium* device as reference. In each case, the 10 bits of sensing range on each side of the device were distributed over the complete bend range, by varying the amplification. Therefore angle resolutions for *Soft*, *Medium*, and *Hard* were respectively 0.022°, 0.007° and 0.004°, on average.

Table 1: Study 1 Target Distances, with required torque and resulting angle of deformation, across the devices.

			Angle (°)		
Target	**Distance**	**Torque**	**Soft**	**Medium**	**Hard**
1	1.2	1.35	3	1.02	0.54
2	1.5	1.69	3.75	1.275	0.675
3	1.87	2.10	4.675	1.5895	0.8415
4	2.34	2.63	5.85	1.989	1.053
5	2.93	3.30	7.325	2.4905	1.3185
6	3.66	4.12	9.15	3.111	1.647
7	4.58	5.15	11.45	3.893	2.061
8	5.72	6.44	14.3	4.862	2.574
9	7.15	8.04	17.875	6.0775	3.2175
10	8.94	10.06	22.35	7.599	4.023

3.1.4 Study 2

In the second study, the target distances were defined in terms of the required deformation angle, which are shown in Table 2, along with the torques required to reach that angle across the devices. For each target distance, the target deformation angle was set to the same angle of deformation from the *Medium* device in Study 1. This would result in *less* required torque for the same bend angle when bending the *Soft* device and *more* required torque for the same deformation angle when bending the *Hard* device.

Table 2: Study 2 Target Distances, with required deformation angle and resulting torque, across the devices.

			Torque (N·m)		
Target	**Distance**	**Angle**	**Soft**	**Medium**	**Hard**
1	1.2	1.02	0.46	1.35	2.55
2	1.5	1.275	0.57	1.69	3.19
3	1.87	1.5895	0.72	2.10	3.97
4	2.34	1.989	0.90	2.63	4.97
5	2.93	2.4905	1.12	3.30	6.23
6	3.66	3.111	1.40	4.12	7.78
7	4.58	3.893	1.75	5.15	9.73
8	5.72	4.862	2.19	6.44	12.16
9	7.15	6.0775	2.73	8.04	15.19
10	8.94	7.599	3.42	10.06	19.00

3.2 Participants & Procedure

24 participants took part, with 12 in each study. Study 1 had 9 males and 3 females, aged from 25 to 42 (mean = 37). Study 2 had 6 males and 6 females, aged from 30 to 43 (mean = 36.33). The experiment lasted approximately 45 minutes and participants were sat in a padded office chair facing a computer monitor sat on a desk approximately 75cm away. They held the devices in both hands and were allowed to rest their elbows on the arms of the chair. They were deliberately stopped from resting the device on their lap/legs, as the friction of the hands rubbing against their legs/clothes could give further tactile feedback as to how much they are bending the device. The positions of the screen and the DUI-RP were such that participants could not see the device bending during the task. We used a within-subjects design for both studies, with all participants using all three DUI-RP devices in a counterbalanced order. Within each device condition, the participant targeted and maintained 40 target distances presented in a random order: each of the 10 distances were targeted twice, in each direction (i.e. bending up and down).

Each trial started with the device in the neutral, flat position. After bending to, and maintaining, a target distance for the full 8 seconds (4 with visual feedback, 4 without), the word "release" appeared onscreen to tell the participant to stop deforming the device to allow the cursor to return to parking. The cursor became visible again upon entering parking and had to remain within parking for 2 unbroken seconds for the next target trial to begin.

The Independent Variables were: *Device Stiffness* (Soft, Medium and Hard), *Target Distance* (10 distances) and *Feedback* (Visual and Non-Visual). The Dependent Variables were: *Error* (average distance of cursor to target distance/deformation), *Variance* (standard deviation of input during the sustain phase only) and *Subjective Workload Estimation* (NASA TLX) ratings, which were taken after each Device condition. For the analysis of the *variance* and *error* data, we ignored the first 500ms of input from the beginning of the sustain phase, to minimise excess movement in the data as the participant transitioned from bending to sustaining. Subjective user reports were also elicited from a post-study interview, which included questions on the *ease of use* of each device and the *difficulty* of any aspect *of the task*; whether they *appreciated bending up and down differently* and whether they had a *preference* for any of the devices.

As some of the data did not fit a normal distribution (infrequent extreme values led to strong positive skew in the data set), we used non-parametric analyses, specifically the Friedman test for non-parametric ANOVA equivalent and Wilcoxon *T* tests for pairwise comparisons. Although the use of non-parametric tests increases the validity of results gained from non-normal data, they are limited by their inability to examine interaction effects. We also add precedence to median values, as the mean is biased by (dragged towards) the skew in the data set. Despite this, in cases where median values were near-equal yet a significant difference exists, means were also shown for illustration. For normally distributed data, ANOVA and means were used.

4. STUDY 1 RESULTS

4.1 Error

Friedman's Test showed no significant main effect of Device Stiffness on Error (χ^2 (2)=0.865, p>.05). Median Error values for each device were 0.1 (SD = 0.467), 0.105 (SD = 0.244), and 0.111 (SD = 0.263), for the Soft, Medium and Hard device respectively. Error box plots can be seen in Figure 4.

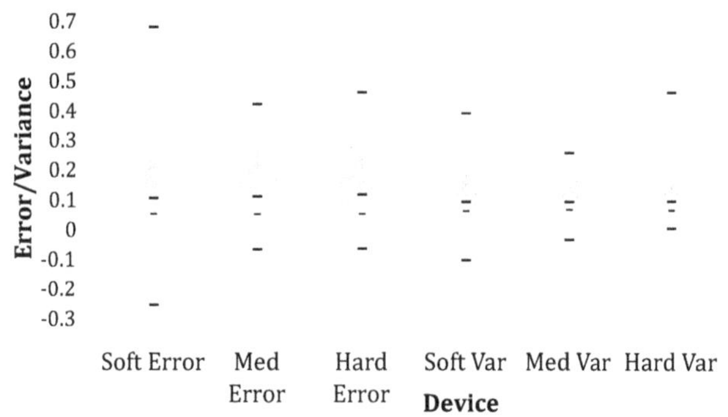

Figure 4: Box plots for Error and Variance across all three devices in Study 1 (tails show 1 SD).

Friedman's Test showed a significant main effect of Distance on Error (χ^2 (9)=27.966, p = .001). Median Error values for each

Distance are shown in Table 3. Post hoc Wilcoxon *T* tests were carried out, adjusting the required alpha for significance to p<=0.0011, and significant differences were found comparing Distance D9 with each of D1, D2 and D7; and D10 with both D1 and D2. In all cases D9 and D10 had higher Error than the others.

Table 3: Median Error and Variance for all Target Distances (TD) in both studies, with standard deviation in brackets.

	Study 1		Study 2	
	Error	Variance	Error	Variance
TD 1	0.108 (0.134)	0.065 (0.064)	0.116 (0.159)	0.062 (0.052)
TD 2	0.110 (0.189)	0.072 (0.072)	0.11 (0.165)	0.065 (0.047)
TD 3	0.091 (0.175)	0.074 (0.094)	0.127 (0.173)	0.068 (0.06)
TD 4	0.106 (0.167)	0.08 (0.119)	0.117 (0.179)	0.068 (0.038)
TD 5	0.093 (0.186)	0.085 (0.076)	0.108 (0.202)	0.077 (0.136)
TD 6	0.090 (0.235)	0.089 (0.123)	0.102 (0.169)	0.08 (0.050)
TD 7	0.103 (0.226)	0.09 (0.108)	0.098 (0.166)	0.088 (0.073)
TD 8	0.102 (0.392)	0.106 (0.180)	0.099 (0.158)	0.086 (0.057)
TD 9	0.134 (0.650)	0.115 (0.182)	0.1 (0.147)	0.091 (0.068)
TD 10	0.125 (0.555)	0.117 (0.443)	0.096 (0.151)	0.082 (0.065)

A Wilcoxon pairwise comparison showed a significant effect of Feedback on Error (T=98484.0, p<.001), as Non-Visual Feedback (median = 0.190, SD = 0.434) produced higher Error than Visual Feedback (median = 0.067, SD = 0.160). Effect size was medium to large, r = 0.49. Effect size was measured using Pearson's correlation coefficient (r), following Cohen's [2] interpretation guidelines of 0.1 for small effect, 0.3 for medium and 0.5 for large.

4.2 Variance

There was also no effect of Device Stiffness on Variance, using Friedman's Test (χ^2 (2)=0.281, p>.05). Median Variance values were 0.087 (SD = 0.246), 0.087 (SD = 0.158), and 0.089 (SD = 0.126), for the Soft, Medium and Hard Devices respectively. Variance box plots can be seen in Figure 4.

Friedman's Test showed a significant main effect of Target Distance on Variance (χ^2 (9)=281.495, p < .001). Median Variance values for each Distance are shown in Table 3. Post hoc Wilcoxon *T* tests were carried out, adjusting the required alpha for significance to p<=0.0011. Significant differences were found between multiple pairs of Distances (D): D1 vs. D4-D10 (inclusive); both D2 and D3 vs. D6-D10; D4 and D5 vs. D8-D10, D6 vs. D9, D10; and D7 vs. D8-D10. In general Variance increased as Distance increased.

A Wilcoxon *T* test showed a significant effect of Feedback on Variance (T=472866.0, p<.05). Non-Visual Feedback had a median Error of 0.083 (SD = 0.193), Visual Feedback had a median Error of 0.090 (SD = 0.174). Effect size was very small, r = 0.04.

4.3 Subjective User Reports

One-way repeated-measures ANOVA showed that Device Stiffness significantly influenced reports of subjective physical demand ($F_{2,22}$= 4.020, p<.05), however post hoc Bonferroni comparisons found no significant differences between Devices. The Medium device produced higher reports of Physical Demand (mean = 9.89) than both the Soft (mean = 8.87) and the Hard (mean = 8.92) Devices. No other TLX scales significantly varied across Devices.

"Getting to near targets was easy but maintaining them was hard, particularly with the [Soft Device]"

11 participants gave this kind of comment. They believed, sometimes for different reasons, that it required little mental or physical effort to move the cursor from parking into close proximity of the nearest targets (by bending the device), but that keeping the cursor as motionless as possible during the sustain phase was more challenging than while sustaining at further target distances. This was attributed to both the Soft device and the Hard device but for different reasons. The Soft device was difficult because being easier to bend led to unintended bending, resulting in overshooting targets at low levels, while the Hard device was difficult because, as it bent so little, it provided little to no haptic feedback concerning input and small changes in deformation angle led to large movements onscreen. In converse, it can be deduced that extra haptic feedback gained from bending the Hard device to further targets may have provided more information concerning input.

"Getting to and maintaining furthest targets was difficult"

6 participants made this, or a similar, comment about the Hard device predominantly. While the nearest targets were difficult to maintain because of too much or too little response from the device, the furthest targets were difficult to maintain due to the physical effort required in bending the devices. This suggests that the middling target distances/torque (approximately 2-6 N·m, 1°-3° rotation for the Hard device) may represent a suitable range for input on more rigid devices.

"The devices felt different but none were "difficult" "

Although a small number of participants reported that they did not notice a physical or mechanical difference between the devices, most reported that they did feel physically different, and most often in terms of stiffness. However, many reported that, although the devices felt perceptually different, they wouldn't consider any device actively "difficult" to use, only comparatively so.

When asked if they had a preference for any device, 6 (50%) said the Soft device, 2 (16.7%) said the Medium device and 1 (8.3%) said the Hard. 3 (25%) had no preference.

5. STUDY 2 RESULTS

5.1 Error

Friedman's Test showed a significant main effect of Device Stiffness on Error (χ^2 (2)=9.231, p=.01). Median Error values for each Device were 0.107 (mean = 0.163, SD = 0.174), 0.1 (mean = 0.151, SD = 0.160), and 0.112 (mean = 0.168, SD = 0.168), for the Soft, Medium and Hard Devices respectively. Post hoc Wilcoxon *T* tests, with an adjusted necessary alpha for significance of p< = 0.0167, showed that the Medium Device differed significantly from both the Soft Device (very small effect size, r = 0.05) and the Hard Device (very small effect size, r = 0.08). Error box plots can be seen in Figure 5.

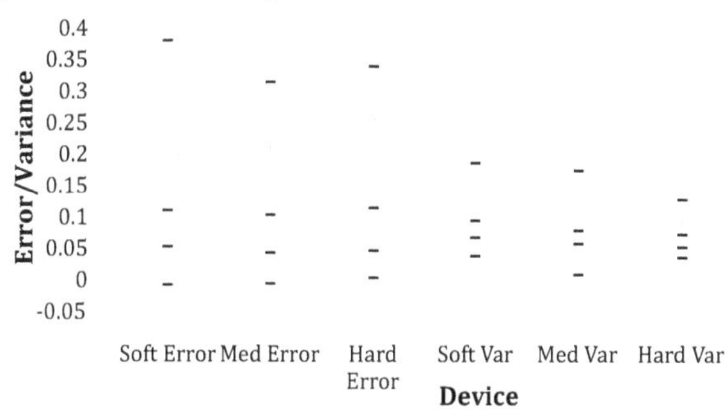

Figure 5: Box plots for Error and Variance across all three devices in Study 2 (tails show 1 SD).

Friedman's Test showed no significant main effect of Target Distance on Error (χ^2 (9)=6.626, p>.05). Median Error values for each Distance are shown in Table 3. A Wilcoxon pairwise comparison showed a significant effect of Feedback on Error (T=107563.0, p<.001), as Non-Visual Feedback (median = 0.182) produced higher Error than Visual Feedback (median = 0.064). Effect size was medium to large, r = 0.48.

5.2 Variance

Friedman's Test showed a significant main effect of Device Stiffness on Variance (χ^2 (2)=189.015, p<.001). Median Variance values for each Device were 0.091 (SD = 0.074), 0.075 (SD = 0.083), and 0.069 (SD = 0.046), for the Soft, Medium and Hard Devices respectively. Post hoc Wilcoxon T tests, with an adjusted necessary alpha for significance of p<=0.0167, showed that all Devices differed significantly from each other, with small to medium effect sizes for Medium vs. Soft (r = 0.24) and Hard vs. Soft (r = 0.3) and a small effect size for Medium vs. Hard Device (r = 0.09). Variance box plots can be seen in Figure 5.

Friedman's Test showed a significant main effect of Target Distance on Variance (χ^2 (9)=219.774, p < .001). Median Variance values for each Distance are shown in Table 3. Post hoc Wilcoxon T tests were carried out, adjusting the required alpha for significance to p<=0.0011, and significant differences were found between multiple pairs of Distances (D): both D1 and D2 vs. D5-D10 (inclusive); D3 and D4 vs. D6-D10; and D5 and D6 vs. D9. In general Variance increased as Distance increased.

Wilcoxon T test showed a significant effect of Feedback on Variance (T=468340.0, p=.001). Non-Visual Feedback (median = 0.079, mean = 0.096) appears to have produced more Variant input than Visual Feedback (median=0.076, mean=0.088). Effect size was very small, r = 0.06.

5.3 Subjective User Reports

One-way repeated-measures ANOVA showed that Device Stiffness significantly influenced reports of subjective physical demand ($F_{2,22}$= 4.434, p<.05), however post hoc Bonferroni comparisons found no significant differences between Devices. Reports of Physical Demand decreased as Device Stiffness decreased, with mean values of 10.25 (SD = 5.36), 8.33 (SD = 3.87) and 6.17 (SD = 3.21) for the Hard, Medium and Soft Devices respectively. No other TLX scales significantly varied across Devices.

"Maintaining furthest targets requires a lot of effort", "the [Hard Device] was hard"

The frequency of this comment and the language used in Study 2 suggest it was a more noticeable issue than in Study 1, although mainly with the Hard device, as well as the Medium device to a lesser extent. In order to reach the furthest targets from parking, a lot of physical effort was needed. Interestingly, in spite of the increased effort, there were conflicting comments on the ease of use, with some believing the Hard device was easier to control, and others believing it was more difficult to control. Whereas it may be more physically challenging to deform, relative changes in deformation angle would have led to less cursor movement than with other devices, providing a more stable input.

"The [Soft Device] felt very sensitive"

In a similar manner to Study 1, the Soft device proved more challenging to maintain nearer targets, due to requiring very little amount of bending, a complaint leveled at the Hard device in Study 1. In fact, the Soft device was frequently considered sensitive in general, with very small changes in input/deformation angle resulting in large changes in cursor position on screen. This made targeting difficult across a wider range of targets, not only the nearest ones to parking, and especially when no visual feedback was present.

In terms of user preference a similar pattern to Study 1 emerged: 5 (41.67%) preferred the Soft device, 3 (25%) preferred the Medium device and 2 (16.67%) preferred the Hard device. 2 (16.67%) had no preference.

Table 4: User preferences for each device, in both studies.

	Soft	Medium	Hard	None
Study 1	6 (50%)	2 (16.7%)	1 (8.3%)	3 (25%)
Study 2	5 (41.67%)	3 (25%)	2 (16.67%)	2 (16.67%)

6. DISCUSSION

6.1 Device Stiffness

The first Research Question (RQ) we sought to answer in this paper was: *"Does device stiffness influence our ability to accurately deform a device?"*. If we consider only the quantitative data and results, it would appear that the answer is generally "no", stiffness did not have a strong impact on user performance, at least concerning the range of material stiffness we used (i.e. 0.45 N·m/rad, 1.3 N·m/rad and 2.5 N·m/rad). There were no significant differences between devices in precision of control when the range of required torque was kept constant in Study 1. Therefore, within the range of 1.35-10.06 N·m, greater or lower device stiffness did not hamper user ability, but neither, it seems, did the potential extra haptic feedback from more physical deformation of the device lead to better performance (remember Soft > Medium > Hard in maximum deformation angle in Study 1).

Regarding Study 2, when the range of deformation angle was kept constant, even though there were statistically significant differences between devices in terms of both Error and Variance, the practical differences were very small. Median Error values were near-equal and median Variance and mean Error values varied by only 0.01-0.03, less than 1% of the interaction space. Therefore, considering only performance and the stiffness ratings used here, device rigidity does not appear to be an important factor. These results echo those from Kildal [12], where small performance differences were found between device stiffness.

However, focusing on participants' subjective reports provides more illuminating information, and goes some way to answering half of *RQ3: "How [does] device stiffness...influence ease, comfort and enjoyment of use?"* An important aspect of our investigation into deformable device design was user perception and preference. In both studies, these did not support equality across the devices, as was suggested by the quantitative results. In Study 1 the majority of participants reported that the devices felt perceptually different in terms of their stiffness, and the significant effect of Device on TLX reports of Physical Demand reinforce this subjective distinctiveness. These participants tended to report similar benefits and liabilities for the Soft and Hard devices. They generally felt that the Soft device was physically easier to bend (and so move the cursor) but that this very softness made it more difficult to maintain a constant angle of bend. Conversely the Hard device was more difficult to bend (particularly to large angles) but that it was easier to maintain target forces.

The common report that none of the devices was considered challenging to use supports the equal quantitative results. However, the subjective opinions, and the finding that 6 (50%) participants expressed preference for the Soft device while only 1 (8.33%) preferred the Hard, suggest that physical comfort and low effort may be more important to users than high precision in deformable device design, a finding that supports Lee *et al.*'s [15] assertion that users naturally prefer softer manipulation devices.

A similar trend emerged from Study 2, where the Hard device required a much larger range of torque values (therefore requiring more effort), but the Soft a much smaller range. In this case stronger negative comments were made about the Hard device, in terms of the physical discomfort, backed up by TLX ratings of Physical Demand, which increased as device stiffness increased. Meanwhile the Soft device was considered by some to be overly sensitive leading to difficulty in maintaining precision across a range of targets. Despite this difficulty, 5 (41.67%) participants still preferred the Soft device, with only 2 (16.67%) preferring the Hard. The Hard device had the lowest Variance of all devices in Study 2 but, again, it appears that physical comfort trumps precision.

Interestingly, there were a small number of hedonic/experiential comments made about the Soft device, such as "the [touch] experience felt nicer" and "more forgiving" and "engaging". These kinds of comments were not made about the Medium or Hard device, so it appears that softer deformable devices are more likely to provide enjoyable and approachable deformable interfaces. Given the apparent trade-off between comfort/physical effort and precision, there is likely to be a balance or compromise, perhaps in the guise of the Medium device, whose stiffness and control gained few negative comments but whose praises were rarely sung as well. At least in our case, a stiffness of 1.3 N·m/rad may be suited to an input range of approximately 1-10 N·m (1°-8° of deformation). Previous focus groups during development of the kinetic DUI-RP also elicited preference for the Medium device for very similar reasons as described here.

Many of these results echo those of Kildal [12]. He also found small performance differences between devices of different stiffness, accompanied by a perception that none of the devices were difficult to use. Participants in that study also strongly preferred softer devices (due to the higher effort levels required to bend the hard device) even though the soft device led to occasional control issues. The congruence of results strongly supports the notion, also put forward by Lee *et al.* [15], that softer devices are more suitable for deformable interaction, although the softest devices may not be optimal from the point of view of perceived sense of control.

6.2 Deformation Range

In answer to *RQ2, 'Does the extent of physical deformation influence our ability to accurately deform a device?'*, there was a pronounced effect of target distance/deformation angle on performance measures. There was no effect of distance/angle on Error in Study 2, however in terms of Error in Study 1 and Variance in both studies, precision of input dropped as the deformation angle increased. In other words greater extents of bend were generally more difficult to apply and maintain accurately. This difficulty was echoed by subjective user comments, which addresses the second half of *RQ3: 'How [does]...deformation extent influence ease, comfort and enjoyment of use?'*.

A point to note is that, even though more comments were made about the difficulty in targeting using the Hard device in Study 2, angle/distance did not affect Error in this study. Even though the Hard device was physically harder to bend, the reduced gain/sensitivity in Study 2 may have made precise targeting easier. Despite the general decrease in precision with increasing target distance, participants also complained at finding the nearest targets difficult to maintain using the Hard device in Study 1. Research has suggested that the Just Noticeable Difference for rotation at both the wrist and elbow joints is 2°C [25], which is likely to be larger than the extent of rotation required to reach the nearer targets. In this case the individual would have had more difficulty in judging the extent of applied torque due to the small differences between targets. As mentioned above, maintaining near targets was also difficult with the Soft device, as high flexibility led to unintended changes in input.

Therefore deformable devices, particularly those made from materials more rigid than perhaps ~2.0 N·m/rad, may do well to require only moderate extents of bend, approximately 1°-3° (with each hand) in our case, in order to support precision and comfort. In contrast, devices made from soft materials (0.45 N·m/rad here) are recommended to require bends greater than approximately 3° (per hand). As user preference for the Soft device testifies, allowing more comfortable interactions may result in more engaged users.

6.3 Feedback

In line with previous HCI and psychophysics research [6, 7, 16, 19], removing visual feedback concerning the extent of input led to significantly higher Error and Variance (although the effect of Variance was weak). From these results it appears that the cutaneous and kinaesthetic feedback gained form bending the device was insufficient to maintain a target force as precisely as when presented with external feedback. One pattern of behaviour is interesting and worthy of note. Recall that proceeding from the visual feedback phase to the non-visual feedback phase is similar to traditional force-matching tasks, where the participant has to judge the magnitude of an externally specified target force and match it with an internally generated force magnitude. The increase in Error without visual feedback was much larger than the increase in Variance, and so it appears that removing visual feedback makes it more difficult to match an abstract externally dictated target force/angle (Error), but maintaining an internally generated force/angle (Variance) is perhaps easier.

Given these results, the answer to *RQ4, 'Is haptic feedback from device deformation sufficient to accurately maintain force output or is external feedback necessary?'* might appear to be a strong "no", however it might depend more on the definition of "sufficient". While the Error more than doubled under non-visual feedback and Variance also suffered, the 'real world' differences were still small, at around 3% of the interaction space. Therefore it is not unreasonable to suggest that eyes-free input on deformable devices such as the Kinetic DUI-RP is feasible, as long as the interaction includes suitable error margins, such as the width of a target. However, our research here did not look at "from-0" non-visual interaction, where the participant would have to move to a target deformation extent from rest/parking with no visual cues at all. This task would better indicate whether eyes-free interaction is possible.

Although there were statistically significant differences, it was surprising that device stiffness [1, 10, 22] and feedback did not have strong real-world influences on control. However it may simply be that the range of stiffness used was not wide enough to significantly influence performance, as we did not have a truly rigid device or a particularly loose device. The comparable performance may also be a product of the task, as non-visual maintenance of a target bend was from a visually-supported position: they simply had to avoid excess movement. Larger performance differences may have been apparent if the task had provided little or no visual feedback, to require participants to rely more on haptic feedback. With these in mind, future work should test a wider range of material stiffness and 'from-0' non-visual interaction with deformable devices, to get a better perspective on whether stiffness and deformation extent truly influence performance, or simply influence user preference. The use of more realistic tasks would also be of benefit, as the task used here was abstract and highly controlled.

7. CONCLUSIONS

This paper presented two studies using a mobile phone-shaped deformable device: Kinetic DUI-RP. It looked at how the device stiffness and the required extent of deformation influenced user precision and preference in a force-matching/targeting task. The purpose was to identify if design materials or interaction requirements might result in inaccurate or undesirable deformable interfaces. It also tested the influence of both external visual feedback and the inherent haptic feedback gained from bending a deformable device by requiring participants to match forces with- and without visual feedback.

It found that, while the range of material stiffness used did not markedly influence performance, user preference was strongly influenced and suggested more rigid/stiff materials were less desirable as they were uncomfortable to bend beyond 3° or 4° per hand, with soft materials allowing for a more comfortable and engaging interface. Also very small (<1° per hand) deformations were difficult to maintain accurately using both soft and stiff materials, so should also be avoided. The removal of external visual feedback resulted in significantly more error-prone control, but performance remained good enough to suggest that haptic-only non-visual interaction might be feasible for deformable devices.

8. REFERENCES

[1] Bergmann Tiest, W.M. & A.M.L. Kappers. Cues for Haptic Perception of Compliance. *IEEE Transactions of Haptics*, 2009. 2: p. 189-199.

[2] Cohen, J. A Power Primer. *Psychological Bulletin*, 1992. 112(1): p. 155-159.

[3] Gallant, D., A. Seniuk, & R. Vertegaal. Towards more paper-like input: flexible input devices for foldable interaction styles. *Proc. of UIST 2008*, p. 283-286.

[4] Hennecke, F., F. Berwein, & A. Butz. Optical Pressure Sensing for Tangible User Interfaces. *Proc. of ITS 2011*, p. 45-48.

[5] Herkenrath, G., T. Karrer, & J. Borchers. Twend: twisting and bending as new interaction gesture in mobile devices. *Proc. of CHI 2008 Extended Abstracts*, p. 3819-3824.

[6] Hong, S., A. Brown, & K. Newell. Compensatory properties of visual information in the control of isometric force. *Perception & Psychophysics*, 2008. 70(2), p. 8.

[7] Jones, L. Visual and Haptic Feedback in the Control of Force. *Experimental Brain Research,* 2000, 130, p. 269-272.

[8] Jones, L. & I. Hunter. Force Sensation in Isometric Contractions - A Relative Force Effect. *Brain Research*, 1982, 244(1), p. 186-189.

[9] Jones, L. & E. Piateski. Contribution of tactile feedback from the hand to the perception of force. *Experimental Brain Research*, 2006, 168, p. 298-302.

[10] Kaim, L. & K. Drewing. Finger force of exploratory movements is adapted to the compliance of deformable objects. *Proc. of Eurohaptics 2009*, p. 565-569.

[11] Kildal, J. Evoked Friction on a Smooth Touch Device. *Proc. of CHI 2011 Extended Abstracts*, p. 2233-2238.

[12] Kildal, J. Interacting with Deformable User Interfaces: Effect of Material Stiffness and Type of Deformation Gesture. *Proc. of HAID 2012*, p. 71-80.

[13] Kildal, J., S. Paasovaara, & V. Aaltonen. Kinetic Device: Designing Interactions with a Deformable Mobile Interface. *Proc. of CHI 2012 Extended Abstracts*, p. 1871-1876.

[14] Lahey, B., A. Girouard, W. Burleson, & R. Vertegaal. PaperPhone: Understanding the Use of Bend Gestures in Mobile Devices with Flexible Electronic Paper Displays. *Proc. of CHI 2011*, p. 1303-1312.

[15] Lee, S., S. Kim, B. Jin, E. Choi, B. Kim, X. Jia, D. Kim, & K. Lee. How users manipulate deformable displays as input devices. *Proc. of CHI 2010*, p. 1647-1656.

[16] Mizobuchi, S., S. Terasaki, T. Keski-Jaskari, J. Nousiainen, M. Ryynanen, & M. Silfverberg. Making an impression: force-controlled pen input for handheld devices. *Proc. of CHI 2005*, p. 1660-1664.

[17] Murakami, T. & N. Nakajima. DO-IT: deformable object as input tool for 3-D geometric operation. *Computer-Aided Design,* 2000, 32, p. 5-16.

[18] Newell, K. & P. McDonald. Information, coordination modes and control in a prehensile force task. *Human Movement Science*, 1994. 13(3-4), p. 375-391.

[19] Ramos, G., M. Boulos, & R. Balakrishnan. Pressure widgets. *Proc. of CHI 2004*, p. 487-494.

[20] Schwesig, C., I. Poupyrev, & E. Mori. Gummi: a bendable computer. *Proc. of CHI 2004*, p. 263-270.

[21] Srinivasan, M., G. Beauregard, & D.L. Brock. The impact of visual information on the haptic perception of stiffness in virtual environments. *Dynamics Systems & Control*, 1996. 58, p. 555-559.

[22] Srinivasan, M. & R. LaMotte. Tactual discrimination of softness. *Journal of Neurophysiology*, 1995, 73(1), p. 88-101.

[23] Stewart, C., M. Rohs, S. Kratz, & G. Essl. Characteristics of Pressure-Based Input for Mobile Devices. *Proc. of CHI 2010*, p. 801-810.

[24] Tajika, T., T. Yonezawa, & N. Mitsunaga. Intuitive page-turning interface of e-books on flexible e-paper based on user studies. *Proc. of Multimedia 2008*, p. 793-796.

[25] Tan, H., B. Eberman, M. Srinivasan, & B. Cheng. Human Factors For The Design Of Force Reflecting Haptic Interfaces. *Dynamic Systems & Control*, 1994. 55, p. 353-359.

[26] Wightman, D., T. Ginn, & R. Vertegaal. BendFlip: Examining Input Techniques for Electronic Book Readers with Flexible Form Factors. *Proc. of INTERACT 2011*, p.117-133.

[27] Wilson, G., S.A. Brewster, M. Halvey, A. Crossan, & C. Stewart. The Effects of Walking, Feedback and Control Method on Pressure-Based Interaction. *Proc. of MobileHCI 2011*, p. 147-156.

[28] Ye, Z. & H. Khalid. Cobra: flexible displays for mobile gaming scenarios. *Proc. of CHI 2010 Extended Abstracts*, p. 4363-4367.

Audible Rendering of Text Documents Controlled by Multi-Touch Interaction

Yasmine N. El-Glaly
Computer Science
Virginia Polytechnic Institute and State University
Blacksburg, VA 24061, USA
yasmineg@vt.edu

Francis Quek
Computer Science
Virginia Polytechnic Institute and State University
Blacksburg, VA 24061, USA
quek@vt.edu

Tonya Smith-Jackson
Industrial and Systems Engineering
Virginia Polytechnic Institute and State University
Blacksburg, VA 24061, USA
smithjac@vt.edu

Gurjot Dhillon
Industrial and Systems Engineering
Virginia Polytechnic Institute and State University
Blacksburg, VA 24061, USA
gurjotsd@vt.edu

ABSTRACT
In this paper, we introduce a novel interaction model for reading text documents depending on situated touch. This interaction modality targets Individuals with Blindness or Severe Visual Impairment (IBSVI). We aim to provide IBSVI with an effective reading tool that enables them to use their spatial abilities while reading. We used an iPad device and augmented it with a static tactile overlay to display the text to serve as a kind of spatial landmark space for the IBSVI. The text is rendered audibly in response to user's touch. Two user studies, with IBSVI participants, were conducted to test the system. The first study was a laboratory-controlled study, and the second one was a longitudinal study. These studies showed that while the approach is new to the users' experience, it is a promising direction to enable self-paced spatial reading for IBSVI.

Categories and Subject Descriptors
H.5.2 [**Information Interfaces and Presentation**]: User Interfaces – *interaction styles, auditory feedback.*

K.4.2 [**Computers and Society**]: Social Issues – *assistive technologies for persons with disabilities.*

General Terms
Algorithms, Design, Human Factors, Standardization, Theory.

Keywords
Audio Rendering, Touch Device, Finite State Machine, Multi-Touch Interaction, Spatial Cognition, Blindness, Reading, Assistive Technology

1. INTRODUCTION
In this paper, we present a novel approach to assist IBSVI users to read text documents by fusing the words touched on a slate-type device with TTS-generated speech. Our Situated Touch Audio Annotator And Reader (STAAR) uses an Apple's iPad as the vehicle to provide IBSVI with the spatially grounded cognitive information that is implicitly and explicitly embedded in the page/document organization of text. Our approach in STAAR is to enable IBSVI to access spatially laid out text through audio rendering of text (word, or line) as the slate screen is touched. A PDF file is loaded and graphically rendered on an iPad. This provides a spatial mapping of the words on the page displayed to the spatial real-estate of the iPad surface. As words on the iPad screen are touched by the user's finger, they are fed to a Text To Speech (TTS) synthesizer [1] that renders them into audible speech. A page description module models the words and text lines on the page. By tracking the user's touch on the iPad and comparing the touch location to the objects in the page model, our system determines which word the user is touching. After detecting the touched word, a Finite State Machine (FSM) algorithm decides if the word should be sent to the TTS. The whole system is dynamic and responsive to each touch of the user to give her instantaneous audio feedback. To help IBSVI move horizontally and keep track of their location on the iPad screen, we augmented the iPad screen with a plastic overlay that has tangible landmarks, as illustrated in Figure 1. The overlay is composed of a vertical ruler at the left margin, a set of horizontal and vertical lines in the 'reading area', and haptic control buttons at the bottom. Although the tactile pattern is static, it can provide the user with the opportunity to map out the space on the iPad surface. The goal is not that the tactile patterns will directly show the structure of the underlying pages – obviously it cannot. Rather, the tactile patterns provide a kind of landmark grid that IBSVI may appropriate to maintain spatial grounding for the document being read. As the IBSVI moves her fingers over the tactilely adorned surface, the words (and sounds) associated with the touch locations are sounded, so that the IBSVI is able to create a spatial index of what is read. Hence, the tactile patterns help to ground the user's mental model of how information is located and organized in the document being read. This mental model serves as a dynamic and persistent reference to enable the IBSVI user to interact more efficiently and effectively with the textual material.

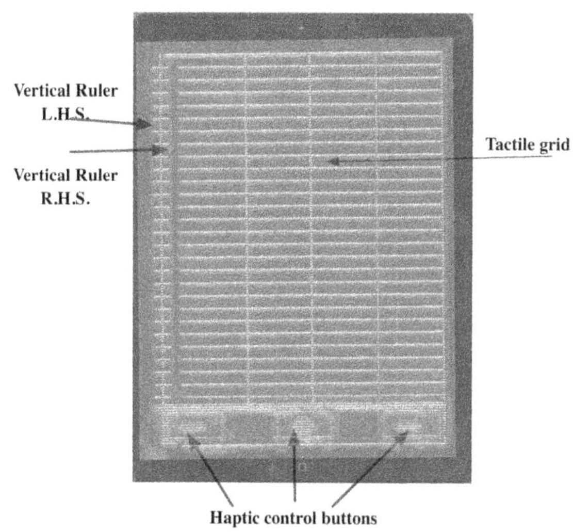

Figure 1. Our tactile overlay on the iPad surface.

2. MOTIVATION

Modern learning and psychology research shows that visual-spatial access [2, 3] is critical to reading of typographical information. Page layout, spacing, and paragraph structure are designed to help sighted readers to keep place while reading, and to revisit critical pieces (e.g., to answer the question "Now, who is the person from whom they got the quote?") The capacity for rapid random access to such page-based information is built right into the very structure of how information is organized in our culture. IBSVI currently have access to reading materials in either Braille or Audio formats. Braille books have limitations because of its weight and non-portability. Moreover, 90% of IBSVI in USA are Braille illiterate according to the American Federation for the Blind [4, 5]. Electronic audio books address these problems as they provide IBSVI with portability without the need to learn Braille. But audio books are sequential in its nature and so they lack spatial indexing. Re-finding a previously read word is difficult even if it exists within the same page because the unsighted user will have to go through the whole page again. Screen readers such as JAWS or Voice Over do not provide IBSVI with enough spatial information [6, 7]. Jaws is a screen reader and does not give the user a sense of information encoded in spatial layout. Voice Over technologies are designed more for screen interaction, and not continuous reading, Our system essentially provides the tactile and spatial support to make Voice-over-type technologies suitable for continuous reading. Moreover, reading is a highly cognitive process requiring simultaneous access to both words and the construction entire sentential units [8], and that can explain why reading Braille activates IBSVI's visual cortex [9]. In sum, reading media are designed for sighted people where they can use visual clues to reacquire recently read piece of information. The ways these media are adapted to be used by IBSVI suffer from linearization that loads IBSVI with the burden of highly depending on their working memory to acquire and keep contextual information. By studying the literature, we found that employing multimodal systems had leveraged accessibility of various interfaces for IBSVI. For example, a group of researchers conducted series of studies to achieve a usable design of accessible multimodal media center for both IBSVI and low vision users [10]. They combined gestures, speech, and haptic feedback as models of interactions. Another study in [11] showed that earcons and speech synthesis could be used in video annotating for IBSVI. The accessibility issues of large touch screens were nicely addressed in [12]. In this paper, we present a novel reading system that enables IBSVI to read spatially. The system is developed on the iPad platform to make use of its tactile and speech capabilities. Our system integrates and fuses these two powerful modalities to achieve our research goals. The critical goal of our approach is to enable IBSVI read with the same self-pacing that individuals with sight have when reading a text.

3. APPROACH

We present a reading system that is composed of five modules: text renderer, audible page mapping, multi-touch handling, reading finite state machine, and speech modeling. Together, the five modules determine which word(s) on the screen is touched by the user and sends this word(s) to the TTS, which in turn speaks it aloud. The development of this system involved two design-test cycles. In the first cycle, we developed an early prototype and engaged a small group of IBSVI consultants to test and give suggestions on the design. The key goals were to explore the interface layout that includes the structure of the tactile overlay, the layout of text to be read, and other general interface design issues. Using the lessons learned from the first cycle, we improved on our prototype, and engaged 16 IBSVI to test different combinations of layout configurations, text layout (i.e., our page model), and overall interaction design. The following describes the design motivated by these two cycles.

3.1 Text Document Renderer

The text document renderer is the most fundamental part of our system. It is the module that renders a PDF document into set of accessible chapters, pages, and words on the iPad. All information about the document size, page size, and bookmark are extracted at this level of the system. Most importantly, text renderer is responsible for representing each page of the targeted document in a format that is accurate enough to be tracked by touch. The idea is to convert a page of text into a set of geometric objects so that each object can be handled independently in case of discrete touches. At the same time, these objects can be computationally grouped for handling continuous touch in real time.

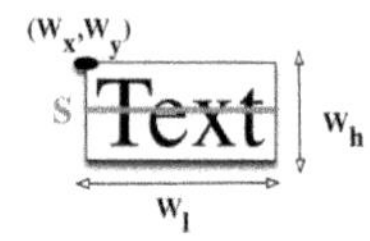

Figure 2. Graphical transformation of a word to segment.

The text renderer scans all the words (W) in page (P) and transforms each word into a segment (S) using the following mathematical model:

— , i={1,..,n} Eq. 1.

where x and y are the coordinates of the top left corner of *W's* bounding box, h and l are the height and length of W respectively, and n is the number of words per page. An illustration of a word's graphical representation is shown Figure 2. We make an exception to this representation for words of one character length such as "I" and "a". A word that is composed of one letter is combined with its successor to form one segment instead of two segments. For example, [Mary has a basket] a sentence of 4 words is rendered by the text renderer into 3 segments: ["~~Mary~~" "~~has~~" "~~a basket~~"]. The reason of merging very small words with the following word is to extend the region of interaction for these small words and consequently facilitate reading by touch for IBSVI. In addition to rendering the text for each page word by word, the text renderer module calculates the "Hot Spots" in the page. A Hot Spot (HS) is the area that corresponds to a whole line of text with an upper and lower margin of 1 point. The margin is added to handle minor differences in words' midlines that occur in some cases, such as when using big and small font at she same line. However, if the difference in words' midlines at the same line is greater than the margin value, the hot spots will not be accurate or complete.

— , i={1,..,n}

Eq. 2.

The reason we pre-calculate Hot Spots is to support smooth reading as the user moves her finger continuously along the line and also to support an additional interaction for speed reading in case the user prefers to read the whole line with a single discrete touch (see Section 3.3.1). Returning to our example: [Mary has a basket], the Hot Spot in this case will look like this: [▬ ~~Mary has a basket~~], where the thin black lines mark the midline of the words and the thick line is the Hot Spot. In summary, the text renderer module transforms each page of text to sets of segments (words representations) and hot spots (line representations). This model could be applied to any language e.g. Arabic or Japanese, as we model words by spatial occupancy and connectivity irrespective of direction or length. The TTS must be changed for different languages.

3.2 Audible Page Mapping

When a sighted person opens a page in a book to read she can see where the lines of text are and can start reading from the start of the line to the end of the line till she finishes reading the whole page. The Audible Page Mapping module of our system conveys this spatial information to BSVI users, in the form of white spaces and end of line information. Given the location of all words per page via the text renderer module, this module furnishes an audible mapping of the page sematic information on the iPad screen. A vertical audible margin is developed at the left of each rendered page. As the user moves her finger along the left margin, she hears a short click whenever she encounters a line of text. This helps the IBSVI user find lines of text easily and accurately.

However, finding the vertical position of line is not enough for smooth reading. Another important information that needs to be conveyed to BSVI users is where white space appears on the page. We chose another audible feedback to represent white space. When the user's finger encounters white space, she hears a sound evocative of a finger rubbing against rough paper. Knowing the presence of empty space helps IBSVI, for example, to find paragraph separations, and page margins, and to contextualize space-separated titles. The bottom of the screen is reserved for control buttons. The user can use these buttons to browse the document by page or by chapter. The intent is that the whole screen of the iPad is responsive and informative to BSVI users. Figure 3 illustrates the page mapping where 90% of the screen space is occupied by text; only 10% of the screen size is used for the vertical margin and the control buttons.

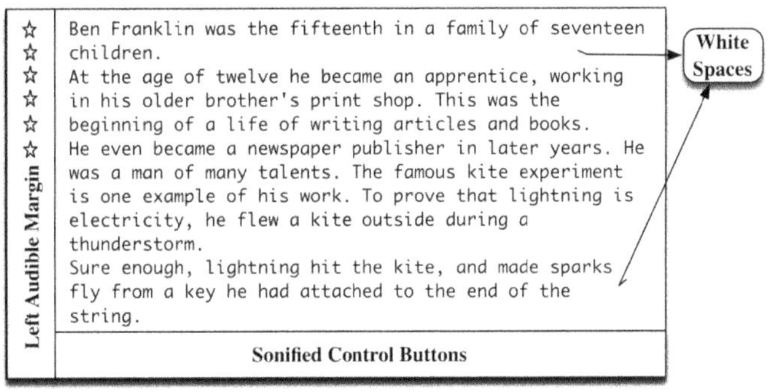

Figure 3. Audible page mapping on iPad screen.

3.3 Multi-Touch Interaction Handling

In this system, we handle two types of touch: reading touch and control gestures. Reading touch refers to a set of touch-configurations that can be used for reading text. Control gestures are the gestures that are used for browsing the document and navigating between pages. Each touch is handled by our system to serve the different modes of interactions that can be initiated by a BSVI user.

3.3.1 Reading Touch-One Touch Interaction

In order to read a single word in a page, the user can simply touch the word. When a single touch is detected, the system determines the closest word represented by its line segment. The distance of a touch point from a word is computed as its distance from the finite line as illustrated in Figure 4. Applying a simple inner-product computation, we determine if the touch point is within the projection of the finite line. If it is, d(C,S) is computed, else the closer of d(A,S) and d(B,S) is distance of the touch point from the line. Additionally, the user can move her finger horizontally from left to right to read a line of text continuously. Further details of how the system interprets the continuous touch are explained in

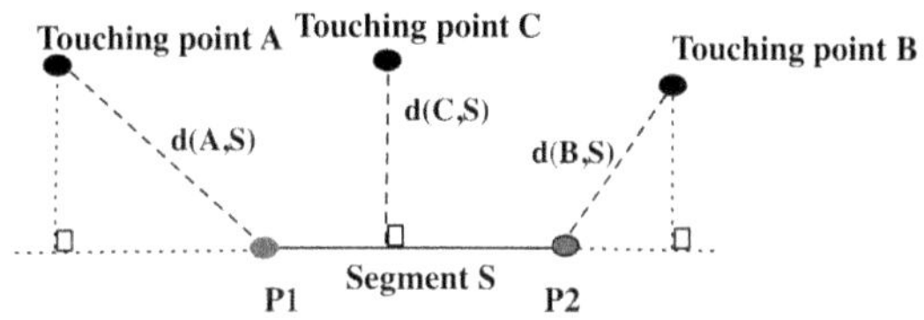

Figure 4. Distance between a segment and a touching point.

Section 3.3.2. Beside single discrete touch and continuous touch, the touch interaction module gives the user the facility to read the whole line at once if the user touches the same location on a text line twice. This gesture is equivalent to double tap for sighted users. When this occurs, the system determines the text line (each associated with a Hot Spot) closest to the touch, and sends the entire line to the TTS to be rendered to speech. To stop reading, the user can issue the 'stop reading touch gesture' by touching the screen with four fingers and then lifting them.

3.3.2 Reading Touch-Multi Touch Interaction

In our pilot studies, we found that IBSVI found it hard to keep place with only the 'reading finger' on the iPad screen. They often need a secondary touch point for spatial reference. This module is responsible for handling two general cases of multi-touch: intended multi-touch and non-intended multi-touch. Figure 5 shows IBSVI using STAAR and interacting with multiple touches.

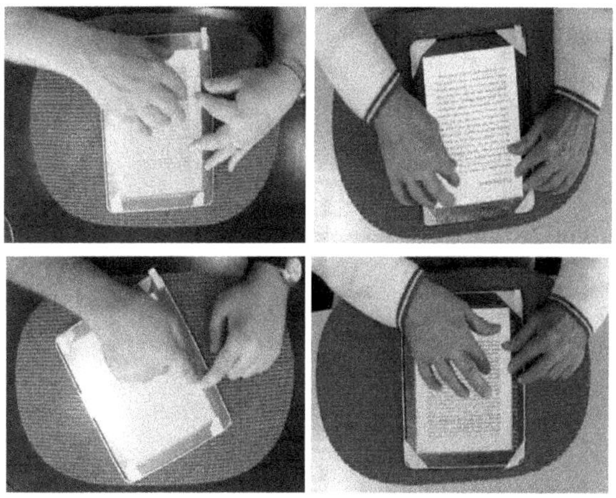

Figure 5. Different multi-touch interactions.

Intended multi-touch is when the user is aware of using more than one touch to read one word or one line. There are three cases of intended multi-touch:

1. The user is resting her palm on the bottom area of the iPad screen and read, with a moving finger, a line at a point higher up on the iPad screen. In this case, the multi-touch interaction module tracks the moving finger and ignores the detected touch that is below the moving finger (Figure 5. top left).
2. The user moves one finger from left to right for reading and moves another adjacent finger that trails the reading finger to the left. As the module detects both touches, it activates the words touched by the most right touch and ignores the touch by the most left touch (Figure 5. top right).
3. The user uses her left hand to move up and down on the left margin, while her right hand moves from left to right on the

text lines. In this case, the system will generate the audible icon of line finding only once when the user hits a text line on the left margin. This will be followed tracking the rightmost finger and sending the touched words to the TTS (Figure 5. bottom left).

Non-intended multi-touch is when the user assumes she is touching the iPad screen with only one finger while she is actually touching the screen with more than one finger (Figure 5. bottom right). That is usually happens when the user has a shaking hand and she accidently touches different points on the screen, or when the user is holding the iPad with one hand and reading with the other hand and then the holding hand accidently touches a point on the active area of the iPad screen. In this case the system will track the consistent finger movement from left to right and ignores any other detected touches. To accomplish this, the module keeps a record of previous touches. If one of the current touches is close to the previous touch, it will be set as the reading point and the other touches will be treated as noise.

3.3.3 Navigational Control Gestures

In order to provide a multimodal interaction for IBSVI, we augmented the haptic buttons on the plastic overlay with gestures. We have appended three virtual buttons beneath the reading area for document navigation. The buttons are used for navigating the rendered document by page and by chapter. These 3 buttons are not typical buttons; they are actually regions that can be entered with a moving touch from outside the region. When a finger first enters the button region, the button label is announced audibly. A second touch with a momentary lifting of the finger activates the button. The rationale for this design is that IBSVI cannot see the button to tap it. Audible announcement of the button on first touch is needed to initiate the interactive task. Hence, we designed control gestures that treat virtual buttons as zones that can be tapped or moved into by the user. The first touch to any of the buttons zones will trigger the button's name similar to the "VoiceOver" function. The second touch to the same button zone will activate the button's function following by announcing the page number of the page moved-to. Speaking aloud the number of the new page gives the user an instantaneous audio feedback, which informs her with her current location in the document.

Alternatively, users can use gestures in the reading area without having to search for the buttons. Swiping with three fingers from left to right will take the user to the next page. Swiping with three fingers from right to left will take the user to the previous page.

3.4 FSM Reading Algorithm

The length of an ordinary English word is in average 4.5 letters [13]. Such words cover a space of 0.5 inches in length. When a user moves her finger from the starting location of the word to its end, she will cross about 100 touching points inside this word. If the system simply speech synthesizes the closest word to the user's touch every time she crosses a word, she will hear the same word repeatedly.

We developed a finite state machine reading algorithm to solve this problem. The diagram shown in Figure 6 illustrates the finite states of a touched word and whether the touched word will be activated or not. A word that is touched by a user will be sent to the TTS or not depending on two variables: history of read words and context of touch. If the user touches a word for the first time, the word will be spoken aloud. If the user continues moving inside the word, the word will not be spoken. However, if the user lifts her finger of the screen and touches the same word again, the history will be cleared and the word will be spoken aloud.

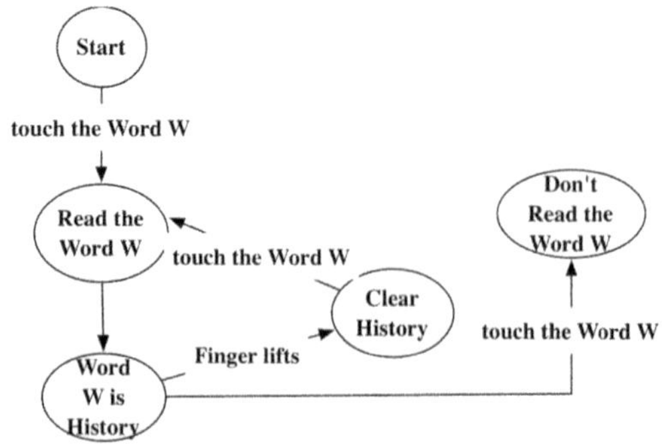

Figure 6. Finite state machine of reading words.

3.5 Speech Modeling

We started designing our system by the idea of sending all touched words to the TTS. A buffer was created to save an ordered list of touched words according to the timing of the touch. Our early user tests with the system revealed a flaw in this approach. When the IBSVI traverses the iPad surface beyond the maximum TTS speech render speed, her reading finger will be distantiated from the word currently spoken. However, she does not know this and may keep moving farther ahead of the system, filling the buffer with yet more words. At some point, she becomes lost and disoriented as the words she hears have little relation with her touch reading activity. The graph in Figure 7 represents the average duration needed by TTS to speak a set of words of average length each, 4.5 letters, and the average time taken by IBSVI to move her finger along the same words in one continuous touch.

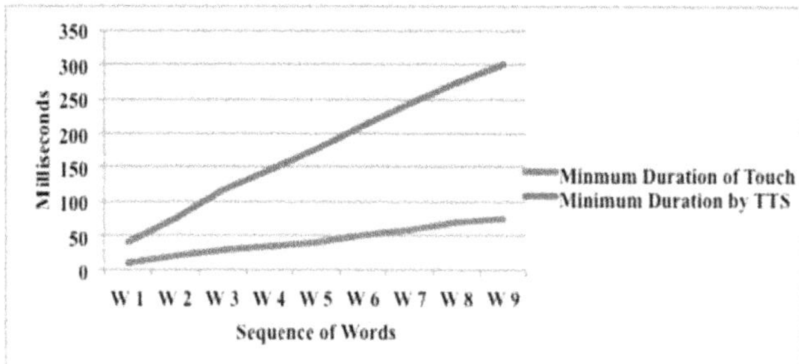

Figure 7. Timeline of touch-speech interaction.

Our current solution is to remove the buffer and to simply read the word that is the user is currently touching. If the user leaves the word that is currently being sounded, and moves into a second word, the first word will complete and the next one will be sounded while the touch is still in this second word. If however, the touch passes through to the third word before the original word is completed, the second word will be elided, and the third word will be sounded because the finger is touching the third word. To inform the user that a word is elided, our system initiates a click sound of 10 milliseconds duration long. The user then can make her decision to either go on and read the rest of the line or go back to read the previous word. The advantage of this interrupting speech technique is that the IBSVI can always know the location of the word in its spatial context. In addition, BSVI user is in control of the reader system, if she wants to read word by word she can move her finger at the appropriate speed. If she wants to jump over the words she can move her finger quickly and she will hear the first couple of letters if it is a long word followed by the click sound, or she will hear only the click sound if the word is too short.

4. STUDY

We designed STAAR with the hypothesis that IBSVI can engage spatial text access by touching and moving their fingers over the iPad screen. This involves the IBSVI actively fusing the activity of spatial touch with rendered speech through TTS technology. But to what extent this is possible? How many words per line can be tracked by the user's finger? How many lines per page can be read by touch without any visual feedback? What is the time needed to read a whole page with a finger? How frequent might the user wander between lines? Does the overlay have any influence on the accessibility of text for IBSVI? Our studies are designed to answer these questions.

4.1 Methodology

We employed two studies. Study 1 was a standard one-shot user study. The system used for the study had no page audio mapping (Section 3.2) except for the white space audio feedback. Also, the speech modeling was in the buffer mode (Section 3.5). The results we obtained from the first study lead to changes in the audio feedback design of STAAR for both the speech and the page semantics sounds. The full audible page mapping was implemented in addition to the speech interruption model. A follow up study with the new audio features was then employed. The second study (Study 2) was a longitudinal study where we provided the technology and reading material to five IBSVI participants for a period of two weeks.

Later, Ponyboy and Johnny talk about killing Bob, and both of them cry out of fear and shock as they discuss the experience. They comfort each other and go back to sleep. When they wake up, both boys feel more relaxed and level-headed. Ponyboy says to Johnny, "We ain't gonna cry no more, are we?" Several days pass. The boys entertain themselves by playing poker and reading aloud from Gone with the Wind. Johnny admires the Southern gentlemen in the novel and says that they remind him of Dally. When Ponyboy doesn't understand, Johnny tells about a time when Dally took the blame for a petty crime committed by Two-Bit. Ponyboy now understands Johnny's deep admiration for Dally, but still feels intimidated by Dally's intensity. One morning, Ponyboy and Johnny watch the sunrise. As they lament that the sunrise's beauty doesn't last, Ponyboy recites the poem "Nothing Gold Can Stay," by Robert Frost. They agree that the poem captures just what they feel, though Ponyboy can't explain the poem's meaning in words. Johnny comments that Ponyboy has made him see the beauty of nature more than he ever had before, and he notes how different Ponyboy is from the other members of his family. #

When Ponyboy gets home, Darry is furious at him for losing track of time and arriving so late. Sodapop tries to intervene, but Darry silences Soda and, losing control, slaps Ponyboy. Darry is immediately remorseful and tries to apologize, but Ponyboy runs out of the house before his brother can say anything. The park is deserted.

As Johnny and Ponyboy walk and talk, the blue Mustang suddenly appears. Bob, his friend Randy, and three other Socs jump out of the car. All of them are drunk. Johnny, terrified, pulls out his switchblade and Ponyboy wishes he had the broken bottle. Bob insults greasers by calling them white trash with long hair. Ponyboy, furious, responds that Socs are white trash with mustangs and madras (plaid) shirts, and spits at the Socs. The Socs attack. One forces Ponyboy's head underwater in a nearby fountain. Ponyboy blacks out. When he comes to, the Socs are gone and he's on the pavement next to Johnny and Bob's dead body. Johnny says, "I killed him."

Johnny's switchblade is covered in blood. Ponyboy panics, but Johnny is calm. He decides that they should go to Dally for help. They find Dally at a party at the house of Dally's rodeo partner, Buck Merril. When he learns what's happened, Dally gives them warm clothes, fifty dollars, a loaded gun, and directions to a hide-out in an abandoned church in the small rural town of Windrixville. He asks Ponyboy if Darry and Sodapop know what happened. Ponyboy tells him not to say anything to Darry. #

Figure 8. Example of "Large" and "Small" page size.

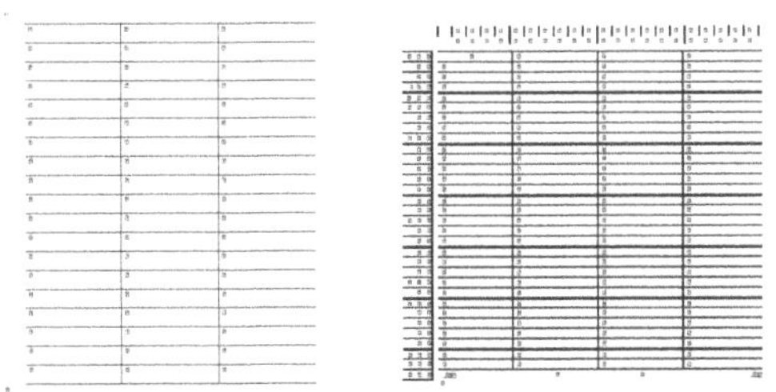

Figure 9. Left is the widely spaced overlay (A), right is the densely spaced overlay (B).

We built STAAR using Objective C, and ran it on iPad 2 with operating system iOS 5.1. We rendered two types of pages of text, which were compiled by MSWord. The first type was written in Arial font with size point equal 14 (Small size), and the second was written in Arial font with size point equal 20 (Large size). An example of a Large and a Small page is shown in Figure 8 at left and right respectively. The Small and the Large pages had 1.5 line spacing. The top, bottom, left, and right margins were set to 1.0 in both Small and Large pages. In order to examine the effect of the overlay on the system accessibility, we designed two overlays: one with wider spacing (Overlay A), and one with denser spacing (Overlay B) as shown in Figure 9. The number of horizontal lines in former overlay is 20 and the distance between the horizontal lines is 0.4 inch. For the denser overlay, the number of horizontal lines is 31 and the distance between them is 0.25 inch.

4.2 The IBSVI Participants

For Study 1, we recruited 16 IBSVI with the help of a local community group. The participants' ages ranged from 34 to 91, with mean age of 69 (*SD* = 33.3). Nine participants were females and 7 were males. Three participants were born blind, 4 participants had total blindness and 8 were legally blind. Six of the participants could read Braille and 15 participants preferred audio as a reading medium. For Study 2, we recruited 5 IBSVI. Participants' ages ranged from 27 to 77 with a mean of 51 (*SD*=18.9). Three participants were females and 2 were males. Four participants had total blindness and 3 of them were born blind. All participants could read Braille.

4.3 Study Description

At Study 1, and at the first meeting with the IBSVI participants of Study 2, the below procedure was followed:

Two researchers met each participant individually. Each participant was first introduced to the iPad and then introduced to STAAR. The researchers gave a page of text on the iPad to the participants to read in order to familiarize themselves with the system. The researchers helped the participants and gave them directions when needed. This familiarization session took between 5 to 10 minutes. Then, each participant was asked to read another page; Large page or a Small page. The Large page has an average number of lines = 21, average number of words = 178, and average number of characters without spaces = 872.5. The Small page has an average number of lines = 24, average number of words = 235, and average number of characters without spaces = 1126.67. The iPads were augmented with either the widely spaced overlay or the densely spaced overlay. The order by which the page type and the overlay type were given to the participants was counterbalanced. During the tasks (reading sessions), the researchers gave no help to the participants. Participants were asked to complete the task independently. At the end of the reading task, each participant was asked 3 questions related to the article she read, and the answers were reported.

At the end of both Study 1 and the end of the second week of Study 2, a semi-structured interview was then conducted to evaluate the overall reading experience using STAAR. The tasks were audio and video recorded for later analysis. During the entire meeting with each of the recruited participants, the researchers observed, took notes, and wrote down the participants' comments. After the conclusion of the sessions of Study 1, the researchers reviewed the observation notes and video and audio recordings to understand how the features of STAAR were used during task execution and how it did or did not help participants to accomplish their goals. We extracted a set of critical incidents from the videos, the incidents were chosen for the goal of answering the research questions stated at the beginning of this section, and to give us insight about the interaction modeling and the interface of the system. A description and an abbreviation for the critical incidents are given in Table 1.

Table 1. Critical incidents extracted from the videos.

Critical Incident	Abbreviation	Description
Whole Line	WL	A whole line of text was read successfully.
Longest Sequence of Words	LSW	The longest sequence of words that was read successfully.
Skip Line	SL	The user skipped a line while moving from line to line.
Wander Between Lines	WBL	The user while reading a line accidentally read the line above or below.
Repeat Same Line	RSL	The user read the same line more than once in a row.

5. DISCUSSION

We divided our discussion into 3 parts. First, we present the results of the studies explained in section 4, and propose answers for the text density questions. Second, we presented our analysis to the users experience for the system as a whole. Finally, we present a comparison between the Braille page and STAAR page in terms of text density.

5.1 The Study Results

There were several missing data points in Study 1. Each participant went through 8 different study conditions (condition A-H). The variations across the trial were fixed (with buffering) or variable (without buffering) speech rate. She was given either overlay A or B over large or small text. Of the total conditions, only two conditions A (fixed speech rate, overlay A, Large text) and E (fixed speech rate, overlay B, Large text) had at least eight observations for most data points to make meaningful comparisons. A Wilcoxon Sign Rank test was used to compare conditions A and E on total knowledge transfer, time (in minutes), mental demand, and frustration ratings. The differences were not significant. Figure 10 illustrates the means for each performance measure (knowledge transfer and time) across all conditions. Figure 11 illustrates mental workload ratings for mental demand and frustration (possible values = 0 to 21). Although no inferential tests could be conducted, upon examination of the data, it was apparent that the fixed speech rate/overlay B/large text yielded the highest knowledge transfer and the fastest response time. However, in terms of mental demand and frustration ratings, the controlled speech rate/overlay A/large text and fixed speech rate/overlay B/small text combinations produced the lowest ratings (perceived ease of use in terms of mental workload).

In Study 1, the researchers observed that the participants were able to operate STAAR to read most of the assigned pages. However, they were not able to answer most of the article-related questions correctly. Further analysis of the knowledge transfer scores was needed to obtain an understanding of these observations. We divided the participants' responses into three categories: correct answers, wrong answers, and no answers. The "No answer" response is the category that includes responses such as: "I do not know" or "I can not remember." By analyzing the responses of the 16 participants, we found that the percentages of correct, wrong, and no answer answers, were 25.35, 39.24, and 35.41, respectively. To better understand the reasons behind these low knowledge transfer results, we decided to analyze the recorded videos. We focused our analysis on 5 participants' videos. Two participants (P01 and P03) reported "no answer" for all the questions. Two participants (P02 and P05) reported relatively high percentage of correct answers, and one participant (P04) reported all her answers wrong. Additionally, in video analysis of Study 1, two researchers coded the critical incidents as described in Table 1. Figure 12 shows the number of occurrences of critical incidents for each of the 5 participants. The abbreviations used in the chart legend are the same as described in Table 1. The first two critical incidents (reading a whole line without errors and longest sequence of read words without errors), are considered incidents of success, while, the other three incidents are considered incidents of no success.

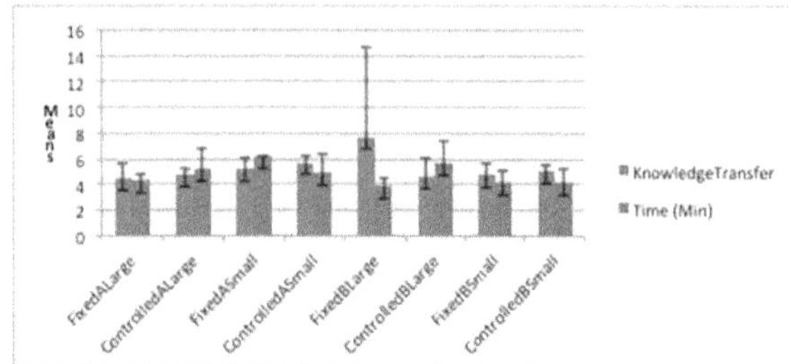

Figure 10. Means and standard deviations of performance variables. The median is shown for the performance time for fixed speech rate, overlay A, small condition due to the size of the variance.

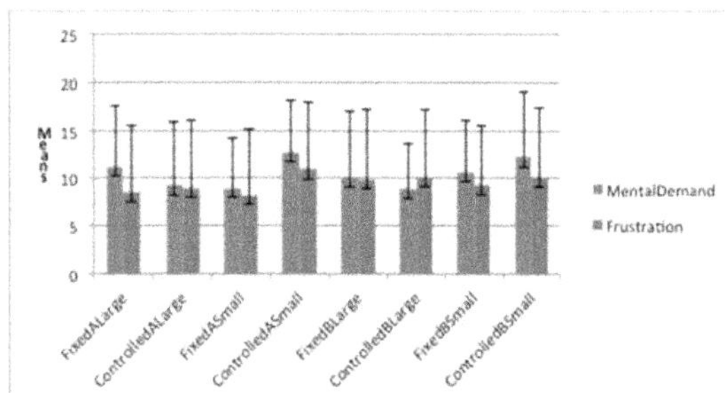

Figure 11. Means and standard deviations of selected mental workload variables.

The critical incidents analysis showed that 3 participants skipped only 1, 2, and 3 lines respectively, while 2 participants (P04 and P05) skipped 9 and 15 lines respectively. We should note here that the high occurrences of failure in critical incidents were observed with the participants who were assigned to read the Small page with the widely spaced overlay. Participant 02 skipped 2 lines and was assigned to a Small page as well; but she had the densely spaced overlay. Based on these data, there is some preliminary evidence that STAAR may enable IBSVI to read text with a density up to 235 words per page, where the dimensions of the page's reading area are 7-inch length and 5.5-inch width, provided that the page has similar dense tactile references. The wandering between lines (WBL) is an important incident because it can reveal the multimodal interaction problems that could exist. Figure 12 shows that WBL occurrences ranged from 2 to 10, (M= 5, SD=3.39). When users could not maintain a horizontal line with the presence of the tactile overlay, it may be necessary to address this problem through the system software. Enabling IBSVI to maintain location on the same text of line without accidently moving to another line is important for an effective reading experience. Since the IBSVI cannot see what she is reading, she also cannot know that she has wandered off the text line she is reading. Hence the words rendered by the TTS as she wanders off the lines will become a confusing jumble if the system provides no appropriate feedback that she has wandered off the horizontal line. In future work, we plan to address this problem by applying advanced statistical techniques that can predict the word meant to be touched and audibly render it. At the same time, an audio feedback should be designed and activated whenever the user's finger deviates from the current horizontal line to provide information about place or location. We investigated the repeating lines (RSL) incidents, and found that it occurred 1 to 3 (M = 1.8, SD=0.8). It is confusing and distracting to users to read the same line more than once consecutively. Although RSL occurred with all of the participants, but it had very low frequency. We do not believe that RSL is a problem within STAAR and it could be avoided when the users gain more experience with using STAAR. By analyzing the successful critical incidents, we found that participants P01 and P03 recorded the highest number of reading whole line (WL) incidents, and they read the Large page with widely spaced overlay. Following them in the third rank is participant P03, who read Small page with the densely spaced overlay. Our conclusion is that the matching between the text density and the overlay density is a critical factor for effective access of the reading material. The results also proved that Large page might be read with fewer errors than the Small page. We started our video coding assuming that there might be instances when a participant could not read a whole line, and that is why we tracked the longest sequence of read words (LSW) incidents.

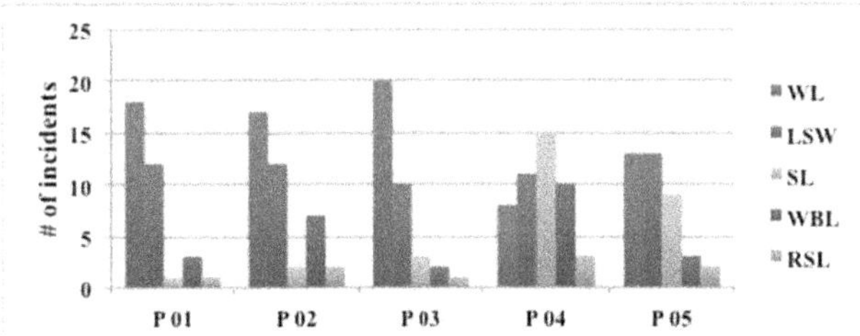

Figure 12. Video coding using critical incidents.

However, all the participants were able to read whole lines. Hence, the LSW is basically the longest read line in terms of number of words per line. The longest LSW was 13 and the shortest was 10 with mean=11.6 (SD=1.14). The time users need to spend in order to read with an acceptable performance should be convenient and at least equivalent to the time needed to read the same amount of information using Braille. As illustrated in Figure 13, the completion time ranged from 125 seconds to 300 seconds with a mean of 237 (SD= 67.5). Relating the time spent to read a whole page to the number of scored success and failure critical incidents, we can see that the more time the user spent on reading the page the more success critical incidents he/she scored and the less failure incidents too. On the contrary, when a participant spent less time reading, her performance is poorer.

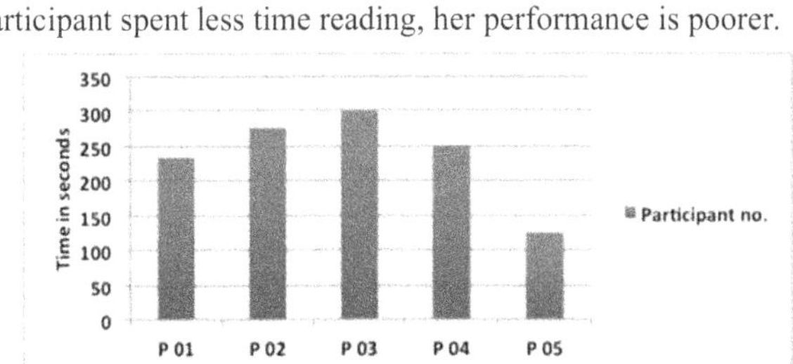

Figure 13. Task completion time.

Four minutes as an average time to read a page can be acceptable as a preliminary timing threshold. However, we plan in our future work to shorten this amount of time. More flexible and coupled integration between the reading touch interaction and the speech generation can lead to more fluent reading with a significant reduction in the time taken. The question now is, if the users were able to let the iPad read most of the displayed pages, why were the knowledge transfer results so low? We explained this by the lack of spatial contextualization in addition to the lack of enough familiarity with the system. The first point was revealed to us as we discovered that the relationship between the static overlay and the rendered text are difficult to correlate without a convenient immediate audio response from the system. The buffering model of the speech led to more spatial confusion to the participants.

Inspired by previous research that introduced new technology to IBSVI [14, 15], we thought that if users were more familiar with the system, their reading performance in terms of knowledge transfer could be highly improved. Hence, we implemented the audio and the speech modeling as described in Sections 4.2 and 4.5 into STAAR, and used it in the longitudinal study. By analyzing the knowledge transfer results for Study 2 at the first meeting, we found that the percentages of correct, wrong, and no answer answers, were 60, 6.67, and 33.33, respectively. While, at the end of the second week, the percentages of correct, wrong, and no answer answers, were 86.67, 6.67, and 6.67, respectively. These results proved our hypothesis; where the addition of spatial cues by the appropriately designed audio feedback had highly leveraged the percentage of the correct answers. Additionally, having longer term of exposure to the system led to a considerable improvement in the knowledge transfer results.

5.2 STAAR Interface Evaluation

Enabling IBSVI to access electronic text spatially is the major aspect of STAAR. However, leveraging access needs integration between the interface components. The critical interface components that are not in the core of the system are the overlay and the speech. The overlay that was laid on the surface of the iPad played a great role in helping IBSVI spatially adapted to the iPad screen. For example, the vertical ruler at the left margin, reduced search space, and leveraged faster and more convenient interaction. It had the advantage of enabling IBSVI to explore the page on the screen effectively. Based on the data collected during the study and from the post interview, we found that the haptic buttons on the overlay were preferred to the control gestures by the BSVI participants. Finding the haptic buttons and activating them were more intuitive and ergonomic for the participants. Two reasons we observed for this finding are mainly interaction problems. The first reason is that the swipe gestures were not performed accurately (3 fingers moved quickly and gently in a horizontal direction across the screen), the gestures could not be recognized by the system, which lead to users frustration. The second reason is that the control gestures were interfered with reading gestures, e.g. swiping with 3 fingers occurred accidentally when the user was just reading with multiple fingers on the iPad.

The second element that highly affected the users experience with STAAR is the speech. Two aspects of the speech caused dissatisfaction to the users, which are familiarity and quality. The speech synthesizer Flite was not familiar to the users, since it is an open source TTS that is usually used for research purposes, and it is not similar to other screen reading applications such as JAWS for Windows or the iPad Voice Over. More importantly, the quality of speech was not satisfying. This is because the speech suffered from choppiness and sharp pauses, which made it difficult to follow and understand. We plan to fix the speech issues in the future versions of STAAR.

5.3 STAAR and Braille

Braille used to be the main approach that provides IBSVI with a spatial medium for reading and enables IBSVI to read, search, and skim text at their own pace. We argue that STAAR could have an advantage over Braille with respect to modality and spatial cognition because:

1. Braille utilizes a single model of information (tactile), while STAAR utilizes a multimodal information representation (tactile and audio).
2. STAAR is more powerful spatially than Braille.

The first point is self-proven as the dimension and the type of both Braille and STAAR modalities are inherited by definition. Braille's tactile information is delivered with the embossed Braille cells, whereas STAAR's tactile information is delivered with the embossed grid on the overlay. Multimodal information representation in reading materials is important because it increases the learning outcomes [16, 17]. However, STAAR cannot compete with Braille in case of the readers are IBSVI with hearing loss. To prove the second point, we compared the space capacity of Braille and STAAR. Braille is accessed through two media: embossed materials and digital Braille. Braille codes characters into six or eight dots in a rectangular array 3×2 or 4x2 called a Braille cell [18]. An A4 sized paper can allow the embossing of 34 to 37 cells per line, and an average of 27 lines per page. Hence, Braille coding utilizes multiplies of spaces of original text. For example, a standard textbook of 300 pages can be transcribed into 1800 Braille pages [19]. This size challenge is inherited by 'Digital Braille' as the needed real-estate makes it typically necessary to restrict the information displayed to a single line. Braille is accessed digitally through piezoelectric Braille displays that display refreshable Braille characters. Commercially-available refreshable Braille displays have a typical limit of 80 Braille cells that can be displayed. Tactobook [19] is an eBook reader with a tactile display. Despite its functionality as a translator from English to Braille, its display area is relatively small (20 x 9.8 x 5 cm), meaning that only a very small window of information may be presented at any time. Compared to these, STAAR presented a practical and efficient solution for accessing reading materials in reasonable dimensions.

6. CONCLUSIONS

In this research, we presented a multimodal reading system for IBSVI. Touch is the primary interaction mode in the presented multimodal system. IBSVI were enabled using STAAR, to use their hands for exploring reading materials on a touch device. The touch channel was used as a substitution for the vision channel to carry the functions of eye glancing in addition to focusing and reading. Complementarity between sonification and audible text, and spatial layout is the major organizational theme of the system's multimodal interaction. STAAR was tested at its different stages of development. The results showed that IBSVI could read in space using STAAR as well as with Braille. IBSVI can consume more significant amount of text in the space provided by STAAR, compared to other spatial media of reading for IBSVI. This research has further opened new research questions that we aim to investigate in our future work. For example, can we further increase the density of text in order to translate the same layout of text as written for the sighted people? In this case, will we need a dynamic haptic overlay? How can we smooth the speech synthesis to cope up with our reading touch-interaction model? What signal processing techniques can be implemented to achieve fast reading interaction?

7. ACKNOWLEDGMENTS

This research is supported by the National Science Foundation under Grant No. IIS1117854. Any opinions, findings, and conclusions or recommendations expressed in this material are those of the authors and do not necessarily reflect the views of the National Science Foundation.

8. REFERENCES

1. *CMU Speech Software*. [cited 2012; Available from: http://www.speech.cs.cmu.edu/flite/.
2. Wildman, D.M. and M. Kling, *Semantic, Syntactic, and Spatial Anticipation in Reading*. Reading Research Quarterly, 1979. **14**(2): p. 128-164.
3. Guthrie, J.T., *Locating Information in Documents: Examination of a Cognitive Model*. Reading Research Quarterly, 1988. **23**(2): p. 178-199.
4. *National Federation of the Blind*. [cited 2012; Available from: http://www.nfb.org.
5. Stephanidis, C., *Universal Access in Human-Computer Interaction. Applications and Services: 5th International Conference, UAHCI 2009, Held as Part of HCI International Applications, incl. Internet/Web, and HCI)* 2009: Springer.
6. Piccolo, L.S.G., E.M.D. Menezes, and B.D.C. Buccolo, *Developing an accessible interaction model for touch screen mobile devices: preliminary results*, in *Proc. 10th Brazilian Symp. on on Human Factors in Comp. Sys. and the 5th Latin American Conf=. on HCI* 2011, Brazilian Comp. Soc.:. p. 222-226.
7. Petit, G., A. Dufresne, and J.-M. Robert, *Introducing TactoWeb: A Tool to Spatially Explore Web Pages for Users with Visual Impairment Universal Access in Human-Computer Interaction. Design for All and eInclusion*, C. Stephanidis, Editor 2011, Springer Berlin / Heidelberg. p. 276-284.
8. Rayner, K., *Eye movements in reading and information processing: 20 years of research*. Psychological Bulletin, 1998. **124**(3): p. 372-422.
9. SADATO, et al., *Activation of the primary visual cortex by Braille reading in blind subjects*. Vol. 380. 1996, London, ROYAUME-UNI: Nature Publishing Group.
10. Turunen, M., et al., *Accessible Multimodal Media Center Application for Blind and Partially Sighted People*. Comput. Entertain., 2010. **8**(3): p. 1-30.
11. Encelle, B., et al., *Annotation-based video enrichment for blind people: a pilot study on the use of earcons and speech synthesis*, in *The Proc. of the 13th international ACM SIGACCESS conference on Computers and accessibility*2011, ACM: Dundee, Scotland, UK. p. 123-130.
12. Kane, S.K., et al., *Access overlays: improving non-visual access to large touch screens for blind users*, in *Proc. of the 24th annual ACM symposium on User interface software and technology* 2011, ACM: California, USA. p. 273-282.
13. Pierce, J.R., *An Introduction to Information Theory: Symbols, Signals and Noise* 1980: Dover Publications.
14. Oliveira, F., et al., *Fun to develop embodied skill: how games help the blind to understand pointing*, in *Proc. of the 3rd International Conference on PErvasive Technologies Related to Assistive Environments*2010, ACM: Samos, Greece. p. 1-8.
15. Quek, F. and F. Oliveira, *Enabling the Blind to See Gestures*. Transactions on Computer-Human Interaction (TOCHI), 2012. **Accepted to appear.**
16. Nugent, G., *Pictures, audio, and print: symbolic representation and effect on learning*. Educational Technology Research and Development, 1982. **30**(3): p. 163-174.
17. Hartman, F., *Recognition learning under multiple channel presentation and testing conditions*. Educational Technology Research and Development, 1961. **9**(1): p. 24-43.
18. Smithmaitrie, P., J. Kanjantoe, and P. Tandayya, *Touching force response of the piezoelectric Braille cell*, in *Proc. ACM 1st Int'l convention on Rehabilitation engineering; assistive technology:*, p. 174-178.
19. Velazquez, R., E. Preza, and H. Hernandez. *Making eBooks accessible to blind Braille readers*. in *Haptic Audio visual Environments and Games, 2008. HAVE 2008. IEEE International Workshop on*. 2008s.

Taste/IP: The Sensation of Taste for Digital Communication

Nimesha Ranasinghe
Department of Electrical and Computer Engineering
Keio-NUS CUTE Center
National University of Singapore
nimesha82@gmail.com

Adrian David Cheok
Graduate School of Media Design
Keio University, Japan
adriancheok@gmail.com

Ryohei Nakatsu
Department of Electrical and Computer Engineering
National University of Singapore
elenr@nus.edu.sg

ABSTRACT

In this paper, we present a new methodology for integrating the sense of taste with the existing digital communication domain. First, we discuss existing problems and limitations for integrating the sense of taste as a digital communication media. Then, to assess this gap, we present a solution with three core modules: the transmitter, form of communication, and receiver. The transmitter is a mobile application, where the sender formulates a taste message to send. Then, for communication, we present a new extensible markup language (XML) format, the TasteXML (TXML) to specify the format of taste messages. As the receiver (actuator), we introduce Digital Taste Stimulator, a novel method for stimulating taste sensations on human. Initial user experiments and qualitative feedbacks were discussed mainly focusing on the Digital Taste Stimulator. We conclude with a brief overview of future aspects of this technology and possibilities on other application domains.

Categories and Subject Descriptors

H.5.m. [**Information Interfaces and Presentation**]: Miscellaneous

General Terms

Design; Measurement; Experimentation

Keywords

Taste; Gustation; Multimodal interaction; User interfaces; Virtual reality; Communication

1. INTRODUCTION

Today, the importance of electronic media is enormous and associate with daily interactions of people. Nevertheless, the electronic media depend on more limited senses or channels for remote communication such as text, sound, image, and video alone or in combinations, whereas, in face-to-face situations, people able to exploit multiple senses (hearing, sight, touch, smell, and taste) along with expressions, gestures, and interaction with the artifacts for communication. Therefore, multisensory digital remote interaction technologies are required to expand existing media technologies [4].

Vision and audition are two of the most applied senses in remote media technologies presently. In addition, the haptic sensation is also explored as a communication media in recent times as in [19, 5]. Conversely, at present, it is harder to integrate taste and smell senses in modern digital communication paradigm due to two main difficulties: unawareness of neurological makeup and the chemical based nature of these two senses. However, there have been a few attempts to develop an integrated and comprehensive approach to stimulate all five basic human senses. For example, the virtual reality helmet ('Virtual Cocoon') developed by British scientists can stimulate five human senses. The helmet releases chemicals in order to stimulate both smell and taste, while hearing, sight, and touch senses are stimulated digitally [3]. The main drawback of these solutions is the use of different chemicals to stimulate the smell and taste senses. Therefore, these solutions are analog and associate with manageability, transferability, and scalability issues due to the use of chemicals.

Taking such issues into account, this paper describes a novel system, Taste over IP (Taste/IP), to remotely and digitally communicate the sensation of taste. The sensation of taste plays a pivotal role in human lives. It is a pleasurable sensation, associates with personal experiences. People prefer to dine together and arrange various food items for events and celebrations in their everyday lives. Thus, the sensation of taste is uniquely valuable to maintain a healthy human body and stronger relationships. However, the sense of taste is given a remarkably little attention as a remote communication media. Therefore, a new methodology is required to digitally stimulate the sense of taste to enable remote communication through the sense of taste.

As illustrated in figure 1, this system consists of three main modules, the transmitter, form of communication, and receiver. A mobile application is developed as the transmitter for facilitating the sender to digitally construct the taste messages. Then, we developed a digital taste actuation system (Digital Taste Stimulator) for delivering the message to the recipient. This taste actuation system is developed based on electrical and thermal stimulation on user's tip of the tongue. The Internet is used as the medium for communication. Furthermore, for digital communication, a

ICMI'12, October 22–26, 2012, Santa Monica, California, USA.
Copyright 2012 ACM 978-1-4503-1467-1/12/10 ...$15.00.

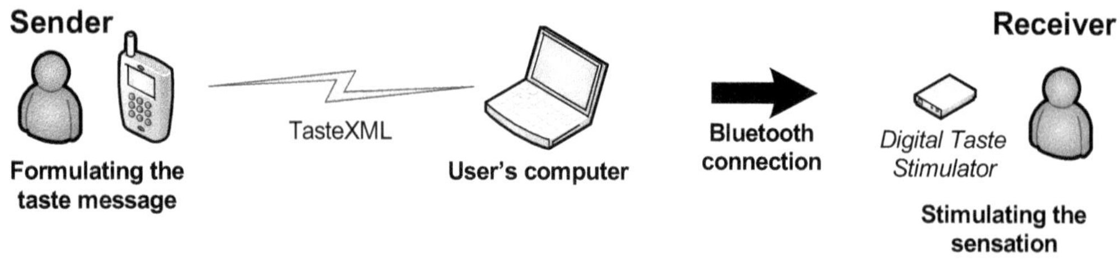

Figure 1: Architecture of the Taste/IP system with transmitter, receiver, and the form of communication

new messaging format is introduced based on the extensible markup language (XML) and named it as TasteXML (TXML).

Being able to communicate taste sensations digitally has distinct advantages in several domains including multisensory communication, mixed and virtual reality, and entertainment. Virtual interactions can be enhanced through this technology by integrating the sense of taste into the virtual environments. In gaming or virtual environments, users' may taste, as they are in a natural environment by incorporating proposed device into their systems. For example, suppose the player is in a virtual kitchen; through the proposed method, the user can taste different dishes prepared in the kitchen.

Rest of the paper is organized as follows. Next section discusses several related research works conducted on taste interfaces. This is followed by the System Description, which presents main components of Taste/IP system with the interactions between those components. Then we conclude with a discussion of initial results and future works of this approach.

2. RELATED WORK

This section presents several scientific research works pertinent to the use of sensation of taste for digital interactions. The review begins with several research works conducted using chemical based approaches; then a section with experiments conducted on non-chemical stimulation methodologies. Since digital communication and stimulation are two of the main focuses, several related works are examined to highlight the possibilities of generating taste sensations through electrical and thermal stimulation methodologies.

2.1 Chemical based approaches

Although using chemicals in an interactive system is fairly complicated, in literature, chemical stimulation of the sensation of taste has been used to develop interactive systems. Besides 'Virtual Cocoon', the 'Food Simulator' uses chemical and mechanical linkages to simulate food-chewing sensations by providing flavoring chemicals, biting force, chewing sound, and vibration to the user [6]. The mechanical section of the device consists of mainly a vibration motor, vibration sensor, and the linkages. This section intended to resist the users' bite thus the motor provides appropriate resistance to the mouth along with chemicals and chewing sound. The study presented in [6] mainly focuses on studying cross sensory interactions of taste with sound, texture, and force.

Another example of using chemicals to stimulate taste sensations is the 'TasteScreen' [10]. The system, which attached to top of the user's computer screen, holds 20 different chemical flavoring cartridges to mix and spray toward the display. Then the user is capable of enjoying the dispensed taste by licking his/her computer screen. However, this approach is unprovable since most users may find this process as unnatural since users should lick their screens. In addition, 'Tag Candy'[1] and 'Meta cookie' [12] systems are using augmented reality based approaches to create different sensations. The Tag Candy is using vibration and hearing through bone conductivity to deliver various sensations while a user enjoys a regular lollipop attached to the system. Conversely, the Meta Cookie system uses visuals and smell information to provide various taste sensations to the user while consuming a regular cookie. The printed augmented reality marker is used to cover the real cookie with a virtual cookie in the system. Furthermore, based on user's choice, smell information is delivered to the user, thus to produce different sensations, although the user consumes same regular cookie in real.

However, there are numerous issues incorporate with chemical based approaches as explained. Chemical stimulation is analogues in nature; using chemicals in an interactive system is impractical since chemicals are difficult to store and transmit. Alternatively, as evident by those prior studies, chemical based solutions have scalability issues for long-term implementations. From the above review, it is evident that a new mechanism is required to achieve the digital controllability of taste.

2.2 Non-chemical based approaches

There are several evidences of taste sensations that occurred through electrical stimulation in medicine, especially in electrophysiology. Alessandro Volta, known for the invention of electric cell and discovery of Voltage, is one of the first scientists that studied the electrical stimulation on the senses of touch and taste. He put two coins, made of different metals, on both sides of his tongue (up and down) and connected them through a wire. He mentioned that he felt salty sensation during that experiment [18].

In [13], single human tongue papillae was electrically stimulated (84 trials) with a silver electrode using five young subjects. They used electrical pulses of both negative and positive with the frequency range of 50 - 800Hertz. The results provided some exciting and effective responses for the sour taste (22.2%) and some small responses for the bitter (3.8%) and salty (1.8%) sensations. Conversely, this experiment was conducted in a controlled environment where it only used single papillae of the tongue.

In addition, another interesting aspect to pursue is the thermal stimulation of the sensation of taste. In "Thermal stimulation of taste" Cruz et al. study the effects on temperature change (heating and cooling) and perceptions of taste sensations [2]. They experimented on anterior edge of

[1]http://www.diginfo.tv/v/10-0245-f-en.php

the tongue and found evidences on sweet, sour, and salty sensations. Furthermore, Talavera et al. examines the thermal activation of TRPM5 ion channel in taste buds of the tongue [17]. TRPM5 ion channel has a key role in the perception of sweet, umami, and bitter tastes. The interesting feature of TRPM5 channels is the activation of this channel could immensely activate the corresponding tastes of that channel due to the activation of G-proteins (guanine nucleotide-binding proteins) associated with taste receptor cells. Furthermore, they have showed that TRPM5 is a highly temperature sensitive and a heat-activated channel thus mapped the thermal-voltage relationship in different temperature levels using whole-cell patch-clamp technique.

Nakamura et al. propose a similar method to augment the taste of foods and drinks by applying small electrical pulses through the food or drink itself [11]. However, their approach is different since we directly stimulate the tongue using electrodes and they did not consider the controllability aspects of the stimuli.

From the above review, it can be seen that the electrical and thermal stimulation are two potential methods to enable the digital stimulation of taste sensations. However, above reported experiments are conducted in controlled environments and in the experimental stage. Whereas, in Taste/IP research one of the most significant aspects is the controllability of generating taste sensations in uncontrolled conditions. Therefore, we introduce a digital control system for stimulating the sensation of taste through electrical, thermal, and hybrid stimulation (hybrid: both electrical and thermal stimulation at the same time), in order to introduce the sense of taste as a new digital media for remote multimodal interactions.

3. SYSTEM DESCRIPTION

In this section, we describe the implementation of Taste/IP system with the three main modules, transmitter, form of communication, and receiver. Currently, in a typical scenario, user formulates a taste message to send using the mobile application. Then, the mobile phone sends the message in TXML format to the recipient's computer, thus to the Digital Taste Stimulator. Figure 1 depicts main steps for sending a taste message. At present, the system uses an intermediate computer as shown in Figure 1 for redirecting the message to the Digital Taste Stimulator. As the immediate next step, we are developing a portable version, which has direct communication through the Internet.

3.1 Transmitter

An android mobile application is developed as the transmitter, which allows the user to create taste messages and transmit them to the receiver. At present, based on the capabilities of Digital Taste Stimulator, we are only focusing on transferring basic taste sensations known as sour, salty, bitter, and sweet. Furthermore, the application allows the user to select the intensity of the taste to be sent.

As shown in Figure 2, the mobile application has three tabs. First for creating the basic taste message (the sensation and the intensity), second for creating a mixed message, and third for network configurations to connect with the user's computer. The second tab is not implemented at the moment. Further studies will be conducted to produce mixed sensations in the future using the Digital Taste Stimulator. The third tab has the properties related to network

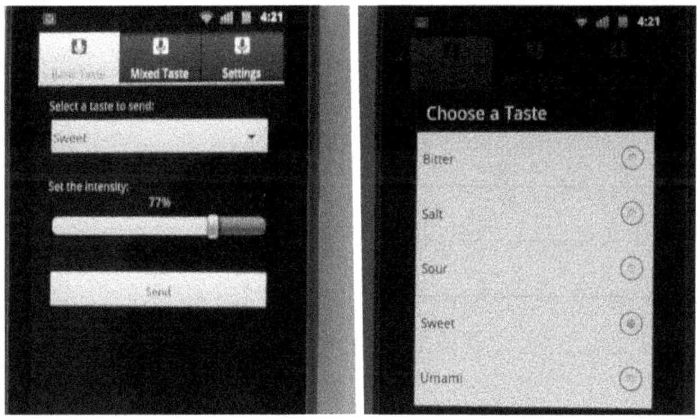

Figure 2: Android application developed for digital taste messaging

communication, the IP of the server (recipient's computer) and the port. Each user is given a client ID for identification purposes.

3.2 Communication

Once the user crafts the taste message, the recipient can be selected by changing the IP address from the settings tab at the moment. The Internet is used as the channel of communication between the sender and the receiver. To transmit a taste message, one of the most important aspects to consider is the form of communication. As a solution, to specify the format of the message created in the mobile application, a new XML format is developed named it as the Taste Extensible Markup Language (TasteXML / TXML).

TasteXML is a Remote Procedure Calling protocol that works over the Internet. TasteXML messages are set of encrypted requests and responses. The body of both request and response are in XML format. When a taste message receives on the server, first it queues until the user is ready to receive the message. Therefore, immediately the server returns a response with the status as "queued". Then later once the recipient consumed the taste message the server returns a success response. We have developed the format in such a way that in the future it can be easily expanded to include other parameters such as parameters for mixed sensations (ex: several sensations and corresponding intensities together) and basic social networking functions (ex: friend-list management). Furthermore, procedure parameters can be scalars, numbers, strings, dates, complex records and list structures. Two samples of TasteXML messages are given below for sending a basic taste message. The intensity of the taste sensation can be represent either in three levels (1: mild, 2: medium, and 3: strong) or as a percentage (ex: 70%). Therefore, in this example, a primary bitter sensation is transferred with the intensity of 70%.

TasteXML - Basic taste message send request

```
<?xml version="1.0" encoding="UTF-8"?>
<TasteXml>
<type>request</type>
<method>SendTasteToFriend</method>
<information>
<ID>T0001</ID>
<FriendID>4</FriendID>
<FriendName>Daniel Jackson</FriendName>
<TasteType>basic</TasteType>
```

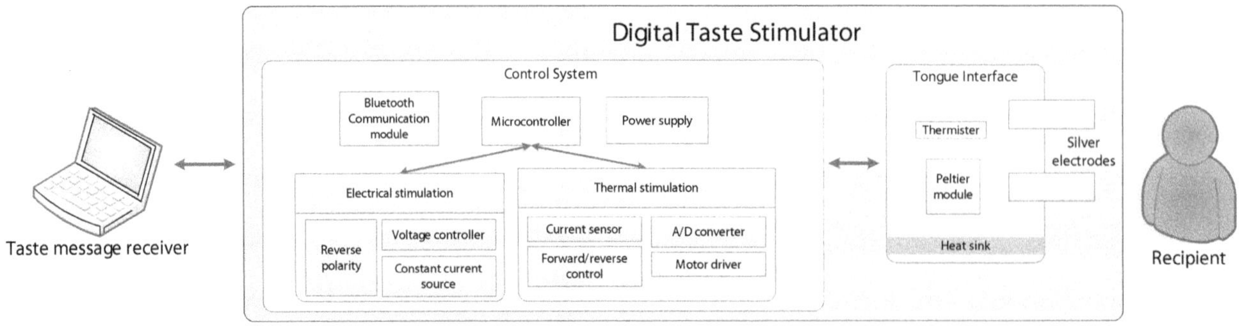

Figure 3: The architecture of the Digital Taste Stimulator. The taste message receiver controls the output of Digital Taste Stimulator based on the sensation and intensity information received

```
<taste intensity="70">Bitter</taste>
</information>
</TasteXml>
```

TasteXML - Basic taste message send response

```
<?xml version="1.0" encoding="UTF-8"?>
<TasteXml>
<type>response</type>
<method>SendTasteToFriend</method>
<information>
<TasteType>basic</TasteType>
<status>queued</status>
</information>
</TasteXml>
```

3.3 Receiver

In this approach for taste communication, the receiver (taste actuator) is recognized as the most significant module. We implemented a novel taste stimulation interface, the Digital Taste Stimulator, based on electrical and thermal stimulation methods. A control system is developed, with a tongue interface, to stimulate the tip of the tongue using small electrical pulses and by changing the temperature.

As can be seen in Figure 3, the Digital Taste Stimulator consists of two main modules, the control system and the tongue interface. The control system acts as the central unit of the Digital Taste Stimulator. It receives command configurations from the computer and configures the output for the tongue interface. The tongue interface is connected to the recipient's tip of the tongue as shown in Figure 4. Two silver electrodes (95%) are used in the tongue interface for stimulating the tongue. Silver is chosen due to high thermal and electrical conductivity of the metal. Communication between the Digital Taste Stimulator and user's computer is implemented using Bluetooth technology. In addition, a wired connection is used between the control system and tongue interface.

The control system consists of two key submodules: the electrical stimulation submodule and thermal stimulation submodule. Furthermore, the tongue interface consists of two silver electrodes (each has dimensions of 40mm x 15mm x 0.2mm), a Peltier module, and a thermister. In addition, it requires a heat sink for effective temperature control through the Peltier module.

At present, the Digital Taste Stimulator stimulates sour, salty, bitter, minty, and spicy sensations on user's tongue; sour, salty, and bitter from electrical stimulation and minty and spicy through thermal stimulation. However, we only managed to control the intensity for sour sensation up to three levels: mild, medium, and strong. In addition, evidences of sweet sensation observed through thermal stimulation. Moreover, we understood the ethical issues behind this research and already secured the necessary approval from the University Institutional Review Board (Approval No: NUS 1049) before the experiments. Next subsections describe technical information on electrical and thermal submodules. Then we present results for each taste sensation stimulated through the Digital Taste Stimulator.

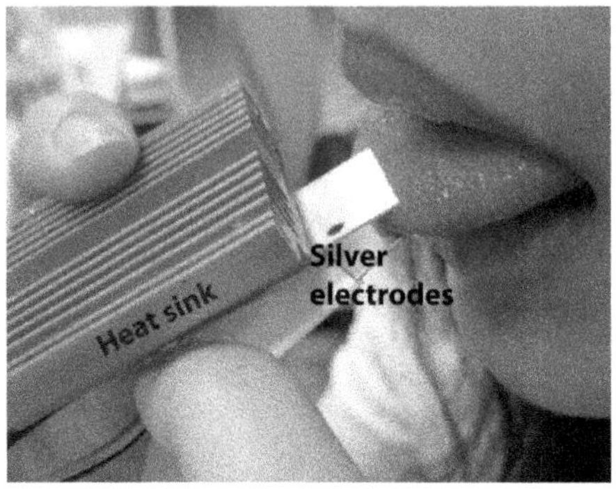

Figure 4: Two silver electrodes of the tongue interface is attached to the user's tip of the tongue

3.4 Electrical stimulation

As shown in Figure 3, the electrical stimulation subsystem has three main modules: the voltage controller, the constant-current source, and the reverse polarity controller. The voltage controller controls the output voltage thus to control the current through the tip of the tongue. The resistance, impedance, as well as the inductance of the tongue for electrical stimulation are based on the structure and the number of papillae on the tongue [7], thus it is different from person to person. Therefore, to maintain constant current levels through the recipient's tongue we implemented a constant-current source. Furthermore, during the initial phase, the device was required to calibrate according to the end user/recipient. Using the constant-current source, this process can be standardized by configuring the device for most apparent configurations. Final implementation of the Digital Taste Stimulator is shown in Figure 5.

Furthermore, in electrical stimulation, the magnitude of

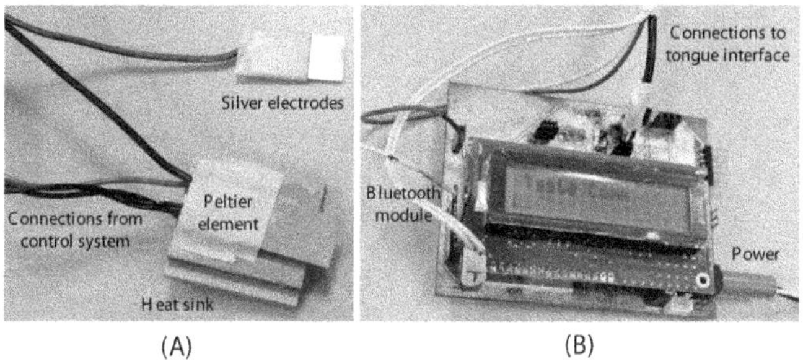

Figure 5: Implementation of the Digital Taste Stimulator: (A) Tongue interface and (B) Control system.

current, the frequency of electric pulses, and the polarity of the stimulation are controlled. Primarily based on literature [14, 16, 13] we finalized the range of frequencies and magnitudes of current as follows,

- Stimulation frequency: the frequency range from 50Hz to 1000Hz was used since lower frequencies have a clear effect on human tissues. The frequency of output signal can be controlled in steps: 50Hz, 100Hz, 200Hz.. up to 1000Hz with 100Hz intervals.
- Magnitudes of current: the output current was chosen from 20μA to 200μA. This range was defined after several initial experiments with users. The control system can control the magnitude of current from 20μA to 200μA with 20μA intervals.
- Both anodic and cathodic stimulation were used to generate taste sensations from the tip of the tongue

To simplify the control system and experiments, currently, we only interested in square wave electrical pulses on the human tongue. The effects of sine, triangle, and sawtooth waveforms will be studied in later stages of this research. Additionally, to implement the voltage controller, a 8-bit (256 positions) digital potentiometer is used with SPI interface with the main microcontroller. The constant-current source is implemented using an op-amp and a transistor similar to [9]. Dependency relationship of the output current and the input voltage of the constant-current source is shown in Figure 6. The input voltage of the constant-current source is adjusted using the digital potentiometer to observe a nearly perfect linear increment of the output current values as required.

The output signal from the tongue interface is monitored using a digital oscilloscope. As can be seen in Figure 7, waveform of the output signal is changing after the human tongue is connected to the constant-current source. The change of the signal waveform indicates that it is low-pass filtered due to the capacitive effect and the inductance of the tongue. However, we will conduct more experiments in the future, to investigate the filtering response of human tongue for electrical stimulation.

3.5 Thermal stimulation

In thermal stimulation, based on the literature, temperature is controlled (both heating and cooling) within 20°C - 35°C. The output of thermal stimulation submodule is connected to a peltier module in the tongue interface, which

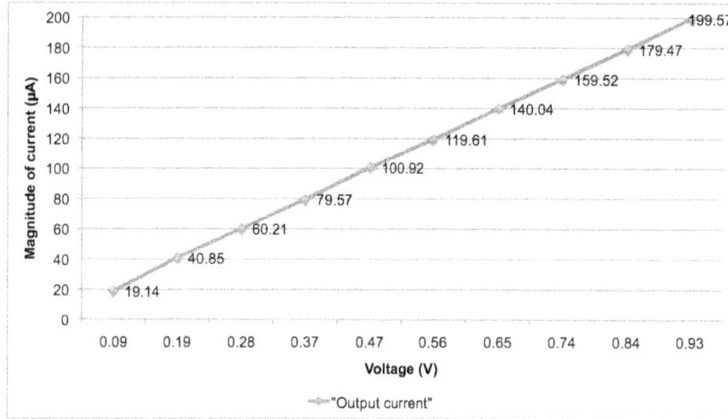

Figure 6: Corresponding output current levels based on input voltage values of the constant-current source

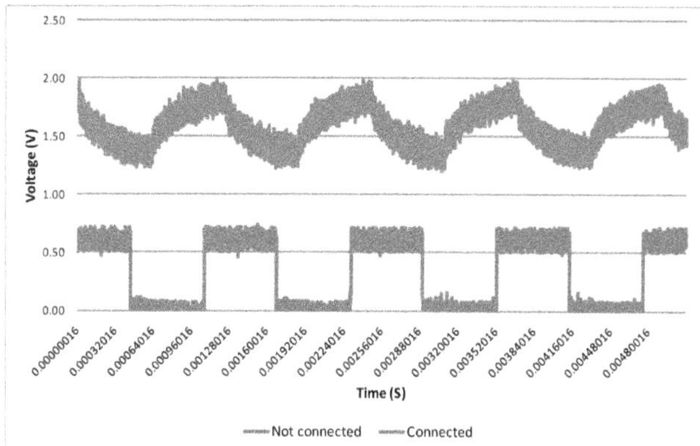

Figure 7: Output current waveforms with and without connecting to the tongue

effectively controls the temperature. In addition, it is noted that the time required to achieve a distinct temperature change is essential, thus implemented a mechanism to control the time required using the Pulse-width modulation (PWM) technique. The performance of heating up and cooling down of the peltier module is depicted in Figure 8. The measurements were obtained with 30% PWM, where duration of achieving a certain temperature change can be controlled by increasing or decreasing the PWM percentage.

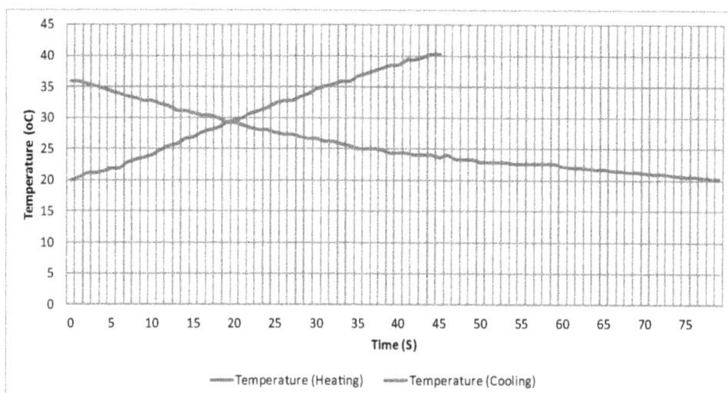

Figure 8: Heating up and cooling down performance of the thermal stimulation module (observed with 30% PWM)

3.6 Experimental results

To investigate and analyze the effectiveness of the Digital Taste Stimulator a user experiment was conducted with eighteen subjects (ten males and eight females, age range from 21-27, M = 23, SD = 2.54). Participants were not trained before the experiment and they were in normal health condition. Electrical pulses with predetermined magnitudes of current (20, 40, 60, 80, 100, 120, 140, 180, 200μA), frequency (50, 100, 200, 400, 600, 800, 1000Hz), temperature (both cooling and heating between 20°C - 35°C), and duration (manual control through computer) of the stimulation are then applied to the tongue through the electrodes (tongue interface) to produce different taste sensations. Participants rinse their mouth with deionized water between each stimulus to prevent bias and reset the tongue. They were asked to provide verbal feedback during the experiments if they perceive taste sensations along with the intensity of the sensation. The level of intensity was recorded in a three level scale: mild, medium, and strong. Likewise, for better analysis of the results, these intensity levels are matched to a numerical scale: mild = 1, medium = 2, and strong = 3. Furthermore, they were instructed not to consume too hot, too cold, or too spicy food/drinks two hours prior to the experiments.

In this paper, we present two experiments, electrical (magnitudes of current / taste), and thermal (temperature change / taste) stimulation. Results from the user experiment are depicted in Figures 9, 11, 12, and 13. Sour, salty, bitter, minty, and spicy are the main sensations reported during the experiments from both electrical and thermal stimulation. Sour sensation has the highest controllability through the electrical stimulation as shown in Figure 9. Furthermore, as illustrated in Figure 10, we were able to identify corresponding three intensities (mild, medium, and strong) for digital sour taste. From the experiment, we found that most of the participants felt mild sour at around 40μA, medium at around 90μA, and strong at around 140μA. Few participants mentioned, although they felt the sour taste, the taste sensation was less similar to the natural (lime) taste. Many of the participants revealed that it was uncomfortable when the current was around or over 180μA. Two participants indicated that they could feel the vibration (tingling sensation) of the tongue around 200μA. One of the most noteworthy comments we received was that some participants felt lower magnitude of currents resulted in more realistic sour taste sensations.

In addition, salty sensation was also reported as illustrated in Figure 9. However, as participants described, the level of intensity was remarkably low. Additionally, by changing the polarity of the electrodes, we stimulated the bitter sensation from the bottom surface of the tongue as illustrated in Figure 11. Another interesting observation through the electrical stimulation was the minimal contribution of the frequency towards taste perception. The sensations have clear relationship with the magnitude of current. However, several participants mentioned that the intensities of taste sensations had a slight increase when the frequency was increased from 50Hz to 1000Hz. As explained, by learning filtering response of the tongue, it will be possible to estimate the frequency response, thus to further study the contribution of frequency for electrical taste perception.

When the temperature was increased from 20°C to 35°C, there were some evidences on sour sensation, though the level of intensity was low. Many participants mentioned that increased temperature resulted slight spiciness on their tongue. These results were shown in Figure 12.

We were most interested on the cooling down sensations since we observed several responses on the sweet sensation as displayed in Figure 13. Few participants mentioned that they could perceive sweet sensation when we rapidly decrease the temperature after heating up to 35°C. Nevertheless, number of responses were low. We believe it deserves more focused experiments on this aspect in the future. Additionally, many participants evident the minty sensation after cooling down the tongue module (below 23°C). Partic-

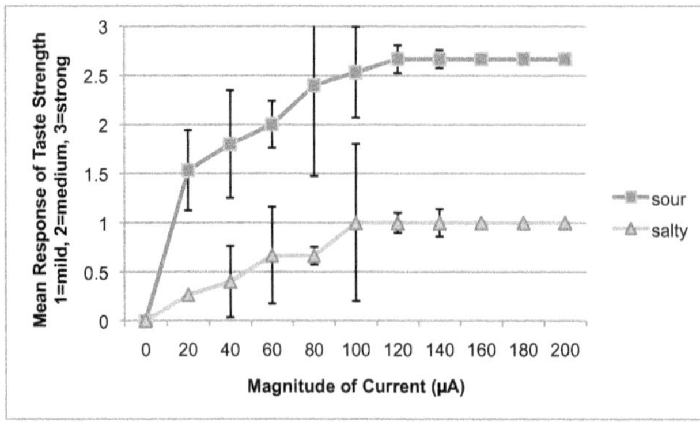

Figure 9: Sour and salty sensations recorded during the experiment. The error bars are showing the standard deviation (SD).

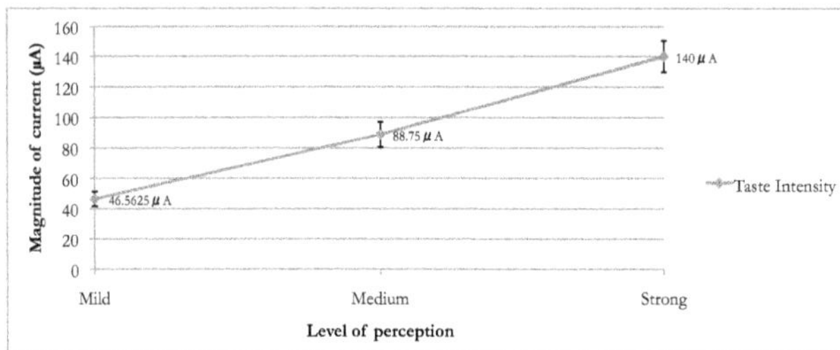

Figure 10: Approximate intensity levels of digital sour taste (Mild: 20μA-38.33μA, Medium: 38.33μA-88.75μA, and Strong: 88.75μA-140μA)

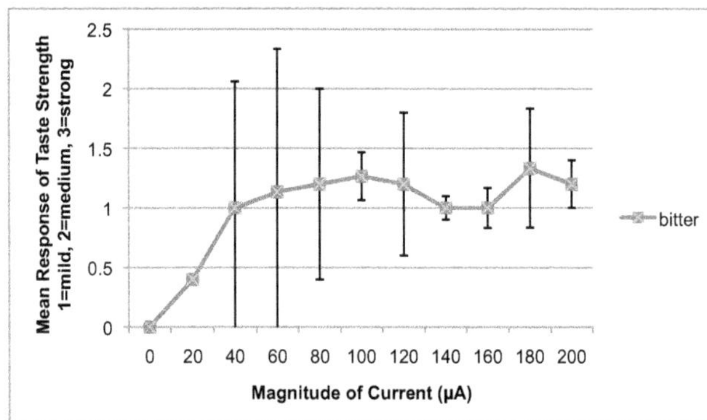

Figure 11: Bitter sensation is recorded from the bottom surface of the tongue. The error bars are showing the standard deviation (SD).

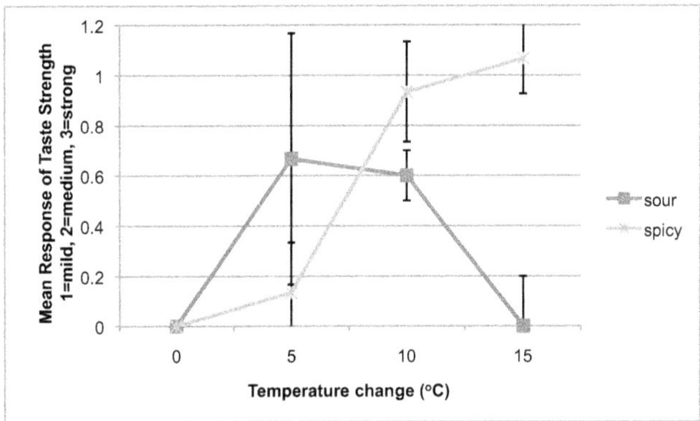

Figure 12: Evidences of sour and spicy sensations when the tongue interface is heating up (from 20°C to 35°C). The error bars are showing the standard deviation (SD).

ularly, two participants mentioned that the sweet sensation they felt was more like a mixed sensation, and they called it "minty sweet".

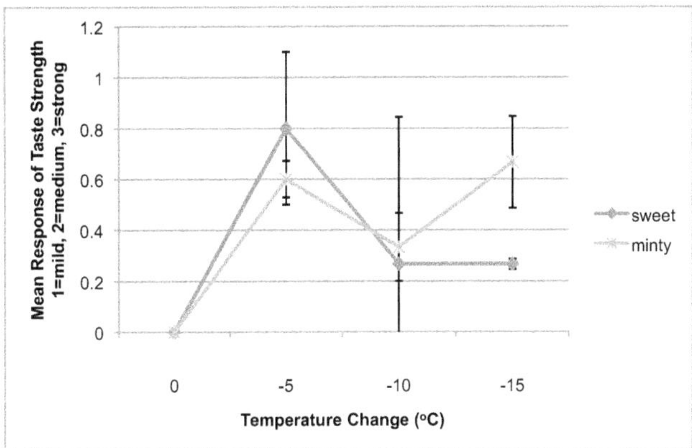

Figure 13: Minty and sweet sensations was reported during the cooling down experiment (from 35°C to 20°C). The error bars are showing the standard deviation (SD).

4. DISCUSSION AND FUTURE WORK

There were several key findings reported in the results section on generating taste sensations digitally using the Digital Taste Stimulator. Although, the conducted experiment has some predictable future directions, it also requires more focused experimental studies. Apart from the stimulation protocol, effects on the material used for stimulation, position on the tongue, and waveform of the electrical pulse require further experiments. For example, platinum and gold materials may have different effects on the tongue for the same stimuli opposed to use silver, because of their material characteristics. Furthermore, we reported the possibility of generating bitter sensation from the bottom surface of the tongue. Therefore, the position on the tongue is also crucial. At this stage, we prefer to use tip of the tongue based on two different properties: 1) easy to access, 2) most sensitive part on the tongue [1]. In the future, we will improve the current tongue interface in order to access other places on the tongue. Furthermore, the waveform of the electrical signal may also affect the results.

In addition to the merits reported in this research, there are several limitations identified. Even though the protocol/format and the sending of the taste message are almost finalized the whole process of taste communication is depended on the capabilities of the Digital Taste Stimulator at this moment. In the future, by experimenting different physiological and psychological aspects of the sensation of taste and by exploring different other digitally controllable mediums, we will continuously improve the results in the same avenue. In addition to the electrical and thermal stimulation, we may also experiment with ultrasonic and infrared stimuli.

Figure 14: Future application of this technology for internet marketing and online shopping technologies

We are already in the process of developing a mobile version of the system (Digital Taste Stimulator) to dispose another limitation in the current setup. The new version will connect to the internet through 3G network and enable the personal use of the device in daily interactions such as 14. Moreover, in the future, this technology may use to implement digital taste based social networking services. Figure 15 shows a possible architecture for a future digital taste based social networking platform called mTaste.

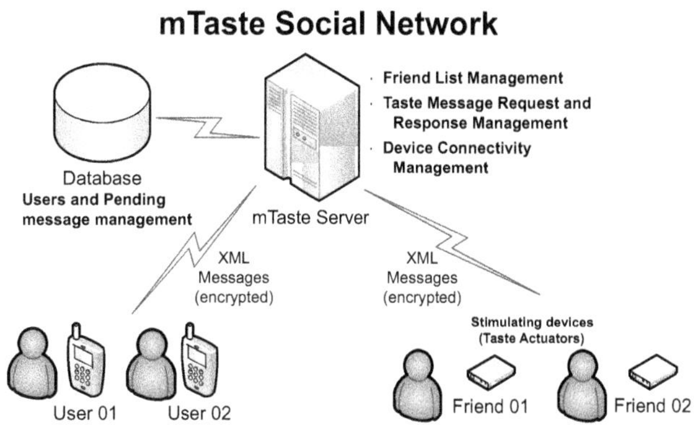

Figure 15: A future digital taste sharing social networking service

Another expected future work is to integrate a new sensing mechanism at the sender's side of the Taste/IP system. Currently, the sender manually formulates the taste message using the mobile application. There are several electronic tongue solutions already developed by research groups [8]. However, it is required to develop more compact and lightweight taste sensing mechanisms to integrate the sensation of taste in a practical communication system. By integrating a sensing mechanism, the sender will be able to capture a taste automatically. In addition, an encoding and decoding mechanism can be developed by extending the TXML to facilitate a complete communication system in the future. For example, if the sender wants to share the taste of his glass of wine with a friend, he/she should be able to automatically capture the taste of that wine in order to send it to the other end. Therefore, it is necessary to integrate a novel sensing apparatus with an advanced encoding mechanism in the future. Moreover, taste is the sense we use the most in perceiving flavor along with the senses of smell, vision, and few other modalities. As explained in [15], we will also explore the possibilities of using brain stimulation mechanisms in the future for multisensory communication methods through flavors (particularly both non-chemical smell and taste).

5. CONCLUSION

In conclusion, this paper presented the Taste/IP, an interactive system to share a taste sensation digitally. As discussed, three main modules were introduced. First, the mobile interface was presented to form a taste message, which includes the sensation of taste and level of intensity. Then, we discussed a novel messaging format to include the taste message with its corresponding properties. Most interestingly, as the third, we discussed a novel method to generate taste sensations digitally, which displays the taste message sent by the sender through the mobile application.

Although the sensation of taste is not facilitated by modern digital media, it is an immensely valuable experience in human life. Thus, in the future, based on the Taste/IP approach, there will be potential applications to incorporate the sensation of taste into the digital communication domain. Furthermore, we believe this paper described current challenges and limitations of this endeavor, while exploring novel methods to enhance digital-mobile multimodal interactions.

6. ACKNOWLEDGMENTS

We would like to thank Prof. P. Gopalakrishnakone and Dr. Hideaki Nii for their invaluable advices and help. This research is supported by the Singapore National Research Foundation under its International Research Centre @ Singapore Funding Initiative and administered by the IDM Programme Office.

7. REFERENCES

[1] R. Brown and D. McNeill. The" tip of the tongue" phenomenon. *Journal of verbal learning and verbal behavior*, 5(4):325–337, 1966.

[2] A. Cruz and B. Green. Thermal stimulation of taste. *Nature*, 403(6772):889–892, 2000.

[3] D. Derbyshire. The headset that will mimic all five senses. *http://www.dailymail.co.uk/sciencetech/article-1159206/The-headset-mimic-senses-make-virtual-world-convincing-real-life.html*, 2009.

[4] T. Eriksen. *Tyranny of the moment: Fast and slow time in the information age.* Pluto Press, 2001.

[5] F. Gemperle, C. DiSalvo, J. Forlizzi, and W. Yonkers. The hug: a new form for communication. In *Proceedings of the 2003 conference on Designing for user experiences*, pages 1–4. ACM, 2003.

[6] H. Iwata, H. Yano, T. Uemura, and T. Moriya. Food simulator: A haptic interface for biting. In *Virtual Reality, 2004. Proceedings. IEEE*, pages 51–57. IEEE, 2004.

[7] I. Lackovic and Z. Stare. Low-frequency dielectric properties of the oral mucosa. In *13th International Conference on Electrical Bioimpedance and the 8th Conference on Electrical Impedance Tomography*, pages 154–157. Springer, 2007.

[8] A. Legin, A. Rudnitskaya, Y. Vlasov, C. Di Natale, F. Davide, and A. D'Amico. Tasting of beverages using an electronic tongue. *Sensors and Actuators B: Chemical*, 44(1-3):291–296, 1997.

[9] L. Loflin. Introduction to constant current circuits. *http://www.bristolwatch.com/ccs/index.htm*, 2011.

[10] D. Maynes-Aminzade. Edible bits: Seamless interfaces between people, data and food. In *Conference on Human Factors in Computing Systems (CHI'05)-Extended Abstracts*, pages 2207–2210. Citeseer, 2005.

[11] H. Nakamura and H. Miyashita. Augmented gustation using electricity. In *Proceedings of the 2nd Augmented Human International Conference*, page 34. ACM, 2011.

[12] T. Narumi, T. Kajinami, T. Tanikawa, and M. Hirose. Meta cookie. In *ACM SIGGRAPH 2010 Posters*, page 143. ACM, 2010.

[13] K. Plattig and J. Innitzer. Taste qualities elicited by electric stimulation of single human tongue papillae. *Pflügers Archiv European Journal of Physiology*, 361(2):115–120, 1976.

[14] A. Pleasonton. Sensitivity of the tongue to electrical stimulation. *Journal of Speech and Hearing Research*, 13(3):635, 1970.

[15] N. Ranasinghe, K. Karunanayaka, A. D. Cheok, O. N. N. Fernando, H. Nii, and P. Gopalakrishnakone. Digital taste and smell communication. In *Proceedings of the 6th International Conference on Body Area Networks*, BodyNets '11, pages 78–84, 2011.

[16] J. Stillman, R. Morton, K. Hay, Z. Ahmad, and D. Goldsmith. Electrogustometry: strengths, weaknesses, and clinical evidence of stimulus boundaries. *Clinical Otolaryngology & Allied Sciences*, 28(5):406–410, 2003.

[17] K. Talavera, K. Yasumatsu, T. Voets, G. Droogmans, N. Shigemura, Y. Ninomiya, R. Margolskee, and B. Nilius. Heat activation of trpm5 underlies thermal sensitivity of sweet taste. *Nature*, 438(7070):1022–1025, 2005.

[18] A. Volta. On the electricity excited by the mere contact of conducting substances of different kinds. *Philosophical Transactions of the Royal Society of London*, 90:403–431, 1800.

[19] Y. Yang, Y. Zhang, Z. Hou, and B. Lemaire-Semail. Adding haptic feedback to touch screens at the right time. In *Proceedings of the 13th international conference on multimodal interfaces*, ICMI '11, pages 73–80, New York, NY, USA, 2011. ACM.

Learning Models for Speaker, Addressee and Overlap Detection from Multimodal Streams

Oriol Vinyals
University of California at Berkeley
1947 Center Street, Suite 600
Berkeley, CA, US
vinyals@eecs.berkeley.edu

Dan Bohus
Microsoft Research
One Microsoft Way
Redmond, WA, US
dbohus@microsoft.com

Rich Caruana
Microsoft Research
One Microsoft Way
Redmond, WA, US
rcaruana@microsoft.com

ABSTRACT
A key challenge in developing conversational systems is fusing streams of information provided by different sensors to make inferences about the behaviors and goals of people. Such systems can leverage visual and audio information collected through cameras and microphone arrays, including the location of various people, their focus of attention, body pose, the sound source direction, prosody, and speech recognition results. In this paper, we explore discriminative learning techniques for making accurate inferences on the problems of speaker, addressee and overlap detection in multiparty human-computer dialog. The focus is on finding ways to leverage within- and across-signal temporal patterns and to automatically construct representations from the raw streams that are informative for the inference problem. We present a novel extension to traditional decision trees which allows them to incorporate and model temporal signals. We contrast these methods with more traditional approaches where a human expert manually engineers relevant temporal features. The proposed approach performs well even with relatively small amounts of training data, which is of practical importance as designing features that are task dependent is time consuming and not always possible.

Categories and Subject Descriptors
H.1.2 **[Models and Principles]:** User/Machine System – *Human Information Processing*; H.5.2 [**Information Interfaces and Presentation**]: Multimedia Information Systems – *Audio input/outputs;* User Interfaces – *Natural Language*

General Terms
Algorithms, Human Factors

Keywords
Multiparty turn taking; multimodal systems; multimodal inference; addressee detection; overlap detection; speaker identification; learning with multimodal temporally streaming data; random forests

1. INTRODUCTION
One of the key challenges in multimodal interactive systems is performing accurate inference from multiple streams of evidence.

Examples include: recognizing activities from joint location information produced by a skeletal tracker, classifying pen or multi-touch gestures, detecting affect from temporal patterns in the acoustic prosodical contour, fusing information from the trajectory and temporal dynamics of visual focus of attention to recognize engagement actions, etc.

A wide array of machine learning techniques have been explored for this type of multimodal inference problems. A simple, commonly used approach for leveraging temporally streaming evidence in classification problems is for a domain expert to manually design features that capture or encode patterns in the temporal streams that may be relevant for the task at hand. These hand-coded features can then be used in conjunction with various machine learning techniques to construct a classification model.

Consider the problem of detecting whether an utterance is addressed to a conversational system or to another participant in a multiparty spoken dialog setting. Apart from basic features that may describe various aspects of the utterance, such as the current dialog state, whether the utterance was correctly understood by the system, the duration of the utterance, etc., a number of *temporally streaming features*, such as the energy in the acoustic signal, its prosodical contour, the frame-by-frame visual focus of attention of the people in the conversation, etc., may also be available. To use the information in these streams with traditional classification approaches, derived features can be manually constructed. Examples include: the average energy at the beginning, middle, and end of the utterance, the percentage of time the speaker maintained their focus-of-attention on the system in the last 100, 200, 500, 1000 milliseconds, prosodical contour statistics like pitch slope, mean, variance, in different segments of the utterance, etc.

This manual feature construction process provides an opportunity for a human expert to infuse deep knowledge into the model by creating complex features that are likely to be relevant to the prediction task. Relying on a manual feature engineering process, however, has several drawbacks: it requires human insight that might not be available for all streams, it makes it more difficult to add additional streams to an existing system, and the expert can never be certain that they have thoroughly explored the space of constructed features.

In this paper we explore the use of discriminative learning techniques on four multimodal inference problems related to speaker, addressee and overlap detection in multiparty human-computer interaction. Developing accurate models for these tasks is critical for enabling physically situated spoken language interaction in open-world settings. We introduce machine learning techniques that aim to shortcut the manual feature engineering process by directly using the raw streaming features. Specifically, we extend the traditional decision tree and random forest algorithms in a manner that allows them to directly incorporate temporally streaming evidence. We compare this novel methodology to the more common manual feature engineering approach. The results suggest that the new approach can learn directly from the stream features. While the approach does not achieve the full performance of models trained on human engineered features, it eliminates the challenging process of manually constructing task-dependent features.

We begin by reviewing related work in the next section. Then, in Section 3, we describe the technical details of the proposed approach. In Section 4 we describe the datasets and multimodal inference problems we used as the empirical test-bed for the proposed techniques, and in Section 5 we present and discuss in detail the results we obtained. Finally, in Section 6 we draw conclusions and present directions for future work.

2. RELATED WORK

The work described in this paper is part of a larger research effort aimed at developing conversational agents that can engage in spoken language interaction in multiparty settings [1, 2]. Specifically, we investigate a number of discriminative learning techniques on the problems of speaker, addressee and overlap detection in multiparty human-computer interactions. The problems of constructing models for addressee and source identification in multiparty settings, as well as other related problems (*e.g.* tracking visual focus of attention) have been previously investigated in various human-computer, *i.a.* [3, 4] and human-human, *i.a.* [5, 6, 7] settings. For instance in [3] the authors interpolate models that use audio and visual cues to determine addressee in a human-human-robot interaction setting. In [4] the authors explore features such as eye gaze, dialogue history and utterance length, and combine them with a Naïve Bayes classifier to identify addressees. In [5] Bayesian Network and Naïve Bayes classifiers are used for addressee identification in face-to-face meetings with four participants. [6] presents a hierarchical generative approach that is used in conjunction with MCMC techniques for jointly tracking the location and speaking activity of multiple participants in a sensor equipped meeting room. In [7] the authors use a generative model for inferring conversational regime (*i.e.* a characterization of the joint gaze patterns) and head directions in a multiparty conversation. Related work in speaker diarization aiming at very short interactions [8] has shown that for extremely short utterances like the ones present in our scenario classic diarization approaches are prone to failure.

We focus on using discriminative techniques to learn from multiparty human-computer interaction data. Some of the main challenges in our domain include integrating temporally streaming features (*e.g.* information from a microphone array or face tracker) with point features (*e.g.* information about dialog state, etc.); the availability of relatively small amounts of training data; and noisy observations.

Almost all applied machine learning uses domain knowledge to extract meaningful features. A good example of this with temporal sequences and Naïve Bayes decision rules can be found in [9]. In [10] the authors present an approach where a manually constructed dictionary of encoding templates is used to create features over sequences that are then filtered in a feature selection process and integrated with a LDCRF model to recognize head gestures.

The use of decision trees in conjunction with sequential data has been previously investigated in other domains. In [11], the authors used acoustic data to predict phonemes as the acoustic model for speech recognition. In their work, each data point in a sequence is treated as an observation, which is equivalent to stacking all the sequences into a large feature vector, and learning a standard decision tree.

[12] also proposed to learn features from sequences of data, and extended the set of classical rules for building a decision tree to include time-aware splitting criterion. This work is more closely related to one of our approaches, presented in Section 3.1.2, but would be computationally prohibitive given the length and nature of our sequences (which mostly consist of continuous real data instead of discrete observations).

3. APPROACH

We focus our attention on two discriminative learning approaches: maximum entropy models and random forests of decision trees. Maximum entropy models are a robust machine learning technique: they are simple, linear models, are easy to train and produce well-calibrated probability outputs. Decision trees can construct more complex decision surfaces by shaping and combining features in non-linear ways. This property can be important for multimodal inference where relationships between information collected across multiple channels is often relevant for the task at hand. A random forest of decision trees [13] typically is resistant to overfitting and often has good generalization error.

A common approach for learning from streaming evidence with these discriminative learning methods is to manually engineer derived features. In an effort to investigate whether we can shortcut this manual feature engineering process, we propose an extension to decision trees that enables them to handle raw, temporally streaming features. Below, we describe this extension, and discuss in more detail the benefits of the random forest approach.

3.1 Stream-enhanced decision trees

Decision trees construct complex decision surfaces by greedily splitting the data according to one feature (dimension) at a time, in a manner that separates data into neighborhoods of increasing purity. The construction of a decision tree is done in a recursive manner. Given a set of labeled data-points, a search is performed to identify the feature, and a corresponding threshold on that feature that "best" splits or partitions the data into subsets. "Best" is typically defined by various entropy-like metrics, such as information gain, that measure the relative purity of the newly formed subsets in contrast to the original set. Once the best split has been identified, the algorithm is recursively applied on the resulting partitions. The sequence of splits on each path from the root of the tree to a leaf allows trees to learn non-linear combinations of features.

Standard decision trees can easily handle real-valued, ordinal, nominal, and Boolean features. In this work we seek to additionally enable decision trees to reason directly about temporally streaming features. Let us denote a *temporally streaming feature* by $f_{\rightarrow}^{s} = \langle f_1^s, f_2^s, \dots, f_n^s \rangle$, where n is a constant[1], and $f_j^s \in \mathbb{R}$. For instance, if $f_{\rightarrow}^{s}$ is the horizontal location of a face in an image, $f_1^s, f_2^s, \dots, f_n^s$ represent the successive real-values of

[1] Here we assume fixed length streams, but this can be generalized to streams of arbitrary length.

the face location at times 1 through n. The challenge then becomes defining a way to partition data based on a temporally streaming feature $f_{\rightarrow}^{s}$. If an informative partitioning can be done, the traditional decision tree methodology can be applied to leverage the raw streaming features. Below, we discuss two mechanisms for creating such partitions.

3.1.1 The Pivot Approach
The first approach we propose is based on selecting a *pivot* data-point, and creating partitions based on the similarity of other data-points to this pivot, where similarity is computed on the given streaming feature $f_{\rightarrow}^{s}$ using a certain metric.

In traditional decision trees, a split on a non-streaming, real-valued point feature f^b is defined by a threshold t. Given the threshold, the data is partitioned into two subsets: one that contains the data-points where $f^b < t$ and the other that contains the data-points where $f^b \geq t$. In contrast, in the proposed *pivot approach*, a split on a temporally streaming feature $f_{\rightarrow}^{s}$ is defined by a pivot data-point p and a threshold t. Given a pivot and a threshold, the data-points are separated into those that are more similar to the pivot (*i.e.* their distance to the pivot is below t), and those less similar to the pivot (*i.e.* their distance to the pivot is above t) – see Figure 1. The pivots are selected from among the data-points at the split, and thresholds are applied to distance metrics that measure how similar the feature stream $f_{\rightarrow}^{s}$ for one point (the pivot) is to another point that will pass into the left or right branch of the test. For example, if the similarity metric is cosine distance, the test measures how similar each data point is to the corresponding stream of the pivot (using cosine distance): the more similar points go down the left branch of the tree and the less similar points go down the right branch. The separation surface is a sphere in distance metric space, centered on the pivot point. For a real-valued point feature f^b the search for the best split involves searching over all possible thresholds, but in the case of a stream feature $f_{\rightarrow}^{s}$, the search must be done over all possible pivots *and* thresholds.

In the approach described so far, similarity is computed on the entire stream, from 1 to n. In reality only certain sub-regions of the stream might be relevant for a given classification problem, so a simple extension of the proposed approach is to compute the similarity on a particular window in the stream $w_s\!:\!w_e$. In this case, search involves finding a pivot p, a window $w = w_s\!:\!w_e$, and a threshold t such that the info-gain of the resulting partitions is maximized. The search can be further extended to include multiple distance metrics.

The pivot approach requires that at each node we save not only the selected feature and threshold but also the data-point used to define the pivot so that the similarity of future test points to the pivots can be measured. In traditional decision trees all training data is discarded once the tree has been trained. One can view pivot-based splits as a form of memory-based learning where distance is measured on a stream feature. A sequence of pivot tests performed on different streams in a path in the decision tree can capture complex within- and cross-stream temporal relationships. One potential disadvantage of pivot-based splits is that the number of possible pivot and threshold combinations can be very large. If multiple windows and distance metrics are used to further refine the similarity measure, the search space grows even larger. While the potential size of the search space is very large, by using a random forest decision tree growing procedure we are able to explore only a fraction of the full search space

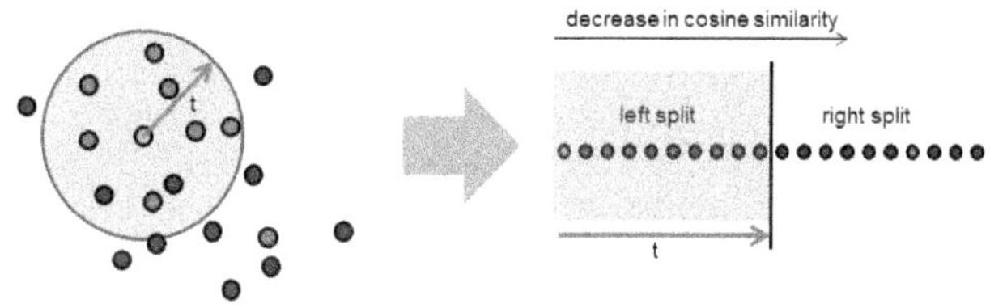

Figure 1. Each point represents a temporal sequence in a high dimensional space. Red and blue are the two classes. The green point is the selected pivot. A metric such as cosine distance is used to measure similarity to the pivot and a radius of threshold t defines the split.

while simultaneously reducing the overfitting of individual trees and increasing the diversity of the tree forest, thus yielding a stream-based decision tree algorithm that is both accurate and reasonably efficient. It is not as efficient as if a human expert had carefully constructed exactly those stream features needed for the task at hand, but it is efficient enough to run on real data and allows one to develop a complete system much faster than when features must be manually constructed.

3.1.2 The Basis-Function Approach
The second approach we investigate does not require memorization of pivot data-points, and is more similar to the traditional feature construction methodology. In order to support the construction of a split on a stream feature $f_{\rightarrow}^{s}$, we compute a set of basis functions within a specific window on the stream, and threshold the result of that function. For example, to create a split on the sound amplitude streaming feature, we might compute the maximum value of the amplitude within the last 200ms in the stream, and search for a threshold on this maximum value. All data points with maximum amplitude in that window below the threshold go down one branch of the tree, while all above the threshold go down the other branch.

Our goal is to develop a small set of basis functions that would be useful across a wide range of problems and streams. We initially used the min, max, and first, second and third moments of the stream. Later we added the second and third *central* moments of the stream (see discussion in section 5).

Unlike the pivot approach, the basis-function approach is equivalent to constructing derived features for each basis function and window in the stream. These features can therefore be pre-computed and then used as regular point features in the decision tree; no extra memorization is required as with pivots. Unlike manually constructed features, once an adequate set of basis functions for temporally streaming features have been established, no manual expertise or insight into the problem or the specific streams is necessary. This makes adding new streams and working with a large number of streams easier.

3.2 Random Forests
A random forest [13] is an unweighted ensemble of decision trees. Each decision tree in the forest is grown on a random subsample of the training data (as with bagging [14]) and uses a randomized split selection procedure that further increases the diversity among the trees. In traditional decision trees, the split selection procedure examines all possible splits and selects the feature and threshold combination that maximizes a measure such as information gain. In random forests, the split selection procedure is only allowed to select from a small random subset of the available features. This randomization makes the decision tree growing process less greedy, increases the diversity of the trees in the ensemble, and

reduces overfitting. Importantly, the random selection of a subset of features from which to select the best split is repeated as each test is installed in the tree, insuring that important attributes and attribute combinations eventually can be discovered on most paths. Although randomization does slightly hurt the accuracy of individual trees, on most problems the gain from the increased diversity of the trees in the ensemble usually more than compensates for this loss, and random forests usually are more accurate than bagged decision trees which do not perform feature randomization prior to selection [15].

In addition to making the ensemble more accurate, a secondary benefit of feature randomization is that far fewer tests need to be considered when deciding what split to install at a node. For example, if only 10% of the available features will be considered for each test, learning will be sped up by a factor of almost 10X. (Because the trees in a random forest are more diverse, one often needs to add more trees to the random forest ensemble, so in practice the gains are somewhat less than this calculation suggests.) We exploit this feature of random forests to partially mitigate the increase in computation required to train trees with the pivot and basis-function approaches outlined above, and to help prevent overfitting from the larger search space over splits.

One advantage of user-constructed features is that complex operations on multiple streams can be crafted prior to learning and are thus available for use in a single split. Tree-based learning methods such as random forests use sequences of tests to combine features. If user-constructed features are not available and the tree must combine multiple streams, the greedy tree-growing process will require multiple steps of learning to construct these higher-order features, and may miss useful combinations if the streams that must be combined do not appear useful individually. Despite this limitation, tree-based ensemble methods are remarkably accurate in many domains [15].

4. DATA

The data for our experiments were collected via a user study that was part of a larger research effort [1, 2] aimed at developing and evaluating computational models for multiparty turn taking. In this experiment, a virtually embodied conversational agent (equipped with a wide-angle camera and a microphone array) engaged in spoken dialog and hosted a trivia questions game with groups of two or three people. The agent asked the questions and mediated the interaction between the participants. The participants could talk to the agent as well as to each other throughout the interactions. Once agreement between participants had been established, the agent indicated if the answer was correct, or provided the correct answer and a short explanation, and then moved to the next question.

The data collection involved 15 groups of four participants each, recruited in pairs of people that knew each other. For each group of four people, all possible subgroups of 2 and of 3 people were formed, and each subgroup played one game with the system. This resulted in a total of 150 dialogs, where in 90 of them the agent played the game with two participants, and in 60 of them the agent played the game with three participants.

The data was transcribed and manually labeled with speaker and addressee information, and an evaluation of the system's turn-taking capabilities was conducted [2]. Lessons learned from this evaluation indicated that major challenges for multiparty turn-taking in these settings include diarization, as well as identifying the speaker and addressees for each utterance. Based on this analysis, we formulated four multimodal inference problems, which we describe below.

4.1 Multimodal Inference Problems

A data-point in each of the problems described below consists of a *detected utterance, i.e.* a continuous segment identified at runtime by the voice activity detector in the system as a single utterance. Given the challenges of diarization in a live, multiparty, interactive setting, each detected utterance may contain speech from a single participant, or concatenated or overlapping speech from multiple participants, or just background noise.

The first problem we defined, which we refer to as the *Target* problem, is a binary classification problem: the goal is to identify whether a detected utterance was addressed to the system or to another participant. When detected utterances contained speech from multiple participants, the addressee for the last spoken segment was considered the target.

The second problem, which we call the *Overlap* problem, is also a binary classification problem: the goal here is to identify whether a detected utterance contains speech from a single, or from multiple participants; the later includes overlapped speech or successive speech from multiple speakers that has been concatenated by the voice-activity detector into a single detected utterance. Detected utterances containing background noise are labeled as single source in the *Overlap* problem.

The third and fourth problems are multiclass problems, and they regard speaker identification. *Source-2* is a 4-way classification problem that was defined on the subset of the data where the system interacted with two participants. The challenge here is to identify whether the detected utterance contains: (1) speech from the first participant, (2) speech from the second participant, (3) speech from both participants, or (4) background noise. Similarly, *Source-3* was defined as a 5-way classification problem on the subset of the data where the system interacted with three participants. The challenge is to identify whether the detected utterance contains (1) speech from the first participant, (2) the second participant, (3) the third participant, (4) a combination of speech from multiple participants, or (5) background noise. The last two problems are closely related to the *Overlap* problem: they refine the *Overlap* detection problem by further separating out the background class and decomposing the "single-source" class to identify the speaker.

4.2 Features

We extracted a set of basic features from seven different modalities and knowledge sources in the system, which we describe below. Some of these features are inherently defined on a per-utterance basis: we refer to them as *basic point features*. Examples include the dialog state at the time the utterance was produced, the speech recognition confidence score for the utterance, whether a non-understanding was triggered, etc. Other features are continuously streaming through time, *e.g.* the microphone array beam direction, or the position of a participant's detected face. We refer to this latter category as *stream features*.

As previously discussed, a common approach for leveraging such streaming evidence is to manually engineer derived point features from the stream features. For instance, computing the standard deviation of the microphone beam location while the utterance is being produced could be informative for predicting whether the detected utterance contains speech from a single source, or overlapping speech from multiple participants. We manually engineered a wide array of such derived features. A large number of these features were designed and used in previous work [16].

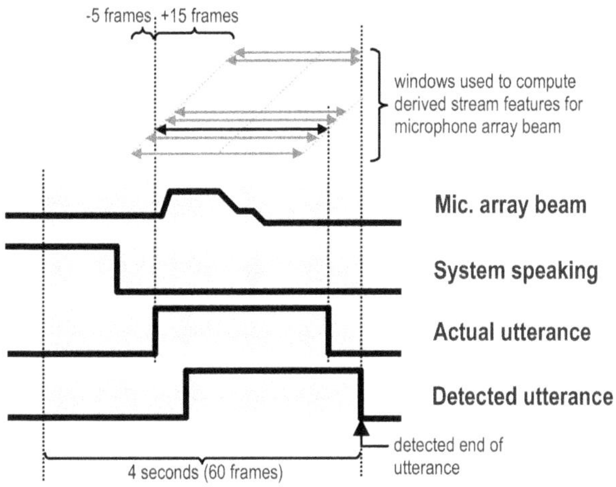

Figure 2. Visualization of four streaming features and windows used to construct derived features for the location of the microphone array beam

To facilitate comparison, both the stream-enabled trees and the manual feature construction were based on the 4-second interval (60 frames at 15fps) prior to the moment the system detected the end of that utterance – see Figure 2. As described below, various sub-regions of this 4-second interval were used to construct derived features.

We now review the set of basic and manually derived features used in the experiments below. They fall into seven classes, according to the knowledge source or modality that originated the feature.

Understanding. This class includes 13 basic point features describing the results of the spoken language recognition and understanding process on the detected utterance. Examples include the speech recognition confidence score, whether or not a non-understanding was triggered, the number of alternates in the n-best list, and average number of words, as well as indicators about whether the top hypothesis or the alternates contain the positive and negative lexical markers *yes* or *no*.

Situation. This class includes one basic point feature indicating whether the agent is interacting with two or three participants.

Dialog. This class includes 8 basic point features that characterize the current dialog state, including classifications at different granularities of the dialog act, whether the last system question was addressed to a single or to multiple participants, whether the previous agent utterance was interrupted by the participant, etc.

Turn-taking. This class includes 3 binary stream features, indicating: (1) when the detected utterance is in progress, (2) when the actual utterance is in progress, and (3) when an agent utterance is in progress. Because of technological delays in the voice activity detection and speech processing pipeline, there is a delay between the moment an utterance actually begins (or ends) until it is detected by the speech engine – see also Figure 2. Based on information available in the 4-second window on these three stream features, we constructed an additional 16 derived features that describe various temporal aspects of turn taking, such as the duration of the detected and actual utterances, and of system speech, the deltas between system speech and the utterances, and the presence of overlaps.

Microphone array. This class includes 3 stream features, which indicate (at two different granularities) the location of the active microphone array beam at any point in time. To construct derived features we considered a set of windows of the same size as the actual utterance but shifted with respect to the actual utterance by -5, -4, -3, … , +14, +15 frames – see Figure 2. If a shifted window extended beyond the boundaries of the 4 second segment, it was cropped to those boundaries. Within the defined windows, we computed the number of distinct active beams, the beam excursion and standard deviation, as well as the average absolute distance from the beam to the location of each actor in the scene, for a total of 126 additional derived features. The intuition for the shifting windows computation is that, like the detection of the utterance, the beam location signal from the microphone array arrives at a certain (unknown) delay from the actual utterance, hence the most informative portion of the signal is in one of these windows.

Acoustic. This class includes a single stream feature that captures the amplitude of the audio signal at any point in time. Based on this stream feature we computed a derived feature which captures the average log energy throughout the actual utterance. In addition, we computed the average log energy (as well as a normalized version with respect to the entire utterance) in a set of windows that cover regions prior to and after the start, and prior to and after the end of the actual utterance. In total, 126 additional derived features were computed to capture the energy of the signal in different regions near the beginning and end of the utterance.

Vision. This class includes 18 stream features (6 per participant), which continuously capture vision information about the participants in the scene. The information includes location, size, and orientation of the tracked faces, the confidence score from the face tracker. In addition, two streams capture information about the inferred visual focus of attention of each participant at two different levels of granularity. One is based on a face detection algorithm and provides information about face orientation in 5 categories: frontal, left, slightly-left, right, slightly-right. The second captures a heuristic that the system uses to classify the face orientation into three categories: left, right, frontal. The information from the face location streams was used in conjunction with the information from the microphone array to construct a set of manually derived features. In addition, we constructed a large set of derived features based on the attentional streams, by computing the mean value the face was oriented in a certain position, throughout various windows prior to and after the beginning, and prior to and after the end of the actual utterance.

5. EXPERIMENTS AND RESULTS

The data collected in the user study described earlier was separated in 15 folds, corresponding to the 15 groups of 4 participants that interacted with the system. We randomly selected 8 of the 15 folds for training/development, and held the other 7 aside as a test set. We developed and analyzed the proposed methods by performing cross-validation experiments on the development set. Once the methods were developed and stable, we evaluated them by training the models on the development set and testing against the test set. For the binary *Target* and *Overlap* problems the training set contained 2101 utterances and the test set contained 2078 utterances. Because the *Source-2* and *Source-3* problems use only the interactions between the system and two or three other participants, respectively, the amount of data is reduced compared to the other two problems. Specifically, for the *Source-2* problem, the train set contained 1218 utterances and the test set contained 1133 utterances; for the *Source-3* problem, the train set contained 871 utterances and the test set contained 941 utterances.

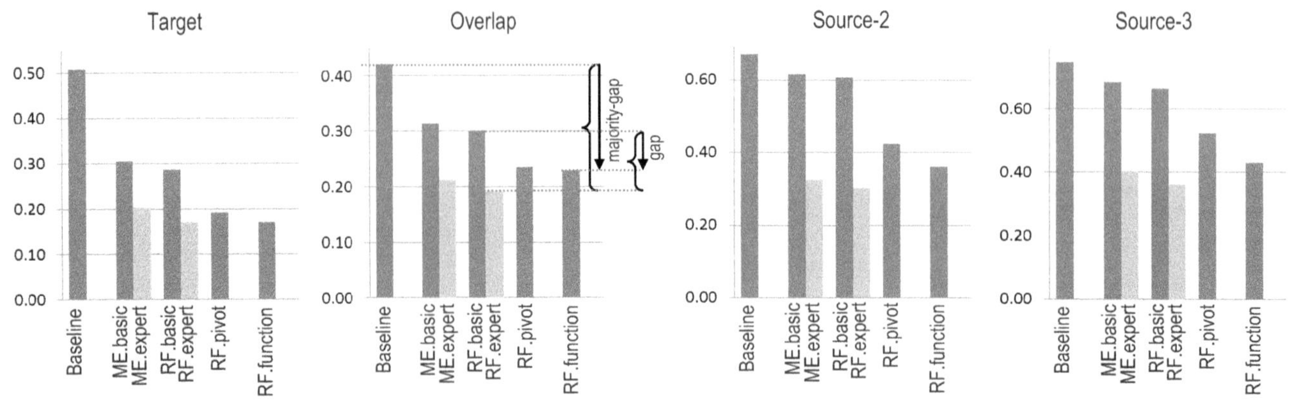

Figure 3. L2 test-set performance of the models on the four multimodal inference problems

The models for inferring speech source, target and overlap that we develop below are to be used in a spoken dialog system in conjunction with decision theoretic approaches for managing turn-taking actions [16]. As such, in addition to accuracy, it is important that these models produce well-calibrated probabilities. We therefore focus the evaluation on the L2-norm (mean squared error of the model's probabilistic output to 0-1 targets), which is a proper scoring rule, and reflects both model refinement and calibration [17]. For completeness, we also report classification error.

We begin by constructing models that only use the basic point features and models that use both the basic and the manually constructed derived features. We refer to the former as *basic* models and the latter as *expert* models. We experimented with maximum entropy models (ME) and random forests (RF). To regularize, the maximum entropy models used standard L1 regularization, with the regularization weight optimized in a 10-fold cross-validation procedure on the train set. For the random forest approach, we trained 200 trees, using information gain as the splitting criterion. We trained each tree with a bootstrap sample from the training set, and at each node randomly sampled 30% of all features to consider for potential splits[2].

The test set results for the *basic* and *expert* models, trained using the maximum entropy and the random forest approach, across all four problems, are shown in Table 1 and illustrated in Figure 3. In each case, the *expert* model improved performance on both L2 and classification error by a significant amount, highlighting the utility of the manually constructed derived features. The random forest approach consistently outperforms the maximum entropy models by a small amount. In contrast to maximum entropy models, random forests are capable of learning non-linear models. The results suggest non-linearity might be useful on these problems. The random forest approach also may be more robust to overfitting.

The *expert* random forest model, which uses manually crafted features, attains a classification error rate of 10.8% on the addressee identification problem (*Target*), and 12.3% on overlap detection. We believe this operating range can enable better decisions for multiparty turn-taking in spoken dialog systems. The error rates are somewhat higher in the Source-2 and Source-3 problems (19.5% and 24.6%, respectively). Recall however that

	Model	L2			Error
		Test	m-gap (%)	gap (%)	Test
Target	**Majority baseline**	**0.51**	**0.0**	**-**	**44.2**
	ME.basic	0.30	60.3	-16.3	21.2
	ME.expert	0.20	90.2	71.4	13.9
	RF.basic	**0.29**	**65.8**	**0.0**	**21.1**
	RF.expert	**0.17**	**100.0**	**100.0**	**10.8**
	RF.pivot	0.19	93.8	81.9	11.8
	RF.basis-function	0.17	100.0	99.9	10.0
Overlap	**Majority baseline**	**0.42**	**0.0**	**-**	**29.2**
	ME.basic	0.31	46.9	-13.6	21.8
	ME.expert	0.21	91.4	81.6	14.2
	RF.basic	**0.30**	**53.3**	**0.0**	**20.2**
	RF.expert	**0.19**	**100.0**	**100.0**	**12.3**
	RF.pivot	0.23	81.4	60.1	16.1
	RF.basis-function	0.23	83.4	64.4	15.4
Source-2	**Majority baseline**	**0.67**	**0.0**	**-**	**60.2**
	ME.basic	0.62	15.0	-3.0	52.9
	ME.expert	0.33	93.7	92.4	20.6
	RF.basic	**0.61**	**17.5**	**0.0**	**51.5**
	RF.expert	**0.30**	**100.0**	**100.0**	**19.5**
	RF.pivot	0.42	67.1	60.1	29.5
	RF.basis-function	0.36	84.7	81.4	23.9
Source-3	**Majority baseline**	**0.75**	**0.0**	**-**	**65.7**
	ME.basic	0.68	16.5	-6.3	60.9
	ME.expert	0.40	89.4	86.5	28.5
	RF.basic	**0.66**	**21.4**	**0.0**	**60.6**
	RF.expert	**0.36**	**100.0**	**100.0**	**24.6**
	RF.pivot	0.52	58.2	46.8	35.6
	RF.basis-function	0.43	81.8	76.9	28.8

Table 1. Test-set comparison of the models on the four multimodal inference problems. The majority baseline and the basic and expert models that define the gap scales are in bold; the best performing stream-based approach is highlighted

these problems are more difficult because these are 4- and 5-way classification problems, we are trying to simultaneously identify both the source and overlaps, and we have less data to train on.

We now turn our attention to the proposed stream random forest models, which use the basic point features and directly leverage the temporally streaming features by using the *pivot* and *basis-function* approaches. Like before, we build 200 trees using bootstrap samples. For the *pivot* approach, we used the cosine similarity metric on windows in the 60 frame stream. To keep the number of windows manageable, we only considered windows that start or stop on every third frame, yielding a total of 210 possible windows. At each node, to create a split, we considered a

[2] To set parameters such as the number of trees in the random forest and the fraction of features to consider at each split, we conducted preliminary cross-validation experiments on the training set. Results indicated that 200 trees were sufficient to asymptote in performance and that the random forest was robust to a wide range of parameter values.

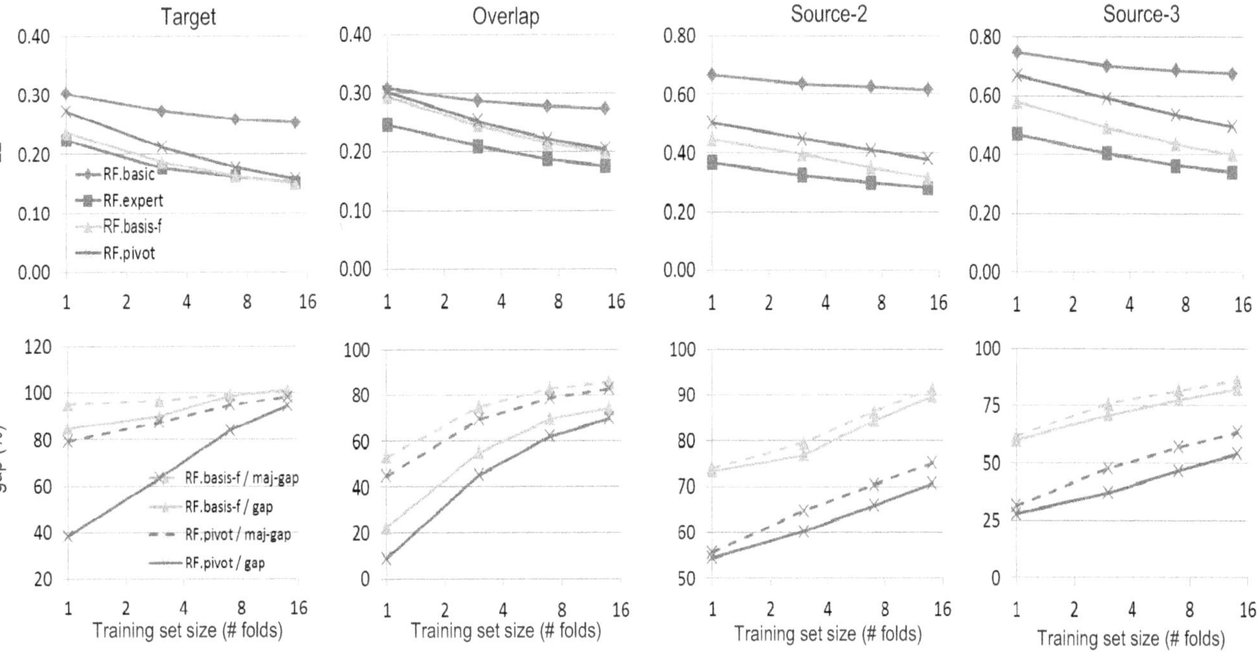

Figure 4. Effect of dataset size on random forest models across the four problems.
Top: L2 error versus number of training folds for basic, expert, pivot, and basis-function models.
Bottom: majority-gap and gap versus number of training folds for pivot and basis-function models.

randomly selected 30% of the point and stream features; for splits on stream features we considered 10% of the data-points that arrive at that node as possible pivots to search over, with 10% of all possible windows.

For the *basis-function* approach we initially considered the min, max, and the first, second, and third moment of the streams. Experiments conducted in cross-validation on the train set revealed the importance of using central moments for the *Overlap* problem: a very informative feature is the standard deviation of the microphone array beam. We therefore added the second and third *central* moments to the set of basis functions. Like in the pivot approach, the split construction algorithm had access to a randomly selected subset containing 30% of the point and stream features, and, in this case, 10% of the possible combinations of basis function and windows for stream feature splits.

We compare these models against the majority baseline, and against the basic and expert models previously constructed using the random forest approach (since they outperformed the maximum entropy models). To facilitate these comparisons, we compute two *gap* measures. The first, denoted *majority-gap* (m-gap in Table 1) indicates how much of the L2 gap between the *majority* baseline and the *expert* model is covered by a given approach (see also Figure 3): 0% indicates that an approach performs no better than the *majority* baseline and 100% indicates that the approach performs as well as the *expert* model, which uses the manually engineered features. The second measure, denoted simply *gap* indicates how much of the reduction in L2 error between the *basic* and *expert* models a given approach covers (see also Figure 3).

The results shown in Table 1 and illustrated in Figure 3 indicate that both the *pivot* and *basis-function* approaches significantly improve upon the *basic* model in all four problems; both methods leverage some of the information in the temporally streaming features. The results also indicate that the basis-function approach outperforms the pivot approach on each problem, improving L2 loss by as little as 0.005 on *Overlap* to as much as 0.09 on *Source-3*. This corresponds to gap scores 4% to 30% better for the basis-function approach.

Comparing the basis function approach to the *expert* model, we see gap scores that range from 64% to 100% and majority-gap scores that vary from 82% to 100%. These results indicate that the basis function random forest method performs almost as well as random forests with manually constructed features (but without requiring human expertise).

5.1 Learning rate experiments

The results discussed in the previous section were obtained by training models on the 8-fold development set and testing on the held-out test set – only half of the available data was used for training. We expect that, with more data, the stream-enabled random forest would further improve performance: as more data is available the trees can grow deeper and the model might capture increasingly more sophisticated cross-stream effects. To explore this hypothesis we performed another experiment where we used cross-validation on the entire dataset (all 15 folds) to train models with varying amounts of data. For each test fold, we randomly selected 1, 3, 7, and 14 of the remaining train folds and built models. To reduce variance in the estimates, we repeated this process 4 times for each test fold, and report the average of the performance of the 4 models.

The results are illustrated in Figure 4: the top row shows the performance of the *basic*, *expert*, *basis-function* and *pivot* random forest models across the four problems, as the amount of training data is increased from 1 to 3 to 7, and finally to 14 folds; the bottom row shows the corresponding gap scores. As is typical for reporting learning curves, the x-axis is shown on a log-scale. The plots indicate that, as more data becomes available, the gap and majority-gap scores increase: the methods learning from the raw streams are approaching the performance of the expert baseline. This suggests that the need to manually construct stream-based features is mitigated as more data becomes available, allowing one to focus on collecting more data (always a good thing) instead of trying to understand the temporal stream data and manually construct effective derived features from them.

5.2 Alternate Methods and Future Work

There are other models that learn directly from sequence data. We have conducted preliminary experiments with both Hidden Markov Models (HMMs) and Recurrent Neural Nets (RNNs).

With HMMs, for each class we use Baum-Welch to train a separate model. Each HMM uses discrete observations derived via vector quantization from the parallel streams. The likelihood scores resulting from HMM decoding of the stream sequences are used as additional point features for learning (*i.e.*, one additional point feature is created for each class). There are many design decisions that must be made to train HMMs and prevent overfitting that must be investigated.

We are also experimenting with using RNNs to create point features that encode the information in the streams. So far, given the small training data, we have been unable to train RNNs successfully from all streams jointly. One potential solution is to train one RNN per stream to construct point features.

Overfitting is a major issue for these models given the amount of training data. Further investigation of these methods is part of future work.

6. CONCLUSION

We investigated discriminative learning approaches (maximum entropy and random forests) for building multimodal inference models for the problems of speaker, addressee, and overlap detection in human-computer interaction. Results indicate that both models perform well on these tasks, with the random forest approach consistently outperforming the maximum entropy method by a small amount.

In an effort to shortcut the manual feature construction process, we developed a novel extension to decision tree learning that enables trees to reason directly about temporally streaming features. The results suggest that the new approach can learn directly from the stream features. While the approach does not achieve the full performance of models trained on the features we manually engineered, it eliminates the often challenging process of manually constructing task-dependent features; results also suggest that adding more data narrows the gap between automatically and manually generated features.

We believe there is room to further improve the stream-based trees. For instance, while selecting stream windows in the pivot and basis-function approaches introduces information about the temporal dimension, the similarity metric and the aggregate statistics we used are not themselves time sensitive. An analysis of the constructed trees can shed more light on the type of within- and cross-stream feature representations that tree can create. An evaluation against features manually engineered by multiple experts on different problems would create a better understanding of the relative performance of this approach. We hope that with further development the stream-based tree construction methods would even be able to learn feature patterns and combinations that human experts might miss.

7. REFERENCES

[1] Bohus, D., and Horvitz, E., (2009). Dialog in the Open World: Platform and Applications, *ICMI'09*, Boston, MA

[2] Bohus D., and Horvitz, E., (2011). Multiparty Turn Taking in Situated Dialog: Study, Lessons, and Directions, *SIGdial'2011*, Portland, OR.

[3] Katzenmaier, R., Stiefelhagen, R., and Schultz, T. 2004. Identifying the addressee in human-human-robot interactions based on head pose and speech. In *Proceedings of ICMI'04*.

[4] Van Turnhout, K., Terken, J., Bakx, I., and Eggen, B. 2005. Identifying the intended addressee in mixed human-human and human-computer interaction from non-verbal features. In *Proceedings of ICMI'05*, 175-182.

[5] Jovanovic, N., Akker, R., and Nijholt, A. (2006). Addressee identification in face-to-face meetings. In *Proceedings of the EACL'06*, 169-176, 2006.

[6] Gatica-Perez, D., Lathoud, G., Odobez, J-M., McCowan, I. 2005. Multimodal multispeaker probabilistic tracking in meetings, In *Proceedings of ICMI'05*.

[7] Otsuka, K., Takemae, Y., and Yamato, J., 2005. A probabilistic inference of multiparty-conversation structure based on Markov-switching models of gaze patterns, head directions, and utterances. In *Proceedings of ICMI'05*.

[8] Imseng, D., and Friedland, G., 2009. Robust Speaker Diarization for Short Speech Recordings, In *Proceedings of ASRU'2009*

[9] Kadous, M.W. 1999. Learning comprehensible descriptions of multivariate time series. In *Proceedings of the International Conference on Machine Learning*.

[10] Morency, L.P. and de Kok, I. and Gratch, J. 2008. Context-based recognition during human interactions: Automatic feature selection and encoding dictionary. In *Proceedings of the 10th international conference on Multimodal interfaces*.

[11] Droppo, J. and Seltzer, M.L. and Acero, A. and Chiu, Y.H.B. 2008. Towards a non-parametric acoustic model: An acoustic decision tree for observation probability calculation. In *Ninth Annual Conference of the International Speech Communication Association*.

[12] Karimi, K. and Hamilton, H.J. 2010. Generation and Interpretation of Temporal Decision Rules. *Arxiv preprint arXiv:1004.3334*.

[13] Breiman, L. (2001). Random forests. *Machine Learning*, 45, 5-32.

[14] Breiman, L. (1996). Bagging predictors. *Machine Learning*, 24, 123-140.

[15] Caruana, R., & Niculescu-Mizil, A. (2006). An empirical comparison of supervised learning algorithms. *ICML '06*, 161-168.

[16] Bohus, D., and Horvitz, E. (2011). Decisions about Turns in Multiparty Conversation: From Perception to Action. *ICMI'2011*, Alicante, Spain

[17] Cohen, I. and Goldszmidt, M., 2004. Properties and benefits of calibrated classifiers. In *Proceedings of EMCL/PKDD*. Pisa, Italy.

Analysis of the Correlation between the Regularity of Work Behavior and Stress Indices Based on Longitudinal Behavioral Data

Shogo Okada
Dept. of Computational Intelligence and Systems Science, Tokyo Institute of Technology
Yokohama, Japan
okada@ntt.dis.titech.ac.jp

Yusaku Sato
Dept. of Computational Intelligence and Systems Science, Tokyo Institute of Technology
Yokohama, Japan
ysato@ntt.dis.titech.ac.jp

Yuki Kamiya
C&C Innovation Initiative NEC Corporation
Ikoma, Japan
y-kamiya@fn.jp.nec.com

Keiji Yamada
C&C Innovation Initiative NEC Corporation
Ikoma,Japan
kg-yamada@cp.jp.nec.com

Katsumi Nitta
Dept. of Computational Intelligence and Systems Science, Tokyo Institute of Technology.
Yokohama, Japan
nitta@ntt.dis.titech.ac.jp

ABSTRACT

Increasingly, longitudinal behavioral data captured by various sensors are being analyzed to improve workplace performance. In this paper, we analyze the correlation between the regularity of workers' behavior and their levels of stress. We used a 23-month behavioral dataset for 18 workers that recorded their use of PCs and their locations in the office. We found that the principal eigenbehaviors extracted from the dataset with PCA represented typical work behaviors such as overwork using a PC and routine times for meetings. We found that more than 80% of each of the 18 workers' individual behaviors could be reconstructed using nine principal eigenbehaviors. In addition, the deviation ranges for the reconstruction accuracies were significantly different for workers in different positions. We conducted the correlation analysis between work behaviors of the workers and their stress level. Our results show a significant negative correlation ($r \geq 0.69$, $p < 0.01$) between the accuracy of reconstructed work behaviors and physical stress levels; and a significant positive correlation between the accuracy of reconstructed behavior and stress dissolution abilities. Our results suggest that the correlation between the stress level of workers and the regularity of their work behavior exists. This correlation will be useful for occupational healthcare.

Categories and Subject Descriptors

I.5.2 [**Pattern Recognition**]: Design Methodology—*Feature evaluation and selection*; H.2.8 [**Database Applications**]: Data mining

General Terms

Algorithms, Experimentation

Keywords

Activity Analysis, Lifelog, Sensor Network, Occupational Healthcare, Stress

1. INTRODUCTION

Various types of low-cost sensor nodes have recently become available, and rapidly changing sensor network technologies hold promise for novel applications using multimodal time series data [11]. One of the great open challenges in this area is understanding human behavior. Significant research has been devoted to analyzing individuals' daily behaviors. Examples of this research include classification of individuals' modes of transportation using a GPS sensor and an ac-celerometer [1], and identification of the contexts correlated with individuals' behaviors in a shopping mall using various kinds of environmental sensors to measure noise level, humidity, and ultraviolet rays [7].

Eagle and Pentland collected a behavioral dataset from smart phones used by 100 individuals, including call logs, location of users, and application usage [6]. They applied eigen-decomposition to extract *eigenbehavior*, which is the principal component of an individual's behavioral data [5].

These studies focus on analyzing observable human behavior. However, to understand the relation between behavior and physiological conditions such as stress, we need to analyze stress and other physiological indices in addition to the observable behavior.

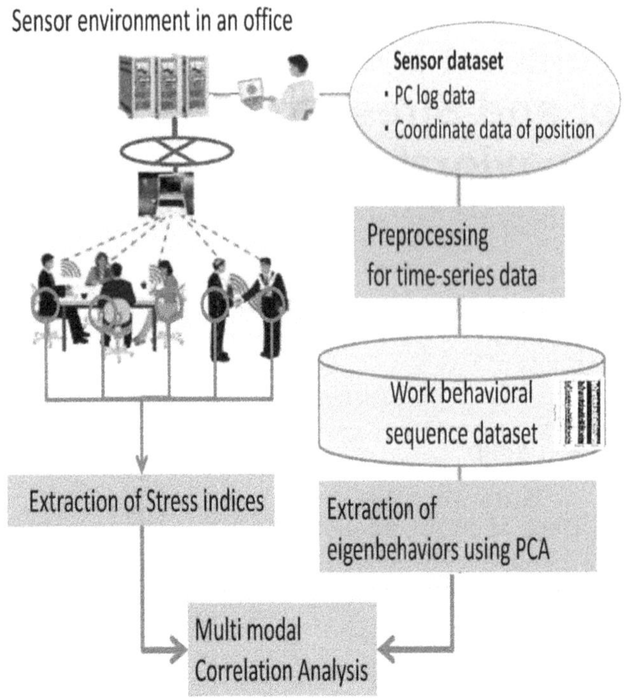

Figure 1: Overview of our proposed approach to multi-modal correlation analysis.

Stress is serious problem for companies that have employees because it has been found that many workers experience stress on the job [13]. Stress is generally related to behavior at work insofar as stress affects individuals' behaviors at work and appropriate behaviors can reduce stress. If we understand the relation between stress and work behaviors that can be extracted by sensors, we can observe workers' stress levels based on their individual work behaviors.

In this paper, we present an analysis of the correlation between stress and behavioral sequences at the workplace. To discover components of workers' activity that are statistically correlated with stress indices, we extracted individual workers' habitual activity patterns from sensor data that captured behavioral sequences over a period of 23 months in the office environment at C&C Innovation Initiative, NEC Corporation.

We represent the habitual activity of a day as a sequence of binary behavioral labels indicating whether a worker had a meeting at a given time and whether a worker used a PC for desk work at a given time. We extracted eigenbehaviors [5] at work from the long-term data and then analyzed the correlation between the eigenbehaviors and stress.

2. RELATED WORK

In this section, we review research that analyzes and recognizes human behavior through sensor networks along with research that analyzes office workers.

2.1 Human activity recognition and analysis using sensor networks

Many researchers have focused on human activities because these are a very important source of information for many computing applications. One main objective of this research is the recognition of daily living activities using sensors [17, 15].

In the systems that have been proposed, the activities that are studied can be predefined by the system designer. In general, the systems have two major components: estimating model parameters from the dataset for the chosen activities and the other is recognizing the sensor input data. Hidden Markov Models (HMM) [12] and Conditional Random Fields (CRF) [10] , are used for activity modeling and recognition.

Another major objective of this research is the ability to identify and analyze activity patterns from large amounts of data obtained from sensors [8, 6, 5]. Hoff et al. proposed an approach for identifying patterns of human activity in hallways and rooms in a large campus building [8]. In their system, the k-means clustering algorithm discovers repetitive patterns, which are spatially and temporally localized. The data are represented by discrete symbols after the clustering, and statistical distribution of the symbols is analyzed using Probabilistic Latent Semantic Analysis (PLSA).

Our research belongs to this second group because its objective is to analyze the correlation between worker behavior (activity) patterns and stress indices in order to discover aspects of worker behavior that are related to stress.

2.2 Analysis of office workers

Much research has focused on analyzing data of office workers. Begloe et al. proposed a way to extract behavioral patterns for both individuals and teams of workers through the analysis of online presence data [4]. Ara et al. proposed a system that can understand human communication processes in an office using wearable sensors [2]. Aral et al. examined the effects of the diffusion patterns on the productivity and performance of information workers using accounting data for project co-work relationships and ten months of email traffic. They found that the effects of these patterns are economically significant, with each additional Ągword seenĄh correlated with approximately $70 in additional revenue generated [3]. Another psychological experiment shows significant moderate correlation between workplace activities extracted by sensors and psychological states [9].

However, none of the researches focus on extraction of typical or routine time-series patterns of work behaviors in an office. Because routine activity patterns show how individuals work and the differences between their work behaviors, it is important to be able to extract and analyze routine activity patterns over the course of a day. Therefore, we have extracted routine activity patterns from longitudinal behavioral data captured by various sensors. In addition, we show the importance of extracting routine activity patterns in our analysis of the correlation between these patterns and stress indices.

3. SENSING ENVIRONMENT FOR DATA COLLECTION IN AN OFFICE

The sensor data, we used in this study, recorded work behavior in C&C Innovation Initiative, NEC Corporation. The data recorded each of 18 workers' locations and PC operations. The data providing the location of each worker was collected with an infrared location management system. The ID transmitters in this system are attached to the ceiling as a grid, and they send individual position coordinates to user terminals every second. Each user terminal receives the location of the closest ID transmitter position along with a time stamp. The temporal resolution is about 3 sec, and the spatial resolution is 1.5-2 m.

The data for each worker's PC operations were collected by a background program. The program can capture the beginning and end of applications and the frequency or number of input operations such as keystrokes, left /right clicks, and mouse cursor motions. In this paper, we focus on the operation of input devices in order to determine whether a worker was using a PC. The time resolution for this data was one second.

3.1 Preprocessing of the time-series work behavior data

We preprocessed the sensor data captured in the office environment for subsequent analysis. The time-series work behavior data were represented with a binary time-series sequence indicating whether the worker performed any of three activities during each time unit. The time unit in this study was set to one min, and the activities were defined as *PC operation*, *Meeting*, and *Other*. Many workers in C&C Laboratory are researchers of Computer Science. Their work is done by using PC. Thus, we choose PC activities and meetings as activity features. As previously noted, we detected the *PC operation* based on input operations such as keystrokes, left/right clicks, and mouse cursor motions. The value for *PC operation* was set to "1" if there were any input operations in the time frame, and "-1" otherwise.

Meetings were detected based on the location data for each worker [14]. The value of *Meeting* was set to "1" if a worker was in an area previously designated for a meeting or if workers were within two meters of one another for longer than five min (except in the case where workers were within two m of one another because of their desk locations); otherwise the value of meeting was set to "-1". Because this was a nonterritorial office, we defined each worker's desk on each day to be the desk where the worker spent most time. About detection of the meeting, actual video data is used to evaluate the result of an algorithm [14]. [14] reports that the algorithm obtains precision of 0.777. *Others* was set to "1" if both *PC operation* and *Meeting* were set to "-1". Otherwise, *Others* was set to "-1".

The time-series work behavior data for a worker on a single day, $\mathbf{\Gamma}$ was represented by a vector of size $\mathbf{\Gamma}$ is represented by $60(minutes) \times 24(hours) \times 3(labels) = 4320(\equiv H)$. The work behavior dataset for a worker, $\boldsymbol{B}$, was given as an $H \times D$ binary matrix

$$\boldsymbol{B} = [\mathbf{\Gamma}_1, \mathbf{\Gamma}_2, \ldots, \mathbf{\Gamma}_D]. \quad (1)$$

where D is the number of days required for sampling the sensor data. Figure 2 shows an example of a worker's time-

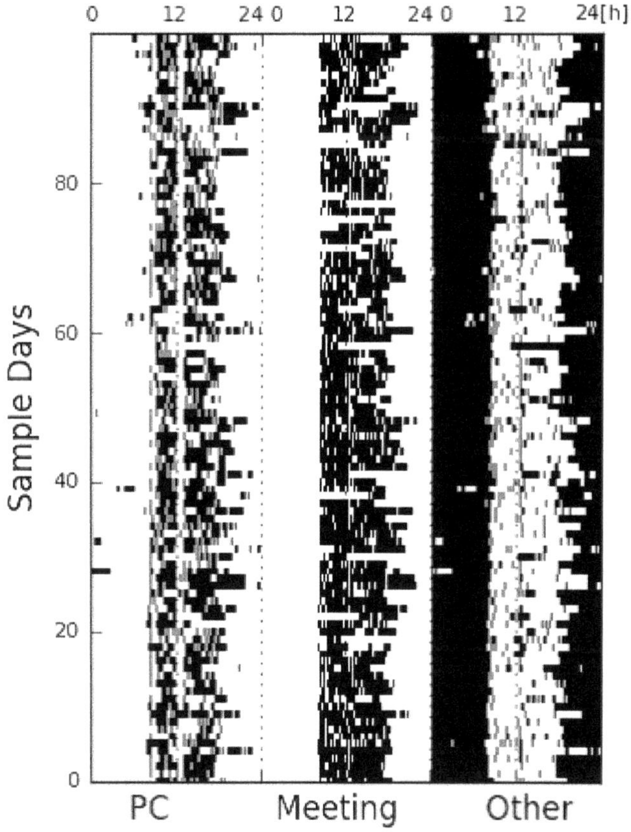

Figure 2: Example of work behavioral data sequence . Example of work behavior data sequence. The sample in each row represents the binary data for a day . (i.e. $\mathbf{\Gamma}^T$ in Equation. 1) Areas of color in black represent that the value of *PC operation*, *Meeting* or *Others* is "1" , and Areas of color in white represent that the value of them is "-1".

series work behavior data. The binary sequence in each row represents the data for a single day (i.e. $\mathbf{\Gamma}^T$). Areas of color in black represent that the value of *PC operation or Meeting* is "1" , and Areas of color in white represent that the value of it is "-1".

In this study, we used long-term work behavior datasets for 18 workers. We used the datasets collected by the sensor for 23 consecutive months. The number of days for each worker D differs because we excluded sampling for days when the data was missing such as holidays and days on which business trips were made. Table 1 shows the number of sampling days. The total number of sampling days was 4844, with an average of 270 sampling days for each single worker.

4. BEHAVIORAL ANALYSIS BASED ON EIGENBEHAVIORS

To individual workers' habitual activity patterns We extracted eigenbehaviors [5] at work from the long-term data Eagle and Pentland used PCA to extract eigenbehaviors from the longitudinal sequential dataset, which are collected

Table 1: Number of sampling days for the sensor data

	# of dates
Total # of dates	4844
Avg. # of dates for a worker	270
Max. # of dates for a worker	353
Min. # of dates for a worker	86

with smart phones [5]. PCA is useful for modeling repetitive behaviors. We assumed that work behaviors would also tend to be repetitive, and thus we used PCA for our behavioral analysis. The eigenvectors are defined as a type of repeated behavior and are called eigenbehavior [5]. The eigenvector corresponding to the eigenvalue of largest magnitude generally represent a type of repeated behavior, such as having meeting in the morning. A linear combination of an individual's eigenbehaviors can accurately reconstruct the behavior from each day

4.1 Extraction of eigenbehaviors with PCA

After preprocessing, our behavioral dataset for each worker $\boldsymbol{B}$, consisted of a time-series behavioral pattern, $\boldsymbol{\Gamma}$ for D days, where $\boldsymbol{\Gamma}$ is a vector of size H, that is, $\boldsymbol{B} = [\boldsymbol{\Gamma}_1, \boldsymbol{\Gamma}_2, ..., \boldsymbol{\Gamma}_D]$. The normalized pattern for each day $\boldsymbol{\Phi}_i$ was represented as;

$$\boldsymbol{\Phi}_i = \boldsymbol{\Gamma}_i - \boldsymbol{\Psi} \quad (i = 1, 2, ..., D) \tag{2}$$

where $\boldsymbol{\Psi}$ is the average vector of the pattern $\boldsymbol{\Gamma}$.

$$\boldsymbol{\Psi} = \frac{1}{D}\sum_{n=1}^{D} \boldsymbol{\Gamma}_n \tag{3}$$

We applied PCA to the normalized patterns to obtain the set of eigenvectors $\boldsymbol{U} = [u_1, u_2, ..., u_H]$ and eigenvalues $\lambda_1, \lambda_2, ..., \lambda_H$. The eigenvectors and the eigenvalues were obtained by eigen-decomposition of the covariance matrix, $\boldsymbol{C}$ of normalized vectors, i.e.,

$$\boldsymbol{C} = \frac{1}{H}\sum_{n=1}^{H} \boldsymbol{\Phi}_n \boldsymbol{\Phi}_n^T \tag{4}$$

$$= \frac{1}{H}\boldsymbol{\Phi}\boldsymbol{\Phi}^T \tag{5}$$

where $\boldsymbol{\Phi} = [\boldsymbol{\Phi}_1, \boldsymbol{\Phi}_2, ..., \boldsymbol{\Phi}_D]$, and

$$\boldsymbol{C} = \boldsymbol{U} \begin{pmatrix} \lambda_1 & & O \\ & \ddots & \\ O & & \lambda_H \end{pmatrix} \boldsymbol{U}^T \tag{6}$$

$$(\lambda_1 > \lambda_2 > \cdots > \lambda_H)$$

The eigenvector $u_1, u_2, \ldots, u_H$ is called an "eigenbehavior". The greater the eigenvalue of the eigenvector, the better is the vector's description of the original behavioral dataset. Thus, the major eigenvectors represent a typical behavioral pattern for the dataset. The eigenvector $\boldsymbol{u}$ was represented by a vector of size $\boldsymbol{u}$ is represented by $60(minutes) \times 24(hours) \times 3(labels) = 4320(\equiv u)$ which equal to an activity pattern in a single day.

4.2 Reconstruction of the work behavior sequence dataset

The work behavior sequence dataset can be reconstructed by projection to the space of eigenbehaviors. We examined the accuracy of behavior reconstruction using N ($N \leq H$) principal eigenbehaviors. The reconstruction accuracy indicates how well the projected dataset in the N-dimensional space describes the original dataset.

The projection of the work behavior sequence dataset, $\boldsymbol{B}'$, is

$$\boldsymbol{B}'^T = \boldsymbol{B}^T \boldsymbol{U}' \boldsymbol{U}'^T \tag{7}$$

where $\boldsymbol{U}' = [u_1, u_2, \ldots, u_N]$. The projected sequence dataset corresponds to the original dataset if $N = H$ (i.e., $\boldsymbol{U}' = \boldsymbol{U}$).

We then binarize the value of each element in $\boldsymbol{B}'$, which might be real numbers. A value was set to "1" if the projected value was positive and "-1" if it was negative. If the projected value of the element was zero, this means there was no deviation of the values in the original dataset. In this case, the original data value was directly used in the reconstructed dataset. Finally, the value of each element of the reconstructed behavior sequence dataset, $\hat{\boldsymbol{B}}$ is;

$$\hat{b}_{ij} = \begin{cases} 1 & b'_{ij} > 0 \\ -1 & b'_{ij} < 0 \\ \psi_{ij} & b'_{ij} = 0 \end{cases} \tag{8}$$

where $\hat{b}_{ij}$ is the value of the element in row i, column j of $\hat{\boldsymbol{B}}$.

Next, we evaluated how well the reconstructed behavior dataset represented the original behavior dataset. We define reconstruction accuracy as the similarity between the original dataset and the projected dataset in the subspace of the principal eigenbehavior, i.e., the reconstruction accuracy, RA, is given as follows:

$$RA = \frac{1}{H \times D}\sum_{i=1}^{H}\sum_{j=1}^{D} match(b_{ij}, \hat{b}_{ij}) \tag{9}$$

$$match(x, y) = \begin{cases} 1 & x = y \\ 0 & x \neq y \end{cases} \tag{10}$$

where b_{ij} and $\hat{b}_{ij}$ are the element of B and $\hat{B}$, respectively, and $= H \times D$ is the number of elements of B.

5. ANALYSIS OF THE EIGENBEHAVIORS

5.1 Eigenbehaviors for the individual workers

We extracted individual eigenbehaviors for 18 workers. Figure 3 shows examples of the top three principal eigenbehaviors for individuals. The graph shows the principal eigenbehaviors for *PC operation*, *Meeting* and *Other* from left to right. Each row in the graph indicates the sequence for an entire day. Each eigenbehavior is represented as a heat map. The dark red and dark blue parts of the sequences represent the notable behavioral patterns.The darkest red color represents the maximum value more than 0. The darkest red color represents minimum value smaller than 0.

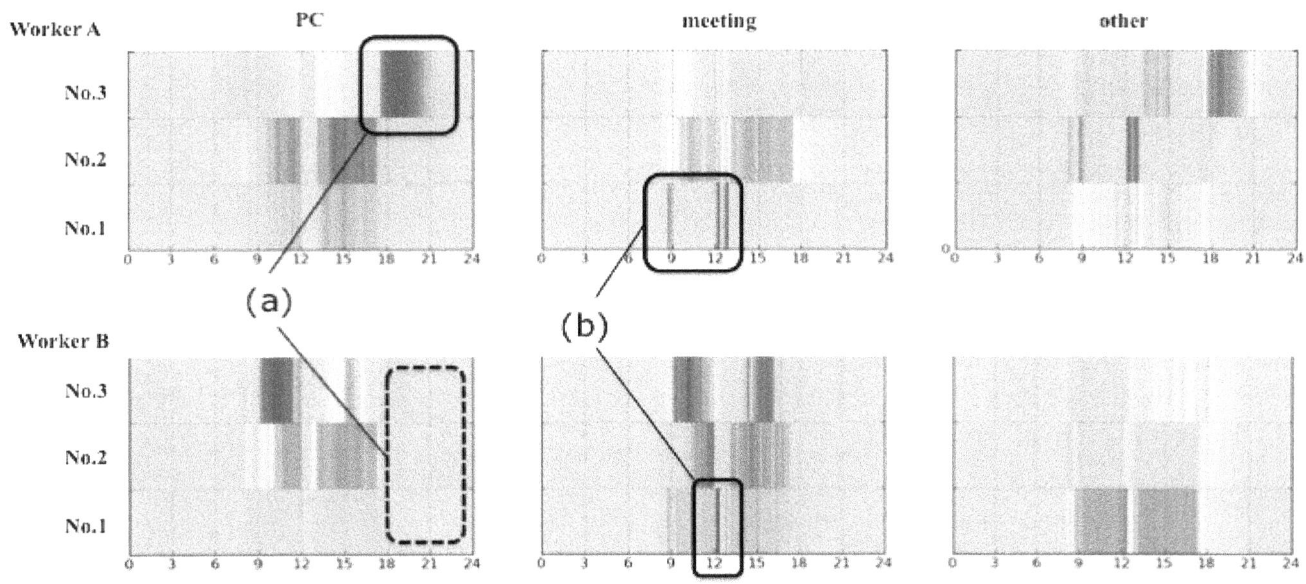

Figure 3: Comparison of individual principal eigenbehaviors: The first to third principal eigenbehaviors (y-axis) of *Worker A* (upper part) and *Worker B* (lower part) in a single day (x-axis). The red and blue parts of a sequence represent noticeable behavior patterns. The principal eigenbehaviors show the difference between the workers' typical behaviors. Here, (a) represents behavior during overwork using a PC and (b) represents behavior during a meeting.

It is important to note that the principal eigenbehaviors for each worker represent his or her own typical work behavior. For example, the third principal eigenbehavior for worker A represents overwork when using a PC ((a) in Figure 3), while Worker B does not exhibit such a behavior. The workers also have different routines during meetings ((b) in Figure 3).

Figure 4 shows the graph with the reconstruction accuracy for 18 workers using a variable number of principal eigenbehaviors for each worker. The graph shows that the average of the reconstruction accuracy for all workers is 87.7% (82.7%–92.2%), with nine principal eigenbehaviors. This means that the linear combination of the nine principal eigenbehaviors can represent 80% of the workers' original behavior. That is, more than 80% of the work behavior sequence for each worker can be described with a combination of only nine types of work behaviors.

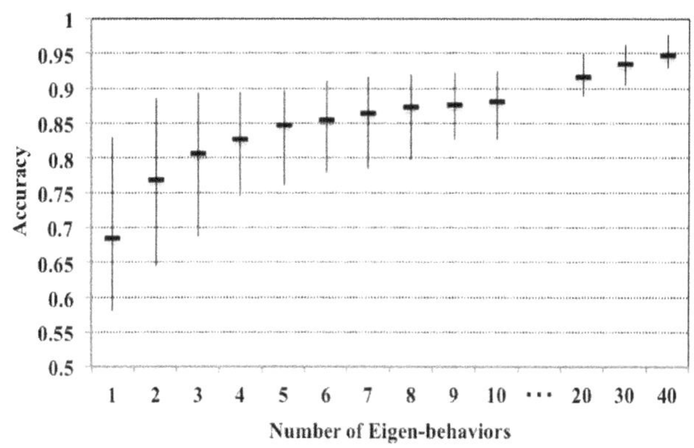

Figure 4: Reconstruction accuracy using a variable number of eigenbehaviors for individual workers. The vertical line represents the deviation of the accuracy and the intersecting horizontal line represents the averaged accuracy.

5.2 Eigenbehaviors for all workers

Common eigenbehaviors for all M workers were extracted by applying PCA to the dataset B_{all} that contains the datasets for all workers, i.e.,

$$B_{all} = [B_1, B_2, \ldots, B_M] \tag{11}$$

Figure 5 shows the principal eigenbehaviors for all workers. Using these eigenbehaviors, we can easily compare the work behaviors of individual workers because all original behavior datasets are projected to the same subspace of the principal eigenbehaviors. The graph in Figure 6 shows the reconstruction accuracy for each worker's behavior using the principal eigenbehaviors for all workers. The result shows that a reconstruction accuracy for all workers that is greater than 80% can be achieved with six principal eigenbehaviors, and an accuracy greater than 90% can be achieved with 14 principal eigenbehaviors. Thus, most of the work behavior for each worker can be described with a set of common principal eigenbehaviors as well as with individual principal eigenbehaviors.

6. ANALYSIS OF THE CORRELATION BETWEEN WORK BEHAVIOR AND STRESS

We analyzed the correlation between work behavior and stress for each worker. We measured the accuracy of the reconstruction of each worker's original work behavior using the principal eigenbehaviors for all workers, as discussed above. From figure 5, it is found that there is a major difference between accuracy of the reconstruction of each worker's behavior. Worker whose reconstruction accuracy is high with a few principal eigenbehaviors takes on the typical behavior in the office and keeps a regular working-style. On the other hand, worker whose reconstruction accuracy is low takes on various behaviors and keeps an irregular working-style, such as irregular working hours, having irregular meetings. We made an assumption that the reconstruction accuracy had a correlation with the stress indices. To obtain a stress index for each worker, we used the average values measured through the procedure described below.

6.1 Data collection of stress levels

To measure stress, we used the Body Checker (Medi-core Co., Ltd.). In the Body Checker, heart rate variability has been used for analyzing an individual's current stress level with the R-R interval (heart beat interval) set to 2 min and 30 s based on the standard reference set by The European Society of Cardiology and The North American Society of Pacing and Electrophysiology in 1996 [16].

Table 2 summarizes the collection of stress level data. The measurements were conducted in the office between work intervals, such as before the beginning of work; during a lunch break; and at the end of the work day on weekdays for two months between August 8, 2011 and September 30, 2011. The subjects for the stress level measurements included 17 of the 18 workers for whom we collected work behaviors. In this paper, we focus on three types of measurement made by the Body Checker: physical stress, mental stress, and stress dissolution ability. Heart Rate Variability is used as a valuable indicator of mental stress. Balance state of instantaneous heartbeats and R-R intervals are used as a valuable indicator of physical stress.

6.2 Result of the correlation analysis

Table 3 shows the Pearson product-moment correlation coefficient with respect to the accuracy of a worker's reconstructed work behavior and his or her stress levels. The reconstruction accuracies is computed by using N_e eigenbehaviors computed in section 5.2. The correlation coefficient were computed by reconstruction accuracies and the average stress levels.

The result indicates significant correlations in which the reconstruction accuracy is negatively correlated with physical stress and positively correlated with stress dissolution ability. In particular strong correlations ($p < 0.01$) are indicated for 12 or more eigenbehaviors. There are no significant correlations between the reconstruction accuracy and mental stress. Therefore, workers who engage in their typical behaviors with a high degree of regularity in their daily work tend to have low levels of physical stress and high stress dissolution abilities.

6.3 Comparative analysis between worker with high stress and worker with low stress

In this section, we focus on worker C which has highest physical stress and worker D which has lowest physical stress and we compared the principal eigenbehaviors of the 2 workers out of the 18 workers, who hold different positions. *Worker C* is a secretary, while *Worker D* is a general manager. The usual business hours for secretaries in the office are well regulated, and their main work is office work using PCs. On the other hand, the business hours of general managers change depending on their business duties and they often do outside work.

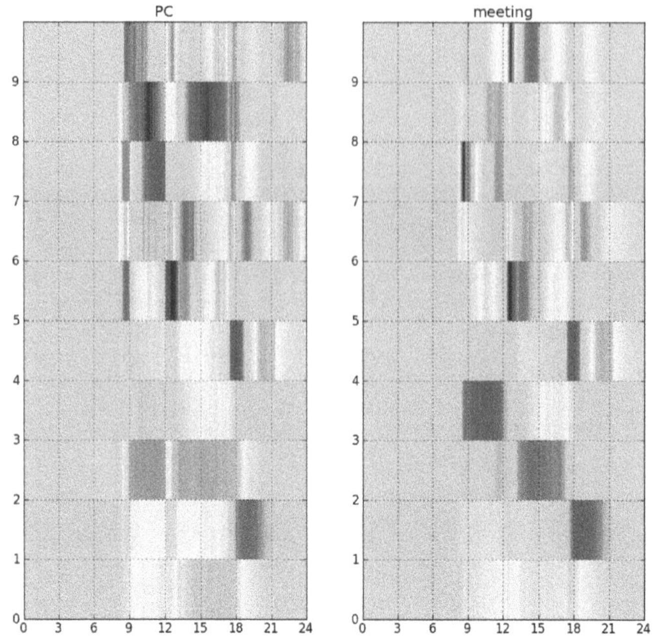

Figure 5: First to tenth principal eigenbehaviors calculated from behavior datasets of all workers. These eigenbehaviors represent typical behaviors as well as eigenbehaviors for the individual workers.

We calculated the accuracies of our behavior reconstruction for each day, as described in Section 5.1. The graph in Figure 7 shows the accuracies of the behavior reconstruction for the daily behavior of the two workers. Compared with the result for *Worker C*, the average accuracy of worker D' s behavior reconstruction is extremely low, with a large difference between the maximum and minimum values. This result suggests that the *Worker C*' s work behavior has a greater regularity than the *Worker D*' s behavior. In fact, the result fits with the intuitive perception about these workers based on the fact that *Worker D* is a general manager and *Worker C* is a secretary.

7. DISCUSSIONS

The result of our correlation analysis shows that the accuracy of behavioral reconstruction is negatively correlated with physical stress, while the accuracy of behavioral reconstruction is positively correlated with stress dissolution ability, using the eigenbehaviors for all workers. In addition, there is not a significant correlation between the reconstruction accuracy and mental stress. This means that workers who engage in typical behavior with a high degree of regularity in their daily work tend to have low physical stress and high stress dissolution ability.

We believe that the eigenbehaviors make it easy to understand the workers' characteristic work behavior. More-

Table 2: Collection of stress level data.

# of workers	17
Term	Weekdays for two months (8/8/2011-9/30/2011)
# of measurements	628
What was measured	Physical Stress Mental Stress Stress Dissolution Ability
When measurements were made	Between intervals of work, such as before the beginning of work; during a lunch break; and at the end of the workday
Where measurements were made	In the office

Table 3: Results of the correlation analysis: The table shows the correlation between the accuracy of work behavior reconstruction and the averages of three types of measures of stress.

		Correlation coefficient between the reconstruction accuracy and the average values of stress on each worker		
		Physical Stress	Mental Stress	Stress Dissolution Ability
The # of principal eigenbehaviors for the reconstruction (N_e)	1	-0.15	0.03	0.18
	3	-0.36	-0.11	0.36
	6	-0.46	-0.10	0.44
	9	**-0.57***	0.00	**0.56***
	12	**-0.71****	-0.11	**0.68****
	20	**-0.70****	-0.14	**0.69****
	40	**-0.68****	-0.02	**0.69****

(*: $p < 0.05$, **: $p < 0.01$, ***: $p < 0.001$)

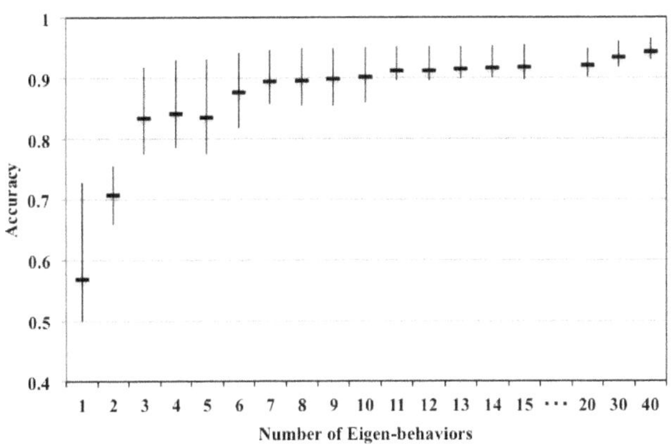

Figure 6: Reconstruction accuracy (y-axis. average(-), max and min) for work behaviors using different numbers of principal eigenbehaviors (x-axis).

over, the behavioral analysis presented in this paper can be applied for behavioral management at various levels. The analysis is also helpful for individual workers who wish to review their own work behaviors.

However, our system has some limitations. First, a large number of work behavior sequences are needed for extracting principal eigenbehaviors, and we do not know how much data is necessary for extracting useful eigenbehaviors. Second, we have not yet established the generality of correlations. In addition, although experimental results shows there is some correlation between work behavior and stress level, causal relationship between the two factors is unknown. For this, we need to conduct more analyses for different groups and different time periods.

8. CONCLUSION

We proposed a method that office administration can use to analyze worker' s stress lebels based on the behavioral data captured by various sensors.

For the analysis, we extracted eigenbehaviors from a longitudinal work behavior dataset. More than 80% of the individual work behaviors of the 18 workers that we studied could be represented using nine principal eigenbehaviors. We also found that the behavior reconstruction accuracies exhibited different deviations for workers in different positions.

We conducted a multi-modal analysis of the correlation between the work behaviors of the workers and their stress levels. The results showed a significant negative correlation ($r \geq 0.69$, $p < 0.01$) between the accuracy of reconstructed work behaviors and physical stress levels along with a significant positive correlation between the reconstruction accuracy and stress dissolution ability. It is believed that an application based on the analysis of behavioral data captured in the office will soon be available to companies so that they can improve their workers' performance and the working environment. Further analyses to address the limi-

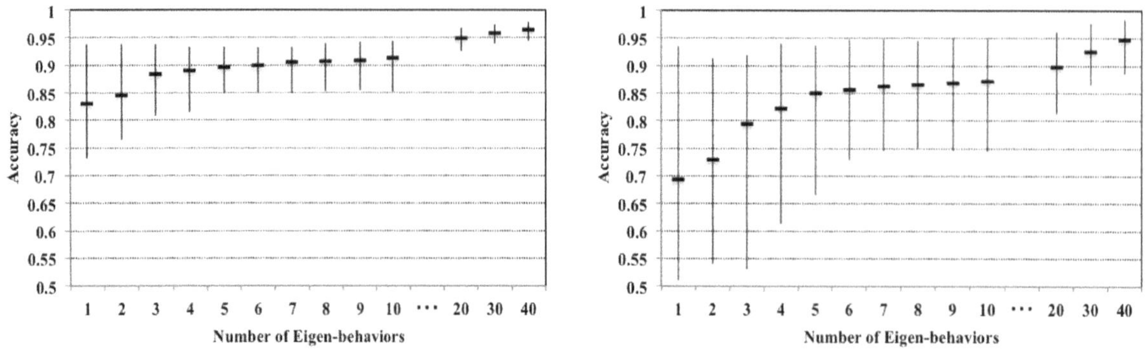

Figure 7: Comparison of behavior reconstruction accuracies (y-axis) using a variable number of eigenbehaviors (x-axis) for two different workers (left: *Worker C* is a secretary; right: *Worker D* is a general manager). Compared with *Worker C*, the average accuracy of behavior reconstruction for *Worker D* was extremely low with a large deviation.

tations described in the previous section are needed to establish a standard framework for the analysis of work behavior datasets for the purpose of improving performance.

Acknowledgements

The authors thank anonymous reviewers for their insightful and worthful comments. This research was partially supported by the Japan Society for the Promotion of Science, Grant-in-Aid for Young Scientists B, 22700146, 2012.

9. REFERENCES

[1] M. A. Abe M., Morinishi Y. A life log collector integrated with a remote-controller for enabling user centric services. *ACM Transactions on Programming Languages and Systems*, 55:295–302, 2009.

[2] K. Ara, T. Akitomi, N. Sato, S. Tsuji, M. Hayakawa, Y. Wakisaka, N. Ohkubo, R. Otsuka, F. Beniyama, N. Moriwaki, and K. Yano. Healthcare of an organization: using wearable sensors and feedback system for energizing workers. In *Proceedings of Asia and South Pacific Design Automation Conference*, pages 567–572, 2011.

[3] S. Aral, E. Brynjolfsson, and M. V. Alstyne. Productivity effects of information diffusion in email networks. In *Proceedings of International Conference on Information Systems*, 2007.

[4] J. B. Begole, J. C. Tang, and R. Hill. Rhythm modeling, visualizations and applications. In *Proceedings of annual ACM symposium on User interface software and technology*, pages 11–20, 2003.

[5] N. Eagle and A. S. Pentland. Reality mining: sensing complex social systems. *Personal Ubiquitous Computing*, 10(4):255–268, mar 2006.

[6] N. Eagle and A. S. Pentland. Eigenbehaviors: identifying structure in routine. *Behavioral Ecology and Sociobiology*, 63(7):1057–1066, 2009.

[7] H. Eiji. Development of behavior context addressable loggers in the shell for travel-activity analysis. *Transportation Research Part C:Emerging Technologies*, 18:55–67, 2010.

[8] W. Hoff and J. Howard. Activity recognition in a dense sensor network. In *Proceedings of International Conference on Sensor Networks and Applications*, 2009.

[9] Y. Kamiya. Sensor-based correlation analysis between office activities and psychological states. In *Book of Abstracts of the European Conference of Positive Psychology*, number 72, 2010.

[10] J. Lafferty, A. McCallum, and F. Pereira. Conditional random fields: Probabilistic models for segmenting and labeling sequence data. In *Proceedings of International Conference on Machine Learning*, pages 282–289, 2001.

[11] E. Pauwels, A. Salah, and R. Tavenard. Sensor networks for ambient intelligence. In *Proceedings of IEEE Workshop on Multimedia Signal Processing, 2007*, pages 13 –16, 2007.

[12] L. R. Rabiner. A tutorial on hidden markov models and selected applications in speech recognition. In *Proceedings of IEEE*, pages 257–286, 1989.

[13] S. Sauter and L. Murphy. *Organizational risk factors for job stress.* American Psychological Association, 1995.

[14] T. Shime, K. Kunieda, K. Yamada, and H. Kawai. Area-based communication detector. In *Proceedings of International Conference on Digital Information Management*, pages 252–257, 2011.

[15] E. Tapia, S. Intille, and K. Larson. Activity recognition in the home using simple and ubiquitous sensors. *Pervasive Computing*, pages 158–175, 2004.

[16] Medicore Co., Ltd.
Body Checker, http://www:medi-core.com.

[17] D. Wilson and C. Atkeson. Simultaneous tracking and activity recognition (STAR) using many anonymous, binary sensors. *Pervasive Computing*, pages 329–334, 2005.

Linking Speaking and Looking Behavior Patterns with Group Composition, Perception, and Performance

Dineshbabu Jayagopi[1] Dairazalia Sanchez-Cortes[1,2] Kazuhiro Otsuka[3]
Junji Yamato[3] and Daniel Gatica-Perez[1,2]
[1] Idiap Research Institute, Martigny, Switzerland
[2] Ecole Polytechnique Fédérale de Lausanne (EPFL), Switzerland
[3] NTT Communication Science Laboratories, Japan.
(djaya,dscortes,gatica)@idiap.ch, otsuka@eye.brl.ntt.co.jp, yamato@brl.ntt.co.jp

ABSTRACT

This paper addresses the task of mining typical behavioral patterns from small group face-to-face interactions and linking them to social-psychological group variables. Towards this goal, we define group speaking and looking cues by aggregating automatically extracted cues at the individual and dyadic levels. Then, we define a bag of nonverbal patterns (Bag-of-NVPs) to discretize the group cues. The topics learnt using the Latent Dirichlet Allocation (LDA) topic model are then interpreted by studying the correlations with group variables such as group composition, group interpersonal perception, and group performance. Our results show that both group behavior cues and topics have significant correlations with (and predictive information for) all the above variables. For our study, we use interactions with unacquainted members i.e. newly formed groups.

Categories and Subject Descriptors

H.5.3 [**Group and Organization Interfaces**]: Collaborative computing

Keywords

Small groups; Nonverbal behavior; Group Mining

1. INTRODUCTION

The automatic analysis of face-to-face group interaction integrates knowledge from signal processing, machine learning, and social psychology. The possibility of recording audio-visual data and extracting multimodal nonverbal cues helps to relate nonverbal behavior with group constructs such as composition, interpersonal perception, and performance [4, 19]. With the global workforce becoming increasingly team-based, understanding group processes, performance, and satisfaction measures has become relevant.

While building supervised learning models to infer interpersonal perception or performance from individual and group behavior has been studied in a few previous works [14, 7, 11, 19], characterizing group behavior in unsupervised frameworks to mine typical behaviors of groups is a relatively unexplored problem [8]. Such an approach can also yield intermediate representations that could help understand some group constructs in a holistic manner, because they describe groups based on co-occurence of observations, rather than directly choosing a measure like performance or satisfaction as it is done in supervised frameworks. The automatically extracted behavioral cues and intermediate representations could serve as complementary information to those measures extracted from self-reports, e.g. personality or interpersonal perception [14].

In this work, we address two research questions: First how to characterize and extract typical speaking and looking patterns; second, to understand how group behavior patterns relate to how group members perform and perceive themselves and other members of their group. In order to address these two questions, we define a data-centric framework as shown in Fig. 1. Specifically, we use LDA, a probabilistic topic model, to extract recurrent nonverbal patterns on five-minute segments of group interactions. We show that the extracted topics are socially meaningful by correlating them with group composition, interpersonal perception, and performance variables obtained from questionnaires. These variables relate to the group input-process-output model in social psychology literature [13]). For this study, we use the Emergent Leadership (ELEA) corpus [17]. This corpus contains, apart from the audio-visual recordings, comprehensive data about self-reported personality (Big-Five traits), interpersonal perception (of dominance, leadership, competence, and liking), and group performance.

Our paper has two contributions. First, mining speaking and gaze behavior patterns in groups is a relatively unexplored problem. While mining approaches have been recently used for audio cues [8], to our knowledge the group-level mining of both speaking and looking patterns has not been addressed. We define turn-taking and gaze-based group behavioral cues. In particular, the proposed gaze-based group cues are novel. The mining framework is powerful as it potentially allows to work with large datasets, make statistical inferences, and validate the results on datasets for which ground-truth is available. Second, relating the cues and the topics with multiple group-level constructs such as group composition, perception, and performance on a single dataset is also novel. Our findings show several interesting correlations between the personality of the group members, how they perceive each other, or how they perform, and the

ICMI'12, October 22–26, 2012, Santa Monica, California, USA.

automatically extracted group's speaking and looking patterns. The ELEA corpus allows us to study this aspect.

Section 2 presents related work. Section 3 introduces the data and the definition of questionnaire variables. Section 4 introduces the group nonverbal cues. Section 5 gives the background for the topic model. In Section 6, we present the correlations between the cues and the questionnaire data. Section 7 presents the topic-based analysis. Section 8 provides conclusions.

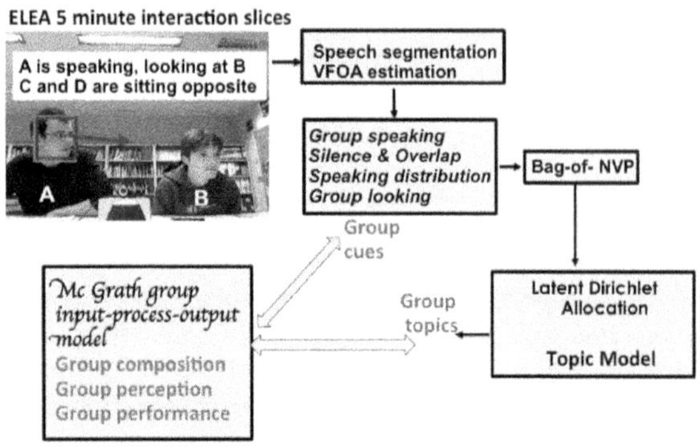

Figure 1: Our approach: Mining and validating group speaking and gaze patterns by defining a bag of nonverbal patterns and employing a topic model.

2. RELATED WORK

The works related to our study belong to either social psychology or social computing.

In social psychology literature, how group composition affects group processes or group performance has been extensively investigated across a variety of group tasks both in lab and field settings. In order to characterize and understand group processes and its effects, self-reports have been used predominantly, as manual annotation of behavior for large interaction datasets is laborious.

A classic framework to study groups was proposed by Mc Grath in 1964, termed the Input-Process-Output model [13]. Group input refers to the characteristics of the group members, including their personality, age, sex, or a formal role. Group process addresses the interpersonal relationship aspects between group members, both perceived as well as observed. This could include both the vertical ('getting ahead') and horizontal ('getting along') facets of relationships. Finally, the outputs could capture performance or satisfaction measured quantitatively or qualitatively. Recent works, such as [1], have validated and reinforced this approach. This study shows that the framework could be used to study teams accomplishing relatively modern tasks such as software development.

Depending on the task characteristics, the relationship between group composition, specifically group personality composition (GPC), and group performance has varied. For example, teams exhibit a significant positive correlation between the personality factor extraversion and software product quality [1]. GPC has been operationalized by considering mean, maximum, or minimum over individual personality scores [2]. The method that computes maximum or minimum score assumes that one person can have significant effect on the group's performance or other group outcomes.

Apart from the individual attributes, the interpersonal perceptions have also been used to predict group outcomes such as performance or satisfaction. Group cohesion and conflict (task or social) have been shown to affect group performance [2]. Also, how the personality of individuals affect group process has also been documented [2]. The relationships among perceived variables such as dominance and leadership or dominance and likeability [18] have also been studied.

In social computing literature concerning small groups, the fact that nonverbal cues are a rich source for automatic social inference about people's traits, or interpersonal perception or performance has been exploited. The existing studies include both individual and group-level inferences. Personality of individuals in groups was estimated in [14]. Formal roles were automatically estimated in [16]. Dominant behavior was inferred in [7] and emergent leadership was studied in [17]. Group level constructs such as group interest and group conversational context (for e.g. cooperative vs competitive behavior and brain-storming vs decision-making behavior) has been studied [7]. Leadership styles were discovered in [8], using a mining framework similar to this work, albeit using only audio cues. The topics were validated with perception annotation using external annotators (unlike our work here that uses self-reported questionnaires from the participants themselves).

The inference of performance in groups using nonverbal behavior has also received attention in recent years [19, 11]. The most comprehensive work been by Woolley et al. [19], in which the effect of collective intelligence (a novel way to characterize group composition) on group performance was studied on a range of cognitive tasks. It was also found that collective intelligence correlated with average social sensitivity of group members and the equality in distribution of conversational turn-taking, which relate to the group composition and processes respectively.

As compared to the literature in social psychology, our work adds the definition of automatic extraction group behavioral cues to the group variables studied. We also propose to mine the group behavior to extract recurrent patterns. Further, as compared to the existing works in social computing, our work explores jointly group composition, perception, and performance. We use both turn-taking and gaze cues. Only few works (such as [6, 12]) have explored gaze cues as compared to the turn-taking cues. Finally, unsupervised approaches to characterize group behavior is still a relatively unexplored direction in group inference [8].

3. INTERACTION DATASET

3.1 Data

We use 18 group interactions from the ELEA corpus [17] to extract and mine group nonverbal behavior and relate it to group-level social psychological constructs (see Fig. 1 for an overview of our approach). Each interaction has 4 unacquainted participants solving the winter survival task [10]. Kickul et al. claim that "the winter survival task allows team members to observe the social or relational skills of others while interacting in this problem solving task." The participants filled a questionnaire about themselves (i.e. their personality using the NEO-FFI inventory [9]) before the interaction started. They were instructed to come up with a ranked list individually before discussing with others and then come up with a joint list after a fifteen-minute discussion. The ranked list would contain twelve items important for surviving a airplane crash in harsh winter conditions.

Later, each of them filled a questionnaire about the behavior of their group members.

The room set-up had a rectangular table, with two people on either side. A Microcone, a commercial array microphone, was used to record the audio and obtain the speech segmentations of participants. The audio sample rate was 16kHz. For video recordings, a portable setup with two webcameras (Logitech R Webcam Pro 9000, 30 fps, 640 by 480) was used. The average duration of an interaction was 14 minutes 8 seconds. The dataset has 4.4 hours of interaction data in total.

3.2 Questionnaire variables

In our work, we operationalize group composition as measured by the personality of individual members. We study group interpersonal perception using dominance, leadership, competence, and liking. Group performance is objectively measured by comparing the joint ranking proposed by the group with that of the experts. Next, we describe the questionnaire data and then define the variables of interest at the level of groups.

Composition (Personality): Personality attempts to capture individual differences i.e. the dimensions along which people differ from each other, and at the same time describe individual persons as unique, integrated wholes [9]. Big Five factors of personality - Agreeableness, conscientiousness, Extraversion, Neuroticism, and Openness to experience have been shown to be a parsimonious and cross-culturally valid approach to personality [9]. We used the NEO-FFI questionnaire commonly used in personality research which has 60 statements measuring these five factors.

Interpersonal perception: After the survival test, participants were asked to answer 16 statements that capture how they perceived each participant. This questionnaire was designed adapting existing questionnaires in leadership with the help of a social psychologist. 16 of the statements were evaluated on a five-point scale. The variables included in these statements are: Perceived Dominance (denoted PDom: dominates, is in a position of power, asserts him- or herself), Perceived Leadership (denoted PLead: directs the group, imposes his or her opinion, is involved), Perceived Competence (denoted PCom: is competent, is intelligent, has a lot of experience), and Perceived Liking (denoted PLike: is kind, friendly, not unpleasant).

Performance: The performance of the group (denoted $GPerf$) was measured by the negative distance between an 'ideal' list created by experts and the list proposed by a group. Therefore higher the performance score, better performing the group is. Zero being the highest score.

Defining group-level variables

Performance is defined at the level of groups. We need to define personality and perception about interaction partners at the group level as well. We compute the *mean*, *maximum*, and *range* (maximum - minimum) over the personality score of the individuals in a group to characterize 'group composition'. This approach is quite standard in the small group literature [5]. Perceived constructs - PDom, PLead, PComp, and PLike are defined at the dyadic level. For example $PDom(i, j)$ denotes what i perceives about j (Note: $PDom(i, i)$ is not defined). Our first four variations are defined by averaging over i, the row variable of PDom.

$$ARDom(j) = \frac{\Sigma_{i=1, i \neq j}^{P} PDom(i, j)}{P - 1} \quad (1)$$

$ARDom(j)$ is what the group (on an average) says about j. Next, we compute *mean*, *maximum*, *toprange* (maximum - second maximum), *range* over ARDom(j) to characterize the perception about the group. *maximum* is abbreviated as $max \rightarrow$.

The final variation is computed by averaging over j.

$$ACDom(i) = \frac{\Sigma_{j=1, j \neq i}^{P} PDom(i, j)}{P - 1} \quad (2)$$

$ACDom(j)$ is what j says about the group (on an average). Next, we compute maximum over ACDom(j), denoted $max \leftarrow$. While $max \rightarrow$ is related to what group perceives about an individual, $max \leftarrow$ is related to what an individual perceives about the group. Also, *mean* is what the group perceives about the group. Finally, *toprange* and *range* is what the group perceives about two individuals, the difference between them to be exact. Similar to PDom, we compute these variations for PLead, PComp, and PLike as well. In total, we have defined 36 group-level variables i.e. group composition(15), group perception (20), and group performance (1) from the questionnaire data.

4. GROUP NONVERBAL CUE EXTRACTION

Nonverbal cues, particularly turn-taking and gaze patterns, are known to reveal social-psychological constructs such as traits [14], interpersonal perceptions [7] and performance [11, 19]. Below, we describe and define the speaking and looking cues that capture a group's turn-taking and gaze behavior in multiple ways.

4.1 Group speaking cues

Individual cues: The Microcone outputs the speaking status - a binary variable indicating speaking (1) and non-speaking (0) - of each of the participant. The speaking status was downsampled to a rate of 5 frames per second (AFps). This rate is sufficient to analyze conversational behavior at the level of turns. Short conversational events, for example backchannels are of the order of 1 or 2 second duration.

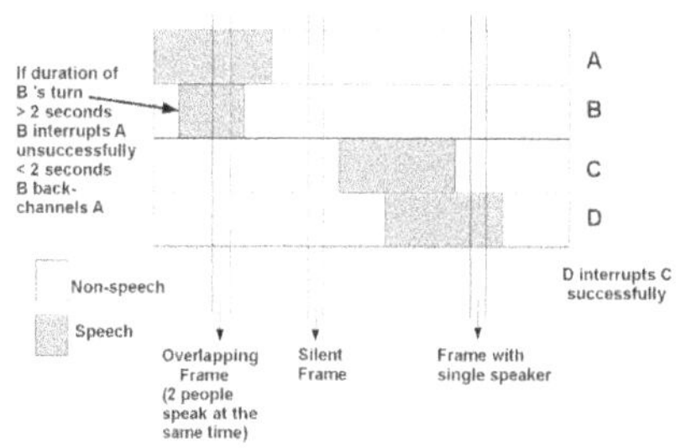

Figure 2: Turn-taking based nonverbal cues.

From the speech segmentation, we compute individual speaking length, speaking turns, successfully interrupting, being unsuccessfully interrupted, and being backchanneled defined below:

Speaking Length (sl): Cumulates the total time that a person speaks according to their binary speaking status.

Speaking Turns (st): Cumulates speaking turns, where a speaking turn is an interval in time for which a person's speaking status is active.

Successfully Interrupting (si) : The feature is defined by the cumulative number of times that speaker $i \in \{1, 2, 3, 4\}$

starts talking while another speaker $j \in \{l : l \neq i\}$ speaks, and speaker j finishes his turn before i does,
Being Unsuccessfully interrupted (ui) : The feature is defined by the cumulative number of times that speaker $i \in \{1, 2, 3, 4\}$ unsuccessfully interrupts (by speaking atleast for 2 seconds) another speaker $j \in \{l : l \neq i\}$
Being Backchanneled (bc) : The feature is defined by the cumulative number of times that speaker $i \in \{1, 2, 3, 4\}$ speaks less than 2 seconds while another speaker $j \in \{l : l \neq i\}$ is talking.

Fig. 2 illustrates the conversational cues at the level of individuals. From these individual cues, three types of group conversational cues are extracted.

Group participation cues: A first set of cues characterize the participation rates of the group by accumulating it over the participants. Let D denote the duration of the meeting in seconds. We compute the following five cues - Speaking Length (SL), Speaking Turns (ST), Successful Interruptions (SI), Unsuccessful Interruptions (UI), Backchannels (BC) - from the individual cues. For e.g. $SL = \Sigma_{i=1}^{P} sl(i)/D$

Silence and Overlap cues: A second set of cues attempts to capture the overlap and silence patterns of a group as a whole. Let $AF = D * AFps$ be the total number of frames in a meeting, S be the number of frames when no participant speaks, M be the number of frames when only one participant is speaking, $O2$ and $O3$ be the number of frames when more than two or three participant talk at the same time. $AFps$ being frames-per-second, the rate at which speaking status is available. Then we define the following four cues - Fraction of Silence(FS), Fraction of Non-overlapped Speech(FN), Fraction of two-people and three-people Overlapped Speech(FO2 and FO3) - defined as follows: $FS = \frac{S}{AF}$, $FN = \frac{M}{AF}$, $FO2 = \frac{O2}{AF}$, $FO3 = \frac{O3}{AF}$.

Speaking distribution cues: A third set of cues characterizes which meeting is more 'egalitarian' with respect to the use of the speaking floor i.e. everyone gets equal opportunities. Let **sl** denote the vector composed of P elements, whose elements are $sl(i)/\Sigma_i sl(i)$ for the ith participant. Employing an analogous notation for **st**, **si**, **ui** and **bc**, these vectors are first ranked (**p**) and then compared with the uniform (i.e. "egalitarian") distribution i.e. a vector of the same dimension with values equal to $\frac{1}{P}$ (**q**). The comparison is done using the Hellinger distance, a measure useful to compare probability distributions and bounded between 0 and 1. The Hellinger distance is defined in terms of the Bhattacharya coefficient as follows: $HD(\mathbf{p}, \mathbf{q}) = \sqrt{1 - BCoeff(\mathbf{p}, \mathbf{q})}$ and $BCoeff(\mathbf{p}, \mathbf{q}) = \Sigma_i \sqrt{p(i) * q(i)}$. Hellinger distance of 0 would correspond to a egalitarian meeting. This results in five cues: Speaking Length Skew (SLS), Speaking Turns Skew (STS), Successful Interruption Skew (SIS), Unsuccessful Interruptions Skew (UIS), Backchannels Skew (BCS).

4.2 Group looking cues

The visual focus of attention (i.e. 'what a participant is looking at') is denoted VFOA and was estimated using the head pose angle as the resolution to track the eye gaze was not enough. The head pose is estimated following the technique described in [15]. Tracking and pose recognition are treated as two coupled problems in a dynamic, probabilistic framework. The method uses a formulation using particle filters, with the state space accounting for the location and scale of the head as well as discretized head pose. The observation model uses both texture [based on Histograms of Oriented Gradients (HOG)] and color features. The left image in Fig. 3 shows the tracker output location which is computed as the mean (in green color) and median (in red color) of all particle filter outputs. The top right part of Fig. 3 shows the estimated pan and tilt head pose angles. The video sampling rate was 30 frames per second (VFps).

Figure 3: Tracking, head-pose estimation, and VFOA estimation for a meeting participant.

Individual cues: Using the head-pose (considering pan and tilt only and not the roll), the VFOA is later estimated using the Maximum Aposteriori (MAP) rule. The MAP rule assumes a Gaussian distribution with mean and standard deviation prespecified manually (in the pan and tilt space), for each of the 5 targets T1 to T5. The bottom right part of Fig. 3 shows the estimated VFOA target. T1, T2 are the participants sitting opposite to the participants shown. T3 is the participant sitting next to the tracked participant. T4 and T5 represent the table area close to tracked participant and participant T3. UN stands for unfocussed.

In order to assess the accuracy, we carried out the annotations for VFOA. For every 15 second, the VFOA of every participant was manually annotated using one annotator for one randomly chosen meeting. This resulted in $61 * 4 = 244$ ground truth samples in total for all four participants. The automatic method had an accuracy of 42% when compared to the manual annotation. The estimation errors were mainly due to tracking failures (which were typically due to background color effects or illumination issues) or inaccuracies in head-pose estimation. Typical VFOA accuracies in group interactions are in this order.

Group Looking cues: From the individual gaze cue i.e. 'what is the visual target of each of the participant', the following group cues are defined, in order to characterize the gaze behavior of the group. Fig. 4 illustrates the visual target and three group cues for an interaction with four participants.

Fraction of People Gaze (FPG): Let $VF = D * VFps$ be the total number of video frames and P1, P2, P3, P4 be the number of frames in an interaction where a participant $i \in \{1, 2, 3, 4\}$ is being looked at. Then $FVTP = \frac{P1+P2+P3+P4}{4VF}$. This feature captures the intution that some groups look at people a lot while some others look at table a lot.

Fraction of Convergent Gaze (FCG): Let C be the number of frames when a participant $i \in \{1, 2, 3, 4\}$ is being looked at by all the other participants $j \in \{l : l \neq i\}$, $FCG = \frac{C}{VF}$.

Fraction of Mutual gaze (FMG): Let MG be the number of frames when two participants look at each other i.e. for a participant $i \in \{1, 2, 3, 4\}$ the visual target is $j \in \{l : l \neq i\}$ and for the participant j the visual target is i, $FMG = \frac{MG}{2VF}$.

Fraction of Shared gaze (FSG): Let SG be the number of frames when two participants look at the same participant.

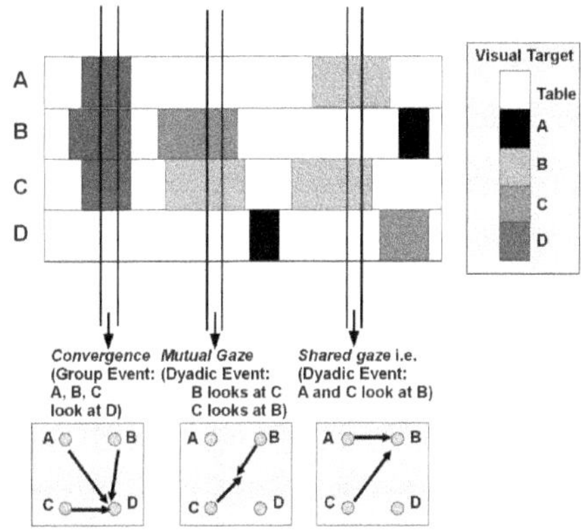

Figure 4: Visual targets and group looking cues

i.e. for a participant $i \in \{1,2,3,4\}$ and $j \in \{l : l \neq i\}$ the visual target is k, $k \in \{l : l \neq i, j\}$, $FMG = \frac{SG}{2VF}$ (see Fig. 4 for an illustration of FCG, FMG, and FSG).

Gaze Skew (GS): This feature follows the definition of distribution measures in audio. First the vector, Total Attention Length (TAL) composed of [P1, P2, P3, P4] is formed, normalized to one, and then compared with the egalitarian vector to obtain a group measure (Definition of this cue follows the speaking distribution cues).

5. TOPIC MODELING OF NONVERBAL GROUP CUES

In order to describe groups using a discrete probabilistic framework, we define the bag-of-NVPs by quantizing the group cues and then employ LDA based topic modeling. Working in the discrete domain helps to describe group behavior in intuitive categorical terms. The categories themselves were constructed using a data-centric approach described in the subsequent subsection. Finally, clustering the group cues in the discrete domain using LDA allows for a probabilistic interpretation of typical group behavior.

5.1 Bag-of-NVP definition

We define our documents as five-minute meeting slices, 163 of them obtained by slicing the 18 group interactions with an overlap of 80%. After computing the group cues in continuous domain, we discretize them to produce a bag-of-NVPs. This quantization was done using K-means procedure for every group cue. We set $K = 5$, rank each of the clusters and assign one of the 5 words corresponding to (HIGHEST, HIGH, AVERAGE, LOW, LOWEST) and color coded with (BLACK, BLUE, GREEN, MAGENTA, RED) for displaying in Figures 5-8.

5.2 LDA based topic extraction

We use LDA, a topic model to cluster our group cues in a discrete space. Topic models are co-occurrence based probabilistic generative models that were originally used in text modeling. In LDA [3], a text document is modeled as a distribution over topics, and a topic as a multinomial distribution over words.

Let there be D documents in a corpus and let a document contain N_d words. Let V denote the total number of unique words in the corpus. The probability of a given word w_i assuming T topics is $p(w_i) = \sum_{t=1}^{T} p(w_i|z_i = t)P(z_i = t)$, where z_i is a latent variable indicating the topic from which the ith word was drawn. Each topic is characterized by a word distribution $p(w|z = t) = \phi_w^{(t)}$ over the vocabulary of words V. Each document is generated by choosing a distribution over topics $p(z = t|d) = \theta_t^{(d)}$. When multiple slices of interaction are available for a particular chosen group g, $d \in D_g$, $p(z|g)$ can be computed by averaging over the multiple slices. This distribution can then be used to characterize and compare groups.

6. CORRELATION ANALYSIS

In this section, we study the correlation among the group behavior cues and the questionnaire variables (group composition, perception, and performance). All variables are 18 dimensional vectors, corresponding to the number of groups. Table 1 gives the significant correlations. For all the results reported below, we compute the Pearson correlation coefficient, hence reporting the r and p values. p-values for Pearson's correlation are computed using a Student's t distribution for a transformation of the correlation. Correlations with $p < 0.05$ are denoted by $*$ and $p < 0.01$ by $**$ in the superscript.

The group participation cues capture one aspect of group composition (extraversion *mean*) and one aspect of group perception (the difference in perceived dominance between top two individuals). Extraversion *mean* had a correlation of 0.56, 0.58, and 0.49 with SL, SI, UI. This means extraverted groups talk more and interrupt more. PDom *toprange* had a correlation of -0.69, -0.66, and -0.55 with ST, BC, and SI. This implies groups with a top-two dominance hierarchy have lesser turns, interruptions, and backchannels.

The silence and overlap cues captured three aspects of group composition (extraversion *mean*, extraversion *max*, and agreeableness *max*) and one aspect of group perception (PDom *toprange*). Extraversion *mean* has a correlation of 0.53 with FO2 and PDom *toprange* has a correlation of -0.64 with FO3. Extraverted groups or groups with lesser hierarchy among top two dominant people have higher overlapping speech. Groups with a disagreeable or an introverted person have a higher fraction of silence, FS (Agreeableness *max* and Extraversion *max* have a negative correlation of -0.57 and -0.5 with FS)

The speaking distribution cues charaterizing the skew in conversational opportunities, expectedly, capture the *range*, *toprange*, and *max* aspects of the perceived constructs. No significant correlation with group composition was found. One of the cue related to group performance. For example, PDom *toprange* had a significant correlation of 0.54, 0.51, 0.55 with SLS, STS, and BCS i.e. groups with top-two dominance hierarchy have unequal speaking time, turns, and backchannels distribution among group members. PLead *toprange* was found to correlate with BCS (r = 0.57). This indicates that groups with a skew in the distribution of backchannels have an emergent leader among the top two scorers on leadership. Group performance had a significant correlation with unsuccessful interruption skew.

The looking cues showed some complementary correlations w.r.t the speaking cues. Several correlations with group perception were found and only one cue captured group composition (Extraversion *max*) and the group performance. While audio cues showed correlation with PDom *max* $\rightarrow$, many of the visual cues were correlated with PDom *max* $\leftarrow$. Particularly, FPG, FCG, GS had correlations of 0.59, 0.52, and 0.61. This implies the likelihood of an individual perceiving the group as dominating is high when there was more people-gaze, convergent gaze, and gaze skew (i.e. everyone are not being looked at equally). The fraction of convergence indicates groups with a competent person and performing groups (FCG had a correlation of 0.63 and 0.57 with PComp *max* $\rightarrow$ and GPerf). Groups with an extraverted person have higher mutual gaze (FMG had a correlation of 0.63 with Extraversion *max*). Group with gaze skew report higher mean dominance score for their team members i.e. in dominant groups everyone is not being looked at equally (PDom *mean* had a correlation of 0.49 with GS).

Group cue	Group variable	r
Group participation cues		
Speaking Length (SL)	Extrav. *mean*	$+0.56^*$
Speaking Turns (ST)	PDom *toprange*	-0.69^{**}
Successful Interruptions (SI)	Extrav. *mean*	$+0.58^*$
	PDom *toprange*	-0.55^*
Unsucc. Interrup. (UI)	Extrav. *mean*	$+0.49^*$
Backchannels (BC)	PDom *toprange*	-0.66^{**}
Silence and overlap cues		
Fr. of Silence (FS)	Agreeab. *max*	-0.57^*
	Extrav. *max*	-0.50^*
Fr. of Non-overlapped Speech (FN)	PLike *toprange*	$+0.53^*$
Fr. 2-people Ovp. (FO2)	Extrav. *mean*	$+0.53^*$
Fr. 3-people Ovp. (FO3)	PDom *toprange*	-0.64^{**}
Speaking distribution cues		
Speaking Length Skew (SLS)	PDom *max* $\rightarrow$	$+0.51^*$
	PDom *toprange*	$+0.54^*$
	PLead *max* $\rightarrow$	$+0.59^*$
	PLead *range*	$+0.58^*$
Speaking Turns Skew (STS)	PDom *toprange*	$+0.51^*$
	PLead *max* $\rightarrow$	$+0.54^*$
Successful Interruptions Skew (SIS)	PLead *max* $\rightarrow$	$+0.59^*$
	PLead *range*	$+0.51^*$
Unsucc. Interruptions Skew (UIS)	PDom *range*	$+0.53^*$
	PComp *max* $\rightarrow$	$+0.59^*$
	PComp *range*	$+0.58^*$
	GPerf	$+0.52^*$
Backchannels Skew (BCS)	PDom *toprange*	$+0.55^*$
	PLead *toprange*	$+0.57^*$
Group looking cues		
Fr. of People Gaze (FPG)	PDom *max* $\leftarrow$	$+0.59^*$
	PLike *toprange*	$+0.51^*$
Fr. of Convergent Gaze (FCG)	PDom *max* $\leftarrow$	$+0.52^*$
	PComp *max* $\rightarrow$	$+0.63^{**}$
	PLike *range*	$+0.54^*$
	GPerf	$+0.57^*$
Fr. Mutual Gaze (FMG)	Extrav. *max*	$+0.50^*$
	PLead *max* $\leftarrow$	$+0.58^*$
Fr. Shared Gaze (FSG)	PLead *max* $\leftarrow$	$+0.50^*$
Gaze Skew (GS)	PDom *mean*	$+0.49^*$
	PDom *max* $\leftarrow$	$+0.61^{**}$
	PComp *range*	$+0.53^*$
	PLike *max* $\leftarrow$	-0.58^*

Table 1: Correlation between group cues and questionnaire variables (: $p < 0.01$, *: $p < 0.05$)**

7. TOPIC-BASED ANALYSIS

For the 163 meeting slices from 18 groups, we systematically study the effect of the data representation on the extracted topics i.e. the Bag-of-NVPs with each set of group cues. The vocabulary size V is five times (corresponding to the five categories from 'highest' to 'lowest') the number of group cues employed to build the bags. We used a symmetric Dirichlet distribution with $\alpha = 1$ and $\beta = 0.01$. We experimented with a small number of topics T, due to limited number of meeting slices or documents. For space reasons, we report the results with $T = 4$ only.

Figures 5-8 shows the top document for each of the four topics as illustration. Table 5-8 documents the correlation between $p(z|g)$ and the questionaire variables (each being a 18 dimensional vector) for various bag representations. Link to couple of demos here: `www.idiap.ch/~djaya/ICMI2012/`

7.1 Topics with group participation cues

The extracted topics with group participation cues are illustrated in Fig. 5 by their top document and in Table 2 by the questionnaire group variables with whom they have significant correlations. Topic 2 represents a group that is extroverted and the group members like each other (correlation with extraversion *mean* is 0.50^* and PLike *mean* is 0.47^*). There is no one perceived to be dominant (correlation with PDom *max* $\rightarrow$ is -0.53^*). Looking at Fig. 5, we see that this group takes more turns, interrupts, and backchannels a lot (i.e. high ST, SI, BC). It is interesting to contrast Topic 2 with Topic 4 in which groups talk even more. Although this topic did not have significant correlations with any variables. Topic 1 captures a group that has a clear hierarchy between the top two dominant people (correlation with PDom *toprange* is 0.68^{**}) and top two liked people (correlation with PLike *toprange* is 0.48^*). The group does not talk or interrupt much.

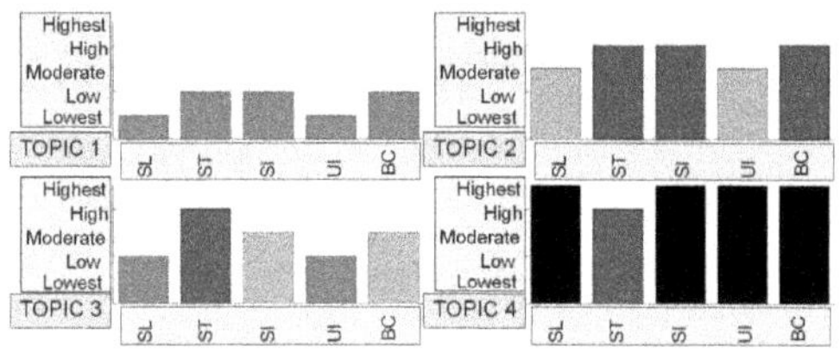

Figure 5: Top documents of four topics using group participation cues

Group cue set (SL, ST, SI, UI, BC)			
Construct	r	Construct	r
TOPIC 1		TOPIC 2	
PDom *toprange*	$+0.68^{**}$	Extrav. *mean*	$+0.50^*$
PLike *toprange*	$+0.48^*$	PDom *max* $\rightarrow$	-0.53^*
		PDom *toprange*	-0.60^{**}
		PDom *range*	-0.47^*
		PLead *max* $\leftarrow$	$+0.47^*$
		PLike *mean*	$+0.47^*$
TOPIC 3		TOPIC 4	
Extrav. *max* $\rightarrow$	-0.52^*		
PLead *max* $\leftarrow$	$+0.63^{**}$		

Table 2: Correlation between the group participation topics and perceived questionnaire variables

7.2 Topics with silence and overlap cues

Fig. 6 shows the top documents and Table 3 lists the significant correlations. Topic 1 represents an agreeable group in which the group members like each other. Correlation with agreeableness *mean* is 0.52* and PLike *mean* is 0.63**. It is to be noted that while group agreeableness is a self-reported quantity, group liking is perception about others. In these groups, the number of silent frames is lowest, with moderate non-overlapping and overlapping speech (see Fig. 6). Topic 4 represents a group that is extroverted and dominating (unlike the Topic 2 with group participation cues in Section 9.1 which is extroverted and group members like each other). Correlation with PDom *mean* is 0.55* and Extraversion *mean* is 0.52*. Topic 3 captures a group with a hierarchy between the top two members (correlation with PDom *toprange* is 0.54). Interestingly, the group members like each other less (correlation with PLike *mean*: −0.50*). Nonoverlapping speech (FN) is highest, which means a lot of monologues (see Fig. 6).

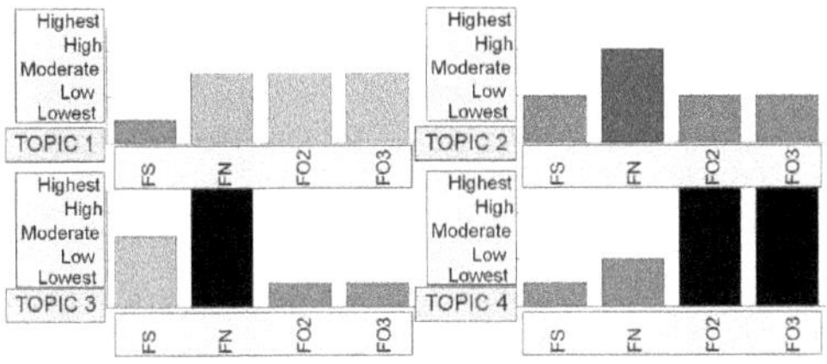

Figure 6: Top documents - silence and overlap cues

Group cue set (FS, FN, FO2, FO3)			
Construct	r	Construct	r
TOPIC 1		TOPIC 2	
Agreeab. *mean*	+0.52*		
PDom *max* →	−0.53*		
PDom *range*	−0.54*		
PDom *max* ←	−0.48*		
PLike *mean*	+0.63**		
PLike *toprange*	−0.49*		
PLike *range*	−0.53*		
TOPIC 3		TOPIC 4	
PDom *toprange*	+0.54*	Extrav. *mean*	+0.52*
PLike *mean*	−0.50*	PDom *mean*	+0.55*
PLike *toprange*	+0.69**	PDom *max* ←	+0.50*

Table 3: Correlation between the silence and overlap topics and perceived questionnaire variables

7.3 Topics with speaking distribution cues

Fig. 7 shows the top documents and Table 4 lists the significant correlations. Topic 1 corresponds to a group with a disagreeable person (correlation with agreeableness *max* → is −0.46*), but no emergent leader (correlation with PLead *max* → is −0.53). Everyone in the group contributes to the conversations as the distribution measures indicate equality i.e. skew is lowest (see Fig. 7). Topic 3 is where the distribution measures indicate inequality (high skew) and in these groups there is a hierarchy. The correlation with PDom *toprange* is 0.55 and correlation with PLead *range* is 0.6.

7.4 Topics with group looking cues

The results are shown in Fig. 8 and Table 5. The group corresponding to Topic 1 is introverted. Correlation with extraversion *mean* is −0.55* and *max* → is −0.47*. Very

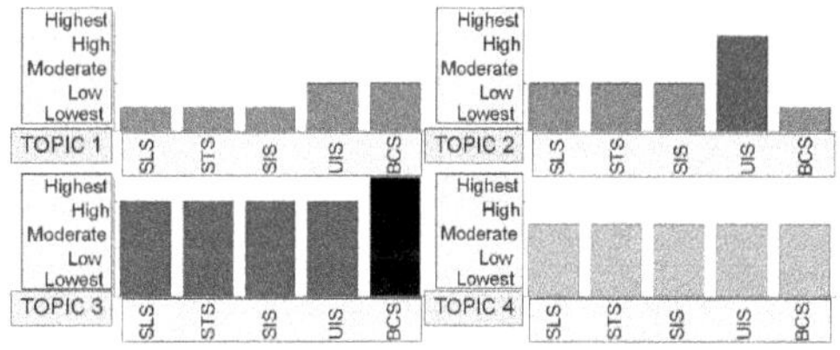

Figure 7: Top documents - speaking distribution cues

Group cue set (SLS, STS, SIS, UIS, BCS)			
Construct	r	Construct	r
TOPIC 1		TOPIC 2	
Agreeab. *max* →	−0.46*	PDom *toprange*	−0.47*
PLead *max* →	−0.53*	PLike *max* ←	−0.48*
TOPIC 3		TOPIC 4	
PDom *toprange*	+0.55*		
PDom *range*	+0.48*		
PLead *max* →	+0.48*		
PLead *toprange*	+0.60**		

Table 4: Correlation between the speaking distribution topics and perceived questionnaire variables

interestingly, the table and not people, is the main visual target, with lowest convergence and mutual gaze (see FCG and FMG in Fig. 8 top left). But everyone is being looked at equally (Gaze skew, GS is lowest). Furthermore, the likelihood of someone perceiving the group members as dominant or taking the lead is less (correlation with PDom *max* ← is −0.54* and PLead *max* ← is −0.48*). The groups corresponding to Topic 2 are in direct contrast. People look at each other a lot, with high mutual and shared gaze (see FMG and FSG in Fig. 8 top left). But the likelihood of someone perceiving the group members as dominant is high (correlation with PDom *max* ← is 0.62**). Furthermore, the group members do not like each other. Topic 3 represents a case where group looking is moderate, the correlation with performance is -0.45 ($p = 0.06$). So this is one signature of a good performing group.

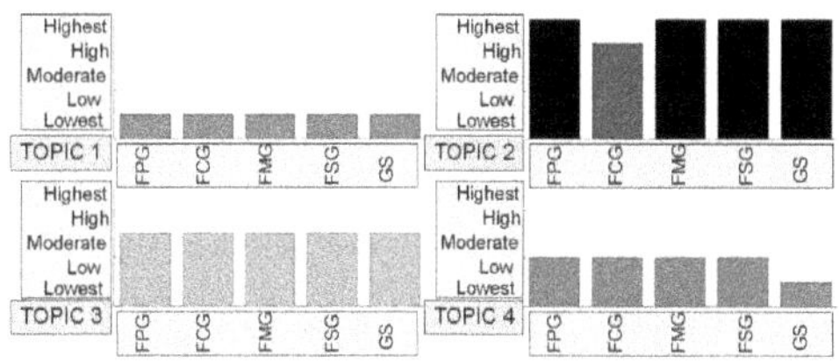

Figure 8: Top documents - group looking cues

7.5 Regression experiments

We used a step-wise linear regression procedure to measure the power of the group cues to predict the questionnaire variables, by combining group cues two sets at a time. We also experimented with group topics. We report the best results here. Regarding group composition, the combination of Group participation cues and Silence-Overlap cues could predict 77% (F = 11.2; p = 0.0004) of the variance in Agreeableness *max*. Regarding perception, the combination of Speaking distribution cues and Silence-Overlap cues could predict 67% (F = 15.3; p = 0.0009) of the variance in PDom

Group cue set (FPG, FCG, FMG, FSG, GS)			
Construct	r	Construct	r
TOPIC 1		TOPIC 2	
Extrav. *mean*	−0.55*	PDom *max* ←	+0.62**
Extrav. *max* →	−0.47*	PLead *max* ←	+0.47*
PDom *max* ←	−0.54*	PComp *range*	+0.50*
PLead *max* ←	−0.48*	PLike *mean*	−0.50*
		PLike *toprange*	+0.52*
TOPIC 3		TOPIC 4	
PLead *max* ←	+0.63**	Op. Exp. *mean*	−0.49*
GPerf	+0.45		

Table 5: Correlation between the group looking topics and perceived questionnaire variables

toprange. Using the topics, a new group composition variable (apart from agreeableness and extraversion) could be modeled. The topics with group looking cues could explain 42% (F = 5.5; p = 0.0089) of the variance in Openness to experience *mean*. Regarding group perception, the topics with Silence-Overlap cues could explain 50% (F = 8.0; p = 0.0054) of the variance in PDom *mean* and 39% (F = 10.3; p = 0.0054) of the variance in PLike *mean*. Group topics show complementary properties compared to the group cues. for certain constructs.

8. CONCLUSION

In this work, we presented a framework to define and extract group behavioral cues characterizing the speaking and looking patterns in face-to-face interactions. We mined these patterns using different bag representations and LDA. First, the relationship between the group constructs and the group cues was documented. Later the correlation with group topics was presented. Group interactions with unacquainted participants, having no prior hierarchy, were used for the study. The group variables were defined using the self-reported questionnaires.

Our study shows multiple significant connections between nonverbal features and variables characterizing the group composition, interpersonal perception, and performance. To summarize, group composition variables such as the average and maximum extraversion of group members, and maximum agreeableness found in the group were significantly related to group participation and the silence-overlap cues. Group perception, like the dominance hierarchy among the top members, and the perceived leadership were captured by many of the group cues. Group performance was captured by two group cues (unsuccessful interruptions skew and convergent gaze). Apart from these trends, it was interesting to observe that higher convergent gaze indicated the presence of a competent group member; that groups with a highly extroverted person have higher mutual gaze; and that gaze skew signalled groups with higher average dominance.

The discovered group topics show certain complementarity as compared to the raw group cues. For instance, while no group cue had significant correlation with mean group liking, a topic with silence-overlap cues correlated well with this construct. It is interesting to note that the topics captured dominance, leadership, and liking aspects more than competence and performance. Also, regarding group composition, the group topics captured the extraversion and agreeableness aspects.

Finally, the regression experiments showed that the group cues and group topics could predict certain constructs, for example the hierarchy between the top two dominant people, and the presence of a highly disagreeable person. For the future, we need to increase the corpus size, and perform classification experiments and model selection to choose the number of topics automatically. Fine-grained gaze cues and speaking cues that capture the dynamics of the interaction over time could also be explored.

Acknowledgments: This research was funded by the NISHA collaborative project between Idiap and NTT, and was also partly supported by the SNSF SONVB project and the EU HUMAVIPS project. We also thank Jean-Marc Odobez (Idiap) for sharing code for VFOA estimation.

9. REFERENCES

[1] S.T. Acuña et al. How do personality, team processes and task characteristics relate to job satisfaction and software quality? *Information and Software Technology*, 51(3):627–639, 2009.

[2] B. Barry and G.L. Stewart. Composition, process, and performance in self-managed groups: The role of personality. *Journal of Applied Psychology*, 82(1):62, 1997.

[3] D. M. Blei et al. Latent Dirichlet Allocation. *J. Machine Learning Research*, 3:993–1022, January 2003.

[4] D. Gatica-Perez. Automatic nonverbal analysis of social interaction in small groups: a review. *IVC*, 2009.

[5] T. Halfhill et al. Group personality composition and group effectiveness. *Small Group Research*, 36(1):83–105, 2005.

[6] H. Hung et al. Investigating automatic dominance estimation in groups from visual attention and speaking activity. In *Proc. ICMI*, pages 233–236. ACM, 2008.

[7] D. Jayagopi. *Computational modeling of face-to-face social interaction using nonverbal behavioral cues.* PhD thesis, École Polytechnique Fédérale de Lausanne, 2011.

[8] D. Jayagopi and D. Gatica-Perez. Mining group nonverbal conversational patterns using probabilistic topic models. *IEEE Trans. Multimedia*, 12(8):790 – 802, 2010.

[9] O. P. John et al. The Big Five trait taxonomy: History, measurement, and theoretical perspectives. In *Handbook of personality: Theory and research.* Guilford, 1999.

[10] J. Kickul et al. Emergent leadership behaviors: The function of personality and cognitive ability in determining teamwork performance and ksas. *JBP*, 2000.

[11] B. Lepri et al. Automatic prediction of individual performance from thin slices of social behavior. In *Proc. ACM MM*, 2009.

[12] B. Lepri et al. Employing social gaze and speaking activity for automatic determination of the extraversion trait. In *Proc. ICMI-MLMI*, page 7. ACM, 2010.

[13] J. E. McGrath. *Groups: Interaction and performance.* Prentice-Hall Englewood Cliffs, NJ, 1984.

[14] F. Pianesi et al. Multimodal recognition of personality traits in social interactions. In *Proc. ICMI*, Greece, 2008.

[15] E. Ricci and J.M. Odobez. Learning large margin likelihoods for realtime head pose tracking. In *Proc. ICIP, Cairo*, 2009.

[16] H. Salamin et al. Automatic role recognition in multiparty recordings: using social affiliation networks for feature extraction. *IEEE Trans. Multimedia*, 11(7), 2009.

[17] D. Sanchez-Cortes et al. An audio visual corpus for emergent leader analysis. In *Proc. ICMI Workshop*, 2011.

[18] J.S. Wiggins. A psychological taxonomy of trait-descriptive terms: The interpersonal domain. *Journal of Personality and Social Psychology*, 37(3):395, 1979.

[19] A.W. Woolley et al. Evidence for a collective intelligence factor in the performance of human groups. *Science*, 2010.

Semi-automatic Generation of Multimodal User Interfaces for Dialogue-based Interactive Systems

Dominik Ertl*
Bosch Engineering GmbH
Hüttenbrennergasse 5
A-1030 Vienna, Austria
dominik@ertl.in

Hermann Kaindl
Vienna University of Technology, ICT
Gusshausstrasse 27-29
A-1040 Vienna, Austria
kaindl@ict.tuwien.ac.at

ABSTRACT

Automation in the course of user-interface (UI) development has the potential to save resources and time. For *graphical* user interfaces, quite some research has been performed on their automated generation. While the results are still not in wide-spread use, at least the problems are well understood meanwhile. In contrast, automated generation of *multimodal* UIs is still in its infancy. We address this problem by proposing a tool-supported process for generating multimodal UIs for dialogue-based interactive systems. For its concrete enactment, we provide tool support for generating a runtime configuration and glue code, respectively. In a nutshell, our approach generates multimodal dialogue-based UIs semi-automatically.

Categories and Subject Descriptors

D.2.2 [**Software Engineering**]: Design Tools and Techniques—*User interfaces*

General Terms

Design

Keywords

Automated UI generation, multimodal user interfaces

1. INTRODUCTION

For automated generation of graphical user interfaces (GUIs), primarily task-based models have been proposed, e.g., see [8], [13]. A more recent approach employs Discourse-based Communication Models for specifying communicative interaction, e.g., see [6], [7], with discourses in the sense of dialogues. From higher-level models, usually model transformations lead to lower-level models and, with the help of templates to final code implementing a GUI. The latter approach has already led to automatic generation of GUIs specifically optimized for smartphones, see [9].

In contrast, we found comparably few approaches in the literature for automated generation of multimodal UIs. Our own approach attempts to be comprehensive by proposing a general *process*. Such a process needs to be tool-supported, of course, for being useful for automated UI generation.

Therefore, we also provide tools for certain aspects, such as for generating configurations for speech interfaces that allow easy use of existing tools for speech processing, both for input and output. For a new modality of interacting with moving robots called *Motion Cue* [2], we had to implement its code manually, of course. However, we show how we can automatically generate the glue code for its integration. Aylet et al. [1] generally present challenges and future perspectives of robot companions.

In order to combine single modalities for a multimodal UI, we had to provide some automation also for *fusion* [5] and *fission* [4], of course. Since this work is published already, we simply build on it in the current paper.

The remainder of this paper is organized in the following manner. First, we discuss previous work. Then we present our process for automated generation of multimodal UIs for dialogue-based interactive systems. Based on that, we elaborate on semi-automatic support for single modalities and present it for speech interfaces and the new modality Motion Cue.

2. PREVIOUS WORK

Previous work deals with certain aspects that are important for semi-automatic generation of multimodal UIs. Here we highlight those that are helpful to better understand this work: what kind of high-level models do we support, how can one combine modalities and which components of runtime architectures are necessary?

Vanderdonckt [14] provides a comprehensive overview of the current state of the art of UI generation. He discusses the advantages and shortcomings of "classical" UI engineering, and compares it with the promising approach of model-driven engineering of UIs. The most common models for this purpose are task models like ConcurTaskTrees [8].

More recently, Discourse-based Communication Models have been proposed, e.g., see [6], [7]. For our work on multimodal UIs, we have chosen such Communication Models as a basis for UI generation. These models are modality-independent and allow a UI designer to specify discourse-based interaction design at a high level, reflecting human-

*Dominik Ertl did this work while being with the Institute of Computer Technology (ICT) of the Vienna University of Technology.

ICMI'12, October 22–26, 2012, Santa Monica, California, USA.

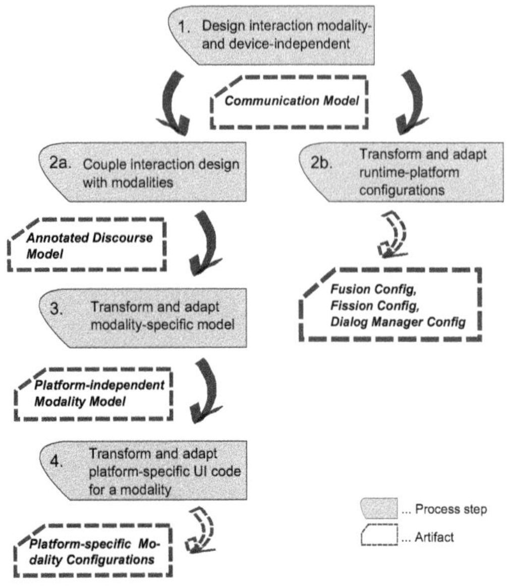

Figure 1: Process of Semi-Automatic Generation of a Multimodal User Interface.

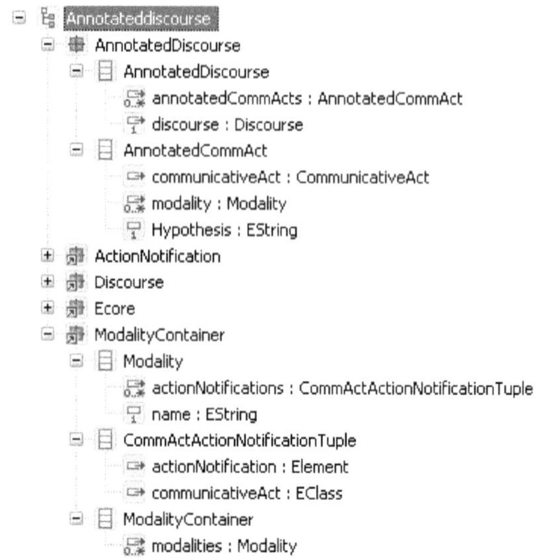

Figure 2: Annotated Discourse Model – Tree-editor.

human-like dialogue structures. These models can also be used to derive a behavior model of a UI.

Stanciulescu et al. [11] show model-based transformations for multimodal UIs from UsiXML. Their resulting multimodal UI consists of GUI and speech, and does not take other modalities into account. Additionally, their Web-based approach does not need an input integration mechanism, since an independent interpretation process is performed for each modality.

We base our work on concepts that support a UI designer in carefully combining modalities (like GUI, speech input/output, gestures, etc.) for a "natural" UI. For example, Bernsen and Tzovaras [12] introduce the concept of modality functionality, which addresses the question which modality or set of modalities to use for a specific interaction purpose. These authors found an essence of 25 modality properties, which are a solid foundation for selecting sets of modalities for a multimodal UI. Another well-established concept of combining modalities in a multimodal UI are the CARE properties (complementarity, redundancy, equivalence, assignment) [3].

In contrast, we present a design-time process for generating multimodal UIs and tool support. From a technical perspective, such a UI is based on an architecture including components for fusion and fission as well as a dialogue manager.

3. OUR PROCESS FOR AUTOMATED GENERATION OF MULTIMODAL UIS

Our process for automated generation of multimodal UIs can be used to generate multimodal UIs for different platforms (smartphones, PCs, etc.) and different kinds of dialogue-based interactive applications. The main properties of the process are:

1. The process guides one to automatically generate modalities like vocal speech input and output from a Discourse-based Communication Model. Moreover, it facilitates coupling of modalities like gesture input via glue code to the multimodal UI.
2. The process guides one to automatically configure an already existing runtime platform, which is able to execute multimodal applications.
3. Tool support is necessary for (semi-)automatic generation, of course.

Figure 1 shows an overview of the process of UI generation. In its first step, *(1) design of interaction modality- and device-independently*, one designs with already existing tool support a Communication Model to define high-level communicative interaction in a machine-readable way.

The outcome of this process step — the Communication Model — is the input for two subsequent steps. In *(2a) coupling of interaction design with modalities*, a UI designer creates the Annotated Discourse Model, which is modality-dependent interaction design for the combination of modalities. This may be informed by guidelines for multimodal UIs like the ones from Reeves et al. [10]. Here, one has to consider the CARE properties, and fusion (for input) and fission (for output) are important when several modalities are combined for interaction. Figure 2 shows a screenshot of an Annotated Discourse Model. There, a UI designer can inspect the elements of a specific Communication Model. Moreover, she can add metadata to the Communication Model, which defines how the communicative interaction is to be rendered into (potentially several) modalities. Here, the UI designer can apply the modality properties of Bernsen [12] or the CARE properties of Coutaz et al. [3] to carefully combine the modalities. This step defines the interplay of the modalities at run-time. The resulting modality specifications are stored in a so-called modality container in a machine-readable XML format. In *(2b) transformation into and adaptation of modality-independent run-time platform configurations*, a UI designer applies editor-based tool support to generate and adapt run-time platform configurations for the fusion, fission and dialogue manager components.

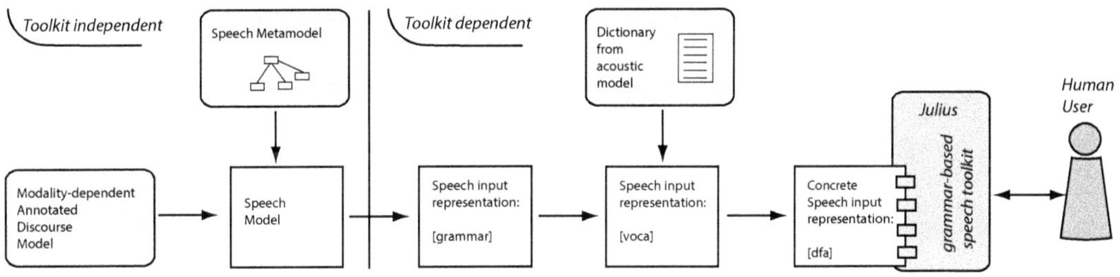

Figure 3: Speech generation process based on the Annotated Discourse Model.

In the subsequent step *(3) transformation into and adaptation of a modality-specific model*, the Annotated Discourse Model is transformed and then adapted via tool support into modality-specific models that are platform-independent. Below we explain how to generate the speech configurations.

Finally, the platform-independent models are *(4) transformed into platform-specific UI code for a concrete modality*. The resulting code can be executed in an already existing run-time platform.

4. FROM A COMMUNICATION MODEL TO SINGLE MODALITIES

Let us present two implemented examples of what we can generate from a Discourse-based Communication Model on the way to implementations of single modalities.[1] The modalities speech input and Motion Cue [2], which we present in the following, are different in their "nature" from a generation point of view and thus require a different kind of code generation. We explain here the generation of *configurations* for speech input and *glue code* for Motion Cue. We also discuss limitations of tool support.

4.1 Generating Speech Input Configurations

For the speech input configuration example, we use the grammar-based Julius[2] speech recognition toolkit because it is Open Source and widely distributed. The Julius speech toolkit is a multi-language speech processing tool for command-based input. The result of the generation process are concrete configuration files for Julius.

The complete generation process to the Julius configuration from a Communication Model is depicted in Figure 3. On the left, the figure shows the generation of a toolkit-independent Speech Model from the Annotated Discourse Model. The Speech Model is an instantiation of the Speech Metamodel. Tool support facilitates the transformation of the parts relevant to speech input into this Speech Model.

In the next step, the Speech Model is transformed (with tool support) into the toolkit- and platform-dependent configuration files. This transformation step requires an acoustic model as input. Julius also requires a template configuration of the physical properties that specifies how to use the toolkit. Our tools also generate this configuration file (shown in the figure as grammar, voca and dfa-files). The tool support for the generation of the configuration files uses XPAND as transformation language. In principle, we specify with XPAND parameterizable templates. The transformation mechanism instantiates the parameters with values from the Speech Model. Finally, each generated configuration file is a fully parameterizable template.

[1]Example code as well as prototypical tooling is available on request.

[2]`http://julius.sourceforge.jp/en_index.php`

4.2 Generating Code for Motion Cue

What is Motion Cue? Inspired by human-human communication, we investigated the modality Motion Cue [2] in the context of communicative interaction between a (prototypical) robot shopping cart and its human user. Whenever they pass in a supermarket incidentally a product on their shopping list not yet taken, the robot cart recognizes this fact and tries to communicate it to its user. As experimentally shown in [2], this message gets across more often to the accompanying user when GUI and speech output are reinforced by the cart slowing down in front of this particular product (as compared to GUI and speech output alone). So, this particular "body" movement serves as a Motion Cue reinforcing GUI and speech output. (Since this robot lacks any "arms", its only possible movements are "body" movements, including speed changes.) If the user does not stop the robot cart, it automatically accelerates again.

How is Motion Cue implemented? In our modality-independent Communication Model, such a scenario is essentially modeled as an *offer* by the robot cart that can be either *accepted* of *rejected* by the human user, and this scenario is to be triggered by an event of approaching a product from the shopping list not yet taken. The concrete rendering for the modality configurations is not defined here, however. This happens in the process step *(2a) coupling of interaction design with modalities*. For example, the designer can select in the Annotated Discourse Model GUI, speech output and Motion Cue for this scenario with a robot. For actually making this Motion Cue possible, the related driving functionality of the robot close to its hardware, including the acceleration and deceleration behavior, is implemented on the robot's operations layer. It is made available through a software interface to be used by the multimodal runtime platform that enacts the discourse model specified in the Annotated Discourse Model.

What can be generated for Motion Cue? Still, some glue code is needed to operate the lower level from the higher-level discourse specification. The glue code is, in essence, code with two functionalities. First, it calls the methods of a modalities' library (e.g., to control a robot). Second, it transfers the return values of the method calls to the runtime platform, which is necessary in the course of dialog events. The mechanism for generation of this glue code uses a list of Communicative Acts as input, which are assigned to the modality Motion Cue, e.g., the Communicative Act *Offer*. The propositional content of the Communicative Act refers to the interface functionality. Using this information, the generation mechanism transforms a code template into concrete code that contains method calls to use the robot's movement functionality. In addition, the resulting class is registered in the multimodal communication platform, so that this platform will call its methods at runtime. The platform also synchronizes these calls with GUI and speech output.

4.3 Limitations of Tool Support

We already provide tool support for generation of the fusion and fission configurations from the Communication Model, of a modality-independent Speech Model, and concrete speech configurations for a specific speech input toolkit. Moreover, there is tool support for the generation of glue code for Motion Cue as described above. Our generation tools are Eclipse-plugins. Manual editing is necessary for combining the modalities in the Annotated Discourse Model and fine-tuning of the configuration files or the glue code. So, this is *semi*-automatic rather than fully-automatic generation of multimodal UIs. In addition, a UI designer who applies this process does not yet have full tool support. In fact, there is a need for tool support not only for the process steps where rule-based transformations are required. For example, UI designers may need to prototype UIs to study modalities, for tools for statistical evaluation, etc.

5. CONCLUSION

In this paper, we address semi-automatic generation of multimodal UIs for dialogue-based interactive systems. In particular, we present a new process for guidance in the course of such a generation. Of course, nothing can be automatically generated here without tool support. So, we partly provide necessary tool support for automated generation and for enacting process steps. In this paper, we show the generation for speech and a new modality named Motion Cue, where we can automate the generation of a runtime configuration and glue code, respectively.

This work contributes to a better understanding of the kind of automation currently possible and, where handcrafting is (still) necessary in the course of generation of multimodal UIs. With our process we can address multimodal UIs both for human-computer interaction (HCI) and human-robot interaction (HRI). In contrast to "pure" HCI, HRI has the embodiment, i.e., the morphology of the robot as a key part of the UI.

6. REFERENCES

[1] R. Aylett, G. Castellano, B. Raducanu, A. Paiva, and M. Hanheide. Long-term socially perceptive and interactive robot companions: challenges and future perspectives. In *Proceedings of the 13th International Conference on Multimodal Interfaces (ICMI)*, pages 323–326, 2011.

[2] C. Bogdan, D. Ertl, H. Hüttenrauch, M. Göller, A. Green, K. Severinsson Eklundh, J. Falb, and H. Kaindl. Evaluation of robot body movements supporting communication: Towards HRI on the move. In *New Frontiers in Human Robot Interaction*, pages 185–210. John Benjamins Publishing Company, 2011.

[3] J. Coutaz, L. Nigay, D. Salber, A. Blandford, J. May, and R. M. Young. Four easy pieces for assessing the usability of multimodal interaction: the CARE properties. In *Proceedings of INTERACT 95*, pages 115–120, 1995.

[4] D. Ertl, J. Falb, and H. Kaindl. Semi-automatically configured fission for multimodal user interfaces. In *ACHI*, pages 85–90, 2010.

[5] D. Ertl, S. Kavaldjian, H. Kaindl, and J. Falb. Semi-automatically generated high-level fusion for multimodal user interfaces. In *Proceedings of the 43nd Annual Hawaii International Conference on System Sciences (HICSS-43)*, Piscataway, NJ, USA, 2010. IEEE Computer Society Press.

[6] J. Falb, H. Kaindl, H. Horacek, C. Bogdan, R. Popp, and E. Arnautovic. A discourse model for interaction design based on theories of human communication. In *Extended Abstracts on Human Factors in Computing Systems (CHI '06)*, pages 754–759. ACM Press: New York, NY, 2006.

[7] J. Falb, S. Kavaldjian, R. Popp, D. Raneburger, E. Arnautovic, and H. Kaindl. Fully automatic user interface generation from discourse models. In *Proceedings of the 13th International Conference on Intelligent User Interfaces (IUI '09)*, pages 475–476. ACM Press: New York, NY, 2009.

[8] G. Mori, F. Paternò, and C. Santoro. CTTE: Support for developing and analyzing task models for interactive system design. *IEEE Transactions on Software Engineering*, 28:797–813, 2002.

[9] D. Raneburger, R. Popp, S. Kavaldjian, H. Kaindl, and J. Falb. Optimized GUI generation for small screens. In H. Hussmann, G. Meixner, and D. Zuehlke, editors, *Model-Driven Development of Advanced User Interfaces*, volume 340 of *Studies in Computational Intelligence*, pages 107–122. Springer Berlin / Heidelberg, 2011.

[10] L. M. Reeves, J. Lai, J. A. Larson, S. Oviatt, T. S. Balaji, S. Buisine, P. Collings, P. Cohen, B. Kraal, J.-C. Martin, M. McTear, T. Raman, K. M. Stanney, H. Su, and Q. Y. Wang. Guidelines for multimodal user interface design. *Commun. ACM*, 47(1):57–59, Jan. 2004.

[11] A. Stanciulescu and J. Vanderdonckt. Design options for multimodal web applications. *Computer-Aided Design Of User Interfaces V*, pages 41–56, 2008.

[12] D. Tzovaras. *Multimodal User Interfaces: From Signals to Interaction (Signals and Communication Technology)*. Springer Publishing Company, Incorporated, 1 edition, 2008.

[13] J. van den Bergh and K. Coninx. From task to dialog model in the UML. In *Proceedings of the 6th International Workshop on Task Models and Diagrams for User Interface Design (TAMODIA 2007), LNCS 4849*, pages 98–111, Toulouse, France, Nov 2007. Springer.

[14] J. M. Vanderdonckt. Model-driven engineering of user interfaces: Promises, successes, and failures. In *Proceedings of 5th Annual Romanian Conf. on Human-Computer Interaction*, pages 1–10. Matrix ROM, Sept. 2008.

Designing Multimodal Reminders for the Home: Pairing Content with Presentation

Julie R. Williamson, Marilyn McGee-Lennon, and Stephen Brewster
Glasgow Interactive Systems Group
The University of Glasgow
Glasgow, United Kingdom
{Julie.Rico, Marilyn.McGee-Lennon, Stephen.Brewster}@glasgow.ac.uk

ABSTRACT

Reminder systems are a specific range of technologies for care at home that can deliver notifications or reminders (such as 'take your medication') to assist with daily living. How to best deliver these reminders is an interesting research challenge. Today's technologies have the potential to deliver the notifications in a range of output modalities. The delivery methods can be selected both by the system (depending on what devices are available in the home) and on the users' needs, capabilities and preferences. This paper describes a user-centred approach to the design of multimodal output for reminders in the home. In a focus group study (N=15), this paper explores how six output modalities could be used to present reminders in a home setting. The results demonstrate user requirements that can be incorporated into the early phases of the design of a multimodal reminder system.

Categories and Subject Descriptors

H5.2. Information interfaces and presentation: User Interfaces (User Centred Design).

General Terms

Human Factors.

Keywords

User-centred design, Multimodal interaction, Reminder systems.

1. INTRODUCTION

Technology that can support or augment care at home is often referred to as assisted or independent living technology and is increasingly accepted as key in continuing to support our ageing population and a general shift towards more self-managed care [7]. Reminder systems are one such technology that can be used to support daily living routines. For example, reminder systems can deliver notifications to the user on upcoming tasks, appointments or reminders about medication [8]. Managing daily life and care regimes with this kind of support can allow older adults to remain independent and in their own homes for longer as they age [7].

It is a significant challenge to design technologies for the home that are easy to set up and use yet configurable by and adaptable to a wide range of people. For example, these technologies may be used by individuals with a wide range of needs and abilities [2], such as older adults, their friends and family and health and social care professionals. Making information accessible and acceptable to such a wide variety of users, and in a wide variety of contexts is a challenge. One way to address this challenge is to make these systems multisensory or 'multimodal' – that is they are able to offer alternative interaction modalities, such as speech, gesture, or touch, for receiving and presenting information [5] [12]. Using multimodal interaction for reminder delivery can provide the opportunity for more flexible and customizable experiences for users. Multimodality allows users to select how they would like different types of reminders presented to them depending on their own preferences, capabilities, social and physical context.

Previous work in the area of assisted living technologies has explored the benefits of using multimodal interactions and including older users in the design process. Although it is clear that the design and development of these technologies is greatly improved by considering multimodality and user-centred design, it is still not clear how multimodal presentations for reminders should actually be presented in the home context for older adults. The most appropriate modality for delivering a message may depend on how important that message is, how private or sensitive the information being delivered is and whether or not the person is alone or sharing the interaction space with a spouse, friends or family. To explore these issues, we completed a focus group study (N=15) that explored how older adults imagined different multimodal presentations working in their own homes. The results demonstrate how these needs and requirements could be incorporated into the design of a multimodal system, for example by distributing multimodal interaction around the home, shifting from implicit to explicit, and augmenting existing practices.

2. PREVIOUS WORK

This paper builds on previous work that looks at how technology can be designed to support assisted living and how multimodal interaction can improve these interfaces. When combined with a user-centred approach, multimodal reminder systems provide a highly flexible platform from which to generate reminders within a home setting.

2.1 Multimodal Reminder Systems

Reminder systems are one of a range of assisted living technologies and can be an important part of an assisted living package [3] [7]. Many people have problems remembering tasks and chores in and around the home as a consequence of ageing [1], the conditions for which they need care [10] or the medications they are taking [7]. Reminder systems can be used to set, manage, and deliver electronic reminders or notifications to someone in or around the home and might include notifications such as 'take your medication'; 'you have an appointment at 2pm' or 'remember to water the plants'. Being able to remember these tasks can be the difference between being moved into residential care and ageing in the comfort of your own home [3] [7].

ICMI'12, October 22–26, 2012, Santa Monica, California, USA.

Recently, researchers have argued that good reminder systems should be multimodal [2] [5], [12]. Multimodality involves the combination of multiple sensory input and output channels for interaction with technology. An additional advantage of multimodal interaction is the option of providing a choice of interaction methods to the user. We would argue that this is particularly important in pervasive health applications where the users are diverse and the context in which applications are used is varied and can change over time [2]. A multimodal reminder system can provide alternative ways to deliver reminders to the user, such visual, auditory, tactile and olfactory [12]. Different output modalities might be selected depending on users' capabilities and impairments, the type of reminder being delivered, user preferences, social context and the output devices available in the home. This multimodality could increase both the accessibility of the information being presented and the likelihood that the delivery method will be pleasant or acceptable to the user without becoming disruptive or annoying [12]. For example, users with sensory impairments can choose to have reminders delivered in a modality appropriate to them. Users with a desire to maintain their own privacy can choose to have reminders delivered discreetly.

Involving users in the design of home care technologies can take many different forms ranging from attitudinal surveys and questionnaires to home tour interviews and co-design sessions with older users. However, many user-centred design techniques still fail to consider the particular challenges of older users [6]. Inclusive design and universal design have become more commonplace and encourage the design of products with accessibility and 'access for all' at the heart of design. This is of particular importance when including older users and users with sensory, physical and cognitive impairment. These methods tend to focus on designers ensuring that products can be used by as wide a range of people as possible, and have produced a range of guidelines and standards to assist designers in achieving this objective [6], [9].

2.2 Reminder Content

Previous work has looked at how users perceive the content of reminders within the home. The survey completed by Williamson *et al.* [13] looked at a variety of factors, such as privacy, importance, helpfulness, and clarity, that might effect users' perception of home reminders. The results of the survey study indicate that the 12 factors explored were significant, with especially interesting implications for design for reminders with differing importance and privacy. Additionally, the results demonstrated that certain factors vary over the content of the message, such as importance and urgency, where other factors vary over the phrasing of the message, such as helpfulness and clarity. These are important factors to consider when designing reminders for the home.

3. MULTIMODAL REMINDERS IN THE HOME

In order to effectively pair multimodal presentations with the content of reminders in the home setting, we completed a focus group study with possible end users in order to incorporate older adults into the early phases of a design process. These focus groups explored participants' preferences for different output modalities and their techniques for pairing those with reminders in the home. Following on from previous work, this focus group study investigated how the privacy and importance of reminders might effect users' chosen presentation of those reminders. These factors were chosen since they were both significant factors in a previous survey study [13], but also because they have interesting implications for the design of these reminders with respect to multimodal interaction. For example, for messages that are highly private, are users more likely to use an abstract presentation modality when others are present? Do they want this message to change to a linguistic presentation when they are alone? With respect to importance, will users accept a more intrusive or annoying reminder if that helps to ensure the message is communicated? These are the kinds of questions these focus groups aimed to address.

	High Importance	Low Importance
High Privacy	Have You Taken Your Pills?	Have You Done Exercise Today?
	Take Your Pills	Do Some Exercise Today
Low Privacy	Do You Have Your Keys?	Have you Watered the Plants?
	Remember Your Keys	Water the Plants

Figure 1. Reminders used in the focus group study.

Each focus group began with a short introduction to the reminders to be used throughout the discussion, as shown in Figure 1. Then, participants were asked to discuss how they would choose to present each reminder in each of the modalities, as described in detail below. The order of reminders was open ended, where participants could discuss these in any order of their choosing. The order of the modalities was randomized for each focus group by the experimenter. For each modality, focus group participants were given a short description of the capabilities of the modality, the aspects of the presentation that could be controlled, and possible places where this could be presented around the house.

3.1 Modalities for Reminders

This study included six possible modalities for multimodal reminder presentation. Of these, 2 were text or speech based and the remaining were abstract, or not based on language. Some examples of how these modalities were demonstrated are shown in Figure 2.

Abstract Visual – This included any visuals that were not based on text. This was demonstrated as flashing lights, images, and icons given using a handheld projector and a tablet PC. The scenarios described to participants included projection of the visuals anywhere in the house, such as on cabinets or walls, and the positioning of the tablet on various surfaces in the house, such as the kitchen counter, hallway table, or mantelpiece.

Olfactory – This modality was demonstrated using a variety of "smell cubes[1]" that can emit a single scent. However, each demonstration included discussion of a deployment scenario where smells would be emitted from a small fan unit that could be plugged into a wall. Participants were told that any smell could be used, and the duration and intensity could be controlled.

Tactile – This modality was demonstrated using a small vibration unit attached to a tablet PC. Each participant was given the chance to experience the vibrotactile sensations, and was told the vibrations could be delivered anywhere on the body such as the back of the wrist as part of a watch, the neck as part of jewellery, or inside one's pockets from their mobile phone.

[1] http://www.daleair.com/

Non-Speech Audio – This included any kinds of sounds that were not based on speech, such as earcons, recorded sounds (such as water dripping or a light switch clicking) and musical tones. These were demonstrated from the tablet PC, but participants were told it could be displayed from any speaker in the house, for example from a TV, radio, or mobile device.

Speech-Based Audio – This included any of a sound based on speech, such as recorded speech, synthesized speech, and spearcons [11]. These were demonstrated using the tablet PC, but participants were told these could be displayed from any speaker in the house. Demonstrations included examples of different types of speech, looking at gender, accent, voice, and volume as qualities of the speech that could be changed.

Text-Based Visual – This modality included visual representations of reminders based on the text of that reminder. These were demonstrated using a handheld projector and a tablet PC, where different scenarios around the house (see abstract visual above) were discussed. Participants were told that the font, colour, size, and duration of the reminder could be changed.

Figure 2. Top: Participants looking at smell cubes for olfactory reminders. Bottom Left: Participant using a small vibrotactile transducer. Bottom Right: Tablet PC and a small portable amplifier used to demonstrate reminders.

4. RESULTS

The results of these focus groups are based on a qualitative analysis of transcripts, for a total of over 7.5 hours of data. The analysis was completed using open, axial, and selective coding [4]. This approach allows researchers to elicit requirements and needs directly from users in order to inform the design of interactive systems. Although this method is limited in that it can only uncover users' imagined needs and desires, it still provides valuable insights that can be incorporated into the early phases of design.

There were 15 participants in this study over 5 focus groups of 1 to 4 participants. They were recruited from local community groups of healthy older adults aged from 60 to 85 in order to reflect possible end users of a home reminder system.

4.1 Designing for Reminders

During the focus groups, participants described how they imagined using reminders in the home as part of a multimodal system. The phrasing of the reminder led to considerable differences in the way that these reminders would be used in the home. When reminders were phrased as a question, participants were unsure when this reminder would be delivered and how they should respond. For example, one participant stated that "well I think because it almost requires an answer, if you know what I mean. Whether or not I'm speaking out loud … because I'm answering that, again, is reminding me." In some cases, participants felt that the question might be delivered too late. Whether or not participants preferred a question or a statement was very much a personal preference. For example, one participant liked the question, stating that "well it was asking me if I'd done a thing rather than telling me to do a thing. Because I actually started thinking I obviously don't like being told what to do." In contrast, another participant liked the clarity of the statement, describing it as "more to the point, the statement, I think." This highlights the necessity of customization in reminder system down to the very phrasing of the messages.

Another aspect of reminders was that unpleasant or annoying reminders were not always undesirable. For example, when describing abstract visual reminders, one participant stated that "the flashing indicator is good because if it does annoy you, you will do the thing you're being reminded to do to cancel the flash." Another participant stated that "it depends if it was important. If it was important then you should interrupt the TV… so no matter whether you like it or not but it's time to do it." In cases where communicating the message was highly urgent or important, users did not always reject the annoying or disruptive presentations.

4.2 Making Existing Reminders Multimodal

Participants discussed in detail their current methods for remembering daily tasks, where some of these approaches could be augmented with multimodal interactions in compelling ways. For example, one participant stated that "I take quite a few tablets and last thing at night I always leave them out on the chopping board that I would do my toast on and I put on tumbler on top of it." This reminder works because the tumbler is visibly out of place in the centre of the kitchen and blocks a future task. In another example, one participant described how they put notes on the back of the door to remember what needed when going out. Using projectors in the home could replicate these kinds of visual reminders and make them more adaptive to the current situation.

4.3 Explicit and Abstract Modalities

One of the most important aspects of multimodal reminder systems is the opportunity to switch between modalities fluidly and effectively. Participants in these focus groups discussed how reminders could be very basic initially in order to keep these reminders simple. This would allow users to make their own judgements about the content of the reminders. For example, participants discussed how a simple prompt would often be enough to remind them of what needs to be done. These "reminders to remember" allow users to add their own interpretation to reminders based on their own context and maintain a greater level of independence from the system. For example, when discussing tactile reminders one participant stated that "I would not probably remember what that was signifying but as an indicator to go and check that there was something that would be fine." Abstract modalities, such as tactile and abstract visual, were often described as a useful starting point for a reminder.

4.4 Distributing Multimodality Around the House

Participants described how a central hub would be the best way to get information easily and quickly. For example, one participant stated that "if it was just mounted somewhere on a wall in the most used room, it could be a wee buzzer, like if I go through and it could buzz when an alarm goes off. It could flash when a reminder comes up, you could go over to it and find out what it's telling you." This kind of central reminder hub was often viewed as a good way to respond to "reminders to remember" that could be delivered on the body or throughout the house.

However, there were some issues that participants brought up if reminders were ubiquitous in the house. With respect to auditory reminders, participants were concerned these could be confused with sounds that already exist within the home. For example, one participant stated that "the cooker buzzes, the oven buzzes, the fryer buzzes, the washing machine buzzes. Everything buzzes these days so I would think you have enough to contend with without having any extra ones." If speech reminders started while the television was on these could be confused as part of the program. For non-speech reminders, participants worried that these might be indistinguishable from other buzzers and tones around the house, such as the microwave or doorbell. In these cases, participants favoured the musical reminders because they were distinct snippets of music that could be easily distinguished from a radio or musical program. The salience of auditory reminders in home soundscapes is an issue that needs further exploration.

Another issue with distributed reminders is that participants were worried they might miss a reminder if it occurred in different places around the house. This could be caused simply because they were not present when the reminder was given or that it would not be noticeable. In this case, participants felt that combining a central point of information and a single on-body point of information would be the most successful distribution.

5. DISCUSSION

This focus group study demonstrates some of the desires and preferences of older users for a multimodal reminder system based on their own self-reported needs and desires. Based on our results, we propose four recommendations for the early phases of design as a initial effort to incorporate user generated requirements.

Increasing Complexity Over Time – Our results indicate that users prefer initial interactions with a reminder to be as simple as possible, where reminders may not initially have any explicitly defined meaning. When reminders begin as simple "prompts to remember," users themselves can try to recall the purpose and content of the message without feeling as though they are being commanded by the reminder system. This could create a greater sense of control and independence, where there is always the option to access more information and increasingly complex combinations of modalities if needed through continued interaction.

Augmenting Existing Remembering Practices – Participants described a variety of their existing practices for remembering daily tasks. Multimodal reminders can be used alongside these practices in order to make them more salient and robust by adapting to the current context. For example, if the reminder involves placing a particular object in a noticeable space then a multimodal reminder system can highlight this space through projections, audio output, or smells until the user notices the object. This allows users to continue with their existing practices with support using one or more additional modalities.

Combining Configuration and Interaction – During these focus groups, we found that the target users often didn't differentiate input and configuration with the system. We recommend that these actions not only be evaluated together but be developed as a single and integrated part of any reminder system. For example, any response to a reminder should also include the option to change and configure that reminder so that input can also be configuration.

Distributing and Centralizing Reminders – Our participants described their desire for a centralized point of information combined with more ubiquitous distributed reminders. We recommend that abstract reminders and "reminders to remember" form the distributed parts of a reminder system and explicitly defined reminders form the central part of a reminder system.

6. CONCLUSION

The results of this focus group study demonstrate how the opinions of older users can be incorporated into the design of a multimodal reminder system. This includes four recommendations based on the qualitative analysis of the focus group discussions. These recommendations demonstrate how older users' preferences and needs can be practically applied to the design of a reminder system. By leveraging multimodal interaction and a user-centred approach to the design of reminder systems, we can create interactions that improve the quality of life for older users and keep them independent and in their own homes longer.

7. REFERENCES

[1] Arking, R. Biology of Aging. Oxford University Press, New York, NY, 3rd edition, 2005.

[2] Clark, J., and McGee-Lennon, M. "A stakeholder-centered exploration of the current barriers to the uptake of home care technology in the UK", Journal of Assistive Technologies, Vol. 5 Issue: 1, (2011) pp.12 – 25.

[3] House of Lords Science and Technology Committee. Ageing: Scientific aspects. The Stationery Office, London, UK (2005).

[4] Miles, M., & Huberman, A. Qualitative data analysis. Sage Publications. (1994).

[5] Naumann, B., Wechsung, I., and Hurtienne, J. "Multimodal interaction: A suitable strategy for including older users?" in Interacting with Computers, (22) 6, 2010 pp. 465-474.

[6] Newell, A. F. and Gregor, P. "Design for older and disabled people where do we go from here?" Universal Access in the Information Society, 2:3–7, 2005.

[7] Ofcom UK. Digital lifestyles – adults aged 60 and over, Report (2009).

[8] Palen, L. and Aaløkke, S. "Of pill boxes and piano benches: home-made methods for managing medication." In Proc. of CSCW '06. Banff, Canada, 2006. ACM. pp. 79-88.

[9] Persad, U., Langdon, P. and Clarkson, J. Characterising user capabilities to support inclusive design evaluation. Universal Access in the Information Society, 6, 2 (2007), 119-153.

[10] SENSE for deafblind people UK. A sense of urgency, Report, 2010.

[11] Walker, B., Nance, A., and Lindsay, J. Spearcons: Speech-Based Earcons Improve Navigation Performance in Auditory Menus. Proc. of HAID '06. London, UK, June 20-23, 2006

[12] D. Warnock, M.R. McGee-Lennon and S. Brewster, "The Role of Modality in Notification Performance". In Proceedings of INTERACT 2011 (Portugal), 2011.

[13] Williamson, J.R., McGee-Lennon, M., and Brewster, S. What colour is 'exercise?' Designing Multimodal Reminders for the Home. In the Extended Abstracts of CHI 2012. Austin, USA. ACM Press.

AVEC 2012 – The Continuous Audio/Visual Emotion Challenge

Björn Schuller
JOANNEUM RESEARCH
Forschungsgesellschaft mbH*
DIGITAL - Institute for
Information and
Communication Technologies
Graz, Austria

Michel Valstar
University of Nottingham
Mixed Reality Lab
Nottingham, UK

Florian Eyben
Technische Universität
München
Institute for Human-Machine
Communication
Munich, Germany

Roddy Cowie
Queen's University
School of Psychology
Belfast, UK

Maja Pantic†
Imperial College London
Intelligent Behaviour
Understanding Group
London, UK

ABSTRACT

We present the second Audio-Visual Emotion recognition Challenge and workshop (AVEC 2012), which aims to bring together researchers from the audio and video analysis communities around the topic of emotion recognition. The goal of the challenge is to recognise four continuously valued affective dimensions: arousal, expectancy, power, and valence. There are two sub-challenges: in the Fully Continuous Sub-Challenge participants have to predict the values of the four dimensions at every moment during the recordings, while for the Word-Level Sub-Challenge a single prediction has to be given per word uttered by the user. This paper presents the challenge guidelines, the common data used, and the performance of the baseline system on the two tasks.

Categories and Subject Descriptors

H.4 [**Information Systems Applications**]: Miscellaneous; D.2.8 [**Software Engineering**]: Metrics—*complexity measures, performance measures*

General Terms

Theory

*The author is further affiliated with Technische Universität München, Munich, Germany

†The author is further affiliated with Twente University, EEMCS, Twente, The Netherlands.

ICMI'12, October 22–26, 2012, Santa Monica, California, USA.

Keywords

Affective Computing, Emotion Recognition, Speech, Facial Expression, Challenge

1. INTRODUCTION

Dimensional affect recognition aims to improve the understanding of human affect by modelling affect as a small number of continuously valued, continuous time signals. Compared to the more limited categorical emotion description (e.g. six basic emotions), and for contemporary computational modelling techniques intractable appraisal theory, dimensional affect modelling has the benefit of being able to: a. encode small changes in affect over time, and b. distinguish between many more subtly different displays of affect, while remaining within the reach of current signal processing and machine learning capabilities.

The 2012 Audio-Visual Emotion Challenge and Workshop (AVEC 2012) will be the second competition event aimed at comparison of multimedia processing and machine learning methods for automatic audio, video and audiovisual emotion analysis, with all participants competing under strictly the same conditions. The goal of the Challenge is to provide a common benchmark test set for individual multimodal information processing and to bring together the audio and video emotion recognition communities, to compare the relative merits of the two approaches to emotion recognition under well-defined and strictly comparable conditions and establish to what extent fusion of the approaches is possible and beneficial.

A second motivation is the need to advance emotion recognition systems to be able to deal with naturalistic behaviour in large volumes of un-segmented, non-prototypical and non-preselected data as this is exactly the type of data that both multimedia retrieval and human-machine/human-robot communication interfaces have to face in the real world.

Following up from AVEC 2011 [16], which used a categorical description of affect in terms of low or high arousal, expectancy, power, and valence, AVEC 2012 aims to accelerate research in automatic continuous affect recognition from audio and/or video. Whereas in AVEC 2011 the dimensional affect recognition problem was essentially reduced to a binary classification problem, for AVEC 2012 it is more naturally posed as a regression problem, and can thus be considered to be both more challenging and rewarding. Another difference between the first and second AVEC is that the first had separate categories for the audio, video, and audio-visual communities to compete in. Instead, for the present challenge we encourage participants to leverage both modalities.

We are calling for teams to participate in emotion recognition from acoustic audio analysis, linguistic audio analysis, video analysis, or any combination of these. As benchmarking database the SEMAINE database of naturalistic video and audio of human-agent interactions [11] will be used, which contains labels for the four target affect dimensions, amongst others. Emotion will have to be recognised in terms of continuous time, continuous valued dimensional affect in the dimensions arousal, expectation, power and valence. The database was recorded as part of the SEMAINE Sensitive Artificial Listener project [13]. Previously a subset of this data was used to perform continuous affect recognition on the dimensions Arousal, Expectancy, Intensity, Power, and Valence [7].

Two Sub-Challenges are addressed in AVEC 2012:

- The *Fully Continuous Sub-Challenge (FCSC)* involves fully continuous affect recognition, where the level of affect has to be predicted for every moment of the recording.

- The *Word-Level Sub-Challenge (WLSC)* requires participants to predict the level of affect at word-level, where a single value of affect has to be predicted per word, and only when the user is speaking.

Four regression problems need to be solved for Challenge participation: the continuous dimensions AROUSAL, EXPECTATION, POWER, and VALENCE. The Challenge competition measure is cross correlation averaged over all character interactions and all four dimensions.

Both Sub-Challenges allow contributors to find their own features to use with their regression algorithm. However, standard feature sets are provided (for audio and video separately), which participants are free to use. The labels of the test partition remain unknown to the participants, and participants have to stick to the definition of training, development, and test partition. They may freely report on results obtained on the development partition, but are limited to five trials per Sub-Challenge in submitting their results on the test partition.

To be eligible to participate in the challenge, every entry has to be accompanied by a paper presenting the results and the methods that created them, which will undergo peer-review. Only contributions with an accepted paper will be eligible for Challenge participation. The organisers preserve the right to re-evaluate the findings, but will not participate in the Challenge themselves.

We next introduce the Challenge corpus (Sec. 2) and labels (Sec. 3), then audio and visual baseline features (Sec. 4), and baseline results (Sec. 5), before concluding in Sec.6.

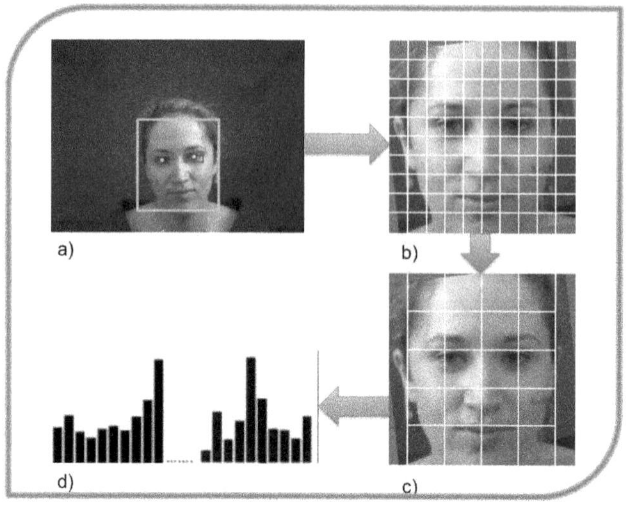

Figure 1: Video feature extraction overview: a) detection of face and eyes b) face normalised based on eye locations, divided in 10 x 10 blocks from which LBP features are extracted c). grid reduced to 5 x 4 to achieve dimensionality reduction d) histograms of separate blocks concatenated into single histogram.

2. SEMAINE DATABASE

The challenge uses the SEMAINE corpus [11] as the source of data. This database was recorded to study natural social signals that occur in conversations between humans and artificially intelligent agents, and to collect data for the training of the next generation of such agents. It is freely available for scientific research purposes from http://semaine-db.eu. The scenario used in the recordings is called the Sensitive Artificial Listener (SAL) technique [4]. It involves a user interacting with emotionally stereotyped "characters" whose responses are stock phrases keyed to the user's emotional state rather than the content of what (s)he says.

For the recordings, the participants are asked to talk in turn to four emotionally stereotyped characters. These characters are Prudence, who is even-tempered and sensible; Poppy, who is happy and outgoing; Spike, who is angry and confrontational; and Obadiah, who is sad and depressive.

Video was recorded at 49.979 frames per second at a spatial resolution of 780 x 580 pixels and 8 bits per sample, while audio was recorded at 48 kHz with 24 bits per sample. To accommodate research in audio-visual fusion, the audio and video signals were synchronised with an accuracy of 25 μs using the system developed by Lichtenauer et al. [10].

In this challenge the 24 recordings of the Solid-SAL part of the database were used, in which the characters are role-played by human operators. There are usually 4 character conversation sessions per recording. This Solid-SAL part was split into three partitions for the AVEC challenge: a training, development, and test partition each consisting of 8 recordings of 8 different users. Because the number of character conversations varies somewhat between recordings, the number of sessions (and thus audio and video files) is different per set: The training partition contains 31 sessions, while the development and test partitions contain 32 ses-

Table 1: Mapping between AVEC 2012 data and corresponding SEMAINE sessions

AVEC train	SEMAINE	AVEC devel	SEMAINE
1	2	1	8
2	3	2	9
3	4	3	10
4	5	4	11
5	29	5	19
6	30	6	20
7	31	7	21
8	40	8	22
9	41	9	34
10	42	10	35
11	43	11	36
12	58	12	37
13	59	13	46
14	60	14	47
15	61	15	48
16	70	16	49
17	71	17	82
18	72	18	83
19	73	19	84
20	76	20	85
21	77	21	94
22	78	22	95
23	79	23	96
24	88	24	97
25	89	25	112
26	90	26	113
27	91	27	114
28	106	28	115
29	107	29	131
30	108	30	132
31	109	31	133
		32	134

sions. Table 2 shows the distribution of data in sessions, video frames, and words for each partition.

The data for the AVEC 2012 was re-organised according to the partitions specified above. To allow researchers to relate the challenge data to the original data, we have provided a mapping in Table 1 for the training and development partitions. The data of the test partition is not available from the SEMAINE web portal. A separate website (`http://AVEC2011-db.sspnet.eu/`) was set up to distribute the AVEC 2012 competition data, which includes pre-computed audio and video features.

3. CHALLENGE LABELS

The affective dimensions used in the challenge were selected based on the available ratings. Dimensions for which all character interactions of the Solid-SAL part are annotated by at least two raters were included. These are the dimensions AROUSAL, EXPECTATION, POWER, and VALENCE, which are all well established in the psychological literature. An influential recent study [8] argues that these four dimensions account for most of the distinctions between everyday emotion categories.

AROUSAL (Activity) is the individual's global feeling of dynamism or lethargy. It subsumes mental activity, and physical preparedness to act as well as overt activity. EXPECTATION (Anticipation) also subsumes various concepts that can be separated as expecting, anticipating, being taken unaware. Again, they point to a dimension that people find intuitively meaningful, related to control in the domain of information. The POWER (Dominance) dimension subsumes two related concepts, power and control. However, people's sense of their own power is the central issue that emotion is about, and that is relative to what they are facing. VALENCE is an individual's overall sense of "weal or woe": Does it appear that, on balance, the person rated feels positive or negative about the things, people, or situations at the focus of his/her emotional state?

All interactions were annotated by 2 to 8 raters, with the majority annotated by 6 raters: 68.4 % of interactions were rated by 6 raters or more, and 82 % by 3 or more. The raters annotated the four dimensions in continuous time and continuous value using a tool called FeelTrace [3], and the annotations are often called *traces*. The annotation process resulted in a set of trace vectors $\{\mathbf{v}_i^a, \mathbf{v}_i^e, \mathbf{v}_i^p, \mathbf{v}_i^v\} \in \mathbb{R}$ for every rater i and dimension a (AROUSAL), e (EXPECTATION), p (POWER), and v (VALENCE). The original traces are binned in temporal units of the same duration as a single video frame (i. e., 1/49.979 seconds). The labels for AROUSAL, POWER, and VALENCE lie in the range $[-1, 1]$, and the labels for EXPECTATION in the range $[0, 100]$.

Due to different ways in which video readers such as quicktime deal with keyframes in the H264 codecs, there are very small differences between the label vector lengths and the actual duration of the recordings. The difference is however very small, with the difference between the number of label instances and actual number of frames in the range of 0-0.04%. Participants are expected to deal with this by clipping/padding the label data as necessary.

In contrast with the first Audio-Visual Emotion recognition challenge (AVEC 2011), we use the fully continuous values as the challenge labels. So, while AVEC 2011 was a binary classification task, AVEC 2012 is a regression task. To obtain a single label per dimension rather than a set of labels with cardinality equal to the number of raters, we take the simple mean over the raters.

Two modes of label segmentation are given, one for each sub-challenge. For the FCSC, the labels that are binned per video frame are used. For the WLSC the traces are binned over the duration of the words uttered by the user, resulting in a single continuous value label per word. To segment the labels for the WCSC the word alignments available with the SEMAINE database were used. These were obtained by running an HMM-based speech recogniser in forced alignment mode on the manual transcripts of the interactions. The recogniser uses tied-state cross-word triphone left-right (linear) HMM models with 3 emitting states and 16 Gaussian mixture components per state. Monophones with 1 Gaussian mixture component per state were bootstrapped on all available speech data (user and operator) of the SEMAINE corpus. The tied-state triphone models were created from these initial monophone models by decision tree based state clustering and the number of Gaussian mixture components was increased to 16 in four iterations of successive mixture doubling. In order to use accessible standard tool kits for maximum reproducibility of results, the Hidden Markov Toolkit (HTK) [19] was used to train the models

Table 2: Overview of dataset make-up per partition

# / (h:m:s) / [ms]	Train	Development	Test	Total
Sessions	31	32	32	95
Frames	501 277	449 074	407 772	1 358 123
Words	20 183	16 311	13 856	50 350
Total duration	2:47:10	2:29:45	2:15:59	7:32:54
Avg. word duration	262	276	249	263

Table 3: Correlation coefficients (CC) for the dimensions at the word and frame level. (e) denotes Expectation, (p) Power, and (v) Valence.

CC	Word level			Frame level		
[%]	E	P	V	E	P	V
Activation	-3.2	22.4	20.7	-3.2	24.5	24.9
Expectation		-35.8	-10.4		-37.3	-7.7
Power			29.7			29.6

and create the alignments. These word timings are provided with the challenge data.

Table 2 lists the number of interactions per data partition, and the number of FCSC instances (i. e., frames) and WLSC instances (i. e., words). It also reports the average word duration, in milliseconds.

Some of the dimensions are highly correlated. For example, in the training and development partitions, at the frame-level, expectation and power are negatively correlated by a factor of 0.373. The full correlation matrices for both word-level and frame-level labels are given in Table 3. All correlations have a p-value << 0.01.

4. BASELINE FEATURES

In the following sections we describe how the publicly available baseline feature sets are computed for either the audio or the video data. Participants could use these feature sets exclusively or in addition to their own features.

4.1 Audio Features

In this Challenge, as was the case for AVEC 2011, an extended set of features with respect to the INTERSPEECH 2009 Emotion Challenge (384 features) [14] and INTERSPEECH 2010 Paralinguistic Challenge (1 582 features) [15] is given to the participants, again using the freely available open-source Emotion and Affect Recognition (openEAR) [5] toolkit's feature extraction backend openSMILE [6]. In contrast to AVEC 2011, the feature set was reduced by 100 features that were found to carry very little information, as they were zero or close to zero most of the time.

Thus, the AVEC 2012 audio baseline feature set consists of 1 841 features, composed of 25 energy and spectral related low-level descriptors (LLD) x 42 functionals, 6 voicing related LLD x 32 functionals, 25 delta coefficients of the energy/spectral LLD x 19 functionals, 6 delta coefficients of the voicing related LLD x 19 functionals, and 10 voiced/unvoiced durational features. Details for the LLD and functionals are given in tables 4 and 5 respectively. The set of LLD covers a standard range of commonly used features in audio signal analysis and emotion recognition.

Table 4: 31 low-level descriptors.

Energy & spectral (25)
loudness (auditory model based), zero crossing rate, energy in bands from 250 – 650 Hz, 1 kHz – 4 kHz, 25 %, 50 %, 75 %, and 90 % spectral roll-off points, spectral flux, entropy, variance, skewness, kurtosis, psychoacousitc sharpness, harmonicity, MFCC 1-10
Voicing related (6)
F_0 (sub-harmonic summation, followed by Viterbi smoothing), probability of voicing, jitter, shimmer (local), jitter (delta: "jitter of jitter"), logarithmic Harmonics-to-Noise Ratio (logHNR)

Table 5: Set of all 42 functionals. [1]Not applied to delta coefficient contours. [2]For delta coefficients the mean of only positive values is applied, otherwise the arithmetic mean is applied. [3]Not applied to voicing related LLD.

Statistical functionals (23)
(positive[2]) arithmetic mean, root quadratic mean, standard deviation, flatness, skewness, kurtosis, quartiles, inter-quartile ranges, 1 %, 99 % percentile, percentile range 1 %–99 %, percentage of frames contour is above: minimum + 25%, 50%, and 90 % of the range, percentage of frames contour is rising, maximum, mean, minimum segment length[1,3], standard deviation of segment length[1,3]
Regression functionals[1] (4)
linear regression slope, and corresponding approximation error (linear), quadratic regression coefficient a, and approximation error (linear)
Local minima/maxima related functionals[1] (9)
mean and standard deviation of rising and falling slopes (minimum to maximum), mean and standard deviation of inter maxima distances, amplitude mean of maxima, amplitude mean of minima, amplitude range of maxima
Other[1,3] (6)
LP gain, LPC 1 – 5

The audio features are computed on short episodes of audio data. Depending on the sub-challenge, these episodes are either whole words (for the WLSC) or 2 second sliding windows (for the FCSC). For the WLSC, one audio feature vector per word is extracted, while for the FCSC feature vectors are extracted at 0.5 second intervals, but only during speech (this includes non-linguistic vocalisations such as sighs and laughs). The first FCSC audio feature vector for every word is timed at the beginning of the word, and this time is thus not necessarily a multiple of 0.5 seconds. They thus do not align perfectly with the FCSC video feature vectors (see below).

Since the timings of the word boundaries were estimated by a speech recogniser with forced alignment using the manually created transcripts of the interactions, it is possible that some of the word boundaries are calculated incorrectly. In particular, some of the words were found to be so short that it is impossible to compute the audio features. To alleviate this problem, for words that were found to be too short we artificially changed the start and end time of the word to attain a segment with a minimum length of 0.25 s. The actual annotated word thereby was placed in the centre of this segment.

4.2 Video Features

The bulk of the features extracted from the video streams of the character interactions are dense local appearance descriptions. The descriptors that generate these features are most effective if they are applied to frontal faces of uniform size. Since the head pose and distance to the camera vary over time in the SEMAINE recordings, we detect the locations of the eyes to help reduce this variance. The information describing the position and pose of the face and eyes are in themselves valuable for recognising the dimensional affect and are thus included with the set of video features together with the appearance descriptors.

To obtain the face position, we employ another open-source implementation – OpenCV's Viola & Jones face detector. This returns a four-valued face position and size descriptor, to wit, the position of the top-left corner of the detected face area (f_x, f_y), followed by its width f_w and height f_h. The height and width output of this detector is rather unstable: Even in a video in which a face hardly moves the values for the height and width vary significantly (approximately 5 % standard deviation). The face detector also doesn't provide any information about the head pose.

To refine the detected face region, and allow the appearance descriptor to correlate better with the shown expression instead of with variability in head pose and face detector output, we proceed with detection of the locations of the eyes. This is again done with the OpenCV implementation of a Haar-cascade object detector, trained for either a left or a right eye. Let us define the detected left and right eye locations as p_l respectively p_r, and the the angle between the line connecting p_l and p_r, and the horizontal as α. The registered image is then obtained by rotating it to set $\alpha = 0$ degrees, scaled to make the distance between the eye locations $||p_l - p_r|| = 100$ pixels, and then cropped to be 200 by 200 pixels, with p_r at position $\{p_r^x, p_r^y\} = \{80, 60\}$ to obtain the registered face image. The eye locations are included as part of the video features provided for candidates.

As dense local appearance descriptors we chose to use uniform Local Binary Patterns (LBP) [12]. They have been used extensively for face analysis in recent years, e. g., for face recognition [1], emotion detection [17], or detection of facial muscle actions (FACS Action Units) [9]. They were also used as the baseline features for the recently held challenge on facial expression recognition and analysis (FERA 2011, [18]). Consisting of 8 binary comparisons per pixel, they are fast to compute. By employing uniform LBPs instead of full LBPs and aggregating the LBP operator responses in histograms taken over regions of the face, the dimensionality of the features is rather low (59 dimensions per image block). In our baseline method and feature extraction implementation we divided the registered face region into 10 x 10 blocks. The LBP histograms of the blocks are concatenated in lexicographic order resulting in the set F of 5 900 features. The video features are thus stored as follows: $\{f_x, f_y, f_w, f_h, p_r, p_l, F\}$, 5 908 features in total.

5. CHALLENGE BASELINES

For transparency and reproducibility, we use Support Vector Machine regression (SVR) without feature selection. We used SVRs with Histogram Intersection Kernels, Sequential Minimal Optimization (SMO) for learning. For evaluation on the test set (which is what the challenge scores are based on), all relevant parameters were optimised on the development partition of the corpus. For evaluation on the development set (which participants may wish to do to pre-evaluate alternative systems they develop), we optimised the parameters on the training set using 5-fold cross-validation. LibSVM for matlab was used throughout our experiments [2].

For the Word-Level Sub-Challenge (WLSC), we trained a single set of regressors using both audio and video features, as for every word there would be both audio and video features present. This is not the case for the Fully Continuous Sub-Challenge (FCSC) however. For the FCSC we consider two conditions: speech and non-speech. As the speaker state is provided with the challenge data as part of the aligned transcripts, we consider the speaker-state known for the training, development, and test partitions. We thus train a separate set of regressors for the non-speech condition using only video features, and another set of regressors for the speech condition where we concatenate the audio and video features into a single feature vector.

The memory consumption of the video features is very large: with over 1.3 million frames and 5 908 features per frame, memory capacity constraints are likely to be exceeded when training a model using all data on a desktop PC. In addition, we need to find a way to fuse the video features with the audio features. For the WLSC, a single audio feature vector is computed for every word, with words having a variable duration, while for the FCSC, a single audio feature vector is computed over every half-second segment. In contrast, video features are computed every $1/49.979 \approx 0.02$ seconds. The simplest thing to do would be to down-sample the video feature rate. But given the histogram nature of the video features, a better opportunity presents itself, and that is to take the histogram of the video features not just for a single frame, but also over multiple frames. The number of frames per segment depends on the sub-challenge: they are defined as 25 frames for the FCSC (to coincide with the audio sampling rate), and have a variable number of frames in the WLSC, defined by the word duration.

To further reduce the memory consumption of the video features, we reduced the dimensionality of the video features

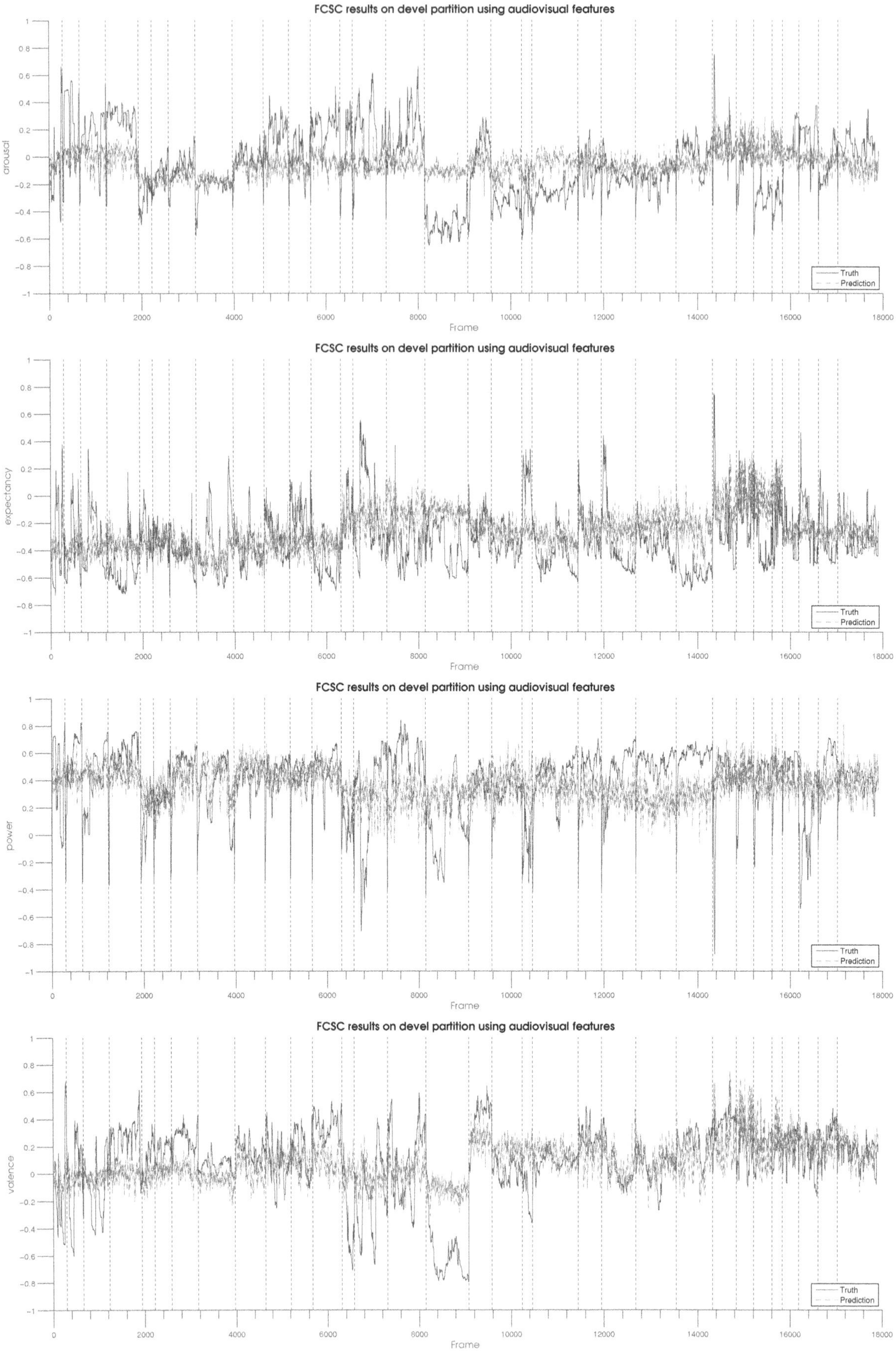

Figure 2: Baseline FCSC results on the development partition, for all four dimensions. Vertical dashed lines delimit consecutive test sessions.

Table 6: **Baseline results. Performance is measured in cross-correlation averaged over all sequences.**

Accuracy	Arousal	Expectation	Power	Valence	Mean
Audio-Visual					
FCSC test	0.141	0.101	0.072	0.136	0.112
WLSC test	0.021	0.028	0.009	0.004	0.015
FCSC development	0.181	0.148	0.084	0.215	0.157
WLSC development	0.018	0.009	0.001	0.002	0.007
Audio only					
WLSC test	0.014	0.038	0.016	0.040	0.027
WLSC development	0.054	0.020	0.019	0.062	0.039
Video only					
FCSC test	0.077	0.128	0.030	0.134	0.093
WLSC test	0.005	0.012	0.018	0.005	0.011
FCSC development	0.151	0.122	0.031	0.207	0.128
WLSC development	0.032	0.013	0.005	0.003	0.014

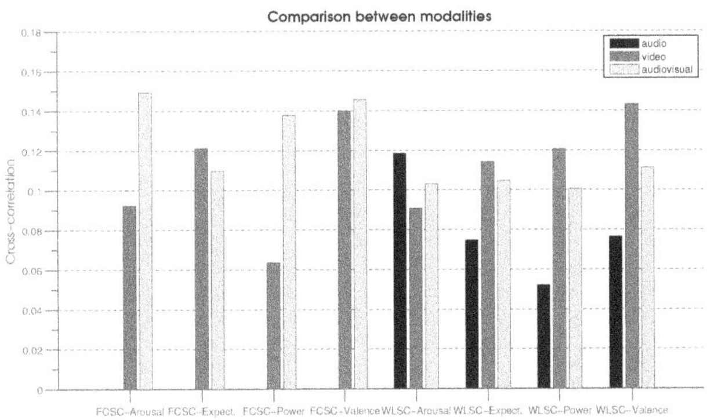

Figure 3: Comparison between the audio only, video only, and feature-level fused audio-visual modalities. Note that there are no results for the audio modality on the FCSC.

by modifying the face partition grid (see Fig 1). We removed the left-and right-most columns, as they often do'nt include the face, or at least not very relevant elements of the face. We further merged blocks in groups of 2×2, resulting in a new grid of 5 rows and 4 columns. The final dimensionality of the video feature vector is then reduced to1188.

Performance is measured in terms of correlation. To be more precise, we calculate the correlation coefficient between the predicted labels and ground truth labels per character interaction (session), per dimension, and calculate the average over all sessions and dimensions. Results for the two Sub-Challenges are given in Table 6. The top two rows are the official baseline results, that is, the FCSC and WLSC results on the test partition using audio-visual features. Participants will be ranked on the mean performance over all four dimensions, i.e. the final column in this table. The table also shows results on the development set, and results obtained on both the test and development partitions using only video or only audio features. Note that for the FCSC it isn't possible to provide audio-only results, as there are large parts of the data where the user isn't speaking. The prediction results on the FCSC development partition using Audio-Visual features is illustrated in Fig. 2.

The baseline results show that for the FCSC on the test partition (i.e. the scores that the participants will be rated on), scores lie between 3% and 14.1% correlation for the four dimensions. It also shows, that scores are consistently highest for the Valence dimension, and most often lowest for the Power dimension. The results also allow a comparison between the audio, video, and audio-visual modalities. This is further illustrated in Fig. 3. The results show that for the FCSC, fusion of audio and video modalities generally increases performance. For the WLSC however, it appears that audio is the dominant modality. This may be because the word boundaries aid forging better audio features on the one hand, and hinder creating affective video features because of mouth movements on the other hand. The fact that for the WLSC the audio and video features are temporally misaligned for a maximum of 0.5 seconds per word is another possibility for the fusion to fail.

Finally, the WLSC scores are significantly lower than the FCSC scores. This is likely due to the nature of the predicted labels, ground truth labels, and the performance measure used. The ground truth labels are a signal with a temporal resolution of 50 Hz, and can vary over the duration of a word. The predicted labels on the other hand have a variable temporal resolution (depending on word duration), and have a constant value during the entire word.

6. CONCLUSION

We introduced AVEC 2012 – the first combined open Audio/Visual Emotion Challenge to be continuous in time and value representation, its conditions, data, baseline features and results. By intention, we preferred to use open-source software and highest transparency and realism for the baselines by refraining from feature space optimisation and optimising on test data. This should improve the reproducibility of the baseline results.

With correlation coefficients on the test partition ranging between 0.03 and 0.141 for the Fully Continuous Sub-Challenge, and between 0.004 and 0.038 for the Word-Level Sub-Challenge, it is evident that continuous affect recognition from audio and/or video is indeed a daunting task. The baseline results indicate that higher scores are attained on the Fully Continuous than on the Word-Level Sub-Challenge.

Importantly, the results show that for the Fully Continuous Sub-Challenge, fusing audio and video is clearly beneficial.

Following the Challenge, we plan to combine all participants' results of the challenge by voting or meta-learning.

7. ACKNOWLEDGEMENTS

The research leading to these results has received funding from the European Community's Seventh Framework Programme (FP7/2007- 2013) under grant agreement No. 289021 (ASC-Inclusion). The authors would further like to thank the sponsor of the challenge, the Social Signal Processing Network (SSPNet). The responsibility lies with the authors.

8. REFERENCES

[1] Ahonen, T., Hadid, A., and Pietikäinen, M. Face description with local binary patterns: Application to face recognition. *IEEE Transactions on Pattern Analysis and Machine Intelligence 28*, 12 (2006), 2037–2041.

[2] Chang, C.-C., and Lin, C.-J. *LibSVM: a library for support vector machines*, 2001. Software available at http://www.csie.ntu.edu.tw/~cjlin/libsvm.

[3] Cowie, R., Douglas-Cowie, E., Savvidou, S., McMahon, E., Sawey, M., and Schröder, M. Feeltrace: An instrument for recording perceived emotion in real time. In *Proc. ISCA Workshop on Speech and Emotion* (Belfast, UK, 2000), pp. 19–24.

[4] Douglas-Cowie, E., Cowie, R., Cox, C., Amier, N., and Heylen, D. The sensitive artificial listener: an induction technique for generating emotionally coloured conversation. In *LREC Workshop on Corpora for Research on Emotion and Affect* (Paris, France, 2008), ELRA, pp. 1–4.

[5] Eyben, F., Wöllmer, M., and Schuller, B. openEAR - Introducing the Munich Open-Source Emotion and Affect Recognition Toolkit. In *Proc. ACII* (Amsterdam, The Netherlands, 2009), pp. 576–581.

[6] Eyben, F., Wöllmer, M., and Schuller, B. openSMILE – The Munich Versatile and Fast Open-Source Audio Feature Extractor. In *Proc. ACM Multimedia (MM)* (Florence, Italy, 2010), pp. 1459–1462.

[7] Eyben, F., Wöllmer, M., Valstar, M., Gunes, H., Schuller, B., and Pantic, M. String-based Audiovisual Fusion of Behavioural Events for the Assessment of Dimensional Affect. In *Proceedings International Workshop on Emotion Synthesis, rePresentation, and Analysis in Continuous spacE, EmoSPACE 2011, held in conjunction with the 9th IEEE International Conference on Automatic Face & Gesture Recognition and Workshops, FG 2011* (Santa Barbara, CA, March 2011), IEEE, IEEE, pp. 322–329.

[8] Fontaine, J., K.R., S., Roesch, E., and Ellsworth, P. The world of emotions is not two-dimensional. *Psychological science 18*, 2 (2007), 1050 – 1057.

[9] Jiang, B., Valstar, M., and Pantic, M. Action unit detection using sparse appearance descriptors in space-time video volumes. In *Proc. IEEE Int. Conf. on Automatic Face and Gesture Recognition* (Santa Barbara, USA, 2011), pp. 314–321.

[10] Lichtenauer, J., Valstar, M. F., Shen, J., and Pantic, M. Cost-effective solution to synchornized audio-visual capture using multiple sensors. *Proc. IEEE Int. Conf. on Advanced Video and Signal Based Surveillance* (2009), 324–329.

[11] McKeown, G., Valstar, M., Cowie, R., Pantic, M., and Schroder, M. The semaine database: Annotated multimodal records of emotionally colored conversations between a person and a limited agent. *IEEE Transactions on Affective Computing 3* (2012), 5–17.

[12] Ojala, T., Pietikainen, M., and Maenpaa, T. Multiresolution gray-scale and rotation invariant texture classification with local binary patterns. *IEEE Transactions on Pattern Analysis and Machine Intelligence 24*, 7 (2002), 971–987.

[13] Schröder, M., Bevacqua, E., Cowie, R., Eyben, F., Gunes, H., Heylen, D., ter Maat, M., McKeown, G., Pammi, S., Pantic, M., Pelachaud, C., Schuller, B., de Sevin, E., Valstar, M., and Wöllmer, M. Building Autonomous Sensitive Artificial Listeners. *IEEE Transactions on Affective Computing 3* (2012), 165–183.

[14] Schuller, B., Steidl, S., and Batliner, A. The INTERSPEECH 2009 Emotion Challenge. In *Proc. INTERSPEECH 2009* (Brighton, UK, 2009), pp. 312–315.

[15] Schuller, B., Steidl, S., Batliner, A., Burkhardt, F., Devillers, L., Müller, C., and Narayanan, S. The INTERSPEECH 2010 Paralinguistic Challenge. In *Proc. INTERSPEECH 2010* (Makuhari, Japan, 2010), pp. 2794–2797.

[16] Schuller, B., Valstar, M., Eyben, F., McKeown, G., Cowie, R., and Pantic, M. AVEC 2011 – The First International Audio/Visual Emotion Challenge. In *Proceedings First International Audio/Visual Emotion Challenge and Workshop, AVEC 2011, held in conjunction with the International HUMAINE Association Conference on Affective Computing and Intelligent Interaction 2011, ACII 2011*, vol. II. Springer, Memphis, TN, October 2011, pp. 415–424.

[17] Shan, C., Gong, S., and Mcowan, P. W. Facial expression recognition based on local binary patterns: A comprehensive study. *Image and Vision Computing 27*, 6 (2009), 803–816.

[18] Valstar, M., Jiang, B., Mehu, M., Pantic, M., and Scherer, K. The first facial expression recognition and analysis challenge. *Proc. IEEE Int. Conf. on Automatic Face and Gesture Recognition* (2011), 921–926.

[19] Young, S., Evermann, G., Gales, M., Hain, T., Kershaw, D., Liu, X., Moore, G., Odell, J., Ollason, D., Povey, D., Valtchev, V., and Woodland, P. *The HTK book (v3.4)*. Cambridge University Press, Cambridge, UK, 2006.

Facial Emotion Recognition With Expression Energy

Albert Cruz
Center for Research in Intelligent Systems
216 Winston Chung Hall
Riverside, CA, 92521-0425, USA
acruz006@student.ucr.edu

Bir Bhanu
Center for Research in Intelligent Systems
216 Winston Chung Hall
Riverside, CA, 92521-0425, USA
bhanu@ee.ucr.edu

Ninad Thakoor
Center for Research in Intelligent Systems
216 Winston Chung Hall
Riverside, CA, 92521-0425, USA
ninadt@ee.ucr.edu

ABSTRACT

Facial emotion recognition, the inference of an emotion from apparent facial expressions, in unconstrained settings is a typical case where algorithms perform poorly. A property of the AVEC2012 data set is that individuals in testing data are not encountered in training data. In these situations, conventional approaches suffer because models developed from training data cannot properly discriminate unforeseen testing samples. Additional information beyond the feature vectors is required for successful detection of emotions. We propose two similarity metrics that address the problems of a conventional approach: neutral similarity, measuring the intensity of an expression; and temporal similarity, measuring changes in an expression over time. These similarities are taken to be the energy of facial expressions, measured with a SIFT-based warping process. Our method improves correlation by 35.5% over the baseline approach on the frame-level sub-challenge.

Categories and Subject Descriptors

H.4 [**Information Systems Applications**]: Miscellaneous; D.2.8 [**Software Engineering**]: Metrics—*complexity measures, performance measures*

General Terms

Experimentation, performance, theory

Keywords

Computer vision, image representation, video analysis

1. INTRODUCTION

Facial emotion recognition has applications in medicine [6], video games, human-machine and computer-interaction and affective computing [4].

Challenge data sets, such as the 2nd International Audio/Visual Emotion Challenge and Workshop (AVEC2012) [11], have advanced state-of-the-art by standardizing the data used by algorithms. This grand challenge provides a common ground with which these algorithms can be compared. However, an algorithm has yet to be revealed that can correctly identify emotions when there is not sufficient training data for an individual, or that individual was not encountered in the training data. This was demonstrated in Maronidis et al. [9] with inter-database experiments, and such is the case in AVEC2012. A conventional approach that classifies the samples solely on their feature vector performs poorly. The decision surface has been trained on particular expressions from the individuals in training data. If a new expression is queried, such as if a previously un-encountered individual expresses an emotion in a different way, it would not be properly labeled by the model. This is a similar situation to the face recognition challenge in the Labeled Faces in the Wild data set, where most individuals have only a single sample in the data. Wolf et al. [12] proposed the use of similarities that captured additional information based on relationships with other samples. That approach and the approach detailed here fall into a specific category of learning titled, "learning with side information" [12], where a discriminating relationship between the samples is learned. We propose the following similarities to improve classification for facial emotion recognition:

Neutral Similarity (Sec. 2.2). This similarity addresses the question, "how intense is the emotion?" When an expression has not been encountered, it may be useful to measure the difference between the current frame and some reference of a face which is not expressive. This similarity is important in measuring the degree of an emotion, which is a new requirement with AVEC2012.

Temporal Similarity (Sec. 2.3). This similarity addresses the question, "how is the expression changing?" If there is a significant difference between the current frame and the previous frame, it may indicate particular emotions. E.g., a neutral expression followed by furrowing of the brows may indicate anger. This similarity also adds temporal information to the approach.

These proposed similarities are inspired by One-Shot and Two-Shot similarities [12], but are substantially different. One-Shot and Two-Shot similarities are both based on unlabeled background data, not deviation from a neutral face or temporal changes. Additionally, we compute these similarities with a SIFT-based warping process, whereas One-Shot and Two-Shots are computed with a vector difference.

The rest of the paper is organized as follows: Sec. 2 details the approach for measuring expression energy, and Sec. 2.5

ICMI'12, October 22–26, 2012, Santa Monica, California, USA.

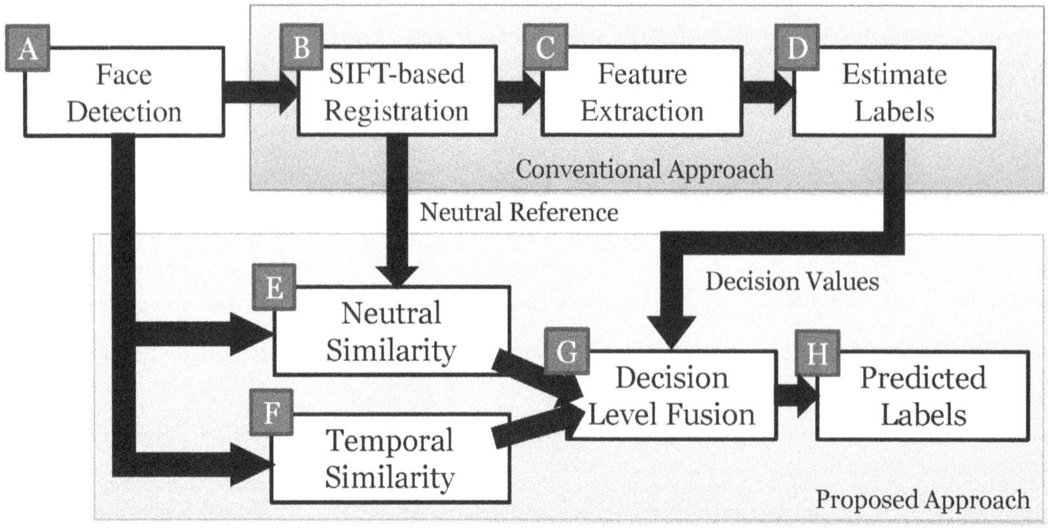

Figure 1: System overview.

details the appearance features also used in the approach. Sec. 3 details the experimental parameters used in the paper and presents the results on AVEC2012. A discussion is given in Sec. 4 that compares the appearance features and also compares the feature space of a conventional approach and the proposed approach. A conclusion is given in Sec. 5.

1.1 Contribution

Our contribution is the following: (1) two novel similarities, neutral and temporal similarity, to be used in unconstrained scenarios where samples in testing were not encountered in training; (2) a novel SIFT-Flow energy function for quantification of these similarities; and (3) improvement of the average correlation of emotion detection on AVEC2012 for both the frame-level and word-level sub-challenges.

2. TECHNICAL APPROACH

The proposed system approach is given in Fig. 1: (A) frames are extracted from the video and face region of interest is detected on a per-frame basis with a cascade of Haar-like features. In a conventional approach, (B) faces would be registered. We register faces with Avatar Image Registration. After registration, (C) an ensemble of low-level appearance features are extracted, re-projected with PCA and then fused at the feature level and (D) a model is trained with Support Vector Regression to estimate labels. With the proposed approach, in a separate pipeline, (E) neutral similarity is measured from a neutral reference that has been estimated during registration, and (F) temporal similarity is measured between frames. (G) These two similarities and the decision values from the conventional approach are fused to calculate (H) the emotion labels.

2.1 Facial Extraction and Registration

Face region of interest (ROI) is detected with Viola and Jones. Within each video, ROI detection errors are pruned with the following schema: a mean face image is generated for that video. If a frame in that video has an L_2 difference from the mean face image of more than four standard deviations away from the mean difference of the mean face image, it is considered an ROI detection error. In training, the frame is removed when training a model. In testing, the frame is not classified; its emotion label is taken to be the nearest frame with a successfully extracted ROI. Four standard deviations was determined empirically, to be robust versus face morphology and slight translation errors from Viola and Jones while removing ROI's that were not a whole face.

The extracted face ROI is aligned with Avatar Image Registration (AIR). In AIR, faces are aligned with SIFT-Flow [7] to an estimated neutral face, titled the Avatar Reference Image. The reader is referred to Cruz et al. [2] for a more in depth explanation of AIR.

2.2 Neutral Similarity

Neutral similarity measures the intensity of an emotion. In the conditions described in the motivation in Sec. 1, the difference of the current frame from a neutral face may provide discriminative information. The metric should indicate when facial expressions are close to neutral, such as in Fig. 2-B, and when facial expressions are intense, such as in C. This is computed by comparing a given frame, $I(\mathbf{x}, t)$, to some reference of a neutral face, such as A. The Avatar Reference Image, a neutrally expressive reference image, is taken to be the neutral reference. It is the mean face image generated from SIFT-registered face ROI's across all training videos and individuals. The reader is referred to Cruz et al. [2] for a proof of this as an estimate of a neutrally expressive face. The similarity is measured with the expression energy function to be described in Sec. 2.4.

2.3 Temporal Similarity

Temporal similarity measures the amount of change between frames. It provides additional information of how expressions are changing temporally. In Fig. 3 there are two pairs of frames taken from the sam video at different times, both spaced 1s apart. Between A and B, the individual is smirking, and the metric should detect the small change. Between C and D, there are many changes in expression, and the metric should reflect this with a higher energy than the energy given to frames A and B. This simi-

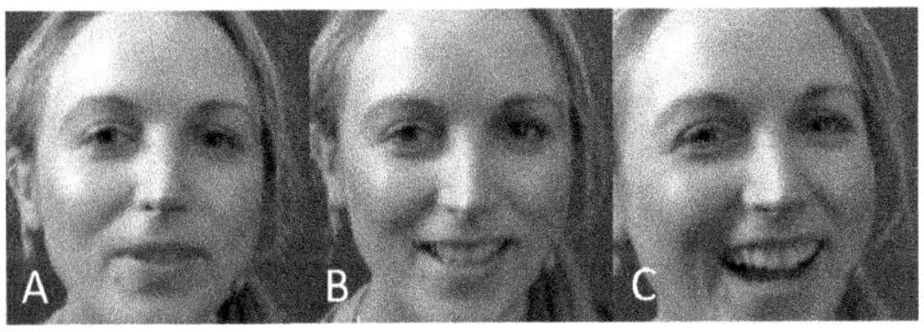

Figure 2: (From left to right): (A) A neutral face. (B) A slightly expressive face. (C) A very expressive face. The energy for C should be higher than B.

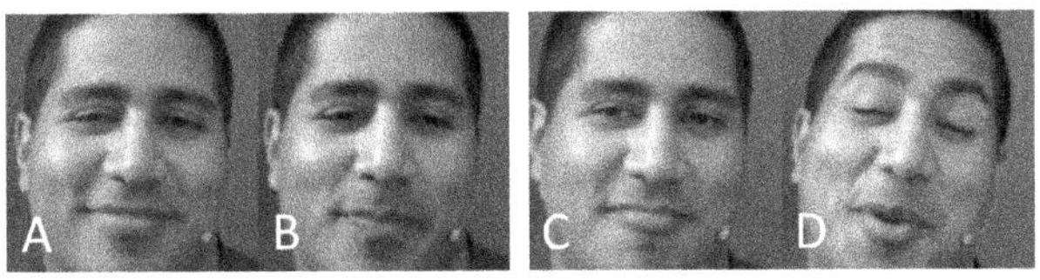

Figure 3: Frames spaced 1s apart. (A-B) A face with slight change in expression. (C-D) A face with large change in expression. The energy of A to B should be lower than for C to D.

larity is computed by comparing $I(\mathbf{x}, t)$ with $I(\mathbf{x}, t-\delta)$. It is also measured with the expression energy function.

2.4 Measuring Expression Energy

Let I_1 and I_2 be two images. We want to quantitatively measure the similarity between two expressive face ROI's. We propose measuring the similarity as the energy of the cost function of a SIFT-based warping process. The energy function used in the warping process can be used as a metric to take this measurement. This similarity is more meaningful than a distance metric between two feature vectors because SIFT-Flow warps the intensity values to match the two images, based on SIFT features. The original SIFT-Flow energy function [7] is as follows:

$$\begin{aligned} E(\mathbf{w}) = & \sum_{\mathbf{x}} \min \|s_1(\mathbf{x}) - s_2(\mathbf{x} + \mathbf{w}(\mathbf{x}))\|_1 \\ & + \gamma \sum_{\mathbf{x}} \left((u(\mathbf{x}))^2 + (v(\mathbf{x}))^2 \right) \\ & + \alpha \sum_{(\mathbf{x},\mathbf{y}) \epsilon N_{\mathbf{x}}} \left(\min |u(\mathbf{x}) - v(\mathbf{y})| \right. \\ & \left. + \min |u(\mathbf{x}) - v(\mathbf{y})| \right) \end{aligned} \quad (1)$$

where $\mathbf{x}$ is a pixel in the image; $\mathbf{w}(\mathbf{x})$ is the motion vector at pixel $\mathbf{x}$ between I_1 and I_2; $\mathbf{w}(\mathbf{x}) = |u(\mathbf{x}), v(\mathbf{x})|$; and s_1 and s_2 are the dense SIFT descriptors of I_1 and I_2 respectively; $\mathbf{y}$ is a pixel that iterates for each member of the $N_{\mathbf{x}}$ neighborhood of $\mathbf{x}$; and γ is a normalization constant. The first summation term measures the L_1 difference between the two SIFT descriptors. The second summation term is the squared magnitude of the motion vector and measures the magnitude of motion in between the two images. The third summation term enforces homogeneity. We propose the following, modified SIFT-Flow energy function:

$$\begin{aligned} E(\mathbf{w}) = & \sum_{\mathbf{x}} \min \|s_1(\mathbf{x}) - s_2(\mathbf{x} + \mathbf{w}(\mathbf{x}))\|_1 \\ & + \gamma \sum_{\mathbf{x}} \left((u(\mathbf{x}) - \mu_u)^2 + (v(\mathbf{x}) - \mu_v)^2 \right) \end{aligned} \quad (2)$$

where μ_u and μ_v are the mean of $u(\mathbf{x})$ and $v(\mathbf{x})$ respectively. Eq. 2 differs from the original SIFT-Flow energy function in the following ways: (1) the second term has the mean vector subtracted from u and v. Viola and Jones is accurate but not precise; the face ROI suffers from translation errors. The mean is subtracted from $\mathbf{w}$ to reduce the impact of a whole-plane translation from the ROI translation errors. (2) There is no term that measures the homogeneity of motion. The homogeneity term in the original implementation of SIFT-Flow is enforced to improve visual quality of the warping result; we seek the similarity between two images and do not care for visualization of the result.

An example of neutral expression energy is given in Fig. 5. The frames are ordered according to neutral similarity, measured with expression energy, from left to right, top to bottom. The faces in the first row have close to neutral expression, whereas the faces in the bottom row have strong expressions. An example of temporal expression energy is given in Fig. 4. Temporal expression energy correctly indicates the amount of change between frames: in Fig. 4A, there is only mouth movement, whereas in I, there is movement of pose, gaze, cheeks, etc.

The energy for neutral and temporal similarities and the decision values from a conventional approach are fused at the decision level with support vector regression (SVR). Temporal smoothing is introduced by aggregating all the similarities in a window: at t, the three similarities about t in a window size of l are concatenated to form the features for the SVR.

2.5 Conventional Approach

We employ four appearance features: (1) Uniform Local Binary Patterns (ULBP). An image is encoded in terms of micro-patterns at the pixel-neighborhood level [1]. (2, 3) Three-Patch (TPLBP) and Four-Patch Local Binary Patterns (FPLBP). These features were proposed by Wolf et al. [12] as features that were complimentary to LBP features. In TPLBP, a pixel's neighborhood is compared to neighborhoods about the pixel. In FPLBP, the pixel's neighborhoods are compared to further neighbors. (4) Discrete Cosine Transform (DCT) [8], the DCT of the face. It was shown that a feature fusion of LBP, TPLBP and FPLBP improved classification rates on the non-trivial Labeled Face in the Wild data set [12]. For that reason, we hypothesize that this fusion captures meaningful facial appearance information, and we employ a similar fusion for facial emotion recognition. We re-project the feature vectors for each feature set with PCA before concatenating them to reduce dimensionality.

2.5.1 Local Binary Patterns

Local Binary Patterns (LBP) are a dense low-level appearance feature that have been used for both face recognition and facial emotion recognition [1]. While the method used to generate the features is commonly referred to as LBP, the features are actually a histogram of an LBP image. In classical 8-neighborhood LBP images, the pixel value $\mathbf{x}$ of a

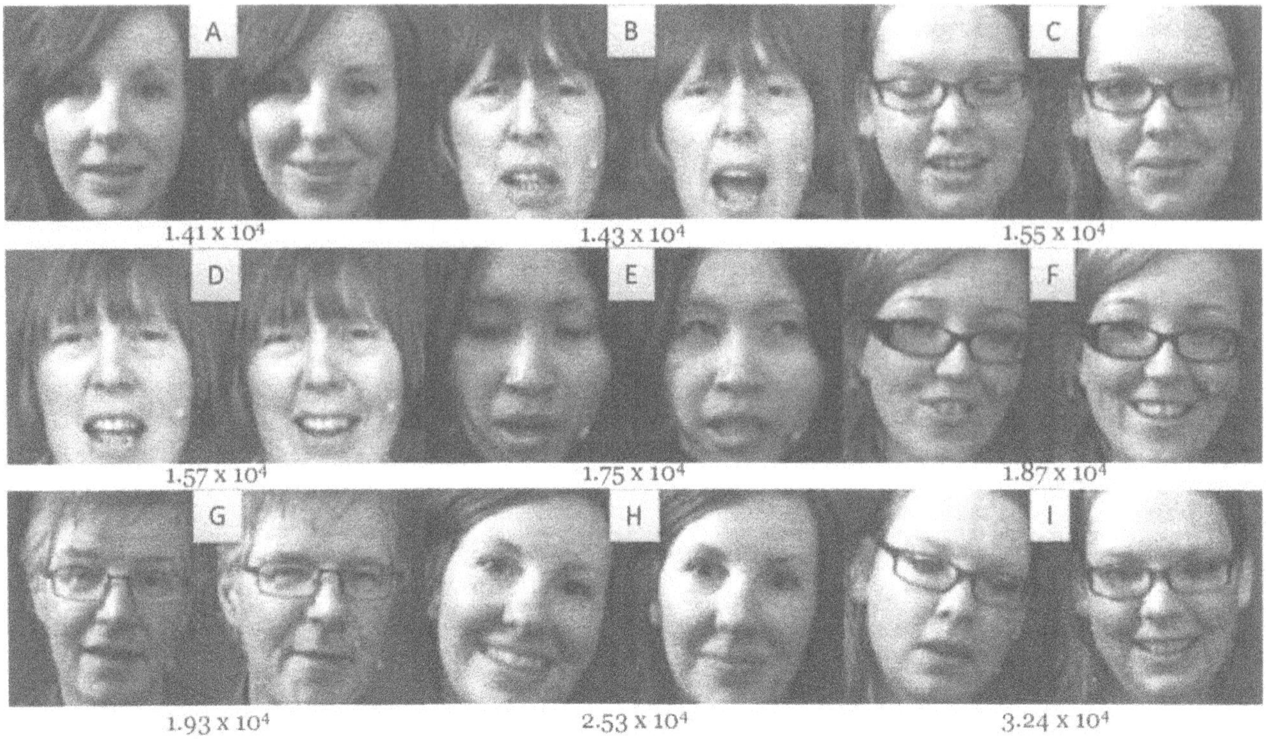

Figure 4: An example of temporal similarity measured with expression energy. Images are sorted from left to right, then top to bottom in order of neutral to most expressive. Beneath the frame is the measured expression energy.

Figure 5: An example of neutral similarity measured with expression energy. Images are sorted from left to right, then top to bottom in order of neutral to most expressive. Beneath the frame is the measured expression energy.

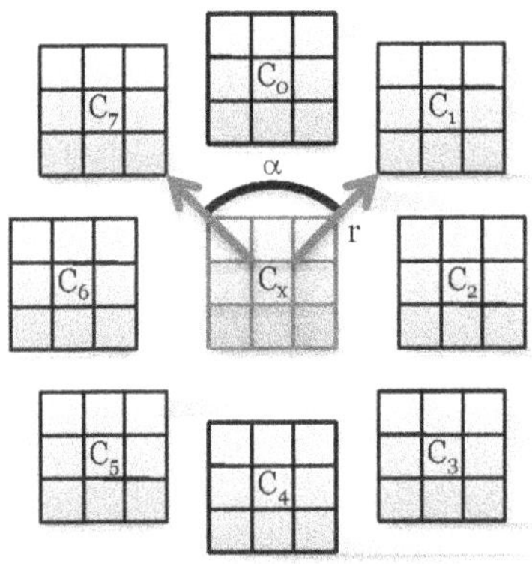

Figure 6: An example of TPLBP.

grayscale image is compared to its 8 member neighborhood $N_{\mathbf{x}}$. It is characterized by three steps: (1) Let $\texttt{LBP}(\mathbf{x})$ be the LBP image. It takes on an 8 bit integer, where each bit reflects whether or not the intensity value at $\mathbf{x}$ is greater than one of its neighbors:

$$\texttt{LBP}(\mathbf{x}) = \sum_{i=1}^{8} 2^{i-1} H\left(\langle N_{\mathbf{x}} \rangle_i - I(\mathbf{x})\right) \tag{3}$$

where $H(.)$ is a step function and $\langle N_{\mathbf{x}} \rangle_i$ is the i-th neighbor of $\mathbf{x}$. (2) Assuming an 8-bit gray level image, a 256-bin histogram is generated from $\texttt{LBP}(\mathbf{x})$. It was found that a simplification to 59-bins results in a rotation invariant property [10], and this simplification is referred to as Uniform Local Binary Patterns (ULBP). (3) To account for face morphology, a face image is reduced to $M \times M$ evenly sized local regions.

2.5.2 *Three-Patch LBP*

Whereas ULBP encodes micropatterns–how a pixel $\mathbf{x}$ compares to its immediately surrounding patch of pixel values C, TPLBP encodes how a the neighboring patches of C are changing with each other, i.e. how homogenous the region about C is in terms of texture. That is, ULBP encodes a micropattern in a compact 8-bit representation and TPLBP encodes a larger pattern and homogeneity, also with a compact 8-bit representation. To compute TPLBP, the values of three patches are compared to produce a single bit value in the code assigned to $\mathbf{x}$. Let $C_{\mathbf{x}}$ be an 8-neighborhood patch of a given pixel. S is the number of patches surrounding $C_{\mathbf{x}}$. The patches are evenly distributed about $\mathbf{x}$ along a circle of radius r. The encoding compares two patches spaced α apart and compares their values to $C_{\mathbf{x}}$. This is done S times, resulting in S bits per pixel. A visual example is given in 6.

$$\texttt{TPLBP}(\mathbf{x}) = \sum_{i=1}^{S} 2^{i-1} H(d(C_i, C_{\mathbf{x}}) - d(C_{i+\alpha \bmod S}, C_{\mathbf{x}}) - \tau) \tag{4}$$

where C_i and $C_{i+\alpha \bmod S}$ are two patches along the ring; $C_{\mathbf{x}}$ is the central patch; the function $d(.)$ is the L_1 distance function between two patches; $H(.)$ is the step function; and τ is an offset to make Eq. 4 robust to small intensity changes due to noise.

2.5.3 *Four-Patch LBP*

FPLBP continues the comparison of texture about $C_{\mathbf{x}}$ by further comparing the neighbors of $C_{\mathbf{x}}$ to their neighbors. It resembles TPLBP, except S patches are examined of a radius r_1 from $\mathbf{x}$, and an additional S patches examined of a radius r_2 from $\mathbf{x}$. Instead of comparing two pairs of patches from the same ring, a pair consists of a patch in ring 1 and a patch in ring 2. The second pair is circularly symmetric to the first pair. A bit is encoded based on which pair has a greater difference. An visual example is given in Fig. 7. The formal definition of the FPLBP code is as follows:

$$\texttt{FPLBP}(\mathbf{p}) = \sum_{i=1}^{S} 2^{i-1} H(d(C_{1,i}, C_{2,i+\alpha \bmod S}) - d(C_{1,i+S/2}, C_{2,i+S/2+\alpha \bmod S}) - \tau) \tag{5}$$

where the variables are the same as in Eq. 4; except $C_{i,j}$ is the ith patch surrounding $C_{\mathbf{x}}$, r_j away from $C_{\mathbf{x}}$.

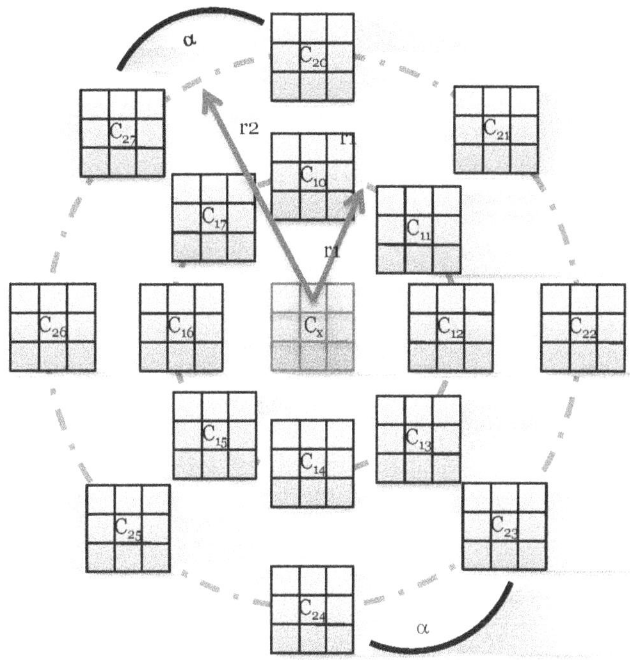

Figure 7: An example of FPLBP.

3. EXPERIMENTATION

The reader is referred to the challenge paper for a description of the data [11]. This is a video only approach that computes features at the frame level. Videos are sub-sampled at 1fps. For training, we use a two-fold cross-validation, where the training set is used to classify the development set, and vice versa. The reported correlation scores are the mean and standard deviation of the correlation of both folds: $E\langle\rho\rangle \pm \text{Std}\langle\rho\rangle$. Avatar Image Registration is run for three iterations, which is empirically selected from previous work [2]. LBP is computed at a radius of 1 and for 8 neighbors, with a 59 bin simplificiation s.t. the feature is rotationally invariant. For TPLBP, $\alpha = 2$, $S = 8$ and $w = 3$. For FPLBP, $\alpha = 2$, $S = 8$ and $w = 3$. For TPLBP and FPLBP, these parameters were empirically selected in previous work. For PCA, we rank the eigenvectors by eigenvalue and retain

Table 1: **Training Results on AVEC2012 for Feature Fusion**

	Arousal	Expectancy	Power	Valence	Avg.					
	With Extreme Learning Machine					With Support Vector Machine				
LBP	.221 ± .096	.027 ± .007	.037 ± .044	.136 ± .030	.105	**.380 ± .006**	.166 ± .007	.031 ± .014	**.263 ± .122**	.210
TPLBP	.064 ± .063	.021 ± .020	.072 ± .067	.058 ± .052	.054	.292 ± .051	.164 ± .019	.046 ± .060	.198 ± .067	.183
FPLBP	.139 ± .098	.022 ± .098	.026 ± .027	.051 ± .010	.059	.311 ± .046	.165 ± .042	**.094 ± .077**	.237 ± .014	.198
DCT	.221 ± .026	.019 ± .007	.007 ± .001	.058 ± .006	.076	.258 ± .026	.170 ± .007	.017 ± .022	.183 ± .103	.163
Fusion	.133 ± .016	.045 ± .011	.022 ± .031	.059 ± .031	.065	.323 ± .034	**.189 ± .027**	.046 ± .012	.219 ± .005	.194

Table 2: Training Results for Proposed Similarities

	Arousal	Expectancy	Power	Valence	Avg.
Video-Only Baseline					
Conventional	.380 ± .160	.189 ± .049	.094 ± .077	.263 ± .126	.231
Proposed	.454 ± .042	.176 ± .043	.139 ± .064	.378 ± .099	.264

Table 3: Official AVEC2012 Testing Results

	Ar.	Exp.	Pow.	Val.	Avg.
Video-Only Baseline					
FCSC	.092	.121	.064	.140	.104
WLSC	.091	.114	.121	.143	.117
Proposed Approach					
FCSC	.227	.093	.102	.141	.141
WLSC	.258	.049	.039	.153	.125

Figure 8: FPLBP encodes large edges.

the eigenvectors that account for 95% of the total variance. For similarity fusion, $\gamma = .008$ and $l = 5$.

3.1 Results

For the conventional method, SVR with a Radial Basis Function kernel and Extreme Learning Machine [5]–a supervised learning algorithm based on a single hidden layer feedforward network–are compared in Tab. 1. Tab. 1 also compares which features are suitable for each class. In Tab. 2, we compare the performance of the best performing features when using a conventional approach versus the proposed similarity fusion. For Arousal and Valence we use LBP features; Expectancy, feature fusion; and Power, FPLBP. All classes employ SVR. The official testing results are given in Tab. 3, where FCSC indicates frame-level scoring and WLSC indicated word-level scoring.

4. DISCUSSION

From Tab. 1, SVR with a radial basis function kernel is the best performer for all classes and features. We postulate that the feature space was not discriminative, and had to be projected into a more highly dimensional space with SVR's radial basis function. Also, from Tab. 1, feature fusion of all the features sets does not always increase performance. Feature fusion of LBP, TPLBP, FPLBP and DCT features gives better classification performance and the least variance for Expectancy. However, for Arousal and Valence, LBP is the best performer. For expectancy, FPLBP is the best classifier. We use best performing feature for each class. FPLBP's performance is surprising because Wolf et al. [12] designed FPLBP to be a complimentary feature to be fused with LBP and TPLBP–their experimental results showed no performance gain when using FPLBP alone for a face recognition task. FPLBP encodes large edges. In Fig. 8, large facial features such as folds in the cheek, eyebrows and lips are encoded. In the Fontaine emotion model [3], anger and sadness are on opposite ends of the spectrum. These two emotions elicit expressions that strongly distort the large facial feature on the face such as the mouth and eyebrows, e.g., in anger the eyebrows are furrowed and the mouth is open with teeth clenched. We posit that FPLBP better encodes these expressions versus other features, leading to the increase in performance.

For the official testing results in Tab. 3, the proposed approach doubles the correlation with arousal and power emotional states. Neutral and temporal similarities provide a more discriminative feature space than feature fusion alone. Note that neutral and temporal similarities are computed pre-registration. In Fig. 9, we provide examples comparing the feature space of a conventional method with feature fusion and the feature space of the proposed neutral and temporal similarities for arousal, expectancy and valence. The conventional feature space has the feature corresponding to the highest eigenvalue along the y-axis and the second highest eigenvalue along the x-axis. The proposed similarity feature space has neutral similarity along the x-axis and temporal similarity along the y-axis. The color indicates a quantized emotional state into bins of high and low, similar to AVEC2011–high is greater than the mean, low is less than the mean value of the label. Note that for all classes the conventional feature space is not very discriminative. It would require a complex decision surface. This is not so

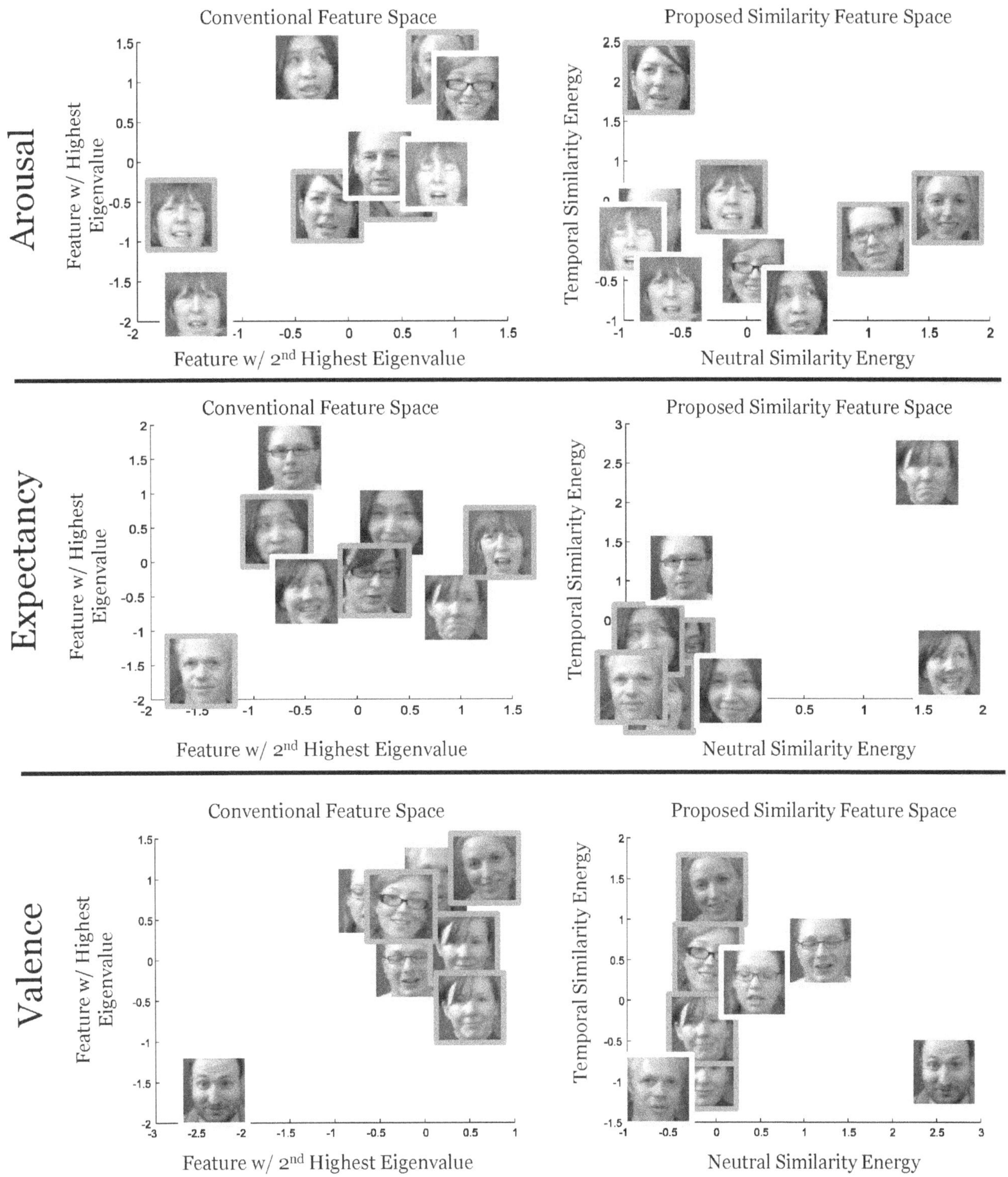

Figure 9: (Left Column) Feature space of feature fusion with the conventional approach and (Right Column) feature space of the propose neutral and temporal similarities. Blue indicates a high value in that emotion, whereas and yellow indicates a low value.

with the proposed methods feature space, the differences of which are described below. Note that in each figure the axes were z-normalized.

For arousal, positive (blue) indicates love and anger, whereas negative (yellow) indicates contentment and disappointment. The proposed method creates a perfectly linearly separable feature space. Note that negative arousal tends to have lower values in neutral and temporal similarities. Intuitively, a person that is content or disappointed will not make as many expressions as a person who is expressing love or anger, two emotions that elicit strong expressions. This is visible in the feature space, as face frames with less than average arousal form a distinctly close to neutral, lacking motion area in the space.

For expectancy, positive (blue) indicates surprise, whereas negative (yellow) indicates guilt and other emotions. It should be noted that while surprise has a high value along this dimension–a value of 3– the majority of big-six emotional states fall densely packed near neutral, zero [3]. This is manifested by in the proposed methods feature space by a very dense concentration of positive expectancy exhibiting less motion and more closeness to neutral than in the previous case with arousal. We can infer from this figure that AVEC2012 contains mostly examples of subtle surprise, e.g., an individual is being mildly impressed or unsure of how to answer the embodied agent. The individual is not shocked; strong surprise would have a high value along the neutral similarity axis. Positive expectancy is located in all other parts of the feature space, corroborating that this emotion is best described as surprise versus other, as defined in the model [3].

For valence, positive (blue) indicates happiness and love, whereas negative (yellow) indicates contempt and disgust. The figure contains examples of happiness ranging from subtle happiness to over happiness. This class is an example of the quality of motion estimation from temporal similarity. The degree of happiness tends to be described by temporal change. A large smile means a large change, as the mouth is moving and it is a large facial feature.

5. CONCLUSION

We proposed novel similarities for facial emotion recognition to be used in scenarios where new individuals are introduced in the testing data. The expression energy measures these similarities with a modified SIFT-Flow energy function. We found that in conventional methods, feature fusion does not always lead to performance increases with AVEC2012. We found that the feature space created by neutral and temporal similarities bears a resemblance to the dimensions defined by the Fontaine emotion model. The proposed method increases correlation over the video-baseline by a ratio of 1.355.

6. ACKNOWLEDGEMENTS

Support for this work was provided for in part by NSF grants 0727129 and NSF IGERT: Video Bioinformatics Grant DGE 0903667. The contents and information do not reflect the position or policy of the U.S. Government.

7. REFERENCES

[1] T. Ahonen, A. Hadid, and M. Pietikainen. Face description with local binary patterns: Application to face recognition. *IEEE Transactions on Pattern Analysis and Machine Intelligence*, 28(12):2037–2041, 2006.

[2] A. Cruz, B. Bhanu, and S. Yang. A psychologically-inspired match-score fusion model for video-based facial expression recognition. In *Affective Computing and Intelligent Interaction*, Lecture Notes in Computer Science. Springer Berlin / Heidelberg, 2011.

[3] J. R. Fontaine, K. R. Scherer, E. B. Roesch, and P. C. Ellsworth. The world of emotions is not two-dimensional. *Psychological Science*, 18(12):1050–1057, 2007.

[4] H. Gunes and M. Piccardi. Automatic temporal segment detection and affect recognition from face and body display. *IEEE Transactions on Systems Science and Cybernetics Part B*, 31(1):64–84, 2009.

[5] G. B. Huang, H. Zhou, X. Ding, and R. Zhang. Extreme learning machine for regression and multiclass classification. *IEEE Transactions on Systems Science and Cybernetics Part B*, 42(2):513–529, 2012.

[6] R. E. Kaliouby and P. Robinson. The emotional hearing aid: an assistive tool for children with asperger syndrome. *Universal Access in the Information Society*, 4(2):121–134, 2005.

[7] C. Liu, J. Yuen, and A. Torralba. Sift flow: Dense correspondence across scenes and its applications. *IEEE Transactions on Pattern Analysis and Machine Intelligence*, 33(5):978–994, 2011.

[8] L. Ma and K. Khorasani. Facial expression recognition using constructive feedforward neural networks. *IEEE Transactions on Systems Science and Cybernetics Part B*, 34(3):1588–1595, 2004.

[9] A. Maronidis, D. Bolis, A. Tefas, and I. Pitas. Improving subspace learning for facial expression recognition using person dependent and geometrically enriched training sets. *Neural Networks*, 24(8):814–823, 2011.

[10] T. Ojala, M. Pietikainen, and T. Maenpaa. Multiresolution gray-scale and rotation invariant texture classification with local binary patterns. *IEEE Transactions on Pattern Analysis and Machine Intelligence*, 24(7):971–987, 2002.

[11] B. Schuller, M. Valstar, F. Eyben, R. Cowie, and M. Pantic. Avec 2012 Ű the continuous audio/visual emotion challenge. In *Proc. Second International Audio/Visual Emotion Challenge and Workshop (AVEC 2012), Grand Challenge and Satellite of ACM ICMI 2012*, 2012.

[12] L. Wolf, T. Hassner, and Y. Taigman. Effective unconstrained face recognition by combining multiple descriptors and learned background statistics. *IEEE Transactions on Pattern Analysis and Machine Intelligence*, 33(10):1978–1990, 2011.

Multiple Classifier Combination Using Reject Options and Markov Fusion Networks

Michael Glodek*
Institute of Neural Information Processing
University of Ulm, Germany
michael.glodek@uni-ulm.de

Martin Schels*
Institute of Neural Information Processing
University of Ulm, Germany
martin.schels@uni-ulm.de

Günther Palm
Institute of Neural Information Processing
University of Ulm, Germany
guenther.palm@uni-ulm.de

Friedhelm Schwenker
Institute of Neural Information Processing
University of Ulm, Germany
friedhelm.schwenker@uni-ulm.de

ABSTRACT

The audio/visual emotion challenge (AVEC) resembles a benchmarking data collection in order to evaluate and develop techniques for the recognition of affective states. In our work, we present a Markov fusion network (MFN) for the combination of different individual classifiers, that is derived from the well-known Markov random fields (MRF). It is capable to restore missing values from a sequence of decisions and can integrate multiple channels and weights them dynamically using confidences. The approach shows promising challenge results compared to the baseline.

Categories and Subject Descriptors

G.3 [**Mathematics of Computing**]: PROBABILITY AND STATISTICS; H.5.2 [**Information Systems**]: INFORMATION INTERFACES AND PRESENTATION—*User Interfaces*; I.4.8 [**Computing Methodologies**]: IMAGE PROCESSING AND COMPUTER VISION—*Scene Analysis*

Keywords

Markov model, information fusion, pattern recognition

1. INTRODUCTION

The emotions expressed by humans differ significantly in non-acted data sets compared to (over-)acted data sets [15, 18, 12]. The expressions are often weak, occur in many variations or appear as mixtures of emotional states and others. Especially emotional expressions in human computer interaction (HCI) situations bear many challenges, since the state of the human interlocutor is in general not accustomed to express emotions in front of a computer. In general, the acquisition of non-acted emotional data does not guarantee the presence of observable emotions, such that a subsequent annotation of the data by experts is required. Since these experts estimate the most probable emotional state based on the observable data, the resulting ground truth for classification will rely on their biased opinions. In summary, the automated recognition of emotional states has to deal with a manifold of challenges, which should be taken into account in the model of the classifier architecture.

Estimating an emotional state of a human being from sensory data is a challenging task for a machine classifier. Unconstrained recordings will lead to weak features and hence to weak classifiers, that will most likely fail in distinct cases. One approach to handle such settings is to assess the quality of a classification, e.g. using uncertainty measures. With this measure for the classification it is now possible to reject a given sample when the risk of misclassification is too high. Furthermore, the combination of different sources can help to improve the classification [14]. Hereby, it is also often useful to have uncertainty values [8]. Additionally one can make smoothness assumptions on the data: It is not likely for an emotional annotation to change very quickly over time. Such assumptions can be influenced by external constraints, e.g. by the turn taking mechanisms in verbal communication.

In order to implement such a strategy, we propose the Markov fusion network (MFN). It is designed to incorporate weak classifiers, weight results from different individual classifiers and to reconstruct missing decisions.

The remainder of this work is organized as follows: Section 2 describes the concept of classifiers making use of an rejection option and the Markov fusion network (MFN) which combines the remaining decisions to obtain a final estimate for every time step. In Section 3 we present the features and the base classifiers utilized. The results are summarized in the Section 4 and the conclusion is drawn in Section 5.

*These authors contributed equally to this work.

ICMI'12, October 22–26, 2012, Santa Monica, California, USA.

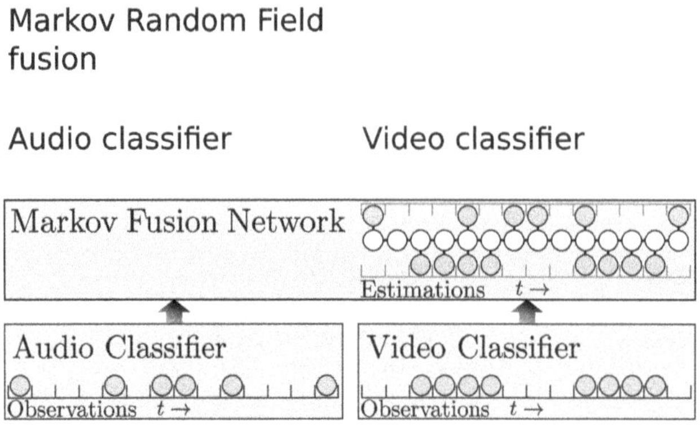

Figure 1: Schematic drawing of the multiple classifier system. Whenever possible, the classifiers of the audio and video channel provide decisions depicted as filled circles for each discrete time step t. In case no decisions are available (e.g. because of a sensor failure or it has been rejected) the corresponding time slot is left blank. The available results are handed over to the Markov fusion network, which estimates a combined decision.

2. METHOD

The approach we propose for the combination of the modalities is able to deal with sensor failures (e.g. missing speech or face is not in the field of view) and noisy signals. Furthermore, the method is capable of weighting decisions dynamically and incorporate knowledge about the speaker turns. Since we expect the classifiers to be relatively weak and we want to avoid mis-classified results in the fusion process, we will furthermore make use of classifiers, which have the additional option to reject a sample. In the following we will describe the details of the developed late fusion.

2.1 Reject Option

In general, loss functions are utilized to reduce the cost of misclassification due to classification errors. However, in applications where classifiers are (still) very weak, it may also be beneficial not to give a decision for a presented sample. This procedure is known as "classification with reject option" [4, 5]. The rejection of samples is usually based on a confidence measure, which can either be obtained by defining a threshold for the posterior probabilities or by measuring the (dis-)agreement of classifier ensembles. Within our work, we make use of the latter principle. Since, we are dealing with a temporal sequences of decisions, the resulting missing decision can be recovered using the decisions, which are not rejected.

2.2 Markov Fusion Network

The recovery of missing decisions and the combination of the channels is performed by the Markov fusion networks (MFN) which is originated from the Markov random field (MRF) commonly used in image processing to reconstruct noisy images [2, 6]. Unlike the MRF, the MFN is designed to handle different streams of one-dimensional sequences as it is the case e.g. in audio-visual information processing (compare Figure 1). The example shows the audio and video channel which provide decisions whenever possible (indicated by filled gray circles). The MFN combines these decisions to obtain an estimated sequence of decisions (filled white circles).

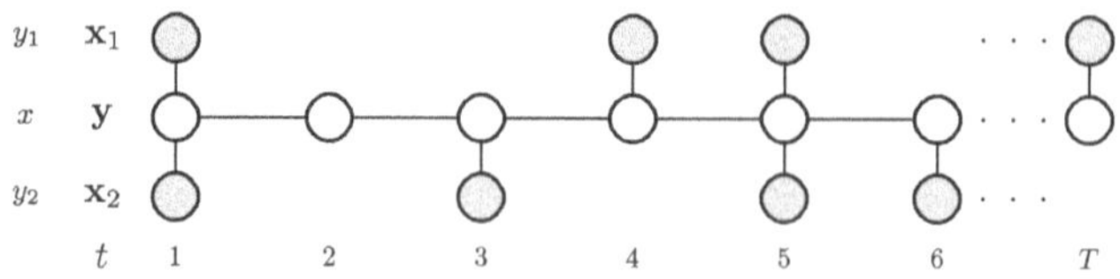

Figure 2: Graphical model of the Markov Fusion Network. The estimates y_t are influenced by the the available decisions x_{tm} of the source m and $t \in \mathcal{L}_m$ and the adjacent estimates y_{t-1} and y_{t+1}.

In Figure 2, a graphical model of a MFN combining two sources is shown. The quantity y_t is defined as the combined result of time step t where $t = 1 \ldots T$. The streams of observed decisions are given by $\mathbf{x}_{tm}$ where $m \in M$ is the index of a source. However, in principle M can be larger than two. The estimates y_t are connected in a Markov chain. Whenever a classifier provides a decision x_{tm}, a link to the estimate y_t is added to the graph.

The MFN is defined by two potentials Ψ and Φ. The potentials Ψ_m of modality $m = 1, \ldots, M$ encourage the outcomes y_t to be equal to the decisions x_{tm} and is given by

$$\Psi = \sum_{m}^{M} \Psi_m = \sum_{m}^{M} \sum_{t \in \mathcal{L}_m} k_{tm}(x_{tm} - y_t)^2,$$

where $\mathcal{L}_{tm}$ is the set of time steps in which a decision for m is available. The *data parameter* $\mathbf{k}_m$ defines the strength of its influence over time. The second potential Φ enforces the lateral similarity of decisions:

$$\Phi = \sum_{t=1}^{T} \sum_{\hat{t} \in N(t)} w_{\min(t,\hat{t})}(y_t - y_{\hat{t}})^2,$$

where the *smoothness parameter* $\mathbf{w} \in \mathbb{R}^{T-1}$ weights the cost of a difference between two adjacent nodes. The set $N(t)$ contains the indices of the immediate neighbors of node t. The parameter $\mathbf{w}$ can be set using domain knowledge at design time, e.g. to weaken similarity in the estimated sequence in case an extraordinary event is induced by the computer. Using these two potentials, the impact of a decision can directly be controlled using the *data parameter*, while the *smoothness parameter* allows to model an additional influence on the adjacent nodes depending on its temporal distance.

The joint distribution of the estimated vector $\mathbf{y}$ given the decisions of the modalities is defined by

$$p(\mathbf{y}|\mathbf{x}_1, \ldots, \mathbf{x}_M) = \frac{1}{Z} \exp\big(-\frac{1}{2}(\Psi + \Phi)\big),$$

where Z is the partition function which normalizes the probability such that the integral is equal to one. Since we are not interested in the probability itself, but in optimizing the mode of the log-posterior probability, the variable $\mathbf{y}$ can be determined using gradient ascent. Because of the problem complexity, the gradient ascent will always lead to the optimal solution However, convergence might get unstable in case the data, parameter and initial estimate give rise to a strong change in the estimate. To prevent the estimate of the model from oscillating the influence of the gradient can be diminished by introducing a learning rate.

2.2.1 Parameter Weighting

To improve the over-all architecture performance, the parameter $\mathbf{w}$ and $\mathbf{k}_m$ can be adapted dynamically. The parameter $\mathbf{w}$ is used to enforce long-time similarity but also can be set to allow quick changes of the result. The effect on lowering the penalty for a time step is illustrated in Figure 3 using a single input channel. The ground truth (thin gray line) has to be reconstructed based on the noisy input decisions (dots). The estimate of the MFN is shown as the black thick line. The dashed line represents the result without the a decrease of the similarity parameter ($k_{t1} = 0.5$ for $t = 1 \dots T$ and $w_t = 128$ for $t = 1 \dots T-1$). The MFN output shows the behavior of a linear curve fitting. The solid black line is based on the same parameter configuration with the exception of time step 50 at which we set $w_{50} = 1$. The resulting MFN estimate makes a steep step downwards in order to minimize the energy function, which obviously is closer to the ground truth function defined.

We use this technique to obtain more reliable estimates based on the assumption that the change of the participant's affective state correlates with each turn-taking of the two speakers, since a shift of topic (and therefore of the affective state as well) is most likely between these events.

The second way to dynamically control the output of the MFN can be realized by adapting k_{tm} to the present input. We assume that the prediction of the base classifiers will have a strong variance in episodes where the classifiers are not reliable. We measure the standard deviation within a distinct time window (we utilized a window of five seconds) around the respective area and use the variance to weight the results (compare Figure 4). The gray curve again represents the ground truth. The decisions (indicated by the dots) are generated using a more complex function. However, the noise in the decisions is directly influenced by the distance to the ground truth function: The greater the distance, the stronger the noise. The dashed black line shows the estimated output using $k_{t1} = 0.5$ for $t = 1 \dots T$ and $w_t = 128$ for $t = 1 \dots T-1$. As a result, all points affect the curve equally. The solid black line shows the resulting estimate using the dynamic weighting as shown in the lower part of the figure. k_{t1} is close to 0.5 in regions of low variance and almost 0.3 in regions in which the MFN input is heavily scattered. The plot shows that the output of the MFN using dynamic weighting is clearly less influenced by the outliers.

2.2.2 On-line and Off-line Processing

The MFN can be evaluated using the complete sequence (off-line processing) or, alternatively, using a time window mechanism (on-line processing) which is as well more eligible for real world applications. The latest decisions within a short time window of five seconds are combined to obtain a new estimate. The closer the estimate taken as the final output is placed to the temporal boundary of known decisions, the more changes to the estimate may occur by unexpected future appearance of new decisions. Figure 5 compares the off-line and on-line procedures. Again the thin gray line corresponds to the ground truth and the orange dots to the available decision. The dashed black line represents the curve estimated using the complete sequence at once (off-line processing). Whereas the solid black line is obtained by determining the estimates in each time window (here 15 time steps of length) which is shifted over the sequence (on-line processing). The final result is embedded five frames "in the past" in the window as indicated by a black circle.

3. DATA COLLECTION AND FEATURES

The recordings of the AVEC 2012 data set show humans having an affectively colored interaction with a remote-controlled intelligent virtual agent. Audio and video channels are provided together with an annotation of the spoken utterances and the respective speaker-turns [17, 11]. The data is labeled in four continuous emotional dimensions, namely *Arousal*, *Expectancy*, *Power* and *Valance* [7]. The challenge is benchmarked using the correlation and the root-mean squared error compared to the ground truth. In this section, the feature extraction and the classification methods for the modalities are described. The classification uses no information which allows inferring the time elapsed after a session started or integrates the content of the dialog (such as the name or the phrases used by the virtual agent etc.).

3.1 Audio Classification

The audio classification is performed using three different types of features:

- The *fundamental frequency* values are extracted using the f_0 tracker available in the ESPS/*waves+*[1] software package. Besides the f_0 track, the *energy* and the *linear predictive coding* (LPC) of the plain wave signal is extracted [13]. All three features types are concatenated to a ten-dimensional early fusion feature vector.
- The *Mel frequency cepstral coefficient* (MFCC) representation is inspired by the biological known perceptual variations in the human auditory system. The perception is modeled using a filter bank with filters linearly spaced in lower frequencies and logarithmically in higher frequencies in order to capture the phonetically important characteristics of speech. The MFCC are extracted as described in [19].
- The *perceptual linear predictive* (PLP) analysis is based on two perceptually and biologically motivated concepts, namely the critical bands, and the equal loudness curves. Frequencies below 1 kHz need higher sound pressure levels than the reference, and sounds between 2 - 5 kHz need less pressure, following the human perception. The critical band filtering is analogous to the MFCC triangular filtering, apart from the fact, that the filters are equally spaced in the Bark scale (not the Mel scale) and the shape of the filters is not triangular, but rather trapezoidal. After the critical band analysis and equal loudness conversion, the subsequent steps required for the relative spectral (RASTA) processing extension, follow the implementation recommendations in [9]. After transforming the spectrum to the logarithmic domain and the application of RASTA filtering, the signal is transformed back using the exponential function.

[1] http://www.speech.kth.se/software/

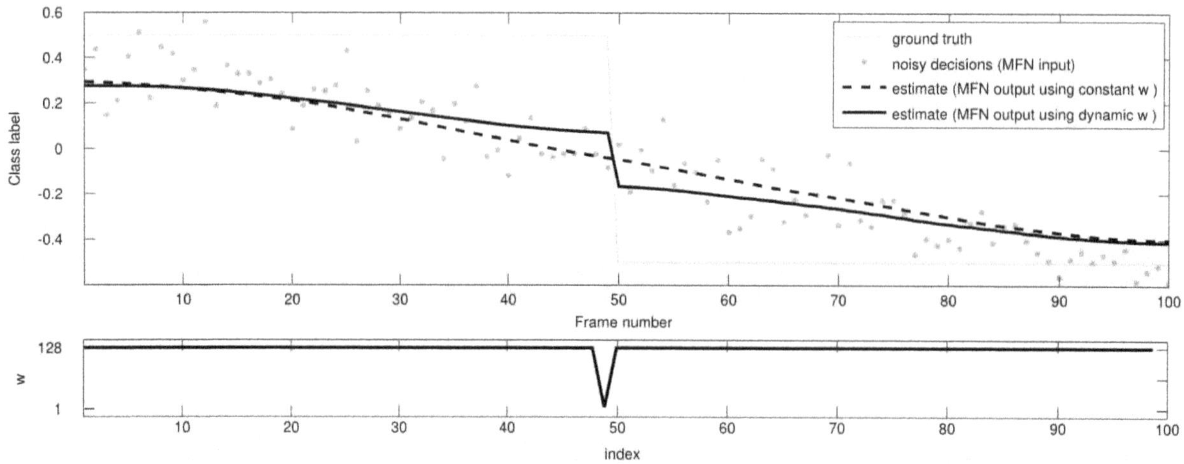

Figure 3: Influence of the smoothness parameter on the estimated decision utilizing the noisy decisions (dots) as input to the MFN. The dynamical parameter setting w has a sudden drop in the smoothness parameter (shown in the lower plot). As a result the estimated decision using the dynamic parameter (solid curve in the upper plot) performs better with respect to the ground truth (light gray curve) than the MFN estimate using no dynamic speaker-turn adaptation (dashed curve).

To classify the speech, the available data is pooled in a word-level granularity and an approach as described in [1] is conducted to overcome different lengths of the data. Herby, "reference" sequences are sampled from the over all data. For every of these sequences one hidden Markov model is constructed. The new representation of the data is now composed of the concatenated log likelihoods for a given sample computed with the different models. The number of reference sequences has to be chosen manually and is set to 75 for the experiments.

The three resulting new feature set are then put together to a new data matrix. The final classification is performed using a random forest with regression trees per dimension [3]. The standard deviation of the individual trees is used as uncertainty measure.

3.2 Video Classification

The features from the video channel are computed using the well-known computer expression recognition toolbox (CERT) [10] which is designed to recognize emotion related facial processes (such as action units or basic emotions) but also general attributes of a subject (e.g. gender, glasses present). The output of modules "Basic Emotions 4.4.3", "FACS 4.4", "Unilaterals" and "Smile Detector" are extracted to obtain high-level features of the AVEC corpus. The extraction resulted in a 36-dimensional vector for a frame. However, sound features are delivered by CERT only in case the face of a subject is successfully recognized. Due to the unrestricted settings of the AVEC corpus (subjects may turn away or leave the visual range of the camera) classification results are missing from time to time. In about 8% of the video frames the toolbox was unable to locate the subject's face, such that no features have been generated for these frames.

The classification is conducted using bagged neural networks. The bagging utilizes 100 individual classifiers for every class dimension. Furthermore, different classifiers are constructed for the frames in which the subject is speaking and for those where the subject is not. All neural networks are set to have two neurons in the hidden layer. Again the standard deviation of the outputs of the individual classifiers is used as uncertainty measure.

4. RESULTS

The smoothness and the data parameters of the MFN, as well as the rejection rates for audio and video, are optimized on the development set for each sub-challenge and label. Preliminary experiments showed that the dynamical setting of the parameters (i.e. decrease of the smoothness parameter in case of a speaker-turn and the weighting of the data parameter based on its reliability) improves the result. Hence the smoothness parameter is set constantly to 8 when the turn in the conversation changes. And within a turn, the values are varied between 64 and 192 during the optimization. Especially for the classes *Arousal* and *Valance* a strong similarity over time of 192 for almost all sub-challenges is preferred. In these cases, the data parameters are set to 0.5 for the video channel, and to 0.3 for the audio channel. However, the impact of the channels are not only determined by these weight but e.g. also by the fact that there are far many results for video available but only comparably few for the audio channel. Also the ratio of rejected samples plays a role, e.g. in case of the audio-visual sub-challenges for the class *Arousal* 90% of the video but only 50% of the audio decisions are rejected. A detailed listing of the rejection rates and parameter settings is shown in Table 1. The parameters of the potential function Ψ are given by the measured uncertainty multiplied by k_{audio} and k_{video}. Lateral similarity is parameterized by w with the exception of the speaker turns which are weighted with w_{turn}. The abbreviation WLSC and FCSC refer to the word-level sub-challenge and the fully continuous sub-challenge.

The on-line processing yielded better results for the labels *Arousal* and *Power*, while the off-line method performed better for the classes *Expectancy* and *Valance*.

Table 2 shows the correlation (CC) and root-mean-squared (RMS) differences of our approach. The base-line results of the audio-visual sub-challenge are clearly out-performed. However, the single channels have only approximately equal or slightly better results. In particular, for the class *Ex-*

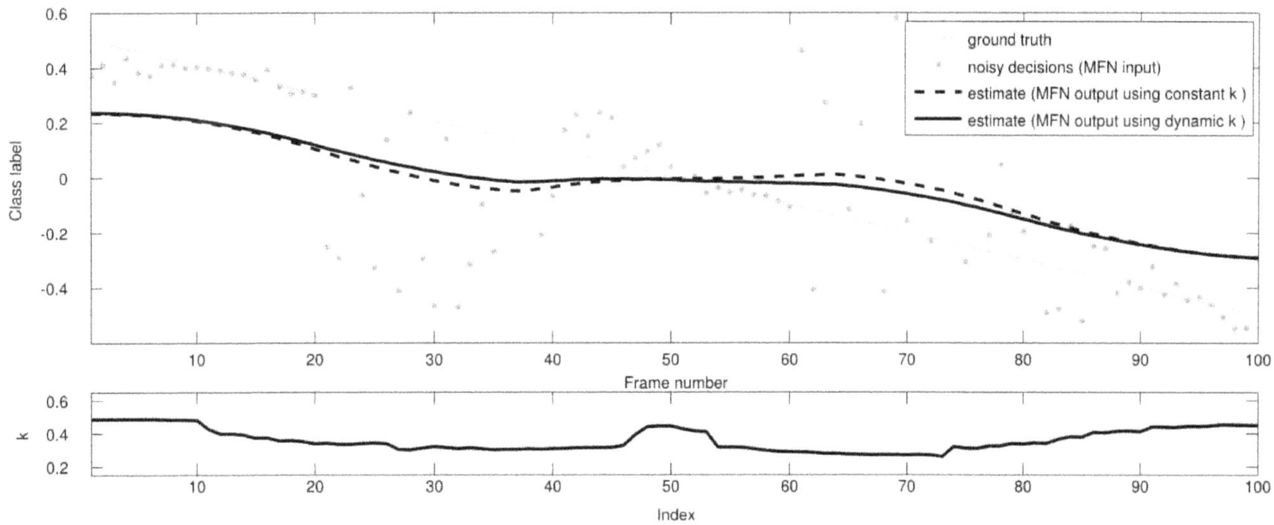

Figure 4: Influence of the dynamic weighting of the parameter k_{tm} to the estimated decisions utilizing noisy decisions (orange dots) as input to the MFN. According to our assumption the decisions of a channel have lower confidence in case they have a strong variance over time. The confidence is determined using a sliding window resulting in a dynamic adaption of the channel weighting parameter (shown in the lower plot). Using the dynamic weighting to obtain the estimated decision (solid curve) performs better with respect to the ground truth (light gray curve) than the MFN estimate using no dynamic weight adaptation (dashed curve).

pectancy and for the word level sub-challenge for the class *valance* an improved performance was obtained. Nevertheless, a remarkable performance increase could be achieved by combining the single modalities.

Figure 6 displays the mean and standard deviation of the original training set class labels for the first 5578 frames (which is the shortest sequence of the set; approximately 110 seconds). The characteristics of the curves appear to be more dependent on the elapsed time than on most other features. In particular Figures 6(a) and 6(c) have a quasi-logarithmic shape.

We evaluated the correlation using $y(t) = \log(t)$ as a predictor for the class labels, where t corresponds to the elapsed time. The results for the training, development and test set are listed in Table 3. Especially the labels *Activation* and *Power* seem to be correlated with the logarithmic function.

Most likely the artifacts observed are originated from the labeling procedure which is based on the annotation tool FEELTRACE [16]. Due to the tool, the annotators are starting all uniformly in one location of the label space and then seem to be moving "upwards". It should be discussed, whether these effects can be computationally eliminated or whether one should restrict oneself to use only the second half of the sequences. These artifacts again show how hard it is indeed to record and annotate a corpus to investigate affective states [12]

5. CONCLUSIONS

We proposed a novel approach for late classifier fusion, which takes the temporal sequence of classifier decisions into account. The so-called Markov fusion network (MFN) is closely related to the Markov random field (MRN) as utilized in image processing to restore noisy images. It can combine an arbitrary number of channels and dynamically weight the impact of the corresponding decisions temporally and between the modalities. The approach has been studied utilizing classifiers, which make use of an additional option to reject samples. The proposed multiple classifier architecture showed a good performance on the sub-challenges provided by the AVEC 2012 corpus. An open issue is still how to choose the initial parameters for the MFN.

6. ACKNOWLEDGMENTS

This paper is based on work done within the Transregional Collaborative Research Centre SFB/TRR 62 Companion-Technology for Cognitive Technical Systems funded by the German Research Foundation (DFG).

We further acknowledge Peter Kurzok, Thilo Hörnle and Sascha Meudt for kindly providing us with CPU time.

7. REFERENCES

[1] M. Bicego, V. Murino, and M. Figueiredo. Similarity-based clustering of sequences using hidden Markov models. In *Proceedings of the International Conference on Machine Learning and Data Mining*, volume 2734 of *LNCS*, pages 95–104. Springer, 2003.

[2] C. M. Bishop. *Pattern Recognition and Machine Learning*. Springer, 2006.

[3] L. Breiman. Random forests. *Machine Learning*, 45(1):5–32, 2001.

[4] C. Chow. On optimum recognition error and reject tradeoff. *IEEE Transactions on Information Theory*, 16(1):41–46, 1970.

[5] C. De Stefano, C. Sansone, and M. Vento. To reject or not to reject: That is the question — An answer in case of neural classifiers. *IEEE Transactions on Systems, Man, and Cybernetics, Part C: Applications and Reviews*, 30(1):84–94, 2000.

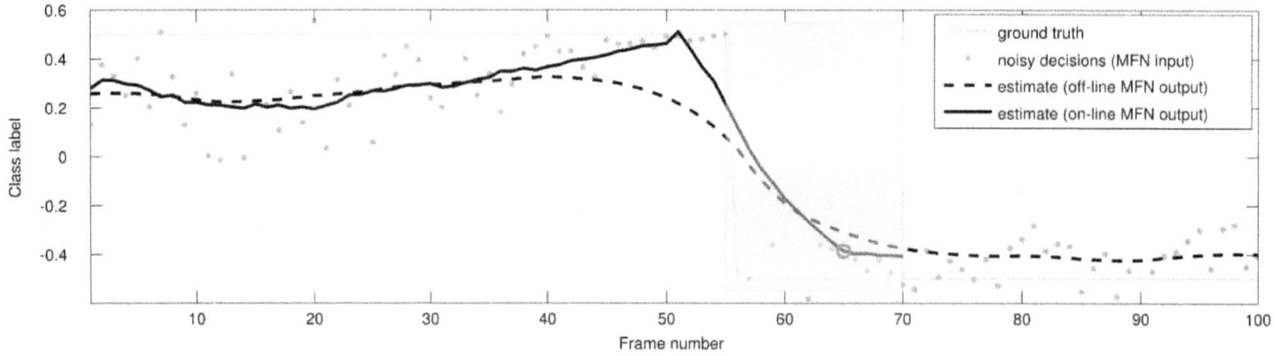

Figure 5: Comparison of on-line and off-line MFN. Again the noisy decisions of a channel (dots) shall be fused over time in order to improve the estimate for the ground truth (light gray curve). The dash curve shows the off-line method with performs the gradient ascent on the whole sequence. To obtain the estimate using an on-line processing (solid curve) a sliding window (yellowish filled square) has been utilized. Only the result of the window marked by the circle is stored to obtain more stable results.

[6] J. Diebel and S. Thrun. An application of Markov random fields to range sensing. In *Proceedings of Advances in Neural Information Processing Systems (NIPS)*, volume 18, pages 291–298. MIT Press, 2006.

[7] J. Fontaine, K. Scherer, E. Roesch, and P. Ellsworth. The world of emotions is not two-dimensional. *Psychological Science*, 18(12):1050, 2007.

[8] M. Glodek, L. Bigalke, M. Schels, and F. Schwenker. Incorporating uncertainty in a layered HMM architecture for human activity recognition. In *Proceedings of the Joint Workshop on Human Gesture and Behavior Understanding (J-HGBU)*, pages 33–34. ACM, 2011.

[9] H. Hermansky, N. Morgan, A. Bayya, and P. Kohn. RASTA-PLP speech analysis technique. In *Proceedings of the International Conference on Acoustics, Speech, and Signal Processing*, volume 1, pages 121–124. IEEE, 1992.

[10] G. Littlewort, J. Whitehill, T. Wu, I. Fasel, M. Frank, J. Movellan, and M. Bartlett. The computer expression recognition toolbox (CERT). In *Proceedings of the International Conference on Automatic Face & Gesture Recognition and Workshops*, pages 298–305. IEEE, 2011.

[11] G. McKeown, M. Valstar, R. Cowie, and M. Pantic. The SEMAINE corpus of emotionally coloured character interactions. In *Proceedings of the International Conference on Multimedia and Expo (ICME)*, pages 1079–1084. IEEE, 2010.

[12] G. Palm and M. Glodek. Towards emotion recognition in human computer interaction. In A. Esposito, S. Squartini, and G. Palm, editors, *Computational Intelligence in Emotional or Affective Systems*, Smart Innovation, Systems and Technologies. Springer, to appear.

[13] L. Rabiner and B. Juang. Fundamentals of speech recognition. *Prentice Hall*, 1993.

[14] M. Schels, M. Glodek, S. Meudt, M. Schmidt, D. Hrabal, R. Böck, S. Walter, and F. Schwenker. Multi-modal classifier-fusion for the classification of emotional states in WOZ scenarios. In *Proceedings of the International Conference on Affective and Pleasurable Design (APD'12)*, Advances in Human Factors and Ergonomics Series, pages 5337–5346. CRC Press, 2012.

[15] S. Scherer, M. Glodek, G. Layher, M. Schels, M. Schmidt, T. Brosch, S. Tschechne, F. Schwenker, H. Neumann, and G. Palm. A generic framework for the inference of user states in human computer interaction: How patterns of low level communicational cues support complex affective states. *Journal on Multimodal User Interfaces*, pages 1–25, 2012.

[16] M. Schröder, R. Cowie, E. Douglas-Cowie, S. Savvidou, E. McMahon, and M. Sawey. 'feeltrace': An instrument for recording perceived emotion in real time. In *Proceedings of the ISCA Workshop on Speech and Emotion: A Conceptual Framework for Research*, pages 19–24. Textflow, 2000.

[17] B. Schuller, M. Valstar, F. Eyben, R. Cowie, and M. Pantic. Avec 2012 — the continuous audio/visual emotion challenge. In *Proceedings of the Second International Audio/Visual Emotion Challenge and Workshop (AVEC 2012), Grand Challenge and Satellite of ACM ICMI 2012*. ACM, 2012.

[18] B. Schuller, M. Valstar, F. Eyben, G. McKeown, R. Cowie, and M. Pantic. AVEC 2011 — the first international audio visual emotion challenges. In *Proceedings of the International Conference on Affective Computing and Intelligent Interaction (ACII)*, volume 6975 of *Lecture Notes in Computer Science (LNCS)*, pages 415–424, 2011. Part II.

[19] F. Zheng, G. Zhang, and Z. Song. Comparison of different implementations of MFCC. *Journal of Computer Science and Technology*, 16(6):582–589, 2001.

Table 1: Rejection rates and parameter setting of each sub-challenge.

Arousal	Audio rejection	Video rejection	k_{audio}	k_{video}	w	w_{turn}
audio WLCS	50%	-	0.3	-	192	8
video WLCS	-	90%	-	0.5	64	8
video FCSC	-	50%	-	0.5	192	8
audio-visual WLCS	50%	90%	0.3	0.5	192	8
audio-visual FCSC	50%	90%	0.3	0.5	192	8
Expectancy						
audio WLCS	10%	-	0.3	-	192	8
video WLCS	-	10%	-	0.5	128	8
video FCSC	-	90%	-	0.5	64	8
audio-visual WLCS	90%	10%	0.5	0.3	128	8
audio-visual FCSC	90%	10%	0.5	0.3	128	8
Power						
audio WLCS	-	-	0.3	-	192	8
video WLCS	-	90%	-	0.5	64	8
video FCSC	-	10%	-	0.5	192	8
audio-visual WLCS	50%	90%	0.3	0.5	192	8
audio-visual FCSC	50%	90%	0.3	0.5	64	8
Valance						
audio WLCS	50%	-	0.3	-	192	8
video WLCS	-	10%	-	0.5	192	8
video FCSC	-	0%	-	0.5	192	8
audio-visual WLCS	0%	10%	0.3	0.5	192	8
audio-visual FCSC	50%	50%	0.3	0.5	192	8

Table 2: Results on all sub-challenges for the development and test set using the MFN multiple classifier system. The correlation measure (CC) is obtained by taking the absolute value of the averaged correlation of the sessions. The root-mean squared measure (RMS) is obtained by averaging the root-mean squared over all sessions.

	Arousal		Expectancy		Power		Valance		Mean	
Measure	CC	RMS	CC	RMS	CC	RMS	CC	RMS	CC	RMS
Audio-Visual										
FCSC test	0.294	32.212	0.268	1178.890	0.268	30.756	0.131	21.664	**0.201**	**315.881**
WLSC test	0.141	4.635	0.223	196.975	0.183	196.975	0.162	4.400	**0.177**	**52.644**
FCSC development	0.202	31.388	0.204	1301.377	0.393	26.991	0.148	26.785	**0.237**	**346.635**
WLSC development	0.088	5.463	0.211	191.140	0.245	4.467	0.150	5.478	**0.174**	**51.637**
Audio only										
WLSC test	0.080	3.778	0.130	189.907	0.048	4.113	0.038	4.275	**0.074**	**50.518**
WLSC development	0.053	4.266	0.180	194.157	0.081	3.841	0.093	5.570	**0.102**	**51.959**
Video only										
FCSC test	0.069	24.709	0.140	1133.402	0.022	27.095	0.180	23.308	**0.103**	**302.128**
WLSC test	0.075	4.276	0.182	200.193	0.012	4.252	0.185	4.553	**0.113**	**53.319**
FCSC development	0.119	22.216	0.198	1073.165	0.182	22.920	0.137	27.781	**0.159**	**286.521**
WLSC development	0.127	4.427	0.195	190.744	0.128	3.901	0.105	5.717	**0.139**	**51.197**

Table 3: Results FCSC on WLSC for the trainings set, development and test set using the function $\log(t)$ having the time step t (i.e. frame number) as input. The correlation (CC) is obtained by taking the absolute value of the averaged correlation coefficients of the sessions.

	Arousal	Expectancy	Power	Valance	**Mean**
Measure	CC	CC	CC	CC	CC
FCSC train	0.4172	0.2172	0.5585	0.0838	**0.3192**
WLSC train	0.3027	0.2582	0.4107	0.0061	**0.2444**
FCSC development	0.3934	0.2385	0.5103	0.0229	**0.2913**
WLSC development	0.3273	0.2496	0.3228	0.1156	**0.2538**
FCSC test	0.3765	0.2503	0.4883	0.0797	**0.2987**
WLSC test	0.2294	0.3036	0.3024	0.0435	**0.2197**

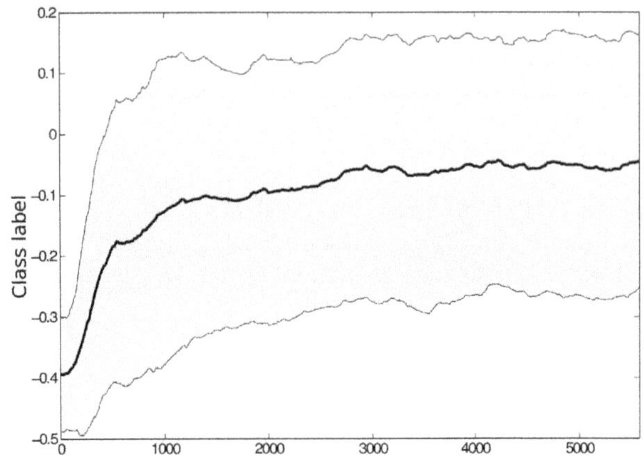

(a) Arousal

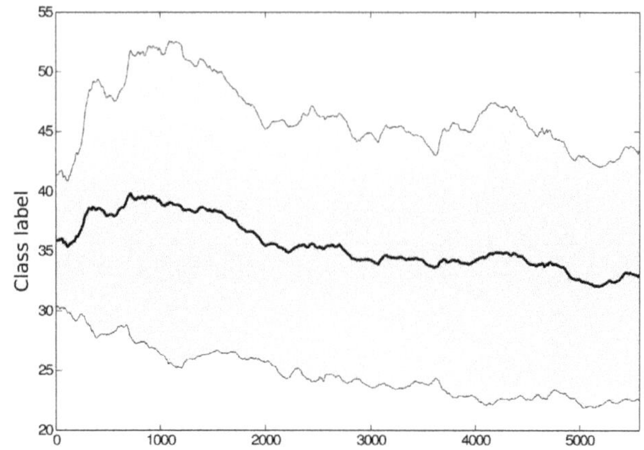

(b) Expectancy

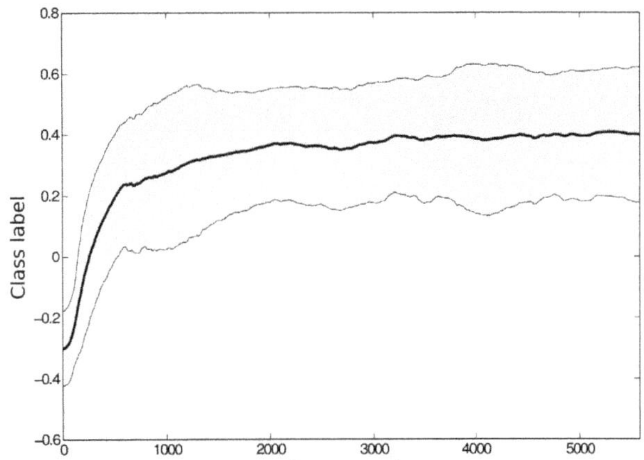

(c) Power

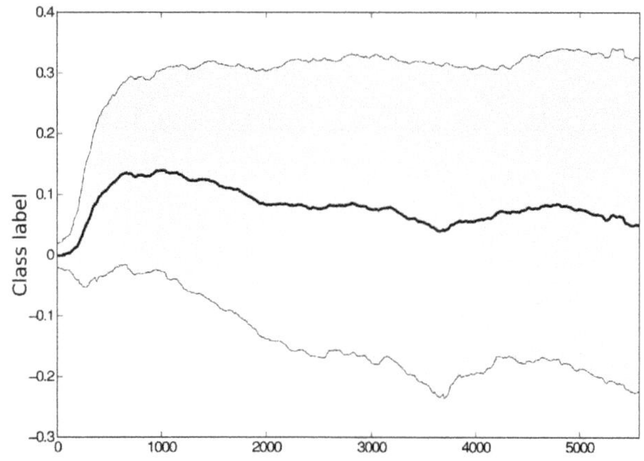

(d) Valence

Figure 6: Frame-wise mean (solid black curve) and standard deviation (gray area around the curve) of the four class labels of the trainings set (inital 5578 frames).

Audio-Visual Emotion Challenge 2012: A Simple Approach

Laurens van der Maaten*
Pattern Recognition and Bioinformatics Group, Delft University of Technology
Mekelweg 4, 2628 CD Delft, The Netherlands
lvdmaaten@gmail.com

ABSTRACT

The paper presents a small empirical study into emotion and affect recognition based on auditory and visual features, which was performed in the context of the Audio-Visual Emotion Challenge (AVEC) 2012. The goal of this competition is to predict continuous-valued affect ratings based on the provided auditory and visual features, *e.g.*, local binary pattern (LBP) features extracted from aligned face images, and spectral audio features.

Empirically, we found that there are only very weak (linear) relations between the features and the continuous-valued ratings: our best linear regressors employ the offset-feature to exploit the fact that the ratings have a dominant direction (more increasing than decreasing). Much to our surprise, only exploitation of this bias already leads to results that improve over the baseline system presented in [10]. The best performance we obtained on the AVEC 2012 test set (averaged over the test set and over four affective dimensions) is a correlation between predicted and ground-truth ratings of 0.2255 when making continuous predictions, and 0.1921 when making word-level predictions.

Categories and Subject Descriptors

I.5 [**Pattern Recognition**]: Applications

Keywords

Social signal processing; Affective computing.

1. INTRODUCTION

Social signal processing aims to automatically identify social cues by inspecting modalities such as facial expressions, human body pose, gestures, non-verbal auditory information, and speech [14]. Whilst the development of systems that automatically recognize basic emotions (see [1] for an overview) or facial action units (*e.g.*, [4, 2, 12]) has seen great improvements over the last decade, the automatic recognition of higher-level social signals such as *arousal*, *expectancy*, *power*, and *valence* is still very difficult. To foster the development of new techniques for the identification of such social signals, Schuller *et al.* [11, 10] recently started organizing the Audio-Visual Emotion Challenge (AVEC). The goal of this competition is to predict ratings of four affective dimensions that were obtained by soliciting human raters (viz. of arousal, expectancy, power, and valence). The ratings are continuous and specified for each frame in the videos, *i.e.* they are measured at 25 frames per second. The competition consists of two main parts, viz. the fully continuous sub-challenge (FCSC) and the word-level sub-challenge (WLSC). In the FCSC challenge, a prediction needs to be made for every frame in the videos, *i.e.* predictions need to be made at 25 frames per second. In the WLSC challenge, word timings are provided and predictions are made of the average rating during the utterance of a single word.

The paper describes our submission to the AVEC 2012 competition, which comprises a very simple system that nonetheless appears to outperform the baseline system described by Schuller *et al.* [10]. Specifically, we use very simple linear regressors because we surmise these are most robust against the large amounts of noise in the input features and because it is straightforward to train on massive databases such as the AVEC 2012 data. We did experiment with more complex models including conditional random fields [3, 7, 13], linear dynamical models [9], and Gaussian Process regressors [8] in preliminary experiments; but we could not establish any performance improvements using these more complicated models. In part, this may be because the relations between the data and the target values appear to be very weak: our best predictors largely ignore the observations when making predictions (see Section 4). In future work, we intend to capture as much of the learning signal as possible using ensemble methods.

In our study, we did not focus on extracting better video or audio features, and we also did not try to use the word annotations in our predictions; we merely tried to maximize the performance whilst using the pre-computed features as provided by the organizers of the challenge [10]. We surmise that the extraction of more elaborate features will, however, be necessary to obtain truly good performances on the AVEC 2012 competition data.

We describe our system in Section 2, and present the results of our experiments in Section 3. We conclude the paper with a discussion in Section 4.

*The website of Laurens van der Maaten can be found at: `http://homepage.tudelft.nl/19j49`

ICMI'12, October 22–26, 2012, Santa Monica, California, USA.

2. SYSTEM

Our system comprises two main parts: (1) a part that performs feature extraction and (2) a part that regresses the resulting features onto the four target dimensions. The two parts are described separately below.

2.1 Features

We adopted the audio and video features that were extracted by Schuller *et al.* [10] from the SEMAINE corpus [5]. The audio features comprise 25 features that are related to the overall energy and the spectrum of the audio signal (*e.g.*, energy per band, entropy, and harmonicity) and 9 features that are voice-related (*e.g.*, F0, jitter, and harmonics-to-noise ratio). The video features were obtained by aligning the face images with the help of a standard Viola-Jones face detector, and densely extracting 8-bit local binary patterns (LBPs; [6]) from the aligned face images in 10×10 pixel blocks. For the WLSC challenge, word timings were measured and the audio and visual features were averaged over the full temporal span of the word [10].

Because previous studies in, *e.g.*, automatic action-unit labeling have found that changes of features over time may be very informative in social signal processing [12], we also compute temporal differences between features. Specifically, on the FCSC challenge, we compute the differences between a feature and its corresponding feature 100 frames earlier (*i.e.* using a differencing window of 4 seconds). On the WLSC challenge, we compute the differences between features and the corresponding features measured during the previous word. In preliminary experiments, we found these window sizes to produce good results.

2.2 Regression

As our regressor of choice, we used a simple l_2-regularized linear least-squares regression. Given a training set $\mathcal{D} = \{(\mathbf{x}_1, y_1), (\mathbf{x}_2, y_2), \ldots, (\mathbf{x}_N, y_N)\}$, where $\mathbf{x}$ represents a feature vector and y the corresponding target, a linear least-squares regressors minimizes the following regularized least-squares criterion:

$$\mathcal{L}(\mathbf{w}; \mathcal{D}) = \frac{1}{N} \sum_{n=1}^{N} \left(\mathbf{w}^{\mathrm{T}} \mathbf{x}_n - y_n \right) + \lambda \|\mathbf{w}\|^2, \tag{1}$$

where $\mathbf{w}$ represents a linear combination of the input features, and λ represents a regularization parameter that needs to be set by the user. It is well-known that the weights $\mathbf{w}^*$ that minimize the regularized quadratic loss are given by:

$$\mathbf{w}^* = \left(\lambda \mathbf{I}_D + \mathbb{E}[\mathbf{x}\mathbf{x}^{\mathrm{T}}] \right)^{-1} \mathbb{E}[\mathbf{x}y] \tag{2}$$

$$= \left(\lambda \mathbf{I}_D + \frac{1}{N} \sum_{n=1}^{N} \mathbf{x}_n \mathbf{x}_n^{\mathrm{T}} \right)^{-1} \left(\frac{1}{N} \sum_{n=1}^{N} \mathbf{x}_n y_n \right), \tag{3}$$

where $\mathbf{I}_D$ represents the $D \times D$ identity matrix. The key advantage of training a linear least-squares regressor is that it scales linearly in N and that it does not require the full data set to be read into memory; the expectations $\mathbb{E}[\mathbf{x}\mathbf{x}^{\mathrm{T}}]$ and $\mathbb{E}[\mathbf{x}y]$ under the data distribution can be computed on-the-fly using a single sweep through the data (*i.e.* requiring only one full read of all the data from disk). This gives us an important advantage over support vector regressors and Gaussian process regressors, which scale quadratically in N, and over gradient-descent learners that require multiple sweeps over the training data. This makes it possible to train a linear least-squares regressor in about 10 minutes on a simple laptop computer (most of which is spent on reading data from disk).

We did notice that there are correlations between some of the target dimensions, *e.g.*, between arousal and valence. We did not exploit such correlations in our predictors, but it is straightforward (and may be helpful) to do so: a simple whitening transform may be applied on the target dimensions. After predicting the whitened targets, the reverse whitening transform needs to be applied to obtain the final prediction. Indeed, it is also possible to incorporate (Gaussian) temporal smoothness constraints on the targets in the quadratic loss, which leads to standard linear dynamical system. We did not use such a Kalman smoother in our study, because the rating sequences are not modeled well by Gaussian dynamics. Instead, the target sequences appear to have been generated by a switching distribution: the targets are approximately constant most of the time, but sporadically, the target values change drastically.

Since the evaluation criterion of the competition is the correlation between the predicted and the true ratings, it is not important that one accurately predicts the actual ratings. Because the target values only sporadically change drastically, it is much more important to accurately predict when a rating is rapidly increasing, when it is rapidly decreasing, or when it is roughly keeping the same value. A simple approach to achieve this is to train the regressors on the derivative of the rating signal instead of on the rating signal itself. In our experiments, we estimate the derivative of the rating signal using the first-order differences of the signal. (Indeed, it may have been helpful to use a smoother derivative estimate that is obtained by, *e.g.*, applying a derivative-of-Gaussian filter.)

On the WLSC challenge, we use regularized linear least squared to train a single regressors that predicts the affective dimensions from the average features for a word (the averaging is over the temporal span of the word). On the FCSC challenge, we follow [10] and use the word timings to train two separate regressors: one regressor for the parts of the video that do contain speech, and one regressor for the parts of the video that do not contain speech.

3. EXPERIMENTS

To evaluate the performance of our approach, we performed experiments on the AVEC 2012 data set. The setup of these experiments is described in 3.1. The results of the experiments are presented in 3.2.

3.1 Experimental setup

In our experiments, we used the pre-processed version of the AVEC 2012 data set as described in [10]. The data is annotated per frame by human raters for arousal, expectancy, power, and valence; the ratings are continuous-valued. The data is subdivided into a of 31 training, 32 validation, and 32 test videos. In total, the data contains 1,358,123 frames (comprising 7.5 hours of video). We used the fixed division of the data in all our experiments. In the paper, we present only results obtained by (1) training on the training data and testing on the development data and (2) training on the combined training and development data and testing on the test data (in which case the organizers measured the performance of our predictors).

Features	Ratings	Arousal	Expect.	Power	Valence	Mean
Normal	*Normal*	0.1550	**0.1599**	0.1193	0.2047	0.1597
Normal	*Derivative*	**0.2733**	0.0695	0.4193	0.1199	0.2205
Derivative	*Normal*	0.0936	0.0914	0.1477	0.0152	0.0870
Derivative	*Derivative*	0.2686	0.0864	**0.4216**	0.1434	0.2300
Baseline system [10]		0.181	0.148	0.084	**0.215**	0.1570
Our best system		**0.2733**	**0.1599**	**0.4216**	0.2047	**0.2649**

Table 1: Correlations between predicted and ground-truth ratings on the AVEC 2012 development set for the FCSC competition (higher is better; best performance is boldfaced).

Features	Ratings	Arousal	Expect.	Power	Valence	Mean
Normal	*Normal*	0.0702	0.1060	0.0219	**0.1833**	0.0953
Normal	*Derivative*	**0.2463**	**0.2662**	0.3501	0.0497	0.2281
Derivative	*Normal*	0.2366	0.2642	0.3477	0.0440	0.2231
Derivative	*Derivative*	0.2407	0.0481	**0.4088**	0.1030	0.2001
Baseline system [10]		0.018	0.009	0.001	0.002	0.0075
Our best system		**0.2463**	**0.2662**	**0.4088**	**0.1833**	**0.2762**

Table 2: Correlations between predicted and ground-truth ratings on the AVEC 2012 development set for the WLSC competition (higher is better; best performance is boldfaced).

We use cross-validation to determine the optimal regularization parameter λ. In all experiments, we allowed our linear predictors to predict an offset by adding a constant feature with a value of 1 to the data; the offset was not regularized.

The quality of the predicted targets is measured via its Pearson correlation with the ground-truth targets. This means that the exact value of the targets does not need to be correct, but that the *direction* of the predicted target signal needs to be correct over time: high correlations are achieved when the predicted target signal goes up if the ground-truth target signal goes up, and the predicted target signal goes down if the ground-truth target signal goes down. (This makes the performance measure invariant under rating offset variations between movies.) The correlations are computed per movie, and subsequently, averaged over all movies in the test data to obtain the final quality measure.

3.2 Results

Table 1 and 2 provide an overview of the results on the development set, obtained using regressors that were trained on the training set. The results are presented separately for the FCSC and WLSC sub-challenges. The results presented in the tables reveal that predicting the derivative of ratings may be beneficial for the prediction of arousal and power, which suggests that human perception of these affective dimensions is for a large part relative to earlier observations of the same individual. For expectancy and valence, the situation is much less clear: these two affective dimensions are much harder to predict, which is reflected in lower average scores and higher variances in the scores between experiments. On the development set, the best mean correlations we obtain are 0.2649 for the FCSC sub-challenge and 0.2762 for the WLSC sub-challenge, which is quite a bit better than the performances of the baseline system (which are 0.157 and 0.039, respectively [10]).

Table 3 and 4 present the results on the AVEC 2012 test set, obtained using regressors that were trained on the combined training and development set (the performance on the test set was measured by the AVEC 2012 competition organizers). Again, the results are presented separately for the FCSC and WLSC sub-challenges. The results on the test set are in line with those on the development set: predicting arousal and power is relatively easy compared to predicting expectancy and valence. In addition, it also appears that predicting rating derivatives is more effective for the former two affective dimensions, although the results are less pronounced than on the development set. For valence, it appears to be best to predict the actual ratings using the standard features, whereas for expectancy, the results vary inexplicably between the two sub-challenges. The best average performances we obtained are 0.2255 for the FCSC sub-challenge and 0.1921 for the WLSC sub-challenge. Whilst these performances are noticeably lower than the results on the development set – despite the fact that they were obtained using regressors that were trained on twice as much data – the performances are still better than the performances of the baseline system (which are 0.112 and 0.027, respectively [10]).

4. DISCUSSION

A curious observation we made is that – when we predict rating derivatives – cross-validating over λ frequently leads to the selection of *extremely* high values of λ (in both competitions). In particular, the value of λ is frequently chosen to be so high that all feature weights are effectively pushed to zero. In this way, the predictor essentially ignores the observations altogether and only uses the offset to make the predictions. The learning then exploits a bias in the data, viz. that ratings are more likely to go up over time than down. Since the offset is in the rating-derivative domain, it can be used to predict a linearly increasing rating. (If we had included a time stamp as a feature with the normal features, we could have obtained a similar effect.). Such a "constant" predictor actually already outperforms the baseline system on the development set.

Features	Ratings	Arousal	Expect.	Power	Valence	Mean
Normal	*Normal*	0.1524	**0.1659**	0.1278	**0.1453**	0.1479
Normal	*Derivative*	0.2809	0.0341	0.2680	0.0517	0.1578
Derivative	*Normal*	0.2056	0.1095	0.1669	0.0684	0.1376
Derivative	*Derivative*	**0.2990**	0.0798	**0.2918**	0.0409	0.1779
Baseline system [10]		0.141	0.101	0.072	0.136	0.1125
Our best system		**0.2990**	**0.1659**	**0.2918**	**0.1453**	**0.2255**

Table 3: Correlations between predicted and ground-truth ratings on the AVEC 2012 test set for the FCSC competition (higher is better; best performance is boldfaced).

Features	Ratings	Arousal	Expect.	Power	Valence	Mean
Normal	*Normal*	0.0861	0.1269	0.0817	**0.1375**	0.1080
Normal	*Derivative*	0.1281	0.0528	0.2123	0.0295	0.1057
Derivative	*Normal*	**0.1669**	0.1269	0.2160	0.0096	0.1299
Derivative	*Derivative*	0.1452	**0.2414**	**0.2225**	0.0255	0.1587
Baseline system [10]		0.021	0.028	0.009	0.004	0.0155
Our best system		**0.1669**	**0.2414**	**0.2225**	**0.1375**	**0.1921**

Table 4: Correlations between predicted and ground-truth ratings on the AVEC 2012 test set for the WLSC competition (higher is better; best performance is boldfaced).

This observation, together with the observations that (1) prediction performances for expectancy and valence are very low and unstable and (2) more complex regression models such as Gaussian process regressors did not produce performance improvements in our preliminary experiments, suggests that there is very little information in the data that is relevant to the prediction of affective dimensions. Next to extracting better features, it thus seems like a sensible approach to combine the results of different approaches via simple ensemble methods such as linear blending to maximally exploit the little bit of learning signal in the data. (Similar approaches have produced good results in other competitions in which the learning signal was very weak, such as the Netflix and Heritage Health Prize competitions.)

5. ACKNOWLEDGMENTS

The author thanks Michel Valstar and David Tax for helpful discussions. Laurens van der Maaten is supported by the EU-FP7 NoE on Social Signal Processing (SSPNet).

6. REFERENCES

[1] B. Fasel and J. Luettin. Automatic facial expression analysis: a survey. *Patt. Recogn.*, 36(1):259–275, 2003.

[2] S. Koelstra, M. Pantic, and I. Patras. A dynamic texture-based approach to recognition of facial actions and their temporal models. *IEEE Transactions on Pattern Analysis and Machine Intelligence*, 32(11):1940–1954, 2010.

[3] J. Lafferty, A. McCallum, and F. Pereira. Conditional random fields: Probabilistic models for segmenting and labeling sequence data. In *Proc. of the Int. Conf. on Machine Learning*, pages 282–289, 2001.

[4] G. Littlewort, M. Bartlett, I. Fasel, J. Susskind, and J. Movellan. Dynamics of facial expression extracted automatically from video. *Image and Vision Computing*, 24(6):615–625, 2006.

[5] G. McKeown, M. Valstar, R. Cowie, M. Pantic, and M. Schröder. The SEMAINE database: Annotated multimodal records of emotionally colored conversations between a person and a limited agent. *IEEE Trans. on Affective Computing*, 3:5–17, 2012.

[6] T. Ojala, M. Pietikainen, and T. Maenpaa. Multiresolution gray-scale and rotation invariant texture classification with local binary patterns. *IEEE Transactions on Pattern Analysis and Machine Intelligence*, 24(7):971–987, 2002.

[7] A. Quattoni, S. Wang, L.-P. Morency, M. Collins, and T. Darrell. Hidden conditional random fields. *IEEE Transactions on Pattern Analysis and Machine Intelligence*, 29(10), 2010.

[8] C. Rasmussen and C. Williams. *Gaussian Processes for Machine Learning*. MIT Press, 2006.

[9] H. Rauch, F. Tung, and C. Striebel. Maximum likelihood estimates of linear dynamical systems. *AIAA Journal*, 3:1445–1450, 1965.

[10] B. Schuller, M. Valstar, F. Eyben, R. Cowie, and M. Pantic. Avec 2012 – the continuous audio/visual emotion challenge. In *Proceedings of the Second International Audio/Visual Emotion Challenge and Workshop*, 2012.

[11] B. Schuller, M. Valstar, F. Eyben, G. McKeown, R. Cowie, and M. Pantic. Avec 2011 – the first international audio/visual emotion challenge. In *Proc. of the First AVEC Workshop*, 2011.

[12] L. van der Maaten and E. Hendriks. Action unit classification using active appearance models and conditional random fields. *Cognitive Processing*, 2012.

[13] L. van der Maaten, M. Welling, and L. Saul. Hidden-unit conditional random fields. In *JMLR W&CP 15*, pages 479–488, 2011.

[14] A. Vinciarelli, M. Pantic, and H. Bourlard. Social signal processing: Survey of an emerging domain. *Image and Vision Computing*, 27:1743–1759, 2009.

Step-wise Emotion Recognition Using Concatenated-HMM

Derya Ozkan
Institute for Creative Technologies
University of Southern California
12015 Waterfron DR
Playa Vista, 90094
ozkan@ict.usc.edu

Stefan Scherer
Institute for Creative Technologies
University of Southern California
12015 Waterfron DR
Playa Vista, 90094
scherer@ict.usc.edu

Louis-Philippe Morency
Institute for Creative Technologies
University of Southern California
12015 Waterfron DR
Playa Vista, 90094
morency@ict.usc.edu

ABSTRACT

Human emotion is an important part of human-human communication, since the emotional state of an individual often affects the way that he/she reacts to others. In this paper, we present a method based on concatenated Hidden Markov Model (co-HMM) to infer the dimensional and continuous emotion labels from audio-visual cues. Our method is based on the assumption that continuous emotion levels can be modeled by a set of discrete values. Based on this, we represent each emotional dimension by step-wise label classes, and learn the intrinsic and extrinsic dynamics using our co-HMM model. We evaluate our approach on the Audio-Visual Emotion Challenge (AVEC 2012) dataset. Our results show considerable improvement over the baseline regression model presented with the AVEC 2012.

Categories and Subject Descriptors

I.2 [**Artificial Intelligence**]: Natural Language Processing

General Terms

Algorithms, Performance

Keywords

Emotion recognition

1. INTRODUCTION

Emotion is one of the fundamental elements of human-to-human interaction [37]. The emotional state of a person effects the way he/she communicates with others [8, 27]. Similarly, emotional state of others affect the way the person reacts to them. Therefore, the area of affective computing attracted a lot of attention from diverse research fields such as computer science, psychology, and cognitive science [38]. Affective computing aims at building systems that can recognize, interpret and produce human emotions. Such emotion sensitive systems can improve the way that the machines communicate with humans [28]. For instance, a virtual human can adjust its behavior based on the emotional state of a user. Other application areas of affect computing include commercial fields such as customer services, call centers, game and entertainment [41].

Earlier work on automated emotion recognition [41] has often focused on analysis of the six discrete basic emotions [12] (happiness, sadness, surprise, fear, anger and disgust), even though in everyday interactions people exhibit non-basic and recognizable mental/affective states such as interest, boredom, and confusion [31]. These emotions are often imprecise. In other words, the emotional state is not always one or the other, but has a level that indicates how strong the expressed feeling is. Furthermore, a single label might not describe the complexity of an affective state well. Therefore, there has been a move to analyze audio and video recordings along a set of small number of emotional dimensions. Examples of such affective dimensions are power (sense of control), valence (pleasant vs. unpleasant), activation (relaxed vs. aroused), and expectancy (anticipation). Fontaine *et al.* [15] argue that these four dimensions account for most of the distinctions between everyday emotion categories, and hence form a good set for analysis.

In this paper, we present an approach based on concatenated Hidden Markov Model (co-HMM) to infer the dimensional and continuous emotion labels from multiple high level audio and visual cues. This approach has the advantage of explicitly learning the temporal relationships among the audio-visual data and the emotional labels. The first step of our approach involves generating a step-wise representation of the continuous emotion dimensions, in which we model the distribution of each emotion dimension by a set of discrete labels (see Figure 2). In the second step, we build a generative model, co-HMM, that can estimate the most likely label at each sample. Using the co-HMM model allows us to learn both the intrinsic dynamics within the same class label and extrinsic dynamics among different classes. The affective dimensions analyzed in our work are arousal, expectancy, power, and valence. Our model is evaluated on the Second International Audio/Visual Emotion Challenge (AVEC 2012) dataset. A complete description of the challenge and the dataset can be found in Schuller *et al.* [3].

We evaluate our method on both set of labels: word-level (WLSC), and fully continuous (FCSC). We see an improvement in performance over existing approaches (Support Vector Machine Regression, and uni-modal co-HMM)

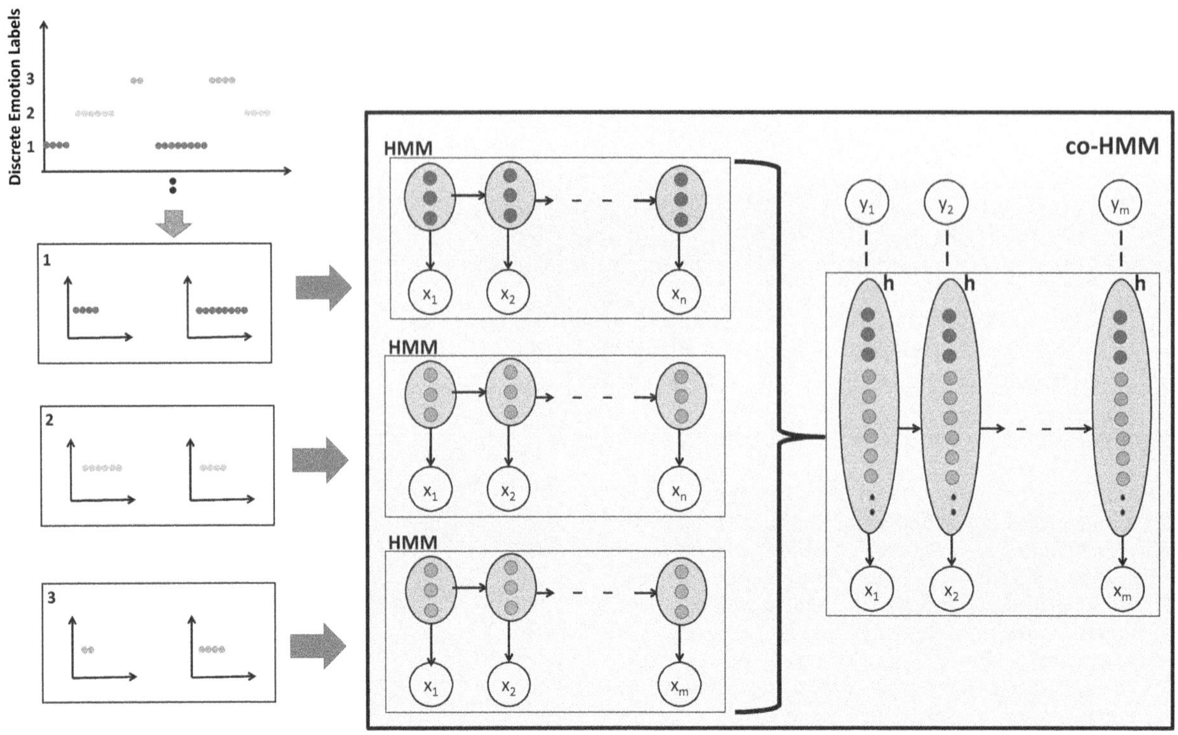

Figure 1: Overview of training procedure for our co-HMM model. First, continuous emotion levels are represented by step-wise labels (see Figure 2). Then, we create sub-datasets containing only sub-sequences with the same label, and one HMM model is learned for each step-wise class label. Finally, the hidden states of these one-label HMMs are concatenated together to form the hidden states of the final co-HMM model. This overview represents our training procedure for one emotional dimension only (i.e. valence) and this same procedure is applied independently on all four dimensions in our dataset.

when evaluating our approach on the development set. Furthermore, when evaluated on the test set our approach considerably improves the baseline results presented from [3].

In the rest of this paper, we first present related works in Section 2. Then, we describe our approach in Section 3. Experimental setup and results are presented in Section 4 and Section 5 respectively. Finally, we conclude in Section 6.

2. RELATED WORK

Several researchers used prosody (i.e pitch, speaking rate, etc.) for speech based emotion recognition [29, 39]. Some studies analyzed visual cues, such as facial expressions and body movements [4, 30, 13]. De Silva et al. [10] and Chen et al. [6] presented one of the early works that integrate both audio and visual information for emotion recognition. We refer readers to following publications on emotion recognition for an extensive survey: [41, 28, 38].

Of special relevance to our work is the work done by Nicolaou *et al.* [25] that presents experiments for classification of spontaneous affect based on Audio-Visual features using coupled Hidden Markov Models. Using coupled-HMMs allow them to model temporal correlations between different cues and modalities. They also show the benefits of using the likelihoods produced from separate coupled-HMMs as input to another classifier, rather than picking the label with a maximum likelihood for audio-visual classification of affective data. Interestingly, their experiments show that visual features contribute more in spontaneous affect classification in the valence dimension.

Wöllmer *et al.* [40] uses Conditional Random Fields (CRF) for discrete emotion recognition by quantising the continuous labels for valance and arousal based on a selection of acoustic features. In addition, they use Long Short-Term Memory Recurrent Neural Networks to perform regression analysis on these two dimensions. Both of these approaches demonstrate the benefits of including temporal information when approaching emotion recognition in dimensional space.

Most of the previous work on emotion recognition (including the studies mentioned above) have focused on classifying human emotional states into discrete labels such as angry, happy or surprised. However, in real life scenarios, human often show imprecise emotions. In other words, emotional have a level of intensity. In this paper, our goal is to not just recognize the binary emotion labels but the strength of the emotion, which we refer to as continuous labels.

Nicolaou et al. [26] recently presented a regression framework for dimensional and continuous emotion recognition. In [22], short term context is used that takes into account the past speech cues. Liscombe et al. [23] showed that using contextual features, such as the structure of spoken dialog and track user state, along with the standard lexical and prosodic features increases the classification accuracy.

In this paper, we present a method for emotion recognition that first builds a step-wise representation of the emotion dimension, and then uses concatenated Hidden Markov Model to learn the dynamics among different class labels of the stepwise representation. Concatenated models, such as concatenated HMMs, have been extensively used in speech recognition and handwriting recognition [19]. For instance, Hu et al. [18] models subcharacter stroke types modeled by HMM's. Then, these HMM models are concatenated together to form letter models for handwriting recognition.

3. APPROACH

In this paper, we propose to use a variant of the Hidden Markov Model (HMM), called concatenated HMM (co-HMM), to recognize affective dimensions in un-segmented video and audio sequences.

We hypothesize that although emotion dimensions are *continuous*, the distribution of these levels of emotion can effectively be modeled by a set of discrete classes for each emotional dimension independently. For example, in Figure 2, originally continuous emotion levels are represented by 6 class labels for arousal. The correlation between original emotion levels and the discrete labels are about 0.8983 on average. Based on that assumption, we use a step-wise label representation of each emotional dimension, in which each continuous emotion level is assigned to a discrete value that can be seen as a class label. This step-wise representation, in practice, provides the most relevant subset of label ranges and helps reducing the effect of noise.

The main idea behind co-HMM is to build a generative model that can estimate the most likely label at each sample (i.e. recognition on unsegmented sequences). We achieve this goal by creating a concatenated HMM model, in which each hidden state is directly associated with a specific label. Figure 1 shows this label-hidden state association through different colors for one emotional dimension. Using the co-HMM model allows us to learn both the intrinsic dynamics within the same class label and extrinsic dynamics among different classes. Intrinsic dynamics are learned through the hidden states of individual HMMs trained on one single class label. By concatenating these individual HMMs, we are able to model the extrinsic dynamics (temporal relationships) among different class labels.

The following section describes the co-HMM model for classification and sub-section 3.2 explains our step-wise label representation process.

3.1 Concatenated HMM

Our concatenated HMM model learns a step-wise representation of continuous emotion dimensions. In the co-HMM, one HMM model is trained for each label class of the step-wise representation and concatenate these one label HMMs. In other words, we train each HMM with segmented subsequences where the frames of each subsequence all belonged to the same label class. For a better understanding of our co-HMM model, we will first briefly introduce Hidden Markov Models and then describe our co-HMM model.

3.1.1 HMMs

Hidden Markov Models are one of the most widely used machine learning technique for modeling sequential data, such as in speech recognition, computational molecular biology, image sequence modeling, and other areas of artificial intelligence and pattern recognition [17]. A Hidden Markov Model learns a probability distribution over a sequence of

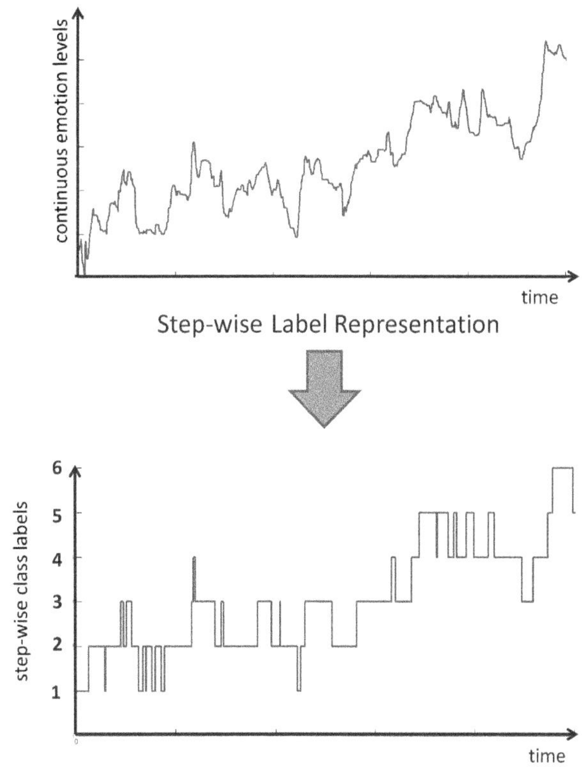

Figure 2: An example of step-wise label representation. The original continuous emotion levels are mapped into 6 label classes for one emotional dimension (i.e. arousal).

observations $\mathbf{x} = \{x_1, x_2, ..., x_m\}$, where each frame observation x_j is represented by a feature vector $\in \mathbf{R}^d$, for example, the audio features at each sample. In a first order HMM, these observations are associated with a set of hidden states $\mathbf{h} = \{h_1, h_2, ..., h_m\}$, where the state of h_t at time t depends only on the previous state t_{t-1} at time $t-1$ and the observation x_t at time t. Graphical representations of HMM models are shown in Figure 1 (middle column).

Based on the above definitions, the joint distribution of state variables and the sequence observations can be found by the following:

$$p(\mathbf{h}, \mathbf{x}) = p(h_1)p(x_1|h_1)\prod_t p(h_t|h_{t-1})p(x_t|h_t) \quad (1)$$

The first two terms are the model priors (distribution over the initial state). Training of an HMM involves finding the probability distribution over the $K * K$ *state transition matrix* that defines $p(h_t|h_{t-1})$, and the output model that defines $p(x_t|h_t)$, which can be modeled in different ways. In our experiments, we use mixtures of gaussians, since our observations–$\mathbf{x}$– are real values. Note that K is the total number hidden states used in the model. In summary, HMMs are represented by 5 types of parameters: priors, transition matrix, mean and variance of gaussian distribution, and mixing values.

Table 1: Correlations between the original and step-wise labels for different number of label classes (3,4,5,and 6) on the training set.

Discretization Level	Emotion Labels				
	arousal	expectacy	power	valence	average
3	0.79092	0.83127	0.75666	0.77554	0.7886
4	0.85866	0.88130	0.82747	0.83778	0.8513
5	0.89305	0.90759	0.85160	0.88595	0.8845
6	0.90992	0.92438	0.85192	0.90691	0.8983

3.1.2 co-HMM

As shown in Figure 1, our co-HMM model is concatenation of multiple HMMs trained on individual labels. In the final co-HMM, the number of hidden states is equal to the sum of hidden states in the one label HMMs. The first step for creating co-HMM model is to divide the dataset into N different sub-datset, where N is the number of label classes (i.e. discrete labels in the step-wise representation). Each sub-datset contains only the sub-sequences of the same class. For example, the third sub-dataset will only contain subsequences from class label 3. Then, for each of these N sub-datsets, we learn a one-label HMM.

In the second step, we concatenate parameters of the one label HMMs. The priors, mean and variance of gaussian, mixture parameters of co-HMM are obtained by simple vector and matrix concatenation. For the transition matrix of the concatenated HMM, we create it in 3 steps. For the first step, we copy the transition matrices of the one label HMMs in a large transition matrix, where the block-wise diagonal of this matrix is the one-label HMM transition matrices. Then, we compute the Viterbi path of each training subsequence using the appropriate one-label HMM, and then count the number of transitions between class labels. In the final step, the counts are inserted in the co-HMM transition matrix,and normalized so that its rows sum to one.

At testing, we apply the forward-backward algorithm on the new sequence, and then sum at each frame the hidden state marginal probabilities associated with each class label y_t.

3.2 Step-Wise Label Representation

In this section, we describe our procedure to create the step-wise label representation and show that these discrete labels correlate with the original continuous emotion levels. As exemplified in Figure 2, we perform label discretization using a percentile approach. For each emotion dimension, we use the labels from the training set to determine the range of continuous emotion levels falling into each discrete label class. This decision depends on the percentage of the continuous levels that have similar (or close) values. For instance, if we want to represent the data with n discrete step-wise labels, then we automatically find 5 thresholds such that each label class contain $1/n$ samples from the training set that have similar continuous levels. These thresholds can then be used to determine the class label for new data (i.e. development set).

The discrete step-wise labels are used to train our co-HMM model. Figure 2 shows an example where the continuous labels are mapped into 6 label classes. To study the effect of the discretization on the accuracy of emotion levels, we computed the correlation between the original continuous emotion levels and the new step-wise labels. Table 1 shows the correlation for different number of discrete class labels. We can see that even with only 3 labels, the correlation is still higher than 0.756 for all dimensions. Note that the baseline models in [3] achieve around 0.112 correlation on average. Therefore, this correlation of 0.756 between step-wise class labels and continuous emotion levels can be considered as high.

In the original data, 66060 unique labels are required to represent the continuous levels. Therefore, this correlation of 0.756 is quiet high considering the amount of labels used in step-wise representation.

4. EXPERIMENTAL SETUP

In this section, we first present our dataset and the audio-visual features used in our experiments. We then describe the training and validation methodology. Finally, we explain how we obtain the word level labels from fully-continuous emotion data.

4.1 Dataset

For all our experiments we used the dataset provided by Schuller *et al.* [3]. The dataset consist of 95 video and audio recorded dyadic interaction sessions between human participants and a virtual agent operated by a human. The dataset consists of upper body video segments with per frame and audio and audio-visual segments with per word binary labels along the four affective dimensions (activation, expectation, power and valence).

The dataset contains two sets of labels: the fully-continuous levels which are sampled at 50Hz and the word-level labels which are only defined during spoken words (see [3] for details).

4.2 Audio-Visual Features

When approaching the challenging problem of recognizing affective dimensions in un-segmented video and audio sequences, one valid approach is to experiment with an extensive set of visual or audio features, where each feature is a low-level representation of the instantaneous appearance of the face or a low level descriptor of the audio signal. The problem with this approach is that the feature space will end up extremely large (5908 dimensions of visual and 1841 of audio features in the case of Schuller *et al.* [3]). This high dimensionality issue can be partially solved by performing dimensionality reduction or feature selection.

In this paper, we approach the problem by using a smaller set of features inspired from previous literature on emotion and human communication. The following three subsections describe the audio, video and time features used in our experiments.

Table 2: Experimental results on the test and devel sets for fully-continuous and word-level datasets.

Sampling	Dataset	Model	Arousal	Expectancy	Power	Valence	Mean
fully-continuous	devel	co-HMM	0.3964	0.2464	0.4755	0.2348	**0.3383**
		SVR [3]	0.181	0.148	0.084	0.215	0.157
	test	co-HMM	0.3248	0.3107	0.4506	0.1825	**0.3171**
		SVR [3]	0.141	0.101	0.072	0.072	0.112
word-level	devel	co-HMM	0.2092	0.2397	0.2893	0.2079	**0.2365**
		SVR [3]	0.018	0.009	0.001	0.002	0.007
	test	co-HMM	0.1431	0.2874	0.2874	0.1699	**0.2003**
		SVR [3]	0.021	0.028	0.009	0.004	0.015

4.2.1 Audio Features

Our audio features include the following measures:

- **Energy (in dB)** is a measure of the intensity of the speech signal. Higher values indicate louder speech.
- **Articulation rate** is calculated by identifying the number of syllables per second. The syllables are detected by identifying vowels in the speech. Articulation rate is extracted following the algorithm in [9].
- **Fundamental frequency (f_0)** is the base frequency of the speech signal. It is the frequency the vocal folds are vibrating at during voiced speech segments. f_0 was extracted following the algorithm in [11].
- **Peak slope** is a measure suitable for the identification of breathy to tense voice qualities. Values closer to zero are considered as more breathy. Peak slope parameters were extracted as explained in [20].
- **Spectral stationarity** is a value that captures the fluctuations and changes in the voice signal. High values indicate a stable vocal tract and little change in the speech (e.g. during a hesitation or sustained elongated vowels). It is a measure of the speech monotonicity and is extracted as explained in [14].

The selection and choice of features is motivated mainly by related work and previous research [32, 7, 33, 34]. Further, they have proven to be robust representatives of the targeted prosodic phenomena. In particular, variations in speech energy have been associated with varying emotional states (e.g. higher energy is related to high activation emotional states and lower energy is associated with low activation and low power emotional states), as mentioned in [32]. Similarly to speech energy, articulation rate, syllable durations and pause variations are related to emotional states [32]. Further, a multitude of emotion recognition and affective computing studies successfully used fundamental frequency (f_0) and its variations in their approaches and evaluations [32, 7]. In [24] and [7] the importance of voice qualities for emotion recognition are investigated and reported. We chose the peak slope parameter for the representation of breathy to tense voice qualities as it has proven to be very robust and successful in voice quality classification tasks [34]. Lastly, the spectral stationarity measure is used as an indicator for monotonicity in speech which is associated with low activity and negative valence [32].

4.2.2 Video Features

We selected a subset of visual communicative signals which were shown to be useful when analyzing dyadic interactions [2, 21, 1] and could be estimated robustly by an off-the-shelf sensing software. In our experiments, we processed each video sequence with the Omron OKAO Vision software library [36] to automatically extract the following four facial features: horizontal eye gaze direction (degrees), vertical eye gaze direction (degrees), smile intensity (from 0-100) and head tilt (degrees). We reason that eye gaze and head movements can help to better recognize emotion [41, 35]. In addition, by using low dimensional visual features, we can better learn the temporal relationships among these features.

4.2.3 Time Feature

It is often observed that the emotional state of a participant is ambiguous at the beginning of a conversation. As the participants perceive the context of the conversation, they start expressing their emotions. The more the participants get engaged to the conversation, the more intense their emotions might get. To take this observation into account, we use the time information as a feature in our models. This feature is in the form of a scalar value that represents the frame number for each single frame observation (i.e. number of frames since the beginning of the video).

4.3 Baseline Models

We compare our co-HMM approach to two baseline approaches as follows:

SVR: The baseline proposed by Shuller et al. [3] uses Support Vector Machine for regression (SVR). Different than the SVR model used there, we trained our baseline SVRs with the 3 sets of features described above (audio, video and time). In our experiments, we use the libSVM library [5].

Uni-modal co-HMMs: We train one co-HMM using uni-modal feature sets. In other words, we learn 3 co-HMM models, where each model is trained using either only the audio, video or the time features. The main purpose of selecting these baseline models is to analyze the effect of combining multimodal information for emotion recognition.

4.4 Methodology

For all our experiments we use the data provided by Schuller *et al.* [3]. The data is divided into 3 subsets: training, development and testing. The training set consists of 31 sessions, while the development set consists of 32 sessions that were used for validation of the model parameters. The test set consists of 32 audio-visual sequences. The test sequences did not have any publicly available labels. The training was

Table 3: Comparison with different models on the development set for fully-continuous data.

Model	Features	Correlations				
		arousal	expectancy	power	valence	average
SVR	audio-visual-time	0.017299	0.0021259	0.0057934	0.020038	0.0113
co-HMM	audio only	0.25846	0.081497	0.34215	0.16722	0.2123
co-HMM	video only	0.11698	076478	0.06298	0.20049	0.1142
co-HMM	time only	0.18634	0	0.048736	0.084662	0.0799
co-HMM	audio-visual-time	0.39640	0.24641	0.47551	0.23482	**0.3383**

Table 4: Comparison with different models on the development set for word-level.

Model	Features	Correlations				
		arousal	expectancy	power	valence	average
SVR	audio-visual-time	0.020329	0.022021	0.0081474	-0.02148	0.0073
co-HMM	audio only	0.14304	0.077095	0.093099	0.13166	0.1112
co-HMM	video only	0.080739	0.087916	0.023905	0.18289	0.0939
co-HMM	time only	0.13474	0	0	0.087367	0.0555
co-HMM	audio-visual-time	0.2092	0.2397	0.2893	0.2079	**0.2365**

performed on the training dataset and validated on development set. We automatically validated the following model parameters: number of hidden states for the co-HMM models was validated with values (2-7), and the number of gaussian mixtures was validated with values (1-4). We also validate the number of label classes (3-6) in the step-wise label representation using the development set.

The co-HMM model is implemented using MATLAB and the uni-modal HMMs were trained using Kevin Murphy Toolbox [16]. The input audio-visual features were computed at 50 frames per second. We first down sample all these input observations to 25 frames per second before training our models to reduce training time and memory requirements. Given the continuous labeling nature of our concatenated-HMM model, prediction outputs are also computed at 25Hz. Once we get these output labels, we up sample them back to the original frame rate of 50fps.

4.5 Word-level Labels

Labels for word-level can be obtained in two ways. In the first approach, we all co-HMM models are trained on the fully-continuous emotion levels. This provides us labels at 50 frames per second. To get the word-level labels, we use the word timings to locate the start and end frames of each word in the output co-HMM labels. Then, the average of these frames are used to assign the corresponding world label. In the second approach, we use word-level co-HMM to directly to learn the word-level labels through word level features and compare it to the first approach in the experiments.

5. RESULTS

In this section, we present an discuss our experimental results on both word-level and fully-continuous dataset in the following two subsections.

5.1 Fully-continuous Data

In our first set of experiments, we compare the co-HMM model with the regression model (SVR) presented in [3]. The correlation values for both test and devel sets are given in Table 2. Remark that the SVR model in [3] uses 1188 video and 1841 audio features that are different than the 11 features that we use in our co-HMM approach. We achieve 0.3171 correlation on average for the test set, whereas the baseline SVR model gives 0.112.

Our second set of experiments on the fully-continuous dataset consist of comparison with our baseline models (see Section 4.3). The main goal of these experiments is to study the influence of different modalities on our results. In these experiments, we learn one regression model (SVR) using the same set of multi-modal features (audio, video and time) as in our co-HMM model. We also train separate co-HMMs using only one of the three modalities. Correlation result for each of these models along with the co-HMM model using all the multi-modal features are given in Table 3. Labels for AVEC 2012 test set are not provided with the dataset; and participants of the challenge had a limited number of 5 submissions to evaluate their model on the test set. Therefore, all these models are tested on the development set.

The co-HMM model outperforms the regression model (SVR) in all emotion dimension even if only the features from one modality is used. This implies that our co-HMM model is able to learn the temporal relationships among input features. Furthermore, our step-wise feature representation allows us to model the most relevant subset of label ranges by removing noise.

Another interesting result is that the performance of our co-HMM approach is the best when all three modalities are used together. This indicates that these features contain complementary information relevant to human emotion recognition.

5.2 Word-level Data

For word-level data, we first compare our co-HMM model with the SVR and uni-modal co-HMM models similar to fully-continuous data. The results are shown in Table 4. These results also implies the importance of modeling temporal relationships among features and combining all 3 different multi-modal information for emotion recognition.

Performance of our co-HMM model and the baseline SVR model in [3] is listed in Table 2. We get 0.2003 correlation by using the co-HMM approach, whereas the baseline is 0.015 on the test set.

Note that all these word-level labels are computed from the fully-continuous output labels as described in Section 4.5.

Another option for word-level label computation would be to use one feature per word and model the word-level labels using the same co-HMM model for fully-continuous data. For this approach, we average all the audio-visual features that fall into the time period where a word is spoken. Then, we use these average audio-visual features to train a co-HMM.

Using this later approach for word-level labels, we get the following correlations for arousal, expectancy, power and valence respectively on the test set: 0.1216, 0.2162, 0.1861, 0.0122. The average of these values is 0.1340, which is not as good as our original word-level correlation of 0.2003. This results shows us that the co-HMM model is able to better learn the temporal relationships on frame level than word level.

6. CONCLUSIONS

In this paper, we proposed an approach that models dimensional and continuous human emotions using concatenated Hidden Markov Models. Our approach relies on the assumption that continuous emotion levels can be model by a set of discrete class labels. Based on this, we first represent our data by some step-wise labels and use them to train our co-HMM model. By using the co-HMM model, we are able to learn both the intrinsic dynamics within each class label, and the temporal relationships among these labels.

We evaluated our approach on the Audio-Visual Emotion Challenge (AVEC 2012) dataset. Our results show considerable improvement over the regression model presented in [3] on the test set. We achieve an average of 0.3171 correlation on the test set, which can be considered as high taking into account that continuous emotion recognition is a difficult problem. Using a step-wise representation, we are able to discover the range of the most relevant subset of label ranges helps reducing the effect of noise. Therefore, we believe that our proposed approach can scale to more realistic settings.

We also compared our model to uni-model co-HMM, and have seen that using all three modalities (audio, video and time) improves the overall recognition process. This shows that our co-HMM model is able to learn the temporal relationships among input features, and these features contain complementary information relevant to human emotion recognition.

7. ACKNOWLEDGMENTS

This material is based upon work supported by the National Science Foundation under Grant No. 0917321 and the U.S. Army Research, Development, and Engineering Command. Any opinions, findings, and conclusions or recommendations expressed in this material are those of the author(s) and do not necessarily reflect the views of the National Science Foundation or the Government.

8. REFERENCES

[1] M. Argyle and J. Dean. Eye-contact, distance and affiliation. *Sociometry*, 28(3):233–304, September 1965.

[2] J. B. Bavelas, L. Coates, and T. Johnson. Listeners as co-narrators. *Journal of Personality and Social Psychology*, 79(6):941–952, December 2000.

[3] Florian Eyben Roddy Cowie Maja Pantic Björn Schuller, Michel Valstar. Avec 2012 Ű- the continuous audio/visual emotion challenge. In *to appear in Proc. of Second International Audio/Visual Emotion Challenge and Workshop (AVEC 2012), Grand Challenge and Satellite of ACM ICMI 2012*. ACM, October 2012.

[4] A. J. Calder, A. M. Burton, P. Miller, A. W. Young, and S. Akamatsu. A principal component analysis of facial expressions. *Vision research*, 41(9):1179–1208, April 2001.

[5] Chih-Chung Chang and Chih-Jen Lin. Libsvm : a library for support vector machines. *ACM Transactions on Intelligent Systems and Technology*, 2(3):1–27, April 2011.

[6] L. S. Chen, T. S. Huang, T. Miyasato, and R. Nakatsu. Multimodal human emotion/expression recognition. In *Proceedings of the 3rd. International Conference on Face & Gesture Recognition*, pages 366–371, Washington, DC, USA, 1998. IEEE Computer Society.

[7] R. Cowie, E. Douglas-Cowie, N. Tsapatsoulis, G. Votsis, S. Kollias, W. Fellenz, and J.G. Taylor. Emotion recognition in human-computer interaction. *IEEE Signal Processing Magazine*, 18(1):32–80, January 2001.

[8] C. Darwin. *The expression of the emotions in man and animals*. University of Chicago Press.

[9] N. H. De Jong and T. Wempe. Praat script to detect syllable nuclei and measure speech rate automatically. *Behavior research methods*, 41(2):385–390, May 2009.

[10] L C De Silva, T Miyasato, and R Nakatsu. Facial emotion recognition using multi-modal information. 1:397–401, September 1997.

[11] T. Drugman and A. Abeer. Joint robust voicing detection and pitch estimation based on residual harmonics. In *Proceedings of 12th Annual Conference of the International Speech Communication Association (Interspeech)*, pages 1973–1976. ISCA, Italy, August 2011.

[12] Paul Ekman. An argument for basic emotions. *Cognition & Emotion*, 6(3):169–200, May 1992.

[13] I.A. Essa and A.P. Pentland. Coding, analysis, interpretation, and recognition of facial expressions. *Pattern Analysis and Machine Intelligence, IEEE Transactions on*, 19(7):757 –763, July 1997.

[14] S. Finkelstein, S. Scherer, A. Ogan, L.-P. Morency, and J. Cassell. Investigating the influence of virtual peers as dialect models on students' prosodic inventory. In *Workshop on Child, Computer and Interaction (WOCCI'12)*. ISCA, Oregon, September, 2012.

[15] J. R. Fontaine, K. R. Scherer, E. B. Roesch, and P. Ellsworth. The world of emotion is not two-dimensional. *Psychological Science*, 18:1050–1057, 2007.

[16] Hidden Markov Model (HMM) Toolbox for Matlab. software. `http://www.cs.ubc.ca/~murphyk/Software/HMM/hmm.html`.

[17] Zoubin Ghahramani. An introduction to hidden markov models and bayesian networks. *IJPRAI*, 15(1):9–42, February 2001.

[18] Jianying Hu, Michael K. Brown, and William Turin. Hmm based on-line handwriting recognition. *IEEE Transactions on Pattern Analysis and Machine Intelligence*, 18:1039–1045, 1996.

[19] Daniel Jurafsky and James H. Martin. *Speech and Language Processing*. Prentice Hall, second edition, 2008.

[20] J. Kane and C. Gobl. Identifying regions of non-modal phonation using features of the wavelet transform. In *Proceedings of Interspeech 2011*, pages 177–180. ISCA, Italy, August, 2011.

[21] Krämer N. C. *Human behavior in military contexts*, chapter Nonverbal Communication, pages 150 – 188. Washington: The National Academies Press, July 2008.

[22] Chi-Chun Lee, Carlos Busso, Sungbok Lee, and Shrikanth S. Narayanan. Modeling mutual influence of interlocutor emotion states in dyadic spoken interactions. In *Proceedings of InterSpeech*, Brighton, UK, September 2009.

[23] Jackson Liscombe and et al. Using context to improve emotion detection in spoken dialog systems. In *Proceedings of Interspeech*, pages 1845–1848, Portugal, September, 2005.

[24] M. Lugger and B. Yang. Cascaded emotion classification via psychological emotion dimensions using a large set of voice quality parameters. In *Proceedings of IEEE International Conference on Acoustics, Speech, and Signal Processing (ICASSP)*, pages 4945–4948. IEEE, Las Vegas, February 2008.

[25] M.A. Nicolaou, H. Gunes, and M. Pantic. Audio-visual classification and fusion of spontaneous affective data in likelihood space. In *ICPR*, 2010.

[26] Mihalis A. Nicolaou, Hatice Gunes, and Maja Pantic. Output-associative rvm regression for dimensional and continuous emotion prediction. In *IEEE International Conference on Automatic Face & Gesture Recognition and Workshops, FG 2011*, pages 16–23, USA, March 2011. IEEE Communications Society.

[27] Keith Oatley, Dacher Keltner, and Jennifer M. Jenkins. *Understanding Emotions*. Wiley-Blackwell, March 2006.

[28] Maja Pantic and Leon J. M. Rothkrantz. Toward an affect-sensitive multimodal human-computer interaction. In *Proceedings of the IEEE*, volume 91, pages 1370–1390, September 2003.

[29] Thomas S. Polzin and Alex H. Waibel. Recognizing emotions in speech. In *The Fourth International Conference on Spoken Language Processing (ICSLP)*, USA, October 1996.

[30] M. Rosenblum, Y. Yacoob, and L.S. Davis. Human expression recognition from motion using a radial basis function network architecture. *Neural Networks, IEEE Transactions on*, 7(5):1121 –1138, September 1996.

[31] Paul Rozin and Adam B. Cohen. High frequency of facial expressions corresponding to confusion, concentration, and worry in an analysis of naturally occurring facial expressions of Americans. *Emotion*, 3(1):68 – 75, March 2003.

[32] K. R. Scherer, T. Johnstone, and G. Klasmeyer. *Handbook of Affective Sciences - Vocal expression of emotion*, chapter 23, pages 433–456. Affective Science. Oxford University Press, January 2003.

[33] S. Scherer. *Analyzing the User's State in HCI: From Crisp Emotions to Conversational Dispositions*. PhD thesis, Ulm University, 2011.

[34] S. Scherer, J. Kane, C. Gobl, and F. Schwenker. Investigating fuzzy-input fuzzy-output support vector machines for robust voice quality classification. *Computer Speech and Language*, June 2012.

[35] Nicu Sebe, T. Gevers, I. Cohen, and T. S. Huang. Multimodal approaches for emotion recognition: A survey. 5670:56–67, November 2004.

[36] OKAO Software. `http://www.omron.com/r_d/coretech/vision/okao.html`.

[37] Fussell SR. *The verbal communication of emotion: introduction and overview*. NJ: Lawrence Erlbaum associates Inc. Publishers, 2002.

[38] Jianhua Tao and Tieniu Tan. Affective computing: A review. In *Affective Computing and Intelligent Interaction*, volume 3784 of *Lecture Notes in Computer Science*, chapter 125, pages 981–995. Springer Berlin / Heidelberg, 2005.

[39] Raquel Tato, Rocío Santos, Ralf Kompe, and J. M. Pardo. Emotional space improves emotion recognition. In *7th International Conference on Spoken Language Processing, ICSLP*, pages 2029–2032, USA, September 2002.

[40] Martin Wöllmer, Florian Eyben, Stephan Reiter, Björn Schuller, Cate Cox, Ellen Douglas-Cowie, and Roddy Cowie. Abandoning emotion classes - towards continuous emotion recognition with modelling of long-range dependencies. In *9th Annual Conference of the International Speech Communication Association (Interspeech)*, pages 597–600. ISCA, Australia, September 2008.

[41] Zhihong Zeng, Maja Pantic, Glenn I. Roisman, and Thomas S. Huang. A survey of affect recognition methods: Audio, visual and spontaneous expressions. *IEEE Transactions on Pattern Analysis and Machine Intelligence*, 31(1):39–58, January 2009.

Combining Video, Audio and Lexical Indicators of Affect in Spontaneous Conversation via Particle Filtering

Arman Savran[♮], Houwei Cao[♮], Miraj Shah[♯], Ani Nenkova[♯], and Ragini Verma[♮]
[♮]Department of Radiology
[♯]Department of Computer & Information Science
University of Pennsylvania
Philadelphia, PA 19104
arman.savran@uphs.upenn.edu, houwei.cao@uphs.upenn.edu, mirajs@seas.upenn.edu,
nenkova@seas.upenn.edu, ragini.verma@uphs.upenn.edu

ABSTRACT

We present experiments on fusing facial video, audio and lexical indicators for affect estimation during dyadic conversations. We use temporal statistics of texture descriptors extracted from facial video, a combination of various acoustic features, and lexical features to create regression based affect estimators for each modality. The single modality regressors are then combined using particle filtering, by treating these independent regression outputs as measurements of the affect states in a Bayesian filtering framework, where previous observations provide prediction about the current state by means of learned affect dynamics. Tested on the Audio-visual Emotion Recognition Challenge dataset, our single modality estimators achieve substantially higher scores than the official baseline method for every dimension of affect. Our filtering-based multi-modality fusion achieves correlation performance of 0.344 (baseline: 0.136) and 0.280 (baseline: 0.096) for the fully continuous and word level sub challenges, respectively.

Categories and Subject Descriptors

I.5.4 [**Computing Methodologies**]: Pattern Recognition—*Applications: Signal processing; Computer vision; Waveform analysis; Text processing*

Keywords

emotion recognition, affective computing, particle filtering, emotion dynamics, multi-modality fusion, local binary patterns, class-spectral features, lexical analysis, adaboost, svm

1. INTRODUCTION

The affective state of a speaker is conveyed in several communication modalities: facial expressions, voice characteristics and intonation and the words the speaker says all contribute useful cues for interpreting the affective state. Even dealing with a single modality is challenging and the complexity of processing increases considerably when multiple modalities are used in automatic affect processing. In this paper, we study facial video, audio and lexical indicators for affect estimation and present results for individual classes of features, as well as combination of all classes for the AVEC2012 challenge [15]. The AVEC2012 challenge follows the dimensional affect modelling theory. The task is to estimate the four affect dimensions—AROUSAL, EXPECTANCY, POWER and VALENCE—of speaker affective states during spontaneous dyadic conversations.

There is a rich literature on automatic emotion recognition independently done with video and speech modalities. For video analysis, almost all prior work [5] focuses on categorical emotion descriptions or detection of facial action units [3] that can be used as intermediate tools for emotion analysis. As far as we know, the only previous video-based work that aims at continuous estimation of the affect states during dyadic conversations uses 20 facial feature points and employs output-associative Relevance Vector Machines [10].

Previous work on acoustic analysis focused on identifying representative features and developing sophisticated classification paradigms[18]. In addition, linguistic and lexical features have been also incorporated in recent years [14].

In contrast, multi-modal affect recognition is limited compared to the richness of single modality studies, partly because of the necessity of interdisciplinary expertise and insufficient number of available databases. A review about previous multi-modal studies is available in [20].

The AVEC2011 challenge [16], where binary classification of affective dimension was performed, was organized in an attempt to bring multidisciplinary researchers together. In AVEC 2012, the objective is the continuous estimation of the affect dimensions rather than binary classification of each dimension. Most of the research teams in AVEC2011 had not considered fusion of audio and video modalities. The only two available fusion studies [2, 6] do not show considerable improvements when audio and video are fused, and even some degradations were observed for several affect dimensions. These prior findings clearly demonstrate the need for improved techniques for fusion.

In our work, we extract rich video, audio and lexical features. Video features comprise the best temporal features amongst the temporal statistics of texture descriptor components (Section 4). Audio features include prosodic, spectral and voice quality features (Section 2). Lexical features are

ICMI'12, October 22–26, 2012, Santa Monica, California, USA.

based on the mutual information between a word and high activation in a specific dimension of affect (Section 3). We then fuse the regressions from the different classes of indicators using a Bayesian filtering approach (Section 5); the algorithm is based on Particle Filtering and makes use of learned dynamics of affect (Section 5.2) in the fusion process. We obtain improved estimations for all three classes of modalities, and our fusion is able to combine these independent estimators effectively, as demonstrated in Section 6.

2. AUDIO REPRESENTATION

Utterances/speaker turns are the unit we use to create the regressors in our experiments with audio. This decision is motivated by the assumption that any changes in audio features within the same turn, creates an effect so that the utterance is perceived as conveying particular affective states, but it is the same mix of emotions conveyed in the entire utterance. In the AVEC challenge data, speaker turns are short, 2–3 seconds on average, so it is reasonable to expect that they have consistent emotion profiles.

Features are calculated to characterize the emotion content in turns and affect dimensions are estimated for each turn. To evaluate word-level or frame-level estimation, we simply assign the estimation obtained for the turn as the value for all constituent words and frames.

We use the openSMILE toolkit [4] to obtain a comprehensive set of acoustic features. In Table 1 we list all of the 26 prosodic and spectral low–level descriptor (LLD) contours used. For each of these, the 19 functional statistics listed in the second column are also computed, as well as the first order delta coefficients.

LLD (26)	Functionals (19)
Prosody features: intensity, loudness, F0, F0 envelope, probability of voicing, zero-crossing rate	max, min, mean, standard deviation, liner regression: offset, slope, linear, quadratic error extremes: value, range
Spectral features: MFCC 1–12, LSF 1–8	relative position, skewness, kurtosis, quartile 1–3, 3 inter-quartile ranges

Table 1: Features used for emotion recognition: low-level descriptors (LLD) and functions

Along with the conventional turn-level acoustic analysis, we also consider class-level spectral features. In the turn-level representation, features are extracted from 20ms frames and values for each feature are summarized as functional statistics of all frames in the utterance. In class-level representation, features are summarized only for the frames that correspond to a particular phoneme class. In order to do this, we perform Viterbi-based forced alignment between the manual transcript and the audio, in order to identify which segments of audio correspond to which phoneme class [19]. In this way we detect the start time and end time of each phoneme, as well as the presence of lexical stress for each vowel in the speech data. After that, for each spoken turn, we group phonemes into three distinct phoneme classes—stressed vowels, unstressed vowels and consonants. Class-level spectral features were extracted by computing statistics of spectral measurements from parts of the spoken turns, corresponding to these classes.

In prior work on categorical emotion estimation, class-level spectral features have proven to be complementary to turn-based features, with superior performance as a standalone class [1][8]. In the work presented here, we analyze the effectiveness of class-based spectral features for the estimation of continuous emotion dimensions. We compute turn-level prosodic, turn-level spectral and class-level spectral features. Later, we will discuss the performance of the following combinations:

TL acoustic: Turn prosodic and spectral

CL acoustic: Turn prosodic and class spectral

3. LEXICAL REPRESENTATION

Many words have strong positive or negative connotations and often what people say (the words they use) carries rich information about the affective state of the speaker. Much work in text processing has shown that subjectivity, opinion and emotion can be successfully estimated simply on the basis of lexical features [11].

In our work we calculate the pointwise mutual information (PMI) between a word and a given affect dimension. PMI has been successfully applied for categorical emotion estimation [9] and is widely used as a measure of association in a range of semantic processing applications [17].

Computing PMI between a word w and a dimension of affect ε is straightforward, when affect is coded as binary presence or absence of a given property. In the AVEC 2012 data, however, AROUSAL, EXPECTATION, POWER and VALENCE are coded as continuous variables. We transform these into binary labels in order to compute PMI. To do this, we computed the average value of each dimension over all words in the dataset. Then the binary labels are assigned depending on whether the continuous label for a word is above or below the overall average. Class 1 is assigned if the original value is above the sample average and class 0 is assigned if the original value is below the average.

Now the PMI between a word and a binary emotion dimension can be calculated as

$$PMI(\varepsilon, w) = \log \frac{P(\varepsilon, w)}{P(\varepsilon)P(w)} = \log \frac{P(\varepsilon|w)}{P(\varepsilon)} \quad (1)$$

$P(\varepsilon)$ is the prior probability of an affect dimension and $P(\varepsilon|w)$ is the conditional probability of the affect dimension given the word w. Both probabilities are computed directly from counts on the data.

For each word w in the training set and for each affect dimension (AROUSAL, EXPECTATION, POWER and VALENCE) we compute two PMI values: one for association between the word and class 0, which corresponds to low values for the affect dimension, and class 1, which corresponds to high values. Table 2 lists examples of the five words with the highest PMI, that are associated with low (class 0) and high (class 1) values of the affect dimensions.

As with audio, the unit of representation and estimation for the lexical models is a speaker turn. We experimented with two turn representations based on the PMI between the words in the turn and affect dimensions.

TL PMI: Turn level PMI

TL Sparse Lex: Turn level sparse lexical representation

The turn-level PMI representation consists of only two features. They are computed as the average of word-level PMI of all the words in the turn. In testing, the values for each turn are calculated by taking the average only for words that appeared in training, ignoring any other word. For turns that consist entirely of words that did not appear in training, we take the values from the preceding turn as features.

The turn-level sparse lexical features are inspired by conventional bag-of-words representations in which texts are represented as sparse vectors of occurrence counts of words from a predefined vocabulary. We use a different set of 1,000 words for each affect dimension. These are the 500 words with highest PMI for class 0 and class 1 respectively. Each turn is represented by 1,000 features with the corresponding PMI values for words that occur in the speaker turn and zeros for words which do not appear in the utterances. Speaker turn in the AVEC dataset consists of 15 words on average, so these representations are indeed sparse.

4. VIDEO REPRESENTATION

In video, unlike in audio, regression is performed directly on the frame level. An immediate complication is that now the size of the training set is prohibitively large, containing more than 500,000 frames. Moreover, neighbouring frames carry redundant information due to the high frame rate (50 fps). To address these problems, we resample the training data. For each emotion dimension, different set of training examples are selected by sampling from frames for which affect value is greater or smaller than half of the standard deviation estimated over the entire training set. Resampling is done randomly by rejection from this set. We empirically determined the rate of the resampling as 40 per minute and rejection neighbourhood size as one second. If a sampled frame falls in the neighbourhood of an already selected frame, it is rejected.

We choose to work with low level image features. However, we employ temporal features as well as spatial features in order to capture temporal cues that can have information about one's affective state, such as fast head and face movements or stable moments. Duration of the visual signals may also correlate with the emotional states. For this reason, we consider temporal features with different durations as well.

Our temporal features are based on still image texture descriptors known as Local Binary Patterns (LBP). We employed the LBP features that are provided within the challenge [15]. These features are extracted after a registration stage that involves face and eye detection and normalization onto a 200×200 pixel image by aligning the eyes. Registered facial images are divided into 10×10 blocks and a histogram with 59 bins is calculated for every block, resulting in 5900 bins to be used as features. Our feature set also involves face and eye detection outputs, resulting in 5908 features of the static face.

For each feature component, we represent temporal information with the mean and standard deviation over fixed length temporal windows. The mean captures the dominant value for each component in a temporal window and smooths out variation, while the standard deviation conveys information about the variability. For each time point, the statistics are computed for five different temporal windows with widths of $\{2^k\}_{k=-1}^{3}$ seconds immediately preceding the time point. The window range is from 25 to 400 frames, given the frame rate of 50 selected for the cuprous. We also include the descriptor bin values of the current frames. Thus, the size of the final feature vector is $(5 \times 2 + 1) \times 5908 = 64988$.

The number of features is too large to include in regression directly, so we perform feature selection. We apply classification AdaBoost, as done in prior work on facial action unit intensity estimation [13], to select compact feature sets (200 features) according to their success at discriminating between high and low values, such that each feature is a binary weak classifier (nearest mean classifier). The high and low values are defined as the values above and below the mean, for each affect dimension.

AdaBoost feature selection is performed on the resampled training set. The selected features are used in epsilon Support Vector Machine regressors (SVR) with linear kernel. Training is also performed on the resampled training set.

5. BAYESIAN FILTERING FOR FUSION

Regression does not incorporate any sequence information. However, prediction of the current state can greatly benefit from the valuable information contained in past estimates from the sequence because emotion sequences are continuous and in most cases emotion states are stable for short intervals of time. In order to take advantage of these temporal dependencies between emotional states, we perform Bayesian filtering via particle filters that adaptively process data to fuse different modalities. The filter operates on the regression outputs of each modality and incorporates prior knowledge about the dynamics of the emotional states.

5.1 Particle Filtering

Particle filtering [12] is an effective Bayesian framework to handle non-linear models and non-Gaussian probability density propagation processes. In our case, an important motivation for using particle filtering is the fusion, because outputs of different regressors can cause multi-modal posterior distributions if they do not agree on the affect state. By propagating the posterior of the states, particle filters can achieve near-optimal estimations. Moreover, the observation model is not completely linear since it is possible that at a given time not all observations are available, as explained in Section 5.3. Estimations with other Bayesian filters that impose strong assumptions, such as linearity and Gaussianity as in Kalman filtering, would be far from optimal.

To define the filtering process, let x_t be our state variable corresponding to an affect dimension at discrete time t. It evolves according to a transition function at t

$$x_t = f_t(x_{t-1}, v_t) \qquad (2)$$

where v_t is an i.i.d. process noise sequence. The objective is to estimate x_t recursively using the measurements

$$\mathbf{z_t} = \mathbf{h_t}(x_t, \mathbf{n_t}) \qquad (3)$$

where n_t is an i.i.d. measurement noise sequence. Here, the components of the measurement vector $\mathbf{z_t}$ are the regression outputs of different modalities at discrete time t.

Particle filtering estimates the posterior distribution of the state given past observations, $p(x_t|\mathbf{z_{0:t}})$, by sequential Monte Carlo method [12]. The posterior is represented by weighted N particles, $\{x_t^i, w_t^i\}_{i=1}^N$ where weights w_t^i are updated at each time step. We use Sampling Importance Resampling (SIR) filter [12], also known as Bayesian Bootstrap filter. The SIR filter uses the prior density as the importance density to draw the particles from. Thus the filter first performs N predictions according to the transition density,

$$x_t^i \sim p(x_t|x_{t-1}^i), \quad (4)$$

and then each prediction is weighted according to the observations in the update step by the likelihood function

$$w_t^i = p(\mathbf{z_t}|x_t^i). \quad (5)$$

Particles are re-sampled according to their weights at each iteration to attain equal weights. This is achieved by re-sampling the same particle multiple times depending on the weight. For inference, we apply minimum mean square error estimation (MMSE) using 50 particles.

5.2 Auto-regressive Emotion Dynamics

During filtering, the current state is predicted according to the transition function f_t (equation 2). A transition model which better approximates the dynamics of the states means we have more realistic prior (prediction) distribution, thus leading to better estimations. Proper predictions can also reduce the number of necessary particles since they may be placed close to the observation likelihood peaks more frequently, i.e., fewer wasted particles.

We find proper models of the emotion dimension dynamics by fitting auto-regressive (AR) models with order K

$$x_t = a_0 + \sum_{k=1}^{K} a_k x_{t-k} + v_t \quad (6)$$

where a_k are the model coefficients and $v_t \sim N(0, \sigma^2)$. AR models are estimated by the Burg method [7]. However, it is important to note that if the model parameters are estimated over the concatenated sequences, spurious signals will appear due to the jumps at the concatenation site. To circumvent this issue, we skip the samples at the concatenation points so that samples from the consecutive sequences are never used in the same iteration, while estimating the autocorrelations.

We chose to use a second order model by analysing the reflection coefficients. We learned AR models for each of the emotion dimensions separately and here was a sharp drop for coefficients of higher order for all emotion dimensions, which suggested that the acceleration model is the most appropriate one. Thus the samples are drawn from the distribution

$$x_t^i \sim N(x_t; a_0 + a_1 x_{t-1} + a_2 x_{t-2}, \sigma^2) \quad (7)$$

5.3 Measurement Model for Fusion

We combine measurements coming from each modality by

$$\mathbf{z_t} = \mathbf{1}.x_t + \mathbf{n_t} \quad (8)$$

where $\mathbf{1}$ is vector of ones, and $\mathbf{n_t}$ is multivariate Gaussian measurement noise with covariance $\mathbf{R}$, $\mathbf{n_t} \sim N(\mathbf{0}, \mathbf{R})$. $\mathbf{z_t}$ is composed of regression outputs of video, audio and lexical indicators. Thus if the variance of error is smaller for one modality, in filtering it will have higher influence than the other modalities. Also, overall higher measurement variance increases the role of predictions for the estimation since posterior distribution becomes more similar to prediction distribution. We estimate full covariance matrices over the error sequences in order to take the correlations between the modalities into account as well.

An issue during fusion is that features for each modality cannot be extracted at every point in time. For instance, audio measurements only exist when the subject is speaking; video measurements are not available if the face is not detected. At times it is even possible that none of the measurements are available. Therefore, for each point in time we use only the available measurements to compute the likelihood of the state. Thus for each combination of measurements we have different likelihood models. In case there is no observation at all, all the particles have the same likelihood, i.e., estimations are based only on the predictions. However, as explained and discussed in Section 6.3 and Section 6.4, we also experiment with a method where we fill missing measurements with values from preceding turns. This can be interpreted as artificial likelihood values over non-speech regions which prevent large deviations from the preceding over-word estimations.

Let the nominal variable c_t represent a measurement combination at time t which indicates a mapping of $\mathbf{z_t}$ to a new observation vector $\mathbf{z_t^{c_t}} \in R^{n_{c_t}}$ where n_{c_t} is the number of available measurements. Then the algorithm is:

- Given: $\{x_{t-1}^i, w_{t-1}^i\}_{i=1}^N, \mathbf{z_t}, c_t$
- Predictions: $x_t^i \sim N(x_t; a_0 + a_1 x_{t-1} + a_2 x_{t-2}, \sigma^2)$
- Update if any measurement exists:
  - $w_t^i = N(\mathbf{z_t^{c_t}} - \mathbf{1}.x_t; 0, \mathbf{R^{c_t}})$
  - $w_t^i \leftarrow w_t^i / \sum_{j=1}^N w_t^j$
  - Resample($\{x_t^i, w_t^i\}_{i=1}^N$)
- Posterior: $p(x_t|\mathbf{z_{0:t}}) \approx \frac{1}{N}\sum_{i=1}^N \delta(x_t - x_t^i)$
- Apply MMSE estimation

6. EXPERIMENTAL RESULTS

6.1 Challenge Datasets

The challenge dataset [15] is composed of 95 sequences of video (upper body video), audio and manual speech transcripts of dyadic interactions between human subjects and virtual agents operated by a human. All frames are annotated for the four dimensions of affect: AROUSAL, EXPECTANCY, POWER and VALENCE. There are four different virtual agents who have unique moods, like angry and cheerful. The subjects have conversations with all of the agents, thus there are four sequences per subject which usually exhibit different combinations of affect states. The total duration of the footage is about 7.5 hours with more than 50 thousands words. The dataset is divided into training, development and test subsets with 31, 32 and 32 sequences respectively. Every subset consist of eight participants, each interacting with all four virtual agents.

There are no subjects that appear both in the training and testing set, however some subjects appear in both training and development data.

For individual classes of features, we use Support Vector Regression (SVR) with linear kernel for regression. SVM parameters are optimized on the development set and the SVR regressors are trained on the training set. For fusion with particle filtering, the training set is used to learn the affect dynamics, and measurement noises are estimated over the regression errors on the development set.

	words associated with class 0	words associated with class 1
AROUSAL	three, plan, alone, change, depressing	car, shopping, around, she, afternoon
EXPECTANCY	plan, their, around, mind, goes	fair, children, question, told, aright
POWER	face, fighting, matter, room, true	afternoon, along, cathy, four, phone
VALENCE	depressing, fighting, room, unnecessarily, angry	afternoon, cathy, four, meet, photograph

Table 2: Examples of the words with the highest PMI for 4 affective dimensions on binary classes

6.2 Analysis of Speech Related Features

Here we discuss the performance and robustness of the audio and lexical features. Table 3 shows the average correlation coefficients of the word-based sub-challenge. Models are trained on the training data and the development sets is used for testing. We analyze the robustness of regression and list both speaker-dependent (SD) and speaker-independent (SI) results in the table. For SD regression, we report results only for the 12 samples from speakers in the development set that also appeared in the training set. For SI regression, we only report on the 20 samples from speakers that did not appear in training.

All our acoustic and lexical models outperform the AVEC12 audio baseline, which we also listed for comparison. The baseline acoustic system relies on features extracted on the word level, unlike ours which works on the turn level. Acoustic features are more sensitive to unseen speakers and performance degrades considerably for all affect dimensions, especially for AROUSAL and VALENCE. The turn level sparse lexical representation is unique because with it, results are higher for speaker independent experiments than for speaker dependent.

In both acoustic and lexical features, different representations lead to best performance on each of the four affect dimensions. The sparse lexical representations are better than the average PMI for AROUSAL and VALENCE, but not for EXPECTANCY and POWER. We observe the same effect for acoustic features. In particular, class-based spectral features will give better regressions on AROUSAL and POWER than turn-level features. These two dimensions are more sensitive to sub-band energy and therefore the more focused class-based spectral-features yield improvements.

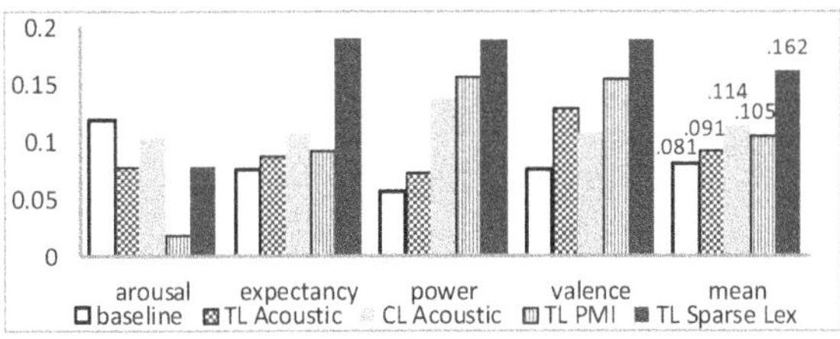

Figure 1: Comparison between the audio baseline and different acoustic and lexical features on the test set. Performance is measured in cross-correlation average over all sequences on the WLSC

Figure 1 gives a comparison of different acoustic and lexical features for the word-level sub-challenge (WLSC) on the test set. The audio baseline results are again shown in the figure for comparison. As in the development set, our audio and lexical features outperform the acoustic baseline by a large margin. Class-level acoustic feature and sparse lexical features achieve correlation coefficients of 0.114 and 0.162 respectively with the gold-standard annotations. The correlation for the audio baseline is only 0.081. On the test set, sparse lexical features prove to be the best individual representation, with 0.2 cross-correlation on all dimensions except AROUSAL. Class-level acoustic features perform notably well for estimating POWER, where they emerge as the best representation that yields more than double improvement over the baseline.

Lexical features appear to be more robust than acoustic features, as performance for them degrades only slightly compared to the results we obtained on the development set. There is a larger performance gap between development and test set for the acoustic features.

6.3 Evaluation of Single Modality Regression Estimations

Here we report both frame-level (FCSC) and word-level (WLSC) correlations with the gold-standard affect annotation. Table 4 shows the averaged correlation coefficient scores (average of correlation coefficients evaluated over each sequence) for both sub-challenges (frame level FCSC and word level WLSC) on development and test sets. We see that on the development set for fully continuous sub-challenge (Table 4.a), our video-only results are above the baseline for all affect dimensions, with 0.283 correlation score on average (baseline video: 0.146). We compute word level video estimates by taking the average values of the frames over the corresponding words, and obtain 0.272 WLSC score (baseline video: 0.124) (Table 4.b).

Our audio (TL acoustic) and lexical indicators (TL Sparse Lex) scores are 0.228 and 0.218 for WLSC (baseline audio: 0.074) (Table 4.b), respectively. To convert speech modality regressions to the frame level, we assume that all frames in a turn have the affect value estimated for the entire turn. Frames that correspond to regions during which the virtual agent speaks (the subject is silent) are assigned the affect value of the preceding turn of the subject. This extrapolation is reasonable if the gaps between the turns are short or if there are still cues, i.e., visual signals, that conform with the current affective state while the subject is listening. Otherwise, extrapolations can cause misleading predictions.

As can be seen in Table 4.a, we obtain 0.295 and 0.263 FCSC correlation scores for audio and lexical indicators, respectively. The extrapolation improves the frame-level POWER estimations dramatically compared to those on word-level, for instance for audio from 0.147 to 0.455. This shows that the POWER of the preceding turn is a great indicator of the affective state of the subject while the subject is listening to their interlocutor in interactive conversations. VALENCE also improves slightly by the extrapolation, but there is slight drop in performance for AROUSAL and EXPECTANCY.

On the test set (Table 4.c and Table 4.d), we observe a

WISC-development	arousal		expectancy		power		valence		average	
Baseline Audio	0.097		0.052		0.061		0.085		0.074	
	SD	SI	SD	SI	SD	SI	SD	SI	SD	SI
Audio features										
TL acoustic	0.340	0.208	0.244	0.235	0.164	0.137	0.340	0.227	0.272	0.202
CL acoustic	0.363	0.216	0.211	0.184	0.170	0.175	0.380	0.203	0.281	0.195
Lexical features										
TL PMI	0.190	0.188	0.260	0.202	0.218	0.171	0.205	0.200	0.218	0.190
TL Sparse Lex	0.268	0.208	0.228	0.204	0.146	0.168	0.216	0.302	0.215	0.221

Table 3: Correlation performances (average of correlation coefficients evaluated over each sequence) of different audio and lexical features in terms of speaker-dependent (SD) and speaker-independent (SI) sequence, on the development set

marked degradation of results for all modalities (our systems and baselines) compared to those on the development set. This may be because all the test subjects are different from the subjects of the training set, while some training subjects are the same in the development set. The mismatch in performance is largest for POWER in the video modality, AROUSAL and EXPECTANCY for audio and AROUSAL for lexical indicators. The reason may be the lack of generalizability on the test set. However, our results are above the baseline: frame level video of 0.178 vs. 0.104, and 0.091 audio and 0.162 lexical vs. baseline audio of 0.081.

6.4 Evaluation of Particle Filtering Based Multimodality Fusion

Correlation scores for several Particle Filtering based fusion types on the development set are shown in Table 4.a. All the fusions are performed at frame level but we convert frame level estimates to word level by taking average over the words. We compare two fusions for the speech only modality, with and without non-speech region extrapolation as explained in Section 6.3. Here, by means of extrapolation, we fill the missing values of the non-speech regions before filtering, thus the particle filter uses the extrapolated values as if they are the current measurements (regression outputs). Actually, both types of fusion over the non-speech regions perform only prediction from the past regression outputs and the learned models of the emotion dimension dynamics (see Section 5.2). However, this extrapolation acts as a mechanism in the filtering process which forces the affect states to become much closer to the preceding speech region estimation.

Fusion results are better than those of the individual modalities being fused, but several other interesting results can be observed in Table 4.a and Table 4.b. When missing values are extrapolated before filtering, we obtain dramatical improvements on POWER estimations compared to when they are not filled, from 0.283 to 0.556. VALENCE fusion is also considerably better when values are filled than when they are not. The same effect is present for word-level fusion. A reason for this peculiarity might be that our assumption that affect states are stable over short periods of time is more applicable to some dimensions than to others. From our results, it appears that AROUSAL and EXPECTANCY are more stable for a person over time, while POWER and VALENCE are more variable, especially depending on whether the subject is speaking or listening. Recall that when values are not extrapolated, only the emotion dynamics leads the estimation. For noisy measurements of highly variable emotion dimensions, the dynamics will cause more deviations over non-speech regions. Therefore, extrapolation improves the correlation performances by reducing these deviations.

We also perform fusion of all three modalities for both sub-challenges, with and without extrapolation for speech indicators. Results are shown in Table 4.a and Table 4.b. For all dimensions, combining video with speech related features leads to results better than those for video only prediction. Again, extrapolation shows similar effects on the scores.

We can see from the results on the development set that each affect dimension should be predicted with a different fusion method. The best results for each dimension are shown in bold in the tables and the last line in the table gives the performance when the best combination is chosen for each dimension (mixed fusion). Motivated by these results on the development data, we also perform mixed fusion on the test data: for AROUSAL and EXPECTANCY video and speech modalities are fused without extrapolation; for VALENCE estimation we fuse video and speech-related features with extrapolation; for POWER we fuse only speech-related features with extrapolation. The mixed fusion gives the best performance on the test set, supporting the observation that different combinations of modalities are appropriate for different affect dimensions.

All of our particle filtering fusion results have higher correlation scores than the baseline results on the development set. In the baseline, feature level fusion is applied, simply combining all features in a single regression. The benefits from particle filtering are clear and can be attributed to the filtering process which is able to propagate multi-modal posterior distribution in time via the learned dynamics.

Finally, we assess our fusion results on the test set (Table 4.c and Table 4.d). The success of our fusion method is validated by FCSC correlation of 0.344 (baseline: 0.136) and WLSC correlation of 0.280 (baseline: 0.096). The contribution of our fusion is much higher. For instance, for WLSC, while we obtain fusion score of 0.280 by combining single modalities with scores 0.178 (video), 0.091 (audio) and 0.162 (lexical), the baseline single modality fusion score is 0.096 after combining single modalities with scores 0.117 (video) and 0.081 (audio).

7. CONCLUSIONS

In this paper, we study estimation of the four dimensions of affect, namely AROUSAL, EXPECTANCY, POWER and VA-

(a) FCSC - development

	Arousal	Expectancy	Power	Valence	Avg.
Single Modality					
Baseline Video	0.157	0.130	0.115	0.186	0.146
Video	0.306	0.215	0.242	0.370	0.283
Audio (Exterp.)	0.215	0.215	0.455	0.297	0.295
Lexical (Exterp.)	0.171	0.176	0.396	0.308	0.263
Speech Modality Fusions					
Audio+Lex. (PF)	0.276	0.208	0.283	0.373	0.285
Audio+Lex. (Exterp., PF)	0.275	0.205	**0.556**	0.423	0.365
Video and Speech Modality Fusions					
Baseline Video+Audio	0.162	0.162	0.111	0.208	0.157
Video+Audio+Lex. (PF)	**0.383**	**0.266**	0.238	0.408	0.324
Video+Audio+Lex. (Exterp., PF)	0.377	0.210	0.477	**0.473**	0.384
Video+Audio+Lex. (Mixed, PF)	0.383	0.266	0.556	0.473	**0.420**

(b) WLSC - development

	Arousal	Expectancy	Power	Valence	Avg.
Single Modality					
Baseline Video	0.145	0.111	0.103	0.137	0.124
Video	0.280	0.202	0.223	0.383	0.272
Baseline Audio	0.097	0.052	0.061	0.085	0.074
Audio	0.257	0.239	0.147	0.270	0.228
Lexical	0.230	0.211	0.160	0.270	0.218
Speech Modality Fusions					
Audio+Lex. (PF)	0.323	0.222	0.192	0.358	0.274
Audio+Lex. (Exterp., PF)	0.329	0.169	**0.296**	0.377	0.293
Video and Speech Modality Fusions					
Baseline Video+Audio	0.113	0.090	0.083	0.114	0.100
Video+Audio+Lex. (PF)	**0.350**	**0.263**	0.209	0.437	0.315
Video+Audio+Lex. (Exterp., PF)	0.384	0.182	0.228	**0.458**	0.313
Video+Audio+Lex. (Mixed, PF)	0.350	0.263	0.296	0.458	**0.342**

(c) FCSC - test

	Arousal	Expectancy	Power	Valence	Avg.
Single Modality					
Baseline Video	0.092	0.121	0.064	0.140	0.104
Video	0.251	0.153	0.099	0.210	0.178
Audio (Exterp.)	0.74	0.032	0.418	0.149	0.168
Lexical (Exterp.)	0.046	0.057	0.426	0.228	0.189
Fusion					
Baseline Video+Audio	0.149	0.110	0.138	0.146	0.136
Video+Audio+Lex. (Mixed, PF)	0.359	0.215	0.477	0.325	**0.344**

(d) WLSC - test

	Arousal	Expectancy	Power	Valence	Avg.
Single Modality					
Baseline Video	0.091	0.114	0.121	0.143	0.117
Video	0.184	0.156	0.146	0.226	0.178
Baseline Audio	0.119	0.075	0.056	0.076	0.081
Audio	0.078	0.087	0.073	0.128	0.091
Lexical	0.078	0.190	0.189	0.189	0.162
Fusion					
Baseline Video+Audio	0.103	0.105	0.066	0.111	0.096
Video+Audio+Lex. (Mixed, PF)	0.302	0.194	0.293	0.331	**0.280**

Table 4: Correlation performances (average of correlation coefficients evaluated over each sequence) of different modalities and their fusions for fully continuous affect dimension state estimation. Results for both sub-challenges (frame level FCSC and word level WLSC) are shown on development and test sets. Extrap. means extrapolation at non-speech regions for the audio and lexical indicators. PF stands for Particle filtering based fusion. Mixed means the use of the best fusion methods for each affect dimension.

LENCE during dyadic conversations on the AVEC 2012 challenge dataset. We first develop single modality regression-based estimators with video, audio and lexical indicators, respectively. For video, we extract temporal statistics of LBP texture descriptor components and consider different time widths to better capture visual clues happening in different time scales better. This makes the number of the possible features impractically large. Also, the total duration of training video is close to three hours. To cope with the excessive amount of video data, we apply automatic video frame selection for training, and discriminative feature selection. Our video regressor obtains 0.178 correlation score compared to the baseline score of 0.104, which highlights the contribution of the temporal features and the effective training frame selection procedure. Video scores of all of the dimensions are above the baseline and are particularly good for the AROUSAL and VALENCE dimensions.

For the speech-related modalities, we exploit both acoustic and lexical information. For the audio modality, we experiment with class-based spectral features for three broad phoneme classes in addition to the conventional turn-based spectral and prosodic features. For the lexical analysis, we computed the word-level mutual-information between words and high and low values for affect dimensions. Words with strongest association are used as the basis for feature space representation of individual turns. Our audio and lexical regressors achieve 0.114 and 0.162 averaged correlation coefficients respectively on test set for the word-level sub-challenge, outperforming the audio baseline of 0.081 by a large margin.

We consider each single modality regression output as an affect measurement in a Bayesian filtering framework. Predictions are done based on past observations and the learned dynamics of the affect states. This is realized by Particle filtering which propagates the multi-modal posterior distributions in time according to the auto-regressive processes.

Our filtering based fusion dramatically improves the scores for single modalities and outperforms baseline fusion which is done on the feature level. This constitutes a major advance compared to the results from the AVEC 2011 challenge where fusion did not appear beneficial [2, 6]. We report fusion correlation scores of 0.344 (baseline: 0.136) and 0.280 (baseline: 0.096) for the FCSC and WLSC, respectively.

8. ACKNOWLEDGMENTS

This work was supported by Grant Number R01-MH-073174 from the NIH.

9. REFERENCES

[1] D. Bitouk, A. Nenkova, and R. Verma. Class-level spectral features for emotion recognition. *Speech communication*, pages 613–625, 2010.

[2] C. M. de Melo, P. Carnevale, D. Antos, and J. Gratch. A computer model of the interpersonal effect of emotion displayed in a social dilemma. In *ACII 2011*, Memphis, TN, Oct. 2011.

[3] P. Ekman, W. V. Friesen, and J. C. Hager. *Facial Action Coding System*. 2002.

[4] F. Eyben, M. Wöllmer, and B. Schuller. Opensmile: the munich versatile and fast open-source audio feature extractor. In *ACM Multimedia*, 2010.

[5] B. Fasel and J. Luettin. Automatic Facial Expression Analysis: A Survey. *Pattern Recognition*, 36(1):259–275, 2003.

[6] M. Glodek, S. Tschechne, G. Layher, M. Schels, T. Brosch, S. Scherer, M. KÃd'chele, M. Schmidt, H. Neumann, G. Palm, and F. Schwenker. Multiple classifier systems for the classification of audio-visual emotional states. In *IJATEM'11*, pages 359–368, 2011.

[7] S. Kay. Prentice Hall, Englewood Cliffs, NJ, 1988.

[8] C. Lee, S. Yildirim, M. Bulut, A. Kazemzadeh, C. Busso, Z. Deng, S. Lee, and S. Narayanan. Emotion recognition based on phoneme classes. In *Interspeech*, pages 205–211, 2004.

[9] C. M. Lee and S. S. Narayanan. Toward detecting emotions in spoken dialogs. *IEEE Transactions on Speech and Audio Processing*, 13:293–303, 2005.

[10] M. Nicolaou, H. Gunes, and M. Pantic. Output-associative rvm regression for dimensional and continuous emotion prediction. In *FG 2011*, 2011.

[11] B. Pang and L. Lee. Opinion mining and sentiment analysis. *Foundations and Trends in Information Retrieval*, 2(1-2):1–135, 2007.

[12] M. K. Pitt and N. Shephard. In N. de Freitas, A. Doucet, and N. J. Gordon, editors, *Sequential Monte Carlo Methods in Practice*. Springer-Verlag, New York, 2001.

[13] A. Savran, B. Sankur, and M. T. Bilge. Regression-based intensity estimation of facial action units. *Image and Vision Computing*, 2011. in press.

[14] B. Schuller, R. Müller, M. K. Lang, and G. Rigoll. Speaker independent emotion recognition by early fusion of acoustic and linguistic features within ensembles. In *INTERSPEECH*, pages 805–808, 2005.

[15] B. Schuller, M. Valstar, F. Eyben, R. Cowie, and M. Pantic. Avec 2012, the continuous audio/visual emotion challenge. In *AVEC 2012 Grand Challenge*.

[16] B. Schuller, M. Valstar, F. Eyben, G. McKeown, R. Cowie, and M. Pantic. Avec 2011, the audio/visual emotion challenge. In *AVEC 2011 Grand Challenge*.

[17] P. D. Turney and P. Pantel. From frequency to meaning: vector space models of semantics. *J. Artif. Int. Res.*, 37(1):141–188, 2010.

[18] D. Ververidis and C. Kotropoulos. Emotional speech recognition: Resources, features, and methods. *Speech communication*, pages 1162–1181, 2006.

[19] S. J. Young, D. Kershaw, J. Odell, D. Ollason, V. Valtchev, and P. Woodland. *The HTK Book Version 3.4*. 2006.

[20] Z. Zeng, M. Pantic, G. I. Roisman, and T. S. Huang. A survey of affect recognition methods: Audio, visual, and spontaneous expressions. *IEEE TPAMI*, 31(1):39–58, January 2009.

A Multimodal Fuzzy Inference System Using a Continuous Facial Expression Representation for Emotion Detection

Catherine Soladié
SUPELEC/IETR, Team SCEE
Avenue de la Boulaie
35576 Cesson-Sévigné
France
catherine.soladie@supelec.fr

Hanan Salam
SUPELEC/IETR, Team SCEE
Avenue de la Boulaie
35576 Cesson-Sévigné
France
hanan.salam@supelec.fr

Catherine Pelachaud
CNRS - Telecom ParisTech
37/39 rue Dareau
75014 Paris France
catherine.pelachaud@telecom-paristech.fr

Nicolas Stoiber
Dynamixyz
80 avenue des Buttes de Coesmes
35700 Rennes France
nicolas.stoiber@dynamixyz.com

Renaud Séguier
SUPELEC/IETR, Team SCEE
Avenue de la Boulaie
35576 Cesson-Sévigné
France
renaud.seguier@supelec.fr

ABSTRACT

This paper presents a multimodal fuzzy inference system for emotion detection. The system extracts and merges visual, acoustic and context relevant features. The experiments have been performed as part of the AVEC 2012 challenge. Facial expressions play an important role in emotion detection. However, having an automatic system to detect facial emotional expressions on unknown subjects is still a challenging problem. Here, we propose a method that adapts to the morphology of the subject and that is based on an invariant representation of facial expressions. Our method relies on 8 key expressions of emotions of the subject. In our system, each image of a video sequence is defined by its relative position to these 8 expressions. These 8 expressions are synthesized for each subject from plausible distortions learnt on other subjects and transferred on the neutral face of the subject. Expression recognition in a video sequence is performed in this space with a basic intensity-area detector. The emotion is described in the 4 dimensions : valence, arousal, power and expectancy. The results show that the duration of high intensity smile is an expression that is meaningful for continuous valence detection and can also be used to improve arousal detection. The main variations in power and expectancy are given by context data.

Categories and Subject Descriptors

G.3 [**Mathematics of Computing**]: Probability and Statistics—*Correlation and regression analysis*; I.4.10 [**Image Processing and Computer Vision**]: Image Representation; I.5.1 [**Pattern Recognition**]: Models

Keywords

Facial Expression Representation, Transfer learning, Fusion Techniques, Fuzzy Inference System, Context in Emotion Recognition

1. INTRODUCTION

Our aim is to develop a method to detect when changes in emotion occur. Among the various signals that can be used to detect emotions, visual and acoustic features play an important part. The context in which the video sequence is recorded also contains key information.

In this paper, we focus on a continuous representation of facial expressions that enables recognizing emotions on unknown subjects. The experiments have been performed as part of the AVEC 2012 challenge [19], which is done over a collection of audio-video sequences, displaying conversations between an emotional agent and an unknown subject. To enhance our results for the challenge, we added acoustic and context features to facial expression features. Context is information specific to AVEC database [19], for example which is the emotional agent that discusses with the subject. The relevant features from audio, video and context are used in a multimodal fuzzy inference system. The emotion is described in the 4 dimensions : valence, arousal, power and expectancy [11] and the changes in emotion are computed for each dimension using cross-correlation with ground truth labels.

Before presenting our system, we will briefly present a state-of-the-art on multimodal emotion recognition systems and on facial expression recognition.

1.1 Multimodal emotion recognition

Multimodal emotion recognition has developed in recent years [30]. The fusion of the modalities can be done at different stages. In early data fusion, that is the fusion of the features before the recognition process, the features are either directly concatenated [2] or the correlation between the features of the different mode is taken into account. This is done for instance by HMM methods [25], neural network methods [12, 14] or Bayesian network methods [21]. In late data fusion, that is the fusion of the recognition results of the various modalities, the recognition results are fused with for example empirical weights [13] or rules [18].

The majority of the systems focus on the classification of discrete emotions [2, 13, 21]. Some systems evolved towards a dimensional representation of emotions (activation, valence, evaluation) but the output value remains discrete [14]. Most systems merge data from the two modalities : acoustic (prosody) and visual (facial expressions). Context is rarely taken into account. Multimodal automatic emotion analysis is still a challenging problem as the last Audio/Visual Emotion Challenge (AVEC 2011 [20]) shows. The results of the challenge were not relevant for some dimensions (especially power) and struggled to perform better than chance.

1.2 Facial expression recognition

Many expressions recognition systems have been proposed in the last decade [10, 27]. Many of them focus on the classification of facial expressions into 6 categories corresponding to the 6 emotions universally associated with distinct facial expressions [8]. Few detect other expressions such as pain [15, 1] or deal with the intensity of the expression [9].

The choice of representation is known to influence the recognition performance. Most systems directly use the appearance features (shape and/or texture features). Other systems extract Action Units defined in the FACS system [7]. In the last few years, some continuous representations of facial expression have been proposed, using manifold learning [3, 23, 4, 26]. The aim is then to represent the whole facial expression space.

As for the multimodal analysis of emotions, challenges were organized to compare the methods on identical databases. The last one, Facial Expression Recognition and Analysis challenge (FERA 2011 [28]) consisted of the recognition of discrete emotion won by [29] and detection of AUs that our team won [22] with the ISIR laboratory. Even if the results were encouraging, the recognition rates remained low : the person-independent discrete emotion recognition did not exceed 75.2% (although the person-specific performance was 100%) and the AU detection only reached 62%.

1.3 Overview of our approach

In this paper, we propose a fully automatic system that extracts relevant features for spontaneous affective audio-video sequences and computes the potentially felt emotional state of the subject. The article focuses on facial expressions detection. The main contribution of the article is that our system adapts to the subject. Its originality is that the neutral face is automatically computed by the mean value of the appearance parameters of the video sequence and that known plausible distortions are applied on this neutral face to create a person-specific appearance space. Another main contribution is the continuous representation of facial expressions, which takes into account the intensity of the expressions, and is invariant across subjects. The particularity of the method is that we did not focus on the appearance space, which carries morphological information of the subject, but on the organization of the expressions with respect to each other. This organization is invariant across the subjects. A facial expression can then be detected with a basic intensity-area detector in this expression space.

The remainder of this paper is organized as follows. In section 2, we describe the global process for multimodal emotion recognition and we define the relevant features extraction. Section 3 focuses on the facial expression extraction. Section 4 presents the training process performed on training and development databases and the resulting fuzzy rules. Section 5 shows and discusses the results of the challenge on the test database. Section 6 concludes the paper.

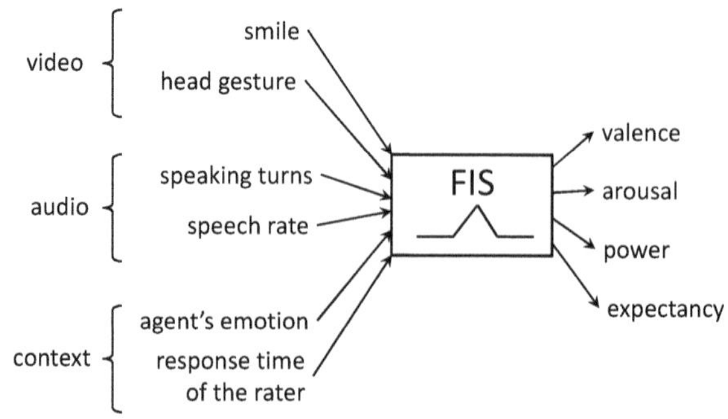

Figure 1: Overall view of the proposed method : a fuzzy inference system transforms the relevant features from video, audio and context into 4 emotional dimensions.

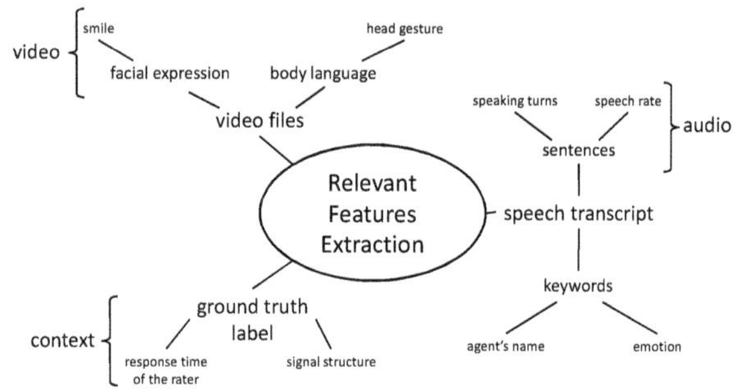

Figure 2: Sources of the relevant features : video files, speech transcripts and emotional labels.

2. A MULTIMODAL FUZZY INFERENCE SYSTEM

This section presents the global system for emotion detection. The system is based on a fuzzy inference system (see subsection 2.1). The relevant features extraction is described in subsection 2.2.

2.1 Global process

The overall process is presented in figure 1. The system is based on a fuzzy inference system that takes in input the relevant features that result from emotional states. The fuzzy inference rules are defined from the analysis of the data of the training and development databases (section 4). The output information is defuzzified to output the 4 emotional dimensions, namely valence, arousal, power and expectancy.

2.2 Relevant features extraction

The choice of the features to extract has been done according to the analysis of the ground truth emotional labels of the training and development databases (annotations of raters using FEELTRACE [6]). The chosen features were those that explain the global trend of the emotion dimen-

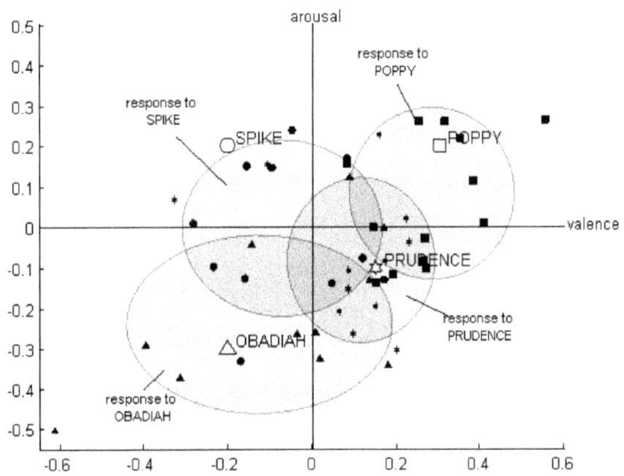

Figure 3: Displayed emotional response of subjects when interacting with agent. The emotion of the agent is showed by an empty marker (Spike is aggressive; Poppy is cheerful; Obadiah is gloomy; and Prudence is pragmatic). The mean ground truth labels of each subject responding to these agents are showed by a filled marker and their distributions are in the ellipses (mean value and standard deviation).

sions and not the small subtle variations of the emotions. The features extraction is made from 3 different data sources : videos, speech transcripts and ground truth labels (see figure 2).

2.2.1 From video files

The extracted features from video files are the facial expressions and the body language.

As the main contribution of this article is about facial expressions, a precise description of the extraction of facial expressions is presented in a dedicated section (section 3).

Concerning the body language, we computed the global movement of the head pose in the scene. The video data are analyzed using a person-independent AAM [5] built on the training and development databases. In the test phase, the pose parameters of the face are computed from the AAM model. The body movement is computed from the standard deviation of the head pose in a video sequence with a sliding temporal window of 40 seconds. The more the subject moves and makes wide movements, the higher this quantity is.

2.2.2 From speech transcripts

The features extracted from audio mode come from the analysis of the sentences and keywords.

The analysis of the sentences gives the length of the sentences pronounced by the subject. In our system, we use binary information. For each speaking turn in a conversation, if the number of words pronounced by the subject is high (above 35 words, empirical data learnt on training and development databases), the sentence is long ; otherwise, the sentence is short.

The analysis of the sentences also gives the speech rate. The speech rate is computed from the transcripts by the rate : number of words by time unit.

The conversations are performed between a subject and an emotional agent, who is set in one of the four quadrants of arousal-valence space (Spike is aggressive; Poppy is cheerful; Obadiah is gloomy; and Prudence is pragmatic). We perform a statistical analysis on the sequences for each emotional agent. Figure 3 shows that the emotional state displayed by the subject matches the one displayed by the agent. For example, if the agent is Poppy, then the subject speaking to Poppy has a tendency to display behaviors of high valence and high arousal. To find automatically which is the emotional agent of the sequences, we extract names from keywords. They provide some contextual information on which emotional agent the subject is speaking to. Indeed, at the beginning of each conversation, subjects select the agent they want to interact with by telling its name; at the end of their conversation, they select the next emotional agent for their next interaction. When the name of the agent is not pronounced, the subjects usually use emotional terms, such as 'angry' or 'annoy' for 'Spike', 'sad' for 'Obadiah' and 'fun' for 'Poppy'. Thus, the keyword 'angry' or 'Spike' appears in conversation with Spike. It is then possible, with the transcripts of a conversation, to automatically find the emotional agent of the sequence, and to deduce a statistical mean value of the subject's valence and arousal for the sequence.

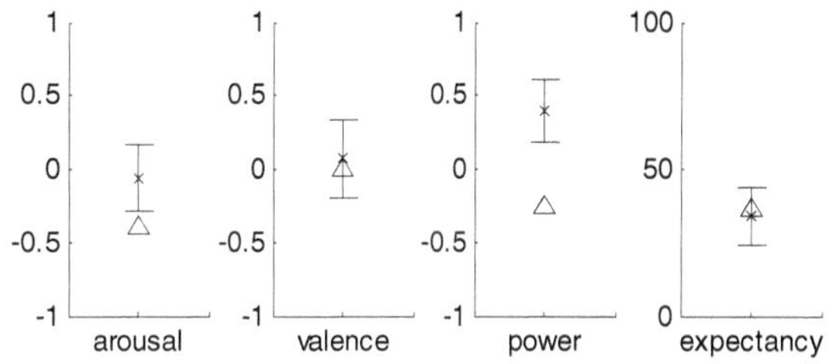

Figure 4: Impact of the response time of the raters on the ground truth labels : the triangle shows the value of the label at the beginning of the sequence and the cross shows the mean and standard deviation of the labels, for each dimension.

2.2.3 From ground truth labels

The analysis of the ground truth labels highlights a delay in the start of annotations. We computed the mean value and standard deviation of the training and development ground truth labels for each emotional dimension. We also extracted the values of the ground truth labels in the beginning of the sequences. First we noticed that the labels in the beginning of the sequences are identical for all the sequences; and secondly that they are very different from the values inside the conversation (see figure 4) for arousal and power. This may be due to the initialization of the tool used to rate and to the response time of the rater, so that the first seconds of the ground truth labels may not be representative of the subject's emotion. Nevertheless, for the challenge, we modeled this behavior with a feature as a decreasing linear function on the first 20 seconds of the conversation.

Finally, the analysis of the labels also highlights that the expectancy varies quite similarly across conversations. In the beginning of the conversation (first minute), the expectancy is low. Then, the expectancy is higher. We modeled this behavior with a square-wave signal (high value the first minute, low value otherwise).

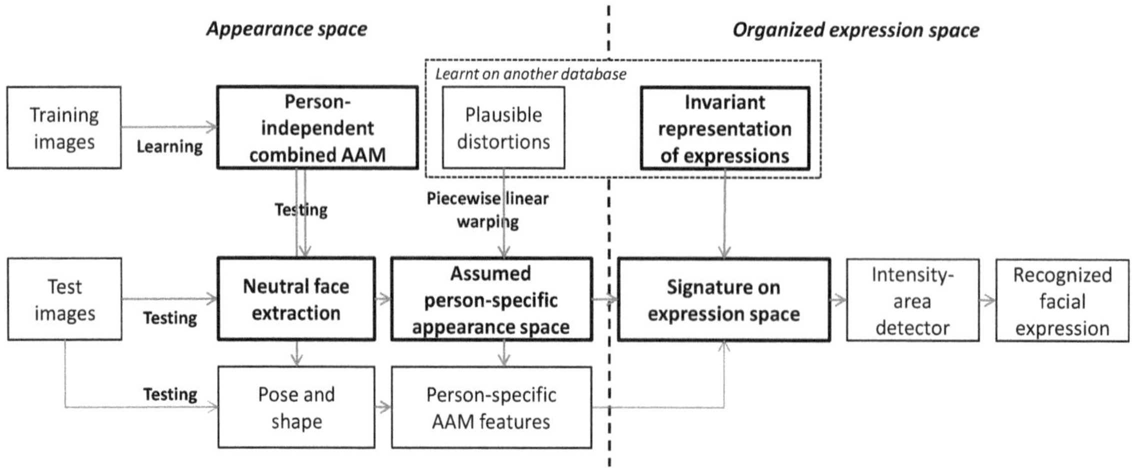

Figure 5: Overall view of the facial expression extraction. The neutral face of each subject and the shape of all the images are extracted using a person-independent combined AAM. An assumed person-specific appearance space is created by applying plausible distortions on the neutral face of the given subject. The person-specific appearance space is transformed into the expression space using an invariant organization of expressions.

3. FACIAL EXPRESSION EXTRACTION

This section presents the main contribution of the article. After a brief description of the overall process (section 3.1), each main step of the facial expression extraction is described (sections 3.2, 3.3, 3.4, 3.5).

3.1 Overview of the process

The global overview of the process is presented in figure 5. The main idea is to take into account the morphology of the subject. The process is composed of 4 steps. The first step concerns the detection of the features of the face by a person-independent AAM (section 3.2). The second step computes a person-specific appearance space (section 3.3). The third step transforms this appearance space into a person-independent expression space (section 3.4). The last step performs the expression recognition (section 3.5).

3.2 Multi-Model AAM

The shape of each face image of each video sequence is extracted using Active Appearance Models (AAM) [5]. For the training and development databases, we use a a Global Face AAM (GF-AAM) which is trained on some images of these two. Regarding the test database, the presence of hair on the face for some persons misleads the GF-AAM in finding a precise localization of the mouth. On the other hand, for other persons in the database (person with beard), a local model fails while the global model does not. So, we propose the Multi-Model AAM (MM-AAM) (cf. figure 6) for this database. This MM-AAM combines the results of a Local Mouth AAM (LM-AAM) (trained on the same images as the GF-AAM) and the GF-AAM. The best shape (between the GF-AAM and MM-AAM) is obtained by computing projection errors on the same global AAM. This permits to take advantage of the precise localization of the mouth by LM-AAM when there is hair covering the face and the ability of the GF-AAM to generalize to new faces by using the correlations between the different parts of the face for the other cases.

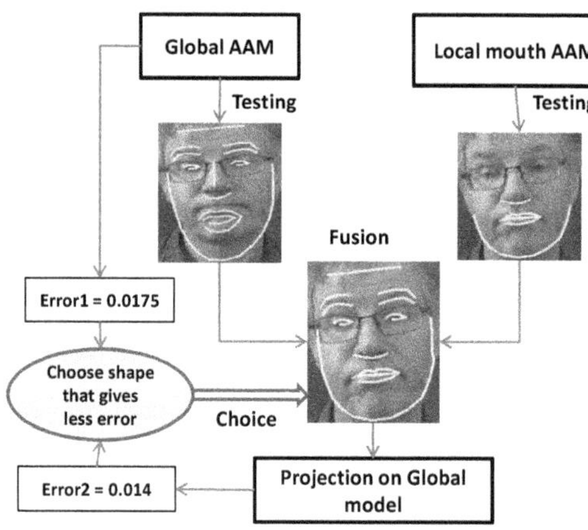

Figure 6: Example of person-independent Multi-Model AAM (MM-AAM).

The algorithm is the following:

1. Train both models: GF-AAM and LM-AAM;
2. Apply both models on the testing videos: Get the global face shape S_{GF} and the local mouth shape S_{LM};
3. Substitute mouth shape from the LM-AAM in the shape from the GF-AAM: get the Multi-Model shape S_{MM};
4. Project S_{MM} on the GF-AAM to obtain the corresponding appearance parameters and the projection error:
   (a) Align the S_{MM} to the mean shape $\bar{s}$ of GF-AAM;
   (b) Find the shape parameters b_s of S_{MM} using $s = \bar{s} + V_s b_s$. V_s are the shape eigenvectors of the GF-AAM;
   (c) Warp the texture under S_{MM} into mean shape ($\bar{g}$);
   (d) Find the texture parameters b_g using $g = \bar{g} + V_g b_g$. V_g are the texture eigenvectors of the GF-AAM;

Figure 7: Examples of neutral faces extracted from the appearance parameters of the person-independent combined AAM. The neutral face is the closest image to the mean value of the appearance parameters when the subject is not speaking.

(e) Concatenate b_s and b_g: $b = \binom{W_s b_s}{b_g}$. W_s is the weighting between pixel distances and intensities.

(f) The projected appearance parameters are then: $c = V_c b$

5. Choose the shape (S_{MM} or S_{GF}) that gives the lowest projection error defined as the difference between the model synthesized image using the appearance parameters and the texture of the real image defined by the shape.

Confidence extraction – After extracting the shapes of all the frames of the videos, each frame is given a binary confidence index. The latter is computed based on the analysis of projection errors of samples of the sequence in question.

3.3 Assumed person-specific appearance space

Our system adapts to the morphology of each subject by creating a person-specific appearance space from the neutral face and plausible expressions.

3.3.1 Neutral face extraction

The neutral face of a subject is automatically extracted from the video sequences of this subject. The extraction is made by computing the mean value of the appearance parameters of the person-independent AAM when the subject is not speaking. The neutral face is the image that has the closest appearance parameters from this mean value. Figure 7 shows some examples of neutral faces.

3.3.2 Assumed shape model

To create a person-specific appearance space, we use 8 plausible expressions of the subject and we compute a person specific shape model by applying PCA on these 8 plausible expressions plus the neutral face. Plausible expressions are computed from known distortions applied on the neutral face of the subject (see figure 8). Each point of each expression is transferred on the neutral face of the subject by piece-wise affine warping. We use 8 known distortions, learnt on another database [1]. Each distortion corresponds to a specific emotional facial expression.

3.4 Organized expression space of an unknown subject

To perform expression recognition, the person-specific appearance space is transformed into a person-independent expression space. This transformation is performed by using

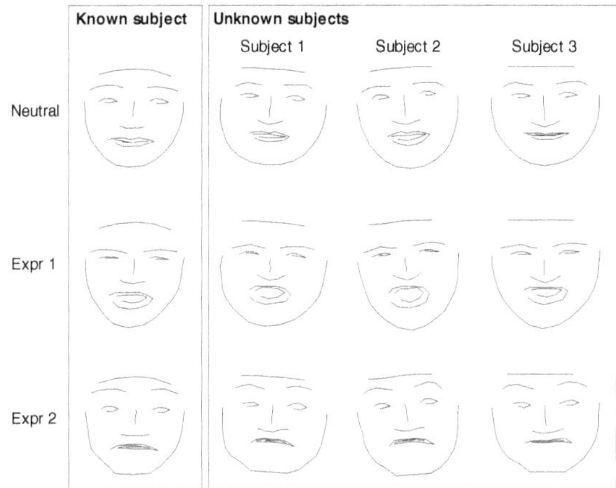

Figure 8: The plausible distortions are learnt from a known subject and applied on the neutral face of the unknown subjects. (Neutral) Neutral face of the known subject and of 3 unknown subjects. (Expr x) Real expression of the known subject and plausible expression of the unknown subjects.

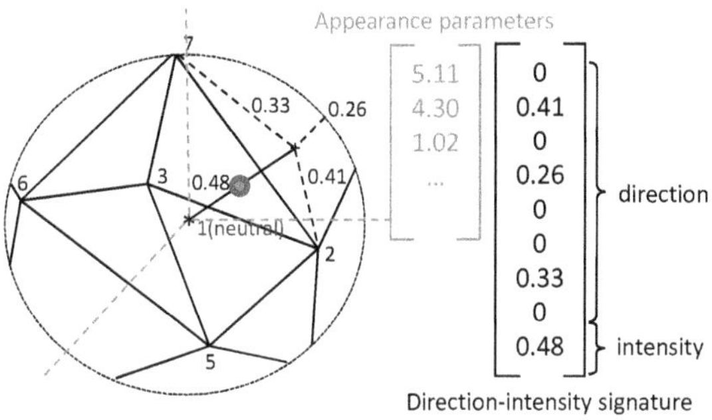

Figure 9: Transformation from appearance parameters to direction-intensity signature.

an invariant representation of facial expressions. Instead of describing one expression by its appearance features (which means taking into account the morphology of the subjects), we describe one expression by its relative position to others. We previously showed [24] that the organization of 8 expressions, with respect to each other, is person-independent.

3.4.1 Signature of an expression

As the organization of expressions is similar between subjects, one expression can be uniquely defined by its relative position to others expressions, for instance, the 8 plausible expressions created in subsection 3.3.

By computing a Delaunay tessellation on the first components of the appearance parameters of these 8 expressions plus neutral face, we get a manifold that approximates the appearance space of the subject. Each new expression is projected onto this manifold and we defined the direction-intensity signature of the new expression by :

- The direction is the barycentric coordinates of the projection on the outer surface of the manifold.

[1]The database is available at `http://www.rennes.supelec.fr/immemo/`.

Table 1: Mean correlation between relevant features and emotions dimensions.

Dimensions	Smile	Body movement	Speaking turns	Speech rate	Response time	Square-wave signal
Arousal	**0.30**	**0.15**	-0.02	0.08	**0.43**	0.19
Valence	**0.41**	0.08	0.09	0.03	0.12	-0.04
Power	0.10	-0.02	-0.13	0.11	**0.56**	0.26
Unexpectancy	0.11	0.03	**0.25**	-0.03	-0.10	**-0.21**

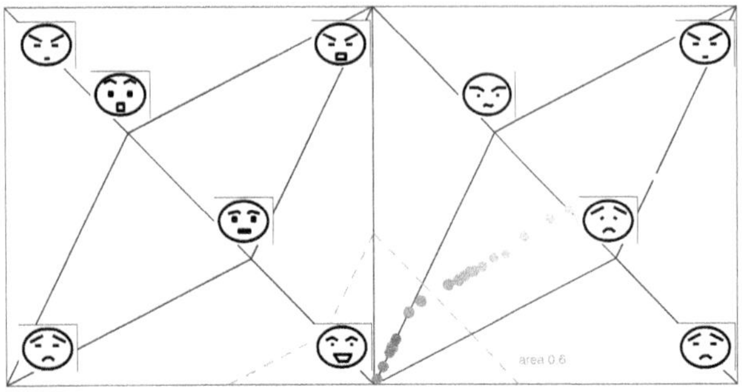

Figure 10: Trajectory of one subject's smile in the person-independent organized expression space.

- The intensity is the Euclidian distance between the neutral and the expression.

Figure 9 shows an example of the computation of the direction-intensity signature.

3.4.2 Person-independent expression space

As the direction-intensity signature is relative, it is independent of the subject. The expression space is the space of the images defined by these signatures. Figure 10 shows an extract of a video sequence that displays a smile in this space. The expression space has been unfolded in 2D. Each point corresponds to one image. The direction is given by the position of the point. The intensity is given by the size of the point.

3.5 Facial expression extraction

As the expression space is person-independent, the recognition of one expression can be achieved by a basic algorithm. For a given window, we define an area and compute the percentage of frames in this area. The direction of one expression is given by barycentric coordinates of the encompassing triangle and the intensity is between 0 (neutral) and 1 (high intensity). In our system, a smile is defined by a direction that is close to the expression E4 (corresponding to a coefficient above 0.6) and an intensity greater than 0.3. The feature 'smile' is defined by the percentage of images representing an expression of smile during a time window of 40 seconds.

4. TRAINING PROCESS

This section presents the training process used to define the fuzzy rules of the global multimodal process.

4.1 Correlation between relevant features and emotional dimensions

To find the source of the main variations of the 4 emotional dimensions, we computed the correlation between the ground truth labels of each sequence of development database and a signal that gives one of the relevant features described in section 2.2. We then compute the average value of these correlation coefficients. A high value of the mean value of the correlation coefficients indicates that the feature can be used to define the global shape of the variations of the emotional dimension. The results are given in table 1. To avoid the impact of the response time of the rater, the first seconds of the sequences have been removed from the computation of the correlation of the features other than response time.

Table 2: Fuzzy rules of the system for each dimension : Valence, Arousal, Power and Expectancy. RT: Response Time of the rater. VL: Very Low, L: Low, AL: Average low, AAL: between AL and A, A: Average, AH: Average High, H:High, VH: Very High.

Rules	Ar.	Va.	Po.	Ex.
During RT	VL	AAL	VL	
Not RT			A	
Not RT and Agent is Poppy	H	H		
Not RT and Agent is Spike	H	AL		
Not RT and Agent is Obadiah	L	L		
Not RT and Agent is Prudence	A	AH		
Not RT and Agent is unknown	A	A		
Not RT and Smile is high	VH	VH		
Sentences are long				VL
Sentences are short				VH
Discourse is beginning				VH
Discourse is established				VL

As expected, the duration of high intensity smile gives relevant information on the valence. We can notice that it also gives information on arousal. Indeed, when subjects smile, they are active. Body movement gives information on arousal. Nevertheless, the correlation is low, even lower than smile. The structure of the speaking turns (long or short sentences) gives information on expectancy. Indeed, when subjects speak (long sentences), they are not surprised (as the agent mainly provides backchannels), whereas when they answer and give short answers (short sentences), that may signify that the conversation is unexpected. Speech rate seems to be linked with power, but the correlation is low. This means that sometimes, when subjects speak fast, they are confident. The response time of the rater characterizes arousal and power with high correlation. This is due to the fact that there is a big difference between the mean value of the signal and the initial value for these two dimensions as shown in figure 4. The square-wave signal at the beginning of the conversation confirms the global change in expectancy during a conversation. High values of this feature for arousal and power are due to the response time of the rater. Finally, the impact of the agent's emotional type cannot be measured in terms of correlation, since it gives a constant value over the entire sequence (figure 3), which is a statistical mean

Table 3: Results (mean correlation coefficients) on training, development and test databases. The first value is computed on the whole sequence, for the second value, the 20 first seconds have been removed from the sequence (to avoid the effect of the response time of the rater). As comparison, the last row shows the mean correlation coefficient between one rater and the other ones.

Dimension	Train.	Devel.	Test	Raters
Arousal	**.40** .22	**.52** .32	**.42** —	**.44** .39
Valence	**.39** .31	**.47** .43	**.42** —	**.53** .50
Power	**.61** —	**.59** —	**.57** —	**.51** .36
Expectancy	**.37** .34	**.30** .29	**.33** —	**.33** .33
Mean	**.44** —	**.47** —	**.43** —	**.45** .39

value of valence and arousal. Nevertheless, this statistical mean value is used in the fuzzy rules to define the offset of the sequence (table 2).

4.2 Rules of the fuzzy system

To fuse the multi-modal features, we used a classical Mamdani type fuzzy inference system [16] where the fuzzy operator AND is product, the fuzzy implication is product, the aggregation is performed by sum and defuzzification by centroid method. The fuzzy rules of the system are listed in table 2. They are directly derived from the above analysis.

5. RESULTS AND DISCUSSION

5.1 Challenge results

Table 3 shows in bold the results on training, development and test databases. The learning has been performed on training and development databases. The results on the test database are the official results of the challenge, computed by the organizers of the challenge.

First we can note the stability of our results over the different databases, which means that our method generalizes correctly. Even if the values remain low (average of about 0.45), they are similar to those of the human raters used for ground truth labelization, which means the human raters often disagree on the variations of the emotion.

The results of the raters also show we get not as good results on valence. To define the valence, we currently use the duration of high intensity smile. Other information on facial expressions such as the lowering of the eyebrows (AU4) could give us information about a decrease in valence and could improve the results.

The difference on arousal and valence between training and development databases is mainly due to smile information. We could not find smile information for one subject in the training database; the face is half out of the screen.

5.2 Context features

As previously said, the ground truth labels of the beginning of the sequences cannot be analyzed in term of emotion (due to the response time of the rater), so that we have also computed the results excluding the 20 first seconds of the sequences. The correlation on power cannot be performed for we only used the response time of the rater for labeling. The results (our results as well as the human raters' ones) are lower especially for arousal and power, for which the response time of the rater plays an important role in the sequence labelization as showed in table 1.

The fact that expectancy rises during conversations has to be confirmed by the analysis of other databases displaying conversations to check if this information can be used in a general context.

The impact of the emotional agent can be interpreted as empathy and emotion contagion, which may be clue information in general case when audio-visual information is not available or uncertain. In our system, the way of extraction is partly specific to the database (name of the agent), and partly generic (theme of the conversation such as 'fun').

5.3 Smile

The impact of smile on arousal can be analyzed by the fact that we compute smile with a high intensity on a long duration, that is the characteristics of laughter. Other kinds of smile could be used to improve the results.

6. CONCLUSIONS

This paper has presented a facial expressions space that takes into account the morphology of the subject, and that can effectively and continuously define facial expressions. It is based on the spatial organization of expressions, one with respect to the others. This organization is invariant among the subjects. As the representation is relevant, expression recognition can then be performed with simple algorithms. Here we used an intensity-area detector.

This facial expression recognition was integrated into a global method for the detection of emotion. A fuzzy inference system is used to merge different modalities (audio, video and context) and calculate 4 emotional dimensions.

Contrary to statistical systems, in which learning must be reprocessed for each new database or context, our system can be easily adapted by removing or adding rules that are specific to the database or to the context for real life scenarios.

The results of correlation between ground truth and the obtained values (correlation coefficient of 0.43 on average on the test set) show that there are still improvements to do in order to determine the variations of emotions, even if we perform in average as good as human raters. Adding other kinds of smile and eye brow movements could improve the results.

7. ACKNOWLEDGMENTS

This research has been conducted with the support of Immemo (french ANR project) and Immersivite (Britanny Region PME project). Portions of the research in this paper use Semaine Database collected for the Semaine project (`www.semaine-db.eu` [17, 19]).

8. REFERENCES

[1] A. B. Ashraf, S. Lucey, J. F. Cohn, T. Chen, Z. Ambadar, K. M. Prkachin, and P. E. Solomon. The painful face-Pain expression recognition using active appearance models. *Image and Vision Computing*, 2009.

[2] C. Busso, Z. Deng, S. Yildirim, M. Bulut, C. Lee, A. Kazemzadeh, S. Lee, U. Neumann, and S. Narayanan. Analysis of emotion recognition using

facial expressions, speech and multimodal information. In *Proceedings of the 6th international conference on Multimodal interfaces*, 2004.

[3] Y. Chang, C. Hu, and M. Turk. Manifold of facial expression. In *Analysis and Modeling of Faces and Gestures, IEEE International Workshop on*, Nice, France, 2003. IEEE Computer Society.

[4] Y. Cheon and D. Kim. Natural facial expression recognition using differential-AAM and manifold learning. *Pattern Recognition*, 2009.

[5] T. Cootes, G. Edwards, and C. Taylor. Active appearance models. *Pattern Analysis and Machine Intelligence, IEEE Transactions on*, 2001.

[6] R. Cowie, E. Douglas-Cowie, S. Savvidou, E. McMahon, M. Sawey, and M. Schroder. Feeltrace : An instrument for recording perceived emotion in real time. In *Proceedings of the ISCA Workshop on Speech and Emotion*, 2000.

[7] P. Ekman and W. V. Friesen. *Facial action coding system: A technique for the measurement of facial movement*. Consulting Psychologists Press, Palo Alto, CA, 1978.

[8] P. Ekman, W. V. Friesen, and P. Ellsworth. *Emotion in the human face*. Cambridge University Press New York, 1982.

[9] N. Esau, E. Wetzel, L. Kleinjohann, and B. Kleinjohann. Real-time facial expression recognition using a fuzzy emotion model. In *Fuzzy Systems Conference, 2007. FUZZ-IEEE 2007. IEEE International*, 2007.

[10] B. Fasel and J. Luettin. Automatic facial expression analysis: a survey. *Pattern Recognition*, 2003.

[11] J. R. Fontaine, K. R. Scherer, E. B. Roesch, and P. C. Ellsworth. The world of emotions is not Two-Dimensional. *Psychological Science*, 2007.

[12] N. Fragopanagos and J. G. Taylor. Emotion recognition in human-computer interaction. *Neural Networks*, 2005.

[13] S. Hoch, F. Althoff, G. McGlaun, and G. Rigoll. Bimodal fusion of emotional data in an automotive environment. In *Acoustics, Speech, and Signal Processing, 2005. Proceedings.(ICASSP'05). IEEE International Conference on*, 2005.

[14] K. Karpouzis, G. Caridakis, L. Kessous, N. Amir, A. Raouzaiou, L. Malatesta, and S. Kollias. Modeling naturalistic affective states via facial, vocal, and bodily expressions recognition. *Artifical Intelligence for Human Computing*, 2007.

[15] G. C. Littlewort, M. S. Bartlett, and K. Lee. Faces of pain: automated measurement of spontaneousallfacial expressions of genuine and posed pain. In *Proceedings of the 9th international conference on Multimodal interfaces*, 2007.

[16] E. H. Mamdani and S. Assilian. An experiment in linguistic synthesis with a fuzzy logic controller. *International journal of man-machine studies*, 1975.

[17] G. McKeown, M. F. Valstar, R. Cowie, and M. Pantic. The SEMAINE corpus of emotionally coloured character interactions. In *Multimedia and Expo (ICME), 2010 IEEE International Conference on*, 2010.

[18] S. Petridis and M. Pantic. Audiovisual discrimination between laughter and speech. In *Acoustics, Speech and Signal Processing, 2008. ICASSP 2008. IEEE International Conference on*, 2008.

[19] B. Schuller, M. Valstar, F. Eyben, R. Cowie, and M. Pantic. Avec 2012 : The continuous Audio/Visual emotion challenge. In *to appear in Proc. Second International Audio/Visual Emotion Challenge and Workshop (AVEC 2012), Grand Challenge and Satellite of ACM ICMI 2012*, Santa Monica, 2012.

[20] B. Schuller, M. Valstar, F. Eyben, G. McKeown, R. Cowie, and M. Pantic. Avec 2011 : The first international Audio/Visual emotion challenge. *Affective Computing and Intelligent Interaction*, 2011.

[21] N. Sebe, I. Cohen, T. Gevers, and T. S. Huang. Emotion recognition based on joint visual and audio cues. In *Pattern Recognition, 2006. ICPR 2006. 18th International Conference on*, 2006.

[22] T. Senechal, V. Rapp, H. Salam, R. Seguier, K. Bailly, and L. Prevost. Combining AAM coefficients with LGBP histograms in the multi-kernel SVM framework to detect facial action units. In *Automatic Face & Gesture Recognition and Workshops (FG 2011), 2011 IEEE International Conference on*, 2011.

[23] C. Shan, S. Gong, and P. W. McOwan. Appearance manifold of facial expression. *Computer Vision in Human-Computer Interaction*, 2005.

[24] C. Soladie, N. Stoiber, and R. Seguier. A new invariant representation of facial expressions : definition and application to blended expressions recognition. In *to appear in Proc. Image Processing (ICIP), 2012 IEEE International Conference on*, 2012.

[25] M. Song, J. Bu, C. Chen, and N. Li. Audio-visual based emotion recognition-a new approach. In *Computer Vision and Pattern Recognition, 2004. CVPR 2004. Proceedings of the 2004 IEEE Computer Society Conference on*, 2004.

[26] N. Stoiber, R. Seguier, and G. Breton. Automatic design of a control interface for a synthetic face. In *Proceedings of the 13th international conference on Intelligent user interfaces*, 2009.

[27] Y. L. Tian, T. Kanade, and J. F. Cohn. Facial expression analysis. *Handbook of face recognition*, 2005.

[28] M. F. Valstar, B. Jiang, M. Mehu, M. Pantic, and K. Scherer. The first facial expression recognition and analysis challenge. In *Automatic Face & Gesture Recognition and Workshops (FG 2011), 2011 IEEE International Conference on*, 2011.

[29] S. Yang and B. Bhanu. Facial expression recognition using emotion avatar image. In *Automatic Face & Gesture Recognition and Workshops (FG 2011), 2011 IEEE International Conference on*, 2011.

[30] Z. Zeng, M. Pantic, G. I. Roisman, and T. S. Huang. A survey of affect recognition methods: Audio, visual, and spontaneous expressions. *Pattern Analysis and Machine Intelligence, IEEE Transactions on*, 2009.

Robust Continuous Prediction of Human Emotions using Multiscale Dynamic Cues

Jérémie Nicolle*
Univ. Pierre & Marie Curie
ISIR - CNRS UMR 7222
F-75005, Paris - France
nicolle@isir.upmc.fr

Vincent Rapp*
Univ. Pierre & Marie Curie
ISIR - CNRS UMR 7222
F-75005, Paris - France
rapp@isir.upmc.fr

Kévin Bailly
Univ. Pierre & Marie Curie
ISIR - CNRS UMR 7222
F-75005, Paris - France
bailly@isir.upmc.fr

Lionel Prevost
Univ. of French West Indies
& Guiana - LAMIA - EA 4540
Guadeloupe - France
lionel.prevost@univ-ag.fr

Mohamed Chetouani
Univ. Pierre & Marie Curie
ISIR - CNRS UMR 7222
F-75005, Paris - France
chetouani@isir.upmc.fr

ABSTRACT

Designing systems able to interact with humans in a natural manner is a complex and far from solved problem. A key aspect of natural interaction is the ability to understand and appropriately respond to human emotions. This paper details our response to the Audio/Visual Emotion Challenge (AVEC'12) whose goal is to continuously predict four affective signals describing human emotions (namely valence, arousal, expectancy and power). The proposed method uses log-magnitude Fourier spectra to extract multiscale dynamic descriptions of signals characterizing global and local face appearance as well as head movements and voice. We perform a kernel regression with very few representative samples selected via a supervised weighted-distance-based clustering, that leads to a high generalization power. For selecting features, we introduce a new correlation-based measure that takes into account a possible delay between the labels and the data and significantly increases robustness. We also propose a particularly fast regressor-level fusion framework to merge systems based on different modalities. Experiments have proven the efficiency of each key point of the proposed method and we obtain very promising results.

Categories and Subject Descriptors

H.4 [**Information Systems Applications**]: Miscellaneous; D.2.8 [**Software Engineering**]: Metrics—*complexity measures, performance measures*

*These authors equally contributed to this work.

Keywords

Affective computing, Dynamic features, Multimodal fusion, Feature selection, Facial expressions

1. INTRODUCTION

In Human-Computer Intelligent Interaction systems, a current challenge is to give the computer the ability to interact naturally with the user with some kind of emotional intelligence. Interactive systems should be able to perceive pain, stress or inattention and to adapt and respond to these affective states, or, in other words, to interact with humans vocally and visually in a natural way. An essential step towards this goal is the acquisition, interpretation and integration of human affective state within the Human-Machine communication system. To recognize affective states, human-centered interfaces should interpret various social cues from both audio and video modalities, mainly linguistic messages, prosody, body language, eye contact and facial expressions.

Automatic recognition of human emotions from both modalities has been an active field of research over the last decade. Most of the proposed systems have focused on the recognition of acted or prototypal emotions recorded in a constrained environment and leading to high recognition rates. These systems usually describe affects via a prototypal modeling approach using the six basic emotions introduced in the early 70s by Ekman [3]. Another standard way to describe facial expressions is to analyze the set of muscles movements produced by a subject. These movements are called facial Action Units (AUs) and the corresponding code is the Facial Action Coding System (FACS) [4]. The first challenge on Facial Expression Recognition and Analysis (FERA'11) focused on these two kinds of affect description. Meta-analysis of challenge results are summarized in [21]. These methods generally use discrete systems whether based on static descriptors (geometrical or appearance features) and/or on static classifiers such as Support Vector Machines [20].

However, these descriptions do not reflect real-life interactions and the resulted systems can be irrelevant to an everyday interaction where people may display subtle and complex affective states. To take this complexity into account, this classical description via prototypal modeling approach has recently evolved to a dimensional approach where emotions are described continuously within an affect space. The choice of the dimensions of this space remains an open question but Fontaine & al. [5] showed that four dimensions cover the majority of affective variability: Valence (positivity or negativity), Arousal (activity), Expectancy (anticipation) and Power (control). The Affective Computing research community has recently focused on the area of dimensional emotion prediction and the first workshop on this topic (EmoSPACE'11, [7]) was organized last year, followed by the first Audio/Visual Emotion Challenge (AVEC'11 [19]).

Usually, the most important parts of multimodal emotion recognition systems are the learning database, the extracted features, the predictor and the fusion method. More precisely, one of the main key points concerns the features' semantic level. Some methods use low-level features. For example, Wollmer et al. [23] propose an approach using features based on the optical flow. Dahmane et al. [2] use Gabor filter energies to compute their visual features. Ramirez et al. [15], conversely, prefer to extract high-level features such as gaze direction, head tilt or smile intensity. Similarly, Gunes et al. [6] focus on spontaneous head movements.

Another key aspect of this new dimensional approach is the need for the system to take the dynamic of human emotions into account. Some methods propose to directly encode dynamic information in the features. For example, Jiang et al. [8] extend the purely spatial representation LPQ to a dynamic texture descriptor called Local Phase Quantisation from Three Orthogonal Planes (LPQ-TOP). Cruz et al. [1] propose an approach that aligns the faces with Avatar Image Registration, and subsequently compute LPQ features. Mcduff et al. [9] predict valence using facial Action Unit spectrograms as features. In this study, we focus on mid-level dynamic features, extracted using different visual cues: head movements, face deformations and also global and local face appearance variations. Most methods use visual cues directly as features. In our method, dynamic information is included by computing the log-magnitude Fourier spectra of the temporal signals that describe the evolution of the previously introduced visual cues. Since an accurate and robust system should take advantage of interpreting signals from various modalities, we also include audio features to bring complementary information.

For the prediction step, different machine learning algorithms can be used. Several methods are based on context-dependent frameworks. For example, Meng et al. [11] propose a system based on Hidden Markov Models. Wollmer et al. [23] investigate a more advanced technique based on context modeling using Long Short-Term Memory neural networks. These systems provide the advantage to encode dynamics within the learning algorithm. Another solution is to base the system on a static predictor as, for instance, the well-known Support Vector Machine [1, 17]. Dynamic information being already included in our features, we chose a static predictor. The proposed method uses a kernel regressor based on the Nadaraya-Watson estimator [12]. For selecting representative samples, we perform a clustering step in a space of preselected relevant features.

To merge all visual and vocal information, various fusion strategies may be relevant. Feature-level fusion (also called early fusion) can be performed by merging extracted features from each modality into one cumulative structure and feeding it to a single classifier. This technique is appropriate for synchronized modalities but some issues may appear for unsynchronized or heterogeneous features. Another solution is decision-level fusion (or late fusion); each extracted feature set feeds one classifier and all the classifier outputs are merged to provide the final response. For example, Nicolaou et al [14] propose an output-associative fusion framework. In our case, the fusion is based on a simple method linearly combining outputs corresponding to the predictions of the four dimensions with different systems to make the final predictions. This way, the system is able to capture the correlations between the different emotion dimensions and to increase robustness by using different modalities.

The designed system is our response to the second Audio/Visual Emotion Challenge (AVEC'12) [18]. This challenge uses the SEMAINE [10] corpus as benchmarking database. Concerning SEMAINE, as Nicolaou et al. [13], we noticed some annotation issues which may directly impact the system performance. This database has been continuously annotated by humans in real-time and a delay between the affect events and the labels has thus been introduced. To avoid this issue, we present in this paper a delay probability estimation method directly used in the feature selection process.

The main contributions presented in this paper for affective signals prediction are the followings:

1. The use of the log-magnitude Fourier spectrum to include dynamic information for human emotions prediction.

2. A new correlation-based measure for the feature selection process that increases robustness to possibly time-delayed labels.

3. A fast efficient framework for regression and fusion designed for real-time implementation.

The proposed framework, presented in Fig. 1, is based on audio-visual dynamic information detailed in section 2. As visual cues, we propose a set of features based on facial shape deformations, and two sets respectively based on global and local face appearance. For each visual cue, we obtain a set of temporal signals and encode their dynamic using log-magnitude Fourier spectra. Audio information is added using the provided audio features. Regarding the prediction, we propose a method based on independent systems for each set of features and for each dimension (section 3). For each system, a new correlation-based feature selection is performed using a delay probability estimator. This process is particularly well-adapted to unsure and possibly time-delayed labels. The prediction is then done by a non-parametric regression using representative samples selected via a k-means clustering process. We finally linearly combine the 16 outputs during a fusion process to take into account dependencies between each modality and each affective dimension (section 4). Section 5 is dedicated to evaluation and analysis. Finally, conclusion and future work are presented in section 7.

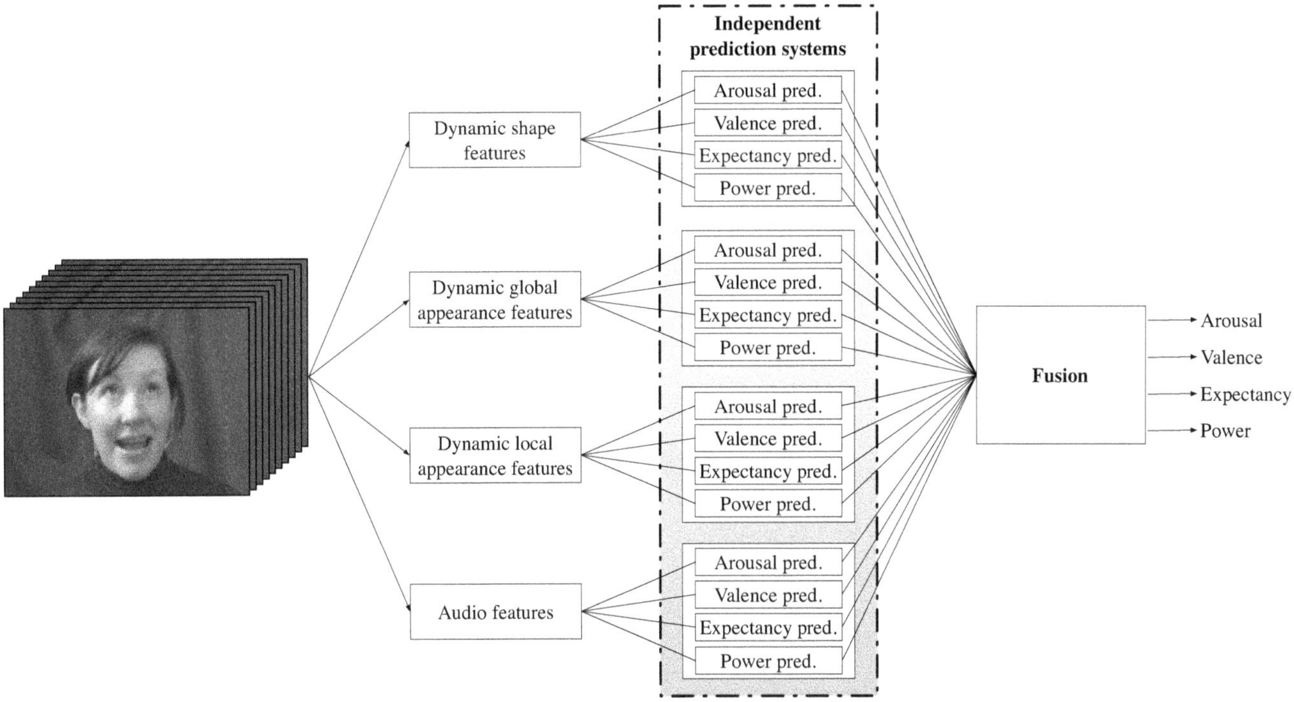

Figure 1: Overview of the proposed framework.

2. FEATURES

In this section, we present the four different sets of features we used. We propose three multiscale dynamic feature sets based on video; the fourth one is based on audio.

For the sets of visual cues, we first extract temporal signals describing the evolution of facial shape and appearance movements before calculating multiscale dynamic features on these signals. The feature extraction process is described in Fig. 2.

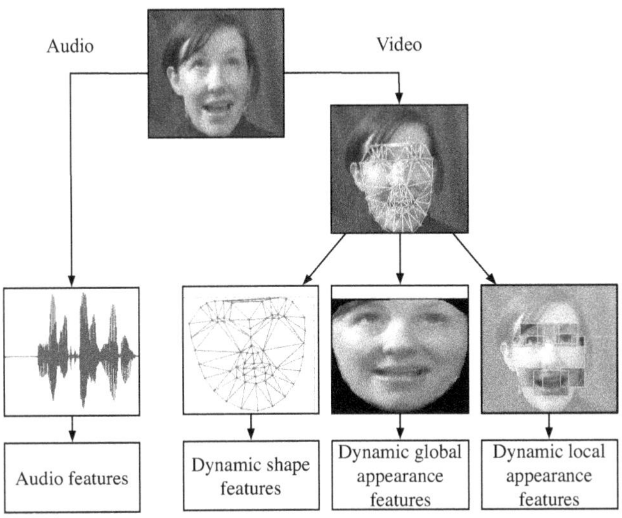

Figure 2: Feature extraction overview.

2.1 Signals extraction

We extract three kinds of signals: one based on shape parameters, and two others based on global and local face appearance.

1. Shape parameters:

   The first set of features we used is based on face deformation shape parameters. The initial step of this feature extraction process is the use of the 3D face tracker proposed in [16]. It detects the face area in the images with a Viola-Jones algorithm [22] before estimating the relative position of 66 landmarks using a Point Distribution Model (PDM). The position of the ith landmark $\mathbf{s}_i$ in the image can be expressed as:

$$\mathbf{s}_i(\mathbf{p}) = s\mathbf{R}(\bar{\mathbf{s}}_i + \mathbf{\Phi}_i\mathbf{q}) + \mathbf{t} \quad (1)$$

   where $\bar{\mathbf{s}}_i$ denotes the mean location of the ith landmark and $\mathbf{\Phi}_i$ the principal subspace matrix computed from training shape samples using principal component analysis (PCA). Here, $\mathbf{p} = \{s, \mathbf{R}, \mathbf{t}, \mathbf{q}\}$ denotes the PDM parameters, which consist of global scaling s, rotation $\mathbf{R}$ and translation $\mathbf{t}$. Vector $\mathbf{q}$ represents the deformation parameters that describe the deformation of $\mathbf{s}_i$ along each principal direction.

   As output of this system, we obtain temporal signals: some of them correspond to the external parameters and give information on the head position, and the others characterize deformations related to facial expressions.

2. Global appearance:

   The second set of features we used is based on global face appearance. First, we warp the faces into a mean model using the point locations obtained with the face tracker. This way, the global appearance will be less sensitive to shape variations and head movements, already encoded in the first set. Then, we select the most important modes of appearance variations using PCA. We obtain a set of temporal signals by projecting the warped images on the principal modes.

3. Local appearance:

   The third set is based on local face appearance. First, we extract local patches of possibly interesting areas regarding deformations related to facial expressions. We extract an area around the mouth in order to capture smiles, areas around the eyes to capture the gaze direction, around the eyebrows to capture their movements, and areas where the most common expression-related lines can appear (periorbital lines, glabellar lines, nasolabial folds and smile lines). We chose to avoid the worry lines area because of the high probability it has to be occulted by hairs. Then, we use PCA as for the global warped images to compute temporal signals corresponding to the evolution of the local appearance of the face during time.

2.2 Dynamic features

For each of these three sets, we calculate the log-magnitude Fourier spectra of the associated temporal signals in order to include dynamic information. We also calculate the mean, the standard deviation, the global energy, and the first and second-order spectral moments. We chose to compute these features every second for different sizes of windows (from one to four seconds). This multiscale extraction gives information about short-term and longer-term dynamics.

2.3 Audio features

The last set of features we used is the audio feature set given to the participants of the AVEC'12 Challenge. It contains the most commonly used audio features for the aimed task of predicting emotions from speech (energy, spectral and voice-related features).

2.4 Feature normalization

Within a set of features, the range of values can be highly different from one feature to another. In order to give the same prior to each feature, we need to normalize them. A global standardization on the whole database would be a solution but we chose to standardize each feature by subject in order to reduce the inter-subject variability. This method should be efficient under the hypothesis that the amount of data for each subject is sufficiently representative of the whole emotion space.

3. PREDICTION SYSTEM

Using each of the four feature sets, we make separate predictions for the four dimensions, leading to a total of 16 signals. The method used for each prediction is described below.

3.1 Delay probability estimation

The SEMAINE database has been continuously annotated by humans. Therefore, a delay exists between videos and labels, which may significantly corrupt the learning system [13]. We introduce in this paragraph a delay probability estimation method to avoid this issue. Let $y(t)$ be the label signal and $\{f_i(t), i \in [\![1,n]\!]\}$ be a set of n features. Making the assumption that the features that are relevant for our prediction will be more correlated to the undelayed label, we can use the sum of the correlations between the features and the τ seconds delayed label signal as a probability indice for the label to be delayed by τ seconds. Thus, we can estimate the delay probability $P(\tau)$ as follows:

$$P(\tau) = \frac{1}{A}\sum_{i=1}^{n} r(f_i(t), y(t-\tau)) \tag{2}$$

where r is the Pearson product-moment correlation coefficient defined, for two random variables X and Y as:

$$r(X,Y) = \frac{E(X-\bar{X})E(Y-\bar{Y})}{\sigma_X \sigma_Y}$$

where σ_X refers to the standard deviation of variable X and $\bar{X}$ refers to its mean. A is the normalization coefficient defined as:

$$A = \int_{-\infty}^{\infty} \sum_{i=1}^{n} r(f_i(t), y(t-\tau))d\tau$$

We calculate $P(\tau)$ for τ varying in a range $[\![0,T]\!]$ where T is the largest expected delay that we fixed at 20 seconds to obtain an estimate of the delay probability distribution in this range. Eq. 2 requires continuous functions. In our case, the data contain different video sequences. We thus estimate the delay probability as the mean of the delay probabilities estimated for the different sequences. To simplify notations, we refer to this estimate as $P(\tau)$.

In Fig. 3, we represent the four different delay probability distributions that have been learned on the training database for the first feature set. By looking at those distributions' maxima, we identify an averaged delay between 3 and 4 seconds for valence and arousal, and between 5 and 6 seconds for expectancy and power. The differences between those delays could be explained by the higher complexity of human evaluation for expectancy and power.

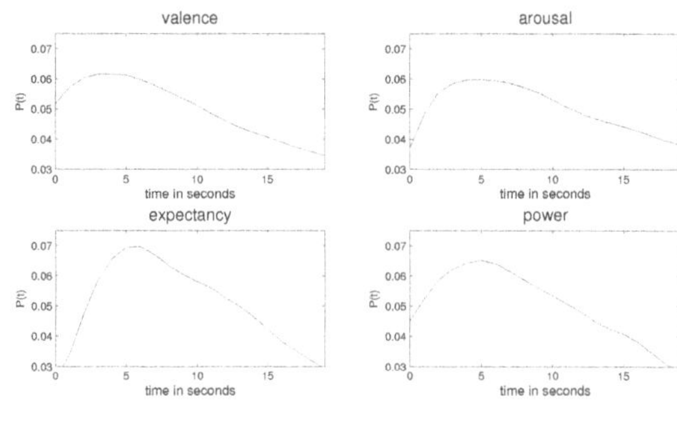

Figure 3: Delay probability distributions

3.2 Correlation-based feature selection

We present in this paragraph a feature selection method adapted to a possibly time-delayed label. The kernel regression proposed in this paper uses a similarity measure based on distances between samples. Using all the features (including the ones that are not useful for our prediction) would corrupt the regression by adding an important noise. We need to identify the most relevant ones and then reduce the number of features that will be used in our distance calculation. In order to only select the features that are correlated to the label knowing the delay probability distribution (Eq. 2), we introduce a time-persistent-correlation-based measure, defined as follows:

$$\rho(f_i(t), y(t)) = \int_{-\infty}^{\infty} r(f_i(t), y(t-\tau))P(\tau)d\tau \qquad (3)$$

This way, we consider the correlation between the feature and the label, but also between the feature and different delayed versions of the label weighted by an estimation of the delay probability. As before, with different separate video sequences, we need to calculate the mean of this measure for the different sequences to obtain a correlation score between the ith feature and the label. To simplify notations, we refer to this score as $\rho(f_i(t), y(t))$. This measure is more robust than a simple correlation measure in the case of possibly time-delayed label (see section 5.3). By selecting features maximizing $\rho(f_i(t), y(t))$, we select a relevant set of features.

3.3 Clustering

We present in this paragraph a clustering step with supervised weighted-distance learning. The feature selection step presented in the previous paragraph gives a correlation score between the label and each selected feature using Eq. 3. We use these scores as the weights of a diagonally-weighted distance d_w, defined as follows:

$$d_w(X, Y) = \sqrt{X^\top WY}$$

where $W \in \mathbb{M}_n(\mathbb{R})$ such as:

$$W_{ij} = \rho(f_i(t), y(t))\delta_{ij}$$

We perform a k-means clustering algorithm to reduce the uncertainty of the label by grouping samples that are close in the sense of the learned distance d_w. We calculate the label of each group as the mean of the labels of the group. In order to initialize the algorithm, we sort out the samples by label values and gather them in k groups of the same size. We calculate the initialization seeds as the means of the features of each group's samples. This initialization is done to ease the repeatability of the clustering and because we expect to gather samples with neighboring labels after the clustering algorithm by using the learned distance d_w. This step leads to the identification of a set of representative samples.

3.4 Kernel regression

After these learning steps, the prediction is done by a kernel regression using the Nadaraya-Watson estimator ([12]). We use a radial basis function (RBF) combined with the previously learned weighted-distance d_w as kernel. Let $\{\mathbf{x_j} \in \mathbb{R}^n, j \in [\![1, m]\!]\}$ be the feature vectors of the m representative samples obtained after the clustering step, and $\{y_j, j \in [\![1, m]\!]\}$ be the associated labels. The prediction for a sample s described by feature vector $\mathbf{x_s} \in \mathbb{R}^n$ is given by the following formula:

$$\hat{y}(s) = \frac{\sum_{j=1}^{m} K_\sigma(\mathbf{x_s}, \mathbf{x_j})y_j}{\sum_{j=1}^{m} K_\sigma(\mathbf{x_s}, \mathbf{x_j})} \qquad (4)$$

where σ is the spread of the radial basis function and K is defined as:

$$K_\sigma(\mathbf{x_s}, \mathbf{x_j}) = e^{-\frac{d_w(\mathbf{x_s}, \mathbf{x_j})^2}{\sigma}} \qquad (5)$$

As a final step, we proceed to a temporal smoothing to reduce the noise of the regressor output.

4. FUSION

Using the regression method described in the previous section, we obtain 16 signals, which are the predictions of the four dimensions using the four different sets of features. In order to fuse these signals and make the final prediction of the four dimensions, we chose to use local linear regressions to estimate linear relationships between the signals and the labels. More precisely, the coefficients of these linear relationships are estimated as the means of the different linear regressions coefficients weighted by the Pearson's correlation between the predicted signal and the label of each sequence. Let $\{y_i^j, i \in [\![1, n_s]\!], j \in \{V, A, E, P\}\}$ be the labels of the n_s video sequences of the learning set. Let $\{S_i, i \in [\![1, n_s]\!]\}$ be the matrices containing the 16 predictions of our system on the n_s sequences of the training set (previously standardized). We estimate the four vectors of coefficients $\alpha_j \in \mathbb{R}^{16}$ of the linear relationships as follows:

$$\alpha_j = \frac{\sum_{i=1}^{n_s} r(\beta_i^j S_i, y_i^j)\beta_i^j}{\sum_{i=1}^{n_s} r(\beta_i^j S_i, y_i^j)} \qquad (6)$$

where $\beta_i^j = (S_i^\top S_i)^{-1} S_i^\top y_i^j$ is the ordinary least squares coefficients vector for sequence i and label j. We can then calculate our final predictions for the four dimensions $\{\hat{y}_j, j \in \{V, A, E, P\}\}$ as: $\hat{y}_j = \alpha_j S_t$ where S_t is a matrix containing the 16 standardized predictions of our regressors on the test sequence we aim to predict.

5. EXPERIMENTS

In this section, we present some experiments we carried out to evaluate the different key points of our method. In order to be robust in generalization, we chose to optimize the hyperparameters in subject-independent cross-validation (each training partition does not contain the tested subject).

As evaluation procedure, we first present the results of the full system (with feature normalization by subject, our time-persistent-correlation measure and our regression framework). Then, we evaluate the contribution of each key point by replacing it by a more commonly used process (global normalization, Pearson's correlation and Support Vector Regression):

1. Normalization by subject, Time-persistent-correlation, Kernel regression (sect. 5.1)

2. Global normalization, Time-persistent-correlation, Kernel regression. (sect. 5.2)

3. Normalization by subject, Standard correlation, Kernel regression. (sect. 5.3)

4. Normalization by subject, Time-persistent-correlation, SVR. (sect. 5.4)

5.1 Fusion evaluation

The proposed fusion method, which is based on a simple linear combination of the inputs learned via local linear regressions, is particularly fast and well-suited for a real-time system. To evaluate the efficiency of this fusion method and the contribution of each feature set, we present the results we obtained by learning on the training set and testing on the development set in Table 1.

Table 1: Pearson's correlations averaged over all sequences of the AVEC'12 development set. Results are given for valence, arousal, expectancy and power. We also indicate the mean of these four dimensions. S corresponds to the shape features. GA to the global appearance features. LA to the local appearance features and A to the audio features. F corresponds to the fusion.

	Val	Aro	Exp	Pow	Mean
S	0.319	0.538	**0.365**	0.429	0.413
GA	0.281	0.498	0.347	0.431	0.389
LA	**0.354**	0.470	0.323	0.432	0.395
A	-0.057	0.445	0.280	0.298	0.241
F	0.350	**0.644**	0.341	**0.511**	**0.461**

We can see that visual features give better results than audio features. Local appearance-based features give a better valence prediction than the other sets. The fusion system significantly improves arousal and power predictions giving a mean score increased by 11.7%. We can notice that when the four predictions (using each set of features) are accurate, the fusion is more successful. On the contrary, the prediction scores of valence and expectancy are lower and the fusion does not improve the system performance.

5.2 Normalization evaluation

In this subsection, we evaluate the effect of the standardization of the features that we performed by subject in order to reduce the inter-subject variability. We compare the results we obtained (presented in the previous table) to those achieved with a global standardization on the whole training set (Table 2).

The normalization by subject has increased the mean score by 9.8%. The effect on valence is more important than on the other dimensions, which can be explained because the selected features for valence predictions are more sensitive to human morphological variations. Most of the features selected for the three other dimensions are high-frequency subbands energies extracted from the temporal signals, which are more robust to morphological variations than the signals' mean values that seem to be useful to predict valence.

Table 2: Pearson's correlations averaged over all sequences of the AVEC'12 development set in the case of a global standardization instead of a standardization by subject.

	Val	Aro	Exp	Pow	Mean
S	0.079	0.526	0.373	0.463	0.361
GA	0.102	0.471	**0.353**	0.416	0.335
LA	**0.314**	0.436	0.311	0.441	0.376
A	-0.069	0.509	0.227	0.254	0.230
F	0.199	**0.633**	0.331	**0.515**	**0.420**

5.3 Time-persistent-correlation evaluation

For evaluating the efficiency of the new proposed correlation-based measure, we compare our results to those we obtain by selecting the features with a standard Pearson's correlation measure which does not take the delay into account. The results are presented in Table 3.

Table 3: Pearson's correlations averaged over all sequences of the AVEC'12 development set in the case of the use of Pearson's correlation instead of our new time-persistent-correlation for feature selection.

	Val	Aro	Exp	Pow	Mean
S	0.299	0.527	0.273	0.413	0.378
GA	0.297	0.489	0.279	0.392	0.364
LA	0.303	0.464	0.294	0.411	0.368
A	0.017	0.426	0.261	0.265	0.242
F	**0.333**	**0.652**	**0.301**	**0.453**	**0.435**

The use of the proposed time-persistent-correlation-based measure has increased the mean score by 6%, which can be explained by the improved robustness of the proposed measure to possibly time-delayed labels.

5.4 Regressor evaluation

Our regression method, which consists of a clustering and a kernel regression, is particularly fast to learn and compute and is therefore suited for real-time implementation. We compare our method to the commonly used Support Vector Regression combined with the kernel defined in Eq. 5. As for our method, the hyperparameters are optimized in subject-independent cross-validation. The obtained results are presented on Table 4.

Table 4: Pearson's correlations averaged over all sequences of the AVEC'12 development set with a Support Vector Regression.

	Val	Aro	Exp	Pow	Mean
S	0.286	0.504	**0.360**	0.442	0.398
GA	0.252	0.393	0.347	0.404	0.349
LA	**0.363**	0.473	0.309	0.411	0.389
A	-0.089	0.400	0.232	0.380	0.231
F	0.275	**0.591**	0.297	**0.493**	**0.414**

The mean score after fusion has increased by 11% by using our method. However, we can see that the fusion is less efficient with SVR than with our regression method. It can be explained by the fact that the fusion coefficients have been estimated using the SVR predictions on the training set. A likely explanation could be that SVR are prone to over-fitting. A solution to this issue would be to learn the fusion coefficients in cross-validation. It is thus not relevant to compare the results after fusion. It is more reliable to compare our regression method to the SVR feature set by feature set. We obtain, in this case, an averaged gain of 5%.

6. RESULTS ON THE TEST SET

We learned our system on the concatenation of the training and the development sets to compute our predictions on the test set. We compare in Table 5 our results to those given in the baseline paper [18]. We can notice that the results obtained on the test set are quite similar to those obtained on the development set. This highlights the high generalization power of the proposed framework. It can be explained by the small number of representative samples for the kernel regression (60 in our system) which limits the flexibility of the model and allows the system to only capture important trends in the data.

Table 5: Pearson's correlations averaged over all sequences of the AVEC'12 test set.

	Val	Aro	Exp	Pow	Mean
Our method	**0.341**	**0.612**	**0.314**	**0.556**	**0.456**
Baseline	0.146	0.149	0.110	0.138	0.136

7. CONCLUSION

We presented a complete framework for continuous prediction of human emotions based on features characterizing head movements, face appearance and voice in a dynamic manner by using log-magnitude Fourier spectra. We introduced a new correlation-based measure for feature selection and evaluated its efficiency and robustness in the case of possibly time-delayed labels. We proposed a fast regression framework based on a supervised clustering followed by a Nadaraya-Watson kernel regression that appears to outperform, for the aimed task, Support Vector Regression. Our fusion method is based on simple local linear regressions and significantly improves our results. Because of the high power of generalization of our method, we directly learned our fusion parameters using our regressors outputs on the training set. In order to improve the fusion for methods that are more prone to over-fitting, we would have to learn these parameters in cross-validation. Our system has been designed for the Audio/Visual Emotion Challenge (AVEC'12) which uses Pearson's correlation as evaluation measure. Therefore, every step of our method has been built and optimized to maximize this measure. An accurate system for everyday interactions would need to be efficient in terms of correlation but also in terms of Root-Mean-Square Error (RMSE). Some modifications on our system would be needed to increase its performance regarding this measure. The SEMAINE database on which our system has been learned and tested contains videos of natural interactions but recorded in a very constraint environment. A perspective for adapting these kinds of human emotion prediction systems to real conditions, as for assistance robotics, would be to learn the system on "in the wild" data

8. ACKNOWLEDGMENTS

This work has been partially supported by the French National Agency (ANR) in the frame of its Technological Research CONTINT program (IMMEMO, project number ANR-09-CORD-012), the French FUI project PRAMAD2 (project number J11P159) and the Cap Digital Business cluster for digital content

9. REFERENCES

[1] A. Cruz, B. Bhanu, and S. Yang. A psychologically-inspired match-score fusion model for video-based facial expression recognition. In *Proc. of Affective Computing and Intelligent Interaction (ACII'11)*, pages 341–350, 2011.

[2] M. Dahmane and J. Meunier. Continuous emotion recognition using gabor energy filters. In *Proc. of Affective Computing and Intelligent Interaction (ACII'11)*, pages 351–358, 2011.

[3] P. Ekman. Facial expression and emotion. *American Psychologist*, 48(4):384, 1993.

[4] P. Ekman and W. Friesen. Facial action coding system: A technique for the measurement of facial action. *Manual for the Facial Action Coding System*, 1978.

[5] J. Fontaine, K. Scherer, E. Roesch, and P. Ellsworth. The world of emotions is not two-dimensional. *Psychological science*, 18(12):1050, 2007.

[6] H. Gunes and M. Pantic. Dimensional emotion prediction from spontaneous head gestures for interaction with sensitive artificial listeners. In *Proc. of Intelligent Virtual Agents (IVA'10)*, pages 371–377, 2010.

[7] H. Gunes, B. Schuller, M. Pantic, and R. Cowie. Emotion representation, analysis and synthesis in continuous space: A survey. In *Proc. IEEE Int'l Conf. Face & Gesture Recognition(FG'11)*, pages 827–834, 2011.

[8] B. Jiang, M. Valstar, and M. Pantic. Action unit detection using sparse appearance descriptors in space-time video volumes. In *Proc. IEEE Int'l Conf. Face & Gesture Recognition(FG'11)*, pages 314–321, 2011.

[9] D. McDuff, R. El Kaliouby, K. Kassam, and R. Picard. Affect valence inference from facial action unit spectrograms. In *Proc. IEEE Int'l Conf. Computer Vision and Pattern Recognition Workshops (CVPRW'10)*, pages 17–24, 2010.

[10] G. McKeown, M. Valstar, R. Cowie, and M. Pantic. The semaine corpus of emotionally coloured character interactions. In *Proc. IEEE Int'l Conf. on Multimedia and Expo (ICME'10)*, pages 1079–1084, 2010.

[11] H. Meng and N. Bianchi-Berthouze. Naturalistic affective expression classification by a multi-stage approach based on hidden markov models. In *Proc. of Affective Computing and Intelligent Interaction (ACII'11)*, pages 378–387, 2011.

[12] E. Nadaraya. On estimating regression. *Theory of Prob. and Appl.*, 9:141–142, 1964.

[13] M. Nicolaou, H. Gunes, and M. Pantic. Automatic segmentation of spontaneous data using dimensional labels from multiple coders. In *Workshop on Multimodal Corpora: Advances in Capturing, Coding and Analyzing Multimodality*, pages 43–48, 2010.

[14] M. Nicolaou, H. Gunes, and M. Pantic. Output-associative rvm regression for dimensional and continuous emotion prediction. *Image and Vision Computing*, 2012.

[15] G. Ramirez, T. Baltrušaitis, and L. Morency. Modeling latent discriminative dynamic of multi-dimensional affective signals. In *Proc. of Affective Computing and Intelligent Interaction (ACII'11)*, pages 396–406, 2011.

[16] J. M. Saragih, S. Lucey, and J. F. Cohn. Deformable Model Fitting by Regularized Landmark Mean-Shift. *International Journal of Computer Vision*, 91(2):200–215, Sept. 2010.

[17] A. Sayedelahl, P. Fewzee, M. Kamel, and F. Karray. Audio-based emotion recognition from natural conversations based on co-occurrence matrix and frequency domain energy distribution features. In *Proc. of Affective Computing and Intelligent Interaction (ACII'11)*, pages 407–414, 2011.

[18] B. Schuller, M. Valstar, F. Eyben, R. Cowie, and M. Pantic. Avec 2012 – the continuous audio/visual emotion challenge. In *Proc. Second International Audio/Visual Emotion Challenge and Workshop (AVEC'12) to appear*, 2012.

[19] B. Schuller, M. Valstar, F. Eyben, G. McKeown, R. Cowie, and M. Pantic. Avec 2011–the first international audio/visual emotion challenge. In *Proc. of Affective Computing and Intelligent Interaction (ACII'11)*, pages 415–424, 2011.

[20] T. Senechal, V. Rapp, H. Salam, R. Seguier, K. Bailly, and L. Prevost. Facial action recognition combining heterogeneous features via multi-kernel learning. *IEEE Transactions on Systems, Man, and Cybernetics–Part B*, 42(4):993–1005, 2012.

[21] M. Valstar, M. Mehu, B. Jiang, M. Pantic, K. Scherer, B. Jiang, M. Valstar, M. Pantic, M. Valstar, B. Jiang, et al. Meta-analysis of the first facial expression recognition challenge. *IEEE Transactions on Systems, Man, and Cybernetics–Part B*, 2012.

[22] P. Viola and M. Jones. Robust real-time face detection. *International journal of computer vision*, 57(2):137–154, 2004.

[23] M. Wöllmer, M. Kaiser, F. Eyben, and B. Schuller. Lstm-modeling of continuous emotions in an audiovisual affect recognition framework. *Image and Vision Computing*, 2012.

Elastic Net for Paralinguistic Speech Recognition

Pouria Fewzee
Centre for Pattern Analysis and Machine Intelligence, University of Waterloo
200 University Ave. W, Waterloo, ON, Canada
spfewzee@uwaterloo.ca

Fakhri Karray
Centre for Pattern Analysis and Machine Intelligence, University of Waterloo
200 University Ave. W, Waterloo, ON, Canada
karray@uwaterloo.ca

ABSTRACT

Given the fact that the length of the feature vector that is being used for the paralinguistic recognition of speech has exceeded some thousands, the importance of a sparse representation of a model becomes notable. The importance of a sparse representation is mainly due to the more interpretability, higher generalization capability, and numerically more efficiency of such a model. In this work, as an endeavor to search for a sparse representation of speech features used for paralinguistic speech modeling, we make use of the elastic net. As for the benchmark, we use the frameworks of the second audio/visual emotion challenge and the Interspeech 2012 speaker trait challenge. Also proposed in this work is the use of part-of-speech tags as syntactic features of speech for emotional speech recognition. Results of this work show that despite the relatively small number of features that is used for the modeling tasks, generalization capability of the suggested models is comparable to those of other models that use thousands of features and more elaborate learning algorithms.

Categories and Subject Descriptors

H.4 [**Information Systems Applications**]: Miscellaneous; G.3 [**Probability and Statistics**]: [Correlation and regression analysis]

General Terms

Algorithms, Experimentation, Theory

Keywords

Affective Computing, Emotion Recognition, Trait Recognition, Speech, Dimensionality Reduction

1. INTRODUCTION

Paralinguistic or nonverbal speech recognition refers to the problem of measuring the qualities of vocal expressions, which do not depend on the actual verbal content of expressions [14]. Also referred to as affective speech recognition, it aims at recognizing not what is said in an utterance, but how it is said. A natural application of this problem is to human-computer interaction (HCI). That is, to enable computers to make use of those qualities, in order to increase operation performance by reducing users' frustration during interactions [12]. In this work, we are interested in measuring some of the qualities of speakers regarding their emotional state, as well as their trait. More specifically, we consider four emotion primitives, namely arousal, expectancy, power, and valence, and three qualities of speaker's trait, including personality, likability, and intelligibility. Therefore, the problem that we are undertaking is to recognize each of those qualities of speech, given a speech sample.

Paralinguistic analysis of speech can be based on acoustic and linguistic features. From the category of acoustic features, prosodic and spectral features have been commonly used by the community [18, 16]. And from the linguistic category, words have been frequently used as semantic cues of speech [15]. In this work, as for the acoustic features, we make use of a sense of binned normalized power spectrum of speech signal, introduced as spectral energy distribution or SED [2]. This set of features is used to model the relative share of spectral intervals in the power spectrum. SED is shown to be efficiently informative for extracting the emotional contents of speech [2]. On the other hand, as for the linguistic features, we propose the use of syntax, as opposed to semantics. For this purpose, we use part-of-speech (POS) tags as a set of linguistic features.

Given a set of features $\mathbf{x}$, the objective of the next step is to find a mapping between $\mathbf{x}$ and the affective content of speech $\mathbf{y}$, which is the objective of supervised learning. That is to say, to capture the sources of variation between $\mathbf{x}$ and $\mathbf{y}$. A part of this problem is to (1) deal with dimensionality reduction, and then to use the reduced set of features $\hat{\mathbf{x}}$ to (2) build a model. Different approaches have been used to deal with the two problems. For dimensionality reduction, the use of wrappers [24], filters [8], and projection methods [10] have been frequently seen in the literature of this problem. On the other hand, for statistical modeling side of the problem, support vector machines [13], decision trees [19], neural networks [25], and different types of probabilistic approaches [26] have been commonly employed. In this work, we are interested in the embedded family of methods, which essentially combine the objectives of the two problems. That is, to perform dimensionality reduction in the body of the learning procedure of a model. For this purpose,

ICMI'12, October 22–26, 2012, Santa Monica, California, USA.

we specifically put the elastic net [27] into practice. Beside the mentioned advantageous characteristic of the elastic net, we use elastic net in this work to make it more known to the speech research community [20, 1].

To investigate the applicability of the acoustic features and the proposed linguistic feature, as well as our choice of model and learning algorithm, we have run some experiments based on the second international audio/visual emotion challenge [17] and the Interspeech 2012 speaker trait challenge [16]. The emotion challenge is based on the continuous notion of emotion primitives, which entails a multidimensional regression problem. On the other hand, for the speaker trait challenge, the presented problem is to recognize the high/low extents of speakers' personality, likability, and intelligibility dimensions, and hence requires solving a multidimensional classification problem.

The rest of this work is organized as follows. In Section two, we talk about dimensionality reduction and different choices for dealing with that problem, and we review the elastic net. Then, in Section three, we present the acoustic and linguistic features that we use in this work. Section four is dedicated to the experimental results of this study; in this section, we present and discuss the results of the experiments. This work is brought to an end by concluding remarks.

2. DIMENSIONALITY REDUCTION

Given explanatory variables $\{\mathbf{x}_1, \dots, \mathbf{x}_p\} = \mathbf{X} \in \mathcal{X}$ and response variable $\mathbf{y}$, the objective of dimensionality reduction is to find a subspace $\hat{\mathcal{X}} \subseteq \mathcal{X}$ with minimal dimensionality d, which can satisfy a particular criterion. In the case of supervised learning, the criterion is to maximize the generalization capabilities of a resulting model. Another common criterion is to minimize the reconstruction error.

Dimensionality reduction algorithms can be categorized as filters, wrappers, or embedded methods [3]. As a few examples, one can think of correlation-based [4] and information theoretic [11] feature selection methods, and Laplacian [5] and Fisher scores from the the filters category; sequential forward selection and backward elimination from the category of wrappers; and ridge regression [6], the Lasso [21], and the elastic net [27] from the embedded category of methods. To explain each of the approaches, we look at those points that make them different. One difference between the three families is the decision criterion that each one uses. Wrappers and embedded methods depend on the prediction performance as their criteria (direct methods), whereas filters use some criteria independent of the prediction accuracy, however relevant in some ways (indirect methods). As another difference, filters and wrappers are considered as preprocessing of the data, whereas embedded methods integrate dimensionality reduction in the body of learning algorithms.

Regardless of the nature of the learning problem, which can be supervised or unsupervised, in the search for the subspace $\hat{\mathcal{X}}$, either to take the response variable $\mathbf{y}$ into consideration or not, is the matter of supervised or unsupervised dimensionality reduction methods. Wrappers and embedded methods are hence essentially supervised methods, however filters can be either of them. As long as the accuracy of prediction is concerned, it is obvious that those algorithms which are supervised and moreover depend on the prediction performance are more likely to suggest a better solution.

From another point of view, dimensionality reduction algorithms can be categorized as feature selection or feature extraction. Feature selection algorithms select a subset of primary features, whereas feature extraction algorithms give out a combination of those. In other words, if we assume $\hat{\mathbf{X}} = \mathbf{XW}$, for selection methods, each of the columns of $\mathbf{W}$ will have all zero entries except one, where the non-zero entry will indicate the index of a selected variable. On the other hand, for projection methods, entries of $\mathbf{W}$ may take values from all over the range. Depending on one's perspective, one of the two approaches might be preferable over the other. A major advantage of the selection algorithms is that they preserve the nature of the original variables, and that makes the interpretation of a model more feasible. Wrappers and embedded methods are variable selection algorithms, however there are filter methods from both selection and extraction categories.

What wrappers do is simply to go over most, if not all, of the possible combinations of features and evaluate their prediction accuracy by employing them in learning tasks. Although they can potentially converge to the globally optimal subset of variables, they can also be very computationally expensive. On the contrary, filter methods are not as computationally demanding, however due to the departure of their selection criteria from minimizing the prediction error, they usually lead to suboptimal solutions. Most appealingly, embedded methods are not as computationally expensive as wrappers and unlike filters they have the potential of finding an optimal subset of features.

As follows, we review the elastic net, which is from the family of embedded methods.

2.1 Elastic Net

Being a linear combination of the ridge regression [6] and the Lasso [21], the elastic net [27, 22] solves the following problem.

$$\min_{(\boldsymbol{\beta},\beta_0)\in\mathbb{R}^{p+1}} \left[\frac{1}{2n}\sum_{i=1}^{n}(y_i - \beta_0 - \mathbf{x}\boldsymbol{\beta})^2 + \lambda \mathbf{P}_\alpha(\boldsymbol{\beta})\right] \quad (1)$$

where

$$\begin{aligned} \mathbf{P}_\alpha(\boldsymbol{\beta}) &= (1-\alpha)\frac{1}{2}||\boldsymbol{\beta}||^2_{\ell_2} + \alpha||\boldsymbol{\beta}||_{\ell_1} \\ &= \sum_{j=1}^{p}[\frac{1}{2}(1-\alpha)\beta_j^2 + \alpha|\beta_j|] \end{aligned} \quad (2)$$

Where n, p, and $\boldsymbol{\beta}$ are the sample size, the dimensionality of the feature space, and the parameters of the linear regression, respectively.

For $\alpha = 0$ and 1 elastic net reduces respectively to the ridge regression and the Lasso. Ridge regression is a shrinkage method and due to the smoothness of the ℓ_2 norm, it always keeps all the explanatory variables in the model. On the contrary, due to the sharp edges of the ℓ_1 constraint, the Lasso provides a compact representation of the feature space. The reason for this behavior and that of the ℓ_2 norm can been found by examining the intersection of the error contour, with respect to the regressors, and the constraints in a solution of the constrained optimization problem. In the case of the ℓ_2 constraint, the intersection can happen arbitrarily wherever on the regressors' hyperplane, whereas in the case of the ℓ_1 constraint, due to the sharp edges of the constraint at the axes, it is more likely to take place in one of the sub-spaces, which implies zero value for all the variables which are independent of the subspace.

Back to the comparison of the ridge regression and the Lasso, despite the sparse representation that the Lasso suggests, it has some limiting attributes. One is that the number of selected variables by the Lasso may not exceed the sample size and this becomes a problem when $p > n$. Also, when a group of variables are highly correlated, Lasso does not make a good selection. It is shown that in such cases, and when $n > p$, the ridge regression results in better prediction performances [21]. The elastic net is therefore proposed [27] to preserve the sparse representation of the Lasso and to alleviate its downsides.

Going back to the choice of α, as the parameter departs zero and gets closer to one, the elastic net behaves more like the Lasso than the ridge regression. For instance, by doing so, for a fixed λ, the resulting answer will become sparser. It is clear that the sparsity of the model also depends on λ: The smaller the parameter, the more number of features will be kept in the model. A proper choice of the two parameters should be set by cross validation.

From a probabilistic point of view, elastic net can be seen as a probability distribution (in the case of Equation 1, a Gaussian distribution) of prediction error, which is constrained with a Gaussian and Laplace prior distributions.

3. SPEECH FEATURES

In this section, we present the acoustic and linguistic features that we use in this work.

3.1 Acoustic

Spectral energy distribution (SED) is shown to be informative for capturing the emotional contents of speech [2]. In this work, we intend to use SED for continuous emotional speech estimation and speaker trait recognition.

Given a speech signal $s[n]$, SED is composed of a set of components, where component i is defined as follows.

$$SED^i = \sum_{i=1}^{N}(H[k - L_i] - H[k - U_i])g(S[k])^2. \quad (3)$$

In this formulation, $S[k]$ denotes the discrete fourier transform of the speech signal $s[n]$, H is the unit step function, L_i and U_i confine the focus of the spectral interval, corresponding to the component, to a specific area in the spectrum, $g(.)$ is a normalizing function, and N is the size of $s[n]$. As for the choice of function $g(.)$, the family of rational exponents is used.

$$g(S) = S^p; 0 < p \leq 1. \quad (4)$$

According to this formulation, SED is a binned normalized power spectrum of $s[n]$ [2].

3.2 Linguistic

Prosodic structure of a spoken sentence is directly affected by intonation. Intonation in turn, depends on various factors, including the syntactic structure of the sentence. In addition, it is known that the emotional characteristics of a spoken sentence is partially derivable from the prosodic features of speech. However, according to our discussion of intonation and the role of syntax, we are required to distinguish between linguistic (verbal) and paralinguistic (nonverbal) prosodic information. Therefore, for the sake of a more accurate model, we are inclined to propose the application of syntactic features of language for emotional speech recognition.

Symbol	RF (%)	Description
CC	2.70	Coordinating conjunction
CD	0.40	Cardinal number
DT	4.89	Determiner
EX	0	Existential *there*
FW	0.00	Foreign word
IN	6.47	Preposition or subordinating conjunction
JJ	2.72	Adjective
JJR	0.23	Adjective, comparative
JJS	0.08	Adjective, superlative
LS	0	List item marker
MD	0.24	Modal
NN	4.37	Noun, singular or mass
NNS	1.56	Noun, plural
NNP	35.10	Proper noun, singular
NNPS	1.24	Proper noun, plural
PDT	0	Predeterminer
POS	0.57	Possessive ending
PRP	7.82	Personal pronoun
PRP$	0	Possessive pronoun
RB	7.99	Adverb
RBR	0	Adverb, comparative
RBS	0	Adverb, superlative
RP	0.29	Particle
SYM	0	Symbol
TO	2.76	*to*
UH	0.41	Interjection
VB	3.67	Verb, base form
VBD	2.15	Verb, past tense
VBG	1.06	Verb, gerund or present participle
VBN	0.52	Verb, past participle
VBP	6.68	Verb, non-3rd person singular present
VBZ	3.27	Verb, 3rd person singular present
WDT	2.26	*wh*-determiner
WP	0.14	*wh*-pronoun
WP$	0	Possessive *wh*-pronoun
WRB	0.41	*wh*-adverb

Table 1: Penn Treebank part-of-speech tags. (RF: relative frequency of appearance in the AVEC 2012 dataset, including training, development, and testing sets)

As for the syntactic features, we will use part-of-speech (POS) tags [7]. POS are lexical categories of a language. Examples of POS are noun, verb, adjective, and adverb. 36 non-symbolic POS tags (excluding punctuations) of Penn Treebank [9] are considered as the syntactic features in this work. A list of those tags along with a short description of eachis shown in Table 1.

Different computational methods are used to approach this problem. To extract the POS tags, we make use of Stanford log-linear POS tagger [23].

4. EXPERIMENTS

In this section, we present the results of our experiments, as well as a discussion on the results. We start by the emotional speech recognition problem and go on with the problem of speaker trait recognition.

4.1 Emotion

In this section, we present the result of our experiments on the two sub-challenges addressed in the second audio/visual emotion challenge (AVEC 2012) [17]. Those two are fully continuous and word-level sub-challenges (FCSC and WLSC). The objective of the FCSC is to predict the emotional content of speech in a continuous manner, regardless of the linguistic boundaries, whereas the objective of the WLSC is to predict the emotional contents of words in an utterance [17]. In this experiment, we suggest a solution for a regression problem, corresponding to each of the four emotion primitives, as addressed in the challenge. As for the database, according to the AVEC 2012, a part of the SEMAINE is considered in this experiment. As follows, we talk about the speech features that we use in this experiment. It is followed by presenting experimental results and a discussion.

4.1.1 *Features*

Three sets of features are used in this set of experiments.

a . This set of features is composed of SED components. Extraction is done from 100 mSec windows of speech signal and the length of the spectral intervals is set to 100 Hz and they cover 0 to 8 kHz. The exponent p, as in Equation 4, is set to 0.2. To set each of these parameters, a line search is performed. As for the statistics, we use the min, max, median, mean, and standard deviation of the features over windows of a speech signal. This feature vector is of 400 dimensions. We use this set of features for both WLSC and FCSC.

b . This set is composed of the provided feature set as the baseline feature vector and it is of 1841 dimensions [17]. We use this set of features for both WLSC and FCSC.

c . This set is composed of part-of-speech tags, as shown in Table 1 and it is of 37 dimensions. Obviously, this set of features is used only for the WLSC.

4.1.2 *Results*

For the FCSC, we have used the elastic net criterion to train three linear models for each of the four emotion primitives, each time using one of the a, b, and a+b feature sets. On the other hand, for the WLSC, we have used the elastic net criterion to train four linear models for each of the four emotion primitives, each time using one of the a, b, c, and a+b+c feature sets. To do the training, we comply with the AVEC 2012 conditions. That is, to use the provided training set for training purposes and predict the emotional contents of the provided development set. Therefore, the development set is not seen in the training stage. The measure of comparison for this experiment is the Pearson's correlation coefficient (CC) of predicted and actual values. The results of this two experiments is presented in Table 2. In this table, we have also included the baseline results of the challenges for the audio, visual, and audio/visual emotion recognition. Table 3 lists the parameters of the elastic net, α and λ, for each one of the tasks, which are set in the process of learning. Figure 4.1 provides an example of how the prediction accuracy (correlation coefficient) and the sparsity of the feature vector change with the changes of α.

4.1.3 *Discussion*

The results of both FCSC and WLSC experiments, although offer a relatively sparse representation of the feature sets, do not show much improvement over the baseline. Except the arousal and expectation dimensions for the FCSC, for which the elastic net results in a more accurate prediction compared to SVM, for the other regression tasks, the contrary is the case. Particularly for those two regression tasks (FCSC arousal and expectation), the size of the feature vector resulting from the elastic net is considerably smaller (less than 1%) than the feature vectors used as the baseline.

According to the obtained results from the application of POS (Table 2), we can see that they show to be informative for modeling expectation and valence emotional dimensions, but not for arousal and power dimensions. It is worthy to notice that for the expectation dimension, the prediction accuracy of the model based on elastic net which uses the POS is equal to the one based on SVM, which uses the feature set b, while the length of the feature vector for the former case is noticeably smaller (less than 1%) than that of the latter.

4.2 Trait

This experiment is conducted in the framework of the Interspeech 2012 speaker trait challenge [16]. The problem that we are dealing with here is to train a classifier for each of the seven dimensions (5 personality dimensions, plus likability and intelligibility), and to use that for predicting the trait of unseen speech samples. In this experiment, a different database is used for each of the personality, likability, and intelligibility challenges: SPC, SLD, and NCSC. As follows, we talk about the feature sets that we use in this experiment. It is followed by the presentation of our results and a discussion.

4.2.1 *Features*

Two sets of features are used for this experiment.

a . This set is composed of SED components, extracted from 100 mSec long windows of signal, the length of spectral intervals are set to 100 Hz and they cover 0-8kHz, and p as in Equation 4 is set to 0.2. All the parameters are optimized by performing line search. Using min, max, median, mean, and standard deviation as for the statistics of the features over windows, makes this feature vector of 400 dimensions.

b . This set is composed of the challenge baseline features and is of 6125 dimensions [16].

4.2.2 *Results*

Using the elastic net criterion, three linear models are trained for each of the seven dimensions, at each time using one of the a, b, and a+b feature sets. As for the conditions of the experiments we abide by the Interspeech 2012 speaker trait challenge [16] rules. That is, provided training set of speech samples is used to train the model and the evaluation of the performance of the prediction is done according to the development set. Therefore, no use of the development set is done at the training phase. The measure of comparison for this experiment is the unweighted average of prediction accuracy, shown as UA. The resulting prediction accuracies on the development set are shown in Table 4. In this table, we also see the baseline results of the challenge on the feature set b, performed by support vector machines (SVM) and random forests (RF). Table 5 lists the parameters as set for the training of those models according to Equations 1 and 2. Table 6 provides the prediction accuracy of the experiment on the test set, put together with the best (between SVM

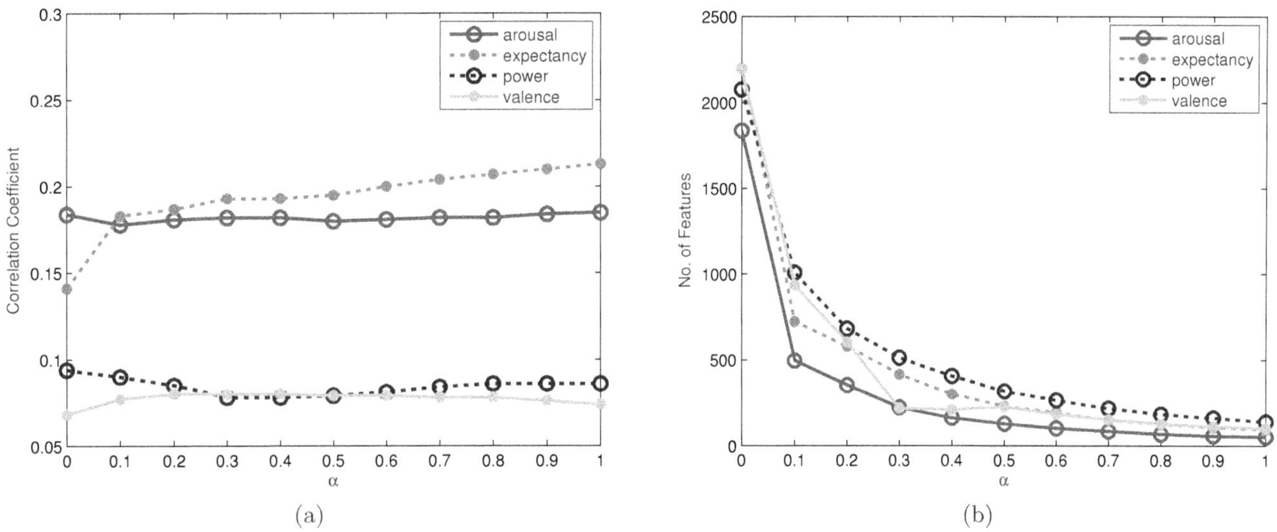

Figure 1: Correlation coefficients and the number of features against the elastic net parameter α, for the case where a+b is employed for the FCSC. (This figure is provided as an example, to show the trend of changes of the correlation coefficient and the number of features with the changes of α.)

Feature Set	Learning Method	Arousal CC	Arousal NF	Expectation CC	Expectation NF	Power CC	Power NF	Valence CC	Valence NF	**mean** CC
				Fully Continuous Sub-Challenge						
a (A)	EN	0.115	15	0.065	25	0.029	214	0.083	19	0.073
b (A)	EN	0.181	51	**0.213**	95	0.094	1726	0.079	409	0.142
a+b (A)	EN	**0.185**	52	**0.213**	94	0.094	2076	0.080	210	0.143
V	SVM [17]	0.157	5908	0.130	5908	**0.115**	5908	0.186	5908	0.147
A/V	SVM [17]	0.162	7749	0.162	7749	0.111	7749	**0.208**	7749	**0.157**
				Word-Level Sub-Challenge						
a (A)	EN	0.066	21	0.029	102	-0.006	159	0.060	16	0.037
b (A)	EN	0.066	132	0.065	114	0.004	228	0.074	213	0.052
	SVM [17]	0.097	1841	0.052	1841	0.061	1841	0.085	1841	0.074
c (A)	EN	0.001	13	0.052	12	0.005	6	0.025	21	0.021
a+b+c (A)	EN	0.071	58	0.073	141	0.007	202	0.077	183	0.057
V	SVM [17]	**0.145**	5908	**0.111**	5908	**0.103**	5908	**0.137**	5908	**0.124**
A/V	SVM [17]	0.113	7749	0.090	7749	0.083	7749	0.114	7749	0.100

Table 2: Prediction accuracy on the development set (A: audio, V: video; CC: correlation coefficient, NF: no. of features; EN: elastic net, SVM: support vector machine)

Feature Set	Arousal α	Arousal λ	Expectation α	Expectation λ	Power α	Power λ	Valence α	Valence λ
			Fully Continuous Sub-Challenge					
a	1	0.0086	1	0.1163	0.1	0.0024	1	0.0043
b	1	0.0103	1	0.2228	0	0.0341	0.3	0.0072
a+b	1	0.0102	1	0.2271	0	0.0374	0.4	0.0102
			Word-Level Sub-Challenge					
a	1	0.0067	0.2	0.0987	0.1	0.0028	1	0.0030
b	0.4	0.0084	1	0.1012	0.7	0.0021	0.1	0.0296
c	1	0.0014	0	63.4225	0.8	0.0029	0	0.7383
a+b+c	0.8	0.0075	0.9	0.1016	0.9	0.0019	1	0.0030

Table 3: Elastic net parameters (as in Equations 1 and 2), corresponding to the results shown in Table 2

and RF) prediction accuracy of the baseline paper on the same set.

4.2.3 *Discussion*

By looking at Table 4 one thing that one may notice is the relatively small number of features that is employed by training using the elastic net. For example, the number of features that is used from the feature set b for modeling the five personality dimensions ranges from 54 to 203, with the average of 118. This number is less than two percent of the number of features that is used from the same feature set for modeling using SVM and RF. This is when the prediction

Feature Set	Learning Method	Personality												Likability		Intelligibility	
		O		C		E		A		N		**mean**					
		UA	NF	UA	NF	UA	NF	UA	NF	UA	NF	UA	NF	UA	NF	UA	NF
a	EN	58.3	**60**	68.5	**31**	78.1	**34**	**70.3**	**17**	70.7	**7**	69.2	**30**	**67.7**	32	60.9	322
b	EN	**62.7**	89	74.3	98	85.8	54	64.5	144	74.3	203	72.3	118	61.8	**18**	62.3	**227**
	SVM [16]	60.4	6K	74.5	6K	80.9	6K	67.6	6K	68.0	6K	70.3	6K	58.5	6K	61.4	6K
	RF [16]	57.7	6K	**74.9**	6K	82.8	6K	67.2	6K	68.9	6K	70.3	6K	57.6	6K	**65.1**	6K
a+b	EN	61.1	85	74.3	98	**86.4**	318	69.2	23	**74.7**	206	**73.1**	146	61.9	212	61.8	353

Table 4: Prediction accuracy on the development set [16] (UA: unweighted average, NF: no. of features; EN: elastic net, SVM: support vector machine, RF: random forests, 6K: 6125; O: openness, C: conscientious, E: extraversion, A: agreeableness, N: neuroticism)

Feature Set	Personality										Likability		Intelligibility	
	O		C		E		A		N					
	α	λ	α	λ	α	λ	α	λ	α	λ	α	λ	α	λ
a	1	0.0065	0.6	0.0389	0.4	0.0548	0.9	0.0236	1	0.0487	0.8	0.0280	1	0.0007
b	1	0.0401	0.3	0.1660	0.6	0.1058	0.2	0.2252	0.1	0.4747	1	0.1289	0.2	0.2069
a+b	1	0.0414	0.3	0.1660	0.1	0.3263	0.1	0.0731	0.2	0.1808	1	0.0293	0.1	0.3249

Table 5: Elastic net parameters (as in Equations 1 and 2), corresponding to the results provided in Table 4 (O: openness, C: conscientious, E: extraversion, A: agreeableness, N: neuroticism)

	Personality						Likability	Intelligibility
	O	C	E	A	N	mean		
baseline [16]	58.8	80.1	75.3	**64.2**	**64.5**	**68.6**	59.0	69.6
this work	**60.1**	**81.6**	**78.4**	63.9	56.1	68.0	**59.3**	**70.0**

Table 6: Prediction accuracy (UA) of the test set [16] (O: openness, C: conscientious, E: extraversion, A: agreeableness, N: neuroticism)

performance of the elastic net is even higher by two percents than those of the SVM and RF. On the other hand, the result of prediction using the feature set a shows comparable accuracy to those performed by the feature set b, and still with considerably smaller size of feature vector. The overall accuracy of the prediction for the personality dimensions shows that in average the best performance is obtained by the elastic net, when the feature set a+b is used. As another example, the best prediction accuracy for the likability dimension is obtained by the elastic net on the feature set a and yet the number of features employed for this task is significantly less than the other four cases. The number of features used for this task is 32 (almost half a percent of the size of the feature set b), however the obtained prediction accuracy is about ten percent higher than those performed on the feature set b. The best prediction accuracy obtained for the intelligibility is that of the RF on the feature set b.

Among the five personality dimensions (Table 4), we can see that for openness and agreeableness the prediction accuracies obtained by one of the two a and b is higher than those of their combinations. This shows that the elastic net has been trapped in a local optimal solution. This also is seen for the likability dimension. Based on this observation and those of the previous studies [1], one may conclude that, in spite of dimensionality reduction, the combination of two or more feature sets does not necessarily result in a more accurate prediction compared to a case where just one of the sets is employed. This is mainly due to the sub-optimality of the dimensionality reduction algorithms. Therefore, a longer vector of features may not necessarily give out a more descriptive model.

The result of this experiment shows that the elastic net provides sparse representations of the feature sets, as expected, while in some cases the prediction accuracy of the suggested model by that also exceeds those of the SVM and RF. Also, according to Table 6, we can see that the prediction accuracy that elastic net obtains is higher than those of the SVM and RF in 5 out of 7 classification tasks.

5. CONCLUSIONS

In this study, we examined the application of elastic net to two paralinguistic recognition problems: emotional speech recognition and speaker trait recognition. For emotional speech recognition, in a comparison with the baseline, although elastic net offered relatively sparse representations in most of the cases the prediction accuracy of the resulting model was not relatively high. However, the application of elastic net to the speaker trait recognition task, not only resulted in a sparse representation, also brought about relatively high prediction accuracies. The reason for these contrary results, we suspect, is due to the difference between the size of the databases. The size of the emotional speech database is very large, and given the fact that elastic net numerically solves an optimization problem, the larger the size of a problem, the more likely it is for the optimization algorithms to trap in locally optimal solutions. Also, the larger a problem, the more computational resources is required to avoid occurrence of such cases. On the other hand, the size of the speaker trait databases are relatively very small, which decreases the possibility of entrapment in sub-optimal solutions. Also, proposed in this work is the application of the part-of-speech (POS) tags as a linguistic feature for emotional speech recognition. The result of our experiments show that this set of features can be useful for expectation and valence emotion primitives, but not necessarily for arousal and power.

6. REFERENCES

[1] P. Fewzee and F. Karray. Dimensionality Reduction for Emotional Speech Recognition. *To appear in Proc. of IEEE SocialCom 2012, Amsterdam, The Netherlands*, 2012.

[2] P. Fewzee and F. Karray. Emotional Speech: A Spectral Analysis. *To appear in Proc. of Interspeech 2012, ISCA, Portland, OR, US*, 2012.

[3] I. Guyon and A. Elisseeff. An Introduction to Variable and Feature Selection. *J. Mach. Learn. Res.*, 3:1157–1182, Mar. 2003.

[4] M. A. Hall. Correlation-Based Feature Selection for Discrete and Numeric Class Machine Learning. In *ICML '00: Proceedings of the Seventeenth International Conference on Machine Learning*, pages 359–366, San Francisco, CA, USA, 2000. Morgan Kaufmann Publishers Inc.

[5] X. He, D. Cai, and P. Niyogi. Laplacian Score for Feature Selection. *In NIPS*, 17, 2005.

[6] A. Hoerl and R. Kennard. Ridge Regression. In *Encyclopedia of Statistical Sciences*, volume 8, pages 129–136. New York: Wiley, 1988.

[7] D. Jurafsky and J. H. Martin. *Speech and Language Processing: An Introduction to Natural Language Processing, Computational Linguistics and Speech Recognition.* Prentice Hall, 2 edition, 2008.

[8] J. Kim, H. Rao, and M. Clements. Investigating the Use of Formant Based Features for Detection of Affective Dimensions in Speech. In *Affective Computing and Intelligent Interaction*, volume 6975 of *Lecture Notes in Computer Science*, pages 369–377. Springer Berlin / Heidelberg, 2011.

[9] M. P. Marcus, M. A. Marcinkiewicz, and B. Santorini. Building a Large Annotated Corpus of English: The Penn Treebank. *Computational Linguistics*, 19(2):313–330, June 1993.

[10] D. Morrison, R. Wang, and L. C. D. Silva. Ensemble Methods for Spoken Emotion Recognition in Call-Centres. *Speech Communication*, 49(2):98 – 112, 2007.

[11] H. Peng, F. Long, and C. Ding. Feature Selection Based on Mutual Information: Criteria of Max-Dependency, Max-Relevance, and Min-Redundancy. *IEEE Transactions on Pattern Analysis and Machine Intelligence*, 27:1226–1238, 2005.

[12] R. W. Picard. Affective Computing for HCI. *Human-Computer Interaction: Ergonomics and User Interfaces*, 1:829–833, 1999.

[13] O. Pierre-Yves. The production and Recognition of Emotions in Speech: Features and Algorithms. *International Journal of Human-Computer Studies*, 59(1-2):157 – 183, 2003.

[14] K. R. Scherer, T. Johnstone, and G. Klasmeyer. Vocal Expression of Emotion. In *Handbook of Affective Sciences*, Series in Affective Science, pages 433–456. Oxford University Press, 2003.

[15] B. Schuller. Recognizing Affect from Linguistic Information in 3D Continuous space. *Affective Computing, IEEE Transactions on*, 2(4):192 –205, oct.-dec. 2011.

[16] B. Schuller, S. Steidl, A. Batliner, E. Nöth, A. Vinciarelli, F. Burkhardt, R. van Son, F. Weninger, F. Eyben, T. Bocklet, G. Mohammadi, and B. Weiss. The Interspeech 2012 Speaker Trait Challenge. In *Proc. of InterSpeech 2012, ISCA, Portland, OR, US*, 2012.

[17] B. Schuller, M. Valstar, F. Eyben, R. Cowie, and M. Pantic. AVEC 2012 – The Continuous Audio/Visual Emotion Challenge. *To appear in Proc. of Second International Audio/Visual Emotion Challenge and Workshop (AVEC 2012), Grand Challenge and Satellite of ACM ICMI 2012*, Oct. 2012.

[18] B. Schuller, M. Valstar, F. Eyben, G. McKeown, R. Cowie, and M. Pantic. AVEC 2011 – The First International Audio/Visual Emotion Challenge. In *Affective Computing and Intelligent Interaction*, volume 6975 of *Lecture Notes in Computer Science*, pages 415–424. Springer Berlin / Heidelberg, 2011.

[19] K. Ślot, J. Cichosz, and L. Bronakowski. Emotion Recognition with Poincare Mapping of Voiced-Speech Segments of Utterances. In *Artificial Intelligence and Soft Computing – ICAISC 2008*, volume 5097 of *Lecture Notes in Computer Science*, pages 886–895. Springer Berlin / Heidelberg, 2008.

[20] Q. F. Tan and S. Narayanan. Novel Variations of Group Sparse Regularization Techniques with Applications to Noise Robust Automatic Speech Recognition. *Audio, Speech, and Language Processing, IEEE Transactions on*, 20(4):1337 –1346, may 2012.

[21] R. Tibshirani. Regression Shrinkage and Selection via the Lasso. *Journal of the Royal Statistical Society: Series B (Methodological)*, 58(1):267–288, 1996.

[22] R. Tibshirani, T. Hastie, and J. H. Friedman. Regularization Paths for Generalized Linear Models via Coordinate Descent. *Journal of Statistical Software*, 33(01), 2010.

[23] K. Toutanova, D. Klein, C. D. Manning, and Y. Singer. Feature-Rich Part-of-Speech Tagging with a Cyclic Dependency Network. In *Proceedings of the 2003 Conference of the North American Chapter of the Association for Computational Linguistics on Human Language Technology - Volume 1*, NAACL '03, pages 173–180, Stroudsburg, PA, USA, 2003. Association for Computational Linguistics.

[24] D. Ververidis and C. Kotropoulos. Fast and Accurate Sequential Floating Forward Feature Selection with the Bayes Classifier Applied to Speech Emotion Recognition. *Signal Processing*, 88(12):2956 – 2970, 2008.

[25] M. Wöllmer, M. Kaiser, F. Eyben, B. Schuller, and G. Rigoll. LSTM-Modeling of Continuous Emotions in an Audiovisual Affect Recognition Framework. *Image and Vision Computing*, 2012.

[26] S. Yun and C. Yoo. Loss-Scaled Large-Margin Gaussian Mixture Models for Speech Emotion Classification. *Audio, Speech, and Language Processing, IEEE Transactions on*, 20(2):585 –598, 2012.

[27] H. Zou and T. Hastie. Regularization and Variable Selection via the Elastic Net. *Journal of the Royal Statistical Society: Series B (Statistical Methodology)*, 67(2):301–320, 2005.

Improving Generalisation And Robustness Of Acoustic Affect Recognition

Florian Eyben
Technische Universität München
Institute for Human-Machine Communication
Munich, Germany

Björn Schuller
JOANNEUM RESEARCH Forschungsgesellschaft mbH*
DIGITAL - Institute for Information and Communication Technologies
Graz, Austria

Gerhard Rigoll
Technische Universität München
Institute for Human-Machine Communication
Munich, Germany

ABSTRACT

Emotion recognition in real-life conditions faces several challenging factors, which most studies on emotion recognition do not consider. Such factors include background noise, varying recording levels, and acoustic properties of the environment, for example. This paper presents a systematic evaluation of the influence of background noise of various types and SNRs, as well as recording level variations on the performance of automatic emotion recognition from speech. Both, natural and spontaneous as well as acted/prototypical emotions are considered. Besides the well known influence of additive noise, a significant influence of the recording level on the recognition performance is observed. Multi-condition learning with various noise types and recording levels is proposed as a way to increase robustness of methods based on standard acoustic feature sets and commonly used classifiers. It is compared to matched conditions learning and is found to be almost on par for many settings.

Categories and Subject Descriptors

H.5.5 [**Information Systems Applications**]: Sound and Music Computing

General Terms

Experimentation, Reliability

Keywords

Emotion recognition, noise robustness, recording level, multi-condition training

*The author is further affiliated with Technische Universität München, Munich, Germany

ICMI'12, October 22–26, 2012, Santa Monica, California, USA.

1. INTRODUCTION

Recently, a shift in emotion recognition research from working with controlled, lab-recorded data to more naturalistic data is observed. Challenges at INTERSPEECH from 2009 to 2011 literally challenged participants with highly naturalistic data for tasks ranging from identification of emotions all the way to identification of speaker states such as intoxication or sleepiness [12]. The reported results are still low, however. Even human agreement on these data-sets is far from perfect, indicating the difficulty of the task and the fuzziness of emotions.

When we want to use affect recognition technology in a live system, either a research demonstrator or a commercial product, robustness and high accuracies are a key factor. For achieving this goal, there are two main factors to consider: (a) optimising the classification performance on given data-sets, and (b) making the system robust to factors, such as background noise. For (a), an optimal choice of features and classifiers are the main research topics, which are dealt with extensively in many other studies such as the INTERSPEECH Challenge contributions. However, experience has shown, that often a system highly optimised for one data-set or task does not perform too well in cross data-set evaluations (cf. [14]), or when external factors such as the environment or the recording equipment change. Thus, we investigate issue (b) – the influence of background noise and level variations – in this paper.

Section 2 gives an overview on related work, section 3 describes our experiments and the proposed method of multi-condition training to build more robust models, section 4 describes the three corpora used for evaluations, and section 5 includes a discussion of the obtained results. A conclusion is drawn in section 6.

2. RELATED WORK

Compared to the large amount of work that has been published on optimising feature sets (e. g., [7]), fusing of modalities (e. g., [5]), and choice of classifiers (e. g., [4]) for affect recognition, few people have investigated the influence of additive noise, and none – to our best knowledge – the effect of level variations. Some work exists on the influence of the environment, specifically the reverberation caused by it (e. g., [15] and [8]).

The effects of additive noise were first investigated on a broad scale on three publicly available databases in [9].

No speaker independent evaluation was performed, however, and features specific to the noise type were selected. A similar study has been performed for noise types occurring in an in-car environment in [11]. Another report on in-car emotion recognition dealing with the effects of in-car noises, such as engine and road noise, is presented in [3]. Weninger et. al, present a method of improving recognition performance in noisy and reverberated settings by using Non-Negative Matrix Factorisation (NMF) based acoustic features in [15].

3. EXPERIMENTS

None of the methods referenced in section 2 have investigated the influence of recording level variations within the test set as well as extensive multi-condition training. Many studies from the ASR field deal with the topic of robustness and background noise, however the findings cannot be transferred to emotion recognition in most cases, as emotion recognition uses different types of features and a different approach to modelling. Low-level signal enhancement and noise reduction can be used in both fields, however this shall not be part of this study.

In previous studies typically matched conditions learning is used, which refers to training on data that is corrupted with the same noise type and Signal-to-Noise Ratio (SNR) as the test data. This is an unrealistic setting for a real-world application, as the noise type in many cases is not known when designing the system and training the models. Mismatched conditions training refers to training on the original, clean data and testing on noisy data. It investigates the performance of a generic model in varying noise conditions. A third alternative is multi-condition training, which combines benefits from matched and mismatched conditions training. Multiple copies of the data overlaid with different noise types at various SNRs are used during training. Thus, a generic model is generated, which is expected to work well in a variety of noise types. [15] investigates multi-condition learning and reports good performance on children's emotional speech from the FAU AIBO corpus.

In this paper, in addition to an extensive study on the influence of additive noise under mismatched, matched, and multi-condition learning, we evaluate the influence of recording level variations for the first time. While the recording level plays a non-significant role in ASR, the correct recordning level is a major factor for the success of current emotion recognition systems. Level variations (scaling of the audio samples) by applying a gain of -20 dB to +10 dB are investigated without noise overlay. We would like to note at this point that this evaluation might seem unnecessary, if the recording level was normalised. However, this requires normalisation of the recording level of speech parts only. This is a non-trivial task if reverberation and esp. background noise are present.

Further, we overlay five noise types without scaling the original audio: babble noise, street noise, office noise, white noise, and music. For babble and street noise we use the Aurora noise samples (cf. [6]). The office noise consists of typical sounds occurring in a busy office environment, such as typing, printer machines, writing, beep sounds, and occasional talk in the background. The noise samples have been sampled from YouTube^{TM} videos which were recorded in office environments. The music noise type has been compiled from a mix of instrumental classic and pop music snippets (no vocals).

Our noise samples have lengths which vary from 1 (street noise) to 47 minutes (office noise). When overlaying an audio chunk with noise a random region of the noise sample is selected, and scaled accordingly to match the desired SNR before adding it to the audio chunk. The SNRs are computed based on Root Mean Square (RMS) amplitudes $A_{sig}^{(rms)}$ and $A_{noise}^{(rms)}$ of signal and noise chunks, respectively, according to the following equation:

$$SNR = 20 \log_{10} \frac{A_{sig}^{(rms)}}{A_{noise}^{(rms)}} \quad (1)$$

Six SNR levels are investigated: -5 dB, 0 dB, 5 dB, 10 dB, 20 dB, 30 dB.

In section 5 we provide and discuss results for matched conditions training, mismatched conditions training, and multi-condition training. Multi-condition training in general refers to the fact that a classifier is trained with target data (e.g. emotional speech sentences), which is repeated in the training material with different conditions applied to it, such as various background noise types or recording level variations. The multi-condition training approach chosen in this paper differs slightly from the one applied in [15]. Weninger et. al create duplicates of the data at all investigated SNRs and for all noise types. In contrast, we synthesise the training data by tripling the amount of original data, applying a random gain between -20 dB and +5 dB to each instance (sentence, phrase), and then adding randomly chosen noise samples from all noise types at random SNRs from the range of 0 dB to 60 dB. 5% of the instances are not overlaid with noise.

All evaluations are performed in a speaker independent manner by leave-one-speaker-out (LOSO) cross validation. We use the INTERSPEECH 2011 Speaker State Challenge acoustic feature set [12] and extract the features with openSMILE [2]. The feature set consists of 4,368 audio features, which are statistical functionals of an exhaustive set of low-level audio descriptors, such as loudness, fundamental frequency, voice quality, Mel Frequency Cepstral Coefficients (MFCC), etc. We use linear kernel Support Vector Machines (SVM) as classifier. The linear kernel allows for fast processing even in a high dimensional space, which is important for live emotion recognition. Results are reported in terms of unweighted average recall rate (UAR), which is the unweighted average of the per-class recall rates.

4. DATABASES

To asses the influence of additive noise and audio gain on different tasks, we present experimental results on three databases: (a) the Berlin Emotional Speech-Database (EmoDB) [1], (b) an acted telephone speech anger corpus, and (c) the TUM Audio-Visual Interest Corpus (AVIC) [10].

The choice of EmoDB is motivated by the fact that often models trained on small, acted data sets which contain prototypical emotions, perform well in cross-validation experiments on the same corpus [13], but show bad performance when evaluated cross-corpus [14] or when used in a live system. The anger database was chosen to asses the effect of audio gain on the discrimination performance between neutral and angry speech. AVIC was chosen to asses the effects of noise and scaling in a natural environment for spontaneous affect.

We briefly describe each of the data sets in the ongoing: EmoDB is a well known set chosen to test the effectiveness of emotion classification. The studio recorded database covers seven emotions: *anger, boredom, disgust, fear, joy, neutral, and sadness.* The spoken content is pre-defined by ten emotionally neutral German sentences. Ten (five female) professional actors speak these sentences multiple times. While the whole set comprises around 900 utterances, only 494 phrases are marked as minimum 60 % natural and minimum 80 % assignable by 20 subjects in a listening experiment. 84.3 % mean accuracy – for identifying the 7 emotions – is the result of this perception study on this limited 'more prototypical' set. As this set is usually used in the manifold works reporting results on the corpus we restrict ourselves to this selection, as well. The 494 phrases have a combined recording length of approx. 23 minutes.

The TUM AVIC corpus contains recordings of personalised commercial product presentations. A product presenter leads each one of 21 subjects (10 female) through an English commercial presentation. The level of interest is annotated for every sub-speaker turn reaching from *boredom* (subject is bored with listening and talking about the topic, very passive, does not follow the discourse; this state is also referred to as level of interest (loi) 1, i.e. loi1), over *neutral* (subject follows and participates in the discourse, it can not be recognised, if she/he is interested or indifferent in the topic; loi2) to *joyful* interaction (strong wish of the subject to talk and learn more about the topic; loi3). Additionally, the spoken content and non-linguistic vocalisations are labeled in the AVIC set, however, not used in this study.

For our evaluation we consider all 3,002 phrases (approx. 108 minutes recording time), in contrast to only 996 phrases with high inter-labeler agreement as e. g. employed in [10]. However, we select a sub-sampled and re-sampled subset of these 3k phrases to eliminate problems caused by the uneven distribution of instances over the three interest levels. The sub-set is created by first sub-sampling the instances with a maximum number of 250 per class and the up-sampling the minority classes with a bias to an even distribution using the re-sampling algorithm implemented in the WEKA data mining toolkit [16]. 243 instances of loi1, 264 of loi2, and 233 of loi3 are retained.

	#	length (m:s)
Anger	319	57:07
Neutral	341	58:33

Table 1: Number of instances and combined recording length for each class in the Anger database.

The Anger database is a private database, which contains telephone quality speech recordings where callers were asked to speak a single English sentence in a neutral and in an acted way multiple times over a land-line telephone connection. There are 9 speakers in total, 4 female and 5 male. The number of instances for each class and the recording times are given in table 1. Unfortunately, the database is not publicly available for research. The mean sentence length is 10.5 seconds, the minimum length is 4.1 seconds and the maximum length 25.3 seconds.

5. RESULTS

The obtained results are summarised in table 4 for noise corruption and in table 2 for recording level variations. The results in table 4 are an average of the individual results of the noise types. They show the general performance degradation for each data-set and each of the three training methods (mismatched condition (*mi*), matched condition (*ma*), and multi-condition (*mu*) training). The result for clean training and testing is given in the 0 dB column in table 2 for *mi* and *ma* evaluation (identical).

UAR [%]	gain/dB					
	-20	**-10**	**-5**	**0**	**+5**	**+10**
EmoDB (*mi*)	77.8	78.1	79.8	80.6	79.6	66.5
EmoDB (*ma*)	81.3	79.9	79.8	80.6	80.7	79.2
EmoDB (*mu*)	78.2	78.3	77.0	78.1	77.5	75.8
Anger (*mi*)	71.1	71.4	70.1	81.7	62.9	56.7
Anger (*ma*)	79.3	82.3	81.5	81.7	82.8	82.0
Anger (*mu*)	80.9	79.5	80.6	69.5	80.0	80.0
AVIC (*mi*)	46.0	45.2	48.8	59.4	53.2	51.7
AVIC (*ma*)	59.2	59.1	57.8	59.4	57.5	60.1
AVIC (*mu*)	58.0	58.5	59.4	56.5	59.2	58.8

Table 2: Results with gain applied to test partitions to simulate varying recording levels. Unweighted Average Recall (UAR) for leave-one-speaker-out cross validation. Training splits with original audio (mismatched condition, *mi*), audio with gain applied (matched condition, *ma*), and noise corrupted and scaled audio with all noise types (multi-condition, *mu*).

By looking at the *mi* results, we can see that recognition performance is heavily affected by additive noise at low SNRs. The effect is much greater as was reported in [9], which could be related to the use of non-hierarchical functionals as features in this paper and the fact that [9] did not perform speaker independent evaluation with leave-one-speaker-out cross validation. At -5 dB SNR the UAR for EmoDB and Anger drop to almost chance level (14.3% and 50% respectively). Performance on AVIC degrades substantially too, however it is still well above chance level (33.3%). A possible explanation is that AVIC contains a minimal amount of background noise and level variations in the training data. EmoDB, for example, has been recorded under studio conditions and the sentences have been normalised to RMS amplitude 1.0, therefore no level variations are present in the training set.

For SNRs of 5 dB and higher multi-condition training performs almost as well as matched conditions training, whereby clean training performs significantly worse (on a level of 0.01). Multi-condition training performance could be further improved for lower SNRs, if data with such SNRs was included in the training set (in our setting the lowest is 0 dB).

Applying a gain to the test data does affect the recognition performance (cf. table 2), but not as strongly as additive noise. The effect is strongest for AVIC (-13.4% for -20 dB gain on test partitions compared to unmodified test partitions) and the Anger database (-25% for +10 dB gain on test compared to unmodified data). A 14.1% decrease is observed for +10 dB gain on EmoDB, however only a 1% decrease for +5 dB is observed. We attribute the large decrease to non-linear distortions introduced through clipping when scaling by the 10 dB factor, as the original (0 dB) samples are already normalised to the maximum peak amplitude. AVIC and Anger databases are recorded at lower levels.

Table 3 shows the confusion matrices for AVIC for LOSO evaluation on the unmodified audio, and -20 and +10 gain applied to the test splits. For the low gain test split (-20 dB) the distinguishability for separating loi3 from loi1 and loi2 decreases, while the distinguishability between loi1 and loi2 does not seem to be affected so much. This can be interpreted in a way that energy/loudness is an important feature for discriminating interested from neutral speech, while pitch and spectral characteristics are more important for neutral vs. boredom. For the high gain test split (+10 dB) the classifier shows a bias towards loi3. This bias is stronger for loi2 instances than for loi1 instances.

For multi-condition training a noteable decrease in performance for 0 dB gain is observable for Anger and AVIC compared to all other gain settings. The only explanation for this behaviour is that the muli-condition training data contains too little actual clean examples at 0 dB gain.

UAR [%]	SNR/dB					
	-5	0	+5	+10	+20	+30
EmoDB (*mi*)	16.4	17.7	23.5	32.9	54.7	71.0
EmoDB (*ma*)	74.6	77.0	78.1	79.5	81.6	80.2
EmoDB (*mu*)	45.2	65.1	72.7	74.9	78.1	78.7
Anger (*mi*)	56.9	59.7	62.3	65.7	62.9	63.1
Anger (*ma*)	74.6	77.0	78.1	79.5	81.6	80.2
Anger (*mu*)	68.7	74.6	77.8	79.6	81.6	81.5
AVIC (*mi*)	44.5	47.5	49.2	51.2	52.0	51.6
AVIC (*ma*)	56.3	57.4	58.2	59.0	59.1	58.5
AVIC (*mu*)	47.3	53.2	55.7	58.3	57.9	58.9

Table 4: Results for testing on noise corrupted audio with SNRs from -5 dB to 30 dB. Unweighted Average Recall (UAR) for leave-one-speaker-out cross validation. Training on original audio (mismatched condition, *mi*), noise corrupted audio (matched condition, *ma*), and noise corrupted and scaled audio with all noise types (multi-condition, *mu*).

Table 5 shows detailed results for each noise type on the AVIC set. As expected, for matched conditions training we see least variation in the results (min. 54.3 % UAR, max. 63.0 % UAR). Noteably, there is even an increase in performance over the clean case for some settings. This is most evident for white noise at an SNR of 30dB. This suggests that adding a small amount of white noise to the training data might improve generalisation performance. Besides that we cannot see a clear, significant trend as to which noise type affects the performance most over all SNRs. However, for both multi-condition and mismatched-condition training, we observe that noise types which degrade performance a lot at low SNRs seem to have the inverse effect at high SNRs (see white noise vs. babble noise).

6. CONCLUSION

We have evaluated the effects of additive noise on automatic affect recognition performance of naturalistic and acted affect. In contrast to previous work we chose a broad variety of emotional content. Moreover, this paper is the first to investigate the effect of recording level variation on

UAR [%]	SNR/dB					
	-5	0	5	10	20	30
Clean training (mismatched condition):						
babble	48.3	48.8	50.3	49.6	52.2	49.8
music	49.0	47.9	49.4	53.6	50.5	51.6
office	41.8	46.9	46.7	48.9	53.5	53.0
street	48.8	52.4	50.0	49.6	52.5	51.1
white	34.7	41.5	49.7	54.5	51.3	52.3
Matched condition training:						
babble	55.7	60.7	58.7	57.9	58.3	56.2
music	57.1	57.5	59.0	58.8	61.4	58.2
office	54.3	58.1	60.1	58.7	58.2	58.5
street	54.4	56.1	56.6	61.3	59.3	56.5
white	59.3	54.5	56.4	58.3	58.1	63.0
Multi-condition training:						
babble	54.8	56.9	52.6	57.8	57.9	57.2
music	48.8	52.3	56.8	60.6	59.8	58.9
office	44.2	49.9	58.7	57.7	58.4	58.6
street	50.3	55.3	53.2	56.5	56.9	59.6
white	38.5	51.4	57.1	58.8	56.3	60.3

Table 5: Detailed results for clean, matched condition, and multi-condition training with 5 noise types and 6 SNR levels. Unweighted Average Recall (UAR) for all noise types and SNRs on AVIC. Leave-one-speaker-out cross validation. For comparison: clean result = 59.4 % UAR.

the recognition performance. We propose a method for robust multi-condition training of a single, robust model, which is able to deal with additive noise and varying recording gain. For SNRs of 5 dB or higher the performance of our multi-condition approach is almost on par with matched conditions training. A significant effect of the recording gain on recognition performance was found for the naturalistic data-set (TUM AVIC), and the task of anger detection. This effect is almost completely eliminated by multi-condition training.

Future work will deal with extending the multi-condition learning approach to reverberation effects and more diverse noise types, as well as an in-depth analysis of which acoustic features are most affected by noise and recording level. This paper helps to better understand the influence of some external factors commonly encountered when building a real-world, speaker independent emotion and affect recognition system from given data-sets and successfully proposed an approach to build more robust models by synthesising new training data.

7. ACKNOWLEDGEMENTS

The research leading to these results has received funding from the European Community's Seventh Framework Programme (FP7/2007- 2013) under grant agreement No. 289021 (ASC-Inclusion).

8. REFERENCES

[1] Burkhardt, F., Paeschke, A., Rolfes, M., Sendlmeier, W., and Weiss, B. A database of german emotional speech. In *Proc. INTERSPEECH 2005, Lissabon, Portugal* (2005), pp. 1517–1520.

[#]	-20 dB			0 dB			+10 dB		
as →	**loi1**	**loi2**	**loi3**	**loi1**	**loi2**	**loi3**	**loi1**	**loi2**	**loi3**
loi1	**140**	65	37	**170**	65	7	**126**	56	60
loi2	95	**111**	57	106	**124**	33	78	**60**	125
loi3	44	100	**88**	27	64	**141**	37	9	**186**
Sum	279	276	182	303	253	181	241	125	371

Table 3: Confusion matrices for AVIC with -20 dB, 0 dB, and +10 dB gain applied to the test split.

[2] EYBEN, F., WÖLLMER, M., AND SCHULLER, B. openSMILE – the munich versatile and fast open-source audio feature extractor. In *Proc. ACM Multimedia (MM), Florence, Italy* (2010), ACM, pp. 1459–1462.

[3] JONES, C., AND JONSSON, I. Performance analysis of acoustic emotion recognition for in-car conversational interfaces. In *Universal Access in Human-Computer Interaction. Ambient Interaction*, vol. 4555 of *Lecture Notes in Computer Science*. Springer, 2007, pp. 411–420.

[4] KOCKMANN, M., BURGET, L., AND CERNOCKY, J. Brno university of technology system for INTERSPEECH 2010 paralinguistic challenge. In *Proc. of INTERSPEECH 2010* (2010), ISCA, pp. 2822–2825.

[5] MOWER, E., LEE, S., MATARIC, M. J., AND NARAYANAN, S. Joint-processing of audio-visual signals in human perception of conflicting synthetic character emotions. In *Proc. of ICME 2008, Hannover, Germany* (June 2008).

[6] PEARCE, D., AND HIRSCH, H.-G. The aurora experimental framework for the performance evaluation of speech recognition systems under noisy conditions. In *Proc. ICSLP '00* (Beijing, China, October 2000).

[7] RAHMAN, T., MARIOORYAD, S., KESHAVAMURTHY, S., LIU, G., HANSEN, J., AND BUSSO, C. Detecting sleepiness by fusing classifiers trained with novel acoustic features. In *Proc. of INTERSPEECH 2011, Florence, Italy* (2011), ISCA.

[8] SCHULLER, B. Affective speaker state analysis in the presence of reverberation. *International Journal of Speech Technology 14*, 2 (2011), 77–87.

[9] SCHULLER, B., ARSIC, D., WALLHOFF, F., AND RIGOLL, G. Emotion recognition in the noise applying large acoustic feature sets. In *Proc. Speech Prosody 2006* (May 2006), ISCA.

[10] SCHULLER, B., MÜLLER, R., EYBEN, F., GAST, J., HÖRNLER, B., WÖLLMER, M., RIGOLL, G., HÖTHKER, A., AND KONOSU, H. Being Bored? Recognising Natural Interest by Extensive Audiovisual Integration for Real-Life Application. *Image and Vision Computing Journal (IVCJ), Special Issue on Visual and Multimodal Analysis of Human Spontaneous Behavior 27*, 12 (November 2009), 1760–1774.

[11] SCHULLER, B., RIGOLL, G., GRIMM, M., KROSCHEL, K., MOOSMAYR, T., AND RUSKE, G. Effects of in-car noise-conditions on the recognition of emotion within speech. In *Proc. DAGA 2007, Stuttgart* (March 2007), DEGA, pp. 305–306.

[12] SCHULLER, B., STEIDL, S., BATLINER, A., SCHIEL, F., AND KRAJEWSKI, J. The INTERSPEECH 2011 speaker state challenge. In *Proc. of INTERSPEECH 2011, Florence, Italy* (2011), ISCA, pp. 3201–3204.

[13] SCHULLER, B., VLASENKO, B., EYBEN, F., RIGOLL, G., AND WENDEMUTH, A. Acoustic emotion recognition: A benchmark comparison of performances. In *Proc. of ASRU* (2009), IEEE, pp. 552–557.

[14] SCHULLER, B., VLASENKO, B., EYBEN, F., WÖLLMER, M., STUHLSATZ, A., WENDEMUTH, A., AND RIGOLL, G. Cross-corpus acoustic emotion recognition: Variances and strategies. *IEEE Transactions on Affective Computing (TAC) 1*, 2 (December 2010), 119–131.

[15] WENINGER, F., SCHULLER, B., BATLINER, A., STEIDL, S., AND SEPPI, D. Recognition of nonprototypical emotions in reverberated and noisy speech by nonnegative matrix factorization. *EURASIP Journal on Advances in Signal Processing 2011* (2011).

[16] WITTEN, I. H., AND FRANK, E. *Data mining: Practical machine learning tools and techniques, 2nd Edition*. Morgan Kaufmann, San Francisco, 2005.

Preserving Actual Dynamic Trend of Emotion in Dimensional Speech Emotion Recognition

Wenjing Han*
School of Computer Science and Technology
Harbin Institute of Technology
150001 Harbin, China
wenjing.han@tum.de

Haifeng Li
School of Computer Science and Technology
Harbin Institute of Technology
150001 Harbin, China
lihaifeng@hit.edu.cn

Florian Eyben
Institute for Human-Machine Communication
Technische Universität München
80290 München, Germany
eyben@tum.de

Lin Ma
School of Computer Science and Technology
Harbin Institute of Technology
150001 Harbin, China
malin_li@hit.edu.cn

Jiayin Sun
School of Humanities and Social Sciences
Harbin Institute of Technology
150001 Harbin, China
sunjiayin@hit.edu.cn

Björn Schuller
Institute for Human-Machine Communication
Technische Universität München
80290 München, Germany
schuller@tum.de

ABSTRACT

In this paper, we use the concept of *dynamic trend of emotion* to describe how a human's emotion changes over time, which is believed to be important for understanding one's stance toward current topic in interactions. However, the importance of this concept - to our best knowledge - has not been paid enough attention before in the field of speech emotion recognition (SER). Inspired by this, this paper aims to evoke researchers' attention on this concept and makes a primary effort on the research of predicting correct dynamic trend of emotion in the process of SER. Specifically, we propose a novel algorithm named Order Preserving Network (OPNet) to this end. First, as the key issue for OPNet construction, we propose employing a probabilistic method to define an emotion trend-sensitive loss function. Then, a nonlinear neural network is trained using the gradient descent as optimization algorithm to minimize the constructed loss function. We validated the prediction performance of OPNet on the VAM corpus, by mean linear error as well as a rank correlation coefficient γ as measures. Comparing to k-Nearest Neighbor and support vector regression, the proposed OPNet performs better on the preservation of actual dynamic trend of emotion.

*This author is also affiliation with Technische Universität München

ICMI'12, October 22–26, 2012, Santa Monica, California, USA.

Categories and Subject Descriptors

I.6.5 [**Model Development**]: Modeling methodologies; H.5.2 [**User Interfaces**]: Voice I/O

General Terms

Algorithms, Experimentation, Human Factors

Keywords

speech emotion recognition, dynamic trend of emotion, loss function, neural network

1. INTRODUCTION

In the field of dimensional Speech Emotion Recognition (SER), the regression-based approach has been widely used [5, 8, 3] nowadays. This approach views the SER problem as a standard regression task, and employs regression algorithms to predict continuous-valued emotions. In the past few years, considerable amount of works have been done in this area. Take *Activation* (a dimension of emotion evaluating how high or low the subject's physiological reaction is) prediction for example, Grimm et al. [5] achieved a mean linear error (MLE) of 0.15 and a correlation coefficient (CC) of 0.82 using the Support Vector Regression (SVR) on the Vera am Mittag (VAM) corpus [6], and Wöllmer et al. [8] reached a mean squared error (MSE) of 0.08 using Long Short-Term Memory Recurrent Neural Networks on the Belfast Sensitive Artificial Listener (SAL) database [2].

However, it could be ill-conceived to directly copy these regression solutions to the case of dimensional SER without appropriate adjustment. This is, as unlike a regular regression task aiming only at numerical approximation between predicted and actual values, the dimensional SER task still has an extra demand for preserving the actual dynamic trend of emotion in the prediction process. The so-called *dynamic trend of emotion* is a description of the emotion change during a fixed period of time. In our daily life, it plays an extremely important role for recognizing one's stance toward the current topic in an interaction. For example, an upward trend of emotion on the valence dimension may indicate an increasingly positive evaluation over the product the speaker is talking about, but a downward trend can mean the opposite. Thus, it is important for an advanced human-machine interface to have the ability of predicting the dynamic trend of human's emotion correctly when deciding a machine's next response. However, although the currently used regression algorithms can also contribute preserving actual dynamic trend of emotion by achieving numerical approximation, such effect is, after all, limited.

Driven by this, this paper focuses on developing an improved approach for dimensional SER, which can reach a common benefit between emotions' numerical approximation and dynamic trend approximation. For our case, the latter term *dynamic trend approximation* is used to define the situation that the predicted emotion trend is very close to the actual one for a given set of instances. And what should be noted is that, when we measure how close the predicted and actual trend is, we consider the pairwise trend (i.e., the emotion trend between every pair of instances in the given dataset). This means we say a predicted emotion trend for a set of instances is the same as the actual one, if and only if the trend for every pair of instances from the set is predicted correctly (cf. Section 6.1).

For this purpose, the trend loss and the numerical loss (e.g., MSE) are both considered to define a prediction loss function. The term *trend loss* is used to refer to the trend difference between the actual and predicted emotion sequences (cf. Section3). Then, a Neural Network model is trained using the gradient descent algorithm to minimize above loss function. The major question then becomes how to define the trend loss part of loss function. An ingenious substitution is proposed in this paper: the measure of trend loss is quantified by calculating another measure of ranking order loss. The so-called ranking order loss denotes the order difference between the list of instances ranked by predicted emotion values and the list of instances ranked by annotations. For its calculation, the top-one probabilistic distribution and cross entropy are also involved. We refer to this proposed approach as an Order-Preserving Network (OPNet) algorithm.

Next, to make a comprehensive evaluation of emotion prediction performance, we also propose employing Goodman and Kruskal's γ with generally accepted MLE as our final evaluation measures. Based on these measures, the performance of the proposed OPNet was then compared with two other baseline methods: k-Nearest Neighbor (k-NN) and SVR on the VAM corpus. The results show that the proposed OPNet algorithm can reach a good trade-off between the dynamic trend approximation and numerical approximation.

The rest of the paper is organized as follows. Section 2 gives a general description of dimensional SER. Section 3 introduces the proposed approach for preserving actual dynamic trend of emotion in SER. Database and acoustic feature extraction are described in Section 4 and Section 5, respectively. Section 6 reports our experimental results before concluding.

2. PROBLEM DESCRIPTION

Let us first give a formalized description of the dimensional SER problem. When representing emotions in a k-dimensional emotion space, each emotional state is associated with k emotion values, correspondingly. Moreover, since these dimensions are independent of each other in the psychological view, the dimensional SER task can be naturally separated into k similar and independent subtasks. For simplified depiction, the following description is given in the context of one of the k subtasks.

In training, a set of speech feature vectors $X = \{x_1, x_2, \cdots, x_n\}$ and its corresponding emotion value set $Y = \{y_1, y_2, \cdots, y_n\}$ are given, where n denotes the number of training samples, X is extracted from speech waves, and Y is obtained by human annotation. Each feature vector x_i and its annotated emotion value y_i then form an instance. The training set can be denoted as $I = \{(x_i, y_i)\}_{i=1}^{n}$.

The goal of dimensional SER is to create a prediction function $f(\cdot)$; for the list of feature vectors X, it outputs a list of predicted emotion values $Z = \{f(x_1), f(x_2), \cdots, f(x_n)\}$. This predication function is designed to approximate the predicted value set Z to the true value set Y as much as possible. Here we formalize this objective as a minimization of the total losses with respect to the training data. To wit, with a loss function L,

$$L(Z, Y), \tag{1}$$

the prediction function $f(\cdot)$ can be denoted as:

$$f(\cdot) = \arg\min_{f} L(Z, Y). \tag{2}$$

In emotion prediction, when a new speech sample is given, we extract feature vector x' and use the trained prediction function $f(\cdot)$ to assign an emotion value to it per dimension.

In brief, when it comes to build a dimensional SER system, two crucial problems need to be solved: 1) how to define the loss function L, and 2) how to model the predication function f to minimize L.

3. APPROACH

3.1 Definition of the loss function

The definition of loss function is a procedure of measuring the difference between predicted result and reference standard. It quite depends on the final purpose of the task. For example, if we aim only at the numerical approximation as normal regression tasks do, the general terms of loss functions, like squared loss, absolute value loss, etc, could be already appropriate. However, if we additionally desire a preservation of actual dynamic trend of emotion during the prediction, there is no doubt that a more comprehensive loss function is demanded. In this work, a linear combination of the numerical loss L_{num} and trend loss L_{trend} is considered to construct the loss function L:

$$L = (1 - \eta) \cdot L_{num} + \eta \cdot L_{trend}, \tag{3}$$

where η *in* $[0, 1]$ is an adjustment factor. With η, the proportion of L_{num} and L_{trend} in the whole loss can then be adjusted as appropriate. Furthermore, for the numerical component L_{num} of loss function L, the widely used squared loss function is chosen:

$$L_{num}(Y, Z) = \frac{1}{2n} \cdot \sum_{i=1}^{n} (y_i - f(x_i))^2, \tag{4}$$

where the y_i and $f(x_i)$ are the human label and predicted label of speech instance x_i, respectively.

The remaining problem then becomes the definition of the trend loss part of loss function: L_{trend}.

3.2 From trend loss to order loss

Supposing given a sequence of emotion values named A with upward trend and another sequence of emotion values named B with downward trend, we can say the dynamic trend of A is entirely different from B's. But now the problem is how to quantify such qualitative description of such difference.

Actually, as we get two trends of training samples X according to Y and Z, namely T_Y and T_Z, two sequences of training samples π_Y and π_Z in descending order can be built as well. There is no doubt that any difference between T_Y and T_Z corresponds to a unique difference between π_Y and π_Z. Inspired by this, we propose to use what we call order loss to quantify the trend loss. To calculate the order loss, a probabilistic method is imported in this work.

Specifically, we map the Y and Z to probability distributions P_Y and P_Z, respectively, using the top one probability model (c.f. **Definition 7** in [1]). For training sample x_i, its top one probability according to Y is defined as

$$P_Y(x_i) = \frac{\exp(y_i)}{\sum_{j=1}^{n} \exp(y_j)}, \tag{5}$$

which represents the probability of the sample x_i being ranked on the top of the descending sequence π_Y. Then $P_Y = \{P_Y(x_i)\}_{i=1}^{n}$ forms a probability distribution over training set X. Likewise, x_i's top one probability according to Z is defined as

$$P_Z(x_i) = \frac{\exp(f(x_i))}{\sum_{j=1}^{n} exp(f(x_j))}. \tag{6}$$

$P_Z = \{P_Z(x_i)\}_{i=1}^{n}$ also forms a probability distribution over training set X.

Then we can take any metric between probability distributions as an order loss function. In this work the cross entropy is chosen, so the order loss function becomes

$$L_{trend}(Y, Z) = -\sum_{i=1}^{n} P_Y(x_i) \log\big(P_Z(x_i)\big). \tag{7}$$

If and only if $P_Y = P_Z$ (i. e., $\pi_Y = \pi_Z, T_Y = T_Z$), the L_{trend} reaches its minimum value. And, the more differences exist between T_Y and T_Z, the larger L_{trend} is. Finally, the total loss function L becomes

$$L = (1-\eta)\cdot\frac{1}{2n}\cdot\sum_{i=1}^{n}(y_i - f(x_i))^2 - \eta\cdot\sum_{i=1}^{n} P_Y(x_i)\log\big(P_Z(x_i)\big). \tag{8}$$

3.3 Order-Preserving Network

We next propose a learning method for optimizing the loss function defined in Eq. (8), with a neural network as model and gradient descent as optimization algorithm. Considering that this method is designed for order (trend) preservation as well as for numerical approximation, we refer to it as Order-Preserving Network (OPNet).

To guarantee the performance of our method, a three-layer nonlinear neural network model was used in the experiments.

Table 1: Learning algorithm of OPNet.

Initialize: weight matrix w and bias b
Input: training instances set $I = \{(x_i, y_i)\}_{i=1}^{n}$, number of iterations T, adjustment rate η, learning rate α and threshold ε
for $t = 1$ **to** T **do**
  Calculate $Z = \{f(x_i)\}_{i=1}^{n}$ using Eq. (9)
  Calculate total loss L using Eq. (8)
  if $L < \varepsilon$
    then Stop network training
  end if
  Calculate Δw and Δb using Eq.(10) and (11)
  Update $w = w - \alpha \cdot \Delta w$, $b = b - \alpha \cdot \Delta b$
end for
Stop network training

However, for the purpose of easy description and space saving, the description presented in this section is based on a two-layer neural network without hidden layer:

$$f(x_i) = \text{tansig}(w^{\text{T}} x_i + b), \tag{9}$$

where w is the weight matrix connecting input layer and output layer, b denotes the bias of output unit, tansig$(\cdot)$ is the transfer function to map network outputs into a range of [-1, 1].

Apparently, the loss function based on Eq. (9) is differentiable, so it can be minimized using gradient descent techniques. The gradient of $L(y, z)$ with respect to parameter $w = \{w_k\}_{k=1}^{m}$ and b can be calculated as follows,

$$\Delta w_k = \frac{\partial L(y,z)}{\partial w_k} = \Big[(1-\eta)\cdot\frac{1}{n}\cdot\sum_{i=1}^{n}\Big(f(x_i) - y_i\Big) + \eta\cdot\sum_{i=1}^{n}\Big(P_Y(x_i) - P_Z\big(f(x_i)\big)\Big)\Big]\Big(1 - f^2(x_i)\Big)x_i, \tag{10}$$

$$\Delta b = \frac{\partial L(y,z)}{\partial b} = \Big[(1-\eta)\cdot\frac{1}{n}\cdot\sum_{i=1}^{n}\Big(f(x_i) - y_i\Big) + \eta\cdot\sum_{i=1}^{n}\Big(P_Y(x_i) - P_Z\big(f(x_i)\big)\Big)\Big]\Big(1 - f^2(x_i)\Big), \tag{11}$$

where $k = 1, 2, \cdots, m$, and m denotes the number of feature's dimensions. Table 1 shows the learning method of the OPNet. From the learning method we can see that: If the adjustment rate η is set to be 0, the OPNet actually becomes equivalent to a normal feed forward neural network, while when η is set to be 1, the OPNet entirely concentrates on emotion ranking.

4. DATABASE

The database used in our work is the audio part of VAM corpus. The data was collected from a German talk-show named Vera am Mittag and consists of spontaneous, unscripted speech from the talk-show guests. All signals were recorded at 16 kHz with 16 bits per sample. It contains 47 speakers (11m/36f), and a total of 947 utterances. All utterances were annotated on three dimensions: ACTIVATION, DOMINANCE and VALENCE by 6 to 17 raters. The self assessment manikins were used as annotation scheme. Final labels for all utterances were given in the normalized range of [-1, 1] in each dimension by application of evaluator weighted es-

Table 2: **Set of 31 low-level descriptors.**

Energy & spectral low-level descriptors (25)
loudness (auditory model based), zero crossing rate, energy in bands from 250 – 650 Hz, 1 kHz – 4kHz, 25%, 50%, 75%, and 90% spectral roll-off points, spectral flux, entropy, variance, skewness, kurtosis, psychoacoustic sharpness, harmonicity, MFCC 1–10
Voicing related low-level descriptors (6)
F_0 (sub-harmonic summation (SHS) followed by Viterbi smoothing), probability of voicing, jitter, shimmer (local), jitter (delta: 'jitter of jitter'), logarithmic Harmonics-to-Noise Ratio (logHNR)

Table 3: Set of all 42 functionals. [1]Not applied to delta coefficient contours. [2]For delta coefficients the mean of only positive values is applied, otherwise the arithmetic mean is applied. [3]Not applied to voicing related LLD.

Statistical functionals (23)
(positive[2]) arithmetic mean, root quadratic mean, standard deviation, flatness, skewness, kurtosis, quartiles, inter-quartile ranges, 1 %, 99 % percentile, percentile range 1%–99%, percentage of frames contour is above: minimum +25%, 50%, and 90% of the range, percentage of frames contour is rising, maximum, mean, minimum segment length[3], standard deviation of segment length[3]
Regression functionals[1] (4)
linear regression slope, and corresponding approximation error (linear), quadratic regression coefficient a, and approximation error (linear)
Local minima/maxima related functionals[1] (9)
mean and standard deviation of rising and falling slopes (minimum to maximum), mean and standard deviation of inter maxima distances, amplitude mean of maxima, amplitude mean of minima, amplitude range of maxima
Other[1,3] (6)
Linear Prediction (LP) gain, LP Coefficients 1 – 5

timate. For more detailed information about the database, please refer to [6].

5. AUDIO FEATURE EXTRACTION

The audio feature set used is the baseline audio feature set adopted in the AVEC 2011 [7] with 1941 features, extracted by the OpenSMILE [4] toolkit at utterance level. It is composed of 25 energy and spectral related low-level descriptors (LLD) × 42 functionals, 6 voicing related LLD × 32 functionals, 25 delta coefficients of the energy/spectral LLD × 23 functionals, 6 delta coefficients of the voicing related LLD × 19 functionals, and 10 voiced/unvoiced durational features. Details for the LLD and functionals are given in Table 2 and Table 3 respectively.

6. EXPERIMENTS AND RESULTS

In order to verify the validity of the proposed OPNet, we launched a series of experiments on the VAM corpus, and compared its performance with two other baseline regression methods: k-NN and SVR as used in [6]. The VAM corpus was split into ten partitions for stratified cross validation purpose as is the standard procedure on this corpus [6]. In the experiment, our OPNet is set with three layers, with 1 unit in the output layer, 100 units in the hidden layer, and 1941 units (i.e., the size of AVEC 2011 acoustic feature set) in the input layer, respectively.

6.1 Measures of prediction

The goal of our approach is to preserve the dynamic trend of emotion for a given set of instances as much as possible. To fully assess the performance of emotion recognition methods, especially their performance on the pairwise trend preservation, we adopt the nowadays commonly used measures MLE in combination with a rank correlation coefficient (RCC) named Goodman and Kruskal's γ. In statistics, this γ test is often used to measure the degree of similarity between two rankings. Considering the close relationship between dynamic trend and ranking order as discussed in Section 3.2, it is a natural choice to employ a RCC to measure the similarity between two dynamic trends. For T_Y and T_Z and their corresponding ranking lists π_Y and π_Z, γ is defined as

$$\gamma = \frac{N_s - N_d}{N}, \tag{12}$$

where N_s denotes the number of instance pairs ranked in the same order on π_Y and π_Z, N_d denotes the number of pairs of instances ranked differently, and $N = N_s + N_d = n(n-1)/2$ is the total number of all instance pairs for a n size dataset. It is inside the interval [-1, 1] and assumes the the value -1 if one ranking is the inverse of the other, 0 if the rankings are completely independent, and 1 if the two rankings are the same.

In other words, we are actually making use of a kind of pairwise emotion trend for γ calculation. We consider the trend for every pair of instances in a given set for performance measure. For each pair of instances, its trend can be one of the following three states: upward, downward and unchangeable. By given this, the N_s becomes to the number of instance pairs which are predicted with correct trends, while the N_d becomes to the number of instance pairs which are predicted with incorrect trends. If and only if the trend for every pair of instances from the set is predicted correctly, the γ equals 1.

6.2 Results and discussion

Table 4 summarizes the MLE and γ between the predicted emotions and actual emotions for the three estimators, for each emotion dimension separately. Especially for the OPNet, to investigate the performance impact when η is changing, the measures obtained as η was assigned to .0, .2, .4, .8 and 1.0 are all shown, respectively. And when η is set to .0, the OPNet becomes a normal neural network actually.

It can be observed that the γs of **Act** (activation) and **Dom** (dominance) prediction are obviously higher than those of **Val** (valence) prediction. However, this is a well-known typical behavior as **Act** (activation) and **Dom** are usually well-assessed by acoustic descriptors, whereas **Val** benefits from linguistic information or additional facial expression information [3, 5].

Comparing the measures for SVR and OPNet ($\eta = 0$), we can see that they show similar performance on each dimension, even their MLE are just the same. In this sense, it seems that our proposed OPNet doesn't outperform SVR as

Table 4: **Performance comparison of k-NN, SVR and OPNet on VAM corpus.**

Measures		k-NN	SVR	OPNet					
				$\eta = .0$	$\eta = .2$	$\eta = .4$	$\eta = .6$	$\eta = .8$	$\eta = 1.0$
Val	MLE	.13	.13	.13	.13	.13	.13	.14	.42
	γ	.274	.301	.297	.313	.336	.357	.362	.418
Act	MLE	.18	.15	.15	.16	.16	.17	.17	.45
	γ	.539	.625	.622	.634	.657	.681	.704	.715
Dom	MLE	.16	.14	.14	.14	.15	.16	.16	.39
	γ	.532	.595	.589	.603	.634	.651	.670	.726

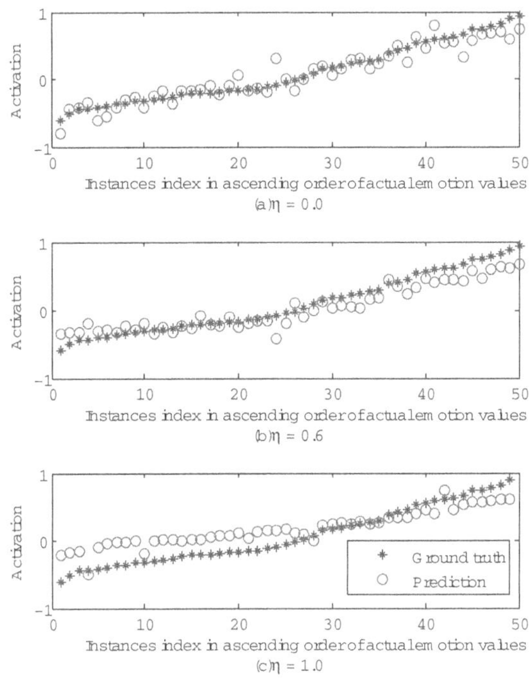

Figure 1: Emotion prediction results by OPNet when $\eta =$ .0, .6 and 1.0: results in comparison with ground truth.

we looked forward to, especially in the task of preserving the dynamic trend of emotion. Actually, this is because when the η is set to 0, our OPNet just becomes to a normal feed forward network. So we need to modify the value of η to adjust the performance of OPNet. We can realize clearly that when the η increases, OPNet's γ becomes higher as well, which means the capability of OPNet for emotion trend preservation becomes better. It has to be noted that when η is less than .8, the γ increases slowly and steadily, but after that point the rise of γ becomes relatively fast.

However, we observe that for the improvement of γ, we pay a cost of deterioration of MLE. Take the **Act** prediction as an example, with an increasing η from .0 to 1.0, the γ is improved from .622 to .715, whereas MLE is increased from .15 to .45. When η equals 1.0, its MLE are even worse than k-NN. But this is reasonable, since OPNet's focus is shifting to trend preservation more and more along with η's increase (cf. Eq. (3)). Moreover, from the table we can see that when η is set to be .4, the OPNet achieves similar MLE with k-NN, and better γ than both the k-NN and SVR.

As a summary of the results, we randomly select 50 instances from the test set, and draw their prediction results in Fig.1. In this figure, the emotion values are arranged in ascending order for clear comparison. We can see clearly that with the growth of η the emotion trend of these 50 instances becomes better.

7. CONCLUSION

In this paper, we believe that a strong capability for predicting correct dynamic trend of emotion can assist a human-computer interface to make correct decisions. Driven by this, our work then mainly focused on the modeling of a dimensional SER approach considering the preservation of actual dynamic trend of emotion in the prediction process. Specifically, the key issue of dimensional SER was formalized to be a minimization task of a loss function. Moreover, numerical loss and trend loss were linearly combined to construct the total loss function in this paper. For trend loss definition, a probability method was used: firstly the sequence of predicted emotion values and the sequence of actual emotion values were mapped to two top one probability distributions, then a metric between probability distributions named cross entropy was calculated as trend loss. Next, the optimization of loss function was implemented by the proposed OPNet algorithm. The core of the OPNet involved a neural network model and a gradient descent optimization. For the experimental verification, a rank correlation coefficient named Goodman and Kruskal's γ was imported to measure the degree of trend similarity between two emotion sequences. With γ, the SER system's capability of preserving the dynamic trend of emotion can be reflected intuitively. The experiment results show that, comparing to normal regression methods, the proposed OPNet expresses better capability on preserving the dynamic trend of emotion with a suitable adjustment rata η.

As to future work, we intend to investigate on the dynamic trend of emotion for each person during a meaningful speech segment instead the whole range of a database. We also plan to try different measures to evaluate the degree of trend similarity between two emotion sequences.

8. REFERENCES

[1] Z. Cao, T. Qin, and T. Liu. Learning to rank: from pairwise approach to listwise approach. In *ICML*, pages 129–136, Corvallis, USA, 2007.

[2] E. Douglas-Cowie, R. Cowie, I. Sneddon, C. Cox, O. Lowry, M. McRorie, J.-C. Martin, L. Devillers, S. Abrilian, A. Batliner, N. Amir, and K. Karpouzis. The HUMAINE database: Addressing the collection and annotation of naturalistic and induced emotional data. *Lecture Notes in Computer Science*, 4738:488–500, 2007.

[3] F. Eyben, M. Wöllmer, A. Graves, B. Schuller, E. Douglas-Cowie, and R. Cowie. On-line emotion recognition in a 3-D activation-valence-time continuum using acoustic and linguistic cues. *Journal on Multimodal User Interfaces*, 3:7–19, 2010.

[4] F. Eyben, M. Wöllmer, and B. Schuller. openSMILE - the Munich versatile and fast open-source audio feature extractor. In *ACM Multimedia*, pages 1459–1462, Firenze, Italy, 2010.

[5] M. Grimm, K. Kroschel, and S. Narayanan. Support vector regression for automatic recognition of spontaneous emotions in speech. In *ICASSP*, volume IV, pages 1085–1088, Honolulu, USA, 2007. IEEE.

[6] M. Grimm, K. Kroschel, and S. Narayanan. The Vera am Mittag German audio-visual emotional speech database. In *ICME*, pages 865–868, Hannover, Germany, 2008.

[7] B. Schuller, M. Valstar, F. Eyben, G. McKeown, R. Cowie, and M. Pantic. AVEC 2011 - the first international audio/visual emotion challenge. *Lecture Notes in Computer Science*, 6975:415–424, 2011.

[8] M. Wöllmer, F. Eyben, S. Reiter, B. Schuller, C. Cox, E. Douglas-Cowie, and R. Cowie. Abandoning emotion classes - towards continuous emotion recognition with modelling of long-range dependencies. In *INTERSPEECH*, pages 597–600, Brisbane, 2008.

Negative Sentiment in Scenarios Elicit Pupil Dilation Response: An Auditory Study

Serdar Baltaci
Informatics Institute
METU
Ankara, TURKEY
90 312 343 15 73
baltaci@ii.metu.edu.tr

Didem Gokcay
Informatics Institute
METU
Ankara, TURKEY
90 312 210 37 50
didem@ii.metu.edu.tr

ABSTRACT
Earlier investigations of pupil size variation during auditory stimulation involved delivery of simple auditory tones. In this study, we investigated pupil size variation in response to auditory stimuli which involved verbal stories. In our study, twenty four participants listened to scenarios with headphones while sitting in front of an eye tracker and rated stories on two bipolar dimensions: emotional valence and arousal. We analyzed pupil data after finishing subjective ratings of scenario. The results showed that the pupil size is significantly large during the story which carried strongly negative sentiment compared to the story with neutral content. To sum up, our results showed that systematically designed scenarios with highly arousing negative sentiment significantly affected the subjects' physiological pupil reaction as well as their subjective experiences. In the future, it might be possible to use pupil size variation as a predictor for sentimental content of scenarios. Auditory emotion-related cues might also be utilized to modulate the users' emotional reactions in affective computing.

Categories and Subject Descriptors
H.1.2 [Models and Principles]: User/Machine Systems - human factors, Human Information Processing. H.5.2 [Information Interfaces and Presentation]: User Interfaces – Evaluation and Methodology

General Terms
Design, experimentation, human factors.

Keywords
Pupil dilation, autonomic nervous system, affective computing, auditory stimuli.

1. INTRODUCTION
Subjective experience, emotional expression, and physical sensation are three distinct but complementary components of emotions. While subjective experience, or in other words, personal feeling of current emotions is hard to investigate, emotional expression is easy to study especially through facial expressions. The third component, physical sensation is manifested through the autonomous nervous system, which in turn modifies physiological arousal. Changes in physiological arousal are quantifiable through skin conductance, thermal camera recordings and pupil dilation [6].

Compared to the measurements of other physiological signals, the measurement of pupil size has important advantages. It is an unobtrusive method because no sensors have to be attached to the user. An important advantage of pupil size measurement is that pupil size variation is an involuntary index of autonomic nervous system (ANS) activity. This means that pupil size variation is not easy to control voluntarily and thus, it identifies real spontaneous activity. It is known from facial expression research that visually observable changes in facial emotional behavior can be and are masked, inhibited, exaggerated, and faked [1,7-9].

In psychological research, pupil size measurements have been used for years. It is known that beside lighting conditions, pupil size will react in response to cognitive effort, mental imagery effects and various forms of stimuli, such as images and sounds [2]. Partala, Jokiniemi, and Surakka [3] reported increased pupil dilation even when participants listened to affectively engaging sounds compared to neutral sounds, suggesting that emotional arousal prompts pupillary dilation even when the perceptual context is not visual. For instance, when auditory tones are used, pupil dilation is detected in a stable way for different tones [11]. In [10], audio and visual features, in [5] visual features and in [1] standardized audio features are used in order to detect emotion. Specific contribution of our study lies in the investigation of pupil dilation in response to the emotional content embedded within stories delivered through only the auditory channel. In our study, users are administered a cognitively engaging story auditorily, while we measured pupil size using a Tobii eye-tracker. The technology needed for the measurement of pupil size is relatively simple. Today's commercial eye tracking systems provide possibility for real time gaze tracking and also pupil size measurement without restraining the head [4]. We used task completion time and subjective ratings of arousal/valence to validate the emotional content of the scenarios in the stories. Our results, as explained in the following sections show that a negative scenario induces higher subjective ratings of arousal and reliably evokes greater pupillary response than a neutral scenario.

ICMI'12, October 22–26, 2012, Santa Monica, California, USA.
Copyright 2012 ACM 978-1-4503-1467-1/12/10...$15.00.

2. EXPERIMENT

2.1 Participants

Twenty-four (10 F, 14 M) 24-42 year-old subjects participated in two experiments. The experiment order was counter-balanced across subjects. Subjects reported their social status as single (29%), married (33.5%) and married with a child (37.5%). The subjects were in good health, free of any pathological condition in their eyes.

2.2 Materials and Design

Two scenarios are administered in two experiments. In each scenario, a single story is vocalized by a woman voice saved in standard sound format (Windows WMV). A 30 second excerpt from a classical soundtrack is added proceeding and succeeding the voice recording. Using Adobe Audition 5.0 application, some sound effects are incorporated. Each story is designed to contain four parts: 1. Music, 2. Introduction with neutral sentiment, 3. Unfolding story (in experiment 1 this part has strong negative sentiment, while in experiment 2 this part has neutral sentiment), 4. Music. During the experiment, the visual input was restricted to a gray blank screen.

Full text of First Story:

(1) Music (2) You are driving on a highway at midnight, in complete darkness. Your spouse is asleep next to you. Your 1.5 year old baby is sitting at the back of the car. (3) Suddenly you brake abruptly when you are about to hit a log on the road. (Brake noise effect) While you are trying to remove the log from the road, two armed men appear in the bushes coming towards you. Your spouse wakes up at that moment, but meanwhile one of the men grabs your child. (crying child and scream effects) Despite your efforts, they restrain your baby. When you make a move they fire at your spouse (gunshot effect) and your spouse collapses on the ground in blood. (Plumping effect) (4) Music

Full text of Second Story:

(1) Music (2) You are a government employee. Your spouse is working in a bank. Your 6 year-old-child will start school this year. You went to your hometown for vacation two weeks ago and you have just returned recently (ocean wave effect) (3) Many errands that should be finished have accumulated. You are trying to readjust to the monotonous daily life. You prepare a to-do list. School supplies will be bought, registration fees will be deposited. You check transactions of your bank accounts while drinking tea. At that time your eyes stick on the calendar. It seems like the next vacation is years away. (4) Music

Between these stories, subjects are given a 5 minute rest in order to reset the influence of emotions. Pupil size and eye movements are recorded during experiments. For the first story, we anticipated a negative reaction in the subjects in terms of increased pupil size, and for the second story, we anticipated no change in the reaction of the subjects.

2.3 Apparatus

Experiments are controlled by an in-house .Net application. Pupil diameter is recorded using a Tobii TX-300 model eye-tracker system, which allows free movement of the head and consists of a video camera and an infrared light source pointed at the participants' right and left eyes. Pupil diameter was sampled at 120 Hz.

2.4 Procedure

The subjects voluntarily participated in the experiment in exchange for candy bars. Participants are introduced to the eye-tracking device and are seated as comfortably as possible. The experimenter informed the subjects that they were about to listen to two different stories and immediately after listening to each story, they would be asked to rate valence and arousal on a scale identified by the self-assessment manikin (SAM) (see Figure 1). On the valence scale, SAM is a graphic figure that ranges from a happy face to frowning face. For the arousal dimension, the SAM scale ranges from excited to relaxed. Participants indicate feeling either happy or unhappy (i.e., neutral), or either calm or aroused, using the midpoint of each scale. In this version of SAM, the participant can fill in any of the figures resulting in a 9-point rating scale for each dimension [5].

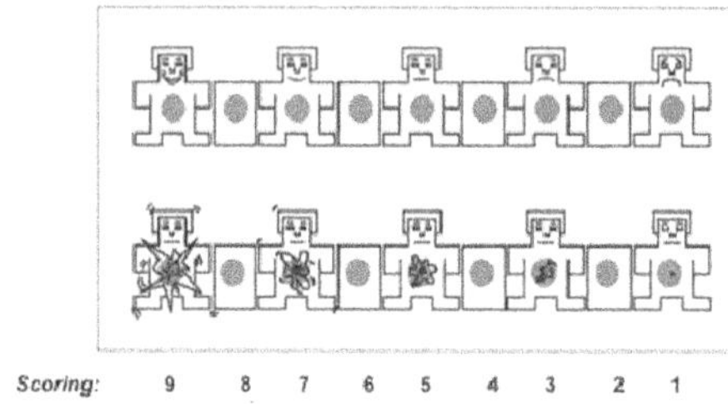

Figure 1. Story evaluation scales: valence (top), arousal (bottom)

2.5 Data Analysis

The data is pre-processed such that when the pupil was obscured due to blinking, linear interpolation is used to estimate pupil size. A 1 second pre-voice baseline average is subtracted from each of the following pupil samples. After pre-processing, only the first three parts of the story are used for future analysis. For these three parts of data in each story, there were unequal sample sizes. So we determined minimum number of samples for each part and then used these in order to compare the same time-length across different parts of the experiment. Between left and right pupil, a strong correlation (0.787) in pupil size is detected. Therefore only left pupil size is considered in our statistical analysis.

3. RESULTS

According to Table 1, the participants evaluated the first story as containing negative emotion with high arousal, while they evaluated the second as neutral on both valence and arousal scales. Therefore we verified that story 1 had strong negative sentiment while story 2 is neutral.

Table 1: SAM Ratings

Experiment	Story 1		Story 2	
	Valence	Arousal	Valence	Arousal
Average	1,375	7,416	4,416	3,541
STD	0,923	1,316	1,248	1,473

Figures 2 and 3 illustrate the change of pupil size with respect to time in scenarios 1 and 2. The first part (shown in blue) has music and second/third parts (shown in green/red) have voice recording enhanced with effects. According to these figures, human voice affects pupil size of participants more than music. In addition, the first scenario which had negative valence and high arousal, contains a steep increase in the pupil size in parts 2 and 3. On the contrary, for the neutral scenario presented in story two, the subjects' pupil exhibits a more or less steady size for parts 2 & 3.

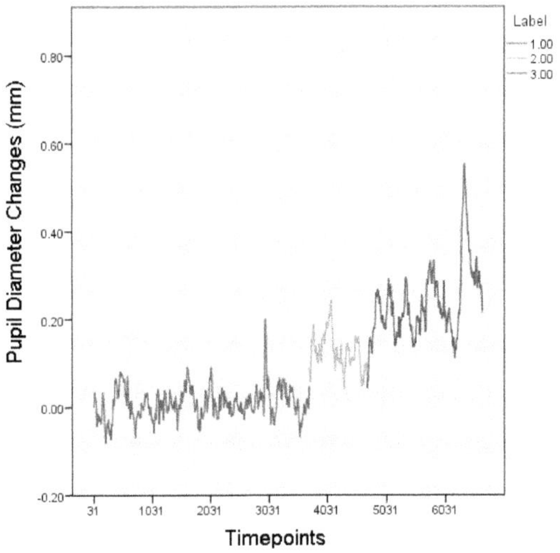

Figure 2. Averaged pupil size for all participants in story 1

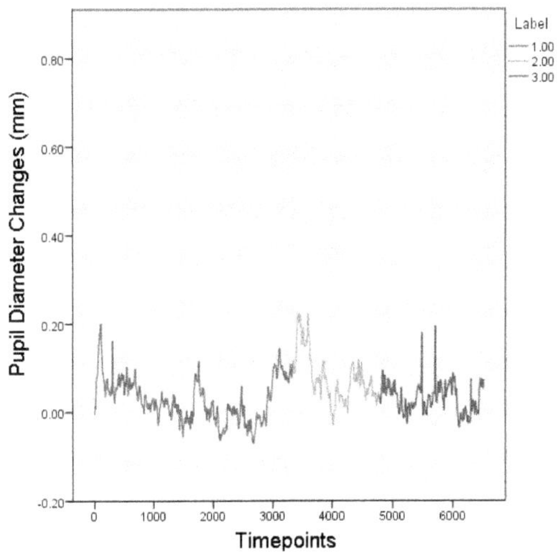

Figure 3. Averaged pupil size for all participants in story 2

In Figure , the mean of pupil diameter values are illustrated for the three separate parts of the stories: 1. Music, 2. Introduction, 3. Unfolding scene. As seen from figure 4, in the first scenario, second and third parts have higher means of pupil size than the first part. In the second scenario, between the first and second part there is a meaningful difference in the pupil size. On the other hand in the third part, pupil size decreases.

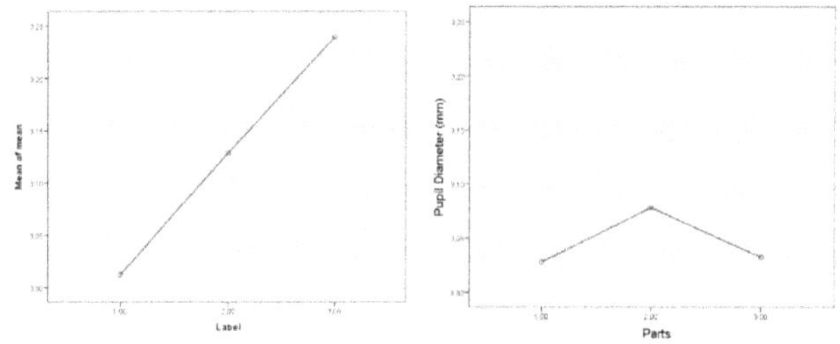

Figure 4. Pupil diameter means for three parts of each scenario

We also investigated gender differences. As seen in figure 5, female's pupil dilation mean for both scenarios is greater than male's.

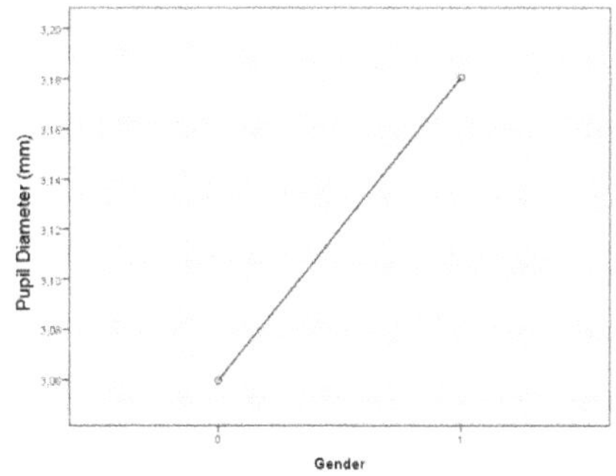

Figure 5. Gender effects in pupil size. 0:Male, 1:Female

Social status is also explored as shown in figure 6. Single subject's pupil diameter mean is greater than married subjects. Married subjects with children have the lowest pupil diameter mean.

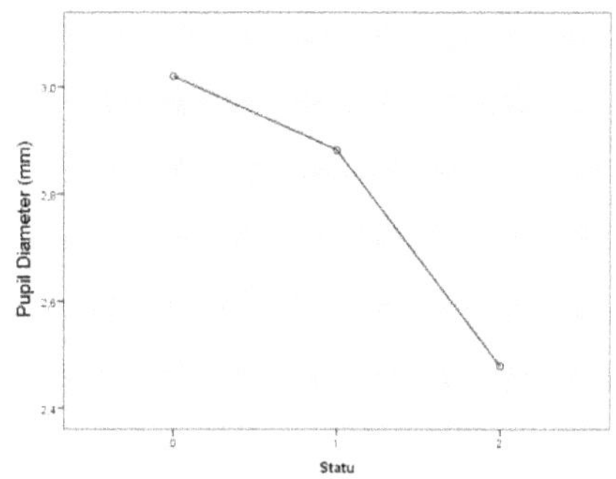

Figure 6. Social status effects on pupil size.

0:Single, 1:Married, 2:Married with a child

Kolmogorov-Smirnov tests are performed to check for deviations from normality of the distributions of these parameters. After checking for normality using Kolmogorov-Smirnov tests in SPSS 20, if p value is below 0.05, then the data significantly deviates from a normal distribution. If also the significance result for homogeneity of variance is less than 0.05, the error variance of the dependent variable is not equal across the groups. Since both of these conditions are met in our data, the assumption of the ANOVA test has been violated, introducing a necessity to perform non-parametric tests.

Since the data does not adhere to normal distribution, we used Wilcoxon-Mann-Whitney test analog to the independent samples t-test. For pupil data, it is concluded that there is a statistically significant difference between story 1 and story 2 ($Z = -71.843$, $p = 0.000$). For pupil data across gender, there is a statistically significant difference ($Z_{left} = -209.786$, $p_{left} = 0.000$, $Z_{right} = -210.118$, $p_{right} = 0.000$) and for pupil data across social status, there is an also statistically significant difference ($Z_{left} = -136.786$, $p_{left} = 0.000$, $Z_{right} = -68.118$, $p_{right} = 0.000$).

Kruskal-Wallis Test (Non-parametric independent group comparisons distribution-free) is used to compare three or more independent groups of sampled data. Unlike the parametric independent group ANOVA (one way ANOVA), this non-parametric test makes no assumptions about the distribution of the data (e.g., normality). For the pupil data with respect to different parts of the story, we can report that there is a statistically significant difference ($H(2) = 4413.567$, $P = 0.000$).

We also investigated receiver operator curve (ROC) characteristics to find out whether pupil size can be used as a sentiment predictor. We joined pupil results from both experiments such that pupil dilation for story 1 indicated a true positive for negative sentiment but pupil dilation for story 2 indicated a false alarm for neutral sentiment. On the other hand, no pupil dilation for story 2 serves as a true negative type of response. Using thresholds based on pupil size change with respect to the average of baseline pupil size, we obtained the ROC for left and right pupil size as shown in figures 7 and 8. From these curves, we conclude that the left pupil size can be used as a negative sentiment predictor. A suitable threshold could be set at a true positive rate of 0.85 and a false alarm rate of 0.32.

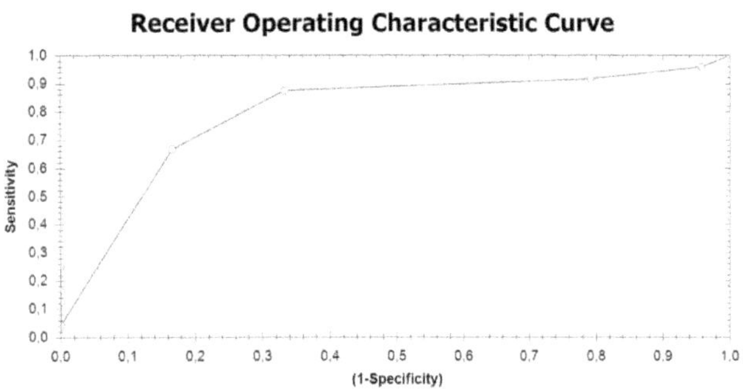

Figure 7. ROC characteristic for left pupil size

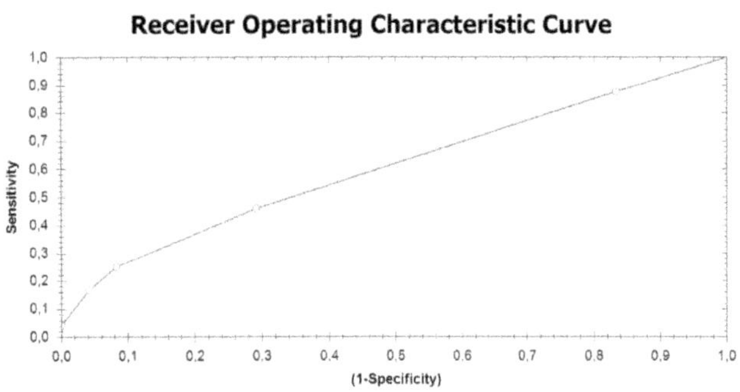

Figure 8. ROC characteristic for right pupil size

4. CONCLUSION

Pupil dilation is a low level response of the autonomic nervous system and it is very sensitive to arousal in emotions, as well as light conditions. We have stabilized the light condition by asking subjects to stare at a gray blank screen. Therefore in our experiments, we captured pupil size change in response to the content of the stories, while stories are delivered verbally through the auditory channel. Auditory scenarios should be well designed and stories should be spoken with great emphasis on emotions in order to affect participants.

From the results of our preliminary study, we conclude that using pupil dilation, negative sentiment induced on the subjects can be detected from auditory scenarios that contain high arousal. The results indicate that pupil dilation occurs when there is a switch from music to talk. In addition, when the content of the story is negatively arousing, pupil dilation is significantly higher in comparison to when the story has a neutral content. Gender and social status also have a meaningful influence on pupil size. Female and single subjects are the most sensitive participants. By generating ROC curves and using a suitable threshold value for pupil dilation, response to a negatively arousing scenario can be predicted approximately with an accuracy of 85% while false alarm stays in the range of 30%.

5. REFERENCES

[1] Partala T. and Surakka V, 2003, Pupil size variation as an indication of affective processing. International Journal of Human-Computer Studies. 59(1–2), 185–98.

[2] Bradley MM, Miccoli L, Escrig MA, Lang PJ (2008) The pupil as a measure of emotional arousal and autonomic activation. Psychophysiology 45:602–607.

[3] Partala, T., Jokiniemi, M., & Surakka, V. (2000). Pupillary responses to emotionally provocative stimuli. In Eye tracking research & application: Proceedings of the 2000 symposium on eye tracking research andapplications (pp. 123–129). New York: ACM Press.

[4] Tobii Technology. http://www.tobii.com/ Website accessed 1/8/2008.

[5] Bradley, M.M., Lang, P.J., 1994. Measuring emotion: the self-assessment manikin and the semantic differential. Journal of Behavioral Therapy and Experimental Psychiatry 25, 49–59.

[6] Didem Gokcay, Serdar Baltaci, Cagri Karahan, Kemal Dogus Turkay, 2011 Prediction of Affective States through Non-invasive Thermal Camera and EMG Recordings. ACII 2, 319-321

[7] Ekman, P., 1985. Telling Lies. W. W. Norton, New York.

[8] Ekman, P., Friesen, W.V., 1982. Felt, false, and miserable smiles. Journal of Nonverbal Behavior 6, 238–252.

[9] Surakka, V., Hietanen, J.K., 1998. Facial and emotional reactions to duchenne and non-duchenne smiles. International Journal of Psychophysiology 29, 23–33.

[10] L. Morency, R. Mihalcea, and P. Doshi, 2011, Towards multimodal sentiment analysis: harvesting opinions from the web, In Proceedings of ICMI., 169-176.

[11] Wang CA, Munoz D and Boehnke S, 2012, Pupil dilation evoked by a salient auditory stimulus facilitates saccade reaction times to a visual stimulus. Journal of Vision, 12 9-1254

Design and Implementation of the Note-taking Style Haptic Voice Recognition for Mobile Devices

Seungwhan Moon
Franklin W. Olin College of Engineering
1000 Olin Way
Needham, MA, U.S.A.
me@shanemoon.com

Khe Chai Sim
National University of Singapore
Computing 1, 13 Computing Drive
Singapore, Singapore 117417
simkc@nus.edu.sg

ABSTRACT

This research proposes the "note-taking style" Haptic Voice Recognition (HVR) technology which incorporates speech and touch sensory inputs in a note-like form to enhance the performance of speech recognition. A *note* is taken from a user via two different haptic input methods - handwriting and a keyboard. A note consists of some of the keywords in the given utterance, either partially spelled or fully spelled. In order to facilitate fast input, the interface allows a shorthand writing system such as Gregg Shorthand. Using this *haptic note sequence* as an additional knowledge source, the algorithm re-ranks the n-best list generated by a speech engine. The simulation and experimental results show that the proposed HVR method improves the Word Error Rate (WER) and Keyword Error Rate (KER) performance in comparison to an Automatic Speech Recognition (ASR) system. Although it generates an inevitable increase in speech duration due to disfluency and occasional mistakes in haptic input, the compensation is shown to be less than conventional HVR methods. As such, this new note-taking style HVR interaction has the potential to be both natural and effective in increasing the recognition performance by choosing the most likely utterance among multiple hypotheses. This paper discusses the algorithm for the proposed system, the results from the simulation and the experiments, and the possible applications of this new technology such as aiding spoken document retrieval with haptic notes.

Categories and Subject Descriptors

I.2.7 [**Artificial Intelligence**]: Natural Language Processing—*Speech recognition and synthesis*; H.5.2 [**Information Interfaces and Presentation**]: User Interfaces—*Haptic I/O*

Keywords

Spoken document retrieval; haptic voice recognition; note-taking style; multi-modal Interface

ICMI'12, October 22–26, 2012, Santa Monica, California, USA.

1. INTRODUCTION

As an increasing number of mobile devices support speech recognition technology as a native application, automatic speech recognition (ASR) technology is becoming a popular method of interaction among smartphone users. ASR technology essentially enables verbal communication between humans and mobile devices, thus providing the most natural interaction experience to users. However, the recognition performance of ASR often does not meet the accuracy to be a primary method of interaction for mobile devices, especially in a noisy environment. As a result, most of the users still choose to use the touch interface as a main input medium.

Haptic Voice Recognition (HVR) is a multi-modal interface that combines speech data with touch sensory inputs via a mobile device to improve voice recognition performance. HVR uses haptic events such as taps or strokes as additional cues, thus filtering away the less probable sequences of words given a speech utterance. Examples of haptic inputs include the Boundary of Sentences (BoS), Boundary of Words (BoW), First Letter of Words (FLoW), etc. Previous research in this field has significantly improved the performance of speech dictation, as shown in the decreased Word Error Rate (WER) and increased Runtime Factor (xRT) performance of HVR, compared to those of conventional Automatic Speech Recognition (ASR). The prior studies however, led to an increased duration of speech and the atypical fluency [9, 10].

In this paper, a different method of combining speech and haptic input, named the *note-taking style* HVR, is examined. In the note-taking style HVR, haptic inputs in the form of a note are used as additional cues to aid in choosing the most likely candidate for a given utterance. In order to maximize the freedom of usability, the note-taking style HVR allows shorthand sequences such as shorthand letters and partially spelled words as haptic inputs. Shorthand writing is a difficult skill to acquire for beginners, but the experts of shorthand systems such as Gregg Shorthand [3], Pitman Shorthand [7], or Teeline Shorthand [2] are known to be able to write five to ten times faster than the average handwriting for the Roman alphabet [3]. In this research, the Gregg shorthand alphabet (Figure 1) is used because of its popularity among journalists and other professionals. This paper defines the rules and algorithms for the note-taking style HVR, and examines its feasibility by conducting simulations and preliminary user studies. Finally, the paper examines the possible applications of the suggested algorithm as well as the future works that may be conducted.

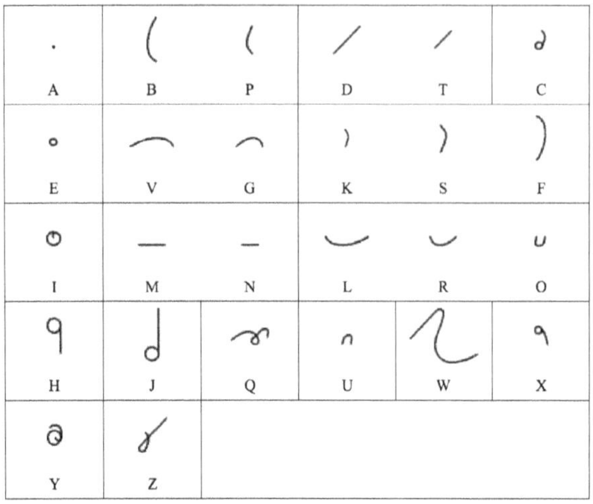

Figure 1: A list of Gregg shorthand letters used in the Note-taking style HVR grouped by their shapes

2. NOTE-TAKING STYLE HAPTIC VOICE RECOGNITION

Note-taking is a natural way of recording information that accompanies verbal communication, which aids in the recognition and retention of both human thoughts and communication. A note is typically taken synchronously with speech, and is usually composed of a series of keywords or shorthand symbols that represent the context of the given speech. As note-taking is a common process widely performed in recording lectures or daily conversations, it is empirically known as a simple task that does not require much cognitive attention.

As such, we design the note-taking style HVR such that it resembles the process of natural note-taking on paper. In the note-taking style HVR, a *note* will be taken synchronously with voice input via touch screen. The optimal interface would thus include both a hand-held touch device and a touch-sensitive stylus pen. A note consists of a sequence of keywords associated with the given speech utterance. Each keyword can be either fully or partially spelled in letters, spelled as common abbreviations, or written in shorthand symbols. Partially spelled words or shorthand symbols add ambiguity, which can be considered as a trade-off for faster input. In this paper, such Partial Lexicon Information (PLI), or a series of partially or fully spelled words that are given by the haptic events is referred to as a *haptic note sequence*. In order to maximize the freedom of usability and the performance of the system , the note-taking style HVR imposes the following rules:

1. An element in a haptic note sequence refers to a partially or fully spelled word in the decoded word sequence.
2. The number and the order of keywords in a haptic note sequence do not need to match those of words in the actual word sequence.
3. The exact time at which a haptic event occurs is ignored.

The first rule ensures that an element of a haptic note sequence is relevant to the actual sequence in terms of its format as well as its context or semantics. The second rule allows users freedom of choosing the context and semantics of the haptic note sequence. The third rule ensures that users will not be concerned about synchronizing the speech and the haptic input. These rules are intended to let users interact in the most natural way possible. Using this haptic information as additional knowledge sources, the algorithm re-ranks the likelihood of the n-best utterances returned by a speech recognition engine. The following sections describe the essential components and the algorithm of the note-taking style HVR in detail.

2.1 Haptic Input Methods

In order to aid the user experience in providing the haptic input, two types of haptic events are allowed: taps and strokes (Figure 2). Tap events are triggered when a user touches the screen with his or her finger, and are defined by the time and location (x, y coordinate of the screen) at which the touch event occurred. Stroke events, on the other hand, are defined by the sequence of times and locations of touch events from the initial touch until the removal of the finger [9]. Therefore, handwritten letters or shorthand symbols can be trained as an ordered sequence of coordinates using Hidden Markov Models (HMM) [4, 5, 12]. For tap events, letters and symbols can be input via a virtual keyboard that consists of a grid layout of letters and symbols.

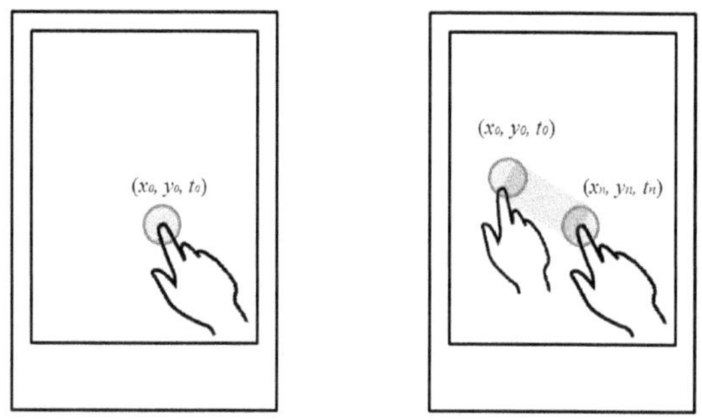

(a) Tap Events (b) Stroke Events

Figure 2: Illustration for a tap event and a stroke event

The series of input letters is split into groups by a white space, each of which is considered as a fully or partially spelled word in a haptic note sequence. For stroke events, words are separated using the simple white space detection algorithm by relative proximity of letters. For tap events, words are separated by an explicit input of a white space.

2.2 Gregg Shorthand Handwriting Recognition for HVR

In order to facilitate fast input, a sequence of words written in Gregg shorthand symbols is accepted as a haptic input as well. Gregg shorthand is completely based on elliptical figures and lines that bisect them, allowing the fastest input possible via handwriting [3]. However, handwriting recognition for Gregg shorthand can be challenging, because some of the letters that have phonetic similarities, such as 'b' and 'p', 'r' and 'l', also have similar shapes (Figure 1). For effective handwriting recognition for HVR, such letters are classified into groups, thus enhancing the overall recognition accuracy. The haptic note sequence written in Gregg symbols thus has to incorporate all the possible permutations of spellings of words as alternatives, which adds ambiguity to the partial lexicon information.

The original Gregg shorthand system has a set of rules that facilitates fast and effective input. For example, the traditional Gregg shorthand system encourages writers to spell words phonetically, which makes writing faster, but significantly harder to retrieve the written document. In order to avoid unnecessary ambiguity added to the haptic note sequence, the Note-taking style HVR specifies users to follow the conventional spelling of words. This paper examines the efficacy and validity of the 'borrowed' Gregg shorthand system optimized for HVR.

2.3 Algorithm Design

Sim [10] defines the haptic voice recognition problem as finding the joint optimal solution for the word sequence, $\hat{\mathcal{W}}$ and the PLI sequence, $\hat{\mathcal{L}}$, given the sequence of observed acoustic features, $\mathcal{O}$, and the sequence of haptic features, $\mathcal{H}$. This definition can be expressed as the following equation:

$$(\hat{\mathcal{W}}, \hat{\mathcal{L}}) = \arg\max_{\mathcal{W},\mathcal{L}} P(\mathcal{W}, \mathcal{L}|\mathcal{O}, \mathcal{H}) \qquad (1)$$

By expanding (1), Sim [10] identifies the four knowledge sources that incorporate HVR, which are the acoustic model score, the language model score, the haptic model score, and the PLI model score. These knowledge sources can be represented as Weighted Finite State Transducers (WFSTs) [6], and the composition operator ($\circ$) can integrate them into a single WFST, of which the shortest path refers to the optimal solution of (1). In the case of the note-taking style HVR, the merged WFST can be expressed as:

$$\bar{\mathcal{F}} = \hat{\mathcal{L}} \circ \bar{\mathcal{P}} \circ \hat{\mathcal{H}} \qquad (2)$$

where $\hat{\mathcal{L}}$, $\bar{\mathcal{P}}$, $\hat{\mathcal{H}}$ denote the WFST representation of the lattice that consists of multiple hypotheses of word sequences decoded by a speech engine, the PLI model, and the lattice of the permutations of the haptic note sequence. Essentially, $\bar{\mathcal{P}}$ serves as the merger that defines the alignment between $\hat{\mathcal{L}}$ and $\hat{\mathcal{H}}$, by assigning non-zero values for *substitution* and *insertion cost*. The distance between a haptic note sequence and a decoded sequence can be determined by computing the edit penalties of $\bar{\mathcal{P}}$. Since the actual order of keywords in a haptic note is ambiguous, all the possible permutations of N words ($N!$) are considered. Finally, the combined WFST ($\bar{\mathcal{F}}$) can be sorted by the computed distances, the process of which is referred to as *lattice rescoring* [10]. Essentially, the whole process can be viewed as re-ranking the n-best list by measuring how probable each decoded word sequence is given the haptic note sequence.

In this research, OpenFST[1], an open source library for performing FST operations [1], was used in order to implement the described process. The n-best list, the PLI model, and the haptic notes were compiled into the WFST representations using `fstcompile` method, which were then composed into a single WFST by executing the `fstcompose` method. Finally, `fstshortestpath` was used to get the n-shortest paths of $\bar{\mathcal{F}}$.

Figure 3 shows an example of the re-ranked n-best list given a haptic note sequence. Note that the best choice

[1]http://www.openfst.org

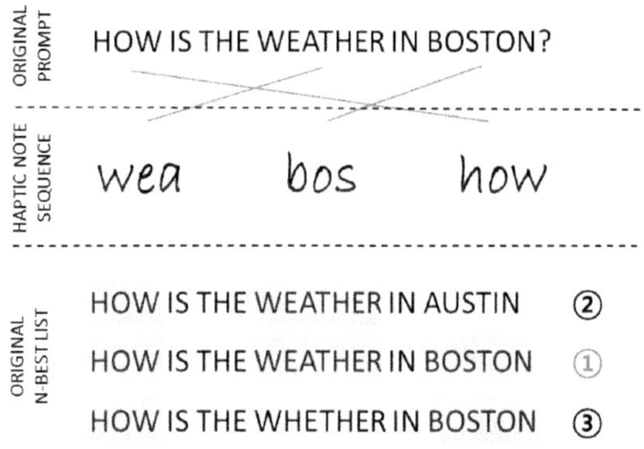

Figure 3: An example of the re-ranked word sequences, given a speech utterance "How is the weather in Boston" and a partially spelled haptic note sequence 'wea bos how.'

after re-ranking has the most number of words matched with the given haptic note sequence, thus having the shortest distance. Note also that if multiple hypotheses have the same distances, they are secondly sorted according to their ranks from the original n-best list.

Note that this method is different from some of the haptic methods which aid in the recognition process by pruning the search space during the decoding process, which is referred to as *haptic pruning*. Haptic events such as First Letter of Words (FLoW) via *integrated decoding*, for example, can effectively prune the search space under the rule that dth haptic input matches the dth word of the decoded sequence of words. If the letter specified by the dth haptic input does not match the first letter of dth word in the Word Link Record (WLR), such word can be pruned away, thereby improving the efficiency of the recognition process. When a WLR is haptically pruned, it improves the runtime factor performance as well as the recognition accuracy [9, 10].

On the other hand, the process of lattice rescoring is independent of a speech engine, and thus it cannot prune away the search space during the decoding process. This is because lattice rescoring is an additional re-validation of the given n-best list. As such, it does not improve the runtime factor of the speech engine itself. It also indicates that the performance of the note-taking style HVR is largely dependent on the quality of the ASR speech engine that it is based on.

3. EXPERIMENTAL RESULTS

In order to investigate the feasibility of the Note-taking Style HVR, the following simulation and experiments were conducted. For each experiment, the Google Speech Recognition API was used to get a 20-best list for each speech input.

3.1 Simulation

The following simulation was performed in order to investigate the theoretical performance improvement over different numbers of haptic input. For each prompt, artificial haptic events were generated by randomly choosing N words from the prompt sentence. In reality, a user would spot and choose the keywords in the sentence, and write or type those keywords by using one of the haptic input interfaces described earlier. This simulated haptic note sequence is then used to find the distance from the n-best list generated by the speech engine.

For each iteration, N words were randomly chosen from each sentence. Two cases were considered for each chosen word: when only the first three letters of the word were provided (partially spelled), and when it was fully spelled. The simulation was repeated from $N = 1$ to $N = 9$, each repeated 100 times, under two different Sound Noise Ratios (SNR) - clean and 15dB. The 15dB sound data were obtained by artificially corrupting the original speech data with the *babble* noise from the NOISEX-92 database [11]. In this simulation, 72 sentences from the Wall Street Journal Database [8] were used. In order to compare the performance with that of other HVR methods, artificial haptic events for FLoW were also generated and tested. Lastly, the Oracle Error Rate, which indicates the lowest WER obtainable from the 20-best list, was measured as a reference for the quality of the speech engine. Figure 4(a) and 4(b) show the simulation results.

As seen in Figure 4(a) and 4(b), the performance of the N-W method reaches its oracle WER at $N = 9$. This shows that the upper boundary for improvement in WER is bounded by the quality of the speech engine that the note-taking style HVR is based on. Note that the differential improvement of WER decreases as N increases. This indicates that the PLI information becomes redundant as the number of the given keywords increases. A user can thus determine the number of keywords to provide, with the trade-off in time duration in mind. Note also that the standard deviations of WER during the 100 simulations on the Note-taking Style HVR are significant. This indicates that the performance of the Note-taking Style HVR greatly depends on the words that a user chooses as their keywords. A user might want to give the words that are often mis-recognized by the speech engine (due to their phonetical or grammatical nature) as keywords, in order to maximize the efficiency of the system. However, this information is not given to users most of the time. Users would rather naturally choose the words that are more important in the context of the sentence. Hence, the results of the actual experiments with more realistic haptic input are presented in the next section.

3.2 Preliminary User Studies

In order to perform preliminary user studies, a prototype interface (Figure 5) was developed for data collection. The data acquisition was conducted under the following protocol: a user provides both speech and haptic note sequence data, given a written prompt and a set of keywords. The experiment is repeated for four different haptic input methods - First Letter of Word (FLoW), haptic note sequence of the first 3 letters of the 3 chosen words (3W3L) inputted by longhand (normal) handwriting, Gregg shorthand handwriting, and touch keyboard. For Gregg shorthand writing, the interface displayed the Gregg symbol representation of the keywords so that a user without expertise in shorthand writing could trace. The 3W3L was performed in this experiment because it showed a good improvement in WER while having the minimal increase in the duration of speech. 72 sentences were randomly selected from WSJ Database, and were recorded by a single user for each haptic input method. The results were compared with the data recorded

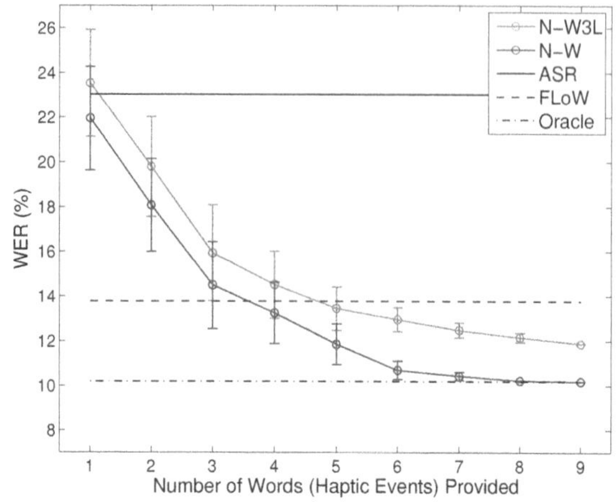

(a) Simulation results (clean)

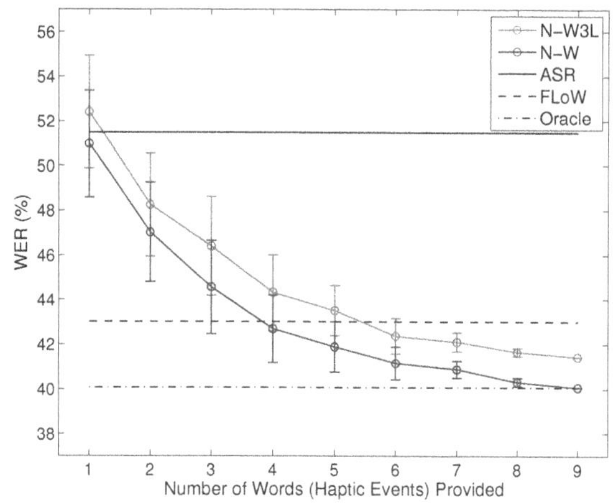

(b) Simulation results (15dB)

Figure 4: Simulation results (a) when performed without any additional noise and (b) when performed with artificial noise at SNR = 15dB. x-axis denotes the number of randomly chosen keywords (N), whereas y-axis denotes the word error rate (WER). The red and the blue lines refer to the Note-taking-style HVR performance with the first 3 letters of N randomly chosen words (N-W3L), and the Note-taking-style HVR performance with N fully-spelled words (N-W). The error bars indicate the standard deviations of the 100 iterations. The ASR performance, FLoW HVR performance, and the Oracle WER performance were represented as the black solid, the dashed, and the dash-dot lines, respectively.

without any haptic events other than the Boundary of Sentences (BoS) which only defines the start and the end of each prompt. The oracle WER and the worst obtainable WER from the given n-best list was also reported, in order to indicate the quality of the speech engine performance.

Table 1: Result of the Experiment. Five haptic methods were applied in this experiment: Boundary of Sentences (BoS), 3 Words and 3 Letters (3W3L) via Shorthand, Longhand, and Keyboard input, and First Letter of Words (FLoW). The table reports the Word Error Rate (WER), the Keyword Error Rate (KER), and the absolute improvement in the error rate from the Automatic Speech Recognition (ASR) results to the Hatpic Voice Recognition (HVR) results.

Haptic Methods	Words Per Minute (WPM)	WER (%)				KER (%)		Absolute Improvement (%)	
		ASR	HVR	Oracle	Worst	ASR	HVR	WER	KER
BoS	110.7	24.9	-	-	-	22.6	-	-	-
Shorthand (3W3L)	94.9	24.8	18.3	12.7	47.5	21.2	12.2	6.6	9.0
Longhand (3W3L)	86.5	23.1	15.8	11.9	46.8	22.2	12.9	7.3	9.3
Keyboard (3W3L)	85.2	25.9	18.6	12.6	51.7	24.4	14.9	7.3	9.4
FLoW	83.9	23.6	14.4	12.0	49.9	23.2	17.5	9.2	5.7

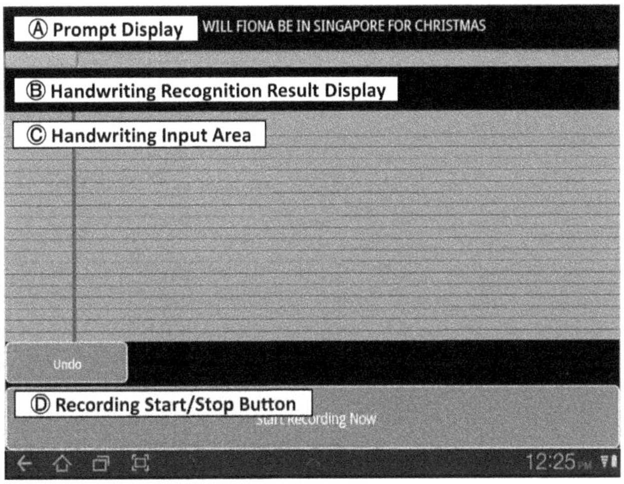

Figure 5: A prototype interface for handwriting data collection. For tap event data collection, a virtual QWRETY keyboard replaced the handwriting area seen in section C.

Table 1 shows the speed of input in Words Per Minute (WPM), WER, and Keyword Error Rate (KER) for each haptic method. WPM is defined as the ratio of the number of words to the total duration of input measured from the start of recording to the end of the last haptic input. KER is defined as the ratio of the number of keywords appearing in the sentence to the total number of keywords provided, where keyword is the word that a user chooses to provide a haptic event for. All the haptic methods showed similar ASR performance, with similar oracle WER and worst obtainable WER. For all the haptic input methods, the algorithm showed improvement in both WER and KER when compared to ASR, although it brought disfluency in speech. Among the haptic methods tried in this experiment, FLoW showed the greatest absolute improvement in WER performance. Although the 3W3L methods showed a smaller improvement in WER, they generally showed a greater improvement in KER than FLoW. This outcome indicates that FLoW chooses the candidate that increases the overall WER, whereas the N-Words haptic methods choose the one that matches the most number of keywords, thus maximizing the KER improvement. As for the speed of input, 3W3L by shorthand handwriting showed the smallest decrease (14.3%) from BoS , whereas FLoW resulted in the largest decrease (24.2%). However, Shorthand 3W3L showed less improvement in WER and KER performance than other 3W3L methods. This decrease is due to the added ambiguity of the shorthand haptic note sequence because of its classified letters.

4. CONCLUSION

The note-taking style of HVR that resembles the process of natural note-taking on paper was examined throughout this study. The simulations and preliminary experiments showed notable improvement in both the Word Error Rate (WER) and the Keyword Error Rate (KER) over ASR. Specifically, the note-taking style HVR showed greater improvement in KER than other HVR methods such as FLoW. When a user writes a note, it is assumed that he or she chooses the keywords of the given speech that best reflect the context and semantics of the speech. Thus, this improvement in KER can enhance the user experience with the speech recognition system, because users expect to see the keywords they choose become corrected in the final output. Although the note-taking style HVR did cause an increased duration of speech compared to ASR, the use of partially spelled words and Gregg shorthand symbols minimized this side-effect. Because the WPM of a haptic method may vary depending on the users' familiarity with the input medium, users can choose the medium that enables the fastest input for them. However, it was shown that users' choice of keywords can significantly affect the performance, as seen in the large standard deviation of WER in the HVR simulation. Therefore, users would have an increased chance of experiencing a better performance if they choose the words that are frequently mis-recognized for their phonetic features or grammatical properties, and vice versa.

It is worthwhile to note that the proposed algorithm can be applied to any speech recognition engine as long as it returns the n-best list for a given speech. As such, the proposed HVR method can easily be augmented to the existing Large Vocabulary ASR services such as Google Speech API for Android devices[2], AT&T's Watson API[3], or wami[4]. This gives developers the opportunity to easily implement applications that make use of this technology.

[2] http://developer.android.com/reference/
[3] http://www.research.att.com/projects/WATSON/index.html
[4] http://code.google.com/p/wami/

The preliminary user studies discussed the case where a user provides both speech and haptic note sequence data synchronously, given a written prompt. As it is shown in the previous research as well, the multi-tasking between speaking and writing is an unusual and thus challenging psychological task. Future work will investigate another application of the same technology, where a user listens to a given speech, and provides an appropriate haptic note sequence synchronously. This task is more natural for a user, of which an example can be found in everyday tasks such as listening to a lecture and taking notes. Such application can aid in spoken document retrieval when a natural note input is given.

5. REFERENCES

[1] C. Allauzen, M. Riley, J. Schalkwyk, W. Skut, and M. Mohri. Openfst: A general and efficient weighted finite-state transducer libraryh. *Lecture Notes in Computer Science*, 4783(11):11–23, 2007.

[2] H. Butler. *Teeline Shorthand.* Butterworth Heinemann, 1991.

[3] J. R. Gregg. *The Basic Principles of Gregg Shorthand.* New York: Gregg Pub, 1923.

[4] S. Gunter and H. Bunke. Hmm-based handwritten word recognition: on the optimization of the number of states, training iterations and gaussian components. *Pattern Recognition*, 37:2069–2079, 2004.

[5] J. Hu, S. G. Lim, and M. K. Brown. Writer independent on-line handwriting recognition using an hmm approach. *Pattern Recognition*, 33(1):133–147, 2000.

[6] M. Mohri, F. Pereira, and M. Riley. Weighted finite-state transducers in speech recognition. *Computer Speech and Language*, 16(1):69–88, 2002.

[7] G. A. Reid, E. J. Thompson, and M. Angus. *Pitman Shorterhand.* New York: Pitman Pub, 1972.

[8] T. Robinson, J. Fransen, D. Pye, J. Foote, S. Renals, P. Woodland, and S. Young. *WSJCAM0 Cambridge Read News.* Linguistic Data Consortium, Philadelphia, 1995.

[9] K. C. Sim. Haptic voice recognition: Augmenting speech modality with touch events for efficient speech recognition. *IEEE Spoken Language Technology Workshop (SLT)*, pages 73–78, 2010.

[10] K. C. Sim. Probabilistic integration of partial lexical information for noise robust haptic voice recognition. In *Proceedings of the 50th Annual Meeting of the Association for Computational Linguistics*, pages 31–39, July 2012.

[11] A. Varga and H. J. Steeneken. Assessment for automatic speech recognition: Ii. noisex-92: A database and an experiment to study the effect of additive noise on speech recognition systems. *Speech Communication*, 12(3):247–251, 1993.

[12] S. Young, D. Kershaw, J. Odell, D. Ollason, V. Valtchev, and P. Woodland. *The HTK Book (for HTK version 3.4).* Cambridge University, December 2006.

Development of the 2012 SJTU HVR System

Hainan Xu
Shanghai Jiao Tong University
800 Dongchuan RD. Minhang
Shanghai, China
xhnwww@sjtu.edu.cn

Yuchen Fan
Shanghai Jiao Tong University
800 Dongchuan RD. Minhang
Shanghai, China
fyc0624@sjtu.edu.cn

Kai Yu
Shanghai Jiao Tong University
800 Dongchuan RD. Minhang
Shanghai, China
kai.yu@sjtu.edu.cn

ABSTRACT

Haptic voice recognition (HVR) is a multi-modal text entry method for smart mobile devices. It employs haptic events generated by speakers during speaking to achieve better efficiency and robustness for automatic speech recognition. This paper describes the detailed design of the 2012 SJTU submission for the HVR Grand Challenge. During the design, a new perplexity metric using conditional entropy is proposed to evaluate the potential search space reduction of a haptic event without speech input. A number of new haptic events are evaluated both theoretically and experimentally in detail. The final submission system uses the haptic event of initial letter plus final letter and reduces word error rate by 76% compared to the baseline initial letter event.

Categories and Subject Descriptors

I.2.7 [**ARTIFICIAL INTELLIGENCE**]: Natural Language Processing—Speech recognition and synthesis

Keywords

haptic voice recognition; multi-modal interface

1. INTRODUCTION

Mobile devices nowadays play an important role in people's lives, yet text entry methods on mobile devices are never satisfying. The most common way to enter text on mobile devices is by tapping on the QWERTY keyboard on the touch screen, and for its lack of haptic feedback, it is highly error prone and slow. As speech is the most natural way of communication of human beings, a great deal of efforts have been made by experts to make automatic speech recognition (**ASR**) possible on mobile devices. However, due to their limited computing resources, large vocabulary continuous speech recognition is nearly impossible to accomplish. What's more, mobile devices are commonly used in noisy environments. No matter what recognition architecture is used, noise will always significantly degrade the recognition performance. Two major solutions have been used to address these problems: First is distributed speech recognition, where the waveform or extracted acoustic vectors are transmitted over the network to the servers where recognition is actually performed and results are sent back. An example of this is Google's speech recognition service. The second solution is that the recognizer predefines the grammar and limit the vocabulary of recognition task so that the search space is reduced, one of the examples is the voice control on iPod touch 4, where the grammar is fixed to be among "play album" followed by an album name, "play songs by" followed by a singer's name, "next song", etc.

Haptic voice recognition (**HVR**)[1] aims to solve the problem by introducing additional information. In HVR, mobile users provide additional haptic inputs on touch screens while they are speaking to the device. Based on different designs of the haptic events, this information could be used by the recognizer in a number of ways to help the recognition, such as reducing search space, helping acoustic model adaptation etc. Among them, search space reduction is the primary advantage of HVR. With a reduced search space, an HVR system requires less computing resource than a standard ASR system does; furthermore, haptic events could potentially compensate for lost or distorted acoustic information due to effect of the noise, making the system more robust in noisy environments. Hence, in this paper, search space reduction is the focus during the design of haptic events.

What a haptic event does to speech recognition is not all positive though. Firstly, the fact that users need to provide haptic inputs to the recognizer while speaking inevitably slows down the input speed, so a trade-off between recognition accuracy and input speed must be made. Secondly, the haptic input provided by the user may contain errors, and thus the system needs to either be less error prone or be able to handle erroneous inputs. Otherwise the erroneous haptic event could prevent the right word or word sequence to be recognized.

This paper describes the design of SJTU submission for the task 1 of the HVR Grand Challenge 2012[2]. The objective of task 1 of the challenge is to design innovative haptic events for HVR and methods for generating these events using touch-screen inputs. This task also imposes a time limit of 80 words per minute (**WPM**) on the overall input. The challenge release contains a baseline HVR system which uses the initial letter sequence of user utterances as the haptic event. Experiments show that the use of haptic events significantly reduces the word error rate (**WER**). In this paper, a number of more informative haptic events

ICMI'12, October 22–26, 2012, Santa Monica, California, USA.

are proposed and achieve further gains. The final submission system obtains 76% relative gain over the baseline HVR system.

The rest of the paper is organized as follows: In section 2, a new metric is proposed to evaluate the effectiveness of a haptic event without speech input. Section 3 describes the design and implementation of the SJTU HVR systems. Experiments are detailed in section 4, followed by the conclusion and future work.

2. EVALUATION OF SEARCH SPACE REDUCTION IN HVR

As indicated in the previous section, the primary advantage of incorporating haptic events into speech recognition process is to reduce the search space so that the search complexity can be reduced and the accuracy can be increased. Although this effect can be evaluated by WER from actual HVR experiments, it is not convenient to do so. To design useful haptic events, it is important to evaluate how much a haptic event can help to predict words without speech input. The evaluation can be done by investigating the effect of haptic events on language model. This section will investigate appropriate metric for the purpose. To simplify the analysis and be consistent with the HVR challenge setup, the language model considered here is just *word loop*, i.e. unigram language model with uniform distribution over all words of the recognition vocabulary. Similar idea can be extended to N-gram language model.

In conventional speech recognition, the prediction power of a language model is measured by perplexity[3]. For a recognition task with vocabulary V, the *perplexity* (**PPL**) of a word-loop language model is defined as

$$PPL = 2^H$$

where H is the entropy of an unigram language model, defined as

$$H = -\sum_{w \in V} P(w) \log_2 P(w)$$

In the case of word-loop, given the number of words of the vocabulary V, denoted as $|V|$, $P(w) = \frac{1}{|V|}$ is a uniform distribution. Hence, the entropy becomes

$$H = \frac{1}{|V|} \sum_{w \in V} \log_2 |V| = \log_2 |V| \tag{1}$$

and consequently the perplexity $PPL = |V|$. From the definition, perplexity is the complexity of the language model, hence, the smaller it is, the more prediction power the language model has.

In HVR, the search space is not only defined by the language model, but also constrained by observed haptic events. Considering the case of offline batch processing, given a haptic event associated with a word, the prior probability of the word in a word-loop language model becomes

$$P(w|e) = \begin{cases} |V_e|^{-1} & w \in V_e \\ 0 & w \notin V_e \end{cases}$$

where V_e denotes the vocabulary associated with haptic event e. Hence, the entropy of the word-loop language model conditioned on the haptic event e is defined as

$$H(e) = -\sum_{w \in V} P(w|e) \log_2 P(w|e) = \log_2 |V_e| \tag{2}$$

The overall entropy of the conditioned language model can then be represented by the expectation of the conditional entropy. Considering that the prior probability of the haptic event is also a uniform distribution, i.e. $P(e) = \frac{|V_e|}{|V|}$, the entropy of haptic event conditioned word-loop language model is defined as

$$H_{hap} = \sum_{e} P(e) H(e) = \frac{1}{|V|} \sum_{e, w \in V_e} \log_2 |V_e| \tag{3}$$

Since V_e is a subset of V, $|V_e| \leq |V|$. By comparing equation (3) to equation (1), it is then easy to find that H_{hap} is always no greater that H, consequently the perplexity $PPL_{hap} = 2^{H_{hap}}$ is no greater than PPL. This demonstrates that incorporating accurate haptic events will almost always help to reduce the perplexity, i.e., increase the prediction power of the corresponding language model.

In addition to the theoretical estimation of perplexity as described before, in practice, it is also useful to estimate how well a particular language model matches the data of a specific test-set. As an analogy of the conventional definition of the perplexity on test-set data, the experimental perplexity for HVR is defined as $PPL_{hap} = 2^{LP_{hap}}$, where LP_{hap} is the log probability of the test data conditioned on haptic events. In the word-loop language model case, it is defined as

$$LP = -\frac{1}{K} \sum_{k=1}^{K} \log_2 \frac{1}{|V_{e(k)}|} \tag{4}$$

which $e(k)$ denotes the haptic event of the kth word, and K is the total number of words in the test-set.

In this paper, both theoretical and experimental perplexity of the conditioned word-loop language model will be used to evaluate the search space reduction.

3. DESIGN AND IMPLEMENTATION OF SJTU HAPTIC EVENTS

During the design of SJTU haptic events, two assumptions are made from the understanding of the HVR challenge rules. Firstly, haptic events are incorporated into speech recognition in an offline mode, i.e. actual speech recognition is performed after receiving all haptic events and speech data. Secondly, word-loop language model is used. With these assumptions, the effect of a haptic event is simply to change the structure of the word network for decoding.

As indicated in section 1, three important factors should be considered when designing a haptic event for HVR:

1. Search space reduction
2. Input reliability
3. Input speed

Previously, *initial letter* has been used as a typical haptic event for HVR, referred to as **IL**. This is also the baseline system provided by the HVR organization committee. In this paper, in addition to **IL**, three haptic events are proposed. The advantage, disadvantage and implementation of each haptic event are discussed in the below sub-sections.

3.1 Initial Letter (IL)

In the baseline system, users need to input the initial letter of each word while speaking. With this haptic inputs, the search space for each word shrinks and only contains the words having the same initial letters.

Taking the development dataset of the HVR challenge as an example, there are altogether 274 words in the vocabulary. Suppose a user wants to input "BUY SOME FRUITS BACK", with a word-loop language model, the search space is formed by the whole vocabulary, as depicted in figure 3.1. The PPL of the word net is 274.

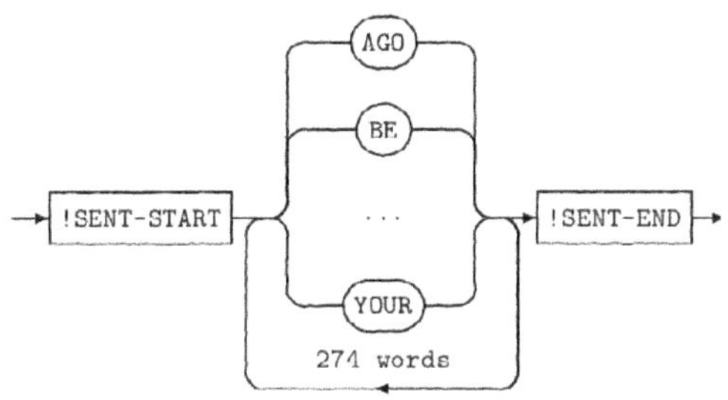

With IL event, the word net changes to:

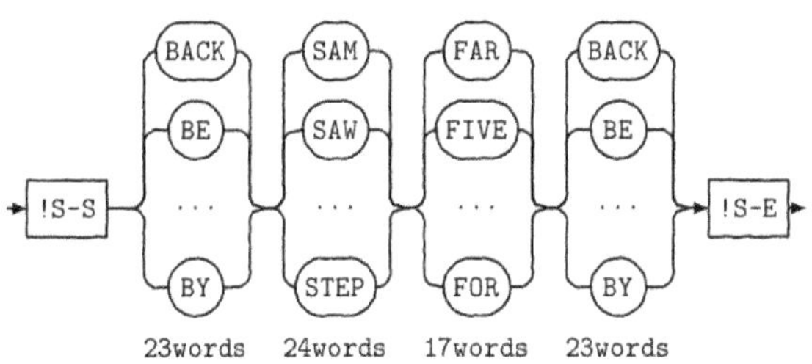

From equation (3), the PPL reduces from 274 to 14. This will result in a significant reduction in search space. What's more, the initial letter information also implies the number of words in the sentence, which helps to reduce the insertion/deletion error as well.

As users only need to input one letter per word, and initial letter of a word is usually directly related to its pronunciation, IL has a pretty good input speed and users are not likely to make input errors. Details of input speed and input reliability will be shown in section 4.

The disadvantage of IL is obvious: IL is far from being sufficiently informative as the recognizer confuses a lot between words with the same initial letter, like "ford" with "for", "like" with "light".

3.2 Initial Letter plus Length

As discussed in the previous section, the baseline HVR system confuses between words with the same initial letter as well. To further reduce the PPL, additional information needs to be added. In this section, word length is investigated as the additional information.

Theoretical analysis shows that, by restricting initial letter and word length information, the PPL of the recognition network is down to 2.78. And also, as longer words generally have longer pronunciations and vice versa, by constricting the length of a word, the recognizer also has implicit knowledge of how long the word is in the recording, and this implicitly gives the recognizer the "boundary of word" information.

Ideally, the accurate length of word information would be most effective in reducing PPL. This is referred to as *Initial Letter plus Accurate Length* (**ILAN**). Although ILAN yields much better PPL than IL, yet a practical problem exists in the that approach: users may not be able to remember the length of a word immediately while speaking, especially for long words, and this would result in more input error and/or slow down the user input. Therefore, it is necessary make compromises.

A series of experiments have been performed to investigate the reliability of the word length event. It is found that in most cases people can remember the exact length of a word when the length is less than 5. Under that assumption, a new event, *Initial Letter plus Fuzzy Length* (**ILFN**) is proposed. Theoretical analysis shows that the PPL of the recognition network is 6.32 on the development data, better than IL. Although it is not as good as ILAN is, this design made this haptic event possible to implement, details about which will be in the following paragraphs.

Once the haptic event is determined, a friendly interface needs to be implemented to efficiently generate it. For most modern mobile devices, the touch screen could handle two types of input: taps and swipes. When these inputs are performed on a QWERTY keyboard, the coordinates of the tapping could be mapped to the English alphabet and the distance of the swiping could represent word length information. Those two types of input are sufficient for us to implement the haptic event introduced above. Fig 1 illustrates how haptic events are interpreted on the QWERTY keyboard.

Figure 1: User Interface for ILFN

For simplicity, all user input on the touch-screen are interpreted as swipes, and the distance of a swipe is defined as the actual distance on touch-screen divided by the width of a key (a quick tap-and-release would be viewed as a swipe with distance 0). The tapping point on the keyboard is recorded as the initial letter of the event. And there are 3 legal swiping directions: left, right and down. For a left or right swipe, the distance plus one denotes the length that the user wants to input; for down swipes, it denotes that the word length is greater or equal to 5. For example, in the picture, if the user wants to input the word "fun", he will tap on the Key F and swipe to the right or left with distance 2, which means he should either release on the Key S or the Key H; for the word "fill", he will tap on the key F and then release on the Key A or J; for the word "family", the user need to tap on F and release on the Key C or the Space. For single-letter words like "I" and "A", the user need to simply tap on the corresponding Key and release on the same key.

Although it seems complicated from the description, in

practice, this input method is highly efficient and easy to learn.

3.3 Initial Letter plus Final Letter (ILFL)

Adding the word length information is not the only solution. Theoretical analysis results show that, restricting both initial letter and final letter further reduces the PPL to 1.99, better than the PPL of ILAN (2.78).

A disadvantage of ILFL is that, unlike the initial letter information of a word which is easy for people to remember, the final letter is relatively harder for people to come up while speaking; another disadvantage is that it requires the user to search for 2 keys for each word in inputting, both of which slow down the input speed and reduce input reliability.

3.4 Initial Letter plus Final Phone (ILFP)

Given the effectiveness of the information about word end, it is useful to find a compromise way with both reliability and speed for ILFL. Unlike the final letter information which may be a little hard to remember immediately, the final phone of a word is easier to come up. However, it is impractical to include all final phones. Considering both the convenience for the users and their effect on reducing PPL, only 4 types of final phones are used:

1. m, n and ng
2. iy and ih
3. s, z, th and dh
4. l

This yields a theoretical PPL of 5.79. Although it is not as low as ILFL, as it does not require information that is hard to remember, combined with the fact that for each word, user only needs to search for one key on the keyboard, the input speed of this method is significant faster than ILFN and ILFL.

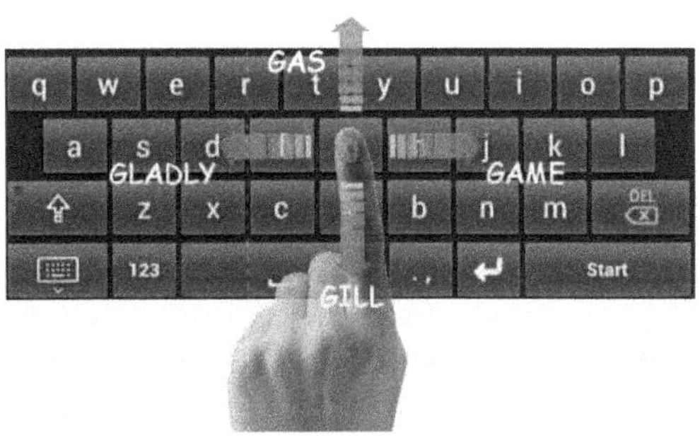

Figure 2: User Interface for ILFP

As shown in Fig 2, the initial letter information is determined by the tapping position on the keyboard. After the tapping, if the final phone of the current word falls in the 4 categories, the user could swipe in the corresponding direction so that this final phone information is added to the event. In any situation if the user is not sure of the final phone, he could always directly release without swiping and then only the initial letter information is recorded in the haptic event.

4. EXPERIMENTS

In this section, experiment results of different haptic events are presented. The ASR (speech recognition without any haptic event) results are also shown so that the effect of haptic events to speech recognition could be clearly seen. The organizer provided an acoustic model for speech recognition, and a recipe script to automatically adapt the acoustic models to different speakers on different noisy environments. These models and scripts are used in both development and evaluation.

The designed haptic events were evaluated on two data sets. The development data consists of both audio recordings and text provided by the organizer of the challenge. There are 80 sentences in the test-set and 243 in the training set, spoken by 6 speakers. 4 sets of data with different noise level were provided: clean, 20dB, 15dB and 10 dB.

As for evaluation, the organizer only provided text prompt. Audio data were recorded by 2 speakers in SJTU. There are 200 sentences in the test set and 40 sentences in the train set which is for adapting the models. Train-data and test-data are made separately. Test recordings are made while the speaker is also inputting the haptic events on the mobile phone, and the haptic events (which contain errors) created in that process are used in recognition.

4.1 Haptic Events Comparison

To choose the best system for the SJTU submission for the challenge, all haptic events were evaluated in terms of search space reduction, recognition performance, input reliability and speed.

4.1.1 Search Space Reduction

The analysis of search space reduction of all haptic events are listed in Table 1. The experimental PPL are calculated using the development and evaluation data with equation 4.

Table 1: Perplexity of Different Haptic Events

PPL	ASR	IL	ILAN	ILFN	ILFL	ILFP
The.		14.05	2.78	6.32	1.99	5.79
Dev.	274	13.18	2.38	4.76	2.03	4.01
Eva.		14.00	2.62	4.20	1.93	6.03

From table 1, all new haptic events obtained significant reduction in PPL. It is expected that the speech recognition performance will be similar.

4.1.2 Recognition Performance

As the development release does not contain data about the haptic events, the newly proposed haptic events were generated from the given transcription in development set (which means that those haptic events do not contain errors). The modified word networks associated with each haptic event were then used for decoding in various noise environments. The results on the artificial data are shown in Fig 3.

From Fig 3, all haptic events help in reducing the WER, and makes recognition less affected by noise. The ordering is also the same as in the PPL table 1.

In addition to the development, similar experiments were also done on the evaluation data. To simulate noisy environments, artificial noise were added to the audio recordings.

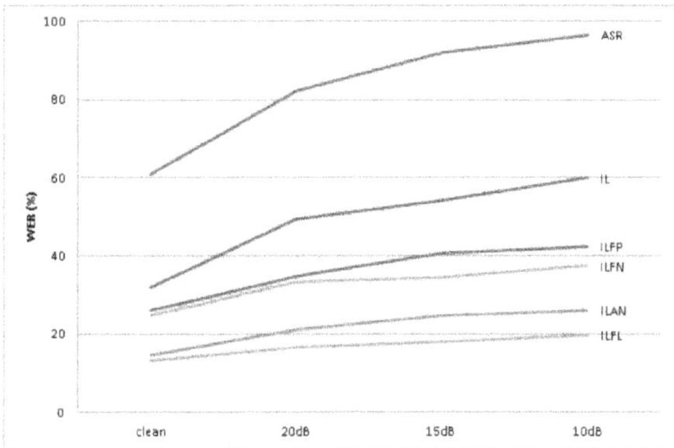

Figure 3: WER On Dev Set With Different Noise Level

The noise added was "babble" from the NOISEX-92 noise database[4], and FAnT tool[5] was used to control the data-noise-ratio. Test results on evaluation data are shown in Fig 4.

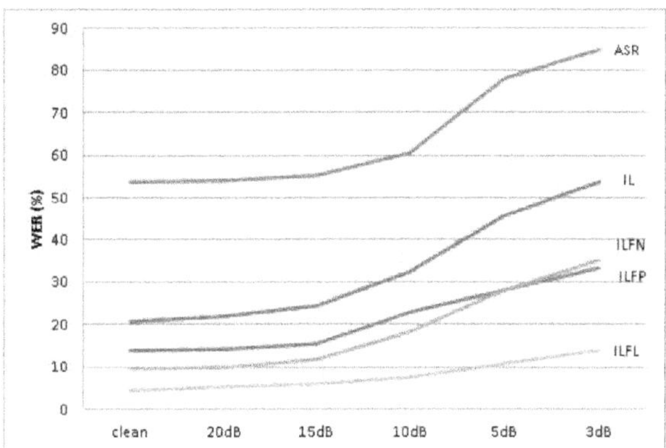

Figure 4: WER On Eval Set With Different Noise Level

The results on the evaluation data have exactly the same trend as the development data. This shows that the proposed haptic events have consistent effect on speech recognition.

4.1.3 Input Speed and Reliability

As discussed before, complex haptic events could slow down the user input. Experiments are conducted to see if our haptic events design satisfies the input speed limit imposed by the challenge.

Input reliability is another important factor. Here input reliability is measured by input error rate (**IER**). IER is defined as the number of errors made during the input divided by the number of total words entered. For instance, in the ILFL haptic event, if the user mistakenly input the word "play" as with initial letter O and final letter T, it will be counted as 2 mistakes.

The experiment is conducted as follows: the subjects first spent enough time in familiarizing themselves with the corresponding haptic event input by exercising random sentences on the mobile phone. After the subjects feel confident, they are asked to input all 200 test sentences on mobile phones during which they also speak the test sentences, and their input speed and input reliability is monitored. Table 2 is our experiment results on those 4 types of haptic events.

Table 2: Input Speed and IER of Different Haptic Events

	IL	ILFN	ILFL	ILFP
Input Speed (WPM)	103	85	83	89
IER (%)	0.63	2.59	1.26	0.91

It could be seen from the table that for their complexity, the other 3 haptic events require more time to input than the baseline haptic event. The slowest is ILFL, for the fact the final letter information is not as easy to remember as other information, and the users need to search for two keys when inputting each word. The IER for ILFL is twice than IL, which is consistent with the fact that ILFL requires 2 key input per word while IL requires 1; ILFP has an IER in between IL and ILFL, and is faster than ILFL. [1]

4.2 Performance of the Final SJTU HVR System

In the previous sections, the performance of different haptic events have been shown. It could be seen that the ILFL has the lowest WER in all settings; although it has the lowest input speed among others as well, it is still higher than the required 80WPM limit; its average IER is acceptable too, so the ILFL system is chosen as our final HVR system for submission.

Table 3: Summary of 2012 SJTU HVR System

	ASR	IL	ILFL
PPL	274	14.05	1.99
WER(% in dev,15dB)	91.89	54.22	18.07
WER(% in eval,15dB)	53.96	24.39	5.89
Input Speed(WPM)	-	103	83
IER(%)	-	0.63	1.26

From table 3, the submitted system has achieved about 76% relative WER reduction compared to the baseline IL system.

4.3 Further Discussion

4.3.1 Recognition Speed

Recognition speed is an important factor for evaluating a speech recognition system, especially when the system works on a resource-limited environment like a mobile phone. We conducted experiments testing how much time it takes the HVR system with different haptic event design to recognize the data provided in the development release. The data contains 80 sentences read by 6 speakers. The PC for testing is on Ubuntu 12.04 32-bit with a Intel Core i3-2120 (3.30GHz) dual processor and 2GB memory.

From the results shown in table 4, it is obvious to see that, by introducing haptic events, the recognition time is greatly reduced in all settings. Compared with standard ASR, the

[1]According to the design of ILFP, the user does not have to provide the final phone information even if the final phone does fall in the 4 categories. In the experiment result, 23 such case occured, while the total number of words whose final phones fall in the 4 categories is 581.

Table 4: Decoding Time (Second) of Different Haptic Events

SNR	ASR	IL	ILAN	ILFN	ILFL	ILFP
clean	523.02	11.92	3.34	5.60	3.17	4.81
20dB	748.90	22.14	4.77	9.36	4.24	7.74
15dB	761.41	25.10	5.37	10.66	4.75	9.01
10dB	759.51	28.74	5.80	11.82	5.14	10.02

ILFL reduced recognition time by a factor of more than 100, which means that the HVR system requires much less computing resources, making it more likely to be able to run on mobile devices.

4.3.2 *Effect of Vocabulary Size*

As so far, all tests have been on a small vocabulary set. Due to the reduction of PPL, haptic events help greatly in reducing WER in recognition. But whether haptic events could still have significant effect on large vocabulary sets remains to be seen. This section adopts the same PPL analysis introduced in section 2 and check whether the gain of haptic event will retain for larger data set.

We did PPL analysis on two larger vocabulary sets: DARPA Resource Management[6] and Wall Street Journal[7]. RM has a vocabulary size of 990 while WSJ has a vocabulary size of 20k. The PPL analysis gives the following results on them:

Table 5: Perplexity on Different Vocabulary Sets

	ASR	IL	ILAN	ILFN	ILFL	ILFP
HVR	274	14.05	2.78	6.32	1.99	5.79
RM	990	50.62	6.08	26.37	5.06	20.33
WSJ	20153	958	107	654	83	348

It could be seen that the effect on reducing PPL of haptic events are still significant in larger vocabulary sets and thus there are reasons to believe that haptic events could still have the significant effect in improving recognition performance in larger datasets. As language models are often used in large vocabulary datasets which also reduces PPL, it could work with haptic and altogether, they can achieve even better results in PPL reduction.

5. CONCLUSIONS

Haptic Voice Recognition (HVR) is useful to achieve highly efficient and robust speech recognition. In this paper, a PPL metric using conditional entropy is proposed to evaluate the effect of haptic events without speech input. The metric has shown consistent results with the final WER in experiments. A number of new haptic events are also introduced in this paper that helps improve speech recognition performance. In the final system we submitted, it reduces WER of recognition by 76% in 15dB recordings compared to the baseline haptic event, while still satisfying the 80WPM limit imposed on input speed.

The future work consists of several subtasks. Research on how to further improve the HVR model and implementation introduced in this paper will be conducted. This includes studies on incorporating haptic events with language models on large-vocabulary speech recognition tasks. We are also going to design an better user-interface to further increase input speed and reduce input error rate by utilizing gesture recognition methods or other technologies. Another aspect of our study is how haptic events could be used in other ways, like those not related to spelling information of words, and haptic events that are not solely aiming for reducing search spaces.

6. ACKNOWLEDGMENTS

The authors would like to thank AISpeech Ltd for providing support for the work.

7. REFERENCES

[1] Khe Chai Sim. Haptic voice recognition: Augmenting speech modality with touch events for efficient speech recognition. In Dilek Hakkani-TÃijr and Mari Ostendorf, editors, *SLT*, pages 73–78. IEEE, 2010.

[2] HVR Grand Challenge 2012. `http://speech.ddns.comp.nus.edu.sg/HVRGrandChallenge2012/index.php`.

[3] Lalit R. Bahl, Frederick Jelinek, and Robert L. Mercer. A maximum likelihood approach to continuous speech recognition. *Pattern Analysis and Machine Intelligence, IEEE Transactions on*, PAMI-5(2):179 –190, march 1983.

[4] Andrew Varga and Herman J. M. Steeneken. Assessment for automatic speech recognition: Ii. noisex-92: A database and an experiment to study the effect of additive noise on speech recognition systems. *Speech Communication*, 12(3):247–251, 1993.

[5] Filtering and Noise Adding Tool. `http://dnt.kr.hsnr.de/download.html`.

[6] P. Price, W. Fisher, J. Bernstein, and D. Pallet. The DARPA 1000-word resource management database for continuous speech recognition. In *IEEE ICASSP-88*, volume 1, pages 651–654, New York, 1988. IEEE.

[7] D. B. Paul and J. M. Baker. The design of the Wall Street Journal-based CSR corpus. *Proc. DARPA Speech and Natural Language Workshop*, 1992.

Improving Mandarin Predictive Text Input by Augmenting Pinyin Initials with Speech and Tonal Information

Guangsen Wang
guangsen@comp.nus.edu.sg

Bo Li
libo@nus.edu.sg

Shilin Liu
shilin.liu@comp.nus.edu.sg

Xuancong Wang
g0801784@nus.edu.sg

Xiaoxuan Wang
wangxx@comp.nus.edu.sg

Khe Chai Sim
simkc@comp.nus.edu.sg

School of Computing, National University of Singapore
Computing 1, 13 Computing Drive, Singapore 117417

ABSTRACT

Recently, a new technology called Haptic Voice Recognition (HVR) was proposed to enhance the speech recognition efficiency and accuracy for modern mobile devices, which has been successfully applied for robust English voice recognition. As both Pinyin and handwriting input methods work quite slow in mobile devices because of typing errors and ambiguity, it is interesting to apply this technology to assist Mandarin predictive text input. However, it is not straightforward because the characteristics of Mandarin significantly differ from alphabetic western languages. In this paper, we investigated what possible haptic inputs are important and how these information can be incorporated to improve Mandarin text input. Various experiments were conducted and results have shown that with the help of acoustic and tonal information, the ambiguity of Pinyin Initial based Mandarin predictive text input is largely reduced and an oracle character error rate of 3.8% for the top 4 candidates could be achieved, which is usually the number of word candidates displayed on mobile devices. Our Mandarin HVR system has also shown its robustness in noisy environments.

Categories and Subject Descriptors

H.5.2 [**Information Interfaces and Presentation**]: User Interfaces—*Haptic I/O, Voice I/O*; I.2.7 [**Computing Methodologies**]: Natural Language Processing—*Speech Recognition and Synthesis*

Keywords

Haptic Voice Recognition, Mandarin Predictive Text Input, Acoustic and Tonal Information

1. INTRODUCTION

Speech is a very natural way for human to communicate with computers. In practice, people do not quite rely on speech recognition technology because of its efficiency and accuracy, which is also the reason why the physical keyboard is still the most popular input device for desktop. However, this situation may be very different for the modern mobile devices with capacitive touch screen, because the virtual keyboard on a tiny screen could produce lots of typing errors so as to slow down the input speed, which encourages voice input for mobile devices.

However, the traditional large vocabulary automatic speech recognition (ASR) system may not be effective for mobile devices because of the high demanding of computing resources [9]. The popular workaround nowadays is Distributed Speech Recognition (DSR) [1] with ability of handling very large scale of recognition problem. However, DSR is strongly subject to the network availability and quality, which may cause long delay to make it impractical. Recently, a new technology called Haptic Voice Recognition (HVR) [5, 6] was successfully applied for improved English voice recognition, in terms of efficiency and accuracy. As Mandarin Chinese language has very different characteristics from alphabetic English language, it is interesting to explore what haptic events are potentially helpful for Mandarin voice input and how these haptic inputs can be incorporated with existing ASR decoding network. This paper conducts a series of experiments to investigate the feasibility of HVR for Mandarin voice input, which includes both user input and true haptic events to form a complete understanding.

In the following sections, firstly a brief introduction of current popular Mandarin input methods is given in Section 2. Then, how the proposed haptic inputs are applied to augment the Mandarin voice recognition is described in Section 3. Mandarin HVR Data collection is detailed in Section 4 and experimental results are reported in Section 5 to justify the importance of various haptic inputs for Mandarin voice recognition.

2. MANDARIN INPUT METHODS

In this section, the popular Pinyin and handwriting input methods in the modern mobile devices are briefly described. Unlike the English input methods whose input is the output, Mandarin input methods are usually interactive: user has to make a selection from the predicted characters after typing the Pinyin or handwriting. Instead of using full Pinyin of characters, using the initial letters of Pinyin to predict the words can further increase the input speed but may dramatically decrease the output speed because of its high ambiguities. For example, if we want to type in the Chinese word "汉字" (*i.e. Chinese character*), the correct Pinyin is "hàn zì"; discarding the tones as all the current input methods do, by typing "han zi" we can get the expected word in the first row with four two-characters candidates "汉字,汉子,汗渍,菡子" in iphone. However, with the initial letters of Pinyin "h z" only, we will have more than 50 candidates shown as "合作,孩子,或者,患者,杭州,会长,汉族...汉字..." according to the word frequencies, where "汉字" is ranked at the 15th place. To compromise, a mix-up of full Pinyin and initial Pinyin is usually adopted, e.g. "h zi", "han z". As the selection is required in most Mandarin input methods, the word boundary, i.e. the number of characters for each word, is naturally given so that the character prediction of the Pinyin initials can be further improved according to the previous words. However, this prediction could be poor considering the weakness of first order language model.

The usual way to apply HVR to improve the Mandarin input methods is to involve fast haptic inputs with the voice inputs. Averagely, using the initial Pinyin letters has fastest input speed which can be obtained by tapping or handwriting. The issue of using initial Pinyin letters as only input is its high ambiguity, which causes too many manual selections. Using additional voice input can reduce such ambiguity because the predicted characters for those initial Pinyin letters are now based on the incorporation of both acoustic model and higher order language model for the whole sentence. As the word boundary information plays a very important role in the current Pinyin input method, it is interesting to evaluate its implication on the Pinyin initials and voice based input method. It is also possibly important to use tonal information as it gives more discriminative information. In the following sections, we will describe how these the Pinyin initials are incorporated with HVR technology and investigate which possible haptic inputs are more feasible to improve the Mandarin input method.

3. INCORPORATION OF HAPTIC INPUTS

The haptic information is incorporated in the decoding network to reduce the search space and guide the decoding. In order to construct a decoding network with the haptic constraints, we need several components: 1) the haptic information which is a sequence of Pinyin initials; 2) mapping from the haptic sequence to Chinese characters or words; 3) the Chinese word language model; 4) the Chinese word to characters mapping. In this section, we will elaborate how to incorporate the haptic information in the final decoding network by representing all the components as WFSTs [3] and combine them using the composition ($\circ$) operation.

The haptic sequence provided by the users is a sequence of Pinyin initials of all the characters in one utterance. This haptic sequence can be represented as a WFST by adding an arc with each haptic event as the input/output labels as shown in Figure 1(a). One of the main differences between Chinese and English is that Mandarin writing does not explicitly denote word boundaries and the Chinese word boundary information can further constrain the search space which may benefit the ASR decoding. Therefore, in addition to the character based haptic sequence, a word haptic sequence is obtained from the character haptic sequence through a longest match algorithm given the word list used in the training of word based language model. For example, the haptic sequence "RMCGG" illustrated in Figure 1(a) is the Pinyin initials for the Chinese character sequence "人们唱国歌". The corresponding word sequence "人们 唱 国歌" is produced by the word segmenter. Note the white spaces are added to illustrate the word boundary. In real Chinese writing, these white spaces do not exist. Thus, the word haptic sequence for the word sequence is "RM C GG" which can also be represented as a WFST shown in Figure 1(b). We denote these WFSTs as H_c and H_w respectively. The next stage requires mapping the character/word haptic sequence to the Chinese characters or words. The WFST mapping from the character haptic sequence "RMCGG" to character sequence "人们唱国歌" is shown in Figure 2(a). Similarly, the mapping from the word haptic sequence "RM C GG" to "人们 唱 国歌" is encoded in the WFST shown in Figure 2(b). These two WFSTs are denoted as M_c and M_w. They are constructed by using the character/word haptic as input and corresponding characters and words as output labels. Given a character or word sequence produced by the previous WFSTs, we need to know the language model scores in order to use the haptic WFSTs for decoding. The word based language model is adopted here and it is converted into WFST using Kaldi [1]. We decode the WFST for the language model as G_w. Note for the HVR, considerable lengthening effects (*i.e.* long pauses are inserted between adjacent characters even within a word) exist because the users are required to simultaneously type/handwrite and speak during the data recording. Thus, it is desirable to use characters as base tokens during recognition to handle the lengthening effects. Therefore, a character based lexicon is used for decoding. However, the output of the word language model WFST G_w is a sequence of words together with their language model scores. In order to use the character based lexicon, a mapping WFST from word sequence to character sequence is needed as shown in Figure 4. This mapping WFST is denoted as L. For a word of length K, there will be K arcs such that the first arc transduces the word to its first character, and all the other arcs transduce "<eps>" (empty string) to following characters. All the word WFSTs are then connected using a union operation and then a closure operation to obtain the mapping WFST L.

Given the four WFSTs, H_c/H_w, M_c/M_w, G_w, L, we can have two different configurations depending on whether word boundary information is available or not:

$\mathcal{FST}_c = H_c \circ M_c \circ L' \circ G_w \circ L$ where L' is the inverse of L by swapping the input and output labels for all the arcs in L. Thus, L' maps from a character sequence to a word sequence. The composition of $H_c \circ M_c$ takes in a character haptic sequence and output a character sequence which is illustrated in Figure 3. Although the word boundary information is assumed unknown, the implicit word boundary information from the lexicon is automatically incorporated through L'. The composition of $H_c \circ M_c \circ L'$ is a mapping from a character haptic sequence to the word sequence. A further composition with the word language model WFST G_w

[1] http://sourceforge.net/projects/kaldi/

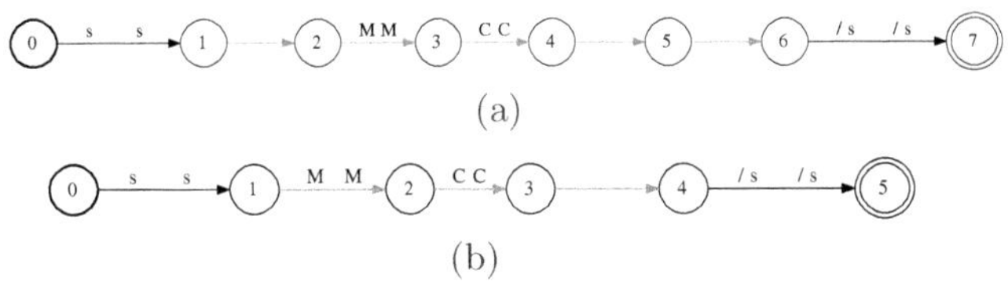

Figure 1: Example character/word haptic WFST for the haptic sequence of "RMCGG"/ "RM C GG".

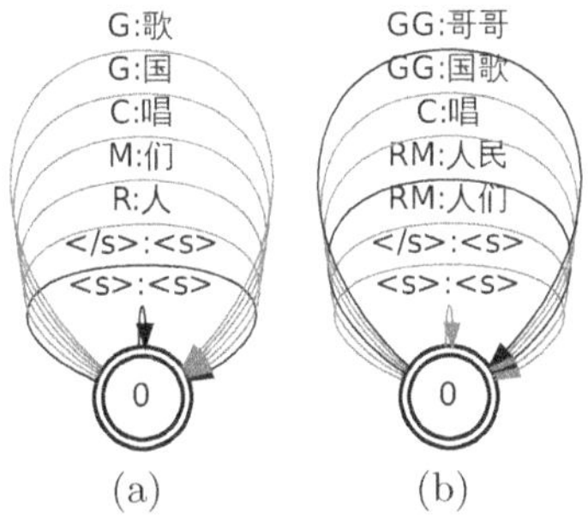

Figure 2: Example mapping WFST from character/word haptic sequence to Chinese character/word sequence.

adds the word language model scores on each arc. Recall that the character based lexicon is needed for decoding, thus a further composition with L is desirable to map the word sequence to character sequence. Note although the word boundary information is unknown, *word* based language model score is used.

$\mathcal{FST}_w = H_w \circ M_w \circ G_w \circ L$ In order to investigate the effectiveness of the word boundary information, a new composition scheme $\mathcal{FST}_w$ is constructed for a comparison with $\mathcal{FST}_c$. The word boundary information is assumed known here thus H_w is used. The composition of $H_w \circ M_w$ is a WFST mapping from word haptic sequence to word sequence as shown in Figure 5. The word language model score is added by composing with G_w. In order to use the character based lexicon, a further composition with L is needed to map the word sequence to the corresponding character sequence with word based language model scores.

4. MANDARIN HVR DATA SET

In order to evaluate the Mandarin HVR system, haptic inputs together with speech recordings are collected from 5 native Mandarin speakers, including 1 female and 4 males. The Mandarin HVR prototype system is implemented on a touch screen device for data collection. The haptic inputs for the Mandarin HVR system in this study are defined as the initial Pinyin letters of each Chinese character in the sentence, which are triggered by either typing using a on-screen soft keyboard or keystroke directly on the touch screen. Each user is required to practice the keystroke until above 70% handwriting recognition accuracy is achieved. Only then will they proceed to the real data collection. The whole process is done under a quiet in-door environment. Two speech

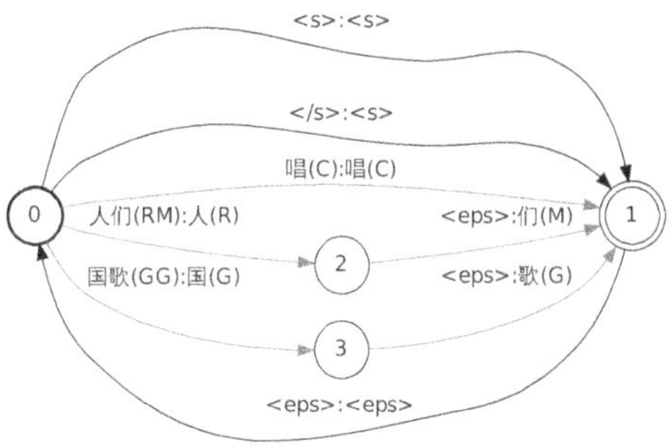

Figure 4: Example word to characters mapping WFST.

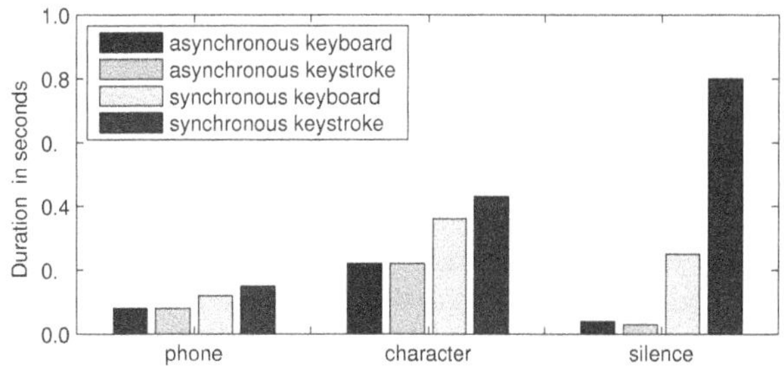

Figure 6: Average phone, word and silence duration statistics.

recording modes (asynchronous and synchronous) and two haptic modes (keyboard and keystroke) mixup into totally four data collection configurations. All the four configurations are recorded for each sentence from all the five speakers. In asynchronous mode, the speaker reads the promoted sentence first, followed by typing or handwriting the corresponding Pinyin letters of each Chinese character sequentially; while in synchronous mode, the speaker is required to type or write them simultaneously with the uttering of each character. During the data collection, haptic errors are allowed unless major fault occurs and then the speaker is required to repeat the process for that specific sentence. In total, 20 sentences per speaker are collected for all the four configurations.

In human-to-human speech communications, haptic events are seldom involved. Hence, the speech recordings an HVR system received may be quite different from the common ones. To understand the effects of haptic inputs on speech, we computed the average duration of phone, character and silence in all the four setups for each speaker. For phone and character duration, silences are excluded. In Figure 6, the four configurations are identified by different colors respectively. The two synchronous modes (the yellow and dark red bars) have much longer durations than the other two modes, clearly illustrate the lengthening effects of incorporating haptic inputs. To further understand whether the lengthening effects is dependent on speaker. Per speaker statistics of the two synchronous modes are plotted in Figure 7. Speakers are labelled as "s1" $\sim$ "s5". All the speakers have similar phonetic lengthening but the silence insertion are quite different especially for the keystroke case, which may correlates with the familiarities of handwriting. Generally speaking, the adoption of haptic inputs both stretches the phone and character to have longer durations and also inserts much longer silences between characters, which must be taken into consideration for decoding those speech data.

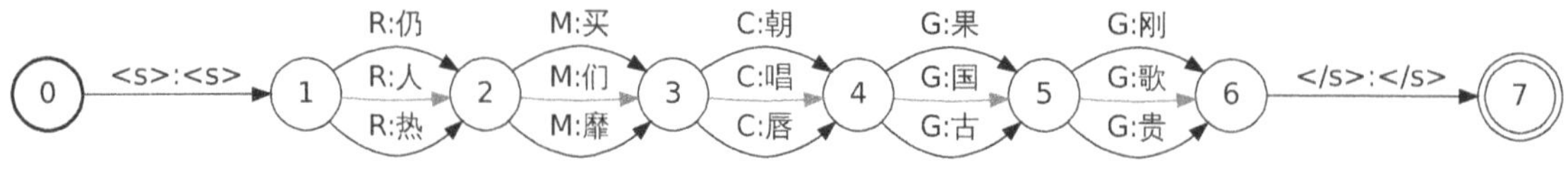

Figure 3: WFST $H_c \circ M_c$ mapping from character haptic sequence to characters for "RMCGG" with unknown word boundary. The red path represents the transcription of the testing utterance. All arcs between two nodes share the same character haptic information.

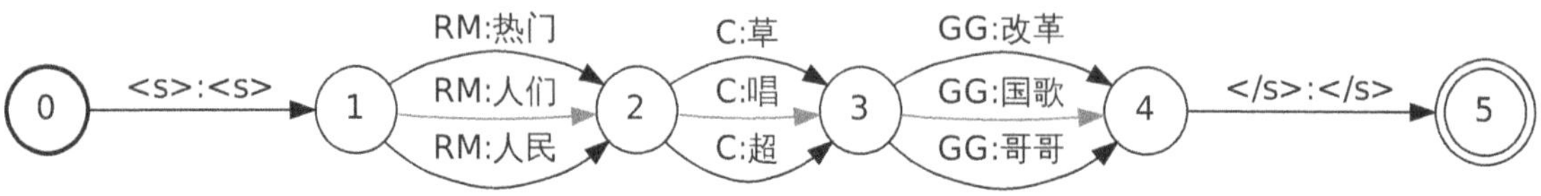

Figure 5: WFST $H_w \circ M_w$ mapping from word haptic sequence to words for "RM C GG" with known word boundary. The red path represents the transcription of the testing utterance. All arcs between two nodes share the same word haptic information.

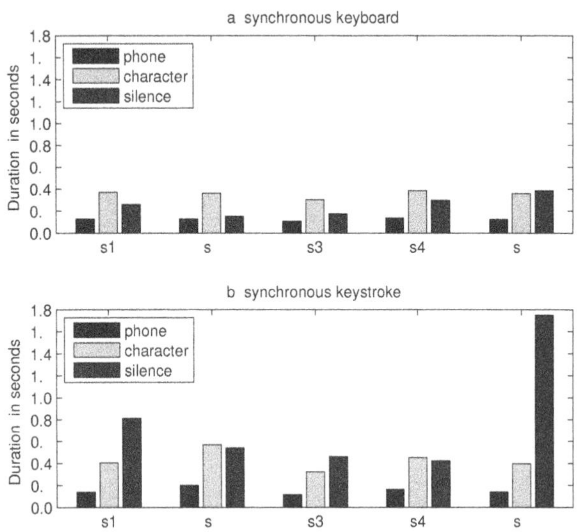

Figure 7: Per speaker average phone, word and silence duration statistics.

Table 1: Letter Error Rate (%) in user generated haptic inputs.

Haptic	Synchronous	Asynchronous
Keyboard	0.9	1.1
Keystroke	5.0	4.5

Additionally, the letter error rates of the haptic inputs collected from users are listed in Table 1. The keystroke haptic inputs have relatively higher error rates compared to the keyboard typing inputs as they involve an extra step of handwriting recognition which may also bring in errors.

5. EXPERIMENTAL RESULTS

This section presents the results from a series of experiments conducted to study the effects of augmenting haptic events for Mandarin HVR. Initial experiments utilizing perfect haptic events artificially simulated for the test speech data are reported, followed by experiments using the real haptic events data collected from users with a prototype HVR interface implemented on a touch-screen device. From the comparison of these two sets of experiments, effects of haptic errors in Mandarin HVR are discussed. Furthermore, as a tonal language, tone information has been shown to be useful for Mandarin speech recognition [4] and thus may also be helpful for the Mandarin HVR performance; hence, the true tonal information is integrated into the Mandarin HVR system as an extra stream of haptic inputs. Additionally, we also investigated the effectiveness of our Mandarin HVR system under various noisy conditions. At the end of this section, we further justified the merit of integrating acoustic and tonal information into the Pinyin initial based Mandarin predictive text input using oracle character error rate (CER) on 1∼4-best outputs.

In our Mandarin HVR system, the haptic inputs are incorporated into the WFST based language models (LMs) (Section 3); while for the acoustic model, we adopt a standard Gaussian Mixture Model (GMM) / Hidden Markov Model (HMM) based cross-word triphone system. The feature vector is 39 dimensional including 13 dimensional MFCC (including 0th component) together with its delta and delta-delta coefficients. Cepstral mean normalization is not applied. The training data consists of 156 hours of 16kHz speech from both TDT2 and TDT3 mandarin speech corpus. The evaluation data collected from 5 native Mandarin speakers consists of totally 0.38 hours' adaptation data and 0.41 hours' test data. In order to investigate the effectiveness of our Mandarin HVR system in noisy conditions, noisy test sets with 20dB, 15dB and 5dB signal-to-noise ratios (SNR) are artificially generated by corrupting the original speech with additive *bubble* noise from the NOISEX-92 database [8]. The acoustic model is trained using the HMM Toolkit (HTK) [10]. There are totally 45 monophones including a silence (`sil`) model and a short pause (`sp`) model. Each HMM has 3 states except for `sp` which has only 1 state. The state of `sp` is tied to the 2nd (*i.e.* middle) state of `sil`. Only

Table 2: **Baseline ASR Recognition CER (%) without Haptic Information.**

Lexicon	Synchronous			Asynchronous		
	bg	tg	fg	bg	tg	fg
Character	71.4	55.0	52.4	56.9	37.1	32.5
Word	86.1	81.3	81.5	41.0	34.6	33.0

Table 3: Recognition CER (%) with Tonal (T), Haptic (H) input and Word Boundary (WB) information for both synchronous and asynchronous speech.

T	H	WB	Synchronous	Asynchronous
×	user	×	33.0	30.6
×	user	✓	22.3	19.8
×	true	×	28.8	26.5
×	true	✓	18.0	16.4
✓	true	×	12.8	11.2
✓	true	✓	8.1	6.5

the `sp` model allows skipping (*i.e.* consuming 0 frames). Tonal information is not utilized for acoustic model building. After cross-word context expansion, standard decision tree clustering is applied on the triphone states to give rise to a total of 6367 physical states. Up to 16 mixture components for each state (32 for `sil` and `sp`) are estimated. Regression tree based `MLLRMEAN` [2] with diagonal covariance transforms are estimated per speaker to capture speaker dependent characteristics. A maximum of 32 transforms are generated for each speaker.

Both word and character based lexicons are evaluated and the performances of the speaker adapted ASR baseline system are presented in Table 2. For asynchronous speech, using either character based lexicon or word based lexicon only differs a lot when using bi-grams (bg). With tri-gram (tg) and four-gram (fg), they have shown similar performances. However, for the synchronous speech, decoding with character lexicon consistently yields better performance than the world lexicon due to the lengthening effects (*i.e.* longer pauses are inserted between adjacent characters even within a word) brought by the requirement of simultaneously typing/handwriting and speaking. This makes the character based lexicon more suitable for recognizing the synchronous speech. Hence, in the following experiments, only results using character based lexicons with the four-gram language model are reported. Due to the distortion incurred by lengthening the sound, there are much larger acoustic variations in synchronous speech than asynchronous one from the speech data we used to build our acoustic model, leading to a much higher Character Error Rate (CER) of 52.4%.

5.1 Mandarin Haptic Voice Recognition

Firstly the Mandarin HVR experiments were conducted on the collected dataset and results in terms of Character Error Rate (CER) are repored in Table 3 with the "user" generated haptic information. The two types of FSTs, *i.e.* with word boundary and without word boundary, were evaluated. From the results, more than 10% CER reduction can be achieved by incorporating word boundary information. To further understand the effects of haptic errors(Table 1), we artificially simulated the haptic events with the true Pinyin Initials. The error reductions from the use of "user" to "true" haptic events correlates well with the haptic input errors in

Table 4: Synchronous HVR Recognition CER (%) without speech (LM) and with speech (LM+AM) in four different noisy conditions (clean, 20dB, 15dB and 10dB) using Tonal (T), Haptic (H) input and Word Boundary (WB) information.

T	H	WB	LM	LM + AM			
				clean	20dB	15dB	10dB
×	user	×	65.3	33.0	41.3	41.4	52.0
×	user	✓	50.9	22.3	28.3	30.2	37.8
×	true	✓	48.3	18.0	23.9	26.4	34.4
✓	true	✓	19.2	8.1	9.6	11.2	14.3

Table 1. Similarly, around 10% CER reduction was brought by incorporating word boundary information.

As a kind of tonal languages, making use of tone information has been shown its importance for Mandarin speech recognition in [4]. We thus further explored the effects of tonal information for Mandarin HVR. We have tried rebuilding a tonal acoustic model which gives relatively small improvements (about 8∼12% CER reduction). In this work we only uses simulated (true) tonal information (not supplied by user during data collection). For practical purposes, possible ways of providing tonal information can be implicit (use a tone recognizer) or explicit (provided by user via touch inputs. e.g. typing an additional key or swipe in different directions after pressing onto the letter key, a fuzzy search method can also be feasible so that if the user is uncertain about the tone, he may just press without sliding).

Experimental results are presented in the last two rows of Table 3. Comparing with using "true" haptic events only, all the CERs are reduced and with word boundary information, we could get the highest accuracy for both synchronous and asynchronous speech, clearly indicating the importance of tonal information for Mandarin speech recognition. When the correct tone of each Chinese character (in practice this can be achieved via explicit user input) is provided to the system, the resultant search space is significantly reduced and thus the CER is reduced by half in most cases. So far for clean speech, incorporating the haptic information together with word boundary information and decoding with character based lexicon is the best setup for Mandarin HVR. Additionally, adding an extra stream of tonal inputs have been shown to be capable of further improving the recognition performance.

5.2 Mandarin HVR In Noisy Conditions

In this set of experiments, we examine the effectiveness of haptic information for Mandarin HVR in noisy conditions. Firstly, the clean acoustic models used in previous experiments are compensated separately for each SNR condition, which is done by Trajectory-based Parallel Model Compensation (TPMC) [7]. Experimental results for synchronous speech are listed in Table 4. For comparison purpose, we also listed the previous HVR performances for clean speech data together with the CERs of the best path of the LMs alone in those tables. Similarly, for user generated haptic inputs, the word boundary information greatly improves the HVR performance for both synchronous and asynchronous speech. With perfect haptic inputs, a relative small improvement could be achieved. The most dramatic error reduction is gained by incorporating tonal information (*i.e.* the last row in Table 4). While from the CER results of using LMs only, the conventional input methods have a CER of 48.3%. If the additional tonal information is also adopted, the decoding searching space is greatly reduced; without any acoustic information, we could already achieve a 19.2% CER. Augmenting with acoustic information, more than half of the errors are further reduced for clean and 20dB speech. Although noisy speech is the one major challenge for state-of-the-art ASR systems and the gain from the extra acoustic information is decreasing, we could still achieve a reasonable good recognition performance. Even for the 10dB case, we are still maintaining a less than 15% CER.

5.3 Interactive HVR Mandarin Input

Furthermore, we investigated the importance of acoustic information and tonal information in ranking the word choices given Pinyin initial letter (with / without tones), the word boundary and the correct word history. Here, we consider an interactive input mode in which the users select their chosen word whenever a word boundary is encountered (this provides word boundary information). Firstly, we build the word WFSTs by constraining the words according to the beginning letter (with / without the true tones) of each character's Pinyin. Then, the per-word N-best list is obtained by rescoring using the LM score of the current word given the correct word history whether or not interpolated with the AM score of that word. We computed the oracle CER of 1 to 4 best output because most mobile devices can only display up to 4 Mandarin words in a row. There are a total of 1240 words (1856 characters). The LM we used here is word-based 4-gram. The interpolation weight between AM and LM is coarsely tuned on the test set and we found that the results are quite insensitive to this weight.

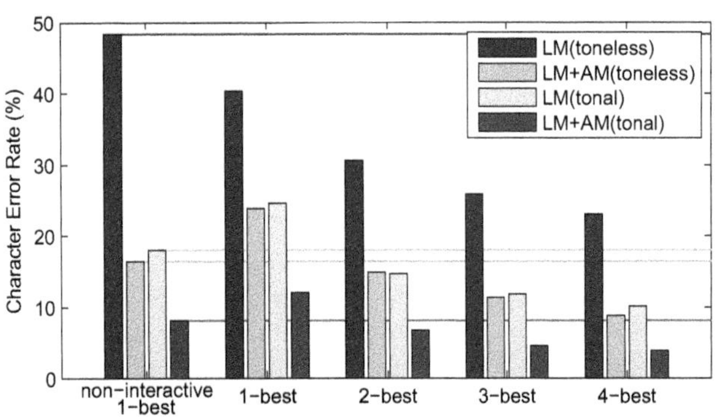

Figure 8: CER(%) of non-interactive inputs and Oracle CER(%) of 1 to 4 best outputs for both interactive inputs.

From the results shown in Figure 8, we can see that both the acoustic information and tonal information play an equally significant role in reducing the CER. And the best result is obtained by making use of both information. One important difference between these results and those in Table 4's clean condition is that here (interactive mode) only previous words information is known exactly because users select their chosen word at every word boundary but future word information is completely unknown; however, in Table 4 (non-interactive mode), both the previous word and future word information are known partially (via Pinyin initials and tones). By comparing the two results without using AM we show that knowing future word information can significantly help predicting previous words better.

6. CONCLUSIONS

In this paper, we investigated augmenting the existing Pinyin initial based predictive text input methods with acoustic and tonal information to speed up typing on mobile devices. Experimental results have shown that adopting acoustic and tonal information could greatly improve conventional input methods by providing the users with target words in the first page of candidates for fast selection. An empirical analysis shows that with our Mandarin Haptic Voice Recognition (HVR) system, we can achieve an oracle character error rate of 3.8% for the top 4 candidates, which is usually the number of word candidates displayed on mobile devices. Moreover, the Mandarin HVR system has also shown its robustness against different noisy conditions which would make this technique more valuable in real world speech applications.

7. REFERENCES

[1] I. Kiss. A comparison of distributed and network speech recognition for mobile communication systems. In *Proceedings of International Conference on Spoken Language Processing*, 2000.

[2] C. J. Leggetter and P. C. Woodland. Maximum likelihood linear regression for speaker adaptation of continuous density hidden markov models. *Computer speech and language*, 9(2):171, 1995.

[3] M. Mohri, F. Pereira, and M. Riley. Weighted finite-state transducers in speech recognition. *Computer Speech & Language*, 16(1):69–88, 2002.

[4] T. Ng, M. Siu, and M. Ostendorf. A quantitative assessment of the importance of tone in mandarin speech recognition. *Signal Processing Letters, IEEE*, 12(12):867–870, 2005.

[5] K. C. Sim. Haptic voice recognition: Augmenting speech modality with touch events for efficient speech recognition. In *Workshop on Spoken Language Technology, IEEE*, pages 73 –78, dec. 2010.

[6] K. C. Sim. Probabilistic integration of partial lexical information for noise robust haptic voice recognition. In *ACL*, pages 31–39, July 2012.

[7] K. C. Sim and M.-T. Luong. A trajectory-based parallel model combination with a unified static and dynamic parameter compensation for noisy speech recognition. In *Proceedings of Workshop on Automatic Speech Recognition and Understanding, IEEE*, pages 107 –112, dec. 2011.

[8] A. Varga and H. Steeneken. Assessment for automatic speech recognition: II. NOISEX-92: A database and an experiment to study the effect of additive noise on speech recognition systems. *Speech Communication*, 12(3):247–251, 1993.

[9] S. Young. Large vocabulary continuous speech recognition: A review. In *ASRU*, pages 3–28, 1995.

[10] S. Young, G. Evermann, M. Gales, T. Hain, D. Kershaw, X. Liu, G. Moore, J. Odell, D. Ollason, D. Povey, et al. The htk book (for htk version 3.4). 2006.

LUI: Lip in Multimodal Mobile GUI Interaction

Maryam Azh[1,2], Shengdong Zhao[1,2]
[1] NUS-HCI Lab
National University of Singapore
13 Computing Drive, Singapore 117417
[2] NUS Graduate School for
Integrative Sciences & Engineering
28 Medical Drive, Singapore 117456
{maryam, zhaosd}@comp.nus.edu.sg

ABSTRACT
Gesture based interactions are commonly used in mobile and ubiquitous environments. Multimodal interaction techniques use lip gestures to enhance speech recognition or control mouse movement on the screen. In this paper we extend the previous work to explore *LUI*: lip gestures as an alternative input technique for controlling the user interface elements in a ubiquitous environment. In addition to use lips to control cursor movement, we use lip gestures to control music players and activate menus. A LUI Motion-Action library is also provided to guide future interaction design using lip gestures.

Categories and Subject Descriptors
H.5.2 [Information Interfaces and Presentation]: User Interfaces - *Interaction styles*

Keywords
LUI, gesture input, multimodal mobile interaction

INTRODUCTION
Mobile interactions often happen in ubiquitous environments, where multi-tasking may prevent the human user to use of all available attentional and physical resources for interaction. There are many cases in which both hands are occupied and cannot be used for interaction with the user interface. For instance, while holding on to the bus handrails with one hand and keeping a tablet with the other, or in case of wearing gloves on both hands while holding a mobile phone, it is challenging to use fingers for interaction. Alternative interaction techniques that leverage multiple modalities can be useful in such scenarios (i.e., [11]). One of the under-utilized input channels is the gestures produced by the mouth, which can potentially be used not only to speak, but also to interact with computer interfaces. With the advancements in computer vision, it is possible to utilize webcam or device-integrated camera capabilities to interact with the user interface through mouth gestures. Our goal is to explore such potential as a complementary modality for interacting with computers.

ICMI '12, October 22–26, 2012, Santa Monica, California, USA.

MOUTH GESTURES FOR MULTIMODAL USER INTERFACES
Deploying mouth information as source of information is widely researched in human computer interaction. Deformation of articulatory organs such as *lips*, *tongue* and *teeth* conveys useful information to complement vocal speech data, can be used solitarily as input modality to interact with the user interface. *Lip* movements are most widely researched as opposed to tongue or teeth, as more dynamic and distinctive shapes can be identified through lip motion [7].

Lip gesture in audio visual speech recognition
Lip movement information is used as complementary visual data to enhance speech recognition. Top-down model-based, or bottom-up feature-based approaches are used to analyze lip image sequences, which utilize various lip movement features such as inner and outer lip contours, shape, color and motion [6]. The four main approaches for extracting visual information for speech recognition, include *image-based*, whereby the mouth image is used as a feature vector, *visual-motion-based*, which assumes relevant speech information within the mouth motion data, *geometric-feature-based*, which bases on height or width of the mouth opening as essential features, and finally *model-based*, which relies on a model of visible speech features such as lip contours [3]. It is expected that the bottom-up approaches prevent systematic model errors and the top-down approaches are more noise resistant.

Lip gesture as the input modality
Lip gestures have been studied as a solution to hands-free control of the user interface. A previous work [10] utilizes six distinctive mouth shapes for handling mouse events. The shapes are identified through vertical and horizontal movements of upper and lower lip centers or mouth corners. Another interesting work [2] tracks lip movements for cursor navigation.

LUI: THE LIP USER INTERFACE
Lip User Interface (LUI) is an application for mobile computers, including laptops, phones and tablets with a built-in front camera, which enables user interaction with the GUI through lip gestures. An overview of the proposed system is illustrated in figure 1.

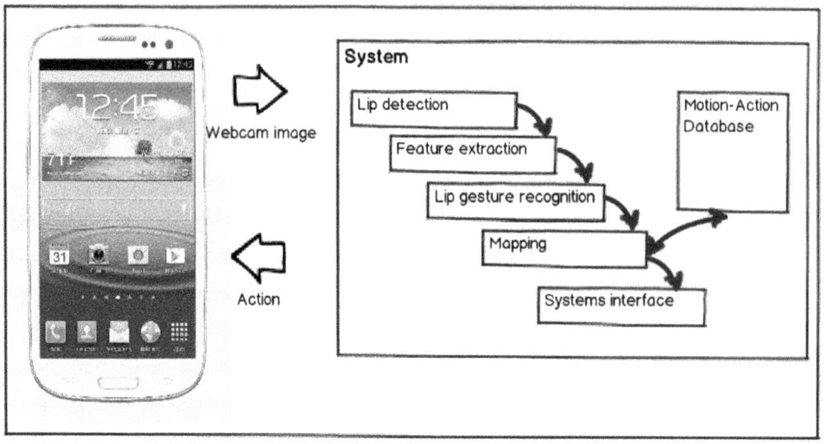

Figure 1. LUI system architecture.

We used an Android-based phone to create a hands-free scenario in a mobile context. The mobile phone built-in camera captures user lip movements in real time. Using the lip detection module implemented in OpenCV library, the frames captured from the video stream are processed and the recognized user lip gestures are mapped to user interface commands, based on the predefined motion-action library.

Table 1 lists some of the predefined motion-action entities. Our system currently supports basic user interface actions such as navigation and selection. A library of distinctive lip gestures can be found in [8] and [4]. The following section provides more detail on the implementation.

Implementation

LUI first detects the lip from the phone camera; processes the lip gesture; and executes action events on the phone user interface. Our system is composed of the following five modules:

Lip detection module: the inner and outer lip contours are identified in OpenCV based on previous work [1, 9].

Feature extraction module is built based on a previous lip feature extraction algorithm [1]. Shape features include lip shape, lip orientation and lip center.

Lip gesture recognition module deploys a Hidden Markov Model for finding the best match between the lip gesture and the image library, which is a commonly used method for lip movement recognition [5].

Mapping module: maps the lip gesture to the *motion* element in the motion-action database. Then the module signals the systems interface module to evoke the corresponding *action* element.

Systems interface module: triggers the action at the Android operating system layer.

User Interface and Interaction

LUI system is developed as an android application and installed on the phone. When the user opens the app, the front camera is activated and lib motions are triggered in real time. The application can be turned off from the Android status bar.

Usage Scenarios

We propose the following navigation and selection scenarios to test our system in the mobile environment.

- *Navigating through the music player interface, including song selection, play, volume change, etc.*
- *Calling a phone number from the contact list.*
- *Opening and scrolling through a PDF document, etc.*

CONCLUSION AND FUTURE WORKS

Our initial implementation of LUI supports basic interactions with lip gestures. In addition to the aforementioned scenarios, LUI can be used for people with hand, vision and speech disabilities as a convenient channel of interaction. User study is yet to be conducted to validate the feasibility of our system for various scenarios in ubiquitous environments.

REFERENCES

1. Çetingül, H. E., Yemez, Y., Erzin, E. and Tekalp, A. M. Discriminative Analysis of Lip Motion Features for Speaker Identification and Speech-Reading. *IEEE Transactions on Image Processing*, *15*(10), 2879-2891 (2006).
2. Dalka, P. and Czyzewski, A. Human-Computer Interface Based on Visual Lip Movement and Gesture Recognition. *IJCSA*, *7*(3), 124-139 (2010)
3. Dupont, S. and Luettin, J. Audio-Visual Speech Modeling for Continuous Speech Recognition. *IEEE Transactions on Multimedia*, *2*(3), 141-151 (2000).
4. Kanade, T., Tian, Y. and Cohn, J. F. Comprehensive Database for Facial Expression Analysis. *FG 2000*, 46-53.

5. Kaynak, M. N., Zhi, Q., Cheok, A.D., Sengupta, K., Zhang, J. and Ko, C.C. Analysis of lip geometric features for audio-visual speech recognition. *IEEE Transactions on Systems, Man, and Cybernetics*, Part A, *34*(4): 564-570 (2004).
6. Matthews, I., Cootes,T. F., Bangham, J. A., Cox, S. and Harvey, R. Extraction of Visual Features for Lipreading. *IEEE Trans. Pattern Anal. Mach. Intell.*, *24*(2): 198-213 (2002).
7. Pantic, M. and Rothkrantz, L. J. M. Automatic Analysis of Facial Expressions: The State of the Art. *IEEE Trans. Pattern Anal. Mach. Intell.*, *22*(12): 1424-1445 (2000).
8. Tian, Y., Kanade, T. and Cohn, J. F. Recognizing Lower Face Action Units for Facial Expression Analysis. *FG 2000*, 484-490.
9. Tian, Y., Kanade, T., and Cohn, J.F. Robust lip tracking by combining shape, color and motion, In *Proc. of ACCV '00*, 1040-1045.
10. Tu, J., Tao, H. and Huang, T. S. Face as mouse through visual face tracking. *Computer Vision and Image Understanding*, *108*(1-2): 35-40 (2007).
11. Zhao, S., Dragicevic, P., Chignell, M.H., Balakrishnan, R., Baudisch, P. earpod: Eyes-free menu selection using touch input and reactive audio feedback. In *Proc. of CHI 2007*, 1395-1404.

Motion		**Action**	
Lip Gesture	**Description**	**Action Event**	**Action Type**
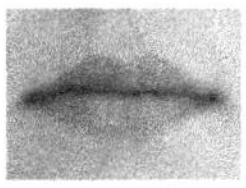	Neutral	-	-
	Lips bitten inward	Home	Main Buttons
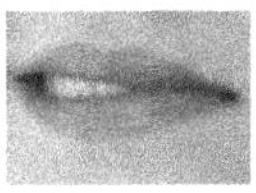	Left corner of the lips open and pulled	Back	
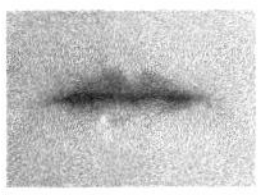	Lips pulled inward	Options	
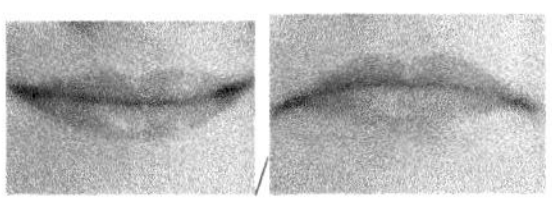	Corner of the lips pulled up/down	Navigate up/down	Navigation
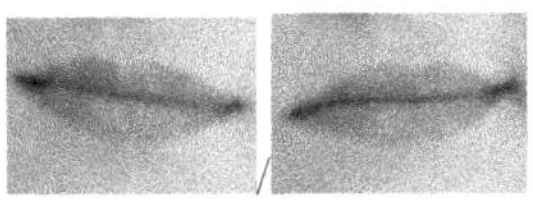	Left/right corner of the lips pulled	Navigate left/right	
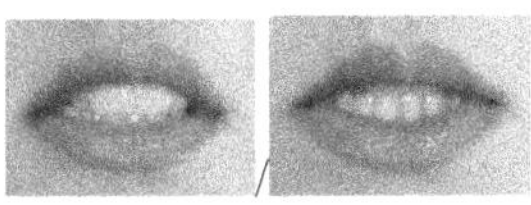	Centre of the upper lip pulled up/ center of the lower lip pulled down	Zoom in/out	
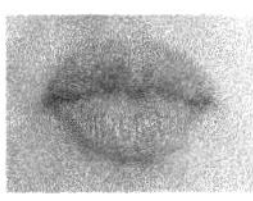	Lips pushed outward with mouth closed	Click	Selection

Table 1: LUI Motion-Action library

Speak-As-You-Swipe (SAYS): A Multimodal Interface Combining Speech and Gesture Keyboard Synchronously for Continuous Mobile Text Entry

Khe Chai Sim
National University of Singapore
Computing 1, 13 Computing Drive
Singapore 117417
simkc@comp.nus.edu.sg

ABSTRACT

Modern mobile devices, such as the smartphones and tablets, are becoming increasingly popular amongst users of all ages. Text entry is one of the most important modes of interaction between human and their mobile devices. Although typing on a touchscreen display using a soft keyboard remains the most common text input method for many users, the process can be frustratingly slow, especially on smartphones with a much smaller screen. Voice input offers an attractive alternative that completely eliminates the need for typing. However, voice input relies on automatic speech recognition technology whose performance degrades significantly in noisy environment or for non-native users. This paper presents Speak-As-You-Swipe (SAYS), a novel multimodal interface that enables efficient continuous text entry on mobile devices. SAYS integrates a gesture keyboard with speech recognition to improve the efficiency and accuracy of text entry. The swipe gesture and voice inputs provide complementary information that can be very effective in disambiguating confusions in word predictions. The word prediction hypotheses from a gesture keyboard are directly incorporated into the speech recognition process so that the SAYS interface can handle continuous input. Experimental results show that for a 20k vocabulary, the proposed SAYS interface can achieve prediction accuracy of 96.4% in clean condition and about 94.0% in noisy environment, compared to 92.2% using a gesture keyboard alone.

Categories and Subject Descriptors

H.5.2 [**Information Interfaces and Presentation**]: User Interfaces—*Voice I/O, Natural language, User-centered design* ; I.2.7 [**Artificial Intelligence**]: Natural Language Processing—*Speech recognition and synthesis*

Keywords

mobile text input; multimodal interface; voice input; gesture keyboard

1. INTRODUCTION

With the proliferation of personal mobile devices, such as the smartphones and tablets, these devices are becoming an important means for human to communicate and obtain information using the Internet. Text entry is one of the most important mode of interaction between human and their mobile devices. However, typing on mobile devices is significantly slower compared to typing on a full-sized keyboard. Studies have shown that the typing speed on a mini-QWERTY keyboard is approximately 58.61 – 61.44 Words Per Minute (WPM); while that on a full-sized keyboard is approximately 86.79 – 98.31 WPM [2]. Voice input offers an attractive alternative to typing because it completely eliminates the need for typing. Voice input is also a more natural and faster way for human to convey messages. However, voice input relies on Automatic Speech Recognition (ASR) technology, which requires high computational resources and is susceptible to performance degradation due to acoustic interference. These are practical issues to be addressed since portable devices typically have limited computation and memory resources. Moreover, ASR systems have to cope with a wide variety of acoustic conditions due to the mobility of these portable devices.

Voice input has also been used as supplementary input where ASR is used as assistive technology in a multimodal interface to improve the efficiency of typing. For example, Haptic Voice Recognition (HVR) [9] was proposed as a multimodal interface that achieves a synchronous combination of voice and touch inputs for mobile text entry. HVR accepts continuous speech input by requiring users to enter only the initial letter of each word. Kristensson *et al.* extended HVR by combining voice input with a gesture keyboard to further enhance the reliability and efficiency of text entry [5]. However, that work focuses on asynchronous input to relief the users from providing voice and touch inputs at the same time.

This paper presents Speak-As-You-Swipe (SAYS), an extension to Kristensson's work by enabling efficient and synchronous input using speech and gesture keyboard. The swipe gesture and voice inputs, together with a statistical language model, provide complementary information that can be very effective in disambiguating confusions in word predictions. The word prediction hypotheses from a gesture keyboard are directly incorporated into the speech recognition process so that SAYS can handle continuous input.

The remaining of this paper is organized as follows. Section 3 introduces the proposed SAYS multimodal interface, focusing on the detailed description of the system architecture. Section 4 presents two interaction designs for SAYS. Section 5 describes the various statistical models used in the SAYS system. Simulation results and analyses are given in Section 6.

2. RELATED WORK

Modern mobile devices are equipped with a touchscreen display where a virtual QWERTY keyboard is commonly used for text entry. For smaller devices, typing on the mini-QWERTY keyboards requires dedicated concentration and precision from the users. Furthermore, it is also more likely for a user to tap incorrectly on neighboring keys. A gesture keyboard allows users to enter words by swiping a finger over a touchscreen keyboard [6]. Gesture keyboards are invented to enhance the text entry experience using the QWERTY keyboard layout. The information provided by the swipe gesture may be ambiguous and an inference has to be made to predict the intended word. A language model can also be incorporated to enhance the prediction accuracy.

On the other hand, voice input has been used as supplementary input where automatic speech recognition is used as assistive technology in a multimodal interface to improve the efficiency of typing. For example, Haptic Voice Recognition (HVR) [9] was proposed as a multimodal interface that achieves a synchronous combination of voice and touch inputs for mobile text entry. The HVR interface accepts both voice and touch inputs concurrently (for synchronous mode). This method uses voice input to provide the main source of information. The touch input is used to provide supplementary cues to reinforce the speech recognition process. The work on HVR in [9] primarily aims at improving the noise robustness of voice input by introducing redundancy using touch input. As an extension to HVR, Kristensson11 *et al.* combines voice input with a gesture keyboard to further enhance the reliability and efficiency of text entry [5]. However, that work focuses on asynchronous input to relief the users from providing both inputs at the same time.

In this paper, the idea of combining voice input and gesture keyboard input is further extended to enable *continuous* and *synchronous* input. A continuous input means that users will utter the entire sentence and using the gesture keyboard continuously, so that the input process is more natural and user-friendly. A synchronous input enables users to speak as they swipe using the gesture keyboard so that it is not necessary to interleave between the voice and touch inputs. The proposed input method is called Say-As-You-Swipe (SAYS). The SAYS interface also shares the same system architecture as HVR, expect that the initial letter inputs are replaced by the swipe gestures. The swipe gestures capture much more information. Therefore, SAYS is expected to be much more efficient computationally at the expense of a much longer time to input the swipe gestures. Hence, there will be greater latency in user input when using the SAYS interface.

3. SPEAK-AS-YOU-SWIPE (SAYS)

Speak-As-You-Swipe (SAYS) is a multimodal interface for text input on mobile devices. SAYS combines voice input with a gesture keyboard to achieve enhanced word prediction accuracy for text entry. A SAYS interface allows users to enter texts verbally, at the same time provide swipe gesture input for each word in the corresponding utterance. A schematic diagram of the system architecture for the SAYS input method is depicted in Figure 1. The SAYS system architecture can be divided into two main parts: 1) the SAYS user interface; and 2) the underlying inference models. When the SAYS interface is active, a soft QWERTY keyboard layout is displayed onscreen (see Figure 1. At the same time, the microphone is also activated to record the user's voice. Therefore, two streams of information are being captured by the SAYS interface and passed on to the back-end inference models for processing. The final predicted words are then returned to the application.

The SAYS inference process consists of two parts. Firstly, the swipe gesture co-ordinates captured by the touchscreen are processed by a swipe gesture recognizer, where a ranked list of predicted words are generated. The ranked list of words are then used to lexically-constrain the speech recognition search. Although the SAYS system appears to be a tandem of two processes, where the predicted words generated by the swipe gesture recognizer are re-ranked using a speech recognizer as a post-processing step, the system can be designed to yield an efficient and flexible continuous input interface.

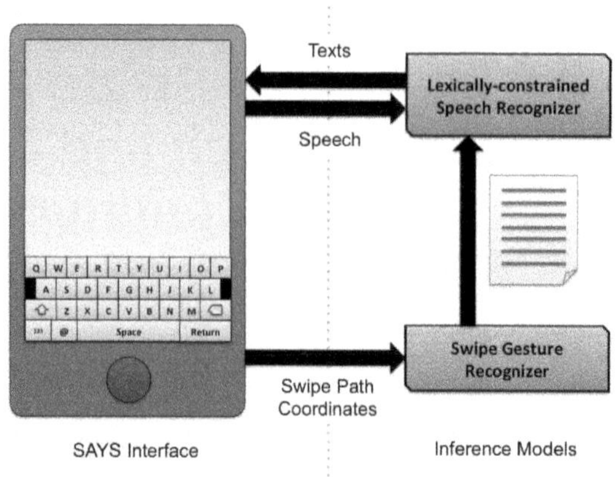

Figure 1: A Schematic Diagram of SAYS Architecture

Table 1: Comparison of Input Systems

Systems	Speech	Touch	Sync.
Speech+GK [5]	Continuous	Swipe	✗
HVR [9]	Continuous	Keyboard	✓
SAYS[1]	Isolated	Swipe	✓
SAYS[2]	Continuous	Swipe	✓

Table 1 summarizes SAYS with several other existing methods. The SAYS system using the isolated and continuous inputs are referred to as SAYS[1] and SAYS[2] respectively. More details about the SAYS interaction designs will be described in the next section. Kristensson's method of combining speech and gesture keyboard is referred to as Speech+GK. Amongst these input methods, only HVR and SAYS[2] offer a continuous and synchronous input, which is much quicker to use. Although synchronous input may increase the cognitive load of using the input interface, with sufficient practice, it is possible that the users will get accustomed to it and be able to handle the cognitive load. It is also interesting to note that the only difference between HVR and SAYS[2] is the kind of additional information provided by the touch inputs. Obviously, the additional swipe gesture of SAYS[2] provided much more information compared to the first letter information. This significantly reduces the recognition search space and the computation requirement. As a result, the SAYS[2] input method can be easily implemented on mobile devices. Fundamentally, Speech+GK and SAYS are based on the same concept of combining voice input and gesture keyboard input to achieve more reliable text entry on mobile devices. The primary difference between these methods is the synchronous input offered by SAYS[2]. Usually, it takes a longer time to complete a swipe gesture for a word then to speak the word. Therefore, 'speak-as-you-swipe' is unlikely to slow down the input speed compared to using the gesture keyboard alone. Moreover, it is not uncommon for some people to mumble or whisper along while typing. In fact, it may come as a natural phenomenon that human, to a certain extend, subconsciously combines speech and keyboard inputs when entering texts. SAYS[2] can be viewed as an intelligent interface that seamlessly picks up the ambient acoustics, locates potential spoken words and uses it to improve the word prediction accuracy.

3.1 Gesture Keyboard

A gesture keyboard [6] allows users to enter a word by performing a swipe gesture (dragging their finger on the touchscreen) such that the path traced by this swipe gesture will pass through all the letters in the same order as the spelling of the word. For example, to enter the word *CHILLED*, users will swipe on the gesture keyboard to trace a path that passes through the "C", "H", "I", "L", "E" and "D" in the same order. An ideal swipe path for the word *CHILLED*, as shown in Figure 2(a), comprises segments of straight lines connecting successive keys. However, in practice, a user will trace a smoother path as illustrated in Figure 2(b). Users do not need to provide explicit cues to indicate repeating letters. Gesture keyboard inputs may be ambiguous as the same gesture may likely to be generated by different words. For example, the swipe path of the word *CHILLED* is every similar to those of the words *CHOKED* and *COOLED*, as illustrated in Figure 2(c) and Figure 2(d) respectively. This is likely to introduce prediction errors to the output. A common way to overcome this problem is to incorporate a language model to improve the prediction accuracy. On the other hand, SAYS uses a speech recognizer to improve the prediction rates using additional complementary features extracted from the accompanying input speech. Instead of using a speech recognizer to *rescore* the N-best hypotheses generated by the swipe gesture recognizer, SAYS uses a *lexically-constrained* decoding algorithm to tightly integrate the two inference processes together.

3.2 Lexically-constrained Speech Recognition

The speech recognition (decoding) process involves searching over all possible word sequences to identify the most likely one. The search space for speech recognition is typically constructed *dynamically* using the acoustic, language and pronunciation models. Search is performed using a dynamic programming [7] approach and beam pruning [8] is commonly applied to avoid exploring word sequences which are unlikely to lead to the optimum solution. This effectively reduces the size of the search space, so that the decoding is more efficient. The recognition search process is complicated and the concept of token passing [12] was introduced to facilitate the understanding and implementation of the decoding algorithm. According to this concept, tokens are used to hold information, such as the likelihood score and time stamp, of the partial search paths. The concept of *haptic pruning* was introduced in [9] to incorporate the constraints imposed by the haptic events. This concept was later generalized to a probabilistic framework [10] where *partial lexical information* (PLI) constraints are incorporated input the standard speech recognition search space by using weighted finite-state transducer operations. Such lexically constrained recognition can be easily extended to SAYS by treating the N-best output from the gesture recognizer as PLI.

The modified lexically-constrained token passing algorithm is given in Algorithm 1. Let $\mathcal{O} = \{o_1, o_2, \ldots, o_T\}$ denote the sequence of acoustic feature vectors for the current utterance and $\mathcal{W} = \{\mathcal{W}_1, \mathcal{W}_2, \ldots, \mathcal{W}_N\}$ be the *lexical constraints* where N is the total number of swipe gestures (which also indicates the total number of words) for the current utterance. For the nth swipe gesture, the K_n word hypotheses given by the swipe gesture recognizer are given by $\mathcal{W}_n = \{w_1^{(n)}, w_2^{(n)}, \ldots, w_{K_n}^{(n)}\}$ where $w_i^{(n)}$ is the ith word hypothesis. The word-transition score is given by:

$$\alpha(w_1, w_2) = \underbrace{\bar{s}\log P(w_2|w_1)}_{\text{Language Model}} + \bar{p} + \underbrace{\bar{\eta}\log p(\mathcal{G}_n|w_2)}_{\text{Gesture Model}}$$

where $\bar{s}$ is the language model scaling factor, $\bar{p}$ is the word insertion penalty and $\bar{\eta}$ is the gesture model factor. n is the depth of w_2 in the word graph. $p(\mathcal{G}_n|w_2)$ is the likelihood of w_2 generating the touch points of the nth swipe gesture, $\mathcal{G}_n$. Further constraint can be imposed by setting $\log p(\mathcal{G}_n|w_2) = -\infty$ for $w_2 \notin \mathcal{W}_n$.

Algorithm 1 Token Passing With Lexical Constraints

Require:
  $\mathcal{O} \leftarrow$ a set of feature vectors for one speech utterance
  $\mathcal{W} \leftarrow$ a set of lexical constraints
Define:
  $\mathcal{H} \leftarrow$ a set of HMMs
  $\mathcal{T}(j) \leftarrow$ a set of tokens for state j
  $\mathcal{P}(j) \leftarrow$ a set of preceding states of state j
  $\mathcal{S}(h) \leftarrow$ a set of succeeding HMMs of HMM h
  $W(h) \leftarrow$ the word in which HMM h belongs to
Algorithm:
  for all feature vector o_t **do**
    for all $h \in \mathcal{H}$ **do**
      (perform internal token propagation)
      for all states j in h **do**
        $p(o_t|j) \leftarrow$ likelihood of state j,
        apply state likelihood, $p(o_t|j)$
        propagate $t \in \mathcal{T}(i)$ to j for all $i \in \mathcal{P}(j)$
      end for
      (perform external token propagation)
      for all exit states j in h **do**
        for all $\hat{h} \in \mathcal{S}(h)$ **do**
          $w_1 \leftarrow W(h)$ *(word of current state)*
          $w_2 \leftarrow W(\hat{h})$ *(word of next state)*
          if $w_1 \neq w_2$ **then**
            apply word transition score, $\alpha(w_1, w_2)$
          end if
          propagate $t \in \mathcal{T}(j)$ to $k \in \mathcal{E}(h)$
        end for
      end for
    end for
  end for

4. INTERACTION DESIGN FOR SAYS

In this section, two different interaction designs of the SAYS interface will be presented. These designs differ in the way voice inputs are (de)activated. For the first design, users will interact with the SAYS interface using isolated word inputs. Users speaks only when the swipe gesture is active. Therefore, users need to be conscious about speaking precisely when they are performing the swipe gesture. For the second design, users can provide natural and continuous inputs. In this case, users do not need to worry about synchronizing their speech precisely with the swipe gesture inputs.

4.1 Design I: Isolated Input

This design adopts the press-hold-release user action to (de)activate voice input. Conveniently, when using a gesture keyboard, each swipe gesture is a press-hold-drag-release action. Therefore, voice input can be activated when the swipe gesture begins and deactivated when the user completes the gesture. Since each swipe gesture corresponds to one input word, this results in an isolated-word

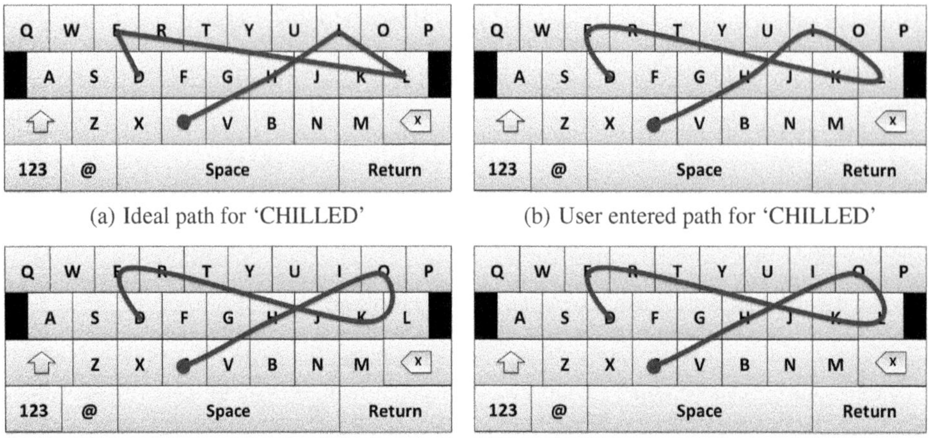

(a) Ideal path for 'CHILLED' (b) User entered path for 'CHILLED'

(c) User entered path for 'CHOKED' (d) User entered path for 'COOLED'

Figure 2: Comparison of various ideal and user-entered key swipe paths. Solid circle indicates start of the swipe path.

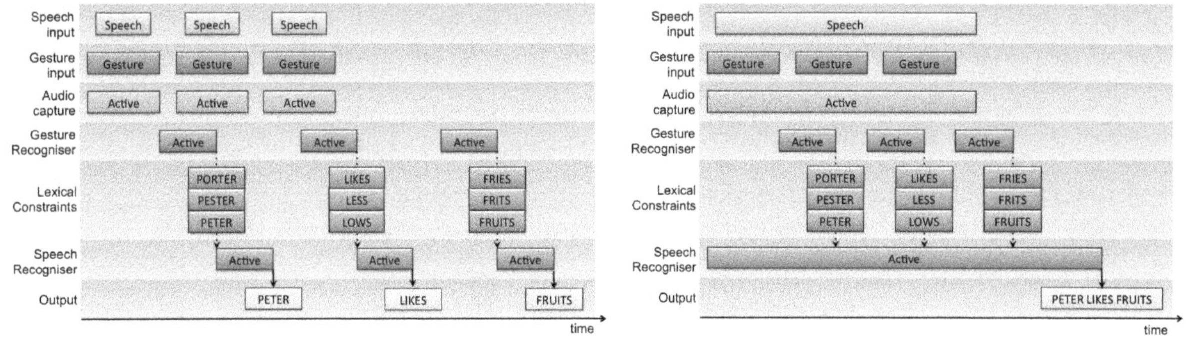

(a) Isolated Input (b) Continuous Input

Figure 3: SAYS Interaction Designs for entering the sentence "PETER LIKES FRUITS"

voice input. Therefore, the (de)activation of voice input can be easily implemented. However, the drawback of this design is that the users need to stay conscious when interacting with the SAYS interface to make sure that they speak precisely when making the swipe gesture input so that the complete utterance of every word is captured. Consequently, users may pause momentarily right after the swipe gesture begins and before it ends to ensure that spoken words are completely captured by the system. This restriction may introduce unnecessary latency and disrupt the natural flow of the input process. Figure 3(a) shows the interaction process flow for isolated word input. The horizontal axis represents time. Each row in this figure shows the status of a particular activity. The first two rows show the activity for the speech and gesture inputs. Note that the speech activity has to be within the period where the audio capture is active (*i.e.* the gesture input is active). At the end of each swipe gesture, a new recognition task is pushed into a queue, where the recognition tasked in the queue will be processed on a separate thread in the same order they were enqueued. Upon finishing one swipe gesture, the user will continue to enter the next word while the system runs the recognition of the previous unprocessed words in the background. For each recognition task, the swipe gesture inputs are first fed into a gesture recognizer to generate an N-best list of word hypotheses. These words are used as lexical constraints to perform isolated word recognition on the corresponding input speech to produce the final word hypothesis. Therefore, words are recognized in sequence and output to the user progressively.

4.2 Design II: Continuous Input

In order to avoid the requirement for the users to carefully synchronize their speech and gesture inputs word by word, the second design allows the users to input both voice and gesture inputs continuously. The voice input of the system remains activated in between consecutive swipe gestures. The interaction process flow of this design is shown in Figure 3(b). Similar to the previous design, the activation of the voice input is also triggered when the user begins a swipe gesture (if it has not already been activated). However, the voice input is not deactivated until a certain period of inactivity in the gesture input is detected. Unlike the previous design, the speech recognizer will be activated as soon as the voice input becomes active. The token passing algorithm will begin to process the speech frames (perhaps even before the user has provided any haptic inputs). Lexical constraints are progressively added to $\mathcal{W}$ upon the completion of each swipe gesture. Since the recognition is performed online, the token propagation algorithm needs to be synchronized with the swipe gesture inputs such that the word graph cannot be propagated beyond depth n until the nth swipe gesture becomes available or when the voice input is deactivated. Therefore, lexical constraints are applied to continuous speech recognition, instead of isolated word recognition. During the continuous speech recognition process, the decoding algorithm will search for the optimum word boundaries, so that speaking outside of the swipe gesture period can be tolerated.

Table 2: **Comparison of input speed (WPM) and WER (%) performance of gesture recognition using a Gesture Keyboard (GK) and a SAYS interface**

Input Methods	Speed (WPM)	WER (%)	
		Gesture Only	Gesture+LM
GK*	28	17.9	7.8
GK	34	19.7	10.2
SAYS	39	22.4	10.8

5. INFERENCE MODELS FOR SAYS

The backend of the SAYS system is the inference models. Let $\mathcal{O} = \{o_1, o_2, \ldots, o_T\}$ denote a sequence of acoustic features and $\mathcal{G} = \{\mathcal{G}_1, \mathcal{G}_2, \ldots, \mathcal{G}_N\}$ is a sequence of swipe gesture path (one for each word). The inference process can be formulated as follows:

$$\hat{\boldsymbol{W}} = \arg\max_{W} P(\boldsymbol{W}|\mathcal{O}, \mathcal{G})$$

where $\boldsymbol{W} = \{w_1, w_2, \ldots, w_N\}$ denotes a word sequence. and

$$P(\boldsymbol{W}|\mathcal{O}, \mathcal{G}) \propto \underbrace{p(\mathcal{G}|\boldsymbol{W})^{\bar{\eta}}}_{\text{Gesture}} \times \underbrace{p(\mathcal{O}|\boldsymbol{W})}_{\text{Acoustic}} \times \underbrace{P(\boldsymbol{W})^{\bar{s}}}_{\text{Language}} \quad (1)$$

where $\bar{\eta}$ and $\bar{s}$ are the gesture model and language model scale factors respectively. As shown above, the proposed SAYS system comprises three statistical inference models: swipe gesture model, acoustic model and language model. In this work, Hidden Markov Models (HMMs) are used to represent the gesture and acoustic models; a statistical n-gram language model is used to model the probability of word sequences. The gesture models are trained on touch points with *normalized*[1] cartesian coordinates. Acoustic models are trained using the Mel Frequency Cepstral Coefficients (MFCC) features [3]. These models are trained using HTK [13].

6. EXPERIMENTAL RESULTS

In order to study the effectiveness of the proposed SAYS interface, a prototype SAYS interface was implemented on the iOS platform. 72 sentences with lengths between 3 to 8 words were selected from the Wall Street Journal test set [4] for data collection. Data was collected from one test user using the prototype interface installed on an iPad. The size of the gesture keyboard is the same as that of the standard soft keyboard available on iPad. 25 sentences were used as development dataset to tune system parameters. The remaining 75 sentences were used as test data. In this study, each sentence was entered twice, once using only the gesture keyboard and a second time using the proposed SAYS input.

First of all, the performance of gesture recognition alone using a gesture keyboard is studied. The variances of the bi-letter models was empirically determined to be $\sigma = 0.2$ by tuning the value on the development dataset. Table 2 shows the effects of providing simultaneous speech and gesture inputs using the SAYS interface in terms of the input speed and Word Error Rate (WER) performance. Two sets of data were collected using gesture keyboard (GK) alone. In one instance, the swipe gestures were carefully performed to make sure that each letter key is properly traced. This is referred to as GK* and the input speed for this data was 28 Words Per Minute (WPM). The second set of data were collected with a quicker swipe gesture. This is faster to input (34 WPM) but the resulting path may only pass the vicinity of certain letter keys. On the other hand, the input speed using both speech and gesture keyboard (SAYS) was 39 WPM, slightly faster than GK, probably due to the tendency of swiping faster to catch up with the speech.

[1]The raw coordinates of the touch points are normalized such that the key button on a gesture keyboard in the normalized coordinate space is a unit square.

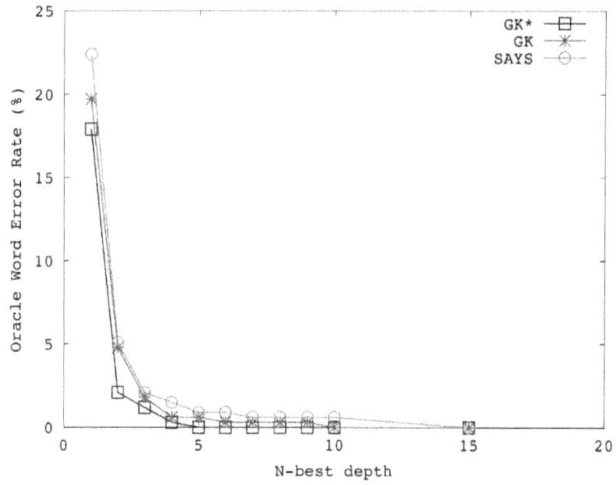

Figure 4: N-best Oracle WER (%) performance of gesture recognition with respect to N with and without concurrent speech input

The WER performance of gesture recognition was also evaluated using data collected with a regular gesture keyboard and the SAYS interface. The gesture recognizer used the 20k vocabulary words from the WSJ0 dataset. Such comparison allows the effect of adding voice input on the quality of the swipe gestures to be studied. The evaluations were done using gesture input alone (Gesture Only) and also gesture input together with a trigram language model (Gesture+LM) trained on the WSJ0 data.

When the swipe gestures were carefully performed, the WER for GK* was 17.9% without using any language model. Adding the trigram language model reduced the WER performance to 7.8% (almost 50% relative improvement). However, the WER performance degraded substantially to 19.7%. and 10.2% without and with a language model respectively, when quicker and sloppier swipe gestures were used. Finally, using the gesture input from Speech+GK, the gesture recognition performance (without using any speech input at this moment) achieved 22.4% WER using gesture features alone and 10.8% with language model boosting. These results are higher than GK. This shows that the effect of '*speak-as-you-swipe*' on the quality of the swipe gestures cannot be ignored. Nevertheless, it will be shown later that the benefit of having the additional speech input outweighs the poorer swipe gesture quality.

In the proposed SAYS system, the gesture recognizer is used to generate the *lexical constraints* in the form of N-best lists to perform lexically-constrained speech recognition. Therefore, one needs to determine the optimum size of the N-best. On one hand, a smaller N will yield tighter constraints, thereby improving the recognition speed. On the other hand, a larger N will reduce the chance of prematurely discarding the correct word hypotheses at the expense of slower recognition speed. Therefore, N needs to be tuned on the development dataset. Figure 4 shows the change in oracle WER (%) performance of gesture recognition with respect to N without (GK) and with (GK+Speech) concurrent speech input. When computing oracle WER, the output is considered correct if the correct word is in the N-best hypotheses. As expected, the oracle WER drops dramatically with increasing N. When $N \geq 5$, the oracle WERs for both input modes dropped below 1.0%. When $N \geq 15$, all the generated hypotheses contain the correct word.

Next, the performance of lexically-constrained speech recognition was evaluated using the N-best word hypotheses generated

Table 3: Comparison of WER (%) performance of lexically-constrained speech recognition using isolated and continuous speech inputs with different signal-to-noise (SNR) ratios

Noise Level (SNR)	WER (%)		
	Isolated	Isolated+	Continuous
Clean	16.4	8.3	3.6
20 dB	15.5	8.7	6.0
10 dB	14.0	8.7	5.4
0 dB	14.3	10.5	6.0

by the gesture recognizer. The acoustic models were HMM-based cross-word triphone models. Decision tree state-clustering was used to control the model complexity. Each HMM state distribution is represented by a Gaussian. Although this is not the best configuration in terms of accuracy, the choice was made to reduce the computational and memory resources required for mobile applications. 39 dimensional MFCC acoustic features (12 static parameters and together with the zeroth coefficient energy term and the first two differential parameters) were used. The results represent the overall WER performance of the SAYS interface, which combines the speech and gesture inputs. The performance of two interaction designs were compared. Table 3 shows the comparison of WER performance for these two interaction designs in different noise conditions. The clean speech data were artificially corrupted with additive babble noise [11] at various signal-to-noise ratios (SNR). The depth of the N-best list ($N = 4$) and the language model weight, $\bar{s} = 50.0$, were empirically found to yield optimum performance on development data. Speech models were also noise-compensated using the widely adopted Vector Taylor Series (VTS) technique [1]. For continuous speech input, the WER in clean condition was 3.6%, significantly lower then using gesture keyboard alone (`Gesture+LM`), which was 7.8% (see Table 2). Moreover, the WER performance in noisy environment were also better than using a gesture keyboard alone. Unlike conventional voice input, the additional speech input was still able to boost the performance even when the speech and noise signals were equally loud (0dB).

Clearly, the results using continuous input are consistently better than those using isolated input. This is largely due to the misalignment between the speech and gesture inputs. As a result, the speech input captured using the isolated interaction may not always correspond to the complete spoken words. To verify this, another set of controlled experiments were conducted using the correct word alignments to perform isolated speech recognition (this is referred to as `isolated+`). The correct word alignments were obtained by performing forced-alignment [13] using the correct transcriptions. Indeed, the performances of `isolated+` were better than `isolated` but still substantially worse than `continuous`. This may be due to the fact that the potential benefit of the cross-word triphone models were not fully exploited since the speech recognition was performed word-by-word in isolation.

7. CONCLUSION

This paper has presented Speak-As-You-Swipe (SAYS), a multimodal interface for efficient continuous text entry on modern mobile devices. The SAYS interface seamlessly integrates voice input into a gesture keyboard and the system can intelligently extract useful cues from the ambient sound to improve the word prediction accuracy. SAYS improves upon the previously proposed Haptic Voice Recognition (HVR) interface by using a gesture keyboard to provide complementary cues to reinforce the speech recognition process. The additional cues provided by SAYS contains much more information about a word compared to the first letter cues of HVR. Although the idea of asynchronously combining the voice input and a gesture keyboard has previously been proposed, this work truly integrates the two inputs concurrently to reduce latency. Experimental results show that the proposed SAYS system is able to utilize the additional concurrent voice input to enhance the accuracy of gesture keyboard input, even in noisy conditions. Furthermore, the results also show that the benefits that '*speak-as-you-swipe*' outweighs the side effect of generating swipe gestures of poorer quality.

8. REFERENCES

[1] A. Acero, L. Deng, T. Kristjansson, and J. Zhang. HMM adaptation using vector Taylor series for noisy speech recognition. In *Proc. of ICSLP*, volume 3, pages 869–872, 2000.

[2] E. Clarkson, J. Clawson, K. Lyons, and T. Starner. An empirical study of typing rates on mini-qwerty keyboards. In *CHI '05 extended abstracts on Human factors in computing systems*, CHI EA '05, pages 1288–1291, New York, NY, USA, 2005. ACM.

[3] S. B. Davis and P. Mermelstein. Comparison of parametric representations for monosyllabic word recognition in continuously spoken sentences. *IEEE Transactions on Acoustic, Speech and Signal Processing*, 28(4):357–366, 1980.

[4] J. Garofalo et al. *CSR-I (WSJ0) Sennheiser*. Linguistic Data Consortium, Philadelphia, 1993.

[5] P. O. Kristensson and K. Vertanen. Asynchronous multimodal text entry using speech and gesture keyboards. In *Proceedings of Interspeech*, 2011.

[6] P. O. Kristensson and S. Zhai. SHARK^2: a large vocabulary shorthand writing system for pen-based computers. In *the 17th Annual ACM Symposium on User Interface Software and Technology*, pages 43–52. ACM Press, 2004.

[7] H. Ney and S. Ortmanns. Dynamic programming search for continuous speech recognition. *IEEE Signal Processing Magazine*, 16(5):64–83, 1999.

[8] S. Ortmanns, H. Ney, H. Coenen, and E. A. Look-ahead techniques for fast beam search. In *ICASSP*, 1997.

[9] K. C. Sim. Haptic voice recognition: Augmenting speech modality with touch events for efficient speech recognition. In *Proc. SLT Workshop*, 2010.

[10] K. C. Sim. Probabilistic integration of partial lexical information for noise robust haptic voice recognition. In *Proceedings of the 50th annual meeting on Association for Computational Linguistics*, ACL '12, 2012.

[11] A. Varga and H. Steeneken. Assessment for automatic speech recognition: II. NOISEX-92: A database and an experiment to study the effect of additive noise on speech recognition systems. *Speech Communication*, 12(3):247–251, 1993.

[12] S. Young, N. Russell, and J. Thornton. Token passing: a simple conceptual model for connected speech recognition systems. Technical report, 1989.

[13] S. J. Young, G. Evermann, M. J. F. Gales, T. Hain, D. Kershaw, X. Liu, G. Moore, J. J. Odell, D. Ollason, D. Povey, V. Valtchev, and P. C. Woodland. *The HTK Book (for HTK version 3.4)*. Cambridge University, December 2006.

Interpersonal Biocybernetics: Connecting through Social Psychophysiology

Alan T. Pope
NASA Langley Research Center
Hampton, VA 23681
USA
757-864-6642
alan.t.pope@nasa.gov

Chad L. Stephens
NASA Langley Research Center
Hampton, VA 23681
USA
757-864-1547
chad.l.stephens@nasa.gov

ABSTRACT
One embodiment of biocybernetic adaptation is a human-computer interaction system designed such that physiological signals modulate the effect that control of a task by other means, usually manual control, has on performance of the task. Such a modulation system enables a variety of human-human interactions based upon physiological self-regulation performance. These interpersonal interactions may be mixes of competition and cooperation for simulation training and/or videogame entertainment.

Categories and Subject Descriptors
H.5.2 User Interfaces: Input devices and strategies; B.4.2 Input/Output Devices: Channels and controllers.

General Terms
Design

Keywords
Physiological modulation, biofeedback

1. INTRODUCTION
The interpersonal biocybernetics concept is an extension of what may be termed an intrapersonal biocybernetics design. In the intrapersonal design, a participant's own physiological signals are made to influence or modulate their manual control of an interface. The intrapersonal design has been implemented by modulating manual videogame controllers and wireless motion videogame controllers.

A key characteristic of this design is the distinction between direct control and modulation of control. This distinction parallels the distinction made by Fairclough [2] between intentional brain-computer interface (BCI) operation and the biocybernetic adaptation paradigm that is based on spontaneous operator functional state. Physiological modulation of manual control differs from the conventional BCI practice of direct control of a task via physiological signals in an important way. A physiologically modulating system is a human-computer interaction system designed such that physiological signals modulate the effect that control of a task by other means, usually manual control, has on task performance. In this way, physiological modulation integrates BCIs as intelligent sensors synergistically with the manual mode of control input.

ICMI '12, October 22–26, 2012, Santa Monica, California, USA.
ACM 978-1-4503-1467-1/12/10.

2. INTRAPERSONAL MODULATION
2.1 Software Modulation
The earliest embodiment of the physiological modulation concept was implemented in game software in a "space battle" scenario [7]. In this modulated prototype, a "difficulty adjuster" was programmed to vary according to an electroencephalographic (EEG) band power ratio, termed an "engagement index" [8]. In one mechanic, the subjective time of the game was correlated with the ratio value. Specifically, a delta time value was calculated based on the value of the EEG ratio. As this ratio value increased, the delta time, or dTime, decreased. This decreased value of dTime caused the subjective time of the game, i.e., the relative speed of target objects, to slow down, thus making it much easier for the player to hit targets and score points. The objective time of the game remained unaffected by the ratio level. Likewise, as the ratio value decreased, the relative speed of the target objects increased, thereby making the game more difficult and discouraging decreases in the ratio. The player is thus encouraged to maintain a high ratio level since the game is easier and his scores are improved. In addition to correlating the subjective time of the game with the ratio level, the prototype altered other parameters. For example, the normal operation of the selected video game introduced an effect termed jitter or evasiveness, which resulted in the position of the targets constantly changing in an unpredictable, seemingly erratic pattern, thereby increasing the difficulty of the game. This jitter effect was conventionally achieved by, e.g., calculating new X and Y positions for the graphic images using a randomly generated incremental change from the previous x and y values establishing position at a particular time. The EEG-modulated prototype inversely related the degree of this incremental change to the EEG band ratio level, i.e., the evasiveness decreased as the level increased and visa versa. In these ways, the player is encouraged to maintain high levels of the ratio index in order to succeed in playing the game.

This approach has the disadvantage of requiring extensive reprogramming of a video game, or the complete construction of a new video game, in order to implement the modulation concept. Because much video game software is proprietary and/or not available in source code, this approach would not be usable for implementing the concept.

2.2 Hardware Modulation
Another approach [6] involves modulation that transforms the controller signals received at the computer's port prior to their being used by the computer simulation or game software. The result can be that the magnitude of the effect of the game or simulation's input device (e.g., joystick, game pad, steering wheel) is modulated by the strength of the physiological signal(s). One implementation modulates the voltage powering a

joystick axis in proportion to a physiological signal. By making the joystick's "control authority" proportional to the physiological signal, the player is encouraged to change the physiological signal according to a programmed criterion (e.g., increase, decrease, or maintain) in order to perform better at the game task. Another implementation pulse-modulates the button presses that a user makes on a controller. The frequency and/or width of the pulses is made proportional to the physiological signal, in effect, imposing a governor on the button's effect on the game or simulation by adjusting the effective closure time of the buttons.

A new type of controller allows a player to make inputs to a video game by moving the entire controller itself, thus requiring a different method of physiological modulation. One implementation exploits these motion-sensing technologies of the wireless Nintendo™ Wii™ videogame remote to modulate the player's movement inputs to the videogame based upon physiological signals. Prototypes of one design [4, 11] enhance the challenge of various games by physiologically modulated attenuation (motion-control dampening) and/or disruption (cursor control perturbation). Games and simulations that are appropriate for this manipulation include first person shooter games using crosshairs position and point of view perturbations, medical simulations that use surgical instrument position perturbation, based on autonomic measures reflecting anxiety, to teach stress management during medical procedures, and sports simulations that adjust golf stroke strength based on electroencephalographic signals reflecting concentration.

These modulation influences can emulate the amplification of nervousness when performing a task under pressure or the increase in the likelihood of error when becoming bored. Or, on the other hand, the enhancement of manual ability when performing a task "in the zone."

In one embodiment, the standard sensor bar of the Wii™ video game system is replaced with an array of infrared light-emitting diodes (LEDs) that are individually controllable on and off. This embodiment turns LEDs in the array on and off in dynamic patterns to produce a disturbance in the player-directed control of the infrared-sensing videogame controller, resulting in a disruption in the stability of the player-controlled object (e.g., a cursor) on the screen. The degree of the disruption is programmed to be proportional to the difference between the player's current momentary physiological signal value and a pre-selected target value. In this way, the player is rewarded for diminishing this difference by an improved ability to accurately position the player-controlled object (e.g., a cursor) on the screen.

A microcontroller samples amplified and processed physiological signals (e.g., cardiotachometer readings), tests the signal levels with programmed conditional instructions, and, in accordance with the physiological signal condition determinations, adjusts the degree of the disruption. A similar scheme dynamically adjusts digitally controlled potentiometers that are configured as voltage dividers to modulate the voltage from the battery supply that powers the controller accelerometers and/or gyroscopes. This manipulation is intended to enhance the challenge of various games by physiologically modulated attenuation (dampening) of a user's motion input (e.g., golf stroke), providing an incentive to produce the target physiological signal(s).

3. INTERPERSONAL MODULATION

Extending intrapersonal modulation to the interpersonal domain is intended to catalyze interaction among participants around physiological self-regulation performance challenge. These interpersonal interactions may be mixes of competition and cooperation for simulation training and/or videogame entertainment.

Physiological modulation technologies that operate by altering the functioning of game controllers, i.e., externally to game consoles, may be readily set up to allow players to interact with the game, and compete with each other, on a psychophysiological level, adding a new dimension to play – as well as expanding the skill set required. Competitive interaction with these intrapersonal modulation functionalities may be implemented with the standard multi-player capability of off-the-shelf game systems.

However, a multiplayer format is also envisioned wherein physiological self-regulation skill contributes to success in ways analogous to traditional game-playing skills, i.e., scoring, power-ups, etc.

3.1 Multi-User Modulation Design

Norris [5] pointed out that:

> Top athletes [...] make excelling in their chosen type of psychophysiological control of the craniospinal system and striate muscles the major focus of their efforts. Here in the West, we value objectivism, material things, and have turned our attention outward toward controlling the external world. In the East, it has been quite different; the orientation of science and society values subjectivism and numinal experiences, and they have turned their attention inward, toward control of the internal world. Therefore, their champion 'acrobats' are those individuals who can assert and demonstrate control over autonomic and other internal processes. [...] in India, they have a sort of autonomic Olympics, where yogis and adepts come from far and wide to demonstrate their prowess at such things...

In the present day, this sort of event could take place in a multi-player environment such as a videogame tournament.

The design of a psychophysiologically competitive, as well as cooperative, environment is proposed in "Physiological Interface for a Multi-User Virtual Environment (MUVE) [9] intended to augment "a computer user's sense of immersion in the computer-generated multi-user virtual environment by adding physiological interactivity to the multi-user virtual environment and by influencing the scoring of performance in the multi-user virtual environment with measured values of a user's physiological functions" (e.g., an EEG-based engagement index [8]).

The aim is to make any multi-user videogame or multi-user computer-simulated task more engaging and hence more effective as a device for teaching physiological self-regulation, by incorporating, as a competitive or cooperative interactive feature, each user's ability to self-regulate aspects of his or her physiology.

This MUVE design is intended as an enhancement of multiplayer videogames that computes physiological scores standardized on an individual's baseline responses - to level the playing field, and compares a selected score with a benchmark target or benchmark normative value. Depending on the results of the comparison, at least one game consequence is selected which may take various forms: a change in a user's point score; or a change in some element in the MUVE, i.e., a "power element" that is important for further success, such as the accrual of virtual fuel, food, ammunition, energy, longevity, shielding; or, a change in some virtual power, capability or function of a user's avatar that is important for further success, such as range of motion, or effect of motion, or duration of activity; or the user's control of the MUVE control input device may be made more or less difficult. Based on the user's performance, game consequences may also take the form of similar competitive or cooperative consequences for the user's opponents or teammates. Each consequence may be made proportional to a functional combination of physiological comparison values.

Additionally, a user may qualify for a gain of a certain advantageous element or game privilege only if the user has attained a threshold score that has been defined for that element or privilege. For example, upon attaining a threshold score, a player may selectably donate or withdraw performance points to or from the score of each other user interacting with the MUVE, adding an additional competitive or a cooperative aspect to the interaction.

One component of a user's performance is determined by each user's skill in using an input device to control the actions of his or her avatar in various scenarios and encounters arising within the MUVE, such as the outcome of combat with an enemy avatar in a videogame embodiment of a MUVE, or the outcome of a cooperative effort with a teammate avatar in a computer-simulated task embodiment of a MUVE. A second component is determined by each user's skill in self-regulating his or her own physiological functioning while controlling his or her avatar using an input device. The second component reflects the competition or cooperation engaged in by each user of the MUVE using measured values of his or her physiologic functions.

A player's physiological performance record accrued in the course of a session in the physiologically modulated MUVE may subsequently be accessed by software or another user. For example, the physiological performance record may subsequently be assigned to another "assignee" avatar whose behavior in the MUVE is thereafter determined and controlled by utilizing the player's performance record, and the player's avatar may be activated while the player is not participating in the MUVE. The assignee avatar assumes the recorded physiological performance of the absent player, and emulates the player's recorded physiological reactions to certain events occurring in the MUVE, such as parrying a sword thrust, thereby effectively serving as a "ghost" of the player with which other users of the MUVE may interact in the absence of the player's actual participation in the MUVE.

3.2 Collaborative Modulation Design

The entertainment value and social interaction experience of electronic gameplay may be enhanced by distributing the control and modulation of inputs to electronic games among two or more players, so that joint game goals are collaboratively pursued and accomplished by separate players who provide different means of control and modulation [10]. For example, one or more players may provide physical activity control via game controller(s) (these players may be termed the physical operators) and one or more other individuals influence the game through physiological activity measured via body sensors (these players may be termed physiological operators). When applied to neurofeedback training, such collaboration encourages the therapist or parent to provide social support by engaging in a training session as the physical operator, while the trainee practices self-regulation as the physiological operator. In a training simulation context, collaboration would consist of a physiological operator (e.g., the pilot-monitoring) practicing a psychophysiological state associated with sustained attention while the physical operator (e.g., pilot-flying) practices manual operation. This interdependent mode of operation could provide novel material for the communication aspect of crew resource management (CRM) training [3].

Some physiologically modulated game designs [6, 7, 11] lend themselves readily to collaborative interaction by having different players assume the physical and physiological operator roles with the same modulated controller [10]. Such an embodiment avoids the problem of movement disruption of physiological sensing by modulating one player's game controller using the physiological signals of another, collaborating player who is physically inactive. This functionality further enables collaborative team play by multiple players with different roles on the team--one or more providing physiological mastery to facilitate game performance and one or more others simultaneously providing manual or physical skills needed to operate the game. This creates richer and more complex gaming opportunities than present games provide, enabling engaging and rewarding team social interactions among people who have different skill sets and interests or who take turns playing different roles on a team—either providing the physiological self-mastery skill or providing physical performance action skills.

This design modulates one or more players' game controller (i.e., game input device operated by physical activity) using the physiological signals of another/other collaborating player(s) who is/are not providing input to the game via a game controller. This function is accomplished by transmitting control signals, either wired or wirelessly, derived from one or more players' physiological signals to modulate the control over the game of one or more other players who are using electronic game controllers, in a way that either limits or boosts the game performance influence of the game controllers.

Alternatively, this shared influence over a game of a physiological operator and physical (game controller) operators can be implemented by blending influences from both into a single control input into the game; in this manner, game action tasks could be operated either via a game controller or particular predefined physiological input, or through pre-defined combinations of both. For instance, a video game task of an avatar game character jumping over a canyon could be initiated by either the game controller operator or by a physiological operator's particular body activity, and the height or length of the jump could then be solely dependent on the physiological activity of the physiological operator whereas the direction of the jump and place of landing on the other side could be controllable only by the game controller input. Thus, the physiological and game controller operators would have to collaborate to succeed at the task of jumping for success in the game.

Two new categories of electronic game play are made possible: 1) modulating one or more player's game controller input using the physiological signals of another/other collaborating individuals; and 2) modulating game activity through joint authority over game actions by game controller input from one or more individuals and physiological sensor input from other separate individuals not using game controllers. Physiological and manual control of electronic games can be allocated in various combinations to several players.

Individuals who are physically challenged may participate in electronic game play by collaborating with a player who is able to manipulate controls that the challenged player cannot, and enables individuals with different skill sets and interests (physiological self-control vs. physical performance skills) to join together in rewarding game play.

Unprecedented electronic games can be created that incorporate a classic motif in superhero comics and movies in which differently-abled protagonists collaborate and/or interact, such as Professor X and his cohorts in the X-Men series, and provides opportunities for new kinds of games where the application of "mental powers" of particular individuals (e.g., particular deliberately produced EEG characteristics) can enable or enrich the performance of other individuals playing a game.

4. DISCUSSION

Certain human physiological states are associated with the optimal performance of certain activities and behaviors, or the attainment of superior states of health. Biofeedback training directed to self-regulating such physiological states seeks to optimize the performance of their associated actions, behaviors, and states of health, thereby facilitating mastery in action and well-being. For example, a self-induced reduction of an elevated heart rate and blood pressure, a rise typically associated with anxiety, may be expected to move a person into a state of superior focus with respect to a challenge and its resolution--a state that is better suited for victory over an opponent in real or simulated combat or completion of a real or simulated task [1].

Biofeedback training techniques for physiological self-regulation are fundamentally grounded upon repetition and the frequency of repetition, techniques for which persons have varying and limiting tolerances, particularly if their practice of biofeedback is undertaken in an environment that is not motivating because it fails to engender excitement, enthusiasm, challenge, stimulation, or curiosity. The absence of such motivating feelings can result in nonadherence to biofeedback training--a persistent and pervasive problem that has limited the prevalence and effectiveness of biofeedback training.

However, biofeedback training programmed into videogames or computer simulations has been limited to single-user videogames or single-user computer simulations, where the user is made aware of only some of his or her own monitored physiological functions, and the user's interaction with the videogame or computer simulation is modulated only by the control of his or her own physiological functions [6, 7, 11]. In effect, the user competes only with himself or herself, and this may limit commitment to play and participation, with a concomitant decline in biofeedback-mediated self-regulation of the user's physiological state.

Recent biofeedback technology innovations have solved this problem to a degree, by blending biofeedback into videogames, and thereby making training inherently motivating,

On the other hand, physiologically modulated videogame or computer simulation systems also enable a variety of human-human interactions based upon physiological self-regulation performance. These interpersonal interactions may be mixes of competition and cooperation for simulation training and/or videogame entertainment.

Physiologically modulating games and simulations has the effect of projecting exaggerated effects of the physiological concomitants of emotion and cognition into the interaction. Incorporating social interactivity into physiologically modulated games and simulations further engages users in human-computer interaction (HCI) experiences that have the capacity to train valuable mental skills beyond hand-eye coordination.

When physiological signal(s) are the target of physiological self-regulation or biofeedback training, modulated game play reinforces therapeutic changes in related physiological processes. However, the reinforcing feedback is implicit in the game play and not explicit in the form of direct feedback (bar graphs, tracings), as in conventional biofeedback training. In this way, contingencies for subtle conditioning of the desirable physiological response(s) are set up.

The added benefit of the physiologically modulated approach is the improvement of self-regulation capabilities that directly impact a player's health in a positive manner. Videogames and simulations can be designed such that success in the virtual world is predicated upon self-regulation skills demonstrative of healthy autonomic function and optimal cognitive states. Evoking certain psychophysiological states is a design choice that developers are currently making de facto, but with the result that games and simulations are often devices that produce frustration and foster poor attention abilities. The decision by designers to incorporate physiological modulation can be considered a next step in a more informed and healthy direction for gaming and simulation products. Making this choice allows users to choose technology that is entertaining as well as beneficial to their physical, mental and interpersonal health.

The approaches to physiological computing described in this paper represent a unique blending of conventional computer interface capabilities with contemporary psychophysiological monitoring and biofeedback techniques. The use of physiologically modulated videogames and simulations involving multiple players using traditional manual control and BCIs as intelligent sensors promises to augment HCI and human-human interaction (HHI) applications. Tapping into the natural social experience that occurs when players compete or collaborate in gaming or simulated environments leverages subtle interpersonal interactions. The addition of the challenge of physiological self-regulation in a social context improves the motivation to perform in order to enable team success or victory over opponents in simulated environments. Further, implementing this challenge in the ways described herein fosters dialogue around self-regulation among the participants. These implementations can require dividing attention between one's own self-regulation performance and that of others, a potentially valuable skill for team settings.

How an interface can adapt to the user to provide support is an important consideration for BCI research. Current BCI technology has specific application and usability goals at the fore. Establishing reliable capabilities is of foremost importance, but, beyond utility, these systems can be designed to inherit the benefit of social experience that occurs between humans. The application of readily available physiological information from BCI technology can be used to enable such a user experience.

5. REFERENCES

[1] Edmonds, W. A. and Tenenbaum, G. (Eds.) (2011) Case Studies in Applied Psychophysiology: Neurofeedback and

Biofeedback Treatments for Advances in Human Performance. West Sussex, UK: Wiley-Blackwell.

[2] Fairclough, S. H. (2008). BCI and Physiological Computing: Differences, Similarities & Intuitive Control. Workshop on BCI and Computer Games, CHI (08), Florence, Italy. http://www.physiologicalcomputing.net/?p=1928

[3] Kanki, B. G., et al. (Eds.) (2010). Crew Resource Management. (2nd ed). San Diego, USA: Elsevier.

[4] NASA's "Mindshift" Biofeedback Gaming Technology Mimics Reality. NASA Tech Briefs, November 1, 2010. http://www.techbriefs.com/component/content/article/8783

[5] Norris, P. (1986). Biofeedback, Voluntary Control, and Human Potential. Biofeedback and Self-Regulation, vol. 11(1), 10-12.

[6] Palsson, O. S., et al. Method and Apparatus for Encouraging Physiological Self-regulation through Modulation of an Operator's Control Input to a Video Game or Training Simulator. U. S. Patent No. 6450820. September 17, 2002.

[7] Pope, A. T. and Bogart; E. H. Method of encouraging attention by correlating video game difficulty with attention level. U.S. Patent No. 5377100. December 27, 1994.

[8] Pope, A. T., Bogart, E. H., & Bartolome, D. S. (1995). Biocybernetic System Validates Index of Operator Engagement in Automated Task. *Biological Psychology*, 40, 187-195.

[9] Pope, A. T. and Palsson, O. S. Physiological User Interface For A Multi-User Virtual Environment. U.S. Patent No. 8062129. November 22, 2011.

[10] Pope, A. T. and Palsson, O. S. Team Electronic Gameplay Combining Different Means of Control. U.S. Patent Application No. 20110300523, December 8, 2011.

[11] Pope, A. T., et al. Physiologically Modulating Videogames or Simulations Which Use Motion-Sensing Input Devices. U.S. Patent Application No. 20120004034. January 5, 2012.

Adaptive EEG Artifact Rejection for Cognitive Games *

Olexiy Kyrgyzov and Antoine Souloumiac
CEA, LIST, Laboratoire d'Outils pour l'Analyse de Données
F-91911, Gif-sur-Yvette, France
{olexiy.kyrgyzov & antoine.souloumiac } at cea.fr

ABSTRACT

The separation of the informative part from an observed dataset is a significant step for dimension reduction and features extraction. In this paper, we present an approach for adaptive artifact rejection from the electroencephalogram (EEG). The main aim of our work is to increase performance of classification algorithms which have a deal with the EEG and are used in cognitive games. We provide a method to separate the EEG into informative and noised parts, select informative one and rank its dimensions. The proposed approach is based on the theoretical relation between classification accuracy, mutual information and normalized graph cut (NC) value. The presented algorithm requires a priori known class labeled EEG dataset that are utilized for a calibration phase of the brain-computer interface (BCI). Experimental results on datasets from BCI competitions show its applicability for cognitive games.

Categories and Subject Descriptors

H.1.2 [**Models and Principles**]: User/Machine Systems

Keywords

Brain-Computer Interfacing, Applied Machine Learning, Multimodal Fusion and Integration

1. INTRODUCTION

Temporal and spatial properties of the EEG do not allow us to read human minds but are sufficient to detect the general cognitive states (recognition, visual evoked potentials, etc.). Due to the low-voltage cognitive signals and high-power distortions, the main problem of such signals is the presence of noise and artifacts [13]. The goal of this project is to determine the intrinsic brain signals that can be used after for the BCI. We refer the reader to a paper on the same problem solution as a starting point for our approach [7], and to a broad literature review which reflects results of the last years [14].

This paper describes results achieved in a part of the global work package on cognitive games implementation managed by INRIA, France. Work team involves both academic groups and industrial companies. The purpose of this collaboration is to release software to the game market. Open Virtual Brain Environment (OpenViBE) is an existing software platform for the BCI. Its main aim is to bind technologies in video game applications and cognitive signal analysis [1]. A common game process consists of 3 components: (a) subject(s); (b) target(s); (c) strategy(s). In the terms of the game process we provide a preprocessing method which separates and improves informative signals from a game subject. Below we provide a brief review of the EEG artifacts, initial conditions of the BCI, and existing solutions on EEG artifact rejection.

1.1 EEG artifacts

Electroencephalography is a registration of electrical cerebral activities measured over the scalp. Along with signals from the brain other artefactual electrical activities are registered. This can significantly distort genuine EEG and influence on decisions in BCI. Artifacts can be divided into two groups according to their origin: physiologic end extraphysiologic [3]. The first ones are generated by the parts of the body different from the brain, e.g., eye blink and movement, muscle activity (hand/foot/body movement, respiration), glossokinetic artifact, ECG signals, skin artifacts. The second ones arise from the external environment, e.g., electrode connections, 50/60-Hz alternating current artifact, movements in the environment around the subject, etc.

The goal of the artifact rejection task is to separate the cerebral signals from the observed EEG, which can be modeled as an unknown linear mixture of the artifacts and the informative cerebral activities. Most of the informative cerebral signals for the BCI (SSVCP, P300, SCP) fall into the range from 0.1 to 20 Hz. Due to the different nature of the EEG generation, the brain waves are classically divided into several frequency bands: (a)Delta band - $0-4Hz$; (b) Theta band - $4-8Hz$; (c) Alpha band - $8-13Hz$; (d) Beta band - $13-30Hz$; (e) Gamma band $> 30Hz$. Each band can contain specific brain waves and artifacts with unique range of frequencies, forms, and amplitudes. Also depending on the nature of origin, artifacts can be located into different registration channels.

*This research has been partially supported by ANR (France) Project OpenViBE, grant ANR-2009-CORD-017.

ICMI'12, October 22–26, 2012, Santa Monica, California, USA.

1.2 Problem statement

Initial conditions of the EEG artifact rejection are common for a wide range of cognitive tasks and can be divided into 5 groups:

1. Unique personal physiology: each person has its own inimitable features of physiological scalp structure that impacts recorded data.
2. Wide range of EEG equipment: there are numerous companies (g.tec, Neurosky, Emotiv, etc.) which produce equipment for cognitive states registration. Their devices differ in the number of the registration electrodes, location on the scalp, type of connection (wet or dry), etc.
3. Electrode position for each session: it is absolutely impossible to place the electrodes precisely on the same part of the scalp. So we can only define approximative regions for EEG electrodes location.
4. External stimulus: they can be divided into two groups (extraphysiologic artifacts and driving signals). The first ones worsen EEG recording and have to be eliminated, the second ones are informative stimulus for the brain.
5. Scenarios: BCI for different tasks (games) involves analysis of different cognitive responses, e.g., P300, SSVEP, motor-visual signals. An artifact rejection procedure has to adapt its parameters both to the behavior of the user and the active conditions of tasks.

Based on the analysis of the initial conditions we can conclude that the final solution for artifact rejection procedure has to be fast, robust, and tunable. It should not depend on personal features of participants, configuration of equipment, and conditions of signal registration.

1.3 Existing solutions for EEG artifact rejection

The accuracy of the EEG signal analysis and interpretation depends significantly on the artifact rejection procedures. In general, data can be corrupted by blinking and eye movement, muscle and heart activities, equipment line noise and environmental signals. One of the most powerful artifacts in the EEG record is generated by eye activity. To eliminate such artifacts one usually utilizes two approaches: (a) discard all EEG epochs where eye blinks or movements are acquired (it can complicate the data acquisition and increase the process time); (b) utilize a regression procedure which involves both EEG and reference signals (we can both eliminate eye artifacts and neglect useful signals from EEG).

Another method for artifact rejection is applying independent component analysis (ICA) to the multichannel EEG records in order to separate cognitive and noise signals [5]. In the ideal case the linear ICA gives us a set of separated brain sources, artifacts and their mixture matrix. An advantage of the ICA approach consists in solving the source separation problem in the whole and we do not need to eliminate each kind of artifacts separately like in the regression approach. The biggest problem of this approach is true sources identification, i.e., how to interpret the ICA results. There are many different methods for ICA implementation. They usually differ in cost functions and used measures. The two broadly used criteria for ICA implementation are minimization of mutual information between sources or maximization of their non-Gaussianity, e.g., Jade (Joint approximate diagonalization of eigen-matrices), FastICA (Maximization of non-Gaussianity as a measure of statistical independence), Sobi (Second-order blind identification), Logistic ICA (Separation super-Gaussian (kurtosis > 0) component activations), Generalized Eigen-Decomposition (involves both the 2nd- and the 4th-order statistics). The last one is widely used and provides fast solution in analytical form but does not involve information on data classes.

ICA recovers linear mixture of sources, $\mathbf{S}$, from observed datarecord, $\mathbf{X}$ [10]:

$$\mathbf{X} = \mathbf{AS} \text{ and } \mathbf{S} = \mathbf{W}^T\mathbf{X}, \tag{1}$$

where matrix $\mathbf{X} = [\mathbf{x}_1; \mathbf{x}_2; \ldots; \mathbf{x}_n]$ and $\mathbf{x}_i$ is i^{th} EEG channel recorded from the appropriate electrodes; $\mathbf{A}$ is a mixture matrix; $\mathbf{S}$ is a matrix of recovered sources. Columns of $\mathbf{X}$ present measurements recorded at the fixed time points. The main aim of the ICA is to define an unmixing matrix, $\mathbf{W}$, which recovers independent components in multi-scale EEG data. Simultaneously, the linear ICA does not allow us to identify: (a) the true number of the sources; (b) the proper sign and scaling factors of the sources; (c) the initial order of the sources (identifiable up to a permutation matrix). These restrictions are issued from the fact that each source in $\mathbf{S}$ is a multiplication of vector times matrix, i.e., $\mathbf{s}_i = \mathbf{w}_i^T\mathbf{X}$, and there are no restrictions on such vectors in $\mathbf{W}$. So to perform the proper ICA as well as source analysis, each data channel must be zero-mean centered and equally normalized by its standard deviation. The same normalization must be performed on recovered sources.

To implement the ICA for the BCI we assume the following properties: (a) brain signals and artifacts are temporally and spatially independent; (b) recorded EEG signals is a constant linear mixture of brain potentials and other signals; (c) delays in propagation of signals are assumed to be insignificant. Since we can change location and conductivity of electrodes on the scalp for each session, it implies performance of the ICA for each person and session independently.

2. METHOD

We propose the following EEG artifact rejection algorithm for cognitive game:

1. Involve gamer into precalibration phase with known EEG classes.
2. Decompose each of the channels in frequency bands.
3. Apply the ICA to concatenated data.
4. Select the most informative sources [7], which maximize classification accuracy, and utilize them for the follow-on game.

To clean the EEG from noise and artifacts one can apply inversion of the ICA and sum signals from all frequency bands. Below we provide a new method for ICA implementation and show how to utilize it for channel selection.

2.1 Mutual information and normalized graph cut

The aim of our method is to increase classification accuracy (CA) in the BCI via artifacts rejection. In the case of the true source separation we need to identify informative EEG sources and reject the other ones. This approach can be applied directly to channels as well. Maximization of the CA is an equivalent problem to the MI maximization of the data. By exploiting the fact that the MI of $\mathbf{S}$ and $\mathbf{X}$ are equal, the MI maximization between sources and class labels is:

$$\max_{\mathbf{X}} I(\mathbf{X}, \mathbf{c}) = \max_{\mathbf{S}} \left(H(\mathbf{S}) - \sum_{c} p_c H(\mathbf{S}|\mathbf{c}) \right), \quad (2)$$

where $\mathbf{S}$ is a set of sources, $\mathbf{c}$ is a vector of class labels, and $H(\mathbf{S})$ is an entropy estimator of the $\mathbf{S}$. In the case of the true source separation we can identify a mixture matrix, $\mathbf{A}$, of the brain waves and artifacts.

A possible method to solve (2) is to apply a linear ICA and perform one-dimensional source ranking [7]. Generalized eigen-decomposition is a widely used linear ICA implementation [4], where the separation matrix $\mathbf{W}$ is achieved via computation of $\mathbf{RW} = \Lambda\mathbf{QW}$, here $\mathbf{Q} = E[\mathbf{X}^T\mathbf{XXX}^T] - \mathbf{R}Tr(\mathbf{R}) - E[\mathbf{XX}^T]E[\mathbf{XX}^T] - \mathbf{RR}$ and $\mathbf{R} = \mathbf{XX}^T$ are fourth-order cumulants and covariance matrix, respectively [11]. This matrix decomposition solves the problem in whole and does not take into account the information about class labels. Such an operation does aim to separate a set of the most informative sources.

In case of the absolutely independent sources the joint and joint-conditional entropies in (2) become the sum of marginal and marginal-conditional entropies, respectively. This assumption allows us to evaluate the MI via one-dimensional sample-space entropy estimation [9]. The method is grounded on the difference between ordered m-samples, where m is typically a square root of the data samples number. Such an estimator is a simple, rapid, and asymptotically converging approach. Due to nonlinear processes in the brain, cerebral signals are not mutually independent. By inversion of the linear ICA model we suppose to recover only two mutually independent subsets of sources: the brain waves and the artifacts. For the multidimensional entropy estimation in (2) we are required to evaluate either Delaunay clusters or hyper-Voronoi regions. The both are complex and time consuming procedures [8].

Instead of the hyper-Voronoi regions we propose to use Parzen-Rosenblatt density estimation. Also instead of the multidimensional entropy we suggest a modified normalized cut value. Knowing class labels of data we can evaluate intra- and inter-class variance via affinity matrix (AM). Such a matrix can be easily implemented in recursive way for source ranking and recovering. In contra to the MI, that monotonically increases with source subset growing in [7], the NC value is minimized only for the most informative sources.

In the literature, the AM is symmetrical which is determined by constant bandwidth for each kernel. It is fair for constant data distribution in each of the data classes. To cover the general case of the data distribution we involve unique kernel bandwidths that converts the AM into asymmetric form. The Fig. 1 provides an example of two data class distributions with different variances and corresponding asymmetric AM. Thus the modified NC is transformed to four summands:

$$nCut = \frac{\sum TR}{\sum TL + \sum TR} + \frac{\sum BL}{\sum TL + \sum BL} + \frac{\sum TR}{\sum BL + \sum TR} + \frac{\sum BL}{\sum TR + \sum BL}, \quad (3)$$

where the letters T, B, L, R specify regions (top, bottom, left, right) of the AM on the Fig. 2(b). We can avoid data overlapping in the AM and reach the global minimal value. Generalizing the properties of vectors in the $\mathbf{W}$ and modified NC we use a new cost function for the linear ICA:

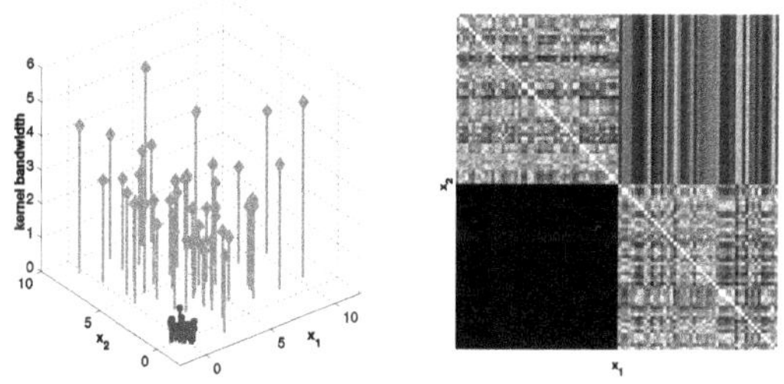

(a) Kernel bandwidths for 2-class data

(b) Asymmetric affinity matrix for data

Figure 1: Modified asymmetric affinity matrix

$$\min_{\mathbf{W}} \left(nCut(\mathbf{S}, \mathbf{c}) + (\mathbf{W}^\mathbf{T}\mathbf{W} - \mathbf{I})^2 \right). \quad (4)$$

Here the first term recovers the most informative sources, the second one avoids singularity in the $\mathbf{W}$ and preserves unit norms of its vectors. In our numerical experiments it outperforms the ICA methods described above that do not involve information on class labels.

2.2 Channel selection

Based on the NC value described above, in the Algorithm 1 we provide a recurrent procedure for channel selection. Proposed algorithm can be implemented in either forward or backward direction. For the forward direction, we incrementally estimate the optimal subset of the most informative channels. For the backward direction we reject the less informative sources from the full set of channels. The global minimum of the NC identifies an optimal subset of the most informative channels. Though the forward direction reaches the global minimum of the NC faster, it does not include the MI for all informative channels until achieving its full set. The advantage of the proposed selection procedure is an ability to rank not only channels in dataset but also samples in channels. In the case of the EEG record with P300 responses, it helps us to identify both the length of the temporal window and its delay.

3. NUMERICAL EXPERIMENTS

To validate the proposed artifact rejection approach we tested and compared it with four different BCI competitions (performances are verified)[1]. In fact, we perform only data preprocessing and do not change classification methods. The following results, which are grounded on the informative source selection procedure, demonstrate accuracy and efficiency of the proposed method.

Dataset I: P300 speller problem is provided by Ulrich Hoffmann [6] as mean values of classification accuracy over 8 subjects. 32 EEG channels were partitioned into groups of 4, 8, 16, 32 channels and were used with LDA algorithm. Classification accuracies provided by the author for electrode configurations against the number of letter representation for 5

[1]Matlab code and datasets are available on the personal web page of the first author: `https://sites.google.com/site/kyrgyzov/bci`

Algorithm 1 Channel selection procedure

$dir = 1$; // direction (1 - forward; -1 - backward)
n // the number of channels (or samples)
$\mathbf{X}$ // dataset consists of n channels and c classes
$\mathbf{U} = [1, \ldots, n]$; // indices of channels
$\mathbf{V} = [\,]$; // ranked indices of channels
while $|\mathbf{U}| \neq 0$ **do**
  for $k = 1 : |\mathbf{U}|$ **do**
    // Evaluate normalized cut
    if $dir = 1$ **then**
      $nC(k) = nCut(\mathbf{X}[\mathbf{V} + \mathbf{U}_k, :], c)$
    else
      $nC(k) = nCut(\mathbf{X}[\mathbf{U} - \mathbf{U}_k, :], c)$
    end if
  end for
  $i = min_i(nC)$
  $\mathbf{V} = \mathbf{V} + \mathbf{U}_i$
  $\mathbf{U} = \mathbf{U} - \mathbf{U}_i$
end while

times (a) are: 86%, 93%, 92%, 94%; for 15 times (b) are: 96%, 99%, 99%, 99%. Classification accuracies obtained in our experiments for 5 times (a) are: 89%, 95%, 93%, 97%; for 15 times (b) are: 97%, 99%, 100%, 100%.
Dataset II: P300 speller problem is provided by Alain Rakotomamonjy and Vincent Guigue [12] (winners of the BCI Competition III, Dataset II) as mean values of classification accuracy over 2 subjects. 64 EEG channels were used with an ensemble of SVMs. Classification accuracies provided by the author against the number of letter representation are 73.5% and 96% for 5 and 15 representations, respectively. Classification accuracies obtained in our experiments are 76% and 97%, respectively.
Dataset III: Self-regulation of slow cortical potentials is provided by Brett Mensh [2] (winner of the BCI Competition II, Dataset Ia) as a value of classification error for one subject. 6 EEG channels were used with a fit of multivariate normal densities to each of the data class. Classification errors given by the author and in our experiments are 11.3% and 10.9%, respectively. Due to the analysis of slow cortical potentials we did not perform the ICA but utilized only the channel selection procedure applied to samples in the EEG channels.
Dataset IV: Motor imagery signals are given by Christin Schafer and Steven Lemm [2] (winners of the BCI Competition II, Dataset III) as a value of classification accuracy for one subject. 3 EEG channels were used with recursive naive Bayes classifier. Implementation of the algorithm described in [2] did not reach published results: 19.2% and 10.7%, respectively. Even so, applying the proposed preprocessing decreased classification errors to 15.7%.

4. CONCLUSIONS

In this paper, we provided an artifact rejection algorithm for BCI application. The method is based on the modified NC value that is involved into both the ICA and the EEG channel/source selection. The algorithm consists of learning and real-time filtering phases. The learning phase exists for each subject, scenario, and use. It requires an initial EEG acquisition from a gamer and takes just a couple of minutes, which is critical for the game market. Thereafter we preform calibration step to adjust parameters and select informative parts of the registered EEG stream. Recursive source ranking procedure based on the NC has a global minimum in contra to the MI approach that is a monotonically growing function. The proposed EEG artifact rejection was applied to the real datasets from the BCI Competitions fairly. Superior classification results and its applicability for different nature of the brain waves were shown. Proposed EEG preprocessing does not depend on the classifiers, does not require re-ranking with modification of external algorithm, and can be utilized for a wide range of data which demands selective analysis. Regarding to the cognitive games in the terms of the OpenVibe project, the presented method does not require any prior information on game environment, strategy and subjects.

5. REFERENCES

[1] Openvibe, INRIA. `http://openvibe.inria.fr/`.
[2] BCI competition II. `www.bbci.de/competition/ii/`.
[3] W. T. at al. Artifact and recording concepts in EEG. *Clinical Neurophysiology*, 28:252–263.
[4] J.-F. Cardoso and A. Souloumiac. Blind beamforming for non-gaussian signals. *IEE Proceedings-F*, 140(6):362–370, December 1993.
[5] A. Delorme and S. Makeig. EEGLAB: an open source toolbox for analysis of single-trial EEG dynamics including independent component analysis. *Journal of Neuroscience Methods*, 134:9–21, 2004.
[6] U. Hoffmann, J. M. Vesin, T. Ebrahimi, and K. Diserens. An efficient P300-based brain-computer interface for disabled subjects. *Journal of Neuroscience Methods*, 167(1):115–125, 2008.
[7] T. Lan, D. Erdogmus, A. Adami, M. Pavel, and S. Mathan. Salient EEG channel selection in brain computer interfaces by mutual information maximization. *Engineering in Medicine and Biology, 27th Annual Conference*, 2005.
[8] E. G. Learned-Miller. A new class of entropy estimators for multi-dimensional densities. *in Proceedings of the ICASSP*, 3:297–300, April 2003.
[9] E. G. Learned-Miller and J. W. F. III. Ica using spacings estimates of entropy. *J. Mach. Learn.*, 4:1271–1295, December 2003.
[10] S. Makeig and T.-P. Jung. EEGLAB. `http://sccn.ucsd.edu/eeglab/`.
[11] L. Parra and P. Sajda. Blind source separation via generalized eigenvalue decomposition. *J. Mach. Learn.*, 4:1261–1269, October 2004.
[12] A. Rakotomamonjy and V. Guigue. BCI competition III: Dataset II - ensemble of SVMs for BCI P300 speller. *IEEE Trans. Biomed Eng*, July 2007.
[13] S. Sanei and J. Chambers. *EEG signal processing.* John Wiley & Sons, 2007.
[14] T. Zander. *Utilizing Brain-Computer Interfaces for Human-Machine Systems.* PhD thesis, TU Berlin, 2012. `http://opus.kobv.de/tuberlin/volltexte/2012/3490/`.

Construction of the Biocybernetic Loop: A Case Study

Stephen H Fairclough
School of Natural Sciences and Psychology
Liverpool John Moores University
Liverpool, UK
+ 44 151 9046311
s.fairclough@ljmu.ac.uk

Kiel Gilleade
School of Natural Sciences and Psychology
Liverpool John Moores University
Liverpool, UK
+44 151 9046314
k.m.gilleade@ljmu.ac.uk

ABSTRACT
The biocybernetic loop describes the data processing protocol at the heart of all physiological computing systems. The loop also encompasses the goals of the system design with respect to the anticipated impact of the adaptation on user behaviour. There are numerous challenges facing the designer of a biocybernetic loop in terms of measurement, data processing and adaptive design. These challenges are multidisciplinary in nature spanning psychology and computer science. This paper is concerned with the design process of the biocybernetic loop. A number of criteria for an effective loop are described followed by a six-stage design cycle. The challenges faced by the designer at each stage of the design process are exemplified with reference to a case study where EEG data were used to adapt a computer game.

Categories and Subject Descriptors
H5.2 [Information Systems]: User Interfaces; K.8.0 [General]: Games; J.3 [Life and Medical Sciences]

General Terms
Measurement, Performance, Design, Experimentation, Human Factors

Keywords
Psychophysiology, physiological computing, adaptation, games.

1. INTRODUCTION
Physiological computing systems receive data from the body, which is subsequently used to adapt the human-computer interface [1, 2]. This category of technology falls into a number of distinct groupings including:- brain-computer interfaces (BCI) [3] that use intentional changes in physiological activity as a form of input control system, and biocybernetic adaptation [4] where spontaneous changes in psychophysiology trigger adaptation at the human-computer interface. All physiological computing systems are constructed upon a biocybernetic control loop where raw physiological data is analysed in near-real time and transformed into input for software control.

This paper is concerned with the design cycle involved in the development of a working biocybernetic control loop. An early loop was developed at NASA where changes in electrocortical activity (EEG) quantified the level of task engagement exhibited by the operator [4, 5]. When the operator was engaged with a simulated aviation task, automation of joystick control was permitted, therefore reducing the mental workload of an alert person. If the level of task engagement fell, automation was terminated, effectively forcing the operator to control the joystick manually and re-engage with the task. This system was designed to manage the psychological state of the operator within acceptable limits. A similar type of biocybernetic control loop that responds to mental workload has been proposed by [6] and [7].

The biocybernetic loop is the elemental concept at the heart of all physiological computing systems. At a basic level, the loop describes the data processing protocol whereby live physiology is converted into control input for a technological system. However, the design of the loop also incorporates an explicit rationale with specific goals, e.g. to sustain a state of engagement, to prevent frustration, to select a desired command; this agenda defines the *modus operandi* of the system.

The loop is initiated by the collection of data from various psychophysiological sensors. Traditionally these sensors have been physically connected to the user, but recent developments in wearable computing [8] and remote sensing [9] demonstrates the availability of unobtrusive monitoring. Physiological data are streamed from sensors to be filtered or corrected for artifacts prior to detailed analysis. These data can be subjected to a range of analysis techniques from simple averaging to more complex analyses, such as Fast Fourier Transform. The output from analysis is used to trigger an adaptive response from the system, either by creating specific criteria or by categorizing data using pattern classification approaches, e.g. [10]; see [11] for review. The response triggered at the interface may fall into a number of categories; it could enable cursor control (move forward, left, right) or trigger specific commands ('select') in the case of BCI applications. Adaptation may trigger a discrete event, e.g. provision of help information, reduction of music volume, or make a covert adjustment to the interface that may not be noticed by the user, e.g. lighting changes to a virtual environment; see [2] for discussion of overt and covert categories of system adaptation.

The biocybernetic loop is designed to promote specific psychological states in the human operator. These states often represent a positive "approach" goal, which is seen to be desirable, such as the promotion of relaxation or productive engagement with activity. Other loops, such as the original version designed at NASA, are negative control loops designed to avoid undesirable operator states, such as disengagement from the task or an extremely high level of mental workload that would jeopardize performance quality. It is important to recognize that the biocybernetic loop must be imbued with a degree of autonomy in order to influence the psychological state of the user in a prescribed fashion.

ICMI'12, October 22–26, 2012, Santa Monica, California, USA.

This paper is concerned with the biocybernetic loop as the essential element at the heart of all physiological computing systems. We wish to consider the challenge of constructing a biocybernetic loop that is both scientifically valid and effective from the perspective of user experience. In order to elaborate on this challenge, we present a case study from our own work.

2. CONSTRUCTION OF A WORKING BIOCYBERNETIC LOOP

The construction of a biocybernetic control loop must be transparent at every stage of development. The rationale and data processing protocol must be open to inspection in order to aid troubleshooting and build a knowledge base for future development. This transparency extends to the rationale and scientific validation of the loop. The goals of the loop, in terms of the intended effects of interaction on the human, should be clearly defined. Furthermore the fundamental process of psychophysiological measurement/inference must have a documented scientific basis.

The biocybernetic loop is a multidisciplinary construction that must satisfy several criteria if it is to work in a satisfactory fashion. If the loop fails to achieve its intended effects on user experience, there are many possible causes from inappropriate selection of measures or insensitive categorisation of data to poor HCI design at the interface. This is why transparency in the design cycle is so important. In the broader context, increased clarity of design will consolidate shared knowledge and understanding as biocybernetic loops are constructed across a wide range of subject domains.

The real challenge of designing a biocybernetic loop is to satisfy a range of criteria that span psychology, signal processing and computer science. In order to examine this issue in greater detail, we have proposed four criteria that must be satisfied in order to ensure that the loop is capable of impacting on user experience in a sensitive and reliable fashion.

1. Psychophysiological inference should be valid

   The complex nature of the psychophysiological inference (i.e. how psychological meaning is inferred from physiological data) has been described in detail [12]. This issue is highly relevant to the biocybernetic loop where physiological measures should correspond to specific psychological concepts across individuals and different environments. The reliability of psychophysiological measures over repeated sessions is a topic that has been relatively under-explored, however, see [13] and [14] for exceptions. It has been argued that biocybernetic loops must be based on valid psychophysiological inference [2], which may be described with reference to previous research. If the measure does not capture the psychological construct with sufficient sensitivity and reliability, the loop will not influence the user state in a predictable fashion.

2. The psychophysiological measures can deliver a sufficient representation of the user state.

   A valid psychophysiological inference delivers a degree of association between measure and construct. These measures must be subsequently translated into a representation of the user state within the loop. For example, we may have evidence that reduced alpha activity in the frontal cortex is related to high mental workload, but this association must be translated into a categorical representation of the user state (e.g. high/low workload) in order for the system to work. This second criteria contains an implication that the representation of user state is sufficiently detailed – but how can we assess the representation in this respect? We argue that the sufficiency of the user representation relates directly to the adaptive repertoire or functional vocabulary of the system, i.e. the number of responses supported by the system.

3. The classification of user representation is accurate

   The representation of the user must be categorised in real-time or near-real time if the loop is to operate dynamically. This criterion is defined by the data processing protocol that converts dynamic and variable streams of physiological data into a representation of the user. The first point to consider is the error rate of the data processing protocol, i.e. how many instances of target states, such as high workload or frustration, are missed? How many instances of non-target states are misclassified? The second point of consideration is related to the time window associated with the data sampling/processing protocol and its relationship to system response at the interface. With respect to latter, the output from a biocybernetic loop may take the form of an adaptation or a form of input control. These outputs are associated with a time window; for input control, this time window may be very short whilst response times may vary considerably in the case of adaptation. Obviously the time window for data analysis and categorisation sets the minimum response time at the interface.

4. The response at the interface has the desired effect on the user

   The output from the biocybernetic loop will largely determine the user experience and the influence of the loop. If interaction at the interface is poorly designed, then the loop will be ineffective, even if the previous three criteria have been satisfied. From the perspective of design, it is important that the adaptive response at the interface has the desired effect on user state and no unintended effects. Therefore, if the loop is designed to enable cursor control, it should do exactly that; if it is designed to minimize frustration, a reduction of negative emotion should be a tangible benefit. The user will expect the system to respond to changes in psychological state in a timely and intuitive manner, i.e. system response should be sensitive and the intention underlying the response should be logical from the users' perspective.

The remainder of this paper will describe six stages in the construction of a working biocybernetic loop that was created in our own laboratory. This loop was designed to detect spontaneous changes in psychophysiology in order to adapt software in near-real time.

3. CASE STUDY

The case study for the construction of a biocybernetic loop is a physiological computing game [15-18]. This category of game is capable of responding to changes in the state of player and tailoring the gaming experience to the individual. The obvious purpose of the loop in this context is to create positive gaming experience, i.e. to minimize sustained periods of frustration and/or boredom and to promote engagement/effort.

In our case study, the loop was designed to manipulate the difficulty of the game in order to drive the experience of the player. We selected the Tetris game for the case study, our reasoning being that there was a relatively simple relationship between speed (of falling blocks) and game difficulty.

The development of the loop is described in six stages, from the conceptual origins to evaluation of a working system. Each stage presents specific challenges and an example is provided in our case study to present how we resolved those issues.

3.1 Stage 1: Conceptual Model

The design of a biocybernetic loop generally rests on two kinds of conceptual model. The first is a psychological model of user behaviour, these models may describe the experience/expression of emotions or the relationship between frustration or fatigue with performance quality. These psychological models will often be derived from existing literature. The second model concerns the rationale behind the loop itself and how the designer anticipates the adaptive logic of the loop will influence the behaviour of the user. This first model is generic whilst the second represents a series of predictions for a specific usage scenario. With respect to the use of psychological models, it is recommended to adopt those models, which are (a) empirical, i.e. constructed on existing measures, and (b) predictive, i.e. associated with specific behavioural outcomes.

One challenge for the designer is how to reconcile the precise design of the biocybernetic loop as defined by the second model with general concepts from psychology. It is easy to describe those behavioural states that should be promoted or prevented by the loop in general terms. The rationale for the biocybernetic loop always seeks to enhance the experience of interaction through the promotion of positive, productive states and mitigation of negative states from boredom to frustration. Such labels serve adequately as a statement of general design goals, however, the biocybernetic loop requires a series of precise and objective formulations in order to achieve those goals.

The first step at this conceptual stage is to define specific categories of user behaviour to be detected; this process sets the context for the adaptive logic of the system. The designer may develop a scheme of desirable vs. undesirable user states; it is equally important to specify the adaptive repertoire of the system within the context of this scheme, i.e. how many states are to be detected and how many different responses must be supported by the loop. If possible, it is sensible to assess the response rate of adaptation to understand how quickly the system must react.

Example: Our basic model was to construct a version of Tetris that engaged the player by controlling the drop speed of pieces to sustain a positive gaming experience. The adaptive mechanic of the loop was straightforward but the definitions of desirable or undesirable states were vague and difficult to assess.

If a biocybernetic system is designed to promote an optimal gaming experience, how should we characterize that state in psychological terms? To be fully engaged with a task to the point that time seems to slip away is known as the *flow state* [19], which is sometimes referred to as being in the zone [20] or total immersion [21]. This state is a desirable experience as the level of challenge is matched with player skill, therefore attention is focused entirely on the game to the exclusion of other forms of mental activity. This type of experience not only provides an optimum level of challenge [22], it also avoids undesirable mental states (e.g. boredom) and promotes a positive emotional experience [23]. These kinds of psychological states represent a transaction between the skills of the player and the objective level of task demand. Representing these states using objective measures (game demand) is problematic because players' response to different Tetris speeds is an interaction between the level of skill and objective task characteristics.

From a psychological perspective, what are the characteristics of an optimal gaming experience? It is reasonable to assume that high levels of game demand would prompt increased mental effort into the game. A high level of effort is also necessary to stimulate skill development and there is evidence that the opportunity to acquire and demonstrate competence/mastery contributes to a positive gaming experience [24]. The relationship between effort investment and the task difficulty is described by motivational intensity model (MIM) [25]. MIM emphasizes a compensatory dynamic where effort is increased in response to rising demand; however, this relationship is nonmonotonic and includes a 'tipping point' where the investment of effort and inclination to continue may abruptly decline due to overload and an appraisal of unachievable demand. Both mental workload (the level of demand experienced by the player) and effort (motivation) are important drivers for optimal gaming experience. Therefore, we adapted the MIM to create four distinct player states: boredom (low effort due to low demand), engagement (increasing effort in line with increasing demand), zone (peak effort at highest level of demand attainable) and overload (low effort due to excessive demand). This scheme is illustrated in Figure 1.

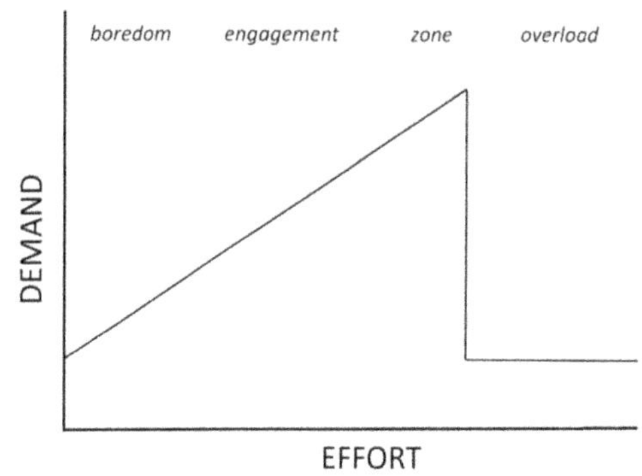

Figure 1. Motivational Intensity Model adapted from [25].

With this scheme in mind, the biocybernetic loop was designed to promote effortful engagement with the Tetris game via states of engagement/zone and to avoid the two states of boredom and overload. The adaptive logic of the loop would be to increase the speed of falling blocks when boredom was detected and to continue to increase speed until effort peaked at the zone. If a zone state was detected, the system was to make no further adjustment. If a combination of high demand and low effort was detected, the loop should reduce the speed of the falling block to take the player out of the overload state. This four-category model corresponds to the model of user representation that would be adopted by our biocybernetic loop.

3.2 Stage 2: Psycho-Physiological Inference

The conceptual model of user behaviour or representation provides an implicit direction for operationalisation. At this stage in the process, the designer must elect to choose a number of psychophysiological measures to represent the user state. The designer should carefully peruse the research literature because it is common for psychological concepts to be associated with more than one physiological measure. By definition, a good psychophysiological measure is sensitive and responds to changes in psychological states in an accurate and reliable fashion. It is also important for the psychophysiological measure to respond specifically to a target psychological state and not be subject to influences from other psychological states.

One important consideration when selecting a psychophysiological measure for the biocybernetic loop is the context used to assess the sensitivity of the measure. A measure may have a proven record of sensitivity in the laboratory but there is often a question about whether the same sensitivity will be apparent in the field. There is also the issue of the task context for sensitivity. Many studies in the psychophysiological literature used standardized stimuli and task protocols that may be very different from the task context for the biocybernetic loop. The designer must also consider several practical issues such as the degree of intrusiveness introduced by the sensor, i.e. a hand-worn sensor would be of little use for a task that required use of both hands.

The designer should at the very least examine the existing research literature from a critical perspective and make an intelligent estimate of whether this research will generalise to the usage scenario of the system. The best way to assess this issue is to run some systematic tests of the psychophysiological measures with the actual task scenario. This kind of testing serves to ensure that sensitivity of the measures is appropriate for the loop, provided that tests are conducted with a reasonable number of participants.

Example: The measurement of effort in the MIM is associated with beta-adrenergic activity in the cardiovascular system, using measures of systolic blood pressure reactivity and the pre-ejection period [26, 27]. These cardiovascular measures are sensitive to movement and were not practical for our purposes. We had already performed an EEG study in our laboratory where increased cognitive demand resulted in enhanced activity in theta band (4-7Hz) power over mid-frontal scalp [28-30]. In addition, the manipulation of cognitive demand leads to a suppression of absolute power in both lower (~7.5-10Hz) and upper (~10.5-13Hz) alpha bands [28]. However, this EEG data was derived from a standard experimental psychology protocol (a working memory task).

We performed a study where 20 participants played Tetris under three conditions: easy/boredom (drop speed of blocks was very low), hard/engagement/flow (drop speed of blocks was fast) and impossible/overload (drop speed of blocks was so fast that playing the game was impossible). The analysis of frontal theta activity at 6Hz revealed an significant effect for task demand [$F(2,18) = 21.89$, $p<.01$]. The observed trend illustrated that frontal theta increased from easy to hard demand and declined when task demand was extremely difficult (see Figure 2). The analysis of upper alpha activity at 11.5Hz revealed a linear trend with increased task demand [$F(1,19)=13.69$, $p<.01$], i.e. greater suppression of alpha activity as game demand increased. This linear effect was localized to the parietal region, e.g. P4.

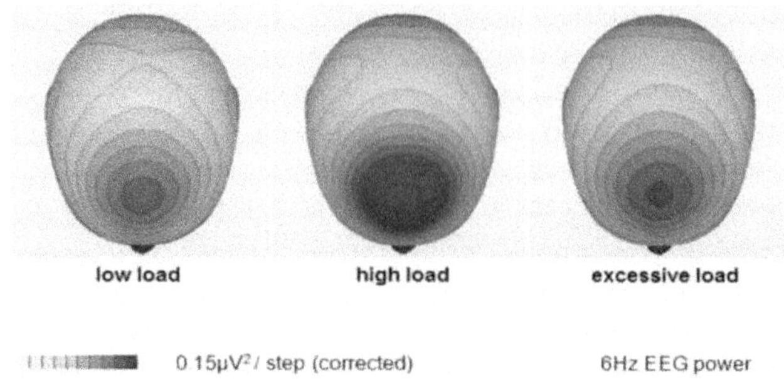

Figure 2. Frontal theta at low, high and excessive demand on Tetris (N=20).

At the end of the experiment, we had two candidate measures; frontal theta to represent effort invested in the game and parietal alpha to capture the level of mental workload/demand experienced by the player. Furthermore, both measures had been validated in the specific usage context of the biocybernetic loop.

3.3 Stage 3: A Quantified Model of User State

Once measures have been validated, the next stage of the process is to recreate the conceptual model of the user state illustrated in Figure 1 in a quantifiable form. The challenge at this stage is to operationalise the conceptual model of the user in an accurate and detailed form. Due to restrictions surrounding the act of measurement (e.g. availability of appropriate sensors, strength of the psycho-physiological inference), there may be a loss of fidelity during the transition from concept to measurement.

This quantifiable model is the way in which the user state or behaviour is represented within the biocybernetic loop. The minimum requirement of the quantified model is that the user is represented with sufficient fidelity to enable the process of adaptation within the loop. In other words, the target states that drive the adaptive logic of the loop should be clearly defined.

Example: The conceptual model of the user was provided by MIM at stage one. We adapted this model by measuring effort/motivation using frontal theta at Fz (Figure 2) whereas the demand dimension was represented by alpha suppression at parietal sites. We made this assumption based upon our experiment as frontal theta demonstrated the shark-fin curve associated with MIM (Figure 1) whilst parietal alpha had a linear relationship with game demand. The combination of both measures, combined with MIM, created the two-dimensional model of user state illustrated in Figure 3 (note: suppressed alpha power = increased demand). The desirable target states of 'zone' and 'engagement' are associated with high effort; undesirable states are defined by high demand in combination with low effort (overload) or low demand/low effort (boredom).

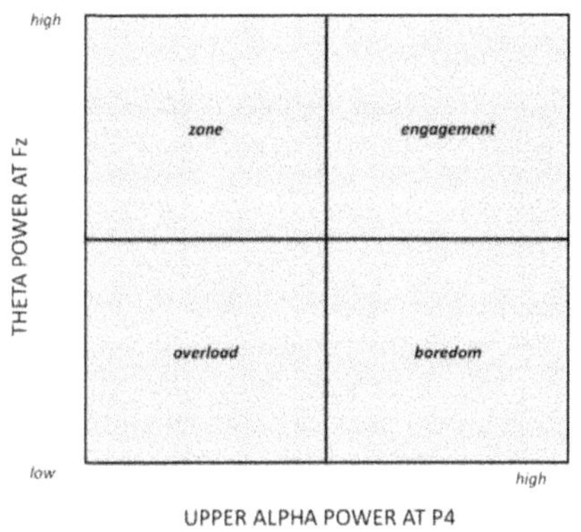

Figure 3. Two dimensional representation of the user state using EEG measures.

3.4 Stage 4: A Real-Time Model of User State

The quantified model of the user state is a generic formulation that defines the 'data space' of the monitoring activity of the loop. In order for the model to trigger adaptation in real-time, this generic model must be populated with classes and criteria that define the four regions of the user representation (Figure 3).

There are many techniques available for the classification of psychophysiological data within the biocybernetic loop, see [11] for review. Many of these machine learning algorithms require training data, i.e. exemplars of psychophysiological data that describe target states. The designer may rely on stage two in order to generate this kind of example data, but often triggers or criteria require a degree of calibration to the individual user. The system may require each user to undergo a calibration process prior to usage. Classification algorithms often require bespoke categories of data to enable training, but there are several approaches to the generation of these training sets. If the biocybernetic loop is designed to detect naturalistic states, such as sleepiness, then it is relatively straightforward to generate example data. e.g. sleep deprivation. Similarly, the generation of data to describe extreme states of high mental workload may be achieved by simply exposing individuals to high cognitive demand. There are a number of emotion induction protocols available that may be used to generate example data for different emotional states. These protocols can involve active manipulation (e.g. asking participants to recall emotional events from the past or placing people in a situation designed to induce a specific emotional state) or passive approaches (e.g. exposure to pictures/movies and/or music designed to induce a particular emotion). Alternatively, psychophysiology may be continuously recorded and participants are required to provide a subjective self-assessment in order to categorise emotional states.

The major obstacle for the generation of example data for the biocybernetic loop is concerned with the context of data collection. Therefore, the real-time model of user state should be calibrated using example data that is fully representative of the context of system usage. The problem with formal protocols is that data obtained may not generalize when the system is being used in a different context. On the other hand, a reliance on subjective self-assessment is complicated by other reasons, e.g. limitations of introspective techniques, retrospective bias, individual differences. However, given that the biocybernetic loop must respond in accordance with subjective perceptions, it is clear that calibration in line with self-reported experiences is an important approach.

Once example data has been translated into a categorization algorithm, the designer must consider the real-time limitations of the model. The response window of the adaptive system has been specified during stage one and the capability of the real-time model to classify data within that response window should be considered.

Example: We developed a number of calibration protocols to deliver trigger values that were tailored to each individual user. Our experimental work had created a version of Tetris where drop speed could be manipulated. We initially created a version with ten different drop speeds from slow to impossibly fast. Prior to system use, we exposed participants to each of ten levels and asked them to indicate a preference for each, i.e. which speed do you enjoy playing the most. This was a standard procedure wherein each person played at each drop speed for two minutes and was asked to deliver a subjective preference. It was relatively straightforward to characterise extreme states of boredom and overload using this manipulation. However this method had two problems: the trigger level depended on the specific characteristics of the connection and two minutes of playing at a constant level was unrepresentative of the game. Baseline levels of frontal theta and parietal alpha were taken to derive a second method of trigger definition. Baseline levels of EEG were collected whilst the participants viewed a relaxing piece of video footage. This second method was based on criteria for triggering adaptation, which were generated relative to baseline levels of EEG activity. For example, if frontal theta activity increased or decreased by a 100% (twice baseline) in any 5 sec window, whilst parietal alpha increased or decreased by 100% then the system adaptation may have been triggered. In our case, if frontal theta increased by 100% whilst parietal alpha fell by 100%, this defined the player as being in the zone (see Figure 3).

We also had to define our criteria within the context of a time window. This represented another design decision. If the time window for the trigger was too short, it was easily influenced by sudden fluctuations in EEG power that were unrepresentative. However, opting for a long time window (>5sec) ran the risk of reducing the sensitivity of the adaptive loop.

3.5 Stage 5: Design of the Adaptive Interface

The biocybernetic loop 'communicates' the results of monitoring/classification to the user via the interface. This may be an overt response that is obvious to the user or the system may adapt in a covert way that may or may not be noticed [2]. The critical concern for the designer at this stage is to ensure that adaptation is perceived as accurate, timely, intuitive and does not have any unintended consequences. User perceptions of interface adaptations are hugely influenced by the visibility of the adaptation. Overt adaptations tend to get noticed and accuracy is assessed in terms of self-appraisal (to what extent does the assessment of my internal state match my actual experience?), timeliness (is this adaptation what I need right now?) and intuition (does this adaptation make sense?). Overt adaptations can have an immediate impact on the state of the user and offer an effective response. However, they do run a risk of drawing attention to system error, which may reduce the trust of the user in the system. Covert adaptations are much less risky in this respect, being inherently ambiguous and involving subtle changes at the interface. The drawback of covert adaptation is that it tends to have a cumulative impact and is less effective than an overt strategy over a short period of time.

The designer may opt to use both overt and covert strategies within the same system. The logical strategy is to use covert adaptation to subtly reach target states and opt for overt forms to manage extreme states.

Example: The adaptive strategy of our Tetris game was relatively simple. The speed of the falling blocks could be increased or slowed. The relationship between the detection of user states and the type of adaptation was also straightforward; speed would be increased during boredom, decreased during overload and sustained during zone and engagement (Figure 3).

Designing the adaptation was principally an issue of magnitude (how much should speed of falling blocks change at each increment) and feedback (should the user be provided with objective feedback of difficulty/drop speed). After a series of pilot tests, we opted for very small adjustments in drop speed and no feedback to the player. This strategy corresponds to the covert designs that were described earlier. The experience of playing the game was that adjustments to drop speed were very subtle and the effect was cumulative and only apparent after playing for several minutes. This strategy was adopted in order to focus players' attentions on the game rather than the activity of the biocybernetic loop.

3.6 Stage 6: Evaluation

The benefits of biocybernetic adaptation for the user may be direct and tangible or nebulous. Like all categories of emerging technology, it is important for the biocybernetic loop to demonstrate some kind of benefit for the user experience, e.g. better performance, greater engagement, reduced frustration.

The final stage of the design process represents the challenge of evaluating and demonstrating the benefits of the biocybernetic loop. There are at least two levels of evaluation for a physiological computing system. The first is designed to answer the issue of relative benefit; in other words, if a biocybernetic system is better, then we can only make this assessment in relative terms, i.e. better compared to what? In the case of adaptive systems, the logical 'control' case is a manual version of the same system, but this kind of comparison tends to be asymmetrical because: (1) manual control systems offer gross control compared to automatic systems, and (2) there is a large novelty effect associated with nascent technology. The issue of novelty may be resolved by longitudinal testing but the nature of the comparison is an intractable issue. The second level of evaluation is to compare different versions of the biocybernetic control loop, i.e. different criteria or control dynamics, random adaptation [31]. This second type of evaluation offers a controlled comparison in a way that the first type does not, but it is only useful for differentiating the impact of different kinds of biocybernetic loop on user perceptions and behaviour.

Once the comparative frame has been established, the designer must decide how to measure outcomes from the evaluation. With respect to comparing the performance of the adaptive system with a 'control' case, there are several options available, such as: performance quality (productivity, efficiency, error rate), psychophysiology (use of measures to index psychological concepts, provided they are subject to direct influence of the loop) and measures related to the properties of the interaction (questionnaires, interviews). The primary choice of outcome measure will be determined by the conceptual basis of the loop as defined at stage one. If the biocybernetic loop is designed to reduce mental workload or reduce errors, these implicit goals set the context for system evaluation. For example, evaluation work conducted on the original biocybernetic loop [31-33] considered a range of outcome measures, including performance quality, subjective mental workload and EEG responses; see [34] for a summary.

When the scope of evaluation includes different kinds of working biocybernetic loops, the designer may also wish to compare the adaptive response of the loop, e.g. frequency of adaptive responses, relative count of different types of adaptive response.

Example: We decided to evaluate the basic prototype with respect to two main questions: (1) does biocybernetic adaptation promote improved player experience compared to manual adjustment of game demand, and (2) how does the reactivity of the biocybernetic loop (i.e. frequent vs. infrequent adjustments) impact on system performance and player experience. The first hypothesis is designed to contrast a covert, automated process of adjustment with a condition where adjustments are overt and at the discretion of the player. The second hypothesis is concerned with the design of trigger events (that activate adjustments) and how psychophysiological criteria impact on the system adaptation and the player experience.

For the current study, we contrasted three types of working biocybernetic loop: (a) a conservative system that only made an adjustment when changes in EEG substantially deviated from baseline (greater than 200%), (b) a liberal system that adjusted game demand in response to a small deviation from baseline levels of EEG (100%), and (c) a "normal" system that responded to moderate changes in EEG (150%) relative to both (a) and (b). It was anticipated that the conservative system would be the least reactive version of the loop, i.e. pushing up demand very gradually and responded to overload very slowly. The liberal system should make frequent adjustments and be faster to respond to the overload scenario. The 'normal' version was included for purposes of comparison with the liberal and conservative systems. For the manual control system, we adopted a 'Wizard of Oz' approach where participants were required to speak aloud an instruction to increase ("higher") or decrease ("lower") the speed of the falling blocks. These adjustments were made in real-time by an experimenter sitting behind a screen in the laboratory.

10 participants (6 females) volunteered for the evaluation session. This was a repeated measures design where each participant encountered four versions of the system (conservative/liberal/normal/manual). Each individual game of Tetris was played for 5 minutes. The order of presentation of each system was counterbalanced and participants had a 5-minute rest break between each game. Participants always started each game on the slowest speed setting. If the blocks reached the top of the board and "game death" occurred, the game always restarted with an empty board on the slowest speed setting.

In order to evaluate player experience, two sets of measures were collected. A mood adjective checklist (UMACL) [35] was administered before and after each game session. This questionnaire assessed three components of mood: energetical arousal (EA: tired-alert), tense arousal (TA: relaxed-tense) and hedonic tone (HT: happy-sad). Participants also completed an immersion questionnaire [21] designed to capture the quality of gaming experience.

The results of the experiment are divided into two areas, behaviour of the system and the influence of system behaviour on the user experience. We captured three aspects of system behaviour: (1) mean frequency of adjustments to task difficulty (increases and decreases of task difficulty), (2) mean frequency of "game deaths" or "resets" (i.e. when blocks reached the top of the board and the game had to be reset), and (3) average difficulty of each game (i.e. game difficulty could vary between 1-10 in accordance with speed of falling blocks). These data were calculated for all three versions of the biocybernetic system and the manual system. Mean values are provided in Table 1 below.

System	Increase Demand	Decrease Demand	Mean Reset	Mean Difficulty
Conservative	63.6	43.2	1.3	3.8
Normal	41.7	56.6	0.6	2.4
Liberal	28.6	62.4	0.4	1.9
Manual	9.4	1.7	0.5	3.3

Table 1. Mean values for measures of system adaptation across all four systems (N=10).

The measures were subjected to a MANOVA analysis (System Type x System Measure) to assess statistical significance. A significant interaction was found between both factors that was subjected to post-hoc t-tests. The number of adjustments to increase task demand was significantly higher for the conservative system compared to the liberal system ($p<.01$); unsurprisingly, all three biocybernetic systems exhibited a higher rate of upward adjustment compared to the manual system ($p<.01$). The latter trend was also apparent in the analysis of downward adjustment ($p<.05$). The analysis of mean difficulty level revealed that difficulty was significantly lower for the liberal system compared to all other systems ($p<.05$).

The impact of system adaptation on the user experience was assessed using two types of subjective questionnaire. The mood questionnaire (UMACL) was administered before and after each game session; this allowed us to calculate a change score (post-game minus pre-game) to assess mood changes in three component of mood: EA (alert-tired), TA (tense-relax) and HT (happy-sad). All three components were subjected to a 2 x 3 MANOVA. Mean values are presented in Table 2.

System	EA	TA	HT	IMM
Conservative	4.3	3.1	0.0	64.7
Normal	2.0	2.4	-1.9	65.5
Liberal	0.2	1.1	-2.0	66.1
Manual	1.1	0.7	-1.6	73.9

Table 2. Mean values for subjective data: EA = energetic arousal, TA = tense arousal, HT = hedonic tone, IMM = immersion (N=10).

Post-hoc t-tests revealed a significant effect for EA only ($p<.05$) – participants found the experience of playing the conservative version of the biocybernetic game to be more alerting compared to the liberal version. The analysis of responses to the immersion questionnaire was insignificant, but a trend was observed that participants found the manual version of the game to be the most immersive.

The goal of the evaluation was to assess how reactivity of the biocybernetic system influenced system performance and user experience. The conservative EEG criteria tended to "push" the player, making the least number of downward adjustments of difficulty and prompting a relatively high frequency of "game death" (Table 1). By contrast, the liberal system required only a small deviation from baseline levels of EEG activity in order to initiate an intervention and made a high number of downward adjustments of difficulty compared to the conservative system. As a result, the liberal system has the lowest level of mean task difficulty out of all four systems. The "normal" system represented a middle path between both extremes of EEG criteria. As expected, the manual system had a much lower frequency of adjustments as participants tended to increase difficulty to a desirable level and make no subsequent adjustments. In terms of average difficulty (Table 1), it was noted that the preferred level of demand was rather low (i.e. maximum difficulty = 10) and fell slightly short of the average demand imposed by the conservative system.

Despite differences in system behaviour, we found little evidence for any substantial effects on the user experience. The "push" provided by the conservative system resulted in enhanced alertness but there were no other significant effects on mood. We were surprised that experience of the game led to an increase of negative affect as this was completely unanticipated. We did speculate that the automated adjustment provided by the biocybernetic loop may have enhanced immersion in the game, compared to the manual version where the person had to 'break' from the experience to indicate an adjustment, but no evidence was found for this effect; in fact, immersion was maximized in the manual condition, presumably because this condition provided an optimal level of challenge.

In hindsight, we felt that the range of EEG criteria adopted to create three versions of the biocybernetic loop was too narrow to create significantly different kinds of user experience. Also, we adopted a 2sec time window for data processing and adaptive responses for all biocybernetic loops. The combination of a 2sec response and small, incremental adjustments to drop speed meant that the system was often unable to prevent "game death" when the game board was filled above two thirds of its height (and drop speed was high). We also felt that players needed longer exposure to the system, preferably in the form of repeated sessions, in order to differentiate the different types of adaptive control

4. SUMMARY

The paper has described the design process of the biocybernetic loop with a case study example. Each stage in the design process contains specific categories of challenge that span psychology, signal processing and human-computer interaction. The most significant challenge for the designer is addressing the multidisciplinary nature of the biocybernetic loop in sufficient detail.

5. ACKNOWLEDGMENTS

This research was performed as part of the REFLECT project (http://reflect.pst.ifi.lmu.de/) and funded by the EU under the Future and Emerging Technologies (FET) Initiative.

6. REFERENCES

[1] Allanson, J. and Fairclough, S. H. 2004. A research agenda for physiological computing. *Interacting With Computers*, 16, 857-878.

[2] Fairclough, S. H. 2009. Fundamentals of Physiological Computing. Interacting With Computers, 21, 133-145.

[3] Allison, B. Z., Wolpaw, E. W. and Wolpaw, J. R. 2007. Brain-computer interface systems: progress and prospects. Expert Review of Medical Devices, 4, 463-474.

[4] Pope, A. T., Bogart, E. H. and Bartolome, D. S. 1995. Biocybernetic system evaluates indices of operator

engagement in automated task. Biological Psychology, 40, 187-195.

[5] Prinzel, L. J., Freeman, F. G., Scerbo, M. W., Mikulka, P. J. and Pope, A. T. 2000. A closed-loop system for examining psychophysiological measures for adaptive task allocation. The International Journal of Aviation Psychology, 10, 4, 393-410.

[6] Wilson, G. F. and Russell, C. A. 2007. Performance enhancement in an uninhabited air vehicle task using psychophysiologically determined adaptive aiding. Human Factors, 49, 6, 1005-1018.

[7] Solovey, E. T., Chauncey, K., et al. 2011. Sensing cognitive multitasking for a brain-based adaptive user interface. In Proceedings of the ACM Conference on Human Factors in Computing Systems CHI'11 (Vancouver, 2011). ACM Press.

[8] Van Laerhoven, K. 2011. ISWC 2010: The latest in wearable computing research. IEEE Pervasive Computing, 10, 1 2011), 8-10.

[9] Poh, M.-Z., McDuff, D. and Picard, R. 2011. A medical mirror for non-contact health monitoring. In Proceedings of the ACM SIGGRAPH Emerging Technologies (Vancouver, 2011). ACM Press.

[10] Baldwin, C. L. and Penaranda, B. N. 2012. Adaptive training using an artificial neural network and EEG metrics for within- and cross-task workload classification. NeuroImage, 59, 1, 48-56.

[11] Novak, D., Mihelj, M. and Munih, M. 2012. A survey of methods for data fusion and system adaptation using autonomic nervous system responses in physiological computing. Interacting With Computers, 24, 153-172.

[12] Cacioppo, J. T. and Tassinary, L. G. 1990. Inferring psychological significance from physiological signals. American Psychologist, 45, 16-28.

[13] Christensen, J. C., Estepp, J. R., Wilson, G. F. and Russell, C. A. 2012. The effects of day-to-day variability of physiological data on operator functional state classification. NeuroImage, 59, 57-63.

[14] Picard, R. W., Vyzas, E. and Healey, J. 2001. Towards machine emotional intelligence: analysis of affective physiological state. IEEE Transactions on Pattern Analysis and Machine Intelligence, 23, 1175-1191.

[15] Fairclough, S. H. 2007. Psychophysiological inference and physiological computer games. Workshop on BCI and Gaming at Advances in Computer Entertainment, Salzburg.

[16] Fairclough, S. H. 2008. BCI and Physiological Computing: Similarities, Differences and Intuitive Control. In Proceedings of the Workshop on BCI and Computer Games: CHI'08 (Florence, 2008).

[17] Gilleade, K. M., Dix, A. and Allanson, J. 2005. Affective videogames and modes of affective gaming: assist me, challenge me, emote me. Paper presented at DIGRA, 2005.

[18] Rani, P., Sarkar, N. and Liu, C. 2006. *Maintaining optimal challenge in computer games through real-time physiological feedback*. In Schmorrow, D. D. (Eds.) Task Specific Information Processing in Operational and Virtual Environments, Foundations of Augmented Cognition, Erlbaum, pp. 184-192.

[19] Csikszentmihalyi, M. 1990. *Flow: The Psychology of Optimal Experience*. Harper Perennial, New York.

[20] Chen, J. 2007. Flow in games (and everything else). Communications *of the ACM*, 50(4), 31-34.

[21] Jennett, C., Cox, A. L., et al. 2008. Measuring and defining the experience of immersion in games. International Journal of Human-Computer Studies, 66, 641-661.

[22] Gilleade, K. M. and Dix, A. Using frustration in the design of adaptive videogame. Paper presented at ACE, 2004. ACM Press, New York, 2004.

[23] Nacke, L. and Lindley, C. A. 2008. Flow and immersion in first-person shooters: measuring the player's gameplay experience. In Proceedings of the Conference on Future Play: Research, Play, Share (Toronto, 2008). ACM, New York.

[24] Ryan, R. M., Rigby, C. S. and Przybylski, A. 2006. The motivational pull of video games: a self-determination approach. *Motivation and Emotion*, 30, 347-363.

[25] Wright, R. A. 2008. Refining the prediction of effort: Brehm's distinction between potential motivation and motivation intensity. Social and Personality Psychology Compass, 2, 682-701.

[26] Richter, M., Friedrich, A. and Gendolla, G. H. 2008. Task difficulty effects on cardiac activity. Psychophysiology, 45, 869-875.

[27] Richter, M. and Gendolla, G. H. E. 2009. The heart contracts to reward: monetary incentives and preejection period. Psychophysiology, 46, 451-457.

[28] Klimesch, W. 1999. EEG alpha and theta oscillations reflect cognitive and memory performance: a review and analysis. Brain Research Reviews, 29, 169-195.

[29] Gevins, A. and Smith, M. E. 2003. Neurophysiological measures of cognitive workload during human-computer interaction. Theoretical Issues in Ergonomic Science, 4, 113-121.

[30] Gevins, A., Smith, M. E., et al. 1998. Monitoring working memory load during computer-based tasks with EEG pattern recognition models. Human Factors, 40, 79-91.

[31] Freeman, F. G., Mikulka, P. J., et al. 2000. Evaluation of a psychophysiologically controlled adaptive automation system, using performance on a tracking system. Applied Psychophysiology and Biofeedback, 25, 103-115.

[32] Bailey, N. R., Scerbo, M. W., et al. 2006. Comparison of a brain-based adaptive system and a manual adaptable system for invoking automation. Human Factors, 48, 693-709.

[33] Prinzel, L. J., Parasuraman, R., et al. 2003. Three experiments examining the use of electroencephalogram, event-related potentials, and heart-rate variability for real-time human-centred adaptive automation design. NASA/TP-2003-212442, NASA, 2003.

[34] Scerbo, M. W., Freeman, F. G. and Mikulka, P. J. 2003. A brain-based system for adaptive automation. Theoretical Issues in Ergonomic Science, 4, 1-2, 200-219.

[35] Matthews, G., Jones, D. M. and Chamberlain, A. G. 1990. Refining the measurement of mood: The UWIST Mood Adjective Checklist. *British Journal of Psychology*, 81, 17-42.

An Interactive Control Strategy is More Robust to Non-Optimal Classification Boundaries

Virginia R. de Sa
Department of Cognitive Science
University of California, San Diego
La Jolla, CA 92122-0515
desa@ucsd.edu

ABSTRACT

We consider a new paradigm for EEG-based brain computer interface (BCI) cursor control involving signaling *satisfaction* or *dissatisfaction* with the current motion direction instead of the usual direct control of signaling *rightward* or *leftward* desired motion. We start by assuming that the same underlying EEG signals are used to either signal directly the intent for *right* and *left* motion or to signal *satisfaction* and *dissatisfaction* with the current motion. We model the paradigm as an absorbing Markov chain and show that while both the standard system and the new *interactive* system have equal information transfer rate (ITR) when the Bayes optimal classification boundary (between the underlying EEG feature distributions used for the two classes) is exactly known and non-changing, the *interactive* system is much more robust to using a suboptimal classification boundary. Due to non-stationarity of EEG recordings, in real systems the classification boundary will often be suboptimal for the current EEG signals. We note that a variable step size gives a higher ITR for both systems (but the same robustness improvement of the interactive system remains). Finally, we present a way to probabilistically combine classifiers of natural signals of *satisfaction* and *dissatisfaction* with classifiers using standard *left/right* controls.

Categories and Subject Descriptors

G.3 [**Probability and Statistics**]: Markov processes; F.1.2 [**Computation by Abstract Devices**]: Modes of Computation —*Interactive and reactive computation*

Keywords

brain-computer interface, BCI, Markov chain, non-stationarity, interactive, EEG, information transfer rate, ITR

1. INTRODUCTION

Brain-computer interface (BCI) systems typically require user training to generate reproducible and distinct brain waves. One popular class of EEG-driven BCI systems is based on imagined movement. In these systems the user interacts with a computer through performing motor imagery such as imagination of hand versus foot movement. The signal is then band-passed to the mu (8-13Hz) and beta (12-30Hz) frequency ranges which are known to show decreased power prior to and during real and imagined movement. Spatial filtering is also used to increase the discriminability between the two classes [2]. The ability of users to control such a BCI is very variable and all the factors involved are not fully understood.

One of the most critical issues in practical BCI use is non-stationarity of the EEG signals [19]. A paper by Shenoy et. al. [19] shows drifts of the optimal classification boundary during online feedback runs on the order of one standard deviation of the individual class densities (see Figure 6 in [19]). Changes between offline training and online use can be much larger due to changes in the user state evoked by the feedback. Online changes are thought to be due to state changes in the user, sweating, movement, and other factors. Drift in EEG can lead to loss of control of the BCI which leads to frustration and a vicious cycle of further drift of EEG signals from their training baselines [10].

Classification boundaries may be sub-optimal due to non-stationarity changing the optimal boundary over time but they may also be non-optimal due to having a small amount of training data with which to train the classifier (and estimate the optimal classification boundary). Thus even if the EEG was stationary, due to finite training set sizes, it is unlikely that the optimal classification boundary is found.

In a standard online BCI, the user receives sensory feedback. For example, if the user is trying to control a 1-Dimensional cursor movement, he would see the progress of the cursor. The feedback is important to inform him of his progress but does not usually or strongly influence his next command (if the cursor is moving left or right, the user will try to give a left signal if he desires a leftward movement regardless of the current feedback until the trial end).

We propose and analyse a more *interactive* way of controlling the BCI where the user changes their intended brain signal depending on the feedback received from the computer. For simplicity we consider the case of binary cursor control, though the ideas could be extended to more complex systems. Rather than imagining "right hand movement" to move the cursor *right* and "foot movement" to move the cursor *left*, we consider these same two signal classes to mean instead *'I approve of the current direction, CONTINUE in the same direction'* and *'I don't like the current direction,*

ICMI'12, October 22–26, 2012, Santa Monica, California, USA.

CHANGE direction'. We will call such a system a D/S (*dissatisfaction/satisfaction*) system and call the first system a R/L (*right/left*) system. Note that while it may seem strange to use hand and foot movement to mean *continue* and *change direction*, R/L motor imagery systems often will pick the most discriminable signals for each user from between "imagine moving your right hand", "imagine moving your left hand", "imagine moving your foot", and "imagine moving your tongue". Once the two most discriminable signals are found, one is mapped to *right* cursor movements and the other to *left* cursor movements. There is no reason that these signals could not be mapped to the intentions *continue moving the cursor in the same direction* and *change cursor direction*. So initially we will assume that the pdfs of the two classes of signals is the same for each system but that they can be used, either in the standard direct (R/L) way, or in a new *interactive* (D/S) way.

2. BCI SYSTEMS AS MARKOV CHAINS

While EEG signals are high dimensional, they are often represented by just a few features before classification. Classification is then usually performed with a linear classifier (often linear discriminant analysis (LDA) or linear support vector machine (SVM)). The relevant dimension for a linear classifier is then the normal distance to the classification boundary. For the numerical computation, we assume that the EEG signals are generated from 1-Dimensional Gaussian probability density functions (pdfs) with different means (μ_1, μ_2) and the same projected variance (σ^2) along this normal dimension. In this formulation, we can represent different discriminabilities thru a single parameter

$$d' = \frac{|\mu_1 - \mu_2|}{\sigma}. \tag{1}$$

The exact form of the probability distributions, however, does not affect the main qualitative findings in the paper.

Single-trial EEG signals are very noisy and it is rare to be able to unambiguously classify a brain state (even from only two options) with a single classification. A common option to increase classification accuracy for online BCIs is to accumulate evidence over several classifications performed on overlapping or adjacent windows of the data. In this work we will consider adjacent windows (of length 500ms). We will assume that these windows are conditionally independent (given the intended class), though this is unlikely to be strictly true. The end result however will show that the D/S system is more robust to non-stationarities that underlie these dependencies and so this independence assumption should only decrease the full effect of the possible improvement with a D/S system.

One common and effective way of combining information between windows is to start with the cursor in the middle of the screen and take a step (left or right) according to the classification of each window of data. When the cursor reaches either of two targets equidistant (left and right) from the starting point, the trial ends. Accuracy can be greatly improved by chaining trials together in this way, though the time to determine an output increases.

The graphical model for state evolution in such a system is shown in Figure 1. As the next position of the cursor depends only on the current position and the classification of the window (which depends probabilistically on the subject's desired goal, the discriminability of their EEG signals, and the classification boundary), the performance of the subject can be considered as a discrete-time Markov process or a Markov chain [8] that takes each step according to a single window classification. As the process will eventually reach one of the endpoints, it is considered an absorbing Markov chain [12]. Once the walk reaches either endpoint the trial terminates and the absorbing (terminating) state determines the classifier output.

When viewed as an absorbing Markov chain, the analysis of the performance of the system is easily obtained [8, 12]. Consider the transition matrix P where p_{ij} is the probability of transitioning from state i to state j (and can be read off from the graphical model). With the transition matrix arranged so that the absorbing states are all at the top, P has the following form

$$P = \left[\begin{array}{c|c} I & 0 \\ \hline R & Q \end{array}\right].$$

If there are r absorbing states from which there are no external transitions (the two end-states in Figure 1) and t transient (non-absorbing) states (5 in Figure 1) then I is an r-by-r identity matrix and 0 is an r-by-t zero matrix. An entry $p_{ij}^{(n)}$ of P^n gives the probability of being in state j after n steps after starting in step i.

$$P^n = \left[\begin{array}{c|c} I & 0 \\ \hline \sum_{i=0}^{n-1} Q^i R & Q^n \end{array}\right].$$

In an absorbing Markov chain we are guaranteed that activity will eventually settle in one of the absorbing states which means that $Q^n \to 0$ as $n \to \infty$. Let $N = \sum_{i=0}^{\infty} Q^i$, then n_{ij} gives the expected number of times that the process is in transient state j when started in transient state i. Also note that N can be easily computed using $N = (I - Q)^{-1}$. This allows for easy analysis of expected accuracy rates for chains with different numbers of cursor positions and for different transition probabilities (which are a function of the discriminability of the signals and the current classification boundary). Nk where k is a column of t ones gives the expected number of steps before the chain is absorbed for each starting state. The entries v_{ij} from the equation $V = NR$ give the probability that the chain will be absorbed in absorbing state j when started in transient state i.

As there is a tradeoff between accuracy and number of steps (time) to completion, it is important to deal with a measure that incorporates both, such as the information transfer rate (ITR). ITR measures the number of bits of information learned about the user's desired class per unit time. For the case of equal accuracy for each class, and equal proportions of each class, the information transfer rate, can be computed using [20]:

$$ITR = (\log_2(C) + p\log_2(p) + (1-p)\log_2((1-p)/(C-1)))/T$$

where p is the classification rate of each class and C is the number of classes to be distinguished and T is the length of time for the computation. We wish to investigate how the ITR varies as the class pdfs drift due to nonstationarity of the EEG. In this work we simulate this with static pdfs but a moving classification boundary. This also simulates the problem of a non-optimal classification boundary due to a noisy estimate of the classification boundary. When the

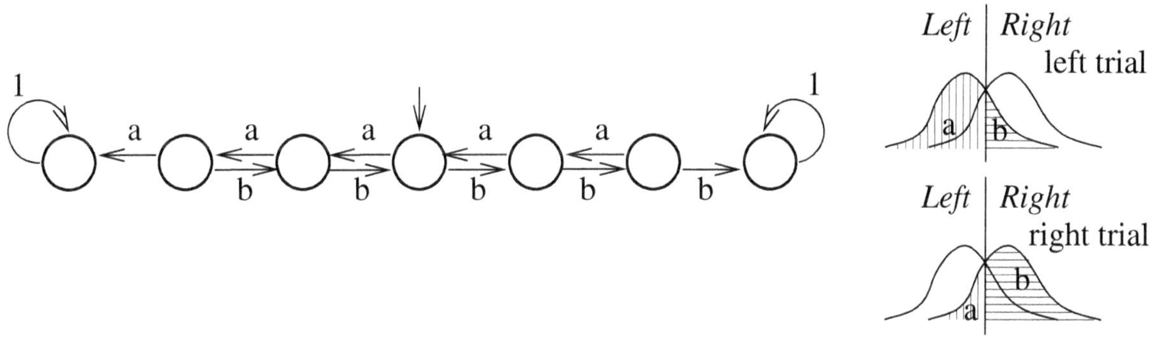

Figure 1: LEFT: The graphical model for system evolution for the standard R/L system. The spatial layout of the states corresponds to spatial cursor location. The rightmost/leftmost state represents hitting the rightmost/leftmost target. The numbers and variables on the arrows represent the transition probabilities between states. For best performance the chain is started in the center state (pointed to by the vertical arrow). This particular model shows a chain with 7 possible cursor positions (NCP=7). RIGHT: Sample 1-D probability density functions (pdfs) show how the transition probabilities a and b relate to the pdfs for the different classes and the classification boundary (shown by the vertical lines separating the hatched areas a and b). When the user intends to give a *left* signal, with probability a he will succeed and the chain will move left, and with probability b he will fail and the chain will move right. The bottom set of pdfs show how a and b are computed in a trial where the user desires to move the cursor right. Note that the classification boundary is shown in the Bayes optimal position. Our analysis investigates how the system performs as the classification boundary moves slightly to the left or right (changing the probabilities a and b).

classification boundary (or the class pdfs) shift the classification rates will differ for the right and left classes with the standard R/L system. In this case, a more general equation for the ITR is used [6]:

$$ITR = \left(\sum_{j=1}^{C} -p(y_j) log_2(p(y_j)) + \sum_{i=1}^{C} \sum_{j=1}^{C} p(x_i) p(y_j|x_i) log_2(p(y_j|x_i)) \right) / T$$

where $p(y_j) = \sum_{i=1}^{C} p(x_i)p(y_j|x_i)$ and x_i represents intended class i and y_j represents decoded class j. (For our example $C = 2$). In order to compare information transfer rates for our systems with different numbers of steps, it is important to also consider the overhead time in setting up the trial (including preparation time and interstimulus interval) thus the time component (T) consists of the sum of the times for each step plus the overhead time in setting up the trial. For this paper we use an overhead time of 5 steps (2.5 seconds). Other reasonable overhead times lead to similar results.

Accuracy, number of steps, and ITR were computed for Markov chains with different numbers of cursor positions (NCP). The results are shown in Figure 3. The black dashed curves represent the performance of R/L systems as the classification boundary is varied over the range shown. Each curve shows the result for a system with a different NCP. Several things can be immediately noticed with the regular R/L system. Accuracy increases with the number of cursor positions between the two absorbing states. Expected time to completion also increases. The best option for maximal information transfer rate, depends on the overhead time. For a d' of 1 and an overhead time of 5 computation steps, the maximal information transfer rate, is achieved for NCP=9. Changing d' for the simulated signals, changes the numeric values and may change the optimal NCP but does not change the general pattern of results. The optimal chain NCP for the best ITR, depends on d' and the overhead.

An analogous D/S system can also be created. In this case the user tries to control the cursor movement with control signals that are not *right* and *left* but *continue (satisfaction)* and *change (dissatisfaction)*. In this case we find that the next cursor position (state) depends not only on the previous cursor position (state) but also the direction the cursor was moving (which can be determined from the state before that). This means that when states represent only cursor positions a D/S system can be considered as a second-order Markov chain since the next state (cursor position) depends on the two previous states. If, however, we duplicate the interior transient states and let a state represent both cursor position and incoming direction, then we once again have a first-order Markov chain where the next state (cursor position and direction) depends on the current state (cursor position and direction) as well as the subject's desired goal, the classification boundary, and the discriminability of their signals. That is, for the the D/S system, the Markov chain is a second order system if only cursor position is considered, but can be considered a first order chain if the state includes the movement direction. The graphical model for this first-order D/S system is shown in Figure 2. The states at the top of the figure represent previous motion from the right and the bottom states represent states that had previous motion from the left. The transitions between the top and bottom rows correspond to cursor direction changes and are triggered by an interpreted *dissatisfaction (change)* signal. Interpreted *satisfaction (continue)* signals result in continuing movement along the current track. For this *interactive* system, if the subject intends to move the cursor to the right then the subject should give a *satisfaction* signal for rightward movements and a *dissatisfaction* signal for leftward movements. The probabilities for the different transitions

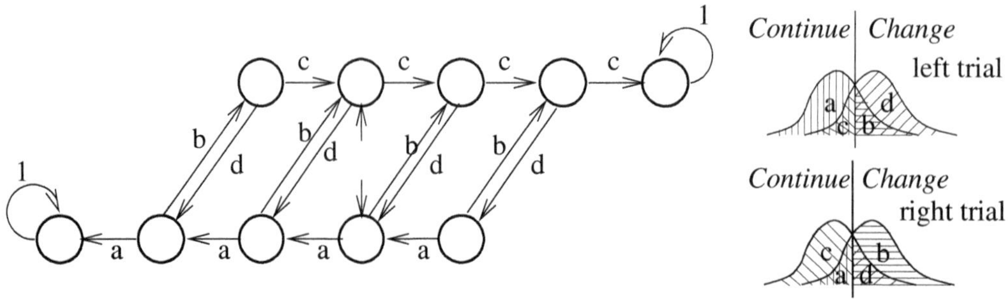

Figure 2: LEFT: The graphical model for system evolution for the proposed D/S system. The horizontal layout of the states corresponds to spatial cursor location. The rightmost/leftmost state represents hitting the rightmost/leftmost target. The numbers and variables on the arrows represent the transition probabilities between states. The vertical layout of the states corresponds to cursor motion direction. The top row of states correspond to states that have cursor movements to the right. The bottom row are the analogous states for cursor movement to the left. The initial cursor direction is randomly selected from between rightward and leftward (with end of first step ending at the center). These two starting states are indicated with the vertical arrows. This particular model shows a chain with 7 possible cursor positions (NCP=7). RIGHT: Sample 1-D pdfs show how the transition probabilities a, b, c, and d relate to the pdfs for the different classes and the classification boundary (shown by the vertical lines separating the hatched areas a and c from b and d). In a trial where the subject desires leftward motion, she generates a signal from the *continue (satisfied)* distribution when the cursor is already moving left (bottom states). This will be correctly detected with probability a and fail to be correctly classified with probability b (resulting in a *change* in cursor direction). When the cursor is going right and the subject desires leftward movement, the user generates a signal from the *change* distribution. This will be correctly classified with probablity d and incorrectly classified with probability c. When a subject desires rightward cursor movement, she should generate a signal from the *continue* distribution when the cursor is already moving right (top-states) and from the *change* distribution when the cursor is already moving left (bottom states). Note that the classification boundary is shown in the Bayes optimal position. Our analysis investigates how the system performs as the classification boundary moves slightly (changing the probabilities a,b,c and d).

are again derived from the assumed pdfs and are shown on the right of Figure 2 for both trials with desired leftward and desired rightward cursor movements.

Performance results for the D/S system are also shown in Figures 3 and 4. The range of high performance is much larger (as a function of classification boundary shift) for the D/S system than the R/L system. The curves show far less sensitivity to the exact boundary in the D/S method. Peak information transfer rates can also be better and are not always at the Bayes optimal classification boundary for distinguishing individual signals for the *continue* and *change* classes. It is interesting to analyze this difference. The R/L system depends crucially on the location of the classification boundary. If the boundary is too far towards the *right* distribution (so that too many windows are classified as *left*), then more left trials are classified correctly but fewer right trials are. The cost to the right trials is larger and the overall accuracy of the classifier goes down. In the D/S method, the classification boundary does not reflect the boundary between *right* and *left* classifications, but between *continue* and *change* classifications. When the classification boundary is moved so that *continue (satisfaction)* is more likely to be interpreted, we decrease the accuracy but also the expected completion time (there are less changes of cursor direction). Note that when the boundary is moved so that *dissatisfaction/change* is made more prevalent, the accuracy actually increases as more decisions are needed to be combined before the cursor reaches a target endpoint. By moving the classification boundary so that *change* is more likely we increase both the convergence time and accuracy. This is very similar to increasing the chain's NCP. Similarly moving the boundary to make *continue* more likely is similar to making the chain shorter. For chains with smaller than optimal NCP for a given d', ITR can be increased by moving the classification boundary so that *change* is more likely to be output. For chains that have a larger than optimal NCP for a given d', ITR can be increased by moving the classification boundary so that *continue* is more likely to be output. This can be seen in the right panel of Figure 3 and the right panel of Figure 4. Note that this means that improvements in the system ITR (for reaching left and right targets) are possible for classification boundaries removed from the Bayes optimal boundary for separating individual signals from the *continue* and *change* classes. Figure 4 also clearly shows that the D/S curves are more parallel to the ITR contours and the R/L curves are more perpendicular which is another way of seeing that the D/S system is much more robust to classification boundary drift. (ITR does not change drastically as the classification boundary drifts). Also note from the state diagram that areas a and d are pushing the cursor right and areas b and c are pushing the cursor left. As the *continue/change* classification boundary is moved, a and d trade off to some extent, as do b and c.

To summarize, in all the simulations, if the classification boundary is optimal (at the crossing point between the class pdfs), the expected number of steps, accuracy, and ITR are the same for both the R/L and D/S system. For the R/L system as the boundary drifts relative to the class pdfs the system will end up over classifying *right* or *left* and the average classification error falls off. In the D/S system differ-

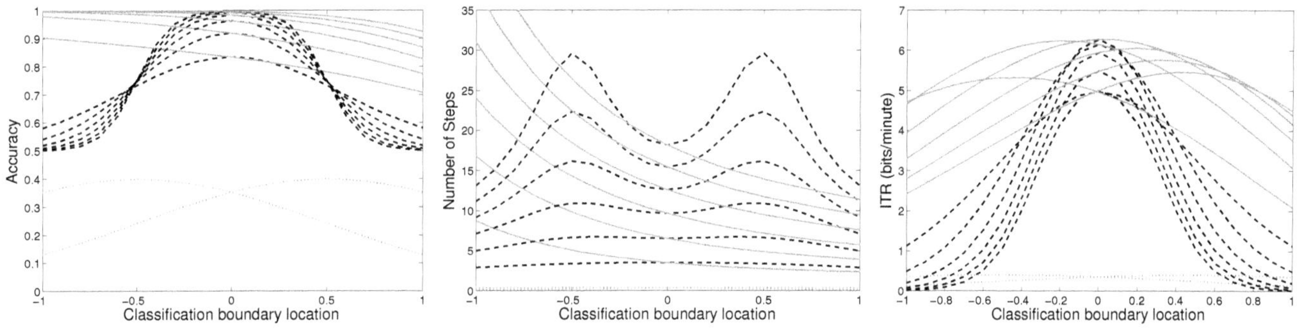

Figure 3: The blue dotted curves at the bottom of each panel show the simulated probability density functions (pdfs) for *left* and *right* for the R/L simulation. They do not have the same units as the other curves but are plotted on the same plot (with the same numeric scaling) so that the classification boundary placement can be seen with respect to the class pdfs. These same pdfs are also used for *continue* and *change* for the D/S simulation (with *change* on the right.) In the left panel, the black dashed curves show the accuracy for the R/L system as a function of classification boundary placement. (Note that optimal placement for a single window classification is at the crossing point of the class pdfs). Positive values for boundary placement mean that the classifier is more likely to output *left*. The magenta curves show the accuracy for the D/S system as a function of the classification boundary placement (between the *continue* and *change* pdfs). Positive values for boundary placement in these curves means that the classifier is more likely to output *continue*. The different curves in each color are for chains with different NCP (5, 7, 9, 11, 13, 15) with the higher accuracies resulting from chains with larger NCP. Note that in the D/S case, system accuracy actually increases as the system is more likely to classify *change* for the observed cursor movement. The middle panel show the number of steps for the same simulations (black dashed R/L, magenta D/S). The curves with more steps are for larger NCP. The final panel shows ITR for the same simulations. In the D/S simulations, for NCP larger than optimal, better ITR is associated with the classifier being more likely to output *continue*; for smaller NCP, better ITR is achieved with the classifier being more likely to output *change*.

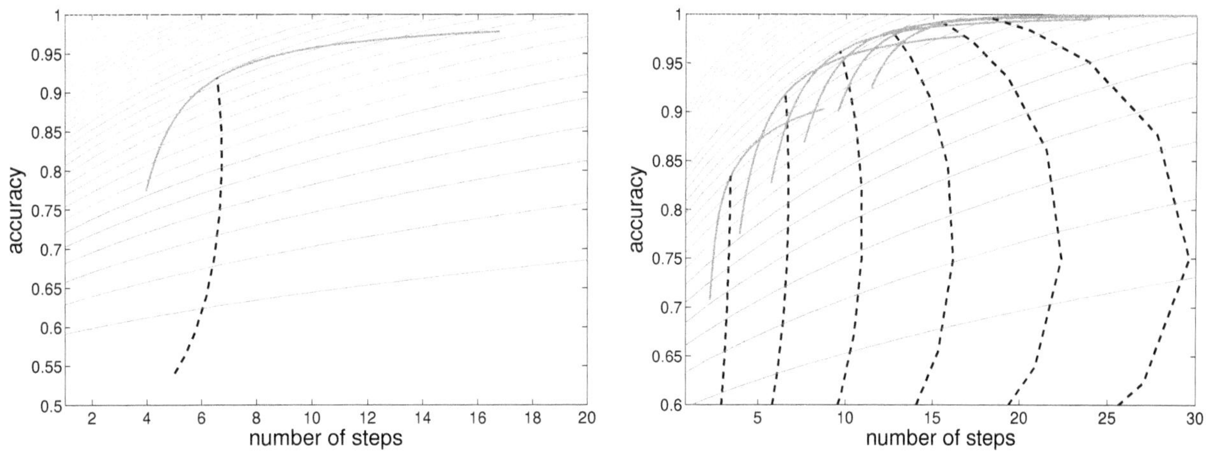

Figure 4: The left plot shows accuracy vs steps for the chains with NCP=7. The black dashed curve shows the values for the standard R/L algorithm as the classification boundary is moved by $\pm 0.5\sigma$ from the optimal boundary with a d' of 1. The magenta curve shows how the D/S values change for the same boundary movement (this time when considered as the boundary between *continue* and *change*). The place where the curves meet represents the values at the optimal classification boundary for distinguishing the single window class pdfs (for *left/right* or *change/continue*). The R/L algorithm performs symmetrically with respect to movements in either direction from this boundary so the curve falls down in the same way as the boundary is moved to the right and left. The thin curves in green show the contours of information transfer rate for an overhead of 5 steps (with higher ITRs in lighter colors and towards the top left corner) and equal classification rates for both classes. The right panel shows the same plots for chains with different NCP (5, 7, 9, 11, 13, and 15) with chains with larger NCP showing more steps and greater peak accuracy. This plot shows the same data presented in Figure 3. For all NCP as the boundary moves away from the single-window optimal boundary, the D/S system does not suffer as much in ITR (and sometimes improves - this is possible because the boundary is only optimal for the single window classification).

ent behavior is experienced if the boundary drifts. If the boundary drifts so that *continue/satisfaction* is more likely, accuracy decreases a little and the expected number of steps also decreases. Note that accuracy falls off much slower than for the R/L system. If the boundary drifts so that *change (dissatisfaction)* is more likely, accuracy will improve and the expected number of steps increases.

2.1 Variable step size is better

A variable step size may be used, so that if the classifier is more confident, the cursor takes a bigger step. This can still be modeled with an absorbing Markov chain where the number of cursor positions is made very large (even the number of pixels between targets) and the probabilities are more finely computed. See for example in Figure 5 a four part option in the R/L system (with NCP=7). Note that analogous modifications can easily be made to the D/S system (Figure omitted because of its visual complexity). Information transfer rate improves with the variable step size for both the standard R/L and *interactive* D/S system. The equality of the solutions at the Bayes optimal classification boundary and the superior robustness of the D/S system are also maintained.

Good performance is obtained with an update rule that performs

$$x = x + k\left(\frac{1}{1+\exp(-\frac{(s-\theta)d'}{\sigma})} \times 2 - 1\right)$$

where x is the cursor position, (s $-\theta$) is the signed normal distance of the sample EEG feature vector from the classification boundary. k is a scale variable that can be set optimally for the given chain NCP. $\frac{1}{1+\exp(-\frac{(s-\theta)d'}{\sigma})}$ computes the probability that the observed sample belongs to the class with larger mean (between μ_1 and μ_2) (assuming Gaussian pdfs with means μ_1, and μ_2, equal class variances of σ^2 and disciminability d' given by Equation (1)). The multiplication by 2 and subtraction of 1 converts the probability into a scaled value from -1 to 1 which can then be multiplied by k to obtain a step size (and direction given by the sign).

3. TOWARDS USING A NATURAL DISSATISFACTION/SATISFACTION SIGNAL

We have shown theoretically that if the *satisfaction* and *dissatisfaction* signals were as equally distinguishable as standardly used signals for right and left desired motion (for example if the same brain states were used to represent these controls), the D/S system would be more robust to error in estimating the optimal boundary and to shifts in this boundary. In a real online system there are other issues. It has been found that users' ITRs decrease with longer trials (possibly due to fatigue or loss of attention) [15]. This means that keeping trials shorter (smaller NCP) may be preferred. The D/S method of control is also not natural for most human users and may be a bit difficult for them at first. Real-time performance can also be strongly affected by feedback. It has been found that a run of bad performance can lead to a much longer term loss of control, possibly due to frustration and the change in signals this causes [10]. Based on these findings, it may be more useful to use a natural *dissatisfaction* signal instead of co-opting a standard motor imagery signal. This *dissatisfaction* signal may involve emotional changes as well as error signals generated in response to seeing the computer incorrectly interpreting their desired signal. It may also have a more active aspect in encoding internal thoughts of "No!" (or a stronger word or expression).

Thus a dissatisfaction signal could arise from both active signals (thinking "No!" including the emotion and the phonation of the word) and passive signals (automatic emotion, error responses). Potentially this may lead to a richer more discriminable signal than the more commonly investigated motor imagery signals (at least for some users). A D/S system using natural *dissatisfaction/satisfaction* signals (as opposed to co-opting the motor imagery of feet and hands) would have the advantage that loss of control should be less of a problem as the system is specifically trained to recognize the frustration and dissatisfaction resulting from loss of control and so natural frustration responses should help the system perform better, rather than working against the system by introducing new untrained factors.

Finally the natural *dissatisfaction* signal could be combined with other more actively generated signals to create a stronger more robust signal. In the next section we briefly discuss a possible hybrid system with a standard R/L system being actively controlled and a more passive D/S system running simultaneously to look for some subset of frustration, errors, and imagined negative words.

4. A HYBRID SYSTEM

Several studies have been performed that use various EEG error (including the error-related negativity (ERN) and other error potential brain signals [18]) to improve performance [9, 5]. Error signals have been used to improve performance on a speeded motor task where the subject physically pushes a button [17], to correct machine-induced errors [11, 21] and to modify the policy (probability of selecting actions) of an automatic agent [3]. Error related signals have also been investigated in motor-imagery based BCIs [7, 1, 13] to change the BCI response after a trial is over [1] or to cancel individual movements [7]. We are not aware, however, of a system that has explored treating error and active signals equivalently and combining the signals in a Markov-chain-like way as we suggest below.

In Section 2 we compared an *interactive* D/S system to a standard R/L system, assuming that both could be used with the same underlying motor imagery signals just used and interpreted differently (as *continue/change* instead of *right/left*). It is also possible to combine the standard active R/L control signal with a passive and reactive D/S signal. In this case the user would be actively controlling the cursor movement to the right and left with motor imagery but passively detected satisfaction or frustration and reactively generated error signals could be used as well. In this system, it is important to weight the signals according to their confidences. This can be done in an online manner using the following formula:

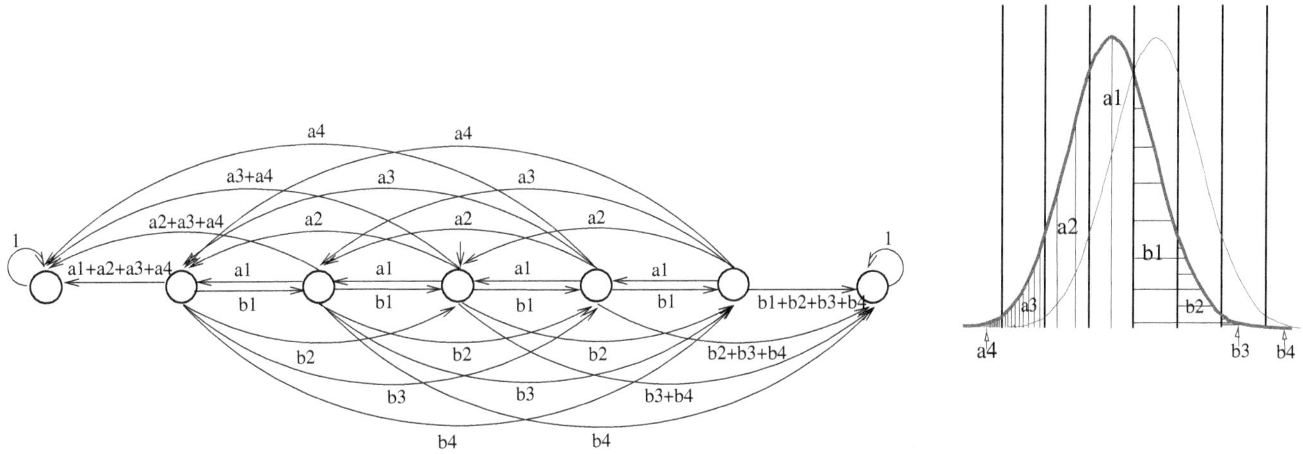

Figure 5: A more fine-scaled R/L Markov chain to allow for variable step size. Larger steps are taken when the classifier is more sure of the class decision. In this figure, the a and b probabilities from Figure 1 are each subdivided into four parts $a1$, $a2$, $a3$, $a4$ and $b1$, $b2$, $b3$, and $b4$. They are drawn at equal intervals along the projected input space but would actually be positioned at equal steps of change in estimated probability for each class. Only the probabilities for a leftward desiring trial are shown to save space. An analogous fine-scaled markov process can be used for a D/S system (not shown due to space limitations).

$$\mathrm{x} = \mathrm{x} + k\left(\frac{1}{1+\exp\left(-\frac{(\,\mathrm{s}-\theta)d'}{\sigma}\right)} \times 2 - 1\right) - r\left(k_{ds}\left(\frac{1}{1+\exp\left(-\frac{(s_{ds}-\theta_{ds})d'_{ds}}{\sigma_{ds}}\right)} \times 2 - 1\right)\right)$$

where x is the current cursor position on the screen, $(s-\theta)$, is the signed normal difference of the EEG R/L feature vector from the *left/right* classification boundary and $(s_{ds} - \theta_{ds})$ is the signed normal difference of the EEG D/S feature vector from the *continue/change* classification boundary. r is a binary variable (-1/+1) that represents the current direction of the cursor (r=1, for cursor moving right, r=-1 for cursor moving left). Scale factors k and k_{ds} may be set equal or optimized on a per-subject basis with cross-validation. Further work will be required to compare this method of integrating natural D/S signals with the previously used approaches.

5. DISCUSSION

The D/S idea works naturally with a two class system and in this paper we have restricted our analysis to a binary cursor control task. It has been found that information transfer rates for people in online systems tend to not improve beyond three or four classes [4, 14]. Kronegg et. al. (2007) state that "increasing the number of mental tasks from two only produces a very limited improvement in terms of information-transfer rate... This observation is in accordance with Dornhege et al. theoretical model [4]...Even if increasing the number of tasks would lead to an increase in ITR, the small gain might not justify the added complexity in terms of protocol design."

Omar and colleagues [16] have shown how to combine binary BCI control signals to generate text and curved trajectories (made from non-binary alphabets). The binary signals in their case are generated from combined evidence from right/left motor imagery. Our paper deals with how best to generate those binary signals.

Though less natural, the D/S idea could be expanded to work with a slightly larger number of classes. A 3 or 4 target D/S system could be set up where the cursor starts to move towards one of the targets at random. It would continue if it interprets a *continue* and it would start towards the clockwise next one when it interprets a *change*. It could also be used for 1-Dimensional cursor control with several targets in a line. Standard R/L systems of 1-Dimensional cursor control with more than two classes in a line have an *interactive* aspect in that to get to a middle target the command is different depending on whether the cursor is currently to the right or left of that target. However this is not the same as a full D/S system because if the classification boundary (on the right/left control signals) has moved so that *left* is overclassified, it will be very hard to hit the rightmost targets. In the D/S system, if the classification boundary has moved so that *continue* is overclassified, accuracy and convergence time will decrease as in the binary system, but ITR will not be as drastically affected. If the boundary has moved so that *change* is overclassified, error rate will decrease and convergence time will increase, and again as in the binary case, the ITR will not be as drastically affected. The D/S system is *interactive* based on both position and direction of motion. A R/L system with three or more classes in a line is just interactive based on position.

The D/S system has another possible advantage. We can recognize drift by noticing that either the average classification time has gone up or down and in each case we know the required direction of change. We also know that we should expect at most one *dissatisfaction* per trial and this may also be used in future work to keep the system tuned in an unsupervised, automatic way.

We have seen that by interacting with the signal, the BCI system can be much less harmed by non-optimal classification boundaries (and thus non-stationarities). By building a control signal that depends intimately on what has already been transmitted, interpreted, and received (and using both direction of motion and position) a much more robust system can be achieved. Future work will involve investigating natural D/S signals and testing both their use (and the use of co-opted standard signals) in online D/S and hybrid BCIs. Finally, while the finding that an *interactive* control signal should result in greater robustness to classification boundary placement was presented in the context of a motor-imagery EEG-based brain computer interface, the result is applicable for any situation where the control signals are noisy (and the optimal classification boundary is unknown or changing) and windows of classification are combined (with feedback of the current progress provided).

6. ACKNOWLEDGMENTS

I would like to thank Eunho Noh and Adam Koerner for helpful discussions and the anonymous reviewers for helpful comments. This research was supported by the National Science Foundation under grants NSF CBET-0756828, NSF IIS-1219200, and NSF SBE-0542013 (to GW Cottrell) and from an innovative research grant from the Kavli Institute for Brain and Mind at UCSD.

7. REFERENCES

[1] X. Artusi, I. K. Niazi, M.-F. Lucas, and D. Farina. Accuracy of a BCI based on movement-related and error potentials. In *Proceedings of the Annual International Conference of the IEEE Engineering in Medicine and Biology Society*, pages 3688–91, 2011.

[2] B. Blankertz, R. Tomioka, S. Lemm, M. Kawanabe, and K.-R. Müller. Optimizing spatial filters for robust EEG single-trial analysis. *IEEE Signal Processing Magazine*, 25(1):41–56, 2008.

[3] R. Chavarriaga and J. del R. Millán. Learning from EEG error-related potentials in non-invasive brain-computer interfaces. *IEEE Transactions on Neural Systems and Rehabilitation Engineering*, 18(4):381–388, 2010.

[4] G. Dornhege, B. Blankertz, G. Curio, and K.-R. Müller. Increase information transfer rates in BCI by CSP extension to multi-class. *Advances in Neural Information Processing Systems*, 16, 2004.

[5] M. Falkenstein, J. Hohnsbein, and J. Hoormann. *Event-related potential correlates of errors in reaction tasks.* Perspectives of event-related potentials research. Amsterdam: Elsevier Science B.V., 1995.

[6] M. Fatourechi, S. G. Mason, G. E. Birch, and R. K. Ward. Is information transfer rate a suitable performance measure for self-paced brain interface systems? In *IEEE International Symposium on Signal Processing and Information Technology*, 2006.

[7] P. W. Ferrez and J. del R Millán. Error-related EEG potentials generated during simulated brain-computer interaction. *IEEE transactions on Biomedical Engineering*, 55(3):923–929, 2008.

[8] C. M. Grinstead and J. L. Snell. Chapter 11: Markov chains. In *Introduction to Probability*, chapter 11. American Mathematical Society, 1997.

[9] S. A. Inverso. Automatic error recovery using P3 response verification for a brain-computer interface. Master's thesis, Computer Science Department, Rochester Institute of Technology, 2004.

[10] S. Jatzev, M. D. Filippis, T. Zander, C. Kothe, S. Welke, and M. Rötting. Towards an heuristic-based approach detecting nonstationarities in BCI features. Abstract presented at BCI 2010, 2010.

[11] S. Jatzev, T. Zander, M. DeFlilippis, C. Kothe, S. Welke, and M. Rötting. Examining causes for non-stationarities: The loss of controllability is a factor which induces non-stationarities. In *Proceedings of the 4th Int. BCI Workshop & Training Course.* Graz University of Technology Publishing House, 2008.

[12] J. G. Kemeny and J. L. Snell. Chapter 3: Absorbing Markov chains. In *Finite Markov Chains*, page 224. Springer-Verlag, New York Berlin Heidelberg Tokyo, second edition, 1976.

[13] A. Kreilinger, C. Neuper, and G. R. Müller-Putz. Error potential detection during continuous movement of an artificial arm controlled by brain-computer interface. *Medical & biological engineering & computing*, 50(3):223–30, Mar. 2012.

[14] J. Kronegg, G. Chanel, S. Voloshynovskiy, and T. Pun. EEG-based synchronized brain-computer interfaces: A model for optimizing the number of mental tasks. *IEEE Transactions on Neural Systems and Rehabilitation Engineering*, 15(1):50–58, 2007.

[15] D. J. McFarland, W. A. Sarnacki, and J. R. Wolpaw. Brain-computer interface (BCI) operation: optimizing information transfer rates. *Biological Psychology*, 63:237–251, 2003.

[16] C. Omar, A. Akce, M. Johnson, T. Bretl, R. Ma, E. Maclin, M. McCormick, and T. P. Coleman. Feedback information-theoretic approach to the design of brain-computer interfaces. *International Journal on Human-Computer Interaction , special issue on Current Trends in Brain-Computer Interface (BCI) Research and Development*, 27(1):5–23, January 2011.

[17] L. C. Parra, C. D. Spence, A. D. Gerson, and P. Sajda. Response error correction - a demonstration of improved human-machine performance using real-time EEG monitoring. *IEEE Transactions on Neural Systems and Rehabilitation Engineering*, 11(2):173–177, 2003.

[18] G. Schalk, J. R. Wolpaw, D. J. McFarland, and G. Pfurtscheller. EEG-based communication: presence of an error potential. *Clinical Neurophysiology*, 111:2138–2144, 2000.

[19] P. Shenoy, M. Krauledat, B. Blankertz, R. Rao, and K.-R. Müller. Towards adaptive classification for BCI. *Journal of Neural Engineering*, 3:R13–R23, 2006.

[20] J. R. Wolpaw, H. Ramoser, D. J. McFarland, and G. Pfurtscheller. EEG-based communication: Improved accuracy by response verification. *IEEE Trans. Rehabil. Eng.*, 6(3):326–333, 1998.

[21] T. Zander and S. Jatzev. Detecting affective covert user states with passive Brain-Computer Interfaces. In I. C. S. Press, editor, *Proceedings of the ACII 2009*, Los Alamitos, CA, 2009.

Improving BCI Performance *after* Classification

Danny Plass-Oude Bos
HMI, Faculty of EEMCS
University of Twente
Enschede, The Netherlands
d.plass@utwente.nl

Hayrettin Gürkök
HMI, Faculty of EEMCS
University of Twente
Enschede, The Netherlands
h.gurkok@utwente.nl

Boris Reuderink
Donders Centre
for Cognitive Neuroimaging
Nijmegen, The Netherlands
b.reuderink@donders.ru.nl

Mannes Poel
HMI, Faculty of EEMCS
University of Twente
Enschede, The Netherlands
m.poel@utwente.nl

ABSTRACT

Brain-computer interfaces offer a valuable input modality, which unfortunately comes also with a high degree of uncertainty. There are simple methods to improve detection accuracy after the incoming brain activity has already been classified, which can be divided into (1) gathering additional evidence from other sources of information, and (2) transforming the unstable classification results to be more easy to control. The methods described are easy to implement, but it is essential to apply them in the right way. This paper provides an overview of the different techniques, showing where to apply them and comparing the effects. Detection accuracy is important, but there are trade-offs to consider. Future research should investigate the effectiveness of these methods in their context of use, as well as the optimal settings to obtain the right balance between functionality and meeting the user's expectations for maximum acceptance.

Categories and Subject Descriptors

H.5.2 [**User Interfaces**]: Input Devices and Strategies

Keywords

Brain-computer interface, multimodal, context-aware, evidence accumulation, user expectations.

1. INTRODUCTION

Brain-computer interfaces (BCIs) do not function as accurately as the keyboard or mouse. This is inherent in the type of signal, which is also why speech recognition and eye movement detection are not perfect, although they have improved a lot over the years [5, 14]. The sensors easily pick up noise. It is very difficult to distinguish between activity intended for control, and other activity. Moreover, there is the challenge of robustness to change in the environment, change in the user, and over different users. These problems are reflected in the way most BCI experiments are set up: the user is preferably put in a shielded room; is instructed to not move or blink, and stay relaxed; and is doing a very simple task.

Is this lack of accuracy of BCIs a problem? BCIs offer a unique input that is private, hands-free, and possibly closer to the user's intent than any other input modality [30]. But the detection accuracy and, related to this, the amount of effort involved, are very important to the user [29]. Users prefer interfaces with allow a high level of control with little effort. Besides, there are some consequences of the current situation. Those limited lab experiments mentioned in the previous paragraph are difficult to translate to the real-world situation, where the user will not be so restricted in context nor behaviour. Additionally, the variety of both mental tasks or states, and their interpretations, are severely limited.

Fortunately, even after the detection phase, there are a lot of ways to boost performance, and make the signal more usable for control[1]. This paper discusses a number of them, divided into two categories: gathering additional, external evidence, and transforming the obtained classification results by themselves. In the end, however, not only the functional properties of the control signal are important, but also how well it matches user expectations. The conclusions provide some recommendations for future research.

2. THE ONLINE BCI CYCLE

To be able discuss when and how to apply the methods that we will describe, first, we need a model of the online BCI cycle. Figure 1 details the different modules, or phases, in the system, and the data streams in between. This model is largely based on the framework by Mason and Birch [19], with some small adjustments which will be discussed.

[1]With control is not only meant intentional control by the user, but also unintentional input based on passive observation of the user. In both cases, the system responds to the information gathered from the user. For simplicity, even in the passive situation, we will therefore talk about 'control'. In the passive situation, there are still correct and incorrect interpretations of the user's mental state by the system, and if there is feedback to the user in some way, there are still user expectations that could be met.

ICMI'12, October 22–26, 2012, Santa Monica, California, USA.

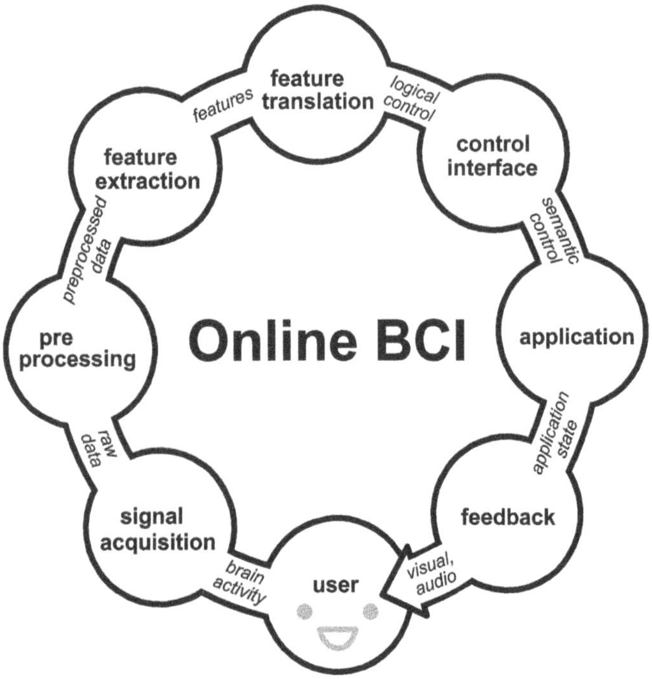

Figure 1: Model of the online BCI cycle, including the data streams between the processes.

The *user* either consciously executes some mental task, or is passively monitored for specific mental states. This brain activity is *acquired* through some brain activity measurement method, such as electroencephalography (EEG, which would consist of electrodes, an amplifier, and likely some additional software by the hardware manufacturer). Here we combined the *electrodes* and *amplifier* modules from Mason and Birch together in one generic module labeled *signal acquisition*.

The raw brain data is *preprocessed*, mainly to improve the signal-to-noise ratio by attenuating the effects of artefacts and noise. Mason and Birch combined this step with *feature extraction*. Many researchers, however, prefer to address this function separately, as is also shown in the model by Van Gerven, et al. [40]. Therefore we also gave it its own module. From this preprocessed data, *features* are then *extracted* that provide information on what the system is supposed to detect.

Feature translation is not a term that is commonly used in this context, but this generic word from the Mason and Birch model appropriately covers the whole range of classification and regression. The results of this module can be hard class labels (e.g. LEFT), soft class labels (80% certainty of LEFT), or some other values that have logical meaning (level of concentration of 0.4)[2].

The *control interface* transforms these logical inputs into semantic control signals that have meaning within the context of the application. This module is often not represented in other models, but Mason and Birch did see the importance of this particular function. It is also particularly relevant to this paper, as many of the proposed methods would be applied in this phase. The resulting semantic control can either be discrete or continuous (for example, key and button presses vs. mouse position and joystick).

On a side note, when both the recognition software (up to and including feature translation) and the application are proprietary, the control interface may be the only way to tie them together in the desired way.

At this point in the pipeline, we deviate from the Mason and Birch model, because of a difference in the context of use of the BCI. Their model reflected the use of BCI to control physical devices, where our model is specified for control of software applications. The functions of Mason and Birch's device controller and the device itself are merged within the application itself (possibly internally modelled according to the model-view-controller design pattern, well explained in [8])

The *feedback* module is simplified here as solely based on data coming from the application. The feedback can however also show representations of output from other modules. Any feedback that helps the user form a suitable mental model of the system could be helpful in improving the level or at least the sense of control. In most cases, the feedback (view) on the application state is handled by the application itself. If the application is adjustable, for example through add-ons, the feedback from other modules can be integrated. If not, it will be necessary to create a separate software application solely to provide this extra information to the user, for example, with overlays on top of the view of the original application.

To conclude, the main modules in which to adjust the control, after classification (or, the more generic: feature translation), are the control interface, and the application.

3. GATHERING EXTERNAL EVIDENCE

Now we have explained the BCI cycle in which the following methods will be used, it is time to give an in-depth explanation of each method, starting with the ones based gathering external evidence, such as from other modalities and the context.

3.1 Multimodality

Multimodal systems process multiple combined user input modalities in a coordinated manner [24]. Multimodality can help in handling errors, improving task performance and broadening the user spectrum with BCI systems [10]. In the BCI community, multimodal BCI systems are referred to as hybrid BCIs [27]. A hybrid BCI not only combines brain data from other modalities, but may also combine different brain responses. For example, a hybrid BCI speller can rely on the P300 response for spelling letters and on the steady-state visually evoked potential (SSVEP) response to switch the spelling on and off [25].

The coordination of the various inputs can be categorized according to two aspects: the treatment of the multimodal data and the temporal relation of the modalities [22]. The multimodal data streams can either be treated *independently*, or they can be *fused*. Fusion can be done at data-, feature- and decision-level, also called early, intermediate, and late fusion. Data-level fusion is performed

[2]Another interesting option, but outside of the scope of this paper to discuss in detail, is to have not only probability information, or strength, but both. In that case, the feature translation could provide information such as 'a level of concentration of 0.9 with a probability of 2%' which can then be translated into an application command that has less effect than if the probability would be higher.

when integrating observations of the same kind, such as the electrical data obtained from EEG and EOG. Feature-level fusion is for modalities which are tightly synchronised, such as frontal EEG and facial audio-visual data. Decision-level (or classifier) fusion, is used for modalities that are not so tightly coupled, such as EEG data and speech or keyboard input. There are also two ways of temporal coordination: the processing can either be sequential or parallel. In either case, the treatment can again be independent, or fused.

For the goal of this paper, the most applicable method is parallel, decision-level fusion, as it is about combining after-classification results from different inputs that happened simultaneously, to obtain a more accurate decision. One of the easier methods to do this, is through majority voting [17], in which the combined result is the one that most classifiers agreed upon. For more complex methods, see [12, 23].

This method could be implemented in the control interface, where it functionally seems to belong. If the application is unadaptable, the control interface is the only option. In case the application also needs to show a response to each input modality by itself, it may be better to implement the fusion in the application directly.

3.2 Context

Another potential source of information is the context, which can be determined from additional sensors, or from the system or application itself. According to Abowd *et al.*: "Context is any information that can be used to characterize the situation of an entity. An entity is a person, place, or object that is considered relevant to the interaction between a user and an application, including the user and applications themselves" [1]. Concrete examples of context are: time of day, location, movement, recent interaction history, the user's emotional state, and the user's focus of attention.

Reducing action space.
Context information can be used to determine what actions the user is probably going to do, therefore reducing the likely action space, which improves the accuracy of the input interpretation. After spelling 'TH', the classifier might return high values for both 'S' and 'E'. Based on the recent actions, in combination with a *language model*, it is easy to determine that 'E' is more likely[3]. Two BCI examples that make use of the predictive properties of text are Dasher [7], and Williamson's Hex-O-Spell [41]. The dynamics of the interaction reflect the level of certainty: it is easier to select more likely options, and more effort is required to select a less likely one. This results in increased accuracy and efficiency.

Similar concepts are *snapping* (when close to a likely target, automatically go to it), and *hysteresis* (the dynamic for changing states depends on what state you come from, to prevent undesirable oscillations from one state to the other; this is also known as debouncing). An example BCI that uses hysteresis is αWoW. In this adaptation of the role-playing game World of Warcraft®, the player's avatar is an elf when relaxed, but changes into a bear when agitated [38]. The relaxation level is based on a transformed level of parietal brain activity in the alpha band. To change to bear, the transformed alpha level needs to be below 0.3, and to change to elf above 0.7. In terms of dynamics based on certainty, this means that once the user is in one state, she is less likely to change to the other. The larger the distance between the two thresholds, the less likely it is that state changes will occur in general.

If certain actions always occur together (the likelihood of the next action is 100%), they can be combined in a *macro*. Back to the case of a P300 speller, instead of spelling single characters, the user now selects a phoneme, word, or whole sentence with one command. Scherer *et al.* use macros to execute more complex and flexible commands [34]. This is also related to the notion of process control (one step forward) versus goal selection (go to the kitchen) [42, 33].

When the implementation of these methods requires knowledge from the application, it is best to implement it in that module. For example, in the case of a speller application, the control interface should not model the effect of the backspace action that deletes the previously-typed character. This is the responsibility of the application. So the knowledge as to what text has actually been spelt so far is only available from the application module. Snapping also requires knowledge about where possible targets are in the application to be able to snap to them. Hysteresis may be implemented in the control interface, as it only requires the knowledge that the actions that belong to the extreme states are opposites and can never occur simultaneously. This logic could be imposed from the mental task or state (i.e. the user cannot be stressed and relaxed at the same time), or by the response from the application (an avatar cannot be a bear and an elf at the same time).

Increasing action space.
Similarly, context can provide the user with a large range of system commands, controlled through a limited set of input actions. Scherer *et al.* give an example of this in World of Warcraft®: when the player is close to a dead enemy, she will loot the corpse. Is the player close to a quest giver, she will talk to him [34]. To read more on how to implement context-aware systems, we recommend the survey by Baldauf *et al.*, which discusses various approaches used in existing systems and presents a design framework [2]. This method obviously requires application knowledge, so that is where it has to be implemented.

Even if context is not used explicitly, it will affect the user's brain activity. It may cause non-stationarity in the signals, which may need to addressed to maintain a good performance [31]. Context could also improve BCI performance, for example, if the situation is more motivating [15]. And perhaps the difference in brain activity can be used as a source of context information by itself.

4. TRANSFORMING CLASSIFICATION

The unsteady feature translation (classification, regression) results can also be transformed by themselves, to increase the certainty of correct detection, and make the characteristics of control better match the expectations of the user given the application. Although the methods below can be adjusted to 'hard' class labels – by giving them a 'soft' probability level of 100% – having access to actual probability information yields more accurate results. Most methods are also applicable to continuous output, for example produced by regression models, such as for the workload or stress level of the user.

[3]More on the redundancy in the English language in [35].

4.1 Accumulating Evidence

A common method to increase BCI detection accuracy is *averaging* over multiple classifications[4]. In Bacteria Hunt, over half of the classifications needs to return true, to eat the target [20]. Averaging smooths the classification results, making it less sensitive to noise. The *moving average* algorithm multiplies the most recent classifications with a smoothing vector, which determines the amount to which newer and older samples contribute to the final result. In αWoW, this simple technique reduces the effect of outliers and provides more smooth interaction [38]. *Smoothing* will slow down the interaction. To reduce this effect, one can use exponential smoothing [11, 26], or IIR filters that have a quick response. This method can be implemented in either the control interface or the application, in which case the control interface is the preferred place for this function.

Similar to BCIs, eye movement data is jittery, noisy, and uncertain. Besides, it is very difficult to distinguish intent from 'normal activity'. Jacob has proposed a solution to this so-called *Midas touch* problem by introducing a *dwell time*: looking at a target for a certain time to select it [13]. In the case of BCIs, the user has to stay in a certain value range for the given duration, to trigger a specific command. This method has been used to select a target with a BCI-controlled cursor [6], to confirm actions in BCI-controlled videogames [34, 38], and to improve classification results in general [36]. From eye movement-based control it is known that the exact duration of dwell time is critical to the flow of the interaction[13]. For brain-computer interaction, the optimal duration is likely to be different and also dependent on the mental tasks used for control. Like most methods mentioned in this paper, dwelling will increase the time to give the command. If application knowledge is required – for example, to know whether the user is hovering over a target – the appropriate place to implement this method is the application.

4.2 Refractory Period

Refractory periods suppress the BCI for a while after a command has been triggered, to reduce the number of false positives [36]. In video games, this is referred to as 'cooldown'. Pfurtscheller *et al.* used it to prevent a device, that enabled a paralyzed patient to grasp a cylinder with his hand, from switching grasping states too quickly [28]. As Bashashati *et al.* rightly observe: "As the debounce period is increased, the false activation rate is decreased for a given true positive rate. However, with increasing this time period, the re-activation time of the BCI system is impacted. The trade-off is clear and one needs to consider this for a given application" [3]. This method needs to know when an action has been triggered as a result of the control signal. It could be implemented in the control interface, but as it is the application that decides what the actual system response is to the input, that might be a better location.

4.3 Class Balancing and Normalization

When the output is biased towards one class, this can occur for a variety of reasons, such as changes in the mental state of the user [4, 31]. Although most solutions to this are applied before classification, it can also be addressed afterwards, by applying normalization methods that balance the output. Adaptive z-score normalization automatically adjusts the system to the user in αWoW. It balances the output with respect to its mean and standard deviation, which avoids a bias towards a specific mental state, and ensures that the user does not get stuck [38].

There is an interesting side effect of adaptive z-score normalization. If the running history contains many samples, as expected, the result is similar to the input, except for the scale (assuming a normal distribution). If the running history is relatively short, however, the transform becomes highly sensitive to changes in the control signal.

A possible danger of class balancing is over-accommodation. The actual class ratios should be investigated in practice. Also, when balancing is done too aggressively, it can make it very difficult for the user to generate brain activity that is extreme enough to trigger the intended action.

This method is best implemented in the control interface. This is functionally the most suitable place, and no semantic knowledge is required.

[4]This assumes the classifications are to some degree independent of each other; otherwise accumulating more predictions does not add new knowledge. This independence is, for example, affected by the overlap of sliding windows.

5. HOW TO CHOOSE

Which method is most suitable in a specific situation mainly depends on two things: (1) Location: what information you can access, and which modules you can modify; and (2) Effects: how to better meet the functional requirements of the application, as well as the user expectations. Table 1 gives an overview the different methods, where to apply them, and how they affect the control signal.

5.1 Location

As we have shown, there are two places to implement these methods after classification or regression: the control interface, and the application. The control interface provides discrete, hard class labels, or continuous values, being soft classification predictions or regression values. It can also maintain a history of these logical control inputs, and the semantic control outputs it has generated. The application has knowledge of its own state, and the semantic control inputs it has received. As both modules have knowledge of the semantic control signal, some methods can be implemented in either. In such a case it is often preferable to put the function in the control interface. Another reason to decide on a particular module is if the other module is simply not modifiable.

5.2 Effects

Each method has a number of effects, and side effects. When applying these methods in order to improve the level of control over the input, one has to take into account the requirements of the application and the expectations of the user.

Bitrates.

Common sacrifices to gain detection accuracy are response time (as the time from action to detection is increased) and bandwidth (as the total time for each detection is increased), both aspects of speed. Similarly, methods that increase robustness inherently decrease sensitivity. To obtain the high-

Method	Location	Effects
Multimodal fusion	CI, App	Higher accuracy, if the other inputs provide new, useful information
(Language) model	CI, App	Higher accuracy, if good model
Snapping	App	Higher efficiency; lower sensitivity
Hysteresis	CI, App	Higher efficiency; lower sensitivity
Macros	CI, App	Higher efficiency; more restrictive
Context-dependent response	App	Higher accuracy if that one input is well-recognized
Smoothing, averaging, dwell time	CI, App	Lower sensitivity; longer response time
Refractory period	App, CI	Lower FP, but possibly also less TP
Normalization, balancing	CI, App	Decreased bias; generalizability over users; adjusted sensitivity

Table 1: Post-processing method comparison. Location: CI = control interface, App = application. Preferred location listed first. FP = false positives (false alarms). Lower sensitivity (also lower FP) implies a debouncing effect and an increase in robustness.

est bitrate[5] [16], the trade-off between accuracy and time per detection needs to be optimized.

Related to bandwidth is the cost of different types of errors. In a first person shooter, if ammunition is abundant, it is best to shoot as often as possible, increasing the chance of hitting the target. False negatives, not shooting when the user tries to, are unwanted. On the other hand, if ammunition is scarce, it is costly to waste bullets, so it is better not to shoot. False positives, shooting when the user does not want to, are undesirable. Thus it is not only the recognition of the BCI that affects the throughput of information. The application also determines how costly it is to make an error and how easy it is to correct one. This provides another angle for improvement. This is also an important consideration in the case of passive interaction. If the system affects the background music, the cost is at worst some annoyance by the user. If the system adjusts the user interface (e.g. to the user's workload), it has to be carefully designed, as errors in detection may directly affect the usability.

Besides the fact that it can be better (or worse) to do nothing than to do the wrong thing, the user will not always be providing actionable input. Adding an idle state, and rejecting classifications with too low confidence levels, may help in increasing the bandwidth and having the interaction better match user expectations [18, 32].

Expectations.

The acceptance of BCI technology does not only depend on its functional properties, but also on how well it matches user expectations. As Jacob mentions "[The human-computer dialogue] should correspond to what the user thinks he or she is doing, rather than what his eye muscles are actually doing" [13]. This is also applicable to brain activity-based interaction. These expectations are highly dependent on the application. When controlling a race car in a racing game, the user will expect fast response times and high accuracies. The situation changes when the input is used to control a hamster. Perfect control may even be unwanted, as it is more interesting if the animal appears to have a will of its own [39]. To address the speed and accuracy issues of BCIs, perhaps controlling a snail is best.

To evaluate how well a particular BCI system as a whole meets expectations[6], the SUXES method is very suitable [37]; particularly the adjusted version for BCI by Gürkök *et al.* [9]. This method consists of two questionnaires, which contain both pragmatic (such as speed and accuracy) and hedonic items (such as naturalness and enjoyability). Each item is rated on a 7-point scale with opposite word pairs at each end (slow – fast). After an introduction to the application, the user indicates a zone of expectations in the first questionnaire. After using the application, the user marks the actual experience in second questionnaire. This makes it easy to compare experiences and expectations.

6. CONCLUSIONS

In a thorough survey of BCI signal processing algorithms of over 200 papers, Bashashati *et al.* observe that "30 BCI designs ... use post-processing algorithms to reduce the amount of error in the output of the BCI system" [3]. This means that, in 2007, for more than 85% of BCI systems, there could still a lot be gained in terms of performance. Although the numbers will have improved somewhat since then, this post-processing is still an under-discussed topic in the field, and deserves more attention.

We described a collection of methods that can be used to improve BCI recognition and sense of control. The methods described above are simple and easy to implement, but it is important to apply them in the right way. Detection accuracy is important, but often there are trade-offs to consider. The application provides another angle to improve the interaction, as its design affects the cost of errors, functional requirements on the interaction, and the user expectations.

Future research should investigate the effectiveness of the methods in their context of use, as well as the optimal settings for these methods to obtain the right balance between functionality and meeting the user's expectations for maximum acceptance.

7. ACKNOWLEDGMENTS

The authors gratefully acknowledge the support of the BrainGain Smart Mix Programme of the Netherlands Ministry of Economic Affairs, the Netherlands Ministry of Education, Culture and Science.

[5]Bitrate is also referred to as information transfer rate. For BCIs this is generally expressed in bits per minute.

[6]However, as Steve Jobs warned us: "People don't know what they want, until you show it to them" [21].

8. REFERENCES

[1] G. Abowd, A. Dey, P. Brown, N. Davies, M. Smith, and P. Steggles. Towards a better understanding of context and context-awareness. In *Handheld and Ubiquitous Computing*, pages 304–307. Springer, 1999.

[2] M. Baldauf, S. Dustdar, and F. Rosenberg. A survey on context-aware systems. *International Journal of Ad Hoc and Ubiquitous Computing*, 2(4):263–277, 2007.

[3] A. Bashashati, M. Fatourechi, R. Ward, and G. Birch. A survey of signal processing algorithms in brain–computer interfaces based on electrical brain signals. *Journal of Neural engineering*, 4:R32, 2007.

[4] B. Blankertz, M. Kawanabe, R. Tomioka, F. Hohlefeld, V. Nikulin, and K. Müller. Invariant common spatial patterns: Alleviating nonstationarities in brain-computer interfacing. *Advances in Neural Information Processing Systems*, 20, 2008.

[5] L. Deng and X. Huang. Challenges in adopting speech recognition. *Commun. ACM*, 47(1):69–75, Jan. 2004.

[6] G. Fabiani, D. McFarland, J. Wolpaw, and G. Pfurtscheller. Conversion of EEG activity into cursor movement by a brain-computer interface (BCI). *Neural Systems and Rehabilitation Engineering, IEEE Transactions on*, 12(3):331–338, 2004.

[7] E. Felton, N. Lewis, S. Wills, R. Radwin, and J. Williams. Neural signal based control of the Dasher writing system. In *Neural Engineering*, pages 366–370. IEEE, 2007.

[8] S. Goderis. *On the separation of user interface concerns: A Programmer's Perspective on the Modularisation of User Interface Code*. PhD thesis, 2008.

[9] H. Gürkök, G. Hakvoort, and M. Poel. Evaluating user experience with respect to user expectations in brain-computer interface games. In *Proceedings of the 5th International Brain-Computer Interface Conference, BCI 2011, Graz, Austria*, pages 348–351. Verlag der Technischen Universität Graz, 2011.

[10] H. Gürkök and A. Nijholt. Brain-computer interfaces for multimodal interaction: A survey and principles. *International Journal of Human-Computer Interaction*, 28(5):292–307, 2012.

[11] C. Holt. Forecasting seasonals and trends by exponentially weighted moving averages. *International Journal of Forecasting*, 20(1):5–10, 2004.

[12] Y. Huang and C. Suen. A method of combining multiple experts for the recognition of unconstrained handwritten numerals. *Pattern Analysis and Machine Intelligence, IEEE Transactions on*, 17(1):90–94, 1995.

[13] R. Jacob. Eye movement-based human-computer interaction techniques: Toward non-command interfaces. *Advances in human-computer interaction*, 4:151–190, 1993.

[14] R. Jacob and K. Karn. Eye tracking in human-computer interaction and usability research: Ready to deliver the promises. *Mind*, 2(3):4, 2003.

[15] S. Kleih, F. Nijboer, S. Halder, and A. Kübler. Motivation modulates the P300 amplitude during brain-computer interface use. *Clinical Neurophysiology*, 121(7):1023–1031, 2010.

[16] J. Kronegg, S. Voloshynovskiy, and T. Pun. Analysis of bit-rate definitions for brain-computer interfaces. In *HCI'05*, volume 12, page 18, 2005.

[17] L. Lam and S. Suen. Application of majority voting to pattern recognition: An analysis of its behavior and performance. *Systems, Man and Cybernetics, Part A, IEEE Trans.*, 27(5):553–568, 1997.

[18] S. Mason and G. Birch. A brain-controlled switch for asynchronous control applications. *Biomedical Engineering, IEEE Trans.*, 47(10):1297–1307, 2000.

[19] S. Mason and G. Birch. A general framework for brain-computer interface design. *Neural Systems and Rehabilitation Engineering, IEEE Transactions on*, 11(1):70–85, 2003.

[20] C. Mühl, H. Gürkök, D. Plass-Oude Bos, M. Thurlings, L. Scherffig, M. Duvinage, A. Elbakyan, S. Kang, M. Poel, and D. Heylen. Bacteria hunt. *Journal on Multimodal User Interfaces*, 4(1):11–25, 2010.

[21] S. Murugesan. What we can learn from steve jobs. *IT Professional*, 13(6):6–8, 2011.

[22] L. Nigay and J. Coutaz. A design space for multimodal systems: concurrent processing and data fusion. In *Proceedings of the INTERACT '93 and CHI '93 conference on Human factors in computing systems*, pages 172–178, New York, NY, USA, 1993. ACM.

[23] R. Nuray and F. Can. Automatic ranking of information retrieval systems using data fusion. *Information Processing and Management*, 42(3):595 – 614, 2006.

[24] S. Oviatt. Multimodal interfaces. In *The human-computer interaction handbook: fundamentals, evolving technologies and emerging applications*, pages 413–428. Lawrance Erlbaum Associates, New York, NY, USA, 2nd edition, 2008.

[25] R. Panicker, S. Puthusserypady, and Y. Sun. An asynchronous P300 BCI with SSVEP-based control state detection. *Biomedical Engineering, IEEE Transactions on*, 58(6):1781 –1788, 2011.

[26] S. Perdikis, H. Bayati, R. Leeb, and J. d. R. Millán. Evidence accumulation in asynchronous BCI. *IJ of Bioelectromagnetism*, 13(3):131–132, 2011.

[27] G. Pfurtscheller, B. Z. Allison, C. Brunner, G. Bauernfeind, T. Solis-Escalante, R. Scherer, T. O. Zander, G. Mueller-Putz, C. Neuper, and N. Birbaumer. The hybrid BCI. *Frontiers in Neuroprosthetics*, 4:30, 2010.

[28] G. Pfurtscheller, G. Müller, J. Pfurtscheller, H. Gerner, and R. Rupp. Thought-control of functional electrical stimulation to restore hand grasp in a patient with tetraplegia. *Neuroscience letters*, 351(1):33–36, 2003.

[29] D. Plass-Oude Bos, M. Poel, and A. Nijholt. A study in user-centered design and evaluation of mental tasks for BCI. *Advances in Multimedia Modeling*, pages 122–134, 2011.

[30] D. Plass-Oude Bos, B. Reuderink, B. L. A. van de Laar, H. Gürkök, C. Mühl, M. Poel, D. K. J. Heylen, and A. Nijholt. Human-computer interaction for BCI games: Usability and user experience. In *CYBERWORLDS*, pages 277–281. IEEE, 2010.

[31] B. Reuderink. *Robust brain-computer interfaces*. PhD thesis, Enschede, the Netherlands, October 2011.

[32] S. Roberts and W. Penny. Real-time brain-computer interfacing: A preliminary study using bayesian learning. *Medical and Biological Engineering and computing*, 38(1):56–61, 2000.

[33] A. Royer and B. He. Goal selection versus process control in a brain-computer interface based on sensorimotor rhythms. *Journal of neural engineering*, 6:016005, 2009.

[34] R. Scherer, M. Proll, B. Allison, and G. Muller-Putz. New input modalities for modern game design and virtual embodiment. In *Virtual Reality Workshops (VR), 2012 IEEE*, pages 163 –164, March 2012.

[35] C. Shannon. The redundancy of english. In *Cybernetics; Transactions of the 7th Conference, New York: Josiah Macy, Jr. Foundation*, pages 248–272. Diaphanes Verlag Berlin/Zurich, 1950. Reprinted 2003.

[36] G. Townsend, B. Graimann, and G. Pfurtscheller. Continuous EEG classification during motor imagery-simulation of an asynchronous BCI. *Neural Systems and Rehabilitation Engineering, IEEE Transactions on*, 12(2):258–265, 2004.

[37] M. Turunen, J. Hakulinen, A. Melto, T. Heimonen, T. Laivo, and J. Hella. SUXES – user experience evaluation method for spoken and multimodal interaction. In *INTERSPEECH*, 2009.

[38] B. van de Laar, H. Gürkök, D. Plass-Oude Bos, M. Poel, and A. Nijholt. BCI as an additional control in an immersive game; a within-subjects comparison. 2012. In submission.

[39] B. van de Laar, D. Plass-Oude Bos, B. Reuderink, M. Poel, and A. Nijholt. How much control is enough? optimizing fun with unreliable input, 2011. CTIT technical report series, TR-CTIT-11-25.

[40] M. van Gerven, J. Farquhar, R. Schaefer, R. Vlek, J. Geuze, A. Nijholt, N. Ramsey, P. Haselager, L. Vuurpijl, S. Gielen, and P. Desain. The brain–computer interface cycle. *Journal of Neural Engineering*, 6(4), 2009.

[41] J. Williamson, R. Murray-Smith, B. Blankertz, M. Krauledat, and K. Müller. Designing for uncertain, asymmetric control: interaction design for brain–computer interfaces. *International Journal of Human-Computer Studies*, 67(10):827–841, 2009.

[42] J. Wolpaw. Brain–computer interfaces as new brain output pathways. *The Journal of Physiology*, 579(3):613–619, 2007.

Emotion-based EEG Control in Music Performance

Rafael Ramirez
Department of Information and Communication Technologies
Universitat Pompeu Fabra
Roc Boronat 138, 08018 Barcelona, Spain
rafael.ramirez@upf.edu

Zacharias Vamvakousis
Department of Information and Communication Technologies
Universitat Pompeu Fabra
Roc Boronat 138, 08018 Barcelona, Spain
zacharias.vamvakousis@upf.edu

Sergio Giraldo
Department of Information and Communication Technologies
Universitat Pompeu Fabra
Roc Boronat 138, 08018 Barcelona, Spain
sergio.giraldo@upf.edu

ABSTRACT

Recently, the study of emotions in human-computer interaction has increased in an attempt to address new user needs. At the same time, current technology allows to record brain activity in real-time and discover patterns to relate it to emotional states. In this paper we present an approach to use brain computer interfaces (BCI) as a sensor to monitor the emotive state of the user and use this information in the context of an interactive music performance system. In particular, we apply machine learning techniques to detect emotion from the user's electroencephalograph (EEG) and use this information to allow a user to interact in real-time with the system during a music performance.

Categories and Subject Descriptors

J.5 [**Computer Applications**]: Arts and Humanities; H.5.2 [**Information Systems**]: User Interfaces

Keywords

Interactive Systems, Emotion, EEG, Music

1. INTRODUCTION

The role of emotions in computer systems has greatly increased in recent years. This is motivated by the need to create computer applications capable of detecting the emotional state of users [16] and use this information to better respond to the user needs. Observing every day interaction among humans, researchers investigating the interaction of users' emotions in computer applications have explored detecting emotions from facial and voice information [17]. However, it has also been noticed that emotions are by no means not always manifested as facial expressions and can be detected from voice information. Hence, other approaches to detect emotion information have been proposed which focus on different physiological data such as heart rate, skin conductance, and pupil dilation [17, 15]. More recently, the use of electroencephalograms (EEGs) for detecting emotions has produced the still relatively new field of research in affective brain-computer interaction [1, 2]. There have been several approaches to EEG-based emotion detection, but the problem of detecting emotion using EEGs is a complex one and there is still little consensus about definite solutions.

In this paper we present an approach to use brain computer interfaces (BCI) as a sensor to monitor the emotive state of the user and use this information in the context of an interactive music performance system. We perform emotion detection from electroencephalogram signals by filtering and processing the signal in order to extract emotion-related features and by applying machine learning techniques to classify emotional states into high/low arousal and positive/negative valence. Contrasting other approaches to emotion detection we do not rely in subject self-reported emotional states during stimuli presentation. Instead, we use a library of emotion-annotated sounds publicly available for emotional research. Once the emotional state of the user is determined, he/she can use this information to interact in real-time with the system during a music performance.

The rest of the paper is organized as follows: Section 2 presents background to this research. In Section 3 we describe how we detect emotion from EEG signals. Section 4 describes our EEG-based music interactive system, while Section 5 presents some conclusions and future research.

ICMI'12, October 22–26, 2012, Santa Monica, California, USA.

2. BACKGROUND

The electrodes of an electroencephalogram headset measure electrical activity corresponding to the field potentials resulting from the combined activity of many individual neuronal cells in the brain cortex. However, the tissue and skull between the electrodes and the neurons introduces noise and reduce the intensity of the recorded signals. In despite of this, EEG measurements are still useful and provide important insight into the electrical activity of the cortex.

The frequency of electroencephalogram signals ranges from

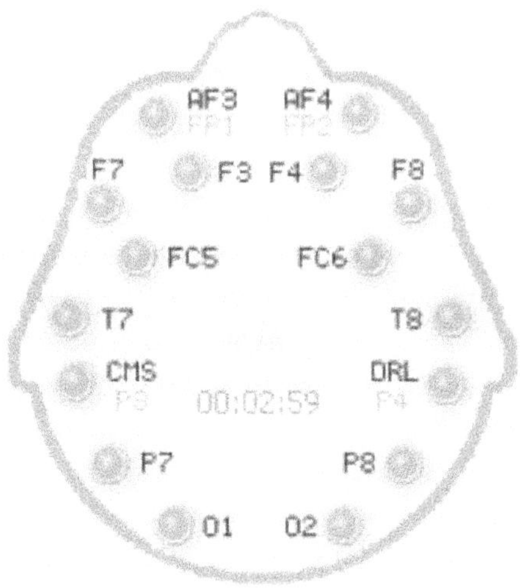

Figure 1: Electrode positioning for the Emotiv Epoc EEG device

1 to 80Hz, with amplitudes of 10 to 100 microvolts [8]. Signal frequencies have been divided into different bands, since specific frequency waves are normally more prominent in particular states of mind. The two most important frequency waves are the alpha waves (8-12Hz) and the beta waves (12-30Hz). Alpha waves predominantly originate during wakeful relaxation mental states, and are most visible over the parietal and occipital lobes. Intense alpha wave activity have also been correlated to brain inactivation. Beta wave activity, on the other hand, is related to an active state of mind, most prominent in the frontal cortex during intense focused mental activity [8].

3. EMOTION DETECTION

3.1 Feature Extraction

Given the nature of this work, the EEG frequency bands of most interest are the alpha (8-12Hz) and beta (12-30Hz). These bands are particularly interesting in emotion research for both valence and arousal [12]. The presence of EOG artifacts (eye movement/blinking) is most dominant below 4Hz, ECG (heart) artifacts around 1.2Hz, and EMG (muscle) artifacts above 30Hz. Non physiological artifacts caused by power lines are normally present above 50Hz [5, 4].

Thus, fortunately by limiting our study to alpha and beta frequencies substantially reduces much of the noise present in EEG signals. We apply bandpass filtering for extracting alpha and beta frequency bands. Using Fourier frequency analysis, the original signal is split up in frequencies in order to remove specific frequencies, before transforming back the signal with only the frequencies of interest. For this research, we apply the bandpass filter implementation provided by the OpenVibe software [14].

From the EEG signal of a person, we determine the level of arousal, i.e. how relaxed or excited the person is, by computing the ratio of the beta and alpha brainwaves as recorded by the EEG. We measure the EEG signal in four locations (i.e. electrodes) in the prefrontal cortex: AF3, AF4, F3 and F4 (see Figure 1). In this study, we used the Emotiv Epoc headset.

As mentioned before, beta waves are associated with an alert or excited state of mind, whereas alpha waves are more dominant in a relaxed state. Alpha activity has also been associated to brain inactivation. Thus, the beta/alpha ratio is a reasonable indicator of the arousal state of a person.

In order to compute the valence level, i.e. negative or positive state of mind, we compare the activation levels of the two cortical hemispheres. This is motivated by psychophysiological research which has shown the importance of the difference in activation between the cortical hemispheres. Left frontal inactivation is an indicator of a withdrawal response, which is often linked to a negative emotion. On the other hand, right frontal inactivation may be associated to an approach response, or positive emotion. An increase in alpha activity together with a decrease in beta waves may be associated with cortical inactivation [12]. F3 and F4 are the most used positions for looking at this alpha activity, as they are located in the prefrontal lobe which plays a crucial role in emotion regulation and conscious experience.

In general, affective valence is related to motivational direction. Therefore, comparing hemispherical activation seems to be a reasonable method to detect valence. Thus, we estimate the valence value in a person by computing and comparing the alpha power a and beta power b in channels F3 and F4. Specifically,

$$valence = a_{F4}/b_{F4} - a_{F3}/b_{F3}.$$

3.2 Learning Task

In this section we describe how we use the descriptors described in the previous section in order to train and evaluate classifiers for the task of detecting the emotional state of mind of a person given the person's observed EEG data. We approach this problem as a two 2-class classification problem. In particular, we apply machine learning techniques to classify high/low arousal and positive/negative valence emotional states. The arousal/valence plane, often used to in emotional research, is a 2D continuous space, with two axes: arousal and valence. Each point, then, denotes a different emotional state. Figure 2 shows the arousal/valence plane with example emotions.

By approaching emotion detection as a high/low arousal and positive/negative valence classification problem we are discretizing the emotion plane into four quadrants: high-arousal/postive-valence, high-arousal/negative-valence, low-arousal/positive-valence, and low-arousal/negative-valence. This is, we are interested in inducing two classifiers, one for detecting high or low arousal, and another for detecting positive or negative valence. In the case of arousal we are interested in obtaining a classifier of the form:

$$ArousalClassifier(EEGdata([t, t+c])) \rightarrow \{high, low\}$$

while in the case of valence we are interested in obtaining a classifier of the form:

$$ValClassifier(EEGdata([t, t+c])) \rightarrow \{positive, negative\}$$

where $EEGdata([t, t+c])$ is the EEG data observed at time interval $[t, t+c]$ and $\{high, low\}$ and $\{positive, negative\}$ are the sets of emotional states to be discriminated. The results reported in this paper are obtained with c=1s and

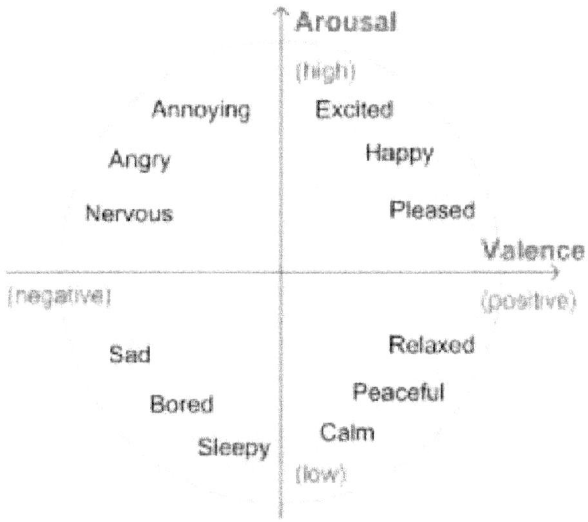

Figure 2: Emotional states and their positions in the valence/arousal plane.

with increments of t of 0.0625s. For each subject in the EEG data sets we train a separate classifier.

3.3 Algorithm

In order to train the described classifiers we apply Support Vector Machines (SVM) [3]. We provide the algorithm with examples of EEG segments together with the corresponding emotion state. The algorithm learns a classifier for predicting the emotion state for each new EEG segment. SVM is one of the most popular supervised learning algorithms for solving classification problems. The basic idea in SVM is to project input data onto a higher dimensional feature space via a kernel transfer function, which is easier to be separated than that in the original feature space. Depending on input data, the iterative learning process of SVM would eventually converge into optimal hyperplanes with maximal margins between each class. These hyperplanes would be the decision boundaries for distinguishing different data clusters. Here, we use linear and radial basis function (RBF) kernel to map data onto a higher dimension space. The results reported are obtained using the SVM implementations in the OpenVibe software [14].

We evaluated each induced classifier by performing 10-fold cross validation in which 10% of the training set is held out in turn as test data while the remaining 90% is used as training data. When performing the 10-fold cross validation, we leave out the same number of examples per class. In the data sets, the number of examples is the same for each class considered, thus by leaving out the same number of examples per class we maintain a balanced training set.

Given that we are dealing with 2-class classification tasks and that the number of instances in each class is the same, the expected classification accuracy of the default classifier (one which chooses the most common class) is 50% (measured in correctly classified instances percentage). For the high-versus-low arousal, and the positive-versus-negative valence classifiers the average accuracies over all participants

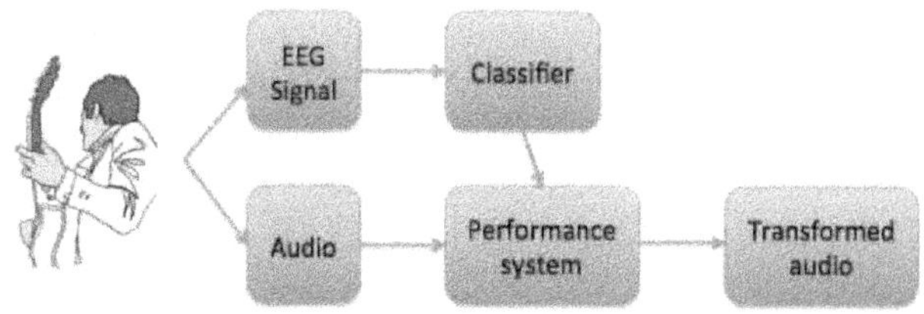

Figure 3: Interactive performance system overview.

(there were 6 participants, 3 male) obtained with SVM were 77.82%, and 80.11%, respectively. For these classifiers the accuracies of the best participant were 83,35%, and 86.33%, respectively.

4. EEG-BASED HUMAN-COMPUTER MUSIC INTERACTION

Once we have trained high-versus-low arousal, and the positive-versus-negative valence classifiers, given a user's EEG activation, we use the classifier predictions to trigger in real-time actions during a music performance. We collect both the user's music output and EEG signal and use the later to apply music transformations to the music output. Figure 3 illustrates the general structure of the system. During music performance, the system obtains both audio and EEG activation from the user. The EEG signal is processed in order to extract the previously described emotion-related features and then fed into the previously trained classifier. The classifier outputs a prediction for arousal (high or low), and for valence (positive or negative). The system then takes into account the classifier predictions to transform the user's audio accordingly.

4.1 Case study: Guitar audio transformation

We have implemented a performance system as described above for guitar performances. The implementation is based on the open source software OpenVibe [14] and Pure Data. Figure 4 illustrates the architecture of the implemented system. We acquire the data stream from the EEG device by

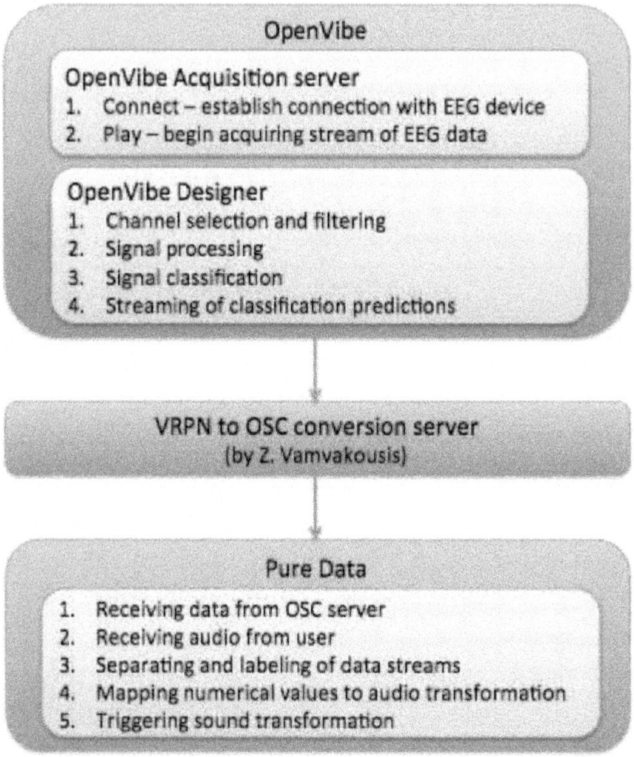

Figure 4: Interactive performance system implementation.

executing the OpenVibe acquisition server, and process the signal using the graphical programming language provided by the OpenVibe designer. First, we select the channels of interest and filter the signal to eliminate artifacts. Once this is done, we compute the emotion-related features described in Section 3 and classify the signal using the previously trained classifiers (also described in Section 3). We then execute a VRPN to OSC conversion server we have implemented to allow the communication of OpenVibe and Pure Data. The rest of the processing is done by Pure Data which receives both the data from the OSC server and the performed audio from the user, separates and labels the two data streams and triggers the sound transformation of the audio according to the OSC data.

We have implemented several audio transformations based on the system emotion predictions and organized a concert involving two traditional music instruments (guitar and flute) and one electronic music instrument (the EyeHarp).We experimented with different audio transformations in one-guitar and two-guitars pieces. For instance, we applied reverberation to to low arousal predictions, and distortion to negative valence predictions. In the two-guitar ensemble, arousal predictions were taken into account to modify the volume of the other guitarist audio, favoring the most aroused performer and thus enhancing his/her performance.

5. CONCLUSIONS

We have presented an approach to use brain computer interfaces (BCI) as a sensor to monitor the emotive state of the user and use this information in the context of an interactive music performance system. We applied machine learning techniques, in particular support vector machines to detect emotion from the user's electroencephalograph (EEG) and use this information to allow a user to interact in real-time with the system during a music performance. We trained classifiers capable of discriminating between high-versus-low arousal and positive-versus-negative valence. We use the trained classifiers' predictions to transform in real-time the performed audio produced by the user.

6. ACKNOWLEDGMENTS

This work is supported by the Spanish TIN project DRIMS (TIN2009-14274-C02-01).

7. REFERENCES

[1] G. Chanel, J. Kronegg, D. Grandjean, and T. Pun. Emotion assessment: Arousal evaluation using eegs and peripheral physiological signals. In MRCS, pages 530-537, 2006.

[2] A. Choppin. Eeg-based human interface for disabled individuals: Emotion expression with neural networks. MasterÕs thesis, Tokyo Institute of Technology, Yokohama, Japan, 2000.

[3] Cristianini N., Shawe-Taylor J. (2000). An Introduction to Support Vector Machines, Cambridge University Press

[4] K. Coburn and M. Moreno. Facts and artifacts in brain electrical activity mapping. Brain Topography, 1(1):37-45, 1988.

[5] M. Fatourechi, A. Bashashati, R. K. Ward, and G. E. Birch. EMG and EOG artifacts in brain computer

interface systems: A survey. Clininical Neurophysiology, (118):480-494, 2007.

[6] Emotiv Systems Inc. Researchers, http://www.emotiv.com/researchers/

[7] E. Harmon-Jones. Clarifying the emotive functions of asymmetrical frontal cortical activity. Psychophysiology, 40(6):838-848, 2003.

[8] E. R. Kandel, J. H. Schwartz, and T. M. Jessell. Principles of Neural Science. Mc Graw Hill, 2000.

[9] Yuan-Pin Lin, Chi-Hong Wang, Tzyy-Ping Jung, Tien-Lin Wu, Shyh-Kang Jeng, Jeng-Ren Duann, and Jyh-Horng Chen (2010). EEG-Based Emotion Recognition in Music Listening, IEEE Transactions on Biomedical Engineering, 57(7).

[10] Mika, S. et al. (1999). "Fisher Discriminant Analysis with Kernels". IEEE Conference on Neural Networks for Signal Processing IX: 41-48.

[11] Ernst Niedermeyer, Fernando Lopes da Silva, Electroencephalography, Basic Principles, Clinical Applications, and Related Fields, page 140, Lippincott Williams & Wilkins, 2004.

[12] C. P. Niemic. Studies of emotion: A theoretical and empirical review of psychophysiological studies of emotion. Journal of Undergraduate Research, 1:15-18, 2002.

[13] Danny Oude Bos, EEG-based Emotion Recognition: The Influence of Visual and Auditory Stimuli,

[14] OpenVibe: An Open-Source Software Platform to Design, Test, and Use Brain-Computer Interfaces in Real and Virtual Environments, MIT Press Journal "Presence," February 2010, Vol. 19, No. 1, pp.35-53

[15] T. Partala, M. Jokiniemi, and V. Surakka. Pupillary responses to emotionally provocative stimuli. In ETRA Õ00: Proceedings of the 2000 Symposium on Eye Tracking Research & Applications, pages 123-129, New York, NY, USA, 2000. ACM Press.

[16] R. W. Picard and J. Klein. Toward computers that recognize and respond to user emotion: Theoretical and practical implications. Interacting with Computers, 14(2):141-169, 2002.

[17] K. Takahashi. Remarks on emotion recognition from bio-potential signals. 2nd International Conference on Autonomous Robots and Agents, pages 186-191, 2004.

Electroencephalographic Detection of Visual Saliency of Motion towards a Practical Brain-Computer Interface for Video Analysis*

Matthew Weiden
mrweiden@hrl.com

Deepak Khosla
dkhosla@hrl.com

Matthew Keegan
mskeegan@hrl.com

HRL Laboratories LLC
3011 Malibu Canyon Rd
Malibu, CA 90265-4797

ABSTRACT

Though Electroencephalography (EEG)-based brain-computer interfaces (BCI) have come to outperform pure computer vision algorithms on difficult image triage tasks, none of these BCIs have leveraged the effects of motion on the human visual attention system. Here we consider the advantages of leveraging the effects of motion by testing a new method for EEG-based target detection using Rapid Serial Visual Presentation (RSVP) of short moving image clips. Comparatively, canonical methods present the operator with still images only. Our experiments show that presenting moving images in RSVP instead of still images significantly increases performance ($p < 0.0005$). In addition, we investigate the effect of increasing target load in RSVP of moving image clips and find some support for the hypothesis that detection will decrease as target load is increased.

Categories and Subject Descriptors

I.2.10 [**Artificial Intelligence**]: Vision and Scene Understanding—*Motion, Perceptual Reasoning, Video Analysis*; J.4 [**Social and Behavioral Sciences**]: [Psychology]

Keywords

Electroencephalography, Brain-Computer Interface, Computer Vision, Image/Video Classification & Triage

1. INTRODUCTION

The integration of BCI technology and the "Rapid Serial Visual Presentation" (RSVP) protocol has proven a useful tool for high-throughput binary classification of images [7]. A human observer views small images, termed 'chips', at high frame rate while the electrical activity of their brain is measured with an electroencephalograph (EEG). Target stimuli generally elicit a P300, a preconscious evoked potential related to the reorientation of attention, making the P300 a reliable indicator of the presence of target stimuli which can be leveraged in image classification.

Leveraging the P300 has three main advantages: reliability, adaptability, and speed. First, with a characteristic waveform, the P300 can be more reliable than conscious observer responses, such as button presses, which often have inconsistent reaction times and are prone to error [4, 7]. Second, though early visual processing associated with the P300 is preconscious, humans can adapt the selectivity of their visual attention to enhance the saliency of target stimuli through selective attention: consciously attending locations where targets appear or their attributes such as motion and orientation can enhance the responses of early visual pathways to target stimuli [8]. Third, detection of the P300 is faster than obtaining conscious observer responses. Even at the high frame rates as high as 10 or 20 Hz, the lower levels of the human visual system perform well in differentiating between target and non-target images, and are far more efficient than conscious inspection [7].

By leveraging these advantages researchers have proven the utility of BCI-enabled RSVP. Huang et. al. [2011] demonstrated the speed of RSVP can be used in efficient image search tasks. Khosla et. al. [2010] fused BCI-enabled RSVP with computer vision algorithms in a scene understanding system capable of searching high resolution, wide field of view video in real-time. Both of these applications make possible the completion of tasks too voluminous for humans alone and too nuanced for computers alone.

BCIs based on P300 differ from the traditional conception of BCIs precisely because the P300 response is preconscious, here the BCI is used more as an intelligent sensor than as conscious input control.

In designing BCIs of this type, there are two challenges discussed here. The first is the problem of representation: what ways is it best to feed information we obtain from the use of BCIs back to the user? The second is that of interpretation: how do we disentangle noisy, high-dimensional BCI data and extract meaningful information? In this work we show that in specific situations these problems are complementary: that by using experimental data from BCI use we can improve our selection of kinds of stimuli and methods of stimuli presentation that will evoke more informative BCI data from the user.

*Approved for Public Release, Distribution Unlimited.

ICMI'12, October 22–26, 2012, Santa Monica, California, USA.

Optimizing BCI-enabled RSVP in these ways is important in applications such as surveillance and scene understanding where high risk is often associated with misclassifying targets and targets can be presented to the system in unpredictable bursts. Providing operator with the ideal type of stimuli will evoke maximally informative BCI data, increasing probability of target detection for consciously perceived targets. Throttling the presentation rate of likely targets would control for attentional blink, reducing number of targets not consciously perceived.

Accordingly, here we demonstrate that selecting moving image stimuli over static image stimuli will evoke more informative BCI data in BCI-enabled RSVP. Additionally, we investigate the affects of target presentation rate in hopes of optimizing stimuli presentation in this paradigm.

1.1 Goals of this work

Fully understanding behavioral variables in BCI-enabled RSVP will help BCI engineers better address the representation and interpretation problems. Accordingly, the goals of this work are to investigate the roles of two variables salient to behavior: motion in stimuli and the presentation rate of salient information on target detection.

First we investigate the effects of motion stimuli on target detection in BCI-enabled RSVP through the use of moving image clips rather than the canonical use of still images. There are several reasons to expect increased detection performance with moving images. Through introspection alone we seem to know that informative motion in objects tends to capture our attention. Several works support this observation. Abrams and Christ [2003] found that targets are most easily detected when the appearance of the target is paired with motion onset. In a similar study Franconeri and Simons [2003] found that disocclusion captures attention. Though the authors' detailed explanations of the underlying mental heuristics may contrast, both suggest that the sudden appearance of a moving target would capture attention. Further, other results suggest that motion may, in fact, be a stronger attractor of attention that other visual features [6].

Our second investigation concerns the effects on RSVP performance as the density of targets in the video condition RSVP sequences increases. It is a well-known phenomenon that P300 responses can be suppressed in the RSVP task if the latency between two targets is less than half a second [5], a phenomenon known as 'attentional blink'. Thus targets in stimulus presentations with a high target density can be difficult to detect. Moreover, the amplitude of the P300 response is heavily dependent on the probability of the target-to-target interval [4]. For this reason many visual-based studies have concentrated on single-target conditions. However, in many applications this is an impractical assumption.

Each of the discussed goals will be explicated through behavioral experiments: First, Experiment A tests for the hypothesized performance gains in RSVP using moving images. Second, Experiment B tests for the hypothesized RSVP performance decrement given higher target densities.

2. EXPERIMENT A: STILL IMAGE VERSUS VIDEO SEQUENCES

In this experiment the EEG signal of participants was recorded while they viewed a number of RSVP sequences. In each sequence the participant was asked to look for vehicles or humans in the sequences of videos or images and to classify them by pressing a button each time they detected a target.

The independent variable in Experiment A varied the type of RSVP sequence. Sequences were comprised of either static images or video clips.

The dependent measure is the Receiver Operating Characteristic Area Under the Curve (Az). This specifies the probability that a true positive, or target stimulus, will be given a higher probability of being a positive than a true negative, non-target stimulus.

2.1 Participants

Seven male and one female participants from HRL Laboratories participated in Experiment A. All had normal to corrected-to-normal vision and reported no history of neurological problems. Informed consent was obtained from all participants in accordance with the guidelines and approval of the DARPA Institutional Review Board.

2.2 Materials

The video and image sequences were created manually using recorded data from military test sites provided by DARPA from the Cognitive Technology Threat Warning System (CT2WS) program (see acknowledgements). The stimuli for both experiments were displayed 512-by-512 pixels against a 50% gray background on a 30" LCD monitor. Participants were positioned approximately 25" away from the display monitor in a quiet room and closely surrounded by a drape to limit external distractions.

EEG data was collected using a 20-channel Advanced Brain Monitoring (ABM) X24 SDK EEG headset connected to an electrode strip with nodes positioned using the international 10-20 system. EEG data were recorded at a sampling frequency of 256 Hz. Timing information was inserted using ABM's External Sync Unit (ESU).

The experimental software used to display sequences and record EEG data was programmed at HRL using C++, OpenCV, and ABM's software SDK. An XBox controller (Microsoft, Redmond WA) was integrated into this software and used to collect participant manual feedback.

2.3 Stimuli

The stimuli used in this experiment were sequences of video clips or static image clips drawn from the DARPA dataset. The component images or video clips in each sequence contained scenes of empty desert, vehicles, or people walking. Vehicles and people walking were designated targets, all other content was considered non-target. The static images consisted of single frames taken from each video clip so that clip quality would not affect the experimental results. Video frames were displayed at 21.4 frames per second and each video clip consisted of 5 frames. Static images were displayed at 4.28 fps. Consequently each clip was displayed for approximately 234ms.

In Experiment A, each participant was shown four sequences, a training sequence and testing sequence for each condition. Each sequence is partitioned into blocks each of which consists of 50 stimuli components (either video clips or static image clips). Each block takes a little less than 12 seconds to display. The training sequences consist of 50 blocks of stimuli and the testing sequences consist of 25 blocks. For the video/static RSVP performance experiment, each block is comprised of one target stimulus and 49 non-target stimuli in each, thus preventing the effects of attentional blink. In addition, the position of the target clip was no less than 10 clips from the beginning or end of each block preventing suppression of the P300 signature caused by novelty effects at the beginning or end of a block. The order of the blocks within each sequence was randomized and the order of presentation of the conditions was varied between participants to control for ordering effects.

2.4 Procedure

First the ABM headset was set up run through an impedance check. The participants were instructed to relax and discouraged from blinking, making sudden movements, and clenching their jaws while viewing the sequences. A red dot was displayed between each block at which point participants were instructed to take breaks if necessary or indicate they were ready to see the next sequence by pressing a button on the XBox controller.

Participants were exposed to 75 sequences total for each sequence type condition. The recorded EEG data from the first 50 sequences were used to train an EEG classifier. The remaining 25 sequences were used to test the classifier. The order of the sequences was counterbalanced between-participants.

Once the data was collected, each channel was centered to have a mean of zero and filtered using a bandpass filter between 0.5 and 100 Hz (elliptic filter) and a 60 Hz notch filter. Support Vector Machine (SVM) classifiers were then applied to the data using MatLab (MathWorks, Natick MA) and LIBSVM [2] software in order to estimate true classifications for target and non-target data.

2.5 Results

As expected, targets were more reliably detected in the video sequence than in the still image sequence. The results of Experiment A are detailed in Table 1 and Figure 1.

The classifier can be trained with the target button responses included or without. Without the button response channel we can see how the classifier performs with the EEG data in isolation. Processing the data using a one-way Analysis of Variance (ANOVA), the separation between the still image and video sequence conditions proves highly significant $F(1,7) = 71.68, p \ll 0.05, \eta^2 = 0.84$. Processing the data with the button response channel yields very similar results: $F(1,7) = 73.73, p \ll 0.05, \eta^2 = 0.84$.

Note that neural correlates of the action of pressing the button will still be present in the EEG data even when the button response channel is not included. Based on prior experience, this neural correlate artifact should not make a substantive change in the results, however. In either case the Az of the still image sequence condition is decidedly lower than that of the video image sequence condition. Participants' performance based on their button responses largely correlated with the results of the analysis of the EEG data. In the video condition, participants showed a high probability of detection, 97%, and low number of false positives, 3 occurrences on average. Comparatively, for the static image condition the average probability of detection dropped precipitously to 42% and the average number of false positives increased to 12 in the still image sequence condition. The results were, again, highly significant ($p \ll 0.05$).

Subject	S1	V1	V3	V5	V7
1	0.55	0.89	0.84	0.78	0.84
2	0.5	0.92	0.83	0.9	0.88
3	0.63	0.97	0.72	0.58	0.55
4	0.6	0.96	0.82	0.72	0.74
5	0.68	0.92	0.82	0.82	0.73
6	0.64	1	0.94	0.94	0.91
7	0.78	0.97	-	-	-
8	0.75	0.95	0.91	0.86	0.84
Mean	0.64	0.95	0.84	0.8	0.78
St. Dev.	0.1	0.04	0.07	0.12	0.12

Table 1: Az for each participant in each condition. Results for Experiment A conditions are labeled S1 and V1 for the static images one target and video one target conditions respectively. Experiment B similarly labeled V3, V5, and V7 for the video three target, video five target, and video seven target conditions respectively.

3. EXPERIMENT B: TARGET LOAD

This experiment differs from the first experiment in that the number of targets per sequence was varied instead of the sequence type. Three target load conditions were tested, with three, five, and seven targets in each video sequence respectively. The single-target classifier from the first experiment was used to assess performance of each multi-target condition. As in the first experiment, the dependent measure was Az.

3.1 Participants

Seven of the eight participants from Experiment A participated in Experiment B. Consequently, the same participant-related precautions taken in Experiment A applied to Experiment B.

3.2 Materials

The materials used in Experiment B were the same as those used in Experiment A.

3.3 Stimuli

All sequences used in Experiment B were comprised of video clips drawn from the same source as Experiment A, but the number of target and non-target stimuli per block was altered according to the target load condition. More specifically, in addition to the single-target training sequences of the first experiment, three, five and seven target sequences were used. These were used as testing data.

3.4 Procedure

The procedure used in Experiment B was identical to that used in Experiment A with the exception of the changes in testing conditions.

The training sessions remained the same with 50 one-target blocks. The testing session was organized with 25 sequences for each of the three target load conditions. The order of the blocks in the training and each test condition were randomly selected and no attempt was made to change the distribution of target clips within RSVP sequences. The order in which the sequences were displayed was counterbalanced between participants.

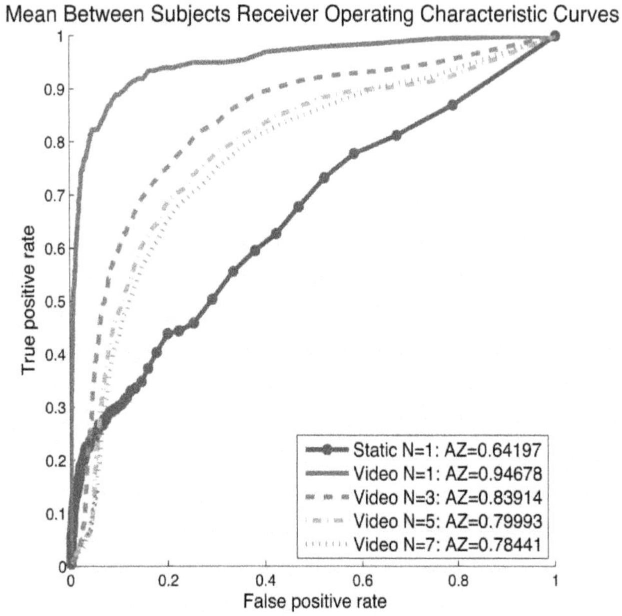

Figure 1: The mean of participants' ROC curves from conditions in both Experiment A and Experiment B are shown above. Though the difference between conditions in Experiment B only suggested significance, comparison to Experiment A conditions is revealing of performance decrements with increased target density in RSVP sequences.

3.5 Results

As the number of targets in each sequence increased Az consistently decreased and the number of false positives in the button responses consistently increased. In a three group one-way ANOVA no group was significantly different than any of the others $F(2,6) = 0.45, p < 0.65, \eta^2 = 0.05$. Trends towards decreasing Az and increasing false positives were observed as shown in Figure 1. The results of Experiment B are detailed in Table 1 and Figure 1.

Participants' button responses again reflected these findings. There were no significant differences between any of the groups $F(1,6) = 1, p = 0.39, \eta^2 = 0.10$. Participants consistently showed high Az for all conditions–$Az = 0.98$ on average with standard deviation 0.018.

Inspection of the mean d' values for each condition make increased target load a less likely cause of the decreasing trend in Az in Experiment B, however. As shown in Table 1, d' as target load was increased from three to five targets d' increased slightly, only decreasing by a small amount once the target load reached seven.

4. DISCUSSION

Our hypothesis for Experiment A was confirmed, the addition of motion to visual stimuli significantly boosts Az in our RSVP classifier's detection of targets. This improvement was directly reflected by participants' subjective judgments indicated by their responses to the stimuli via button presses. These results agree with psychological research on the importance of motion onset or object disocclusion found in visual attention literature [6, 8, 1, 3]. This result clearly underlines the significance of motion-based salience to RSVP performance. Thus by leveraging this phenomenon, we can improve the detection of oddball stimuli in electroencephalographic data.

Condition	S1	V1	V3	V5	V7
d'	1.78	2.45	1.43	1.45	1.34

Table 2: d' scores for the data between subjects. From Experiment A d' reflects the large advantage of video over static stimuli. The lack of significance in the Experiment B ANOVA is mirrored in the flat d' measurements across conditions. Further, the lack of a downward trend as the targets increase may indicate the the performance loss reported in Az measurements may be due to the relative proportions of target and non-target test data.

The results of Experiment B are not concrete but are still potentially informative. A decline in performance was observed as target load was increased but not enough to demonstrate statistical significance among all cases. While the proper experimental controls are not in place to make a concrete comparison between data from Experiment A to Experiment B, it is possible to form hypotheses for future work based on such a comparison. Notably, if we include the single-target video sequence data from Experiment A, we do observe significant differences between the conditions. In a four group one-way ANOVA with the four target load conditions excluding button responses from the classifier, we observe a significant difference $F(3,6) = 4.01$, $p < 0.05$. This hypothesis is further reinforced when taking into account the d' values in Table 2 where there is a precipitous drop in d' between the one target and multiple target video conditions. Based on this observation we hypothesize that increased target loads do, in fact, decrease BCI performance in RSVP tasks. Testing this hypothesis and thereby further understanding the effects of target load on BCI performance in RSVP will be important in future work since using overly conservative or liberal target loads directly limits the utility of the BCI-enabled RSVP.

The findings of this research suggests some basic guidelines for future applications of BCI-enabled RSVP. First, when choosing stimuli, use video or other types that the human visual system is well adapted to searching. Second, optimize the number of targets in RSVP presentation to maximize the throughput of the system. This work underscores the importance of optimizing BCIs by leveraging the strengths of the human neurological system.

Future work will explore the performance and fatigue associated with the task so as to determine ideal working conditions. Other work will simplify the use of EEG devices, refine the algorithms behind decoding their signals, and reduce the cost of the equipment. With these improvements EEG-based brain-computer interfaces have the potential to become a more attractive option for solving a multitude of both specialized and everyday tasks.

5. ACKNOWLEDGMENTS

This work was partially supported by the Defense Advanced Research Projects Agency Cognitive technology Threat Warning System (CT2WS) program (contract No. W31P4Q-08-C-0264). The views and conclusions contained in this document are those of the authors and should not be interpreted as representing the official policies, either expressly or implied, of the Defense Advanced Research Projects Agency or the U.S. Government.

6. REFERENCES

[1] R. A. Abrams and S. E. Christ. Motion onset captures attention. *Psychological Science*, 14(5):427–432, 2003.

[2] C.-C. Chang and C.-J. Lin. LIBSVM: A library for support vector machines. *ACM Transactions on Intelligent Systems and Technology*, 2:27:1–27:27, 2011. Software available at `http://www.csie.ntu.edu.tw/~cjlin/libsvm`.

[3] S. Franconeri and D. Simons. Moving and looming stimuli capture attention. *Attention, Perception, and Psychophysics*, 65:999–1010, 2003.

[4] C. J. Gonsalvez and J. Polich. P300 amplitude is determined by target-to-target interval. *Psychophysiology*, 39(3):388–396, 2002.

[5] C. Kranczioch, S. Debener, and A. K. Engel. Event-related potential correlates of the attentional blink phenomenon. *Cognitive Brain Research*, 17(1):177 – 187, 2003.

[6] D. Mahapatra, S. Winkler, and S.-C. Yen. Motion saliency outweighs other low-level features while watching videos. In B. E. Rogowitz and T. N. Pappas, editors, *Human Vision and Electronic Imaging XIII*, volume 6806. SPIE-IST Electronic Imaging, 2008.

[7] S. Thorpe. Speed of processing in the human visual system. *Nature*, 381(6582):520–522, 1996.

[8] S. K. Ungerleider and L. G. Mechanisms of visual attention in the human cortex. *Annual Review of Neuroscience*, 23(1):315–341, 2000.

Workshop on Speech and Gesture Production in Virtually and Physically Embodied Conversational Agents

Ross Mead
Interaction Lab
University of Southern California
Los Angeles, CA, USA
+1 213 740-6245
rossmead@usc.edu

Maha Salem
Faculty of Technology
Bielefeld University
D-33594 Bielefeld, Germany
+49 521 106-67107
msalem@techfak.uni-bielefeld.de

ABSTRACT

This full day workshop aims to bring together researchers from the embodied conversational agent (ECA) and sociable robotics communities to spark discussion and collaboration between the related fields. The focus of the workshop is on co-verbal behavior production – specifically, synchronized speech and gesture – for either virtually or physically embodied platforms. It elucidates the subject in consideration of aspects regarding planning and realization of multimodal behavior production. Topics discussed highlight common as well as distinguishing factors of their implementations within each respective field.

Categories and Subject Descriptors

I.2 [**Artificial Intelligence**]: General—*Cognitive simulation*; Robotics—*Kinematics and dynamics, manipulators, operator interfaces*; J.4 [**Social and Behavioral Sciences**]: Psychology.

General Terms

Human Factors, Languages, Standardization.

Keywords

Multimodal communication, speech and gesture for artificial communicators, sociable human-agent interaction.

1. INTRODUCTION

To successfully engage in social interactions with humans, artificial communicators such as embodied conversational agents (ECAs) or sociable robots should provide communicative functionality that is both natural and intuitive [1, 2]. Given their embodiment and potentially humanoid design, they are typically expected to exhibit human-like communicative behaviors, using their bodies for non-verbal expression just as humans do [1]. Representing an integral component of human communication [5, 7], co-verbal gestures are frequently modeled and implemented to extend the non-verbal expressiveness of sociable agents [6, 8, 9].

ICMI'12, October 22–26, 2012, Santa Monica, California, USA.
ACM 978-1-4503-1467-1/12/10.

The work of two research communities is most relevant to this full-day workshop: firstly, in the area of computer animation, researchers have developed frameworks to realize multimodal communication behavior in virtually embodied conversational agents; secondly, in the field of robotics, researchers have explored various approaches to generate non-verbal behaviors along with speech in sociable robots. The challenges are similar in that both research areas demand a high degree of control and flexibility so that human-like motion can be adapted to a system with non-human kinematics. The levels of complexity encountered in each field, however, are not equivalent. Although the range of different body types found in virtually embodied agents is manifold and hence challenging, character animation has less restrictive motion than even the most state-of-the-art humanoid robots. For example, animation of virtual agents reduces or even eliminates the problems of handling joint and velocity limits; for a robot body, however, these have to be explicitly addressed given real physical restrictions.

Generally, computational approaches to synthesizing multimodal behavior can be modeled as three consecutive tasks as illustrated in Figure 1: firstly, determining *what* to convey (i.e., content planning); secondly, determining *how* to convey it (i.e., behavior planning); finally, *conveying* it (i.e., behavior realization). These tasks can be outlined as two major stages of behavior generation: **planning** and **realization**. In an attempt to identify intersections between the two above mentioned research fields, approaches on both the planning and the realization levels are considered and discussed within the scope of this workshop.

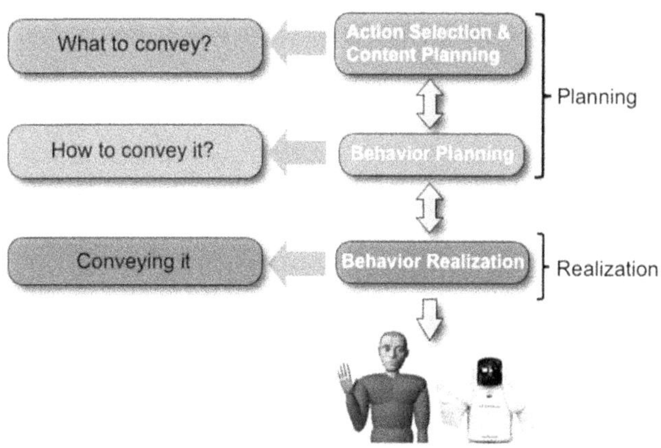

Figure 1. Behavior generation pipeline comprising two main stages: *planning* and *realization* (adapted from [9]).

2. OBJECTIVES

This workshop elicits participation from those interested in the general conference themes of multimodal interaction design and system development. Specifically, it aims to bring together researchers from the ECA and sociable robotics communities to spark discussion and collaboration between the related fields. The focus of the workshop is on co-verbal behavior production – specifically, synchronized speech and gesture – for either virtually or physically embodied platforms.

The workshop elucidates the subject in consideration of aspects regarding planning and realization of multimodal behavior production. Topics discussed in the workshop highlight common and distinguishing factors of their implementations within each respective field. An interactive panel discussion provides participants with the opportunity to learn about related state-of-the-art research from a group of experts with diverse backgrounds. The breakout session as part of the workshop aims to focus on the definition and development of common standards for both the specification and realization of multimodal behaviors. Ideally, such standards target solutions that are suitable for both ECAs and sociable robots by identifying interfaces that can bridge the gap between these unequally embodied platforms.

3. TOPICS

Under the focus of speech-gesture-based multimodal human-agent interaction, the workshop covers original work, either completed or still in progress, related to one or more of the following topics:

- Computational approaches to:
  - Content and behavior planning, e.g., rule-based or probabilistic models
  - Behavior realization for virtual agents or sociable robots (one or the other, or both)
- From ECAs to physical robots: potential and challenges of cross-platform approaches
- Behavior specification languages and standards, e.g., FML [3, 6], BML [10, 6, 8], and MURML [4, 9]
- Speech-gesture synchronization, e.g., open-loop vs. closed-loop approaches
- Situatedness within social/environmental contexts
- Feedback-based user adaptation
- Cognitive modeling of gesture and speech

4. ACKNOWLEDGMENTS

The *ICMI-2012 Workshop on Speech and Gesture Production in Virtually and Physically Embodied Conversational Agents* is sponsored in part by the Center of Excellence "Cognitive Interaction Technology" of Bielefeld University, Germany. We thank the invited speaker, Stefan Kopp, as well as the workshop program committee: Dan Bohus, Kerstin Dautenhahn, Jonathan Gratch, Alexis Heloir, Takayuki Kanda, Jina Lee, Stacy Marsella, Maja Matarić, Louis-Philippe Morency, Bilge Mutlu, Victor Ng-Thow-Hing, and Catherine Pelachaud. We also thank the workshop chairs: Toyoaki Nishida and Rainer Stiefelhagen.

5. REFERENCES

[1] Breazeal, C. 2002. *Designing Sociable Robots*. MIT Press, Cambridge, Massachusetts.

[2] Cassell, J., Prevost, S., Sullivan, J., Churchill, E. 2000. *Embodied Conversational Agents*. MIT Press, Cambridge, Massachusetts.

[3] Heylen, D., Kopp, S., Marsella, S.C., Pelachaud, C., Vilhjálmsson, H. 2008. The next step towards a function markup language. *Proceedings of the 8th International Conference on Intelligent Virtual Agents*, Tokyo, Japan, 270-280.

[4] Kranstedt, A., Kopp, S., and Wachsmuth, I. 2002. MURML: a multimodal utterance representation markup language for conversational agents. *Proceedings of the AAMAS-02 Workshop on Embodied Conversational Agents – Let's Specify and Evaluate Them*, Bologna, Italy.

[5] Kendon, A. 1986. Current issues in the study of gesture. Nespoulous, J.-L., Perron, P., and Lecours, A. R., (eds.), *Biological Foundations of Gestures: Motor and Semiotic Aspects*, Lawrence Erlbaum Associates, Hillsdale, New Jersey, 23-47.

[6] Lee, J. and Marsella, S. 2006. Nonverbal behavior generator for embodied conversational agents. *Proceedings of the 6th International Conference on Intelligent Virtual Agents*, Marina del Rey, California.

[7] McNeill, D. 1992. *Hand and Mind: What Gestures Reveal about Thought*. University of Chicago Press, Chicago, Illinois.

[8] Mead, R., Wade, E.R., Johnson, P., St. Clair, A., Chen, S., and Matarić, M.J. 2010. An architecture for rehabilitation task practice in socially assistive human-robot interaction. *Proceedings of The 19th IEEE International Symposium in Robot and Human Interactive Communication*, Viareggio, Italy, 404-409.

[9] Salem, M. 2012. *Conceptual Motorics – Generation and Evaluation of Communicative Robot Gesture*. Doctoral Thesis. Bielefeld University.

[10] Vilhjálmsson, H., Cantelmo, N., Cassell, J., Chafai, N. E., Kipp, M., Kopp, S., Mancini, M., Marsella, S., Marshall, A. N., Pelachaud, C., Ruttkay, Z., Thorisson, K. R., van Welbergen, H., and van der Werf, R. J. 2007. The behavior markup language: recent developments and challenges. Pelachaud, C., Martin, J.-C., Andre, E., Collet, G., Karpouzis, K., and Pele, D., (eds.), *Proceedings of the 7th International Conference on Intelligent Virtual Agents, Lecture Notes in Computer Science* 4722, Berlin, Germany, 99–111.

1st International Workshop on Multimodal Learning Analytics

[Extended Abstract]

Stefan Scherer
USC Institute for Creative Technologies
15012 Waterfront Dr.
Playa Vista, CA
scherer@ict.usc.edu

Marcelo Worsley
Stanford University
520 Galvez Mall
Stanford, CA
worsley@stanford.edu

Louis-Philippe Morency
USC Institute for Creative Technologies
15012 Waterfront Dr.
Playa Vista, CA
morency@ict.usc.edu

ABSTRACT

This summary describes the 1st International Workshop on Multimodal Learning Analytics. This area of study brings together the technologies of multimodal analysis with the learning sciences. The intersection of these domains should enable researchers to foster an improved understanding of student learning, lead to the creation of more natural and enriching learning interfaces, and motivate the development of novel techniques for tackling challenges that are specific of education.

Categories and Subject Descriptors

H.4 [**Information Systems Applications**]: Miscellaneous; K.3 [**Computers and Education**]: General

Keywords

Multimodal Learning Analytics, Machine Learning, Statistical Analysis

1. INTRODUCTION

Multimodal learning analytics, learning analytics, and educational data mining all are emerging disciplines concerned with developing techniques to more deeply explore unique data in educational settings. They use the results based on these analyses to understand how students learn. Among other things, this includes how they communicate, collaborate, and use digital and non-digital tools during learning activities, and what the impact of these tools is on acquiring new skills and knowledge. Past research on learning analytics has aimed to model studentsâĂŹ knowledge and motivation during learning, to contribute to understanding learning dynamics during computer-supported and collaborative exchange, to diagnose studentsâĂŹ failure to progress during learning activities, and to adapt learning activities to studentsâĂŹ limitations and learning status. More generally, advances in learning analytics are expected to contribute new empirical findings, theories, methods, and metrics for understanding how students learn. They also can contribute to improving pedagogical support for studentsâĂŹ learning through assessment of new digital tools, teaching strategies, and curricula.

The most recent direction within this area is multimodal learning analytics, which emphasizes the analysis of natural rich modalities of communication during situated learning activities. This includes studentsâĂŹ speech, writing, and nonverbal interaction (e.g., gestures, facial expressions, gaze). A primary objective of multimodal learning analytics is to analyze coherent signal and activity patterns in order to uncover entirely new learning-oriented phenomena. Another is to develop a better collection of converging metrics for learning-related behavior and landmarks. These include metrics that eventually could be analyzed unobtrusively, continuously, automatically, and in natural classroom environments and mobile settings.

Progress in these areas will transform our ability to identify and stimulate effective learning, support more rapid feedback and responsive intervention, and facilitate learning in more diverse students and contexts.

2. KEYNOTE SPEAKERS

Prof. Sharon Oviatt (Incaa Designs) She is internationally known for her work in human-centered interface design and evaluation, educational interfaces, mobile interfaces, and pen, speech, and multimodal interfaces. She has been a lifelong educator and prolific scientist, with over 130 scientific publications in a wide range of venues. In 2000, she received a National Science Foundation Creativity Award for pioneering research on interfaces.

Prof. Paulo Blikstein (Stanford University) He is an Assistant Professor at the Stanford University School of Education and (by courtesy) the Computer Science department. He directs the Transformative Learning Technologies Lab which focuses on researching how new technologies can deeply transform the learning of science, engineering, and mathematics. His work involves cutting-edge, multi-modal technologies for constructionist learning environments where students learn science and mathematics by building sophisticated projects and devices. Paulo is a recipient of the prestigious NSF Early Career Award and is also the director of the Lemann Center for Educational Entrepreneurship and Innovation in Brazil.

ICMI'12, October 22–26, 2012, Santa Monica, California, USA.
ACM 978-1-4503-1467-1/12/10.

4th Workshop on Eye Gaze in Intelligent Human Machine Interaction: Eye Gaze and Multimodality

Yukiko I. Nakano
Dept. of Computer and Information Science, Seikei University
3-3-1 Kichijoji-kitamachi, Musashino-shi, Tokyo 180-8633 Japan
y.nakano@st.seikei.ac.jp

Kristiina Jokinen
Institute of Behavioural Sciences, University of Helsinki
Siltavuorenpenger 20 A, PO Box 9, FIN-00014 University of Helsinki
Kristiina.Jokinen@helsinki.fi

Hung-Hsuan Huang
Department of Information & Communication Science, Ritsumeikan University
Noji-higashi 1-1-1, Kusatsu-shi, Shiga 525-8577 Japan
hhhuang@acm.org

ABSTRACT

This is the fourth workshop in a series of workshops on Eye Gaze in Intelligent Human Machine Interaction, in which we have discussed a wide range of issues for eye gaze; technologies for sensing human attentional behaviors, roles of attentional behaviors as social gaze in human-human and human-humanoid interaction, attentional behaviors in problem-solving and task-performing, gaze-based intelligent user interfaces, and evaluation of gaze-based user interfaces. In addition to these topics, this year's workshop focuses on eye gaze in multimodal interpretation and generation. Since eye gaze is one of the facial communication modalities, gaze information can be combined with other modalities or bodily motions to contribute to the meaning of utterance and serve as communication signals.

Categories and Subject Descriptors

H.1.2 [User/Machine Systems] - Information Systems - MODELS AND PRINCIPLES (includes Human factors and Human information processing), H.5.1 [Multimedia Information Systems] - Information Systems - INFORMATION INTERFACES AND PRESENTATION (I.7)

General Terms

Algorithms, Design, Experimentation, Human Factors, Languages, Measurement.

Keywords

Eye gaze, multimodal communication.

1. INTRODUCTION

Eye gaze is one of the most important aspects in modeling human-human communication, and has great potential in improving human-humanoid interaction. In human face-to-face communication, eye gaze plays an important role in floor management, grounding, and engagement in conversation. In human-robot interaction research, social gaze, gaze directed at an interaction partner, has been a subject of increased attention.

This is the fourth workshop on Eye Gaze in Intelligent Human Machine Interaction. In the previous workshops, a wide range of issues for eye gaze has been discussed: technologies for sensing human attentional behaviors, roles of attentional behaviors as social gaze in human-human and human-humanoid interaction, attentional behaviors in problem-solving and task-performing, gaze-based intelligent user interfaces, and evaluation of gaze-based user interfaces.

The first workshop held at IUI 2010 [1] addressed issues of eye-tracking technologies, analyses of human eye-gaze behaviors, multimodal interpretation, user interfaces using an eye-tracker, and presenting gaze behaviors in humanoid interfaces. Following the first workshop, the second workshop, which was held at IUI2011, covered wider topics from eye-tracking technologies to building gaze-based interactive intelligent user interfaces including educational systems [2]. The third workshop was held at HRI 2012 to approach the problems of understanding the role of social gaze in human-robot interaction, and discussed how to measure social gaze behavior by humans and how to implement it in robots that interact with them. In addition to the topics discussed at previous workshops, this year's workshop focuses on eye gaze in multimodal interpretation and generation. Since eye gaze is one of the facial communication modalities, gaze information can be combined with other modalities or bodily motions to contribute to the meaning of utterance and serve as communication signals.

The workshop aims to continue exploring this growing area of research by bringing together researchers including human sensing, multimodal processing, humanoid interfaces, intelligent user interface, and communication science. We will exchange ideas to develop and improve methodologies for this research area with the long term goal of establishing a strong interdisciplinary research community in "attention aware interactive systems".

2. OBJECTIVES AND TOPICS

The research areas and questions that will be targeted in the workshop are as follows;

(1) Technologies for sensing human attentional behaviors

- Sensing attentional behaviors using bodily motions such as pupil movements, head movements and torso directions
- Sensing attentional behaviors using brain activities
- Issues in tracking attentional behaviors in intelligent user interfaces

(2) Eye gaze in multimodal interpretation

- Eye gaze as multimodal communicative signals in human-human and human-humanoid interaction
- Eye gaze in multimodal understanding

ICMI' 12, October 22-26, 2012, Santa Monica, California, USA.
ACM 978-1-4503-1467-1/12/10.

- Eye gaze in interpreting user's intentions, attitude, grounding, and engagement in conversational interactions

(3) Eye gaze in multimodal generation and behavior selection in conversational humanoids

- Selecting appropriate eye-gaze behaviors for virtual agents and communication robots
- Effective multimodal expressions by combining eye gaze and other modalities

(4) Empirical study for human attentional behaviors

- Attentional behaviors in interaction with computer systems including humanoids
- Attentional behaviors in dyads and multiparty face-to-face conversations
- Implications of analysis of human attentional behaviors towards HCI design

(5) Evaluation and design issues for using eye gaze in multimodal interfaces

- Evaluation method for gaze-based multimodal interfaces
- Designs of user studies to identify the real impact of eye gaze in multimodal interfaces

3. PROGRAM COMMITTEE

We would like to thank our Program Committee members for their precious time and great effort in reviewing papers.

Thomas Bader (Karlsruhe Institute of Technology, Germany)

Roman Bednarik (University of Eastern Finland, Finland)

Ralf Biedert (German Research Center for Artificial Intelligence (DFKI) GmbH, Germany)

Frank Broz (University of Plymouth, UK)

Justine Cassell (Carnegie Mellon University, USA)

Joyce Chai (Michigan State University, USA)

Cristina Conati (University of British Columbia, Canada)

Andrew Duchowski (Clemson University, USA)

Patrick Jermann (Ecole Polytechnique Fédérale de Lausanne (EPFL), Switzerland)

Yoshinori Kuno (Saitama University, Japan)

Hagen Lehmann (University of Hertfordshire, UK)

Bilge Mutlu (University of Wisconsin-Madison, USA)

Toyoaki Nishida (Kyoto University, Japan)

Elizabeth Peinsipp-Byma (Fraunhofer Institute for Optronics, Systems Engineering and Image Analysis IOSB)

Christopher Peters (Coventry University, UK)

Zahar Prasov (U.S. Army Research Laboratory)

Matthias Rötting (University of Berlin)

Candy Sidner (Worcester Polytechnic Institute, USA)

4. REFERENCES

[1] Elisabeth André and Joyce Y. Chai. Workshop: Eye Gaze in Intelligent Human Machine Interaction. In *Proc. IUI 2010*, ACM Press (2010), p431.

[2] Yukiko Nakano, Cristina Conati, Thomas Bader: 2nd workshop on eye gaze in intelligent human machine interaction. In *Proc. IUI 2011*, ACM Press (2011), pp479-480.

The 3rd International Workshop on Social Behaviour in Music (SBM2012)

Antonio Camurri, Donald Glowinski, Maurizio Mancini, Giovanna Varni, Gualtiero Volpe
Casa Paganini - InfoMus
DIBRIS – University of Genoa
Viale Causa 13, 16145, Genoa, Italy
+39 010 3532201
{toni, donald, maurizio, giovanna, gualtiero}@infomus.org

ABSTRACT

Since its first edition in 2009, the International Workshop on Social Behaviour in Music (SBM) has been an occasion for researchers and practitioners for discussing recent advances in automated analysis of social behaviour, being music the selected test-bed and application scenario. The first edition of SBM was held in Vancouver, Canada, in the framework of the 2009 IEEE International Conference on Social Computing (SocialCom 2009). The second one was held in Genova, Italy, in the framework of the 4th International ICST Conference on Intelligent Technologies for Interactive Entertainment (Intetain 2011). SBM is now at its third edition, which takes place in the framework of the 14th International Conference on Multimodal Interaction (ICMI 2012), Santa Monica, California, USA. Again, SBM aims at providing a picture of current research breakthrough and issues, giving at the same time directions for future works and collaborations.

Categories and Subject Descriptors

H.5.2 **[Information Interfaces and Representation (HCI)]**: User Interfaces

H.5.5 **[Information Interfaces and Presentation]**: Sound and Music Computing

General Terms

Algorithms, Measurement, Design, Experimentation, Human Factors, Theory

Keywords

Social behaviour, music performance, social signal processing.

1. GOALS

Human-Computer Interaction has recently seen a growing interest of researchers toward social interaction. New disciplines emerged, such as, for example, Social Signal Processing [1][2] (see also http://sspnet.eu). Human-Computer Interaction, that traditionally faced the development of (natural and multimodal) interfaces for the single user, is thus in front of a new research challenge, i.e., how to support the natural and multimodal interaction of multiple users with the computer, including the social interaction among these users.

ICMI'12, October 22–26, 2012, Santa Monica, California, USA.
ACM 978-1-4503-1467-1/12/10.

Research in Sound and Music Computing (SMC) can provide a great help in facing such a challenge. For example, current work on embodied coordination for social active listening to music tries to recover the embodied and social dimension of music listening (see for example [3]). Foundational research on social interaction also founds in music an important test-bed for developing theories, validating models, and implementing algorithms.

The 3rd International Workshop on Social Behaviour in Music (SBM2012) is an occasion for researchers and practitioners to meet and discuss about computational models and techniques for analysis and processing of social behaviour and emotion in music. The goal is to discuss current research, to identify research challenges, to show results, and to foster collaborations and future projects.

The workshop is partially supported by the EU-ICT-FET Project SIEMPRE (http://www.siempre.infomus.org/). The goal of the SIEMPRE project is to develop novel research theoretical and methodological frameworks, computational models, and algorithms for the analysis of creative communication within groups of people. Research in SIEMPRE is focused on small and large ensemble musical performance and audience experience. These are taken as an ideal test-bed for the development of models and techniques for measuring creative social interaction and related emotions in an ecologically valid framework. In particular, the focus is on exploring interpersonal interaction in (i) musician-musician, (ii) conductor-musicians, and (iii) musician-listener scenarios. Recently, SIEMPRE was extended to include non-European partners from US and Japan. The workshop starts from the knowledge acquired in the initial two years of SIEMPRE and is open to new perspectives and experiences on social and emotional communication in music.

2. TOPICS

The workshop focuses on the social signals and their features that are most significant for a qualitative and quantitative analysis of social behaviour and experience in music, including the emotional dimension. It addresses scenarios where the distinction between listeners and performers fades out and users become producers and consumers of music experience.

Research questions the workshop addresses include, for example: which are the multimodal signals characterising social experience in performers and listeners interplay? How to model interaction in groups of performers, in the audience, between audience and performers? Which is the minimal set of low-level features describing interaction in performance? Which are the social signals that better describe social interaction in music? How do these social signals induce specific emotions in performers and listeners?

These topics typically require a research methodology grounded on analysis and processing of non-verbal multimodal signals. Indeed, analysis of social behaviour of music ensembles (from the smallest ones, e.g., string quartets, to the biggest ones, e.g., symphonic orchestras) encompasses analysis of signals from different modalities (e.g., audio, video, motion capture, and biometric signals) and the multimodal fusion of the information from the single modalities. Analysis of social behaviour in music is thus a specific though significant test-bed for multimodal signal processing as well as a valuable source for future multimodal interfaces. Moreover, multidisciplinary expertise is needed, integrating research in engineering and physics, as well as in human sciences, e.g., social psychology and affective sciences.

This edition of the workshop includes presentation of original work in the field and a final round-table, drawing conclusions and discussing directions for future research.

3. ACKNOWLEDGMENTS

Our thanks to the SBM scientific committee and reviewers for their precious help in preparing the workshop. The workshop is partially supported by the EU-ICT-FET Project SIEMPRE. The project SIEMPRE acknowledges the financial support of the Future and Emerging Technologies (FET) programme within the Seventh Framework Programme for Research of the European Commission, under FET-Open grant number: 250026-2.

4. REFERENCES

[1] Vinciarelli, A., Pantic, M., Bourland, H., and Pentland, A. 2008. Social signals, their function, and automatic analysis: a survey. In *Proceedings of the 10th International Conference on Multimodal Interfaces*, (Chania, Crete, Greece, October 20-22, 2008). ICMI'08. ACM, New York, NY, 61-68. DOI=http://doi.acm.org/10.1145/1452392.1452405.

[2] Pentland, A. 2007. Social signal processing. *IEEE Signal Proc. Mag*. 24, 4 (July 2007), 108-111. DOI=10.1109/MSP.2007.4286569

[3] Volpe, G., and Camurri, A. 2011. A system for embodied social active listening to sound and music content. *ACM Journal on Computing and Cultural Heritage*, 4, 1, 2-23. DOI=http://doi.acm.org/10.1145/2001416.2001418

Smart Material Interfaces: "A Material Step to the Future"

Anton Nijholt
Human Media Interaction
University of Twente, NL
a.nijholt@utwente.nl

Leonardo Giusti
MIT - Mobile Experience Lab
Massacchussets,USA
lgiusti@mit.edu

Andrea Minuto
Human Media Interaction
University of Twente,NL
a.minuto@twente.nl

Patrizia Marti
Department of Social, Political and Cognitive Sciences
University of Siena
marti@unisi.it

ABSTRACT

Over the past years the technology push and the creation of new technological materials made available on the market many new smart materials. Smart Material Interfaces (SMIs) want to take advantage of these materials to overcome traditional patterns of interaction, leaving behind the "digital feeling" by a more continuous space of interaction, tightly coupling digital and physical world by means of the smart materials' properties. With this workshop about SMIs, we want to draw attention to the emerging field, stimulating research and development in interfaces that make use of smart materials and encourage new and different modalities of interaction.

Categories and Subject Descriptors

H.5.2 [**Information Interfaces and Presentation**]: User Interfaces - Interaction styles

General Terms

Design.

Keywords

Smart material interface, Reality-based interface, Tangible interface, Organic interface

1. INTRODUCTION

Every day we are getting closer to Mark Weiser's [14] vision of Ubiquitous Computing that motivated researchers to augment everyday objects and environments with computing capabilities to provide Tangible User Interfaces (TUIs) [4], organic interfaces [11] and reality-based [5] interaction possibilities. That is, HCI researchers are developing a wide range of new interfaces that tend to separate from the "window, icon, menu, pointing device" (WIMP).

We can find many different examples of these post-WIMP interaction styles such as: mixed and augmented reality, tangible interaction, ubiquitous and pervasive computing, handheld and mobile interaction, perceptual and affective computing etc. [5]. As mentioned in [5], many of these interaction styles seem to proceed in different and unrelated ways, but they share a common important knowledge. All of these interaction styles try to take advantage on users' preexisting knowledge of everyday life. They employ themes of reality such as users' understanding of naïve physics, their own bodies, the surrounding environment, and other people trying to mimic the real world for making the users more comfortable, creating an interaction more close to what they are used to do already.

To foster and experiment new kinds of interfaces and interaction styles, a vision called Smart Material Interfaces (SMIs) (see e.g. [8]) has been introduced. This vision takes advantage of the latest generation of engineered materials that has special properties defined "smart". Partly introduced to provide an answer to the limitations present in common TUIs, SMIs try to overcome traditional patterns of interaction and leave behind the "digital feeling" by a more analogical and continuous space of interaction, tightly coupling digital and physical world by means of the materials' properties. And not just to copy reality-based patterns, but also to create new possible ways to reach the users' needs and satisfaction.

The main focus of a SMI is being able to make changes in the physical and material properties, creating channels for new input/output modalities. SMI proposes the use of materials that have inherent or "self-augmented" capabilities of changing physical properties such as color, shape and texture, under the control of some external stimulus such as, among other things, electricity, magnetism, light, pressure or temperature.

2. EXAMPLES OF SMI

Considerable efforts have been made to explore the possibilities of applying smart materials in interfaces. For example, Surflex [1] consists of a foam with coiled nitinol muscle wires embedded. The muscle wires can be used to reshape the foam into different shapes. This principle has been applied as a way to use SpeakCup [3], a device used to record and replay messages by physically manipulating its shape (shape-changing interfaces [3]). Parkes and Ishii [9] presented a design tool for motion prototyping and form finding,

ICMI'12, October 22–26, 2012, Santa Monica, California, USA.
ACM 978-1-4503-1467-1/12/10.

named Bosu. Bosu consists of a number of flexible modules that can be physically manipulated (e.g. bending, twisting). The physical manipulations can then be played back thanks to nitinol muscle wires embedded in the modules. Smart materials have been used in the creation of novel ambient displays. Shutters [2]) is a curtain with a grid of shutters that are actuated by nitinol wires. Shutters can be used to regulate the amount of light and air flow that enters a room, as well as serves as an ambient display by creating patterns using the grid of shutters. An ambient display that aims for a more tangible experience is Lumen [10]. A grid of cylindrical physical pixels is actuated to move up and down, using nitinol wires. The physical pixels contain LED's that allow Lumen to display animations both visually, and physically. While nitinol is by far the most widely applied smart material, others have used ferrofluids to create physical ambient interfaces as well as thermo-chromic materials. WeMe [7] for example, is an ambient display that visualizes the presence of members of remote families represented by bubbles of ferrofluid. Another display that makes use of magnetic fluids is Programmables Blobs [12] by Wakita, that try to force the blobs to change shape using electromagnets. Wakita [13] also notes how in design the materials and colors are felt as part of the emotional communication of the interface. Using the property (in this case colors) of the material directly, their aim is to communicate mood by changing the color of Jello Display-Keyboard using IR-chromic material. Several other examples can be found in arts and design installations, as for example Kodama's artwork with ferrofluid [6].

3. WORKSHOP THEMES AND TOPICS

We invited original contributions in a variety of areas related to Interaction design and development of interfaces that make use of SMART MATERIALS. Main topic of interest was the application of smart materials in designing and building interfaces of everyday life. Interfaces that communicate information to the user or allow the user to manipulate information, using different modalities provided by the material's properties. Such as deforming or changing shape of the interface, ambient modifications or interactive textiles. The proposed topics for the workshop included but were not limited to the following: *reality-based interfaces, tangible Interfaces, organic user interfaces, programmable matter, electronic textiles, computational textiles, smart textiles robotics.*

4. WORKSHOP FOCUS

The workshop discussion focuses on three categories about how SMIs can change our environment, i.e., by using shape, color or interactive textiles. The design of Everyday Computational Things allows new materials to enter in our daily life.

For example, SMIs can change shape through movement to suggest information at the right moment or change shape to create interaction or better comfort in everyday condition. Or SMIs can make houses more energy efficient by changing the thermal transmittance of surfaces (windows, facades, etc...). In this way the material change influences both the appearance and the impact of sunlight. SMIs can also enhance experience on embodied interaction using smart textiles.

5. REFERENCES

[1] M. Coelho, H. Ishii, and P. Maes. Surflex: a programmable surface for the design of tangible interfaces. In *CHI '08 extended abstracts on Human factors in computing systems*, CHI EA '08, pages 3429–3434, New York, NY, USA, 2008. ACM.

[2] M. Coelho and P. Maes. Shutters: a permeable surface for environmental control and communication. In *Proc. conf. on Tangible and Embedded Interaction*, TEI '09, pages 13–18, New York, NY, USA, 2009. ACM.

[3] M. Coelho and J. Zigelbaum. Shape-changing interfaces. *Personal Ubiquitous Comput.*, 15(2):161–173, Feb. 2011.

[4] H. Ishii. Tangible bits: beyond pixels. In *proc conf Tangible and Embedded Interaction*, TEI '08, pages xv–xxv, New York, USA, 2008. ACM.

[5] R. J. Jacob, A. Girouard, L. M. Hirshfield, M. S. Horn, O. Shaer, E. T. Solovey, and J. Zigelbaum. Reality-based interaction: a framework for post-wimp interfaces. In *Proc. conf. SIGCHI on Human factors in computing systems*, CHI '08, pages 201–210, New York, NY, USA, 2008. ACM.

[6] S. Kodama. Dynamic ferrofluid sculpture: organic shape-changing art forms. *Commun. ACM*, 51(6):79–81, June 2008.

[7] N. Masson and W. E. Mackay. Weme: Seamless active and passive liquid communication. In J. A. Jacko, editor, *HCI (2)*, volume 5611 of *Lecture Notes in Computer Science*, pages 694–700. Springer, 2009.

[8] A. Minuto, D. Vyas, W. Poelman, and A. Nijholt. Smart material interfaces: A vision. In *Proc. 4th International ICST Conference on Intelligent Technologies for Interactive Entertainment (INTETAIN)*, LNICST 78, pages 57–62. Springer, 2011.

[9] A. Parkes and H. Ishii. Bosu: a physical programmable design tool for transformability with soft mechanics. In *Proc. conf. on Designing Interactive Systems*, DIS '10, pages 189–198, New York, NY, USA, 2010. ACM.

[10] I. Poupyrev, T. Nashida, S. Maruyama, J. Rekimoto, and Y. Yamaji. Lumen: interactive visual and shape display for calm computing. In *ACM SIGGRAPH 2004 Emerging technologies*, SIGGRAPH '04, pages 17–, New York, NY, USA, 2004. ACM.

[11] R. Vertegaal and I. Poupyrev. Introduction. *Commun. ACM*, 51(6):26–30, June 2008.

[12] A. Wakita, A. Nakano, and N. Kobayashi. Programmable blobs: a rheologic interface for organic shape design. In *Proc. conf. Tangible, embedded, and embodied interaction*, TEI '11, pages 273–276, New York, NY, USA, 2011. ACM.

[13] A. Wakita, M. Shibutani, and K. Tsuji. Emotional smart materials. In J. A. Jacko, editor, *HCI (3)*, volume 5612 of *Lecture Notes in Computer Science*, pages 802–805. Springer, 2009.

[14] M. Weiser. The computer for the 21st century. *Scientific American*, 3:94–104, 1991.

Author Index

www.ingramcontent.com/pod-product-compliance
Ingram Content Group UK Ltd.
Pitfield, Milton Keynes, MK11 3LW, UK
UKHW051417290926
15471UKWH00009B/1657

9 781450 319270